Skip·Beat!

Shojo Beat

Skip·Beat!

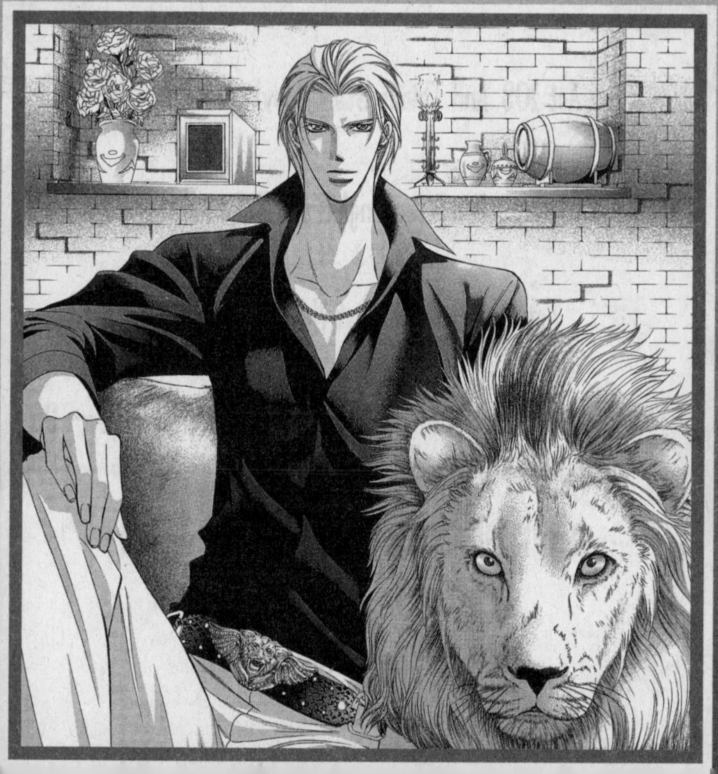

Skip·Beat!

Volume 19

CONTENTS

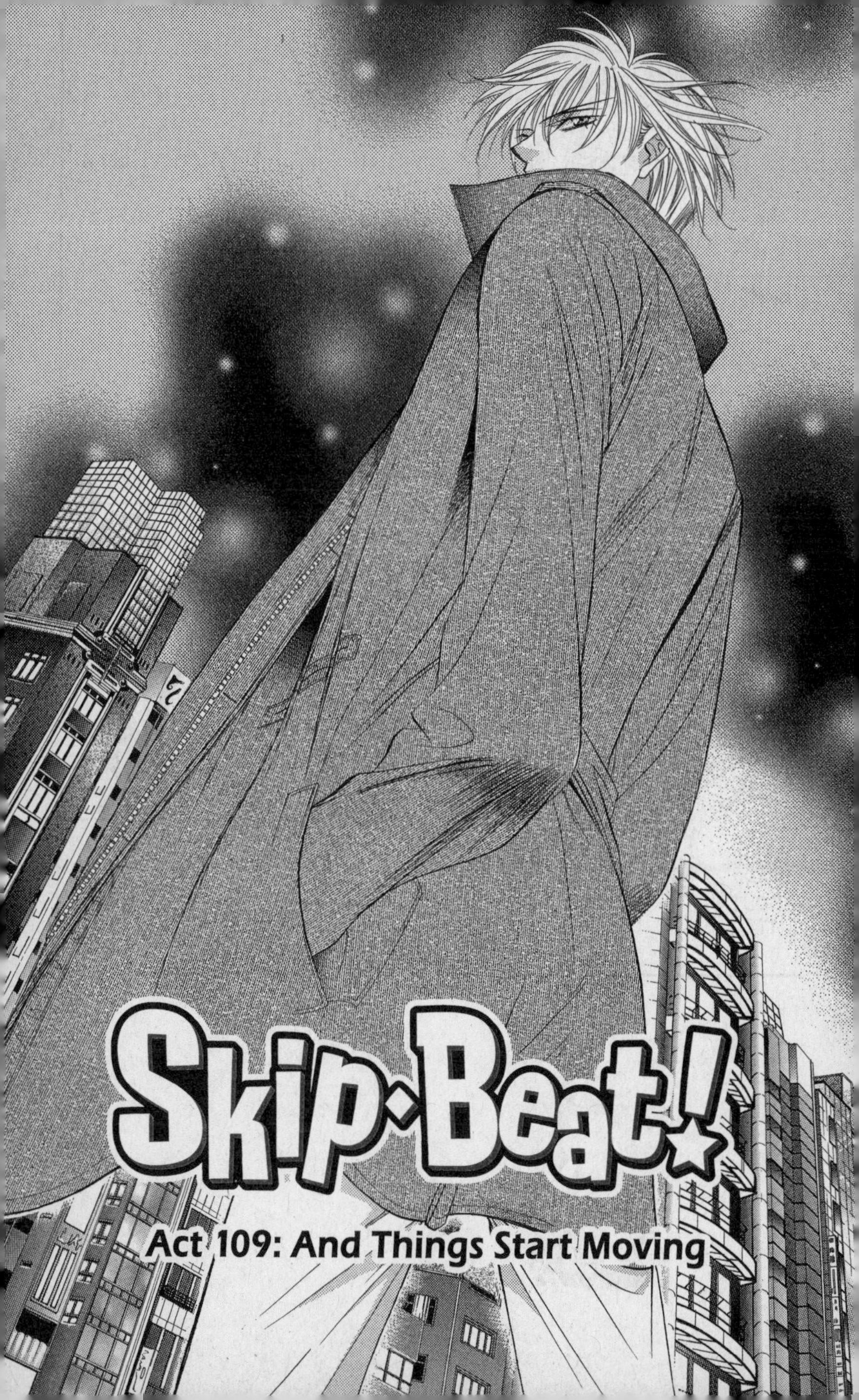
Skip·Beat!
Act 109: And Things Start Moving

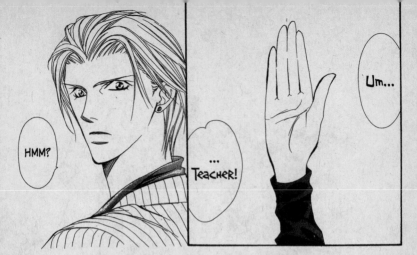

Um...
...Teacher!
HMM?
WHAT IS IT?
You look scary.
UH...
ABOUT MY ROLE-CREATING!
Hmm?
YEAH, WHAT ABOUT IT?

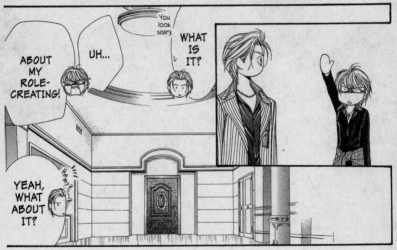

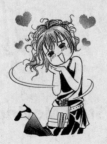

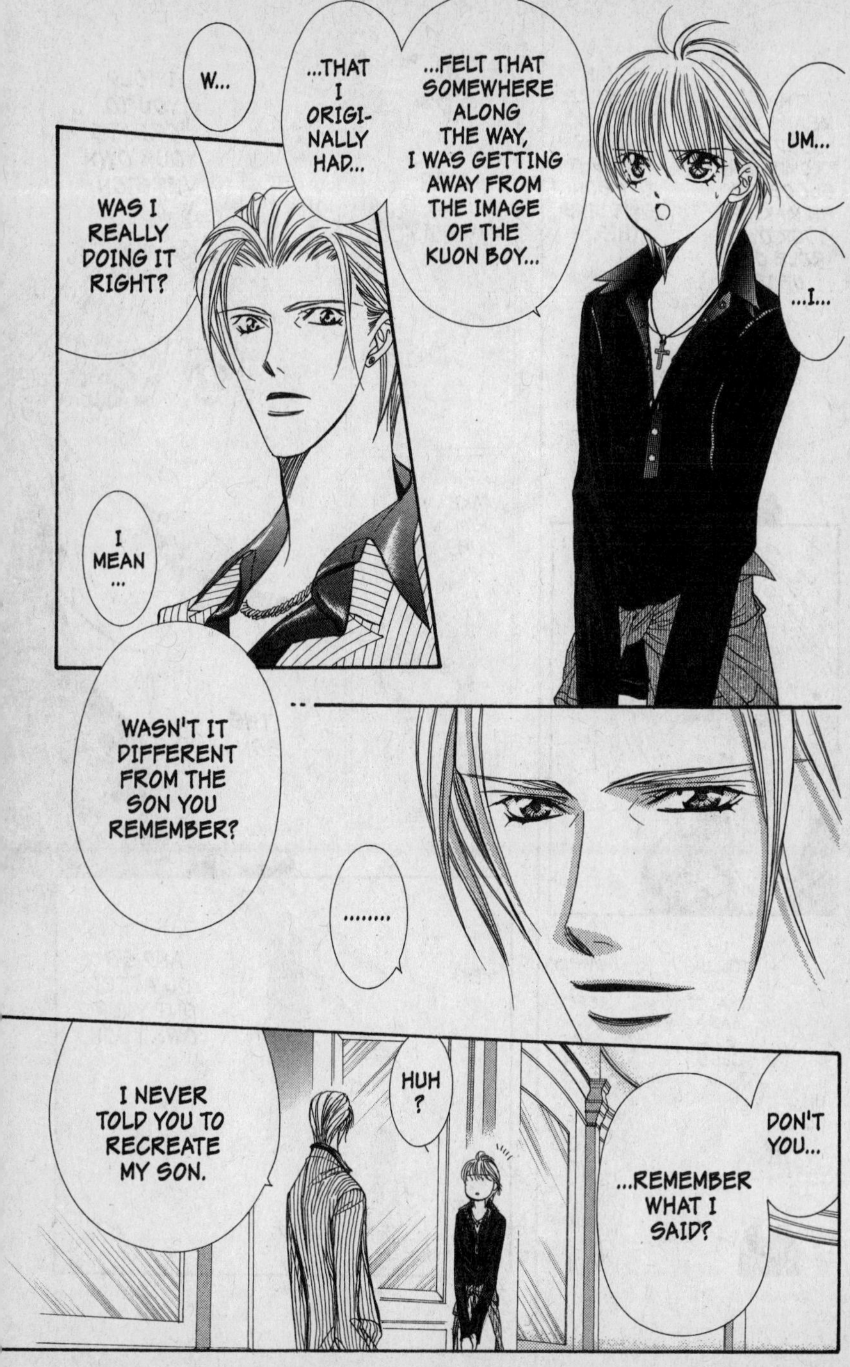
UM...
...I...
...FELT THAT SOMEWHERE ALONG THE WAY, I WAS GETTING AWAY FROM THE IMAGE OF THE KUON BOY...
...THAT I ORIGINALLY HAD...
W...
WAS I REALLY DOING IT RIGHT?
I MEAN...
WASN'T IT DIFFERENT FROM THE SON YOU REMEMBER?
....
DON'T YOU...
...REMEMBER WHAT I SAID?
HUH?
I NEVER TOLD YOU TO RECREATE MY SON.

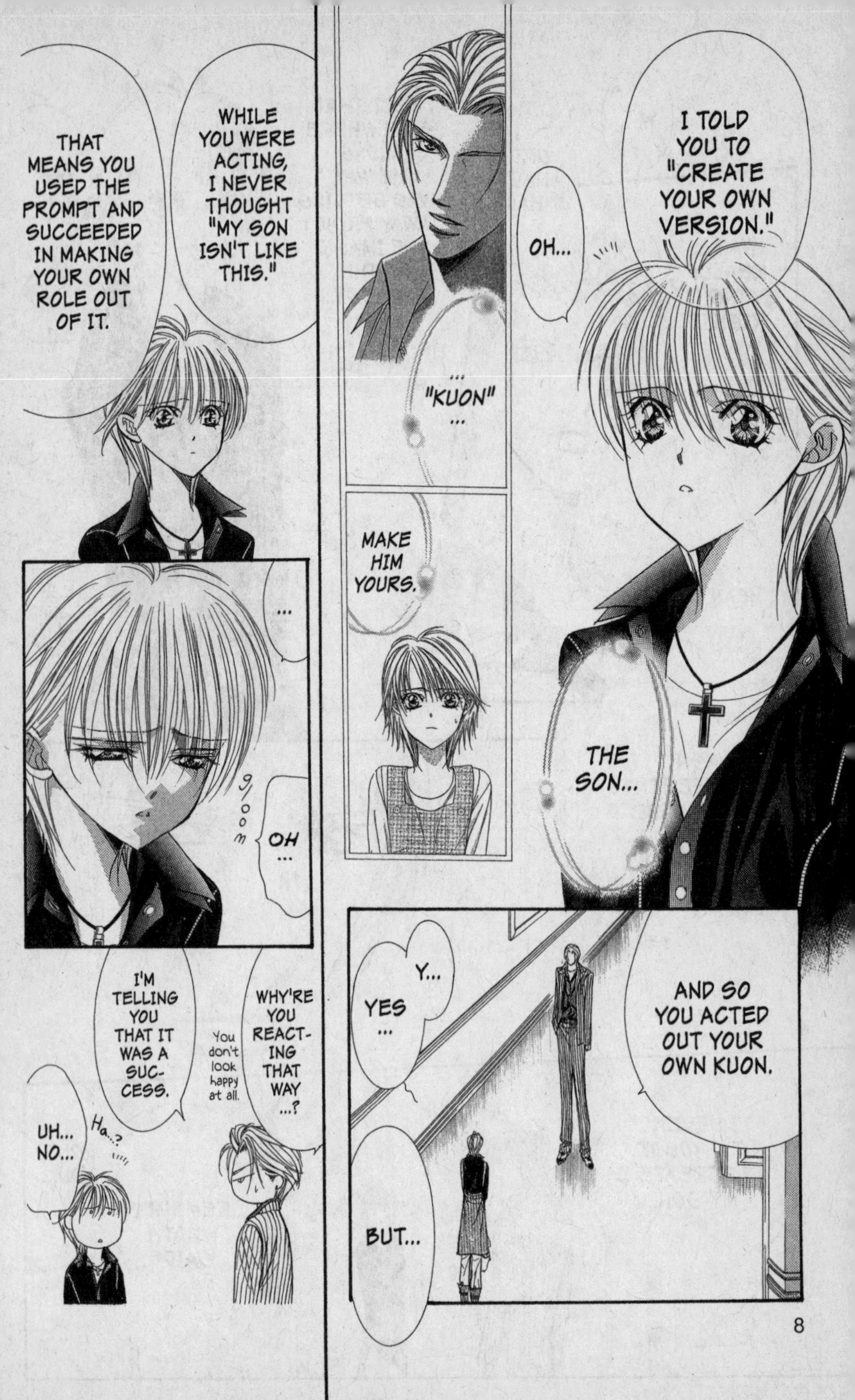
I TOLD YOU TO "CREATE YOUR OWN VERSION."
THE SON...
OH...
... "KUON" ...
MAKE HIM YOURS.
AND SO YOU ACTED OUT YOUR OWN KUON.
Y... YES ...
BUT...
WHILE YOU WERE ACTING, I NEVER THOUGHT "MY SON ISN'T LIKE THIS."
THAT MEANS YOU USED THE PROMPT AND SUCCEEDED IN MAKING YOUR OWN ROLE OUT OF IT.
...
gloom
OH ...
WHY'RE YOU REACT-ING THAT WAY ...?
You don't look happy at all.
I'M TELLING YOU THAT IT WAS A SUC-CESS.
Ha...?
UH... NO...

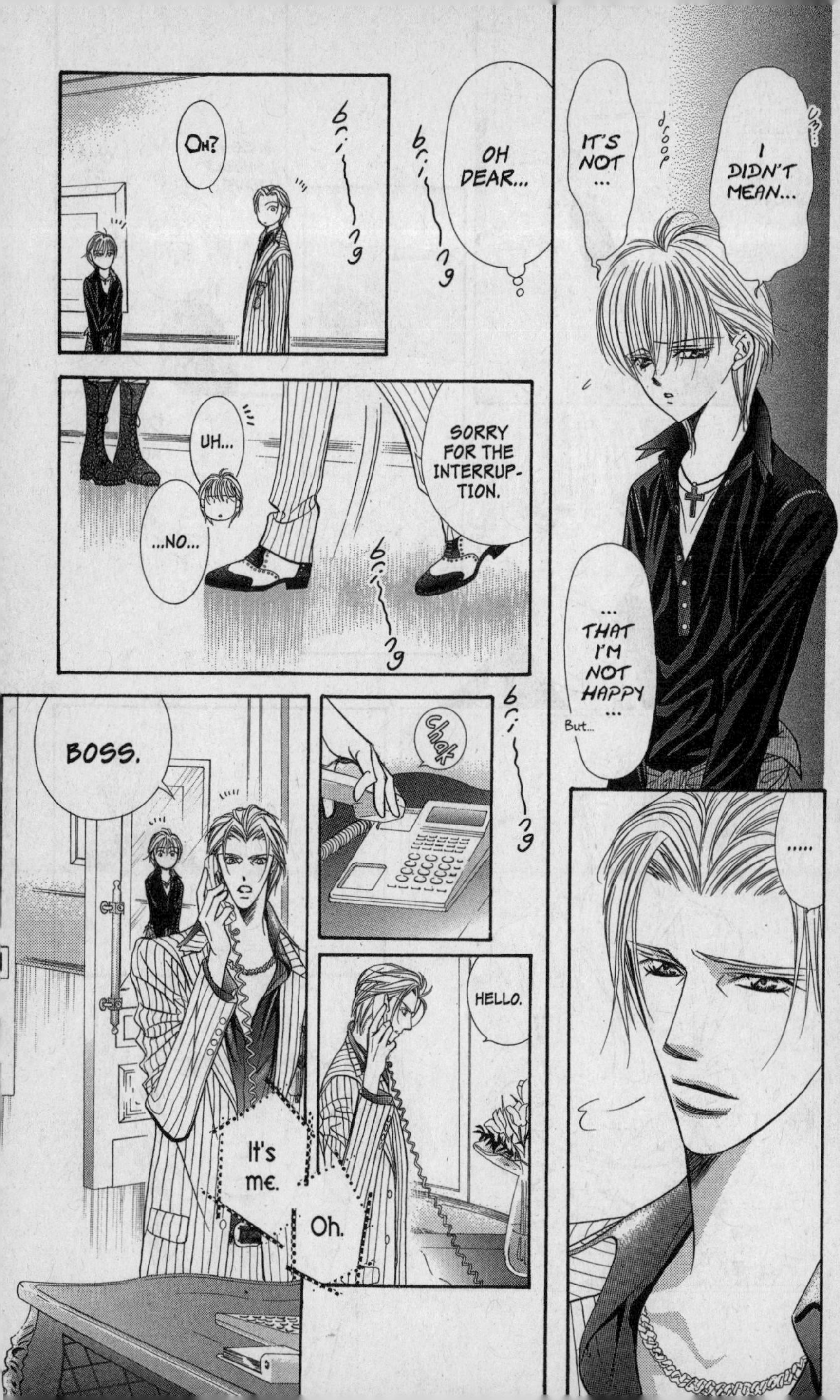
Um...
I DIDN'T MEAN...
droop
IT'S NOT ...
... THAT I'M NOT HAPPY ...
But...
.....
OH DEAR...
bring
bring
OH?
SORRY FOR THE INTERRUPTION.
bring
UH...
...NO...
bring
Chak
HELLO.
BOSS.
It's me.
Oh.

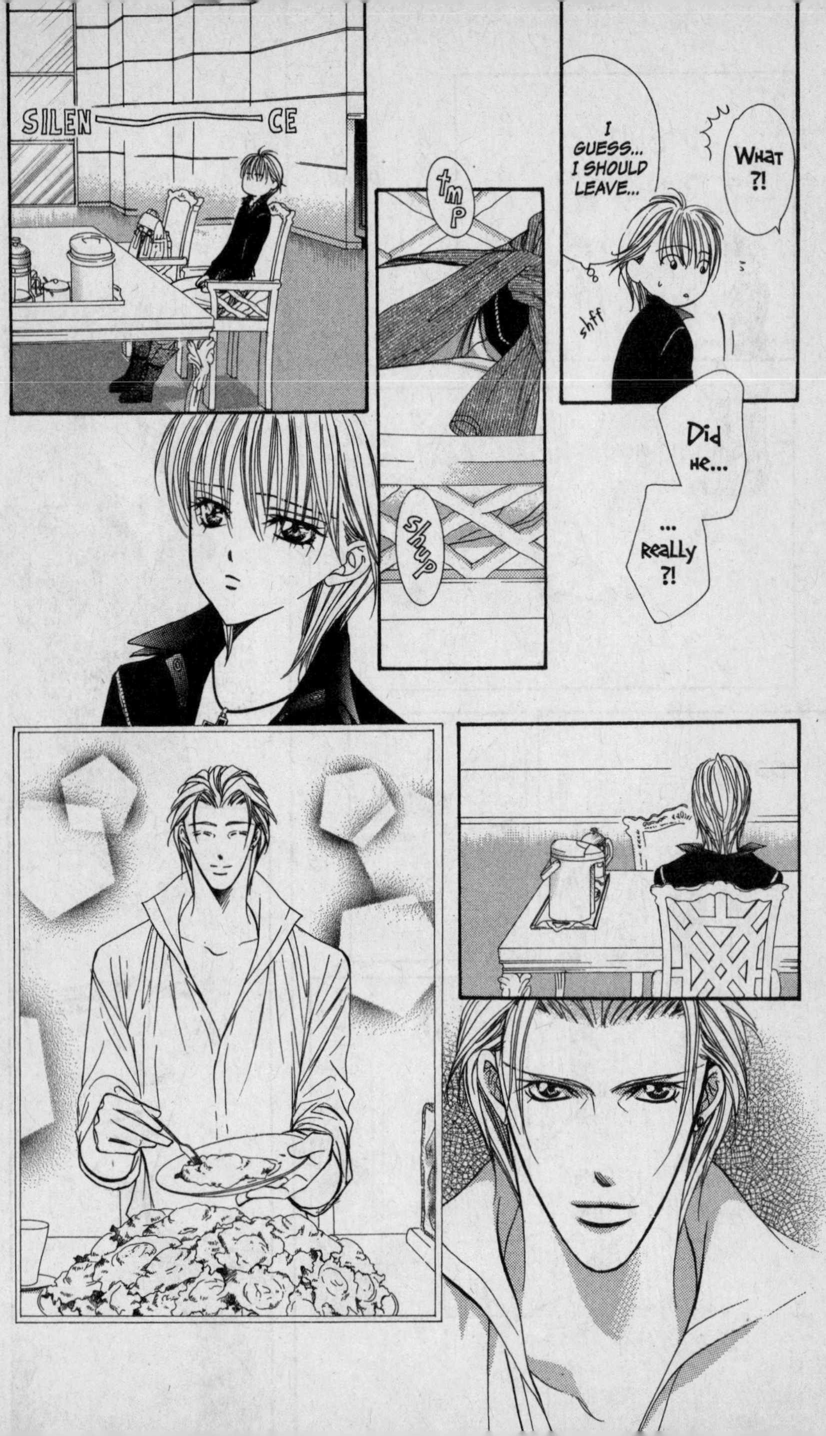
I GUESS... I SHOULD LEAVE...
WHAT ?!
shff
Did he... ...really ?!
tmp
shup
SILEN— CE

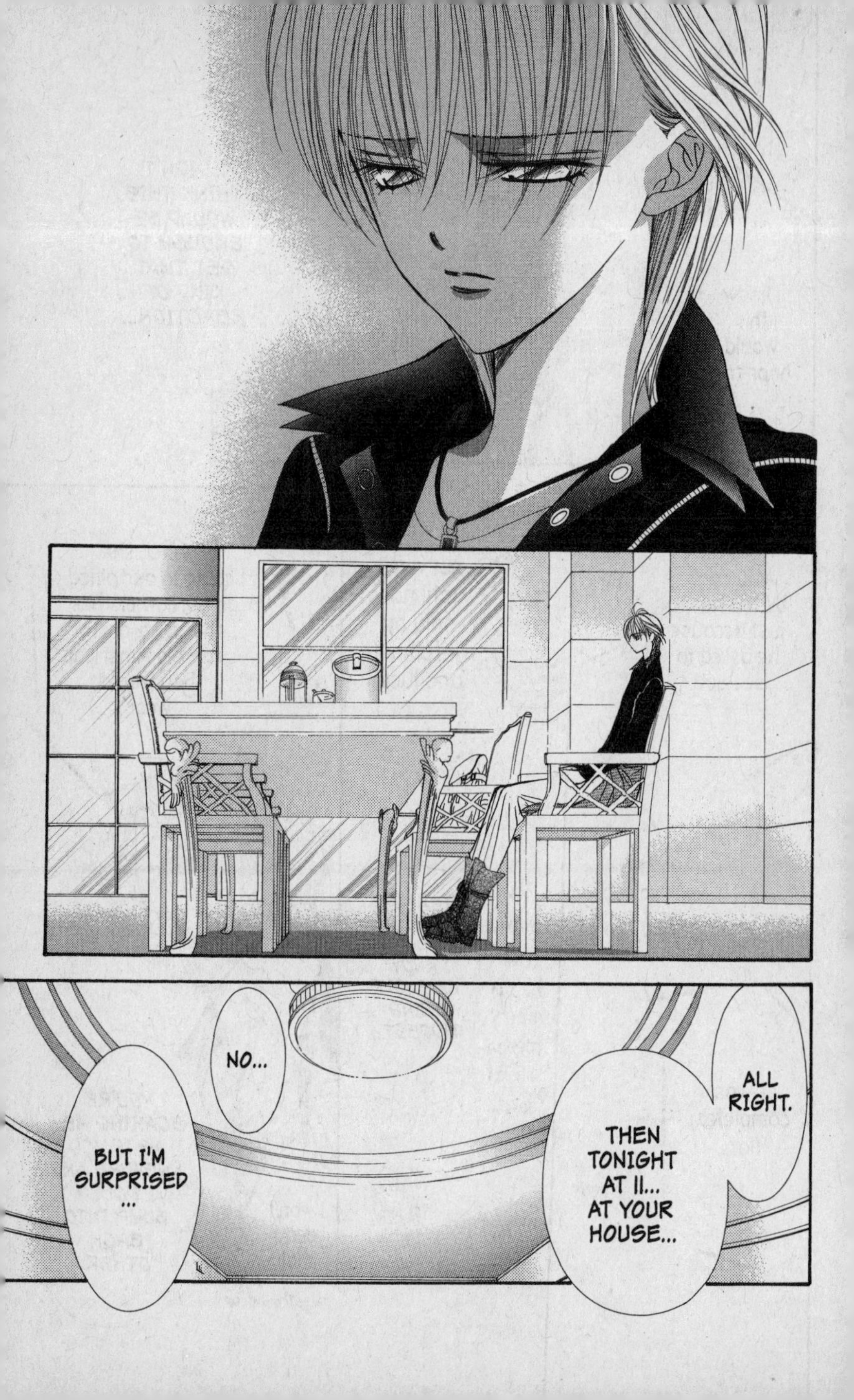
ALL RIGHT.
THEN TONIGHT AT 11... AT YOUR HOUSE...
NO...
BUT I'M SURPRISED ...

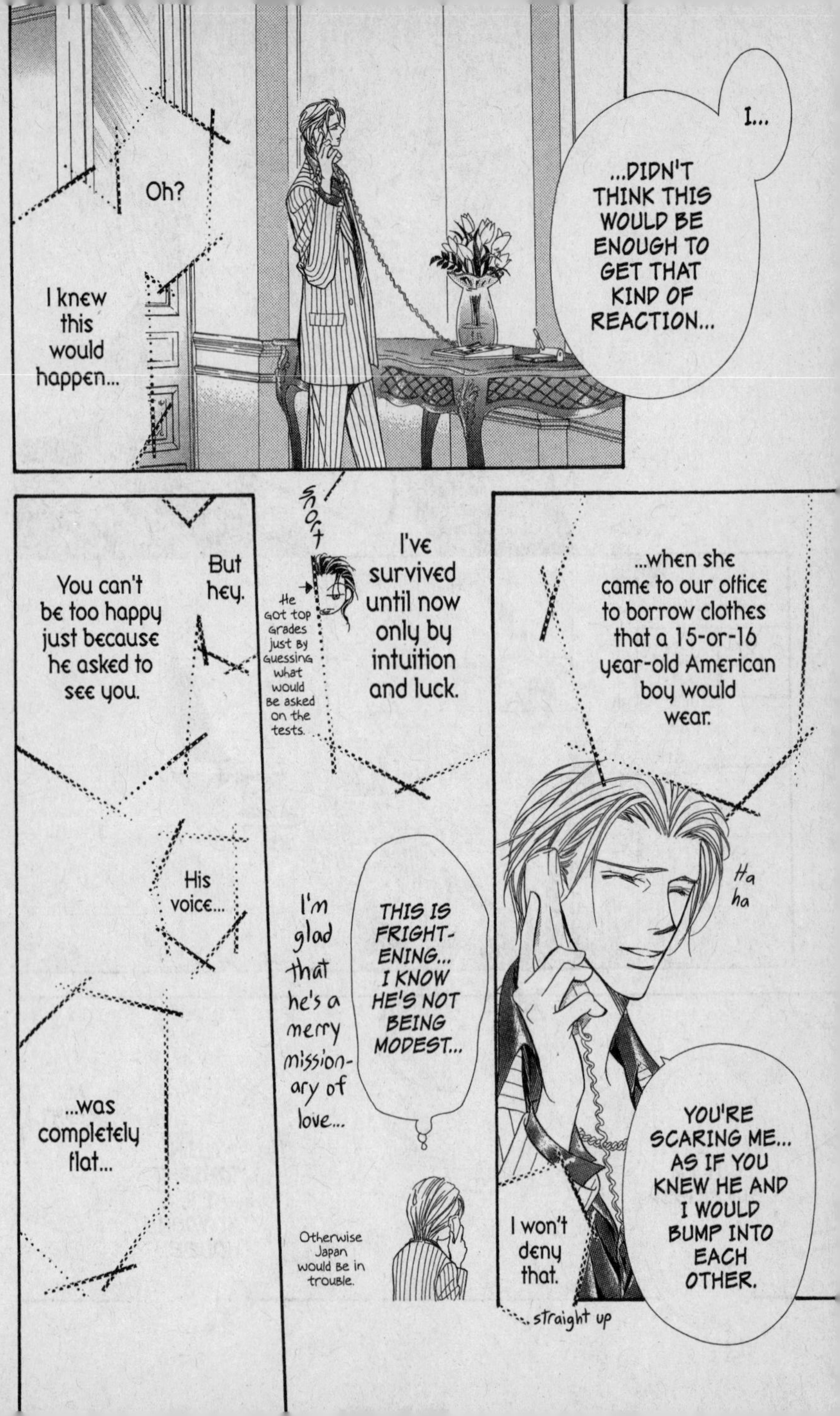
I...
...DIDN'T THINK THIS WOULD BE ENOUGH TO GET THAT KIND OF REACTION...
Oh?
I knew this would happen...
...when she came to our office to borrow clothes that a 15-or-16 year-old American boy would wear.
Ha ha
YOU'RE SCARING ME... AS IF YOU KNEW HE AND I WOULD BUMP INTO EACH OTHER.
I won't deny that.
straight up
I've survived until now only by intuition and luck.
snort
He got top grades just by guessing what would be asked on the tests.
THIS IS FRIGHTENING... I KNOW HE'S NOT BEING MODEST...
I'm glad that he's a merry mission-ary of love...
Otherwise Japan would be in trouble.
But hey.
You can't be too happy just because he asked to see you.
His voice...
...was completely flat...

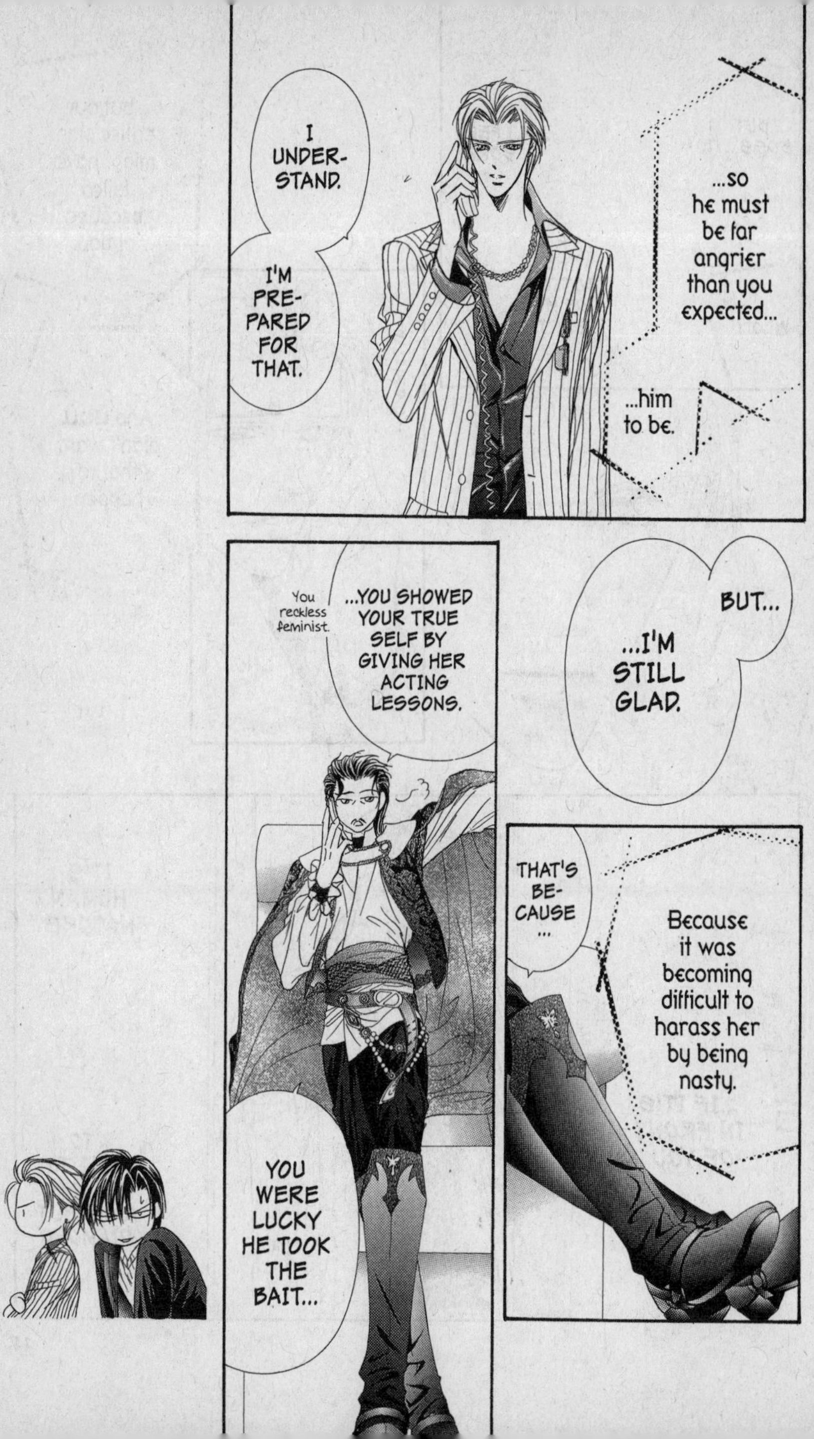
...so he must be far angrier than you expected...
...him to be.
I UNDER-STAND.
I'M PRE-PARED FOR THAT.
BUT...
...I'M STILL GLAD.
THAT'S BE-CAUSE...
Because it was becoming difficult to harass her by being nasty.
...YOU SHOWED YOUR TRUE SELF BY GIVING HER ACTING LESSONS.
You reckless feminist.
YOU WERE LUCKY HE TOOK THE BAIT...

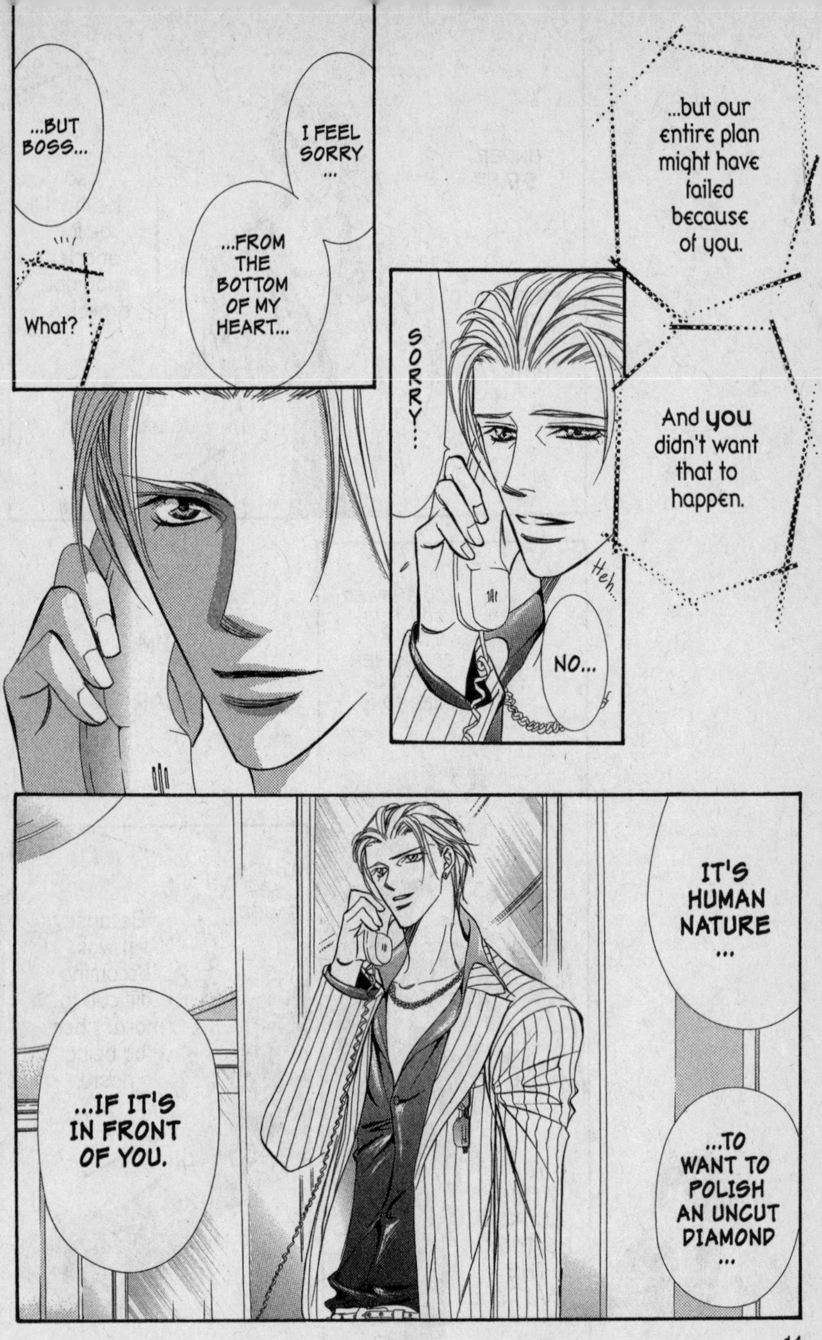

...but our entire plan might have failed because of you.
I FEEL SORRY...
...FROM THE BOTTOM OF MY HEART...
...BUT BOSS...
What?
And you didn't want that to happen.
SORRY...
Heh...
NO...
IT'S HUMAN NATURE...
...TO WANT TO POLISH AN UNCUT DIAMOND...
...IF IT'S IN FRONT OF YOU.

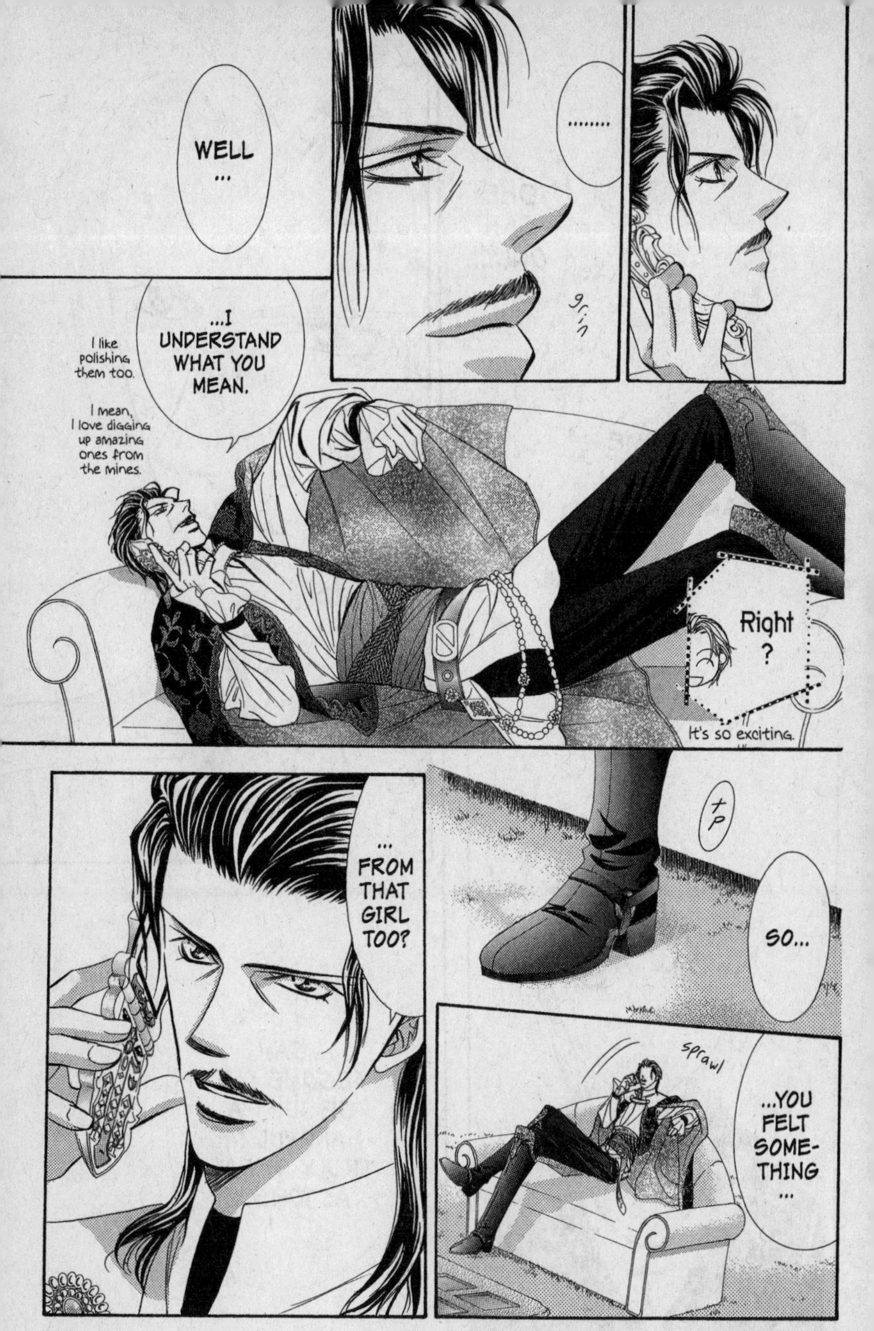
....
grin
WELL ...
...I UNDERSTAND WHAT YOU MEAN.
I like polishing them too.
I mean, I love digging up amazing ones from the mines.
Right?
It's so exciting.
tp
SO...
sprawl
...YOU FELT SOMETHING ...
... FROM THAT GIRL TOO?

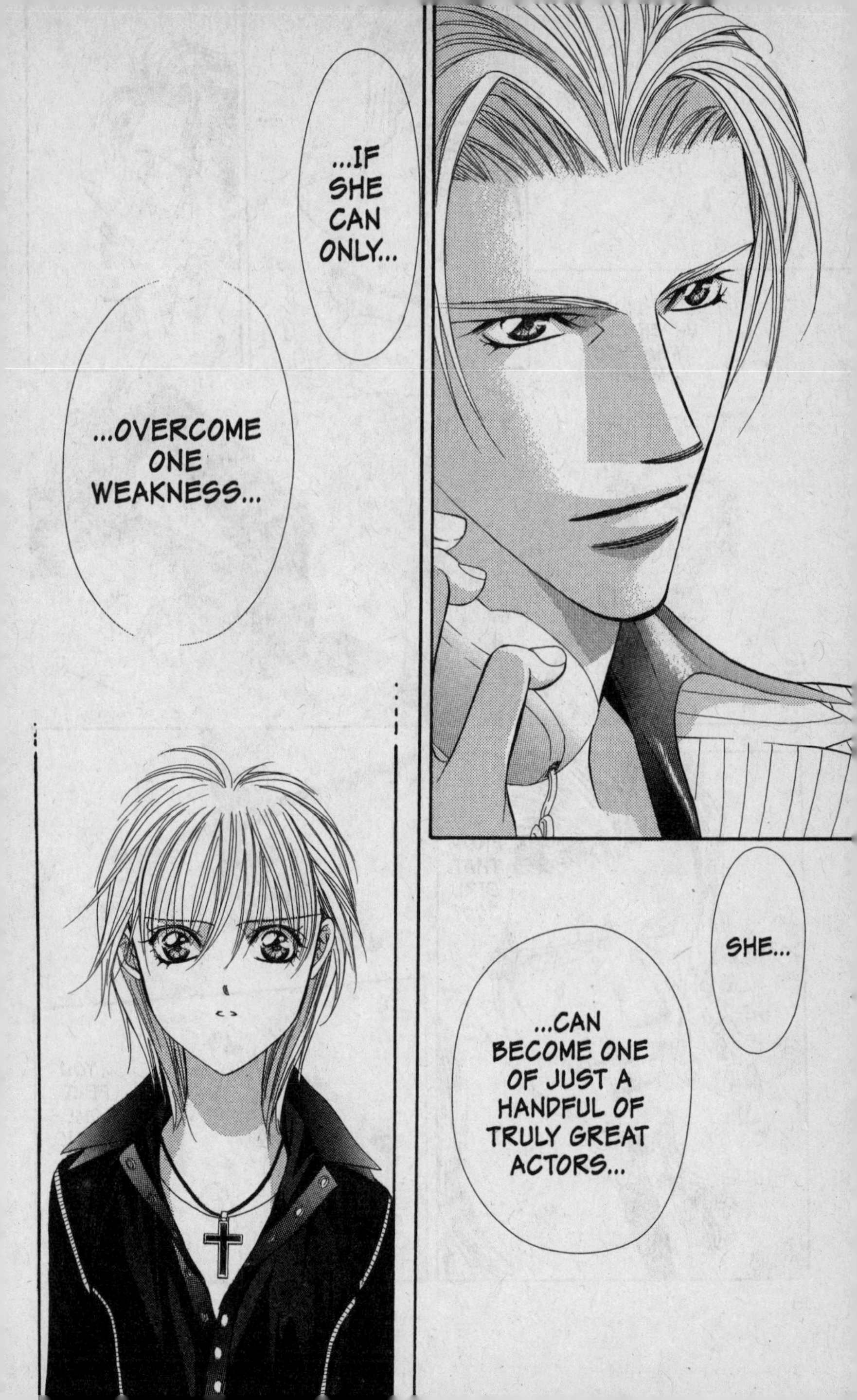
...IF SHE CAN ONLY...
...OVERCOME ONE WEAKNESS...
SHE...
...CAN BECOME ONE OF JUST A HANDFUL OF TRULY GREAT ACTORS...

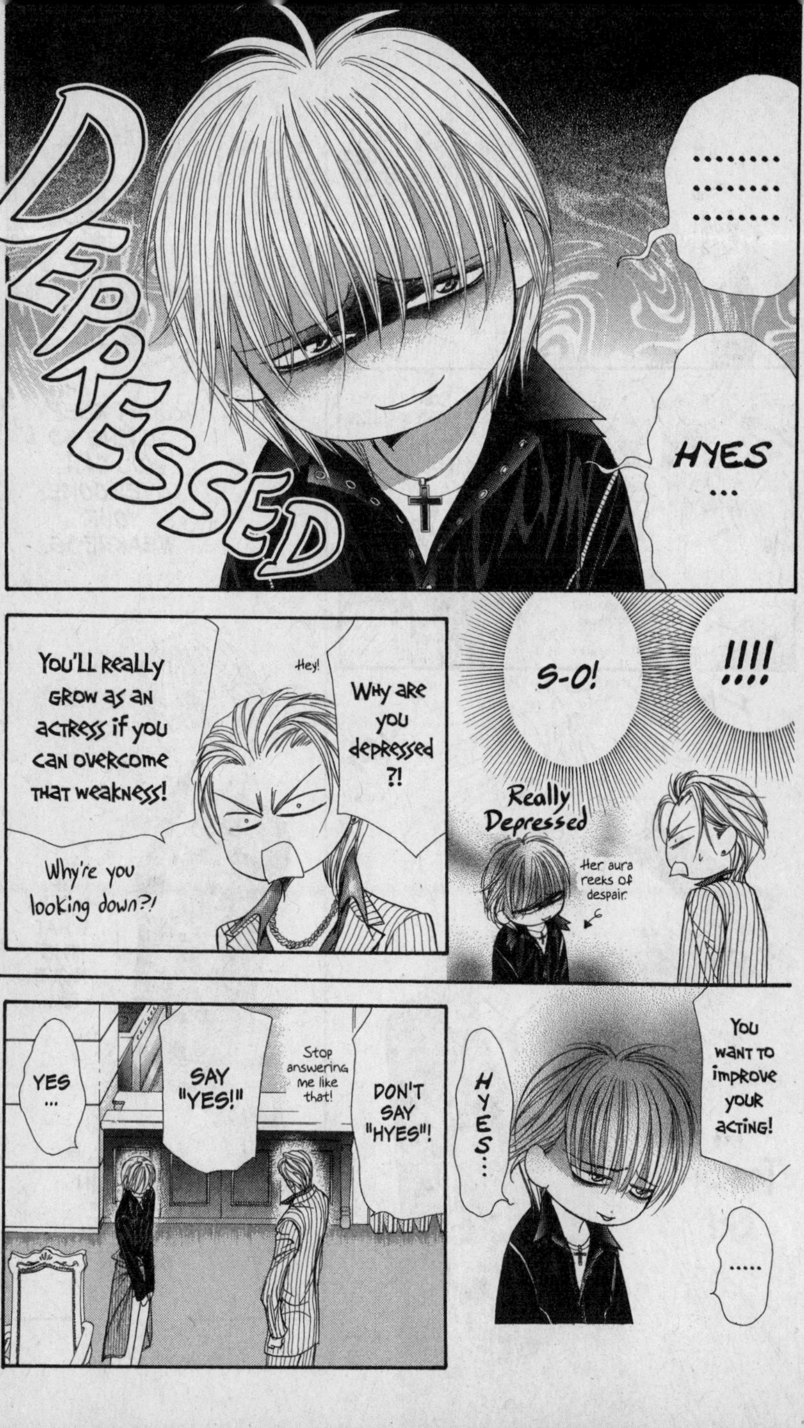
....
HYES ...
DEPRESSED
!!!!
S-O!
Really Depressed
Her aura reeks of despair.
Why are you depressed?!
Hey!
You'll really grow as an actress if you can overcome that weakness!
Why're you looking down?!
You want to improve your acting!
HYES...
.....
DON'T SAY "HYES"!
Stop answering me like that!
SAY "YES!"
YES ...

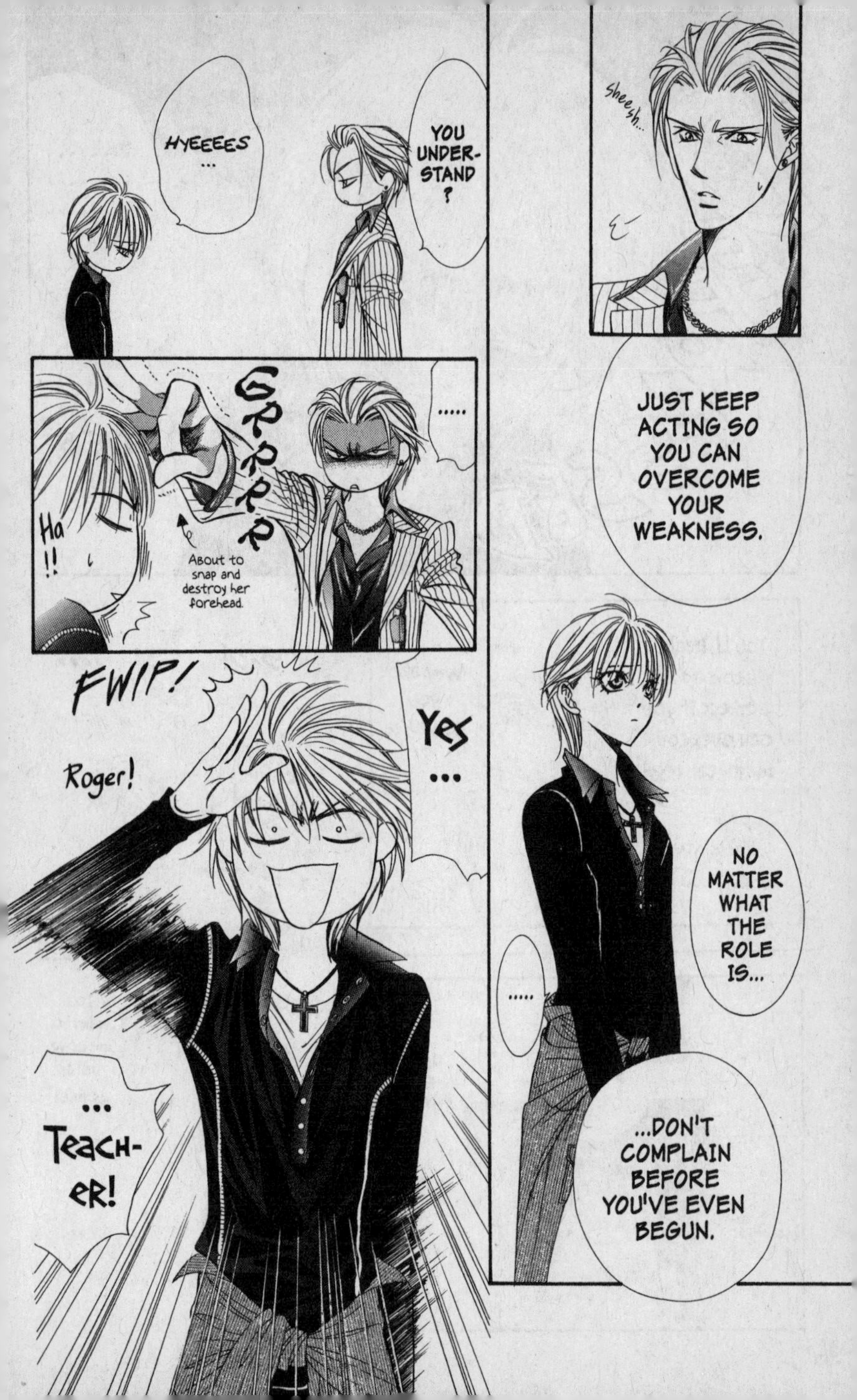
Sheesh...
JUST KEEP ACTING SO YOU CAN OVERCOME YOUR WEAKNESS.
NO MATTER WHAT THE ROLE IS...
.....
...DON'T COMPLAIN BEFORE YOU'VE EVEN BEGUN.
YOU UNDERSTAND?
HYEEEES...
.....
GRRRR
About to snap and destroy her forehead.
Ha!!
Yes...
Roger!
FWIP!
...Teacher!

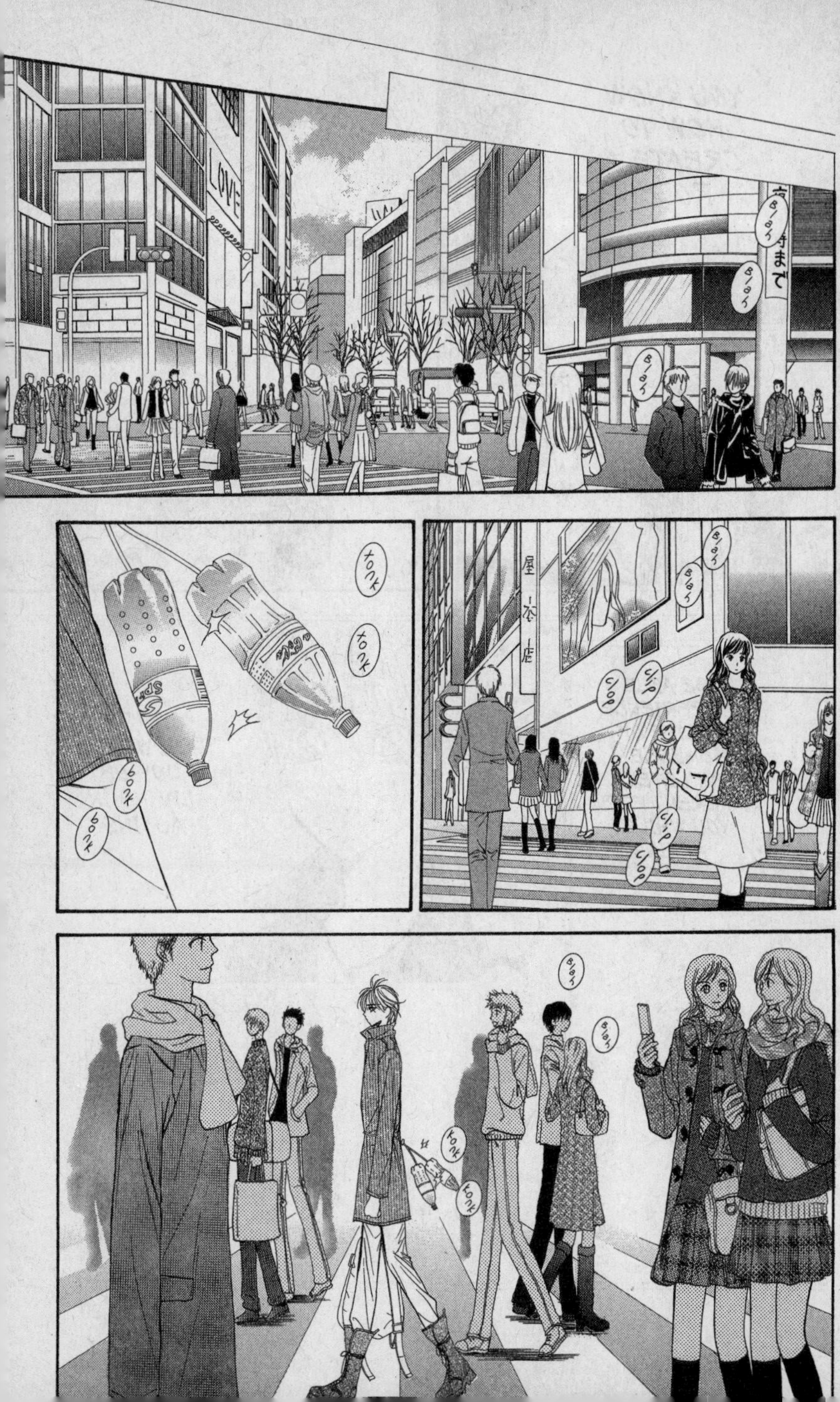
Blah
Blah
Blah
LOVE
Blah
Blah
屋本店
clip
clop
clip
clop
konk
konk
bonk
bonk
Blah
Blah
konk
konk

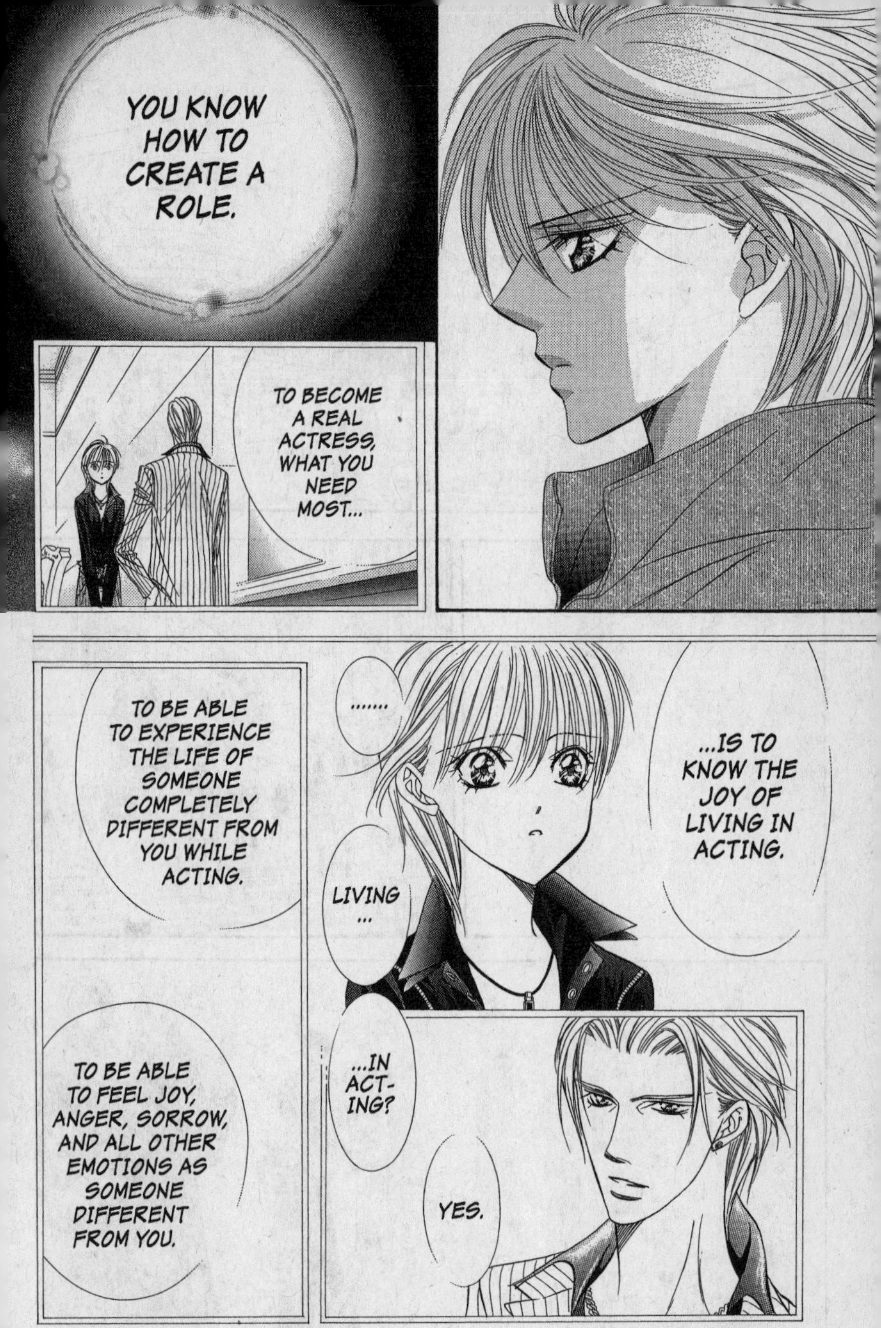
YOU KNOW HOW TO CREATE A ROLE.
TO BECOME A REAL ACTRESS, WHAT YOU NEED MOST...
...IS TO KNOW THE JOY OF LIVING IN ACTING.
....
LIVING ...
...IN ACT-ING?
YES.
TO BE ABLE TO EXPERIENCE THE LIFE OF SOMEONE COMPLETELY DIFFERENT FROM YOU WHILE ACTING.
TO BE ABLE TO FEEL JOY, ANGER, SORROW, AND ALL OTHER EMOTIONS AS SOMEONE DIFFERENT FROM YOU.

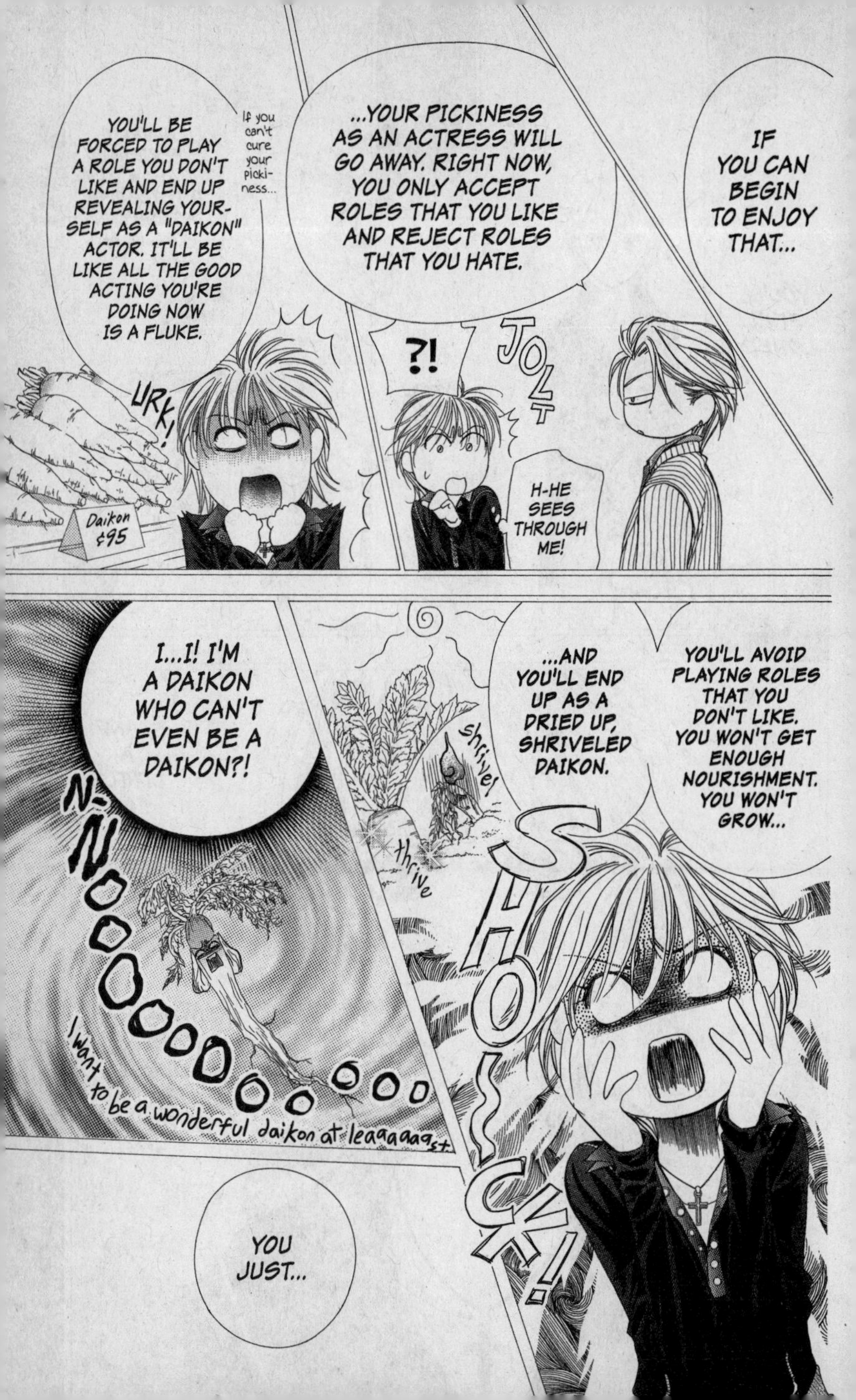
IF YOU CAN BEGIN TO ENJOY THAT...
...YOUR PICKINESS AS AN ACTRESS WILL GO AWAY. RIGHT NOW, YOU ONLY ACCEPT ROLES THAT YOU LIKE AND REJECT ROLES THAT YOU HATE.
?!
JOLT
H-HE SEES THROUGH ME!
If you can't cure your picki-ness...
YOU'LL BE FORCED TO PLAY A ROLE YOU DON'T LIKE AND END UP REVEALING YOURSELF AS A "DAIKON" ACTOR. IT'LL BE LIKE ALL THE GOOD ACTING YOU'RE DOING NOW IS A FLUKE.
URK!
Daikon ¢95
YOU'LL AVOID PLAYING ROLES THAT YOU DON'T LIKE. YOU WON'T GET ENOUGH NOURISHMENT. YOU WON'T GROW...
...AND YOU'LL END UP AS A DRIED UP, SHRIVELED DAIKON.
SHOCK!
shrivel
thrive
I...I! I'M A DAIKON WHO CAN'T EVEN BE A DAIKON?!
N-NOOOOOOOO...
I want to be a wonderful daikon at leaaaaaast.
YOU JUST...

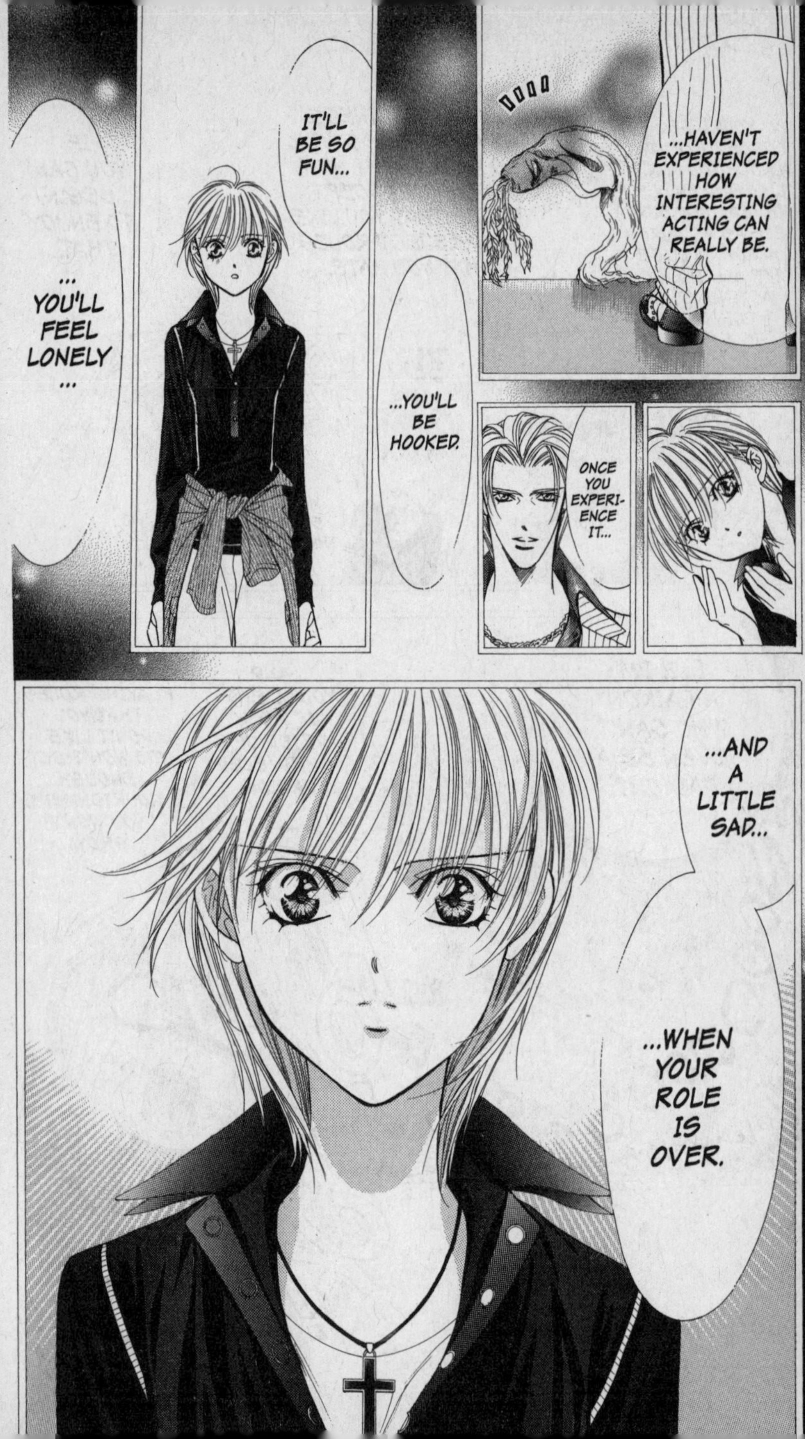
...HAVEN'T EXPERIENCED HOW INTERESTING ACTING CAN REALLY BE.
ONCE YOU EXPERIENCE IT...
...YOU'LL BE HOOKED.
IT'LL BE SO FUN...
...YOU'LL FEEL LONELY...
...AND A LITTLE SAD...
...WHEN YOUR ROLE IS OVER.

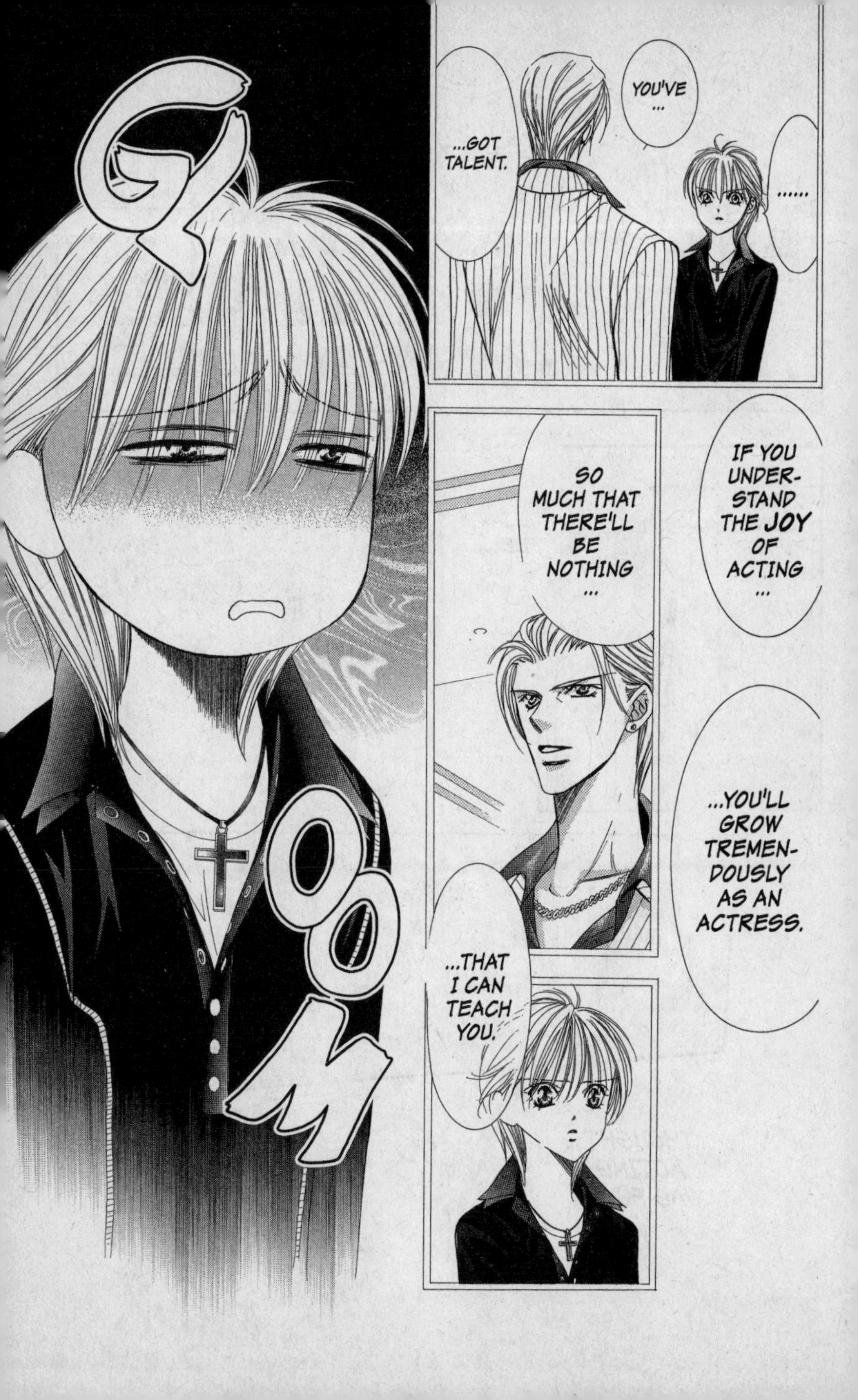

......
YOU'VE ...
...GOT TALENT.
IF YOU UNDER-STAND THE JOY OF ACTING ...
...YOU'LL GROW TREMEN-DOUSLY AS AN ACTRESS.
SO MUCH THAT THERE'LL BE NOTHING ...
...THAT I CAN TEACH YOU.
GLOOM

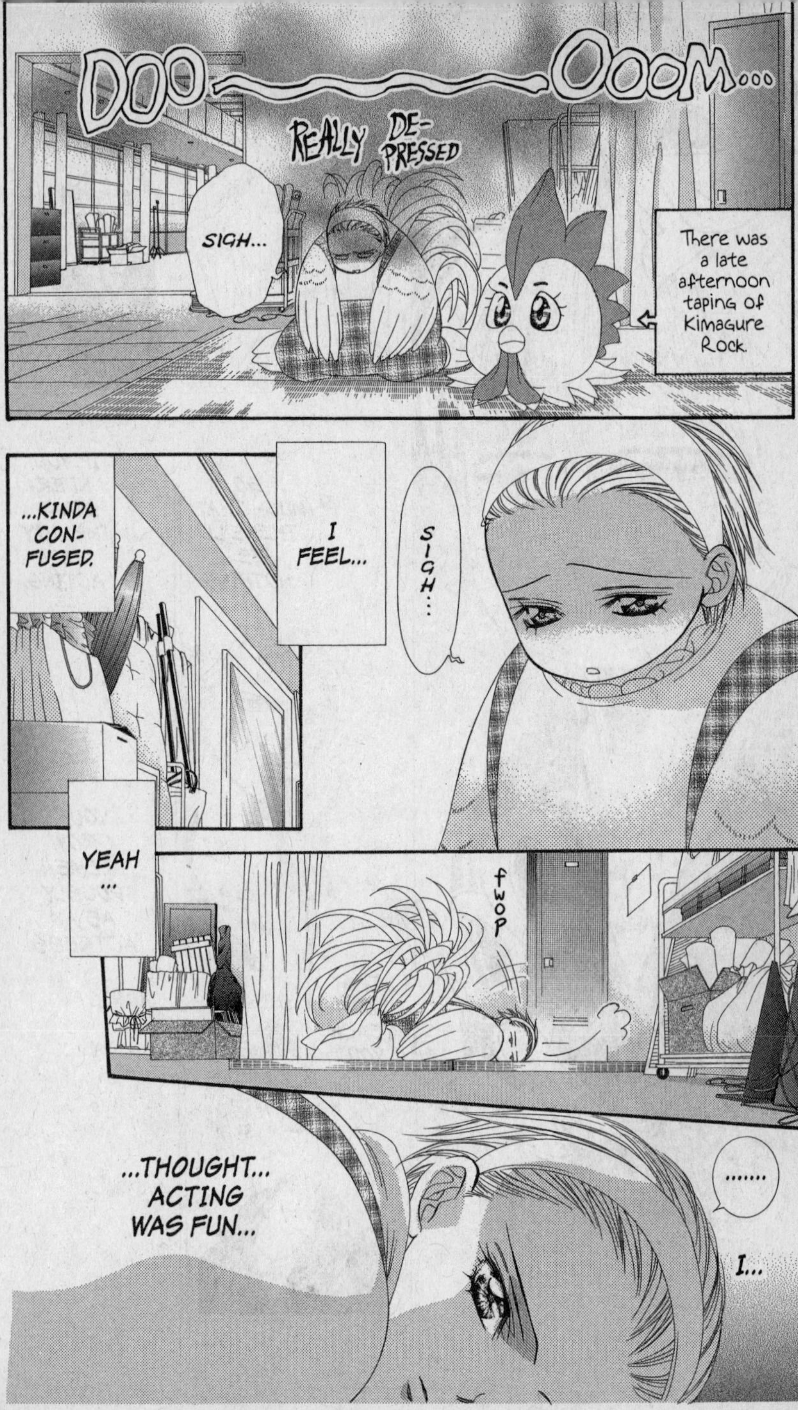

DOO——OOOM...
REALLY DE-PRESSED
There was a late afternoon taping of Kimagure Rock.
SIGH...
SIGH...
I FEEL...
...KINDA CONFUSED.
YEAH...
fwop
....
I...
...THOUGHT... ACTING WAS FUN...

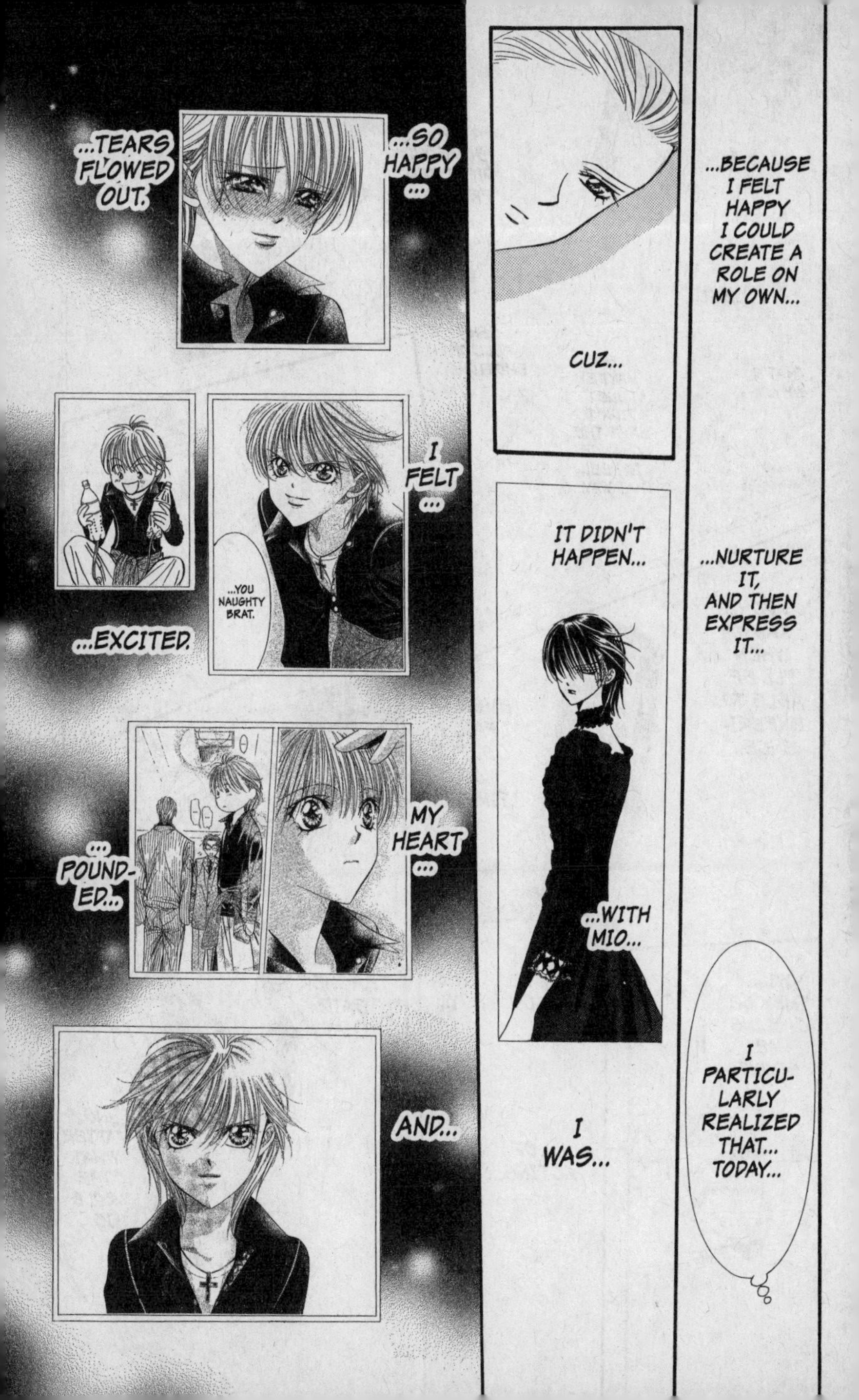
...BECAUSE I FELT HAPPY I COULD CREATE A ROLE ON MY OWN...
...NURTURE IT, AND THEN EXPRESS IT...
I PARTICULARLY REALIZED THAT... TODAY...
CUZ...
IT DIDN'T HAPPEN...
...WITH MIO...
I WAS...
...SO HAPPY...
...TEARS FLOWED OUT.
I FELT...
...YOU NAUGHTY BRAT.
...EXCITED.
MY HEART...
...POUNDED...
AND...

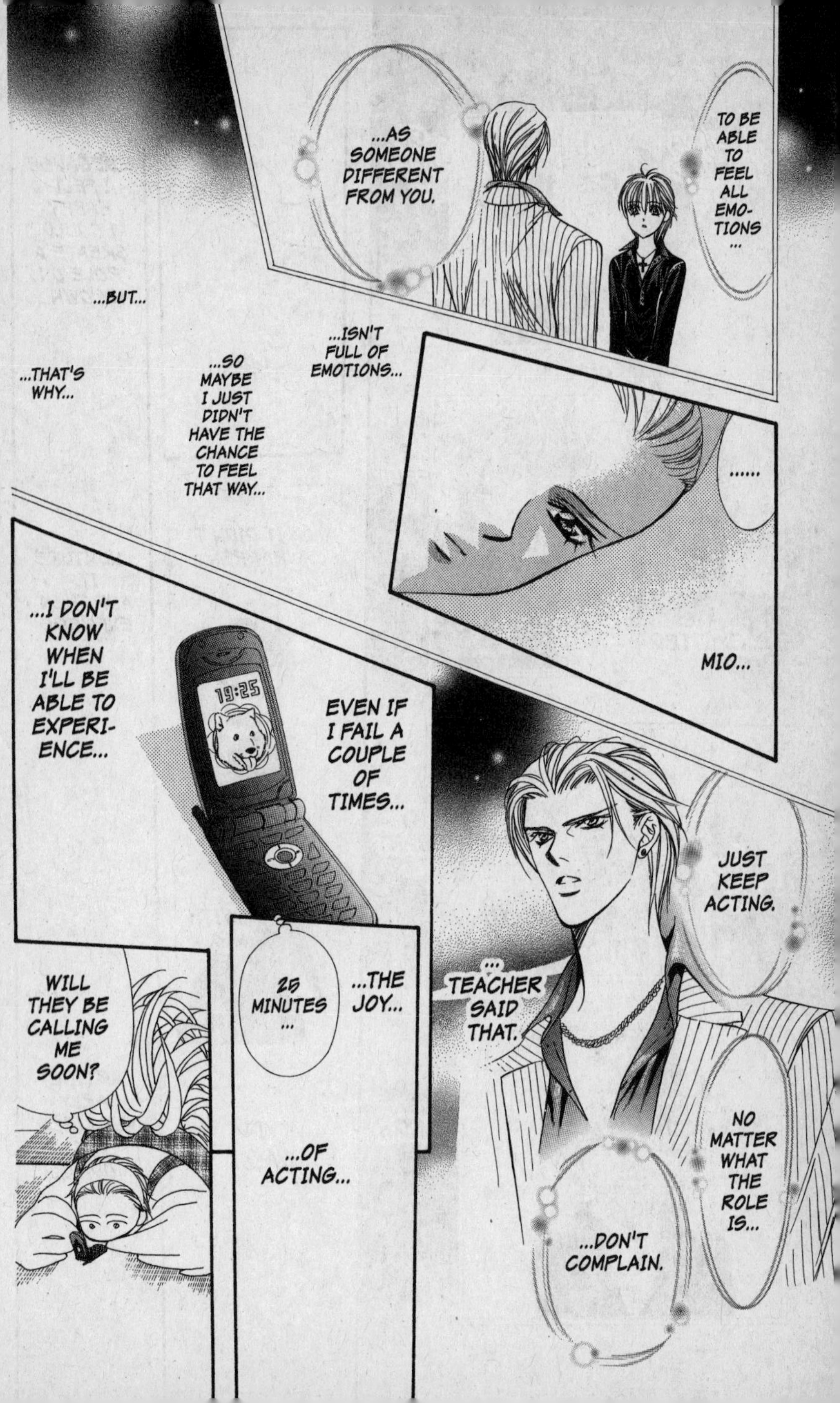
TO BE ABLE TO FEEL ALL EMOTIONS...
...AS SOMEONE DIFFERENT FROM YOU.
...BUT...
......
...ISN'T FULL OF EMOTIONS...
...SO MAYBE I JUST DIDN'T HAVE THE CHANCE TO FEEL THAT WAY...
...THAT'S WHY...
MIO...
JUST KEEP ACTING.
NO MATTER WHAT THE ROLE IS...
...DON'T COMPLAIN.
...TEACHER SAID THAT.
EVEN IF I FAIL A COUPLE OF TIMES...
...I DON'T KNOW WHEN I'LL BE ABLE TO EXPERIENCE...
19:25
...THE JOY...
...OF ACTING...
25 MINUTES ...
WILL THEY BE CALLING ME SOON?

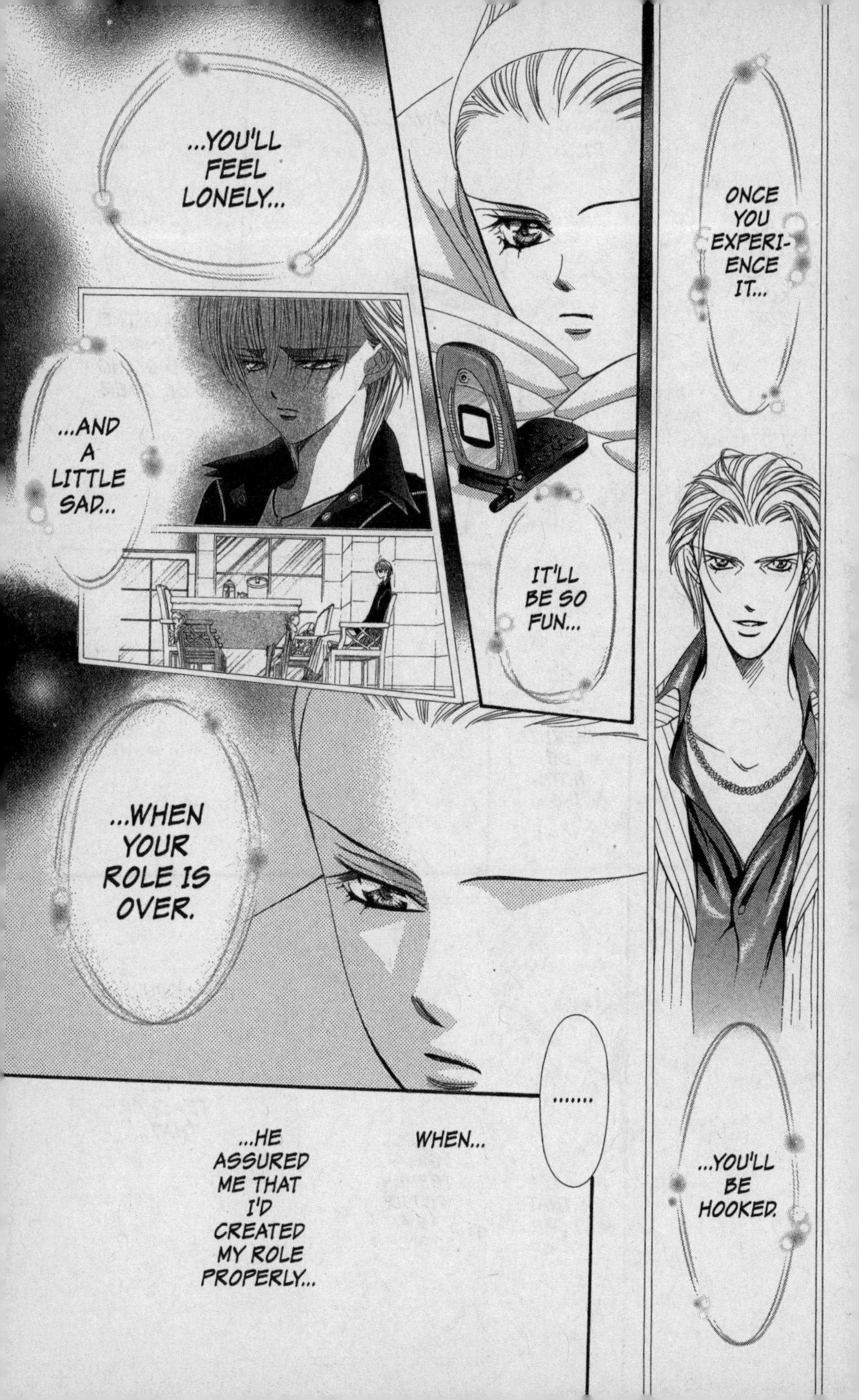

ONCE YOU EXPERIENCE IT...
...YOU'LL BE HOOKED.
IT'LL BE SO FUN...
...YOU'LL FEEL LONELY...
...AND A LITTLE SAD...
...WHEN YOUR ROLE IS OVER.
......
WHEN...
...HE ASSURED ME THAT I'D CREATED MY ROLE PROPERLY...

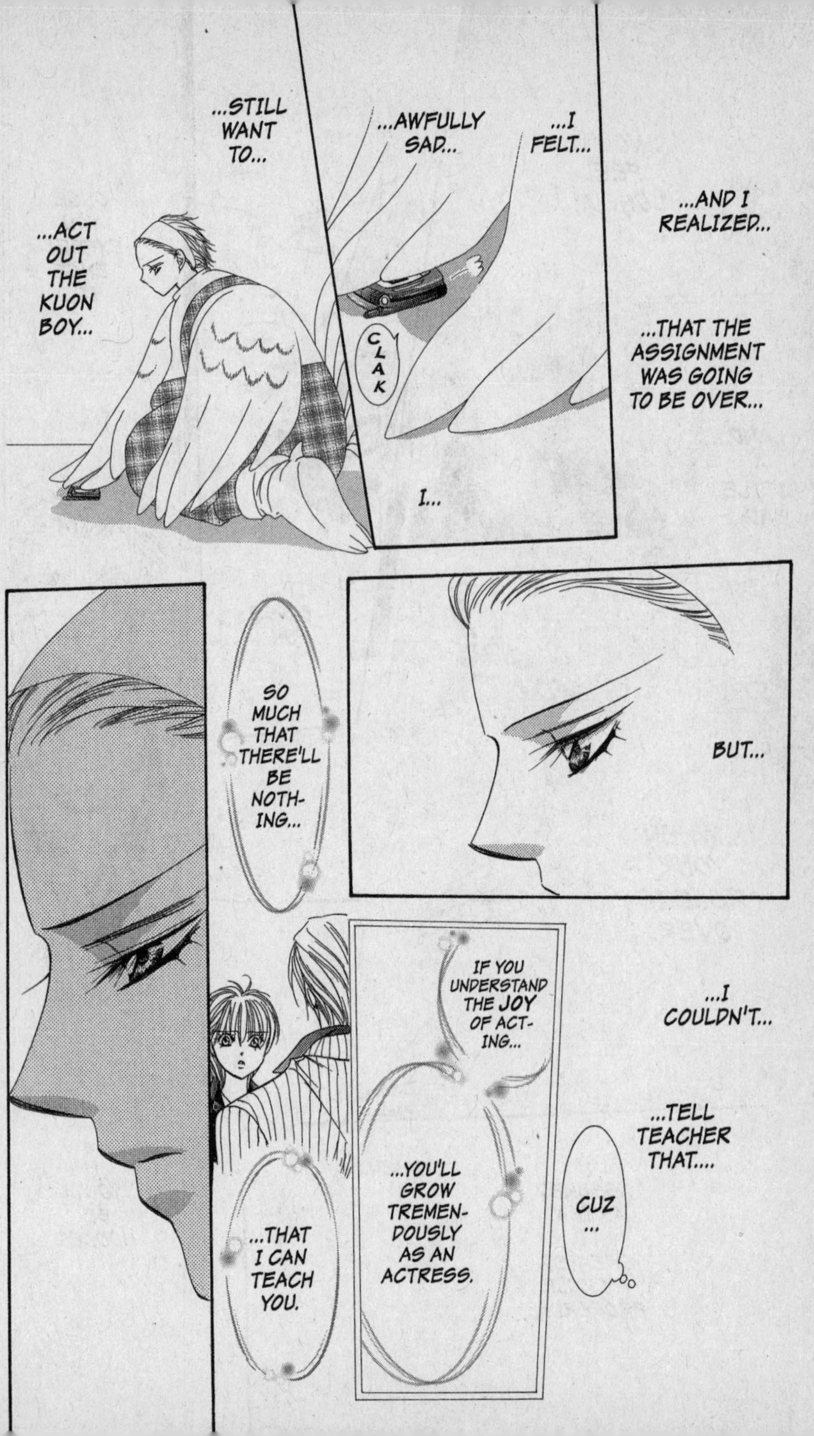
...AND I REALIZED...
...THAT THE ASSIGNMENT WAS GOING TO BE OVER...
I...
...I FELT...
...AWFULLY SAD...
CLAK
...STILL WANT TO...
...ACT OUT THE KUON BOY...
BUT...
...I COULDN'T...
...TELL TEACHER THAT....
CUZ ...
IF YOU UNDERSTAND THE JOY OF ACT-ING...
...YOU'LL GROW TREMEN-DOUSLY AS AN ACTRESS.
SO MUCH THAT THERE'LL BE NOTH-ING...
...THAT I CAN TEACH YOU.

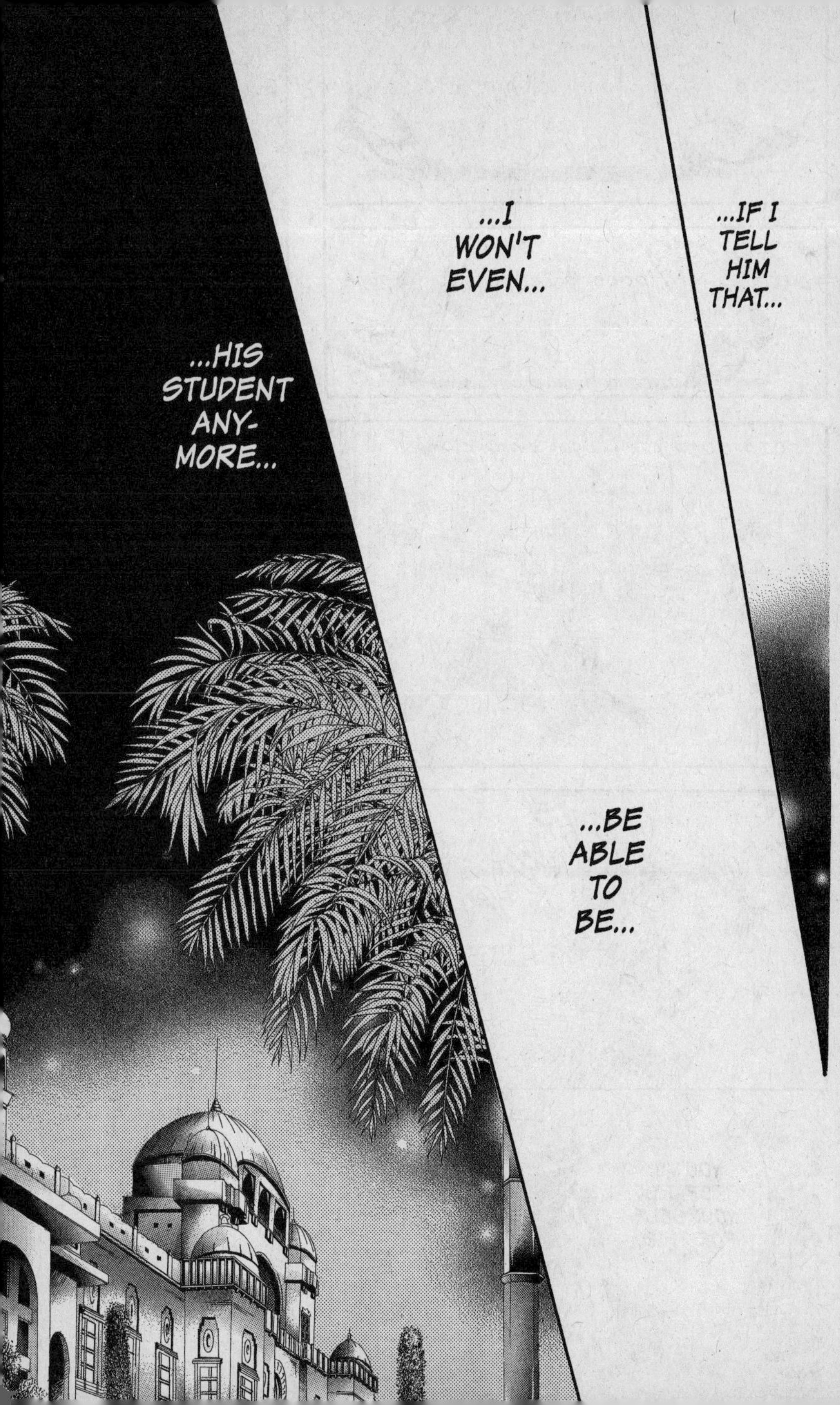
...IF I TELL HIM THAT...
...I WON'T EVEN...
...BE ABLE TO BE...
...HIS STUDENT ANY-MORE...

clomp   clomp clomp clo   om

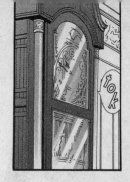
tok

pace   pace pace pace   pace

clomp clomp clomp clomp clomp clomp

...

pace pace pace   pace pace

KOO.

HURK!

FWAP

← Sedative

FWUU

YOU'RE IRRITAT-ING ME.

YOU'VE PREPARED YOURSELF FOR THIS.

JUST COOL IT.

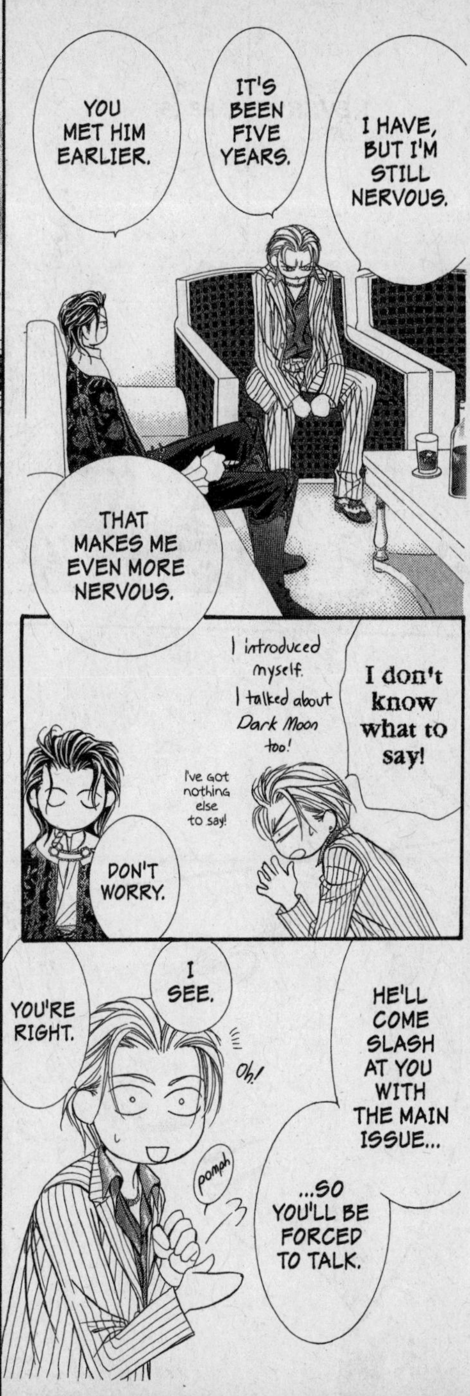
I HAVE, BUT I'M STILL NERVOUS.
IT'S BEEN FIVE YEARS.
YOU MET HIM EARLIER.
THAT MAKES ME EVEN MORE NERVOUS.
I don't know what to say!
I introduced myself. I talked about Dark Moon too!
I've got nothing else to say!
DON'T WORRY.
HE'LL COME SLASH AT YOU WITH THE MAIN ISSUE...
...SO YOU'LL BE FORCED TO TALK.
I SEE.
Oh!
pomph
YOU'RE RIGHT.

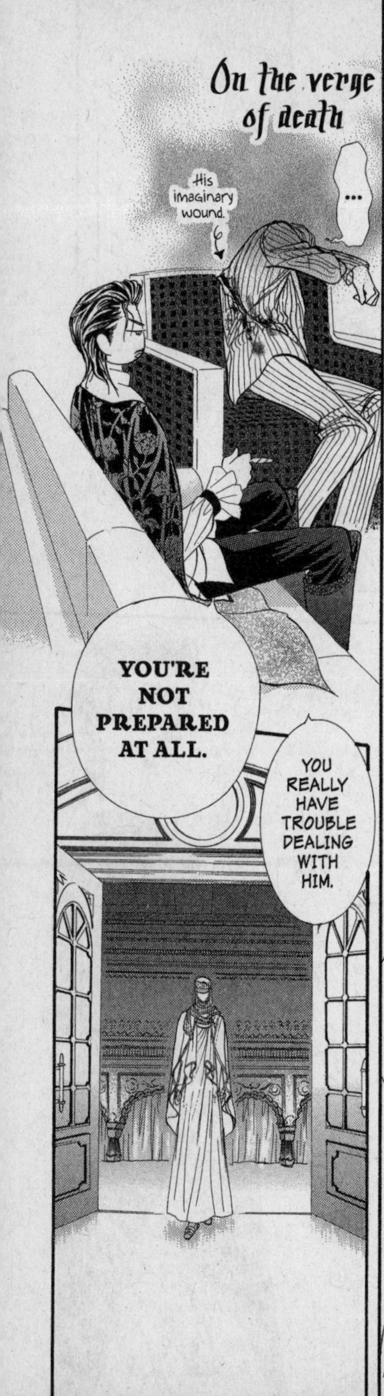
On the verge of death
...
His imaginary wound.
YOU'RE NOT PREPARED AT ALL.
YOU REALLY HAVE TROUBLE DEALING WITH HIM.

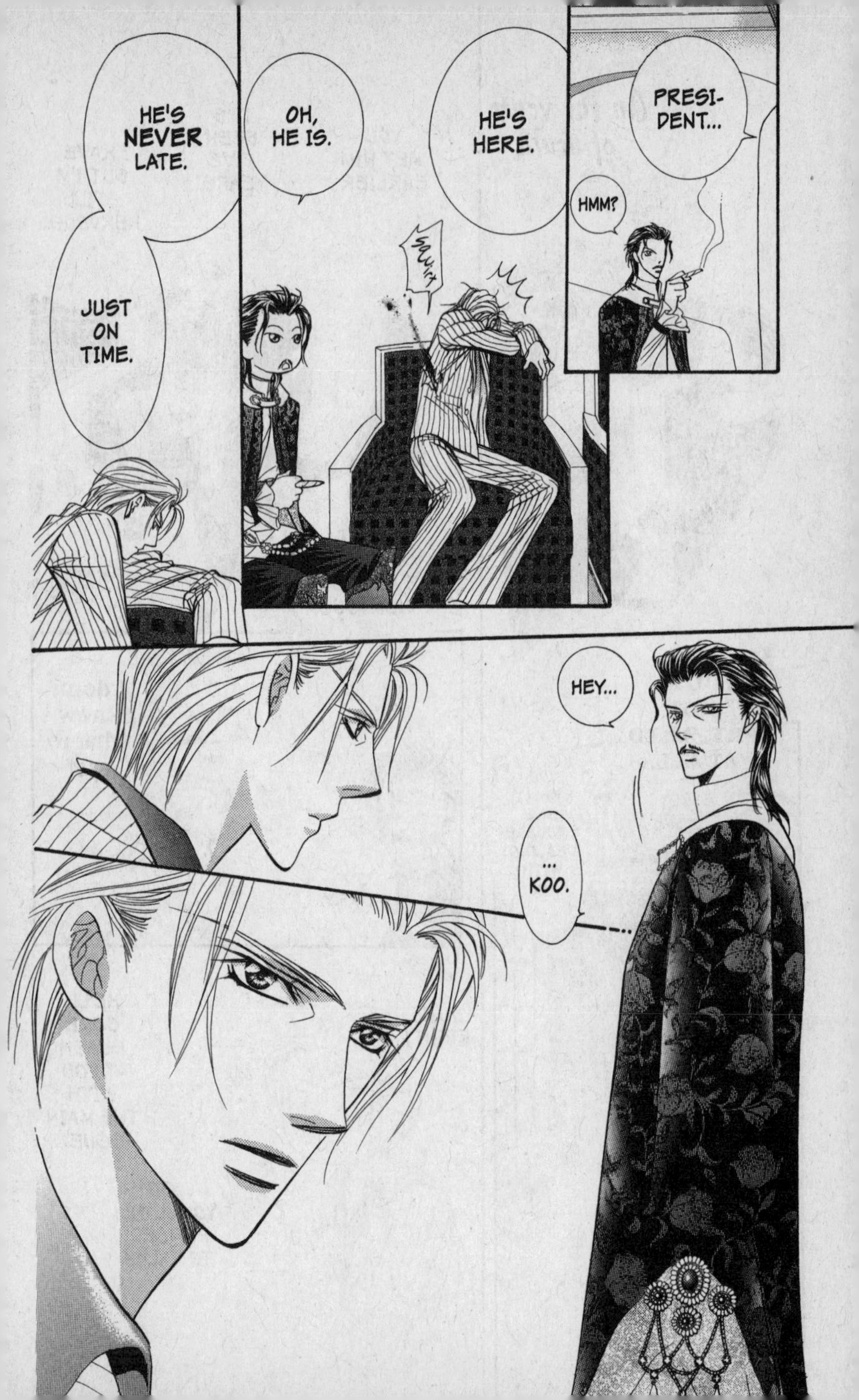
PRESI-DENT...
HMM?
HE'S HERE.
SQUIRT
OH, HE IS.
HE'S NEVER LATE.
JUST ON TIME.
HEY...
...KOO.

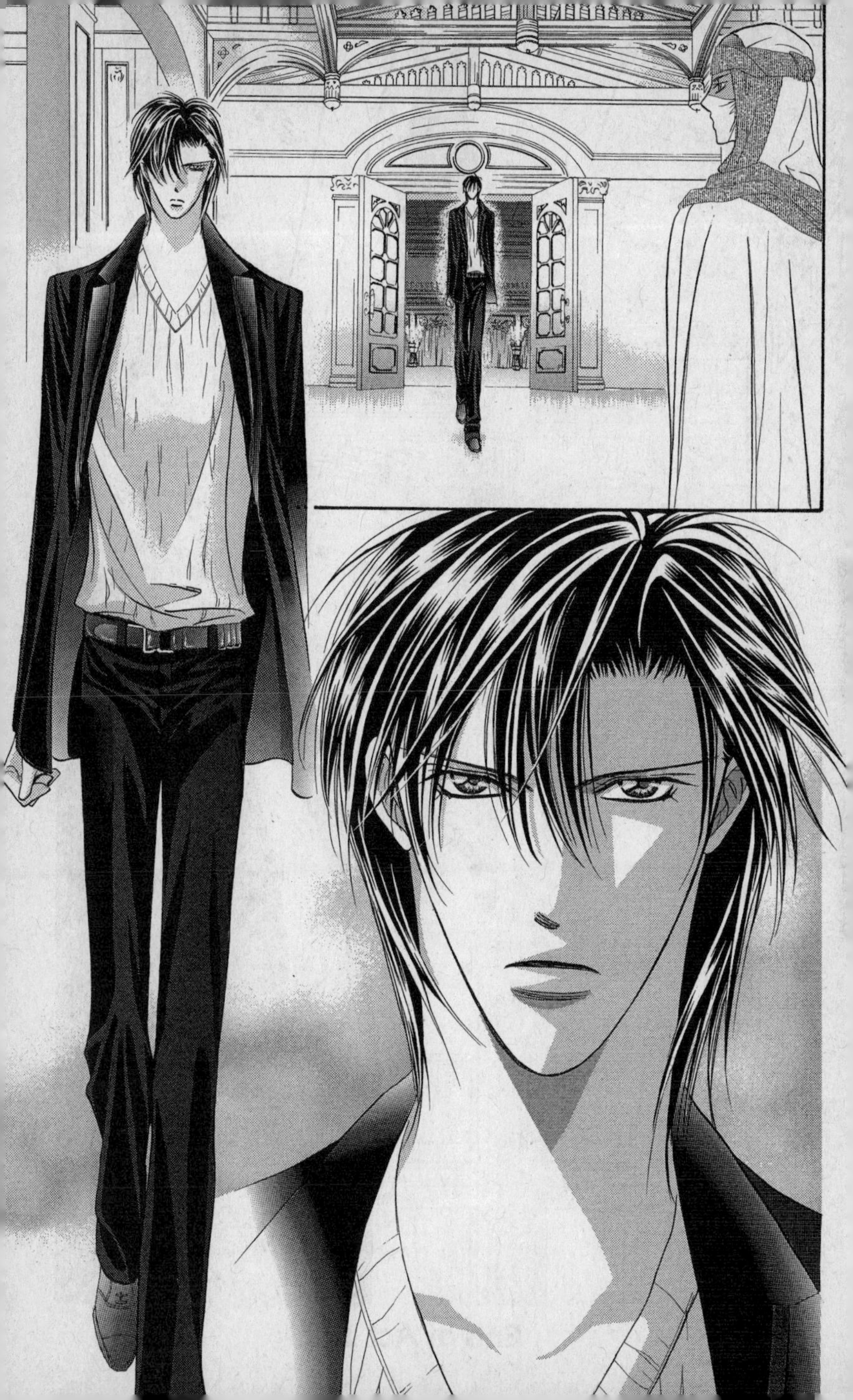

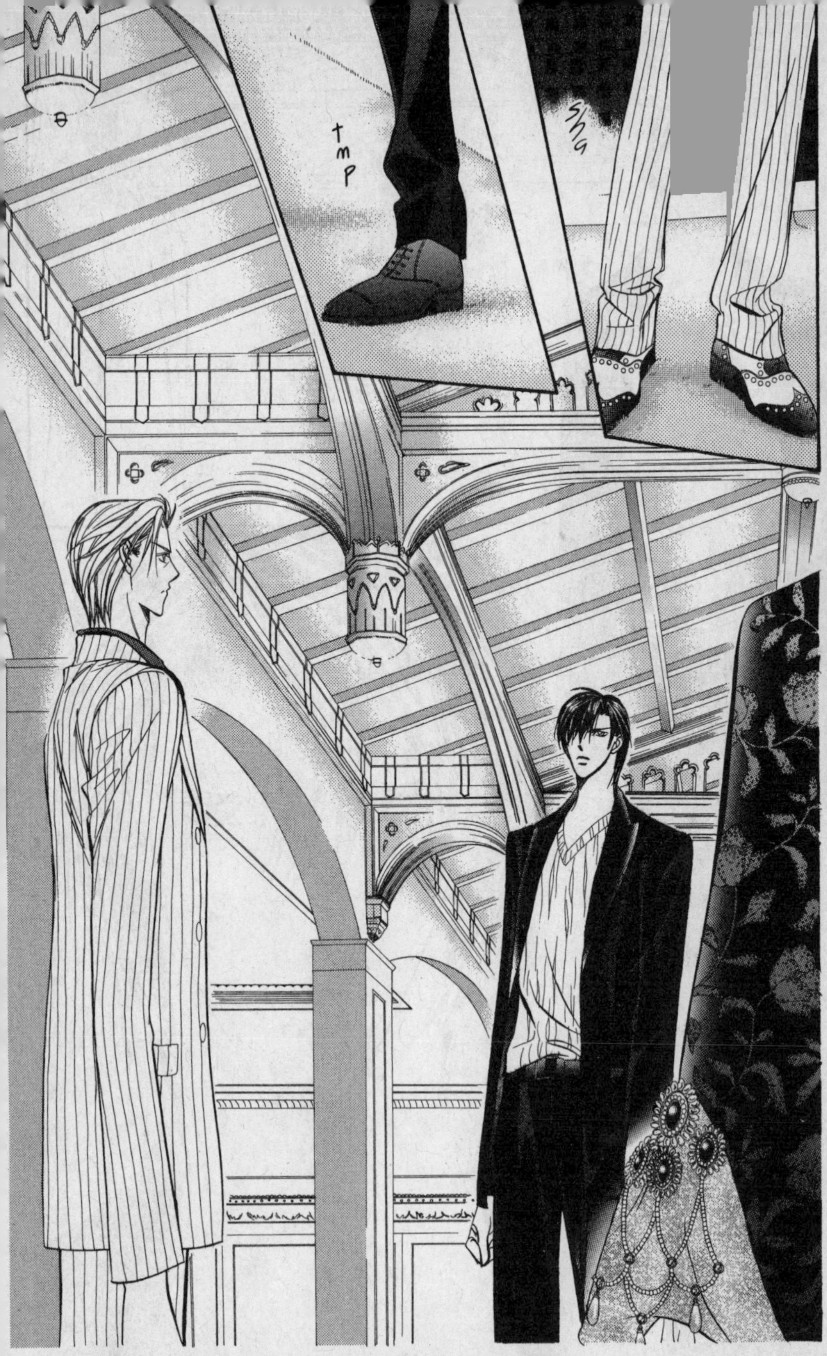
sng
tmp

End of Act 109

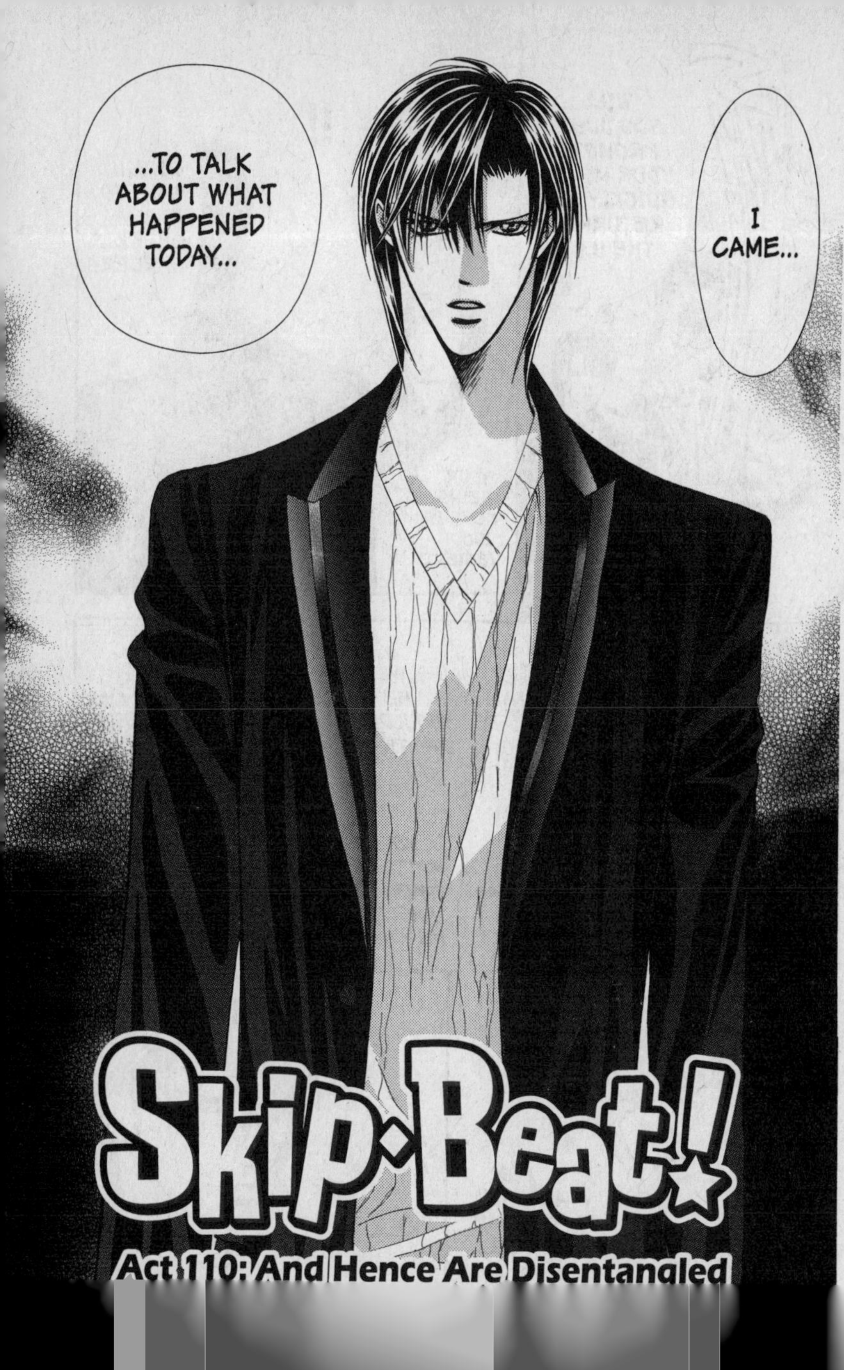
I CAME...
...TO TALK ABOUT WHAT HAPPENED TODAY...
Skip·Beat!
Act 110: And Hence Are Disentangled

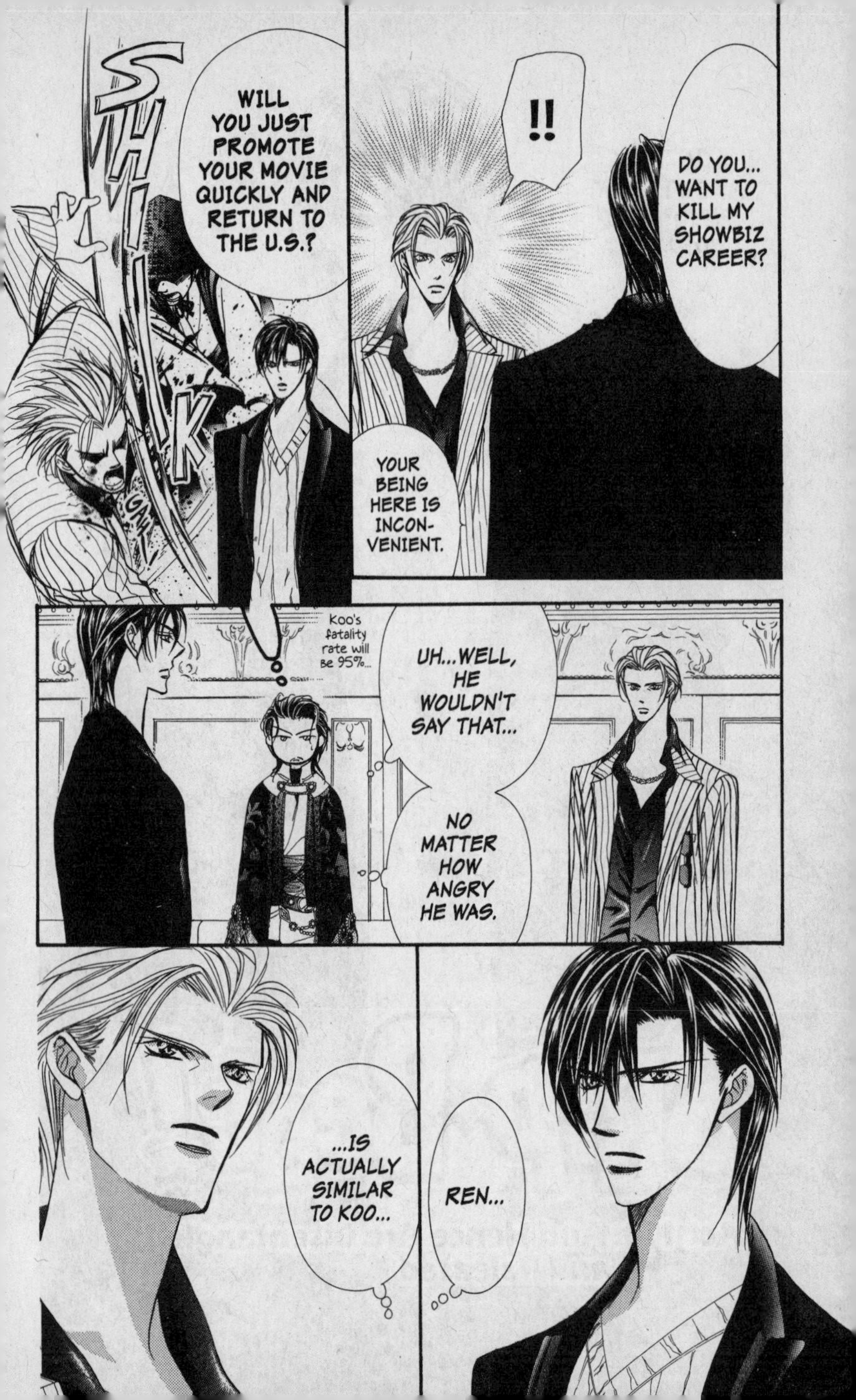
DO YOU... WANT TO KILL MY SHOWBIZ CAREER?
!!
YOUR BEING HERE IS INCON-VENIENT.
WILL YOU JUST PROMOTE YOUR MOVIE QUICKLY AND RETURN TO THE U.S.?
UH...WELL, HE WOULDN'T SAY THAT...
NO MATTER HOW ANGRY HE WAS.
Koo's fatality rate will be 95%...
REN...
...IS ACTUALLY SIMILAR TO KOO...

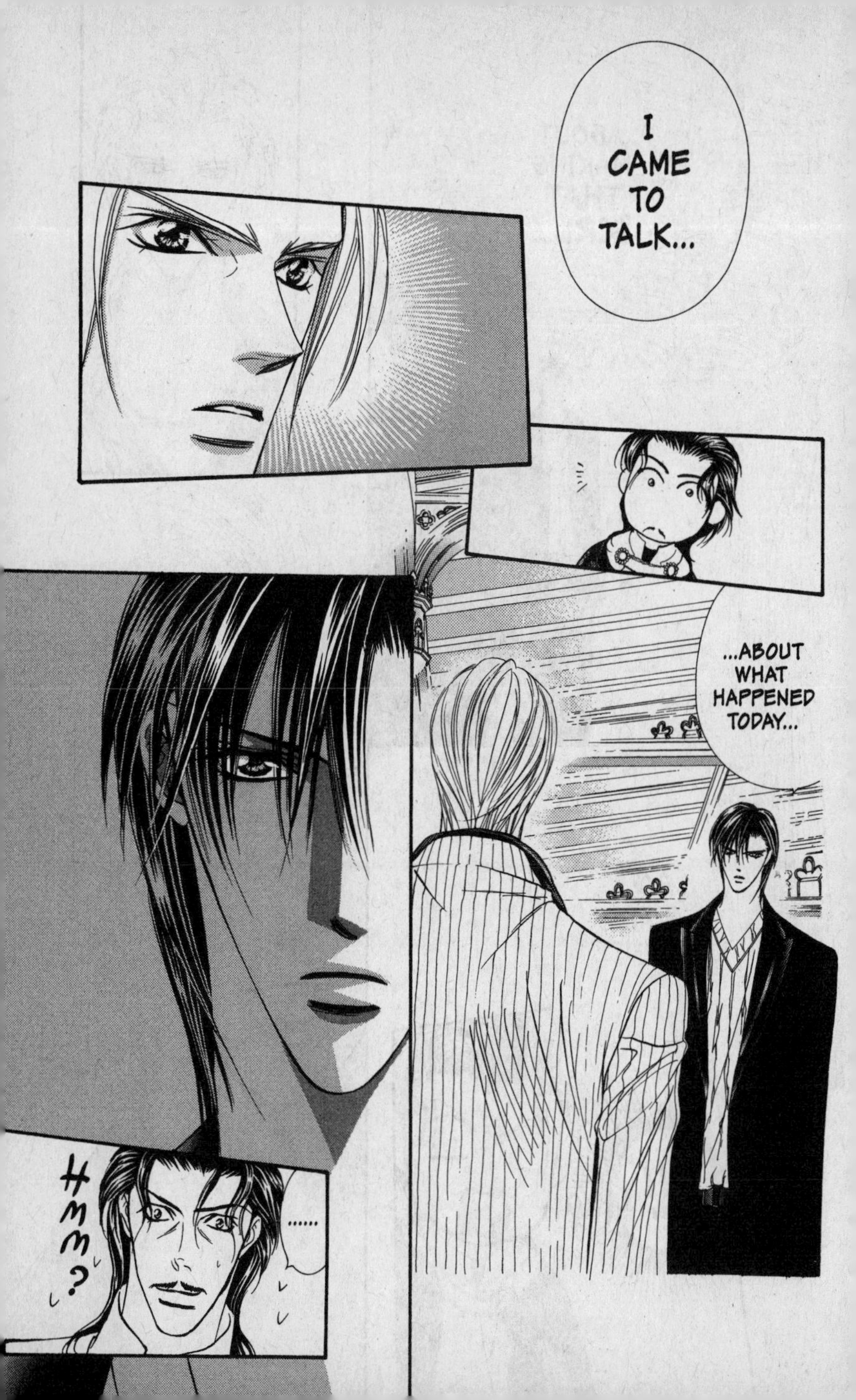
I CAME TO TALK...
...ABOUT WHAT HAPPENED TODAY...
......
HMM?

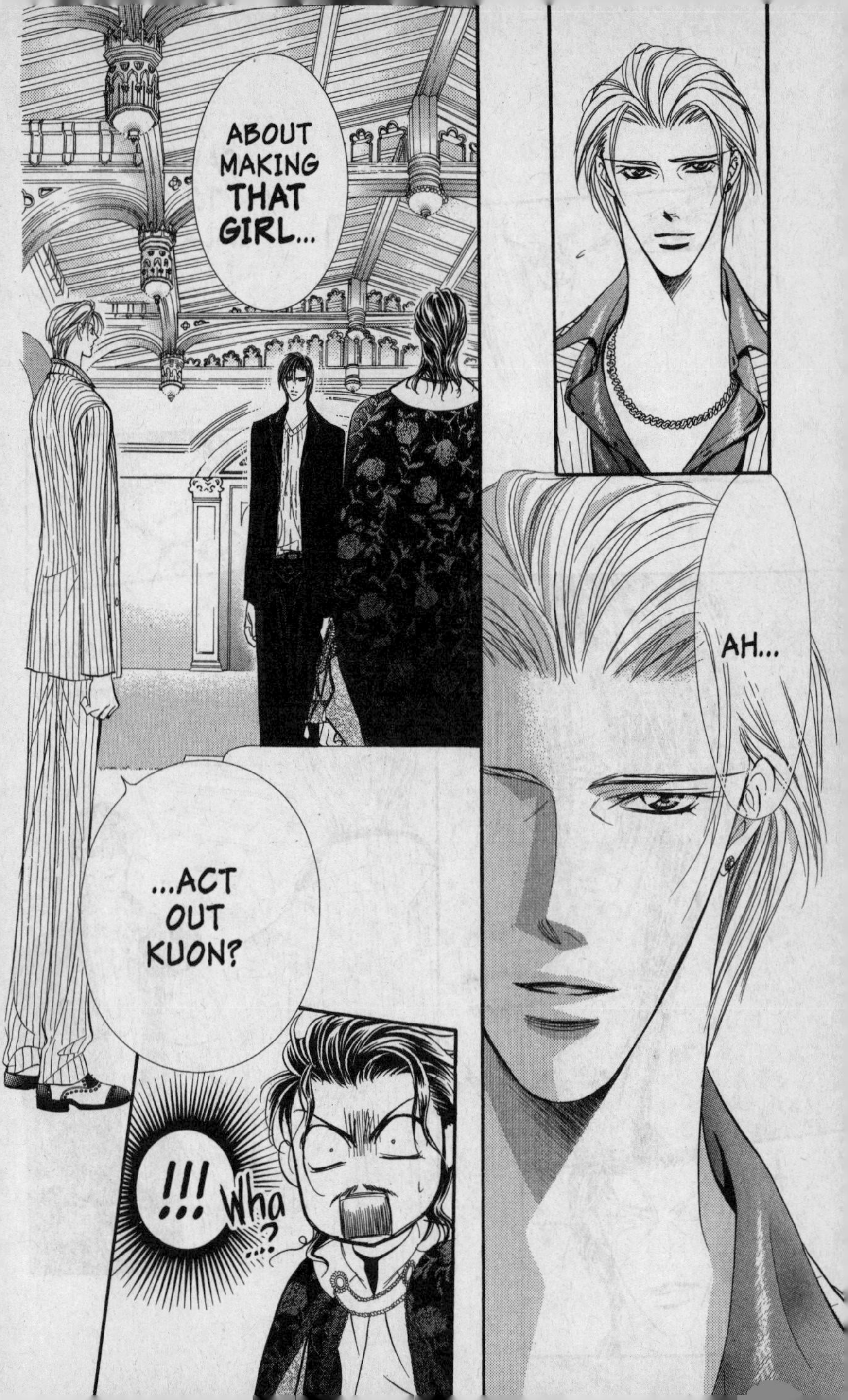
ABOUT MAKING THAT GIRL...
...ACT OUT KUON?
!!!
Wha...?
AH...

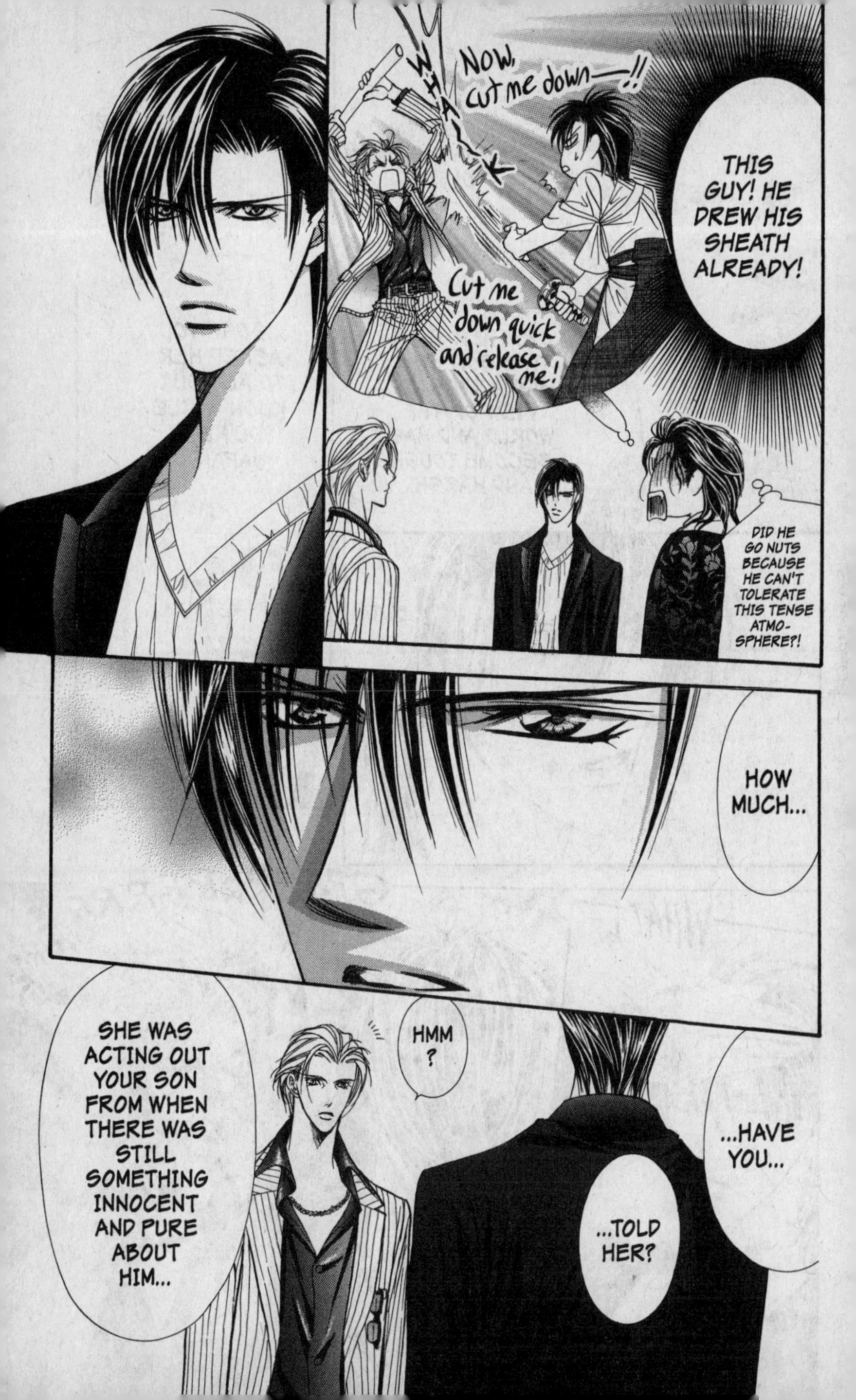
THIS GUY! HE DREW HIS SHEATH ALREADY!
Now, cut me down—!!
WHAK
Cut me down quick and release me!
DID HE GO NUTS BECAUSE HE CAN'T TOLERATE THIS TENSE ATMOSPHERE?!
HOW MUCH...
...HAVE YOU...
...TOLD HER?
HMM?
SHE WAS ACTING OUT YOUR SON FROM WHEN THERE WAS STILL SOMETHING INNOCENT AND PURE ABOUT HIM...

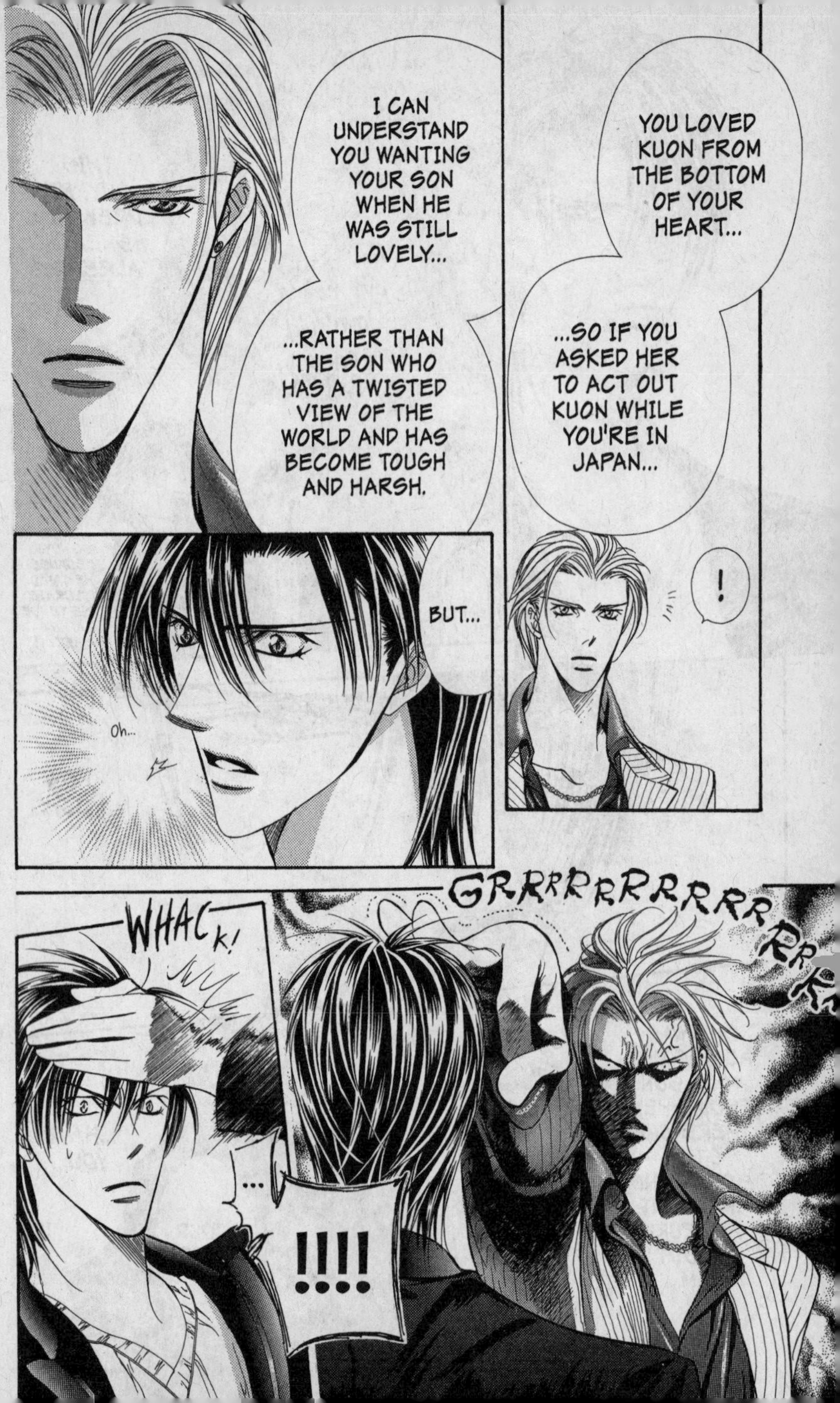
YOU LOVED KUON FROM THE BOTTOM OF YOUR HEART...
...SO IF YOU ASKED HER TO ACT OUT KUON WHILE YOU'RE IN JAPAN...
!
I CAN UNDERSTAND YOU WANTING YOUR SON WHEN HE WAS STILL LOVELY...
...RATHER THAN THE SON WHO HAS A TWISTED VIEW OF THE WORLD AND HAS BECOME TOUGH AND HARSH.
BUT...
Oh...
GRRRRRRRRRRRRRRK
WHACK!
...
!!!!

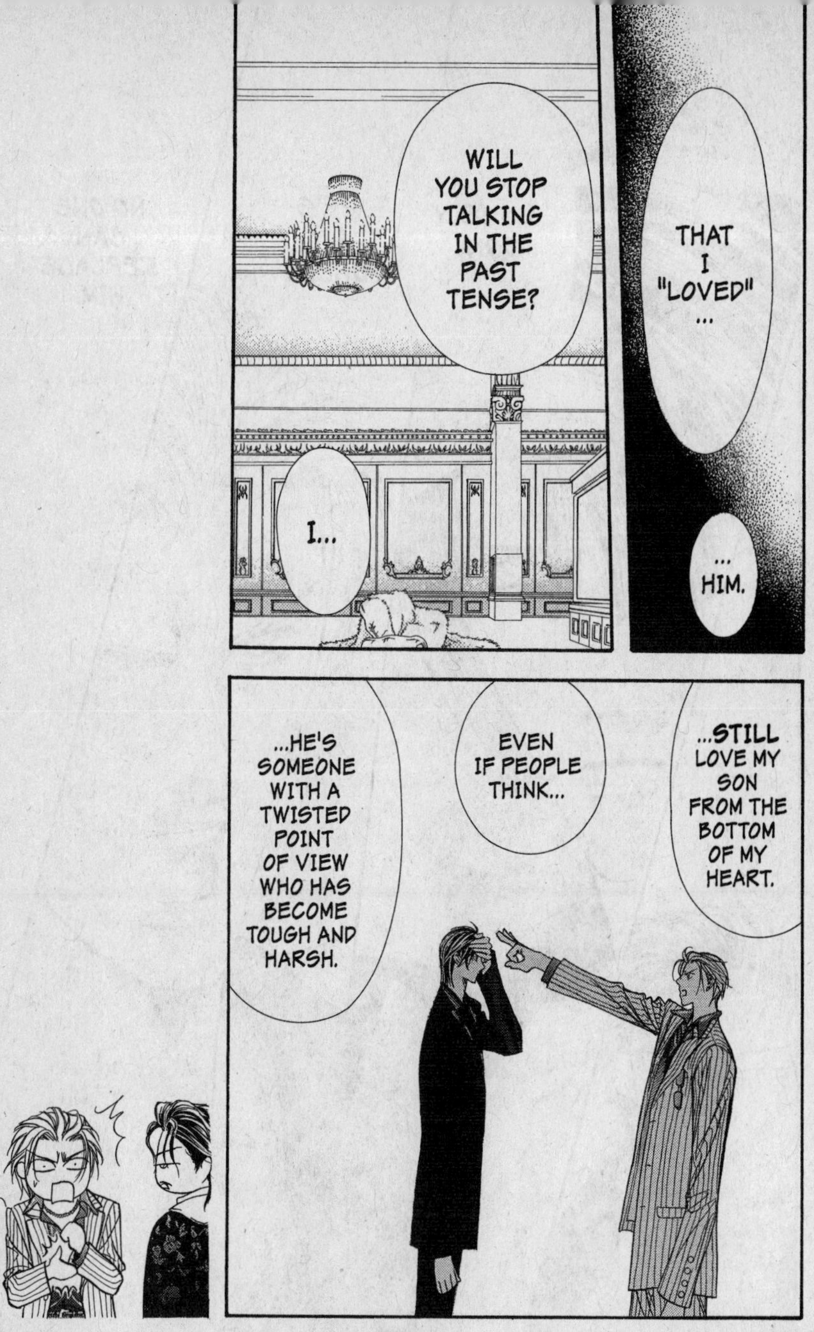
THAT I "LOVED"...
...HIM.
WILL YOU STOP TALKING IN THE PAST TENSE?
I...
...STILL LOVE MY SON FROM THE BOTTOM OF MY HEART.
EVEN IF PEOPLE THINK...
...HE'S SOMEONE WITH A TWISTED POINT OF VIEW WHO HAS BECOME TOUGH AND HARSH.

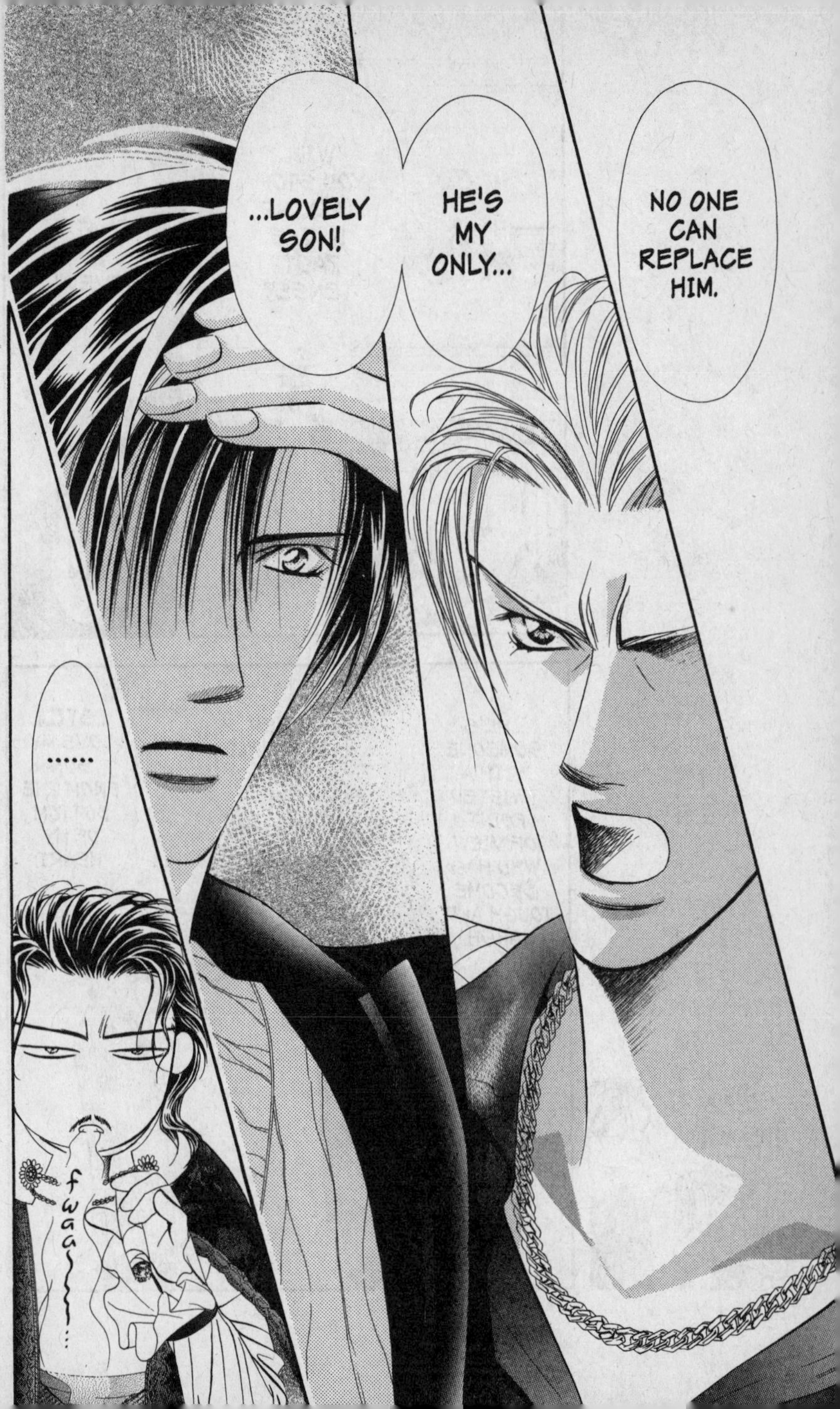
NO ONE CAN REPLACE HIM.
HE'S MY ONLY...
...LOVELY SON!
......
fwaa~~...

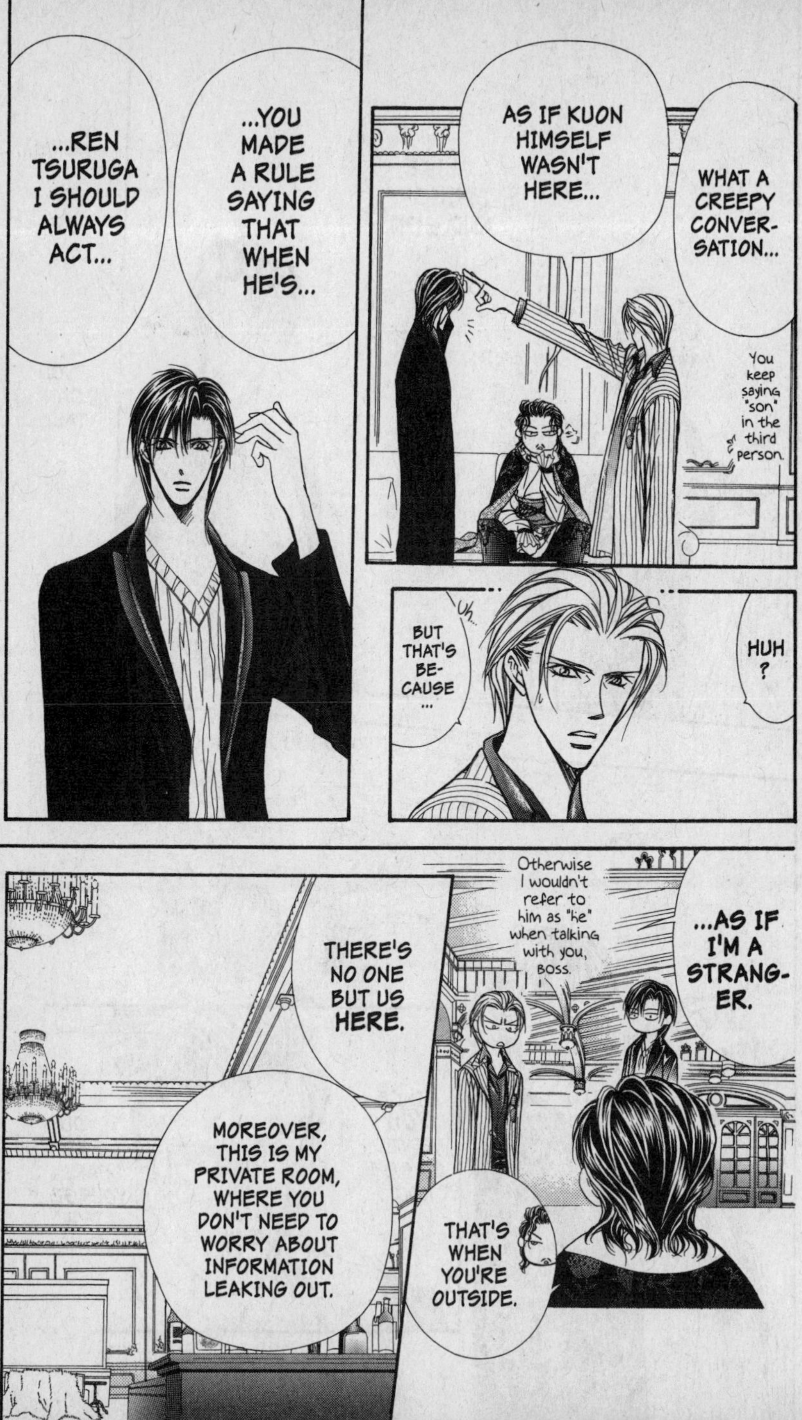
WHAT A CREEPY CONVER-SATION...
AS IF KUON HIMSELF WASN'T HERE...
You keep saying "son" in the third person.
HUH?
Uh...
BUT THAT'S BE-CAUSE...
...YOU MADE A RULE SAYING THAT WHEN HE'S...
...REN TSURUGA I SHOULD ALWAYS ACT...
...AS IF I'M A STRANGER.
Otherwise I wouldn't refer to him as "he" when talking with you, BOSS.
THAT'S WHEN YOU'RE OUTSIDE.
THERE'S NO ONE BUT US HERE.
MOREOVER, THIS IS MY PRIVATE ROOM, WHERE YOU DON'T NEED TO WORRY ABOUT INFORMATION LEAKING OUT.

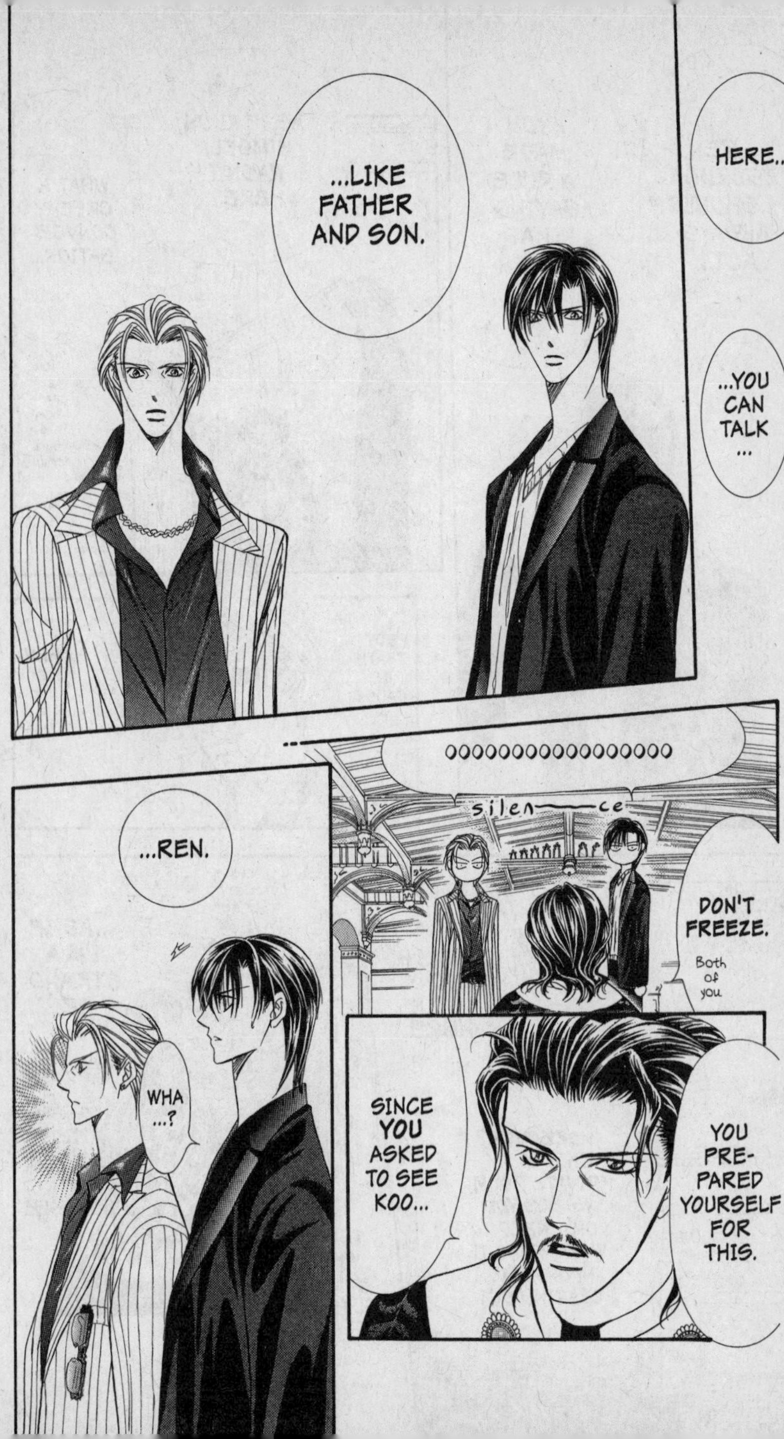
HERE...
...YOU CAN TALK ...
...LIKE FATHER AND SON.
--OOOOOOOOOOOOOOOOOO
silen——ce
DON'T FREEZE.
Both of you
YOU PRE-PARED YOURSELF FOR THIS.
SINCE YOU ASKED TO SEE KOO...
...REN.
WHA ...?

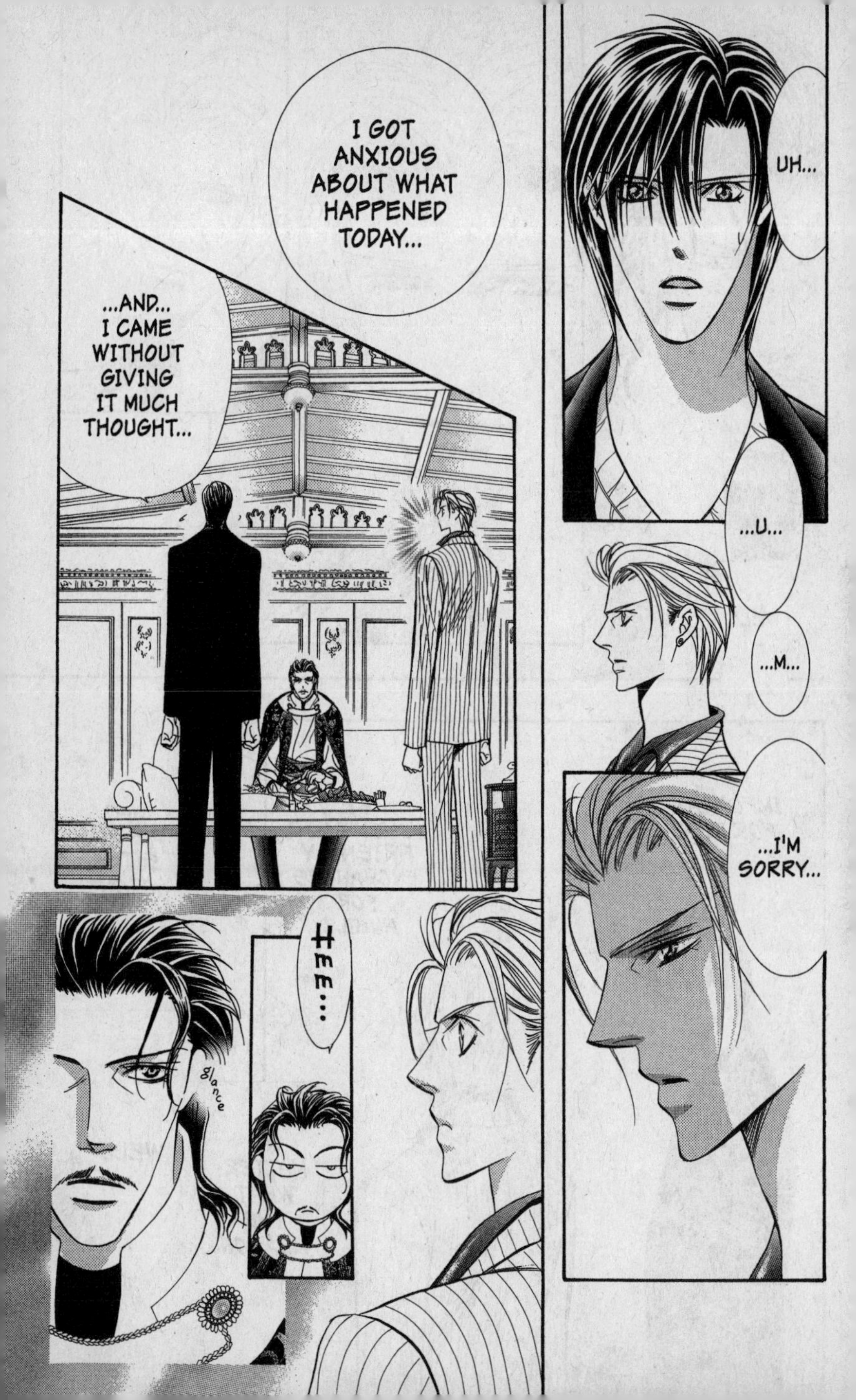
UH...
...U...
...M...
...I'M SORRY...
I GOT ANXIOUS ABOUT WHAT HAPPENED TODAY...
...AND... I CAME WITHOUT GIVING IT MUCH THOUGHT...
Hmm...
glance

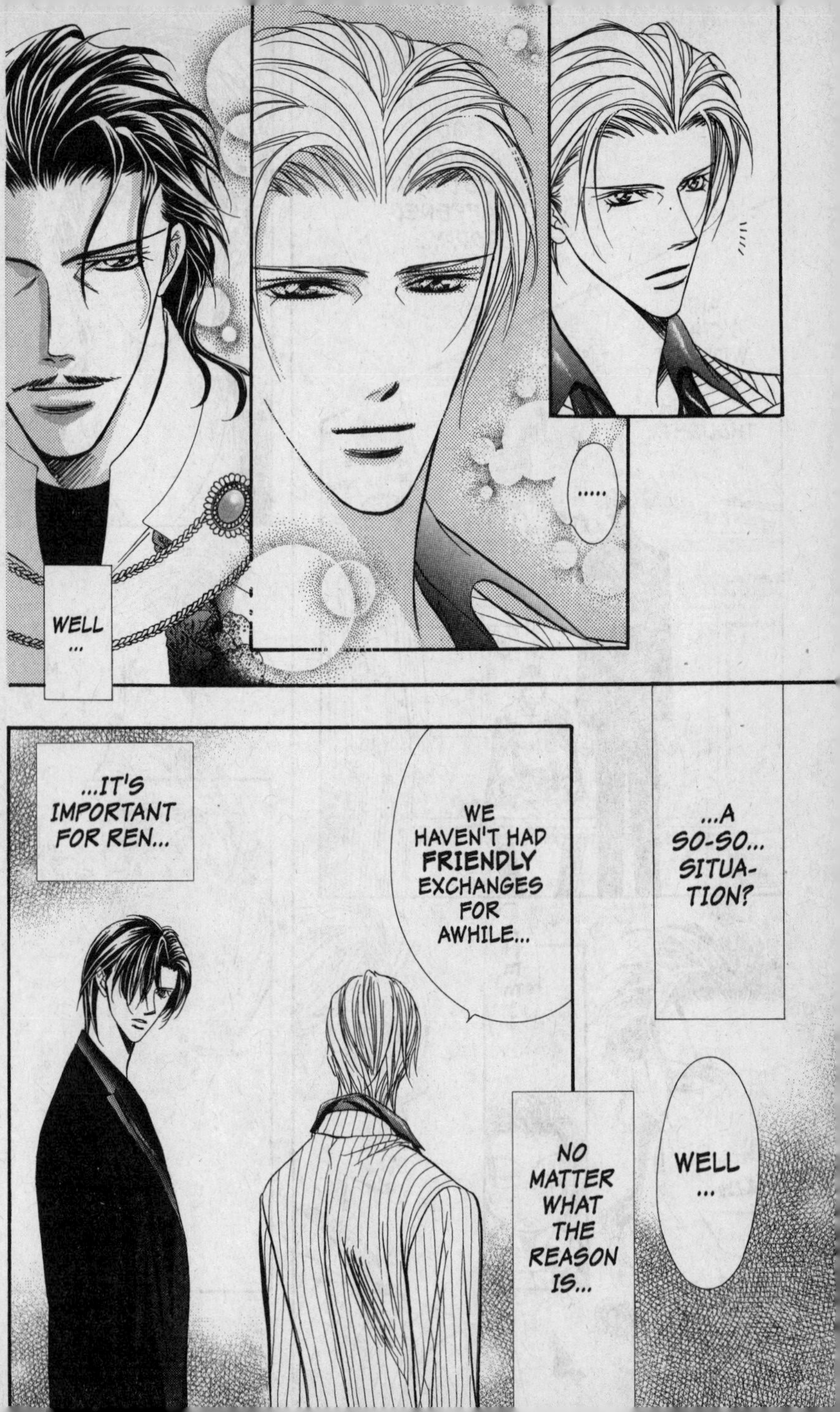
.....
WELL ...
...A SO-SO... SITUATION?
WELL ...
WE HAVEN'T HAD FRIENDLY EXCHANGES FOR AWHILE...
NO MATTER WHAT THE REASON IS...
...IT'S IMPORTANT FOR REN...

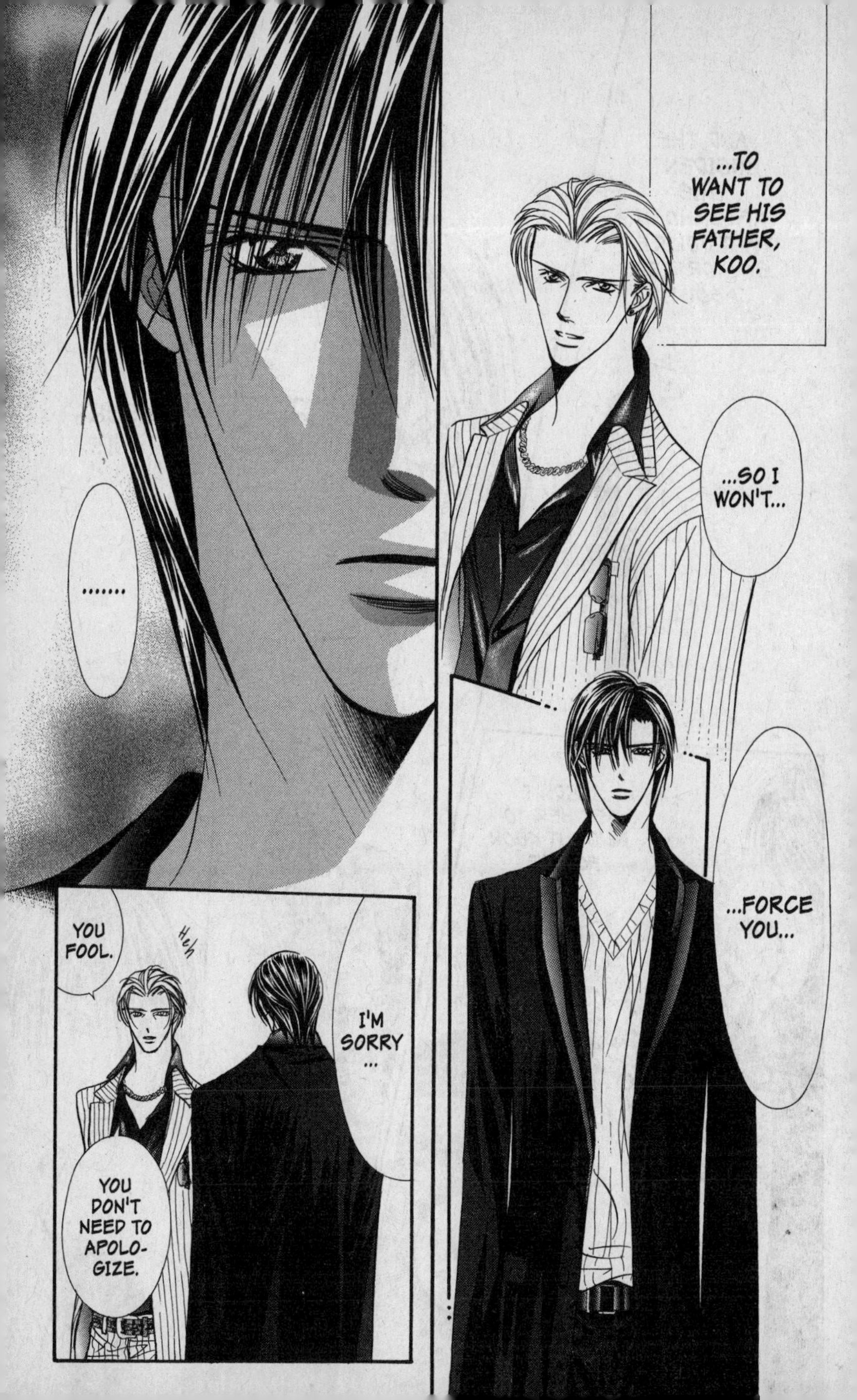
...TO WANT TO SEE HIS FATHER, KOO.
...SO I WON'T...
...FORCE YOU...
....
I'M SORRY ...
YOU FOOL.
Heh
YOU DON'T NEED TO APOLO-GIZE.

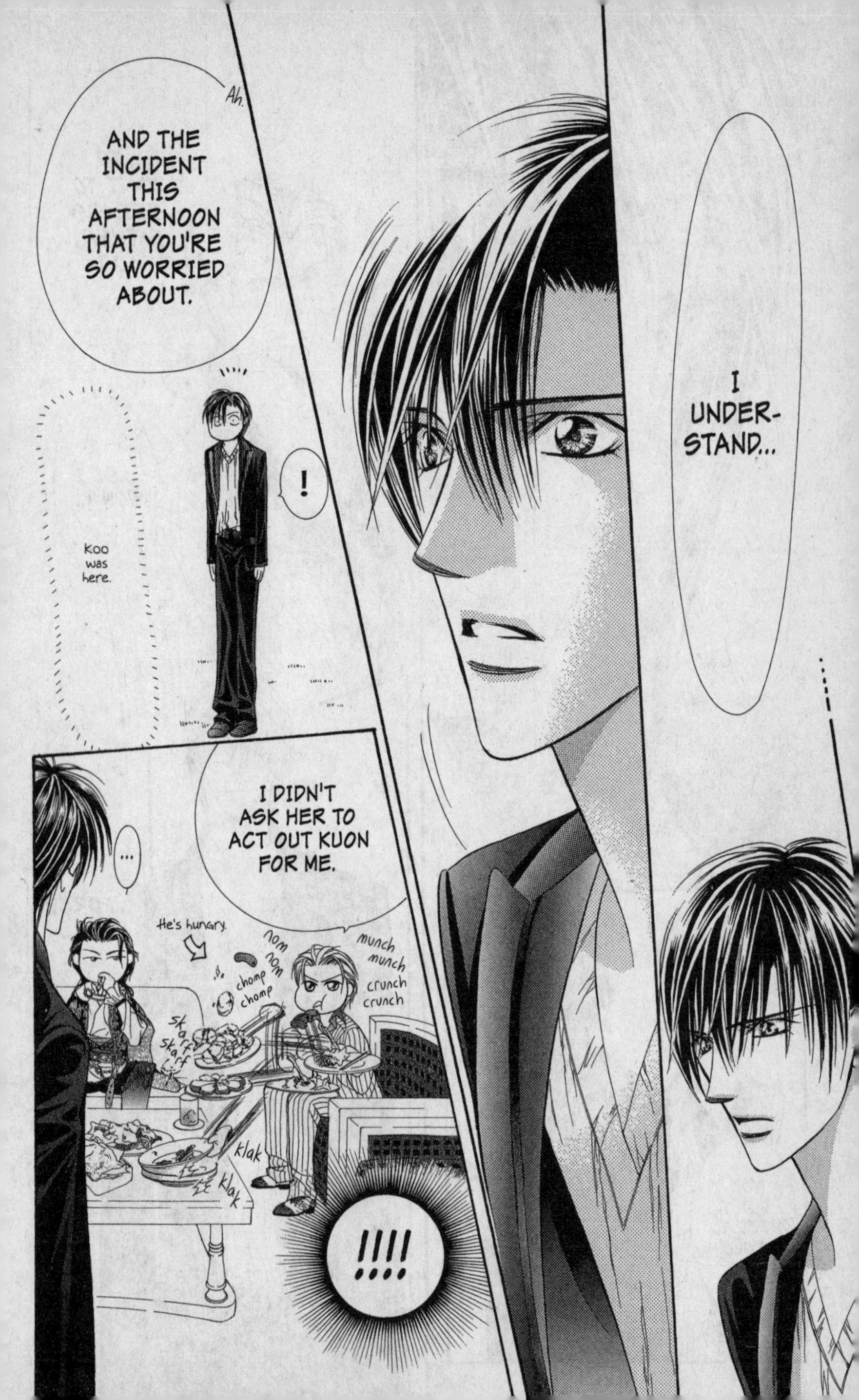

I UNDERSTAND...
Ah.
AND THE INCIDENT THIS AFTERNOON THAT YOU'RE SO WORRIED ABOUT.
!
Koo was here.
I DIDN'T ASK HER TO ACT OUT KUON FOR ME.
...
munch munch
crunch crunch
nom nom
He's hungry.
chomp chomp
skarf skarf
klak klak
!!!!

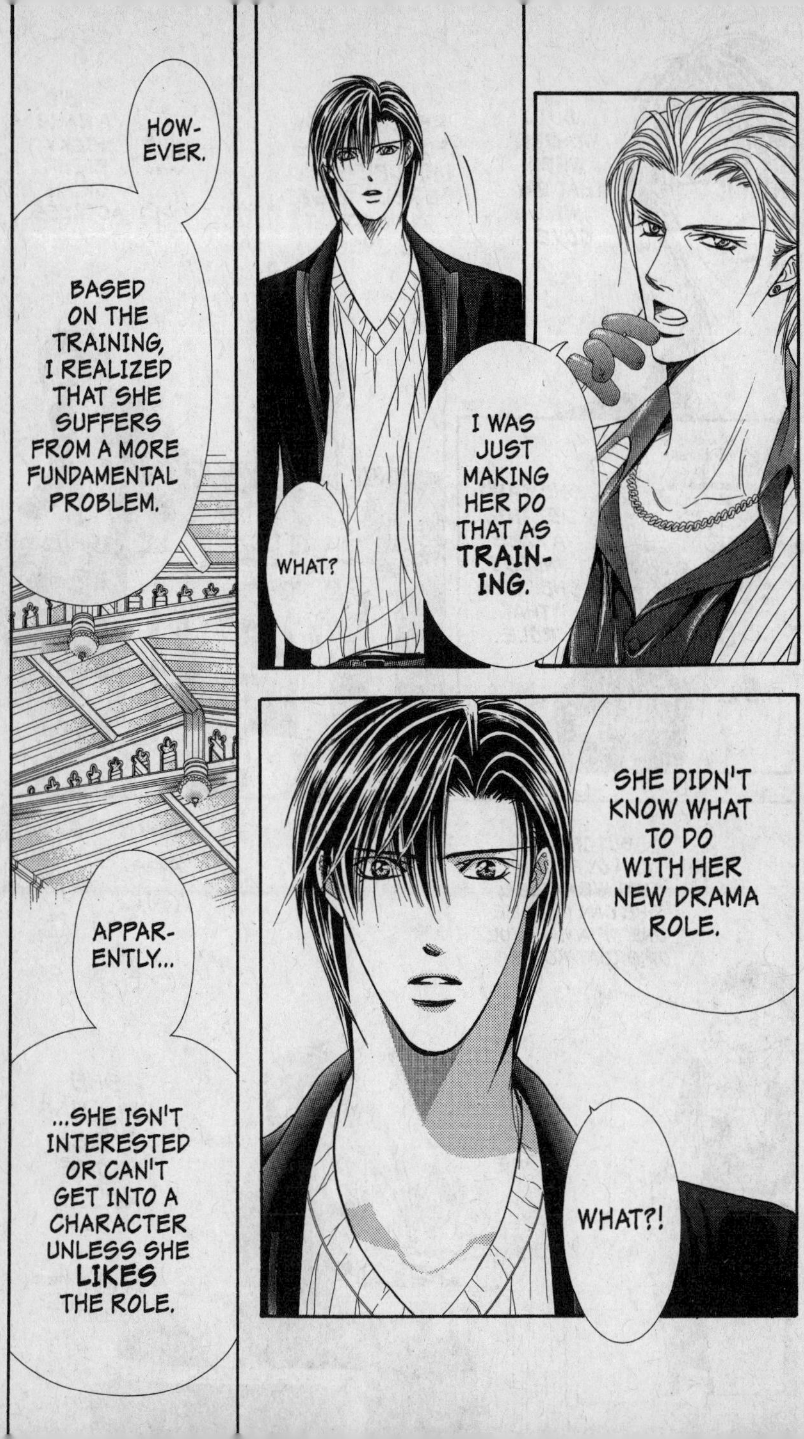
I WAS JUST MAKING HER DO THAT AS TRAINING.
WHAT?
SHE DIDN'T KNOW WHAT TO DO WITH HER NEW DRAMA ROLE.
WHAT?!
HOW-EVER.
BASED ON THE TRAINING, I REALIZED THAT SHE SUFFERS FROM A MORE FUNDAMENTAL PROBLEM.
APPAR-ENTLY...
...SHE ISN'T INTERESTED OR CAN'T GET INTO A CHARACTER UNLESS SHE LIKES THE ROLE.

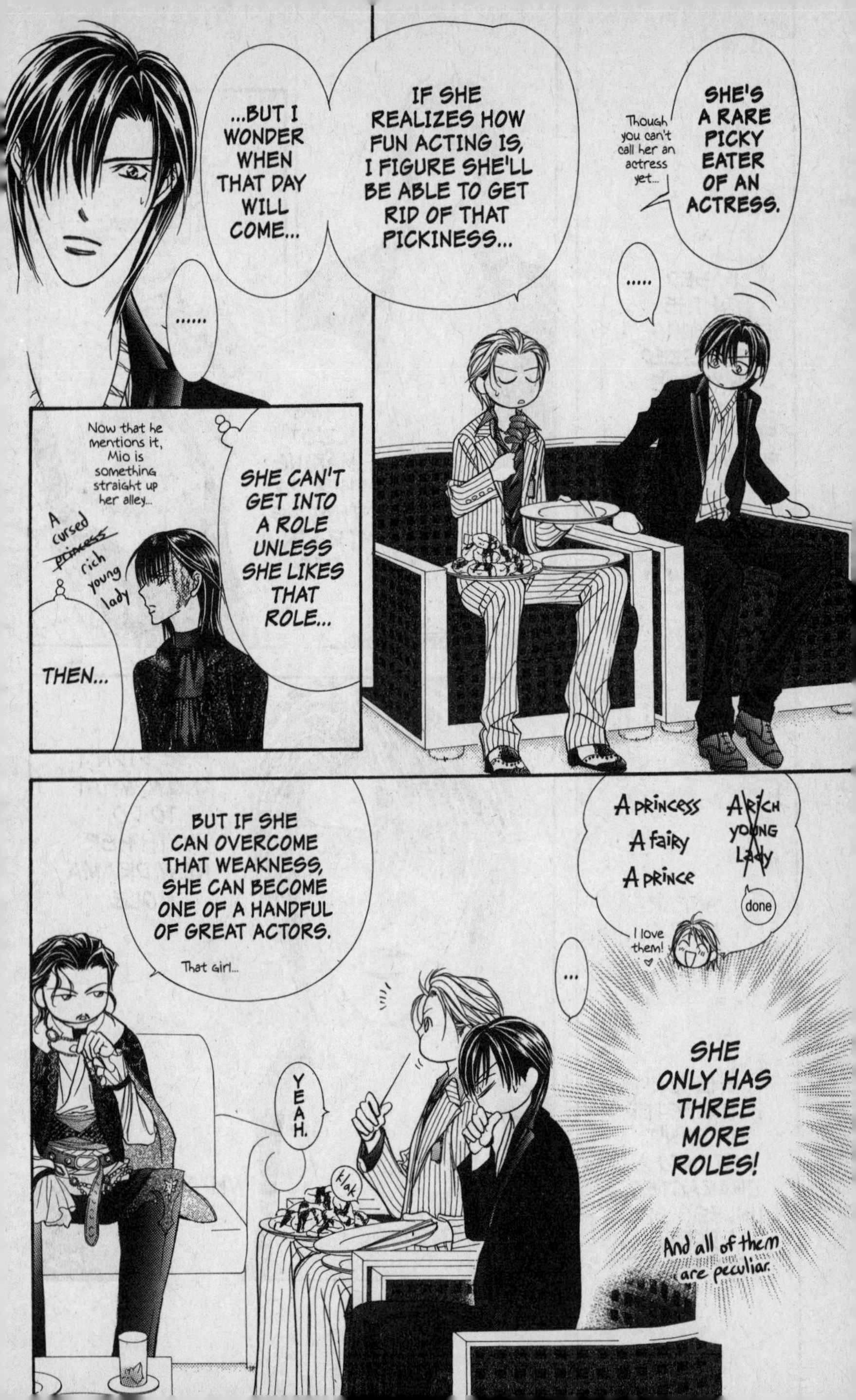

SHE'S A RARE PICKY EATER OF AN ACTRESS.
Though you can't call her an actress yet...
.....
IF SHE REALIZES HOW FUN ACTING IS, I FIGURE SHE'LL BE ABLE TO GET RID OF THAT PICKINESS...
...BUT I WONDER WHEN THAT DAY WILL COME...
......
SHE CAN'T GET INTO A ROLE UNLESS SHE LIKES THAT ROLE...
Now that he mentions it, Mio is something straight up her alley...
A cursed ~~princess~~ rich young lady
THEN...
A princess
A fairy
A prince
A rich young lady
done
I love them! ♥
...
SHE ONLY HAS THREE MORE ROLES!
And all of them are peculiar.
YEAH.
klak
BUT IF SHE CAN OVERCOME THAT WEAKNESS, SHE CAN BECOME ONE OF A HANDFUL OF GREAT ACTORS.
That girl...

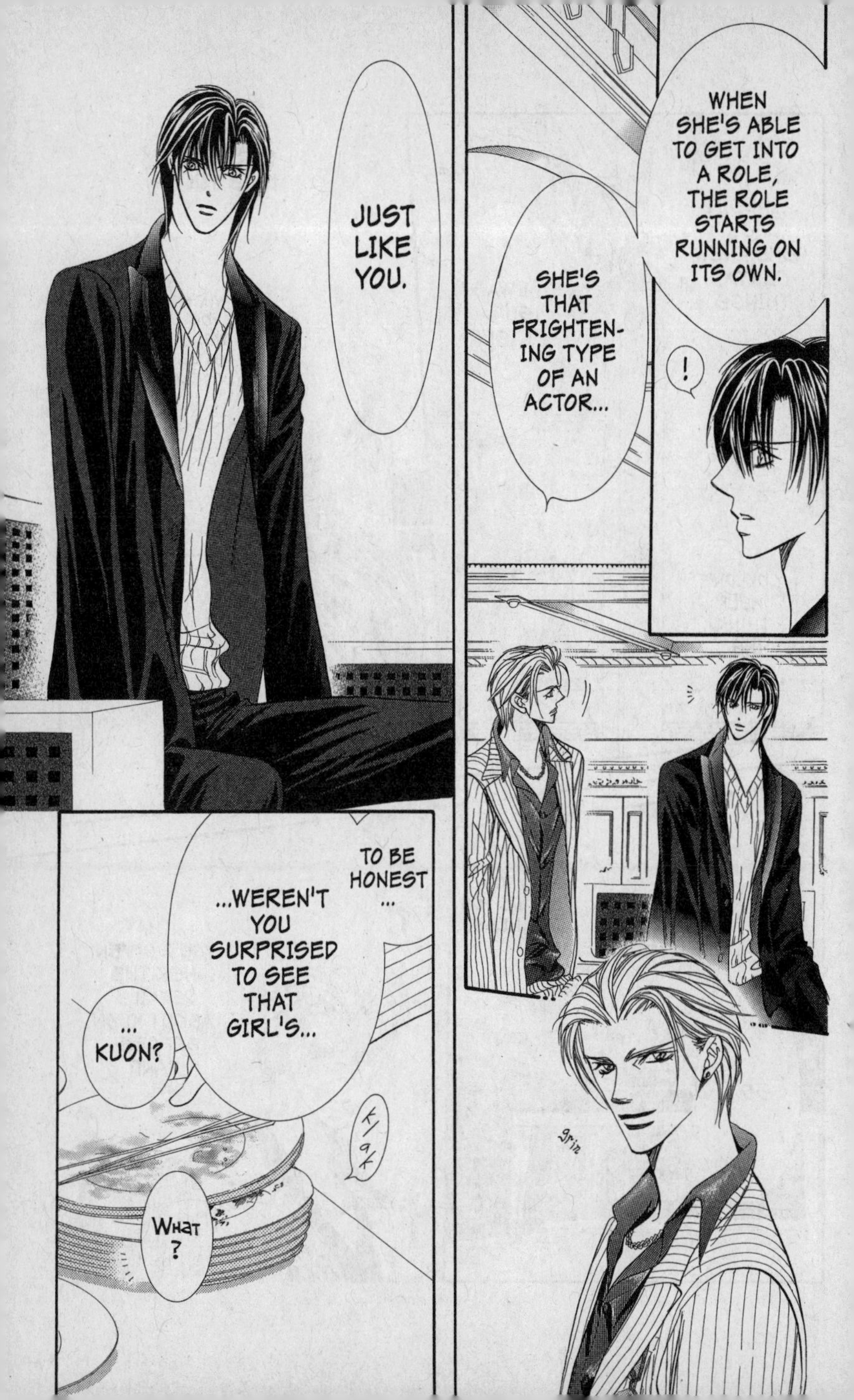
WHEN SHE'S ABLE TO GET INTO A ROLE, THE ROLE STARTS RUNNING ON ITS OWN.
SHE'S THAT FRIGHTENING TYPE OF AN ACTOR...
!
grin
JUST LIKE YOU.
TO BE HONEST ...
...WEREN'T YOU SURPRISED TO SEE THAT GIRL'S...
... KUON?
Klak
What ?

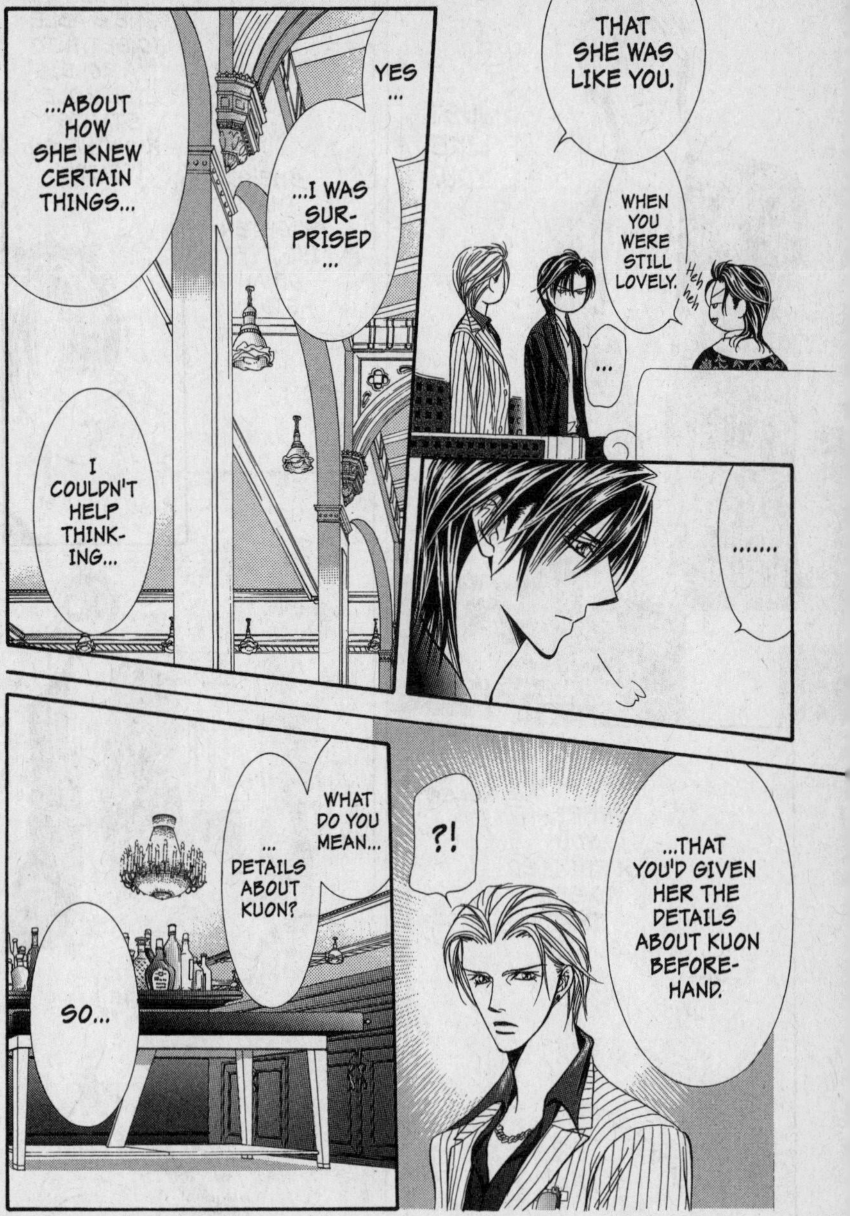
THAT SHE WAS LIKE YOU.
WHEN YOU WERE STILL LOVELY.
Heh heh
...
....
YES...
...I WAS SUR-PRISED...
...ABOUT HOW SHE KNEW CERTAIN THINGS...
I COULDN'T HELP THINK-ING...
...THAT YOU'D GIVEN HER THE DETAILS ABOUT KUON BEFORE-HAND.
?!
WHAT DO YOU MEAN...
...DETAILS ABOUT KUON?
SO...

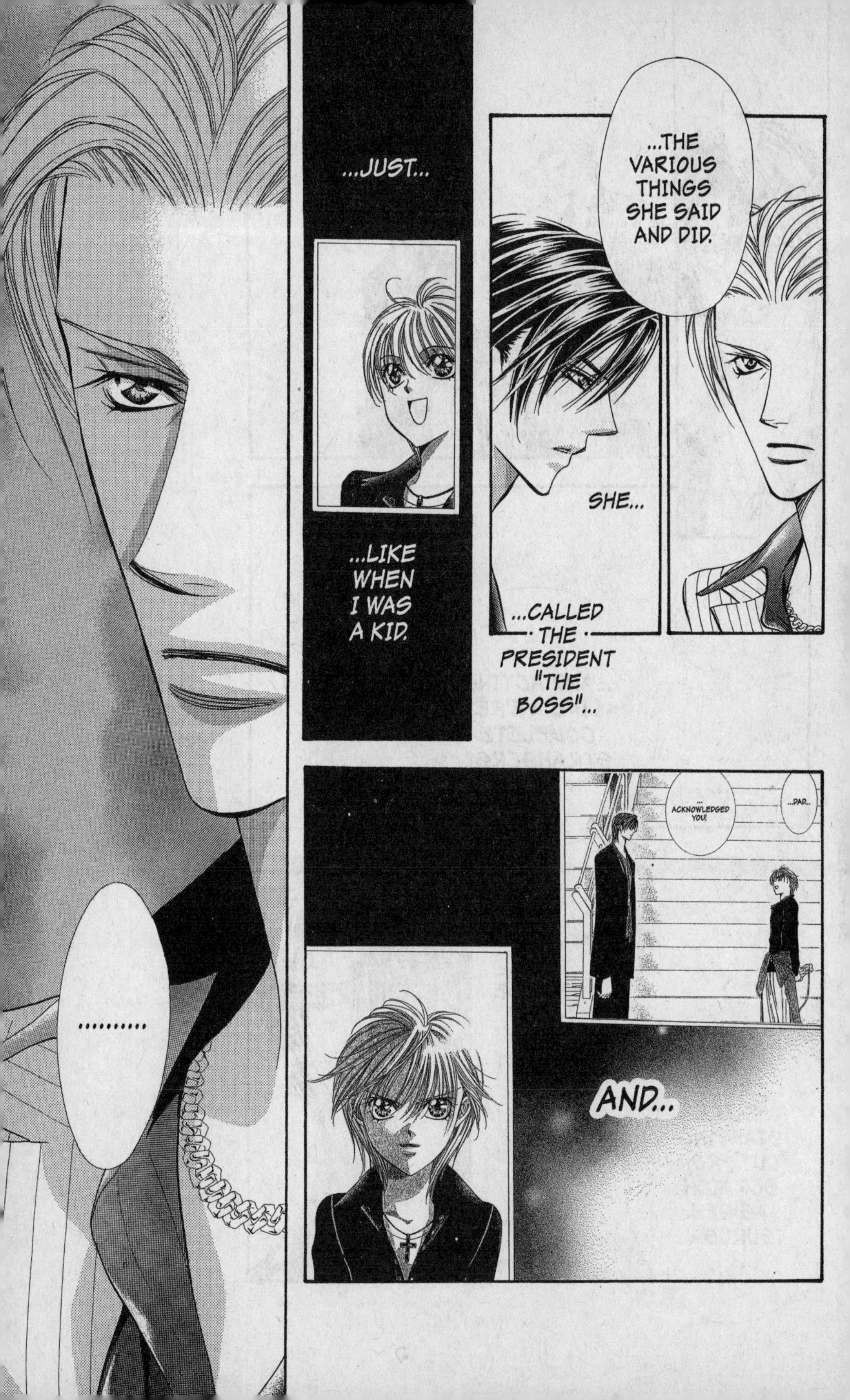
...THE VARIOUS THINGS SHE SAID AND DID.
SHE...
...CALLED THE PRESIDENT "THE BOSS"...
...JUST...
...LIKE WHEN I WAS A KID.
...DAD...
...ACKNOWLEDGED YOU!
AND...
....

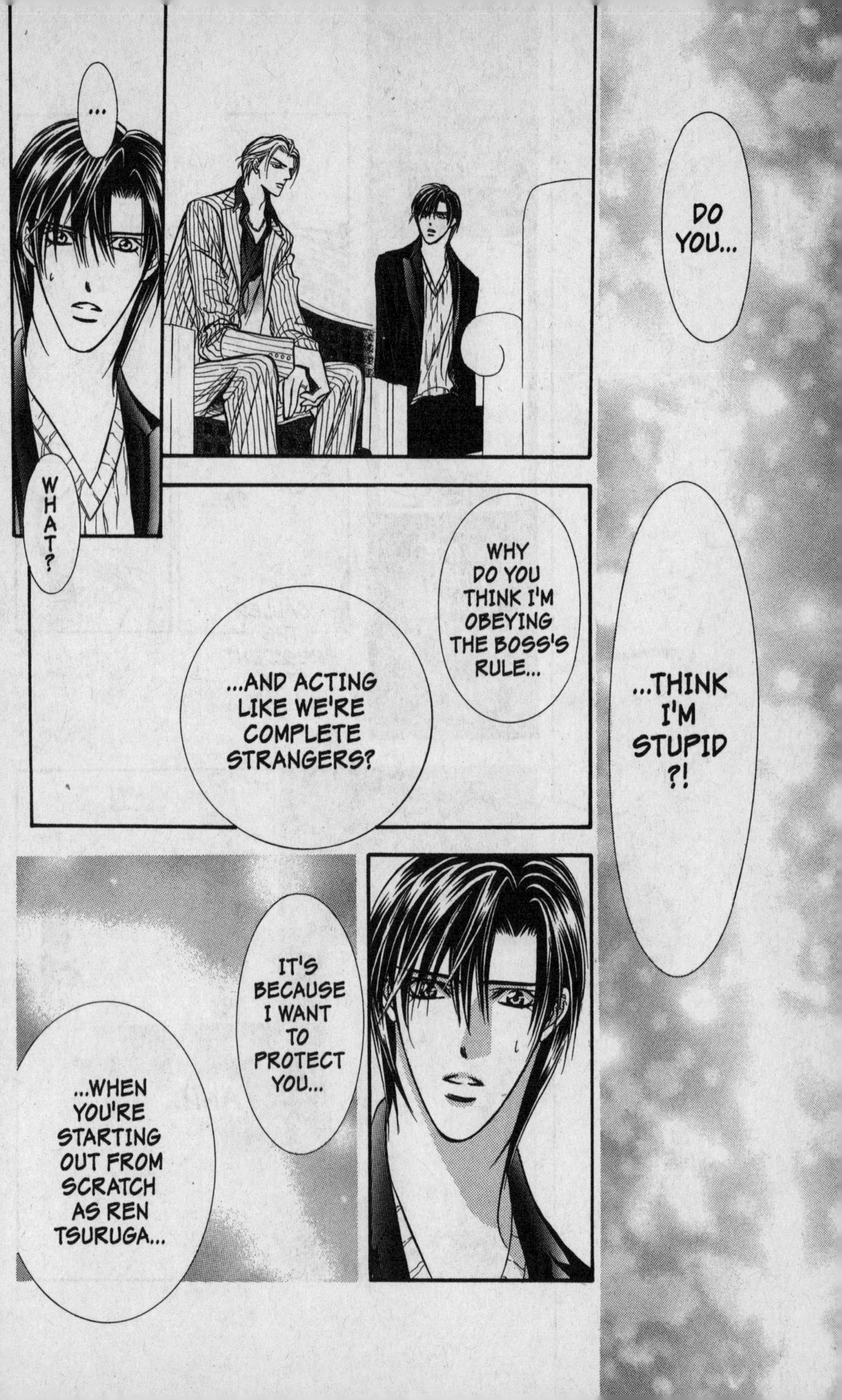
DO YOU...
...THINK I'M STUPID?!
...
WHAT?
WHY DO YOU THINK I'M OBEYING THE BOSS'S RULE...
...AND ACTING LIKE WE'RE COMPLETE STRANGERS?
IT'S BECAUSE I WANT TO PROTECT YOU...
...WHEN YOU'RE STARTING OUT FROM SCRATCH AS REN TSURUGA...

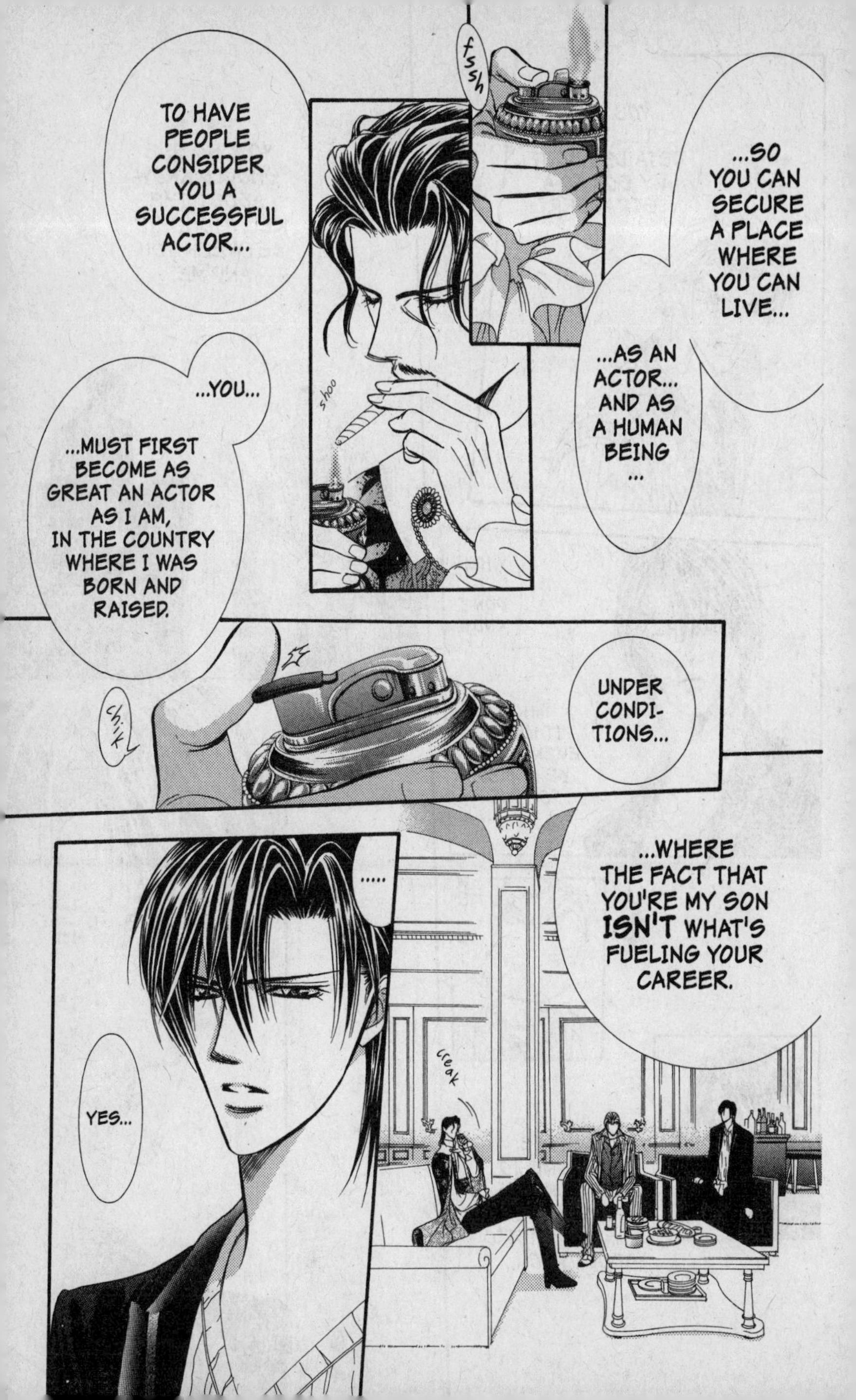
fssh
...SO YOU CAN SECURE A PLACE WHERE YOU CAN LIVE...
...AS AN ACTOR... AND AS A HUMAN BEING ...
shoo
TO HAVE PEOPLE CONSIDER YOU A SUCCESSFUL ACTOR...
...YOU...
...MUST FIRST BECOME AS GREAT AN ACTOR AS I AM, IN THE COUNTRY WHERE I WAS BORN AND RAISED.
UNDER CONDI-TIONS...
chik
...WHERE THE FACT THAT YOU'RE MY SON ISN'T WHAT'S FUELING YOUR CAREER.
.....
creak
YES...

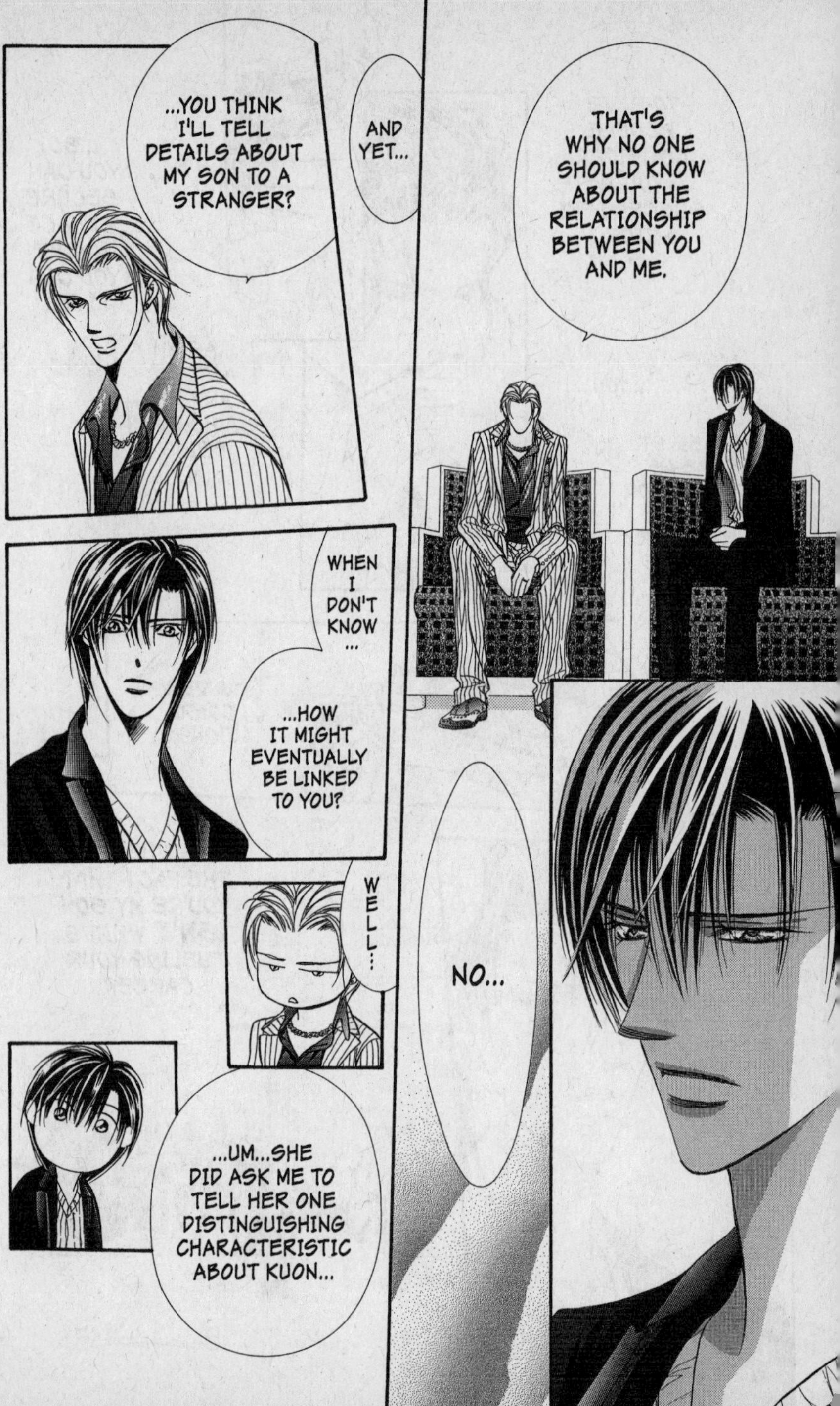
THAT'S WHY NO ONE SHOULD KNOW ABOUT THE RELATIONSHIP BETWEEN YOU AND ME.
AND YET...
...YOU THINK I'LL TELL DETAILS ABOUT MY SON TO A STRANGER?
WHEN I DON'T KNOW ...
...HOW IT MIGHT EVENTUALLY BE LINKED TO YOU?
WELL...
...UM...SHE DID ASK ME TO TELL HER ONE DISTINGUISHING CHARACTERISTIC ABOUT KUON...
NO...

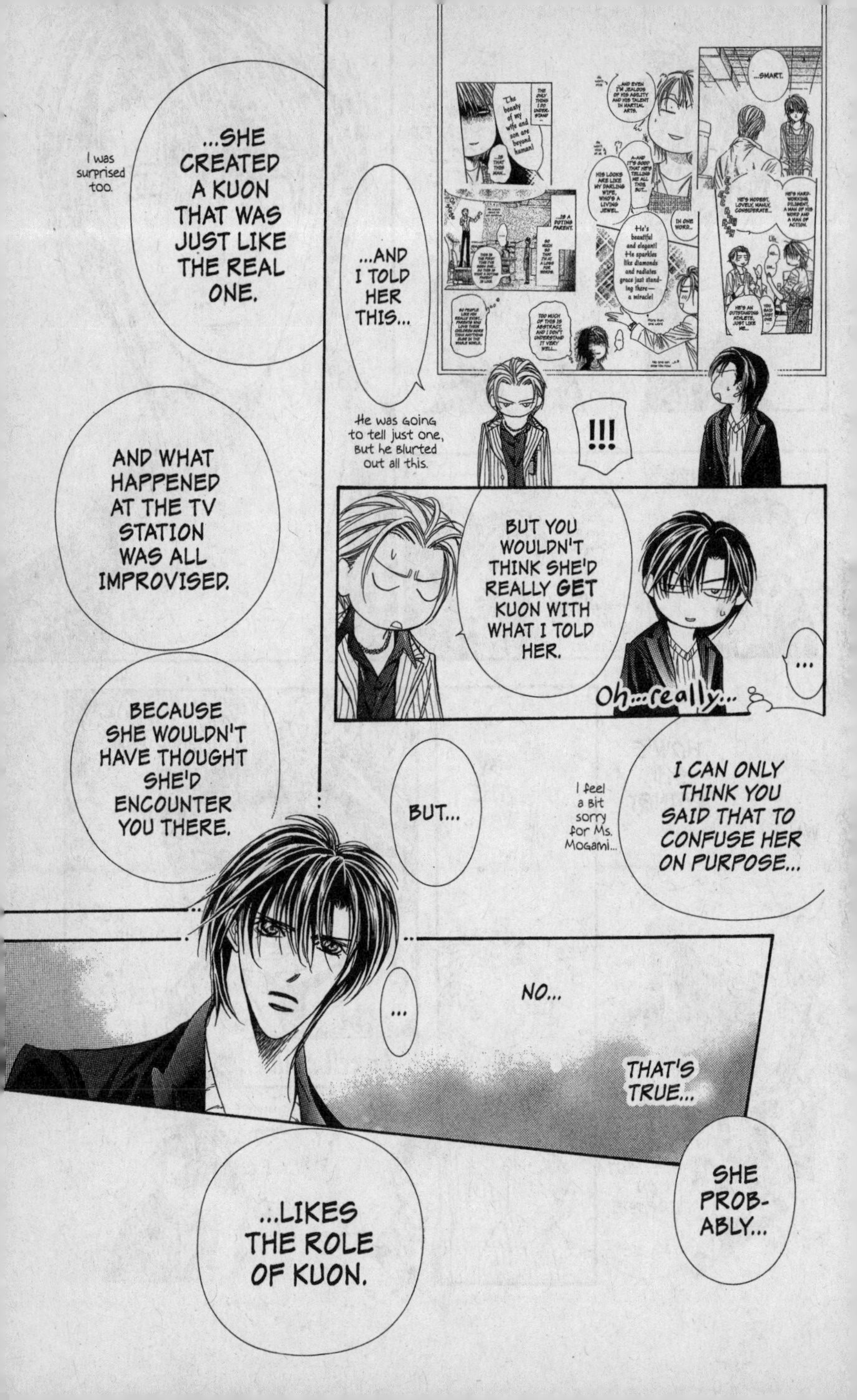
...AND I TOLD HER THIS...
!!!
He was going to tell just one, but he blurted out all this.
...SHE CREATED A KUON THAT WAS JUST LIKE THE REAL ONE.
I was surprised too.
AND WHAT HAPPENED AT THE TV STATION WAS ALL IMPROVISED.
BECAUSE SHE WOULDN'T HAVE THOUGHT SHE'D ENCOUNTER YOU THERE.
...
BUT YOU WOULDN'T THINK SHE'D REALLY GET KUON WITH WHAT I TOLD HER.
Oh...really...
I CAN ONLY THINK YOU SAID THAT TO CONFUSE HER ON PURPOSE...
I feel a bit sorry for Ms. Mogami...
BUT...
NO...
...
THAT'S TRUE...
SHE PROBABLY...
...LIKES THE ROLE OF KUON.

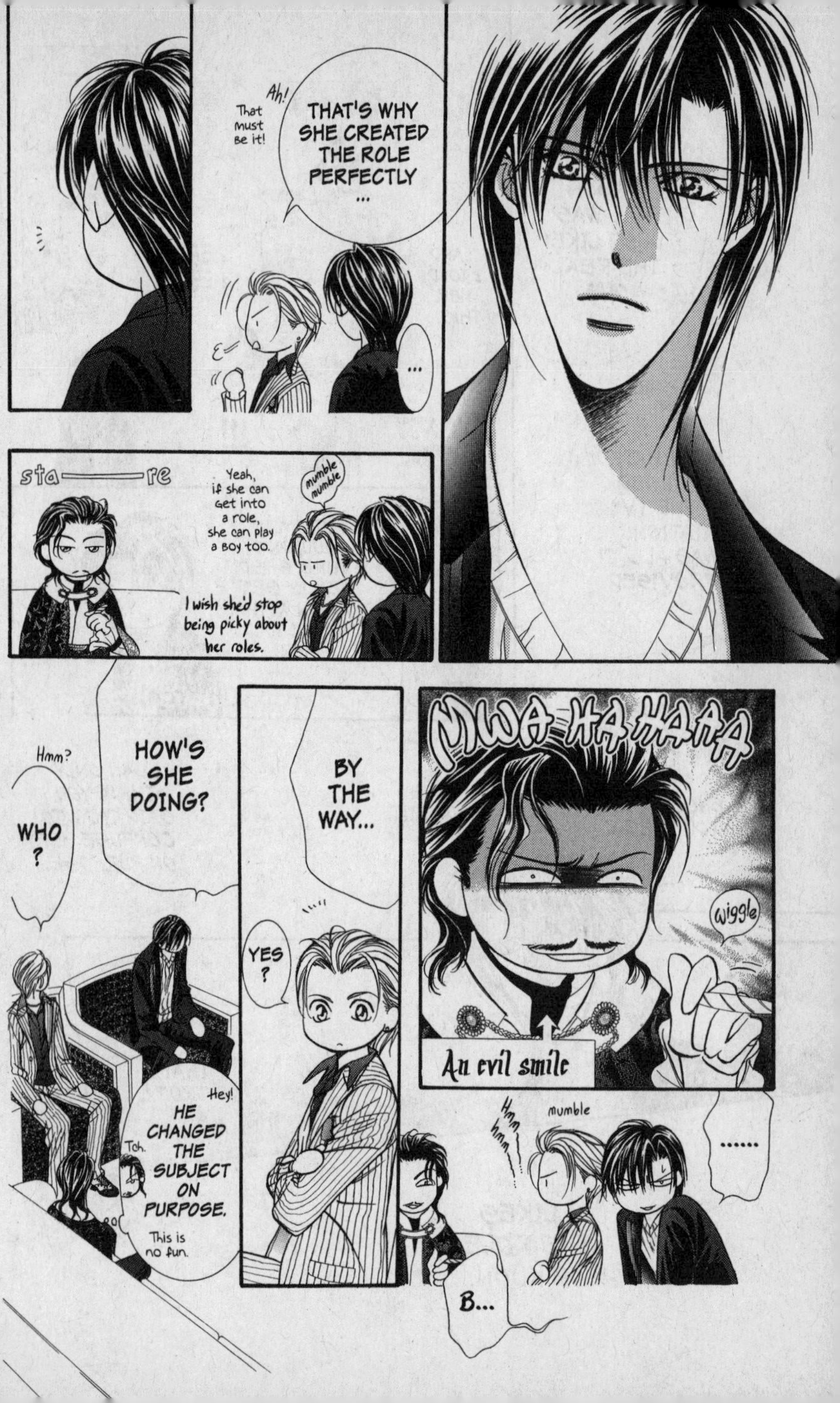
THAT'S WHY SHE CREATED THE ROLE PERFECTLY ...
Ah!
That must be it!
...
mumble mumble
Yeah, if she can get into a role, she can play a boy too.
sta——re
I wish she'd stop being picky about her roles.
MWA HA HAAA
wiggle
An evil smile
......
mumble
Hmm hmm
B...
BY THE WAY...
YES?
HOW'S SHE DOING?
Hmm?
WHO?
Hey!
HE CHANGED THE SUBJECT ON PURPOSE.
Tch.
This is no fun.

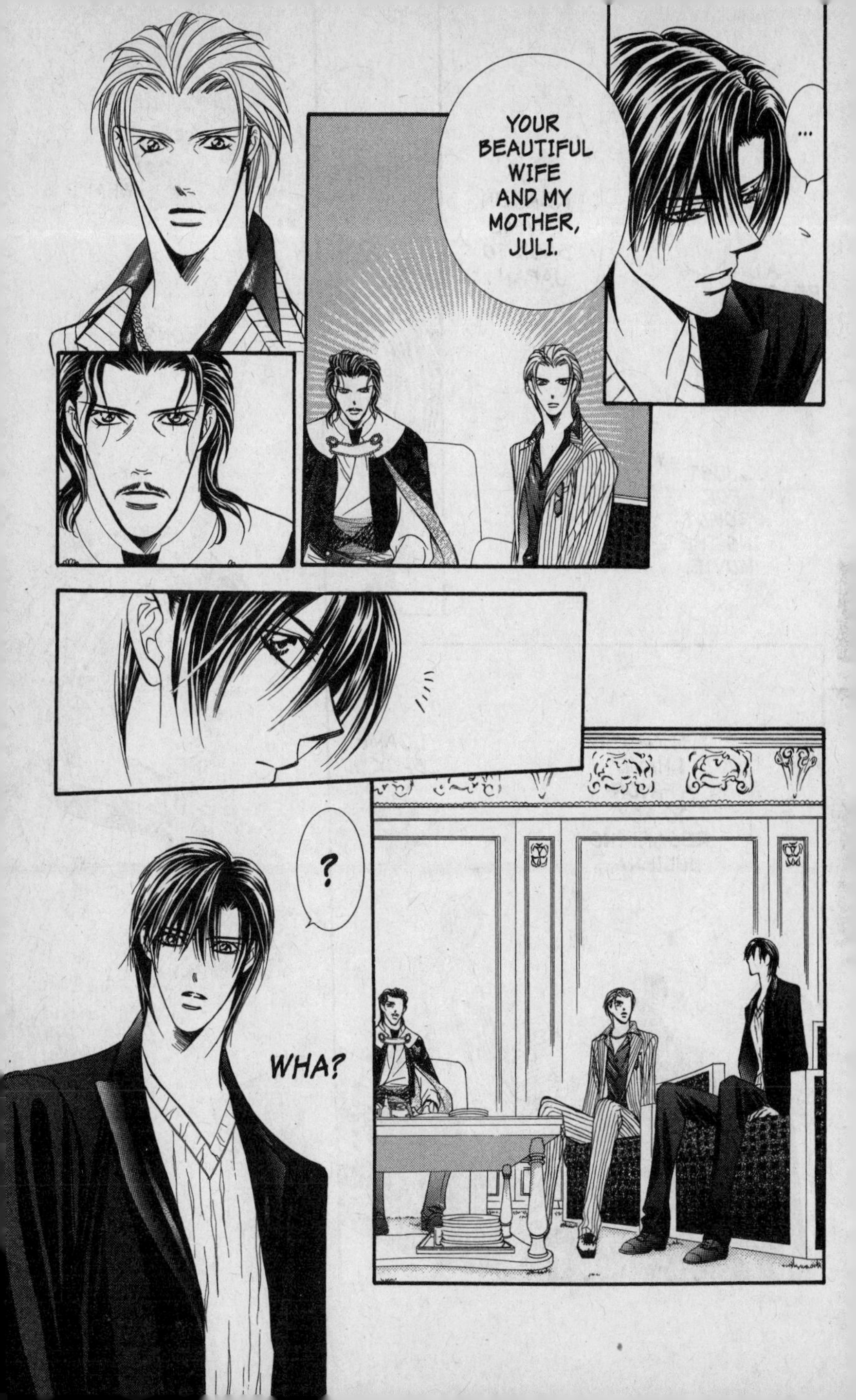
...
YOUR BEAUTIFUL WIFE AND MY MOTHER, JULI.
?
WHA?

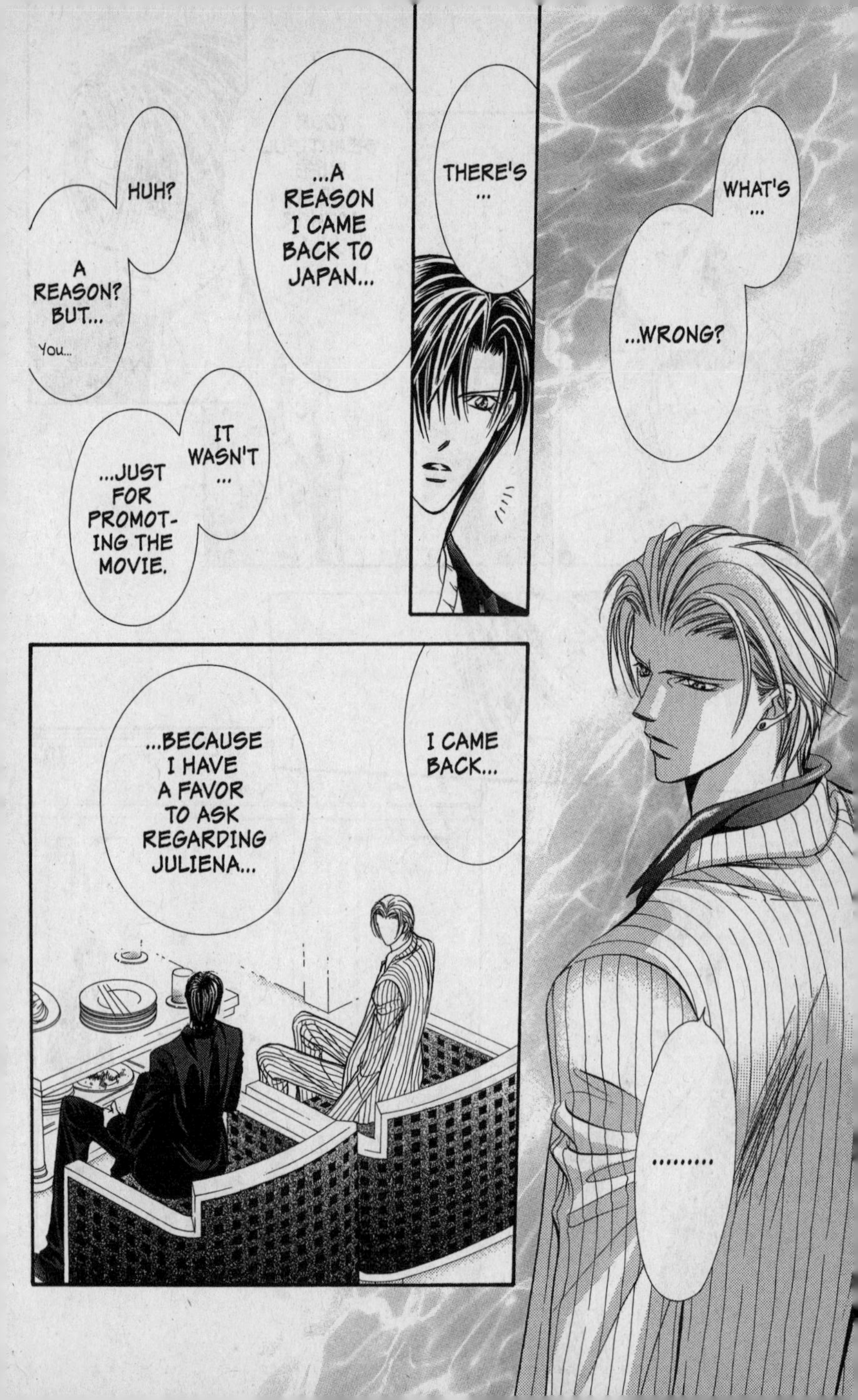
WHAT'S ... ...WRONG?
....
THERE'S ...
...A REASON I CAME BACK TO JAPAN...
HUH?
A REASON? BUT...
You...
IT WASN'T ...
...JUST FOR PROMOTING THE MOVIE.
I CAME BACK...
...BECAUSE I HAVE A FAVOR TO ASK REGARDING JULIENA...

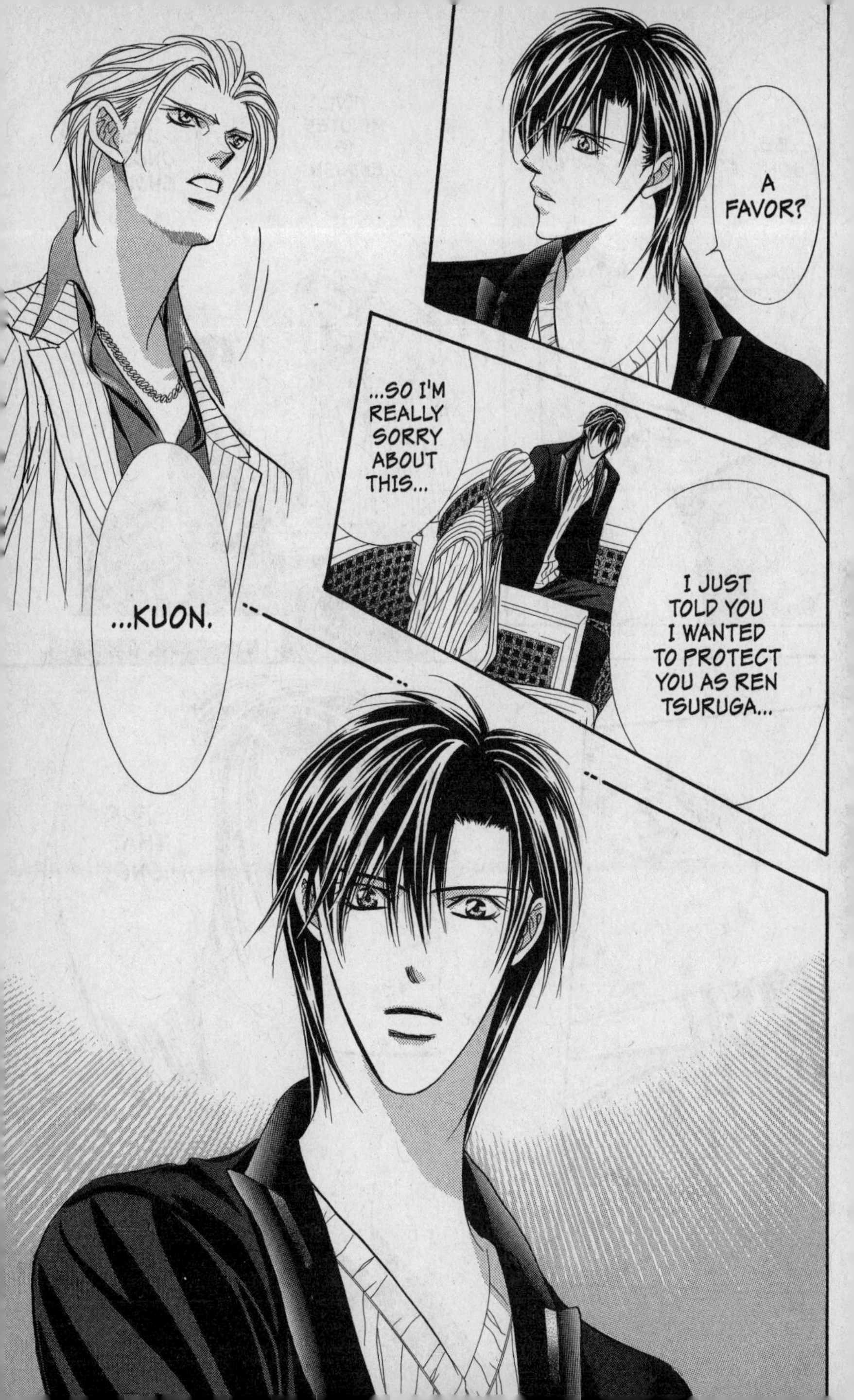
A FAVOR?
I JUST TOLD YOU I WANTED TO PROTECT YOU AS REN TSURUGA...
...SO I'M REALLY SORRY ABOUT THIS...
...KUON.

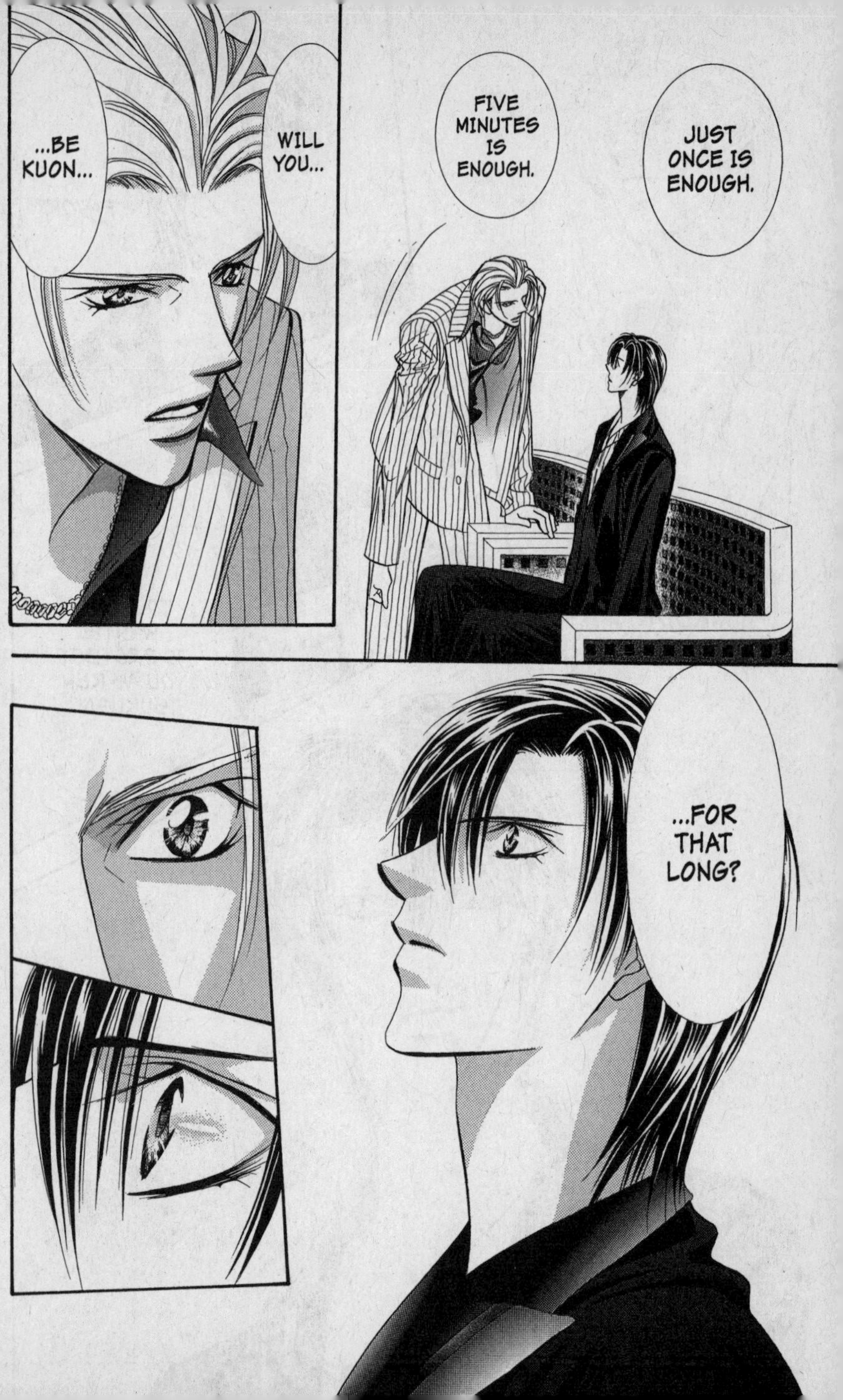
JUST ONCE IS ENOUGH.
FIVE MINUTES IS ENOUGH.
WILL YOU...
...BE KUON...
...FOR THAT LONG?

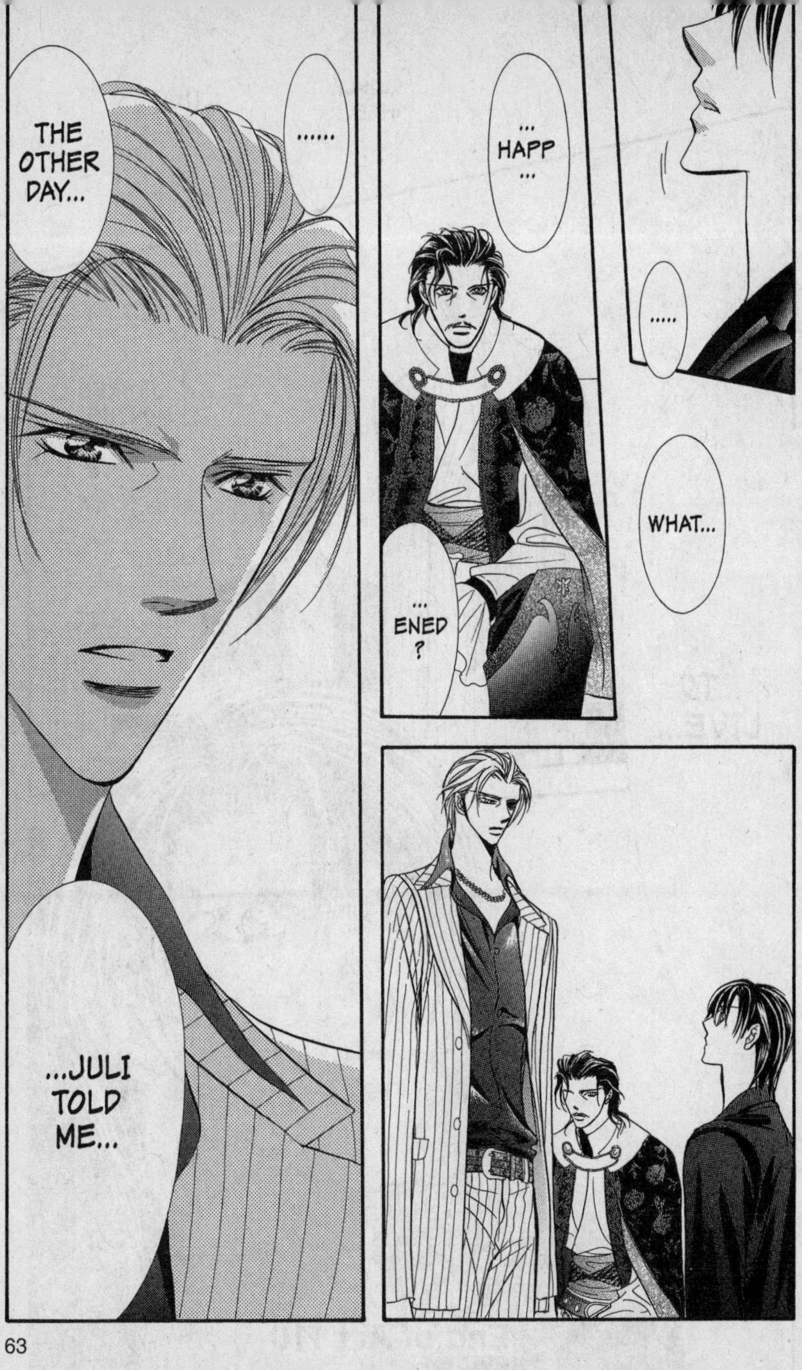
.....
WHAT...
... HAPP ...
... ENED ?
......
THE OTHER DAY...
...JULI TOLD ME...

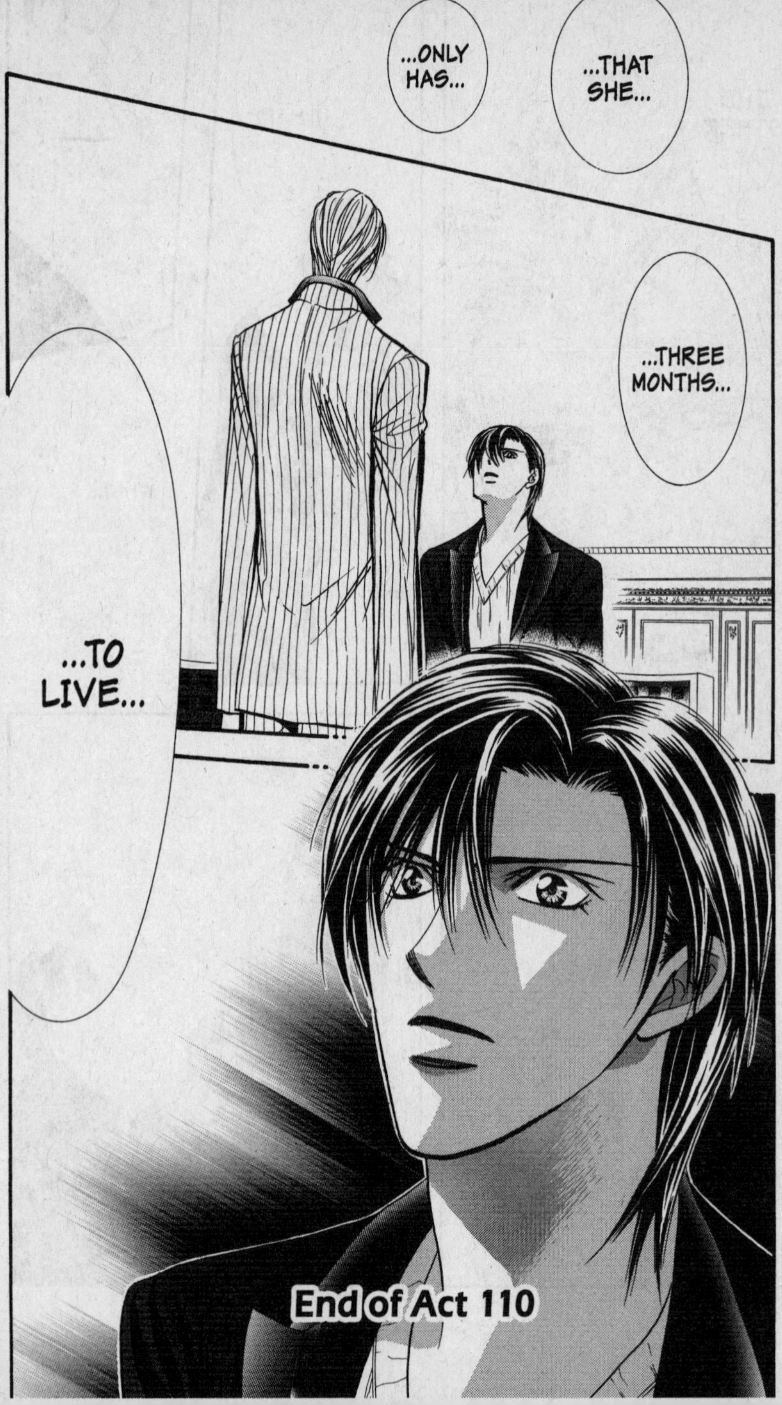
...THAT SHE...
...ONLY HAS...
...THREE MONTHS...
...TO LIVE...
End of Act 110

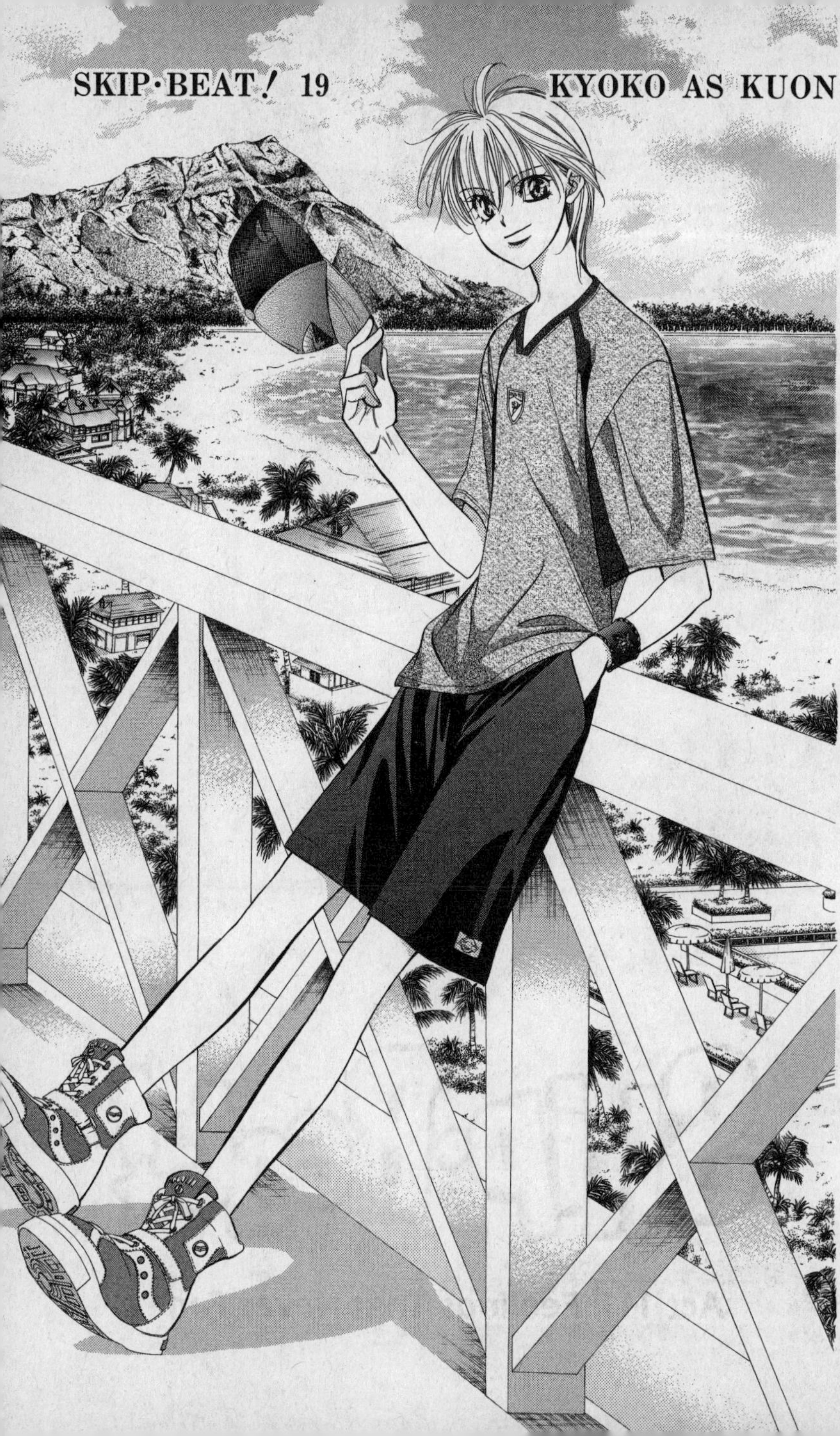
SKIP·BEAT! 19
KYOKO AS KUON

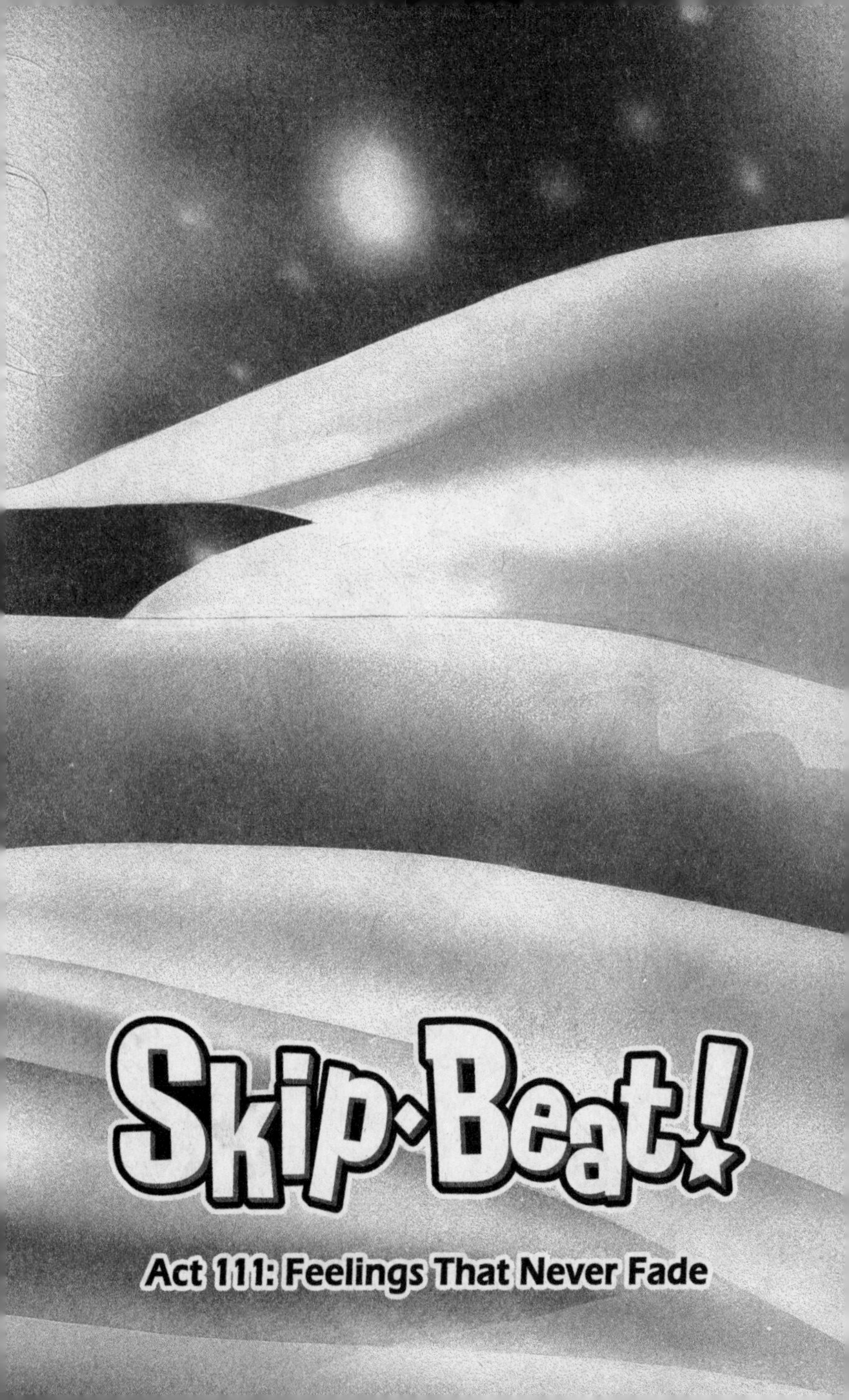
Skip·Beat!
Act 111: Feelings That Never Fade

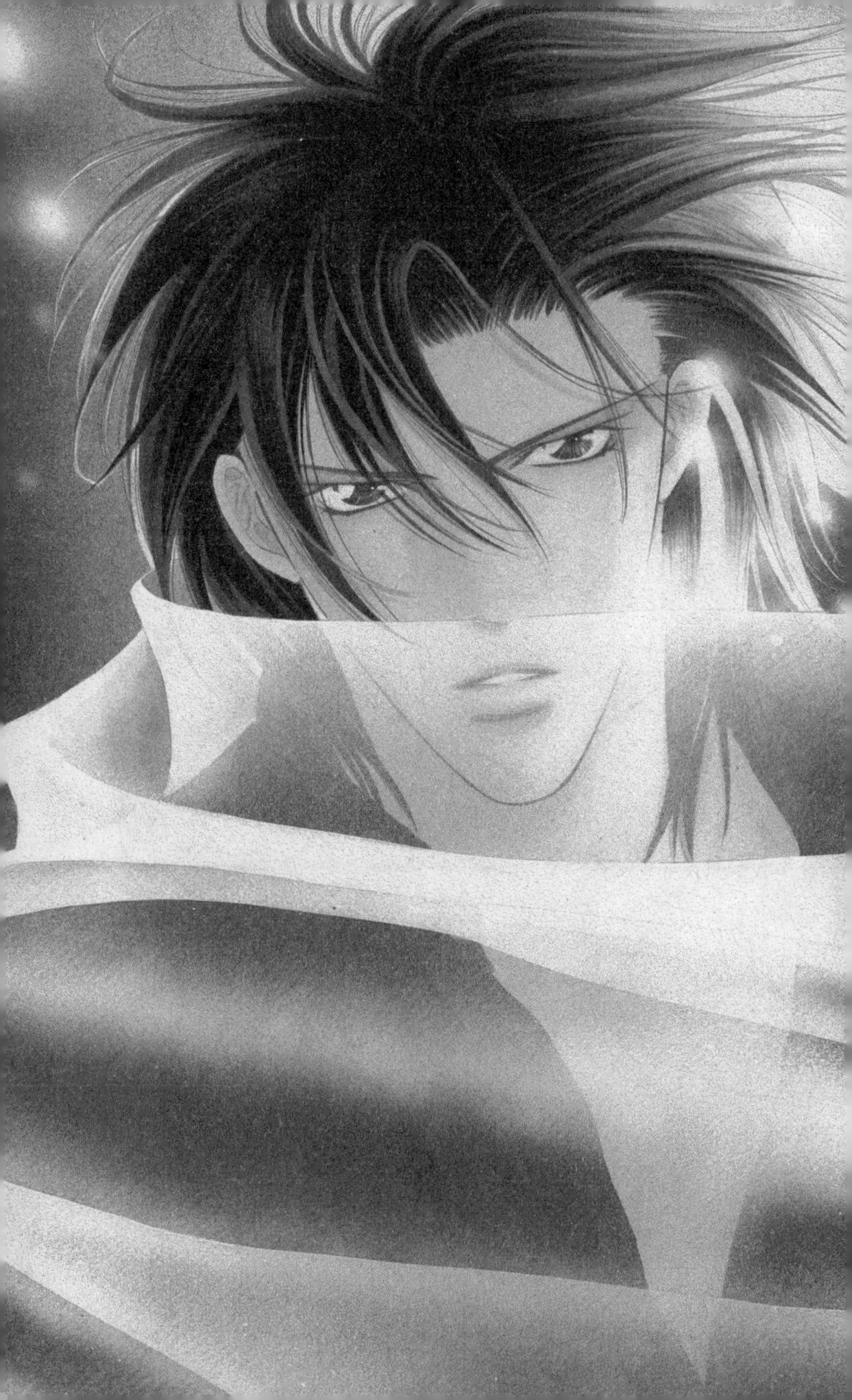

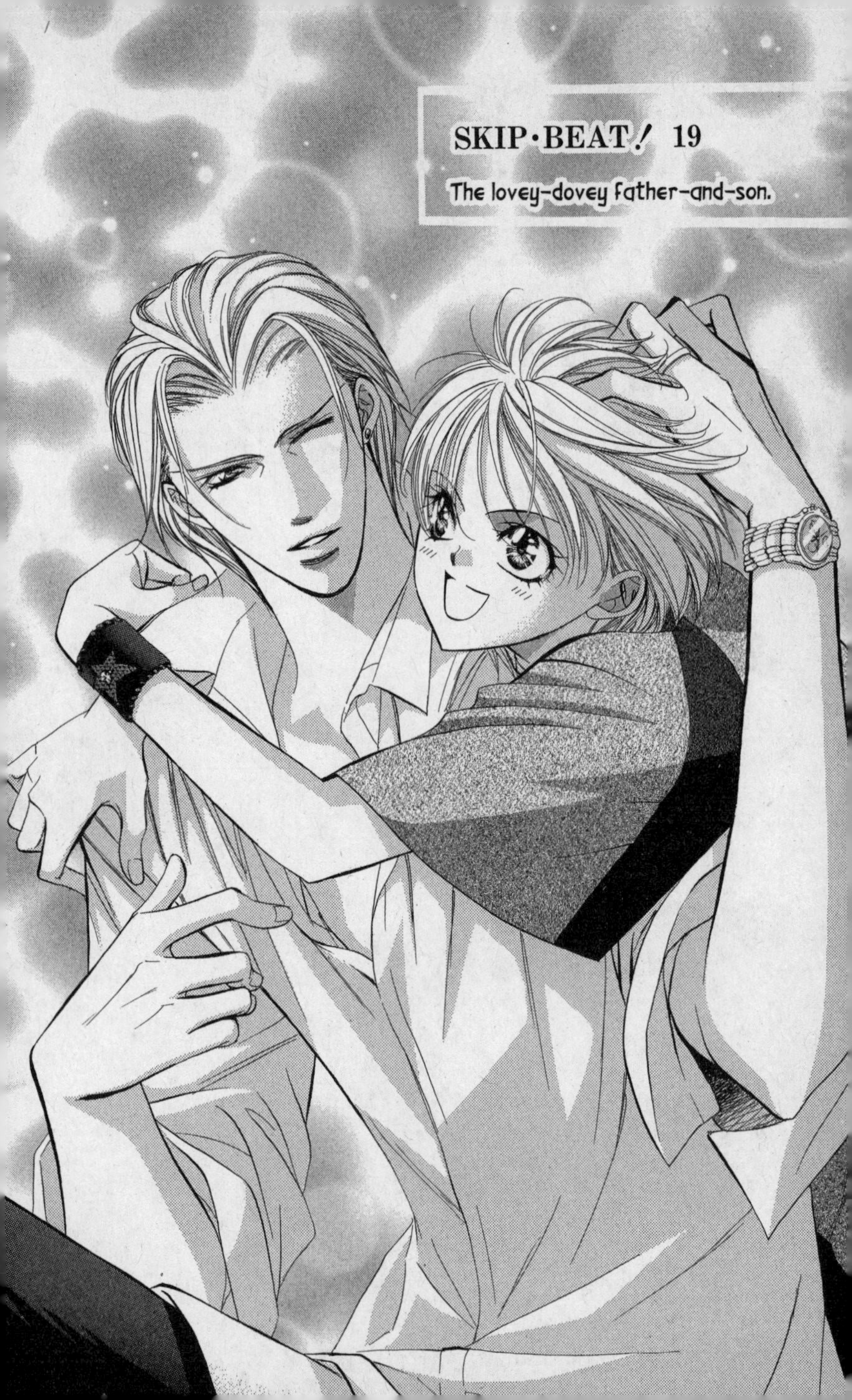
SKIP·BEAT! 19
The lovey-dovey father-and-son.

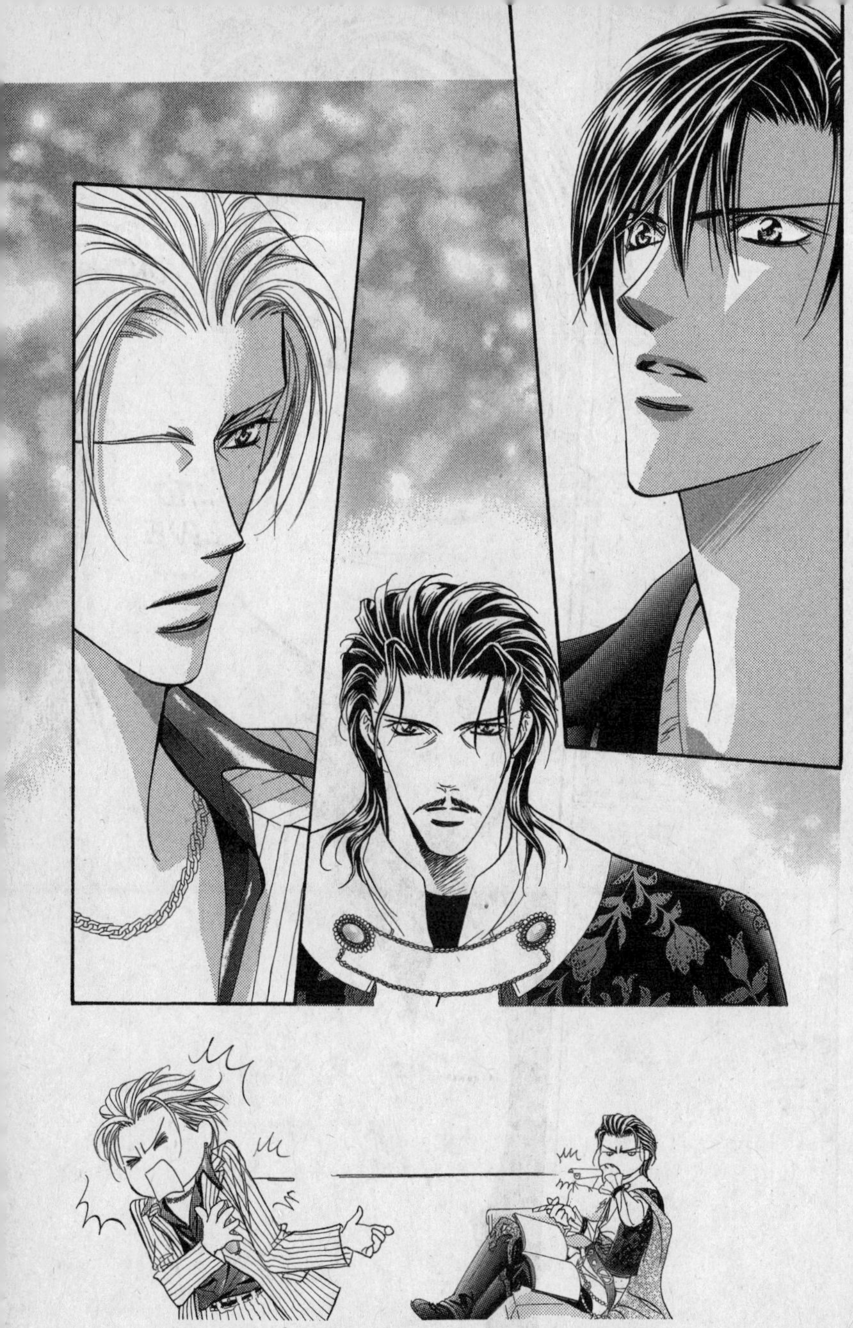

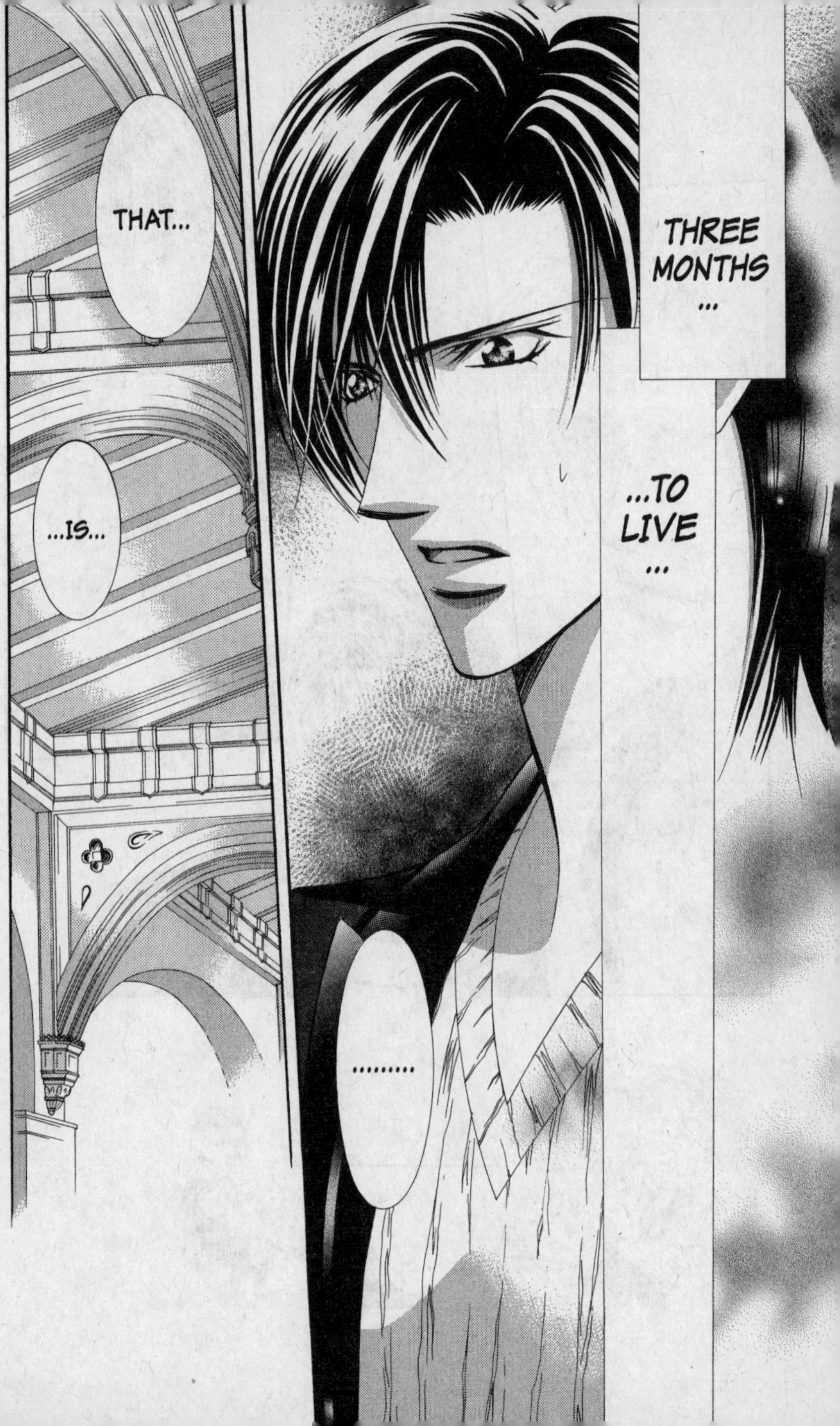
THREE MONTHS ...
...TO LIVE ...
....
THAT...
...IS...

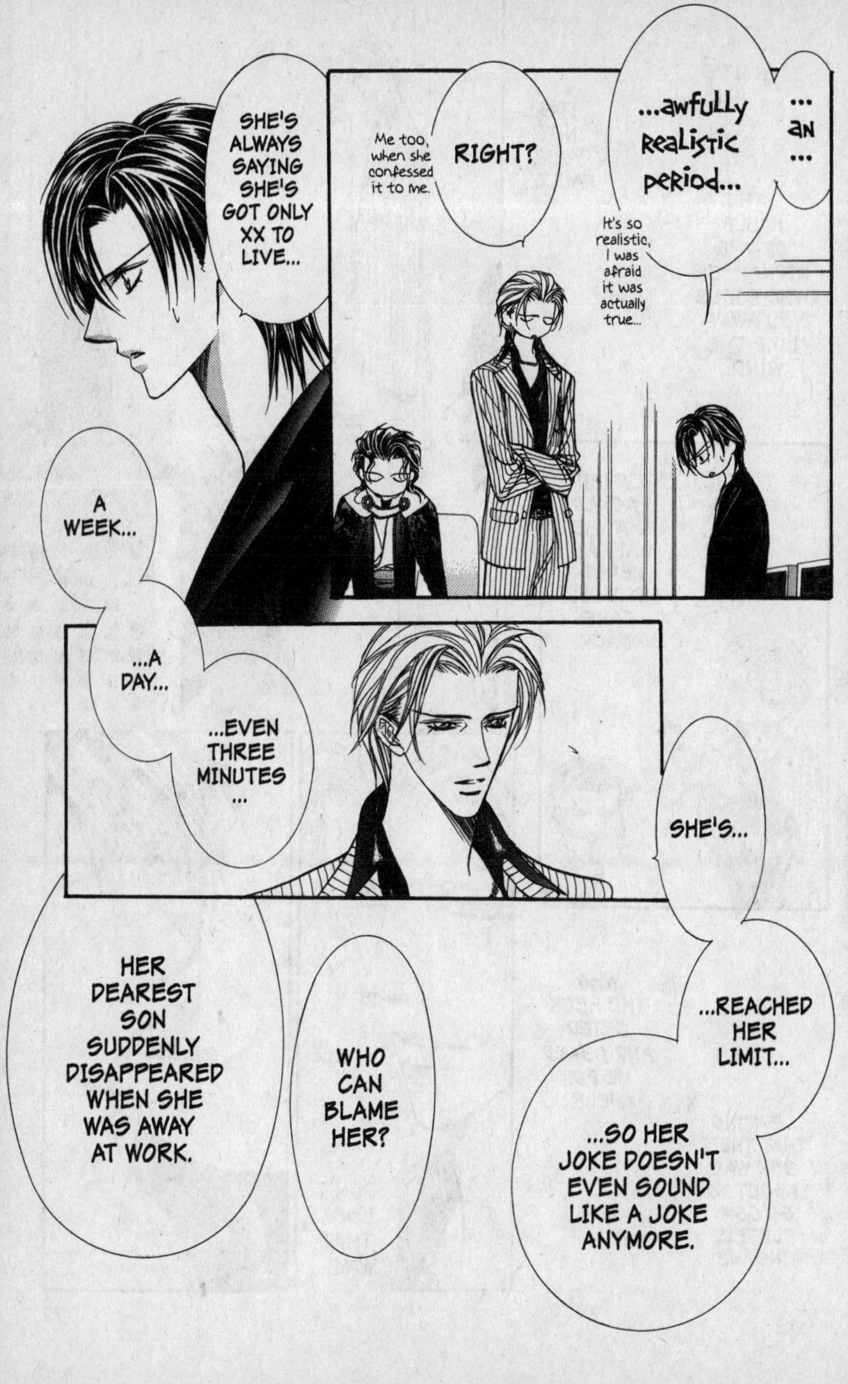
...an...
...awfully realistic period...
It's so realistic, I was afraid it was actually true...
RIGHT?
Me too, when she confessed it to me.
SHE'S ALWAYS SAYING SHE'S GOT ONLY XX TO LIVE...
A WEEK...
...A DAY...
...EVEN THREE MINUTES...
SHE'S...
...REACHED HER LIMIT...
...SO HER JOKE DOESN'T EVEN SOUND LIKE A JOKE ANYMORE.
WHO CAN BLAME HER?
HER DEAREST SON SUDDENLY DISAPPEARED WHEN SHE WAS AWAY AT WORK.

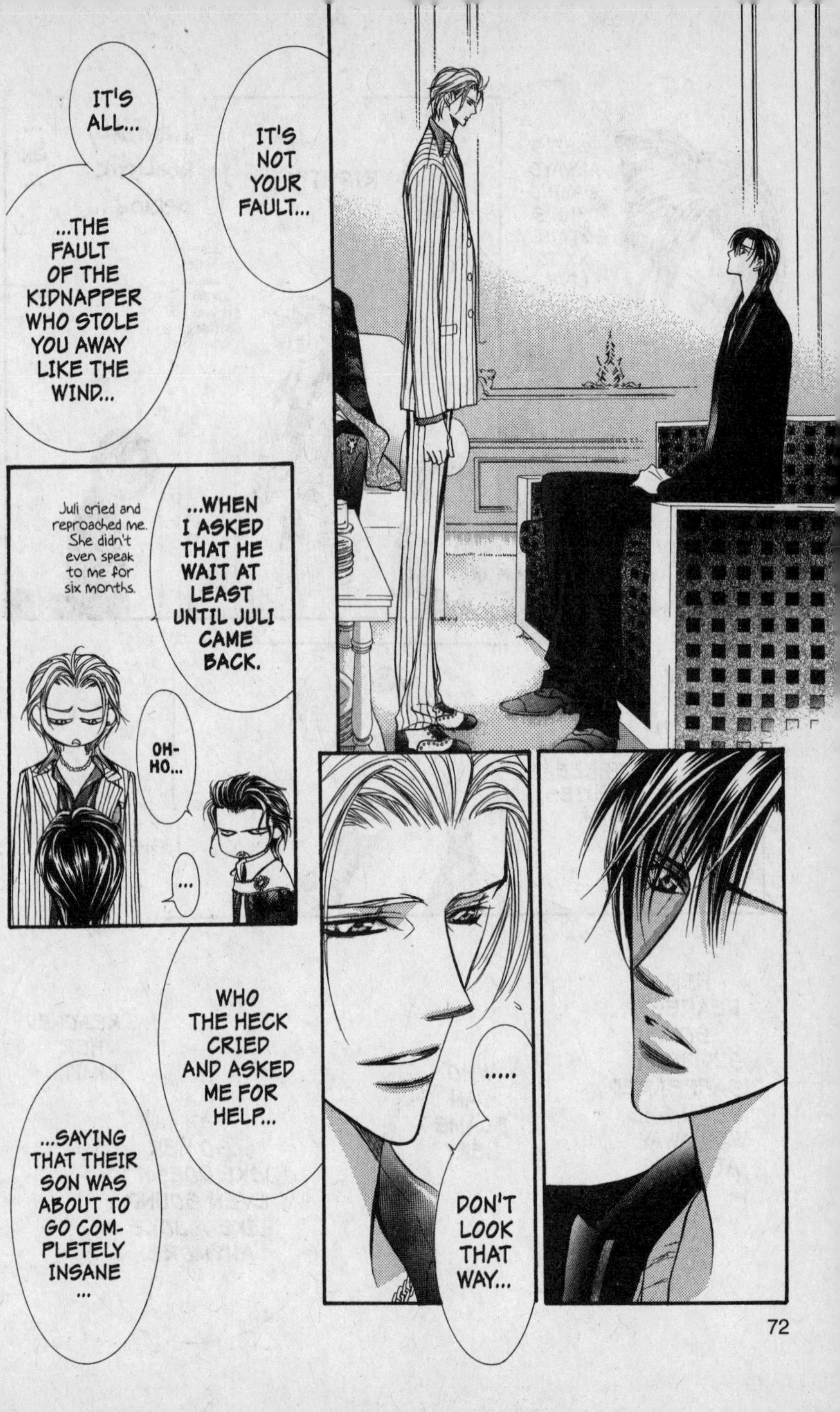
IT'S NOT YOUR FAULT...
IT'S ALL...
...THE FAULT OF THE KIDNAPPER WHO STOLE YOU AWAY LIKE THE WIND...
...WHEN I ASKED THAT HE WAIT AT LEAST UNTIL JULI CAME BACK.
Juli cried and reproached me. She didn't even speak to me for six months.
OH-HO...
...
.....
WHO THE HECK CRIED AND ASKED ME FOR HELP...
...SAYING THAT THEIR SON WAS ABOUT TO GO COMPLETELY INSANE ...
DON'T LOOK THAT WAY...

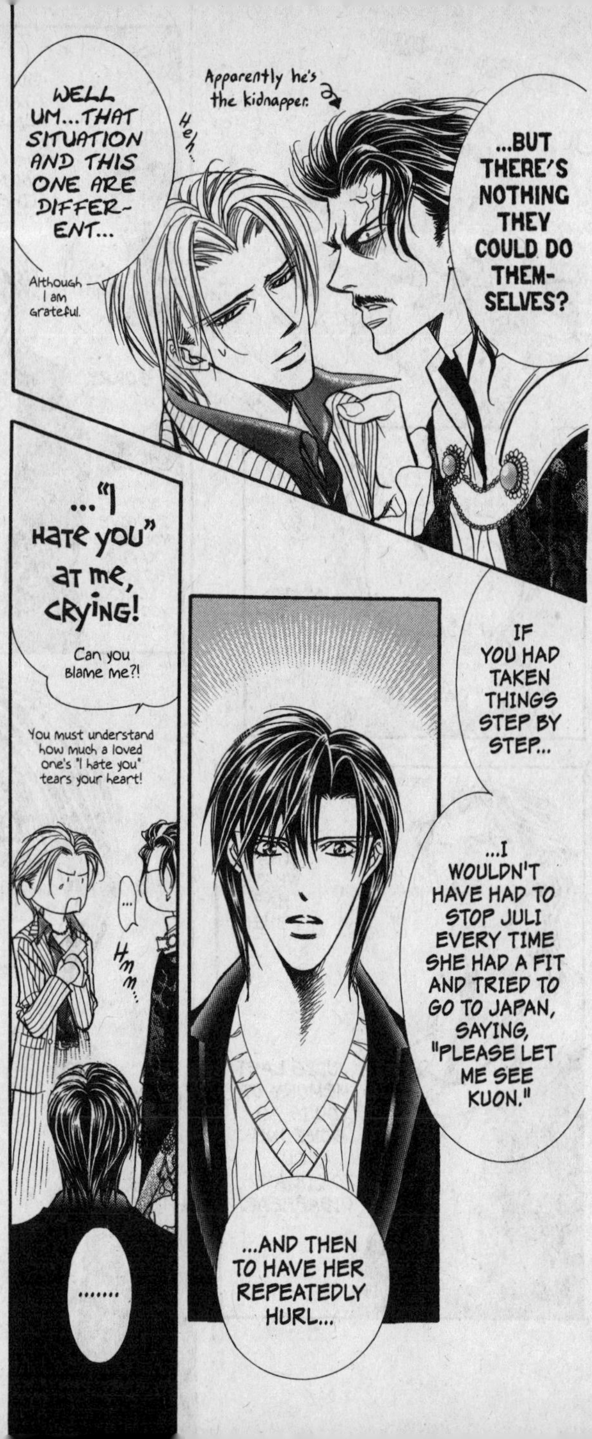
...BUT THERE'S NOTHING THEY COULD DO THEMSELVES?
Apparently he's the kidnapper.
Heh...
WELL UM...THAT SITUATION AND THIS ONE ARE DIFFERENT...
Although I am grateful.
IF YOU HAD TAKEN THINGS STEP BY STEP...
...I WOULDN'T HAVE HAD TO STOP JULI EVERY TIME SHE HAD A FIT AND TRIED TO GO TO JAPAN, SAYING, "PLEASE LET ME SEE KUON."
...AND THEN TO HAVE HER REPEATEDLY HURL...
..."I hate you" at me, crying!
Can you blame me?!
You must understand how much a loved one's "I hate you" tears your heart!
...
Hmm...
....

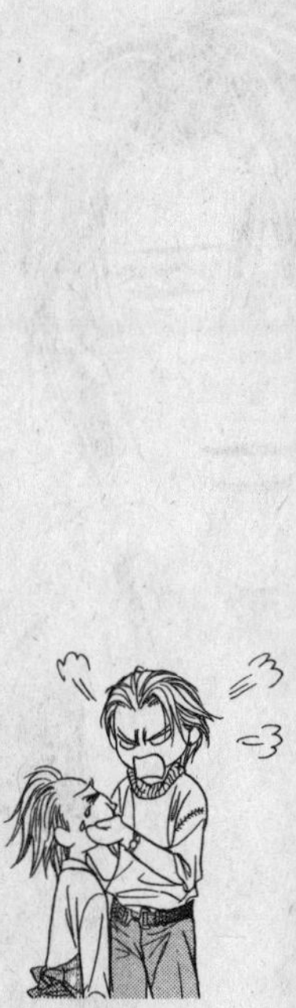

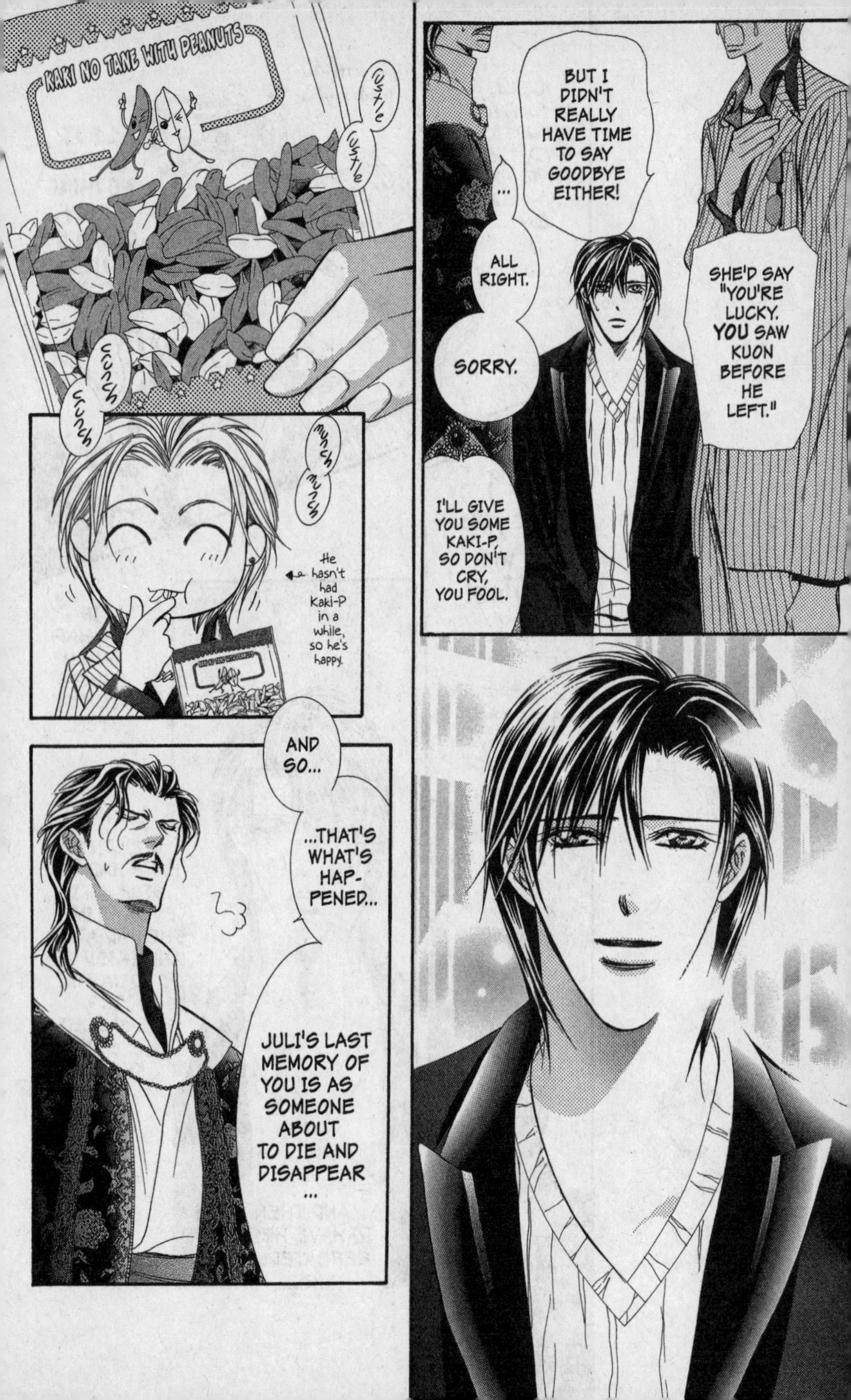
SHE'D SAY "YOU'RE LUCKY. YOU SAW KUON BEFORE HE LEFT."
BUT I DIDN'T REALLY HAVE TIME TO SAY GOODBYE EITHER!
...
ALL RIGHT.
SORRY.
I'LL GIVE YOU SOME KAKI-P, SO DON'T CRY, YOU FOOL.
KAKI NO TANE WITH PEANUTS
rustle
rustle
crunch
crunch
munch munch
He hasn't had Kaki-P in a while, so he's happy.
AND SO...
...THAT'S WHAT'S HAPPENED...
JULI'S LAST MEMORY OF YOU IS AS SOMEONE ABOUT TO DIE AND DISAPPEAR ...

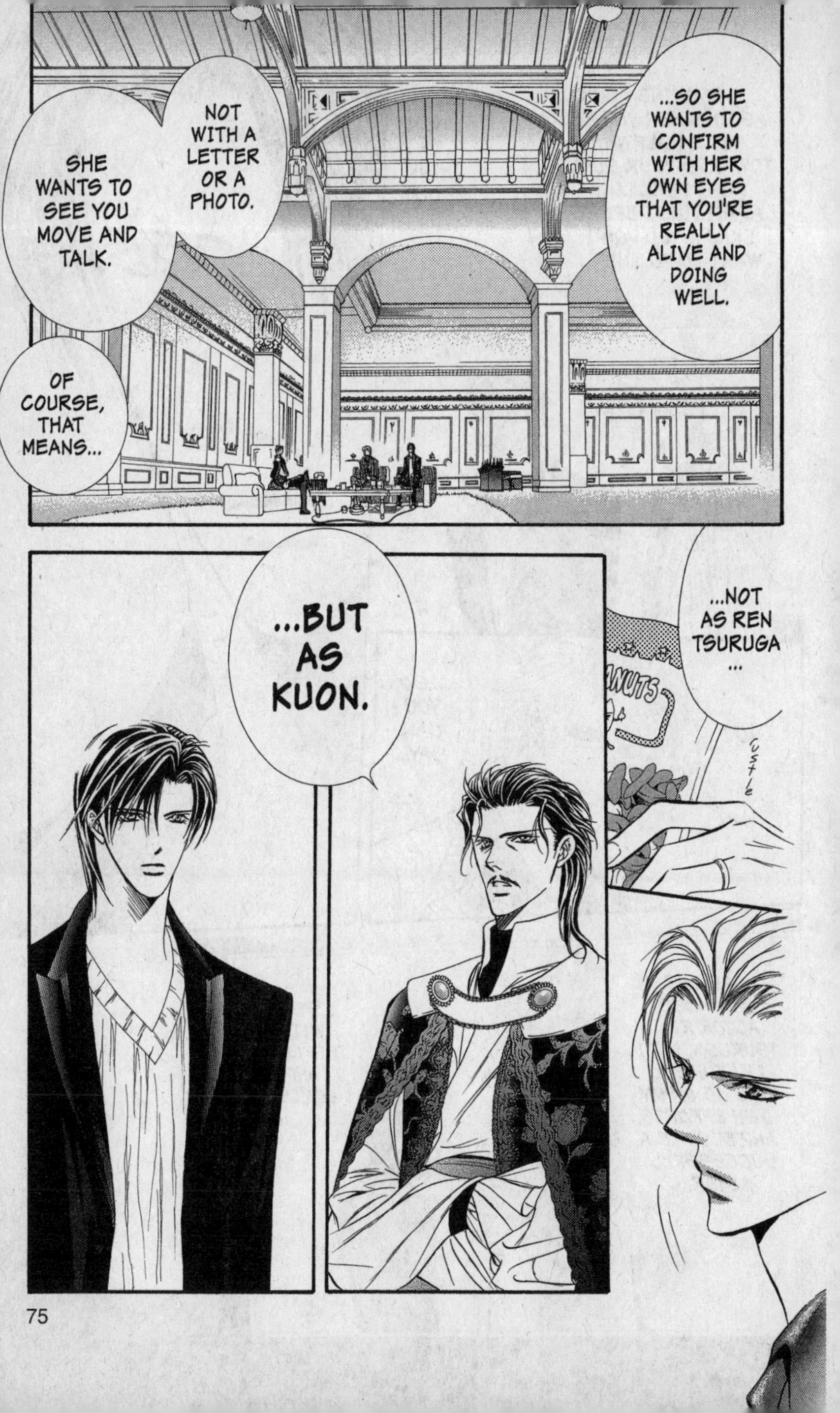
...SO SHE WANTS TO CONFIRM WITH HER OWN EYES THAT YOU'RE REALLY ALIVE AND DOING WELL.
NOT WITH A LETTER OR A PHOTO.
SHE WANTS TO SEE YOU MOVE AND TALK.
OF COURSE, THAT MEANS...
...NOT AS REN TSURUGA ...
rustle
...BUT AS KUON.

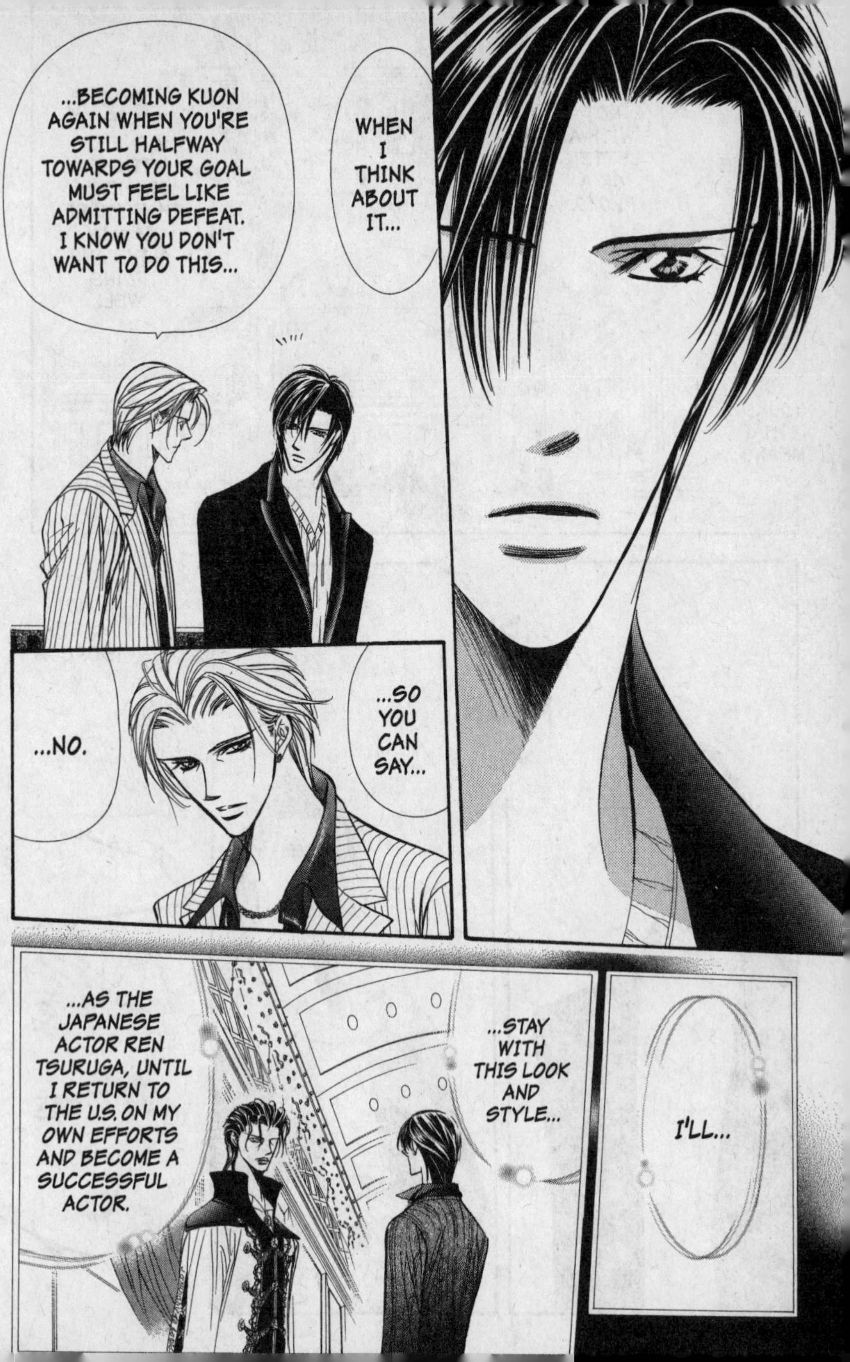
WHEN I THINK ABOUT IT...
...BECOMING KUON AGAIN WHEN YOU'RE STILL HALFWAY TOWARDS YOUR GOAL MUST FEEL LIKE ADMITTING DEFEAT. I KNOW YOU DON'T WANT TO DO THIS...
...SO YOU CAN SAY...
...NO.
I'LL...
...STAY WITH THIS LOOK AND STYLE...
...AS THE JAPANESE ACTOR REN TSURUGA, UNTIL I RETURN TO THE U.S. ON MY OWN EFFORTS AND BECOME A SUCCESSFUL ACTOR.

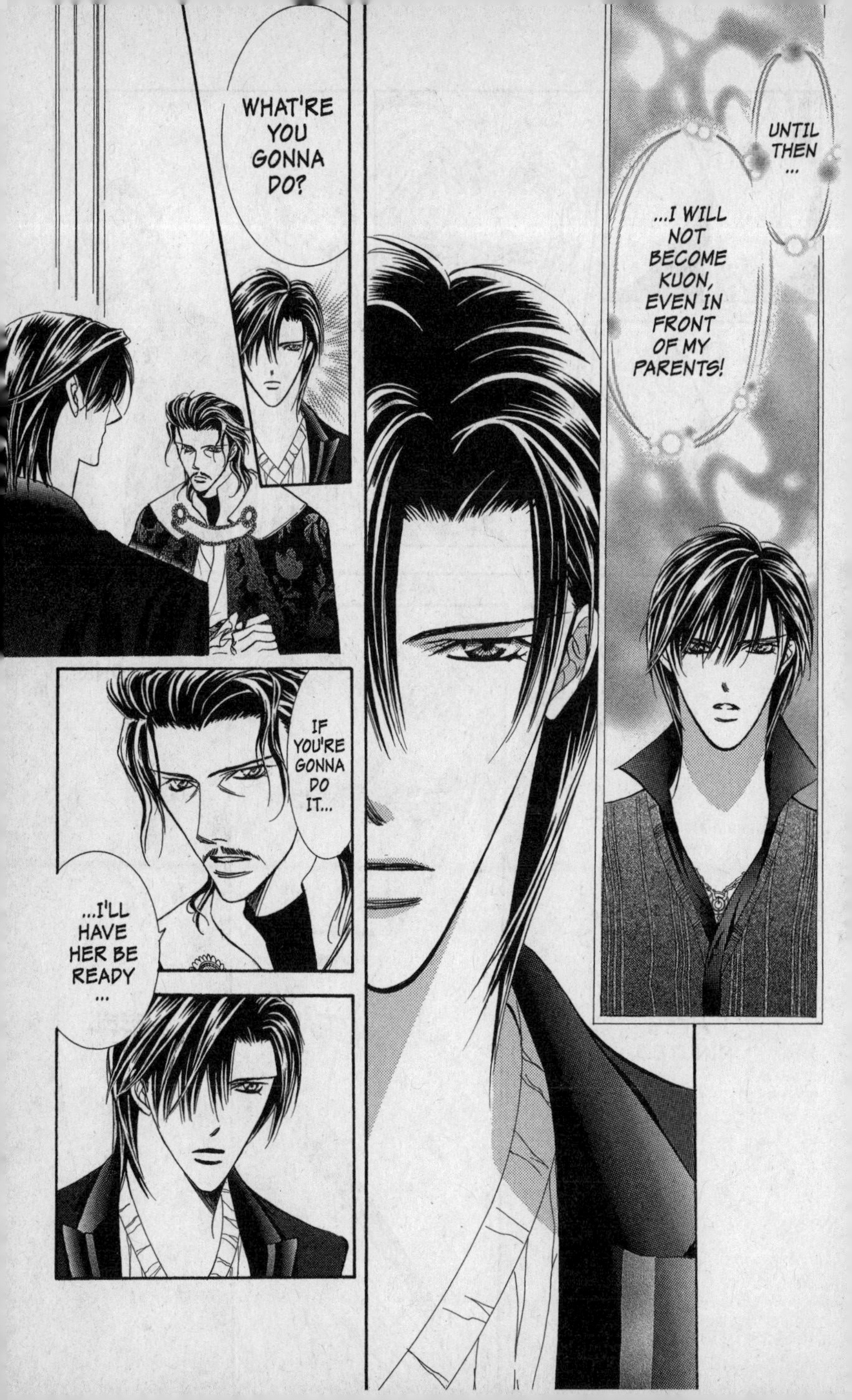
UNTIL THEN ...
...I WILL NOT BECOME KUON, EVEN IN FRONT OF MY PARENTS!
WHAT'RE YOU GONNA DO?
IF YOU'RE GONNA DO IT...
...I'LL HAVE HER BE READY ...

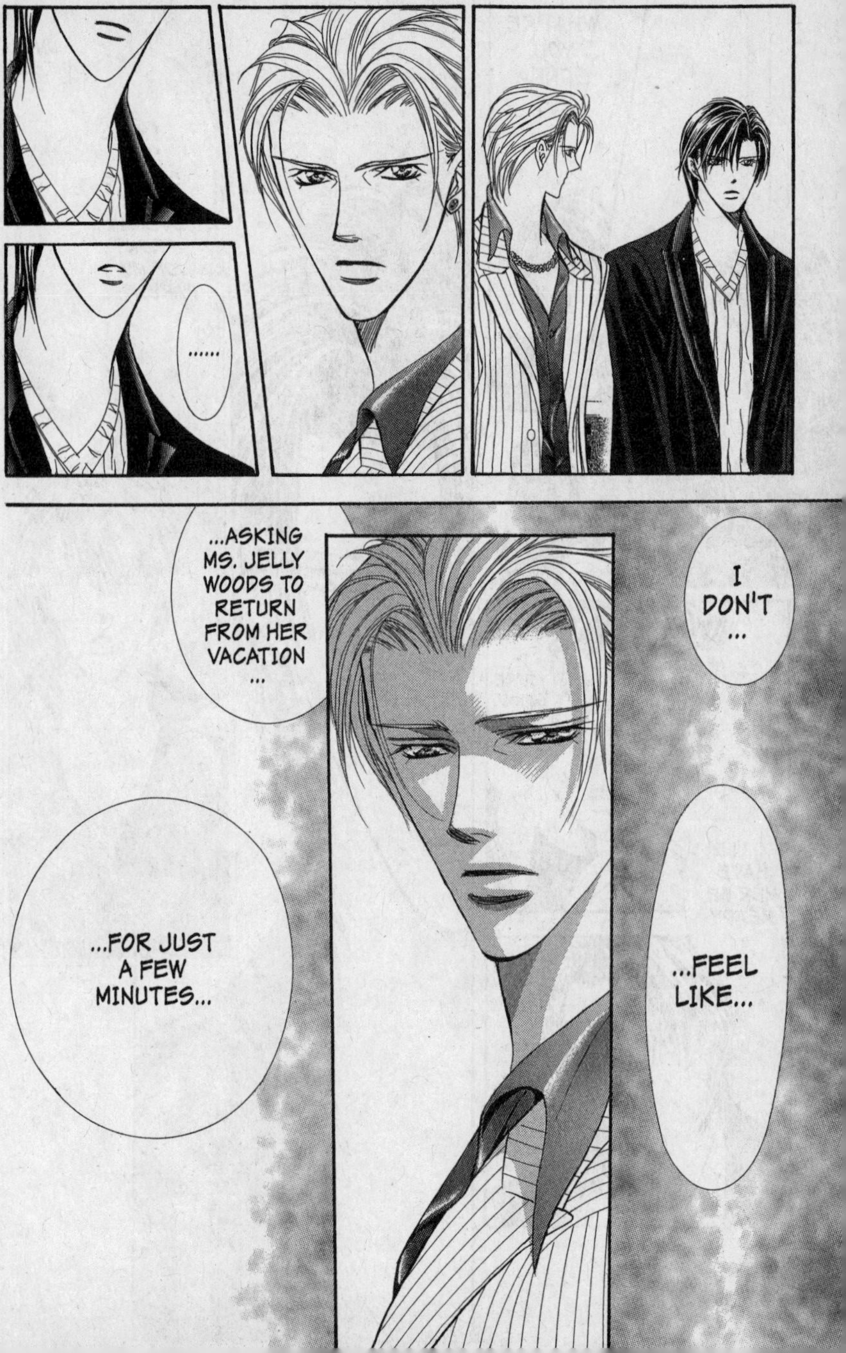
......
I DON'T ...
...FEEL LIKE...
...ASKING MS. JELLY WOODS TO RETURN FROM HER VACATION ...
...FOR JUST A FEW MINUTES...

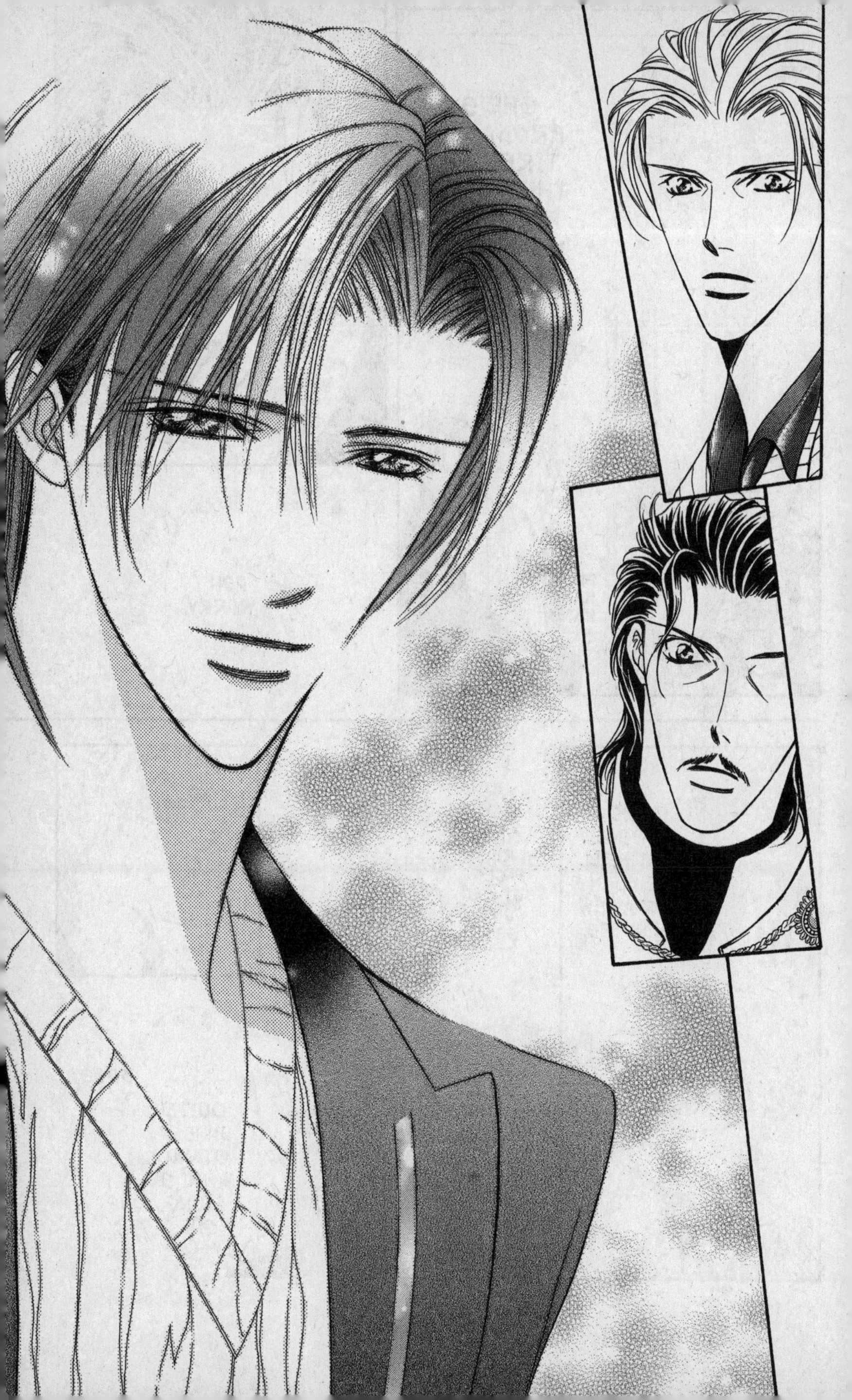

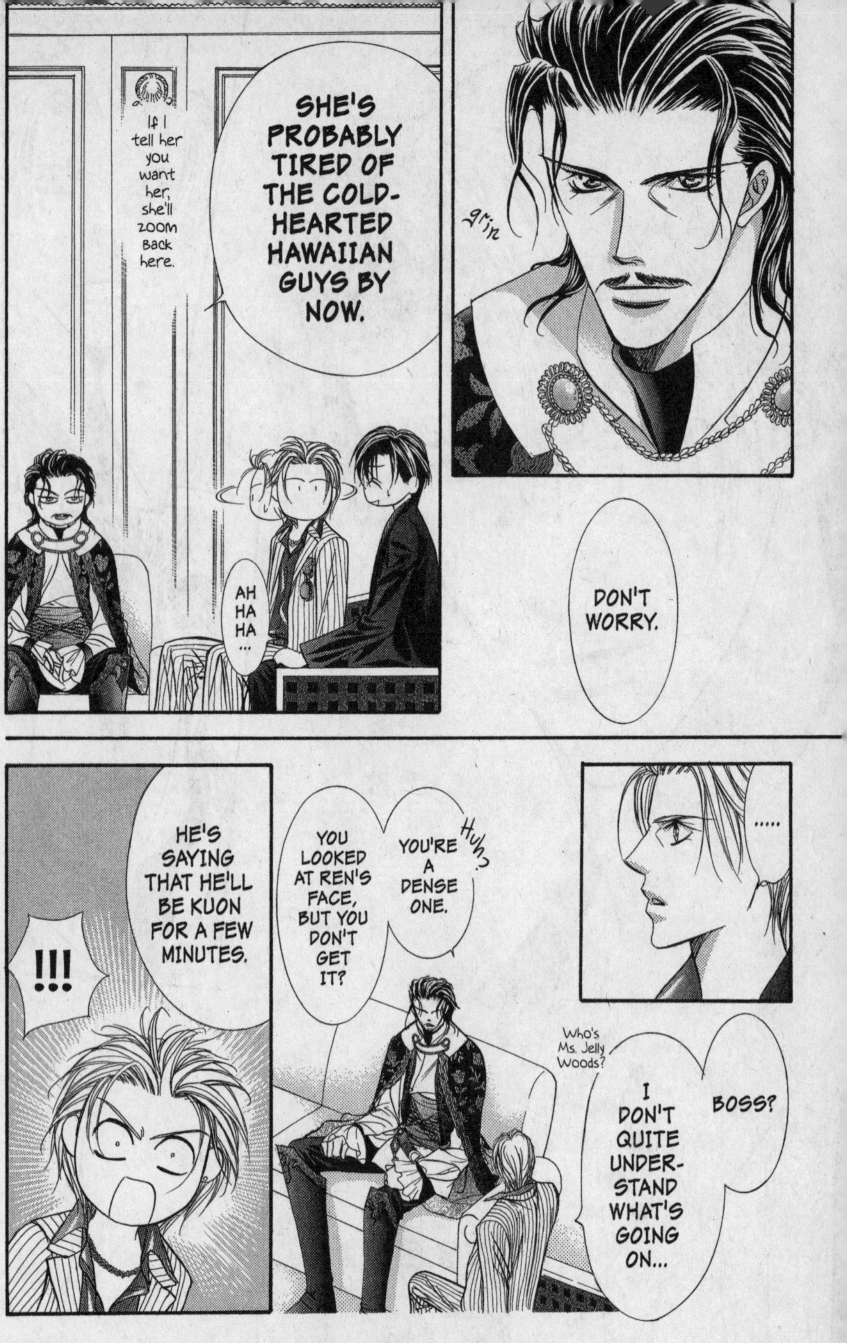
grin
DON'T WORRY.
SHE'S PROBABLY TIRED OF THE COLD-HEARTED HAWAIIAN GUYS BY NOW.
If I tell her you want her, she'll zoom back here.
AH HA HA...
.....
BOSS?
I DON'T QUITE UNDERSTAND WHAT'S GOING ON...
Who's Ms. Jelly Woods?
YOU'RE A DENSE ONE.
Huh?
YOU LOOKED AT REN'S FACE, BUT YOU DON'T GET IT?
HE'S SAYING THAT HE'LL BE KUON FOR A FEW MINUTES.
!!!

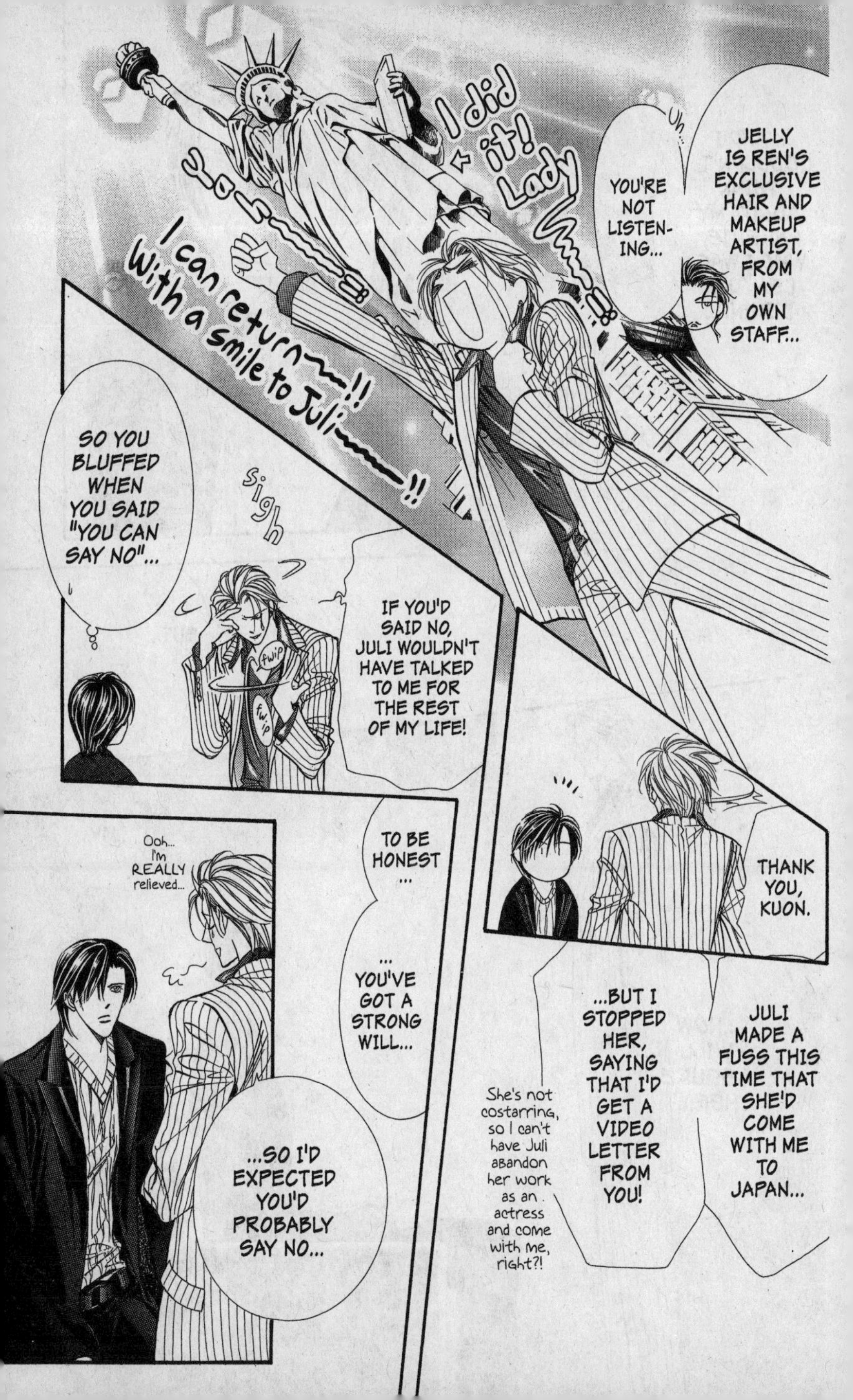
JELLY IS REN'S EXCLUSIVE HAIR AND MAKEUP ARTIST, FROM MY OWN STAFF...
Uh...
YOU'RE NOT LISTENING...
I did it! Lady
I can return~~!! With a smile to Juli~~!!
THANK YOU, KUON.
IF YOU'D SAID NO, JULI WOULDN'T HAVE TALKED TO ME FOR THE REST OF MY LIFE!
sigh
fwip
fwip
SO YOU BLUFFED WHEN YOU SAID "YOU CAN SAY NO"...
JULI MADE A FUSS THIS TIME THAT SHE'D COME WITH ME TO JAPAN...
...BUT I STOPPED HER, SAYING THAT I'D GET A VIDEO LETTER FROM YOU!
She's not costarring, so I can't have Juli abandon her work as an actress and come with me, right?!
TO BE HONEST...
...YOU'VE GOT A STRONG WILL...
Ooh... I'm REALLY relieved...
...SO I'D EXPECTED YOU'D PROBABLY SAY NO...

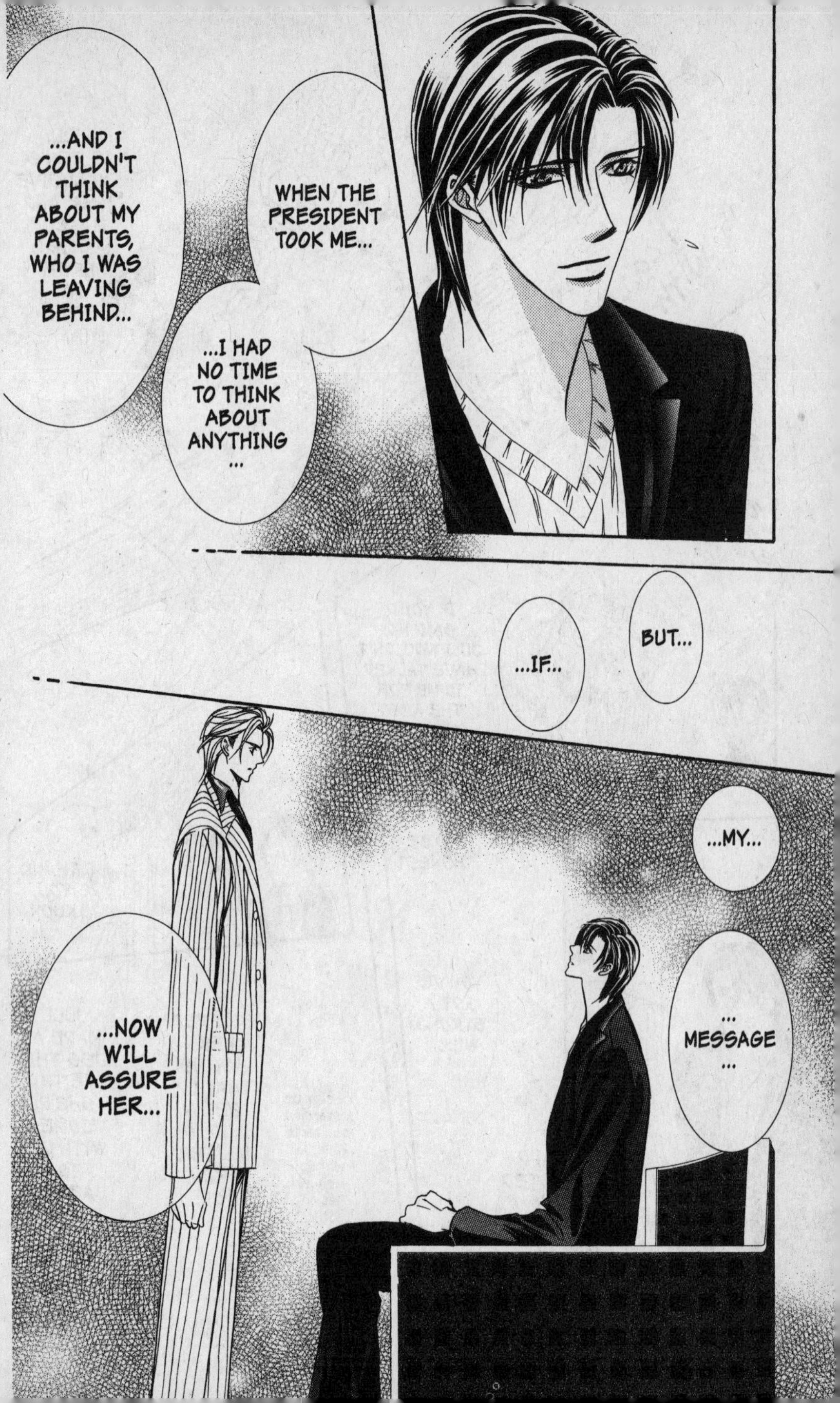
WHEN THE PRESIDENT TOOK ME...
...I HAD NO TIME TO THINK ABOUT ANYTHING...
...AND I COULDN'T THINK ABOUT MY PARENTS, WHO I WAS LEAVING BEHIND...
BUT...
...IF...
...MY...
...MESSAGE...
...NOW WILL ASSURE HER...

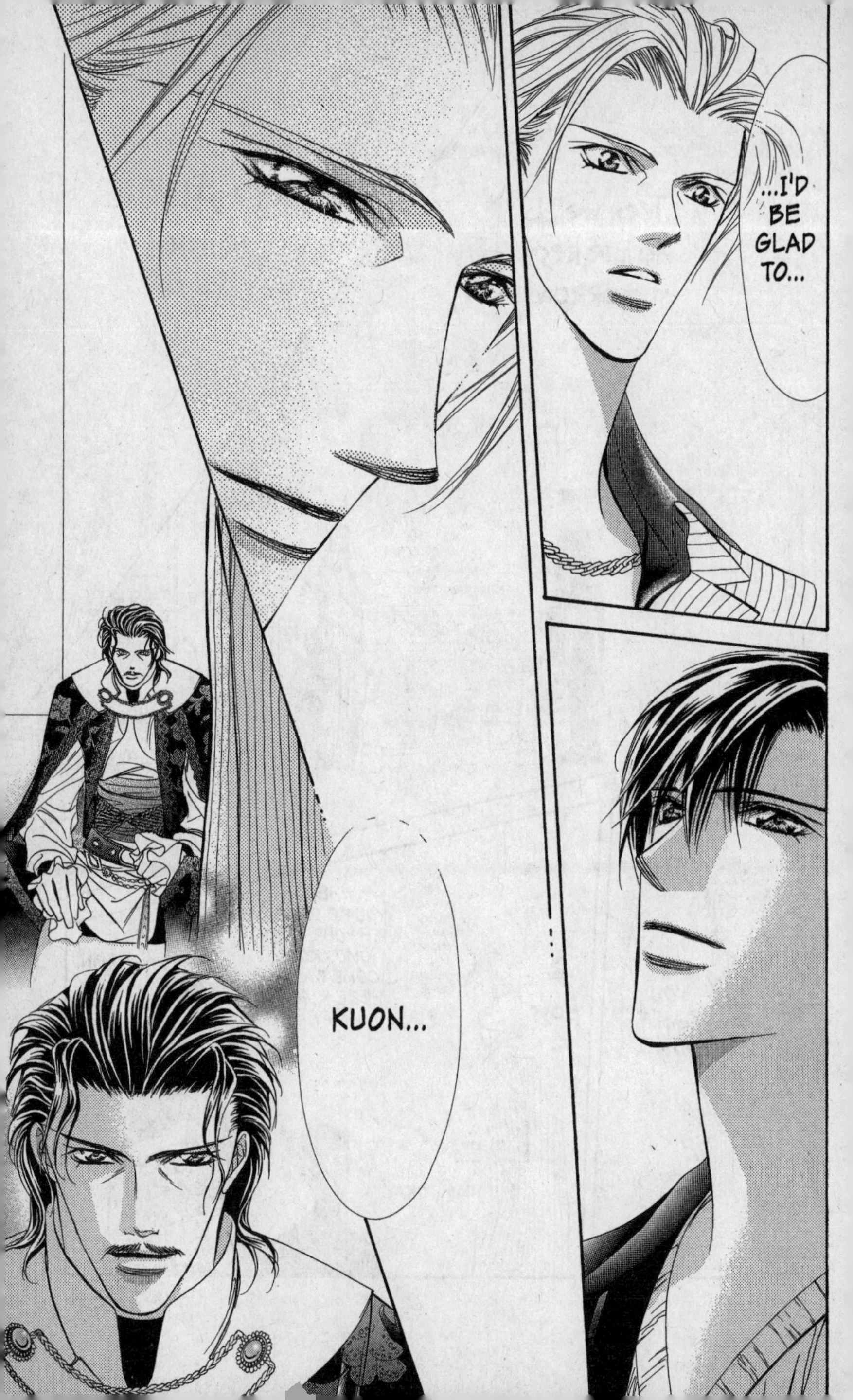
...I'D BE GLAD TO...
KUON...

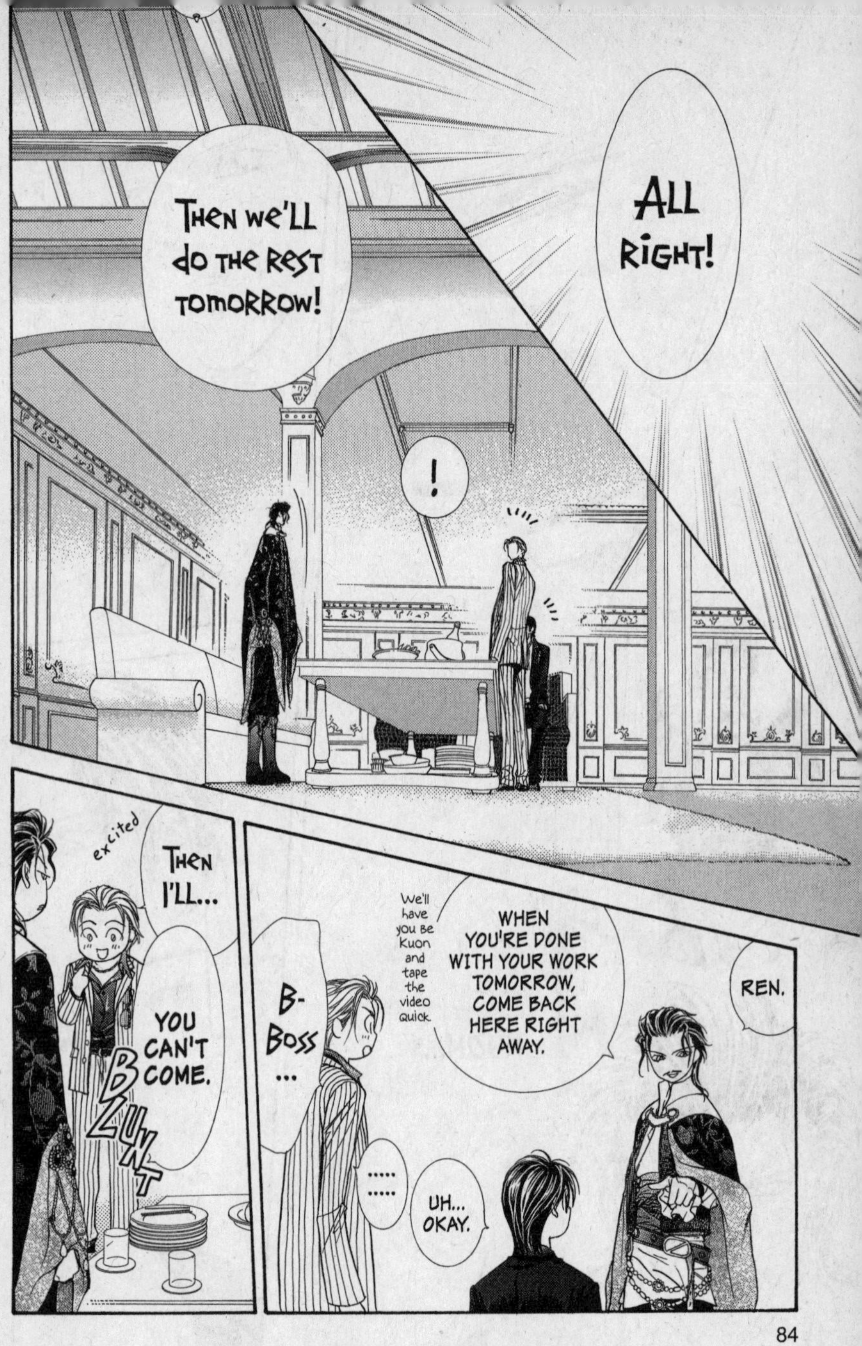

ALL RIGHT!
THEN WE'LL DO THE REST TOMORROW!
!
REN.
WHEN YOU'RE DONE WITH YOUR WORK TOMORROW, COME BACK HERE RIGHT AWAY.
We'll have you be Kuon and tape the video quick
B-BOSS...
UH... OKAY.
......
......
excited
THEN I'LL...
YOU CAN'T COME.
BLUNT

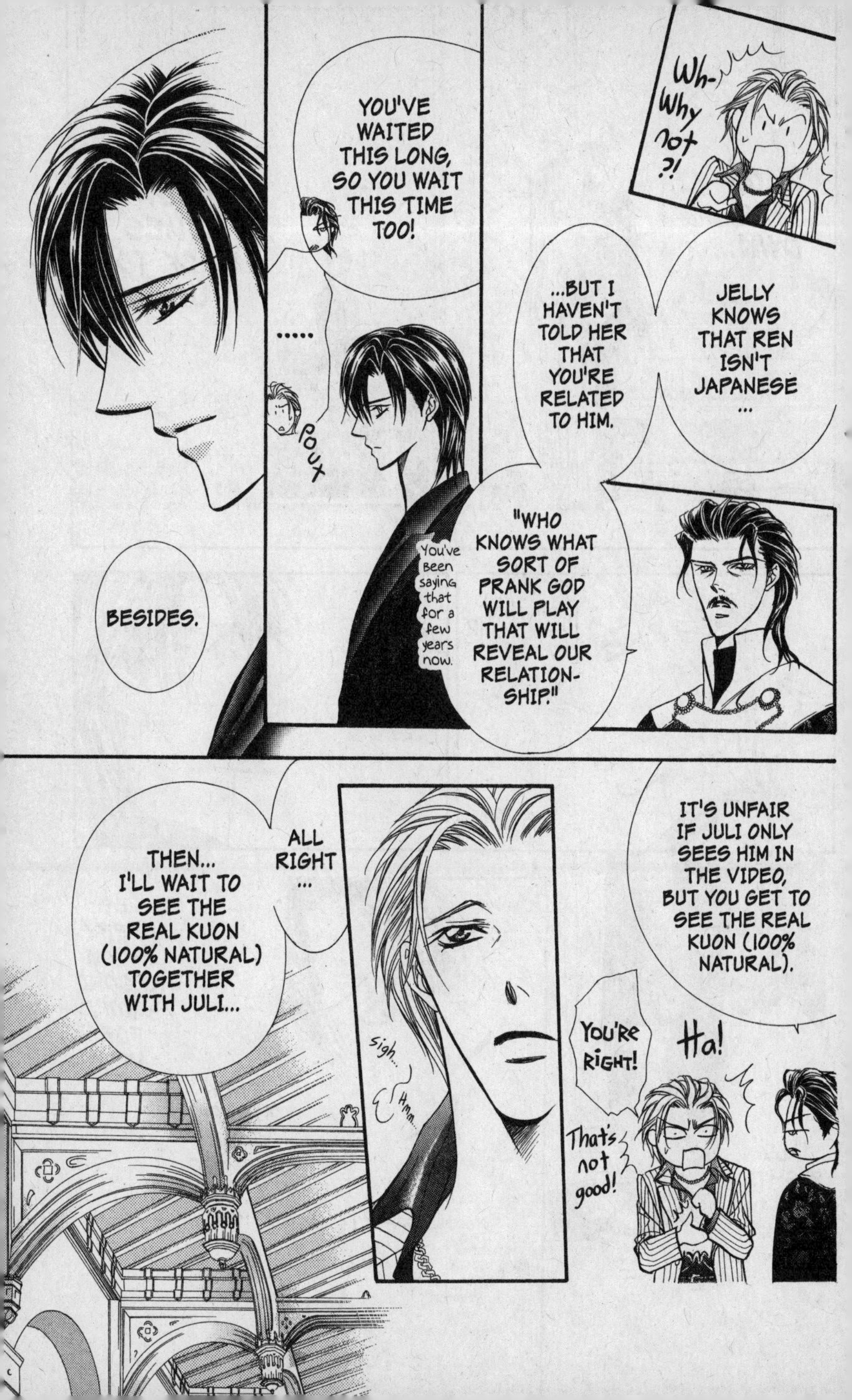

Wh-Why not?!
JELLY KNOWS THAT REN ISN'T JAPANESE...
...BUT I HAVEN'T TOLD HER THAT YOU'RE RELATED TO HIM.
"WHO KNOWS WHAT SORT OF PRANK GOD WILL PLAY THAT WILL REVEAL OUR RELATIONSHIP."
You've been saying that for a few years now.
YOU'VE WAITED THIS LONG, SO YOU WAIT THIS TIME TOO!
.....
Pout
BESIDES.
IT'S UNFAIR IF JULI ONLY SEES HIM IN THE VIDEO, BUT YOU GET TO SEE THE REAL KUON (100% NATURAL).
Ha!
You're right!
That's not good!
sigh...
Hmm...
ALL RIGHT...
THEN... I'LL WAIT TO SEE THE REAL KUON (100% NATURAL) TOGETHER WITH JULI...

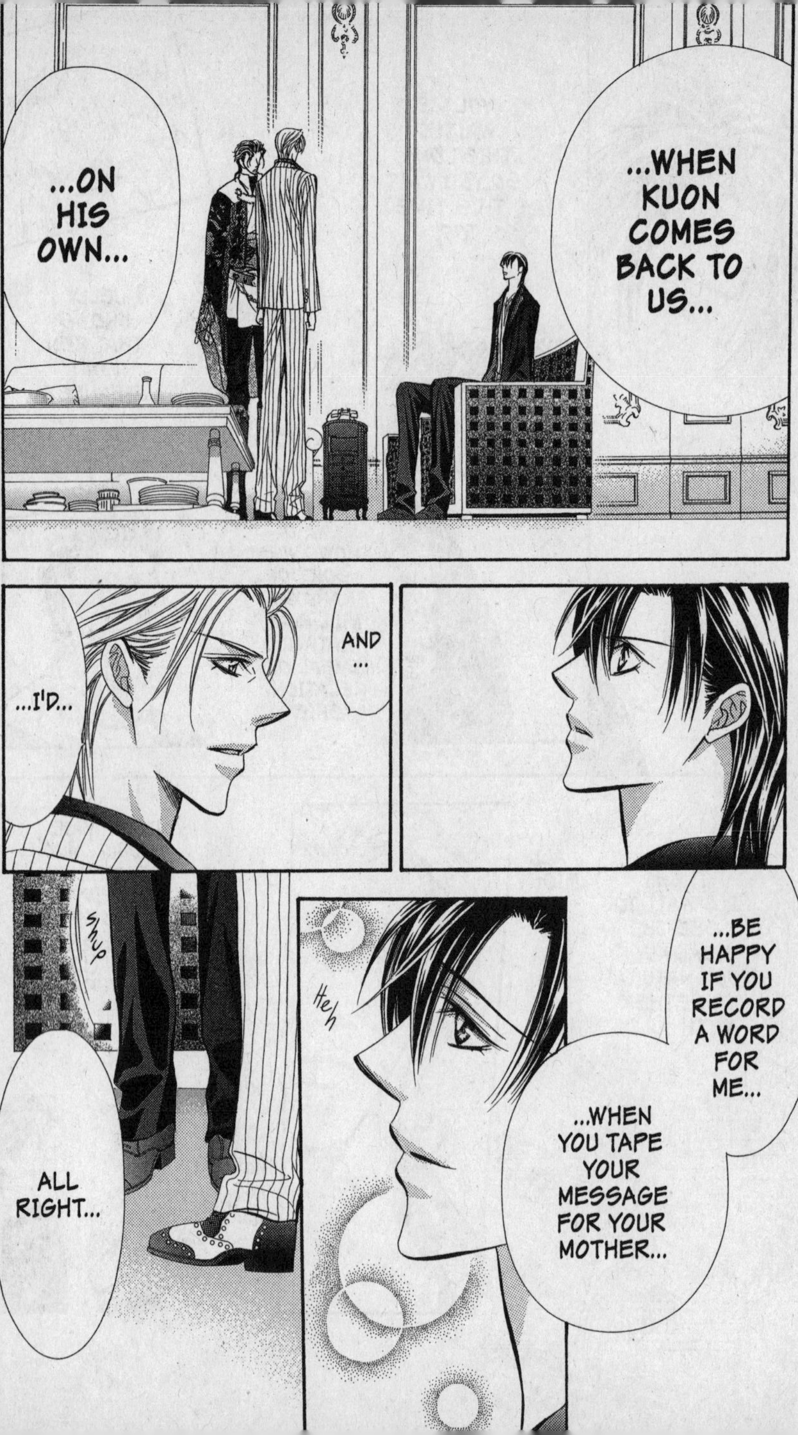
...WHEN KUON COMES BACK TO US...
...ON HIS OWN...
AND ...
...I'D...
...BE HAPPY IF YOU RECORD A WORD FOR ME...
...WHEN YOU TAPE YOUR MESSAGE FOR YOUR MOTHER...
Heh
Shup
ALL RIGHT...

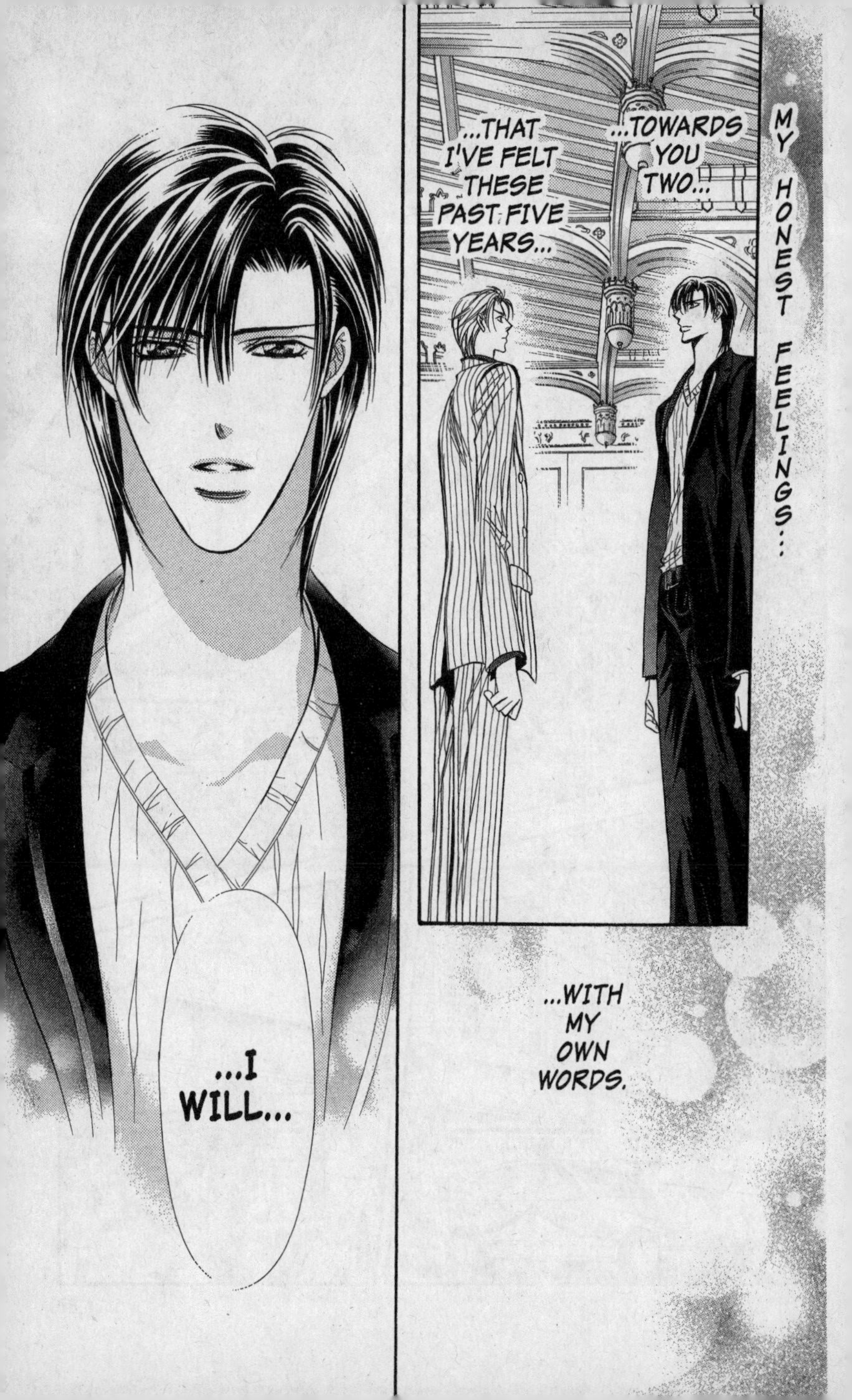
MY HONEST FEELINGS...
...TOWARDS YOU TWO...
...THAT I'VE FELT THESE PAST FIVE YEARS...
...WITH MY OWN WORDS.
...I WILL...

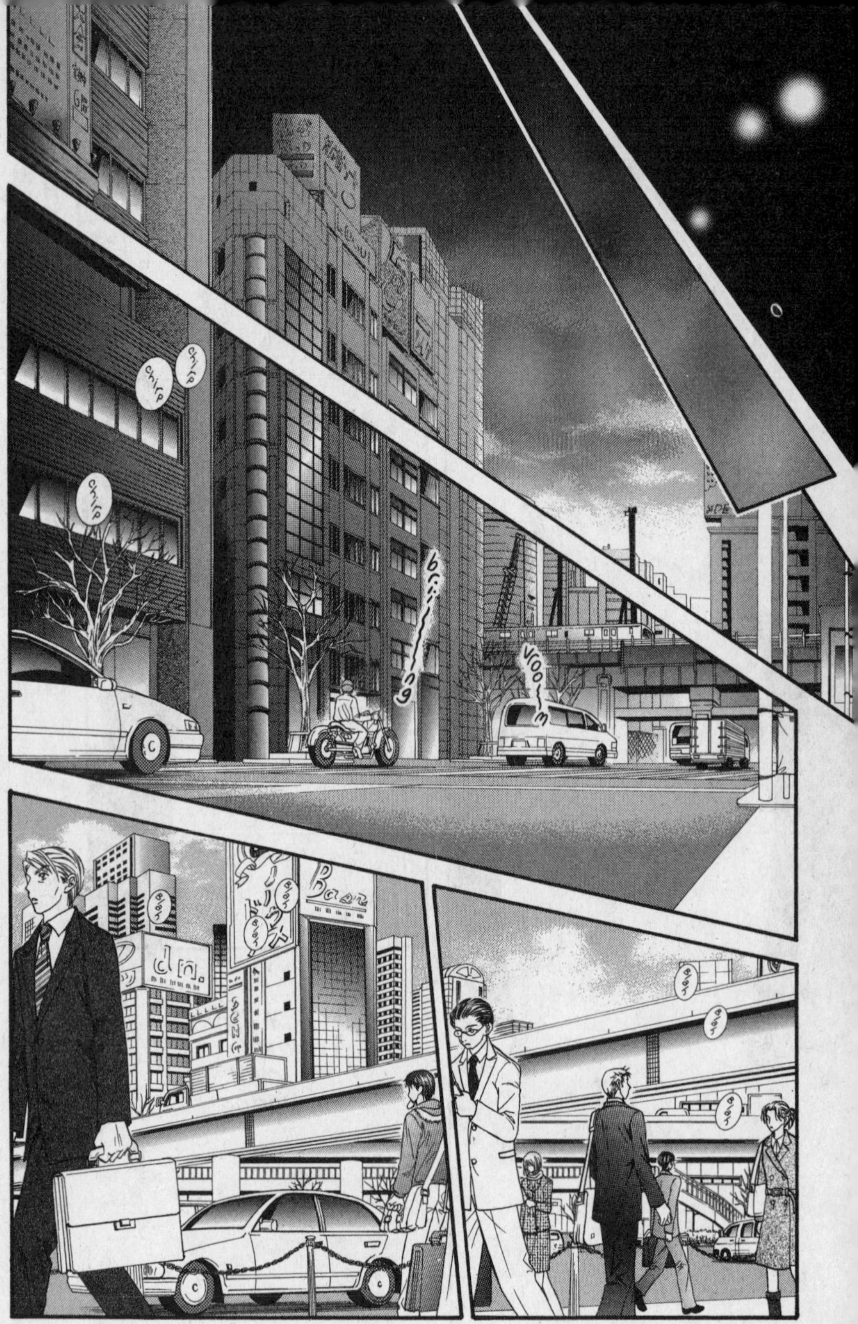
vroo~m
brrr~ng
chirp
chirp
chirp

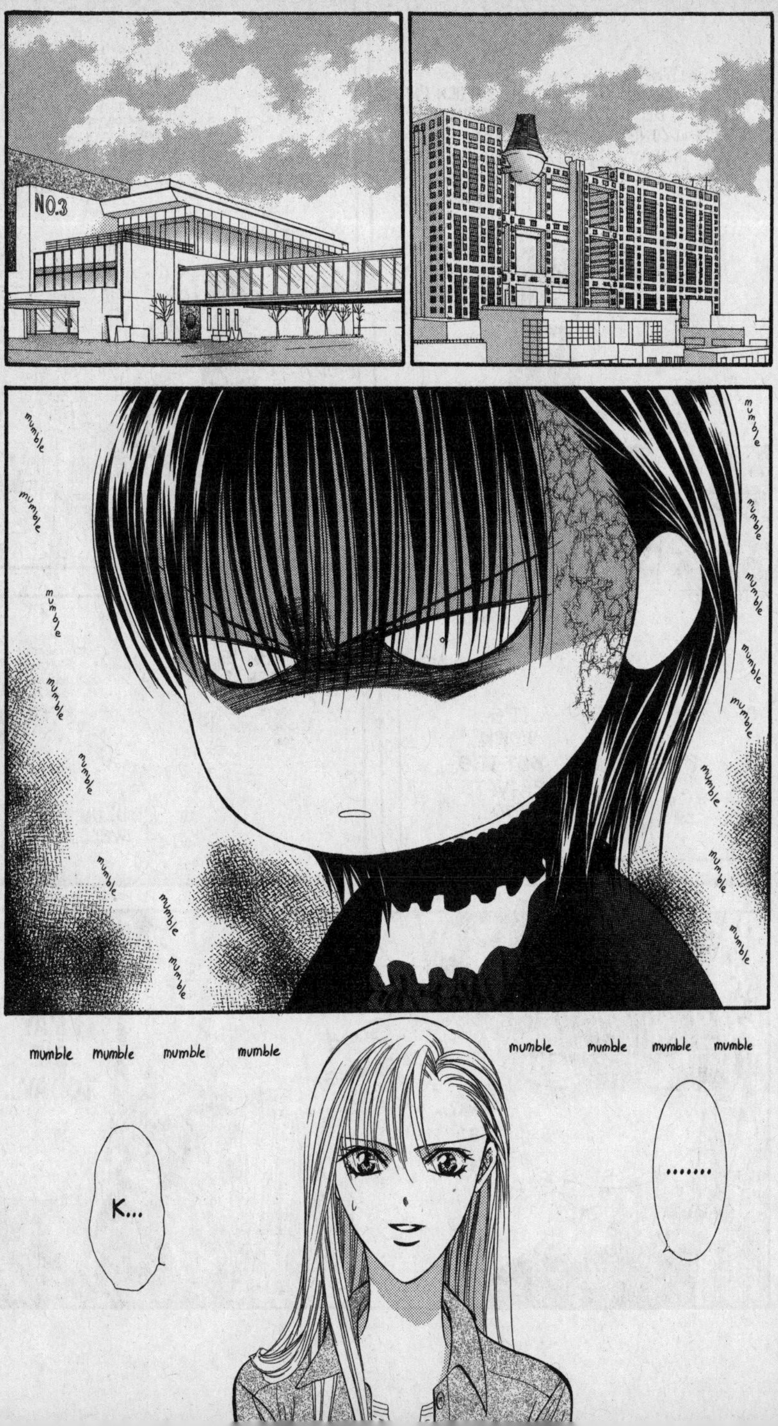
mumble
mumble
mumble
mumble
mumble
mumble
mumble
mumble
mumble
mumble
mumble
mumble
mumble
mumble
mumble
mumble
mumble
mumble mumble mumble mumble
mumble mumble mumble mumble
....
K...

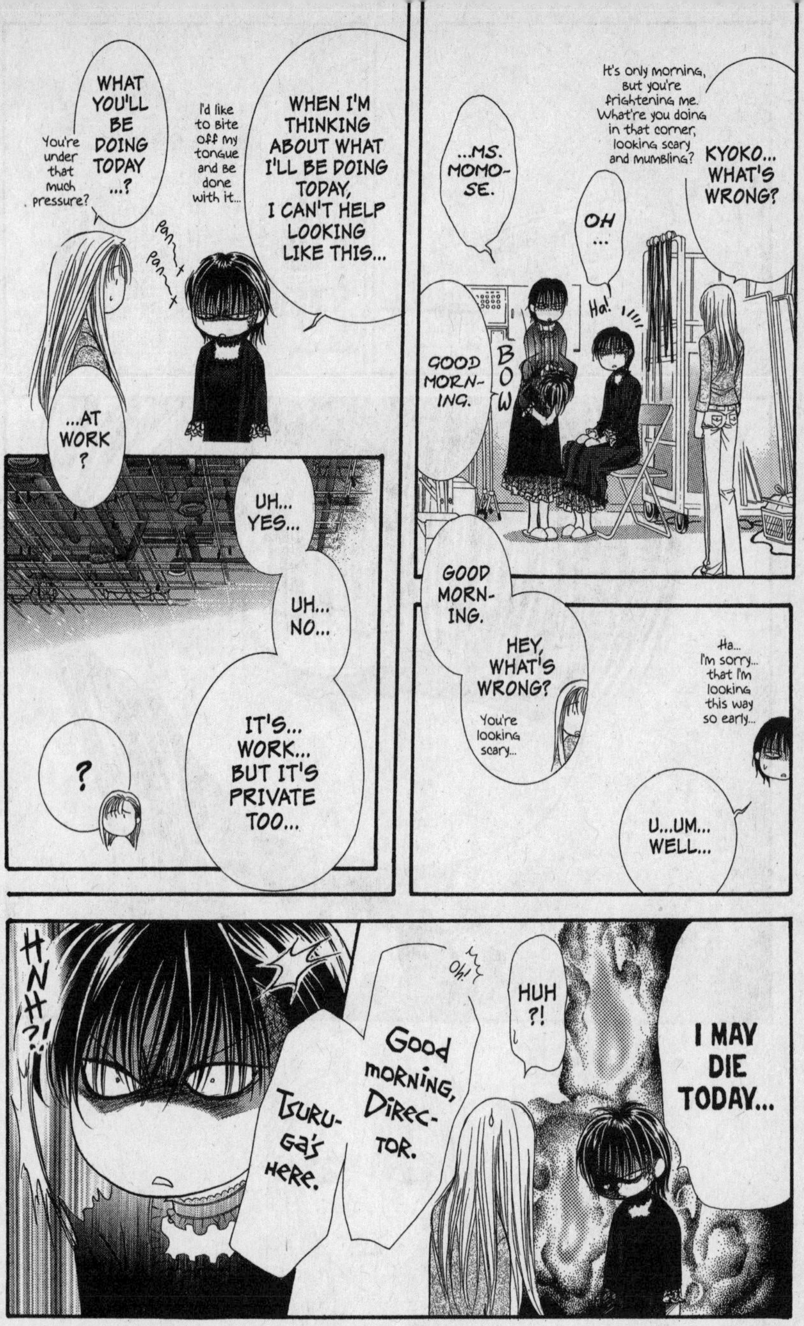
KYOKO... WHAT'S WRONG?
It's only morning, but you're frightening me. What're you doing in that corner, looking scary and mumbling?
OH...
...MS. MOMOSE.
Ha!
GOOD MORNING.
BOW
WHEN I'M THINKING ABOUT WHAT I'LL BE DOING TODAY, I CAN'T HELP LOOKING LIKE THIS...
I'd like to bite off my tongue and be done with it...
Pant Pant
WHAT YOU'LL BE DOING TODAY...?
You're under that much pressure?
...AT WORK?
GOOD MORNING.
HEY, WHAT'S WRONG?
You're looking scary...
Ha... I'm sorry... that I'm looking this way so early...
U...UM... WELL...
UH... YES...
UH... NO...
IT'S... WORK... BUT IT'S PRIVATE TOO...
?
I MAY DIE TODAY...
HUH?!
Oh!
Good morning, Director.
Tsuruga's here.
HNH?!

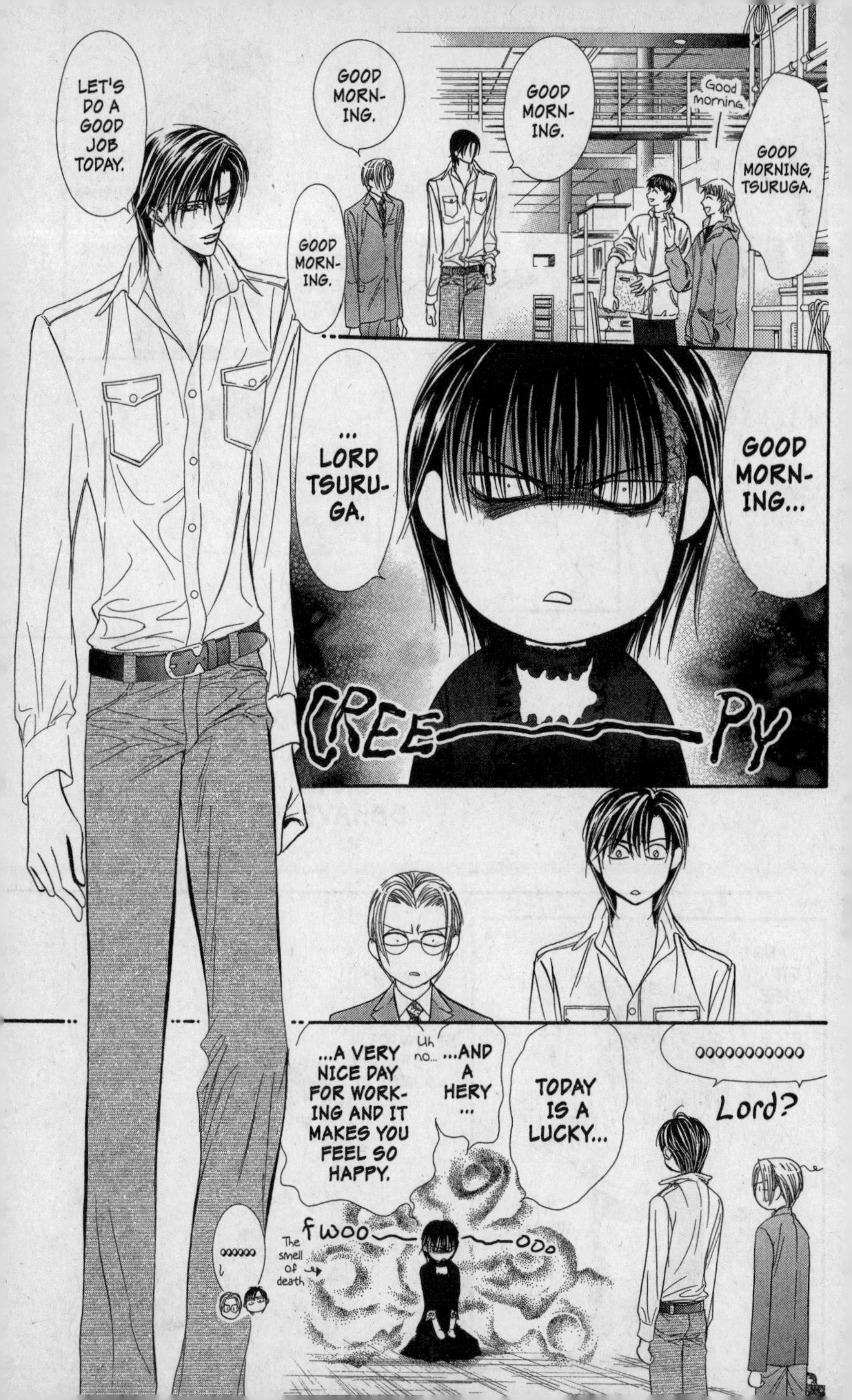
GOOD MORNING, TSURUGA.
Good morning.
GOOD MORN-ING.
GOOD MORN-ING.
GOOD MORN-ING.
GOOD MORN-ING...
...LORD TSURU-GA.
CREE—PY
oooooooooooo
Lord?
TODAY IS A LUCKY...
...AND A HERY...
Uh no...
...A VERY NICE DAY FOR WORK-ING AND IT MAKES YOU FEEL SO HAPPY.
FWOO——OOO
The smell of death
oooooo
LET'S DO A GOOD JOB TODAY.

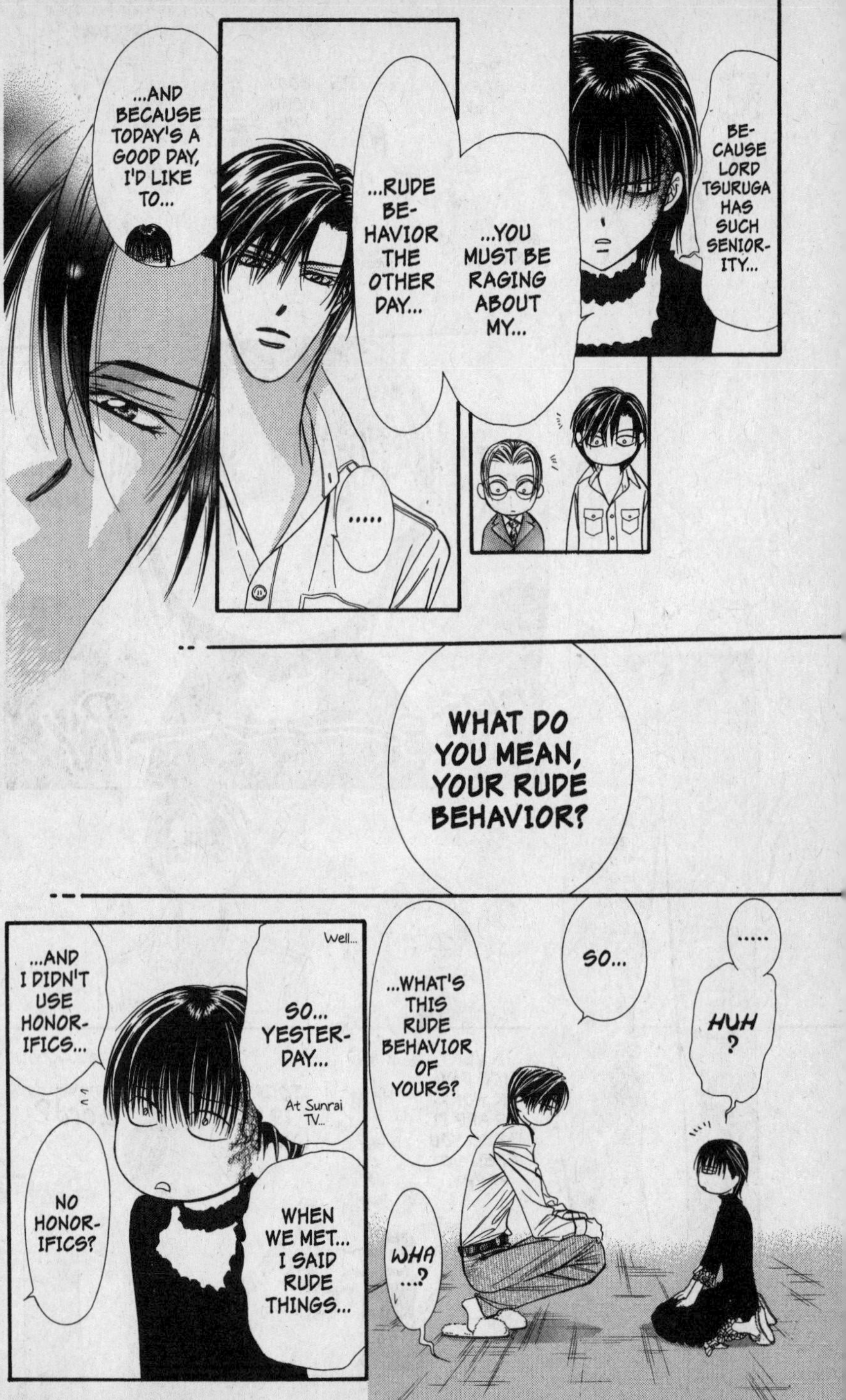
BE-CAUSE LORD TSURUGA HAS SUCH SENIOR-ITY...
...YOU MUST BE RAGING ABOUT MY...
...RUDE BE-HAVIOR THE OTHER DAY...
.....
...AND BECAUSE TODAY'S A GOOD DAY, I'D LIKE TO...
WHAT DO YOU MEAN, YOUR RUDE BEHAVIOR?
.....
HUH?
SO...
...WHAT'S THIS RUDE BEHAVIOR OF YOURS?
WHA...?
Well...
SO... YESTER-DAY...
At Sunrai TV...
...AND I DIDN'T USE HONOR-IFICS...
WHEN WE MET... I SAID RUDE THINGS...
NO HONOR-IFICS?

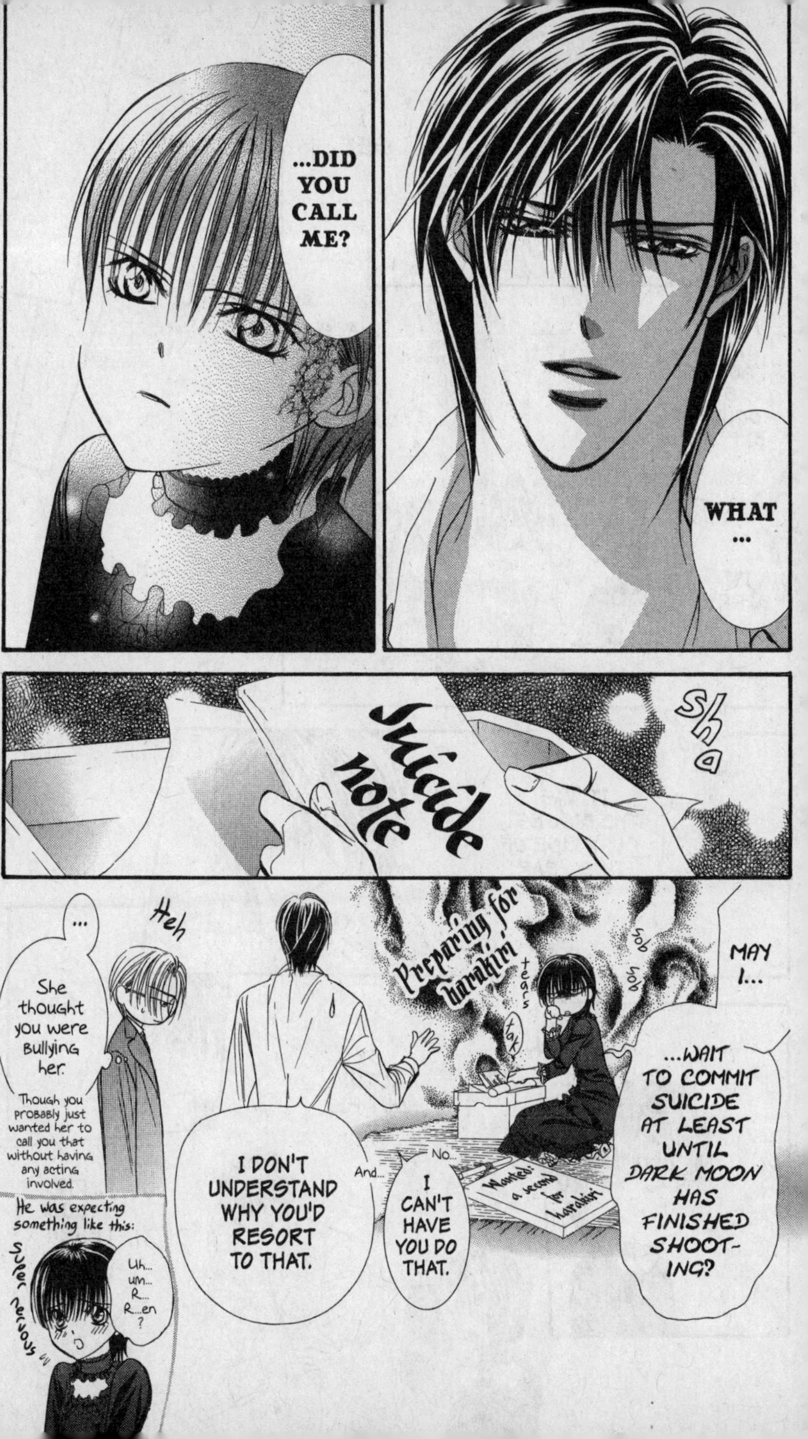
WHAT ...
...DID YOU CALL ME?
Sha
Suicide note
MAY I...
...WAIT TO COMMIT SUICIDE AT LEAST UNTIL DARK MOON HAS FINISHED SHOOTING?
Sob Sob
Preparing for harakiri
tears
Yak
Wanted: a second for harakiri
No...
I CAN'T HAVE YOU DO THAT.
And...
I DON'T UNDERSTAND WHY YOU'D RESORT TO THAT.
Heh
...
She thought you were bullying her.
Though you probably just wanted her to call you that without having any acting involved.
He was expecting something like this:
Super nervous
Uh... um... R... R...en?

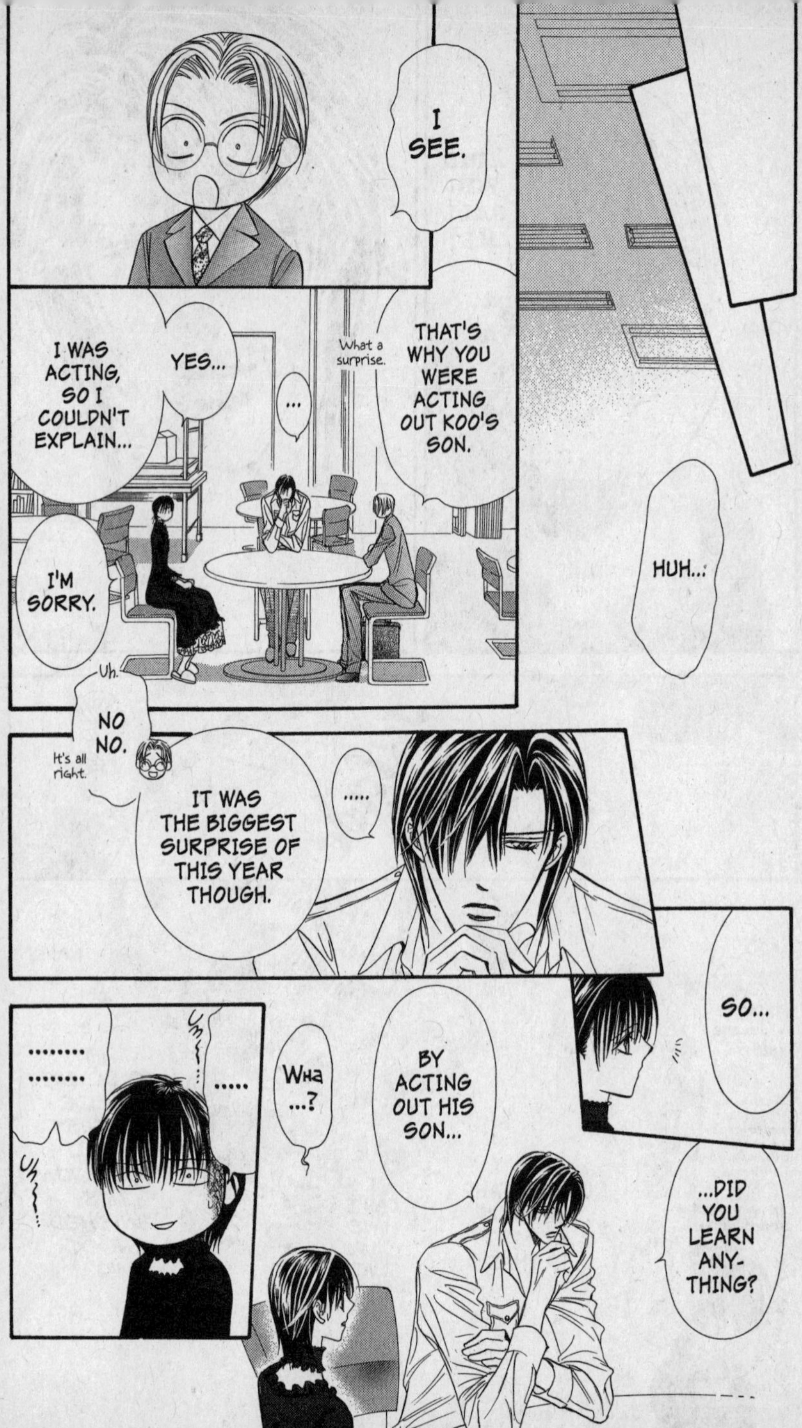
HUH...
I SEE.
What a surprise.
THAT'S WHY YOU WERE ACTING OUT KOO'S SON.
...
YES...
I WAS ACTING, SO I COULDN'T EXPLAIN...
I'M SORRY.
.....
IT WAS THE BIGGEST SURPRISE OF THIS YEAR THOUGH.
Uh.
NO NO.
It's all right.
SO...
BY ACTING OUT HIS SON...
...DID YOU LEARN ANYTHING?
WHA ...?
.....
....
....

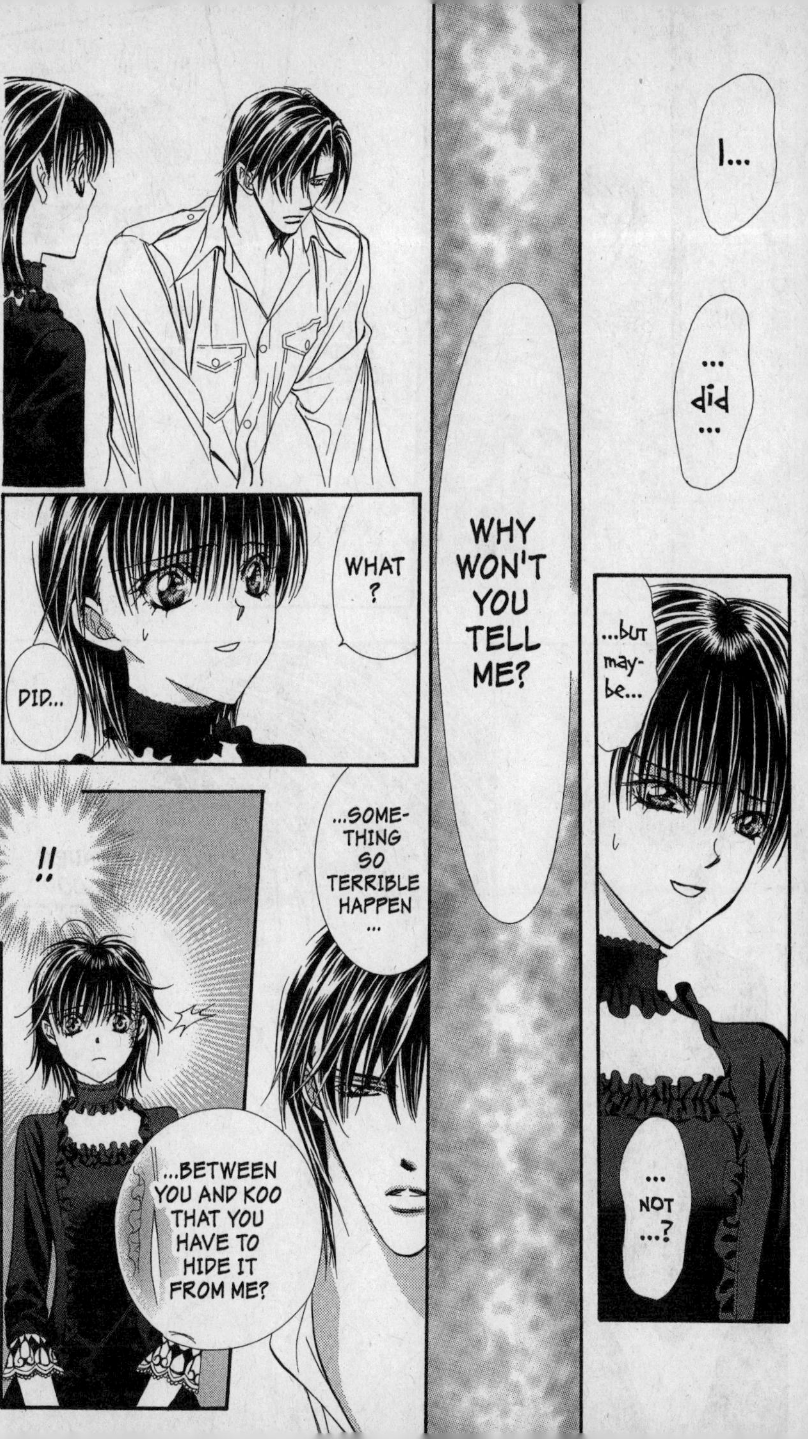
I...
...did...
...but maybe...
...NOT...?
WHY WON'T YOU TELL ME?
WHAT?
DID...
...SOMETHING SO TERRIBLE HAPPEN...
!!
...BETWEEN YOU AND KOO THAT YOU HAVE TO HIDE IT FROM ME?

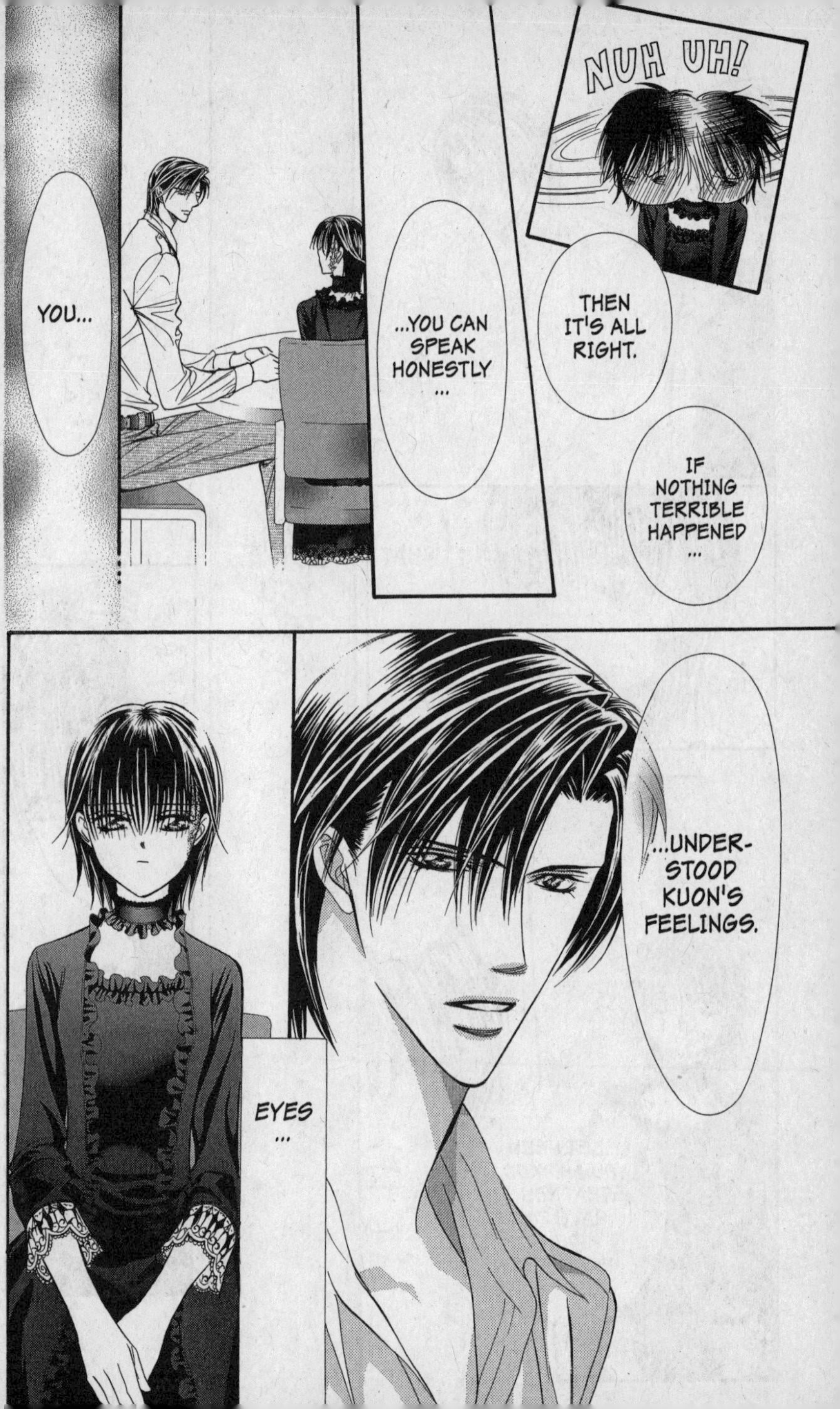
NUH UH!
THEN IT'S ALL RIGHT.
IF NOTHING TERRIBLE HAPPENED...
...YOU CAN SPEAK HONESTLY...
YOU...
...UNDER-STOOD KUON'S FEELINGS.
EYES...

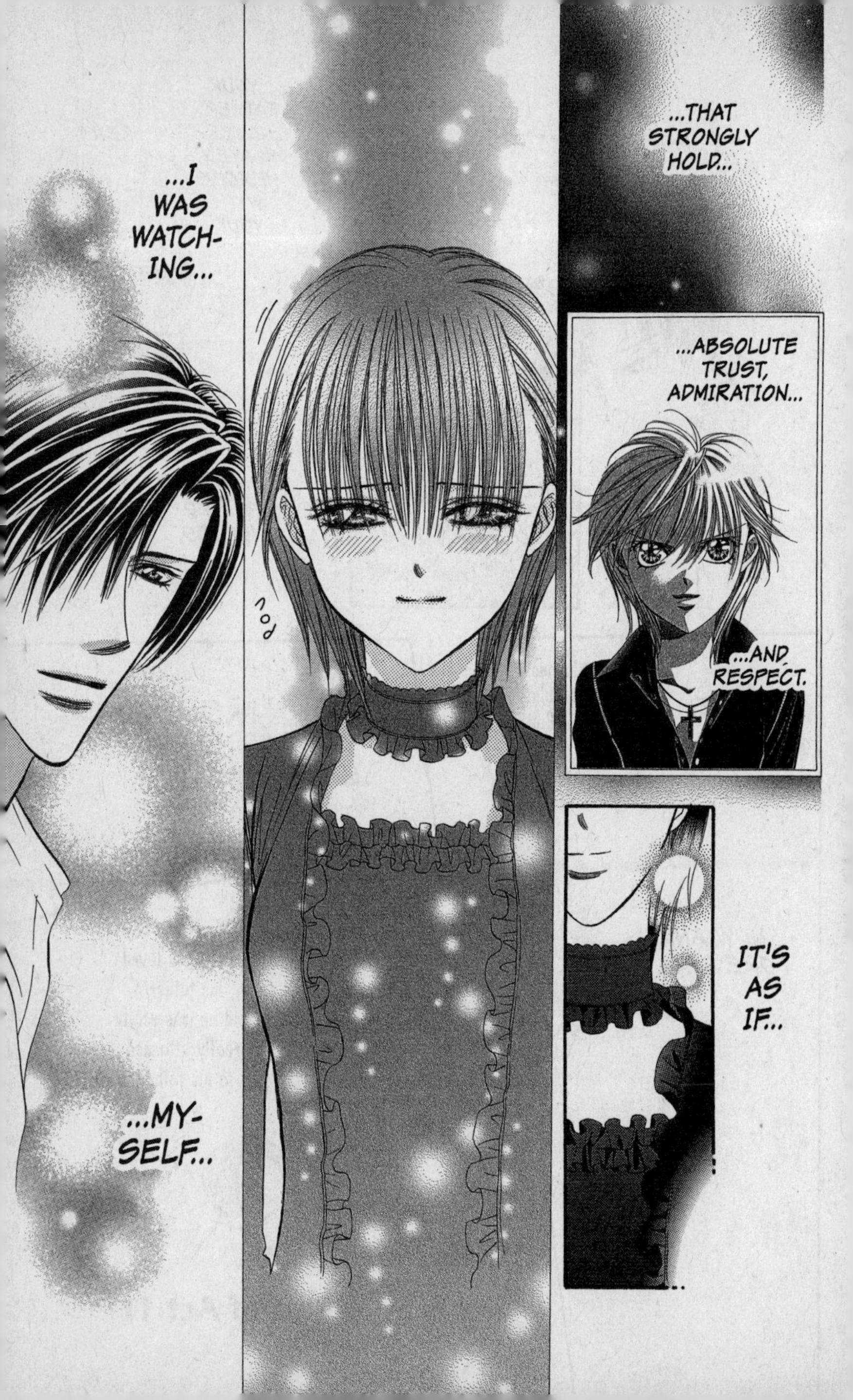
...THAT STRONGLY HOLD...
...ABSOLUTE TRUST, ADMIRATION...
...AND RESPECT.
IT'S AS IF...
nod
...I WAS WATCHING...
...MYSELF...

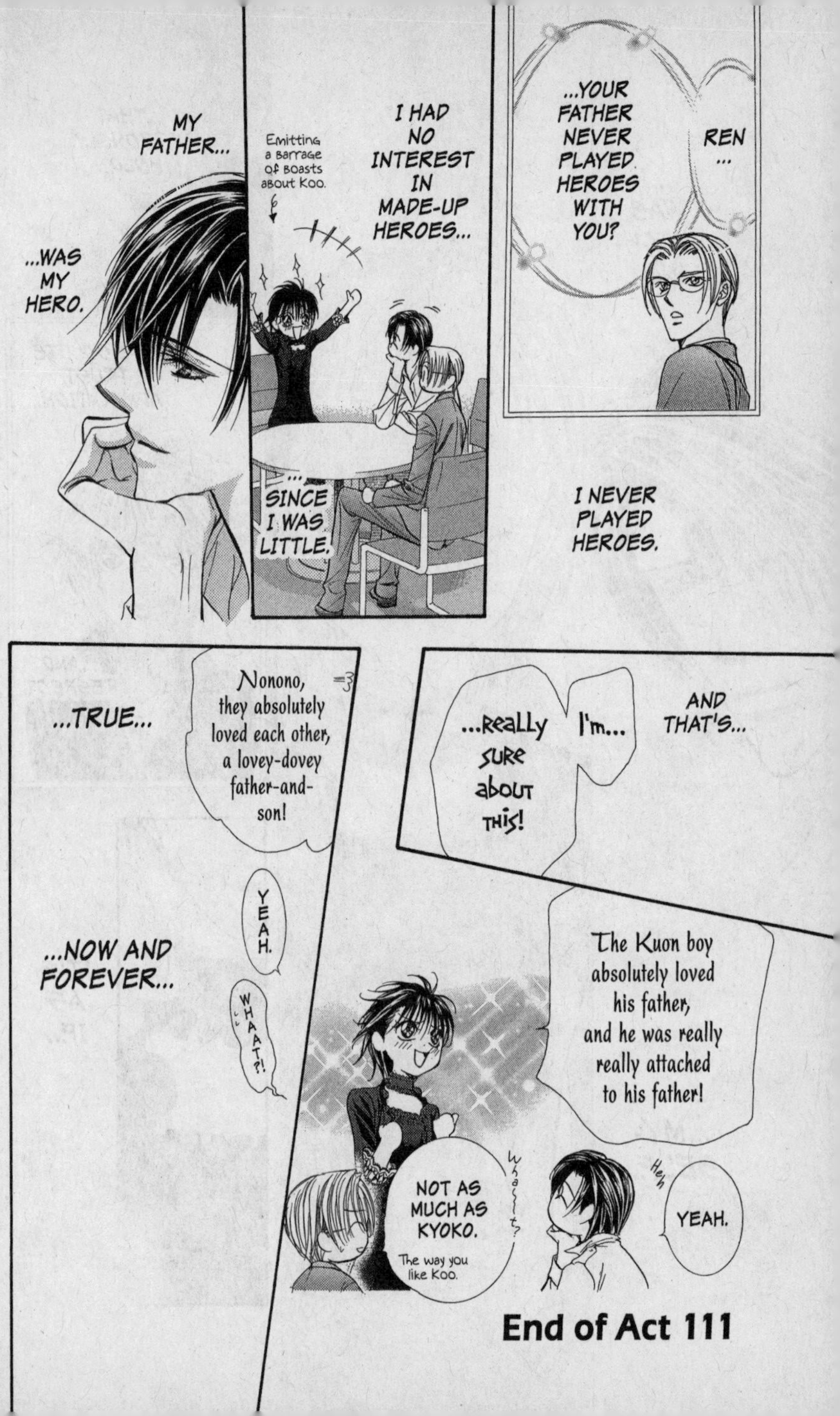
REN...
...YOUR FATHER NEVER PLAYED HEROES WITH YOU?
I NEVER PLAYED HEROES.
I HAD NO INTEREST IN MADE-UP HEROES...
Emitting a barrage of boasts about Koo.
...SINCE I WAS LITTLE.
MY FATHER...
...WAS MY HERO.
AND THAT'S...
I'm...
...really sure about this!
Nonono, they absolutely loved each other, a lovey-dovey father-and-son!
...TRUE...
The Kuon boy absolutely loved his father, and he was really really attached to his father!
YEAH.
...NOW AND FOREVER...
WHAAT?!
Heh
YEAH.
Wha~t?
NOT AS MUCH AS KYOKO.
The way you like Koo.

End of Act 111

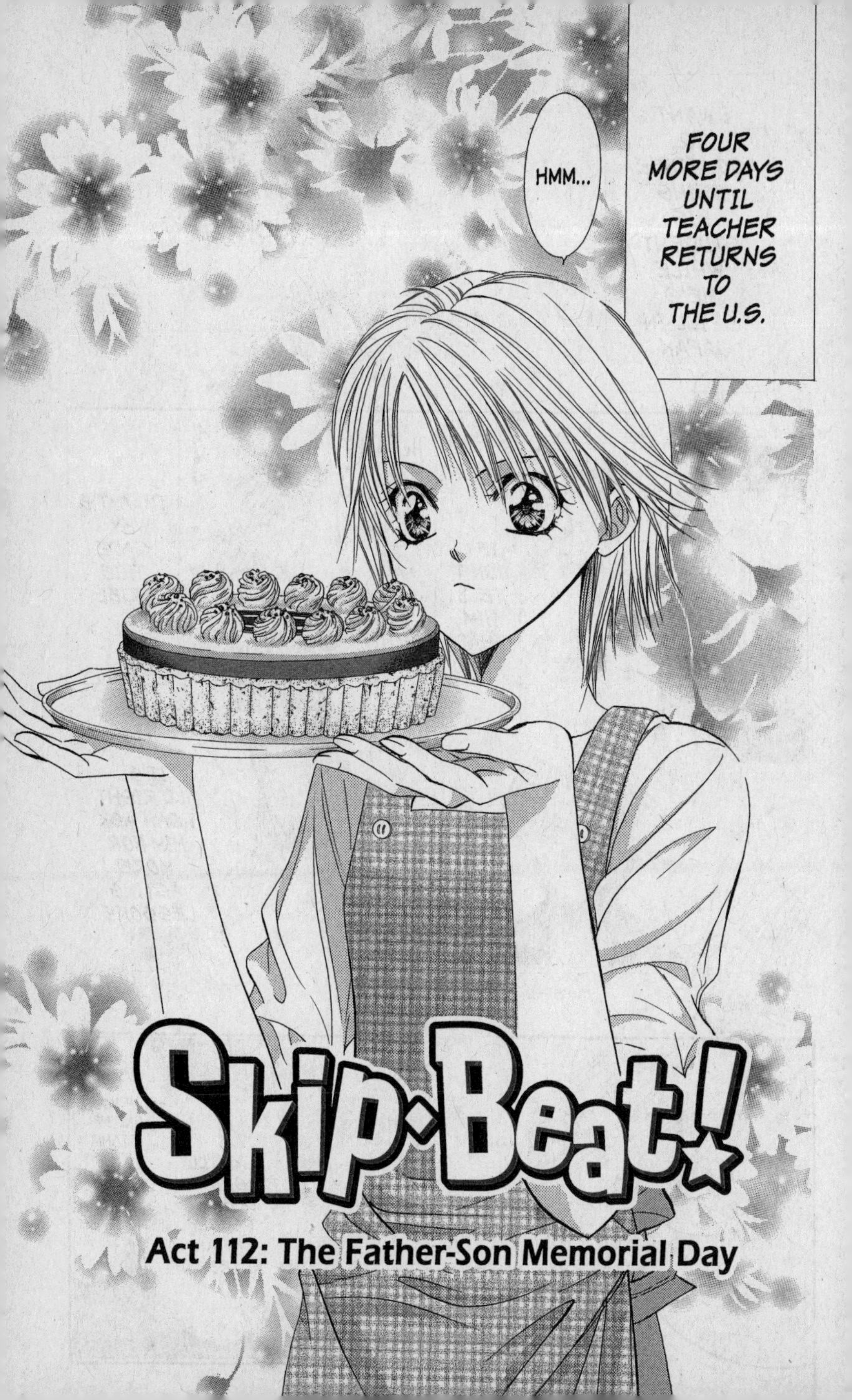
FOUR MORE DAYS UNTIL TEACHER RETURNS TO THE U.S.
HMM...
Skip·Beat!
Act 112: The Father-Son Memorial Day

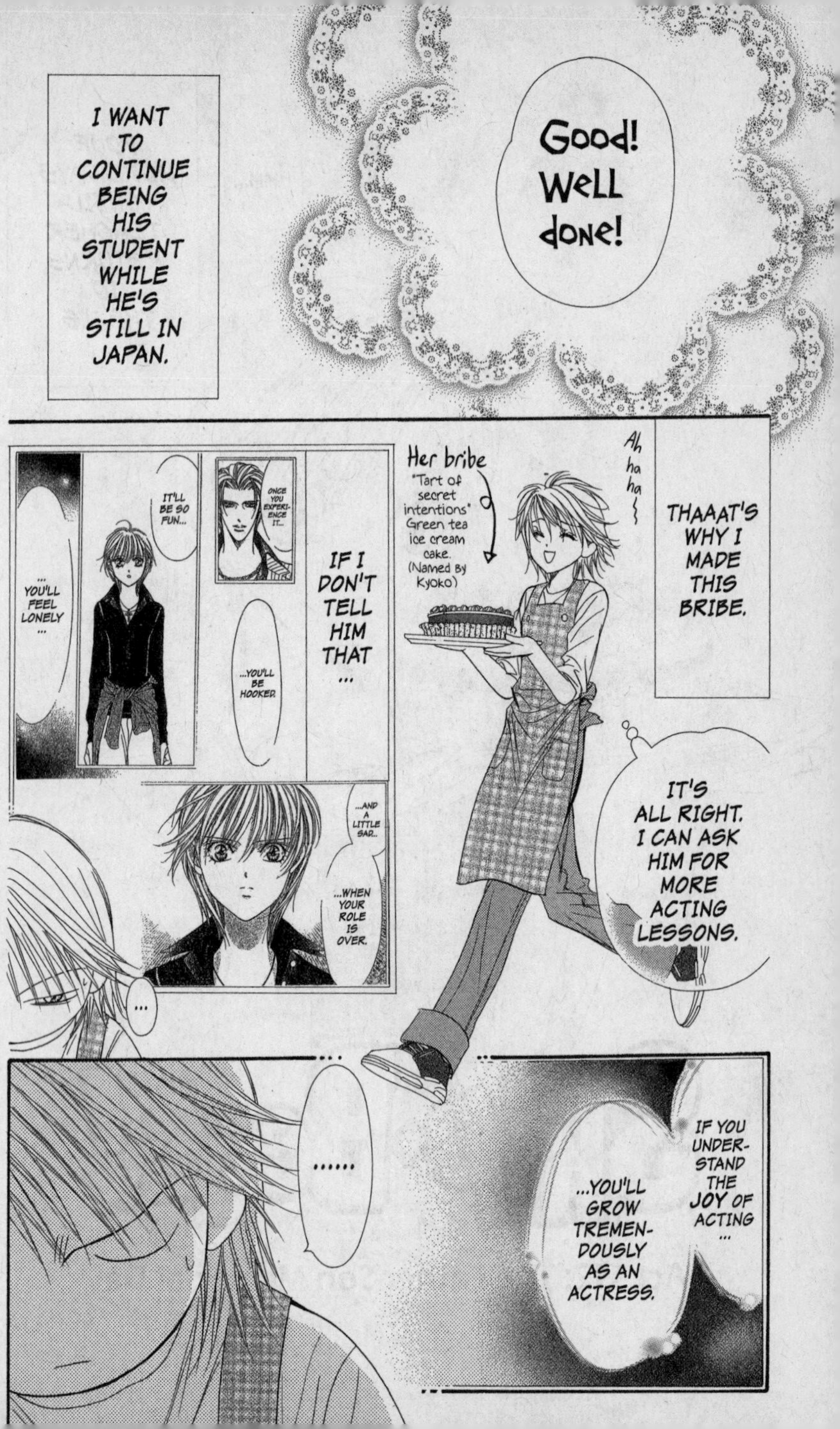
Good! Well done!
I WANT TO CONTINUE BEING HIS STUDENT WHILE HE'S STILL IN JAPAN.
THAAAT'S WHY I MADE THIS BRIBE.
Ah ha ha~
Her bribe
"Tart of secret intentions" Green tea ice cream cake. (Named By Kyoko)
IT'S ALL RIGHT. I CAN ASK HIM FOR MORE ACTING LESSONS.
IF I DON'T TELL HIM THAT...
ONCE YOU EXPERIENCE IT...
...YOU'LL BE HOOKED.
IT'LL BE SO FUN...
...YOU'LL FEEL LONELY...
...AND A LITTLE SAD...
...WHEN YOUR ROLE IS OVER.
...
IF YOU UNDERSTAND THE JOY OF ACTING...
...YOU'LL GROW TREMENDOUSLY AS AN ACTRESS.
......

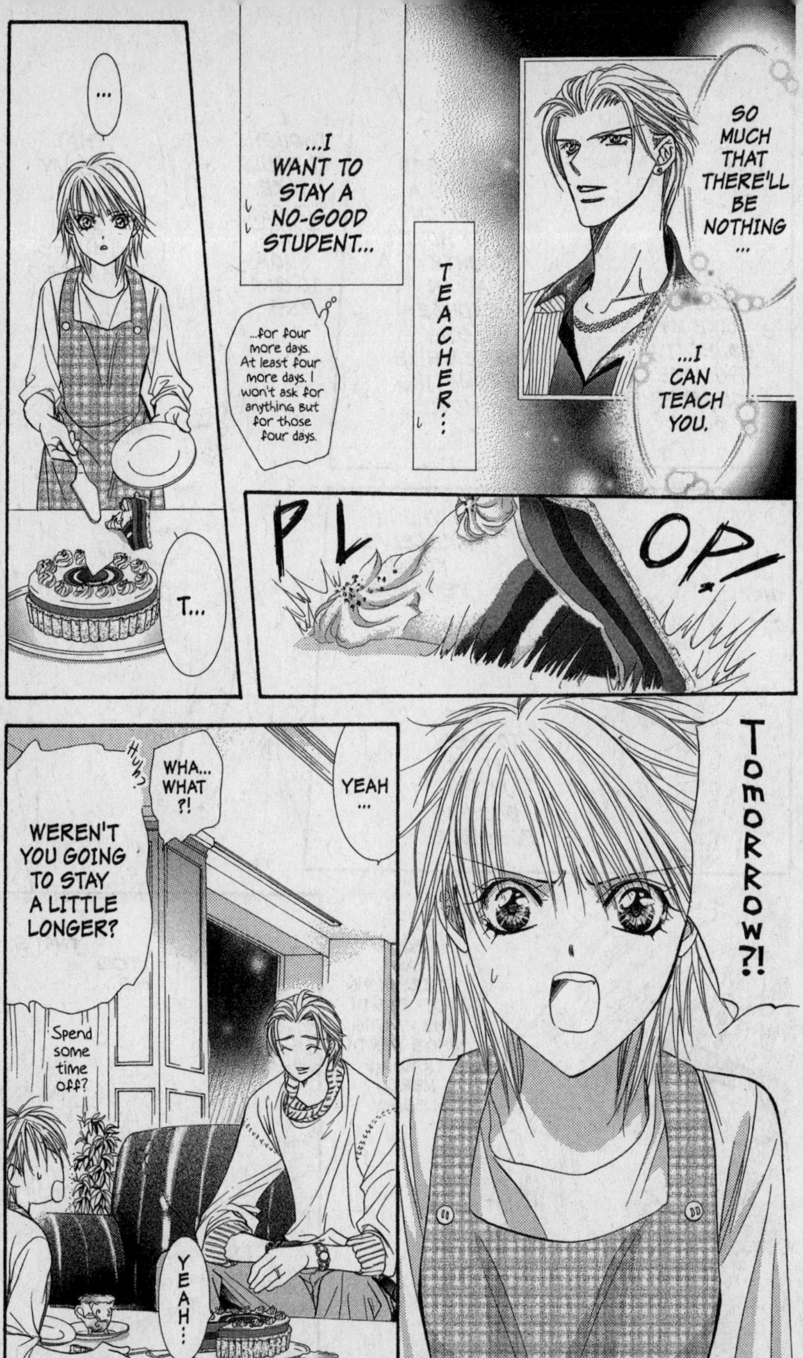
SO MUCH THAT THERE'LL BE NOTHING ...
...I CAN TEACH YOU.
TEACHER...
...I WANT TO STAY A NO-GOOD STUDENT...
...for four more days. At least four more days. I won't ask for anything but for those four days.
PLOP!
...
T...
TOMORROW?!
YEAH ...
WHA... WHAT ?!
Huh?
WEREN'T YOU GOING TO STAY A LITTLE LONGER?
Spend some time off?
YEAH...

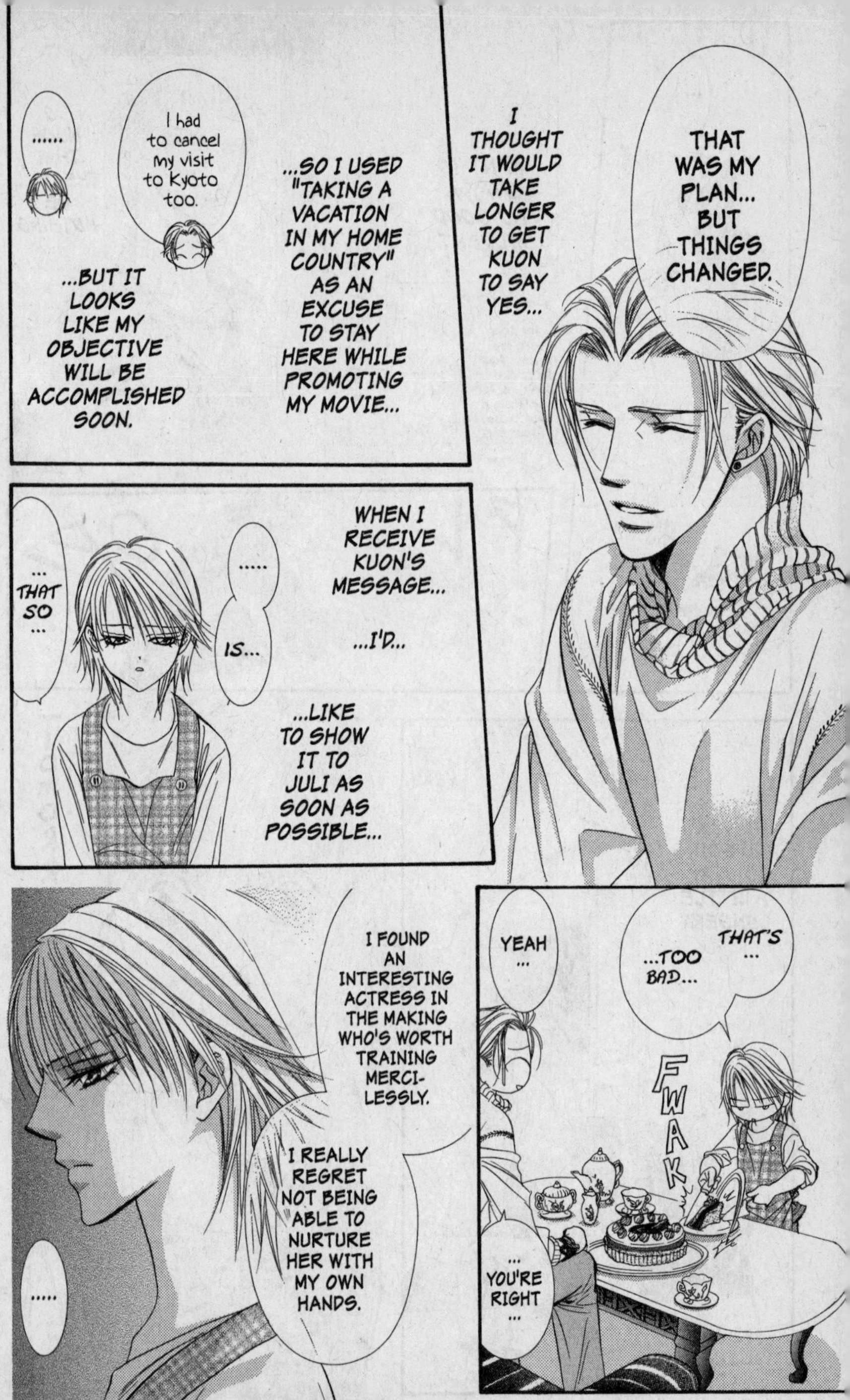
THAT WAS MY PLAN... BUT THINGS CHANGED.
I THOUGHT IT WOULD TAKE LONGER TO GET KUON TO SAY YES...
...SO I USED "TAKING A VACATION IN MY HOME COUNTRY" AS AN EXCUSE TO STAY HERE WHILE PROMOTING MY MOVIE...
I had to cancel my visit to Kyoto too.
......
...BUT IT LOOKS LIKE MY OBJECTIVE WILL BE ACCOMPLISHED SOON.
WHEN I RECEIVE KUON'S MESSAGE...
...I'D...
...LIKE TO SHOW IT TO JULI AS SOON AS POSSIBLE...
......
IS...
...THAT SO...
THAT'S...
...TOO BAD...
YEAH...
FWAK
...YOU'RE RIGHT...
I FOUND AN INTERESTING ACTRESS IN THE MAKING WHO'S WORTH TRAINING MERCILESSLY.
I REALLY REGRET NOT BEING ABLE TO NURTURE HER WITH MY OWN HANDS.
......

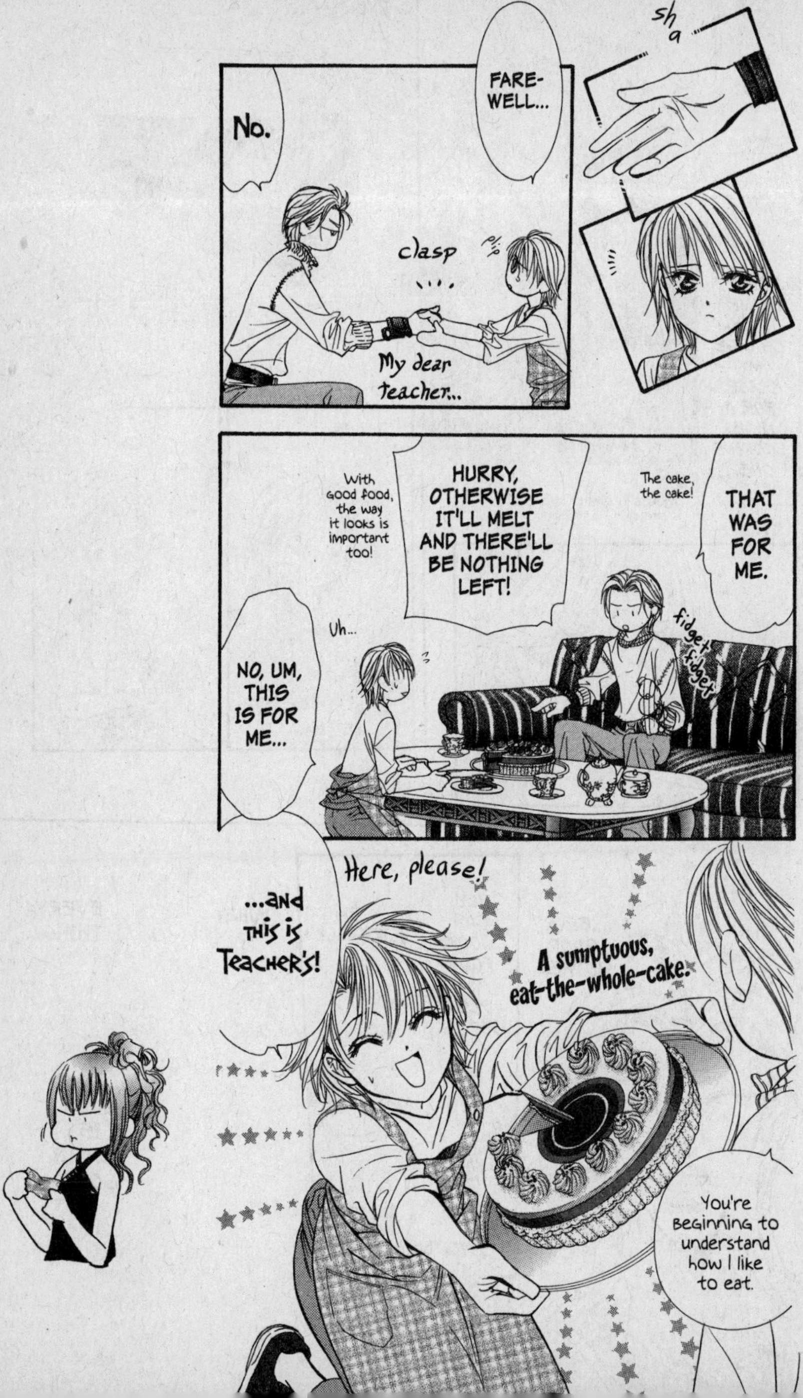
sha
FARE-WELL...
No.
clasp
My dear teacher...
THAT WAS FOR ME.
The cake, the cake!
fidget fidget
HURRY, OTHERWISE IT'LL MELT AND THERE'LL BE NOTHING LEFT!
With good food, the way it looks is important too!
Uh...
NO, UM, THIS IS FOR ME...
Here, please!
A sumptuous, eat-the-whole-cake.
...and THIS is TEACHER'S!
You're beginning to understand how I like to eat.

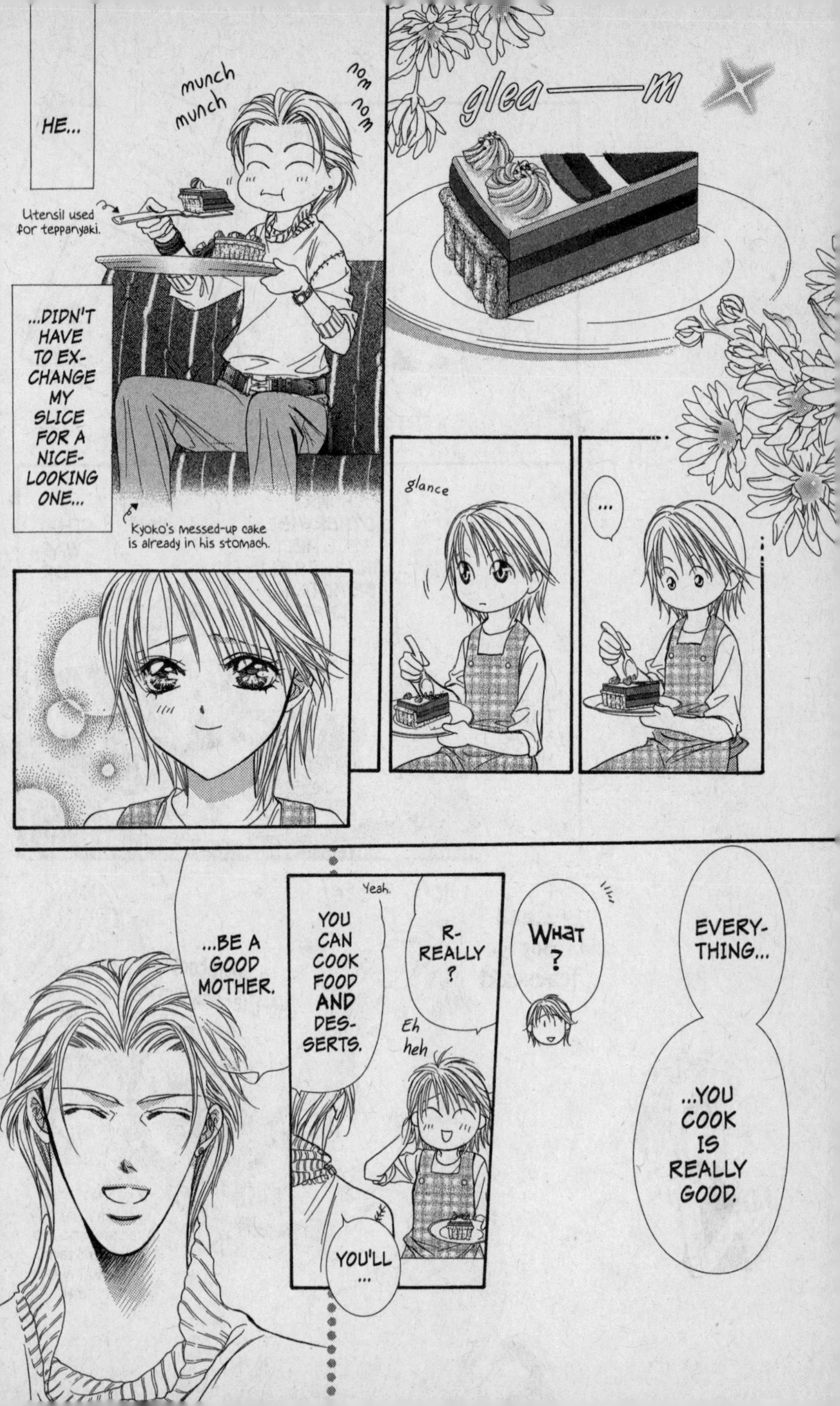
glea—m
HE...
munch munch
nom nom
Utensil used for teppanyaki.
...DIDN'T HAVE TO EX-CHANGE MY SLICE FOR A NICE-LOOKING ONE...
Kyoko's messed-up cake is already in his stomach.
...
glance
EVERY-THING...
...YOU COOK IS REALLY GOOD.
WHAT?
R-REALLY?
Yeah.
YOU CAN COOK FOOD AND DES-SERTS.
Eh heh
YOU'LL...
...BE A GOOD MOTHER.

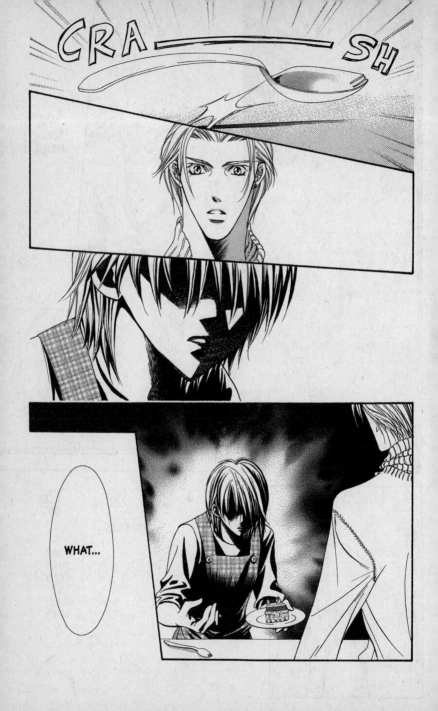

CRA ———— SH

WHAT...

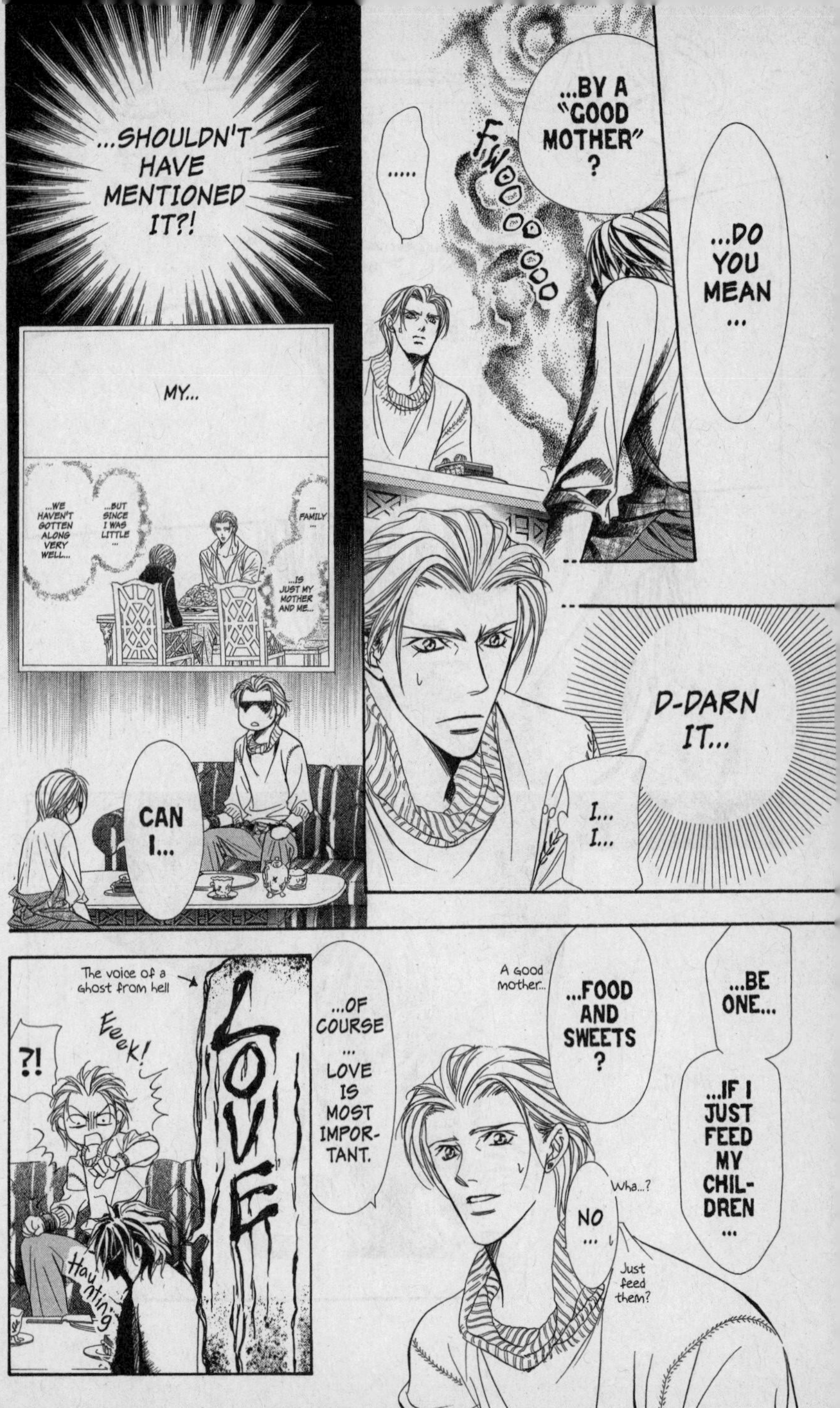

...DO YOU MEAN...
...BY A "GOOD MOTHER"?
FWOOOOOOOO
.....
D-DARN IT...
I... I...
...SHOULDN'T HAVE MENTIONED IT?!
MY...
...FAMILY...
...IS JUST MY MOTHER AND ME...
...BUT SINCE I WAS LITTLE...
...WE HAVEN'T GOTTEN ALONG VERY WELL...
CAN I...
...BE ONE...
...IF I JUST FEED MY CHIL-DREN...
A good mother...
...FOOD AND SWEETS?
Wha...?
NO...
Just feed them?
...OF COURSE... LOVE IS MOST IMPOR-TANT.
LOVE
The voice of a ghost from hell
Eeek!
?!
Haunting

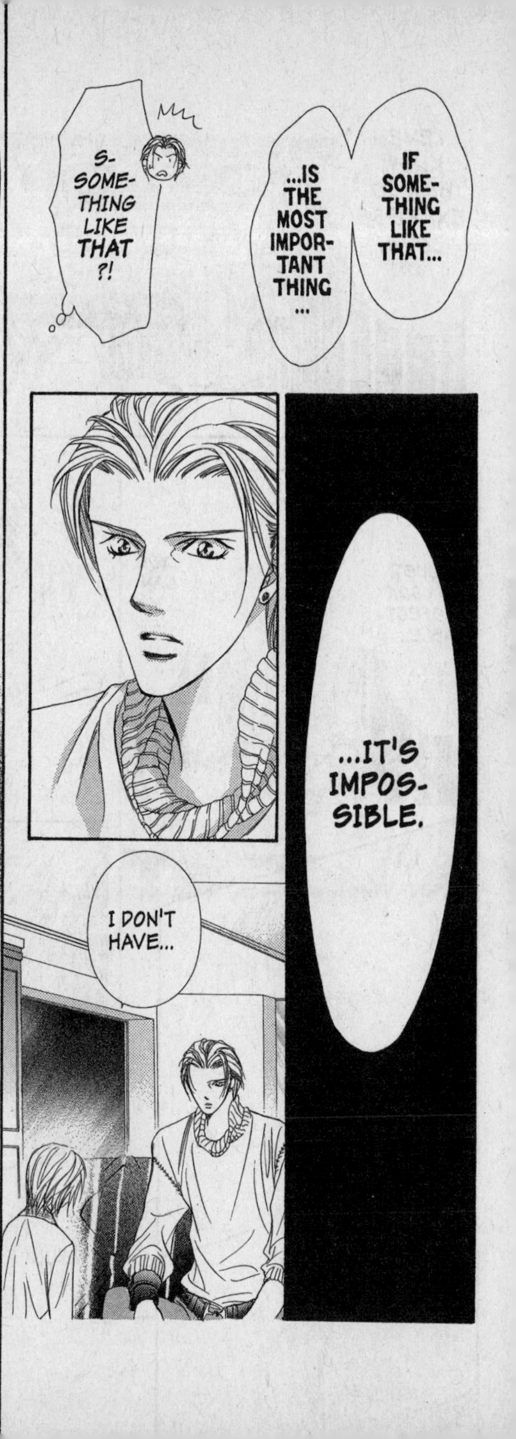
IF SOMETHING LIKE THAT...
...IS THE MOST IMPORTANT THING...
S-SOMETHING LIKE THAT?!
...IT'S IMPOSSIBLE.
I DON'T HAVE...

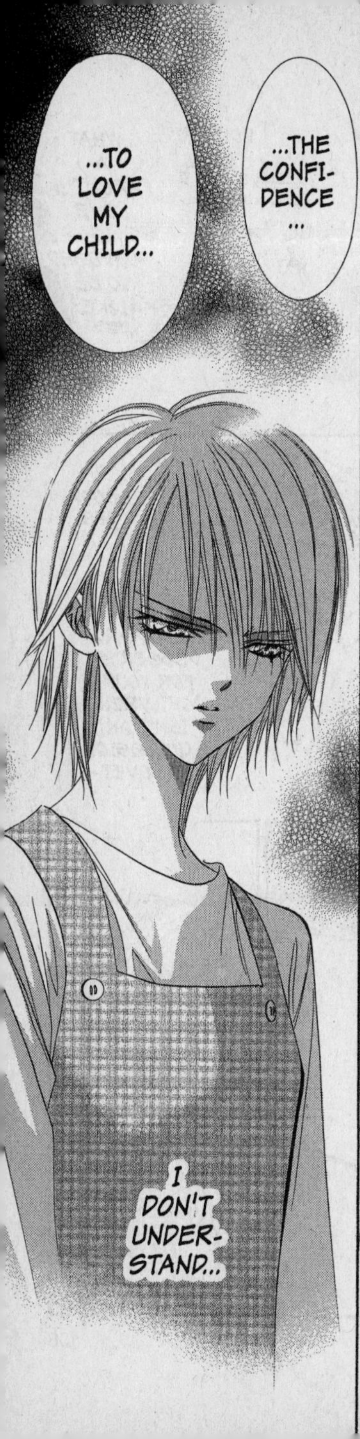
...THE CONFIDENCE...
...TO LOVE MY CHILD...
I DON'T UNDERSTAND...

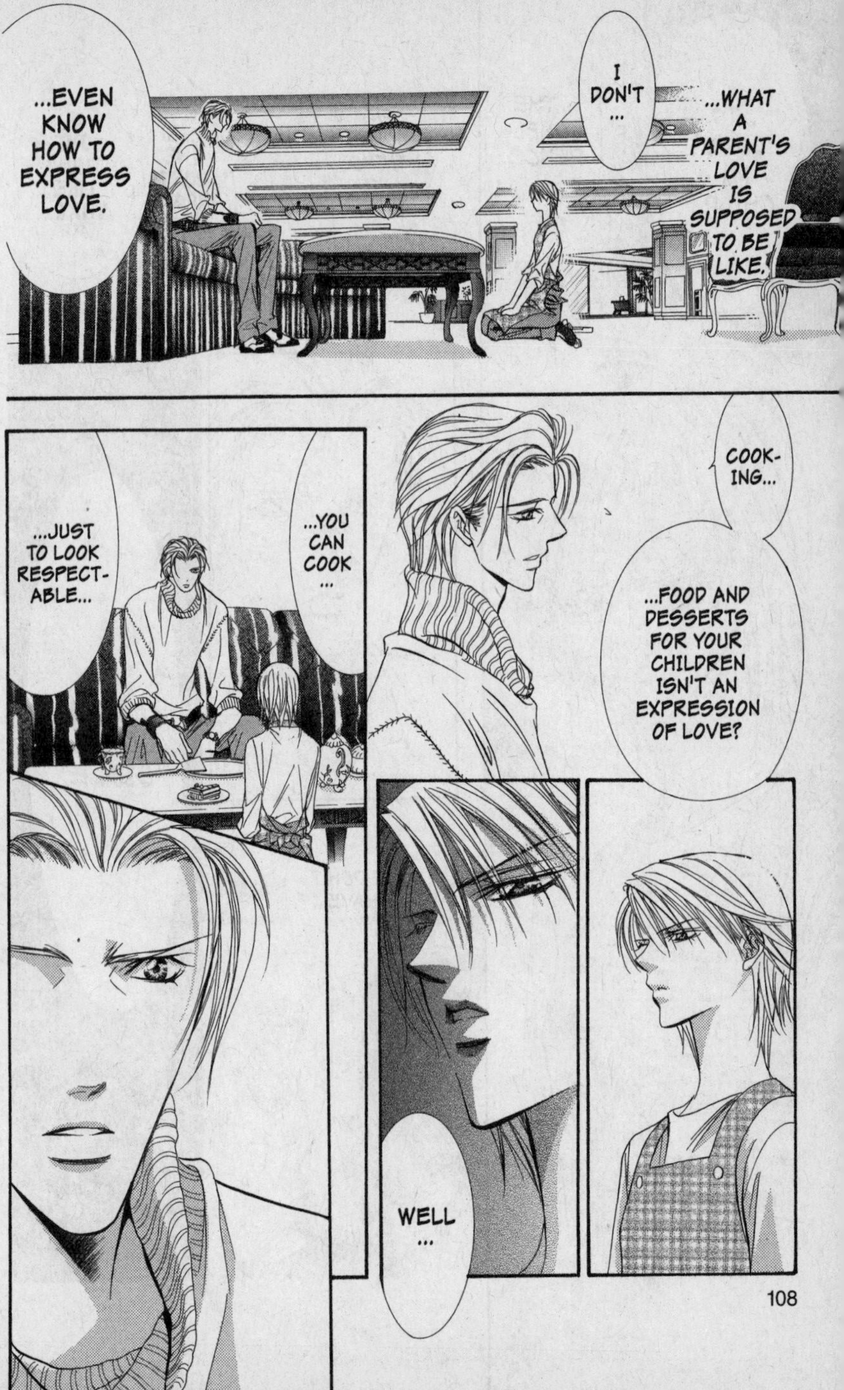
I DON'T ...
...WHAT A PARENT'S LOVE IS SUPPOSED TO BE LIKE.
...EVEN KNOW HOW TO EXPRESS LOVE.
COOK-ING...
...FOOD AND DESSERTS FOR YOUR CHILDREN ISN'T AN EXPRESSION OF LOVE?
...YOU CAN COOK ...
...JUST TO LOOK RESPECT-ABLE...
WELL ...

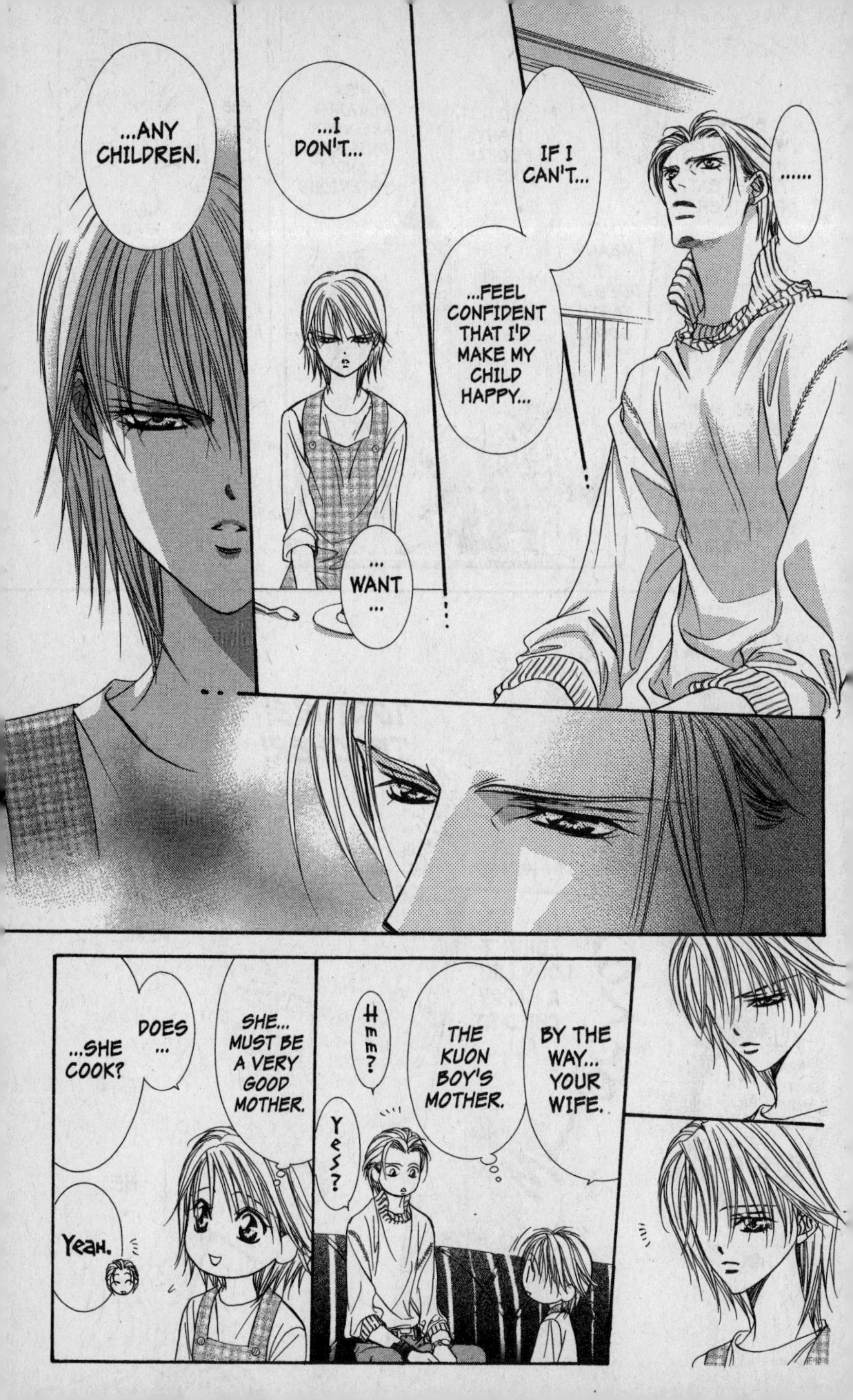
......
IF I CAN'T...
...FEEL CONFIDENT THAT I'D MAKE MY CHILD HAPPY...
...I DON'T...
... WANT ...
...ANY CHILDREN.
BY THE WAY... YOUR WIFE.
THE KUON BOY'S MOTHER.
Hmm?
Yes?
SHE... MUST BE A VERY GOOD MOTHER.
DOES ...
...SHE COOK?
Yeah.

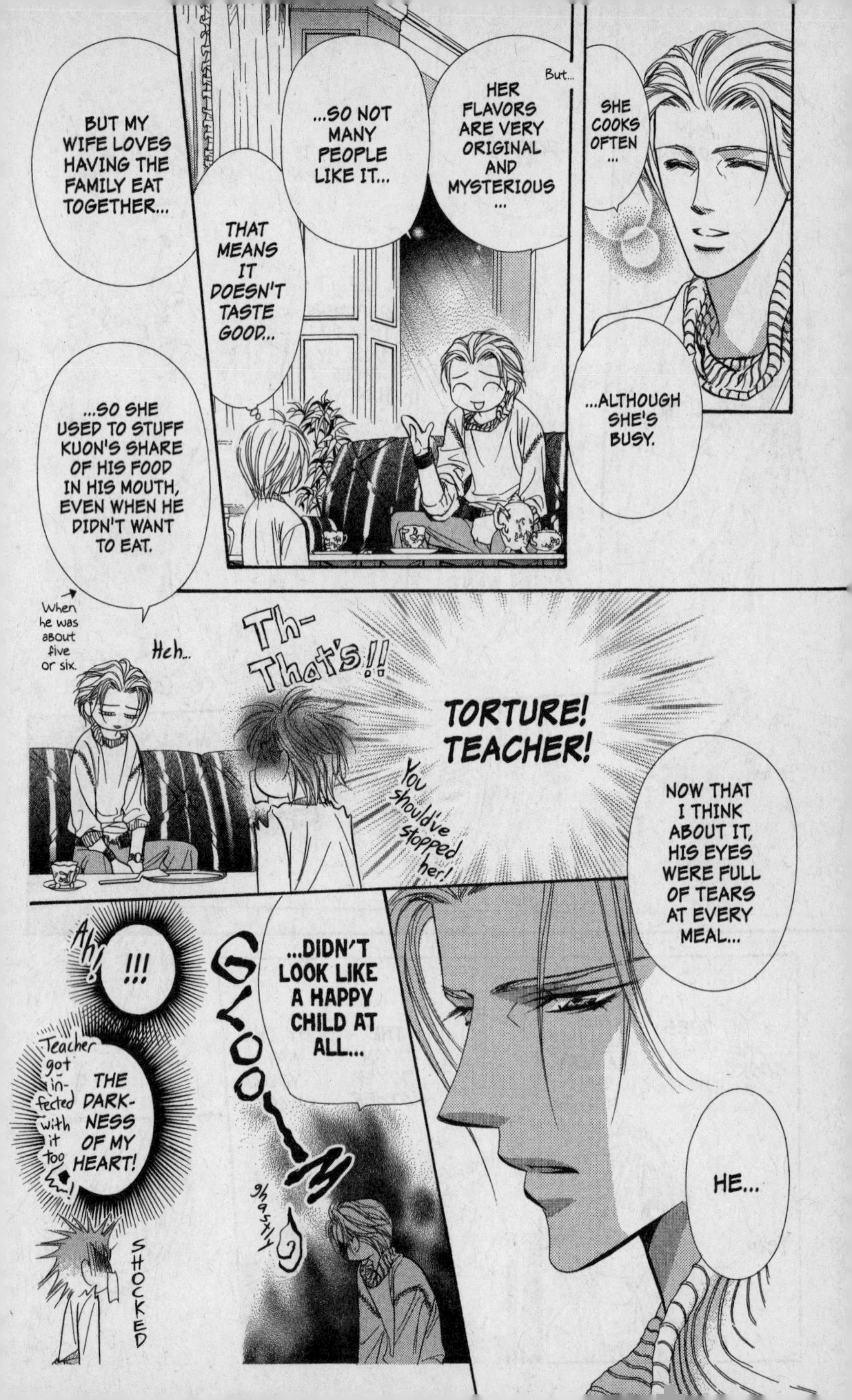
SHE COOKS OFTEN ...
...ALTHOUGH SHE'S BUSY.
But...
HER FLAVORS ARE VERY ORIGINAL AND MYSTERIOUS ...
...SO NOT MANY PEOPLE LIKE IT...
THAT MEANS IT DOESN'T TASTE GOOD...
BUT MY WIFE LOVES HAVING THE FAMILY EAT TOGETHER...
...SO SHE USED TO STUFF KUON'S SHARE OF HIS FOOD IN HIS MOUTH, EVEN WHEN HE DIDN'T WANT TO EAT.
When he was about five or six.
Heh...
Th- That's!!
TORTURE! TEACHER!
You should've stopped her!
NOW THAT I THINK ABOUT IT, HIS EYES WERE FULL OF TEARS AT EVERY MEAL...
HE...
...DIDN'T LOOK LIKE A HAPPY CHILD AT ALL...
GLOO—M
ghastly
Ah!
!!!
THE DARKNESS OF MY HEART!
Teacher got in-fected with it too
SHOCKED

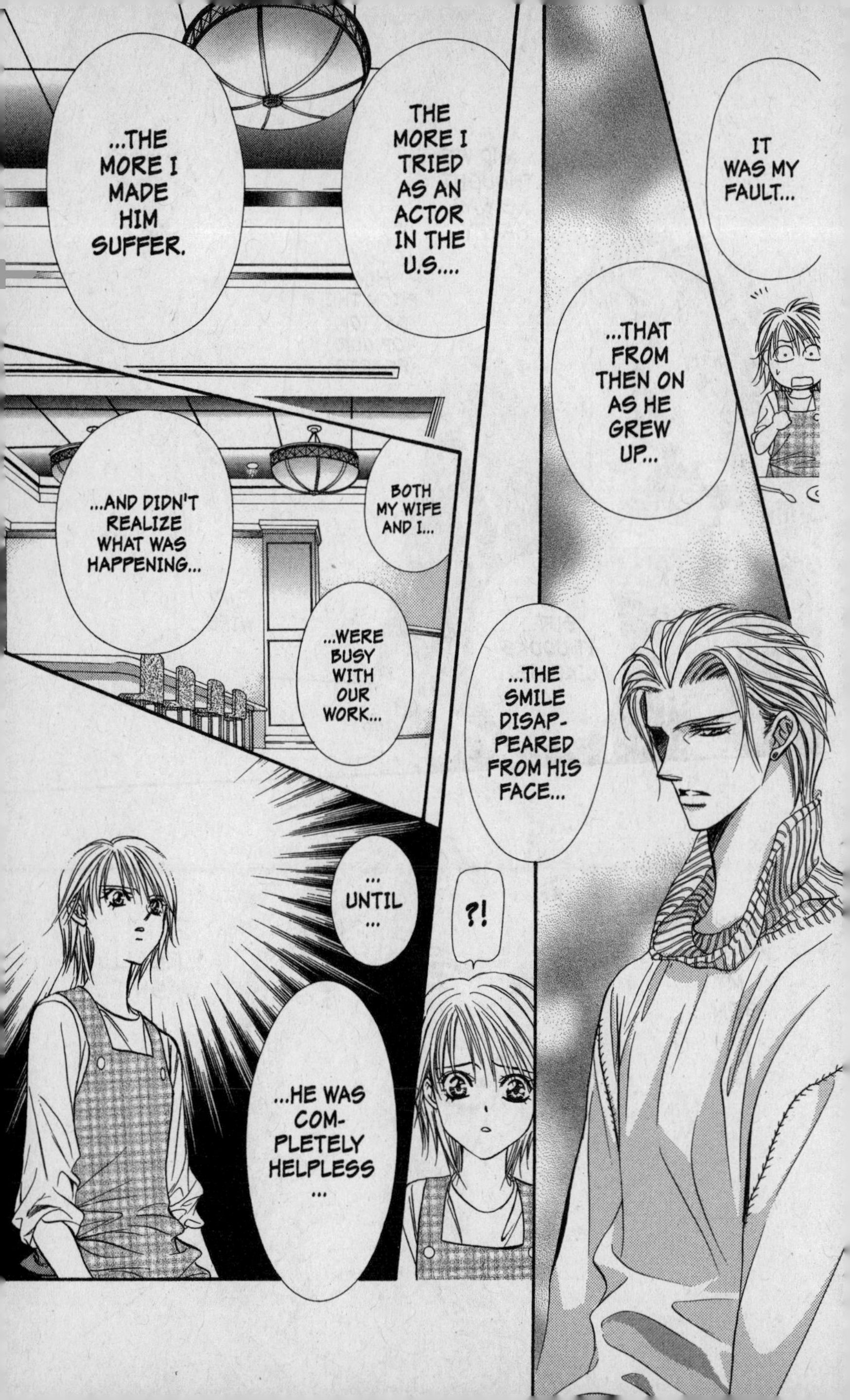
IT WAS MY FAULT...
...THAT FROM THEN ON AS HE GREW UP...
...THE SMILE DISAP-PEARED FROM HIS FACE...
THE MORE I TRIED AS AN ACTOR IN THE U.S....
...THE MORE I MADE HIM SUFFER.
BOTH MY WIFE AND I...
...WERE BUSY WITH OUR WORK...
...AND DIDN'T REALIZE WHAT WAS HAPPENING...
?!
... UNTIL ...
...HE WAS COM-PLETELY HELPLESS ...

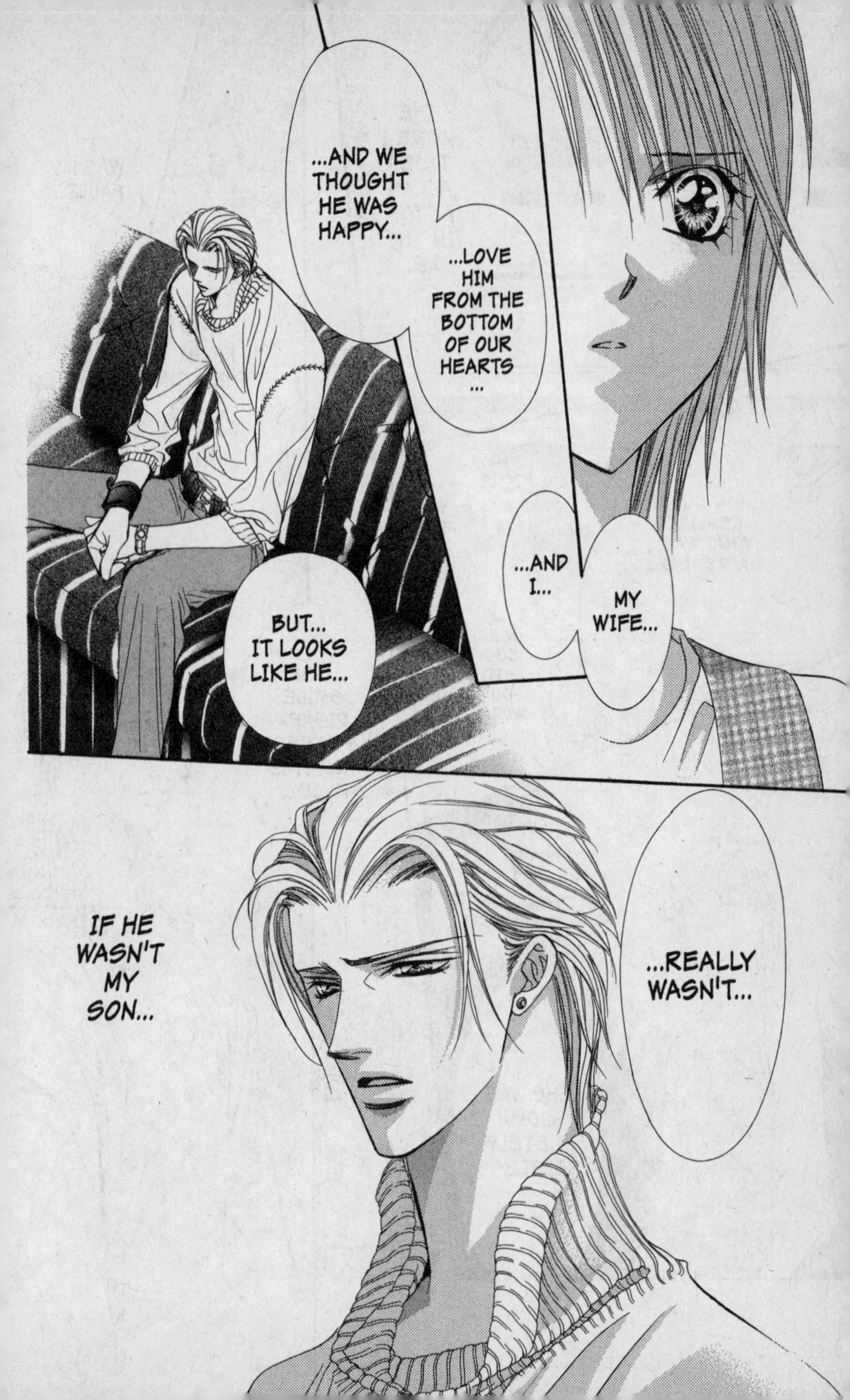
MY WIFE...
...AND I...
...LOVE HIM FROM THE BOTTOM OF OUR HEARTS...
...AND WE THOUGHT HE WAS HAPPY...
BUT... IT LOOKS LIKE HE...
...REALLY WASN'T...
IF HE WASN'T MY SON...

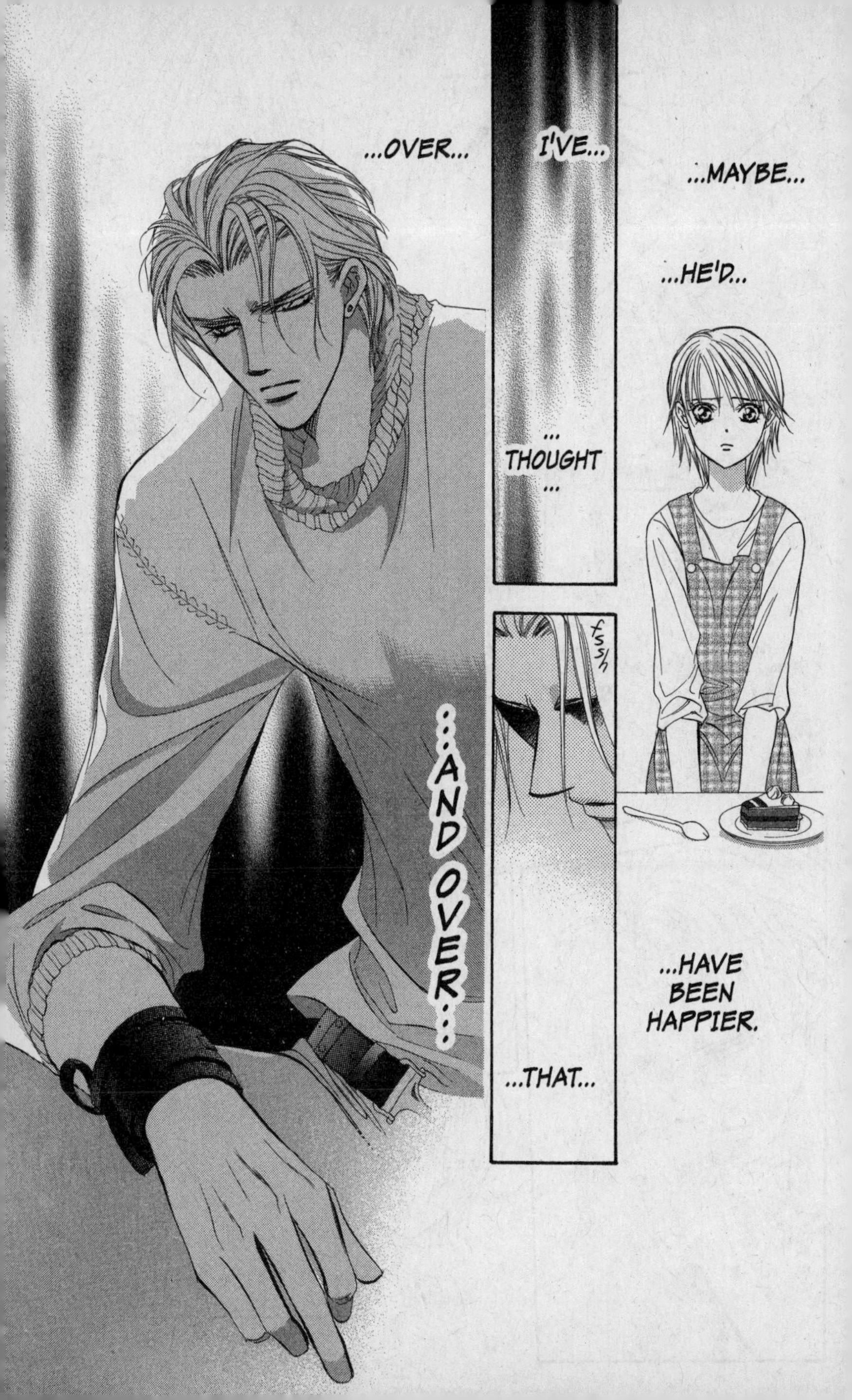
...MAYBE...
...HE'D...
...HAVE BEEN HAPPIER.
I'VE...
...THOUGHT...
fssh
...THAT...
...OVER...
...AND OVER...

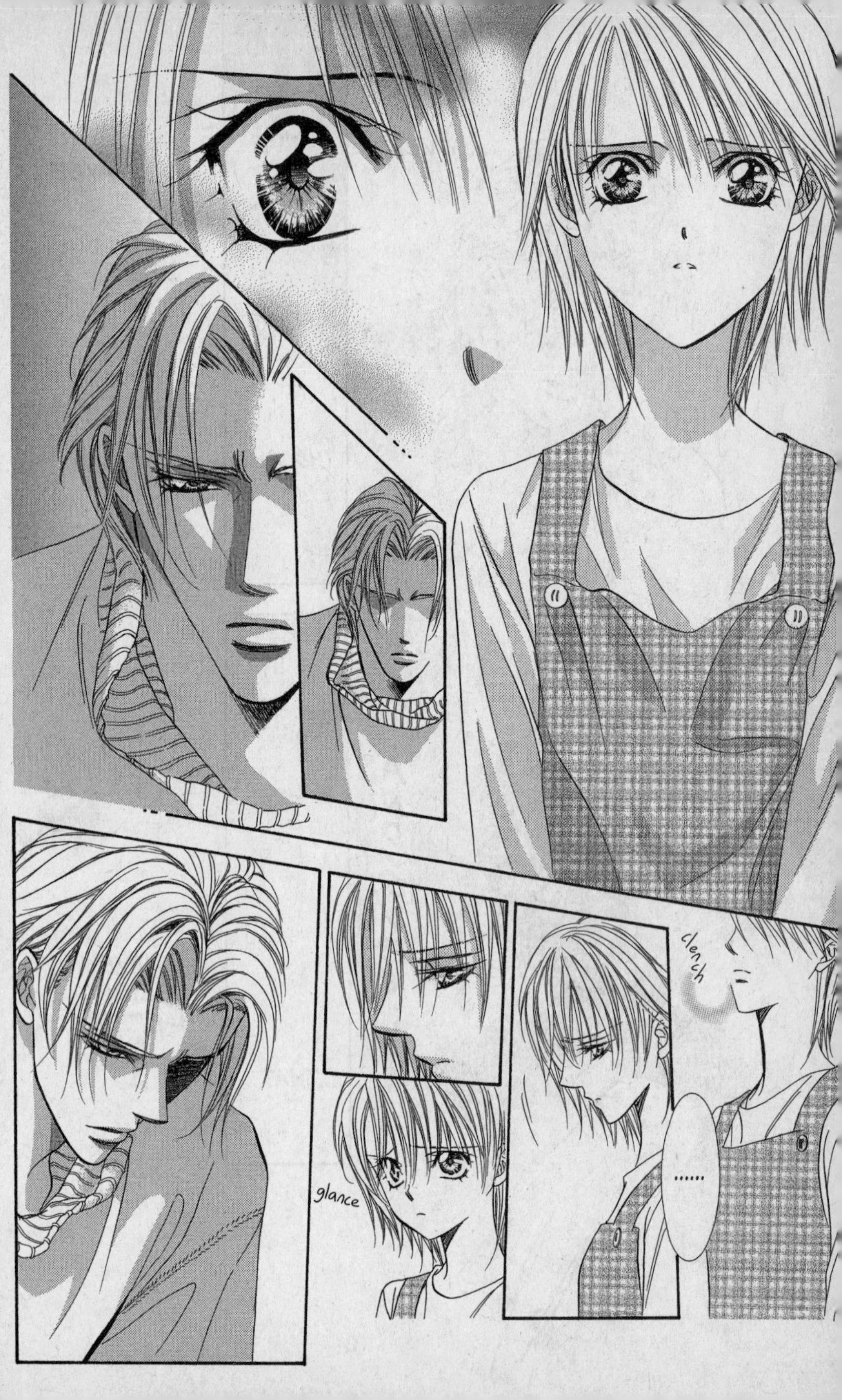
clench
......
glance

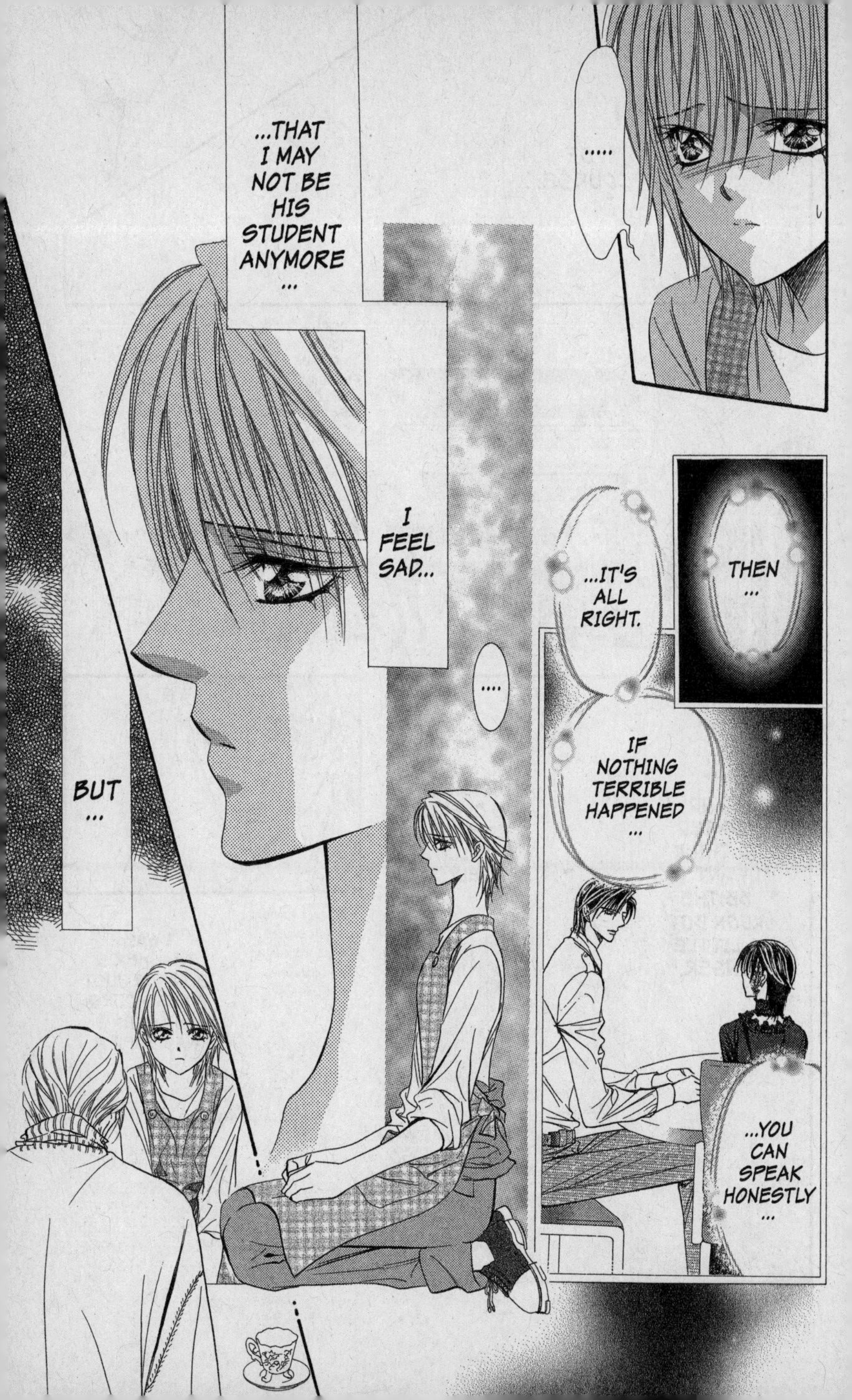
.....
THEN ...
...IT'S ALL RIGHT.
IF NOTHING TERRIBLE HAPPENED ...
...YOU CAN SPEAK HONESTLY ...
...THAT I MAY NOT BE HIS STUDENT ANYMORE ...
I FEEL SAD...
....
BUT ...

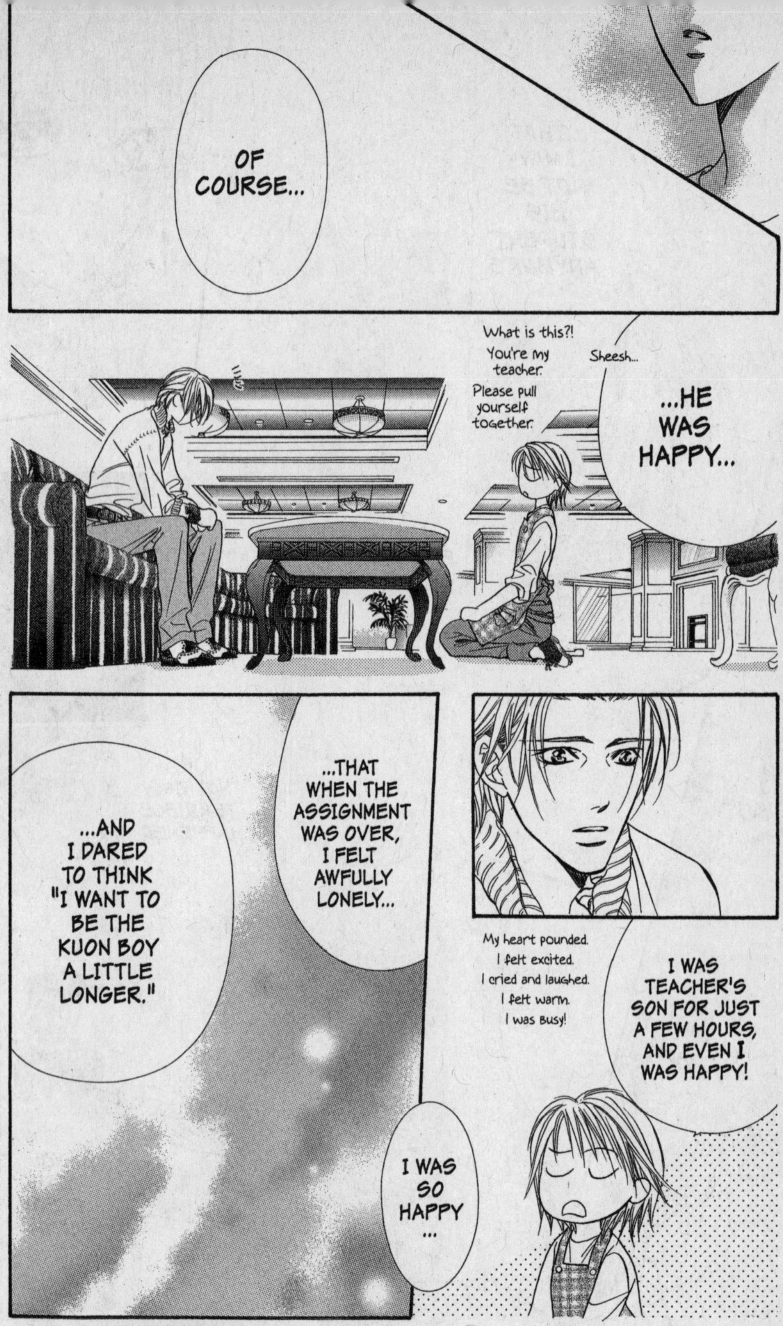
OF COURSE...
...HE WAS HAPPY...
Sheesh...
What is this?!
You're my teacher.
Please pull yourself together.
I WAS TEACHER'S SON FOR JUST A FEW HOURS, AND EVEN I WAS HAPPY!
My heart pounded.
I felt excited.
I cried and laughed.
I felt warm.
I was busy!
I WAS SO HAPPY ...
...THAT WHEN THE ASSIGNMENT WAS OVER, I FELT AWFULLY LONELY...
...AND I DARED TO THINK "I WANT TO BE THE KUON BOY A LITTLE LONGER."

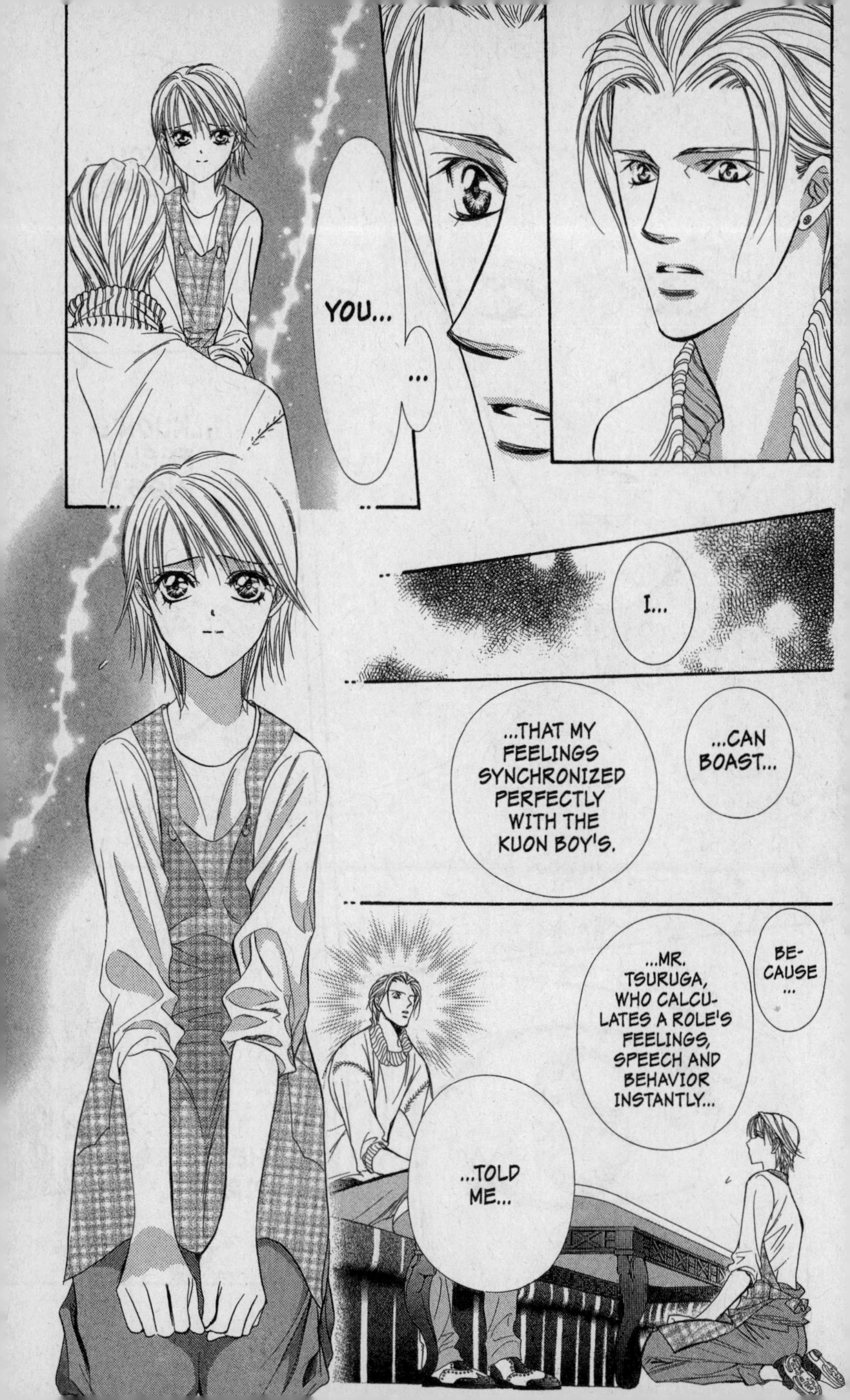
YOU...
...
I...
...CAN BOAST...
...THAT MY FEELINGS SYNCHRONIZED PERFECTLY WITH THE KUON BOY'S.
BE-CAUSE...
...MR. TSURUGA, WHO CALCU-LATES A ROLE'S FEELINGS, SPEECH AND BEHAVIOR INSTANTLY...
...TOLD ME...

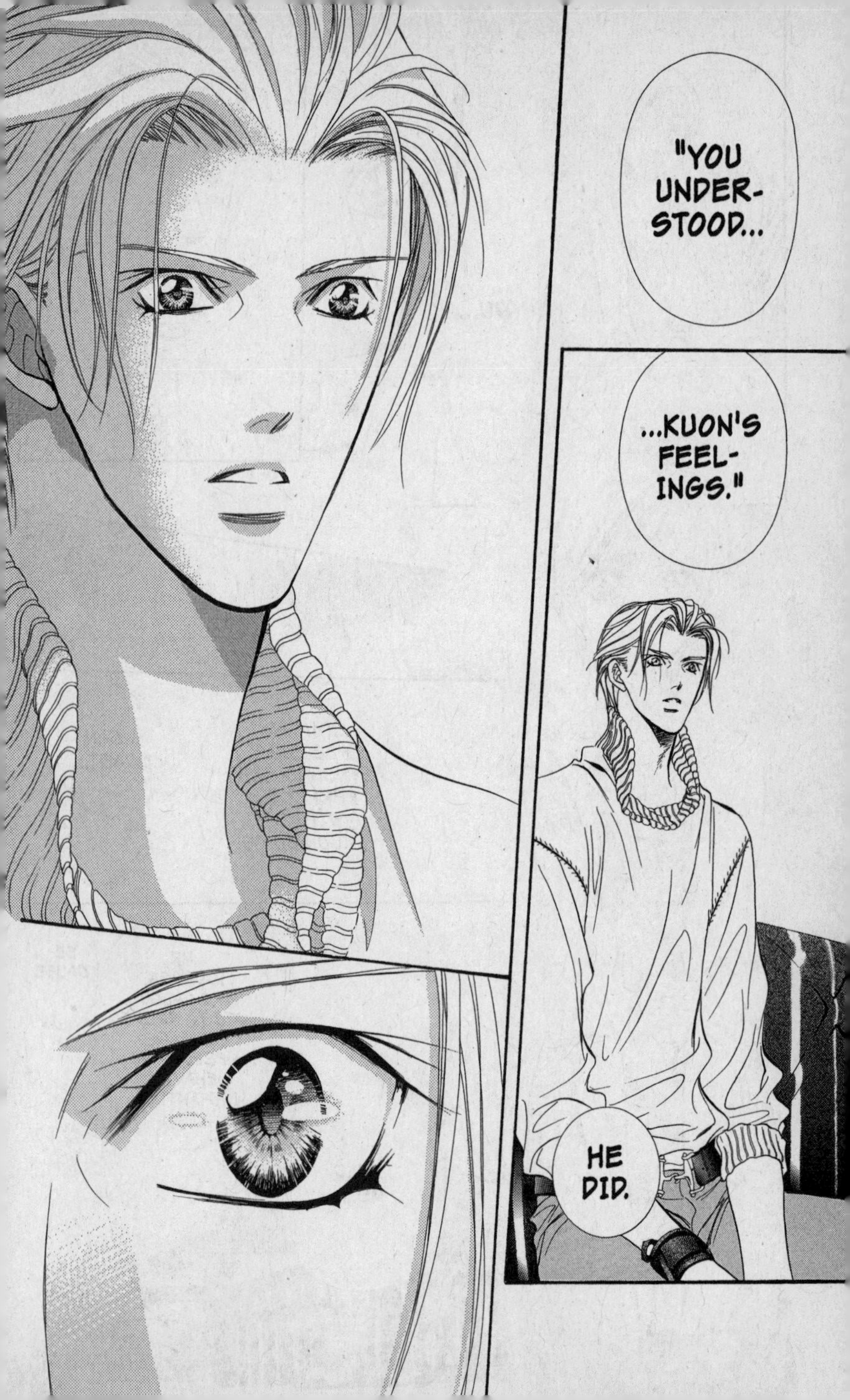
"YOU UNDER-STOOD...
...KUON'S FEEL-INGS."
HE DID.

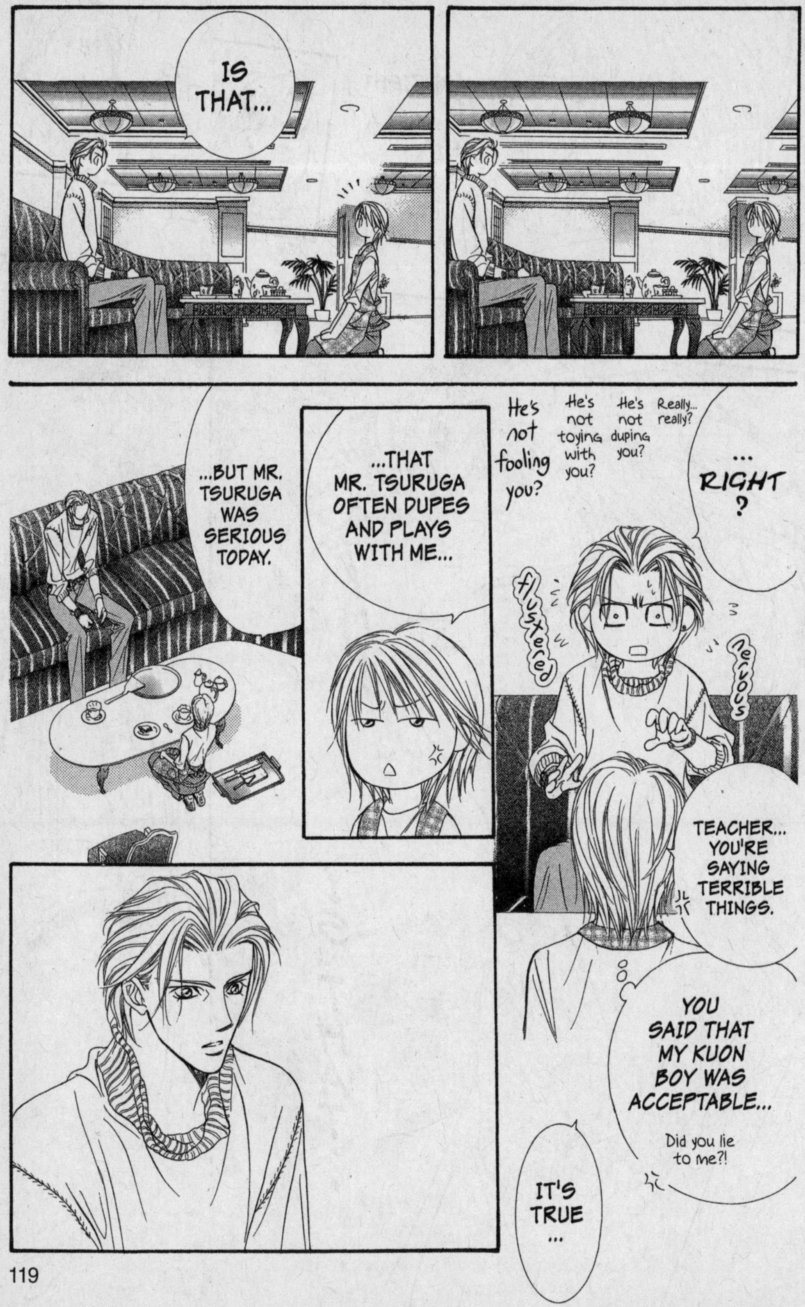
IS THAT...
...RIGHT?
Really... really?
He's not duping you?
He's not toying with you?
He's not fooling you?
flustered
nervous
TEACHER... YOU'RE SAYING TERRIBLE THINGS.
YOU SAID THAT MY KUON BOY WAS ACCEPTABLE...
Did you lie to me?!
...THAT MR. TSURUGA OFTEN DUPES AND PLAYS WITH ME...
...BUT MR. TSURUGA WAS SERIOUS TODAY.
IT'S TRUE...

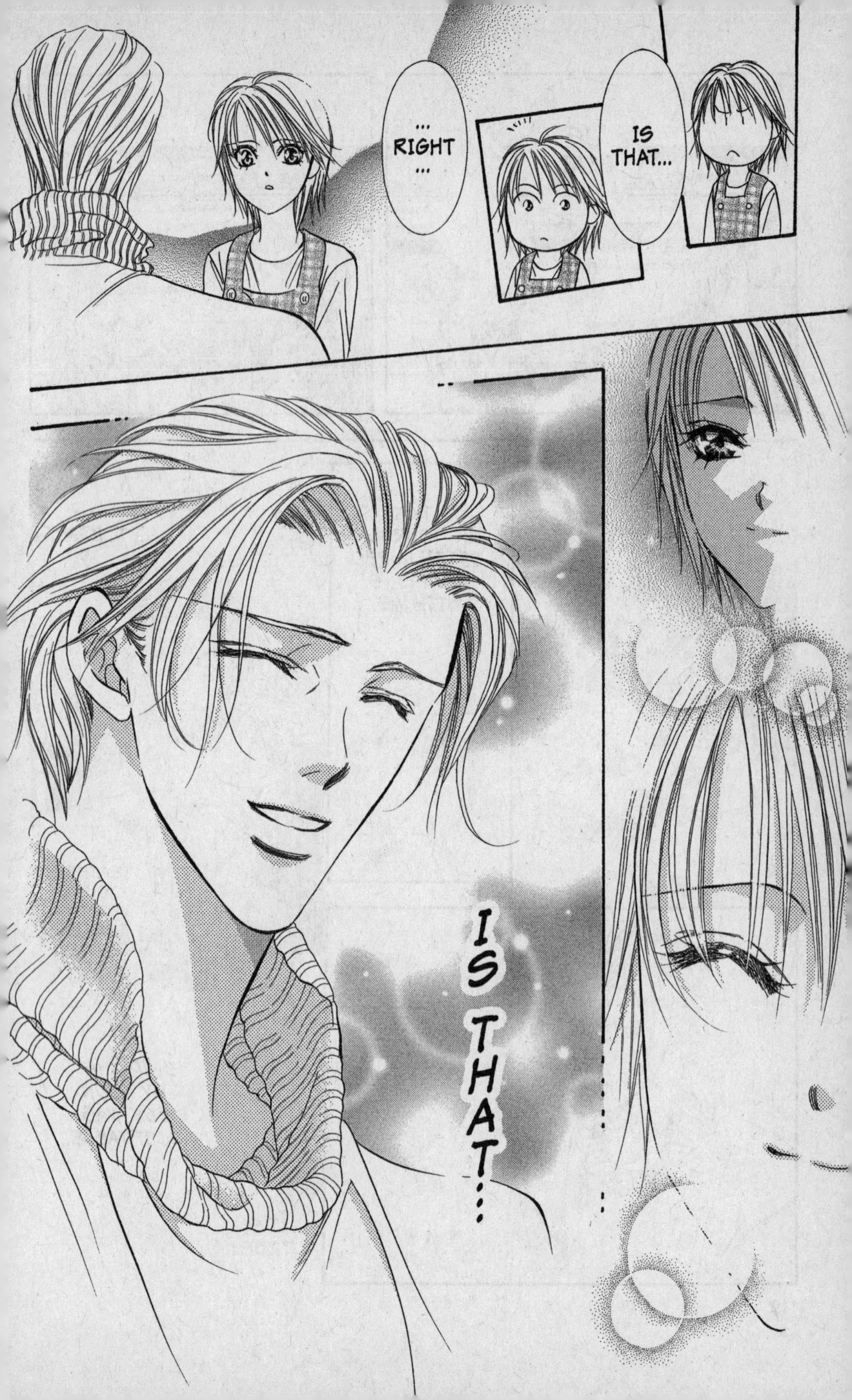
IS THAT...
...RIGHT...
IS THAT...

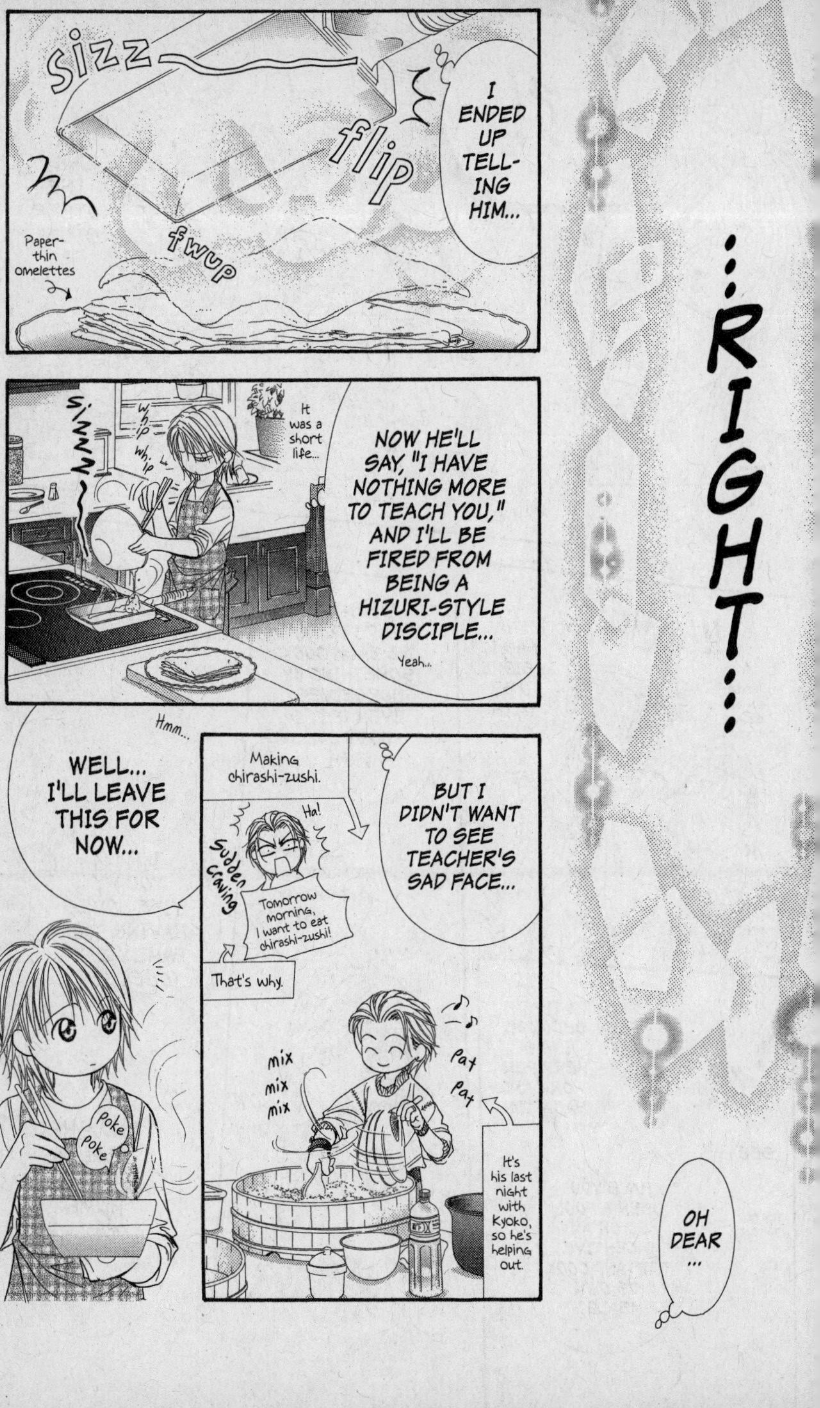
...RIGHT...
OH DEAR...
sizz
I ENDED UP TELLING HIM...
flip
fwup
Paper-thin omelettes
NOW HE'LL SAY, "I HAVE NOTHING MORE TO TEACH YOU," AND I'LL BE FIRED FROM BEING A HIZURI-STYLE DISCIPLE...
Yeah...
It was a short life...
whip whip
sizzz
BUT I DIDN'T WANT TO SEE TEACHER'S SAD FACE...
Making chirashi-zushi.
Ha!
Sudden craving
Tomorrow morning, I want to eat chirashi-zushi!
That's why.
Pat Pat
mix mix mix
It's his last night with Kyoko, so he's helping out.
Hmm...
WELL... I'LL LEAVE THIS FOR NOW...
Poke Poke

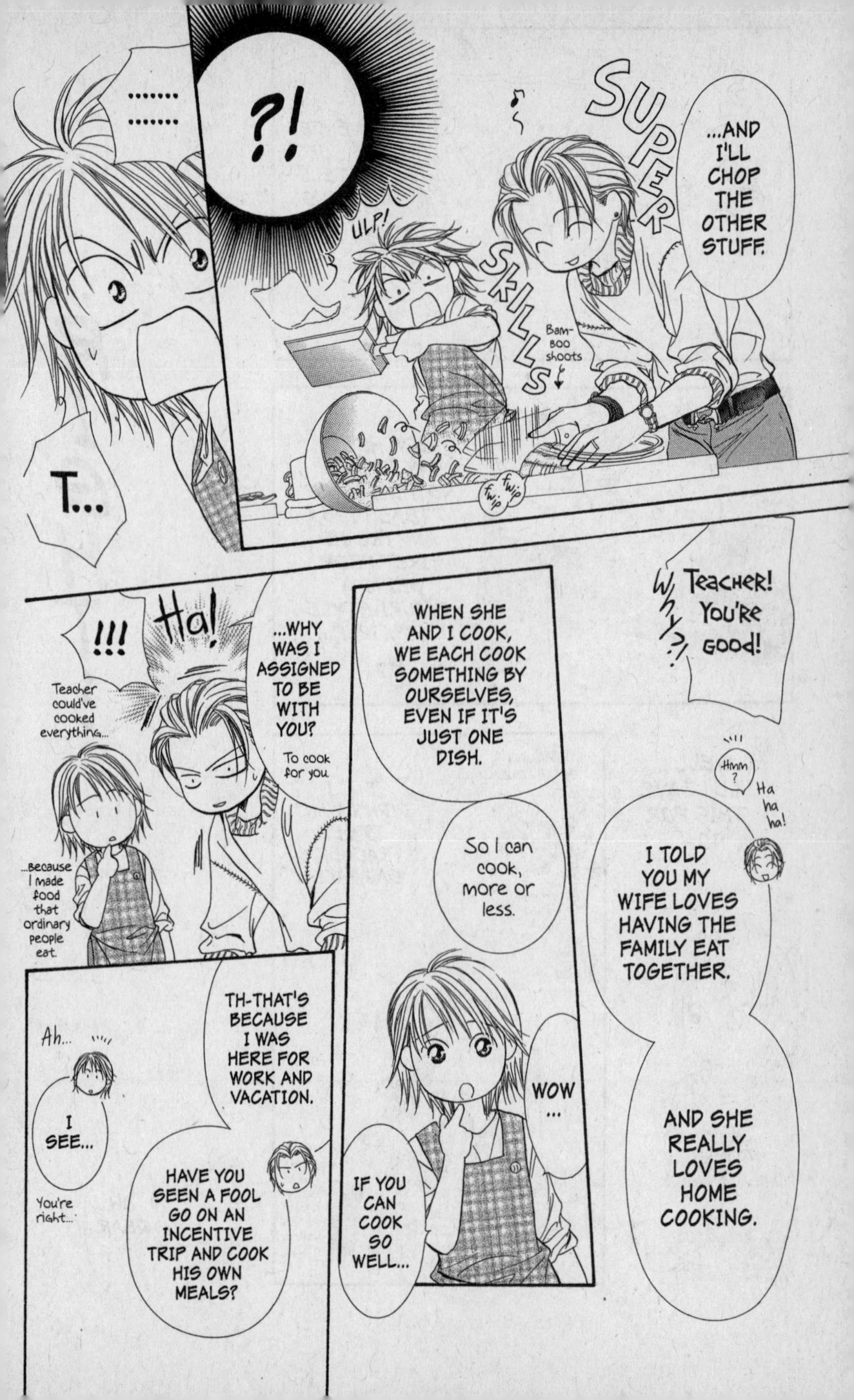
...AND I'LL CHOP THE OTHER STUFF.
SUPER SKILLS
ULP!
Bamboo shoots
fwip fwip
?!
......
......
T...
Why?!
Teacher! You're good!
Hmm?
Ha ha ha!
I TOLD YOU MY WIFE LOVES HAVING THE FAMILY EAT TOGETHER.
AND SHE REALLY LOVES HOME COOKING.
WHEN SHE AND I COOK, WE EACH COOK SOMETHING BY OURSELVES, EVEN IF IT'S JUST ONE DISH.
So I can cook, more or less.
WOW...
IF YOU CAN COOK SO WELL...
...WHY WAS I ASSIGNED TO BE WITH YOU?
To cook for you.
Ha!
!!!
Teacher could've cooked everything...
...Because I made food that ordinary people eat.
TH-THAT'S BECAUSE I WAS HERE FOR WORK AND VACATION.
HAVE YOU SEEN A FOOL GO ON AN INCENTIVE TRIP AND COOK HIS OWN MEALS?
Ah...
I SEE...
You're right...

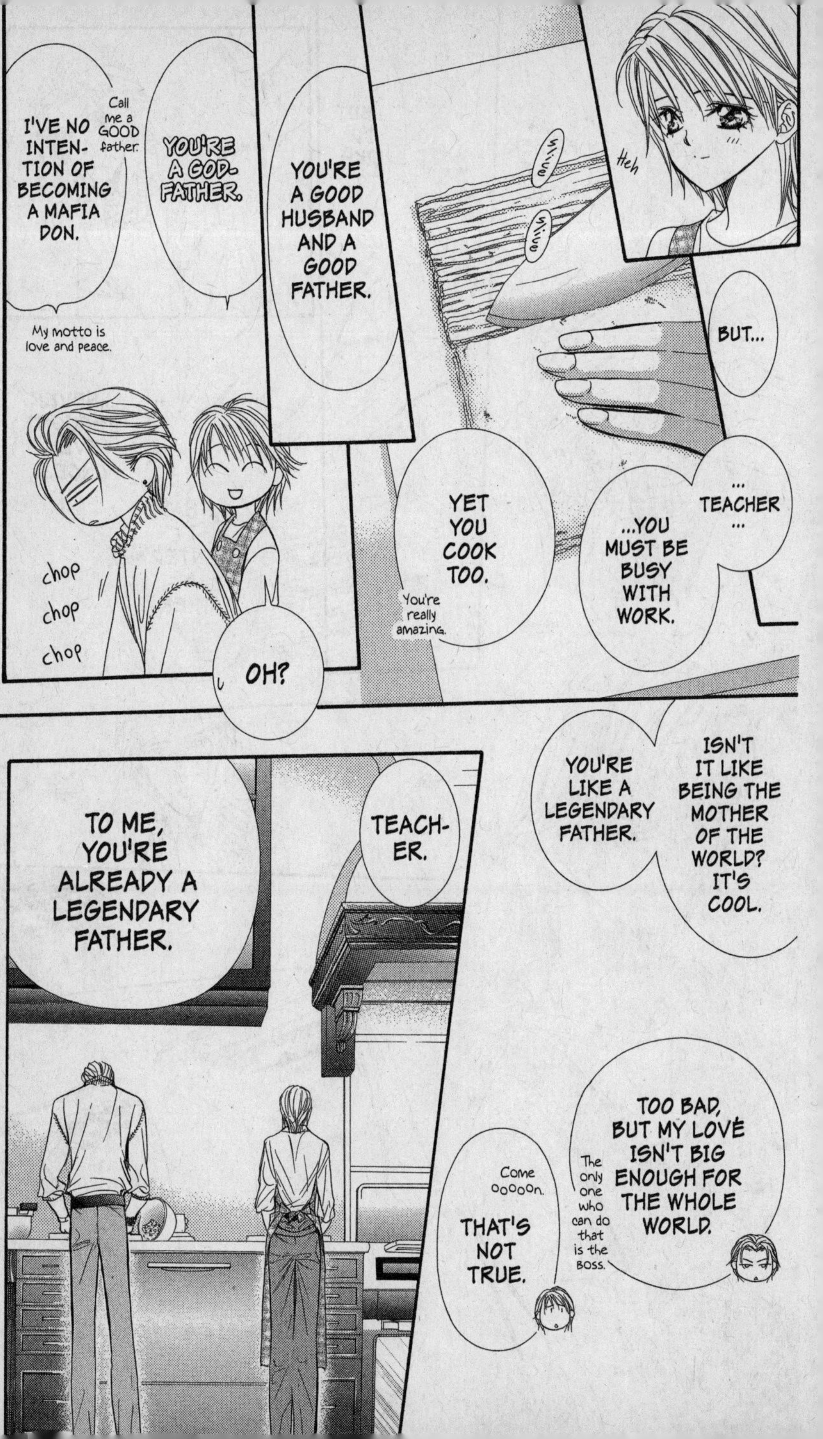
Heh
slice
slice
BUT...
... TEACHER ...
...YOU MUST BE BUSY WITH WORK.
YET YOU COOK TOO.
You're really amazing.
YOU'RE A GOOD HUSBAND AND A GOOD FATHER.
OH?
YOU'RE A GOD-FATHER.
Call me a GOOD father.
I'VE NO INTEN-TION OF BECOMING A MAFIA DON.
My motto is love and peace.
chop
chop
chop
ISN'T IT LIKE BEING THE MOTHER OF THE WORLD? IT'S COOL.
YOU'RE LIKE A LEGENDARY FATHER.
TOO BAD, BUT MY LOVE ISN'T BIG ENOUGH FOR THE WHOLE WORLD.
The only one who can do that is the Boss.
THAT'S NOT TRUE.
Come oooOOn.
TEACH-ER.
TO ME, YOU'RE ALREADY A LEGENDARY FATHER.

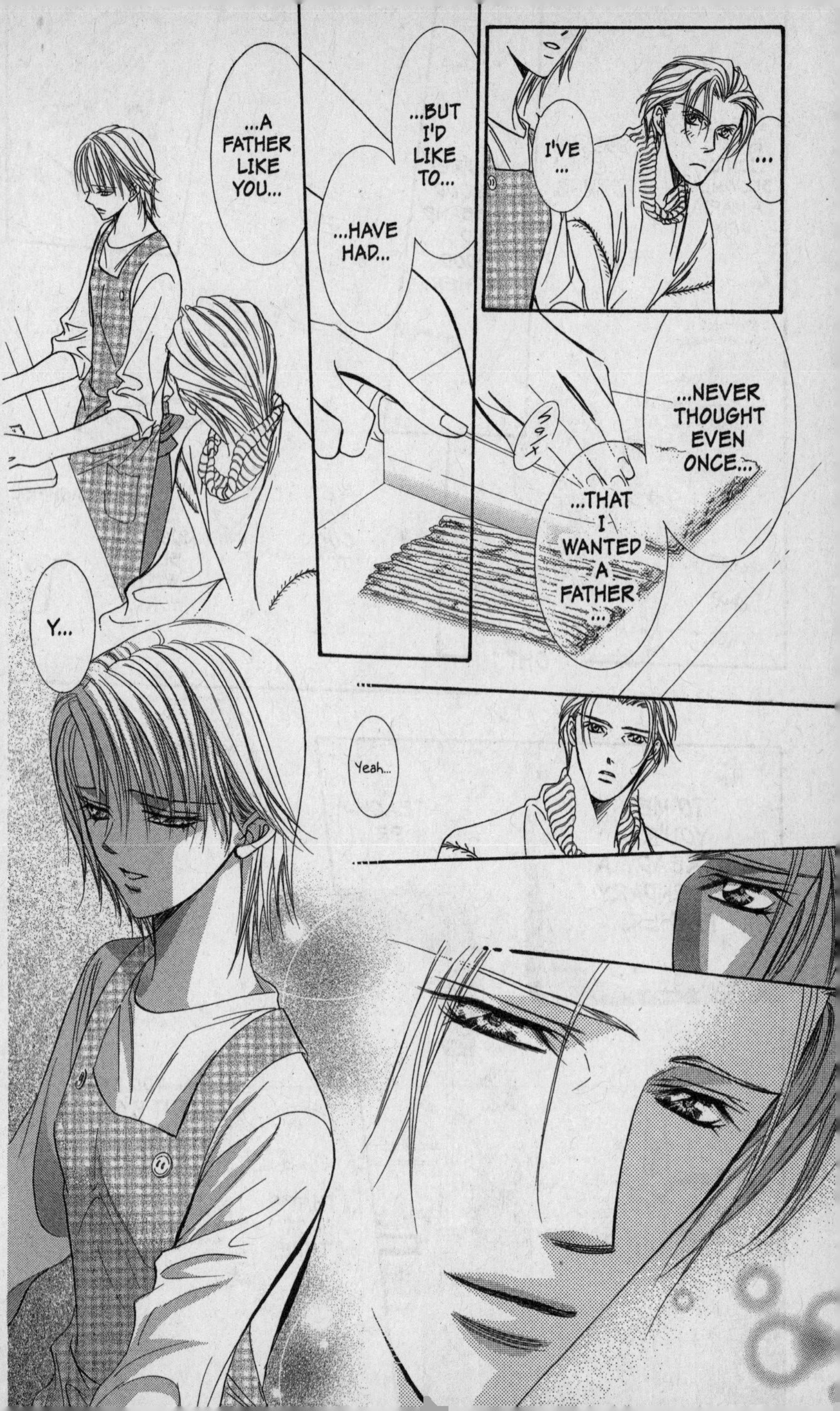
...
I'VE ...
...NEVER THOUGHT EVEN ONCE...
...THAT I WANTED A FATHER ...
...BUT I'D LIKE TO...
...HAVE HAD...
...A FATHER LIKE YOU...
Yeah...
Y...

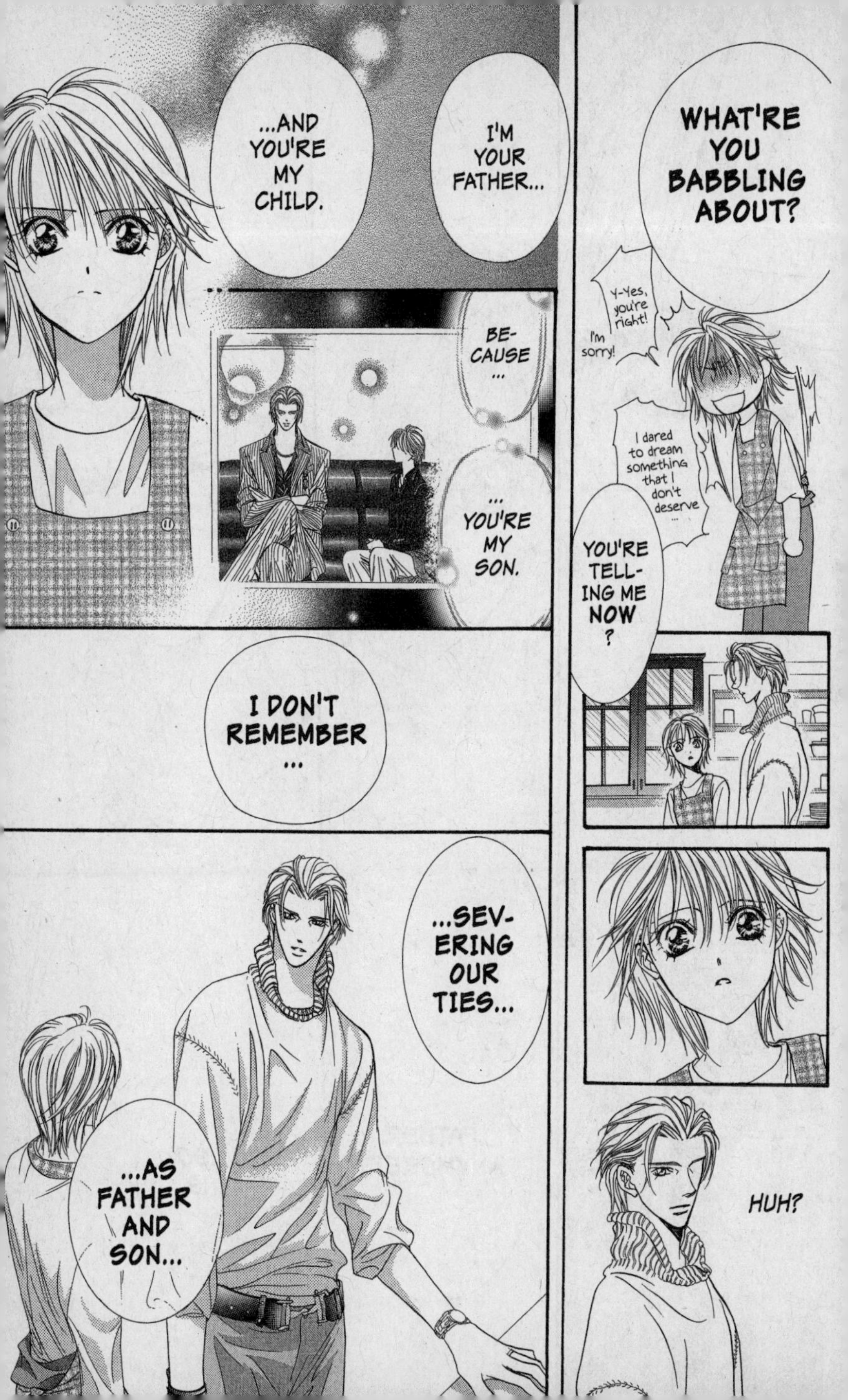
WHAT'RE YOU BABBLING ABOUT?
Y-Yes, you're right!
I'm sorry!
I dared to dream something that I don't deserve ...
YOU'RE TELLING ME NOW ?
HUH?
I'M YOUR FATHER...
...AND YOU'RE MY CHILD.
BE-CAUSE ...
... YOU'RE MY SON.
I DON'T REMEMBER ...
...SEV-ERING OUR TIES...
...AS FATHER AND SON...

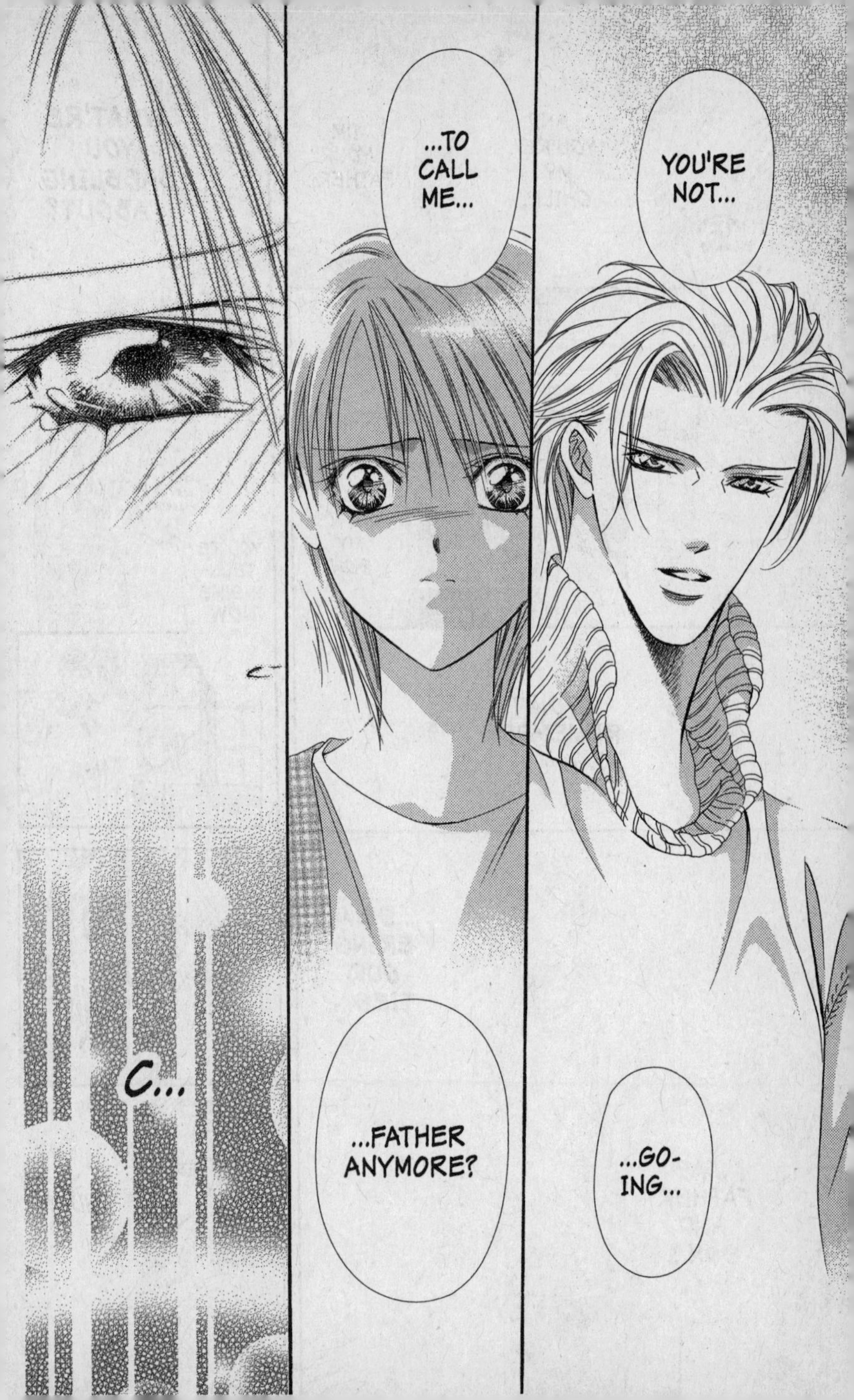
YOU'RE NOT...
...GO- ING...
...TO CALL ME...
...FATHER ANYMORE?
C...

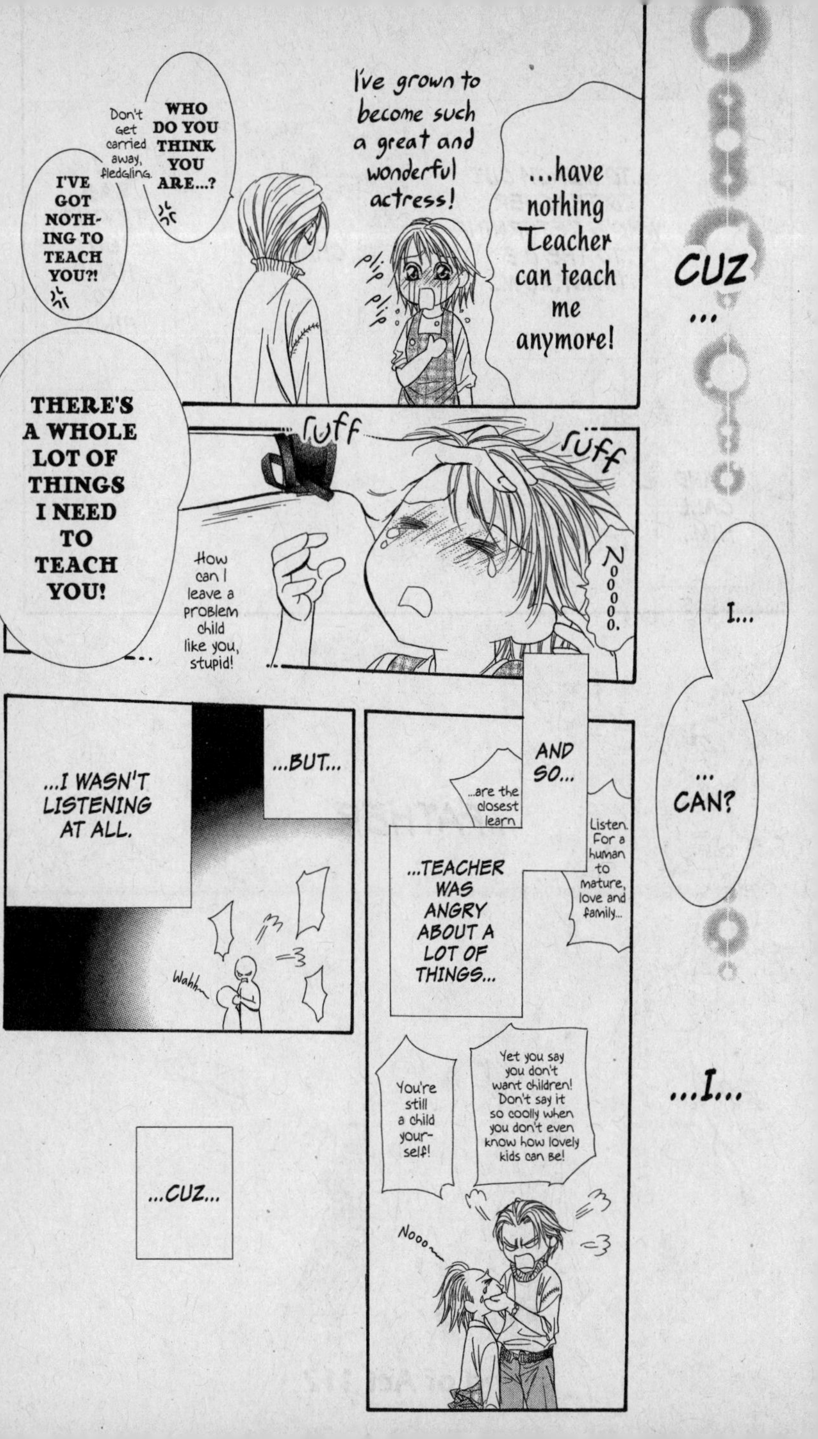
CUZ...
I...
...CAN?
...I...
...have nothing Teacher can teach me anymore!
I've grown to become such a great and wonderful actress!
plip plip
WHO DO YOU THINK YOU ARE...?
Don't get carried away, fledgling.
I'VE GOT NOTHING TO TEACH YOU?!
ruff
Noooooo.
ruff
How can I leave a problem child like you, stupid!
THERE'S A WHOLE LOT OF THINGS I NEED TO TEACH YOU!
AND SO...
...are the closest learn
Listen. For a human to mature, love and family...
...TEACHER WAS ANGRY ABOUT A LOT OF THINGS...
Yet you say you don't want children! Don't say it so coolly when you don't even know how lovely kids can be!
You're still a child your-self!
Nooo~
...BUT...
...I WASN'T LISTENING AT ALL.
Wahh~
...CUZ...

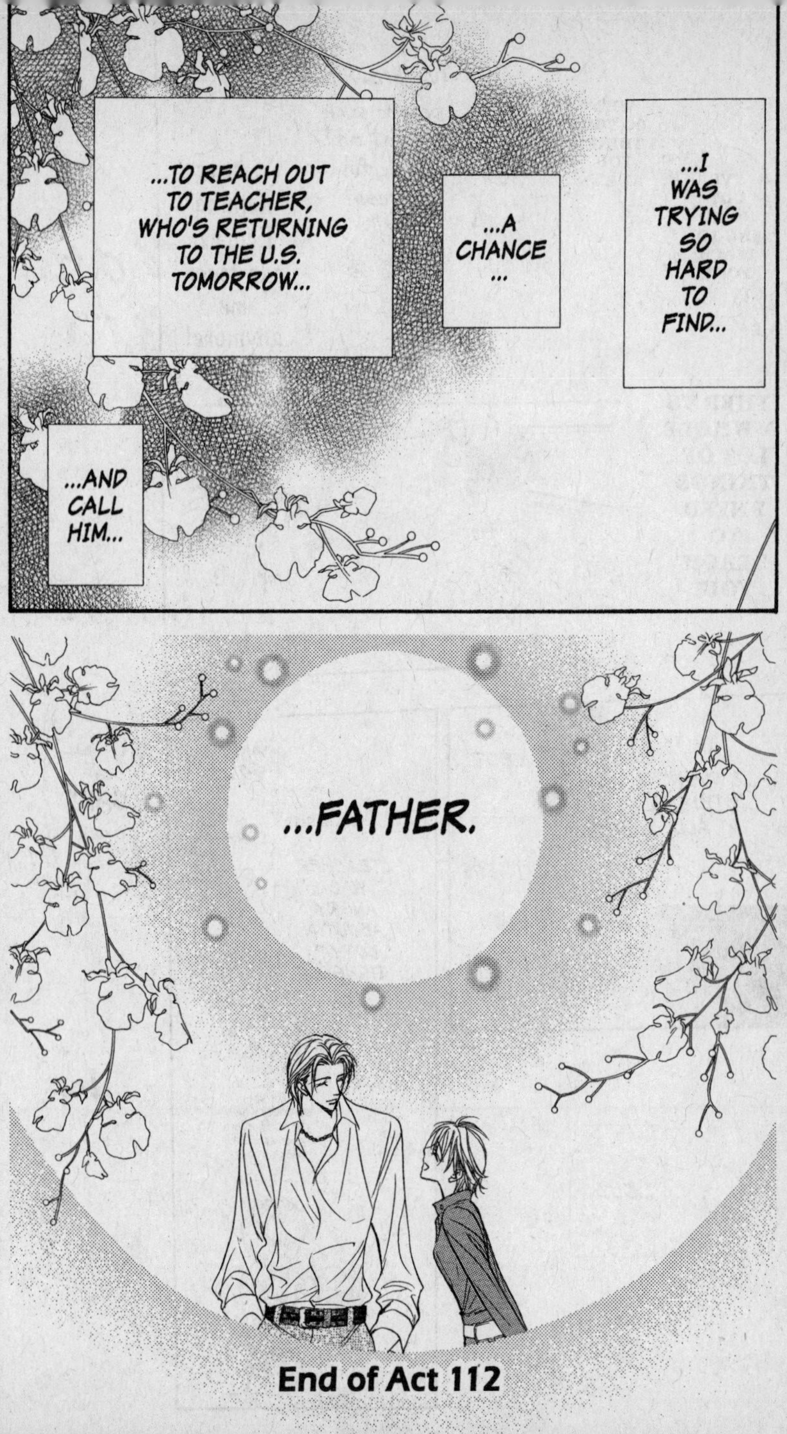
...I WAS TRYING SO HARD TO FIND...
...A CHANCE...
...TO REACH OUT TO TEACHER, WHO'S RETURNING TO THE U.S. TOMORROW...
...AND CALL HIM...
...FATHER.

End of Act 112

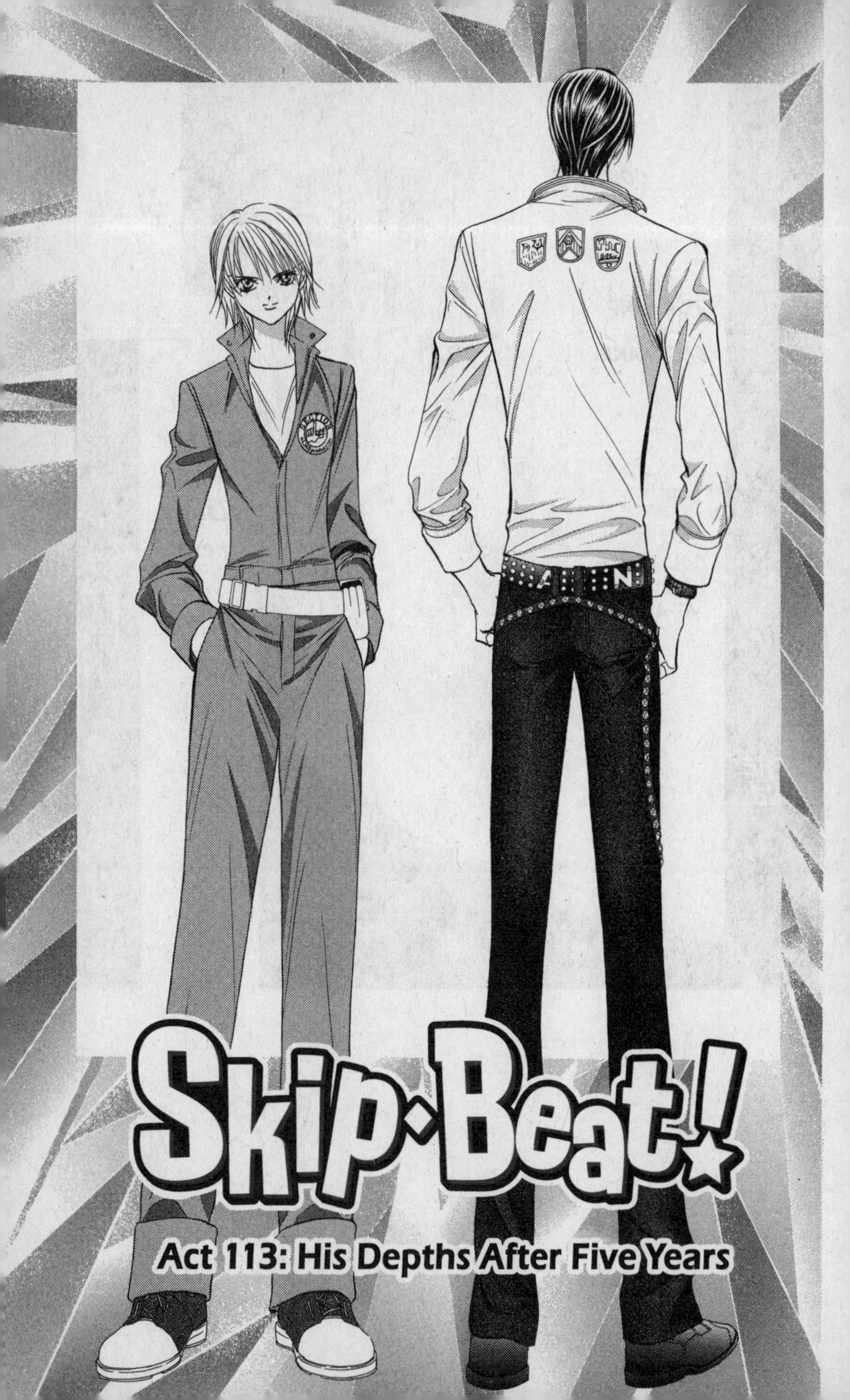
Skip·Beat!
Act 113: His Depths After Five Years

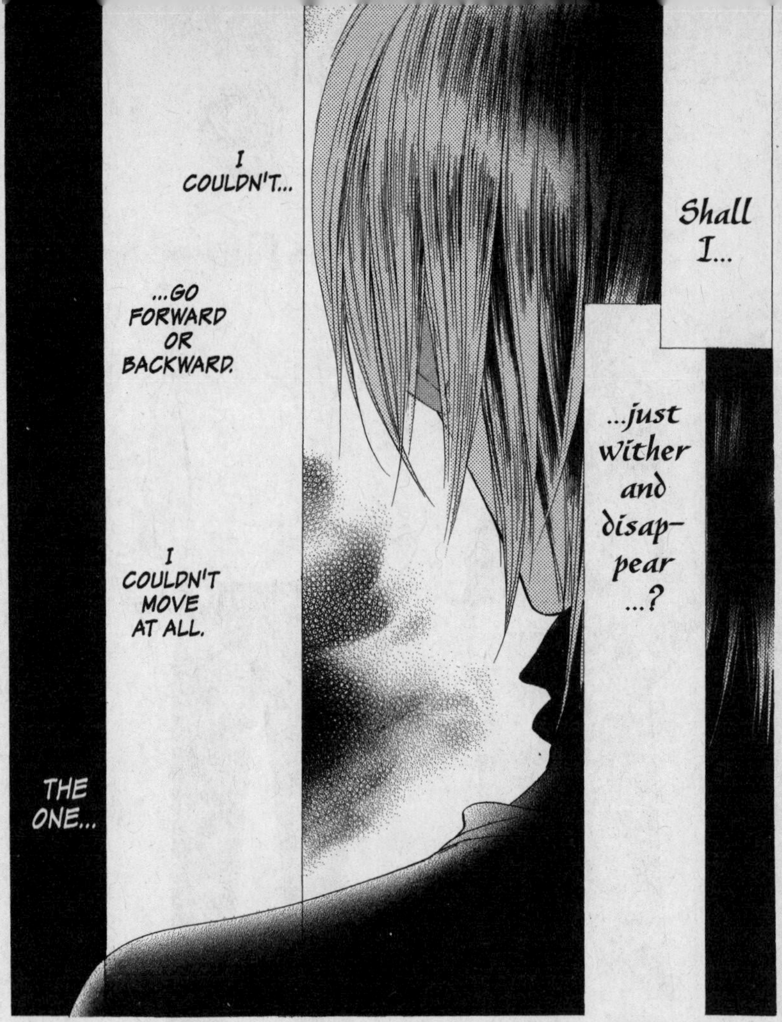
Shall I...
...just wither and disap-pear ...?
I COULDN'T...
...GO FORWARD OR BACKWARD.
I COULDN'T MOVE AT ALL.
THE ONE...

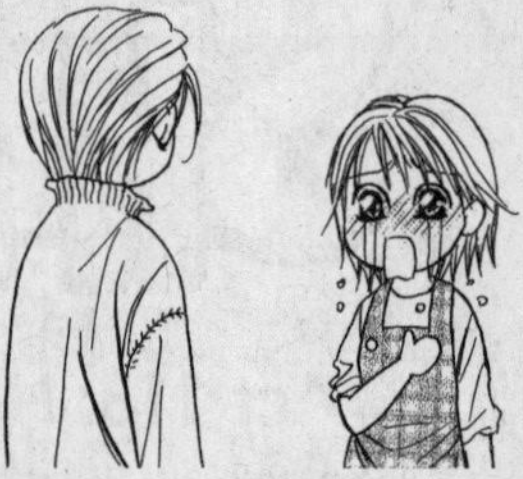

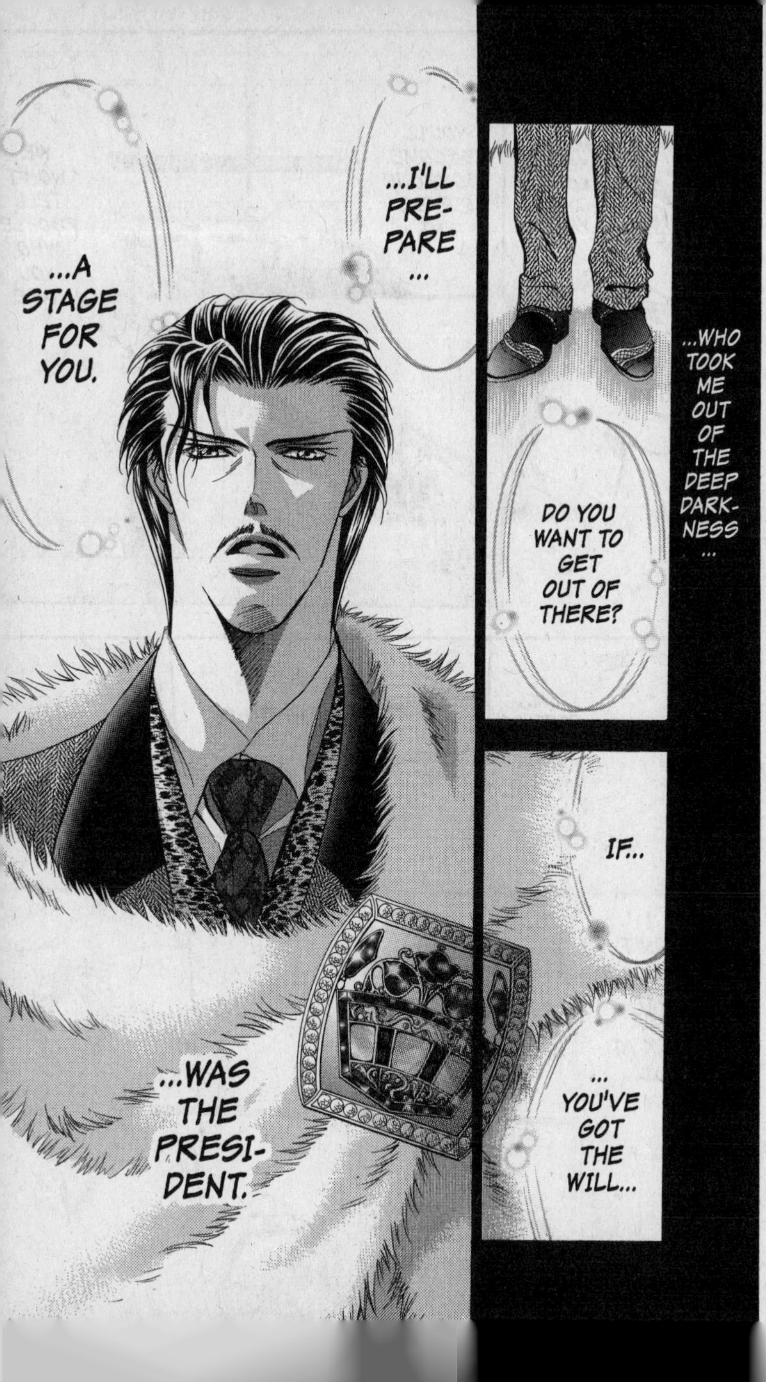
...WHO TOOK ME OUT OF THE DEEP DARKNESS...
DO YOU WANT TO GET OUT OF THERE?
IF...
...YOU'VE GOT THE WILL...
...I'LL PREPARE...
...A STAGE FOR YOU.
...WAS THE PRESIDENT.

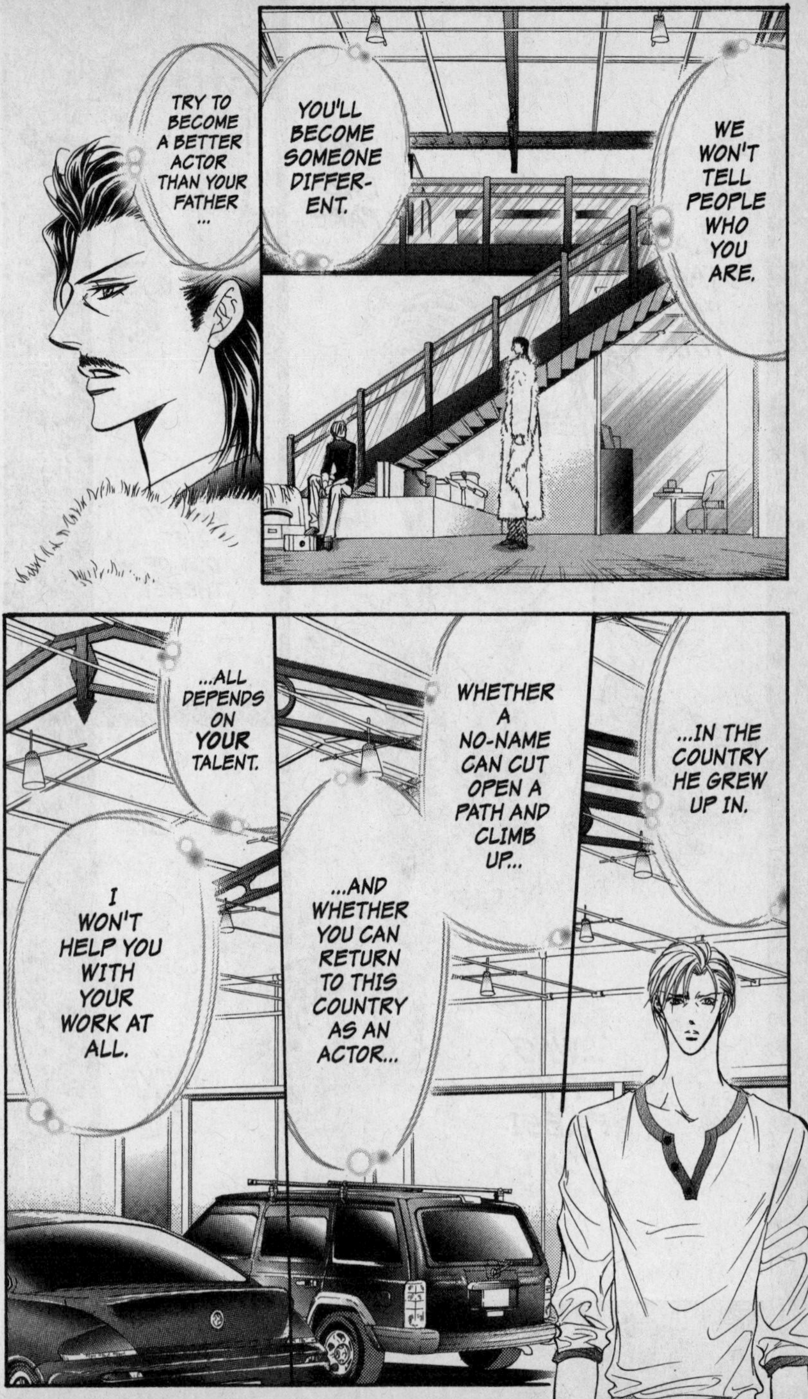
WE WON'T TELL PEOPLE WHO YOU ARE.
YOU'LL BECOME SOMEONE DIFFER-ENT.
TRY TO BECOME A BETTER ACTOR THAN YOUR FATHER...
...IN THE COUNTRY HE GREW UP IN.
WHETHER A NO-NAME CAN CUT OPEN A PATH AND CLIMB UP...
...AND WHETHER YOU CAN RETURN TO THIS COUNTRY AS AN ACTOR...
...ALL DEPENDS ON YOUR TALENT.
I WON'T HELP YOU WITH YOUR WORK AT ALL.

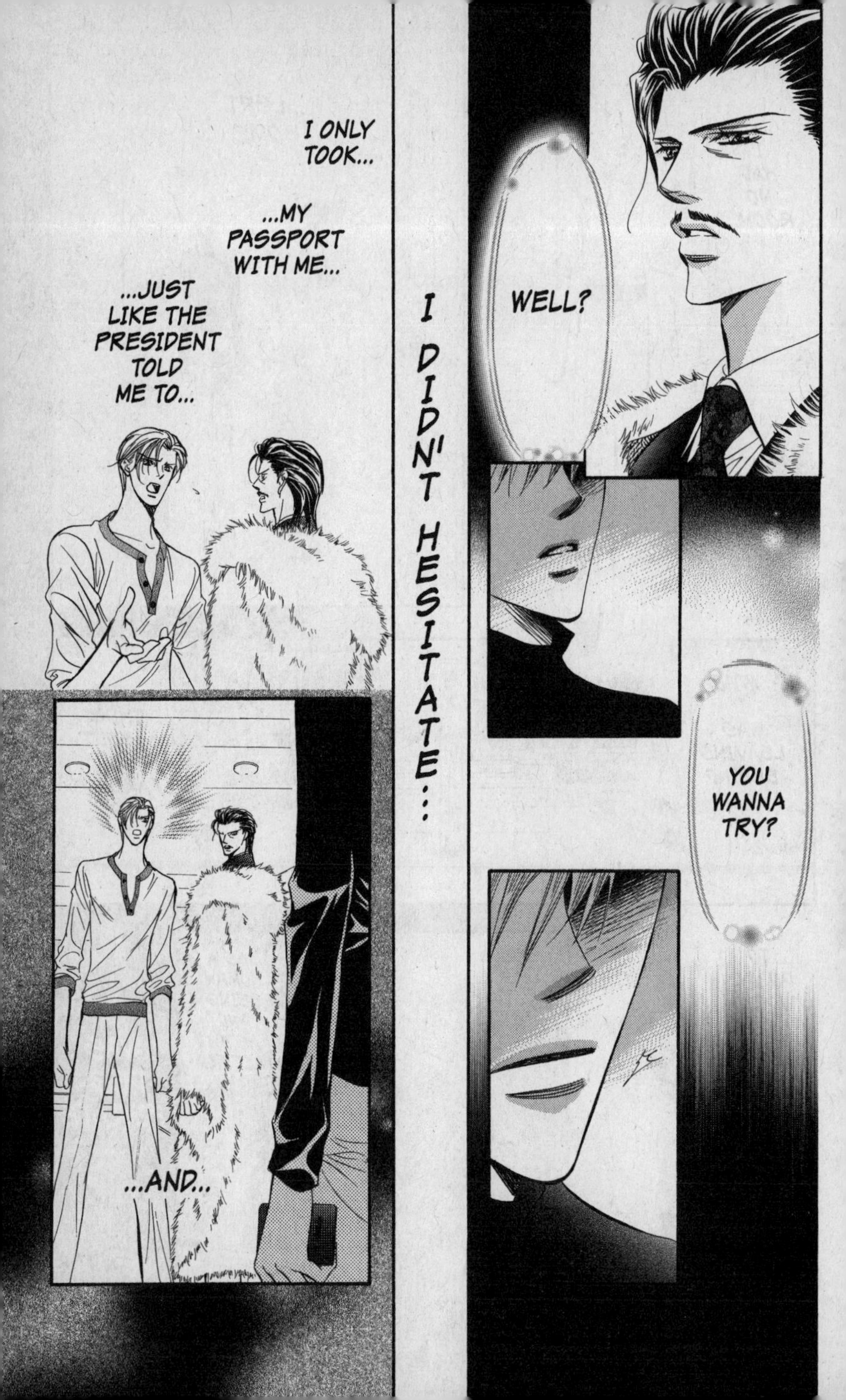
WELL?
YOU WANNA TRY?
I DIDN'T HESITATE...
I ONLY TOOK...
...MY PASSPORT WITH ME...
...JUST LIKE THE PRESIDENT TOLD ME TO...
...AND...

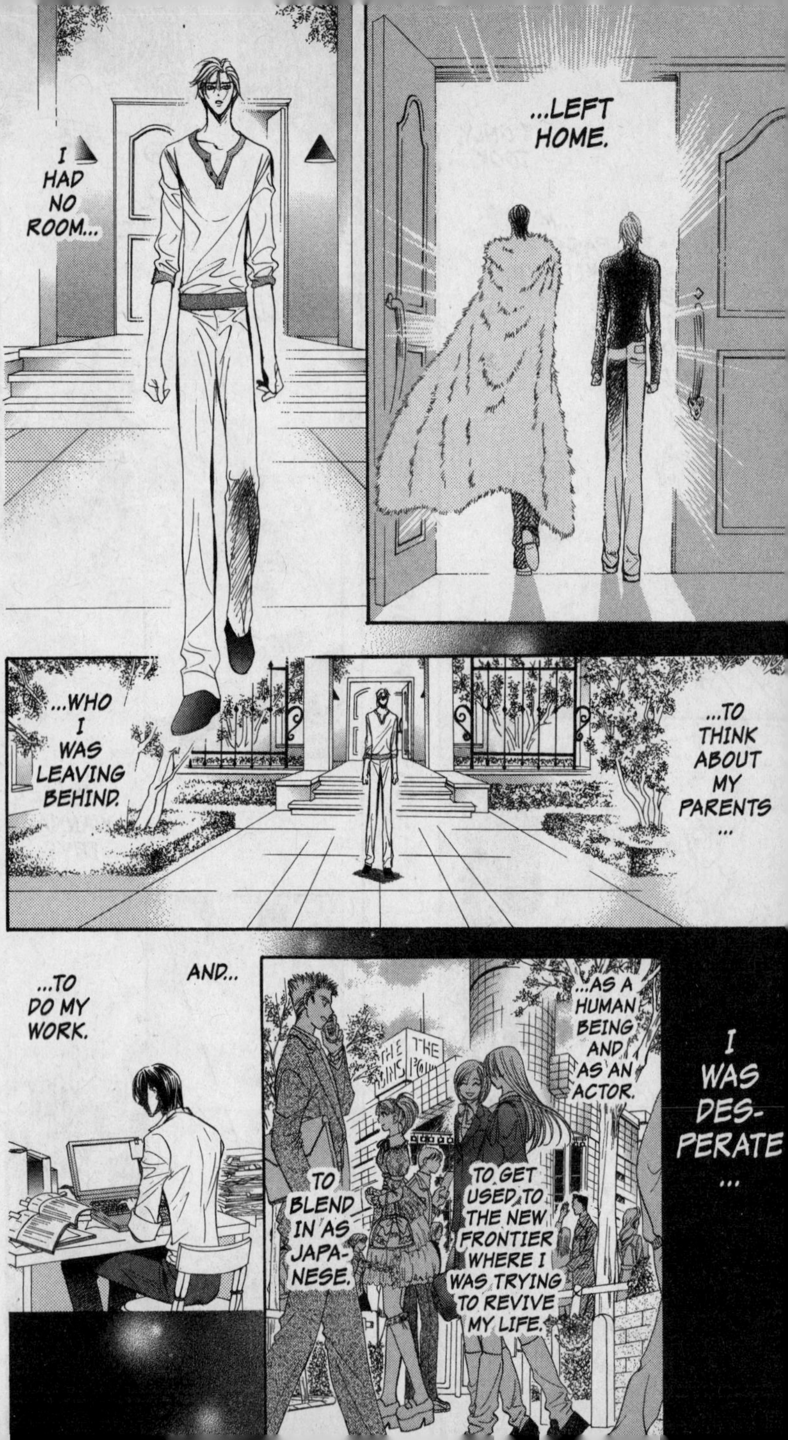
...LEFT HOME.
I HAD NO ROOM...
...TO THINK ABOUT MY PARENTS...
...WHO I WAS LEAVING BEHIND.
I WAS DES-PERATE...
...AS A HUMAN BEING AND AS AN ACTOR.
TO GET USED TO THE NEW FRONTIER WHERE I WAS TRYING TO REVIVE MY LIFE.
TO BLEND IN AS JAPA-NESE.
AND...
...TO DO MY WORK.

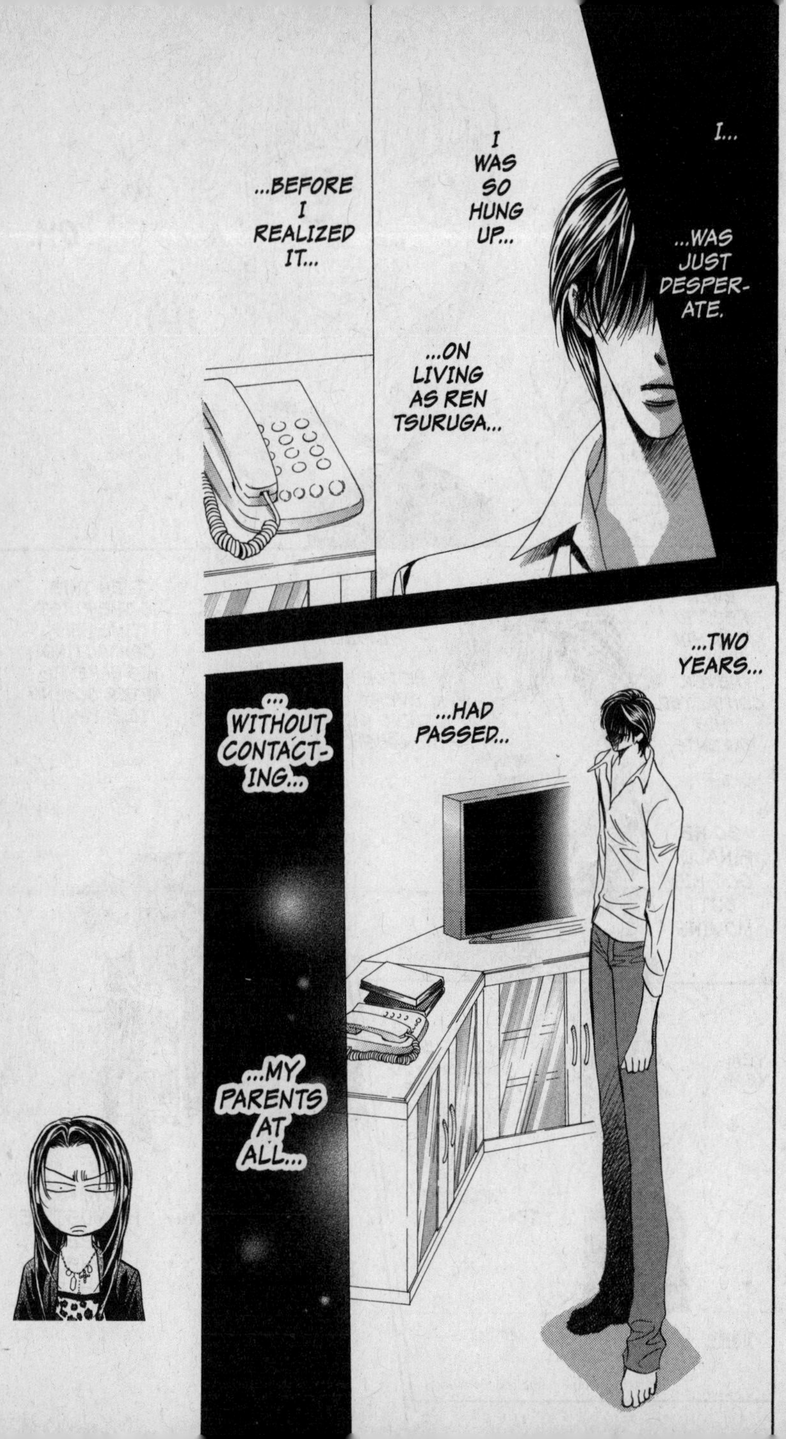
I...
...WAS JUST DESPERATE.
I WAS SO HUNG UP...
...ON LIVING AS REN TSURUGA...
...BEFORE I REALIZED IT...
...TWO YEARS...
...HAD PASSED...
...WITHOUT CONTACTING...
...MY PARENTS AT ALL...

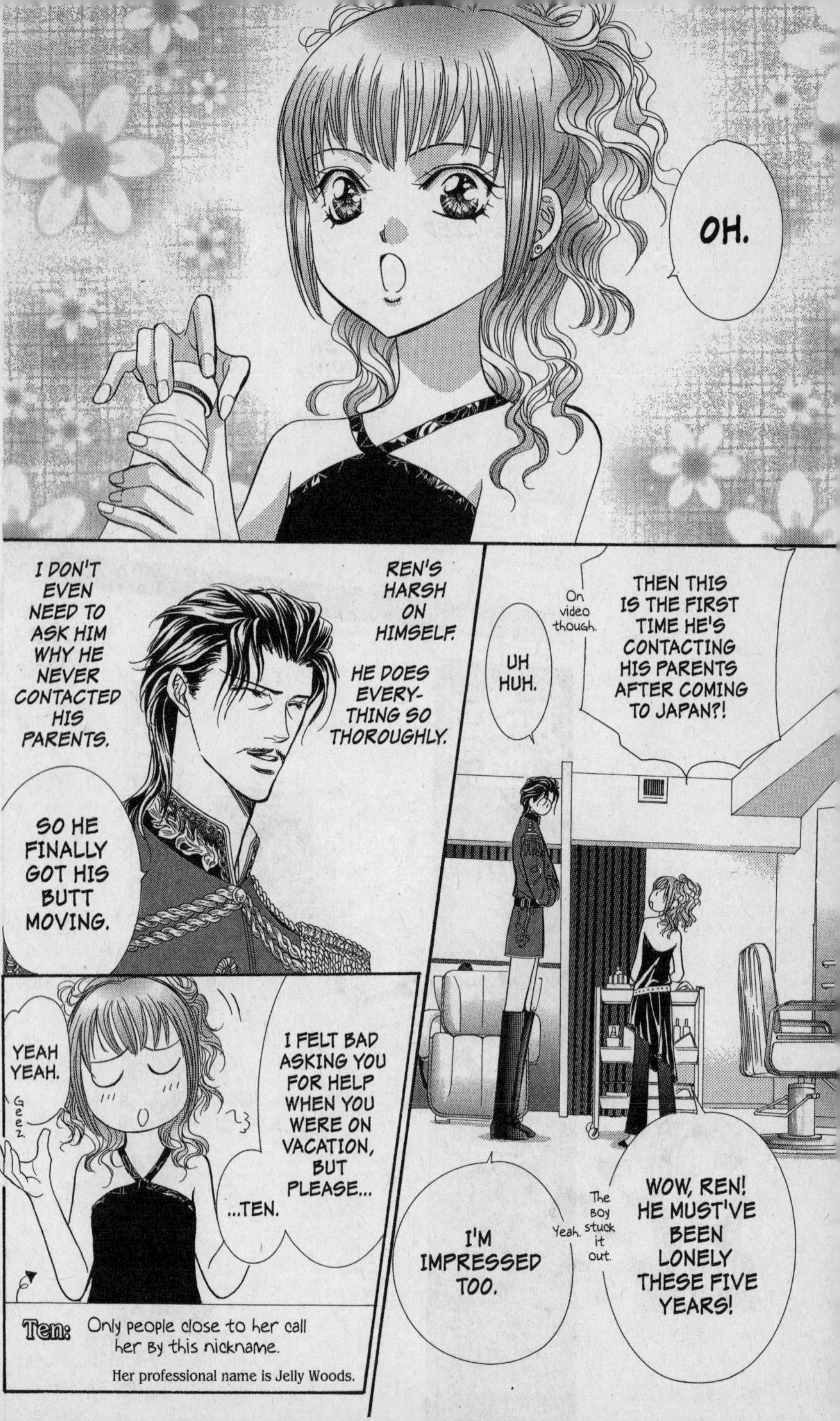
OH.
THEN THIS IS THE FIRST TIME HE'S CONTACTING HIS PARENTS AFTER COMING TO JAPAN?!
On video though.
UH HUH.
WOW, REN! HE MUST'VE BEEN LONELY THESE FIVE YEARS!
The Boy stuck it out.
Yeah.
I'M IMPRESSED TOO.
REN'S HARSH ON HIMSELF.
HE DOES EVERY-THING SO THOROUGHLY.
I DON'T EVEN NEED TO ASK HIM WHY HE NEVER CONTACTED HIS PARENTS.
SO HE FINALLY GOT HIS BUTT MOVING.
I FELT BAD ASKING YOU FOR HELP WHEN YOU WERE ON VACATION, BUT PLEASE...
...TEN.
YEAH YEAH.
Geez.
Ten: Only people close to her call her By this nickname.
Her professional name is Jelly Woods.

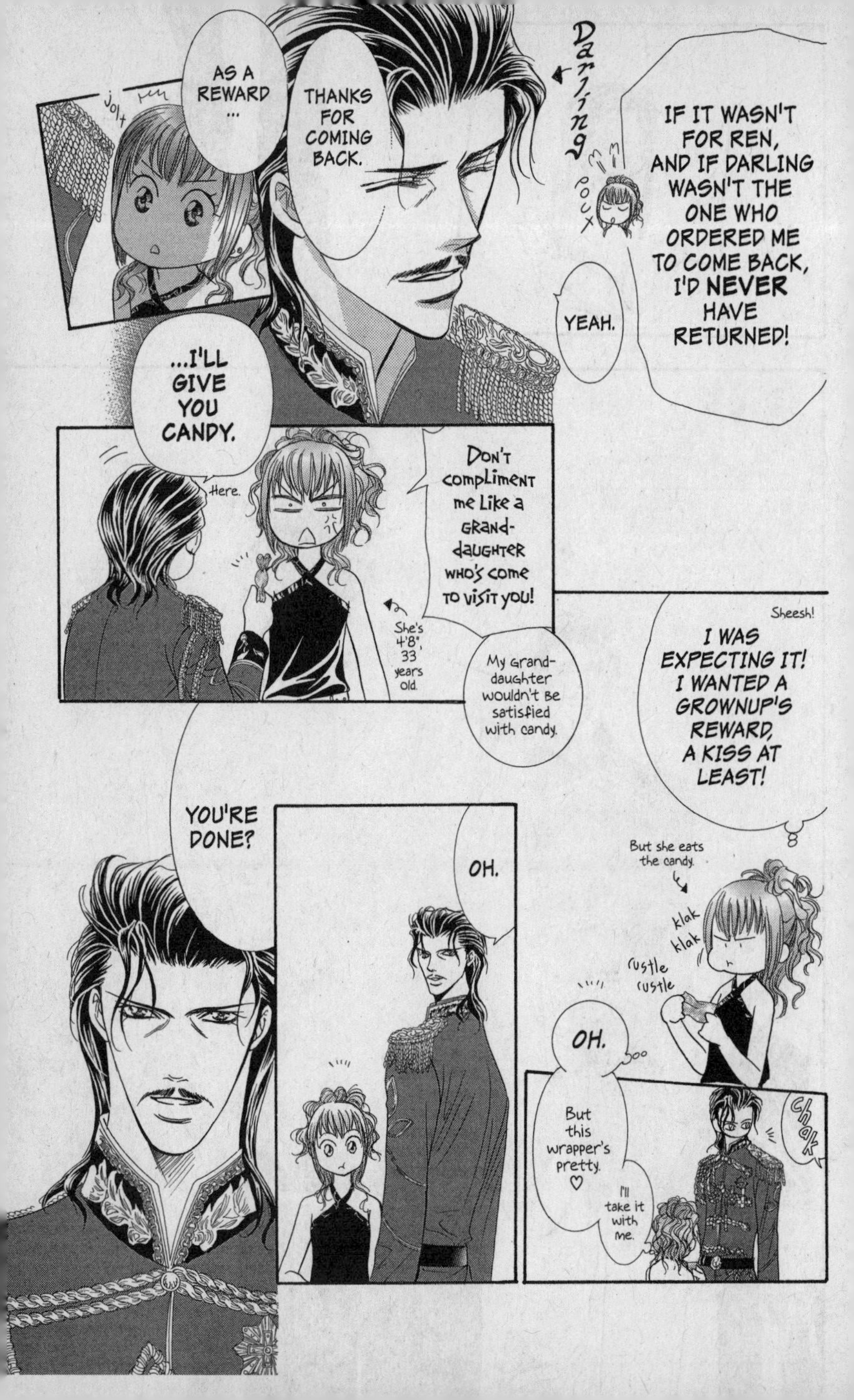
Darling
IF IT WASN'T FOR REN, AND IF DARLING WASN'T THE ONE WHO ORDERED ME TO COME BACK, I'D NEVER HAVE RETURNED!
pout
YEAH.
THANKS FOR COMING BACK.
AS A REWARD ...
jolt
...I'LL GIVE YOU CANDY.
Here.
Don't compliment me like a grand-daughter who's come to visit you!
She's 4'8", 33 years old.
My grand-daughter wouldn't be satisfied with candy.
Sheesh!
I WAS EXPECTING IT! I WANTED A GROWNUP'S REWARD, A KISS AT LEAST!
But she eats the candy.
klak klak
rustle rustle
OH.
But this wrapper's pretty. ♡
I'll take it with me.
Chak
OH.
YOU'RE DONE?

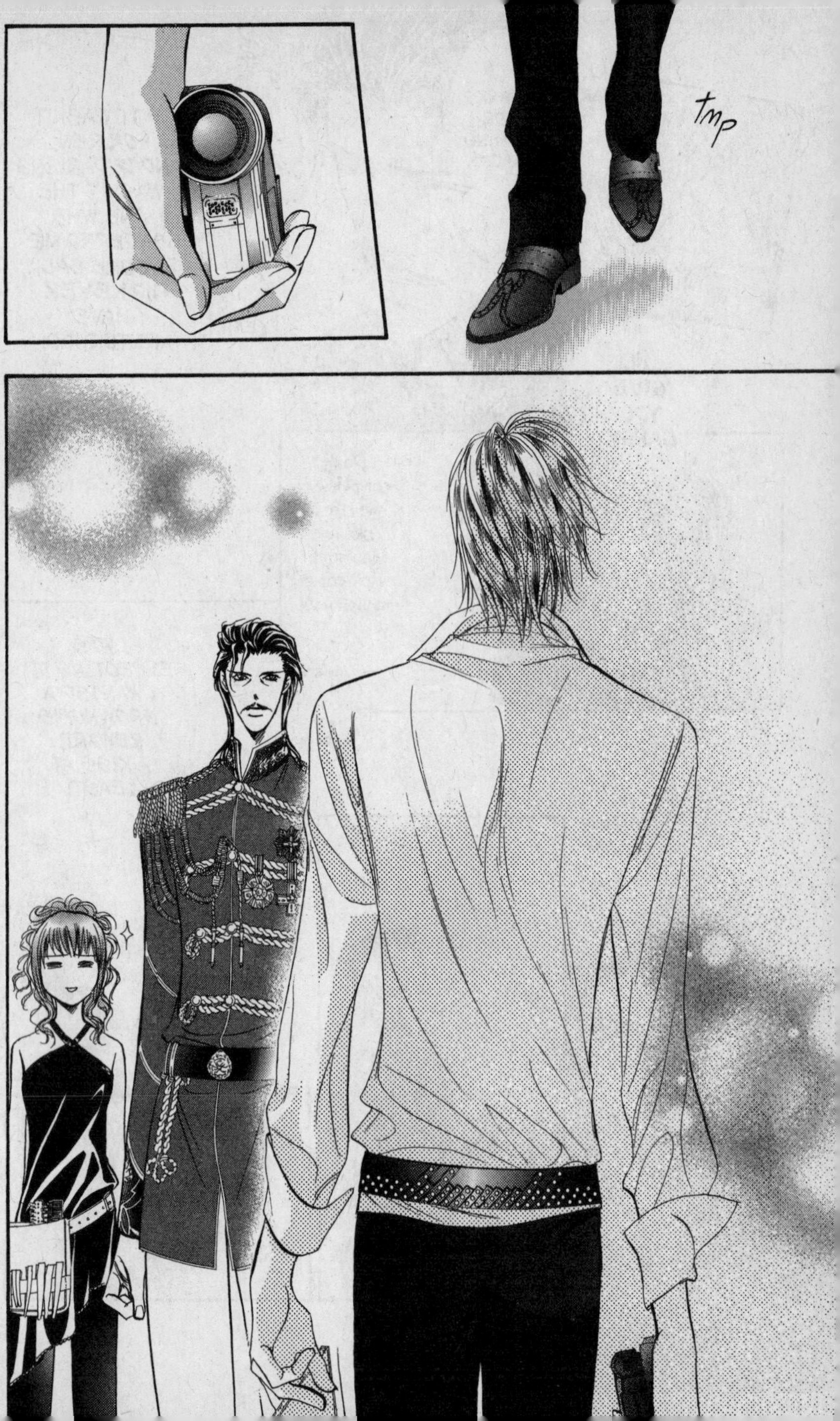
tmp

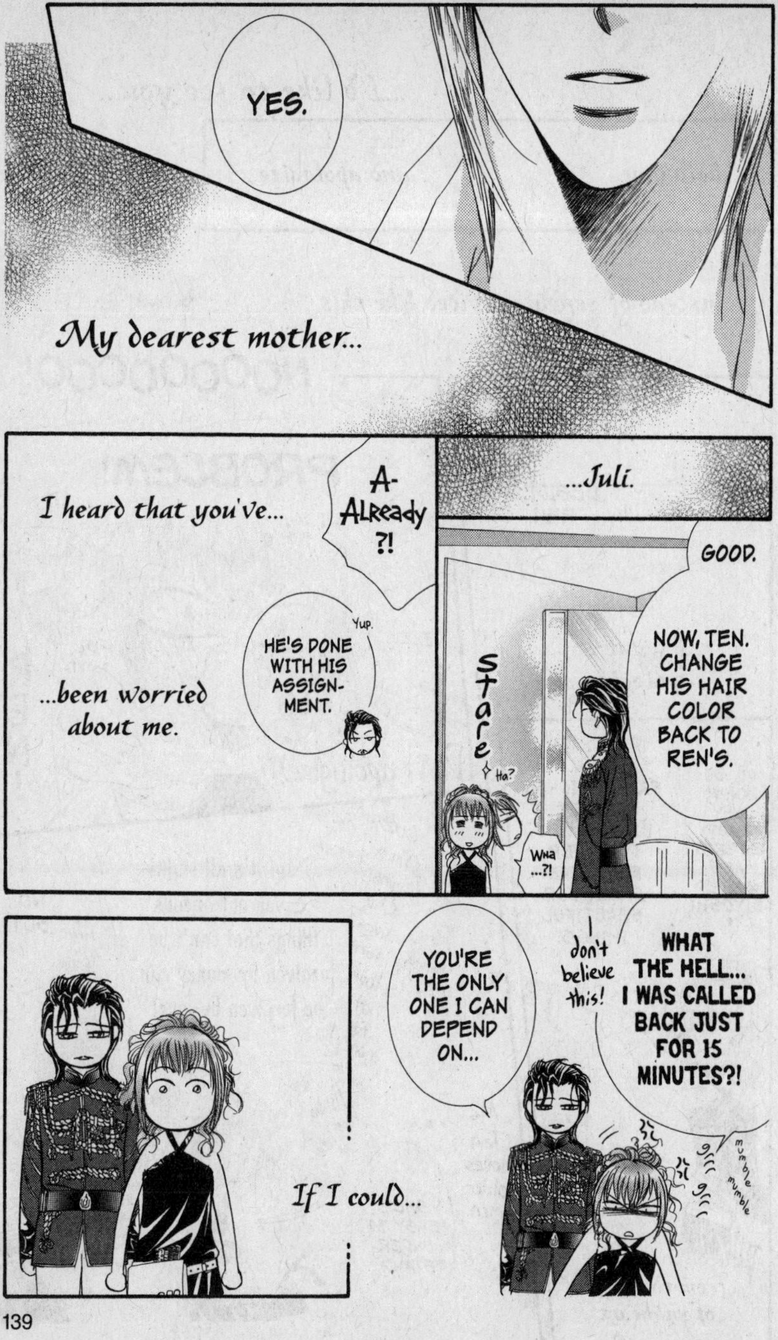
YES.
My dearest mother...
...Juli.
GOOD.
NOW, TEN. CHANGE HIS HAIR COLOR BACK TO REN'S.
Stare
Ha?
Wha ...?!
A- Already ?!
I heard that you've...
Yup.
HE'S DONE WITH HIS ASSIGNMENT.
...been worried about me.
WHAT THE HELL... I WAS CALLED BACK JUST FOR 15 MINUTES?!
I don't believe this!
YOU'RE THE ONLY ONE I CAN DEPEND ON...
grr grr grr
mumble mumble
If I could...

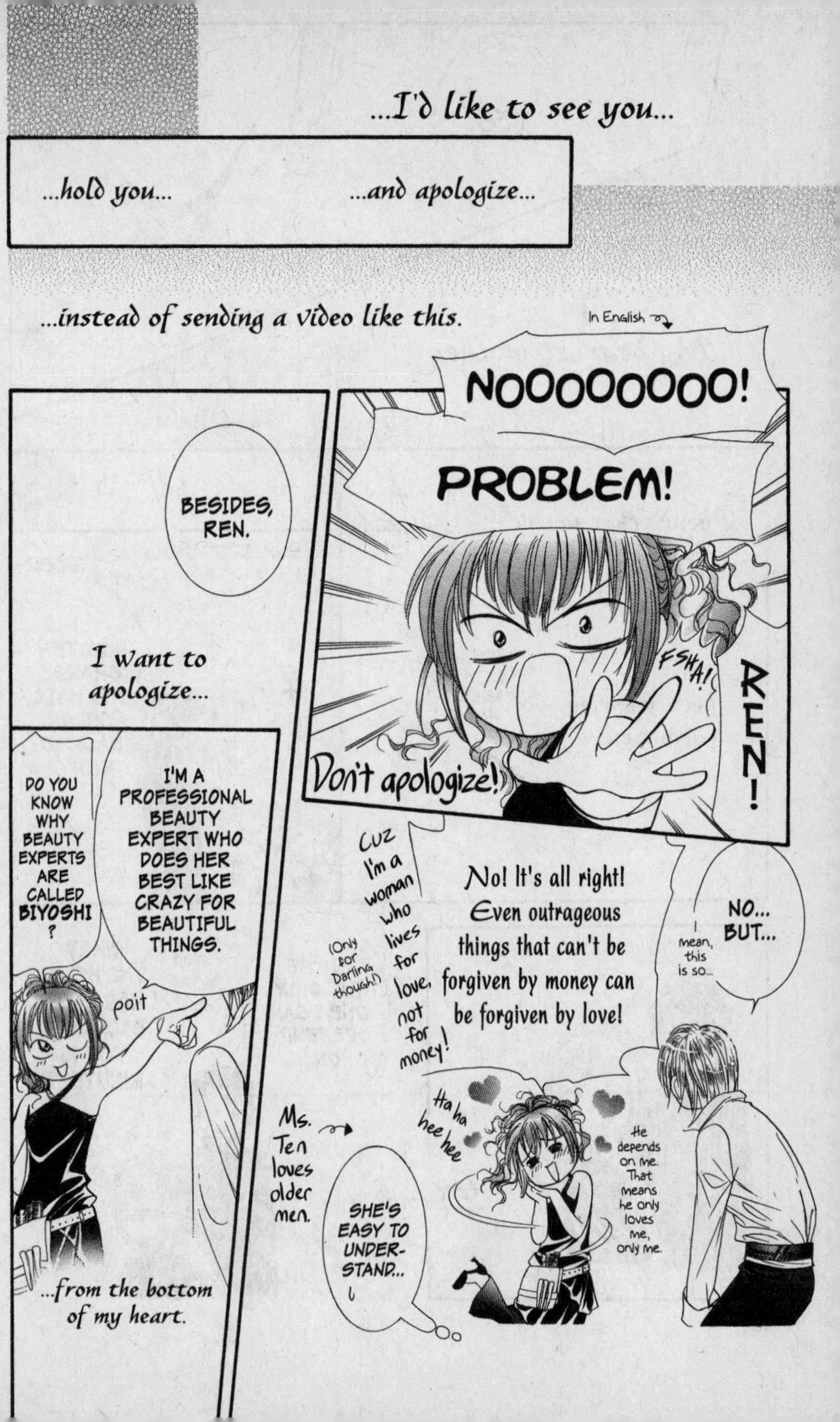
...I'd like to see you...
...hold you... ...and apologize...
...instead of sending a video like this.
In English
NOOOOOOOO!
PROBLEM!
REN!
FSHA!
Don't apologize!
BESIDES, REN.
I want to apologize...
NO... BUT...
I mean, this is so...
No! It's all right! Even outrageous things that can't be forgiven by money can be forgiven by love!
Cuz I'm a woman who lives for love, not for money!
(Only for Darling though!)
He depends on me. That means he only loves me, only me.
Ha ha hee hee
Ms. Ten loves older men.
SHE'S EASY TO UNDER-STAND...
I'M A PROFESSIONAL BEAUTY EXPERT WHO DOES HER BEST LIKE CRAZY FOR BEAUTIFUL THINGS.
DO YOU KNOW WHY BEAUTY EXPERTS ARE CALLED BIYOSHI?
poit
...from the bottom of my heart.

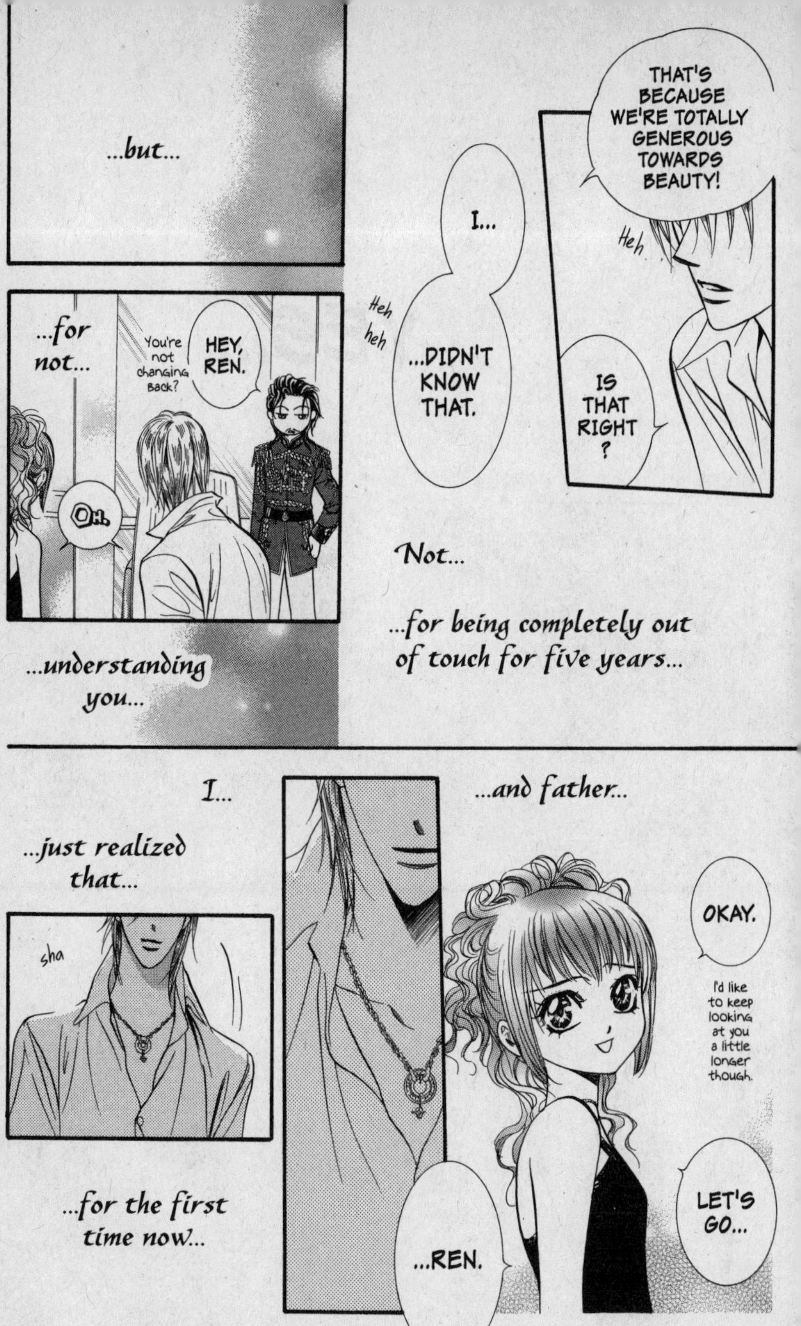
THAT'S BECAUSE WE'RE TOTALLY GENEROUS TOWARDS BEAUTY!
Heh
IS THAT RIGHT?
I...
...DIDN'T KNOW THAT.
Heh heh
Not...
...for being completely out of touch for five years...
...but...
...for not...
HEY, REN.
You're not changing back?
OH.
...understanding you...
OKAY.
I'd like to keep looking at you a little longer though.
LET'S GO...
...REN.
...and father...
I...
...just realized that...
sha
...for the first time now...

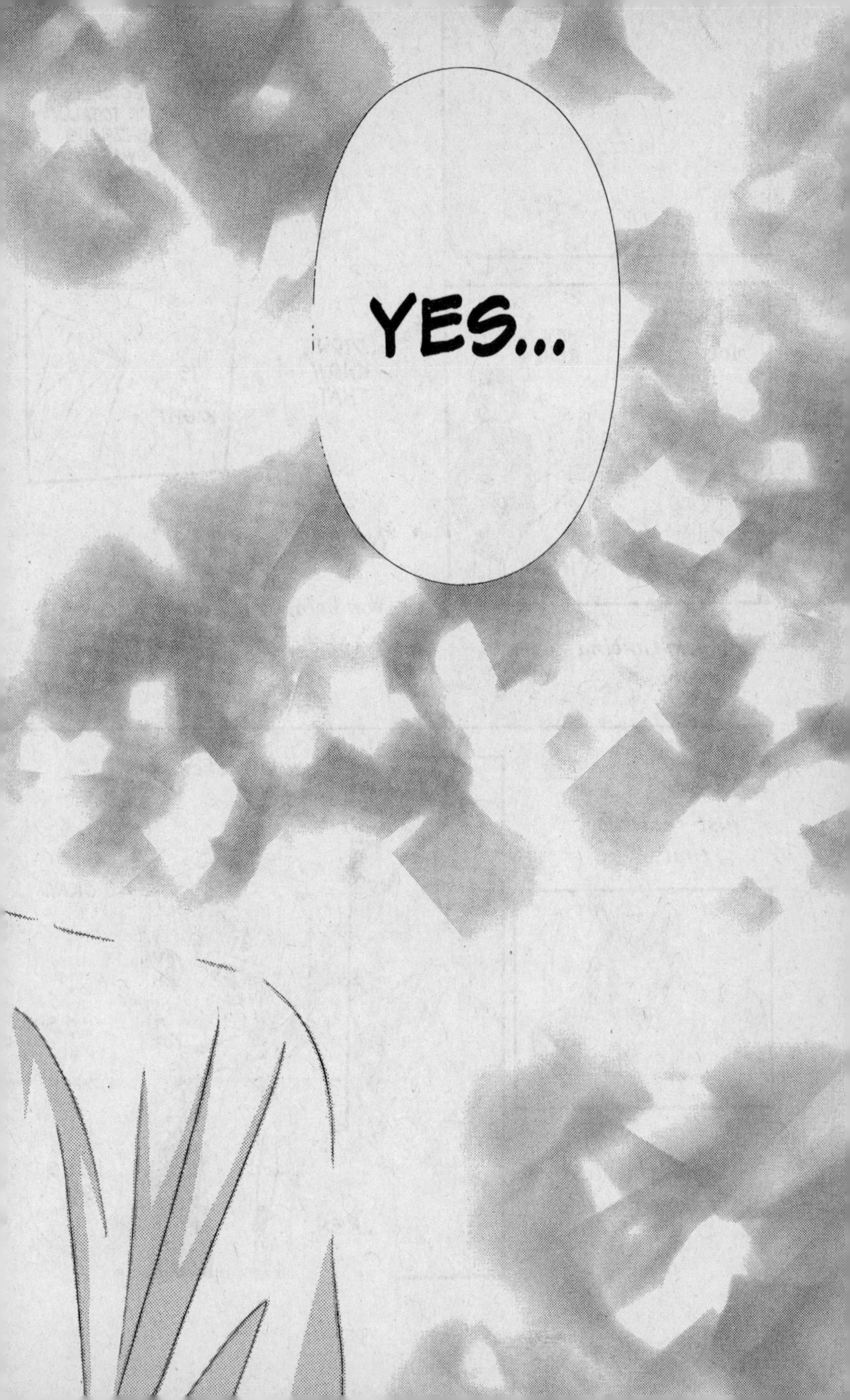
YES...

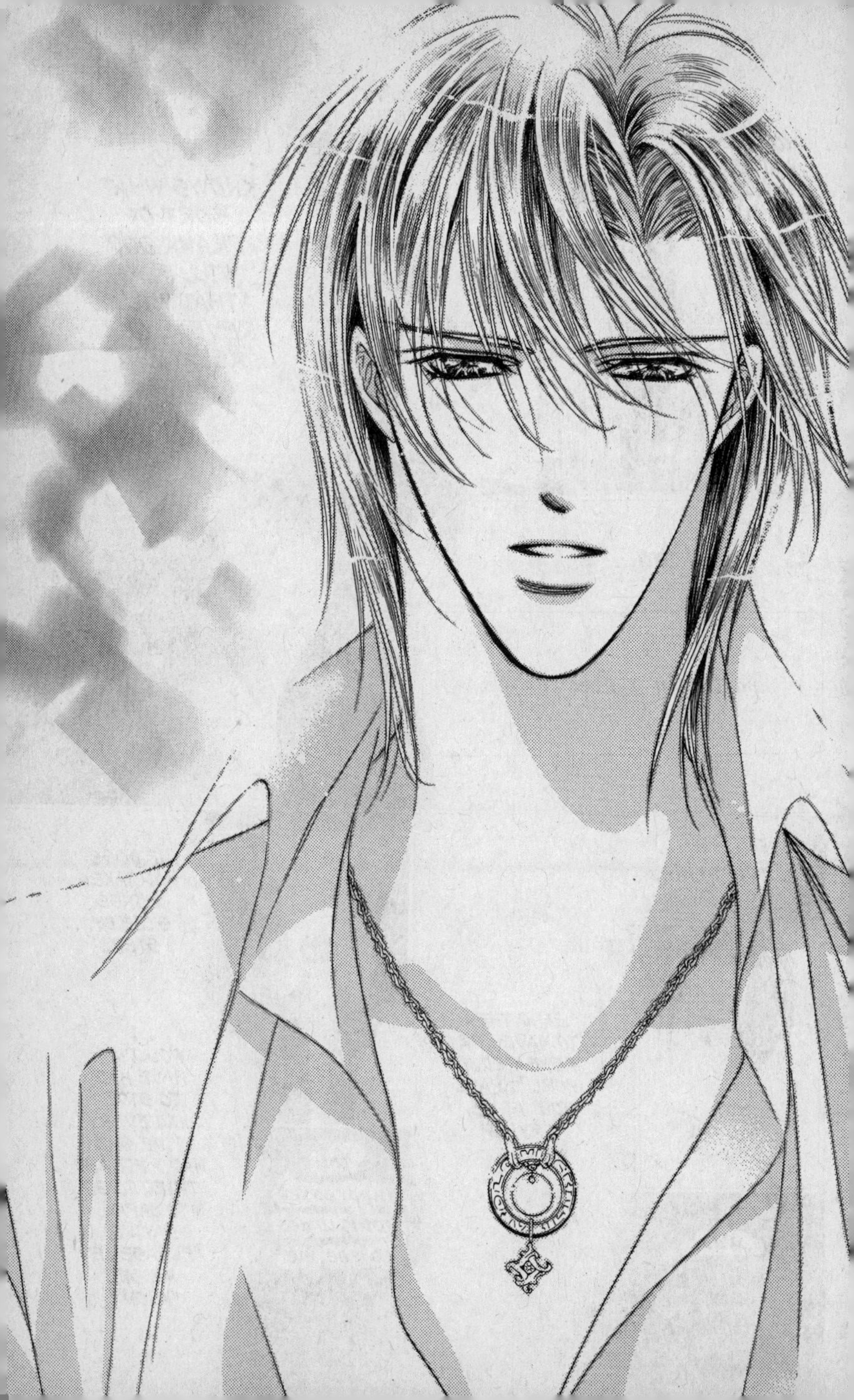

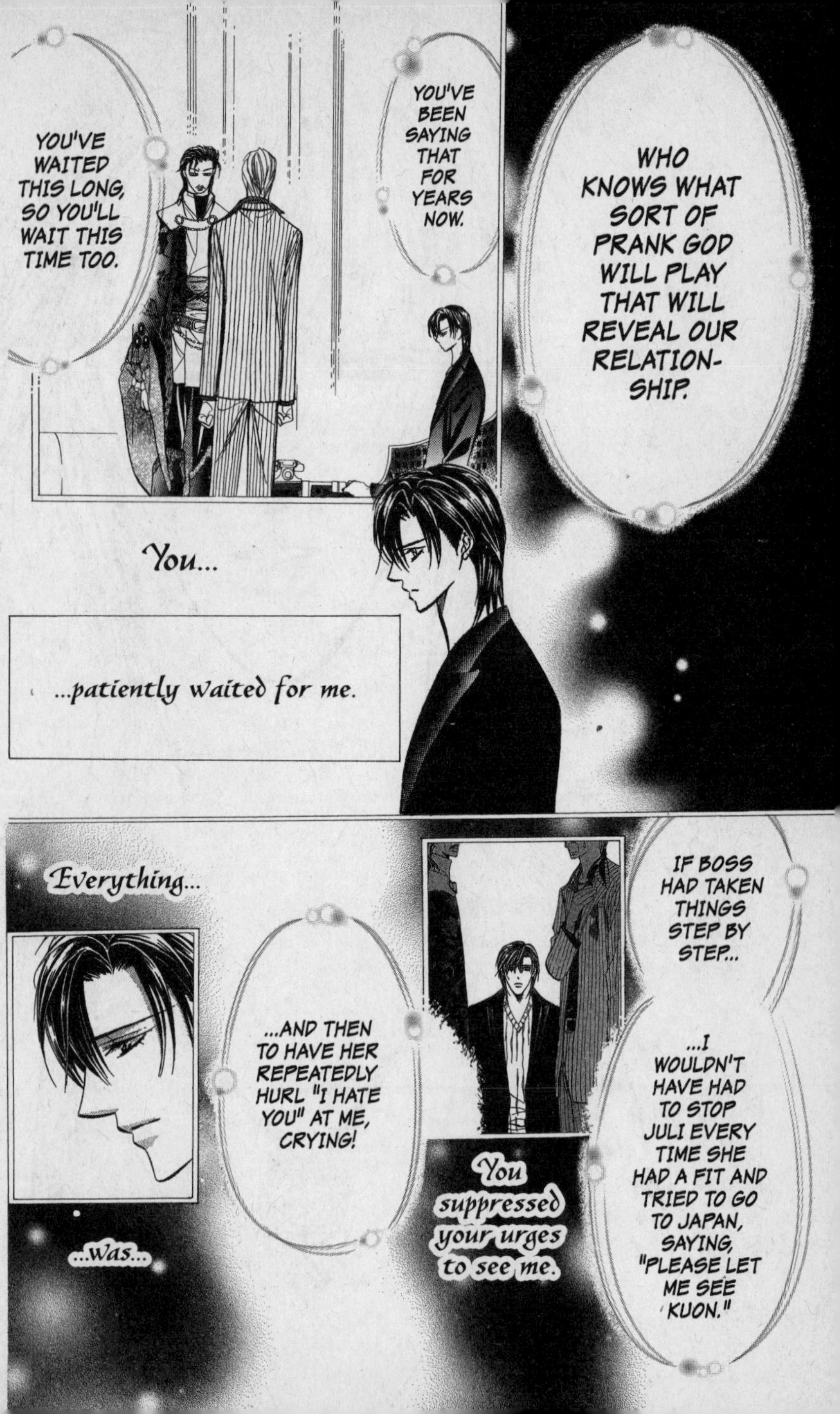
WHO KNOWS WHAT SORT OF PRANK GOD WILL PLAY THAT WILL REVEAL OUR RELATION-SHIP.
YOU'VE BEEN SAYING THAT FOR YEARS NOW.
YOU'VE WAITED THIS LONG, SO YOU'LL WAIT THIS TIME TOO.
You...
...patiently waited for me.
IF BOSS HAD TAKEN THINGS STEP BY STEP...
...I WOULDN'T HAVE HAD TO STOP JULI EVERY TIME SHE HAD A FIT AND TRIED TO GO TO JAPAN, SAYING, "PLEASE LET ME SEE KUON."
You suppressed your urges to see me.
...AND THEN TO HAVE HER REPEATEDLY HURL "I HATE YOU" AT ME, CRYING!
Everything...
...was...

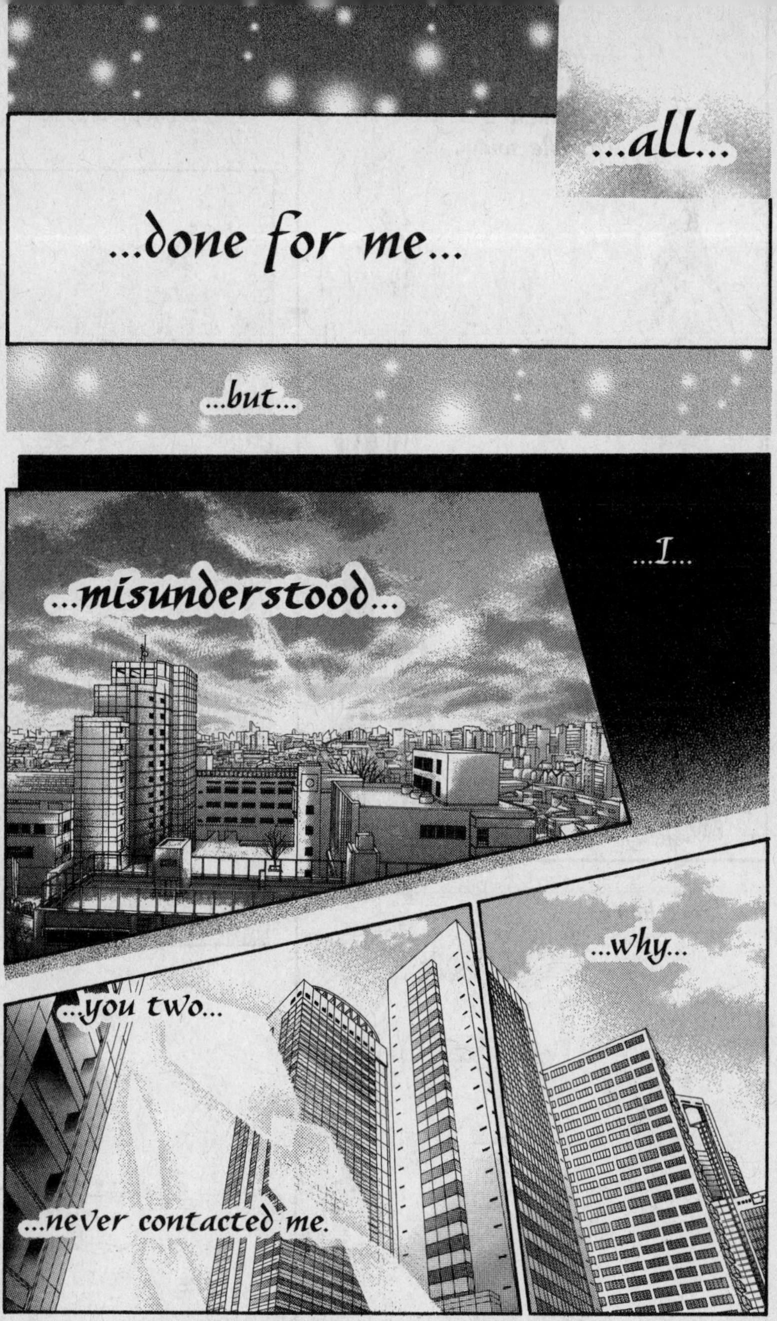
...all...
...done for me...
...but...
...I...
...misunderstood...
...why...
...you two...
...never contacted me.

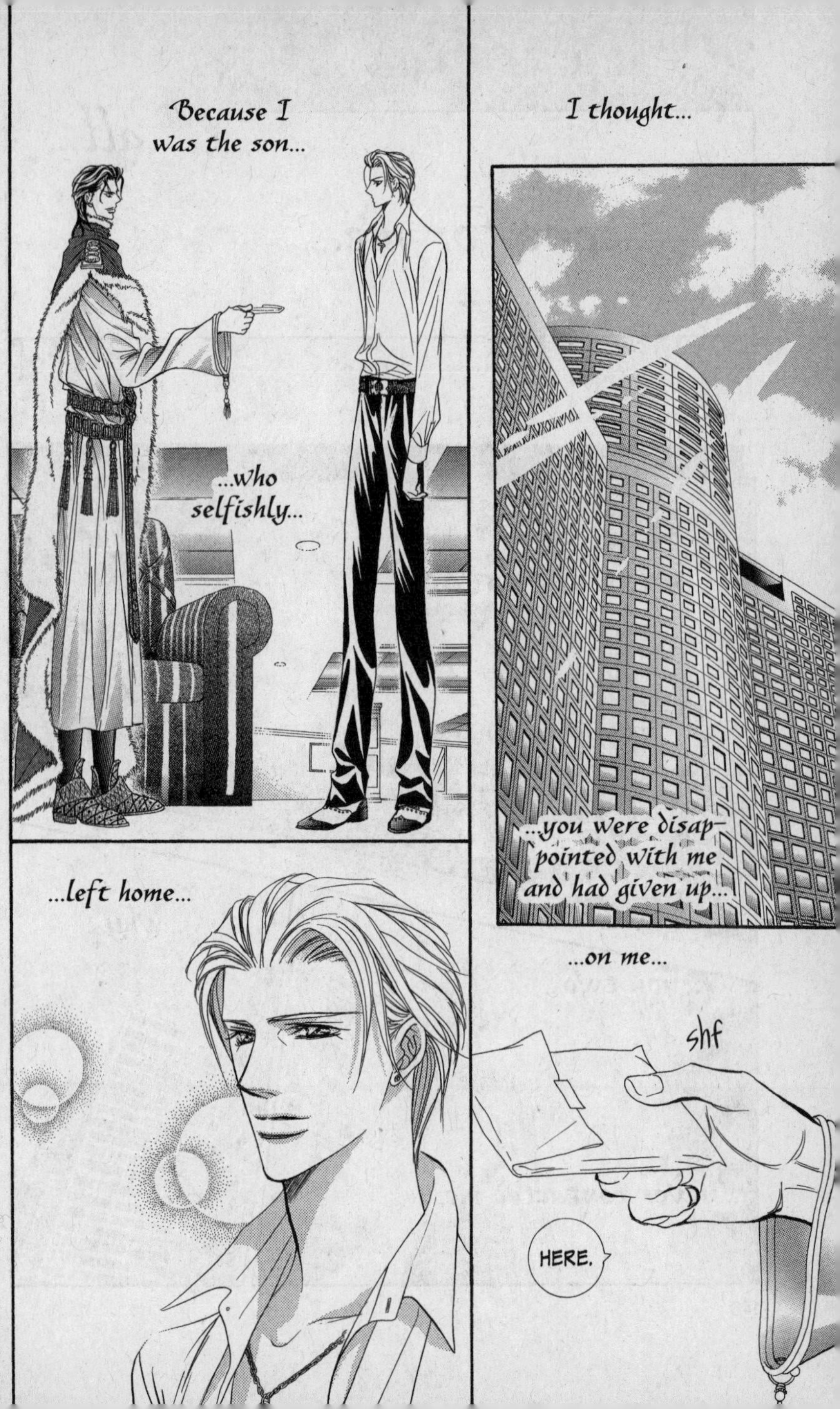
Because I was the son...
...who selfishly...
...left home...
I thought...
...you were disap-pointed with me and had given up...
...on me...
shf
HERE.

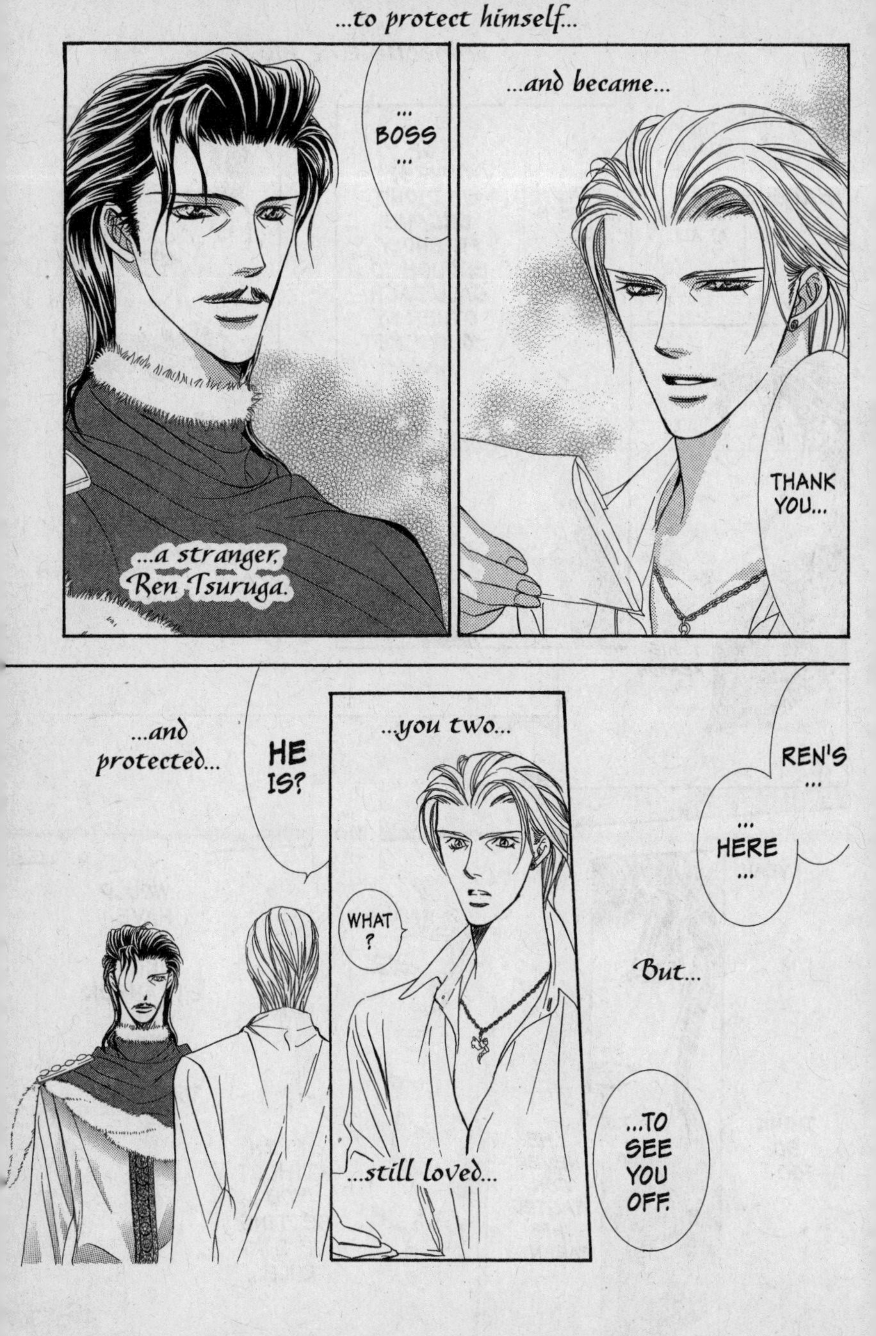
...to protect himself...
...and became...
THANK YOU...
... BOSS ...
...a stranger, Ren Tsuruga.
REN'S ...
... HERE ...
But...
...TO SEE YOU OFF.
...you two...
WHAT ?
...still loved...
...and protected...
HE IS?

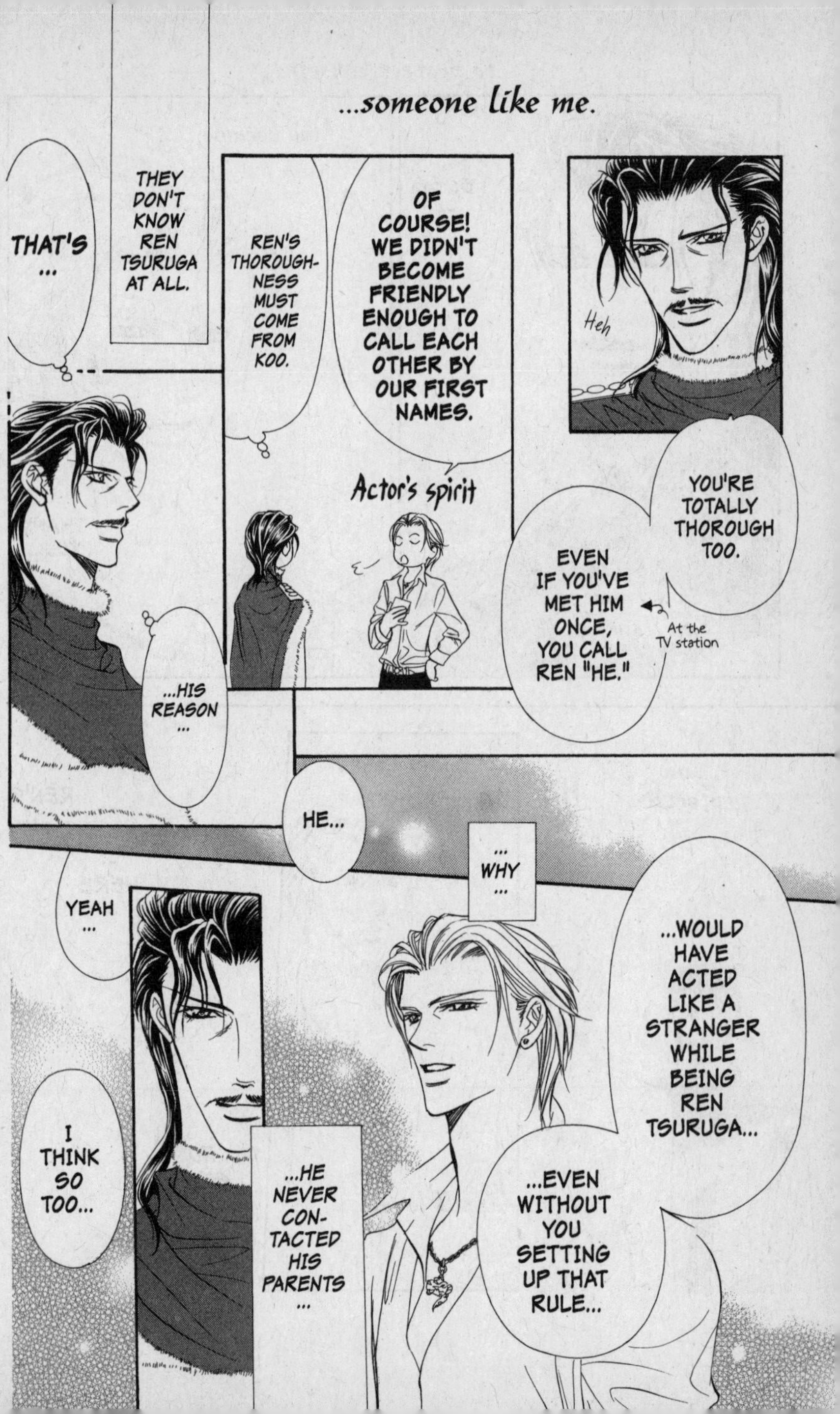
...someone like me.
Heh
OF COURSE! WE DIDN'T BECOME FRIENDLY ENOUGH TO CALL EACH OTHER BY OUR FIRST NAMES.
REN'S THOROUGHNESS MUST COME FROM KOO.
Actor's spirit
YOU'RE TOTALLY THOROUGH TOO.
EVEN IF YOU'VE MET HIM ONCE, YOU CALL REN "HE."
At the TV station
THEY DON'T KNOW REN TSURUGA AT ALL.
THAT'S...
...HIS REASON...
HE...
...WHY...
...WOULD HAVE ACTED LIKE A STRANGER WHILE BEING REN TSURUGA...
...EVEN WITHOUT YOU SETTING UP THAT RULE...
...HE NEVER CONTACTED HIS PARENTS...
YEAH...
I THINK SO TOO...

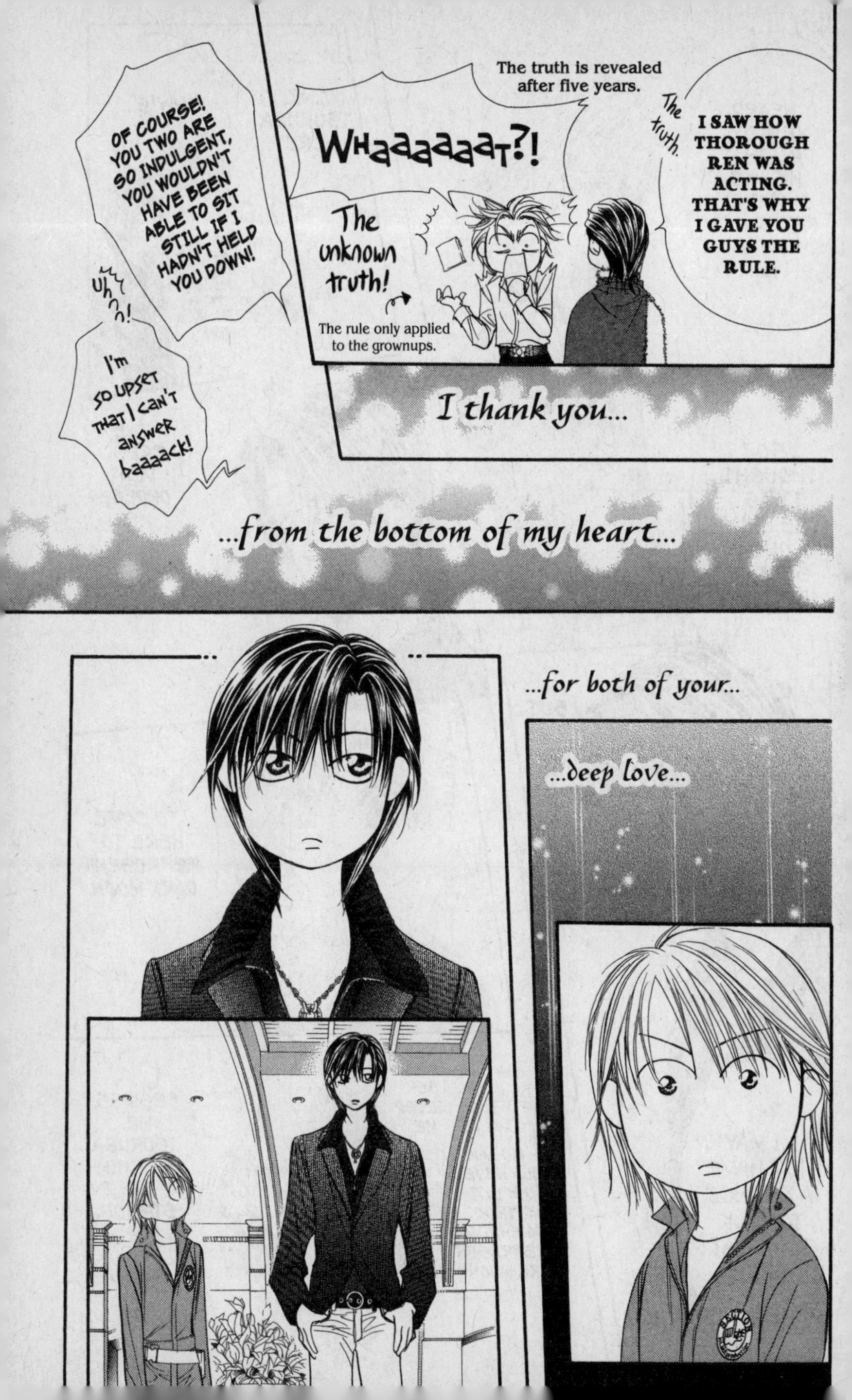
The truth.
I SAW HOW THOROUGH REN WAS ACTING. THAT'S WHY I GAVE YOU GUYS THE RULE.
The truth is revealed after five years.
Whaaaaaaat?!
The unknown truth!
The rule only applied to the grownups.
OF COURSE! YOU TWO ARE SO INDULGENT, YOU WOULDN'T HAVE BEEN ABLE TO SIT STILL IF I HADN'T HELD YOU DOWN!
Uh?!
I'm so upset that I can't answer baaaack!
I thank you...
...from the bottom of my heart...
...for both of your...
...deep love...

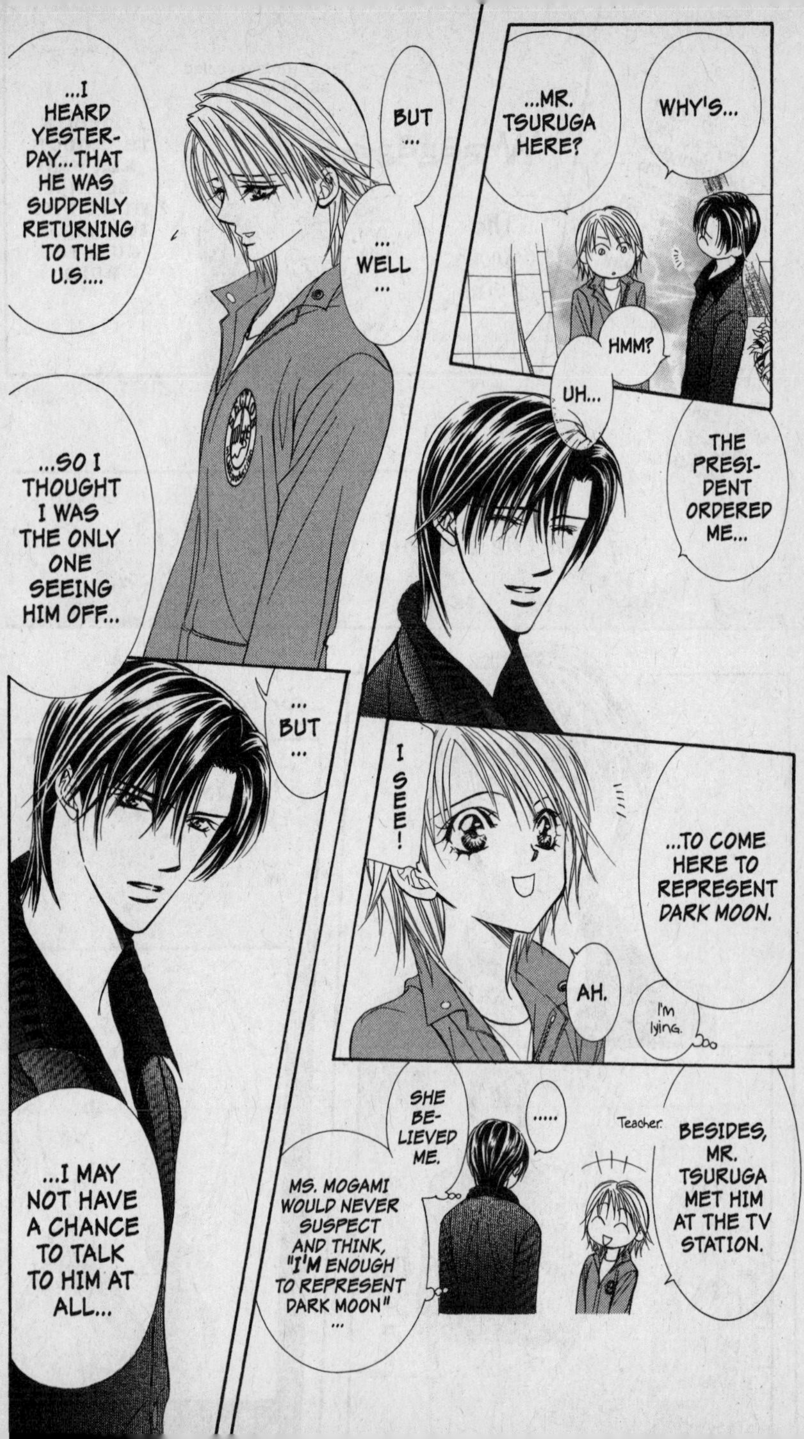
WHY'S...
...MR. TSURUGA HERE?
HMM?
UH...
THE PRESIDENT ORDERED ME...
...TO COME HERE TO REPRESENT DARK MOON.
I SEE!
AH.
I'm lying.
BESIDES, MR. TSURUGA MET HIM AT THE TV STATION.
Teacher.
.....
SHE BELIEVED ME.
MS. MOGAMI WOULD NEVER SUSPECT AND THINK, "I'M ENOUGH TO REPRESENT DARK MOON"...
BUT...
...WELL...
...I HEARD YESTERDAY...THAT HE WAS SUDDENLY RETURNING TO THE U.S....
...SO I THOUGHT I WAS THE ONLY ONE SEEING HIM OFF...
...BUT...
...I MAY NOT HAVE A CHANCE TO TALK TO HIM AT ALL...

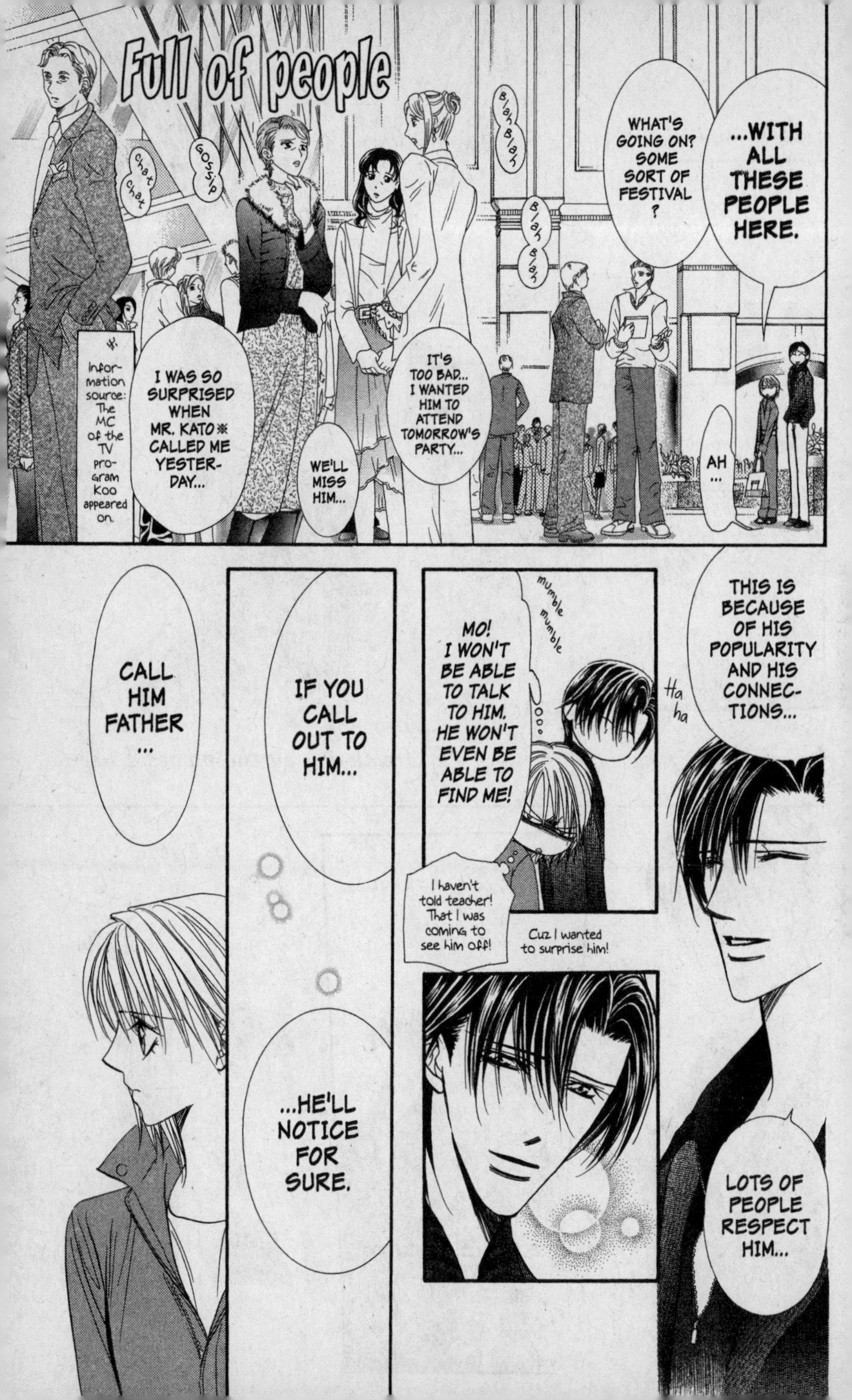
...WITH ALL THESE PEOPLE HERE.
WHAT'S GOING ON? SOME SORT OF FESTIVAL?
Blah Blah
Blah Blah
Full of people
GOSSIP
Chat Chat
AH...
IT'S TOO BAD... I WANTED HIM TO ATTEND TOMORROW'S PARTY...
WE'LL MISS HIM...
I WAS SO SURPRISED WHEN MR. KATO※ CALLED ME YESTERDAY...
※ Information source: The MC of the TV program Koo appeared on.
THIS IS BECAUSE OF HIS POPULARITY AND HIS CONNECTIONS...
LOTS OF PEOPLE RESPECT HIM...
Ha ha
mumble mumble
MO! I WON'T BE ABLE TO TALK TO HIM. HE WON'T EVEN BE ABLE TO FIND ME!
I haven't told teacher! That I was coming to see him off!
Cuz I wanted to surprise him!
IF YOU CALL OUT TO HIM...
...HE'LL NOTICE FOR SURE.
CALL HIM FATHER...

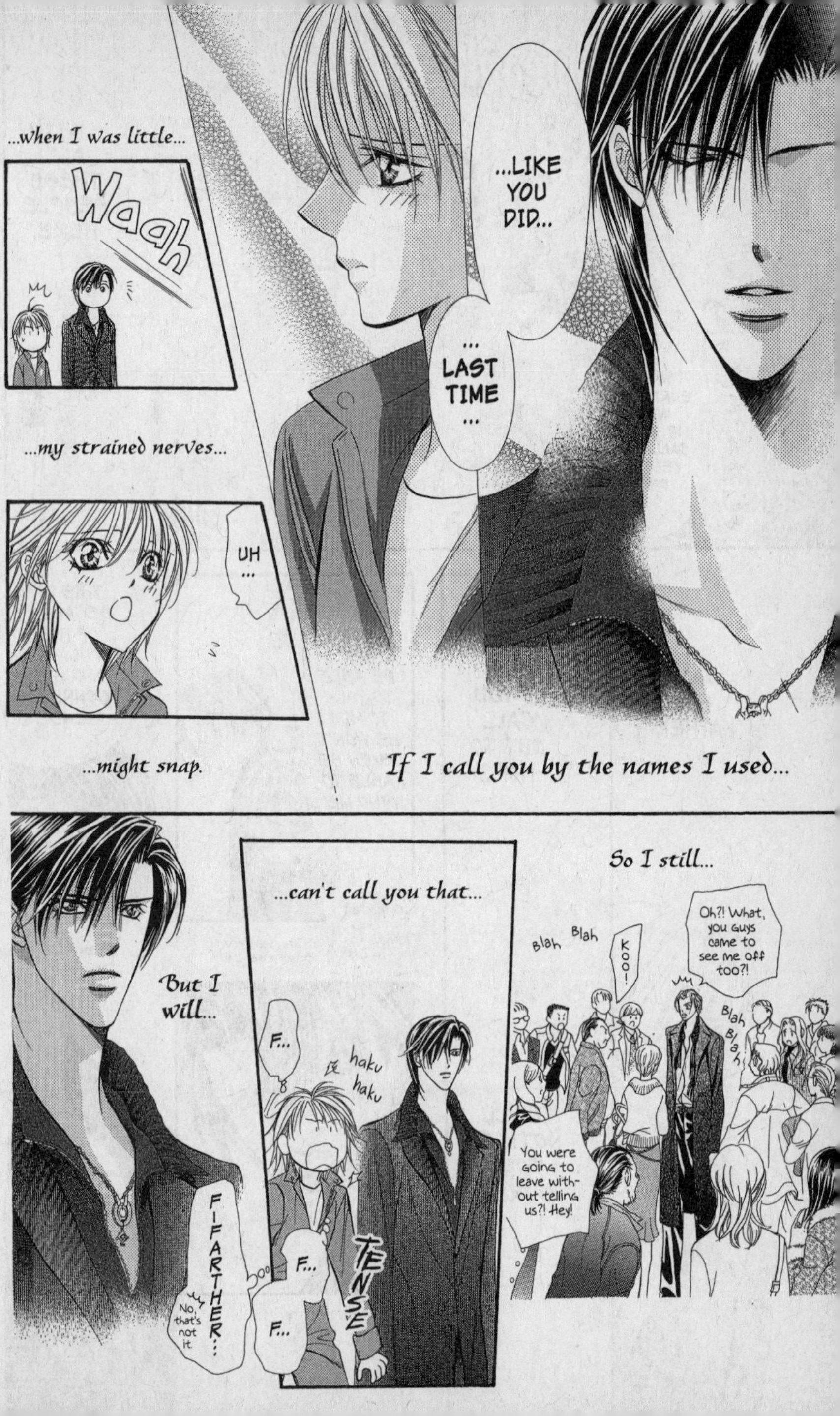

...LIKE YOU DID...
... LAST TIME ...
If I call you by the names I used...
...when I was little...
Waah
...my strained nerves...
UH ...
...might snap.
So I still...
Oh?! What, you guys came to see me off too?!
KOO!
Blah Blah
Blah Blah
You were going to leave with-out telling us?! Hey!
...can't call you that...
F...
haku haku
F...
F...
TENSE
But I will...
FIFARTHER...
No, that's not it.

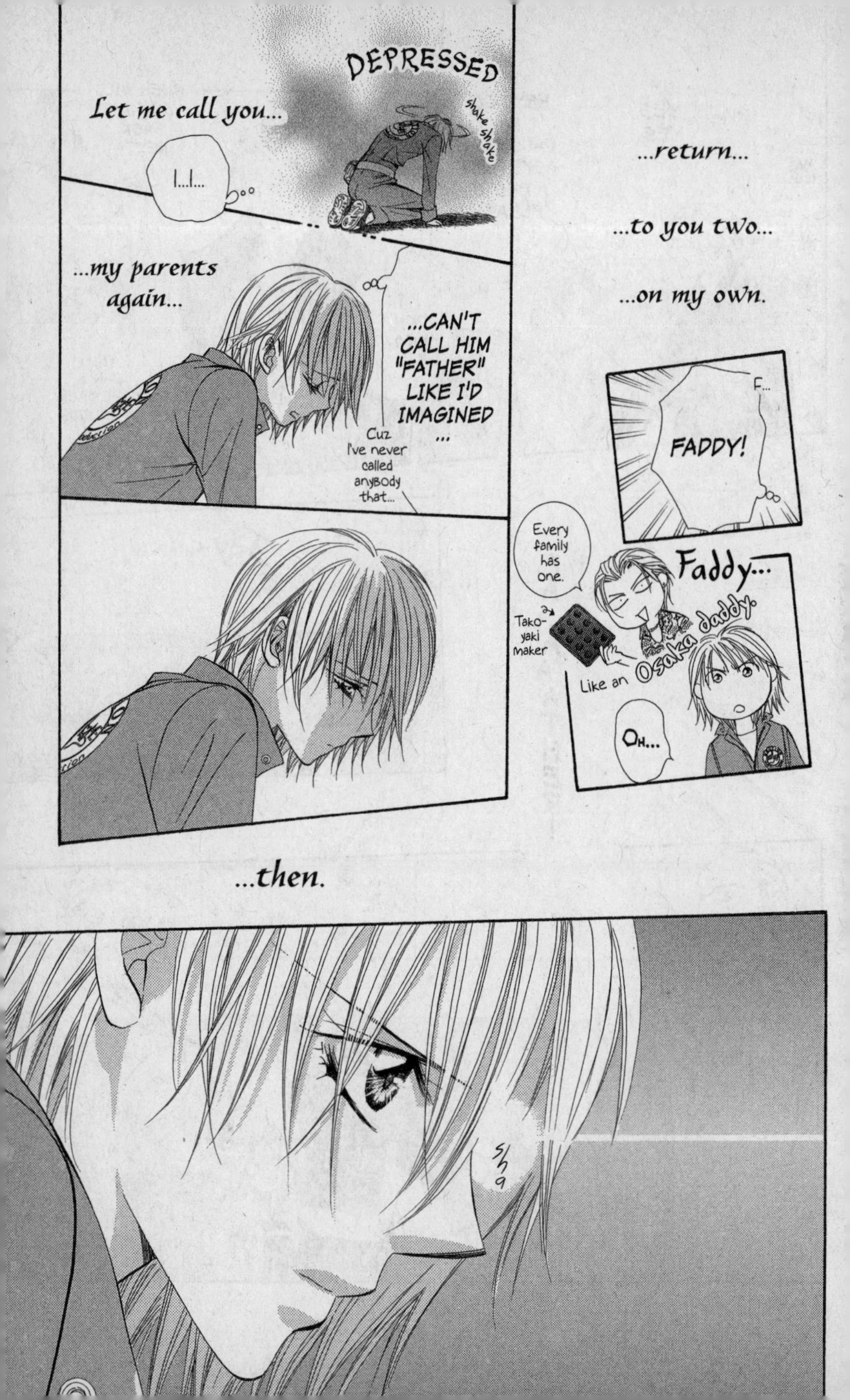
...return...
...to you two...
...on my own.
F...
FADDY!
Every family has one.
Faddy...
Like an Osaka daddy.
Tako-yaki maker
Oh...
Let me call you...
DEPRESSED
shake shake
I...I...
...my parents again...
...CAN'T CALL HIM "FATHER" LIKE I'D IMAGINED...
Cuz I've never called anybody that...
...then.

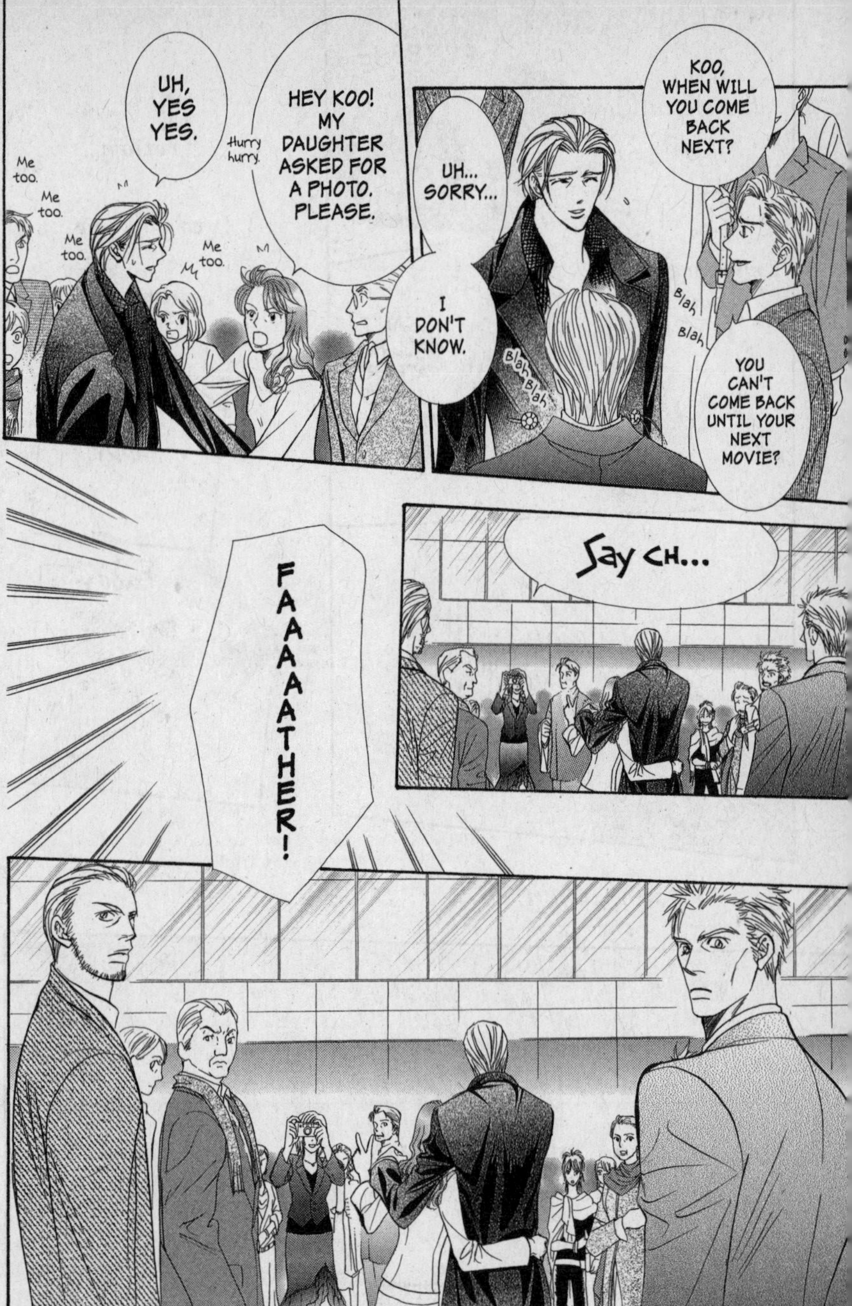
KOO, WHEN WILL YOU COME BACK NEXT?
UH... SORRY...
Blah Blah
YOU CAN'T COME BACK UNTIL YOUR NEXT MOVIE?
I DON'T KNOW.
Blah Blah
HEY KOO! MY DAUGHTER ASKED FOR A PHOTO. PLEASE.
Hurry hurry.
UH, YES YES.
Me too.
Me too.
Me too.
Me too.
Say CH...
FAAAAATHER!

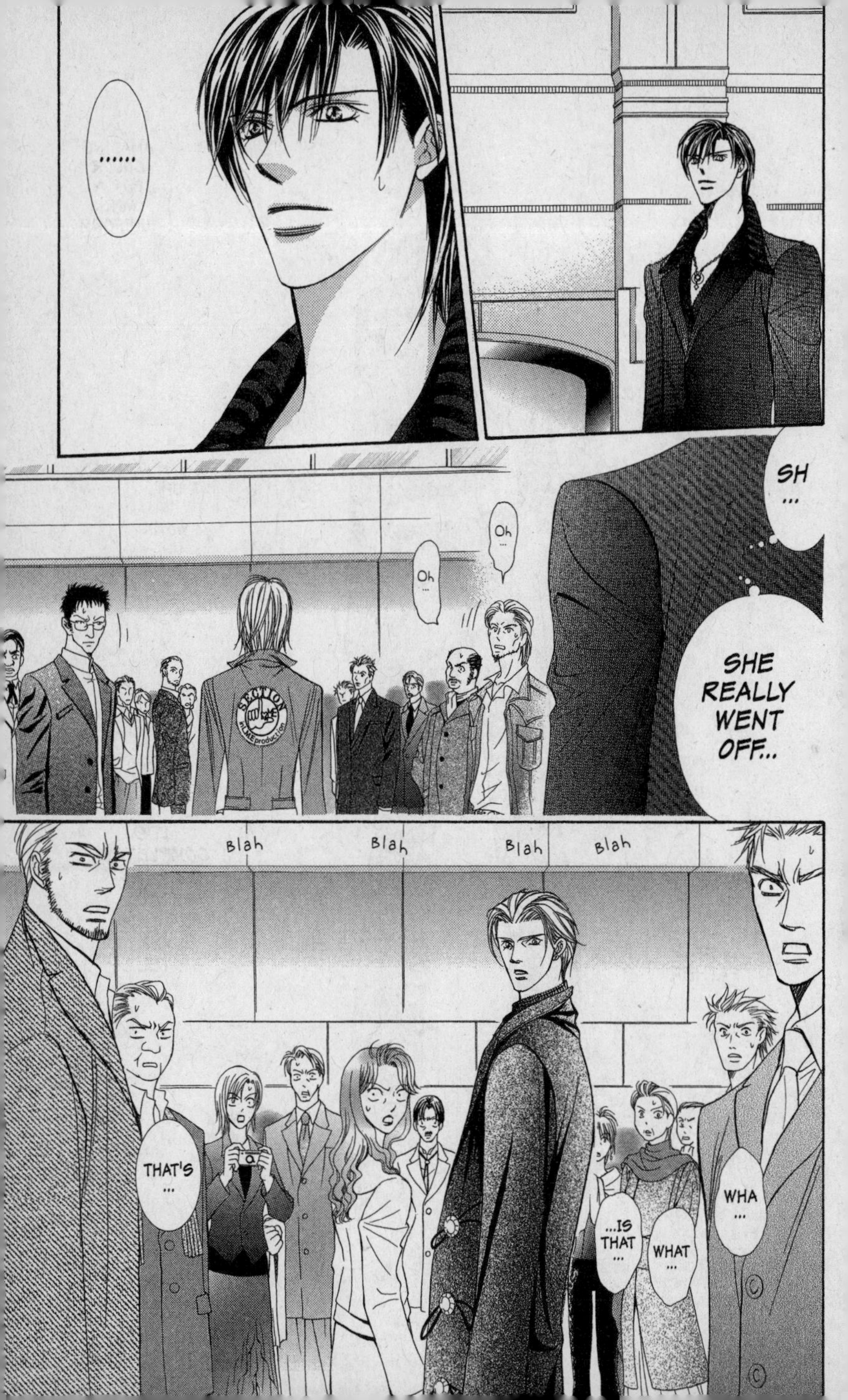
......
SH...
SHE REALLY WENT OFF...
Oh...
Oh...
Blah
Blah
Blah
Blah
WHA...
WHAT...
...IS THAT...
THAT'S...

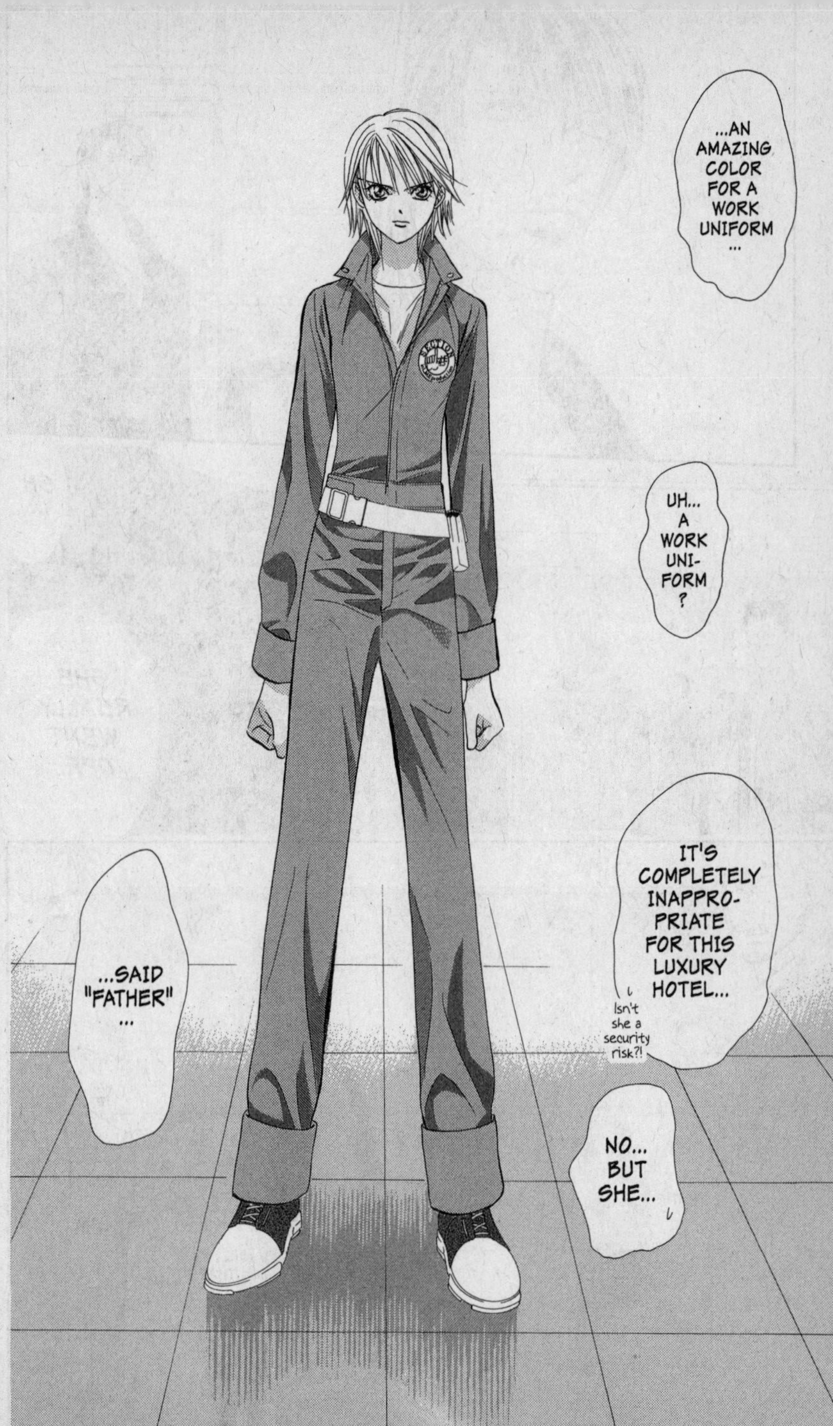
...AN AMAZING COLOR FOR A WORK UNIFORM ...
UH... A WORK UNI-FORM ?
IT'S COMPLETELY INAPPRO-PRIATE FOR THIS LUXURY HOTEL...
Isn't she a security risk?!
NO... BUT SHE...
...SAID "FATHER" ...

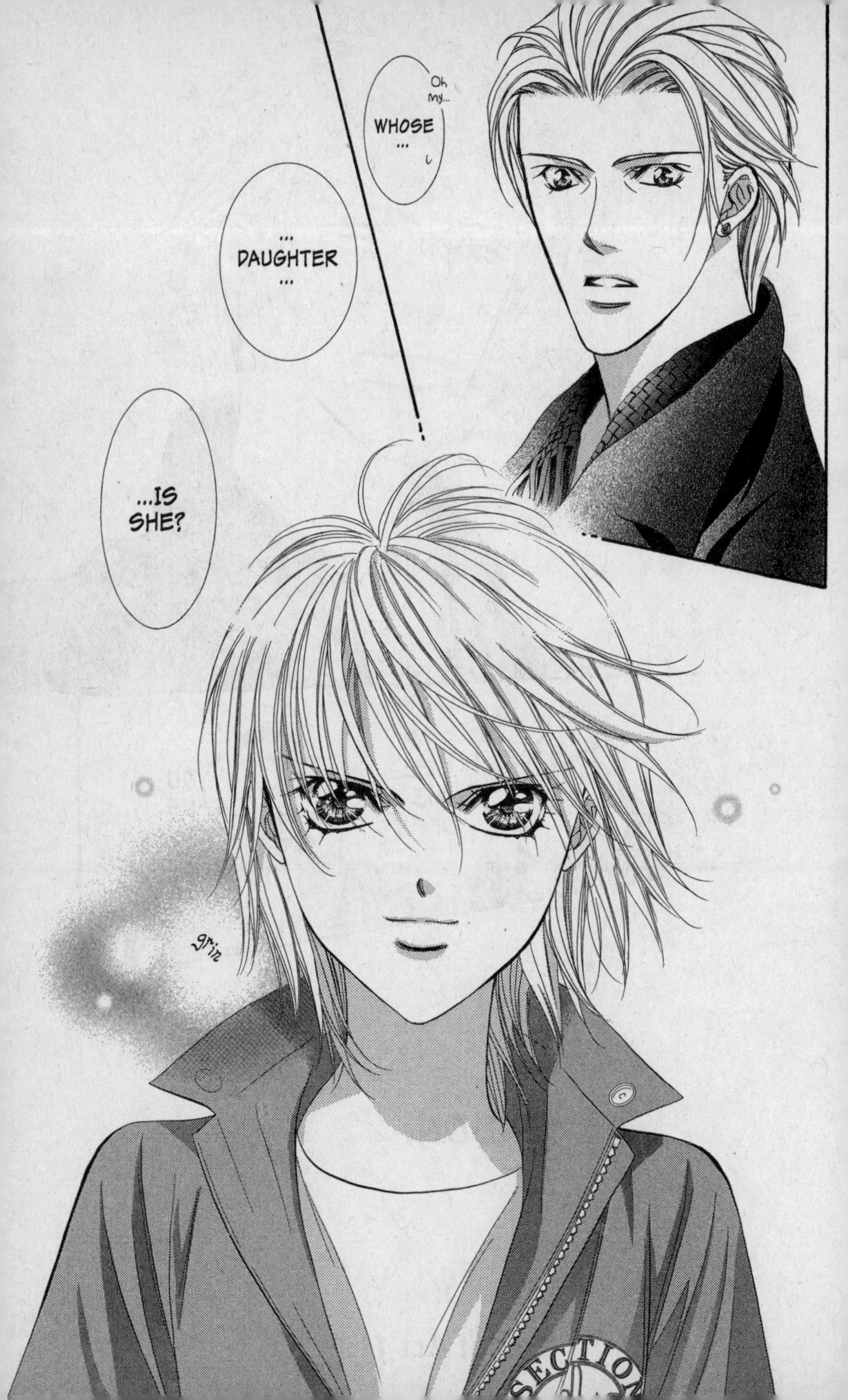
Oh my...
WHOSE ...
... DAUGHTER ...
...IS SHE?
grin

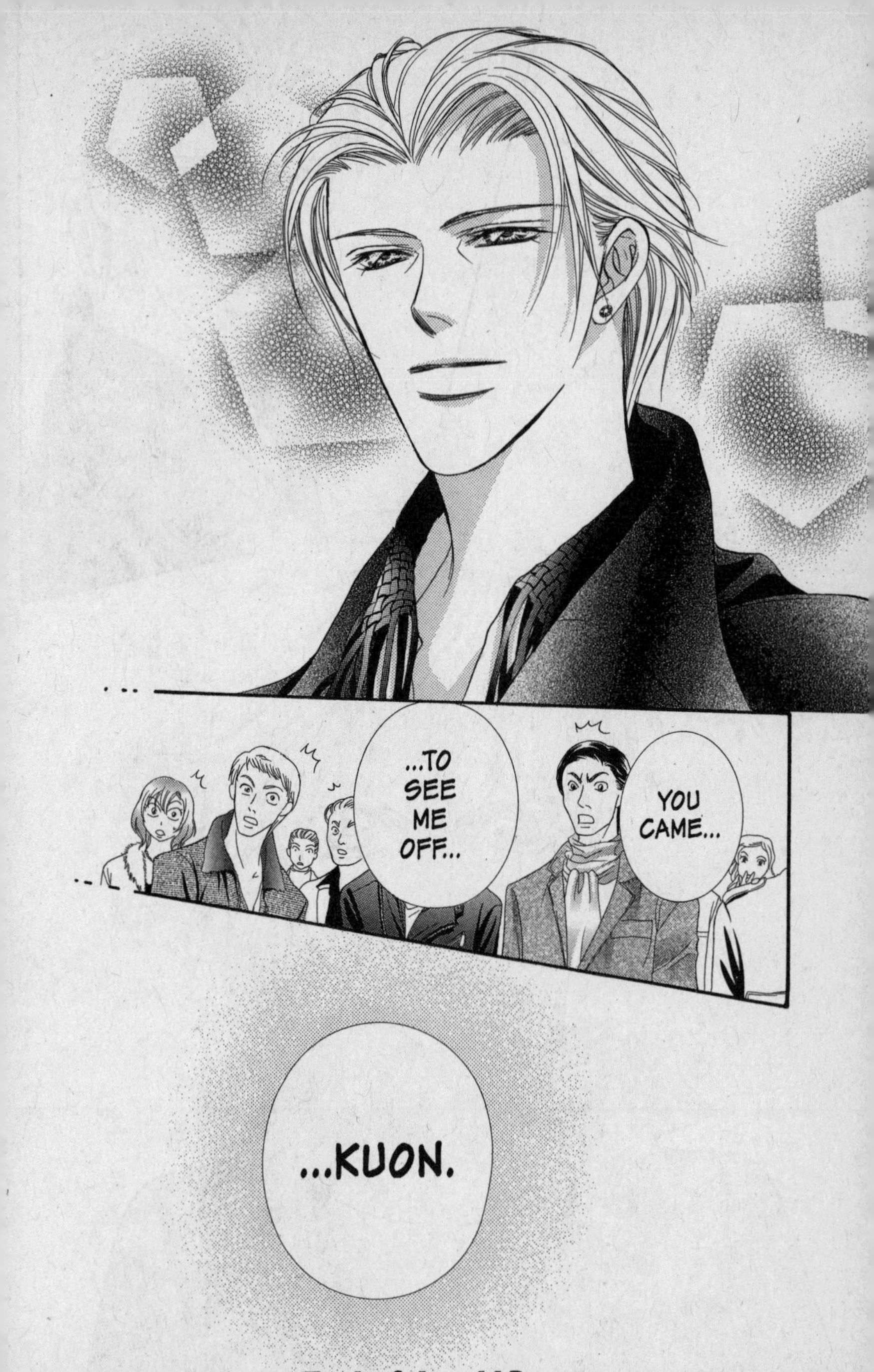
YOU CAME...
...TO SEE ME OFF...
...KUON.

End of Act 113

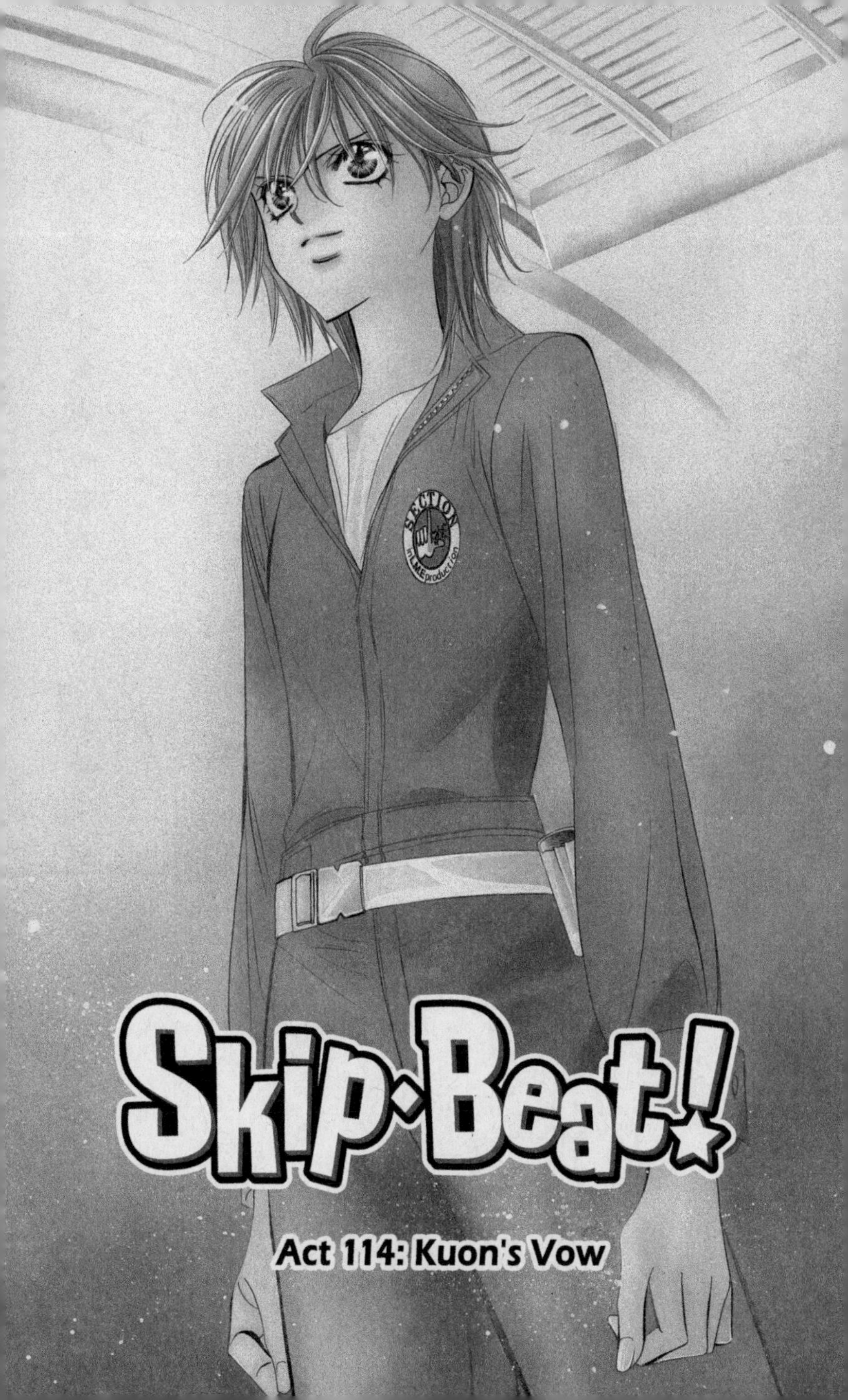
SECTION
Skip·Beat!
Act 114: Kuon's Vow

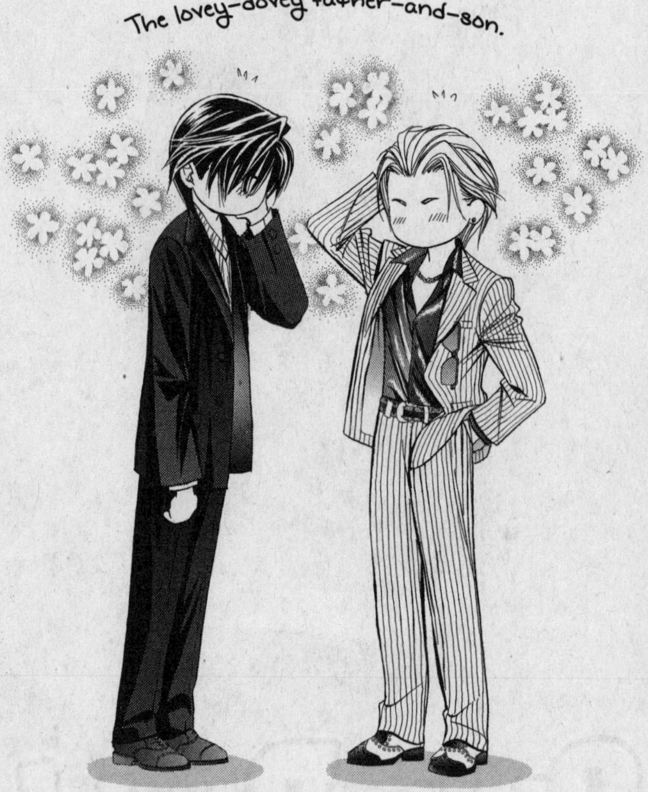

The lovey-dovey father-and-son.

SKIP・BEAT! 19

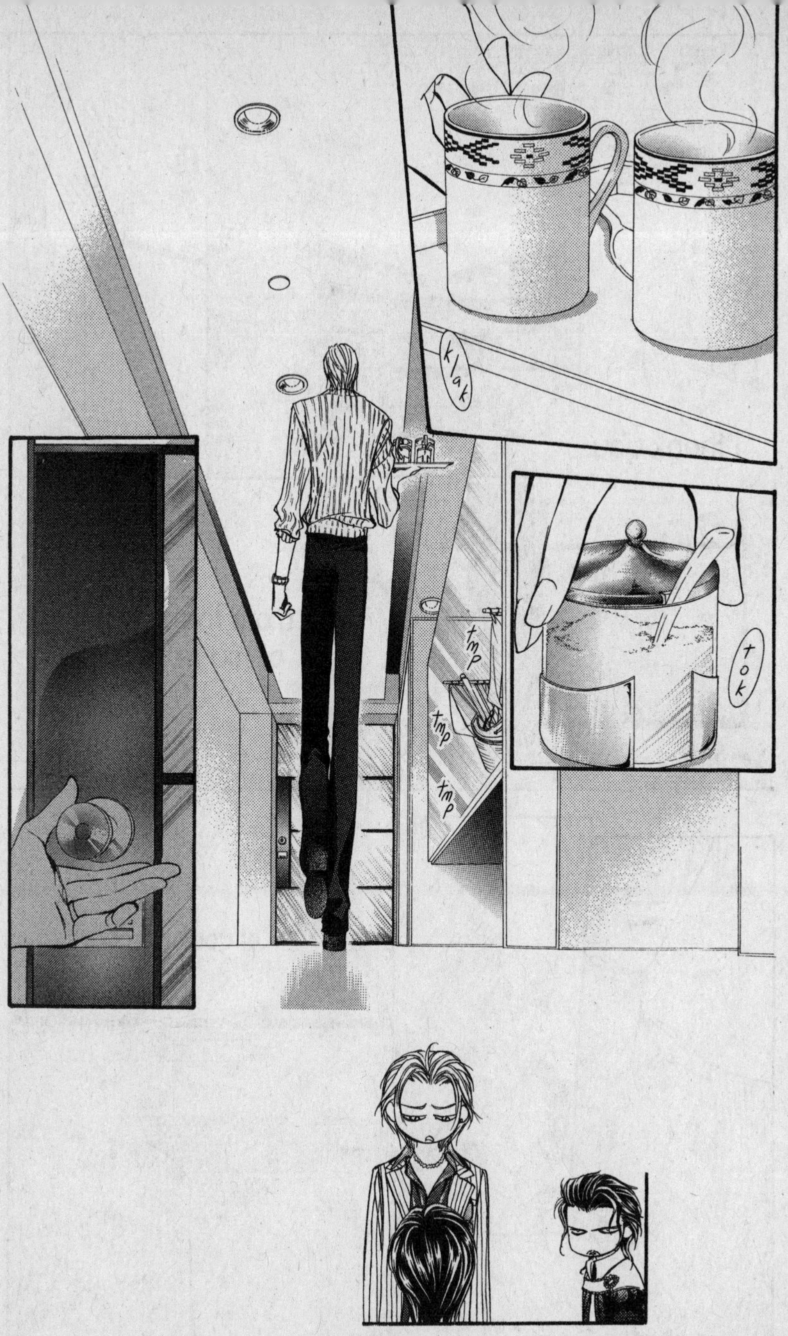
klak
tok
xmp
xmp
xmp

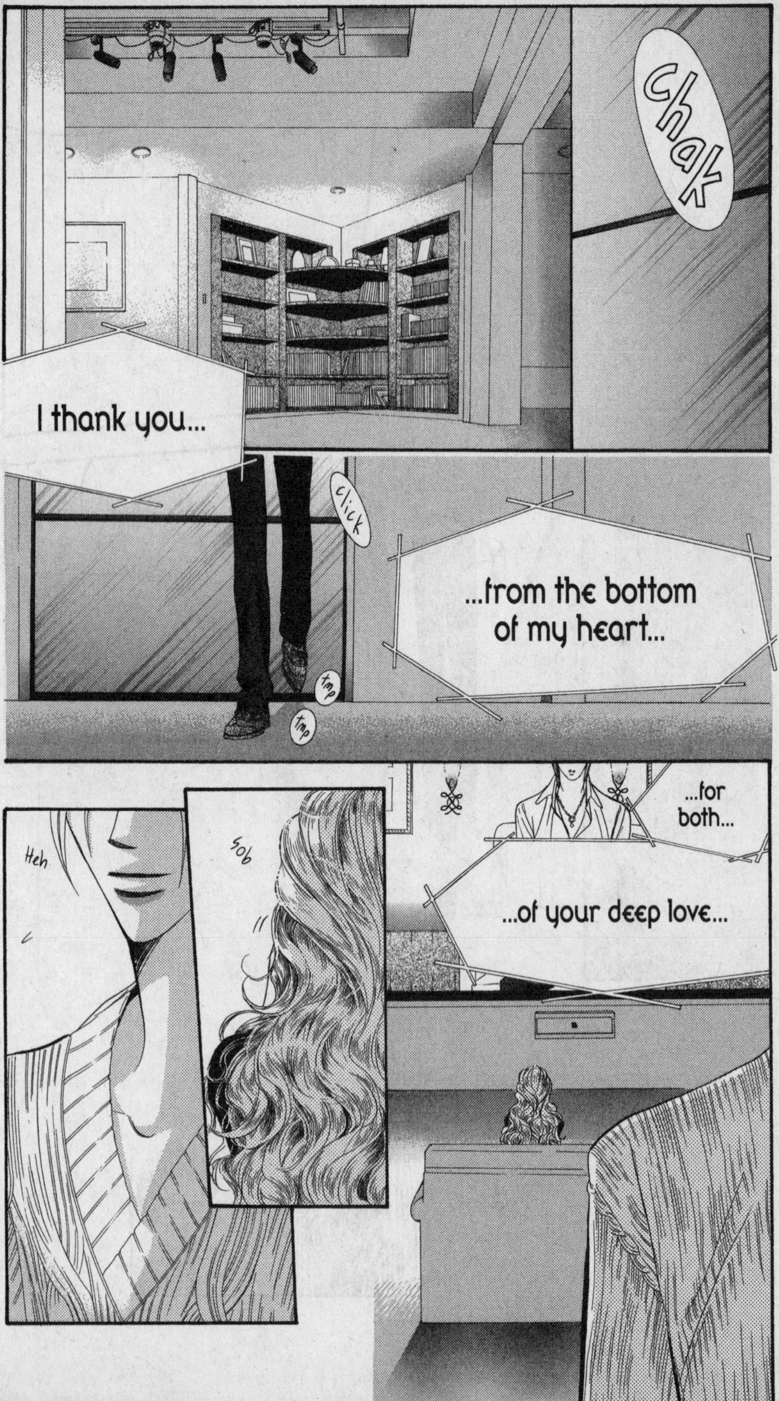
Chak
I thank you...
...from the bottom of my heart...
click
tmp
tmp
...for both...
...of your deep love...
sob
Heh

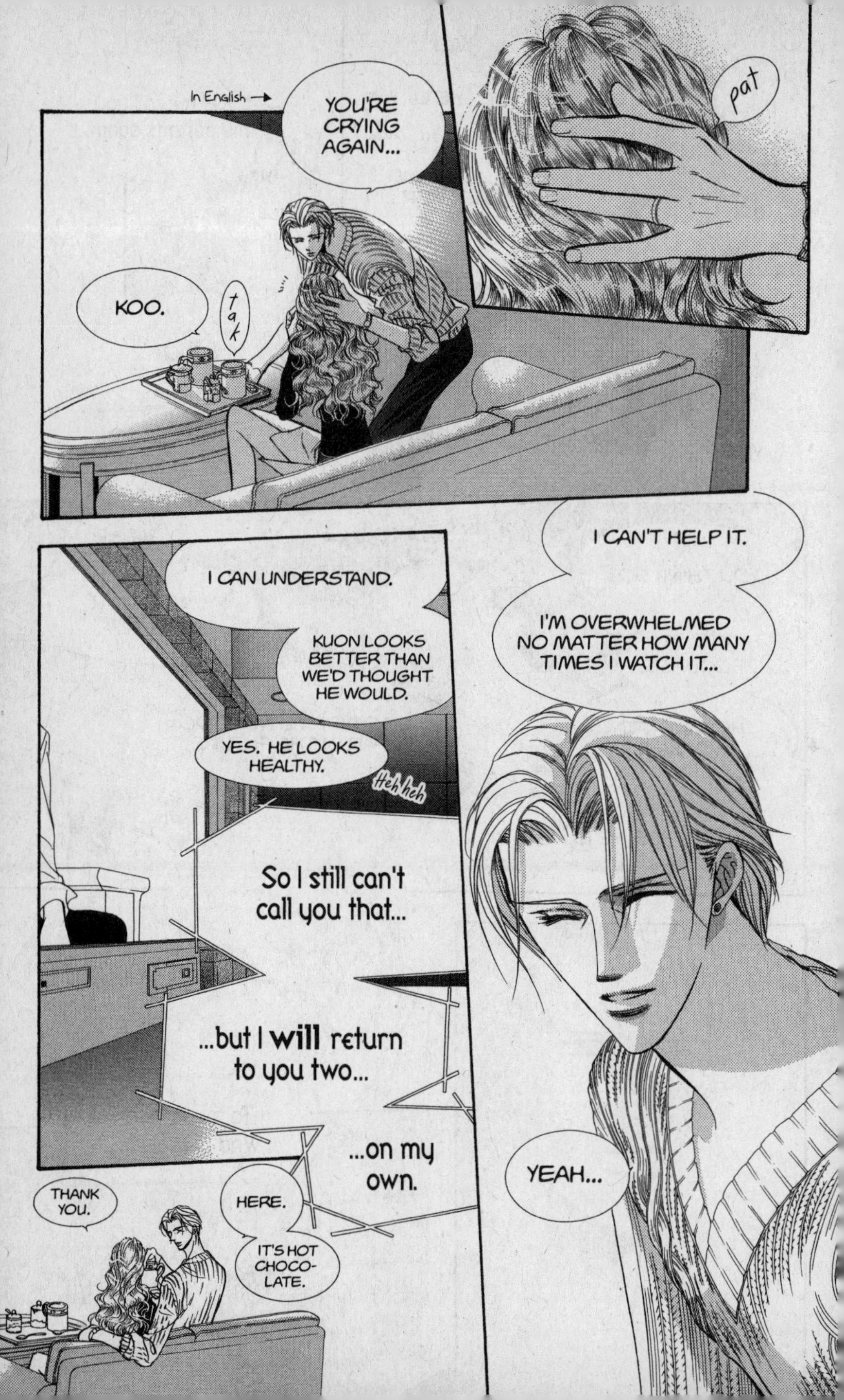
pat
In English →
YOU'RE CRYING AGAIN...
tak
KOO.
I CAN'T HELP IT.
I'M OVERWHELMED NO MATTER HOW MANY TIMES I WATCH IT...
YEAH...
I CAN UNDERSTAND.
KUON LOOKS BETTER THAN WE'D THOUGHT HE WOULD.
YES. HE LOOKS HEALTHY.
Heh heh
So I still can't call you that...
...but I will return to you two...
...on my own.
HERE.
IT'S HOT CHOCOLATE.
THANK YOU.

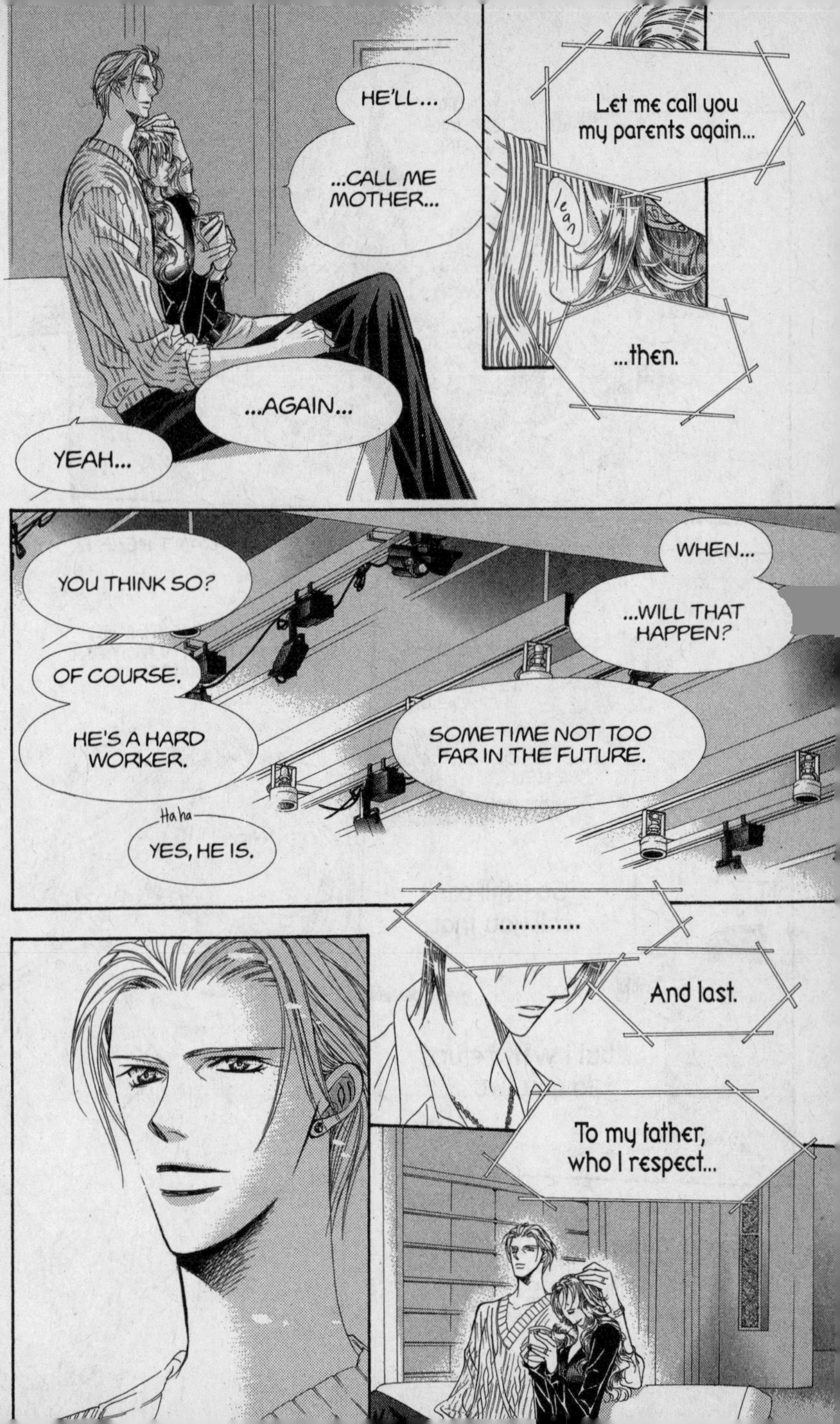
Let me call you my parents again...
lean
...then.
HE'LL...
...CALL ME MOTHER...
...AGAIN...
YEAH...
WHEN...
...WILL THAT HAPPEN?
SOMETIME NOT TOO FAR IN THE FUTURE.
YOU THINK SO?
OF COURSE.
HE'S A HARD WORKER.
Ha ha
YES, HE IS.
....
And last.
To my father, who I respect...

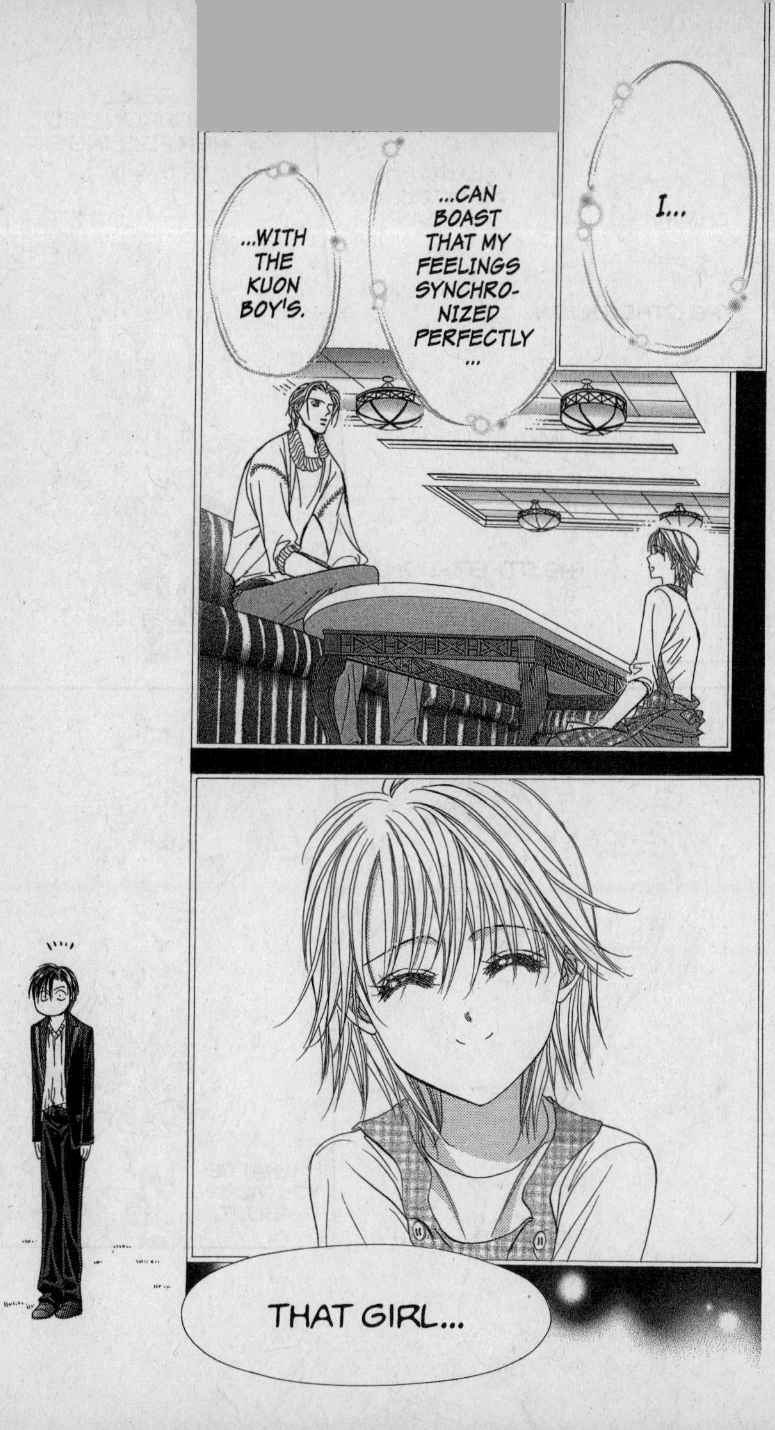
I...
...CAN BOAST THAT MY FEELINGS SYNCHRO-NIZED PERFECTLY...
...WITH THE KUON BOY'S.
THAT GIRL...

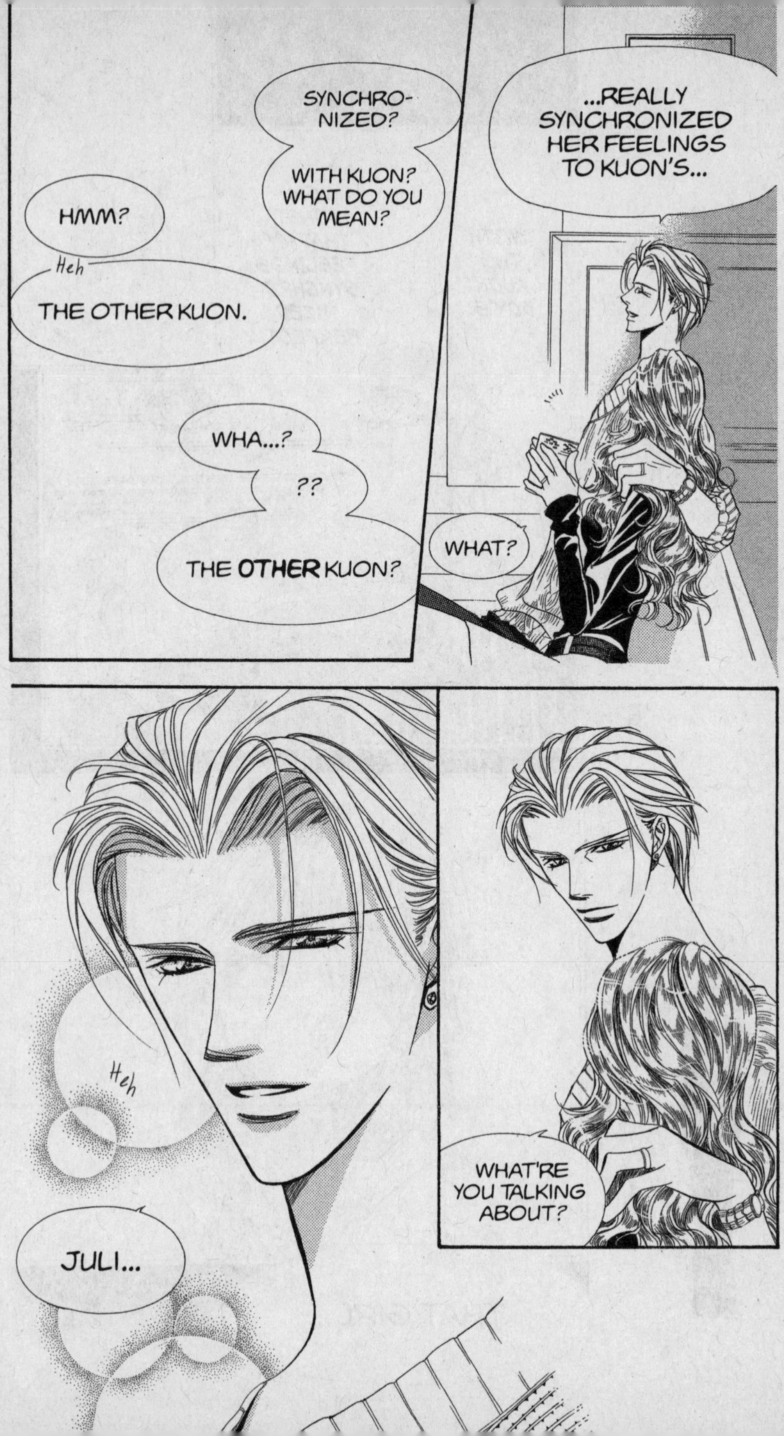
...REALLY SYNCHRONIZED HER FEELINGS TO KUON'S...
WHAT?
SYNCHRONIZED?
WITH KUON? WHAT DO YOU MEAN?
HMM?
Heh
THE OTHER KUON.
WHA...?
??
THE **OTHER** KUON?
WHAT'RE YOU TALKING ABOUT?
Heh
JULI...

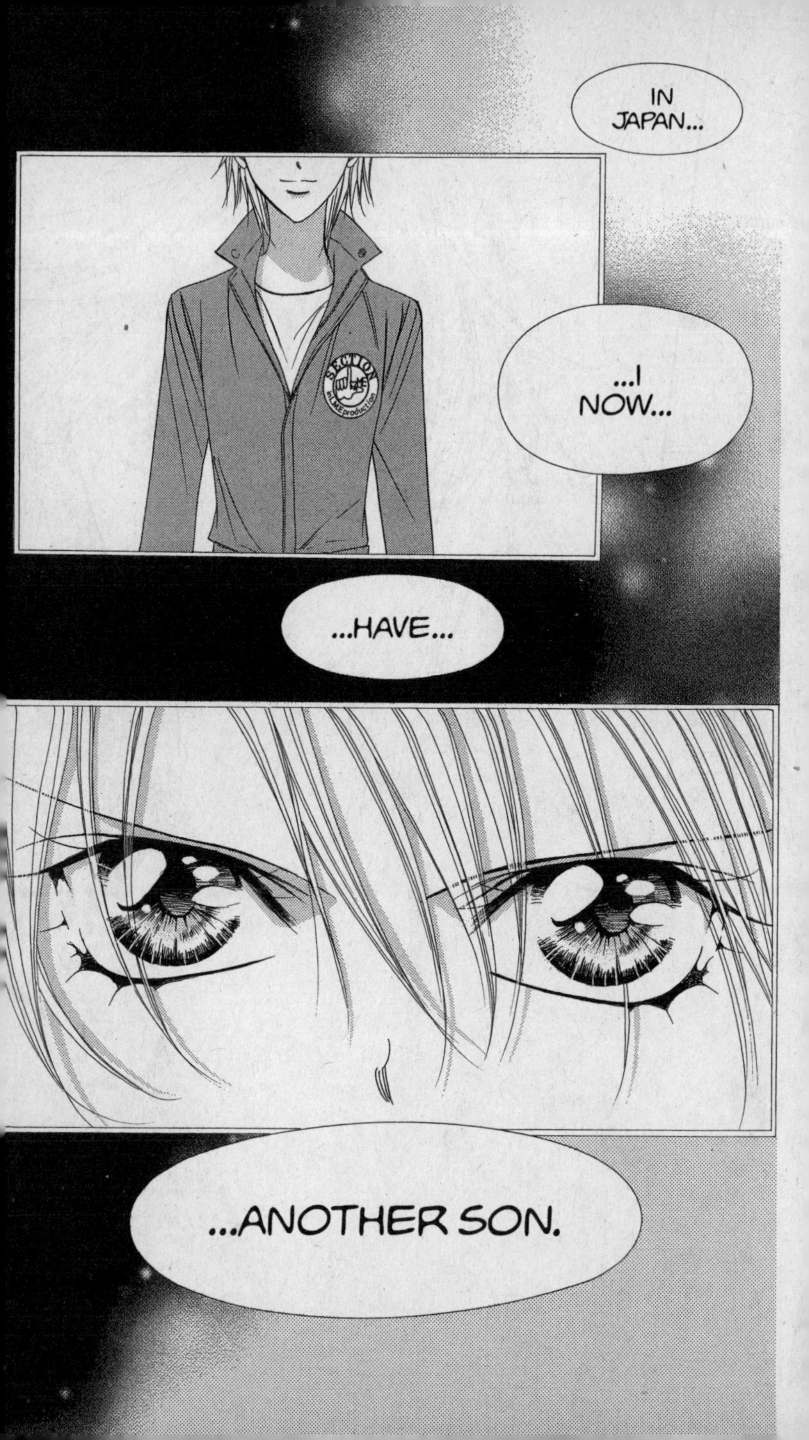
IN JAPAN...
...I NOW...
...HAVE...
...ANOTHER SON.

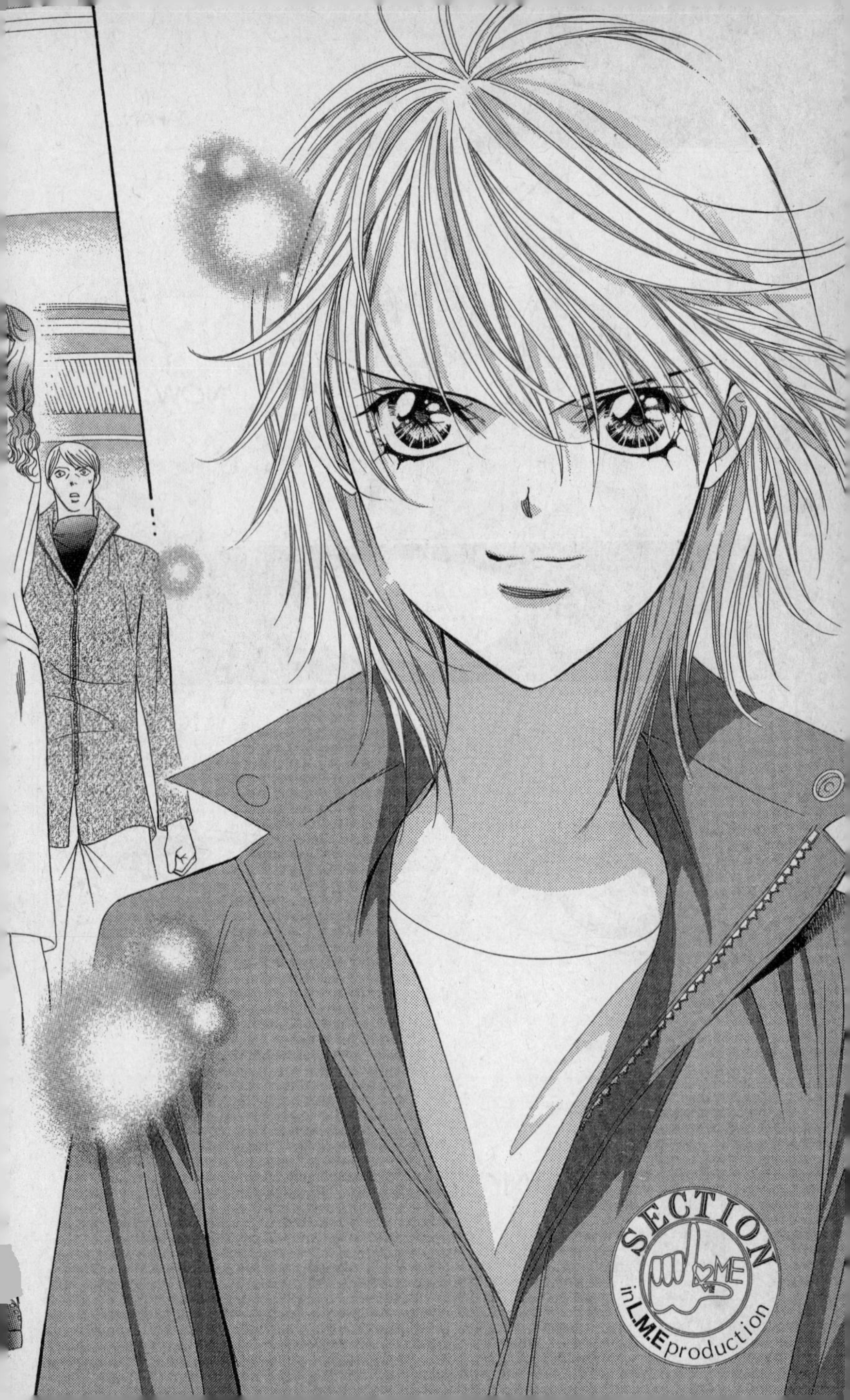
SECTION
in L.M.E production

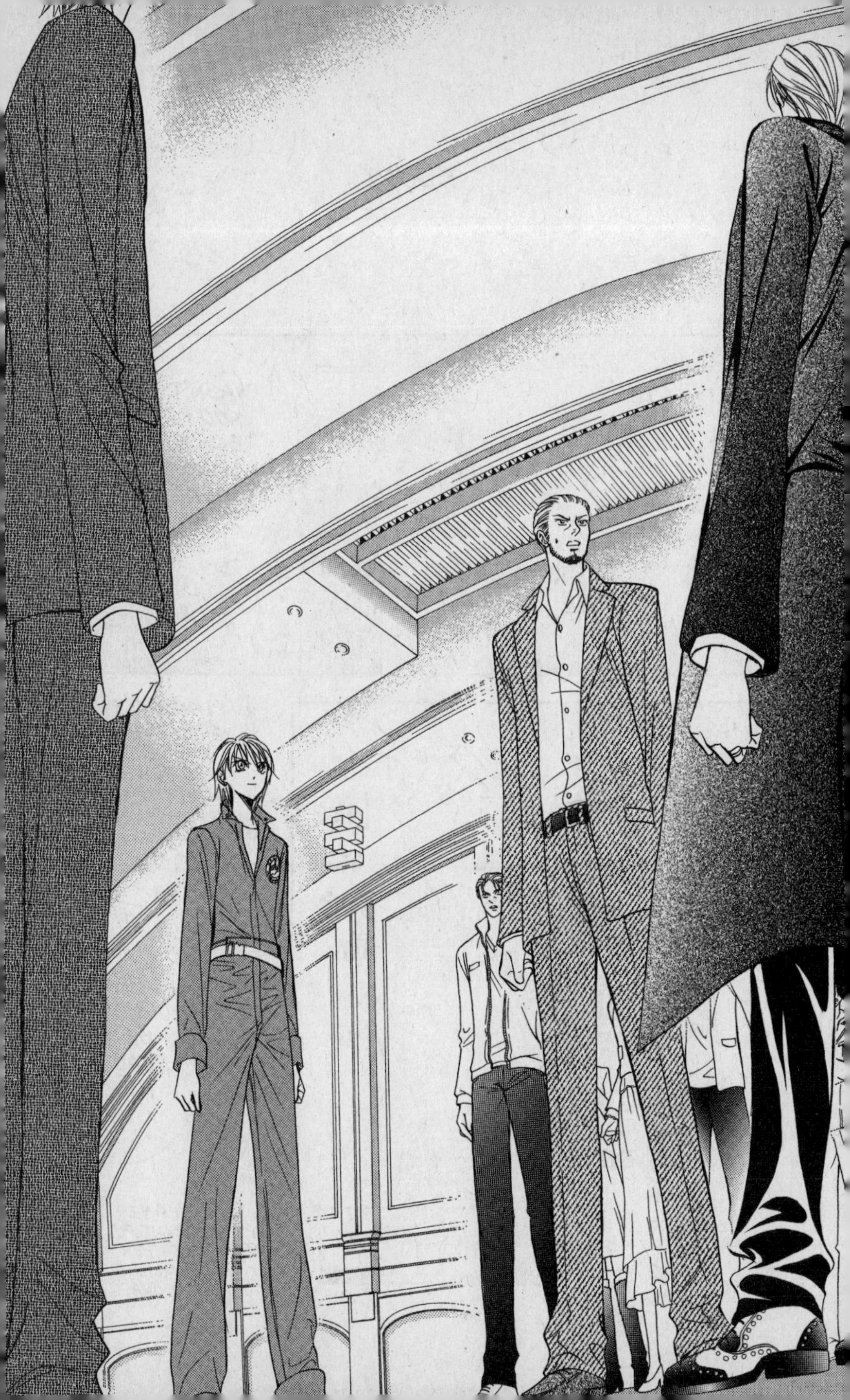

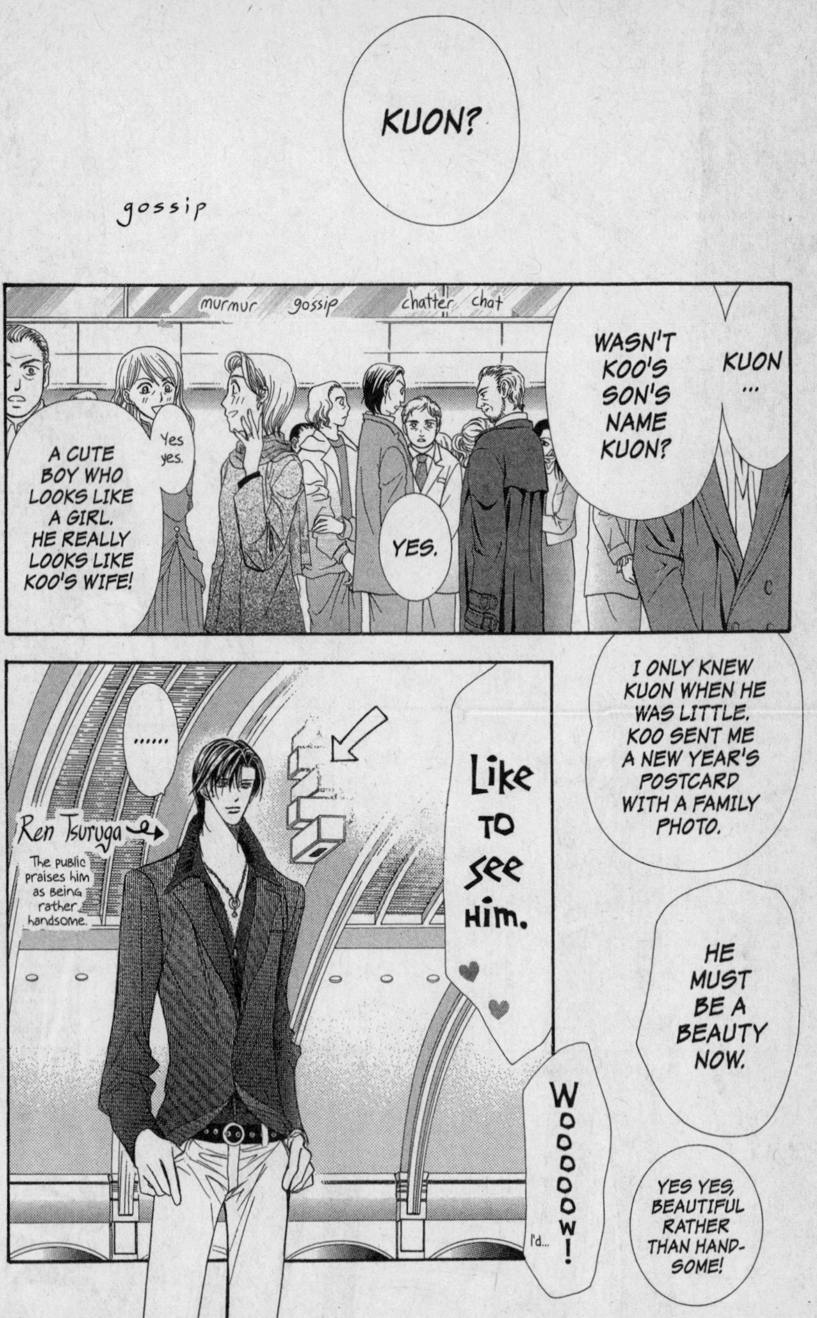
KUON?
gossip
KUON ...
WASN'T KOO'S SON'S NAME KUON?
murmur gossip chatter chat
YES.
Yes yes.
A CUTE BOY WHO LOOKS LIKE A GIRL. HE REALLY LOOKS LIKE KOO'S WIFE!
I ONLY KNEW KUON WHEN HE WAS LITTLE. KOO SENT ME A NEW YEAR'S POSTCARD WITH A FAMILY PHOTO.
HE MUST BE A BEAUTY NOW.
YES YES, BEAUTIFUL RATHER THAN HANDSOME!
Like to see him.
WOOOOOW!
I'd...
......
Ren Tsuruga
The public praises him as being rather handsome.

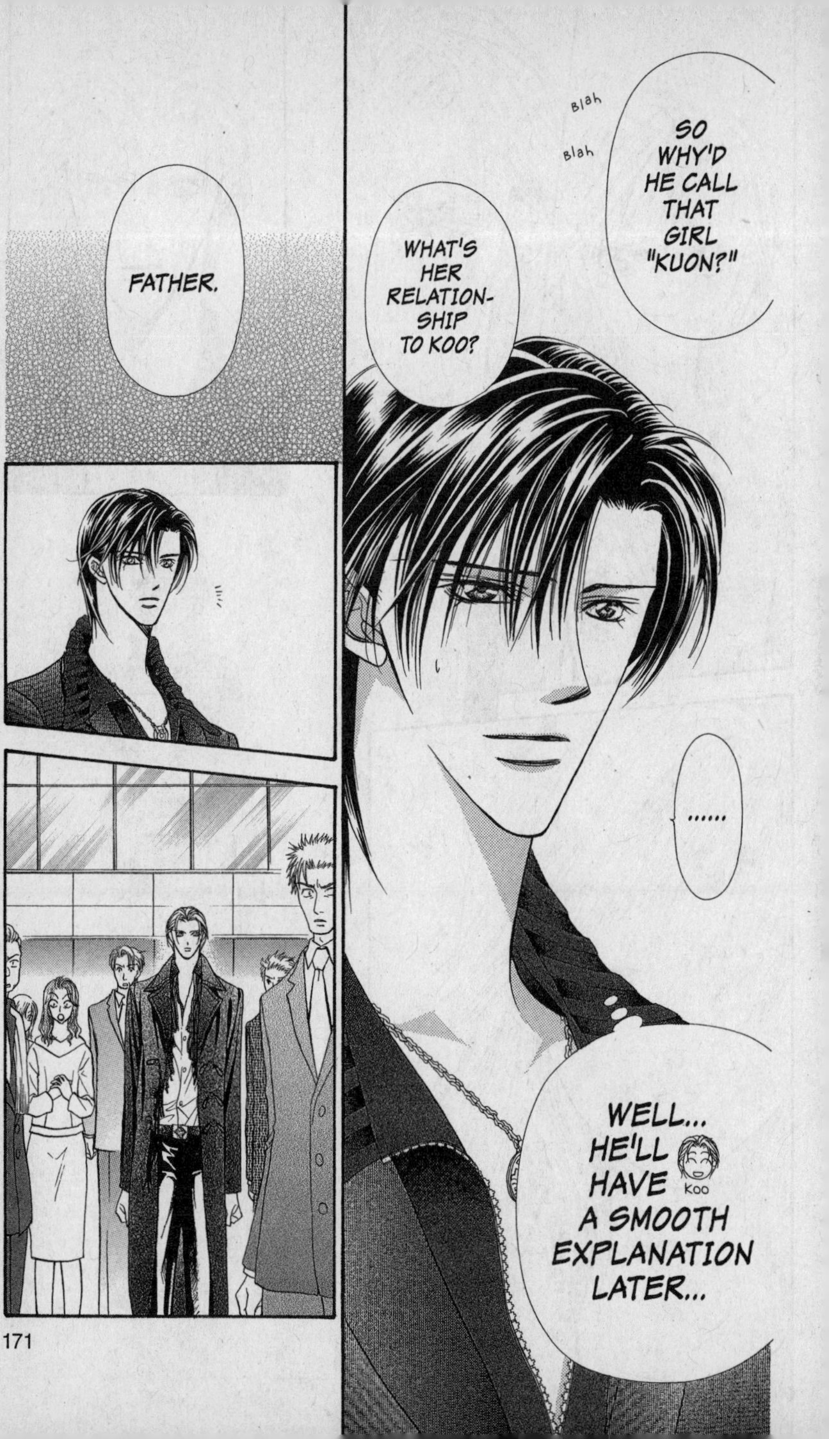
Blah
Blah
SO WHY'D HE CALL THAT GIRL "KUON?"
WHAT'S HER RELATION-SHIP TO KOO?
......
WELL... HE'LL HAVE A SMOOTH EXPLANATION LATER...
Koo
FATHER.

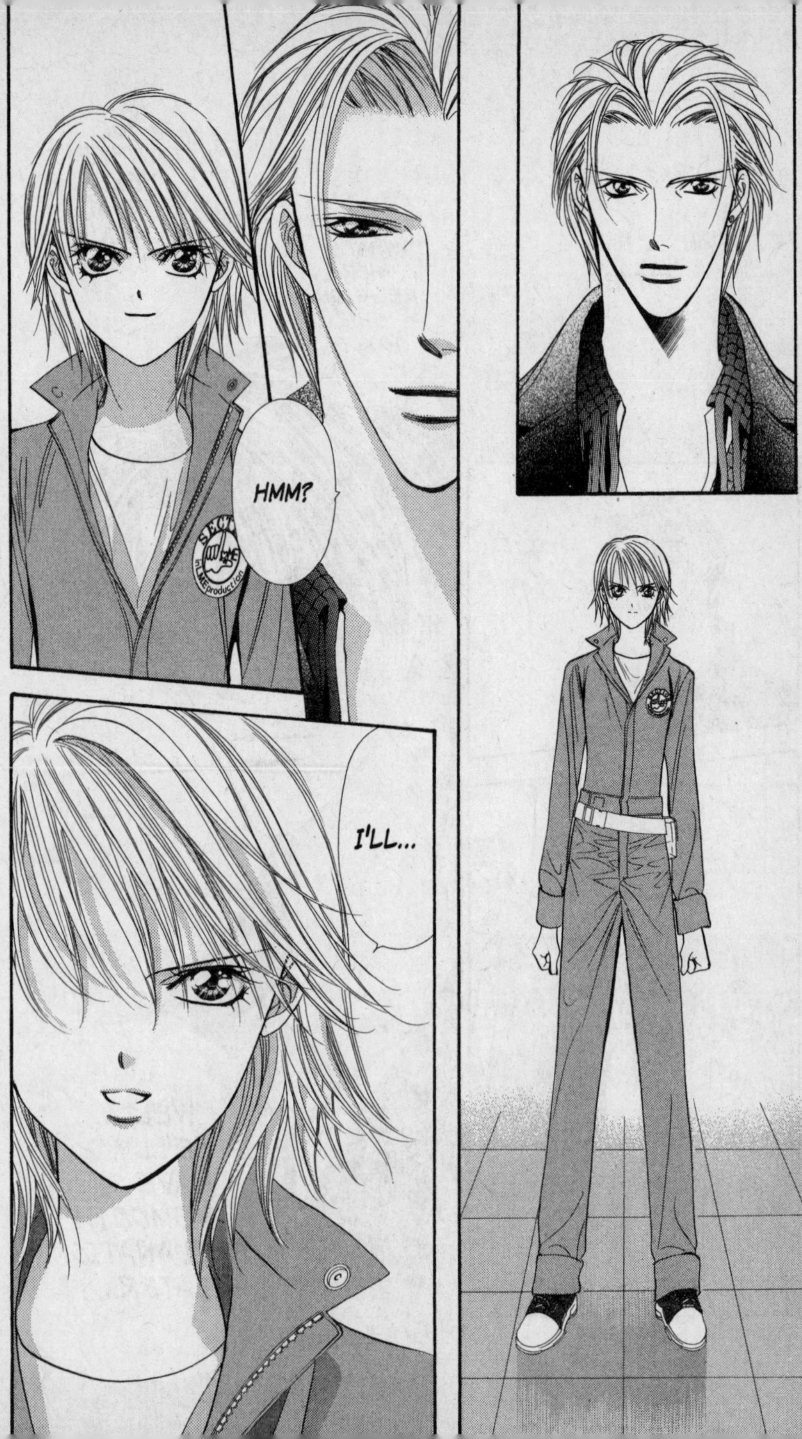
HMM?
I'LL...

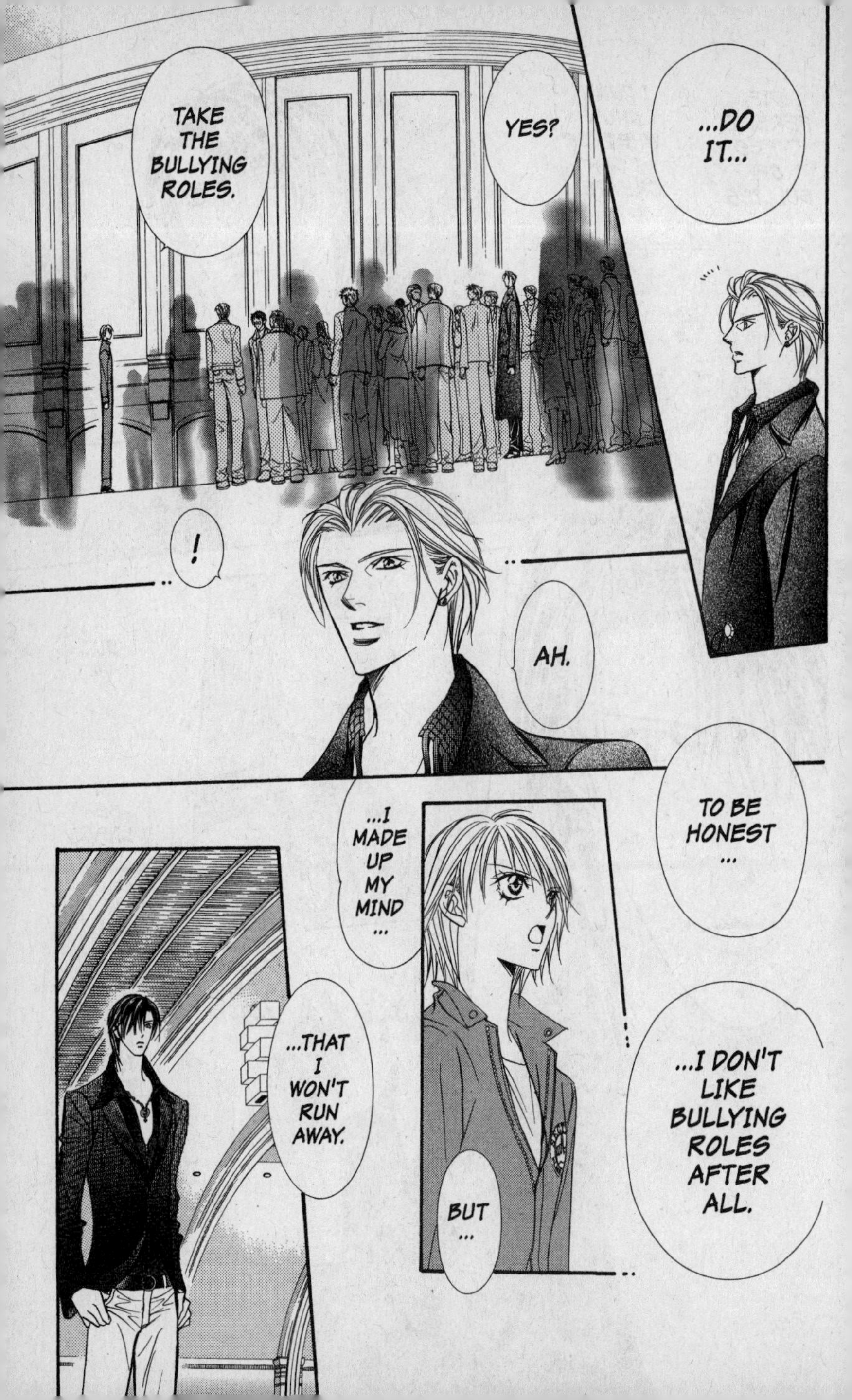
...DO IT...
YES?
TAKE THE BULLYING ROLES.
AH.
!
TO BE HONEST...
...I DON'T LIKE BULLYING ROLES AFTER ALL.
BUT...
...I MADE UP MY MIND...
...THAT I WON'T RUN AWAY.

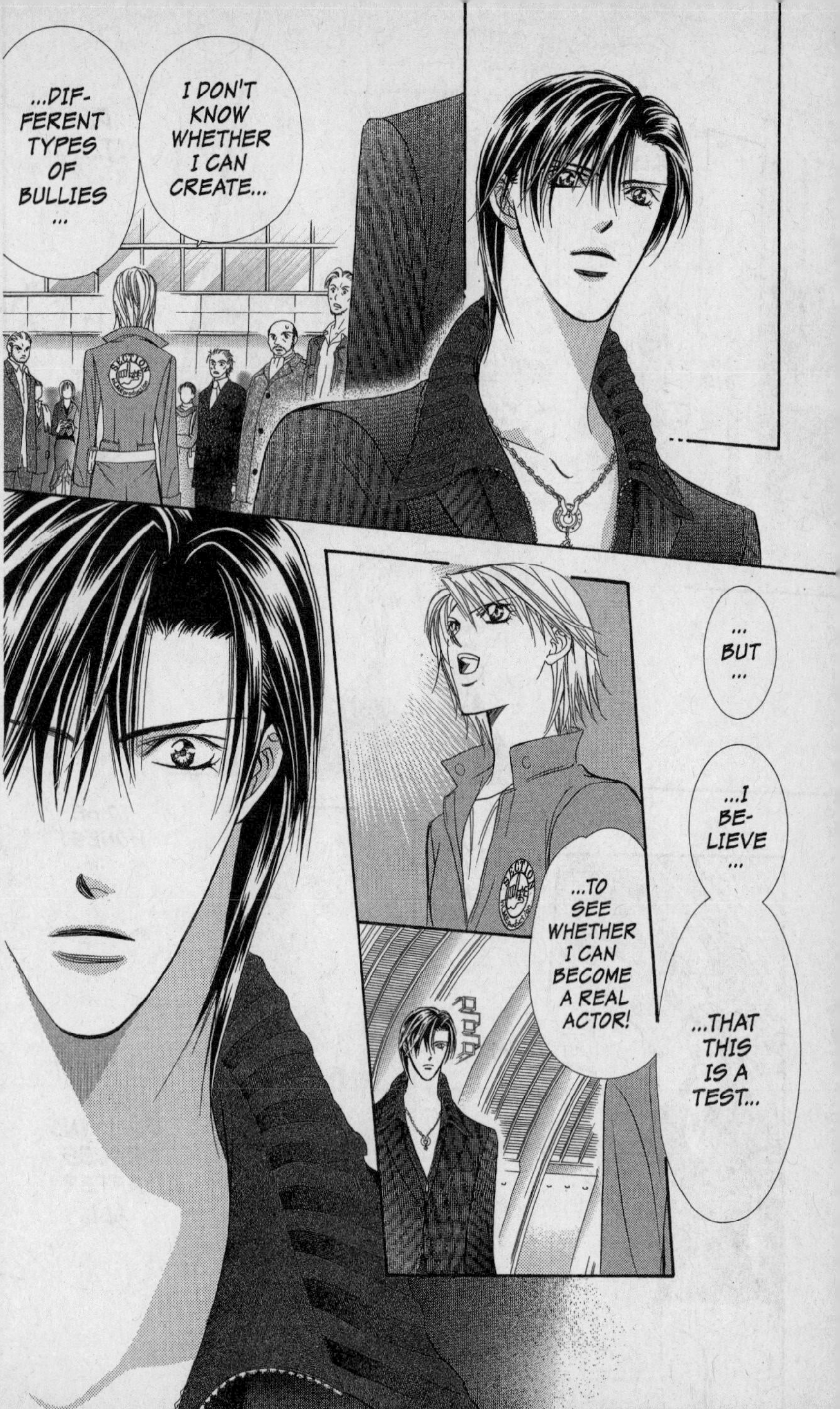
I DON'T KNOW WHETHER I CAN CREATE...
...DIF-FERENT TYPES OF BULLIES...
...
...BUT...
...I BE-LIEVE...
...THAT THIS IS A TEST...
...TO SEE WHETHER I CAN BECOME A REAL ACTOR!

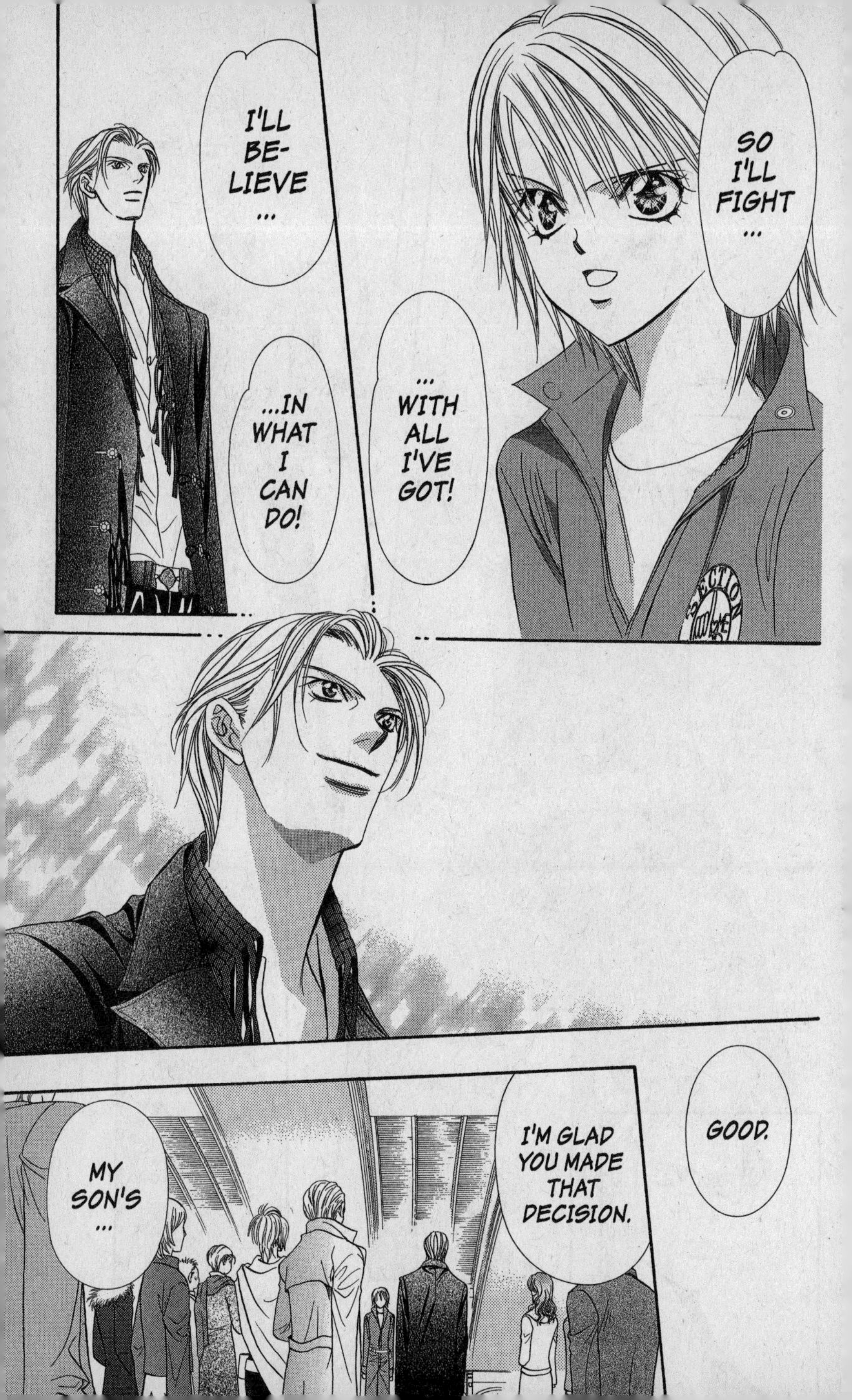
SO I'LL FIGHT ...
... WITH ALL I'VE GOT!
I'LL BE-LIEVE ...
...IN WHAT I CAN DO!
GOOD.
I'M GLAD YOU MADE THAT DECISION.
MY SON'S ...

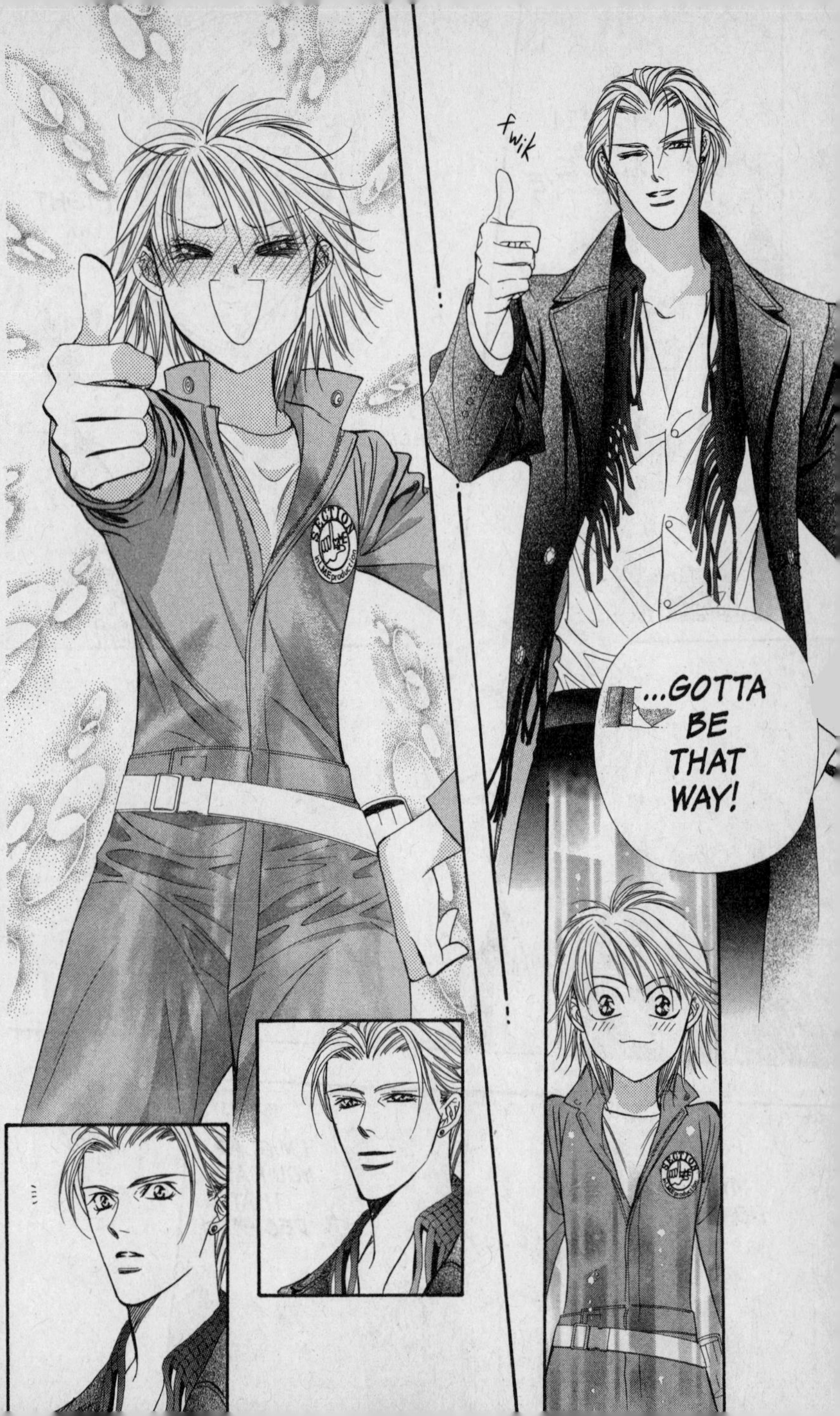
fwik
...GOTTA BE THAT WAY!

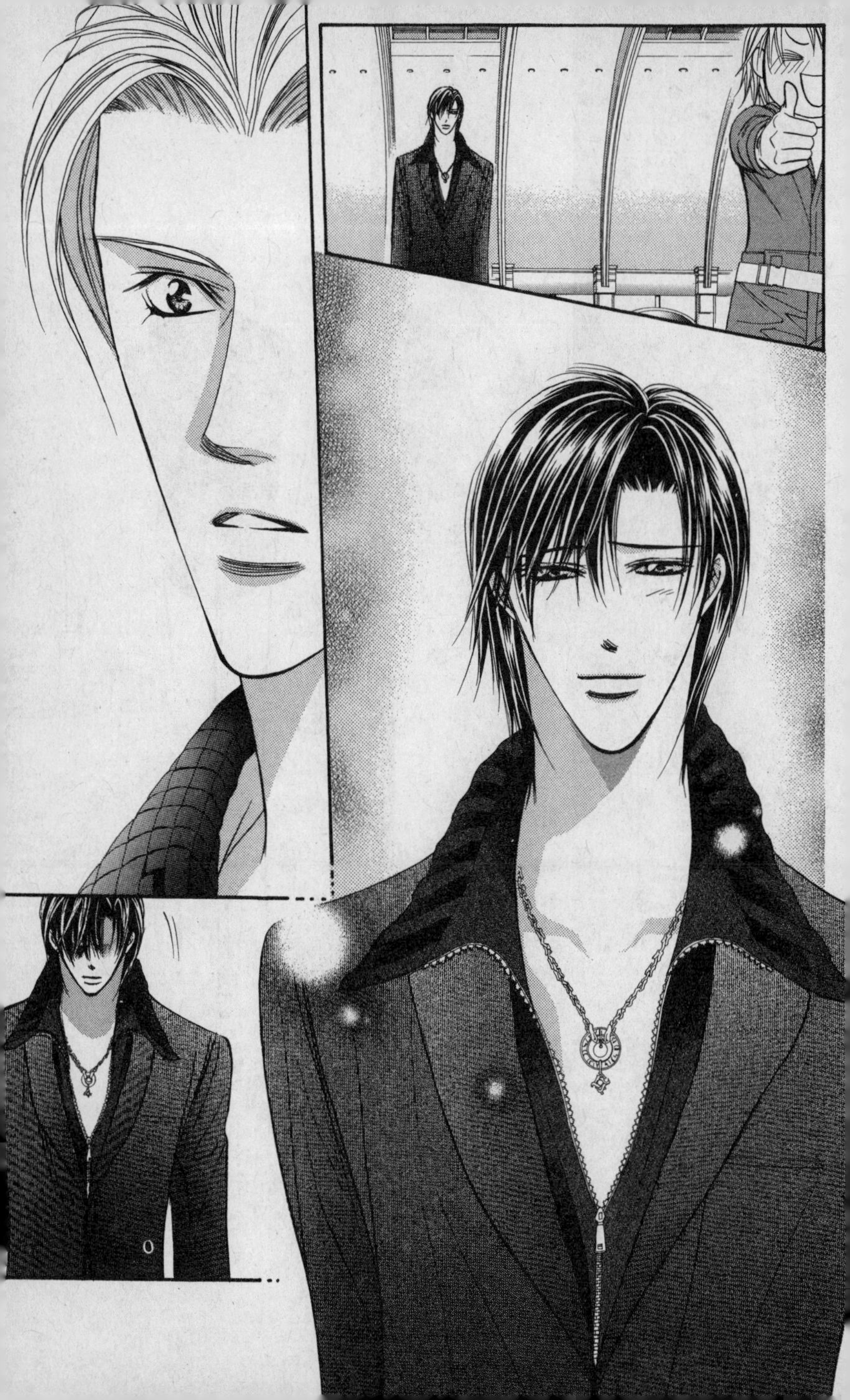

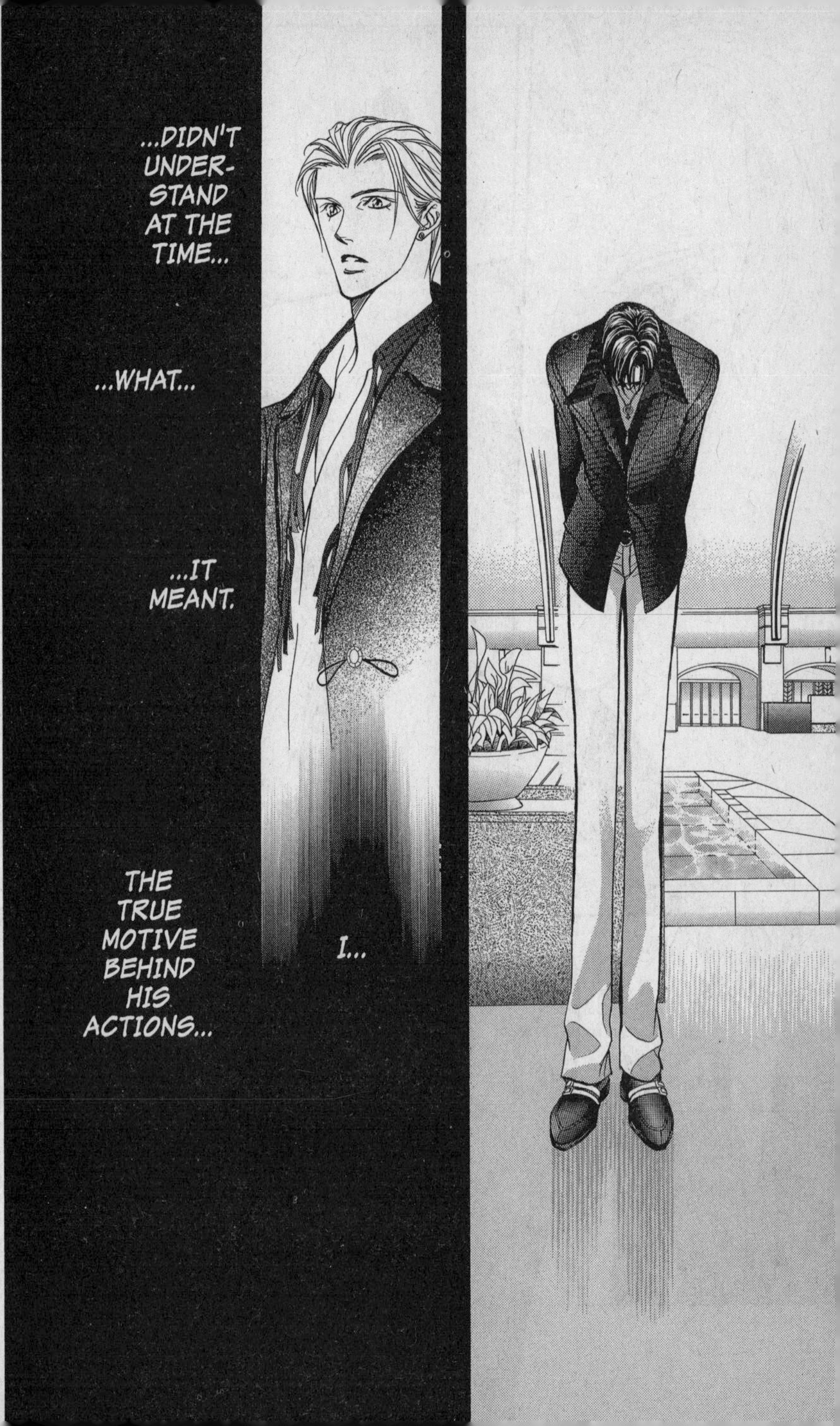

...DIDN'T UNDERSTAND AT THE TIME...

...WHAT...

...IT MEANT.

THE TRUE MOTIVE BEHIND HIS ACTIONS...

I...

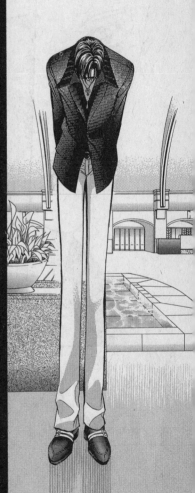

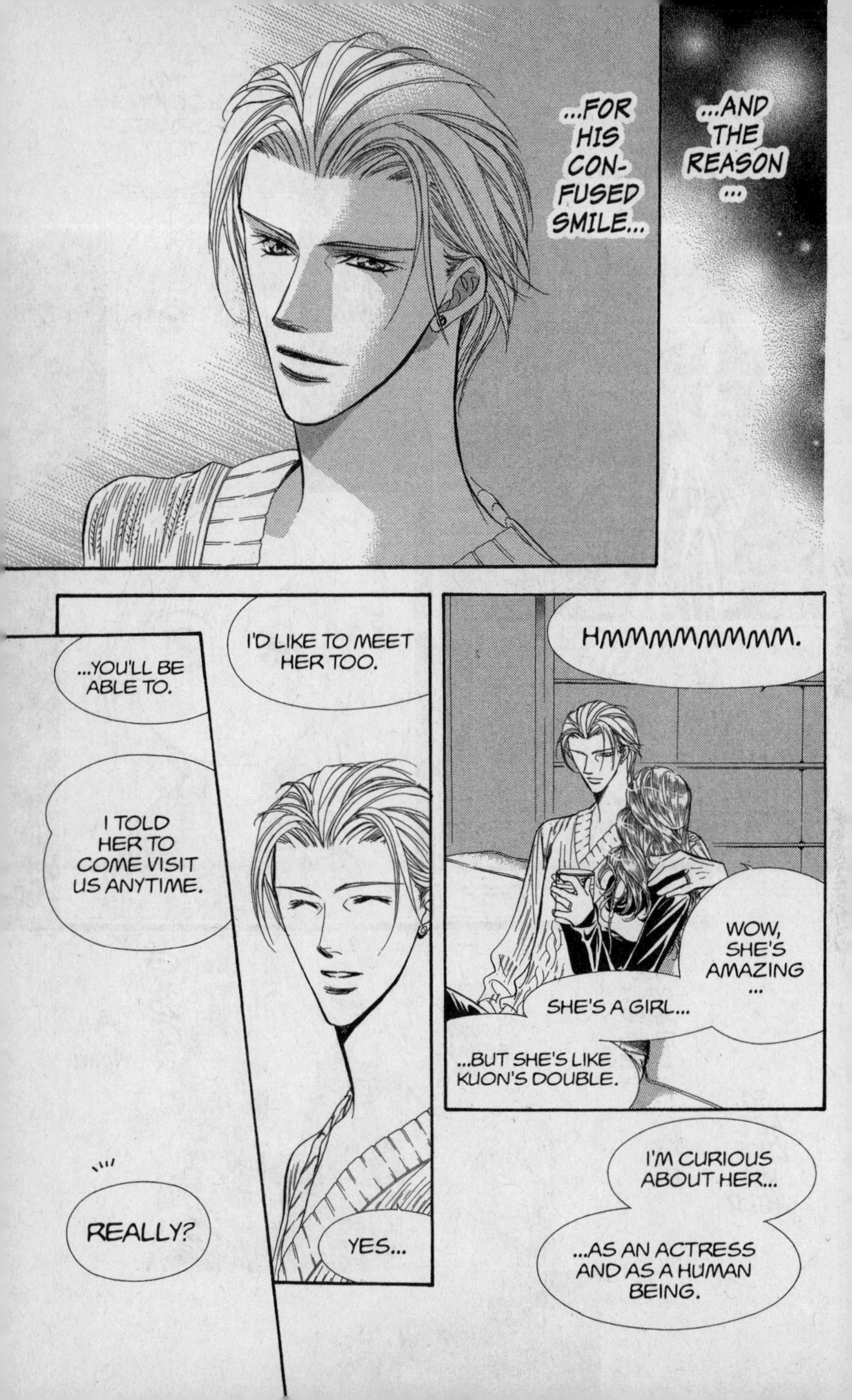
...AND THE REASON ...
...FOR HIS CONFUSED SMILE...
HMMMMMMMM.
WOW, SHE'S AMAZING ...
SHE'S A GIRL...
...BUT SHE'S LIKE KUON'S DOUBLE.
I'M CURIOUS ABOUT HER...
...AS AN ACTRESS AND AS A HUMAN BEING.
I'D LIKE TO MEET HER TOO.
...YOU'LL BE ABLE TO.
I TOLD HER TO COME VISIT US ANYTIME.
REALLY?
YES...

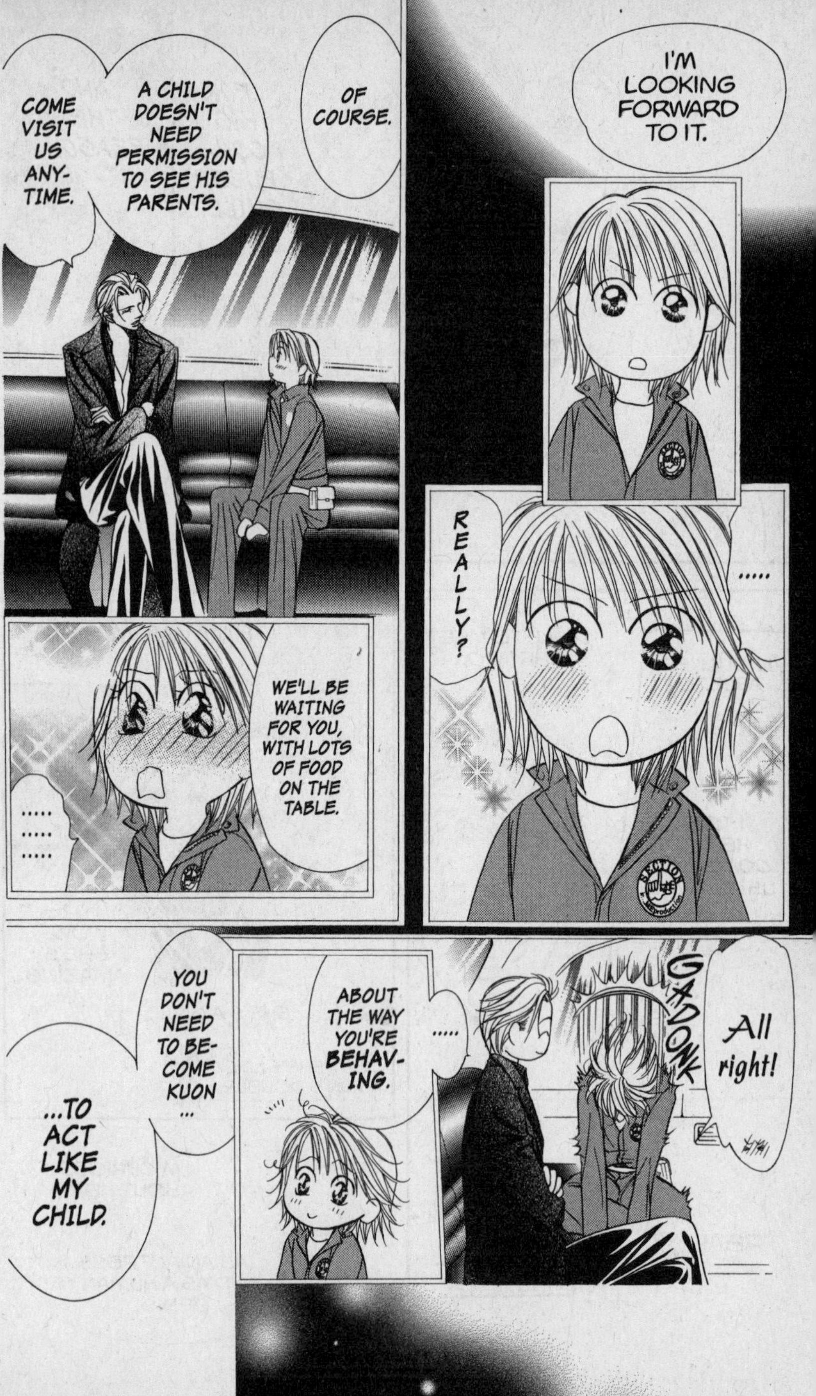
I'M LOOKING FORWARD TO IT.
REALLY?
.....
OF COURSE.
A CHILD DOESN'T NEED PERMISSION TO SEE HIS PARENTS.
COME VISIT US ANY-TIME.
WE'LL BE WAITING FOR YOU, WITH LOTS OF FOOD ON THE TABLE.
....
All right!
GADONK
.....
ABOUT THE WAY YOU'RE BEHAV-ING.
YOU DON'T NEED TO BE-COME KUON...
...TO ACT LIKE MY CHILD.

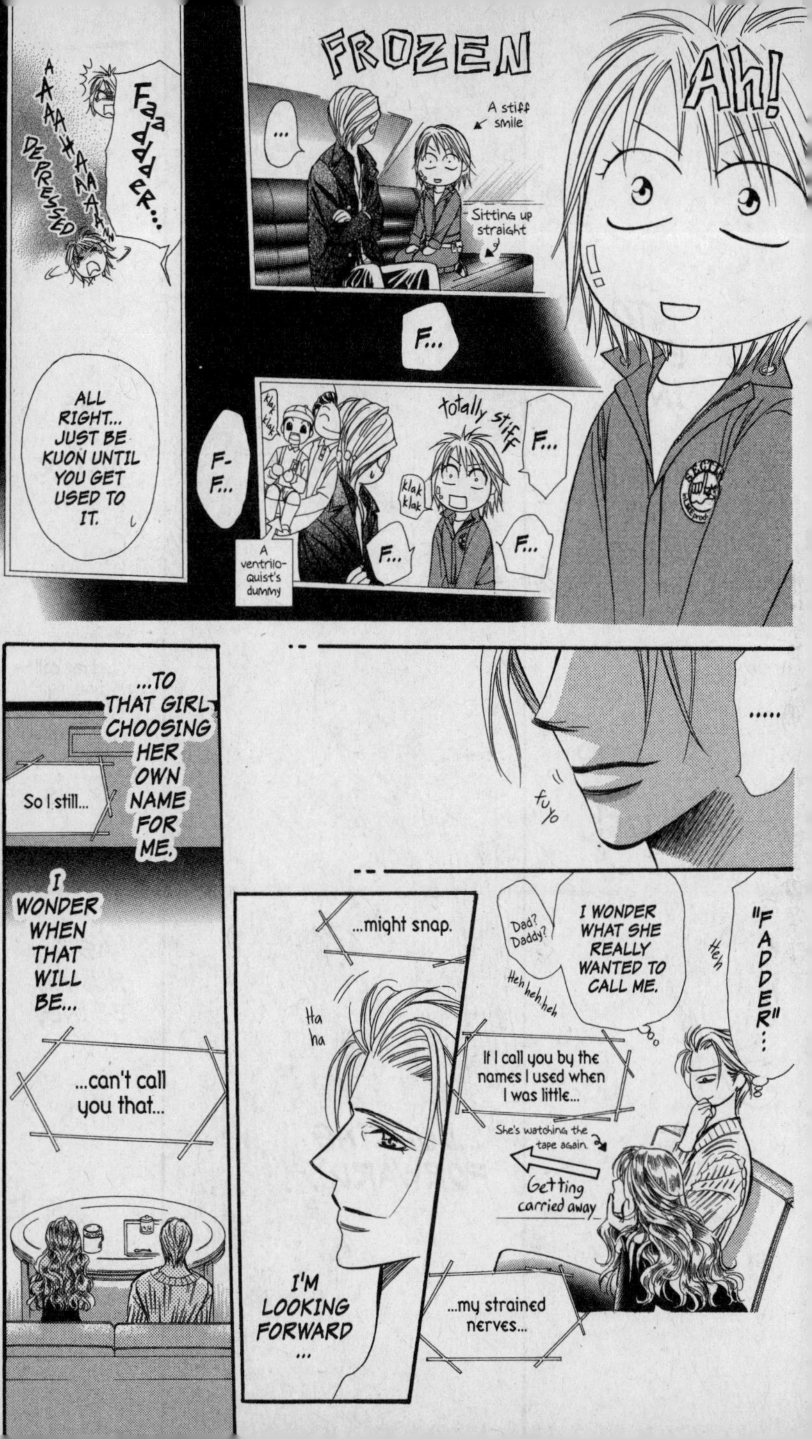

Ah!
FROZEN
...
A stiff smile
Sitting up straight
F...
F...
totally stiff
klak klak
klak klak
F...
F-F...
A ventriloquist's dummy
F...
Faaadder...
AAAAHAAAAAANN
DEPRESSED
ALL RIGHT... JUST BE KUON UNTIL YOU GET USED TO IT.
.....
fuyo
...TO THAT GIRL CHOOSING HER OWN NAME FOR ME.
So I still...
"FADDER"...
Heh
I WONDER WHAT SHE REALLY WANTED TO CALL ME.
Dad? Daddy?
Heh heh heh
If I call you by the names I used when I was little...
She's watching the tape again.
Getting carried away
...my strained nerves...
...might snap.
Ha ha
I'M LOOKING FORWARD ...
I WONDER WHEN THAT WILL BE...
...can't call you that...

...but I **will** return to you two on my own.
AS AN ACTOR.
Let me call you my parents...
AS A HUMAN BEING.
...again then.
I'M REALLY...
...LOOKING FORWARD...
...TO SEE-ING...
And last.

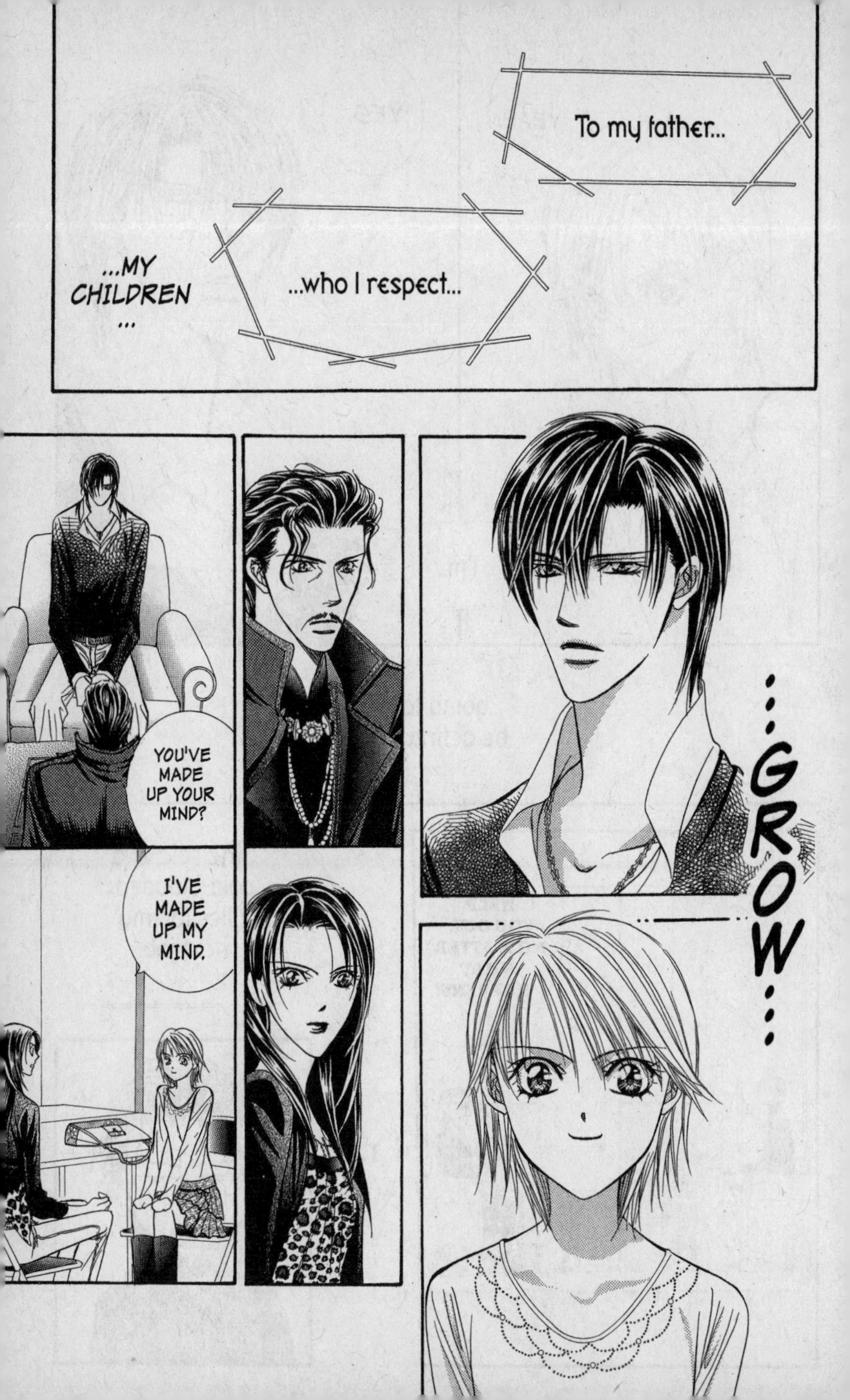
To my father...
...who I respect...
...MY CHILDREN ...
...GROW...
YOU'VE MADE UP YOUR MIND?
I'VE MADE UP MY MIND.

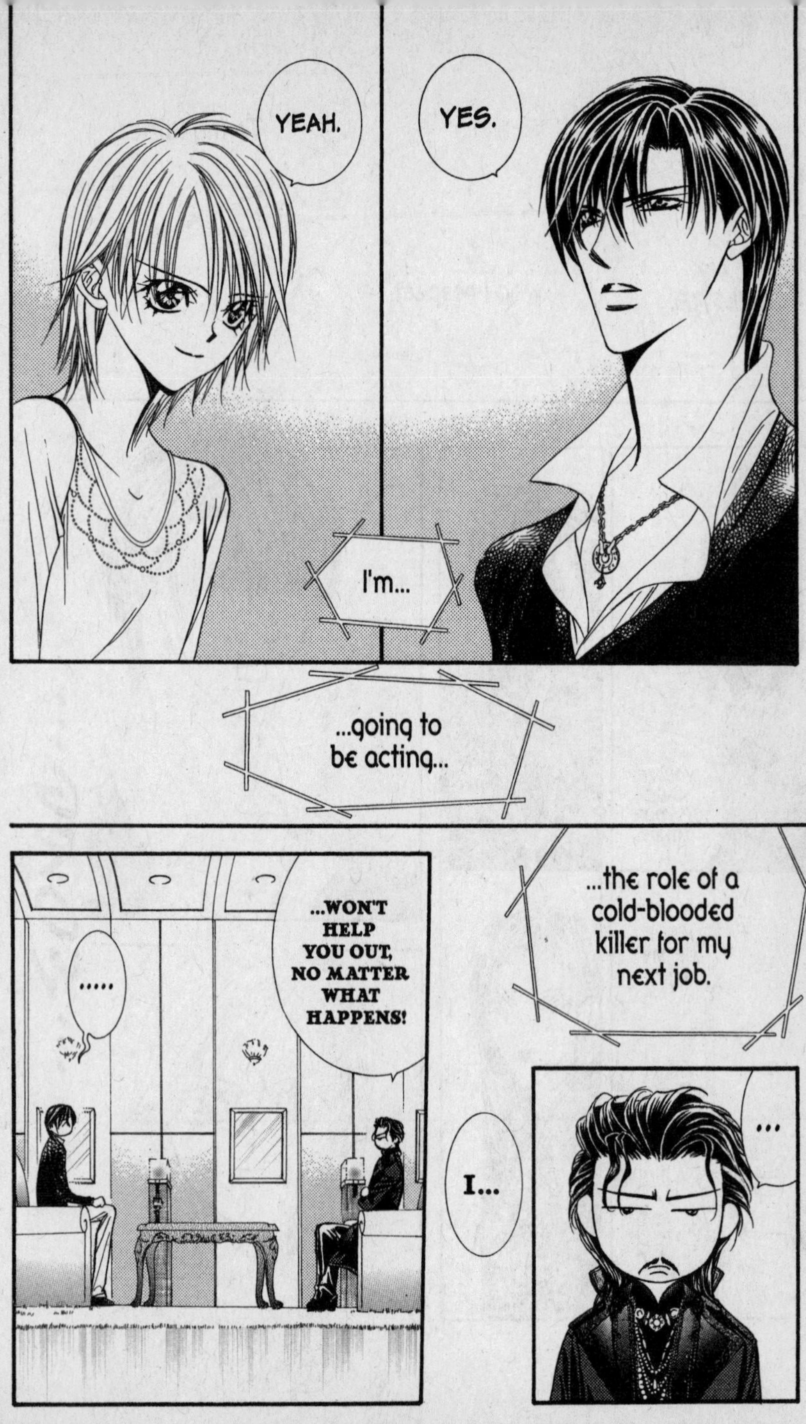
YES.
YEAH.
I'm...
...going to be acting...
...the role of a cold-blooded killer for my next job.
...
I...
...WON'T HELP YOU OUT, NO MATTER WHAT HAPPENS!
......

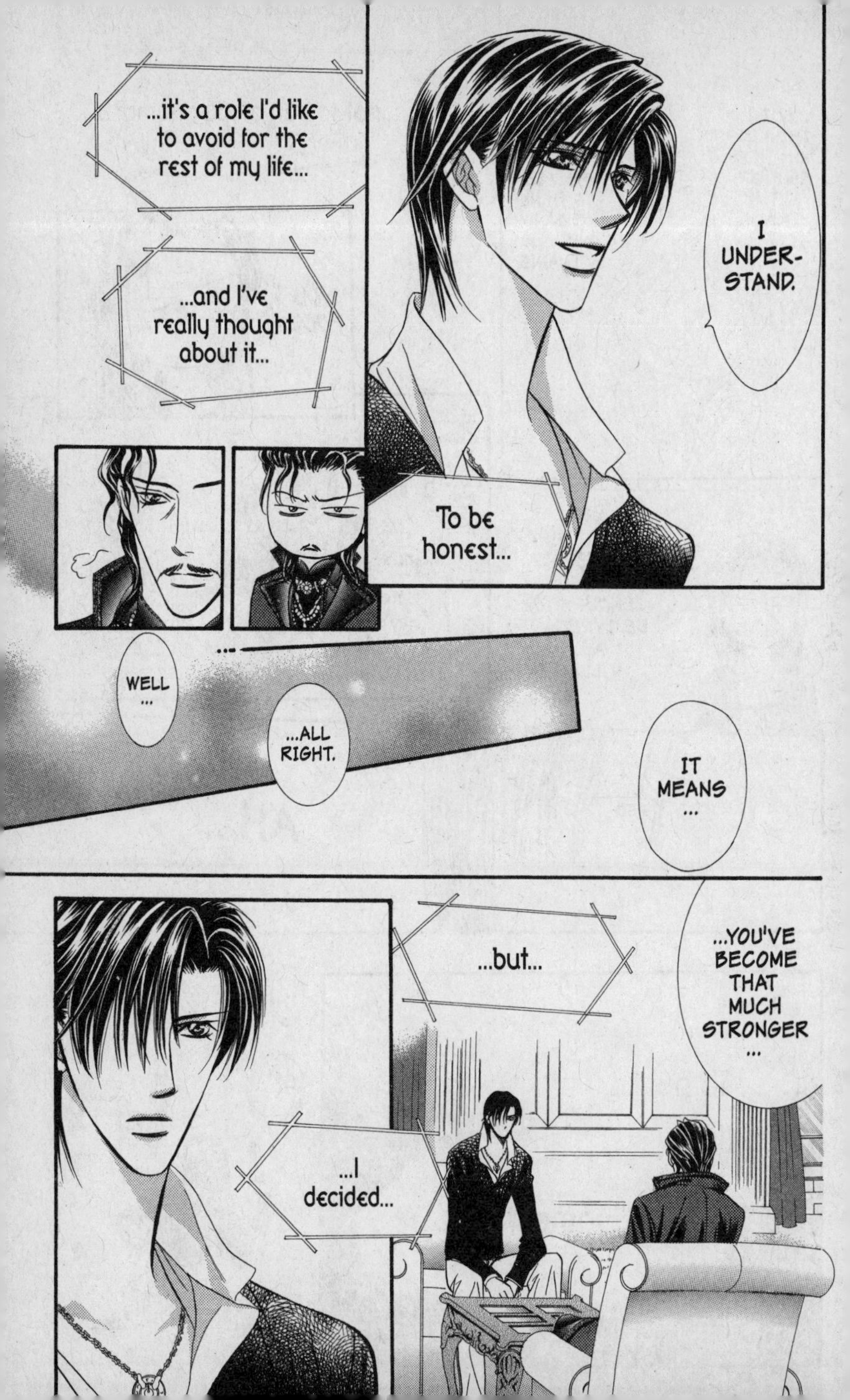
I UNDERSTAND.
To be honest...
...it's a role I'd like to avoid for the rest of my life...
...and I've really thought about it...
...
WELL...
...ALL RIGHT.
IT MEANS...
...YOU'VE BECOME THAT MUCH STRONGER...
...but...
...I decided...

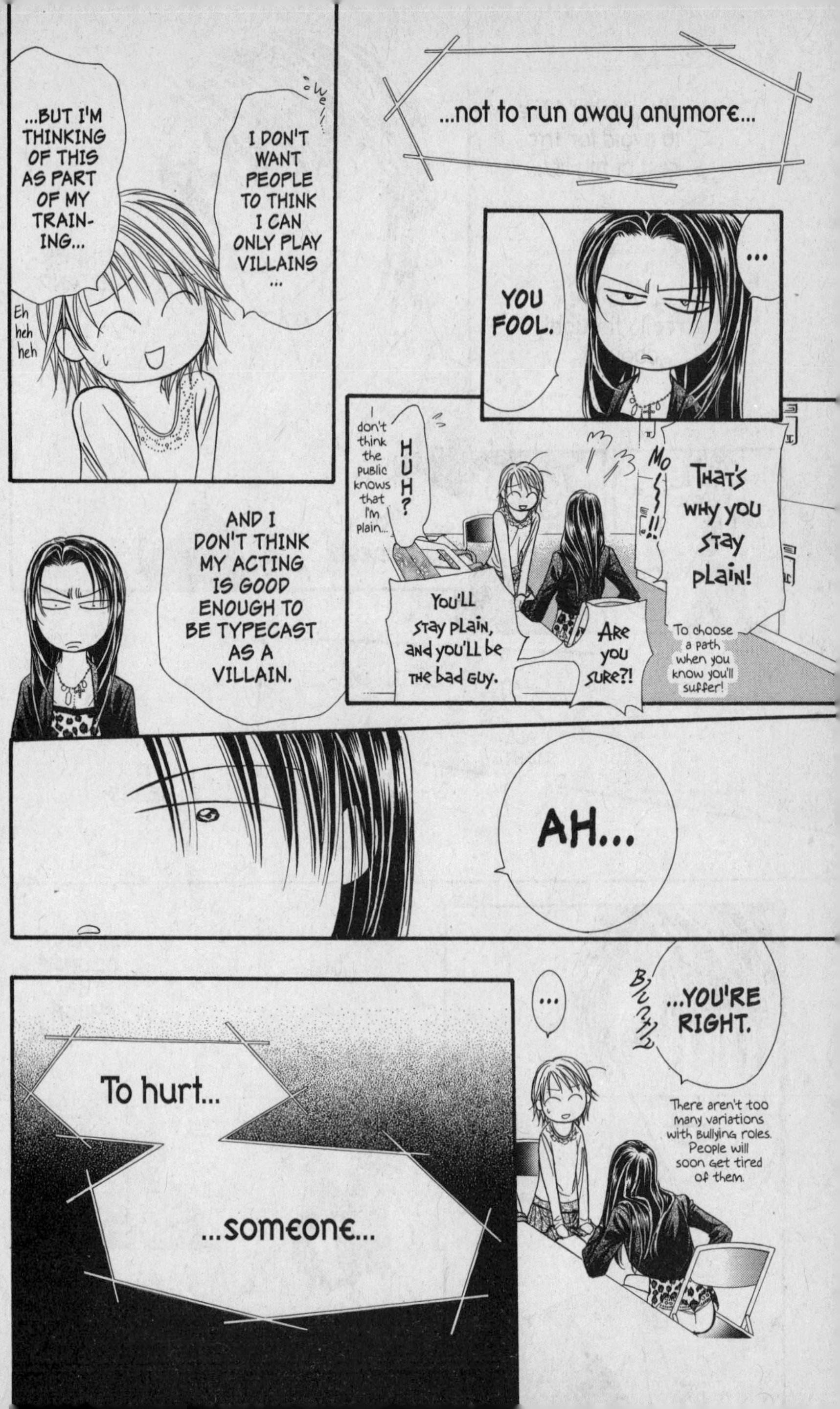

...not to run away anymore...
Well...
I DON'T WANT PEOPLE TO THINK I CAN ONLY PLAY VILLAINS...
...BUT I'M THINKING OF THIS AS PART OF MY TRAIN-ING...
Eh heh heh
AND I DON'T THINK MY ACTING IS GOOD ENOUGH TO BE TYPECAST AS A VILLAIN.
...
YOU FOOL.
MO~!!
THAT'S WHY YOU STAY PLAIN!
To choose a path when you know you'll suffer!
HUH?
I don't think the public knows that I'm plain...
Are you sure?!
You'll stay plain, and you'll be the bad guy.
AH...
...YOU'RE RIGHT.
...
There aren't too many variations with bullying roles. People will soon get tired of them.
To hurt...
...someone...

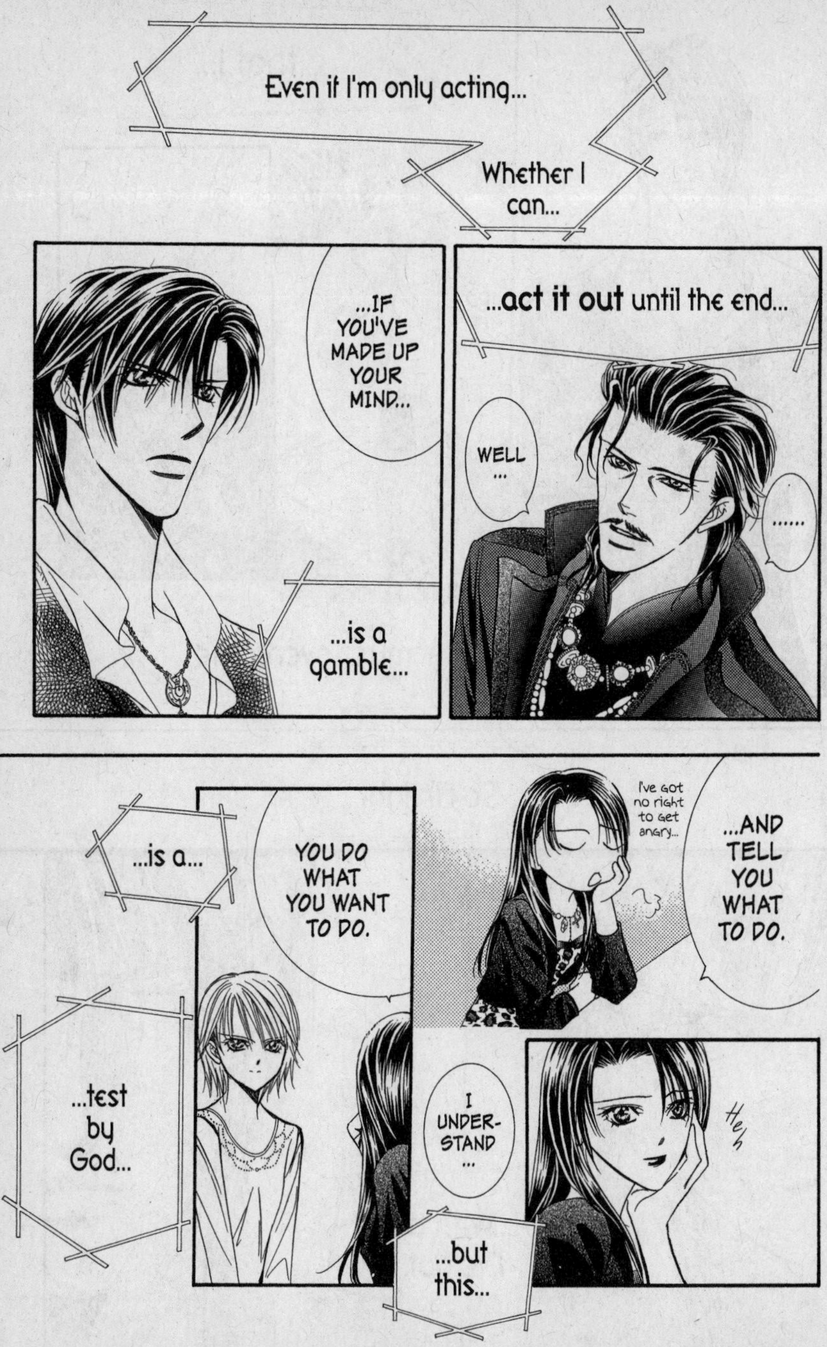
Even if I'm only acting...
Whether I can...
...act it out until the end...
WELL ...
......
...IF YOU'VE MADE UP YOUR MIND...
...is a gamble...
...AND TELL YOU WHAT TO DO.
I've got no right to get angry...
Heh
I UNDER-STAND ...
...but this...
YOU DO WHAT YOU WANT TO DO.
...is a...
...test by God...

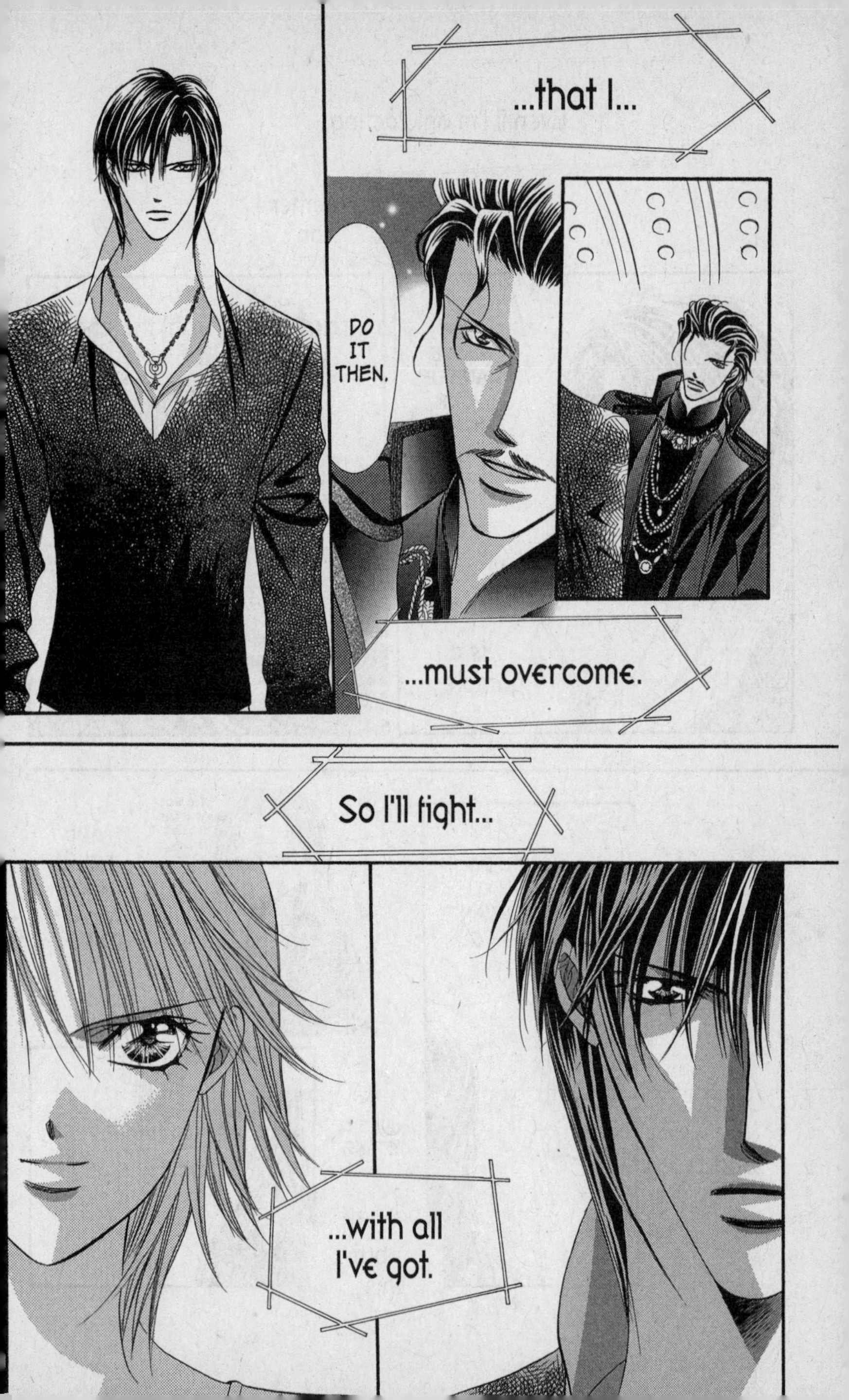
...that I...
DO IT THEN.
...must overcome.
So I'll fight...
...with all I've got.

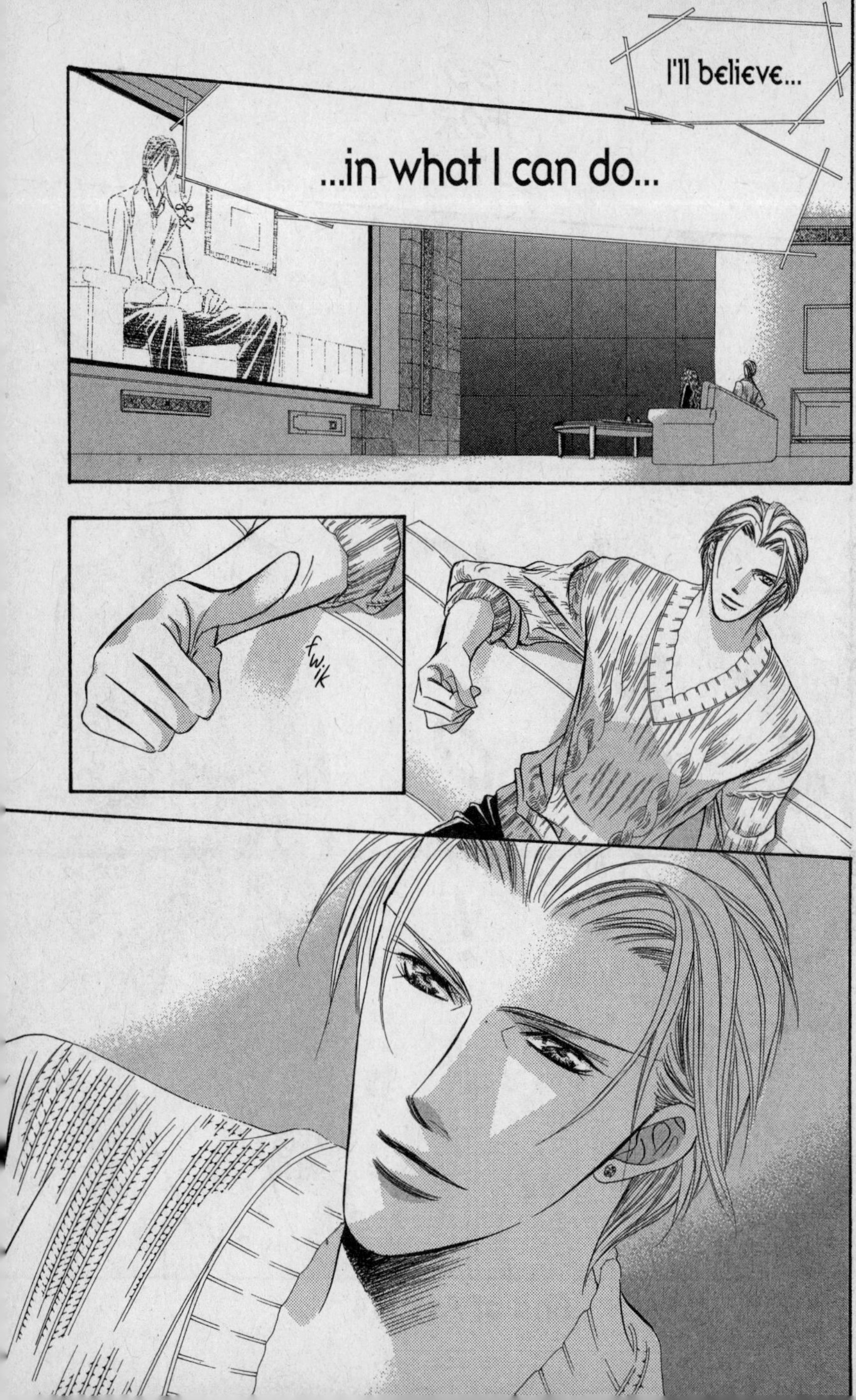

I'll believe...
...in what I can do...
fwik

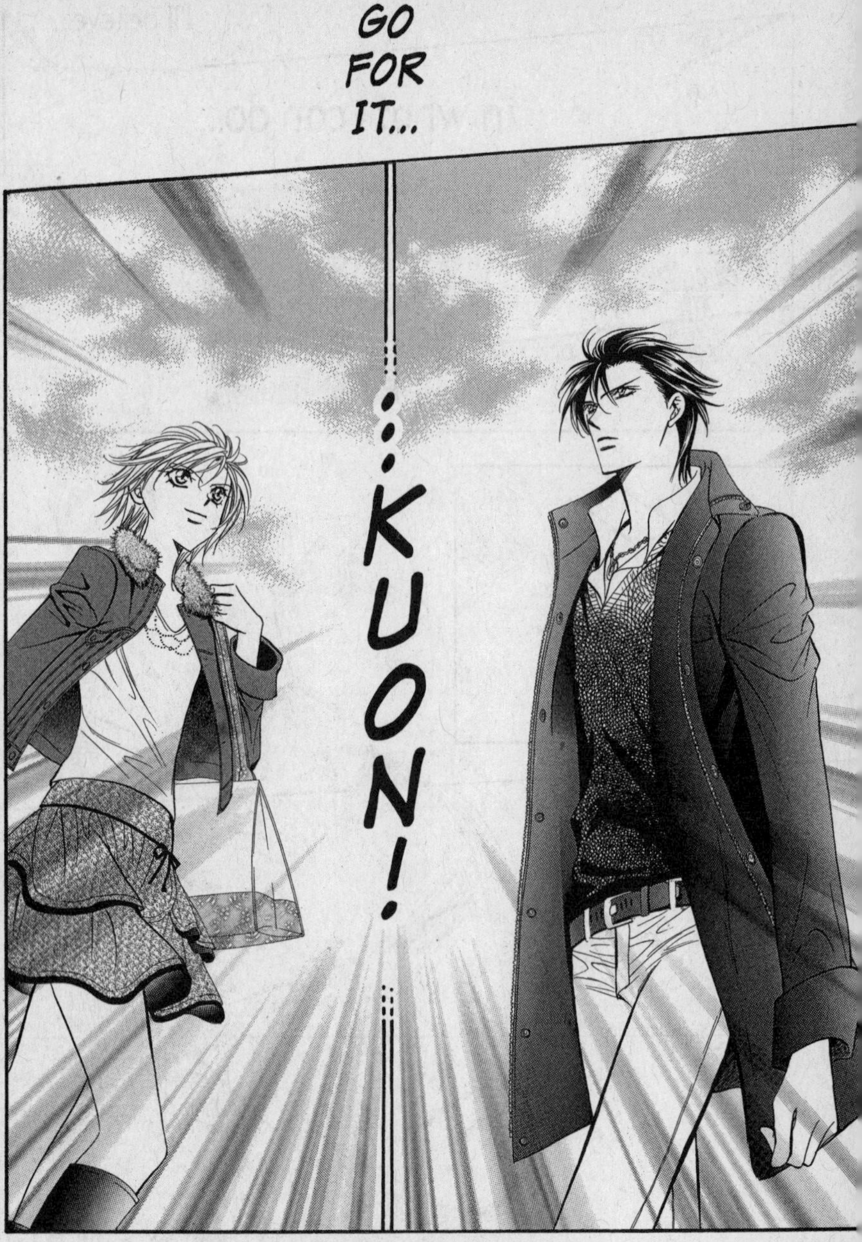
GO FOR IT...
...KUON!

End of Act 114

Skip-Beat! End Notes

Everyone knows how to be a fan, but sometimes cool things
from other cultures need a little help crossing the language barrier.

Page 21, panel 3: Daikon actor
One meaning is similar to that of the phrase "ham actor" in English. In
Japanese, the word used for an actor's success and the way bad food affects
your system is the same—*ataru* or "shock." But daikon is considered a safe
food that will never make you sick, and likewise a daikon actor will never
gain success.

Page 74, panel 3: Kaki no tane
Literally means "persimmon seeds," and here refers to spicy orange crackers
in the shape of persimmon seeds.

Page 93, panel 4: Harakiri
Ritual suicide by slitting the stomach. Traditionally used by samurai to regain
honor in the face of defeat or after some disgrace. It is also known as *seppuku*.

Page 93, panel 4: Second for harakiri
The Japanese is *kaishakunin*, or the person who administered the coup d'
grace by cutting off the head of the person committing harakiri. It was a
trusted position, since otherwise death by harakiri could be a long and
painful affair.

Page 104, panel 4: Teppanyaki
Teppanyaki is a type of Japanese cuisine in which ingredients such as meat,
seafood or vegetables are cooked on an iron griddle, and was introduced
sometime around 1945. The word comes from *teppan* (iron plate) and *yaki*
(grilled).

Page 121, panel 4: Chirashi-zushi
Sushi rice served with thin strips of egg, pieces of raw fish, vegetables and
other things arranged on top. In the U.S., chirashi-zushi is usually served as a
bowl of rice with sashimi on top.

Page 153, panel 2: Faddy
Here Kyoko slips and says *oton*, which is a much more casual way of saying
father. The Kansai dialect is considered more informal than Standard
Japanese.

Page 153, panel 3: Takoyaki maker
Takoyaki are fried octopus balls, a popular street food that originated
in Osaka.

Shojo Beat

Skip·Beat!

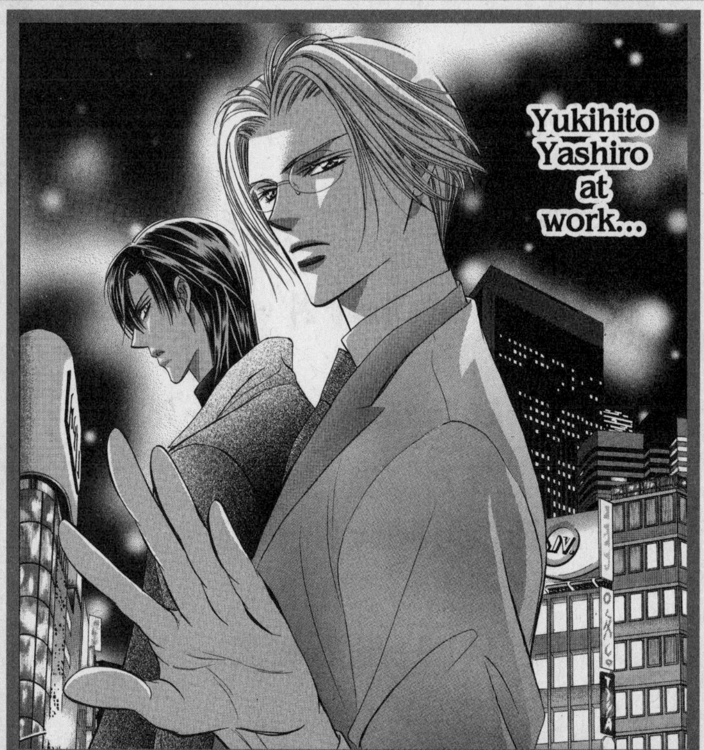
Yukihito Yashiro at work...

Skip·Beat!

Volume 20

CONTENTS

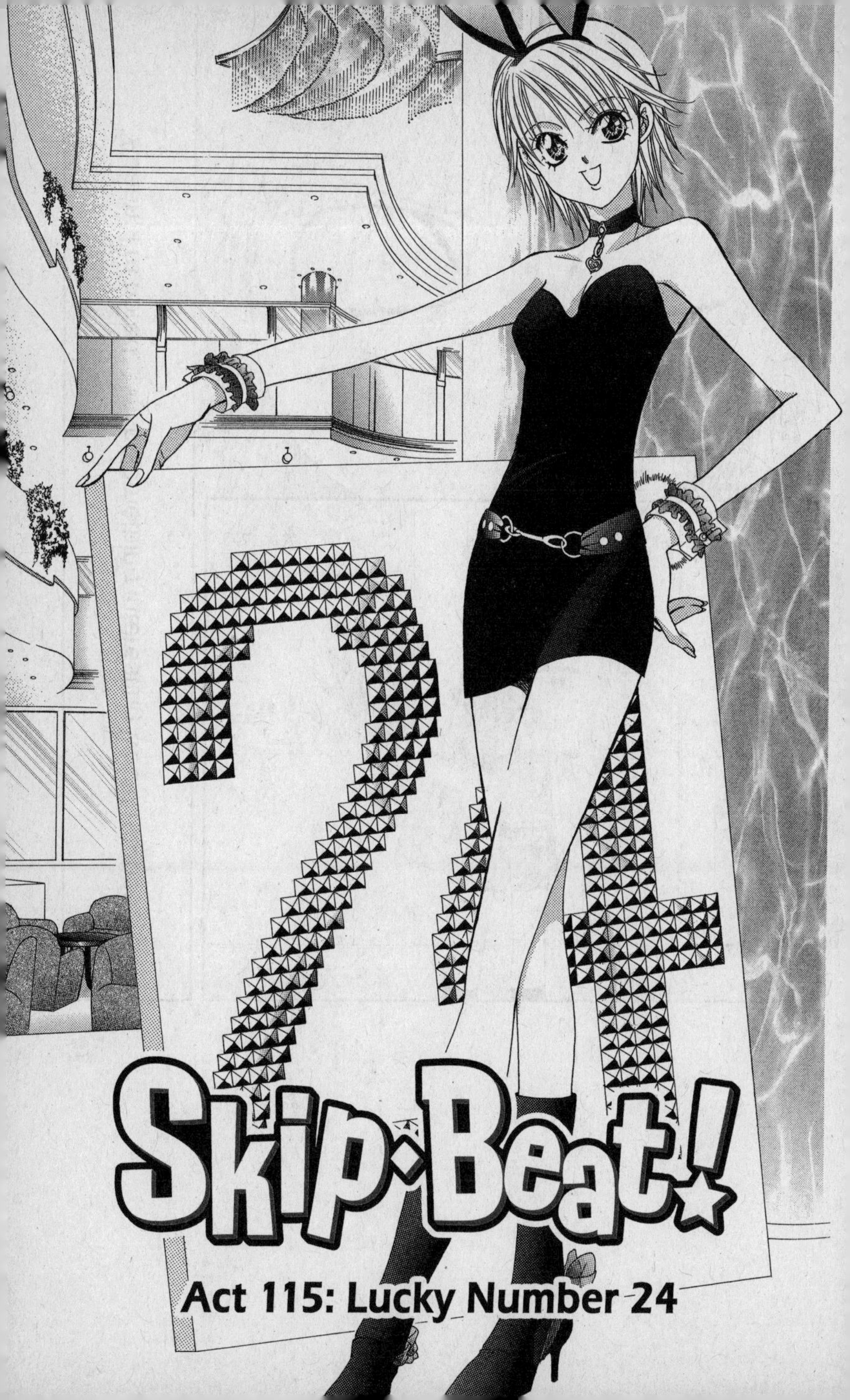
24
Skip·Beat!
Act 115: Lucky Number 24

"Aaaah, I'm bored. I wish something interesting would happen."

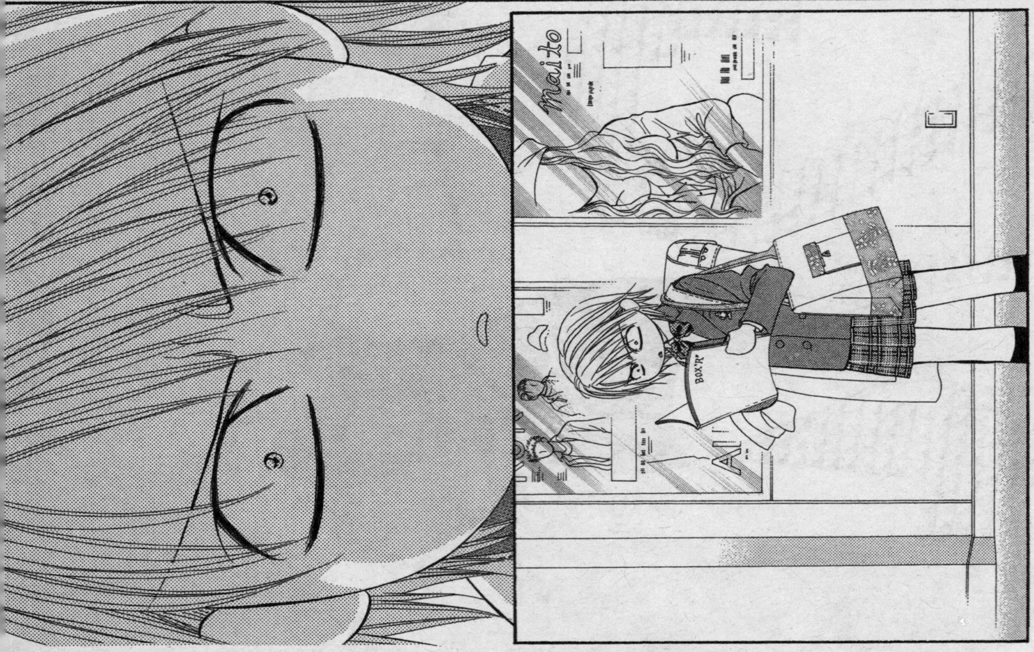

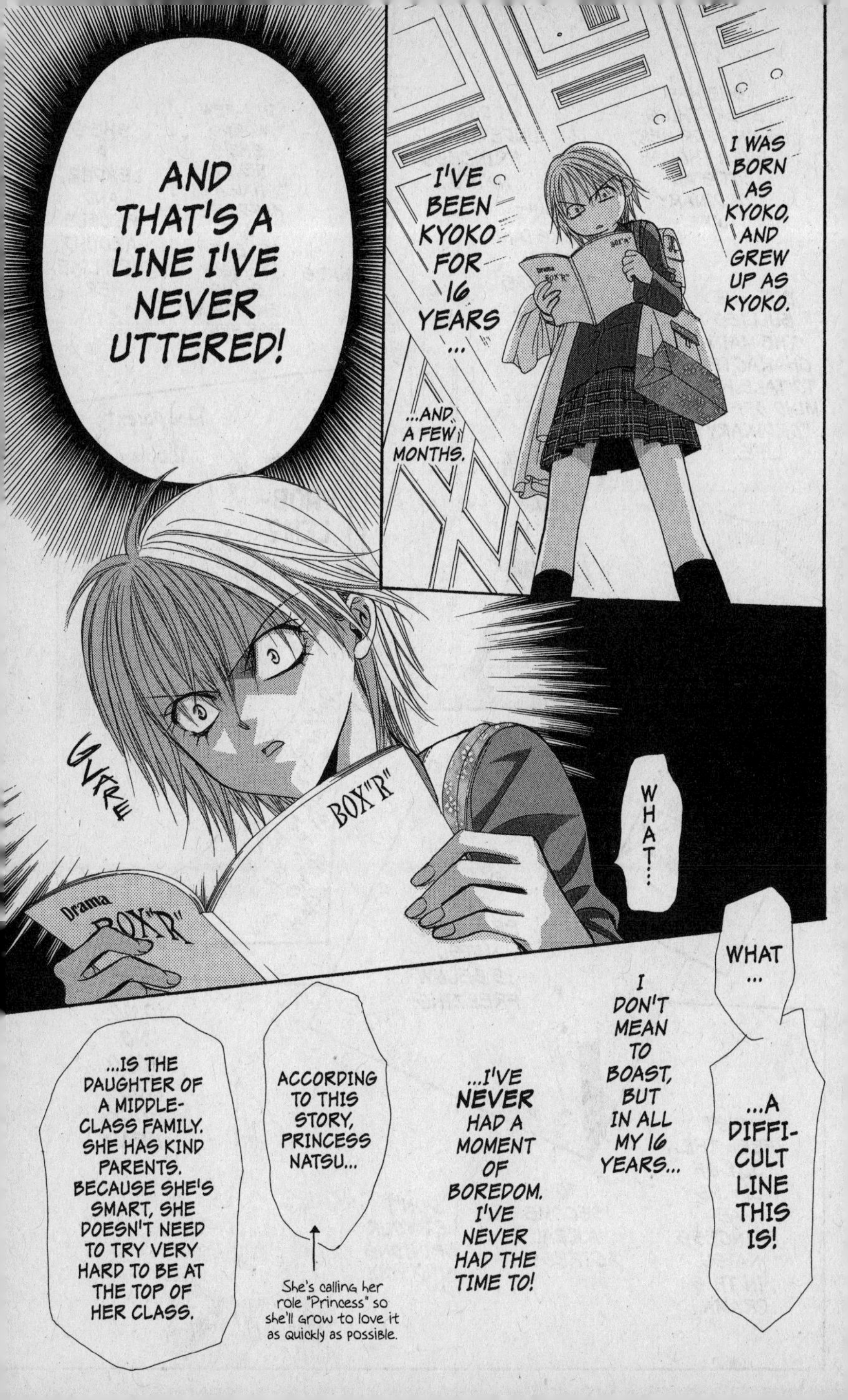
I WAS BORN AS KYOKO, AND GREW UP AS KYOKO.
I'VE BEEN KYOKO FOR 16 YEARS...
...AND A FEW MONTHS.
AND THAT'S A LINE I'VE NEVER UTTERED!
WHAT...
GVARE
BOX"R"
Drama BOX"R"
WHAT...
...A DIFFICULT LINE THIS IS!
I DON'T MEAN TO BOAST, BUT IN ALL MY 16 YEARS...
...I'VE NEVER HAD A MOMENT OF BOREDOM. I'VE NEVER HAD THE TIME TO!
ACCORDING TO THIS STORY, PRINCESS NATSU...
She's calling her role "Princess" so she'll grow to love it as quickly as possible.
...IS THE DAUGHTER OF A MIDDLE-CLASS FAMILY. SHE HAS KIND PARENTS. BECAUSE SHE'S SMART, SHE DOESN'T NEED TO TRY VERY HARD TO BE AT THE TOP OF HER CLASS.

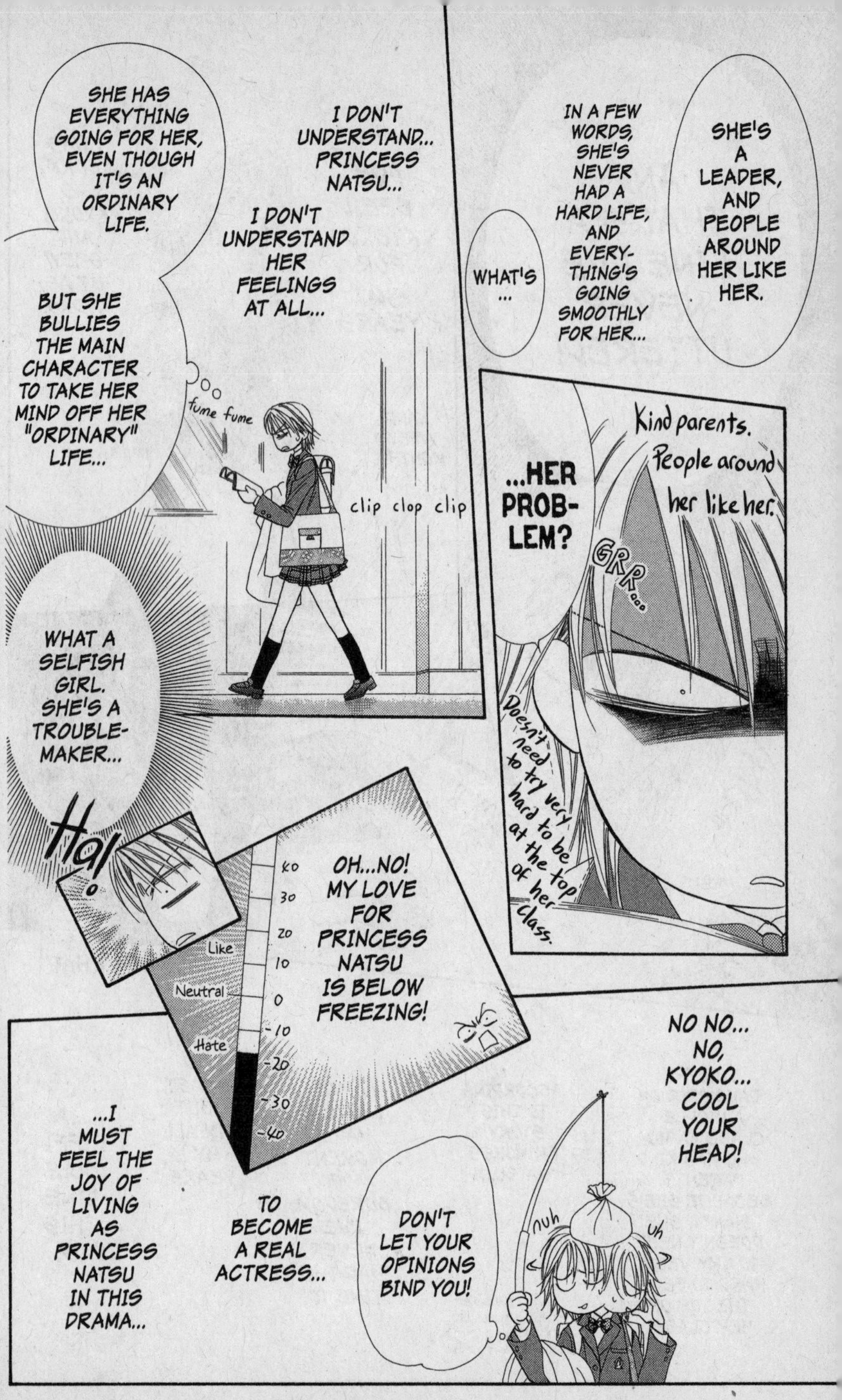
SHE'S A LEADER, AND PEOPLE AROUND HER LIKE HER.
IN A FEW WORDS, SHE'S NEVER HAD A HARD LIFE, AND EVERY-THING'S GOING SMOOTHLY FOR HER...
WHAT'S...
I DON'T UNDERSTAND... PRINCESS NATSU...
I DON'T UNDERSTAND HER FEELINGS AT ALL...
SHE HAS EVERYTHING GOING FOR HER, EVEN THOUGH IT'S AN ORDINARY LIFE.
BUT SHE BULLIES THE MAIN CHARACTER TO TAKE HER MIND OFF HER "ORDINARY" LIFE...
Kind parents. People around her like her.
...HER PROB-LEM?
GRR...
Doesn't need to try very hard to be at the top of her class.
fume fume
clip clop clip
WHAT A SELFISH GIRL. SHE'S A TROUBLE-MAKER...
Ha!
40
30
20
10
0
-10
-20
-30
-40
Like
Neutral
Hate
OH...NO! MY LOVE FOR PRINCESS NATSU IS BELOW FREEZING!
NO NO... NO, KYOKO... COOL YOUR HEAD!
nuh uh
DON'T LET YOUR OPINIONS BIND YOU!
TO BECOME A REAL ACTRESS...
...I MUST FEEL THE JOY OF LIVING AS PRINCESS NATSU IN THIS DRAMA...

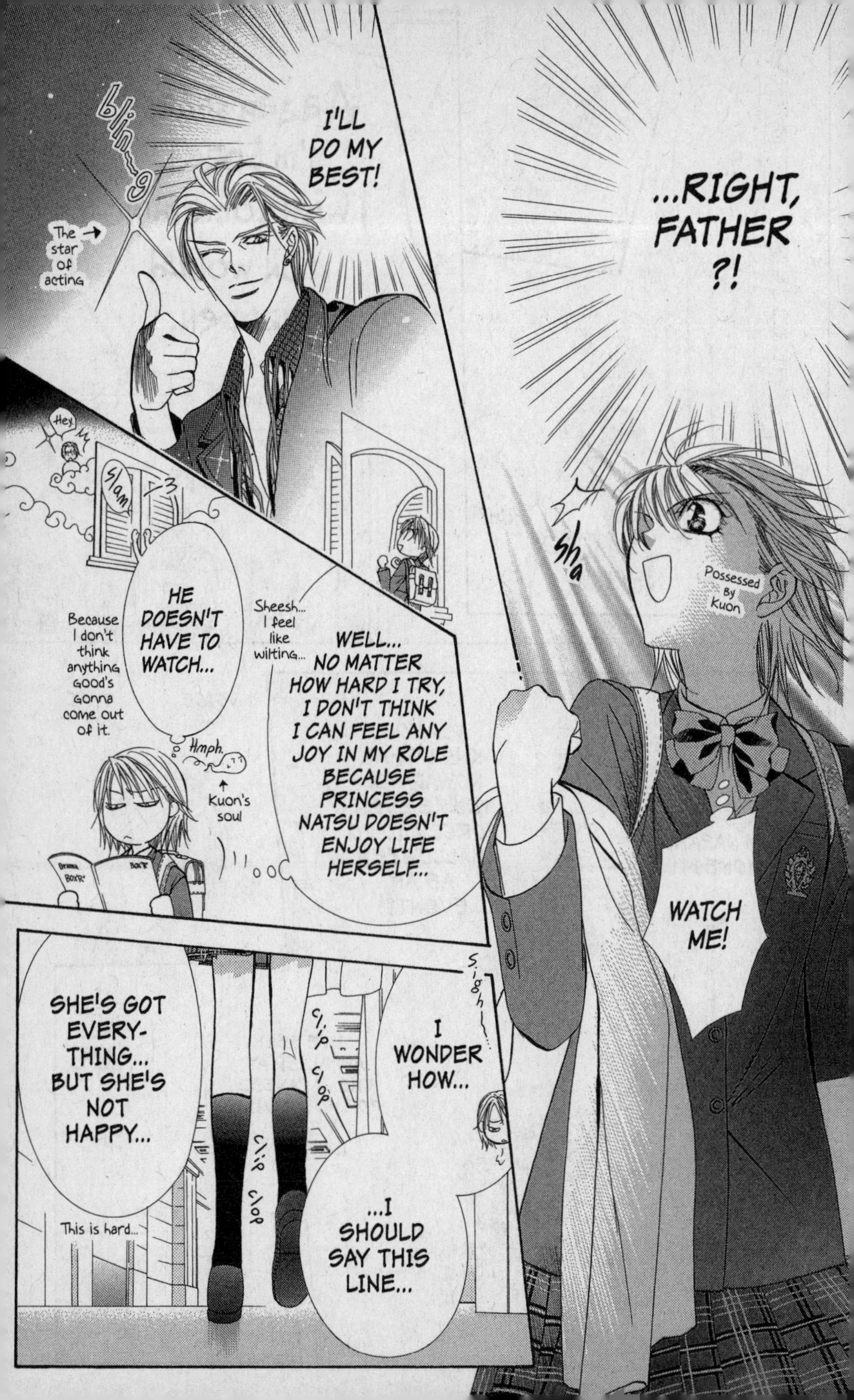
...RIGHT, FATHER ?!
sha
Possessed By Kuon
WATCH ME!
I'LL DO MY BEST!
blin~g
The star of acting
Sheesh... I feel like wilting...
WELL... NO MATTER HOW HARD I TRY, I DON'T THINK I CAN FEEL ANY JOY IN MY ROLE BECAUSE PRINCESS NATSU DOESN'T ENJOY LIFE HERSELF...
slam
Hey.
HE DOESN'T HAVE TO WATCH...
Because I don't think anything good's gonna come out of it.
Hmph.
Kuon's soul
Sigh
I WONDER HOW...
...I SHOULD SAY THIS LINE...
clip clop
clip clop
SHE'S GOT EVERY-THING... BUT SHE'S NOT HAPPY...
This is hard...

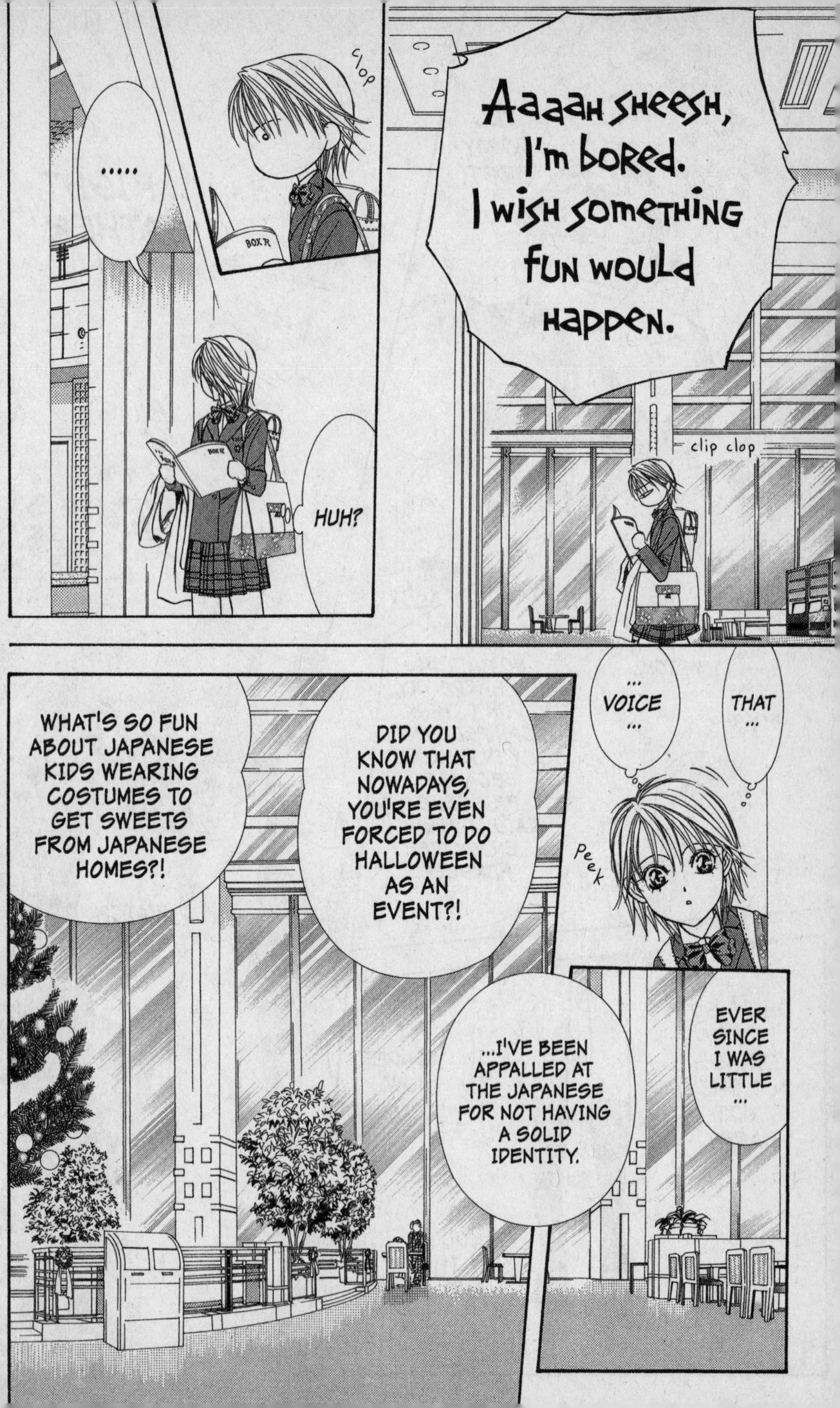
Aaaah sheesh, I'm bored. I wish something fun would happen.
clip clop
clop
.....
BOX R
HUH?
THAT ...
... VOICE ...
Peek
EVER SINCE I WAS LITTLE ...
...I'VE BEEN APPALLED AT THE JAPANESE FOR NOT HAVING A SOLID IDENTITY.
DID YOU KNOW THAT NOWADAYS, YOU'RE EVEN FORCED TO DO HALLOWEEN AS AN EVENT?!
WHAT'S SO FUN ABOUT JAPANESE KIDS WEARING COSTUMES TO GET SWEETS FROM JAPANESE HOMES?!

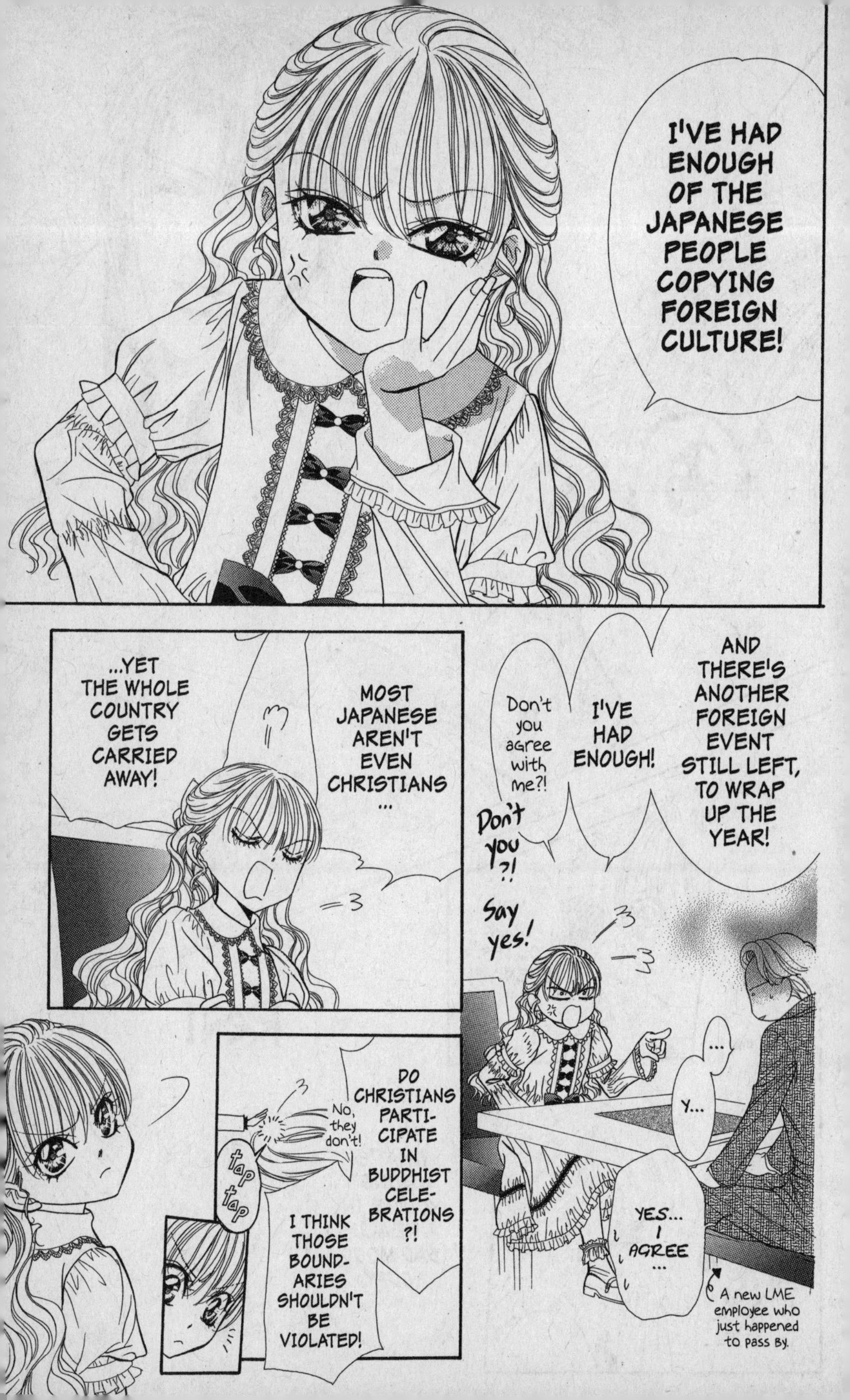
I'VE HAD ENOUGH OF THE JAPANESE PEOPLE COPYING FOREIGN CULTURE!
AND THERE'S ANOTHER FOREIGN EVENT STILL LEFT, TO WRAP UP THE YEAR!
I'VE HAD ENOUGH!
Don't you agree with me?!
Don't you?!
Say yes!
...
Y...
YES... I AGREE ...
A new LME employee who just happened to pass by.
MOST JAPANESE AREN'T EVEN CHRISTIANS ...
...YET THE WHOLE COUNTRY GETS CARRIED AWAY!
DO CHRISTIANS PARTICIPATE IN BUDDHIST CELEBRATIONS?!
No, they don't!
tap tap
I THINK THOSE BOUNDARIES SHOULDN'T BE VIOLATED!

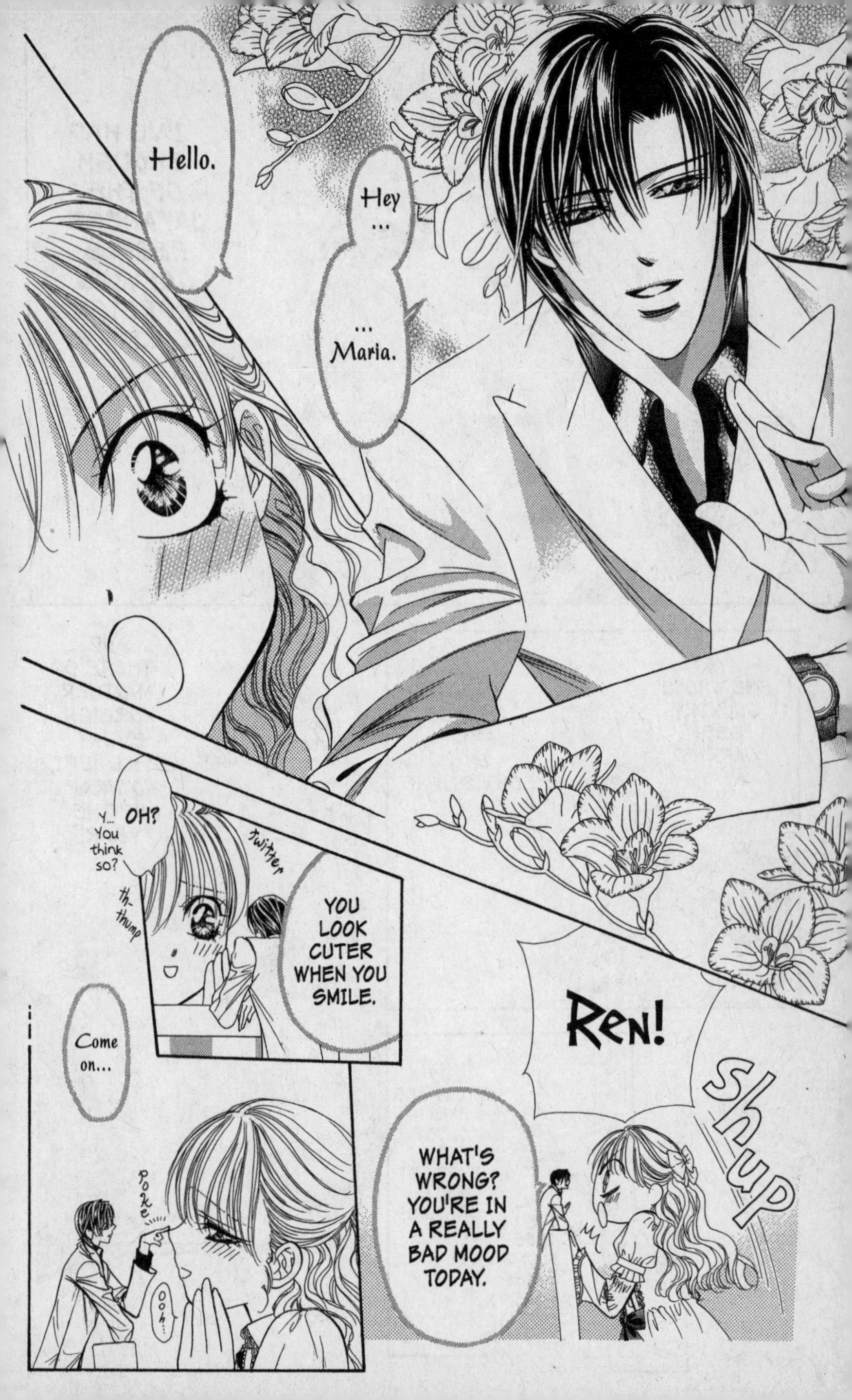

Hey ... ... Maria.
Hello.
Ren!
Shup
WHAT'S WRONG? YOU'RE IN A REALLY BAD MOOD TODAY.
YOU LOOK CUTER WHEN YOU SMILE.
OH?
Y... You think so?
twitter
th-thump
Come on...
poke
Ooh...

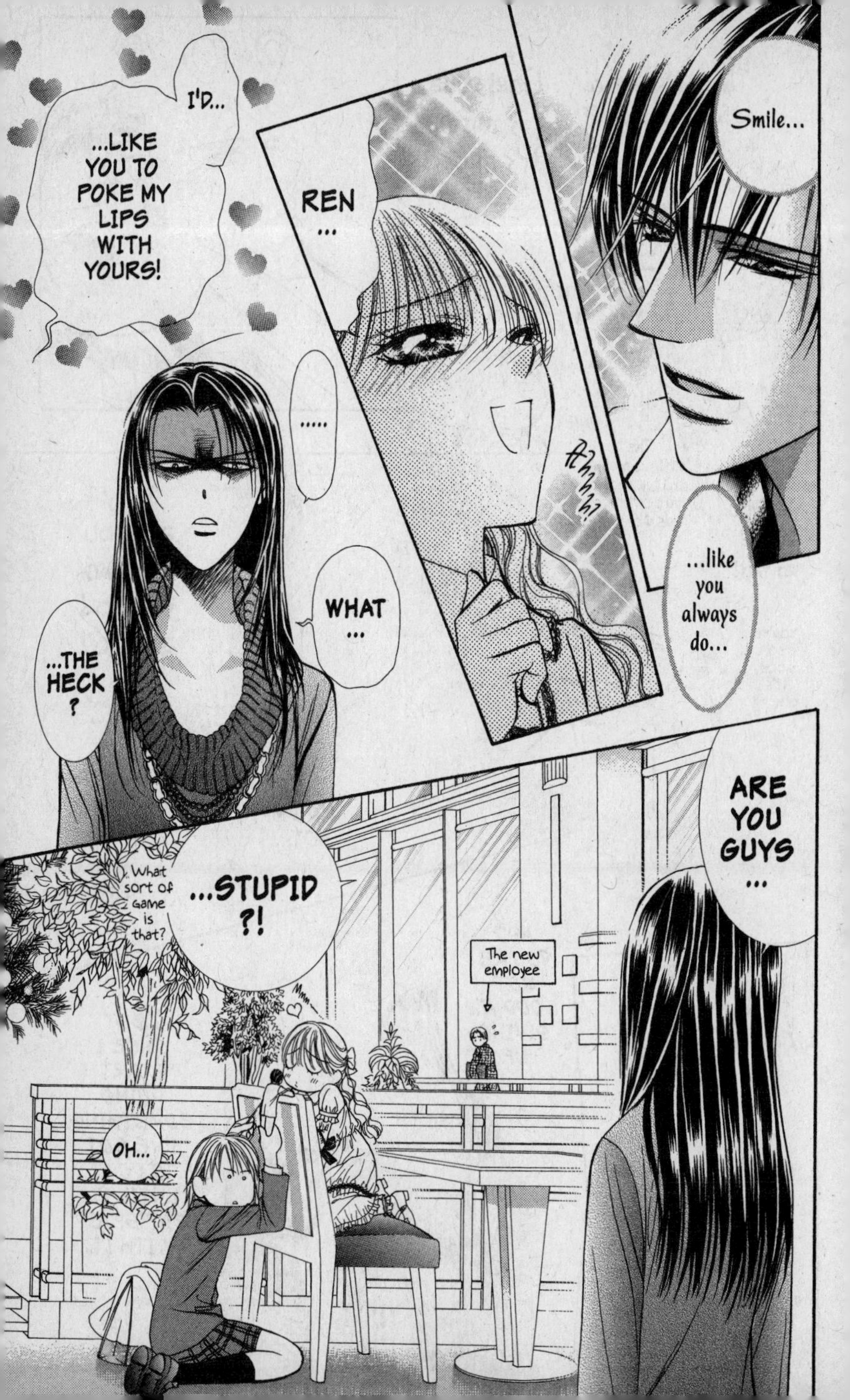
Smile...
...like you always do...
REN...
I'D...
...LIKE YOU TO POKE MY LIPS WITH YOURS!
.....
WHAT...
...THE HECK?
ARE YOU GUYS...
...STUPID?!
What sort of Game is that?
The new employee
Mmm
OH...

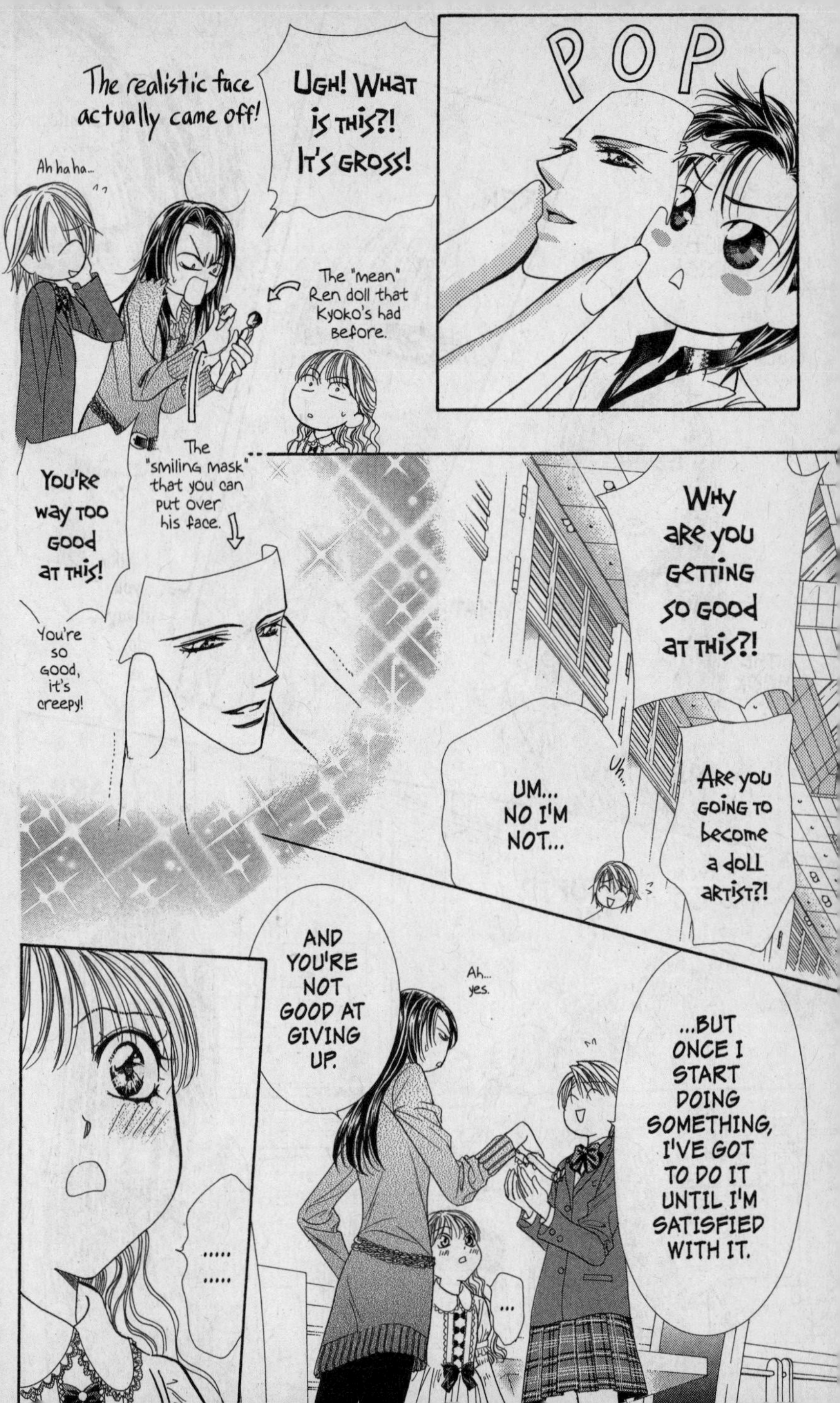
POP
UGH! WHAT IS THIS?! IT'S GROSS!
The realistic face actually came off!
Ah ha ha...
The "mean" Ren doll that Kyoko's had before.
The "smiling mask" that you can put over his face.
WHY are you GETTING SO GOOD AT THIS?!
Are you GOING TO become a doll ARTIST?!
Uh...
UM... NO I'M NOT...
YOU'RE way TOO GOOD AT THIS!
You're so good, it's creepy!
...BUT ONCE I START DOING SOMETHING, I'VE GOT TO DO IT UNTIL I'M SATISFIED WITH IT.
Ah... yes.
AND YOU'RE NOT GOOD AT GIVING UP.
...
....

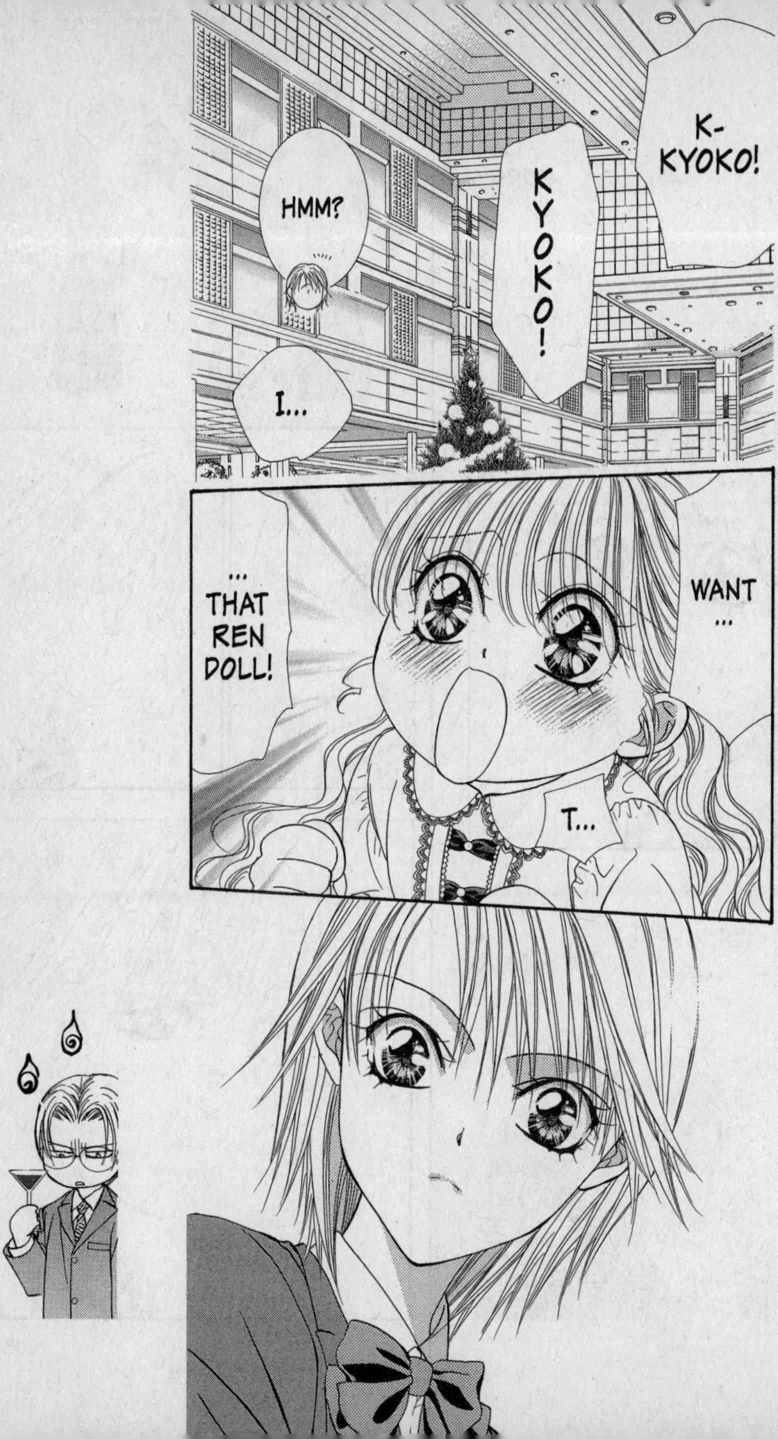
K-KYOKO!
KYOKO!
HMM?
I...
WANT ...
T...
... THAT REN DOLL!

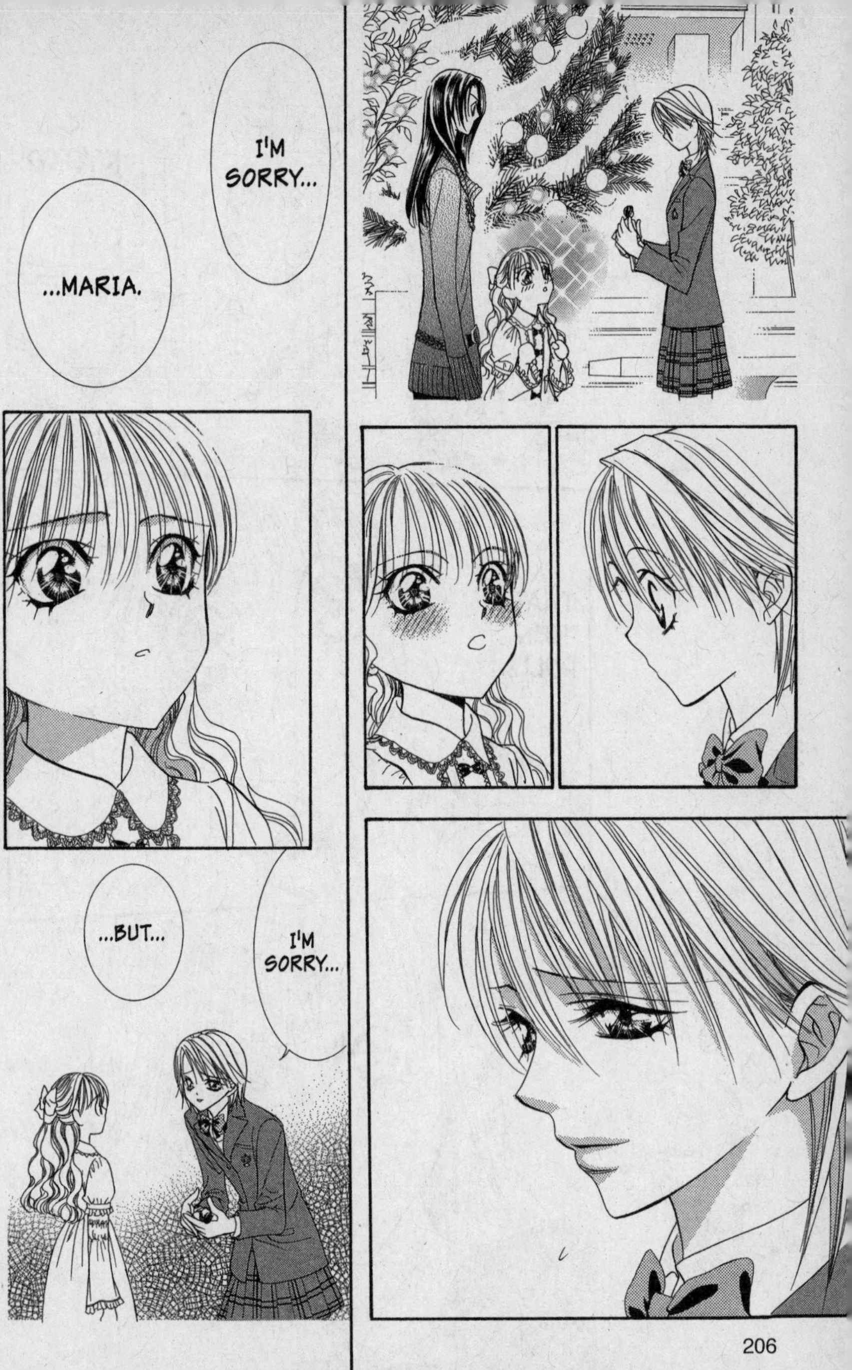
I'M SORRY...
...MARIA.
I'M SORRY...
...BUT...

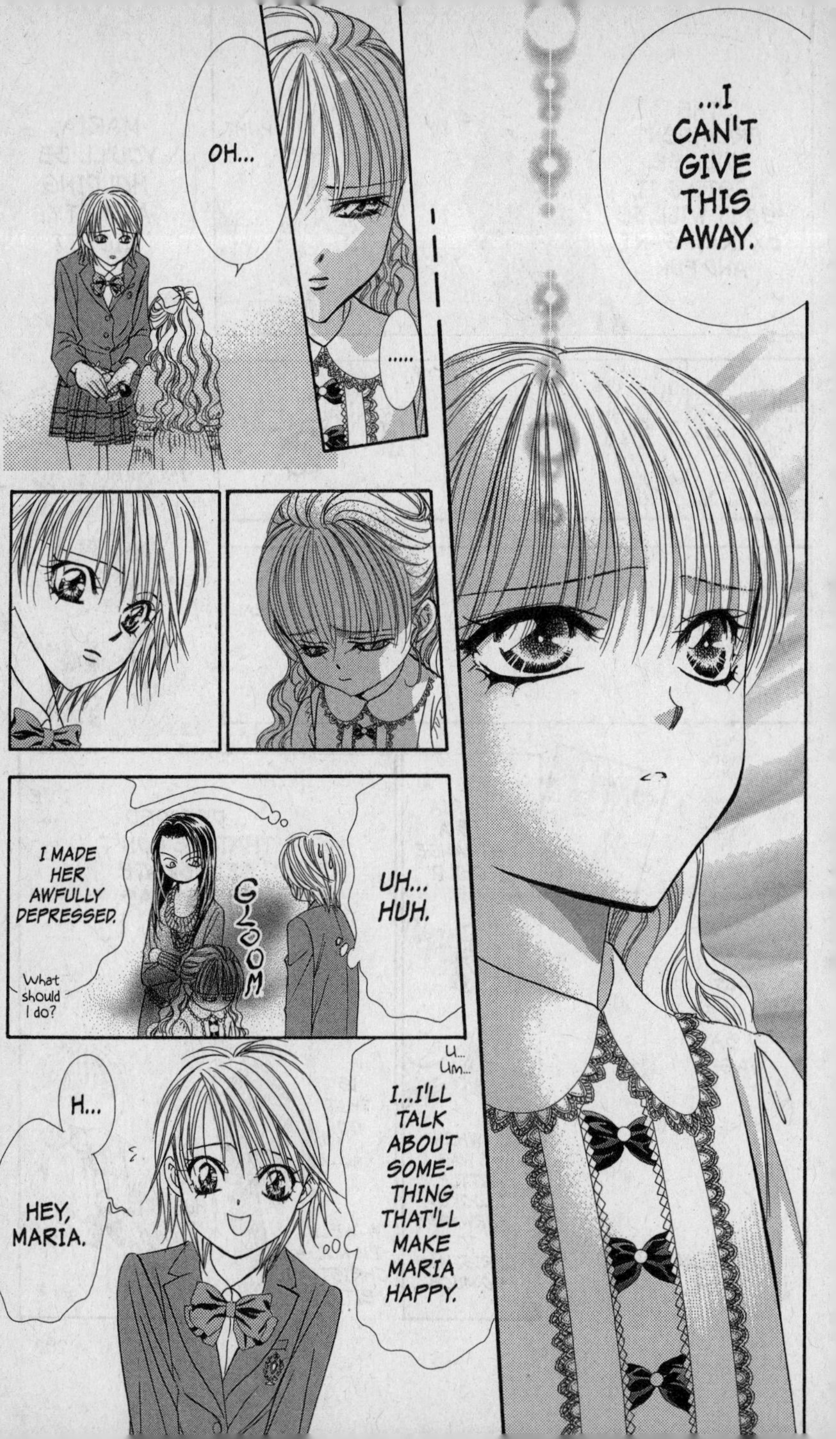
...I CAN'T GIVE THIS AWAY.
.....
OH...
UH... HUH.
GLOOM
I MADE HER AWFULLY DEPRESSED.
What should I do?
U... Um...
I...I'LL TALK ABOUT SOME-THING THAT'LL MAKE MARIA HAPPY.
H...
HEY, MARIA.

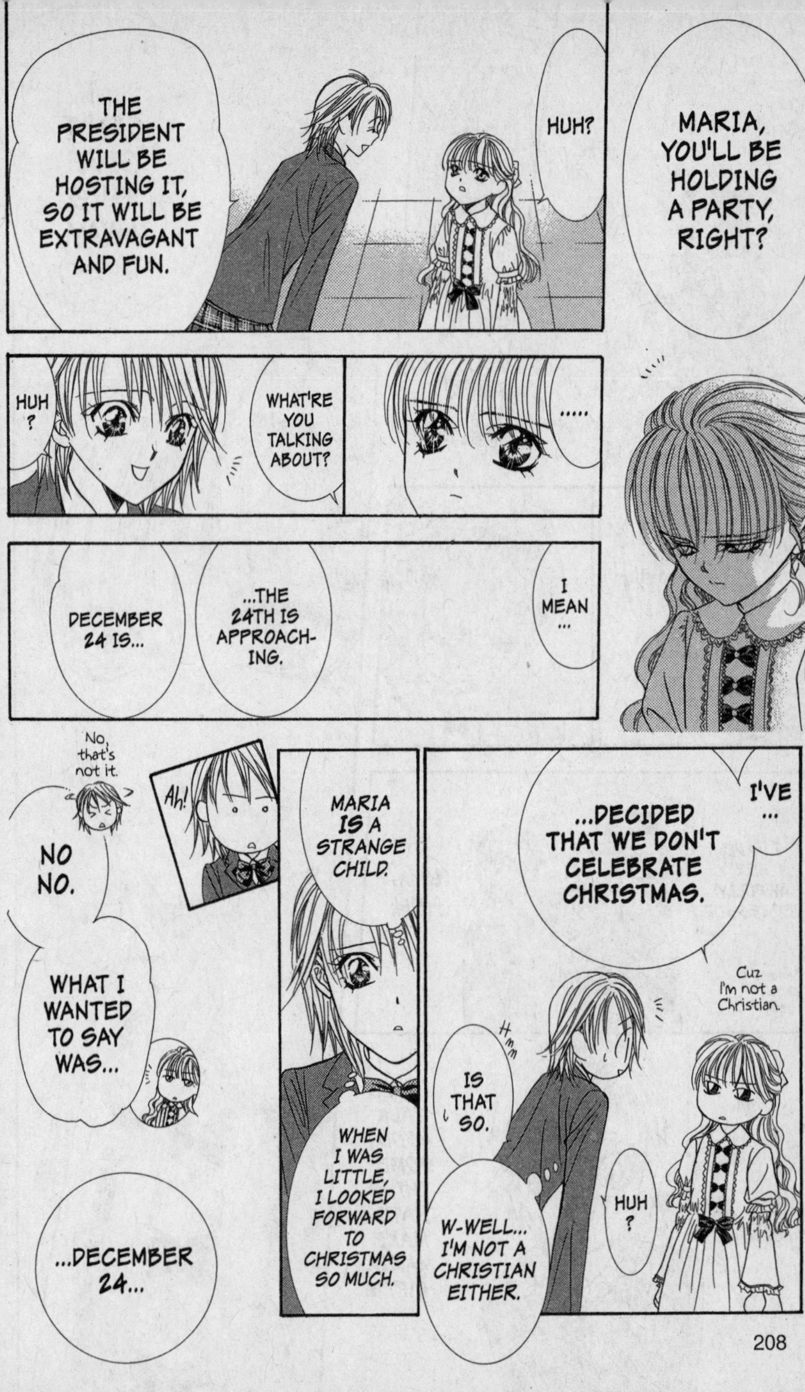
MARIA, YOU'LL BE HOLDING A PARTY, RIGHT?
HUH?
THE PRESIDENT WILL BE HOSTING IT, SO IT WILL BE EXTRAVAGANT AND FUN.
.....
WHAT'RE YOU TALKING ABOUT?
HUH ?
I MEAN ...
...THE 24TH IS APPROACH-ING.
DECEMBER 24 IS...
I'VE ...
...DECIDED THAT WE DON'T CELEBRATE CHRISTMAS.
Cuz I'm not a Christian.
Hmm
IS THAT SO.
HUH ?
W-WELL... I'M NOT A CHRISTIAN EITHER.
MARIA IS A STRANGE CHILD.
WHEN I WAS LITTLE, I LOOKED FORWARD TO CHRISTMAS SO MUCH.
Ah!
No, that's not it.
NO NO.
WHAT I WANTED TO SAY WAS...
...DECEMBER 24...

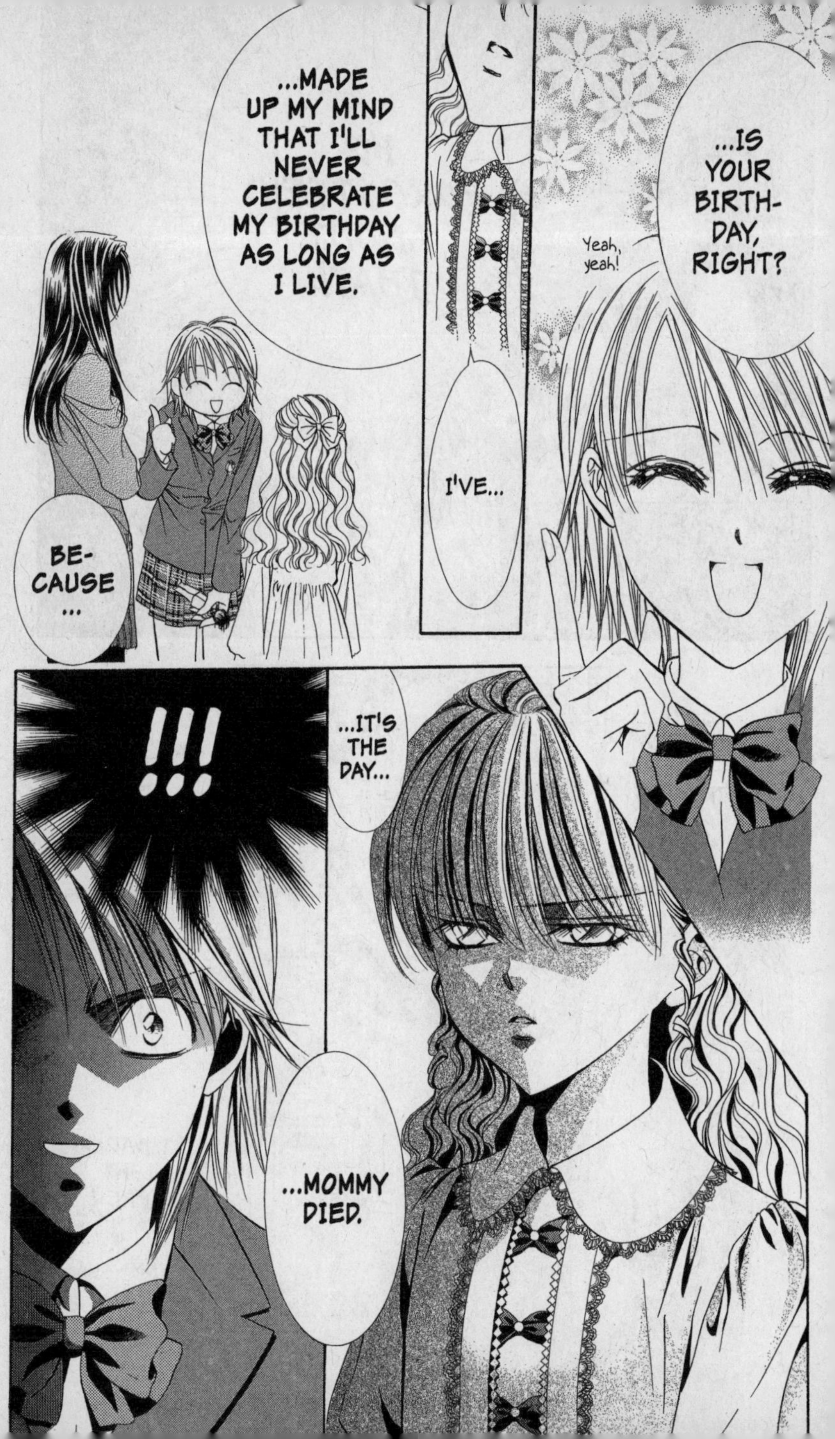
...IS YOUR BIRTH-DAY, RIGHT?
Yeah, yeah!
I'VE...
...MADE UP MY MIND THAT I'LL NEVER CELEBRATE MY BIRTHDAY AS LONG AS I LIVE.
BE-CAUSE...
...IT'S THE DAY...
...MOMMY DIED.
!!!

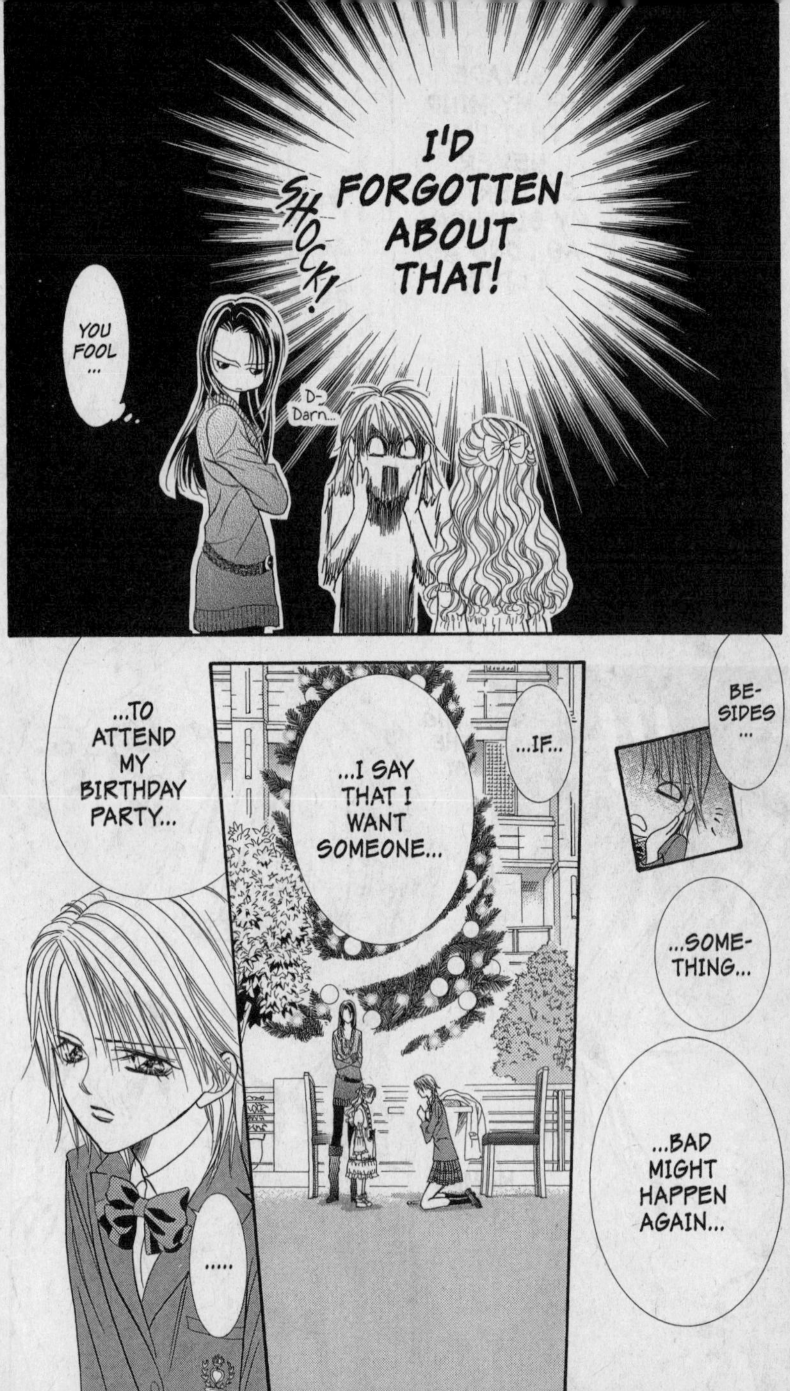
I'D FORGOTTEN ABOUT THAT!
SHOCK!
D-Darn...
YOU FOOL...
BE-SIDES...
...IF...
...I SAY THAT I WANT SOMEONE...
...TO ATTEND MY BIRTHDAY PARTY...
...SOME-THING...
...BAD MIGHT HAPPEN AGAIN...
.....

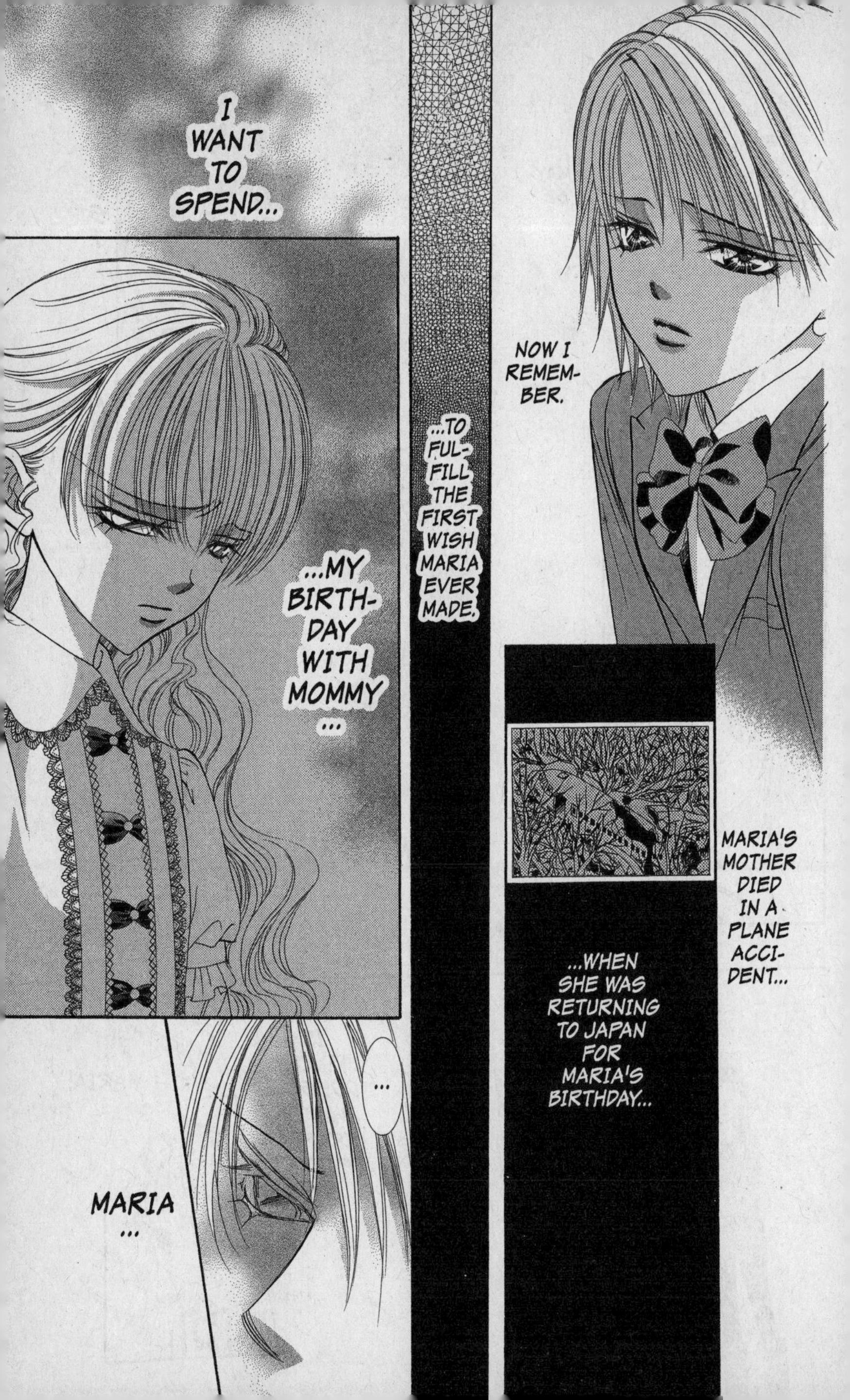
NOW I REMEMBER.
MARIA'S MOTHER DIED IN A PLANE ACCIDENT...
...WHEN SHE WAS RETURNING TO JAPAN FOR MARIA'S BIRTHDAY...
...TO FULFILL THE FIRST WISH MARIA EVER MADE.
I WANT TO SPEND...
...MY BIRTHDAY WITH MOMMY...
...
MARIA...

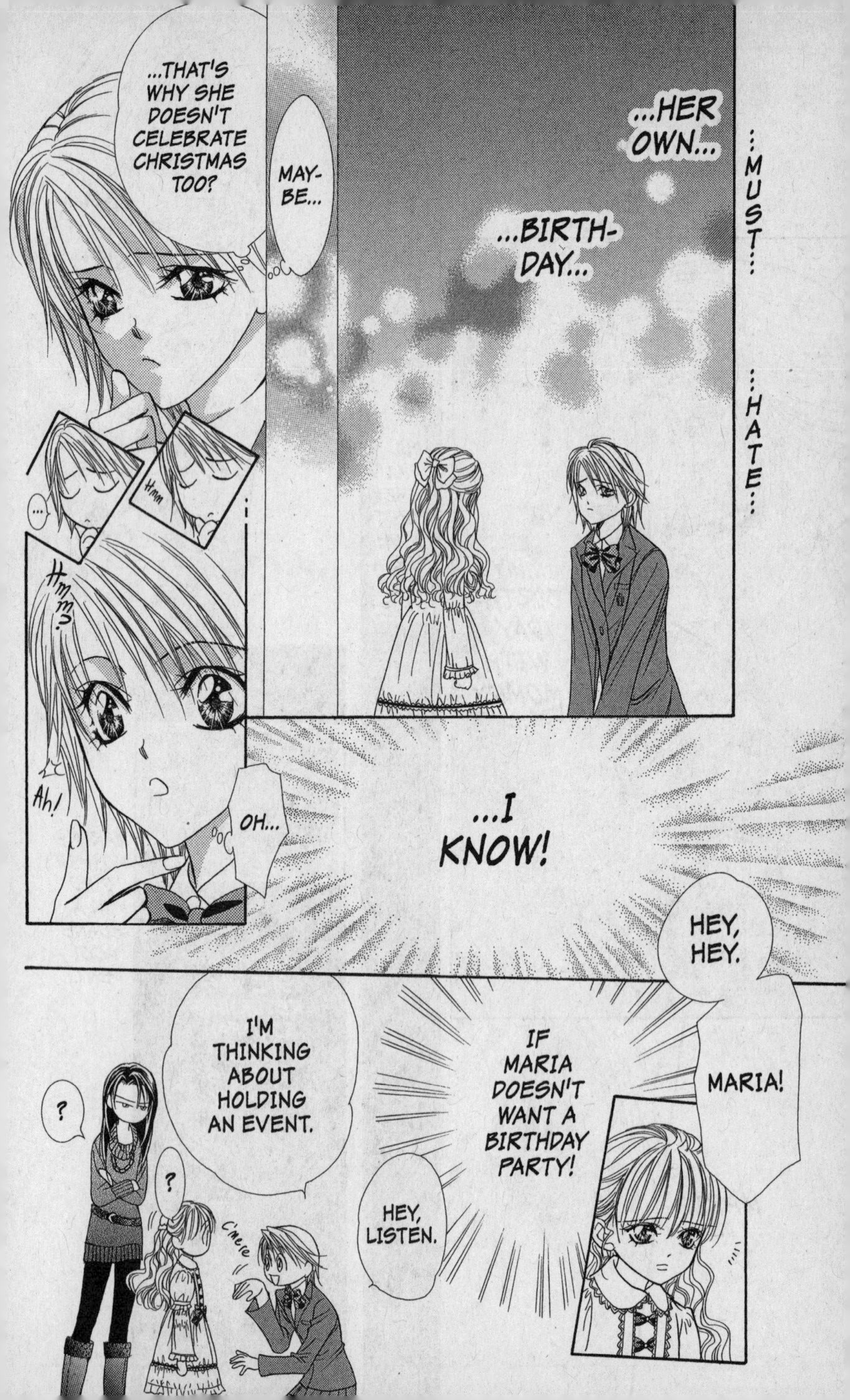
...MUST...
...HATE...
...HER OWN...
...BIRTH-DAY...
...THAT'S WHY SHE DOESN'T CELEBRATE CHRISTMAS TOO?
MAY-BE...
...
Hmm
Hmm?
Ah!
OH...
...I KNOW!
HEY, HEY.
MARIA!
IF MARIA DOESN'T WANT A BIRTHDAY PARTY!
HEY, LISTEN.
I'M THINKING ABOUT HOLDING AN EVENT.
C'mere
?
?

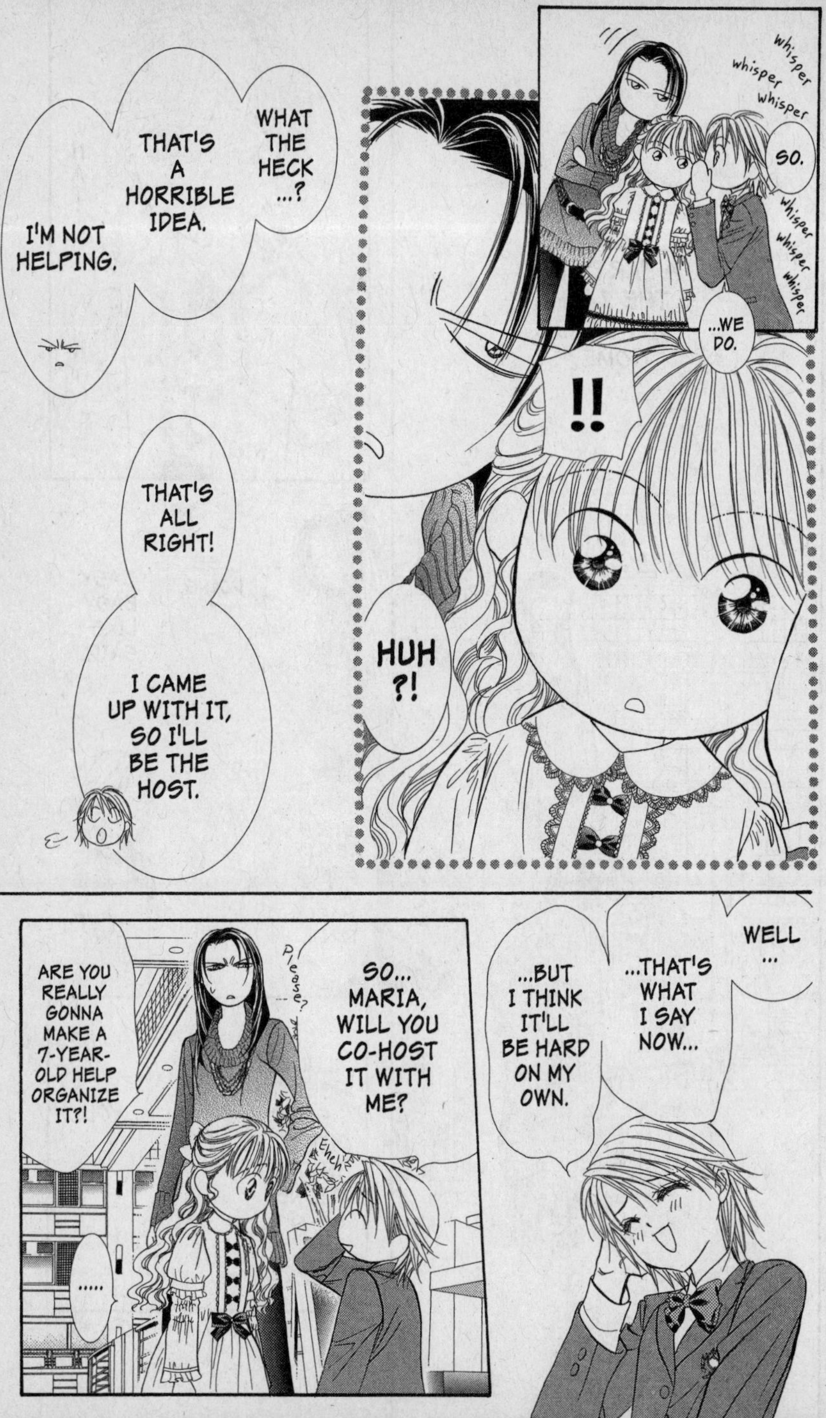
whisper whisper whisper
SO.
whisper whisper whisper
...WE DO.
!!
HUH?!
WHAT THE HECK...?
THAT'S A HORRIBLE IDEA.
I'M NOT HELPING.
THAT'S ALL RIGHT!
I CAME UP WITH IT, SO I'LL BE THE HOST.
WELL...
...THAT'S WHAT I SAY NOW...
...BUT I THINK IT'LL BE HARD ON MY OWN.
SO... MARIA, WILL YOU CO-HOST IT WITH ME?
Please?
Eheh
ARE YOU REALLY GONNA MAKE A 7-YEAR-OLD HELP ORGANIZE IT?!
.....

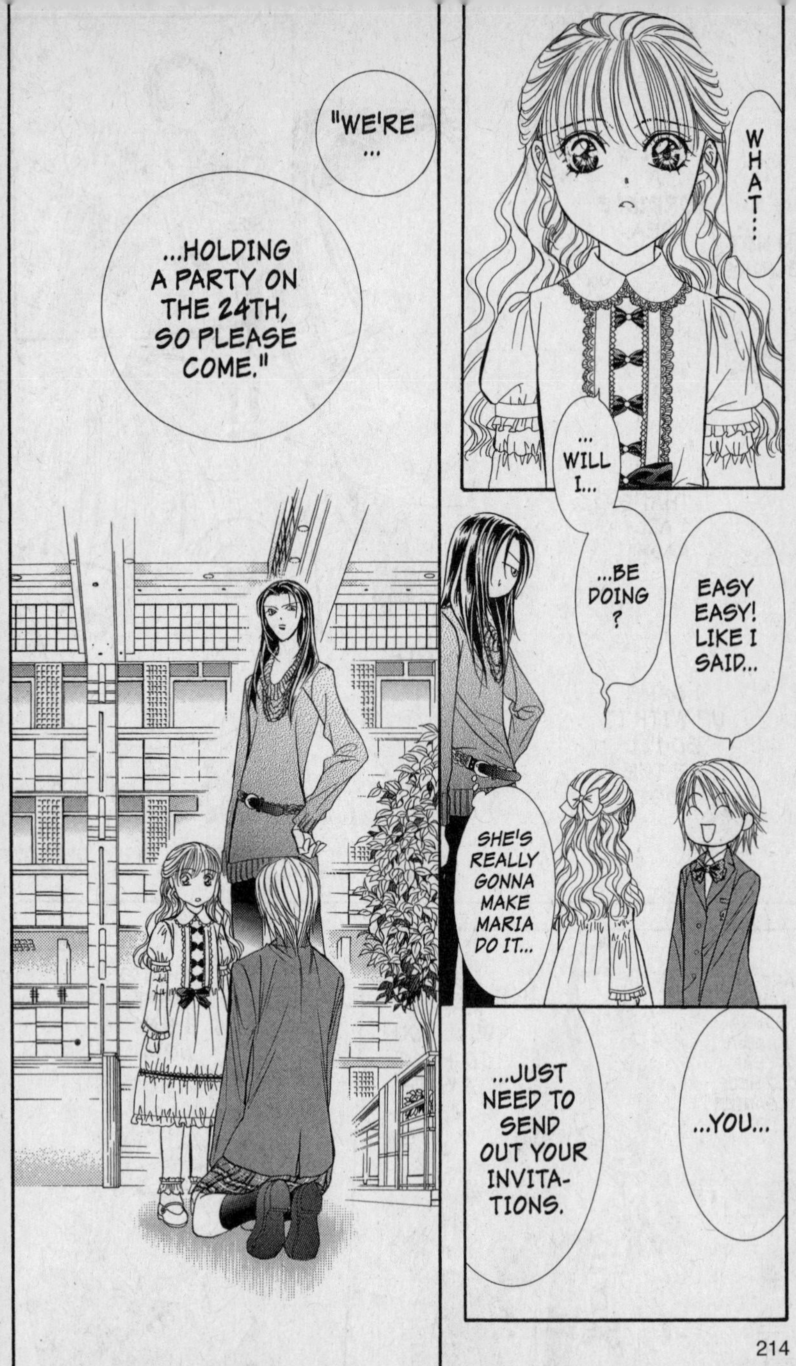
WHAT...
...WILL I...
...BE DOING?
EASY EASY! LIKE I SAID...
SHE'S REALLY GONNA MAKE MARIA DO IT...
...YOU...
...JUST NEED TO SEND OUT YOUR INVITATIONS.
"WE'RE ...
...HOLDING A PARTY ON THE 24TH, SO PLEASE COME."

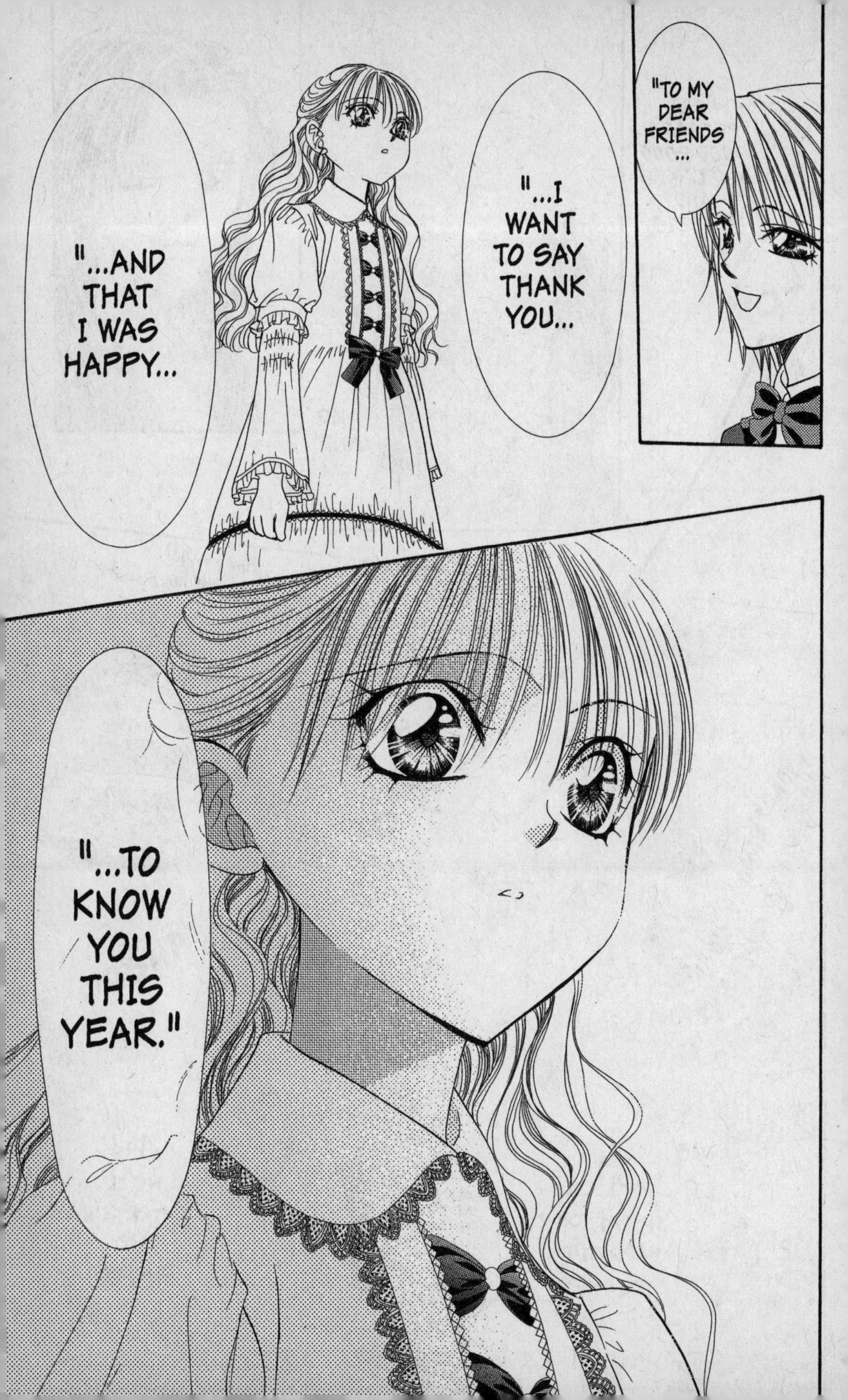
"TO MY DEAR FRIENDS...
"...I WANT TO SAY THANK YOU...
"...AND THAT I WAS HAPPY...
"...TO KNOW YOU THIS YEAR."

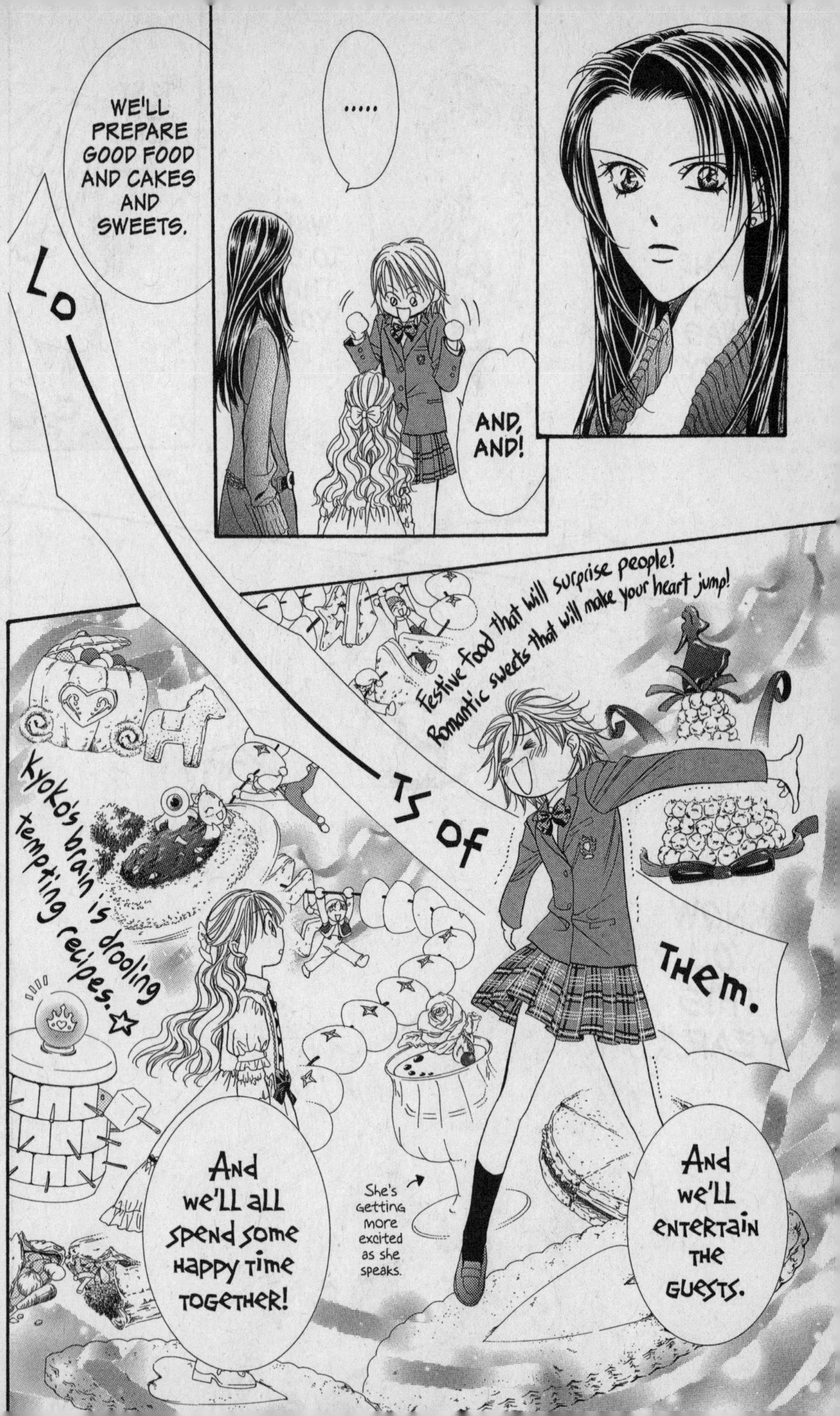
.....
AND, AND!
WE'LL PREPARE GOOD FOOD AND CAKES AND SWEETS.
LO
TS OF
THEM.
Festive food that will surprise people!
Romantic sweets that will make your heart jump!
And we'll entertain the guests.
She's getting more excited as she speaks.
And we'll all spend some happy time together!
Kyoko's brain is drooling tempting recipes.☆

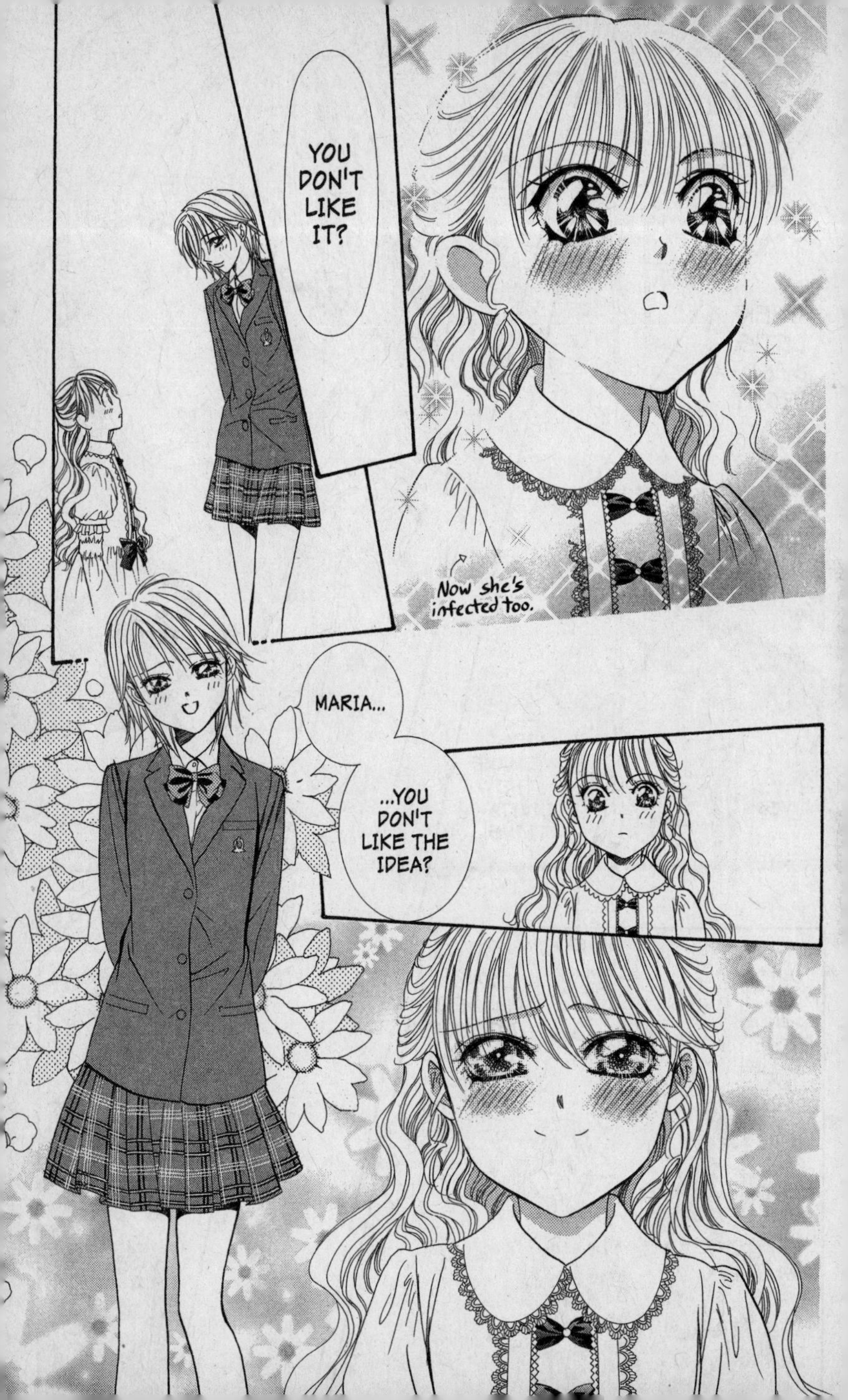
Now she's infected too.
YOU DON'T LIKE IT?
MARIA...
...YOU DON'T LIKE THE IDEA?

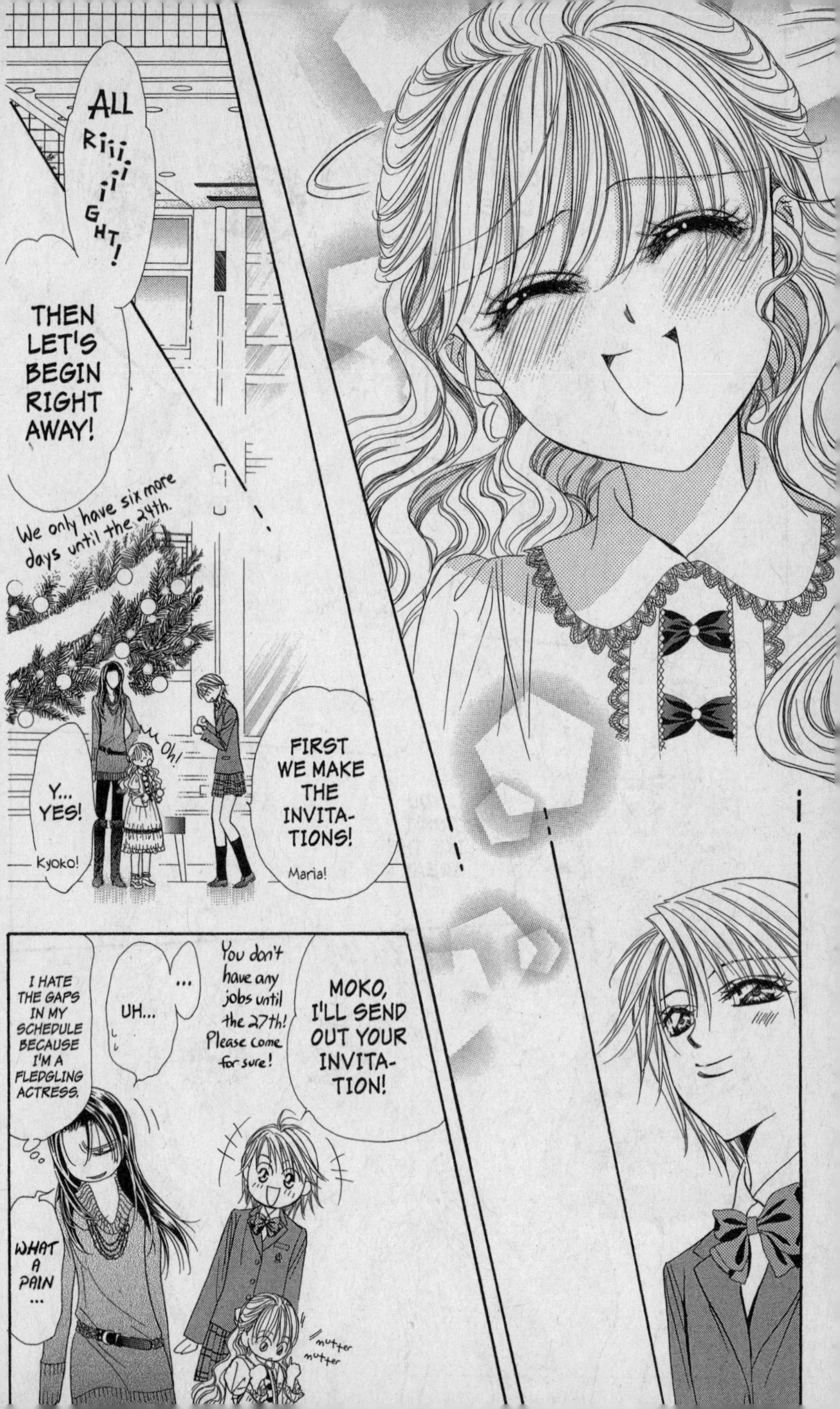
ALL RIIIIIGHT!
THEN LET'S BEGIN RIGHT AWAY!
We only have six more days until the 24th.
FIRST WE MAKE THE INVITATIONS!
Maria!
Oh!
Y... YES!
Kyoko!
MOKO, I'LL SEND OUT YOUR INVITATION!
You don't have any jobs until the 27th! Please come for sure!
...
UH...
I HATE THE GAPS IN MY SCHEDULE BECAUSE I'M A FLEDGLING ACTRESS.
WHAT A PAIN...
mutter mutter

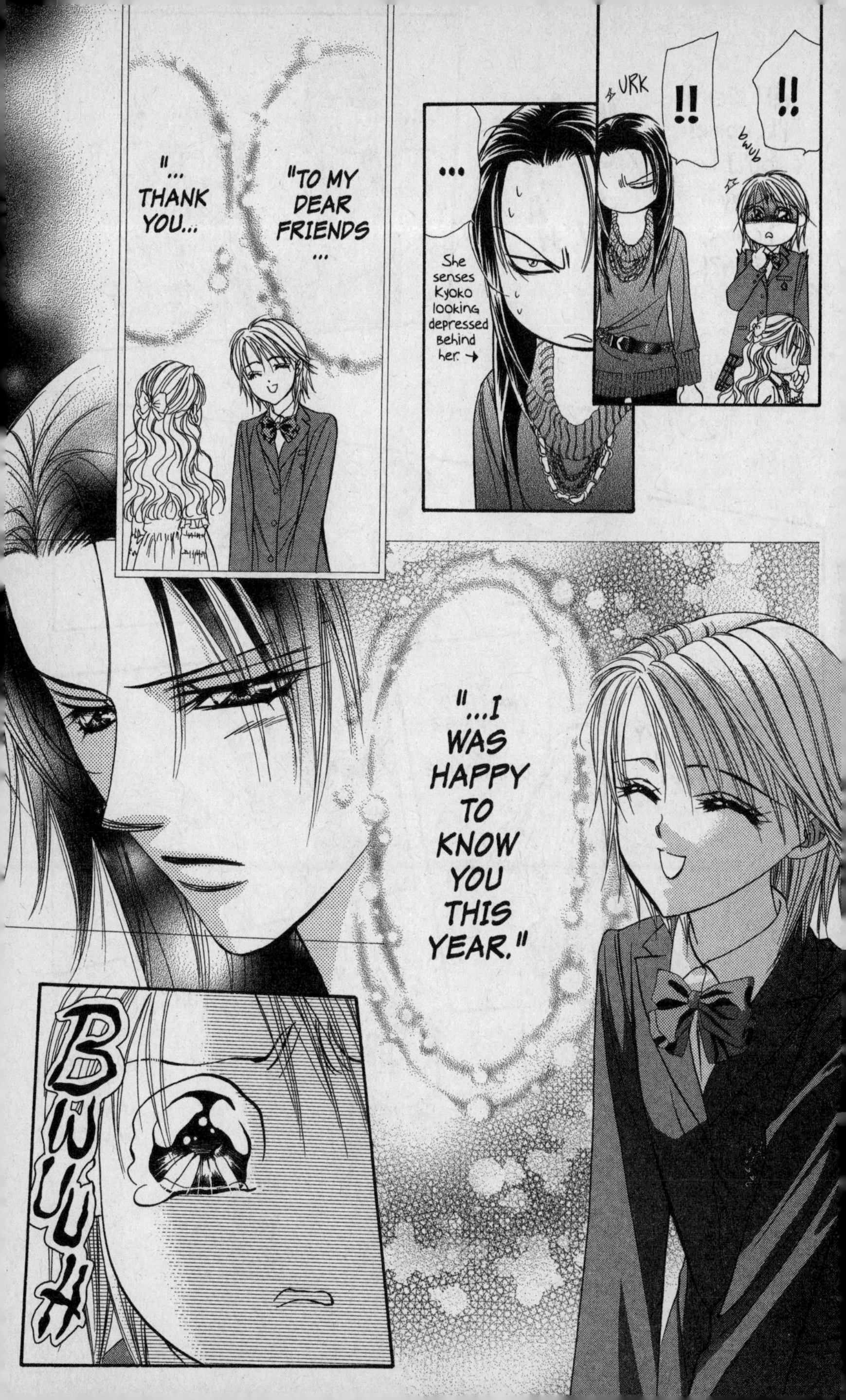

!!
!!
URK
bwub
...
She senses Kyoko looking depressed behind her. →
"TO MY DEAR FRIENDS ...
"... THANK YOU...
"...I WAS HAPPY TO KNOW YOU THIS YEAR."
BWUUH

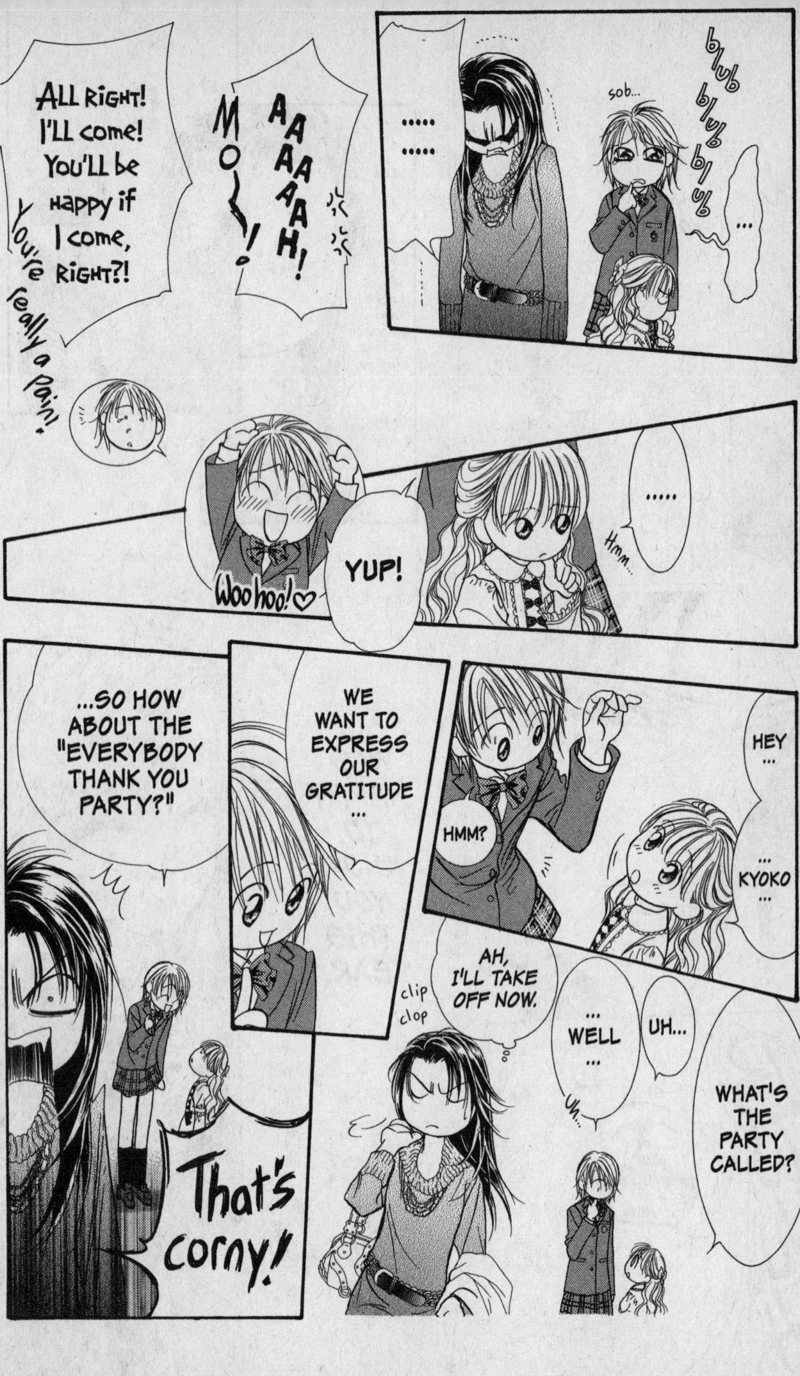
blub blub blub
sob...
......
......
...
AAAAAAAH!
MO~!
ALL RIGHT! I'LL come! You'LL be happy if I come, RIGHT?!
You're really a pain!
.....
Hmm...
YUP!
Woohoo!♡
HEY ...
... KYOKO ...
HMM?
WE WANT TO EXPRESS OUR GRATITUDE ...
...SO HOW ABOUT THE "EVERYBODY THANK YOU PARTY?"
WHAT'S THE PARTY CALLED?
UH...
... WELL ...
Uh...
AH, I'LL TAKE OFF NOW.
clip clop
That's corny!

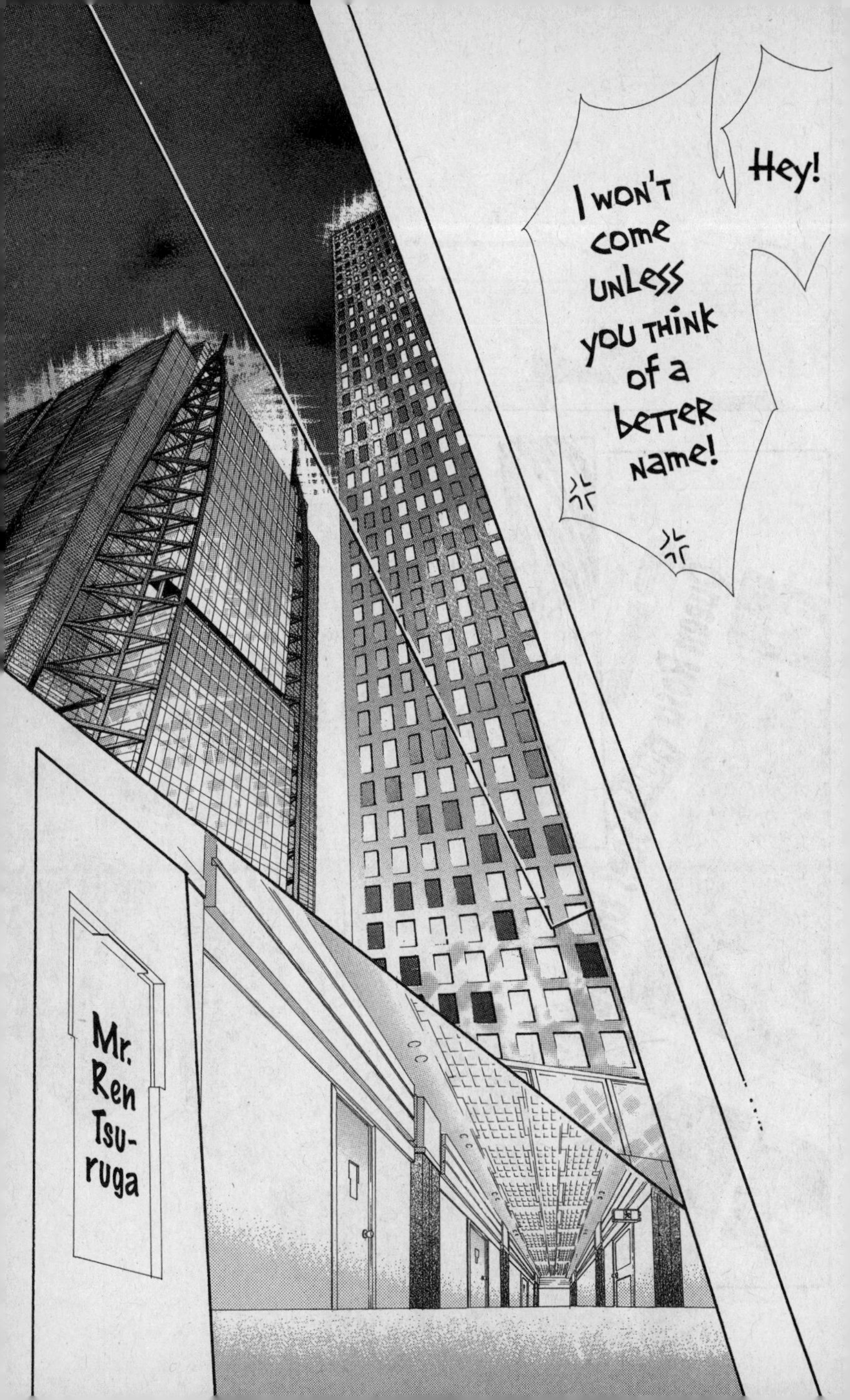
Hey!
I won't come unless you think of a better name!
...
Mr. Ren Tsuruga

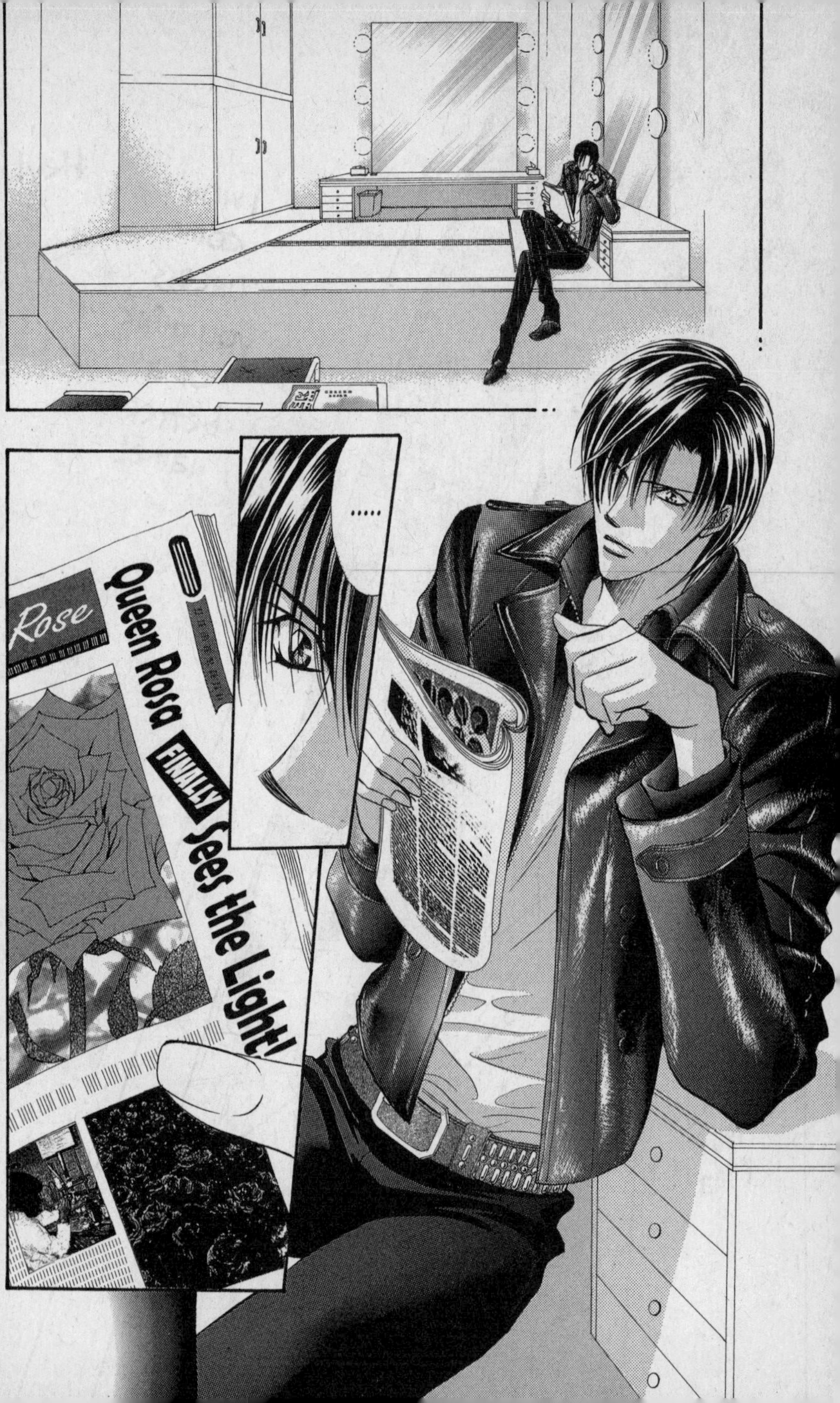

.....
Rose
Queen Rosa FINALLY Sees the Light!

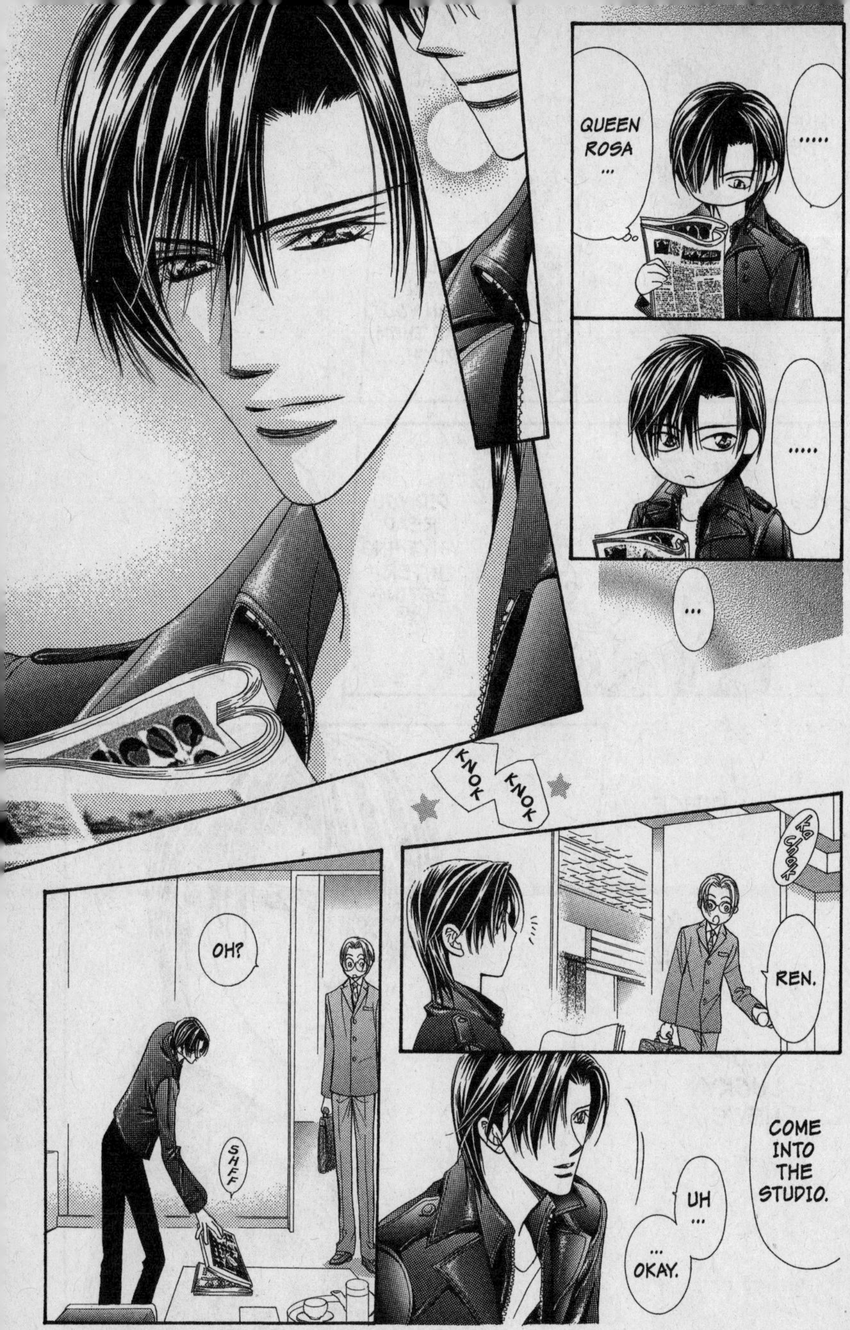
.....
QUEEN ROSA ...
......
...
KNOK KNOK
KA CHAK
REN.
COME INTO THE STUDIO.
UH ...
... OKAY.
OH?
SHFF

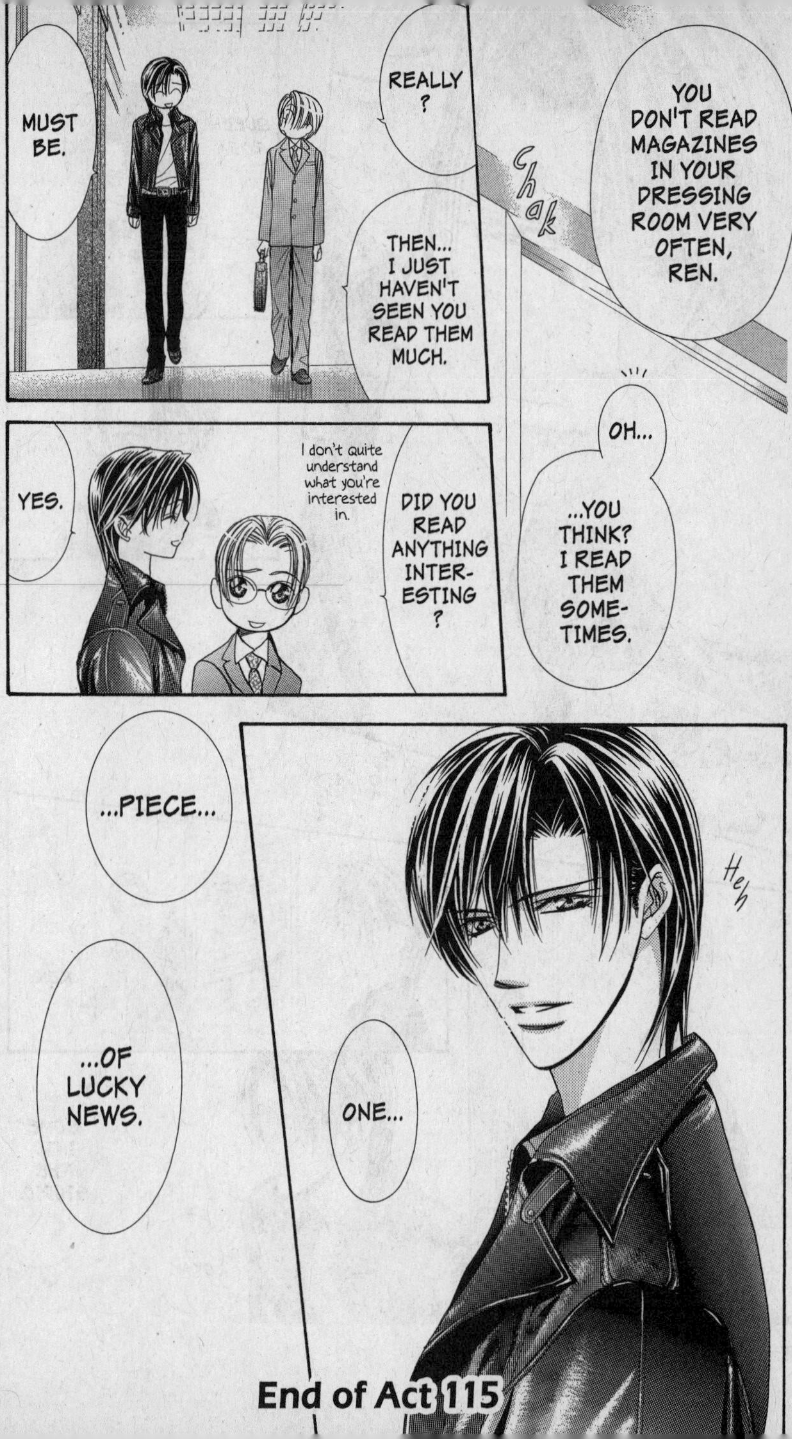
YOU DON'T READ MAGAZINES IN YOUR DRESSING ROOM VERY OFTEN, REN.
Chak
OH...
...YOU THINK? I READ THEM SOME-TIMES.
REALLY?
THEN... I JUST HAVEN'T SEEN YOU READ THEM MUCH.
MUST BE.
DID YOU READ ANYTHING INTER-ESTING?
I don't quite understand what you're interested in.
YES.
Heh
ONE...
...PIECE...
...OF LUCKY NEWS.
End of Act 115

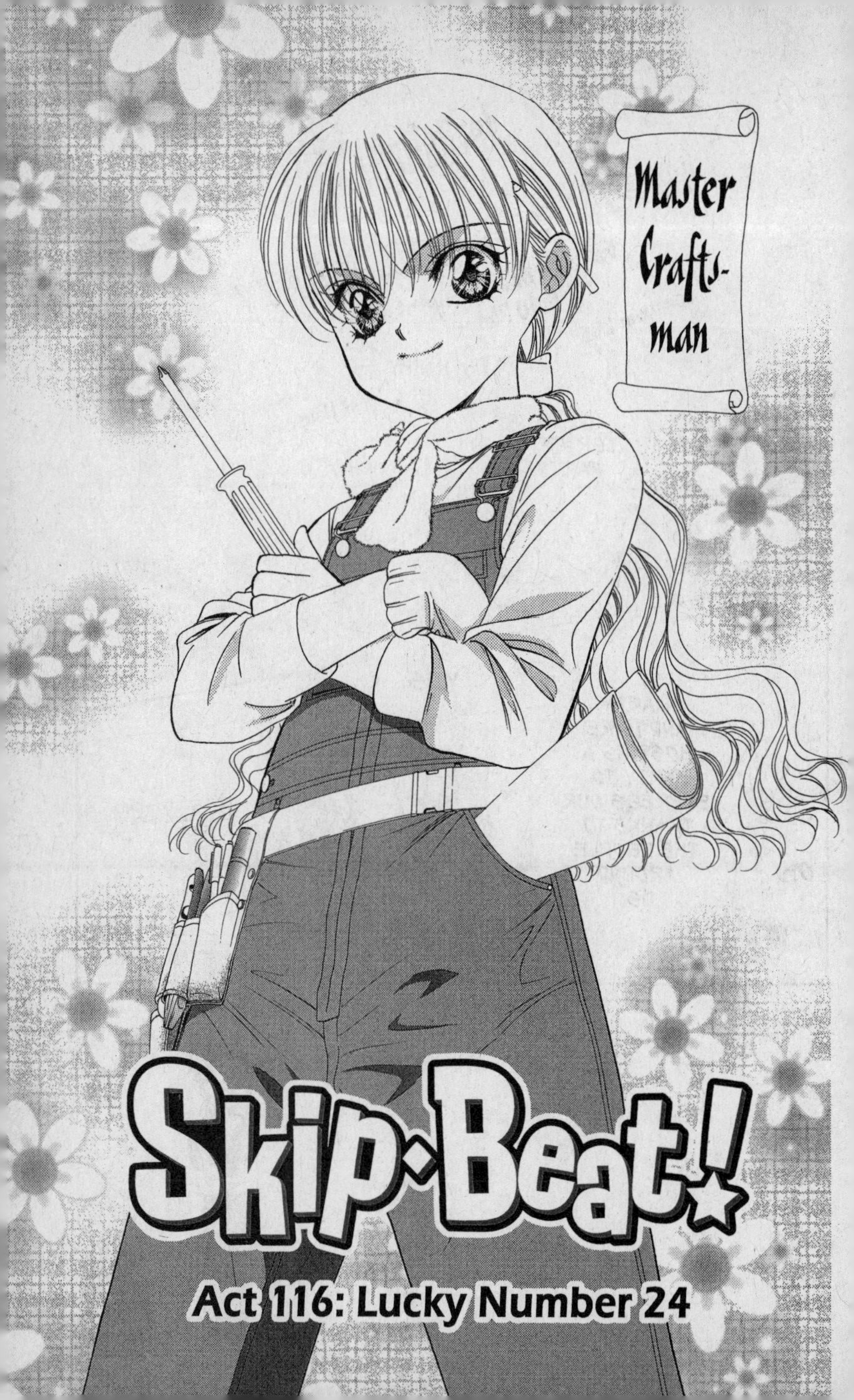
Master Crafts-man
Skip·Beat!
Act 116: Lucky Number 24

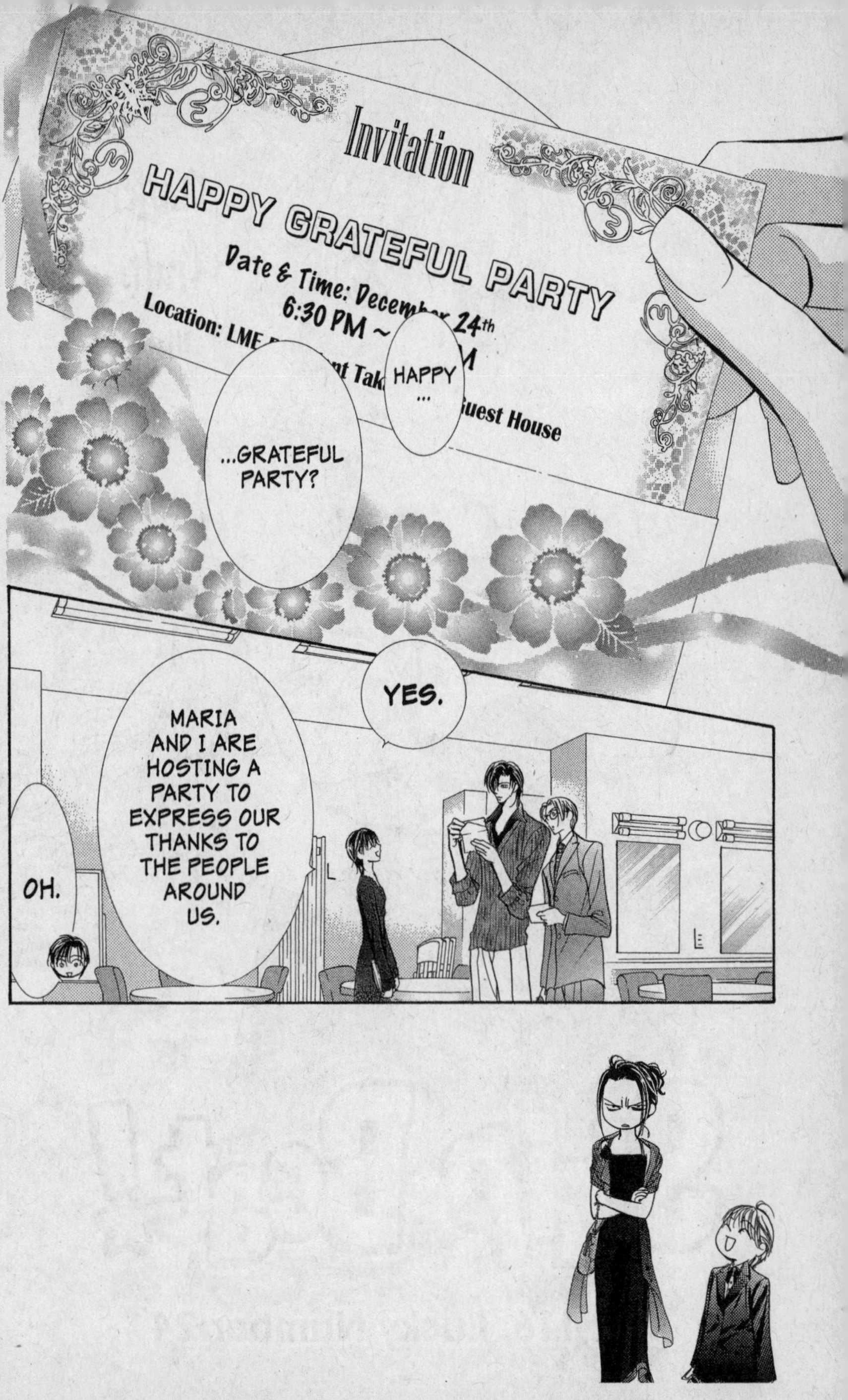
Invitation
HAPPY GRATEFUL PARTY
Date & Time:
6:30 PM ~
Location:
HAPPY ...
...GRATEFUL PARTY?
YES.
MARIA AND I ARE HOSTING A PARTY TO EXPRESS OUR THANKS TO THE PEOPLE AROUND US.
OH.

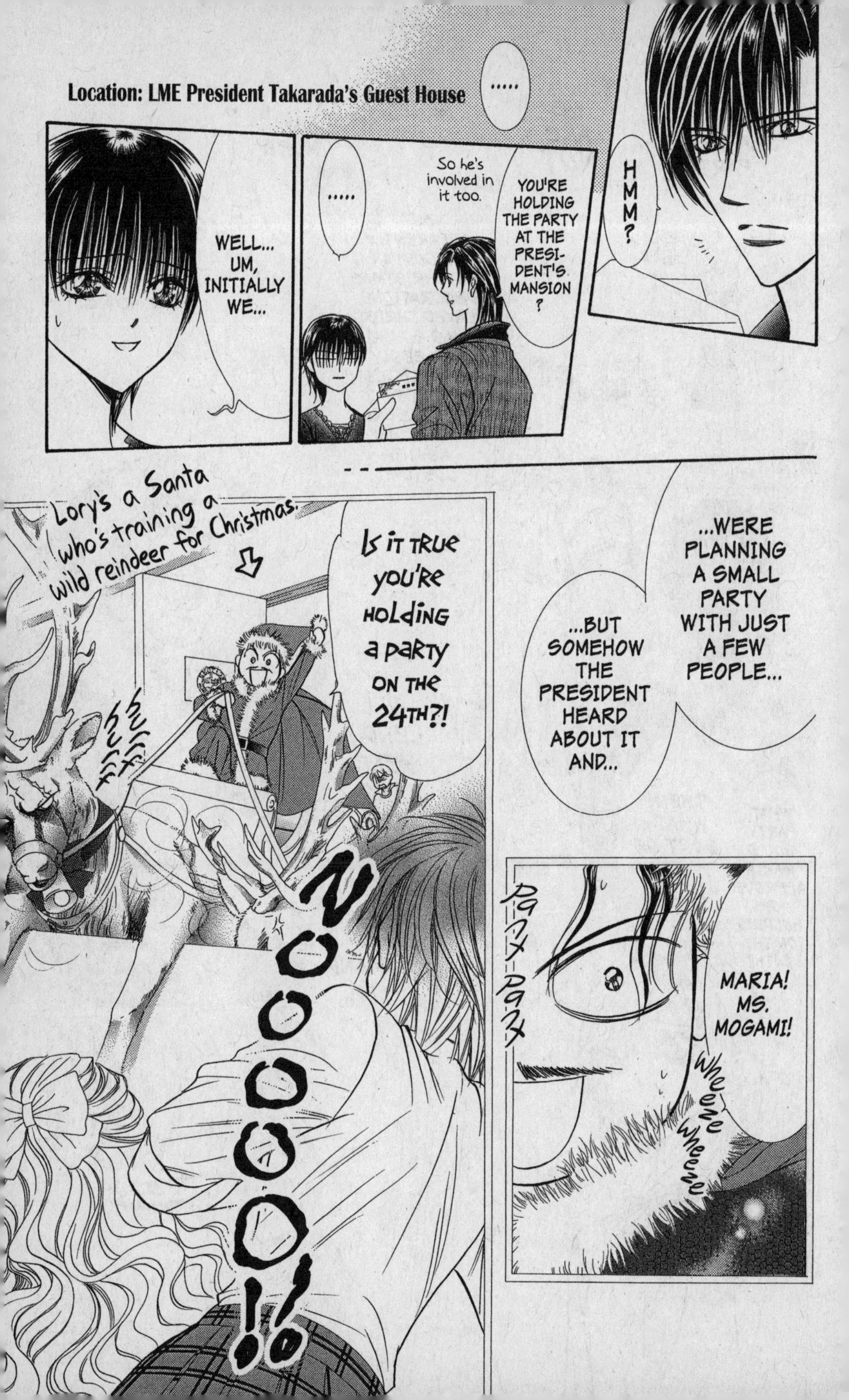

Location: LME President Takarada's Guest House
HMM?
.....
YOU'RE HOLDING THE PARTY AT THE PRESIDENT'S MANSION?
So he's involved in it too.
.....
WELL... UM, INITIALLY WE...
...WERE PLANNING A SMALL PARTY WITH JUST A FEW PEOPLE...
...BUT SOMEHOW THE PRESIDENT HEARD ABOUT IT AND...
MARIA! MS. MOGAMI!
Pant pant
wheeze wheeze
Is it true you're holding a party on the 24th?!
Lory's a Santa who's training a wild reindeer for Christmas.
huff huff
NOOOOO!!

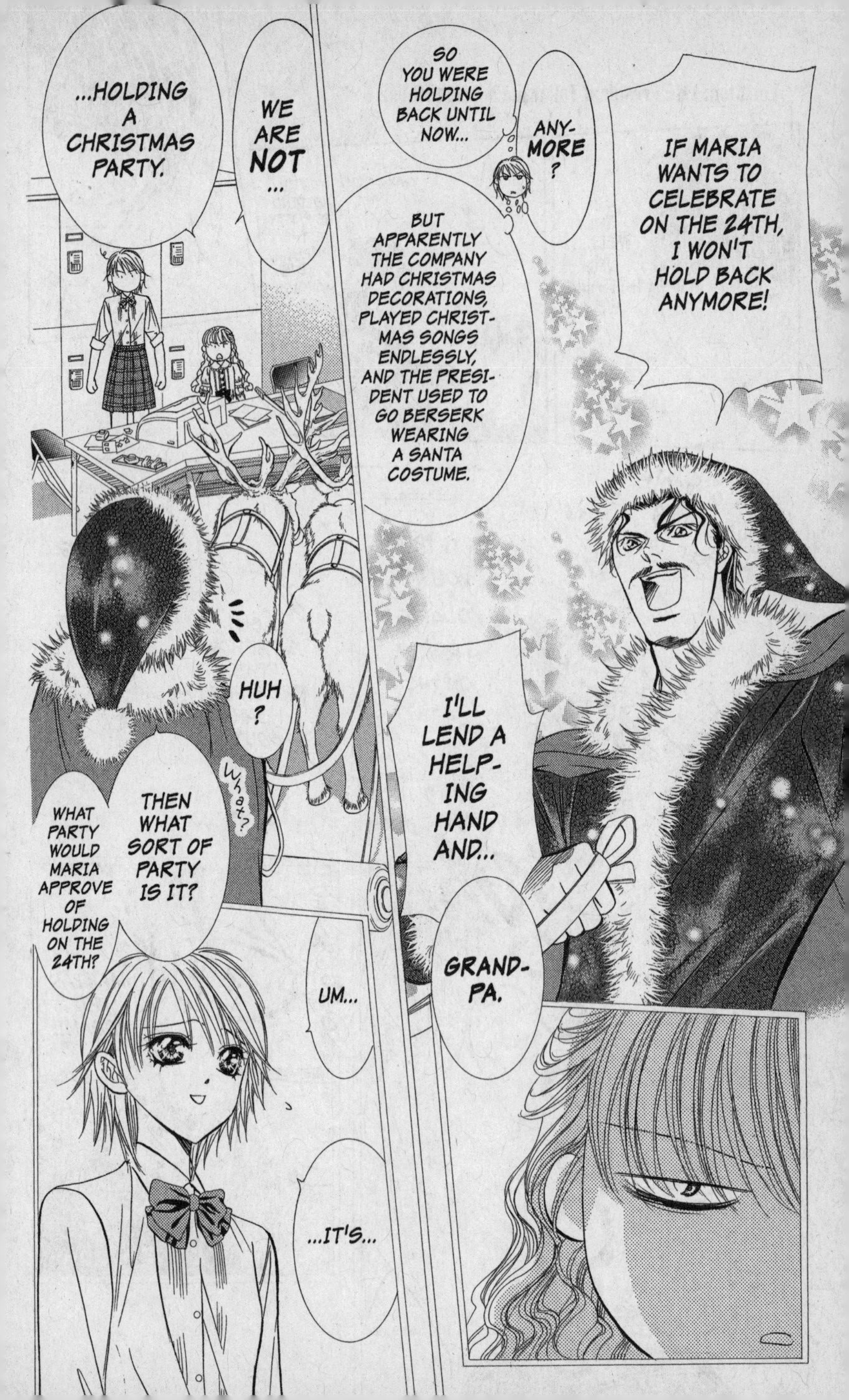
IF MARIA WANTS TO CELEBRATE ON THE 24TH, I WON'T HOLD BACK ANYMORE!
ANY-MORE?
SO YOU WERE HOLDING BACK UNTIL NOW...
BUT APPARENTLY THE COMPANY HAD CHRISTMAS DECORATIONS, PLAYED CHRIST-MAS SONGS ENDLESSLY, AND THE PRESI-DENT USED TO GO BERSERK WEARING A SANTA COSTUME.
I'LL LEND A HELP-ING HAND AND...
GRAND-PA.
WE ARE NOT...
...HOLDING A CHRISTMAS PARTY.
HUH?
What?
THEN WHAT SORT OF PARTY IS IT?
WHAT PARTY WOULD MARIA APPROVE OF HOLDING ON THE 24TH?
UM...
...IT'S...

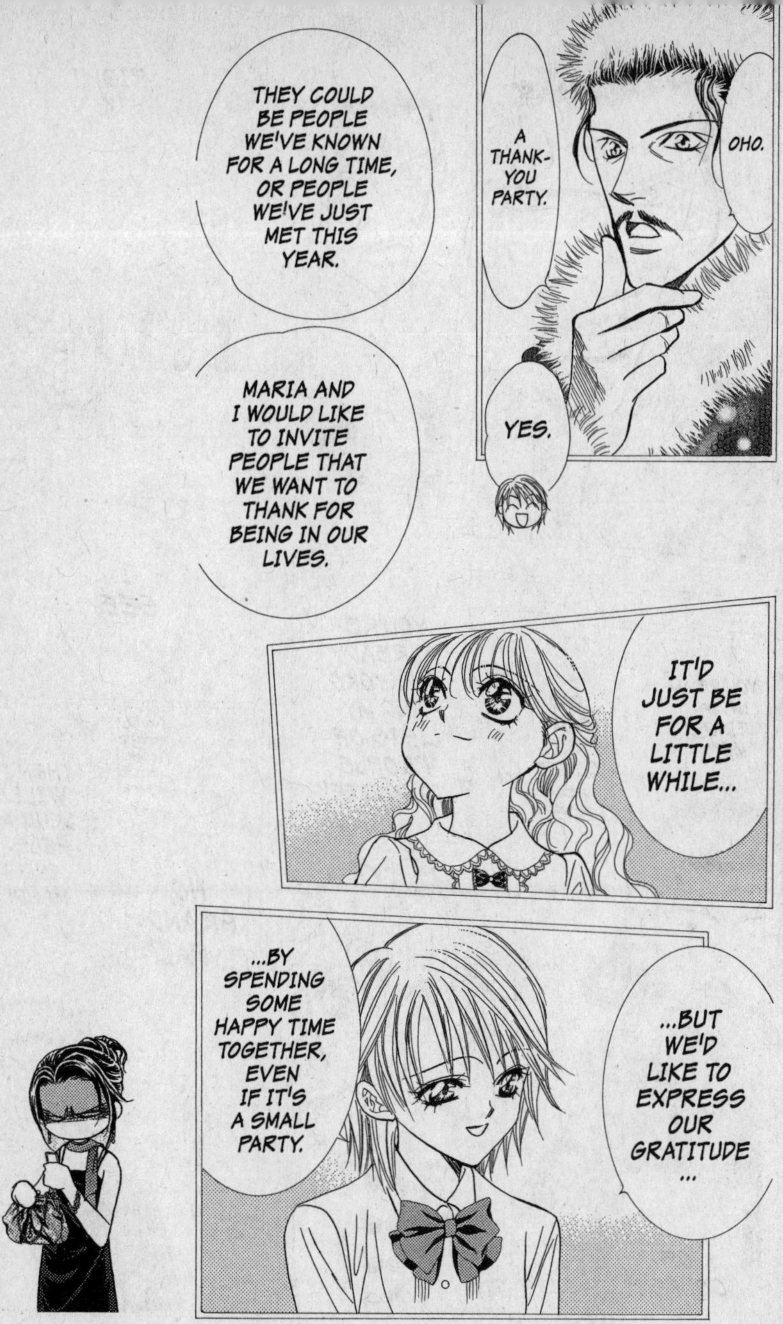
OHO.
A THANK-YOU PARTY.
YES.
THEY COULD BE PEOPLE WE'VE KNOWN FOR A LONG TIME, OR PEOPLE WE'VE JUST MET THIS YEAR.
MARIA AND I WOULD LIKE TO INVITE PEOPLE THAT WE WANT TO THANK FOR BEING IN OUR LIVES.
IT'D JUST BE FOR A LITTLE WHILE...
...BUT WE'D LIKE TO EXPRESS OUR GRATITUDE...
...BY SPENDING SOME HAPPY TIME TOGETHER, EVEN IF IT'S A SMALL PARTY.

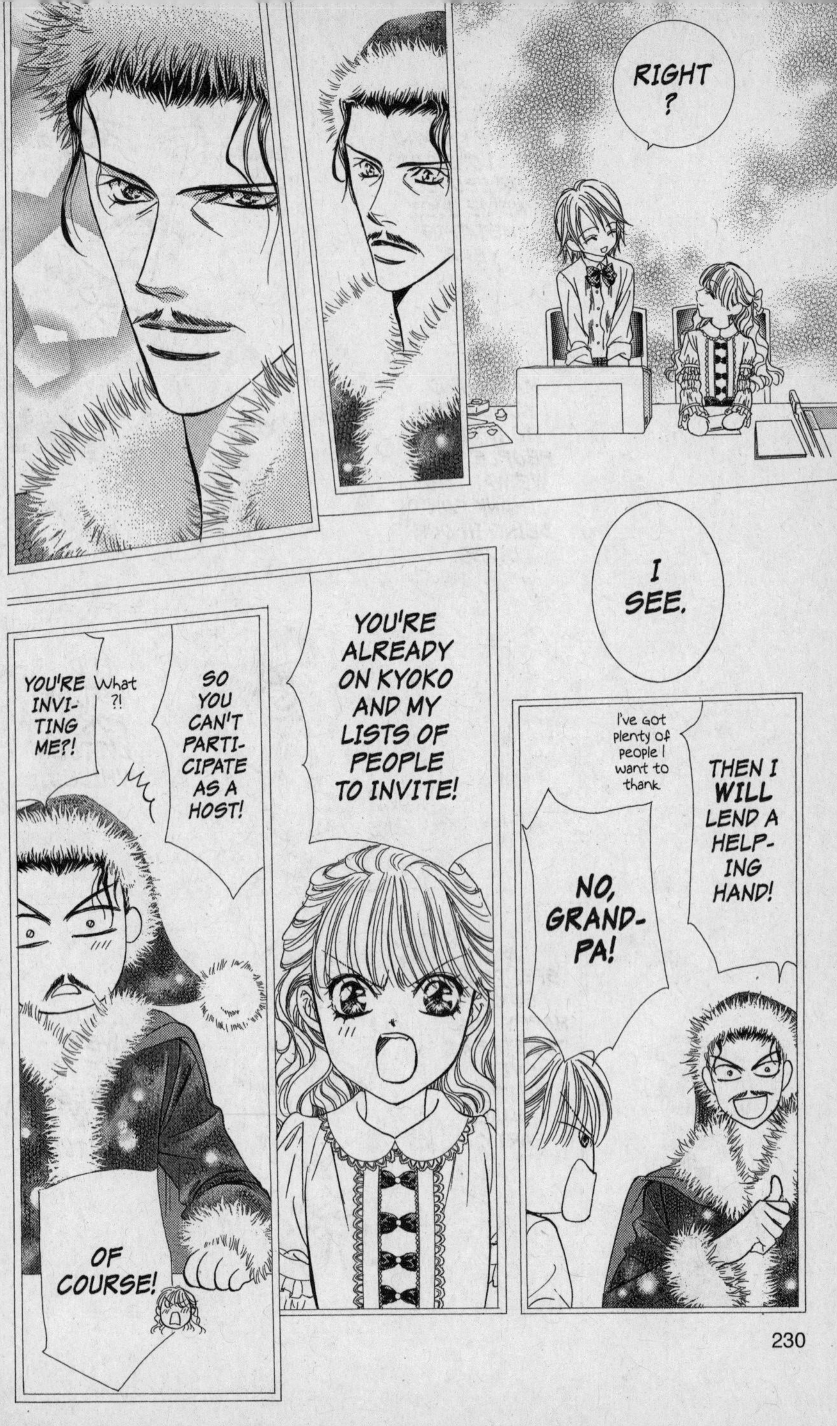

RIGHT?
I SEE.
THEN I WILL LEND A HELPING HAND!
I've got plenty of people I want to thank.
NO, GRANDPA!
YOU'RE ALREADY ON KYOKO AND MY LISTS OF PEOPLE TO INVITE!
SO YOU CAN'T PARTICIPATE AS A HOST!
What?!
YOU'RE INVITING ME?!
OF COURSE!

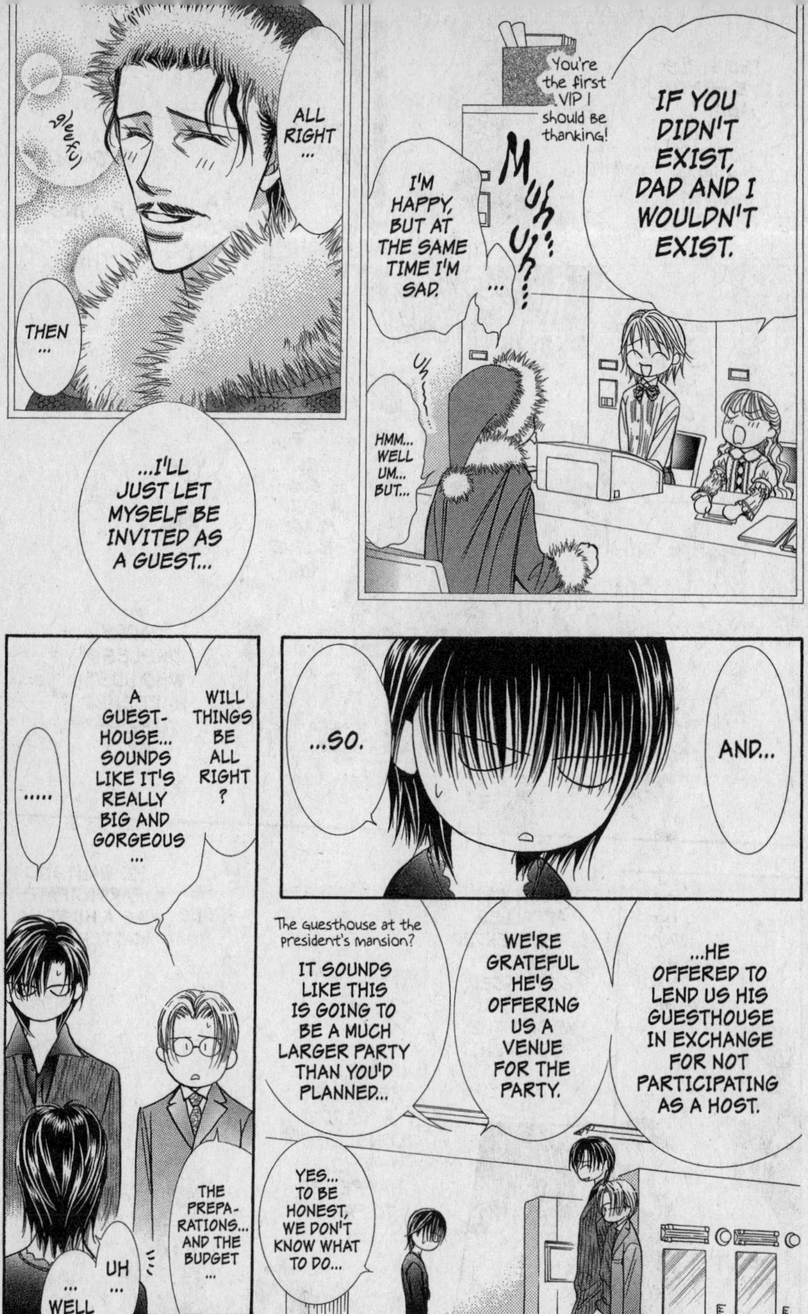
IF YOU DIDN'T EXIST, DAD AND I WOULDN'T EXIST.
You're the first VIP I should be thanking!
Muh uh...
I'M HAPPY, BUT AT THE SAME TIME I'M SAD.
...
Uh—
HMM... WELL UM... BUT...
ALL RIGHT ...
gleeful
THEN ...
...I'LL JUST LET MYSELF BE INVITED AS A GUEST...
AND...
...SO.
...HE OFFERED TO LEND US HIS GUESTHOUSE IN EXCHANGE FOR NOT PARTICIPATING AS A HOST.
WE'RE GRATEFUL HE'S OFFERING US A VENUE FOR THE PARTY.
The guesthouse at the president's mansion?
IT SOUNDS LIKE THIS IS GOING TO BE A MUCH LARGER PARTY THAN YOU'D PLANNED...
YES... TO BE HONEST, WE DON'T KNOW WHAT TO DO...
WILL THINGS BE ALL RIGHT?
A GUEST-HOUSE... SOUNDS LIKE IT'S REALLY BIG AND GORGEOUS ...
.....
THE PREPA-RATIONS... AND THE BUDGET ...
UH ...
... WELL ...

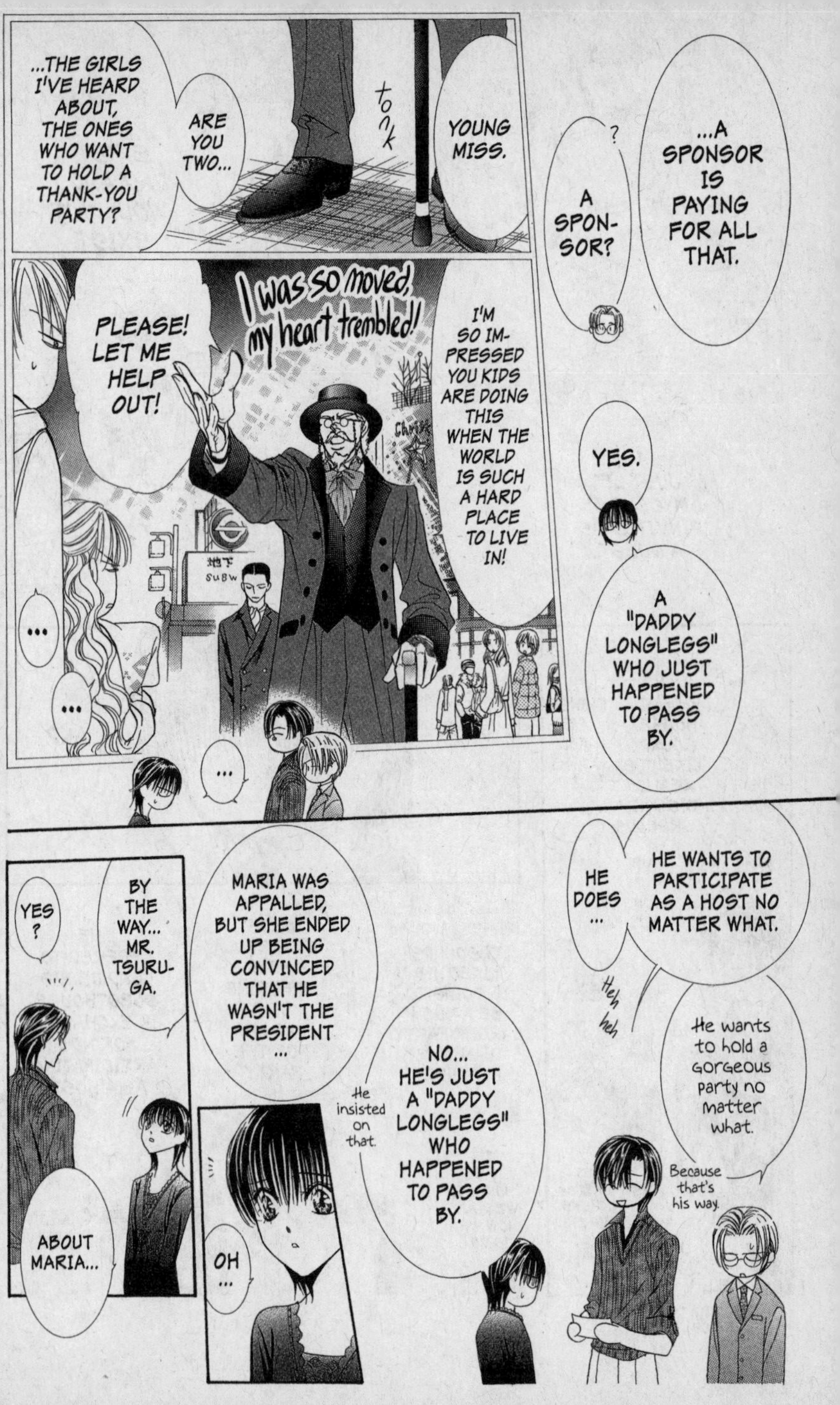
...A SPONSOR IS PAYING FOR ALL THAT.
?
A SPON-SOR?
YES.
A "DADDY LONGLEGS" WHO JUST HAPPENED TO PASS BY.
YOUNG MISS.
tonk
ARE YOU TWO...
...THE GIRLS I'VE HEARD ABOUT, THE ONES WHO WANT TO HOLD A THANK-YOU PARTY?
I'M SO IM-PRESSED YOU KIDS ARE DOING THIS WHEN THE WORLD IS SUCH A HARD PLACE TO LIVE IN!
I was so moved, my heart trembled!
PLEASE! LET ME HELP OUT!
...
...
...
HE WANTS TO PARTICIPATE AS A HOST NO MATTER WHAT.
HE DOES...
Heh heh
He wants to hold a gorgeous party no matter what.
Because that's his way.
MARIA WAS APPALLED, BUT SHE ENDED UP BEING CONVINCED THAT HE WASN'T THE PRESIDENT...
NO... HE'S JUST A "DADDY LONGLEGS" WHO HAPPENED TO PASS BY.
He insisted on that.
OH...
BY THE WAY... MR. TSURUGA.
YES?
ABOUT MARIA...

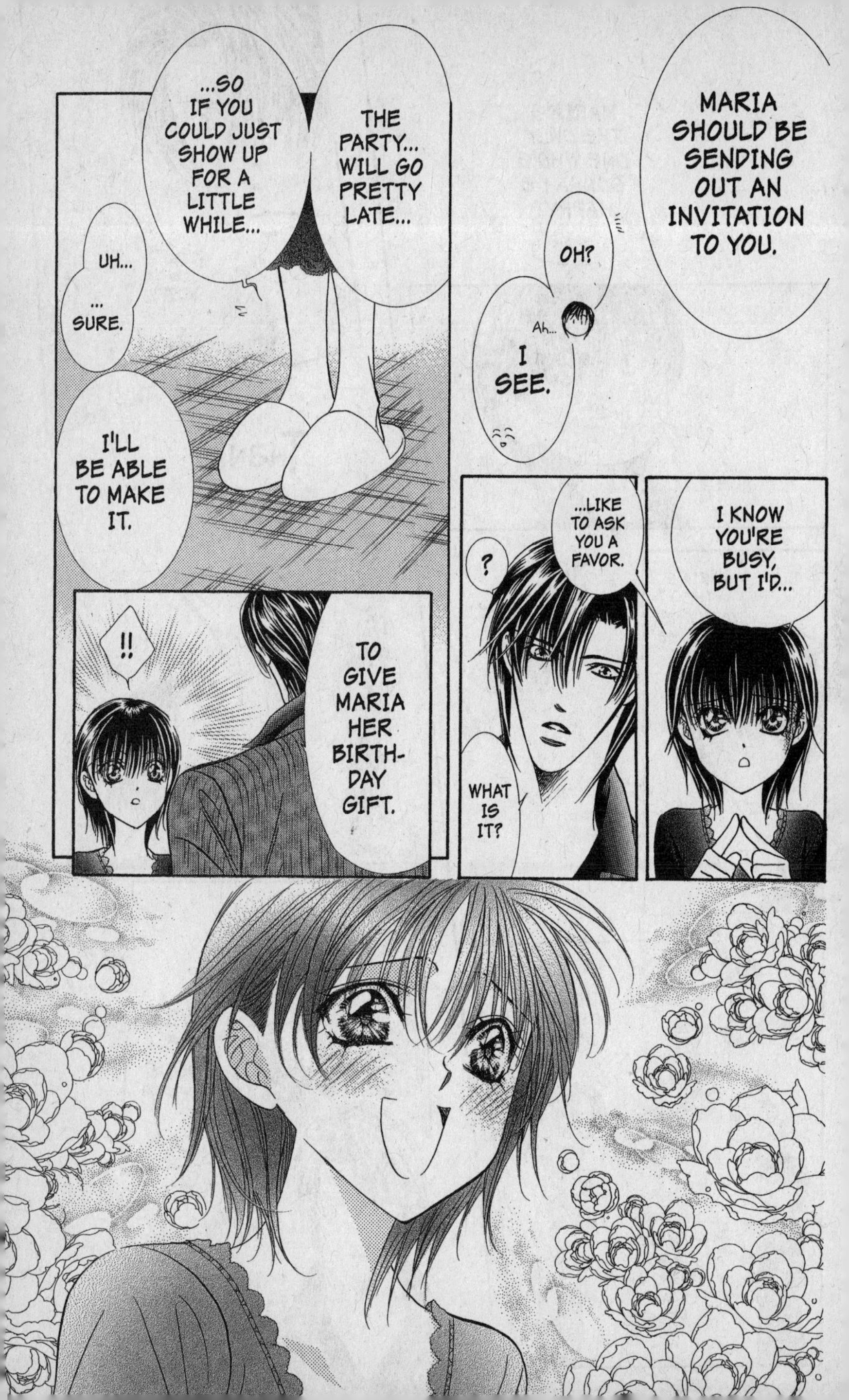
MARIA SHOULD BE SENDING OUT AN INVITATION TO YOU.
OH?
Ah...
I SEE.
THE PARTY... WILL GO PRETTY LATE...
...SO IF YOU COULD JUST SHOW UP FOR A LITTLE WHILE...
UH...
... SURE.
I'LL BE ABLE TO MAKE IT.
I KNOW YOU'RE BUSY, BUT I'D...
...LIKE TO ASK YOU A FAVOR.
?
WHAT IS IT?
TO GIVE MARIA HER BIRTH-DAY GIFT.
!!

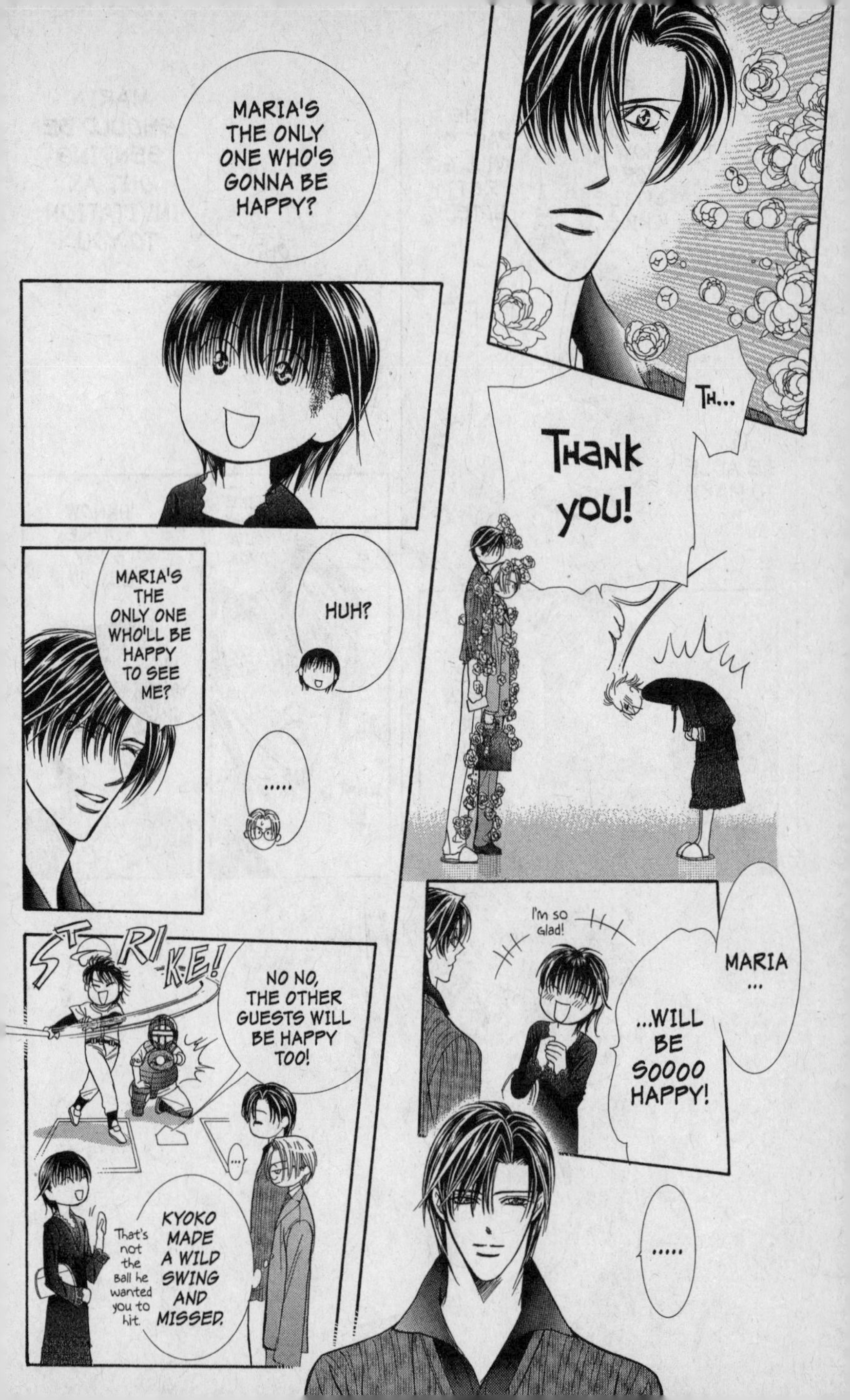
TH...
THANK you!
MARIA ...
...WILL BE SOOOO HAPPY!
I'm so Glad!
.....
MARIA'S THE ONLY ONE WHO'S GONNA BE HAPPY?
HUH?
MARIA'S THE ONLY ONE WHO'LL BE HAPPY TO SEE ME?
.....
NO NO, THE OTHER GUESTS WILL BE HAPPY TOO!
STRIKE!
...
KYOKO MADE A WILD SWING AND MISSED.
That's not the Ball he wanted you to hit.

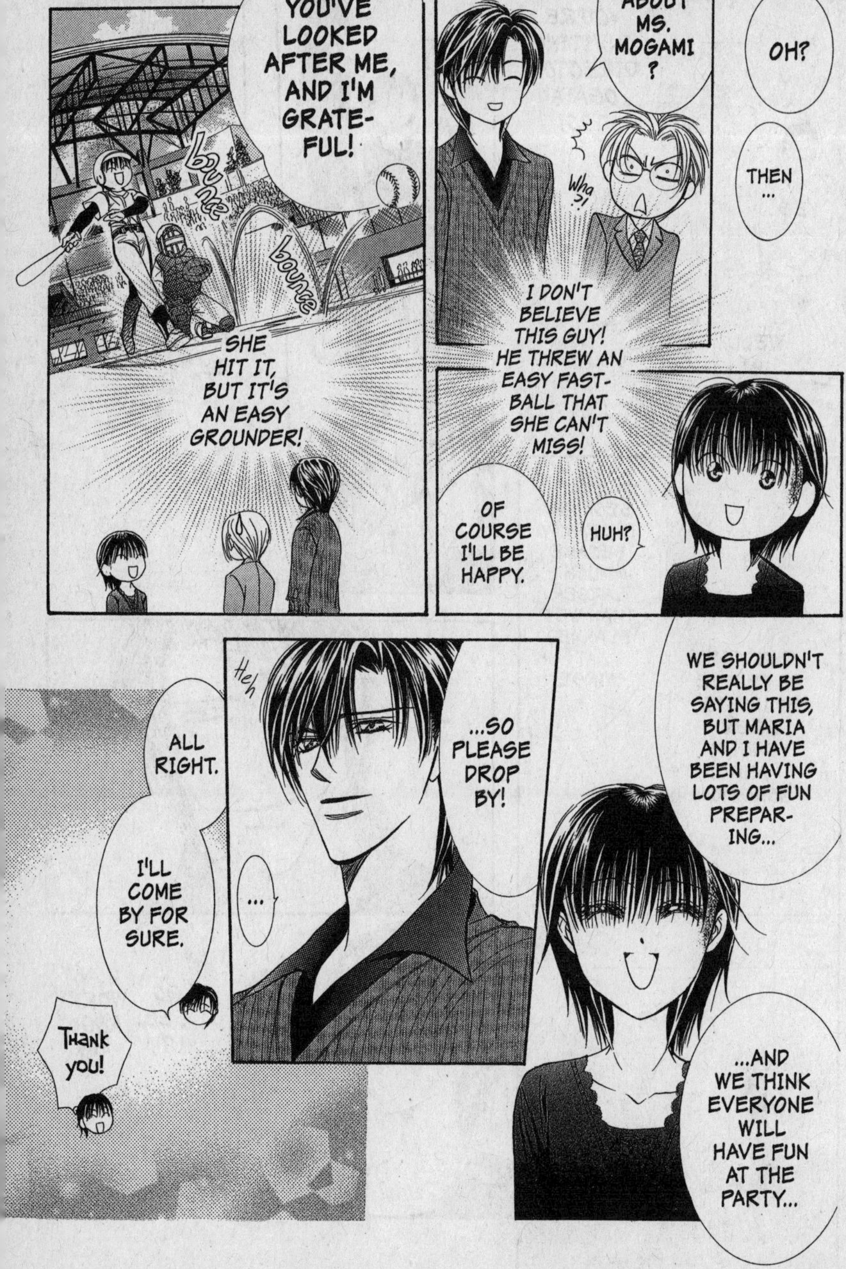
OH?
THEN...
...WHAT ABOUT MS. MOGAMI?
Wha?!
HUH?
OF COURSE I'LL BE HAPPY.
I DON'T BELIEVE THIS GUY! HE THREW AN EASY FASTBALL THAT SHE CAN'T MISS!
YOU'VE LOOKED AFTER ME, AND I'M GRATEFUL!
bounce
bounce
SHE HIT IT, BUT IT'S AN EASY GROUNDER!
WE SHOULDN'T REALLY BE SAYING THIS, BUT MARIA AND I HAVE BEEN HAVING LOTS OF FUN PREPARING...
...AND WE THINK EVERYONE WILL HAVE FUN AT THE PARTY...
...SO PLEASE DROP BY!
Heh
...
ALL RIGHT.
I'LL COME BY FOR SURE.
Thank you!

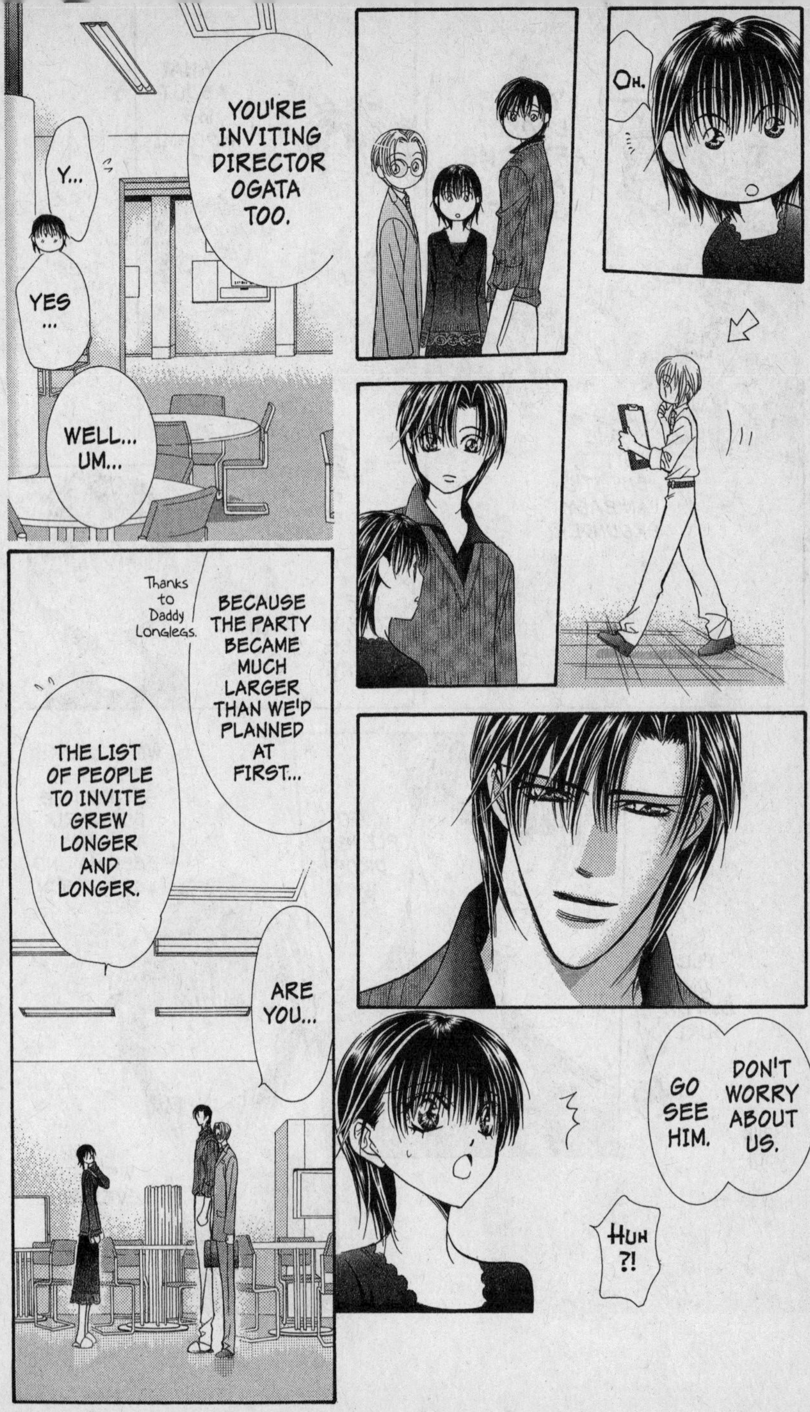
OH.
DON'T WORRY ABOUT US.
GO SEE HIM.
HUH ?!
YOU'RE INVITING DIRECTOR OGATA TOO.
Y...
YES ...
WELL... UM...
BECAUSE THE PARTY BECAME MUCH LARGER THAN WE'D PLANNED AT FIRST...
Thanks to Daddy Longlegs.
THE LIST OF PEOPLE TO INVITE GREW LONGER AND LONGER.
ARE YOU...

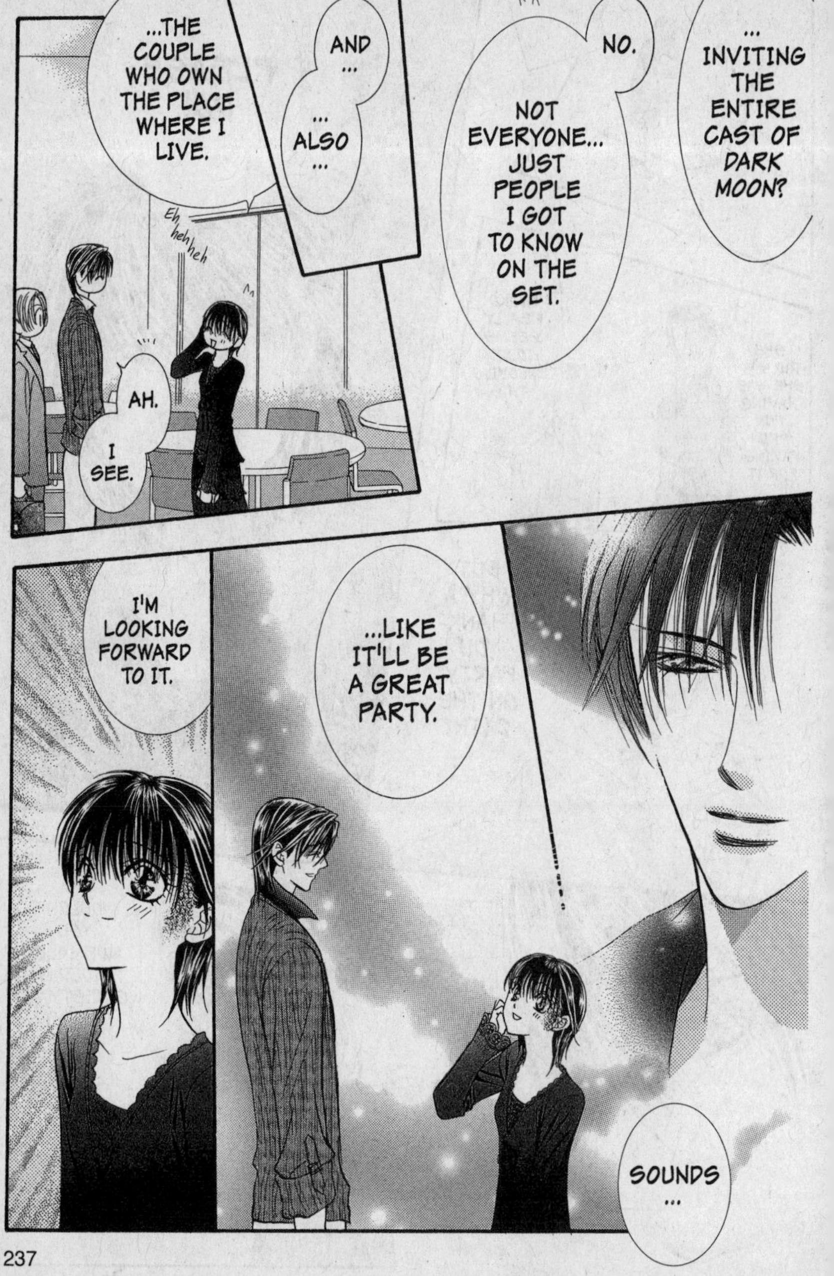
... INVITING THE ENTIRE CAST OF DARK MOON?
NO.
NOT EVERYONE... JUST PEOPLE I GOT TO KNOW ON THE SET.
AND ...
... ALSO ...
...THE COUPLE WHO OWN THE PLACE WHERE I LIVE.
Eh heh heh
AH.
I SEE.
SOUNDS ...
...LIKE IT'LL BE A GREAT PARTY.
I'M LOOKING FORWARD TO IT.

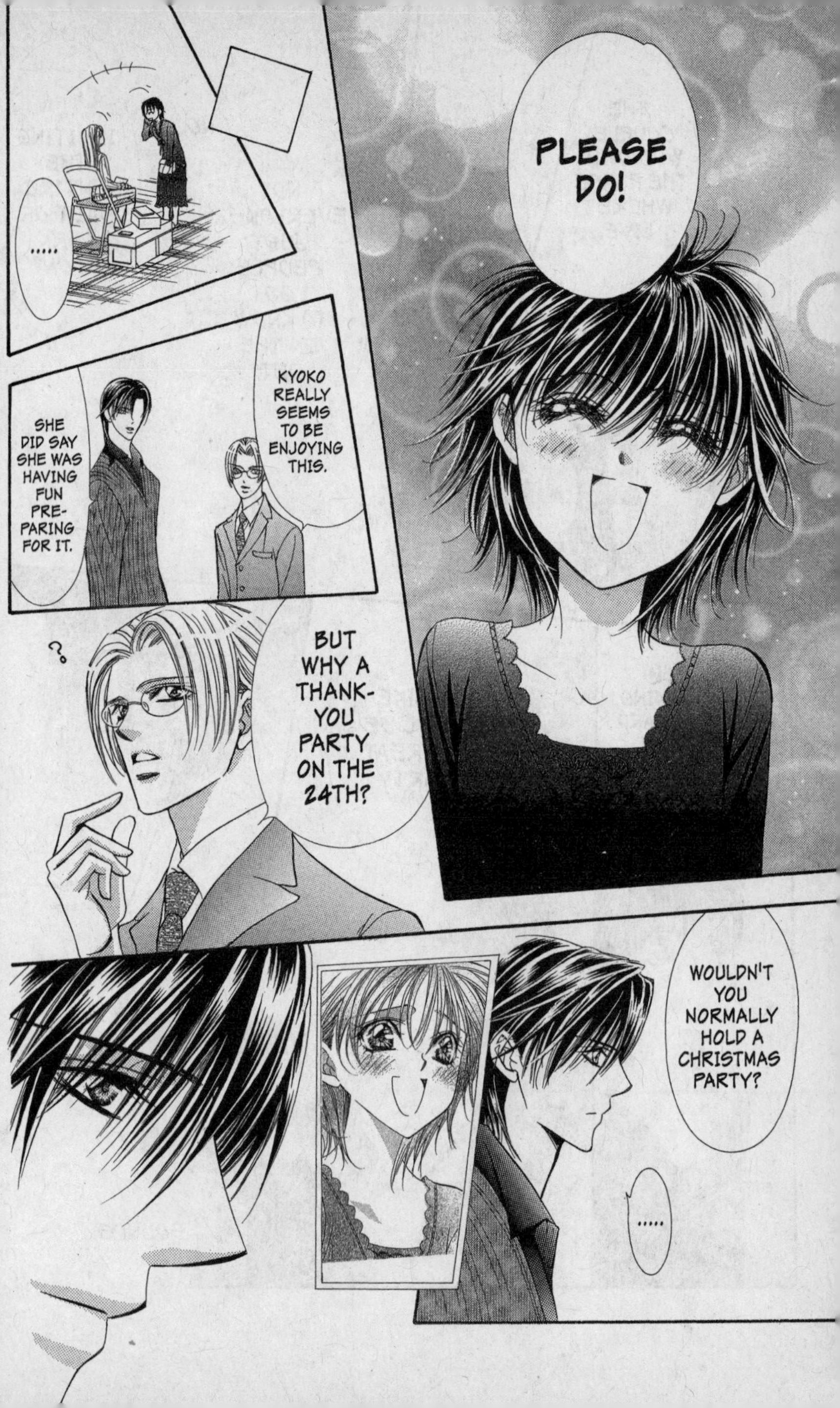
PLEASE DO!
.....
KYOKO REALLY SEEMS TO BE ENJOYING THIS.
SHE DID SAY SHE WAS HAVING FUN PRE-PARING FOR IT.
BUT WHY A THANK-YOU PARTY ON THE 24TH?
WOULDN'T YOU NORMALLY HOLD A CHRISTMAS PARTY?
.....

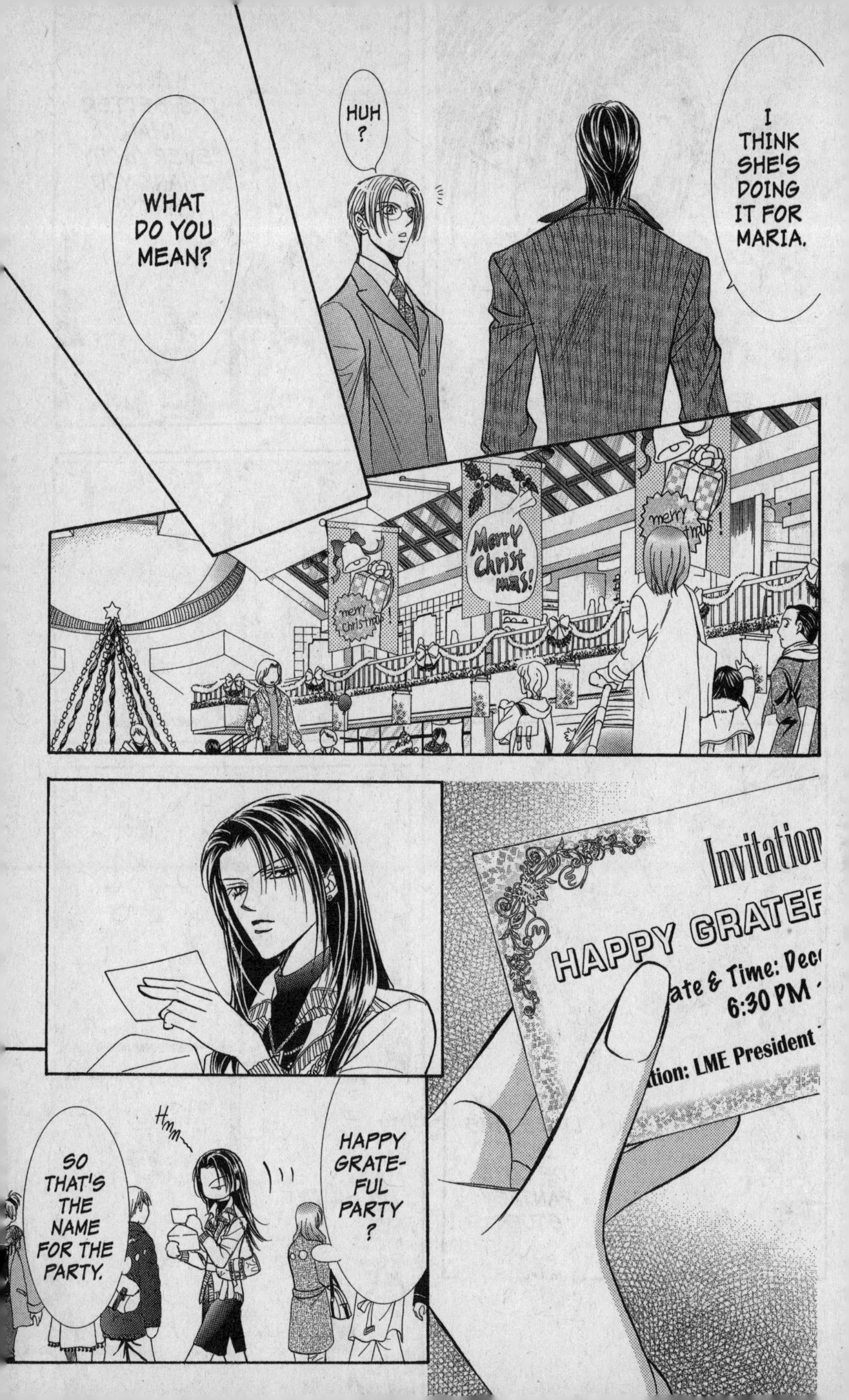
I THINK SHE'S DOING IT FOR MARIA.
HUH?
WHAT DO YOU MEAN?
merry Christmas!
Merry Christmas!
merry Christmas!
Invitation
HAPPY GRATEF
ate & Time: Dec
6:30 PM
tion: LME President
HAPPY GRATEFUL PARTY?
Hmm~
SO THAT'S THE NAME FOR THE PARTY.

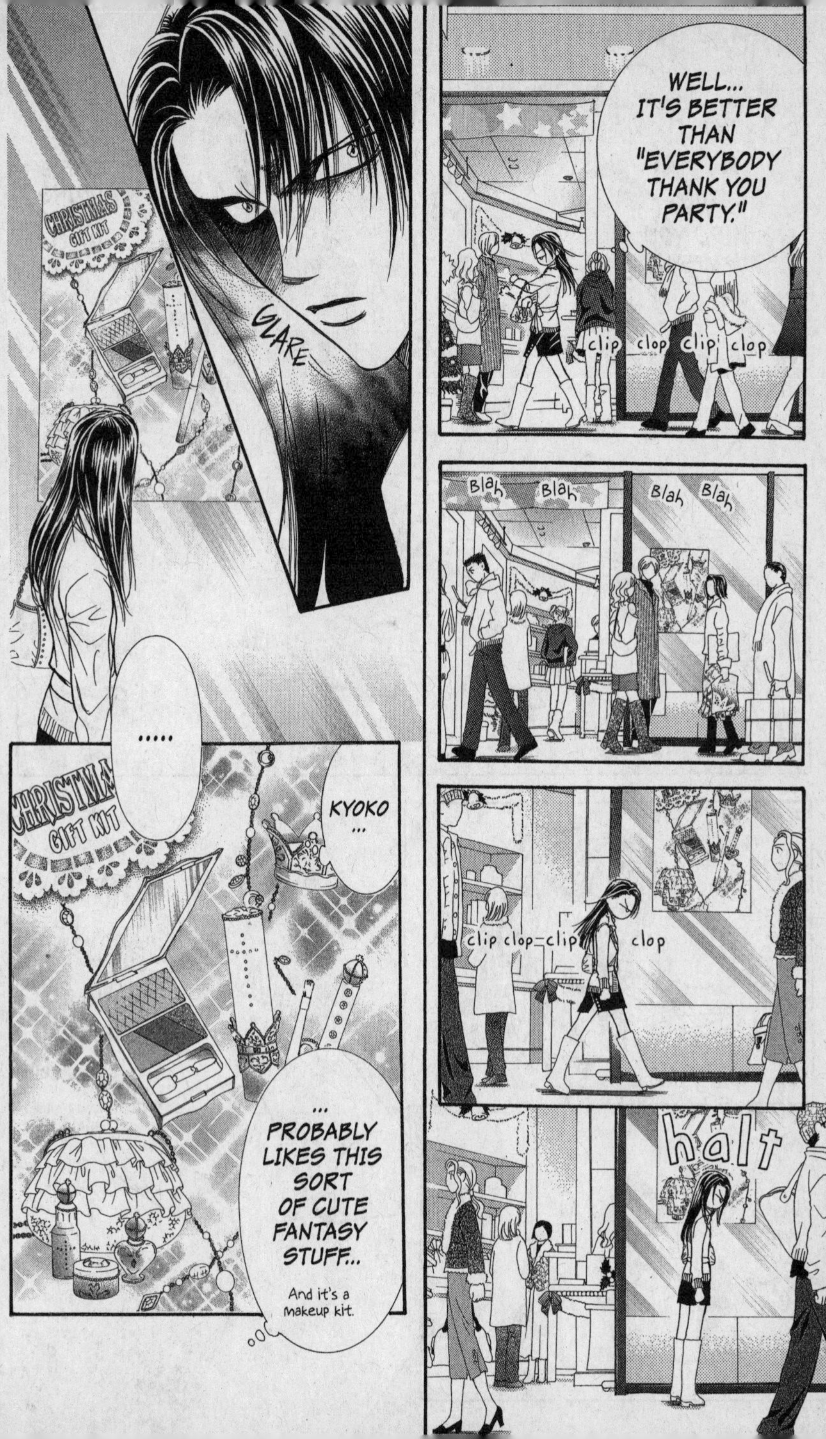
WELL... IT'S BETTER THAN "EVERYBODY THANK YOU PARTY."
clip clop clip clop
Blah Blah Blah Blah
clip clop clip clop
halt
CHRISTMAS GIFT KIT
GLARE
.....
KYOKO ...
CHRISTMAS GIFT KIT
... PROBABLY LIKES THIS SORT OF CUTE FANTASY STUFF...
And it's a makeup kit.

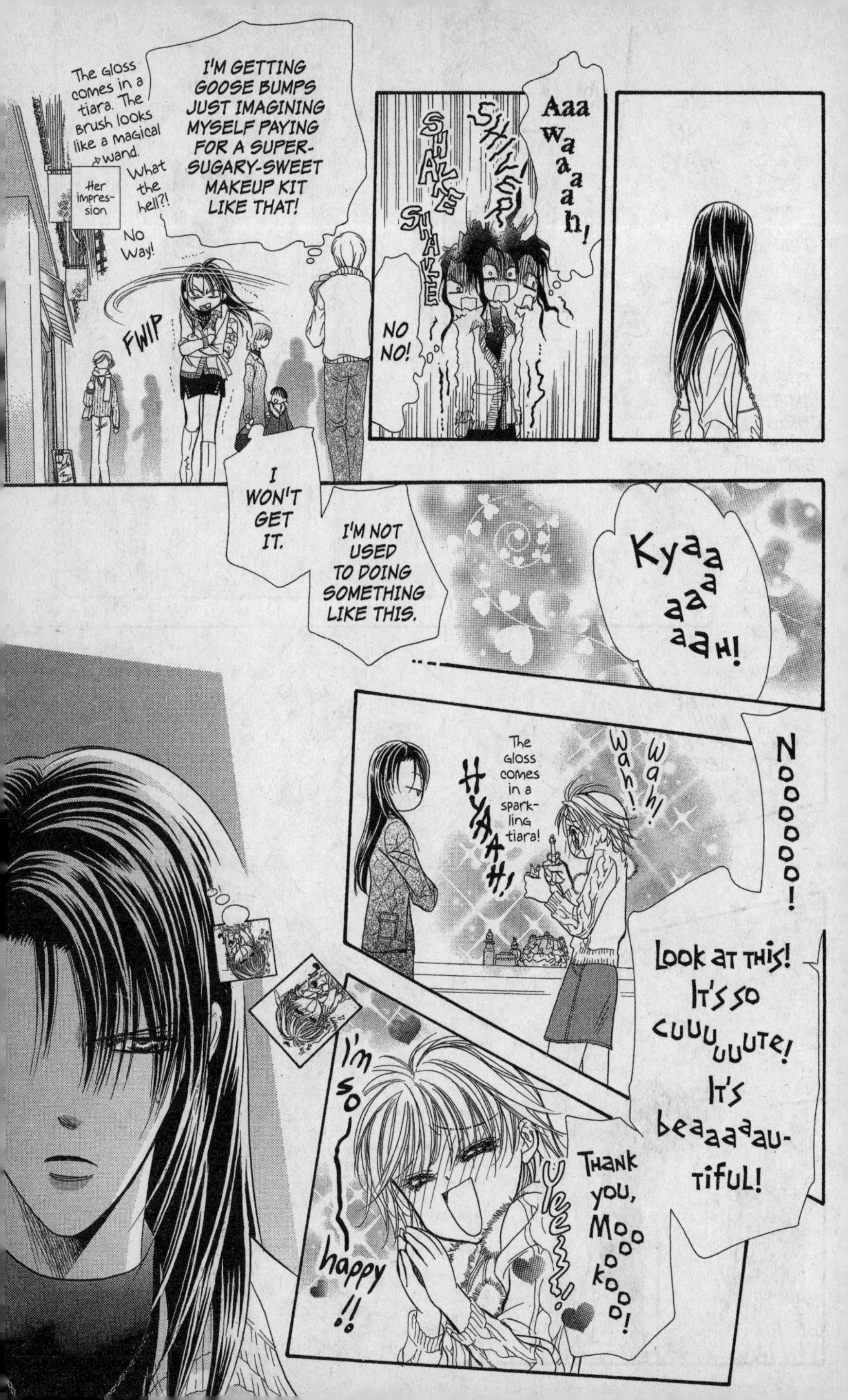
Aaa waaaah!
SHIVER!
SHAKE SHAKE
NO NO!
I'M GETTING GOOSE BUMPS JUST IMAGINING MYSELF PAYING FOR A SUPER-SUGARY-SWEET MAKEUP KIT LIKE THAT!
The gloss comes in a tiara. The brush looks like a magical wand.
Her impression
What the hell?!
No Way!
FWIP
Kyaaaaaaah!
I'M NOT USED TO DOING SOMETHING LIKE THIS.
I WON'T GET IT.
Noooooo!
Wah! Wah!
The gloss comes in a sparkling tiara!
HYAAAH!
Look at this! It's so cuuuuute! It's beaaaaau-tiful!
Thank you, Mooooookooo!
Yeeey!
I'm so---happy!!

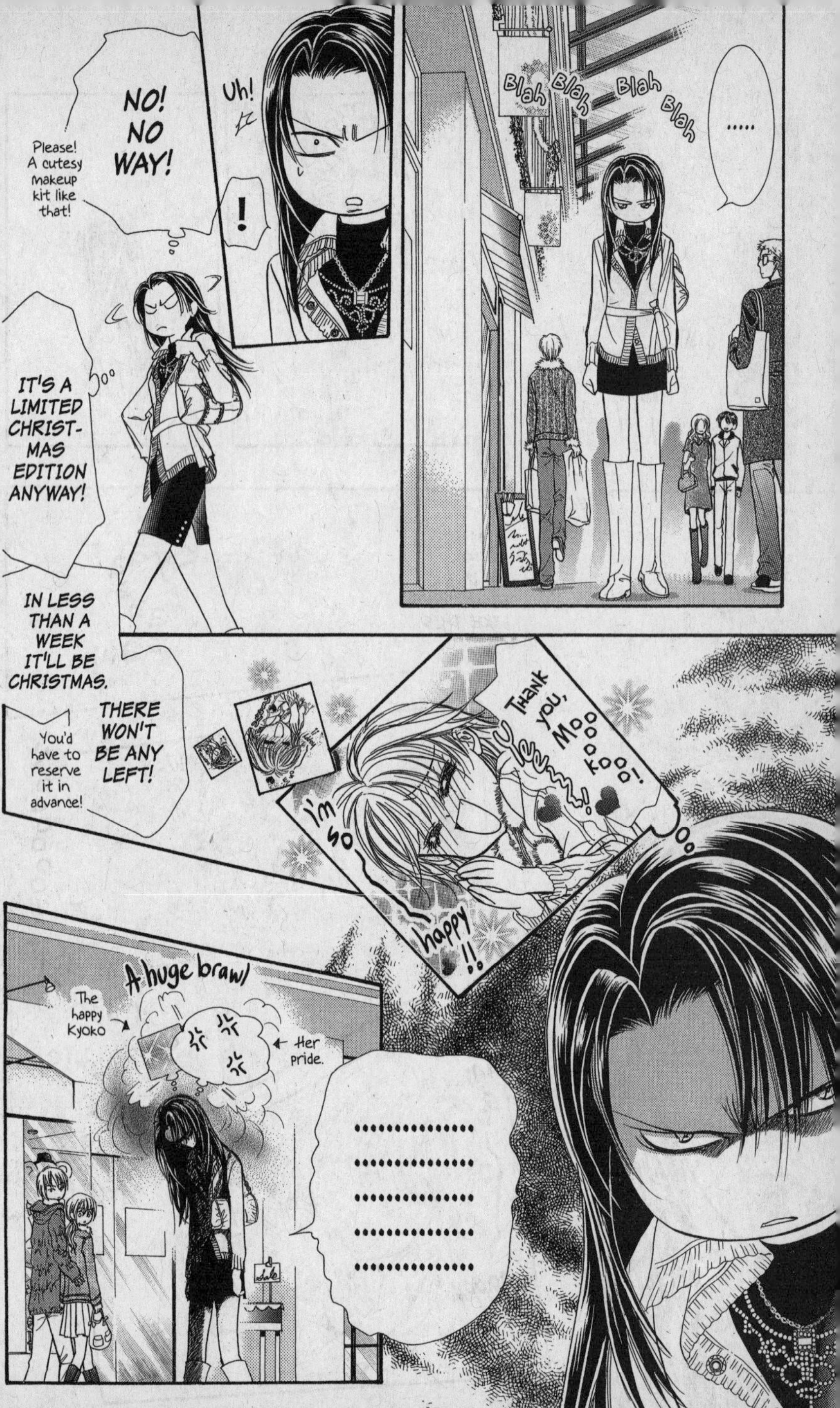

Blah Blah Blah Blah
.....
Uh!
!
NO! NO WAY!
Please! A cutesy makeup kit like that!
IT'S A LIMITED CHRISTMAS EDITION ANYWAY!
IN LESS THAN A WEEK IT'LL BE CHRISTMAS.
THERE WON'T BE ANY LEFT!
You'd have to reserve it in advance!
Thank you, Mooooko!
I'm so happy!!
....
A huge brawl
The happy Kyoko
Her pride.

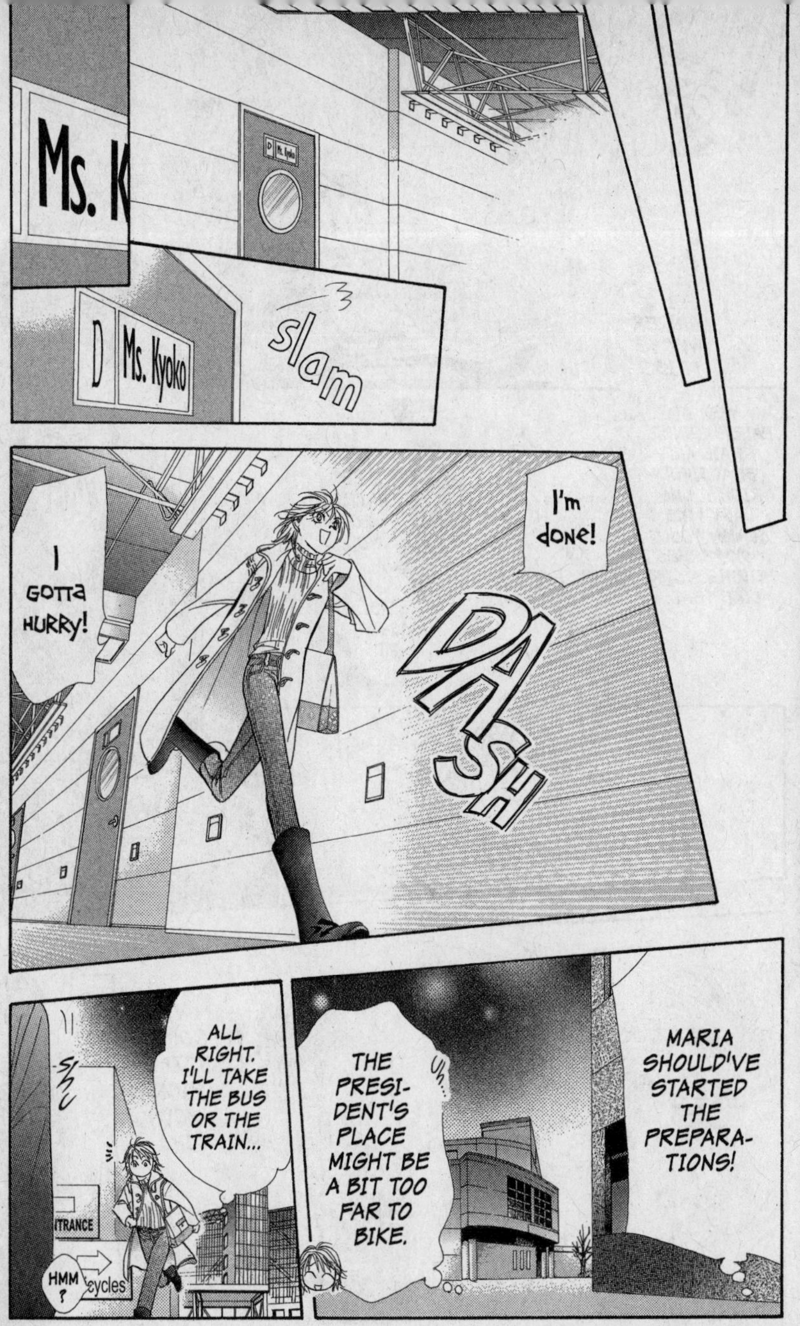
Ms. K
D Ms. Kyoko
slam
I'm done!
DASH
I gotta hurry!
MARIA SHOULD'VE STARTED THE PREPARATIONS!
Uh...
THE PRESI-DENT'S PLACE MIGHT BE A BIT TOO FAR TO BIKE.
ALL RIGHT. I'LL TAKE THE BUS OR THE TRAIN...
HMM ?

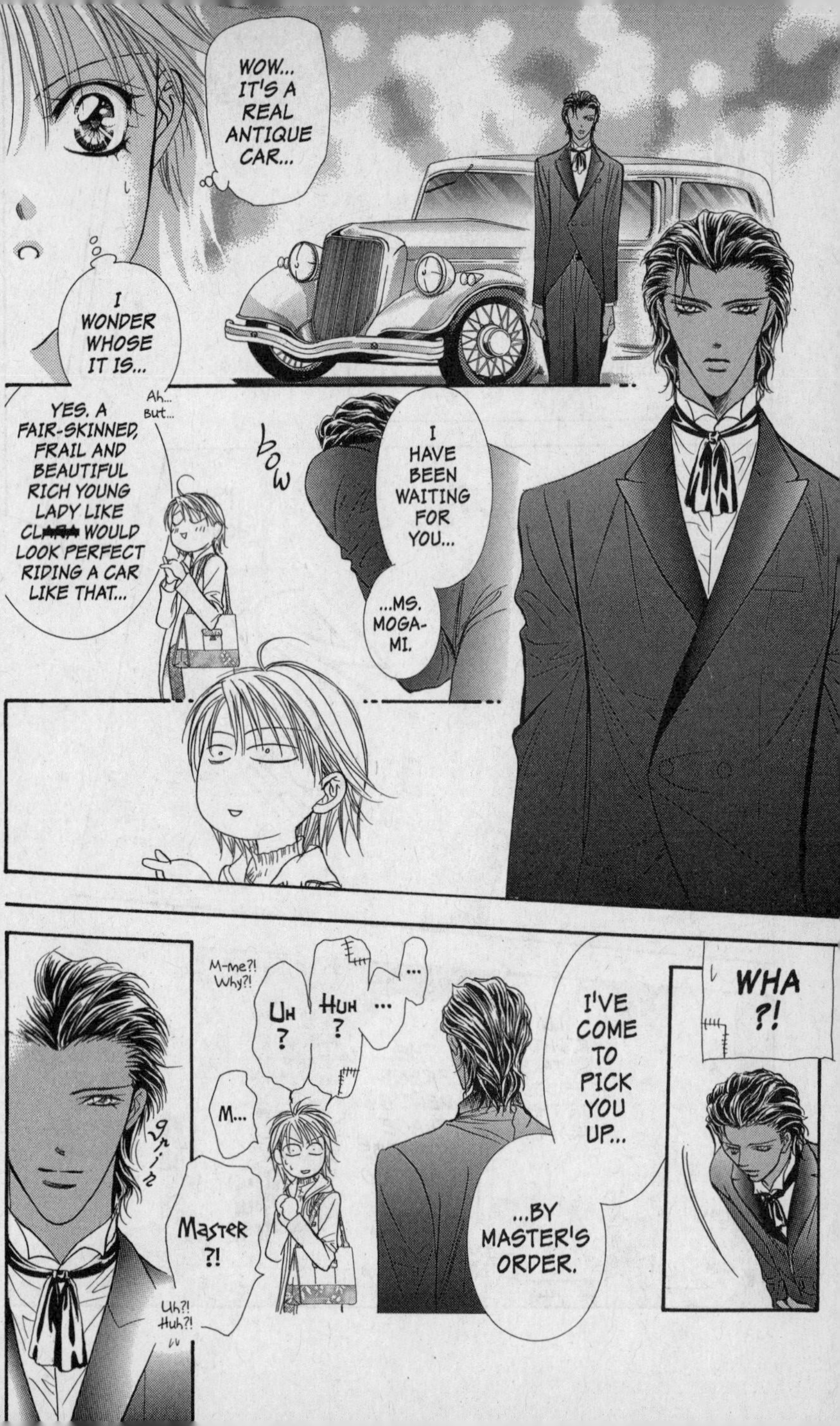
WOW... IT'S A REAL ANTIQUE CAR...
I WONDER WHOSE IT IS...
Ah... But...
YES. A FAIR-SKINNED, FRAIL AND BEAUTIFUL RICH YOUNG LADY LIKE CL[redacted] WOULD LOOK PERFECT RIDING A CAR LIKE THAT...
bow
I HAVE BEEN WAITING FOR YOU...
...MS. MOGAMI.
WHA ?!
I'VE COME TO PICK YOU UP...
...BY MASTER'S ORDER.
...
HUH ? ...
UH ?
M-me?! Why?!
M...
Master ?!
Uh?! Huh?!
grin

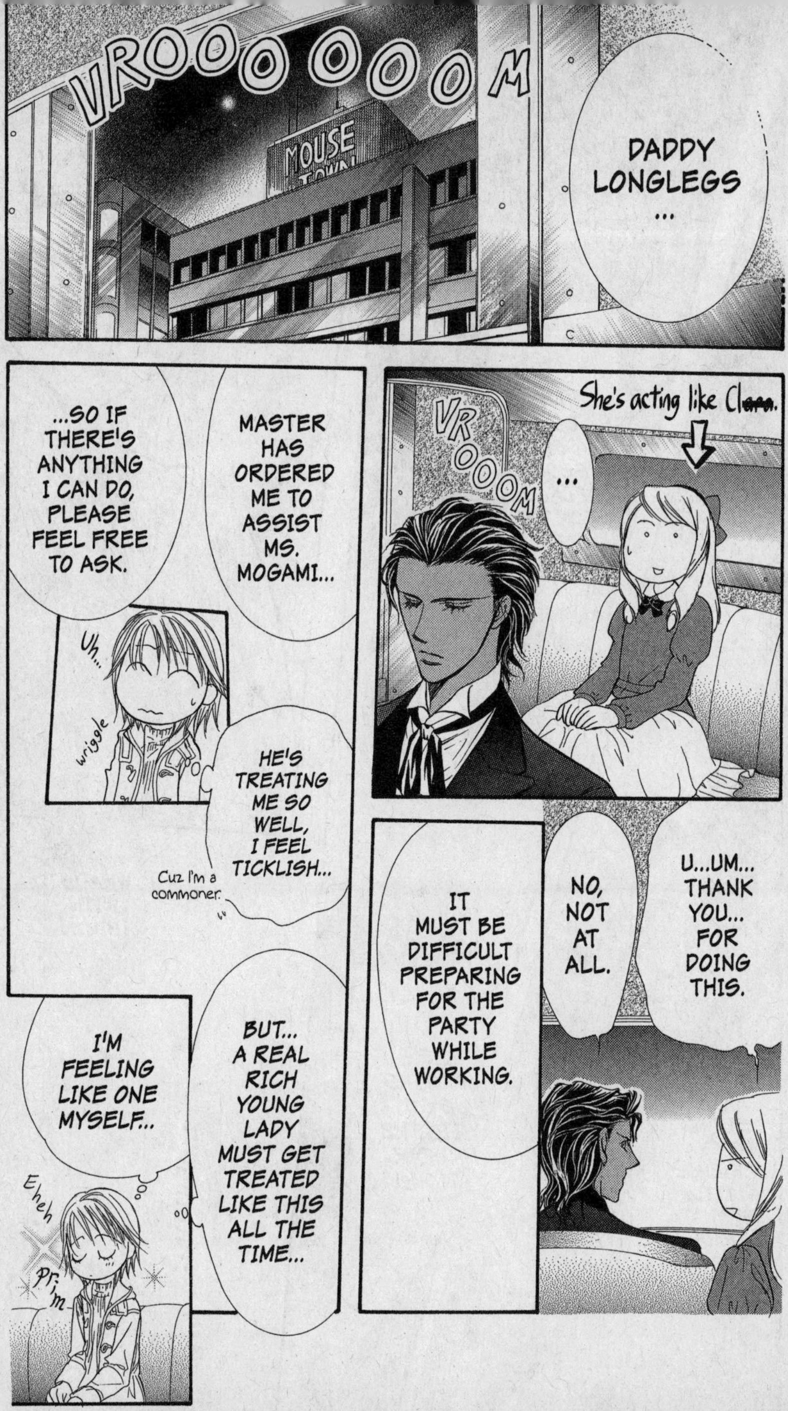
DADDY LONGLEGS ...
VROOOOOOOM
MOUSE TOWN
She's acting like Cl.
VROOOM
...
MASTER HAS ORDERED ME TO ASSIST MS. MOGAMI...
...SO IF THERE'S ANYTHING I CAN DO, PLEASE FEEL FREE TO ASK.
Uh...
wriggle
HE'S TREATING ME SO WELL, I FEEL TICKLISH...
Cuz I'm a commoner.
U...UM... THANK YOU... FOR DOING THIS.
NO, NOT AT ALL.
IT MUST BE DIFFICULT PREPARING FOR THE PARTY WHILE WORKING.
BUT... A REAL RICH YOUNG LADY MUST GET TREATED LIKE THIS ALL THE TIME...
I'M FEELING LIKE ONE MYSELF...
Eheh
Prim

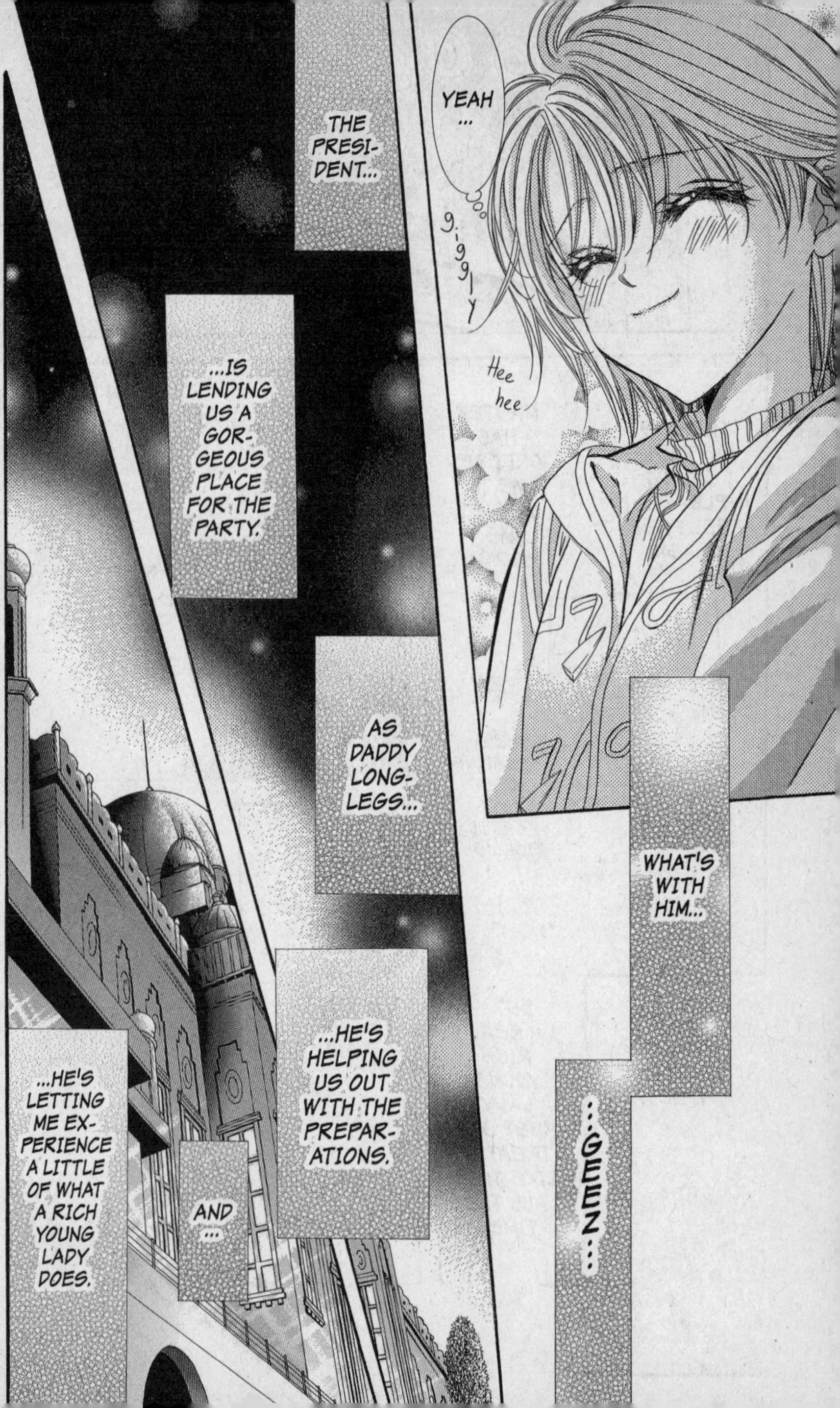
YEAH...
giggly
Hee hee
WHAT'S WITH HIM...
...GEEZ...
THE PRESIDENT...
...IS LENDING US A GORGEOUS PLACE FOR THE PARTY.
AS DADDY LONG-LEGS...
...HE'S HELPING US OUT WITH THE PREPARATIONS.
AND...
...HE'S LETTING ME EXPERIENCE A LITTLE OF WHAT A RICH YOUNG LADY DOES.

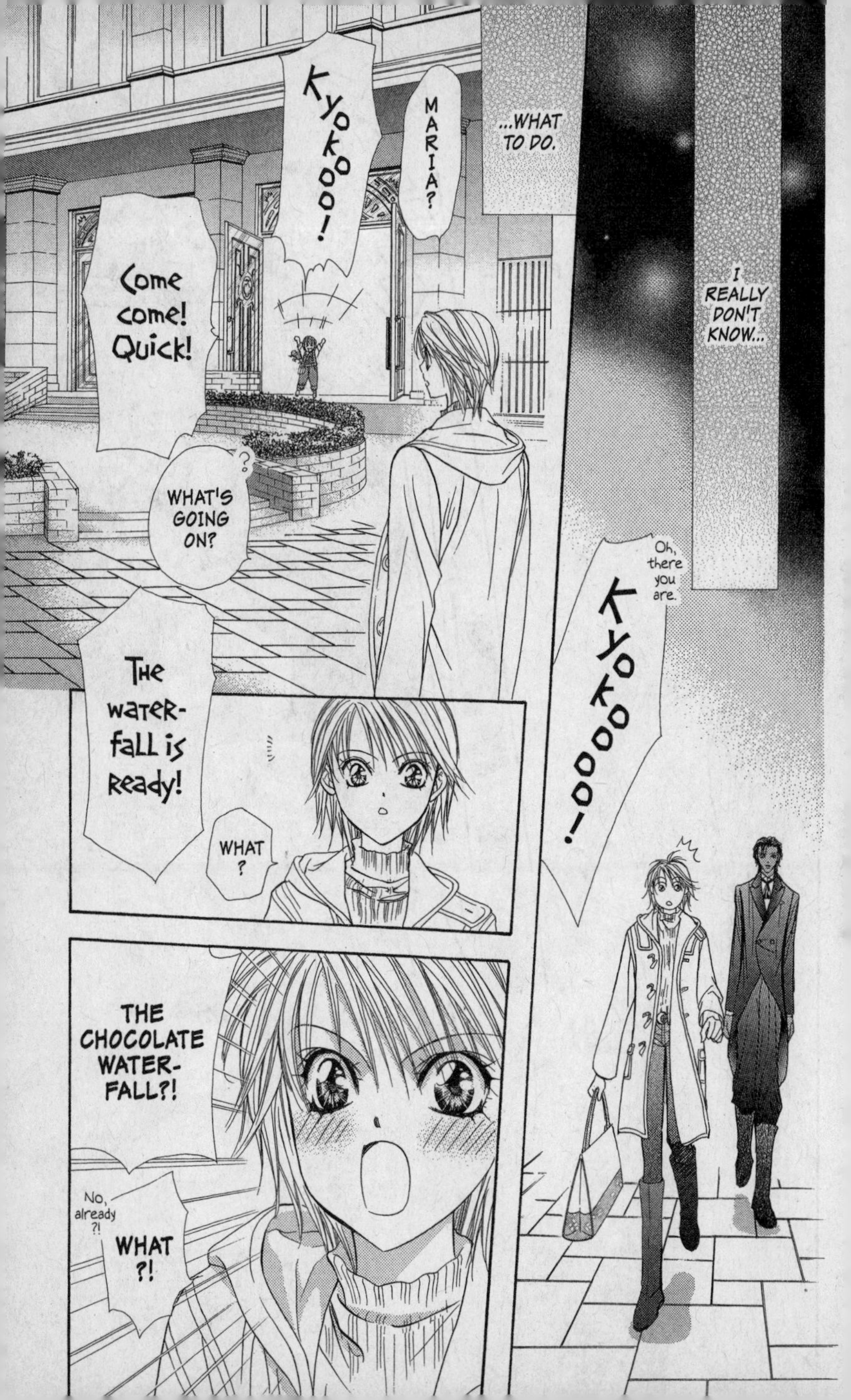
...WHAT TO DO.
I REALLY DON'T KNOW...
KYOKOOOO!
Oh, there you are.
MARIA?
KYOKOOO!
Come come! Quick!
WHAT'S GOING ON?
The waterfall is ready!
WHAT?
THE CHOCOLATE WATERFALL?!
WHAT?!
No, already?!

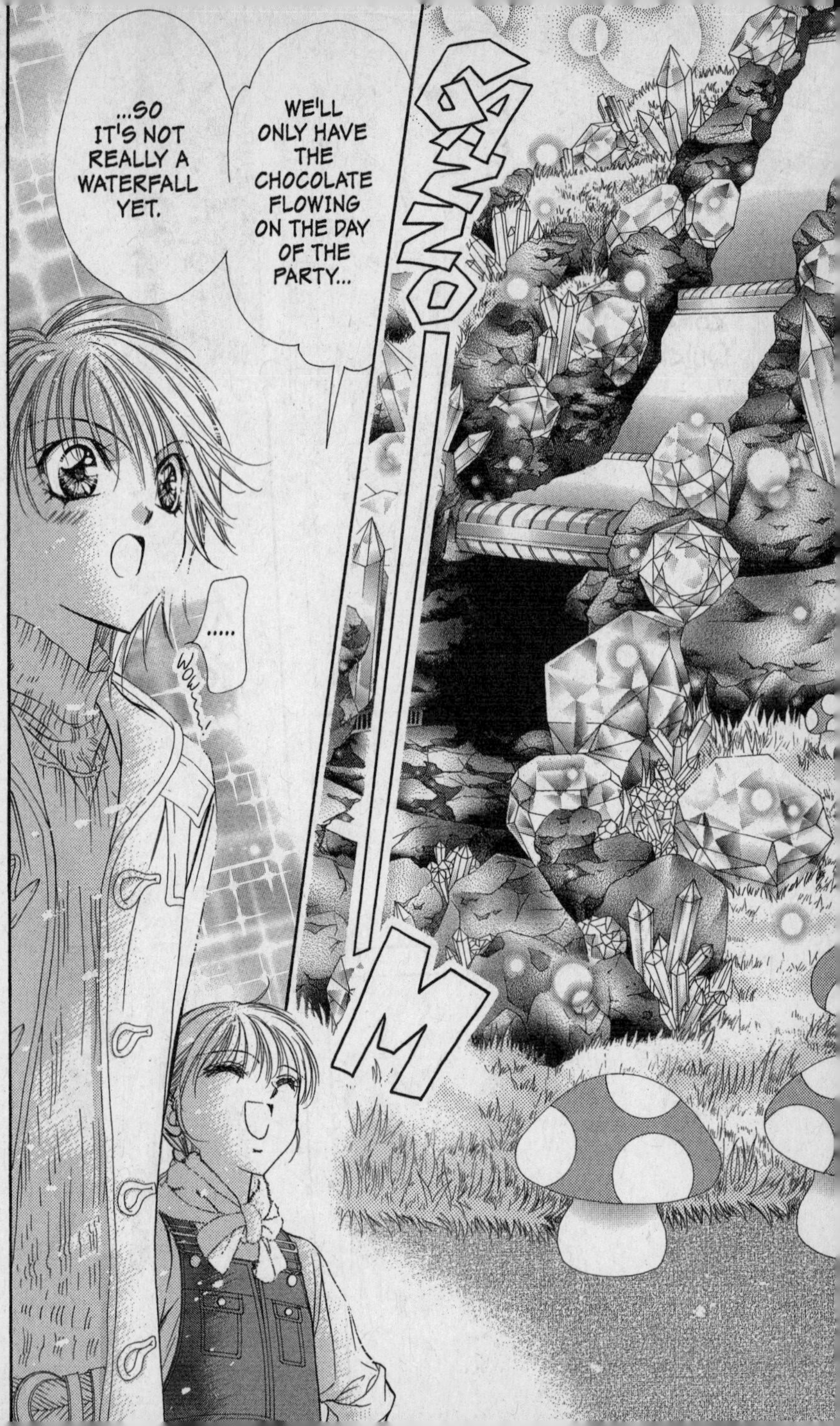
GAWWO—M
WE'LL ONLY HAVE THE CHOCOLATE FLOWING ON THE DAY OF THE PARTY...
...SO IT'S NOT REALLY A WATERFALL YET.
.....
WOW...!

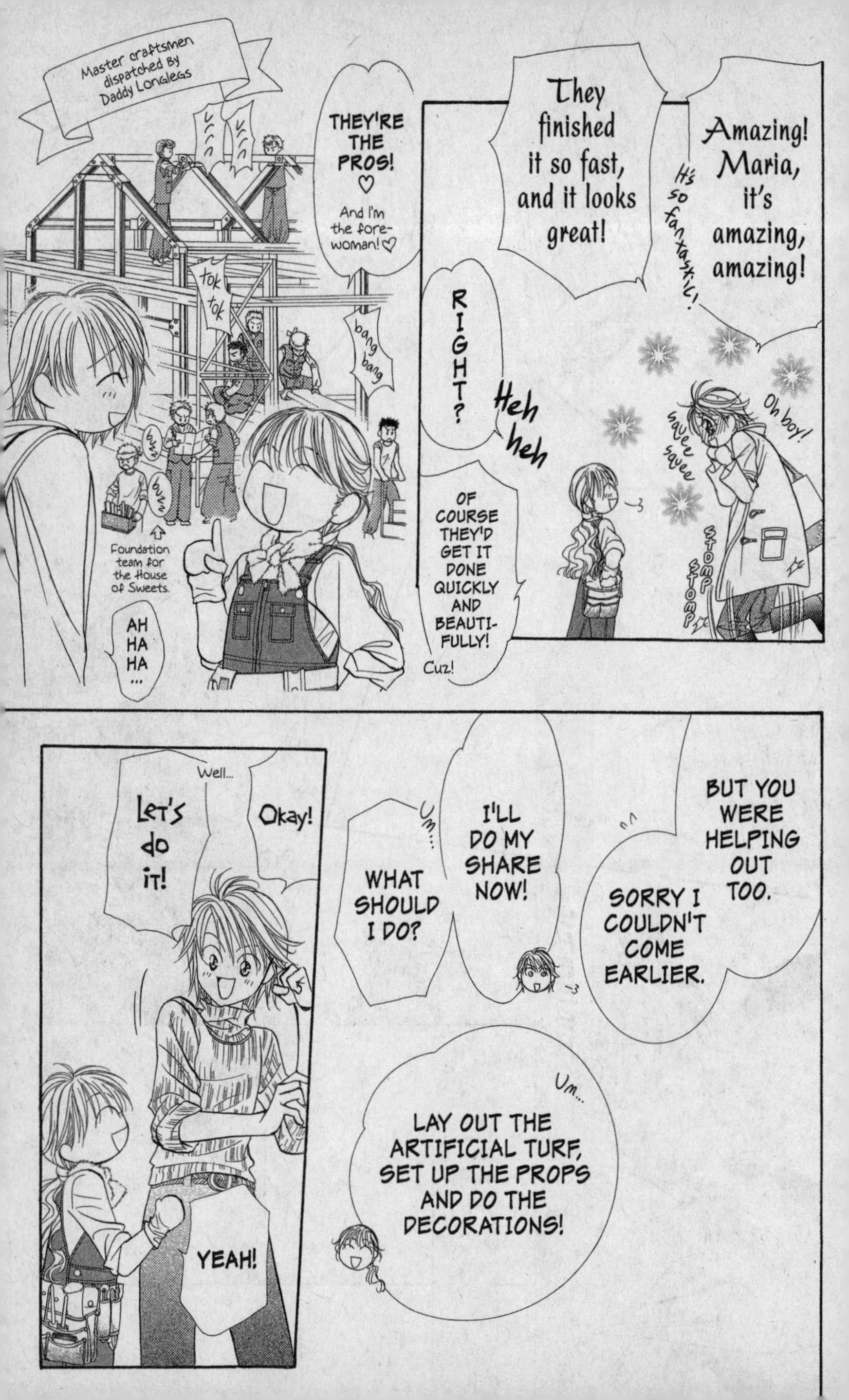
Amazing! Maria, it's amazing, amazing!
It's so fantastic!
They finished it so fast, and it looks great!
Oh boy!
squee squee
STOMP STOMP STOMP
RIGHT?
Heh heh
OF COURSE THEY'D GET IT DONE QUICKLY AND BEAUTIFULLY!
Cuz!
Master craftsmen dispatched by Daddy Longlegs
THEY'RE THE PROS! ♡
And I'm the fore-woman! ♡
tok tok
bang bang
buzz
buzz
Foundation team for the House of Sweets.
AH HA HA...
BUT YOU WERE HELPING OUT TOO.
SORRY I COULDN'T COME EARLIER.
I'LL DO MY SHARE NOW!
Um...
WHAT SHOULD I DO?
Um...
LAY OUT THE ARTIFICIAL TURF, SET UP THE PROPS AND DO THE DECORATIONS!
Okay!
Well...
Let's do it!
YEAH!

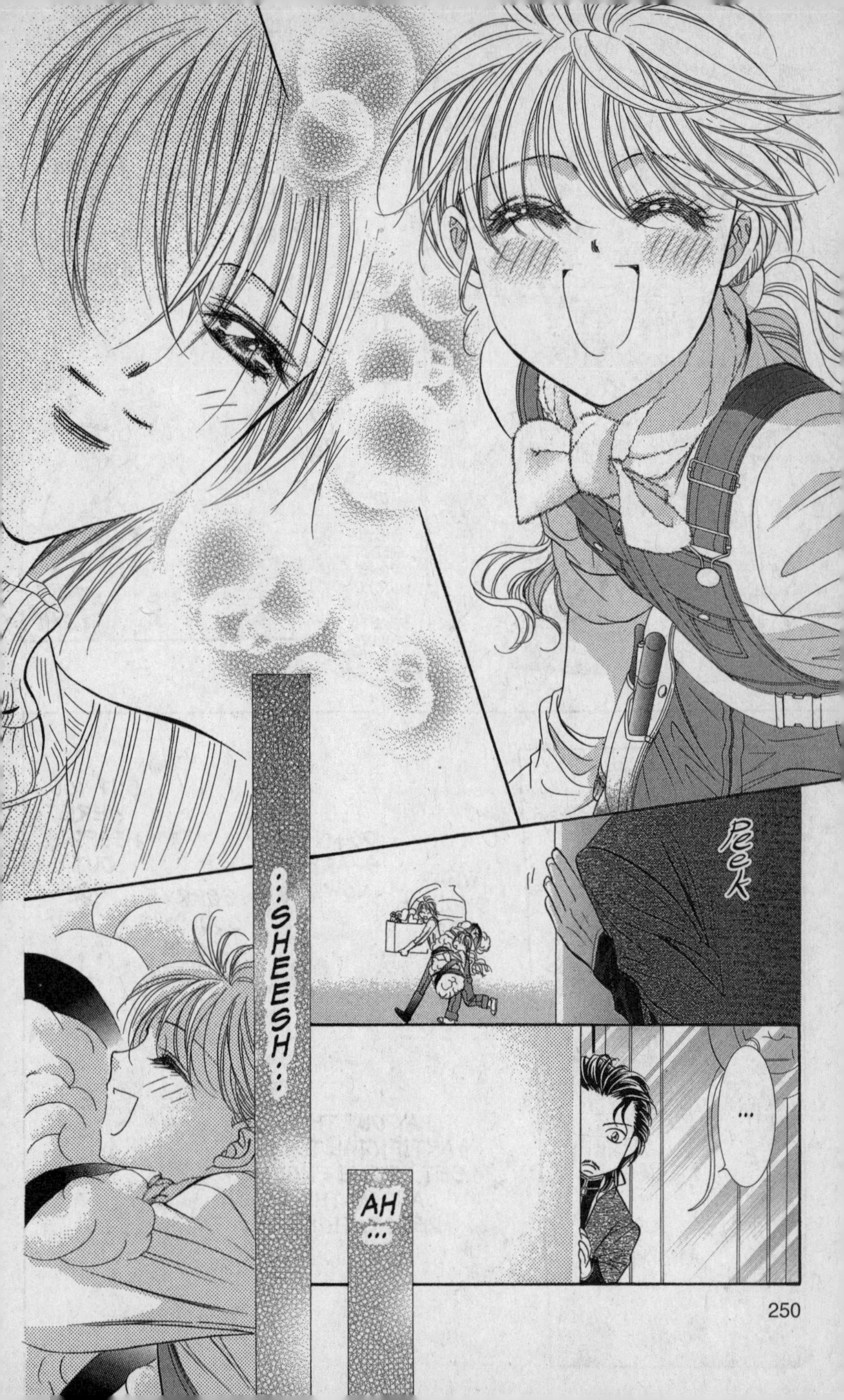
PEEK
...SHEESH...
...
AH ...

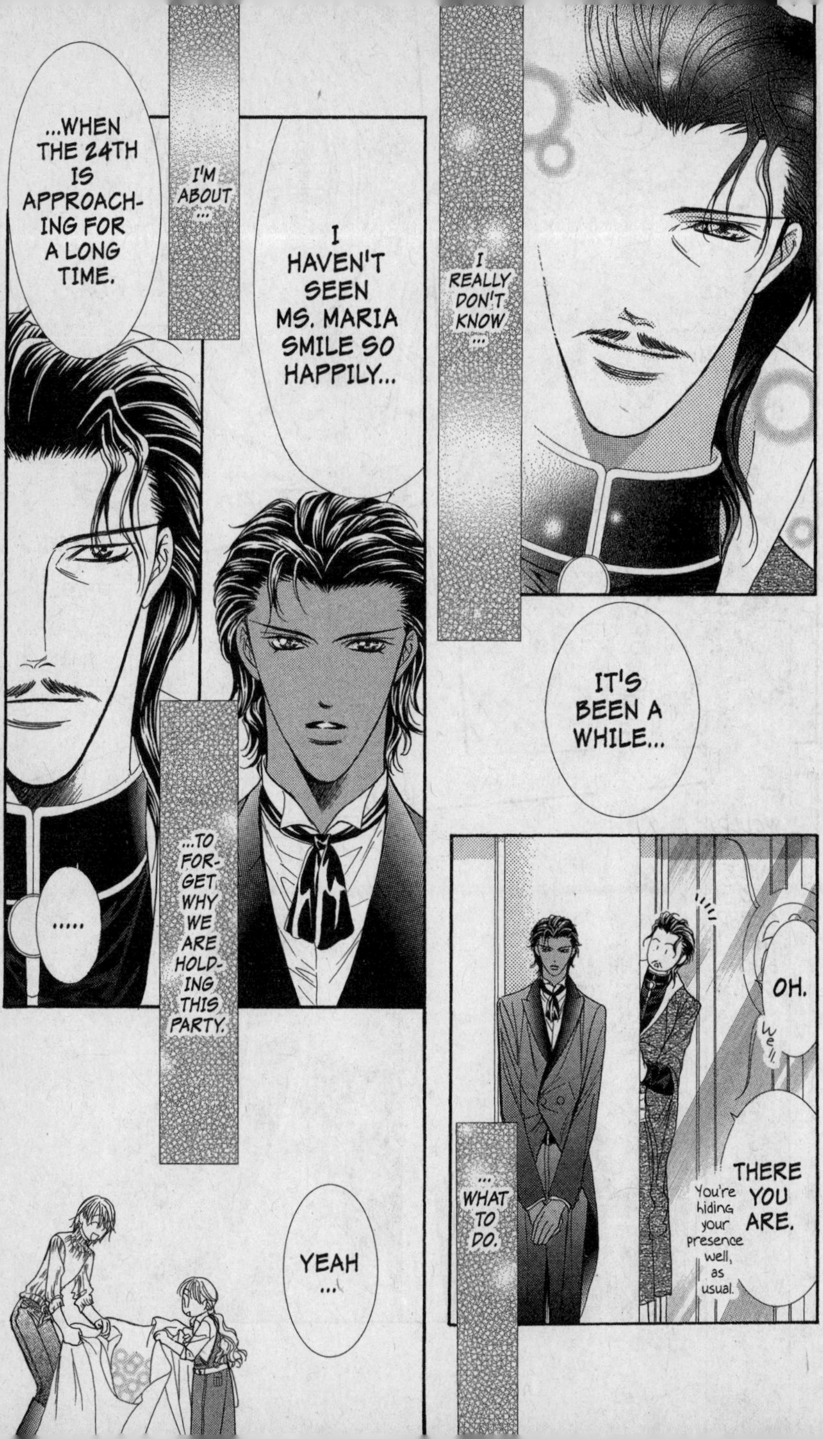
I REALLY DON'T KNOW ...
I HAVEN'T SEEN MS. MARIA SMILE SO HAPPILY...
I'M ABOUT ...
...WHEN THE 24TH IS APPROACHING FOR A LONG TIME.
.....
...TO FORGET WHY WE ARE HOLDING THIS PARTY.
IT'S BEEN A WHILE...
OH.
Well...
THERE YOU ARE.
You're hiding your presence well, as usual.
... WHAT TO DO.
YEAH ...

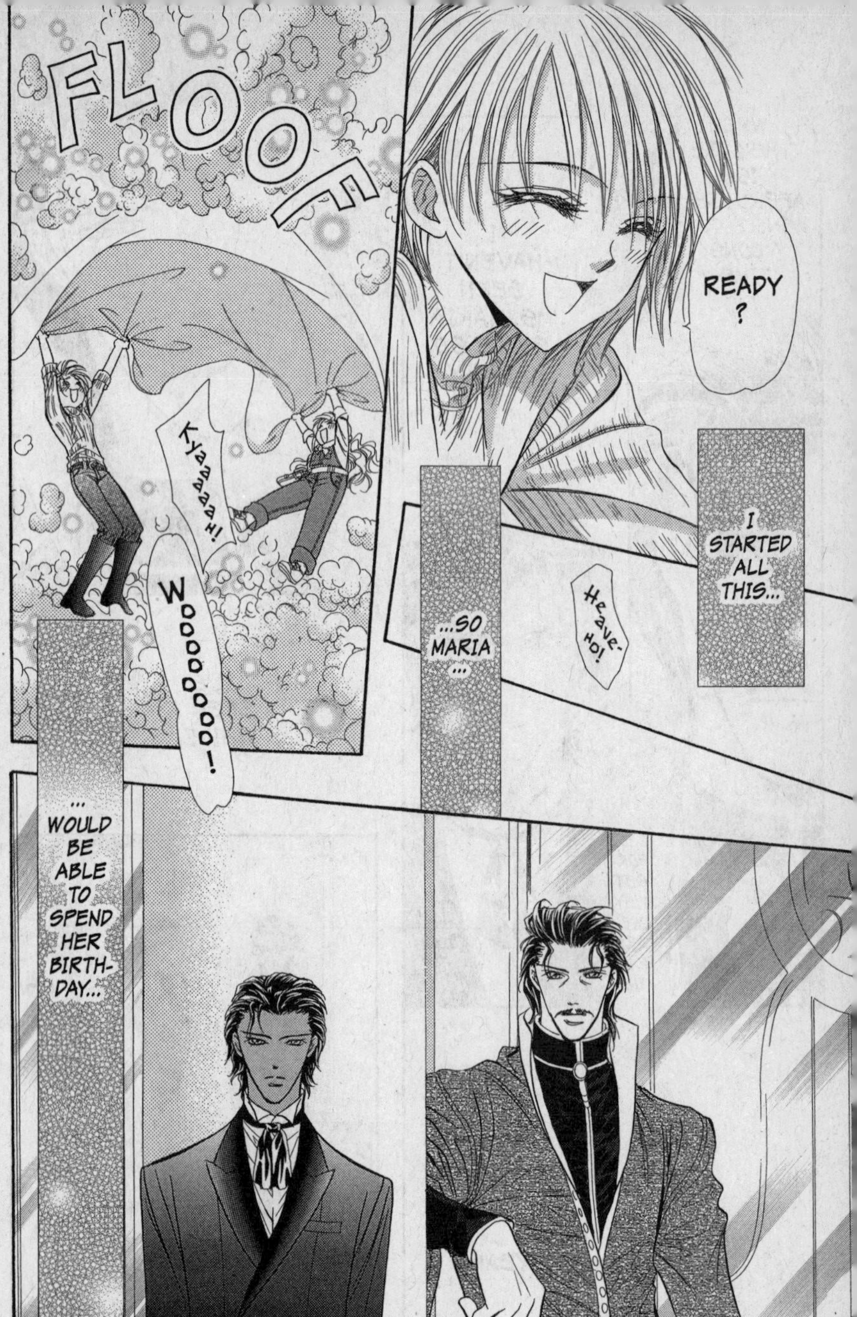
READY?
I STARTED ALL THIS...
Heave-ho!
...SO MARIA...
FLOOF
Kyaaaaaah!
Wooooooooo!
...WOULD BE ABLE TO SPEND HER BIRTHDAY...

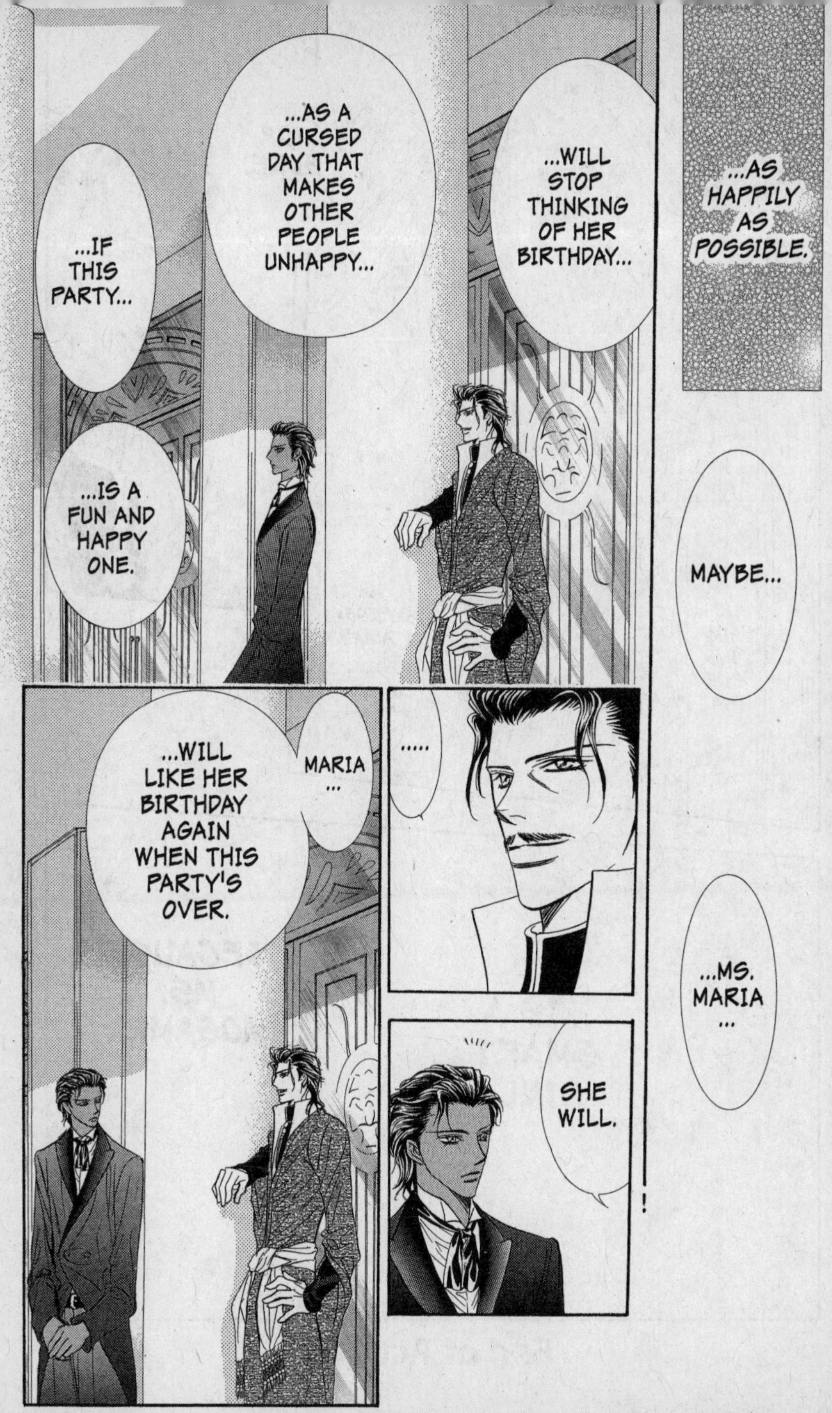

...AS HAPPILY AS POSSIBLE.
MAYBE...
...MS. MARIA ...
...WILL STOP THINKING OF HER BIRTHDAY...
...AS A CURSED DAY THAT MAKES OTHER PEOPLE UNHAPPY...
...IF THIS PARTY...
...IS A FUN AND HAPPY ONE.
.....
SHE WILL.
MARIA ...
...WILL LIKE HER BIRTHDAY AGAIN WHEN THIS PARTY'S OVER.

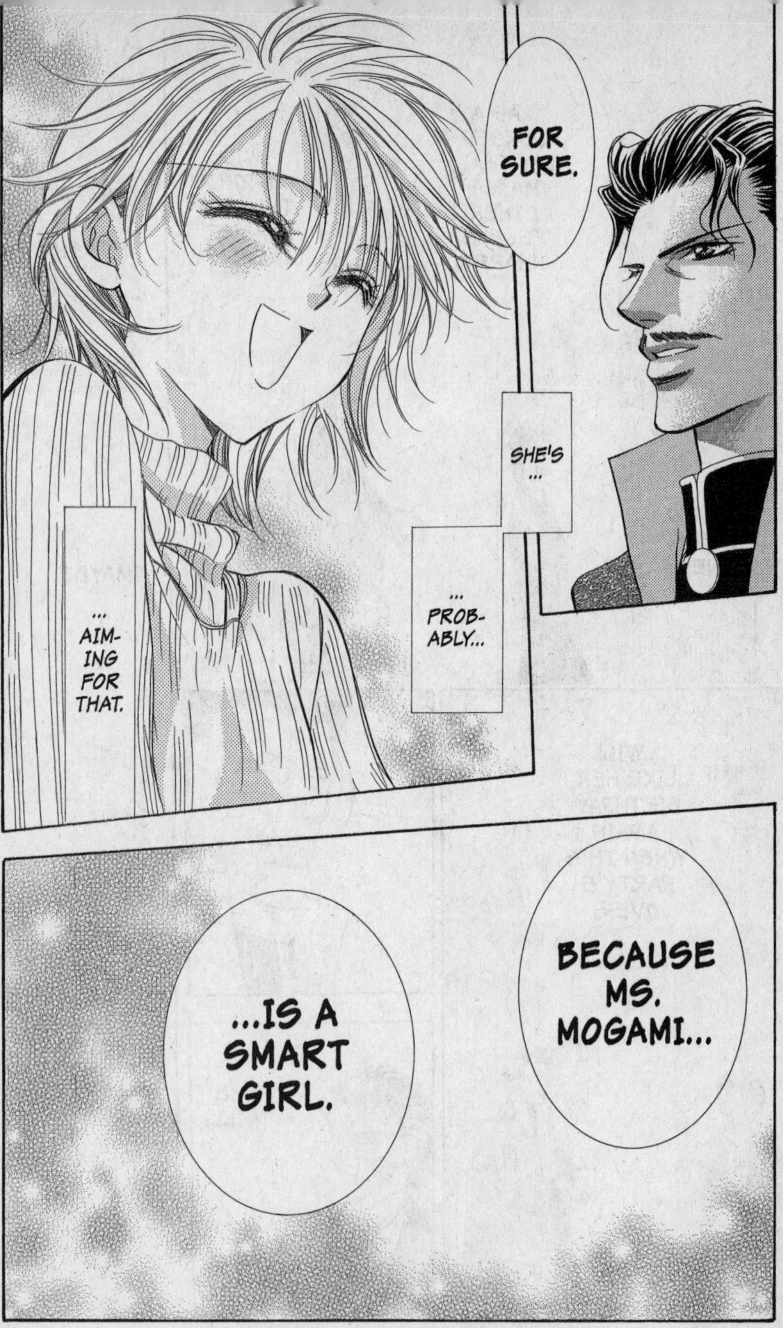
FOR SURE.
SHE'S ...
... PROBABLY...
... AIMING FOR THAT.
BECAUSE MS. MOGAMI...
...IS A SMART GIRL.

End of Act 116

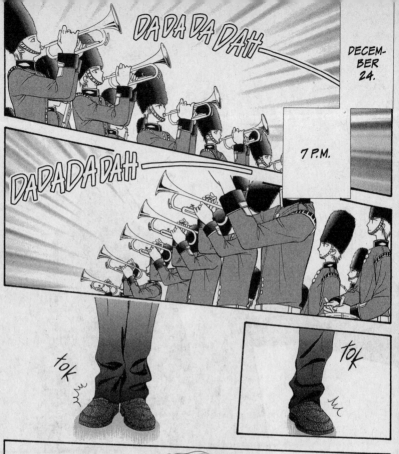

DADADADAH

DECEM-BER 24.

7 P.M.

DADADADAH

tok

tok

...FOR COMING...

THANK YOU...

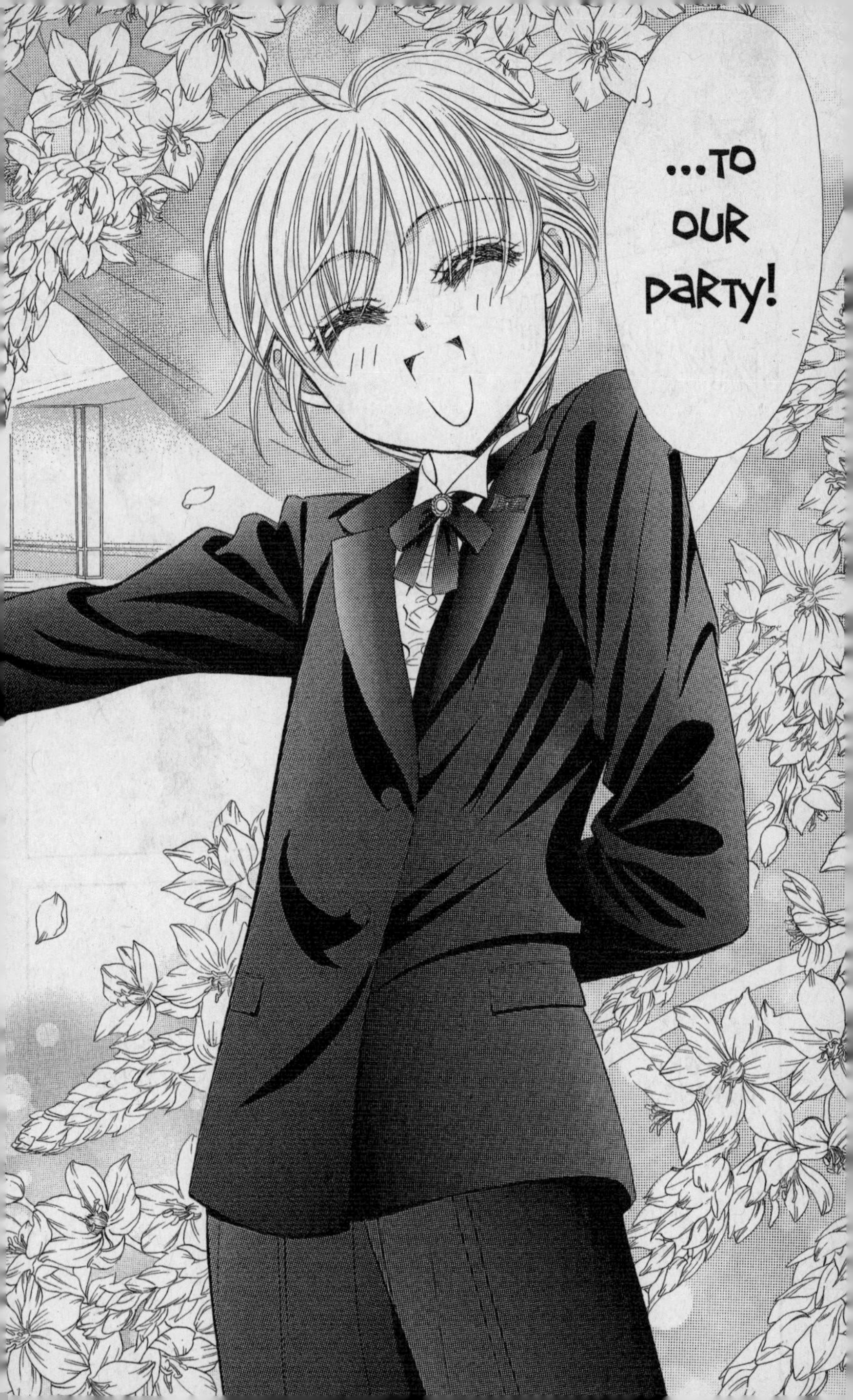
...TO OUR PARTY!

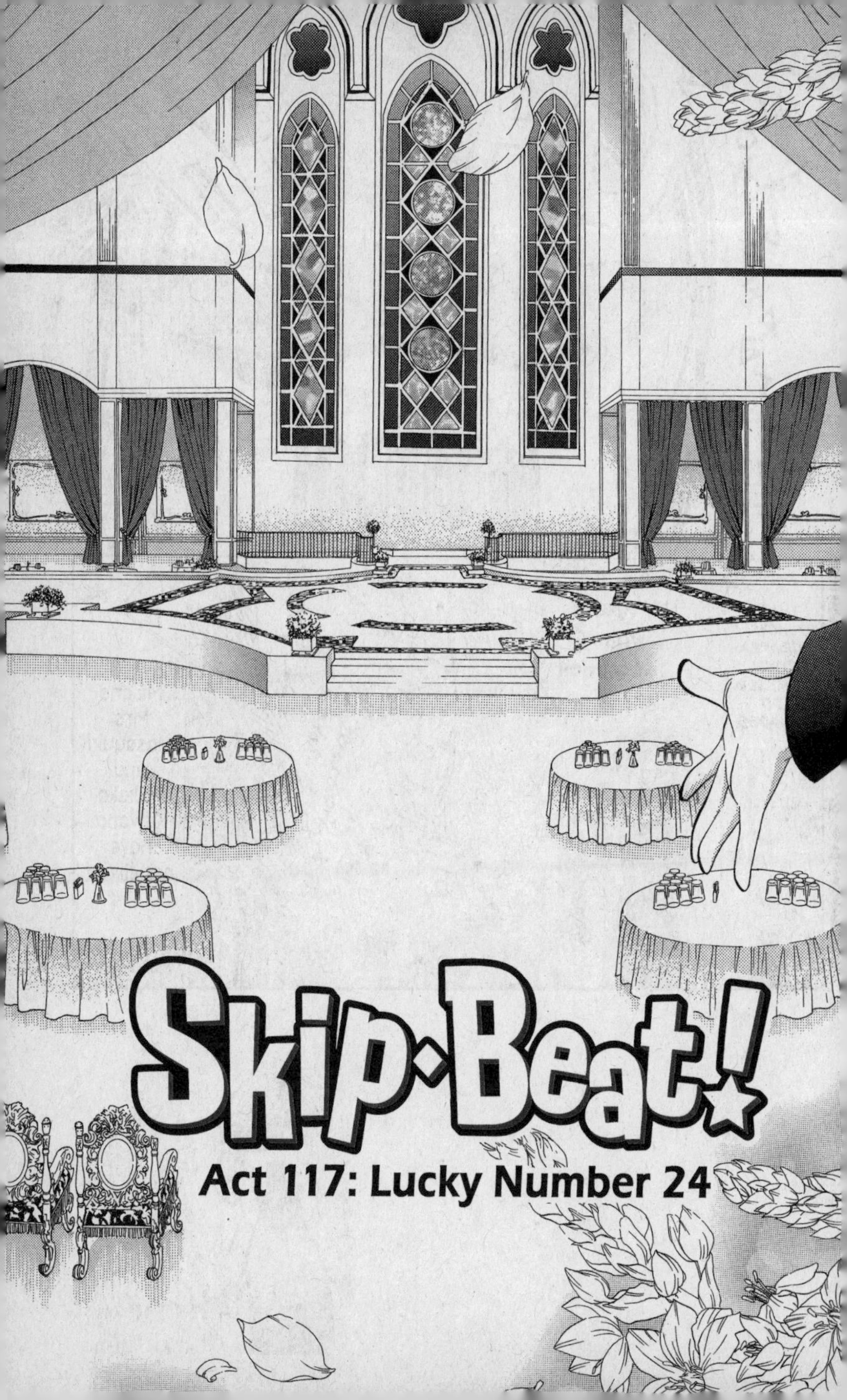
Skip·Beat!
Act 117: Lucky Number 24

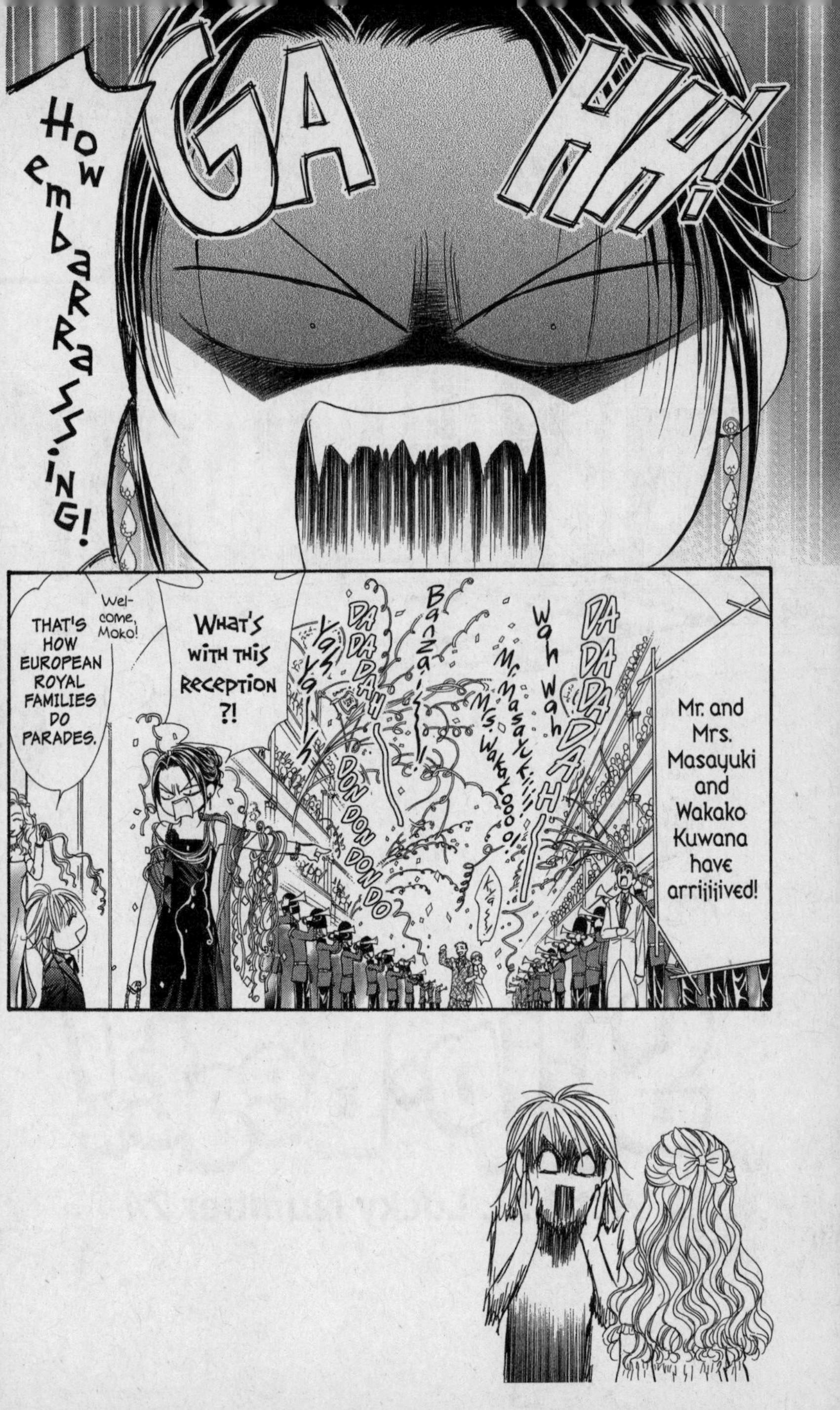
GAHH!
How embarrassing!
Mr. and Mrs. Masayuki and Wakako Kuwana have arriiiiived!
DA DA DA DA DAH!
Wah wah
Mr. Masayuki!! Mrs. Wakakooo!
Banzai!
DA DA DAH
DON DON DON DO
What's with this reception?!
Wel-come, Moko!
THAT'S HOW EUROPEAN ROYAL FAMILIES DO PARADES.

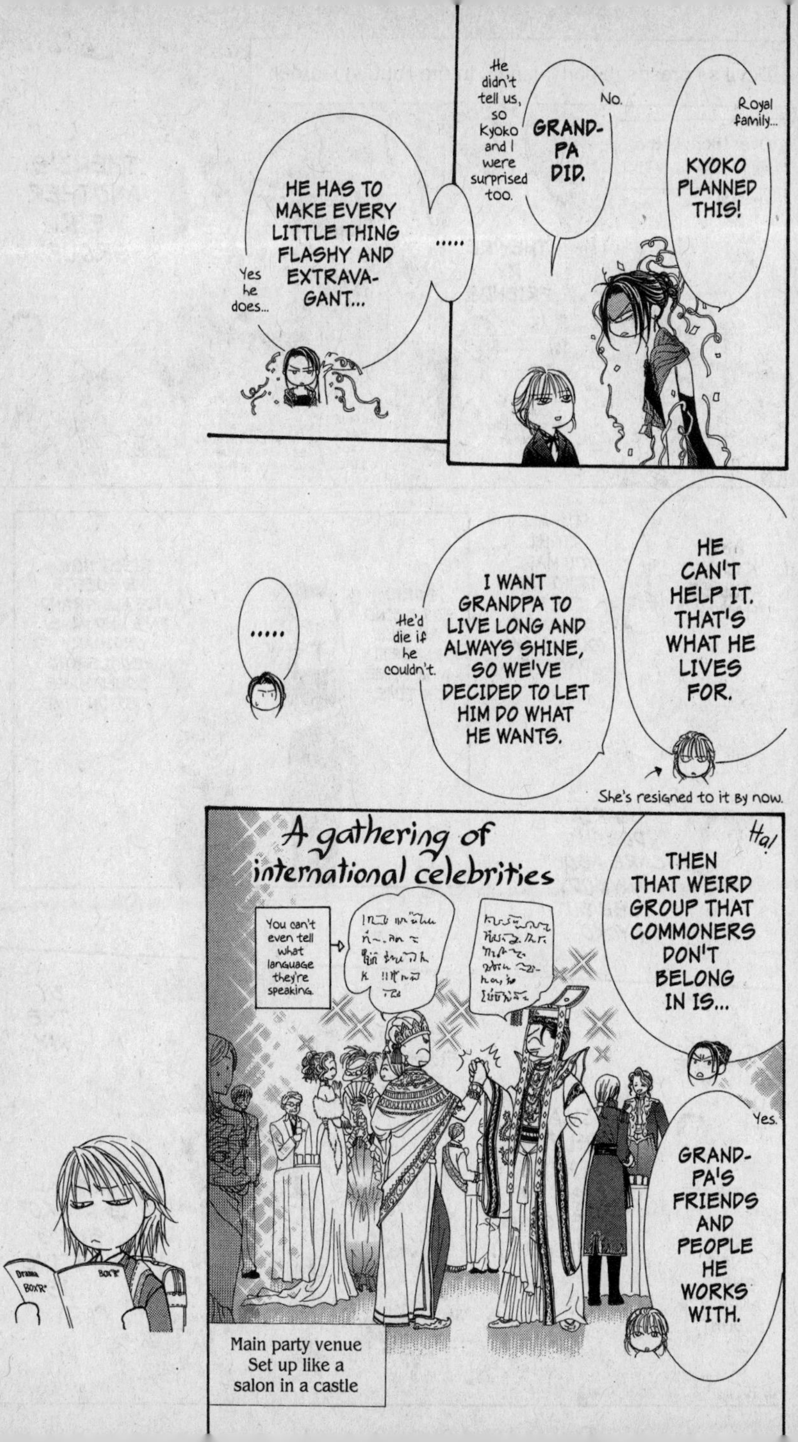
Royal family...
KYOKO PLANNED THIS!
No.
GRAND-PA DID.
He didn't tell us, so Kyoko and I were surprised too.
.....
HE HAS TO MAKE EVERY LITTLE THING FLASHY AND EXTRAVA-GANT...
Yes he does...
HE CAN'T HELP IT. THAT'S WHAT HE LIVES FOR.
I WANT GRANDPA TO LIVE LONG AND ALWAYS SHINE, SO WE'VE DECIDED TO LET HIM DO WHAT HE WANTS.
He'd die if he couldn't.
......
She's resigned to it by now.
Ha!
THEN THAT WEIRD GROUP THAT COMMONERS DON'T BELONG IN IS...
Yes.
GRAND-PA'S FRIENDS AND PEOPLE HE WORKS WITH.
A gathering of international celebrities
You can't even tell what language they're speaking.
Main party venue Set up like a salon in a castle

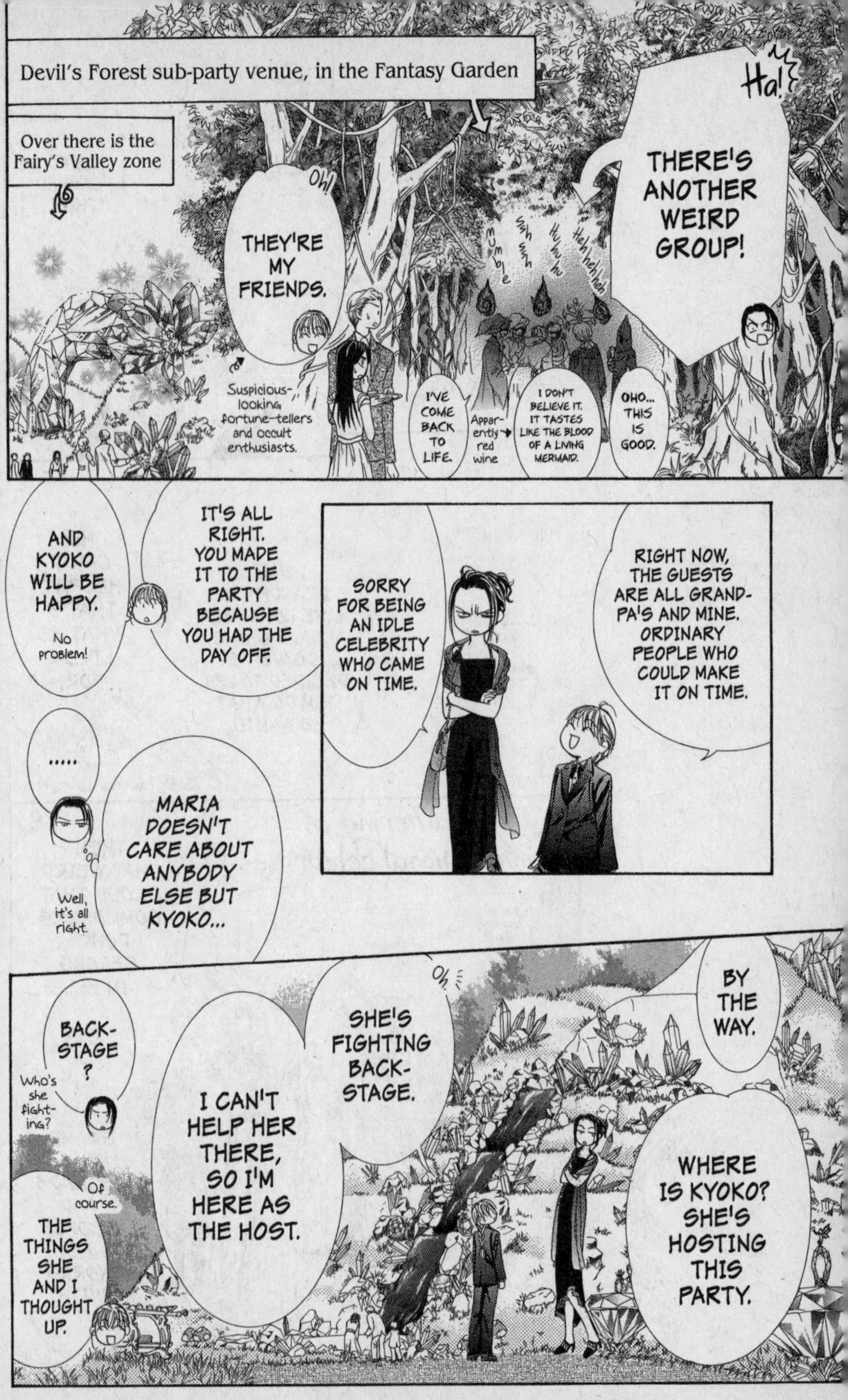
Devil's Forest sub-party venue, in the Fantasy Garden
Ha!
THERE'S ANOTHER WEIRD GROUP!
Heh heh heh
Hu hu hu
Ssh ssh
mumble
OHO... THIS IS GOOD.
I DON'T BELIEVE IT. IT TASTES LIKE THE BLOOD OF A LIVING MERMAID.
Apparently red wine
I'VE COME BACK TO LIFE.
Oh!
THEY'RE MY FRIENDS.
Suspicious-looking fortune-tellers and occult enthusiasts.
Over there is the Fairy's Valley zone
RIGHT NOW, THE GUESTS ARE ALL GRANDPA'S AND MINE. ORDINARY PEOPLE WHO COULD MAKE IT ON TIME.
SORRY FOR BEING AN IDLE CELEBRITY WHO CAME ON TIME.
IT'S ALL RIGHT. YOU MADE IT TO THE PARTY BECAUSE YOU HAD THE DAY OFF.
AND KYOKO WILL BE HAPPY.
No problem!
......
MARIA DOESN'T CARE ABOUT ANYBODY ELSE BUT KYOKO...
Well, it's all right.
BY THE WAY.
WHERE IS KYOKO? SHE'S HOSTING THIS PARTY.
Oh.
SHE'S FIGHTING BACK-STAGE.
I CAN'T HELP HER THERE, SO I'M HERE AS THE HOST.
BACK-STAGE?
Who's she fighting?
Of course.
THE THINGS SHE AND I THOUGHT UP.

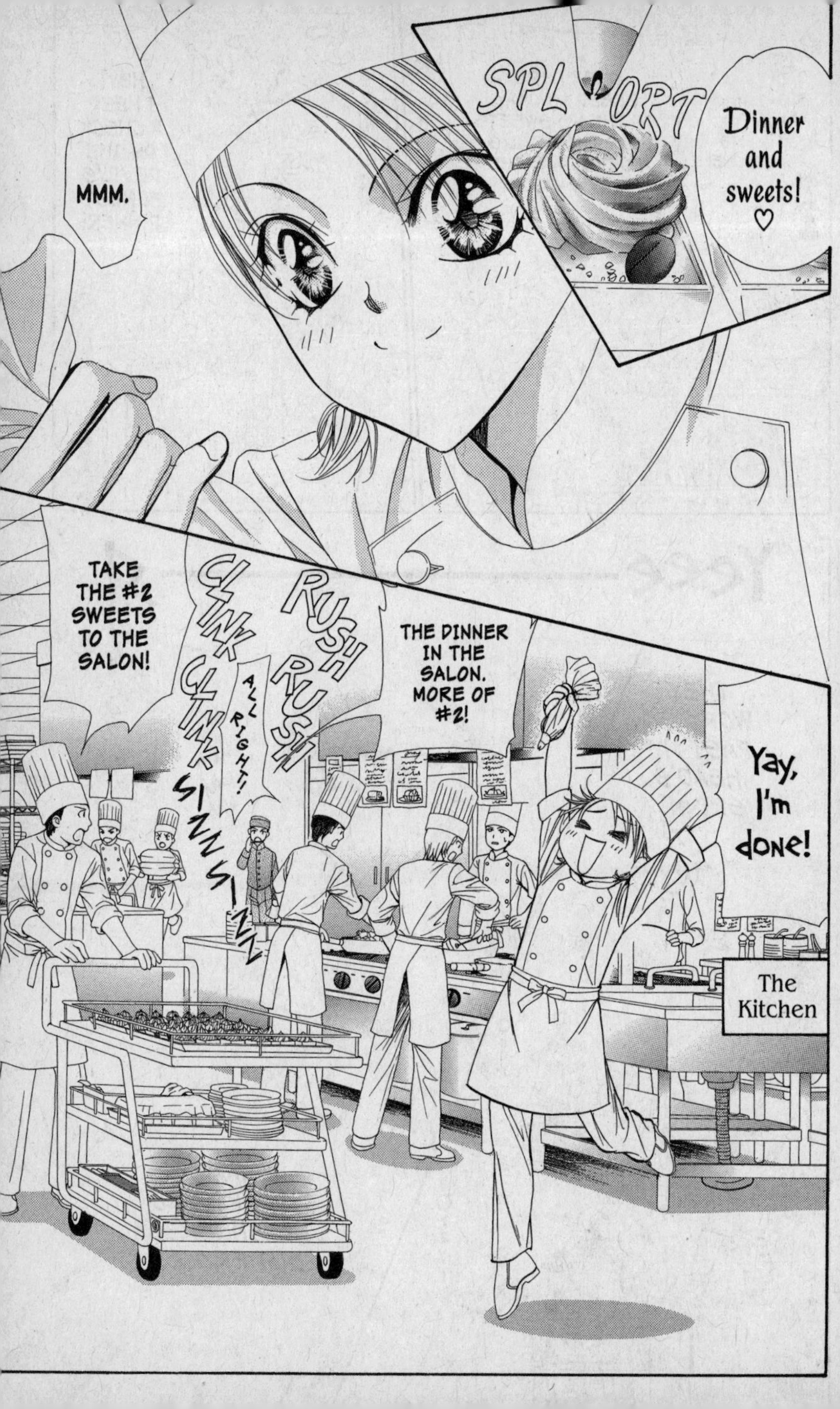
SPLORT
Dinner and sweets! ♡
MMM.
Yay, I'm done!
The Kitchen
THE DINNER IN THE SALON. MORE OF #2!
RUSH RUSH
ALL RIGHT!
CLINK CLINK
SIZZZ SIZZZ
TAKE THE #2 SWEETS TO THE SALON!

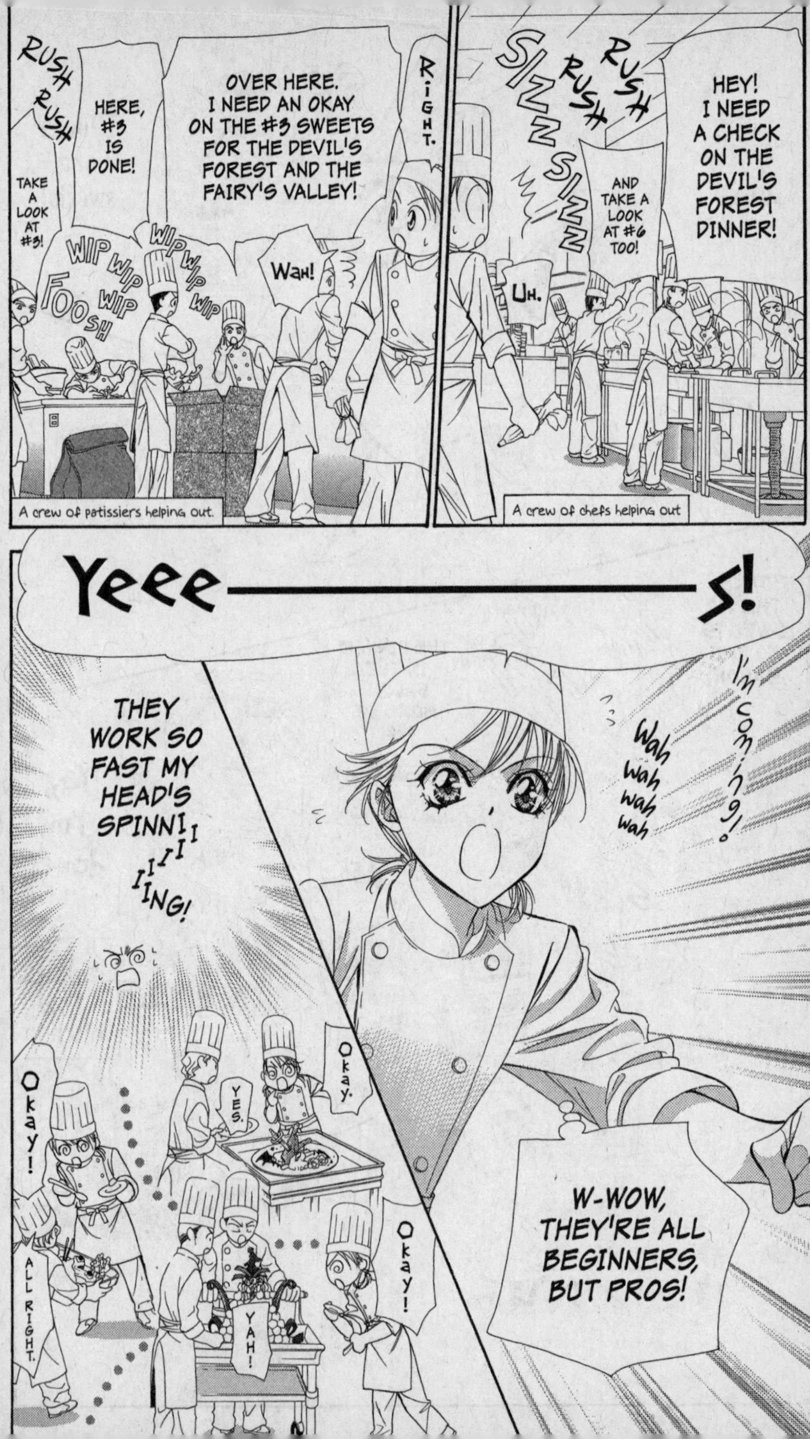
RUSH RUSH
SIZZ SIZZ SIZZ
HEY! I NEED A CHECK ON THE DEVIL'S FOREST DINNER!
AND TAKE A LOOK AT #6 TOO!
UH.
A crew of chefs helping out
RIGHT.
OVER HERE. I NEED AN OKAY ON THE #3 SWEETS FOR THE DEVIL'S FOREST AND THE FAIRY'S VALLEY!
HERE, #3 IS DONE!
RUSH RUSH
TAKE A LOOK AT #3!
WAH!
WIP WIP WIP WIP
WIP WIP
FOOSH
A crew of patissiers helping out.
Yeee————s!
I'm coming!
Wah wah wah wah
THEY WORK SO FAST MY HEAD'S SPINNIIIIIING!
Okay.
YES.
Okay!
W-WOW, THEY'RE ALL BEGINNERS, BUT PROS!
Okay!
YAH!
ALL RIGHT.

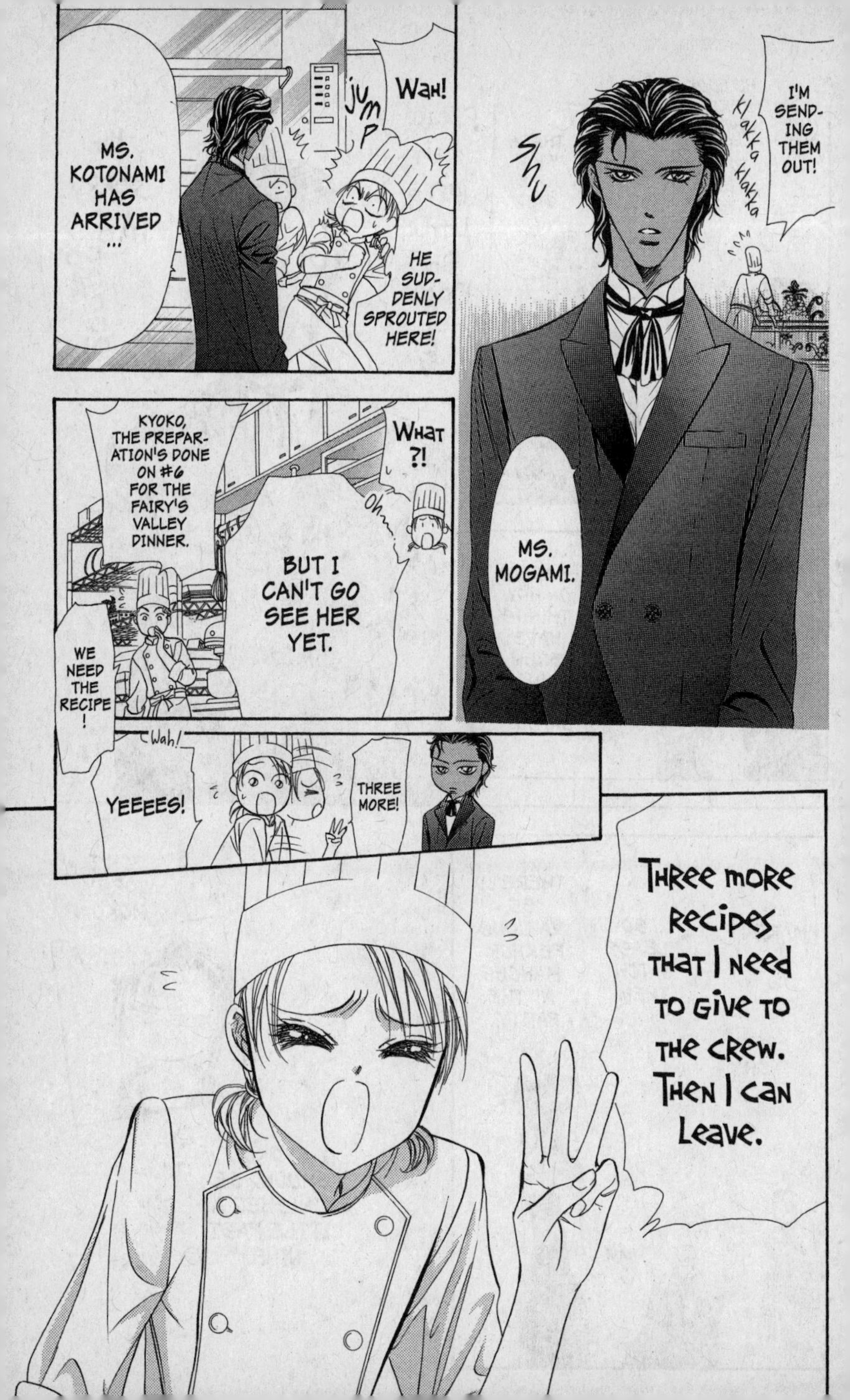

I'M SENDING THEM OUT!
klakka klakka
shu
MS. MOGAMI.
WAH!
jump
MS. KOTONAMI HAS ARRIVED ...
HE SUDDENLY SPROUTED HERE!
WHAT ?!
Oh...
KYOKO, THE PREPARATION'S DONE ON #6 FOR THE FAIRY'S VALLEY DINNER.
BUT I CAN'T GO SEE HER YET.
WE NEED THE RECIPE!
THREE MORE!
Wah!
YEEEES!
Three more recipes that I need to give to the crew. Then I can leave.

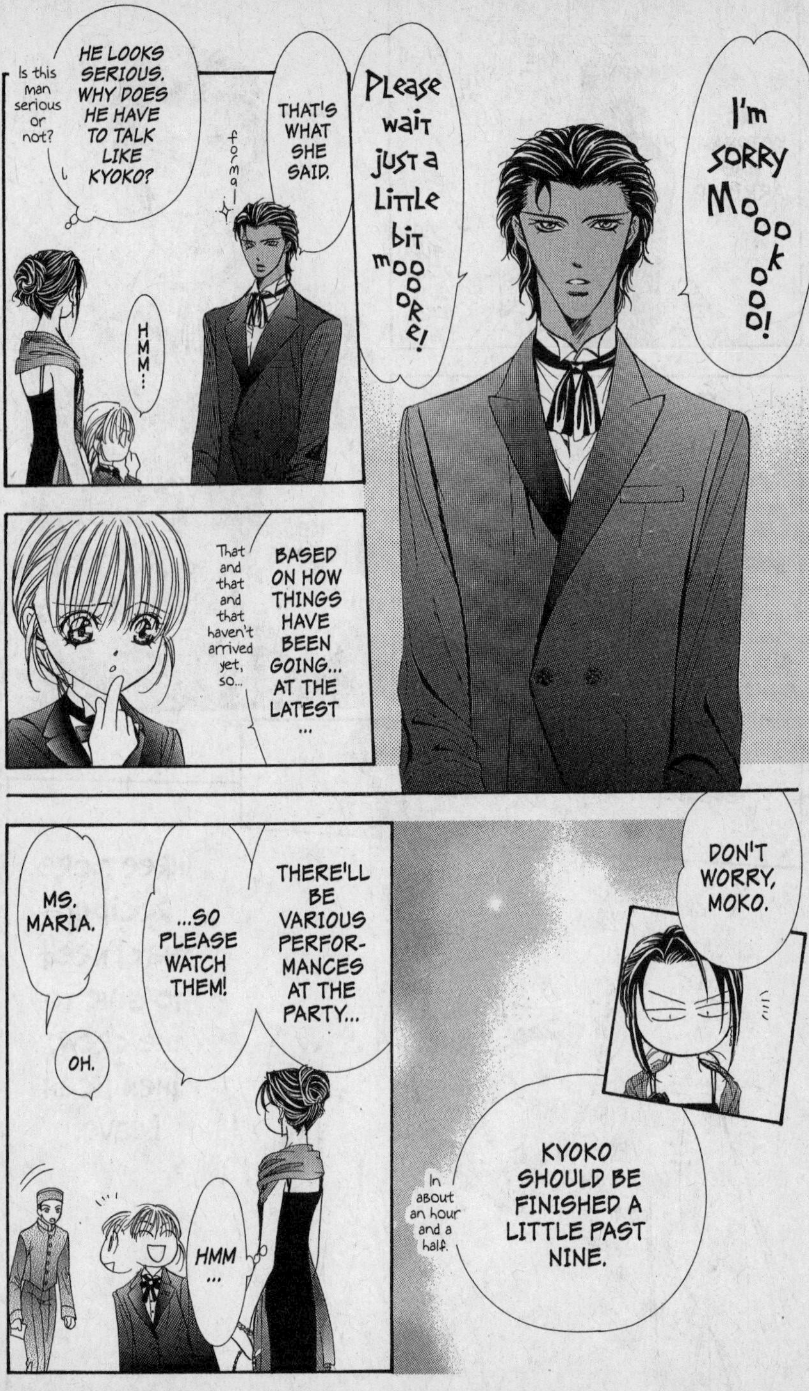
I'm SORRY MOOOKOOO!
Please wait just a little bit moooore!
THAT'S WHAT SHE SAID.
formal
HE LOOKS SERIOUS. WHY DOES HE HAVE TO TALK LIKE KYOKO?
Is this man serious or not?
HMM...
BASED ON HOW THINGS HAVE BEEN GOING... AT THE LATEST...
That and that and that haven't arrived yet, so...
DON'T WORRY, MOKO.
KYOKO SHOULD BE FINISHED A LITTLE PAST NINE.
In about an hour and a half.
THERE'LL BE VARIOUS PERFORMANCES AT THE PARTY...
...SO PLEASE WATCH THEM!
MS. MARIA.
OH.
HMM...

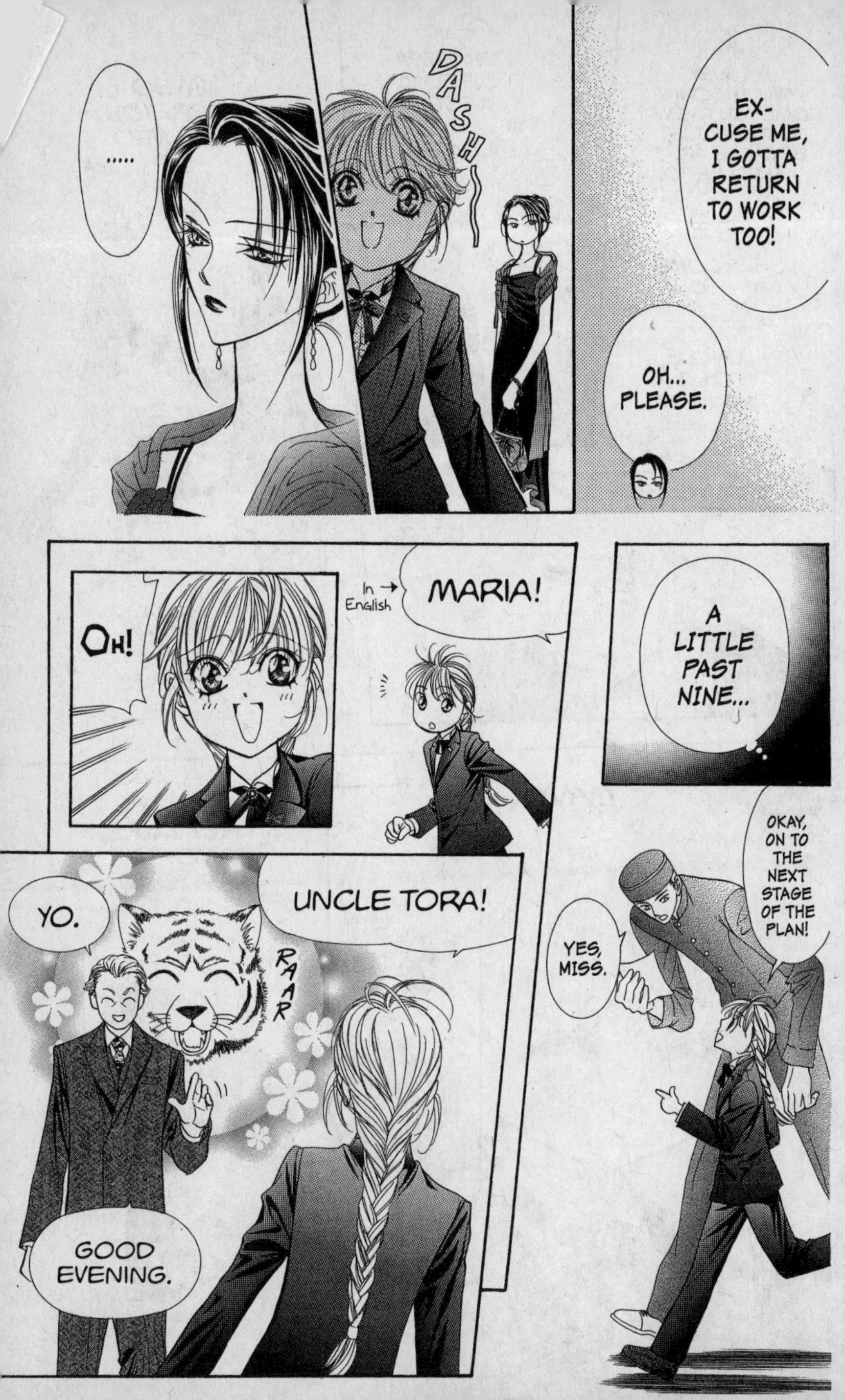
EX-CUSE ME, I GOTTA RETURN TO WORK TOO!
OH... PLEASE.
DASH
.....
A LITTLE PAST NINE...
MARIA!
In → English
OH!
OKAY, ON TO THE NEXT STAGE OF THE PLAN!
YES, MISS.
UNCLE TORA!
RAAR
YO.
GOOD EVENING.

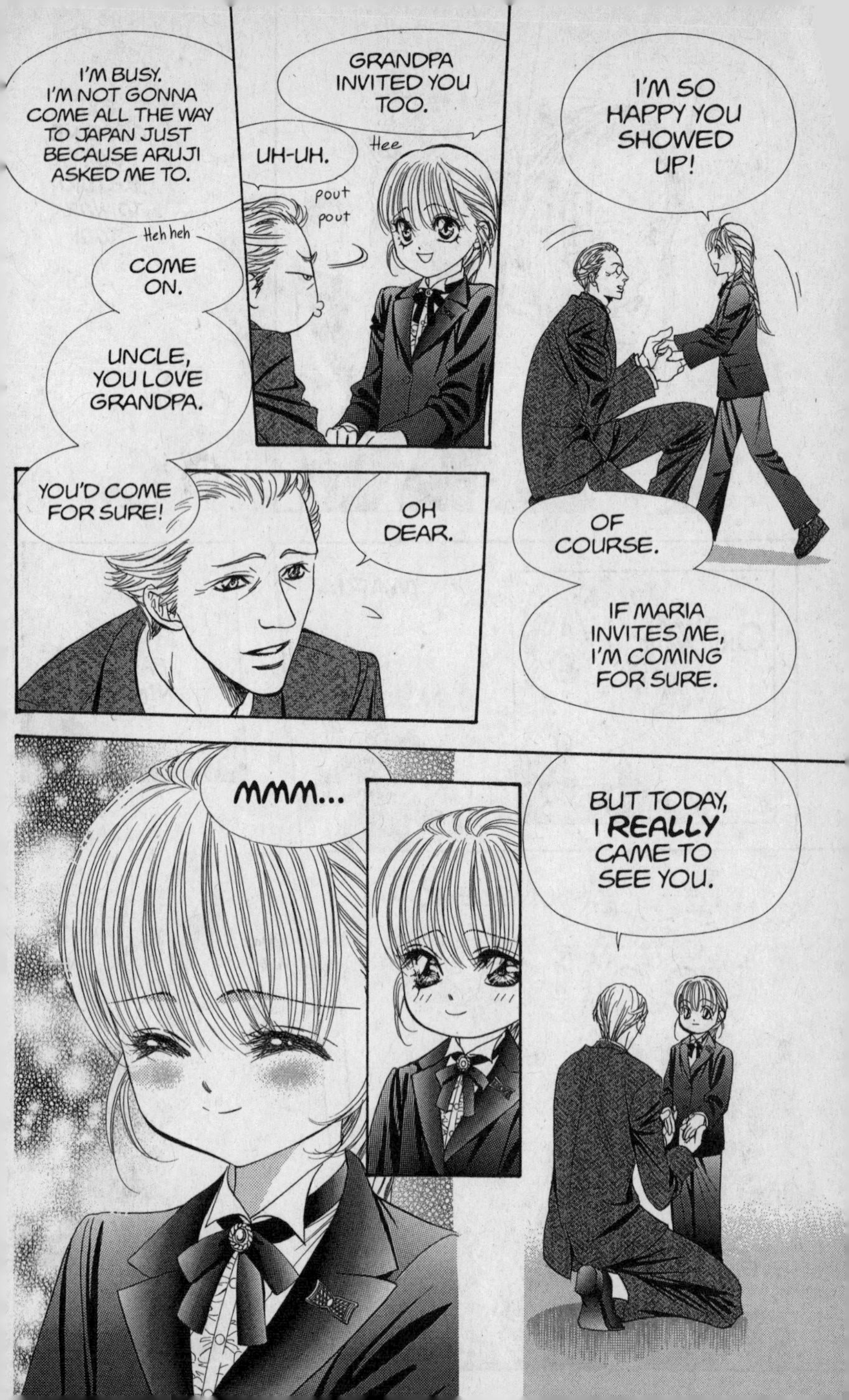

I'M SO HAPPY YOU SHOWED UP!
GRANDPA INVITED YOU TOO.
Hee
UH-UH.
pout pout
I'M BUSY. I'M NOT GONNA COME ALL THE WAY TO JAPAN JUST BECAUSE ARUJI ASKED ME TO.
Heh heh
COME ON.
UNCLE, YOU LOVE GRANDPA.
YOU'D COME FOR SURE!
OH DEAR.
OF COURSE.
IF MARIA INVITES ME, I'M COMING FOR SURE.
BUT TODAY, I REALLY CAME TO SEE YOU.
MMM...

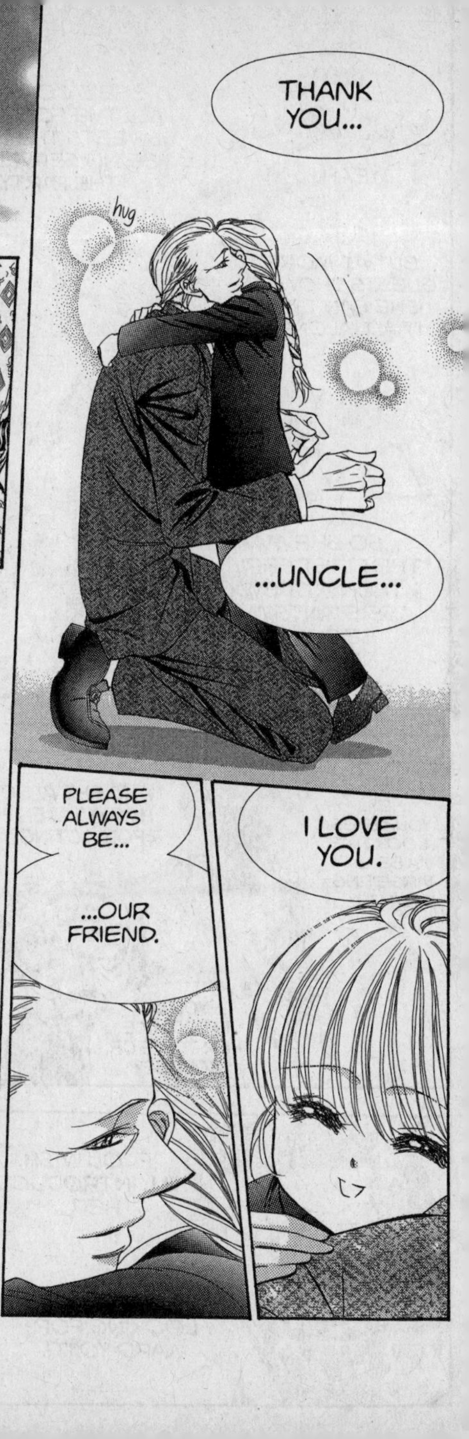
THANK YOU...
hug
...UNCLE...
I LOVE YOU.
PLEASE ALWAYS BE...
...OUR FRIEND.

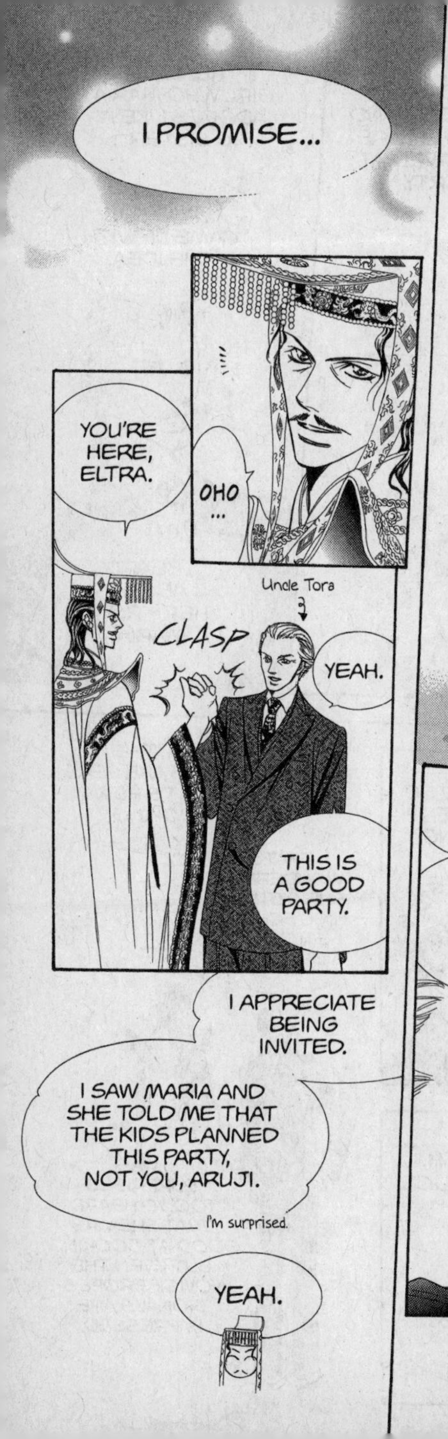
I PROMISE...
YOU'RE HERE, ELTRA.
OHO...
Uncle Tora
CLASP
YEAH.
THIS IS A GOOD PARTY.
I APPRECIATE BEING INVITED.
I SAW MARIA AND SHE TOLD ME THAT THE KIDS PLANNED THIS PARTY, NOT YOU, ARUJI.
I'm surprised.
YEAH.

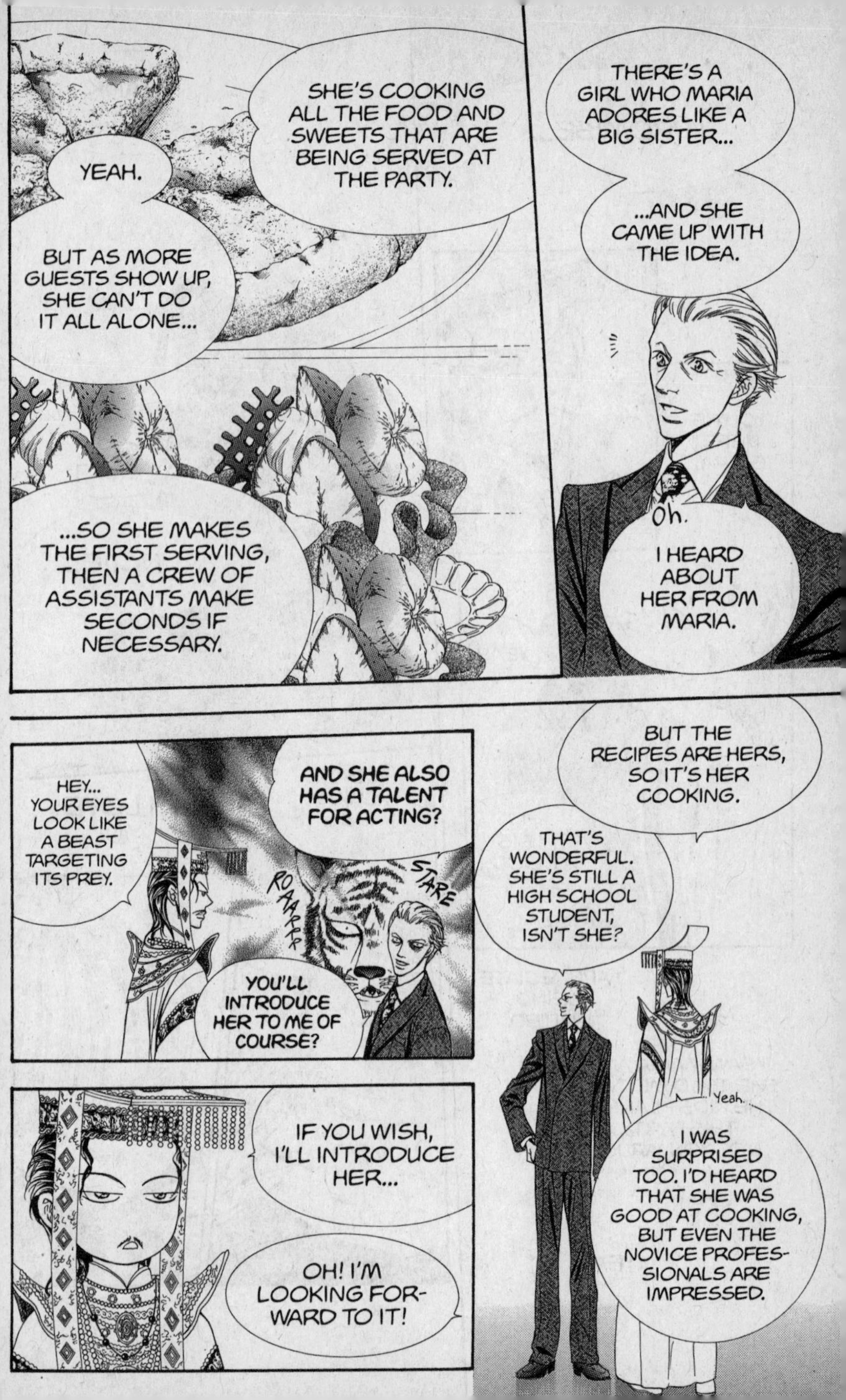
THERE'S A GIRL WHO MARIA ADORES LIKE A BIG SISTER...
...AND SHE CAME UP WITH THE IDEA.
Oh.
I HEARD ABOUT HER FROM MARIA.
SHE'S COOKING ALL THE FOOD AND SWEETS THAT ARE BEING SERVED AT THE PARTY.
YEAH.
BUT AS MORE GUESTS SHOW UP, SHE CAN'T DO IT ALL ALONE...
...SO SHE MAKES THE FIRST SERVING, THEN A CREW OF ASSISTANTS MAKE SECONDS IF NECESSARY.
BUT THE RECIPES ARE HERS, SO IT'S HER COOKING.
THAT'S WONDERFUL. SHE'S STILL A HIGH SCHOOL STUDENT, ISN'T SHE?
Yeah.
I WAS SURPRISED TOO. I'D HEARD THAT SHE WAS GOOD AT COOKING, BUT EVEN THE NOVICE PROFES-SIONALS ARE IMPRESSED.
AND SHE ALSO HAS A TALENT FOR ACTING?
STARE
ROAAARRR
HEY... YOUR EYES LOOK LIKE A BEAST TARGETING ITS PREY.
YOU'LL INTRODUCE HER TO ME OF COURSE?
IF YOU WISH, I'LL INTRODUCE HER...
OH! I'M LOOKING FOR-WARD TO IT!

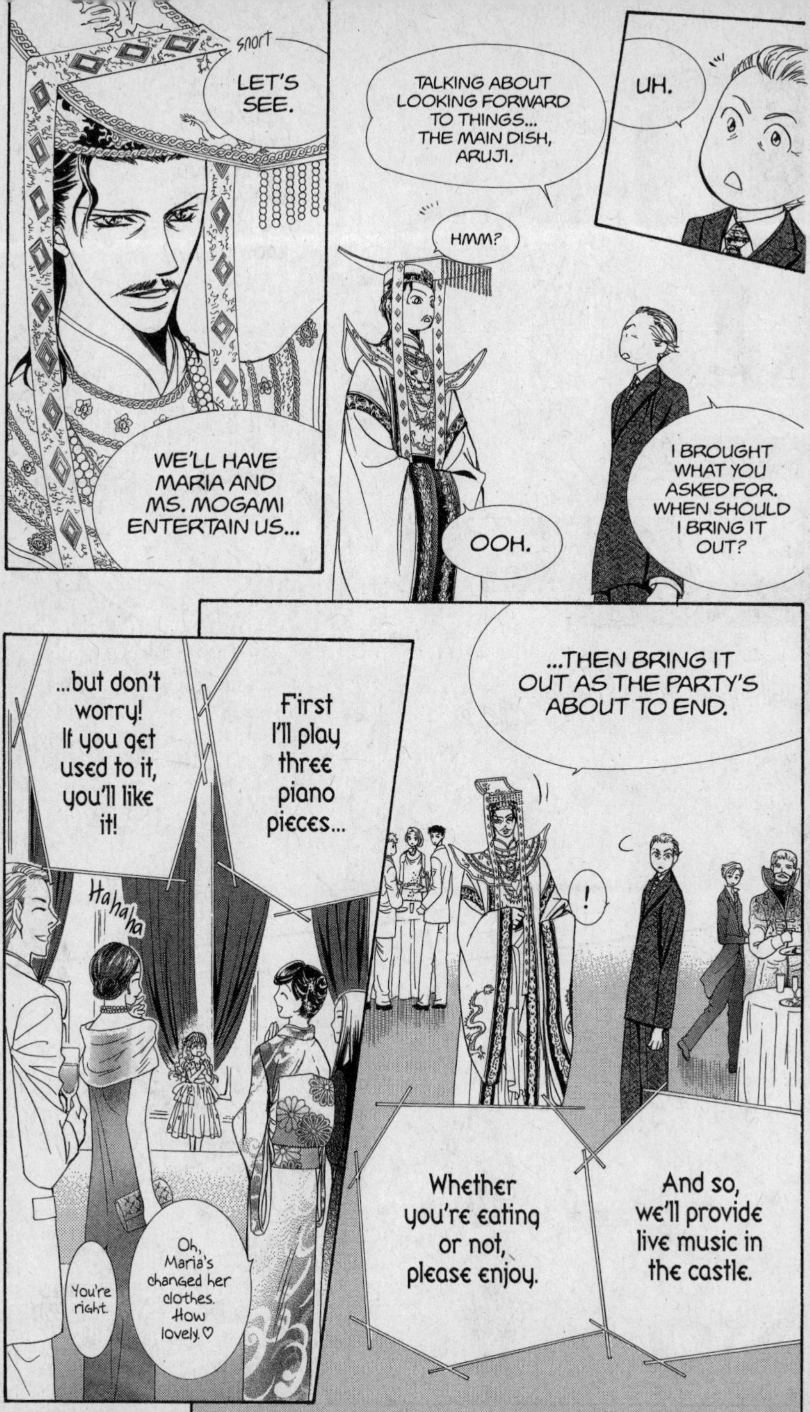
UH.
TALKING ABOUT LOOKING FORWARD TO THINGS... THE MAIN DISH, ARUJI.
HMM?
I BROUGHT WHAT YOU ASKED FOR. WHEN SHOULD I BRING IT OUT?
OOH.
Snort
LET'S SEE.
WE'LL HAVE MARIA AND MS. MOGAMI ENTERTAIN US...
...THEN BRING IT OUT AS THE PARTY'S ABOUT TO END.
!
And so, we'll provide live music in the castle.
Whether you're eating or not, please enjoy.
First I'll play three piano pieces...
...but don't worry! If you get used to it, you'll like it!
Hahaha
Oh, Maria's changed her clothes. How lovely.♡
You're right.

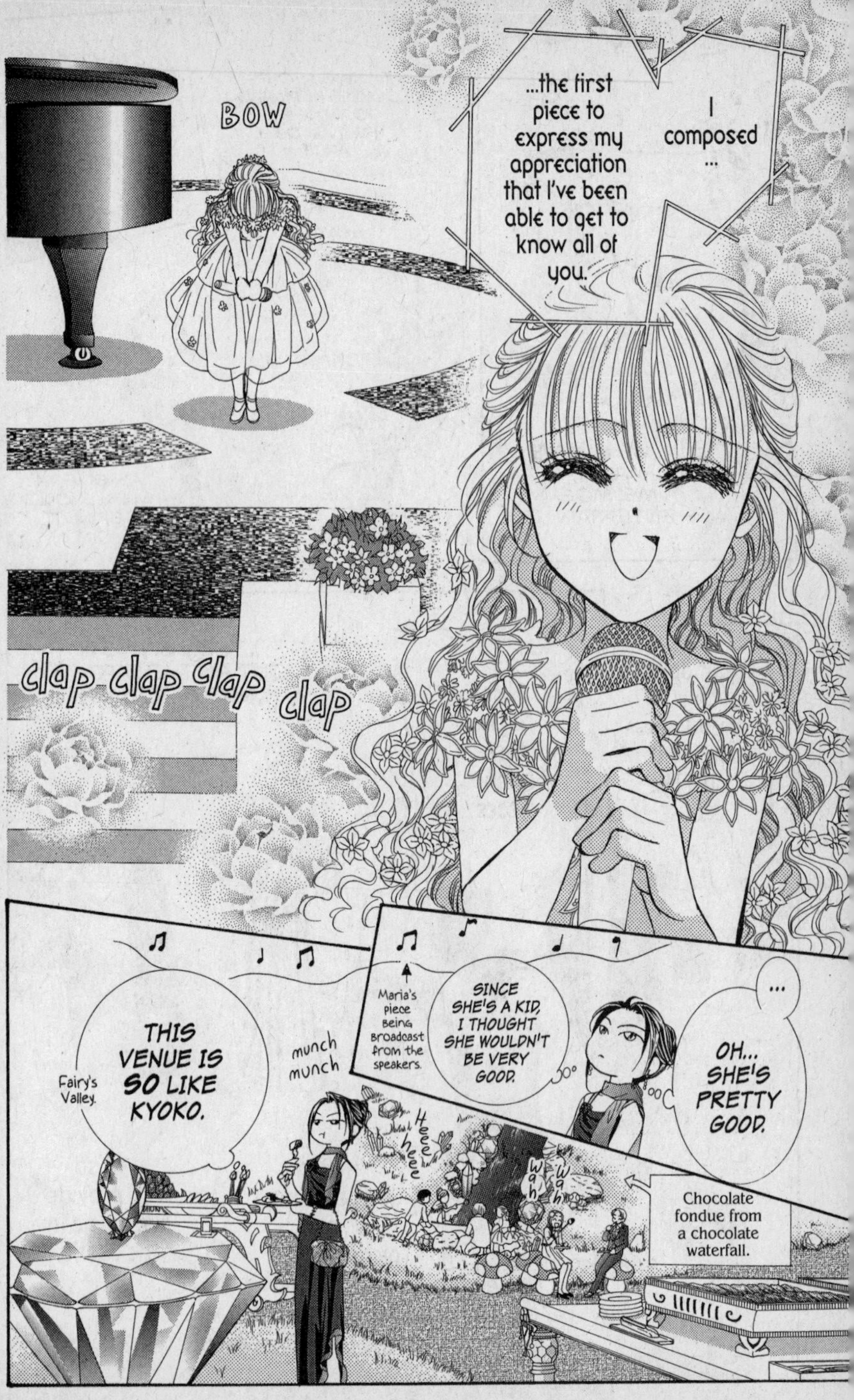
I composed ...
...the first piece to express my appreciation that I've been able to get to know all of you.
BOW
clap clap clap clap
...
OH... SHE'S PRETTY GOOD.
SINCE SHE'S A KID, I THOUGHT SHE WOULDN'T BE VERY GOOD.
Maria's piece being broadcast from the speakers.
Chocolate fondue from a chocolate waterfall.
Wah wah
Heee heee
munch munch
THIS VENUE IS SO LIKE KYOKO.
Fairy's Valley.

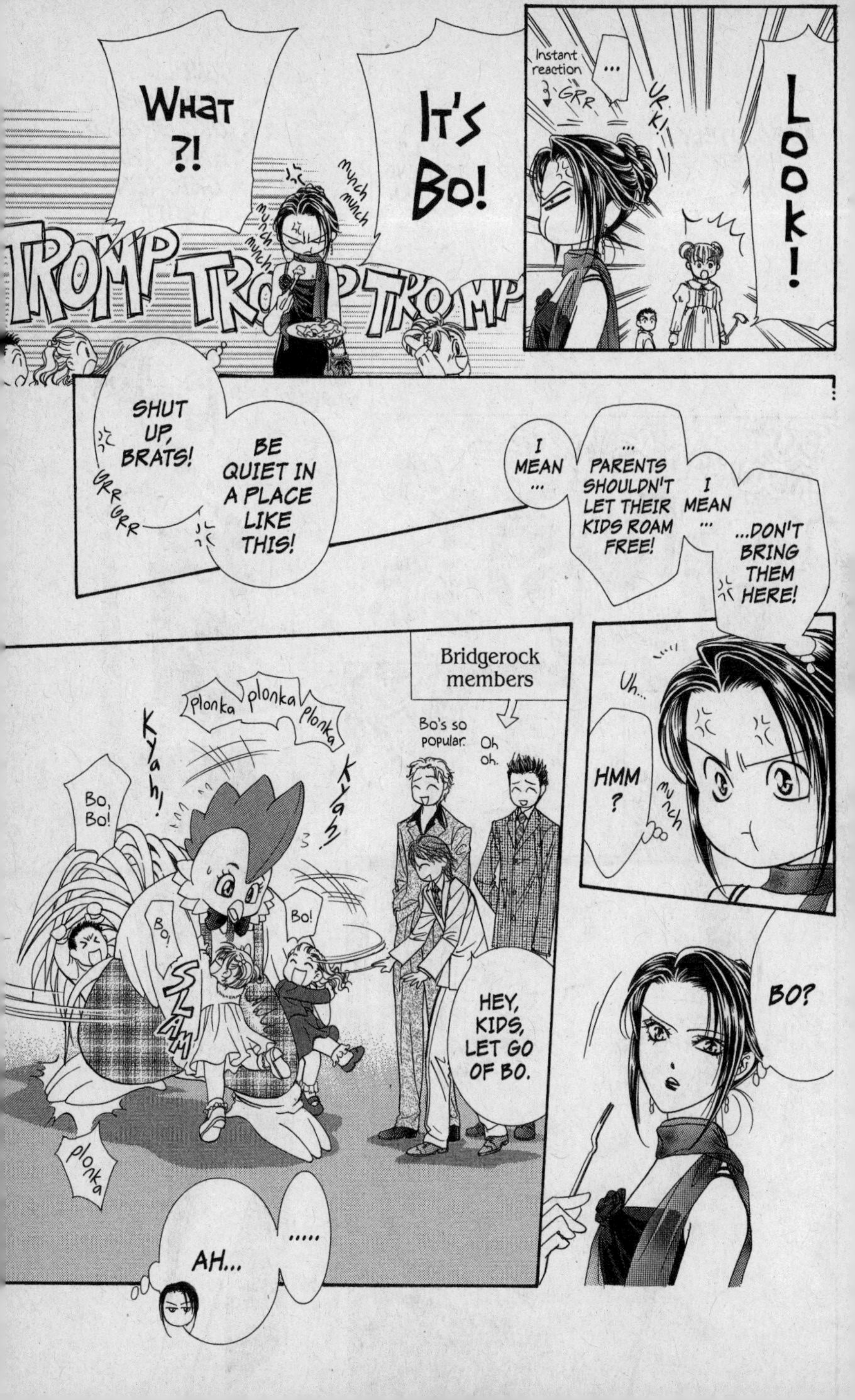
LOOK!
URK!
Instant reaction
GRR
...
IT'S BO!
munch munch munch munch
WHAT ?!
TROMP TROMP TROMP
I MEAN ...
...DON'T BRING THEM HERE!
... PARENTS SHOULDN'T LET THEIR KIDS ROAM FREE!
I MEAN ...
BE QUIET IN A PLACE LIKE THIS!
SHUT UP, BRATS!
GRR GRR
Uh...
HMM ?
munch
BO?
Bridgerock members
Oh oh.
Bo's so popular.
HEY, KIDS, LET GO OF BO.
plonka plonka plonka
Kyah!
Kyah!
Bo, Bo!
Bo!
Bo!
SLAM
plonka
.....
AH...

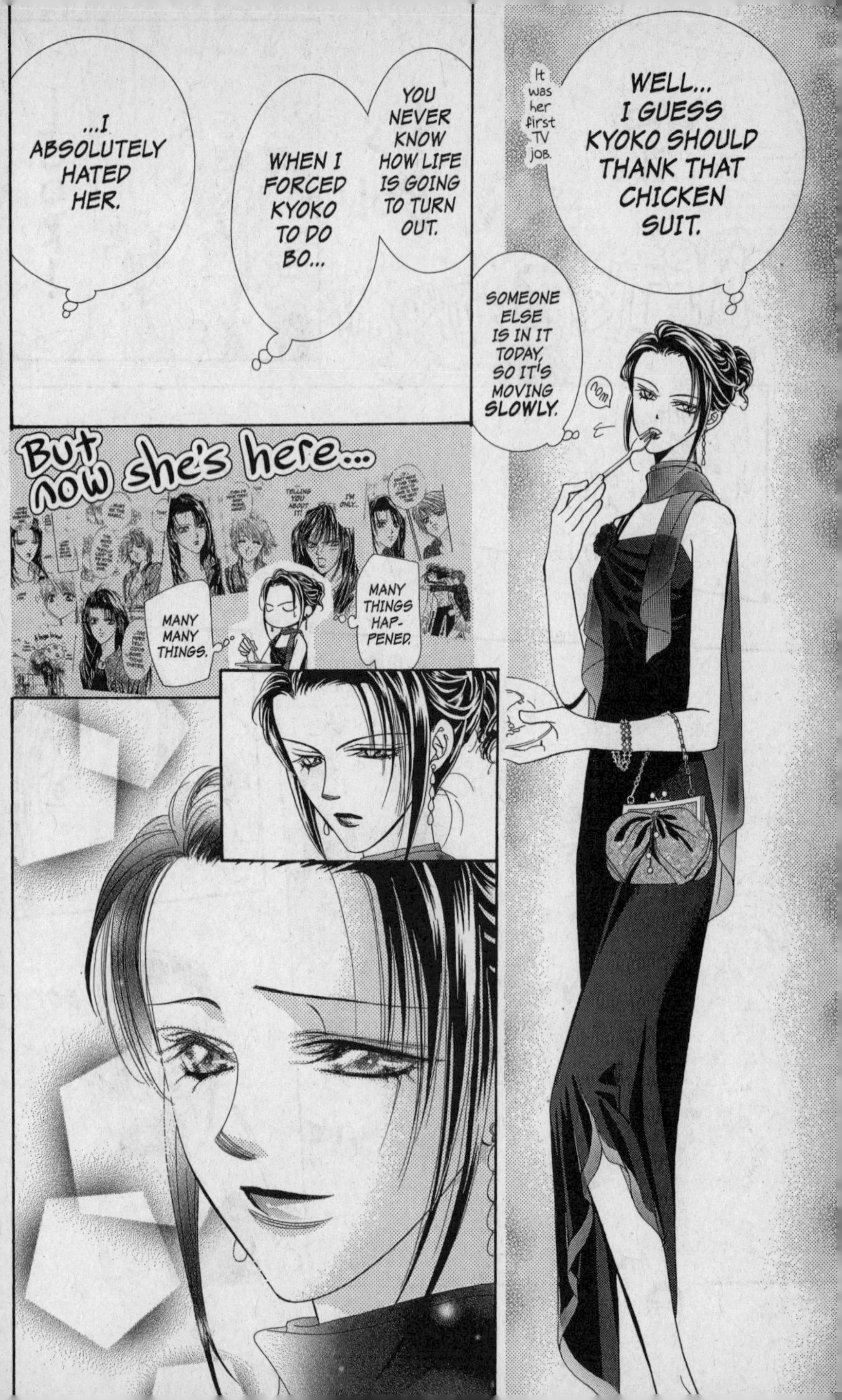
WELL... I GUESS KYOKO SHOULD THANK THAT CHICKEN SUIT.
It was her first TV job.
SOMEONE ELSE IS IN IT TODAY, SO IT'S MOVING SLOWLY.
nom
YOU NEVER KNOW HOW LIFE IS GOING TO TURN OUT.
WHEN I FORCED KYOKO TO DO BO...
...I ABSOLUTELY HATED HER.
But now she's here...
MANY THINGS HAP-PENED.
MANY MANY THINGS.

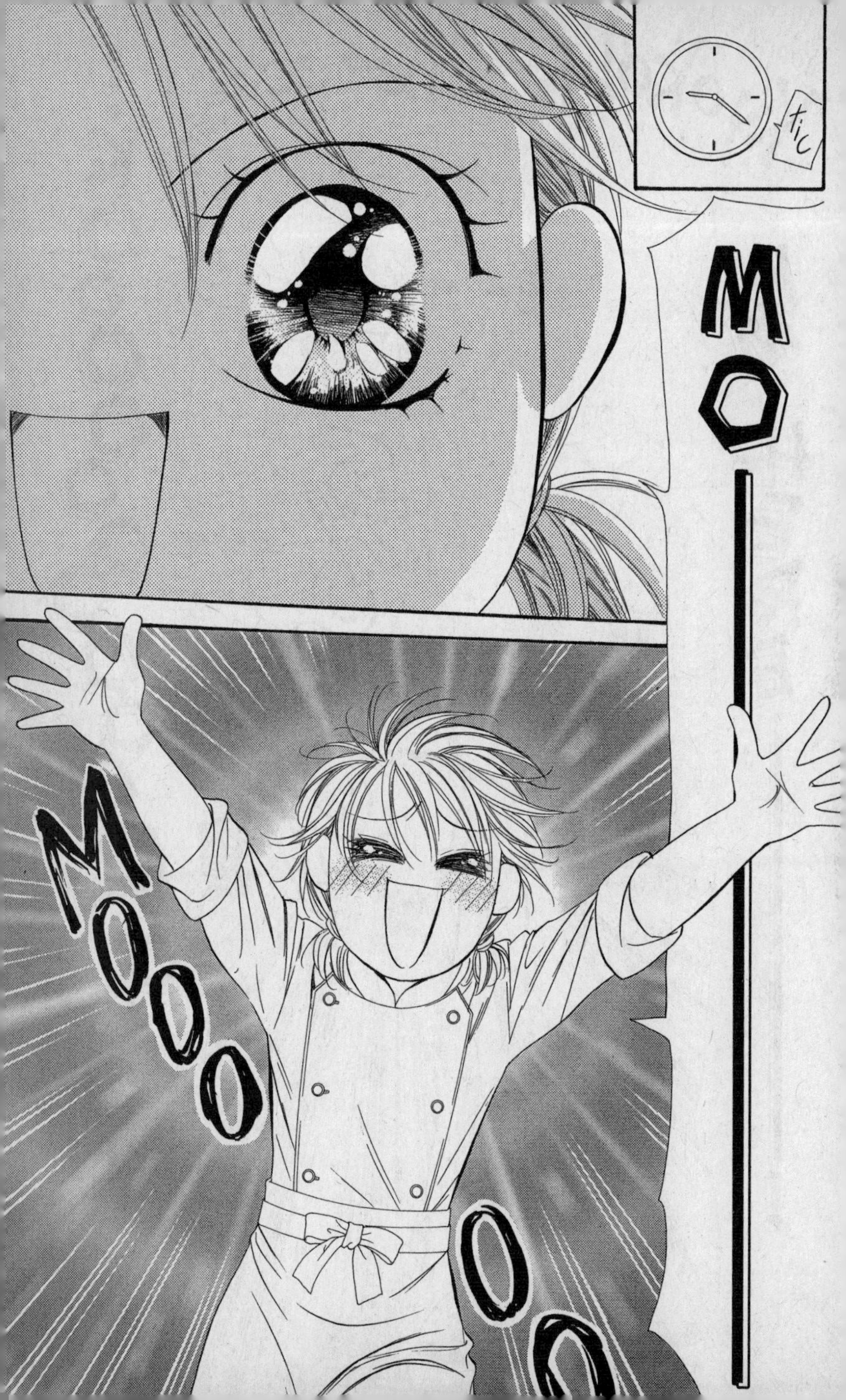
tic
MO—
MOOOOOO

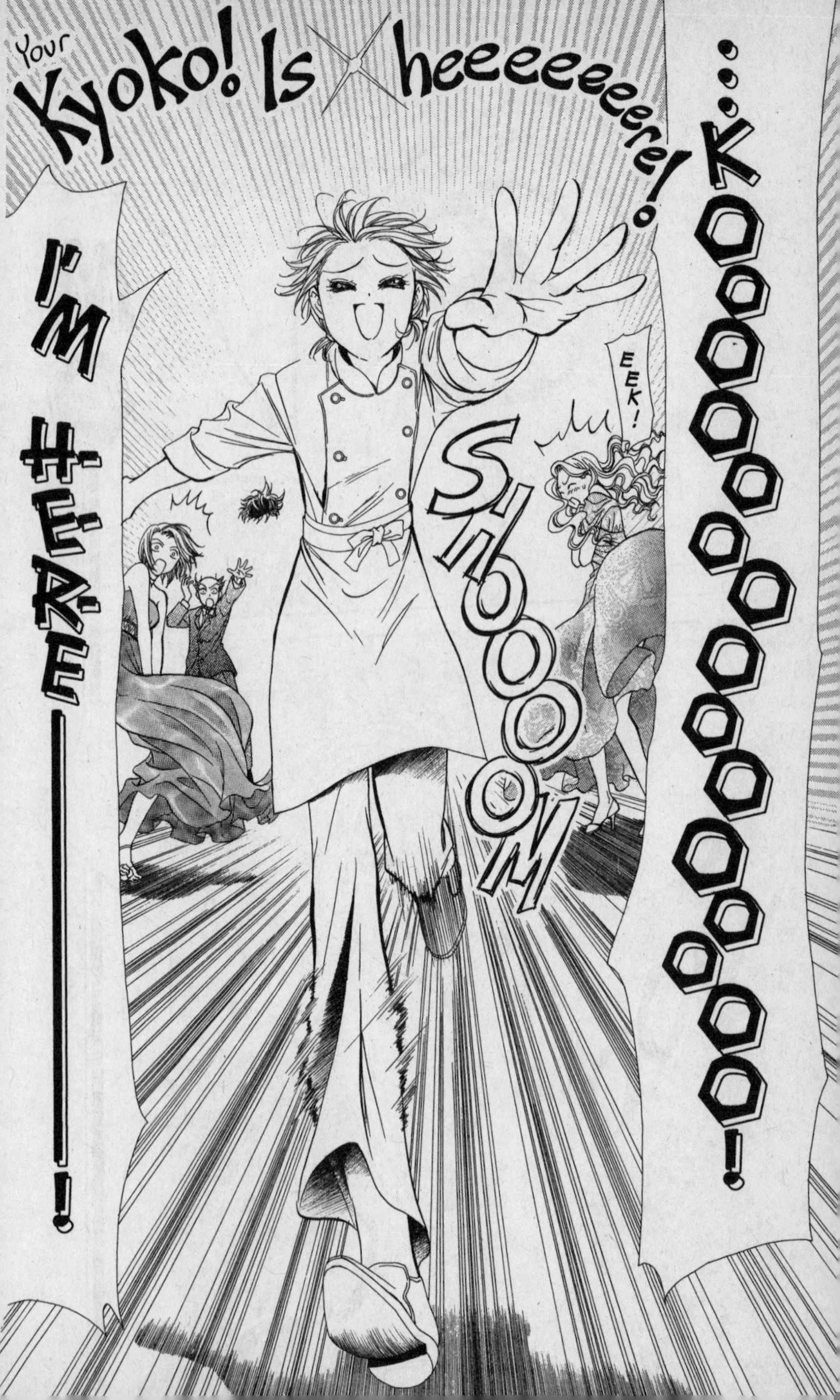
Your Kyoko! Is heeeeeeeere!
...KOOOOOOOOOOOOOOOO!
EEK!
SHOOOOOM
I'M H-E-R-E——!

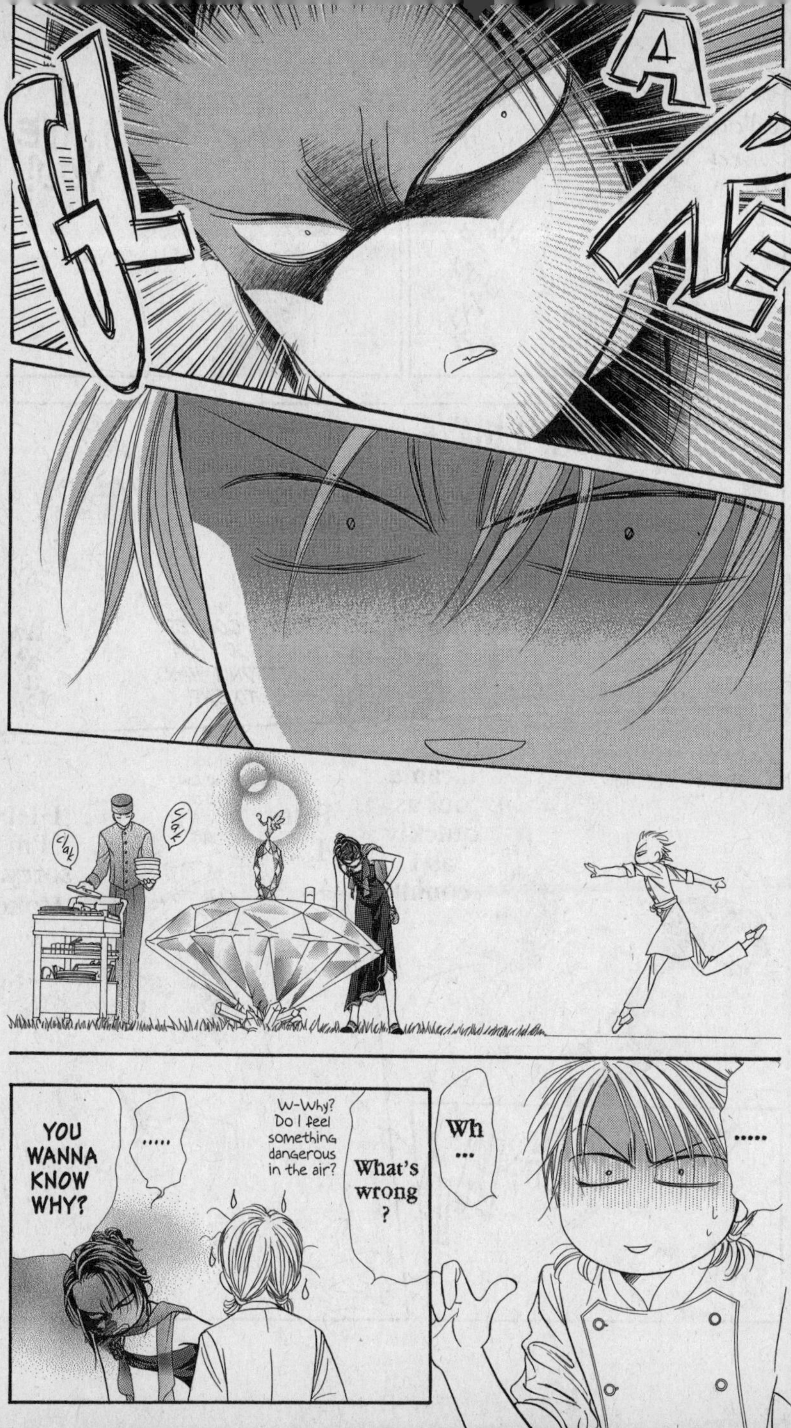
GLARE
clak
clak
.....
Wh...
What's wrong?
W-Why? Do I feel something dangerous in the air?
.....
YOU WANNA KNOW WHY?

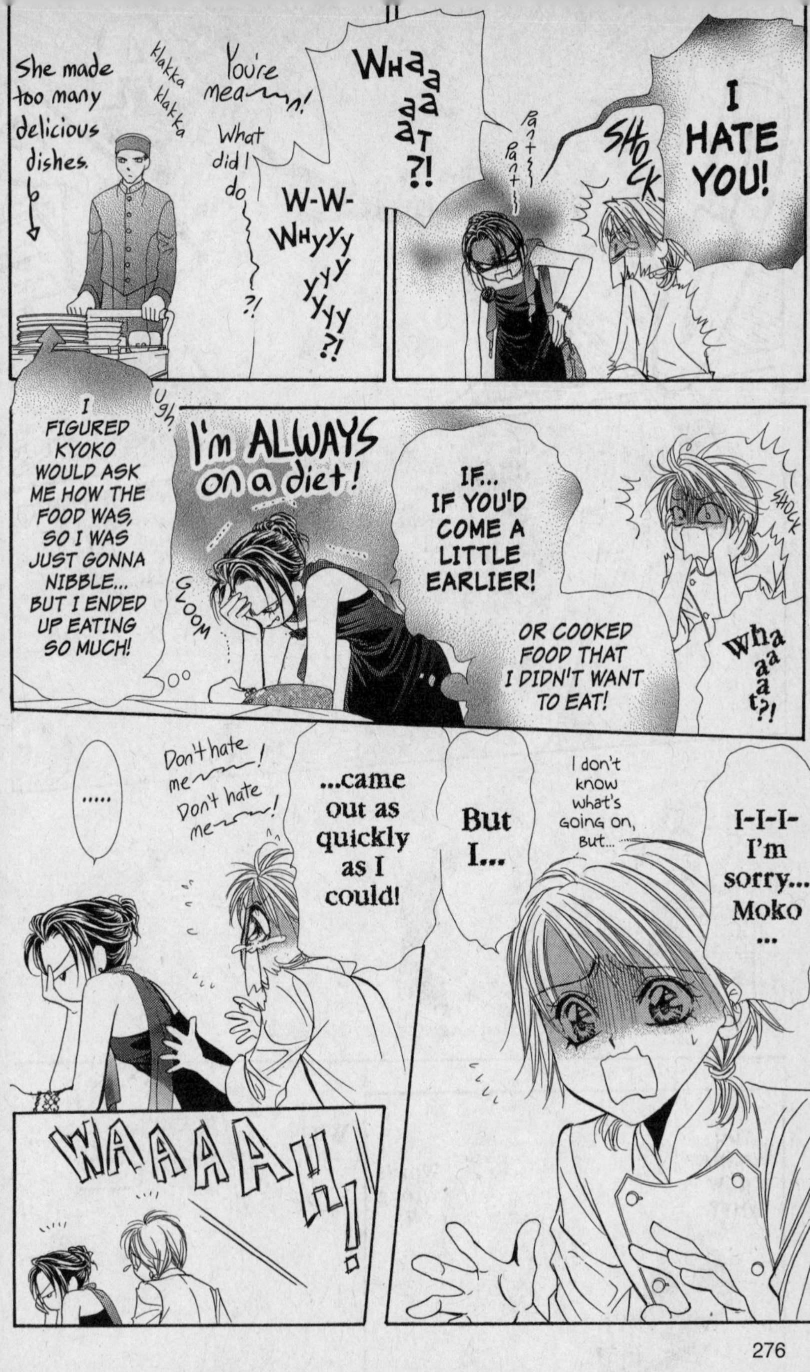
I HATE YOU!
SHOCK
Pant pant
WHAAAAT?!
W-W-WHYYYYYYY?!
You're meaaan!
What did I do?!
klakka klakka
She made too many delicious dishes.
Whaaaat?!
SHOCK
IF... IF YOU'D COME A LITTLE EARLIER!
OR COOKED FOOD THAT I DIDN'T WANT TO EAT!
I'm ALWAYS on a diet!
GLOOM
Ugh
I FIGURED KYOKO WOULD ASK ME HOW THE FOOD WAS, SO I WAS JUST GONNA NIBBLE... BUT I ENDED UP EATING SO MUCH!
I-I-I- I'm sorry... Moko ...
I don't know what's going on, but...
But I...
...came out as quickly as I could!
Don't hate me! Don't hate me!
.....
WAAAAH!

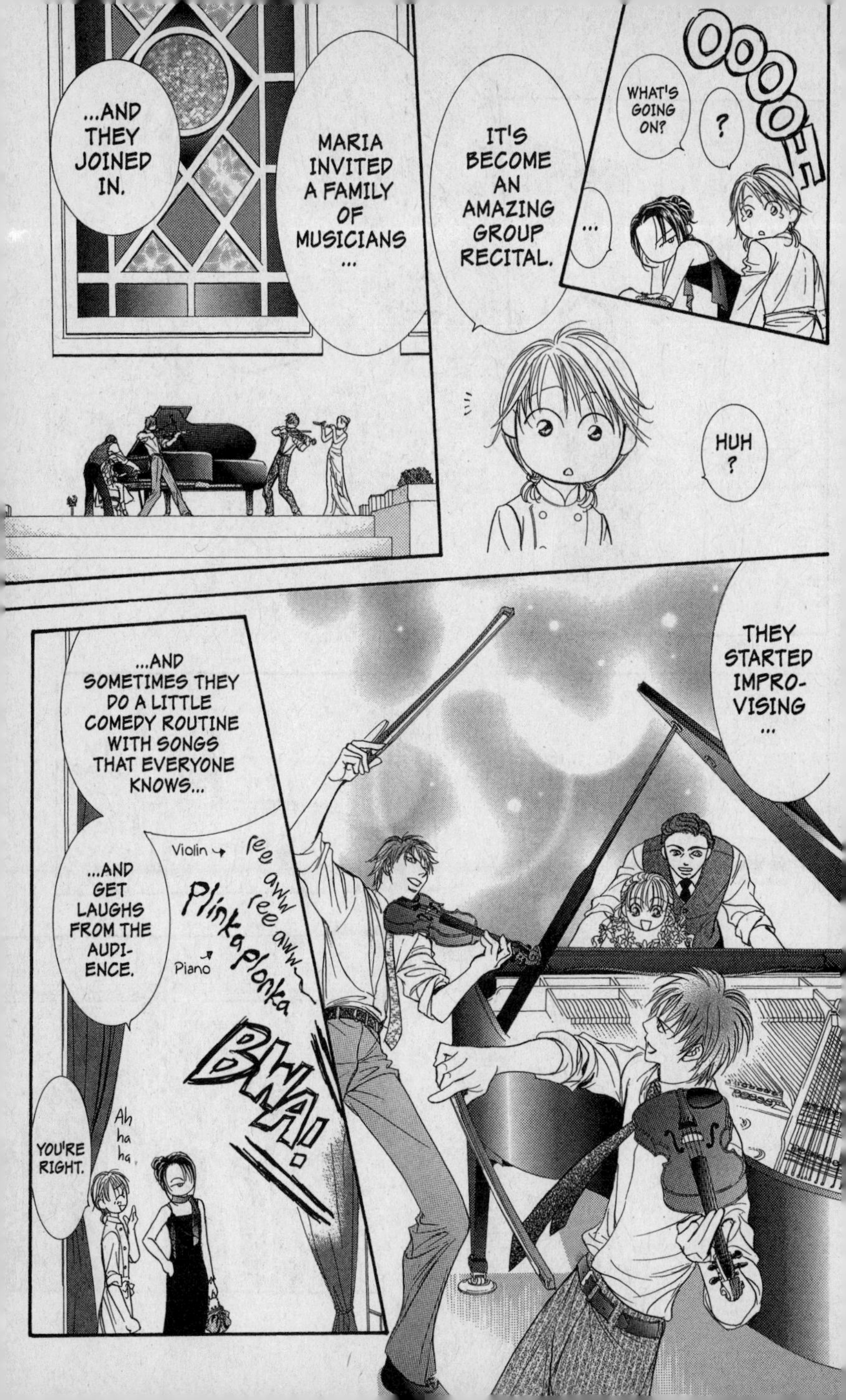
OOOOH
WHAT'S GOING ON?
?
...
IT'S BECOME AN AMAZING GROUP RECITAL.
MARIA INVITED A FAMILY OF MUSICIANS...
...AND THEY JOINED IN.
HUH?
THEY STARTED IMPRO-VISING...
...AND SOMETIMES THEY DO A LITTLE COMEDY ROUTINE WITH SONGS THAT EVERYONE KNOWS...
Violin
ree aww ree aww
Piano
Plinka plonka
...AND GET LAUGHS FROM THE AUDI-ENCE.
BWAA!
Ah ha ha
YOU'RE RIGHT.

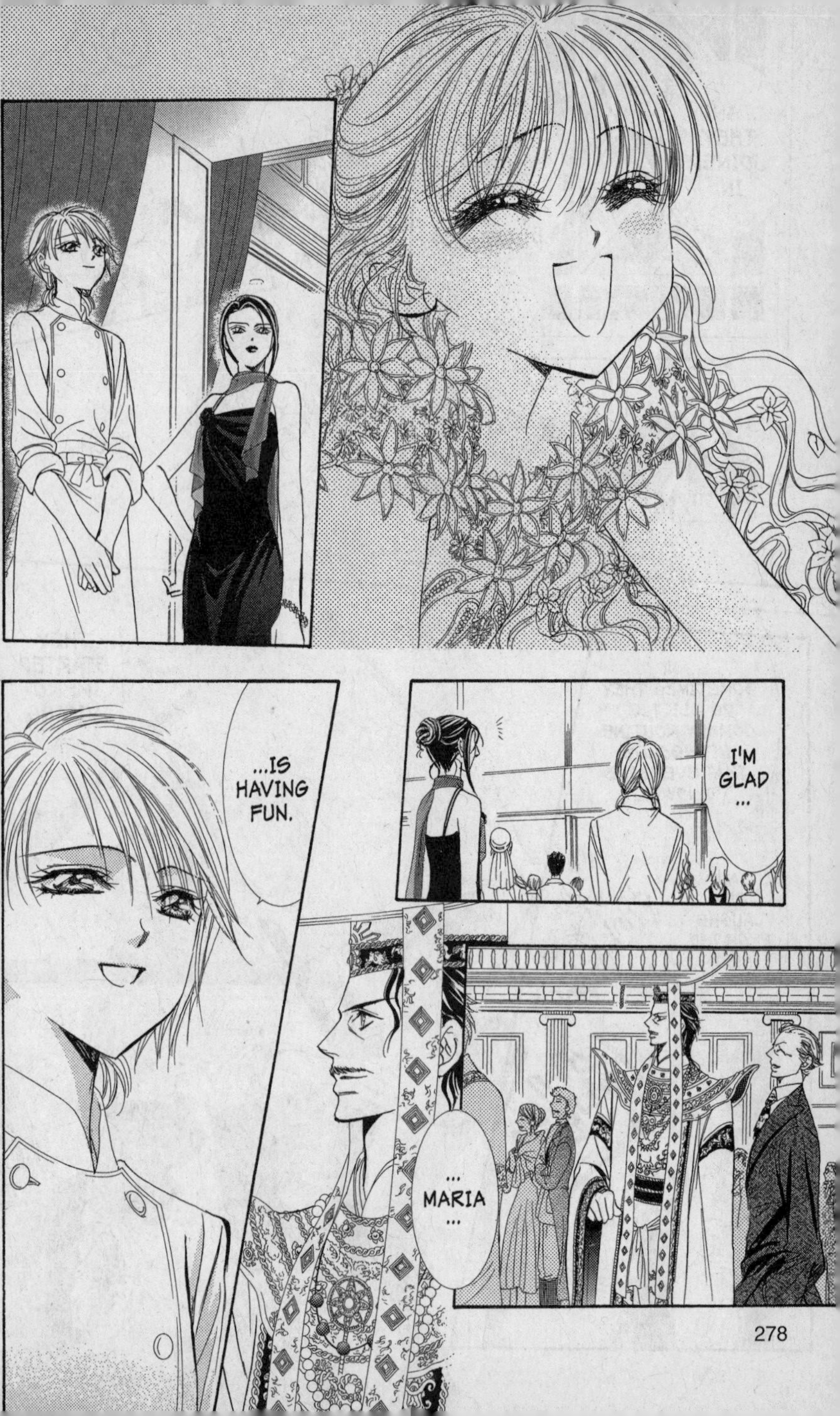
I'M GLAD ...
... MARIA ...
...IS HAVING FUN.

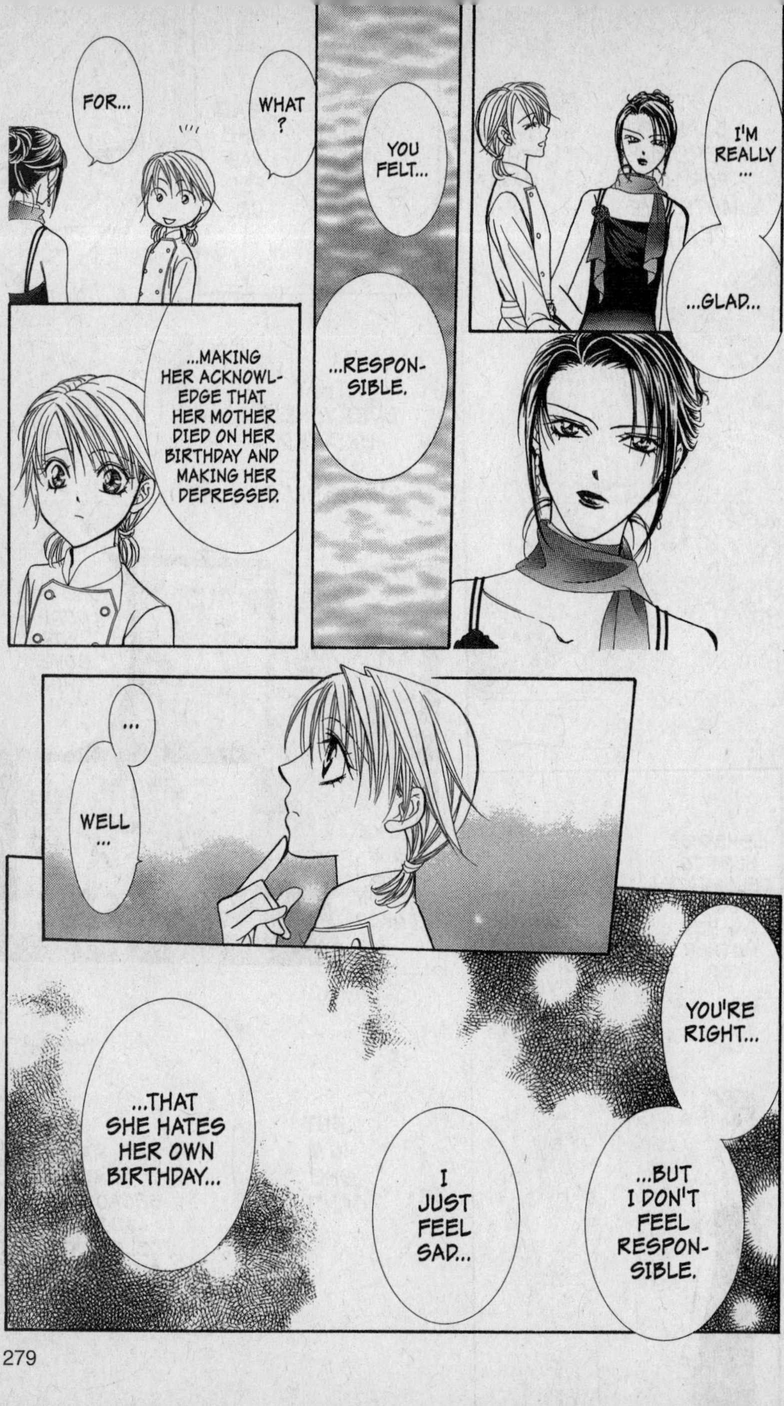
I'M REALLY ...
...GLAD...
YOU FELT...
...RESPON-SIBLE.
WHAT ?
FOR...
...MAKING HER ACKNOWL-EDGE THAT HER MOTHER DIED ON HER BIRTHDAY AND MAKING HER DEPRESSED.
...
WELL ...
YOU'RE RIGHT...
...BUT I DON'T FEEL RESPON-SIBLE.
I JUST FEEL SAD...
...THAT SHE HATES HER OWN BIRTHDAY...

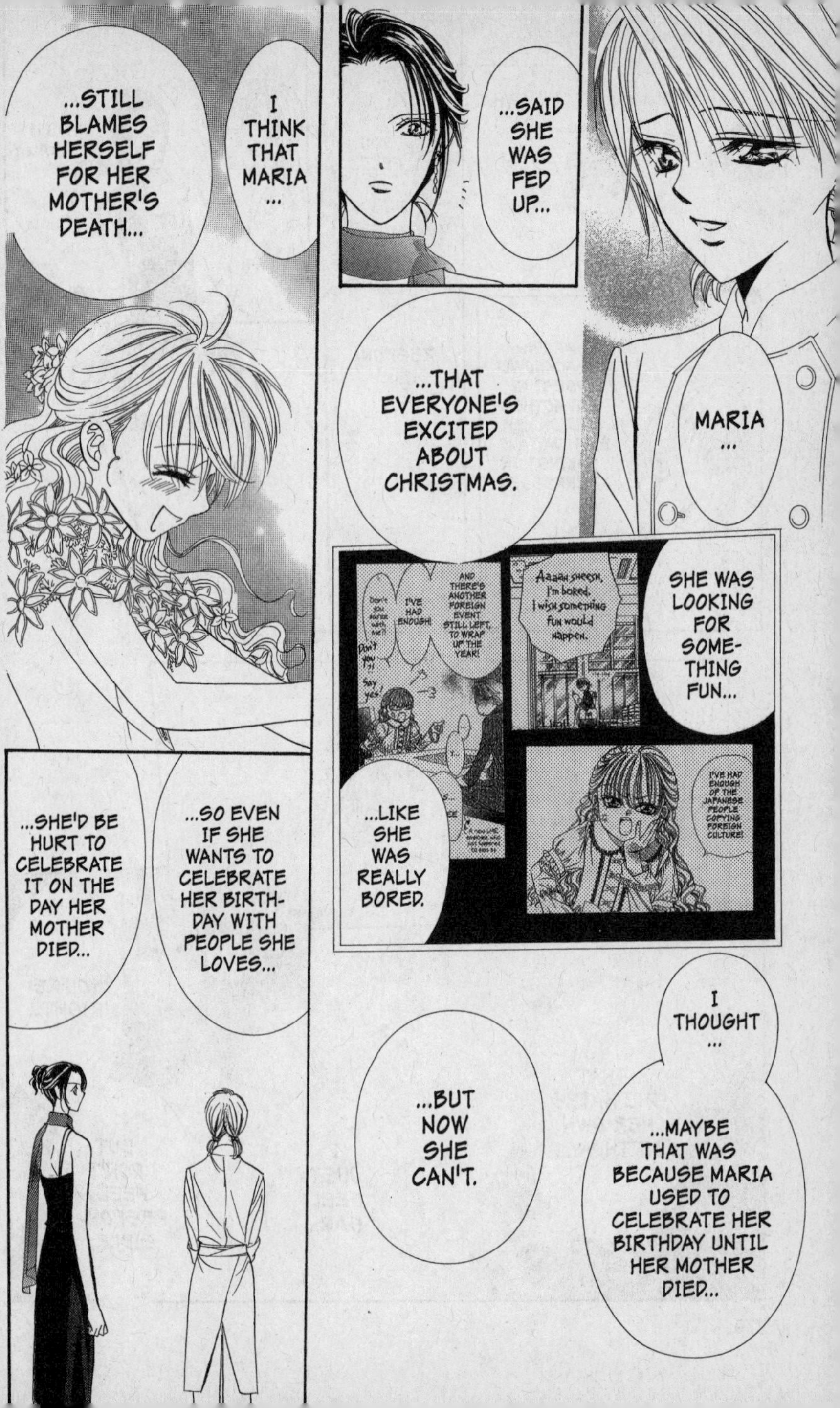
MARIA ...
...SAID SHE WAS FED UP...
...THAT EVERYONE'S EXCITED ABOUT CHRISTMAS.
SHE WAS LOOKING FOR SOME-THING FUN...
Aaaah sheesh, I'm bored. I wish something fun would happen.
AND THERE'S ANOTHER FOREIGN EVENT STILL LEFT TO WRAP UP THE YEAR!
I'VE HAD ENOUGH!
Don't you agree with me?!
Don't you?!
Say yes!
I'VE HAD ENOUGH OF THE JAPANESE PEOPLE COPYING FOREIGN CULTURE!
...LIKE SHE WAS REALLY BORED.
I THOUGHT ...
...MAYBE THAT WAS BECAUSE MARIA USED TO CELEBRATE HER BIRTHDAY UNTIL HER MOTHER DIED...
...BUT NOW SHE CAN'T.
I THINK THAT MARIA ...
...STILL BLAMES HERSELF FOR HER MOTHER'S DEATH...
...SO EVEN IF SHE WANTS TO CELEBRATE HER BIRTH-DAY WITH PEOPLE SHE LOVES...
...SHE'D BE HURT TO CELEBRATE IT ON THE DAY HER MOTHER DIED...

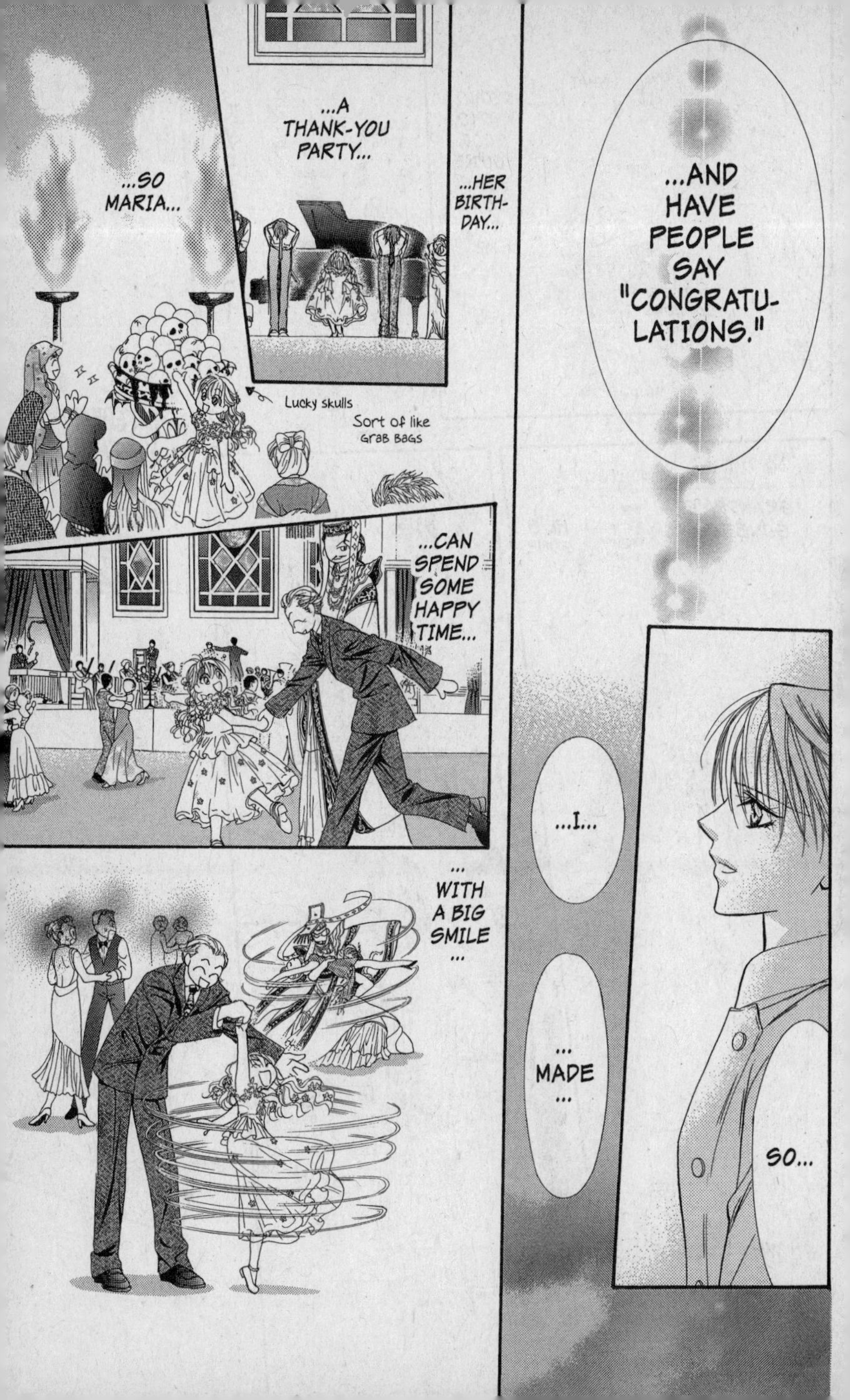
...HER BIRTH-DAY...
...A THANK-YOU PARTY...
...SO MARIA...
Lucky skulls
Sort of like Grab Bags
...CAN SPEND SOME HAPPY TIME...
...WITH A BIG SMILE...
...AND HAVE PEOPLE SAY "CONGRATU-LATIONS."
SO...
...I...
...MADE...

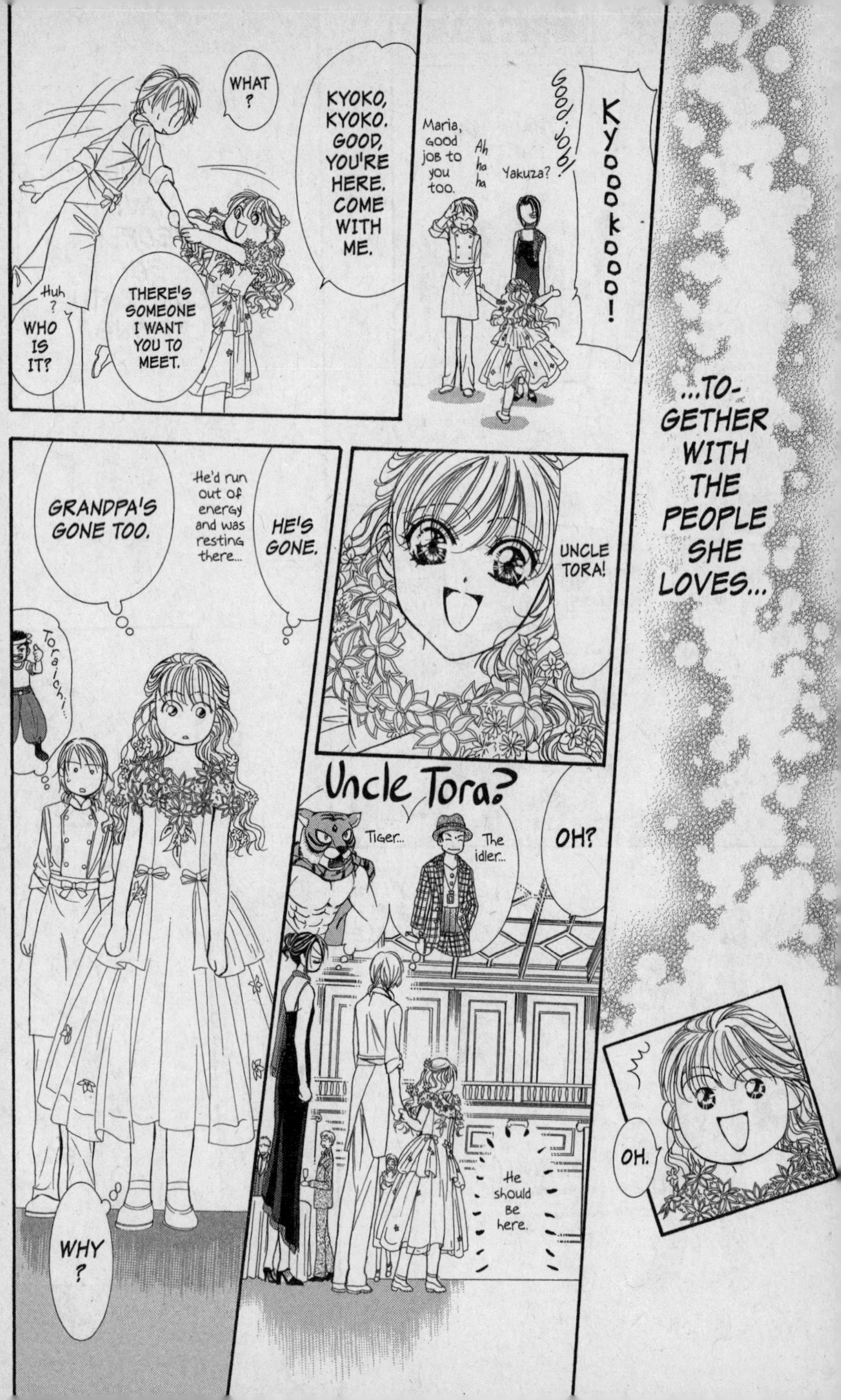
...TO-GETHER WITH THE PEOPLE SHE LOVES...
KYOOOKOOOO!
Good job!
Yakuza?
Ah ha ha
Maria, good job to you too.
KYOKO, KYOKO. GOOD, YOU'RE HERE. COME WITH ME.
WHAT?
THERE'S SOMEONE I WANT YOU TO MEET.
Huh?
WHO IS IT?
UNCLE TORA!
OH?
Uncle Tora?
Tiger...
The idler...
He should be here.
HE'S GONE.
He'd run out of energy and was resting there...
GRANDPA'S GONE TOO.
Toraichi...
WHY?
OH.

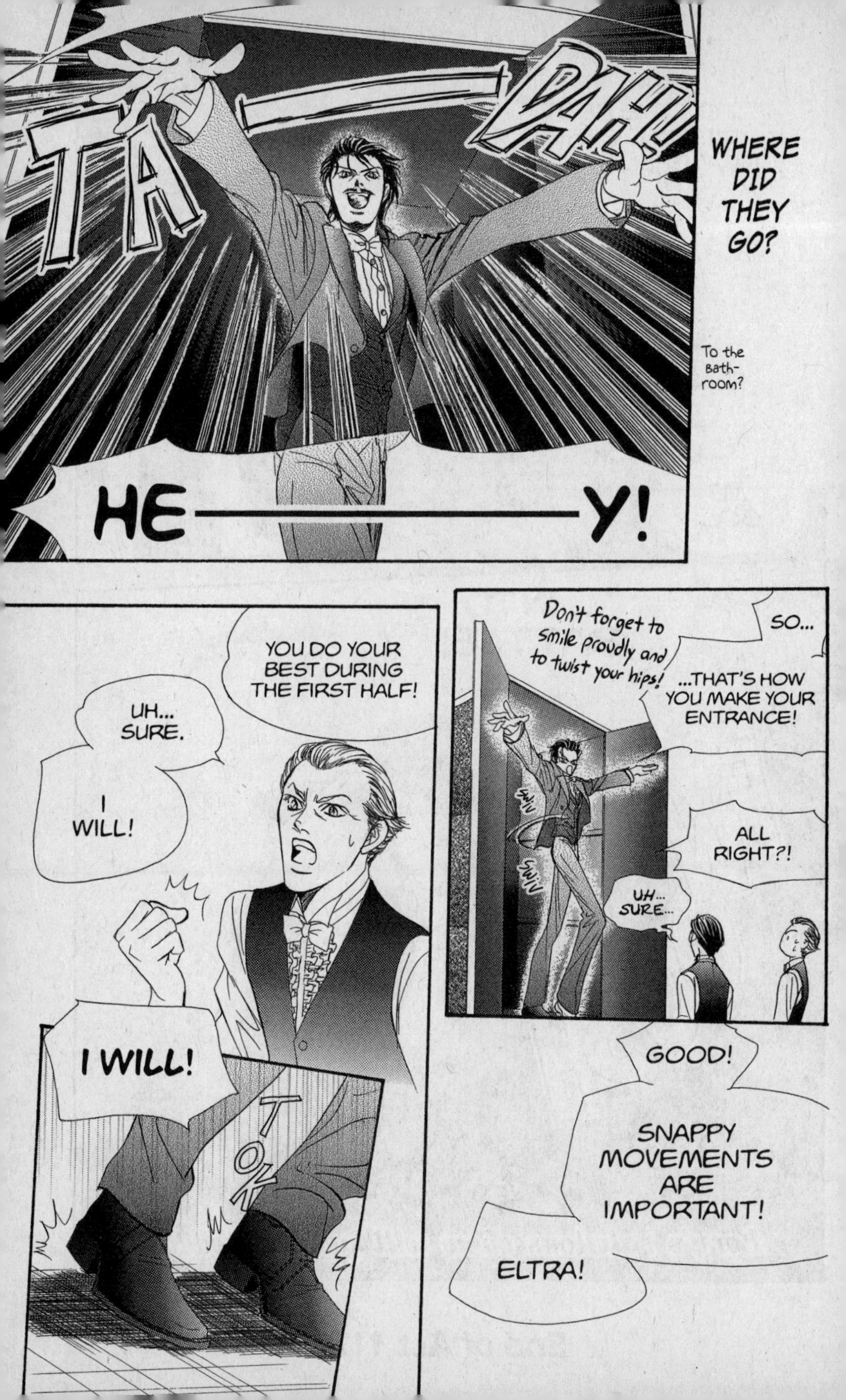
WHERE DID THEY GO?
To the Bath-room?
TA DAH!!
HE———Y!
SO...
...THAT'S HOW YOU MAKE YOUR ENTRANCE!
Don't forget to smile proudly and to twist your hips!
SWIV
SWIV
ALL RIGHT?!
UH... SURE...
GOOD!
SNAPPY MOVEMENTS ARE IMPORTANT!
ELTRA!
YOU DO YOUR BEST DURING THE FIRST HALF!
UH... SURE.
I WILL!
I WILL!
TOK

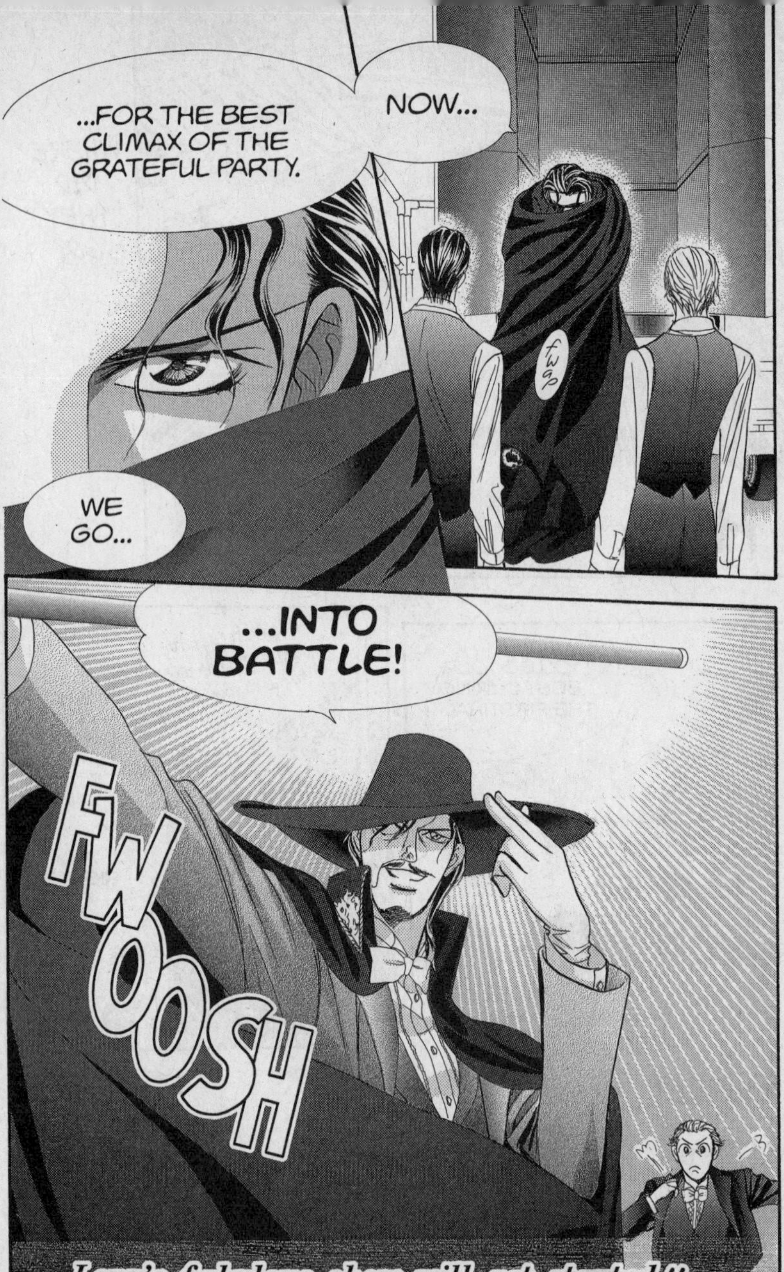
NOW...
...FOR THE BEST CLIMAX OF THE GRATEFUL PARTY.
WE GO...
...INTO BATTLE!
FWOOSH
Lory's fabulous show will get started!!

End of Act 117

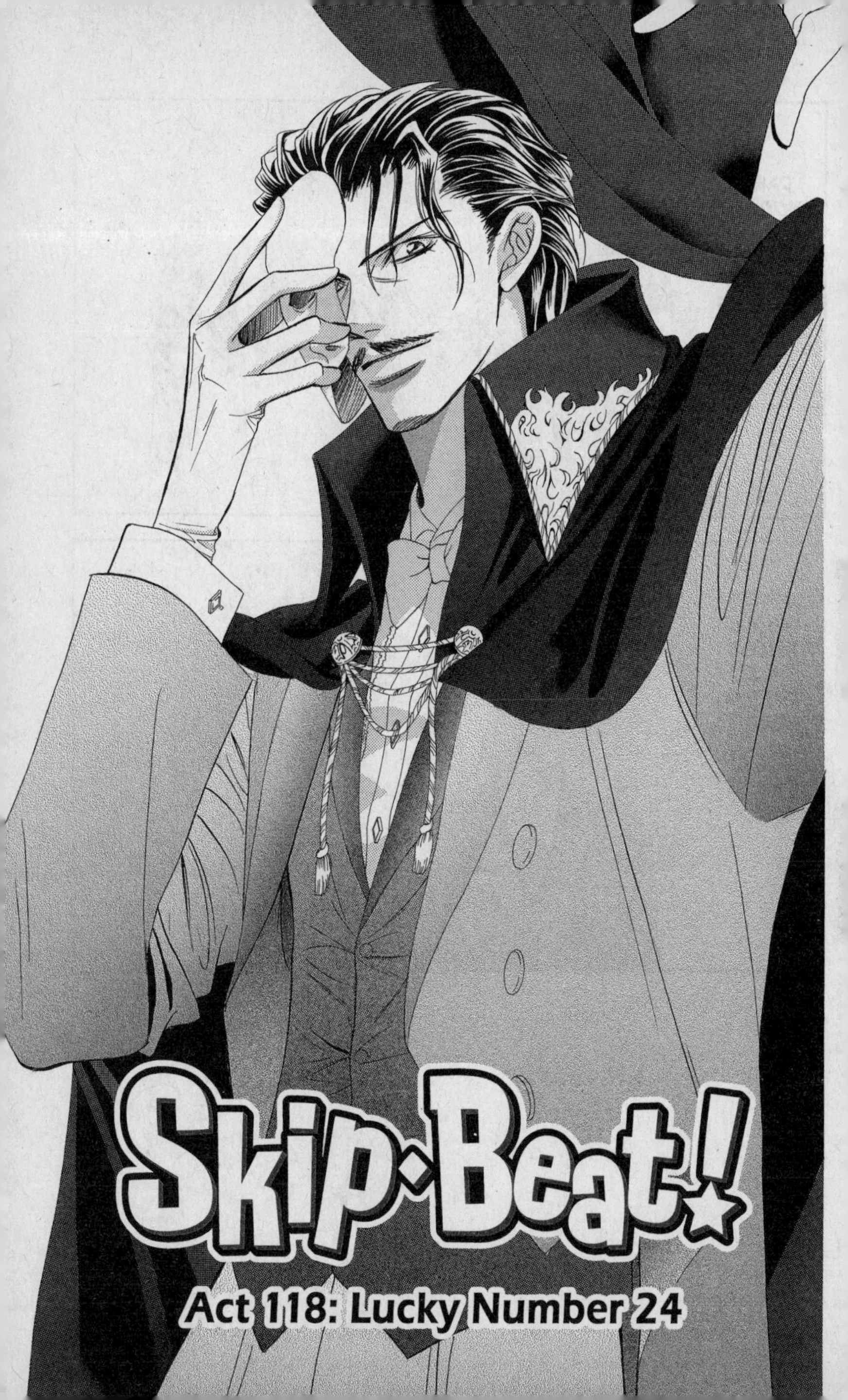
Skip·Beat!
Act 118: Lucky Number 24

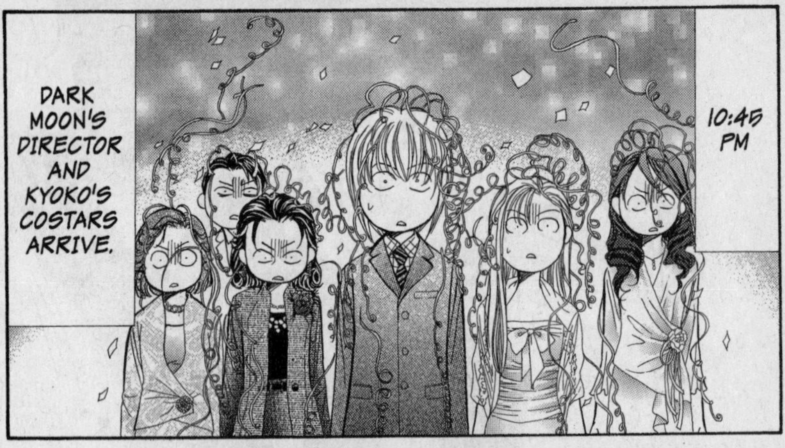
10:45 PM
DARK MOON'S DIRECTOR AND KYOKO'S COSTARS ARRIVE.

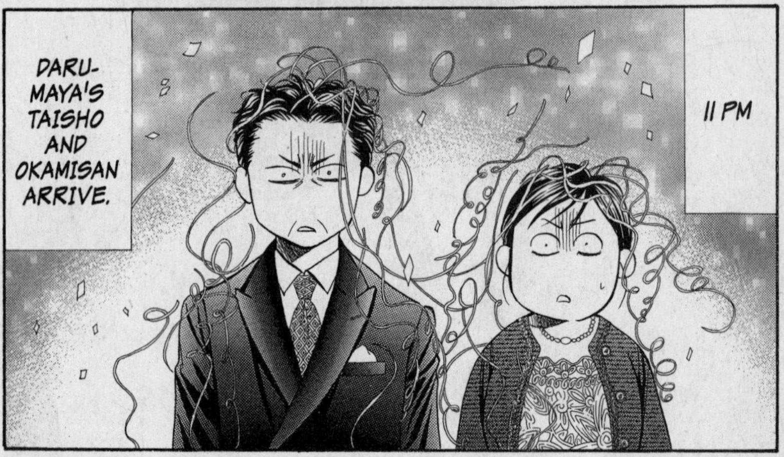
11 PM
DARU-MAYA'S TAISHO AND OKAMISAN ARRIVE.

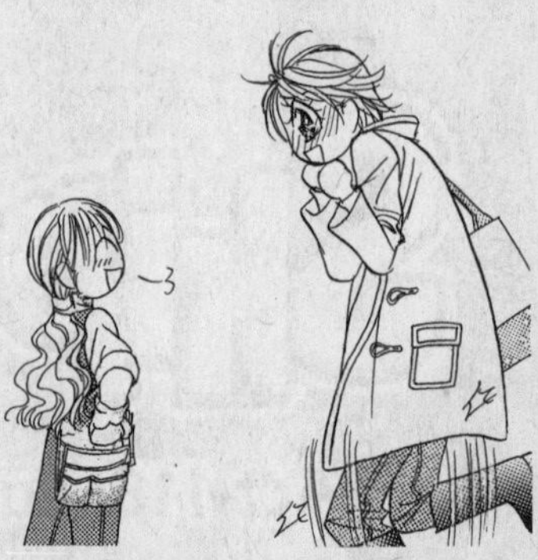

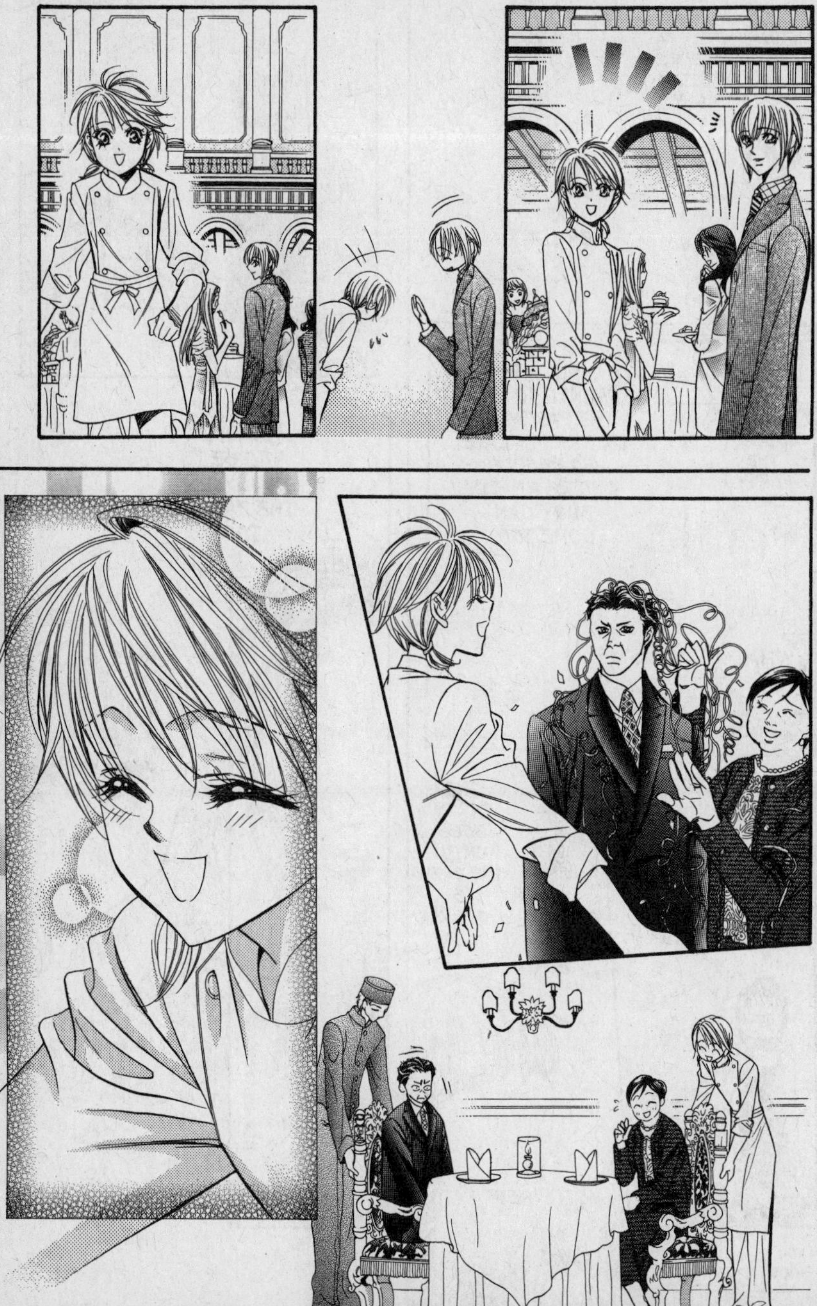

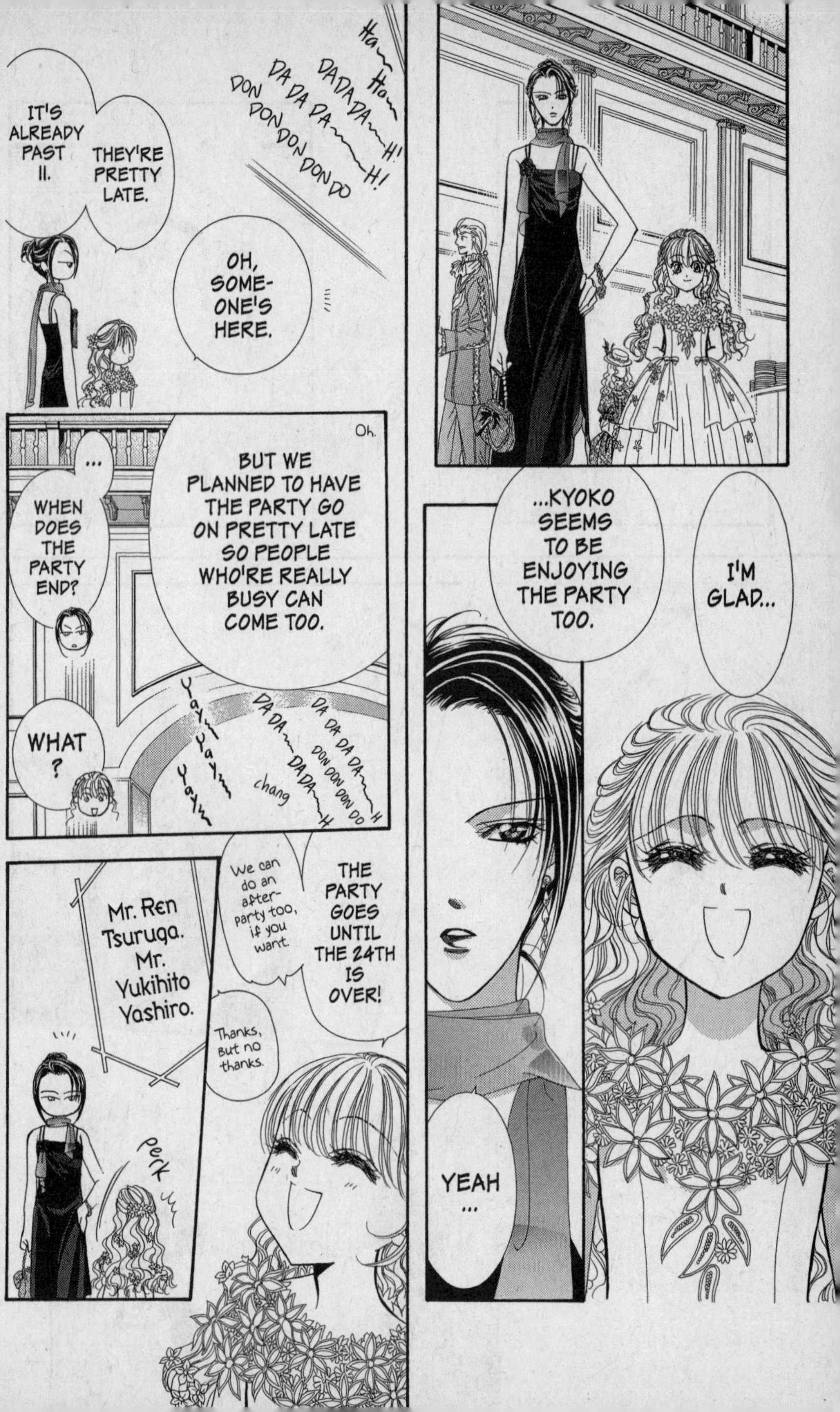
I'M GLAD...
...KYOKO SEEMS TO BE ENJOYING THE PARTY TOO.
YEAH ...
Ham Ham
DADADADA~H!
DA DA DA DA~H!
DON DON DON DON DO
IT'S ALREADY PAST 11.
THEY'RE PRETTY LATE.
OH, SOMEONE'S HERE.
Oh.
BUT WE PLANNED TO HAVE THE PARTY GO ON PRETTY LATE SO PEOPLE WHO'RE REALLY BUSY CAN COME TOO.
...
WHEN DOES THE PARTY END?
DA DA DA DA~H
DON DON DON DO
DA DA~DA DA~H
chang
Yay Yay Yay
WHAT?
THE PARTY GOES UNTIL THE 24TH IS OVER!
We can do an after-party too, if you want.
Thanks, but no thanks.
Mr. Ren Tsuruga. Mr. Yukihito Yashiro.
Perk

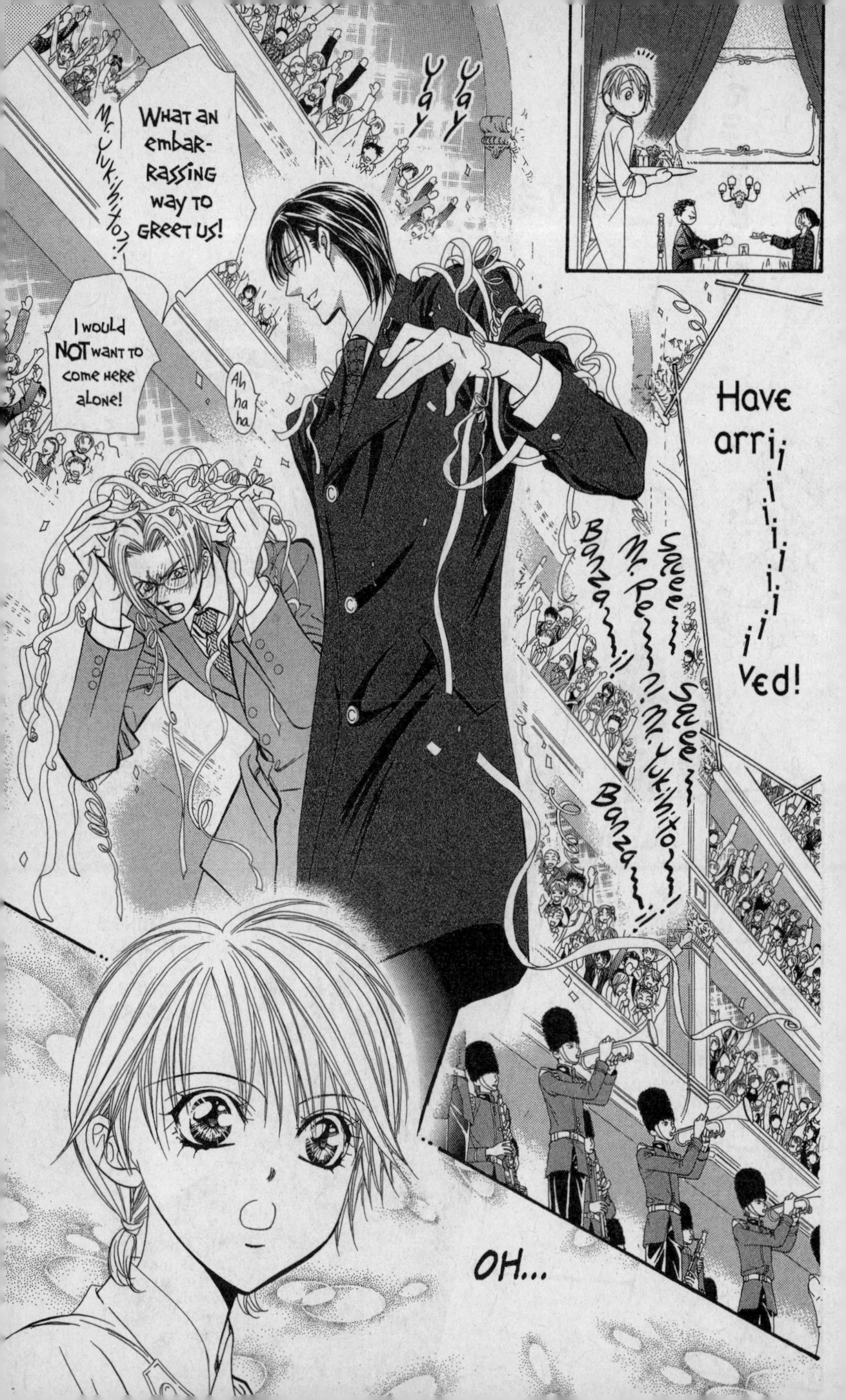

Have arriiiiiiiiived!
Saee~ Saee~
Mr. Ren~!! Mr. Yukihito~!
Banza~i!! Banza~i!!
Yay Yay
Mr. Yukihito?!
What an embar-rassing way to greet us!
I would NOT want to come here alone!
Ah ha ha.
OH...

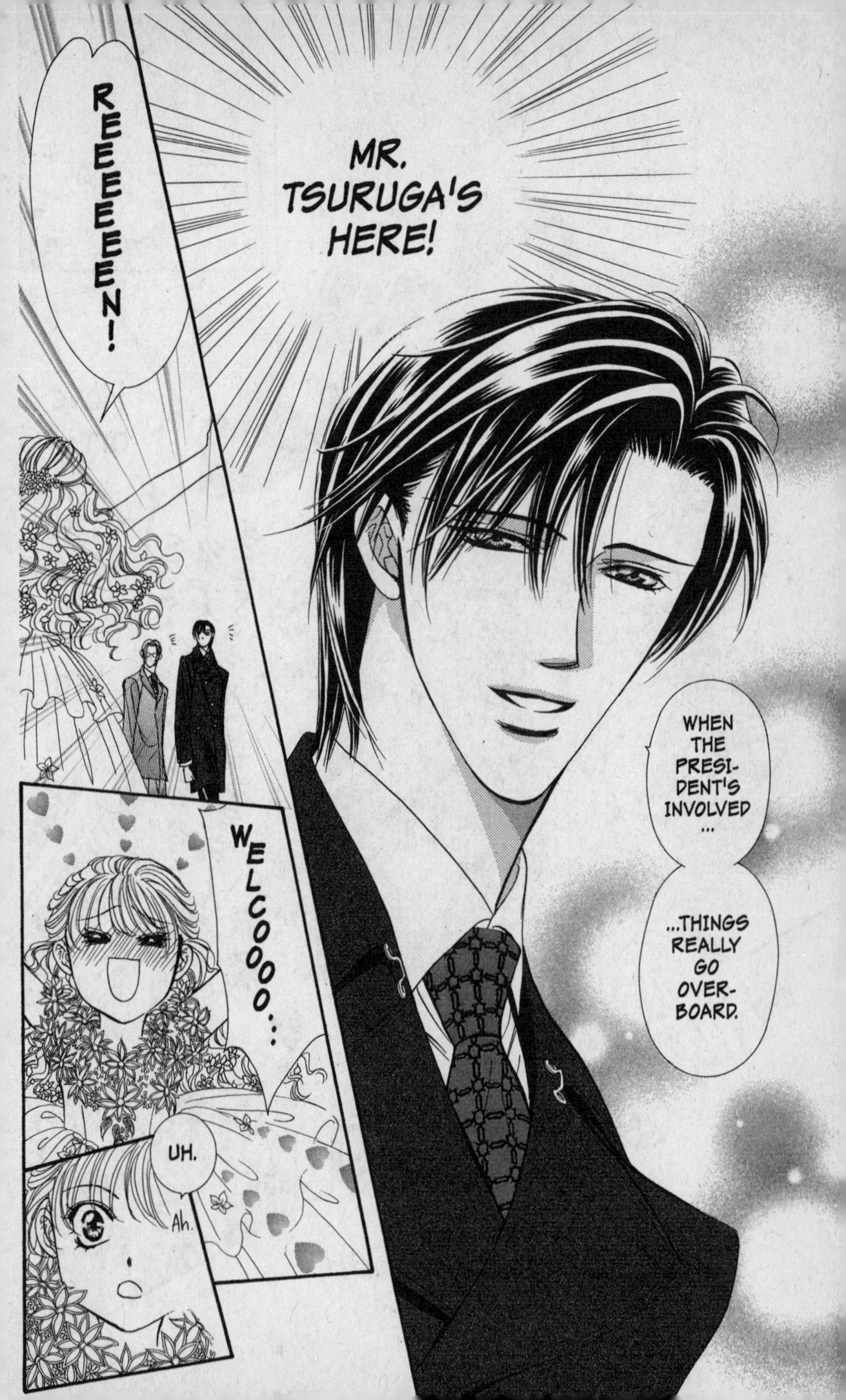
MR. TSURUGA'S HERE!
WHEN THE PRESI-DENT'S INVOLVED...
...THINGS REALLY GO OVER-BOARD.
REEEEEEEN!
WELCOOOO...
UH.
Ah.

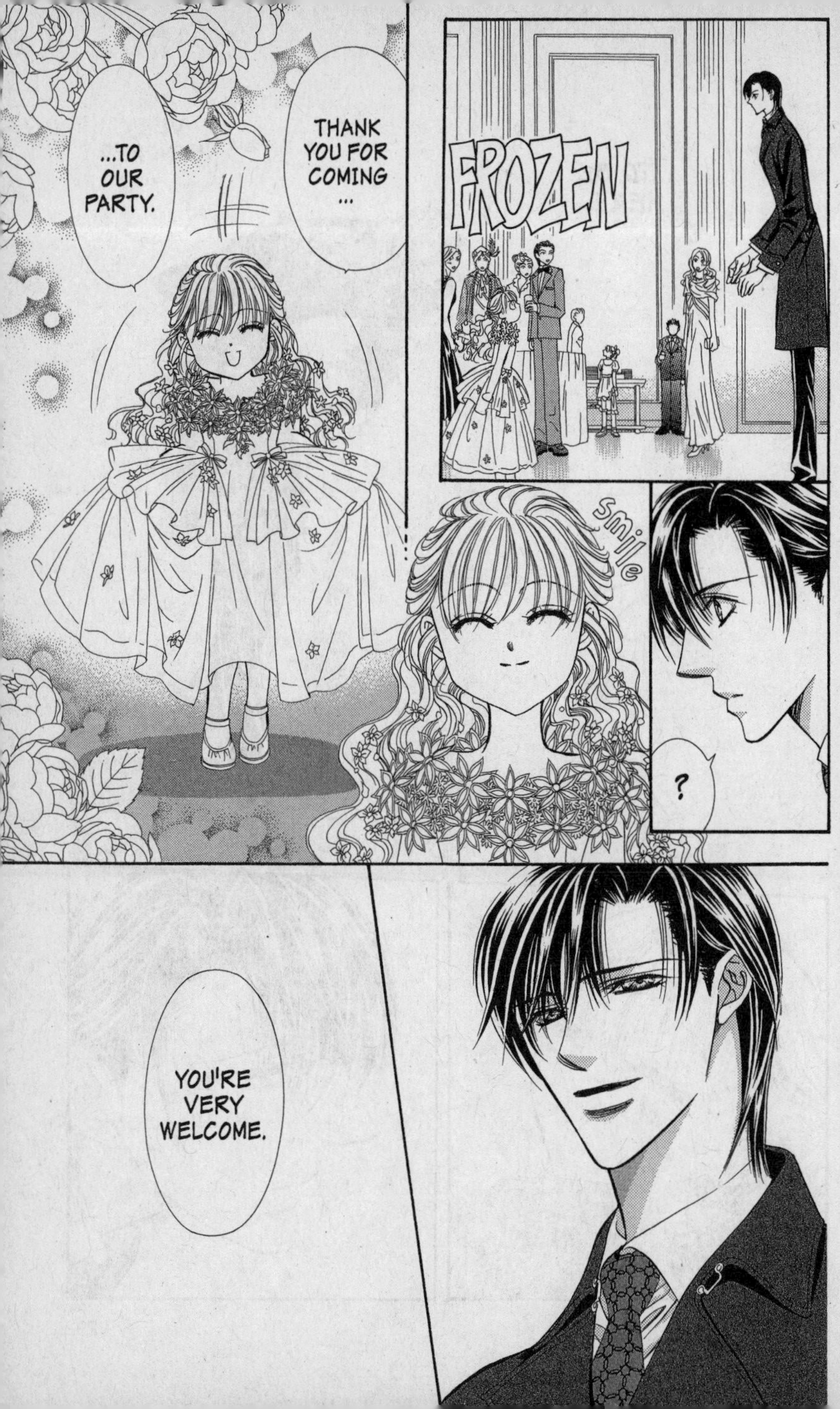
FROZEN
?
Smile
THANK YOU FOR COMING ...
...TO OUR PARTY.
YOU'RE VERY WELCOME.

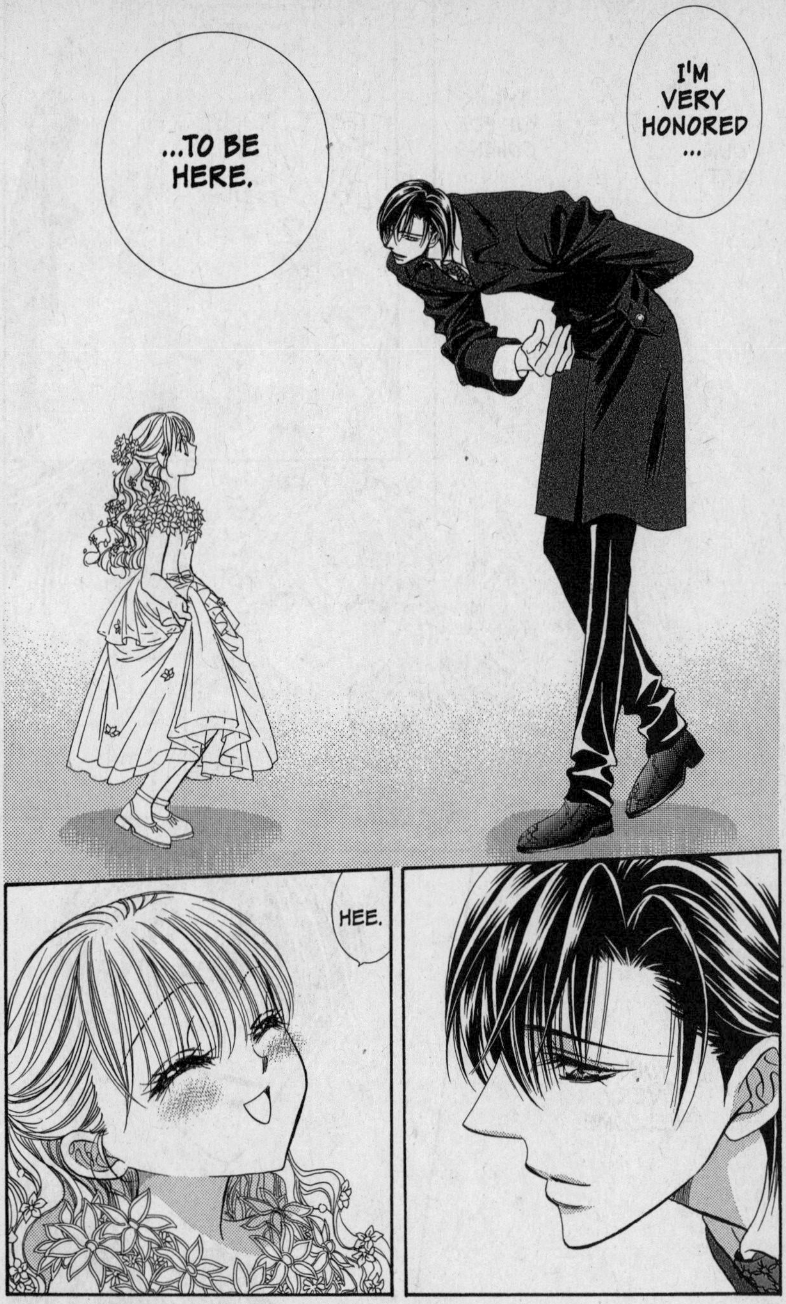
I'M VERY HONORED ...
...TO BE HERE.
HEE.

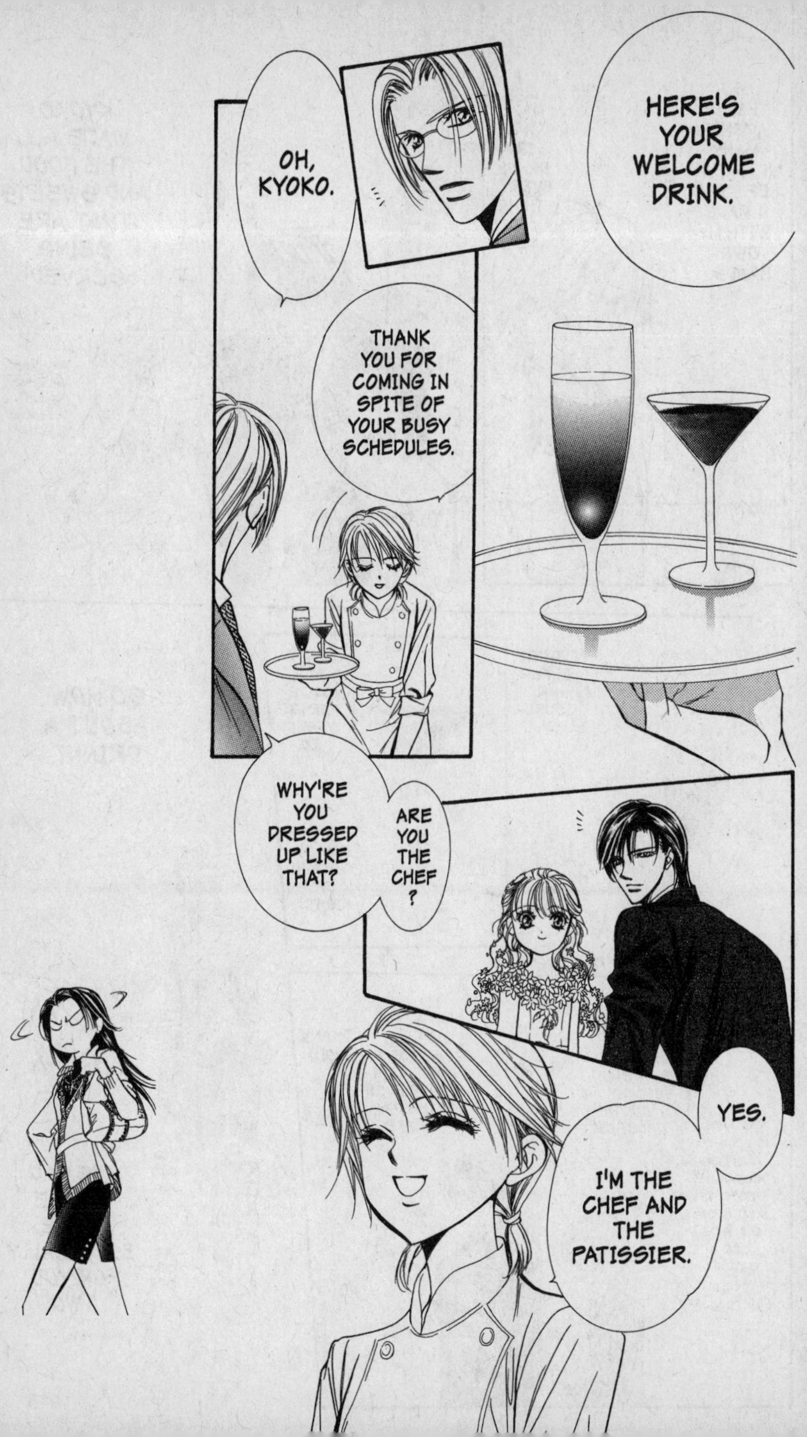
HERE'S YOUR WELCOME DRINK.
OH, KYOKO.
THANK YOU FOR COMING IN SPITE OF YOUR BUSY SCHEDULES.
ARE YOU THE CHEF?
WHY'RE YOU DRESSED UP LIKE THAT?
YES.
I'M THE CHEF AND THE PATISSIER.

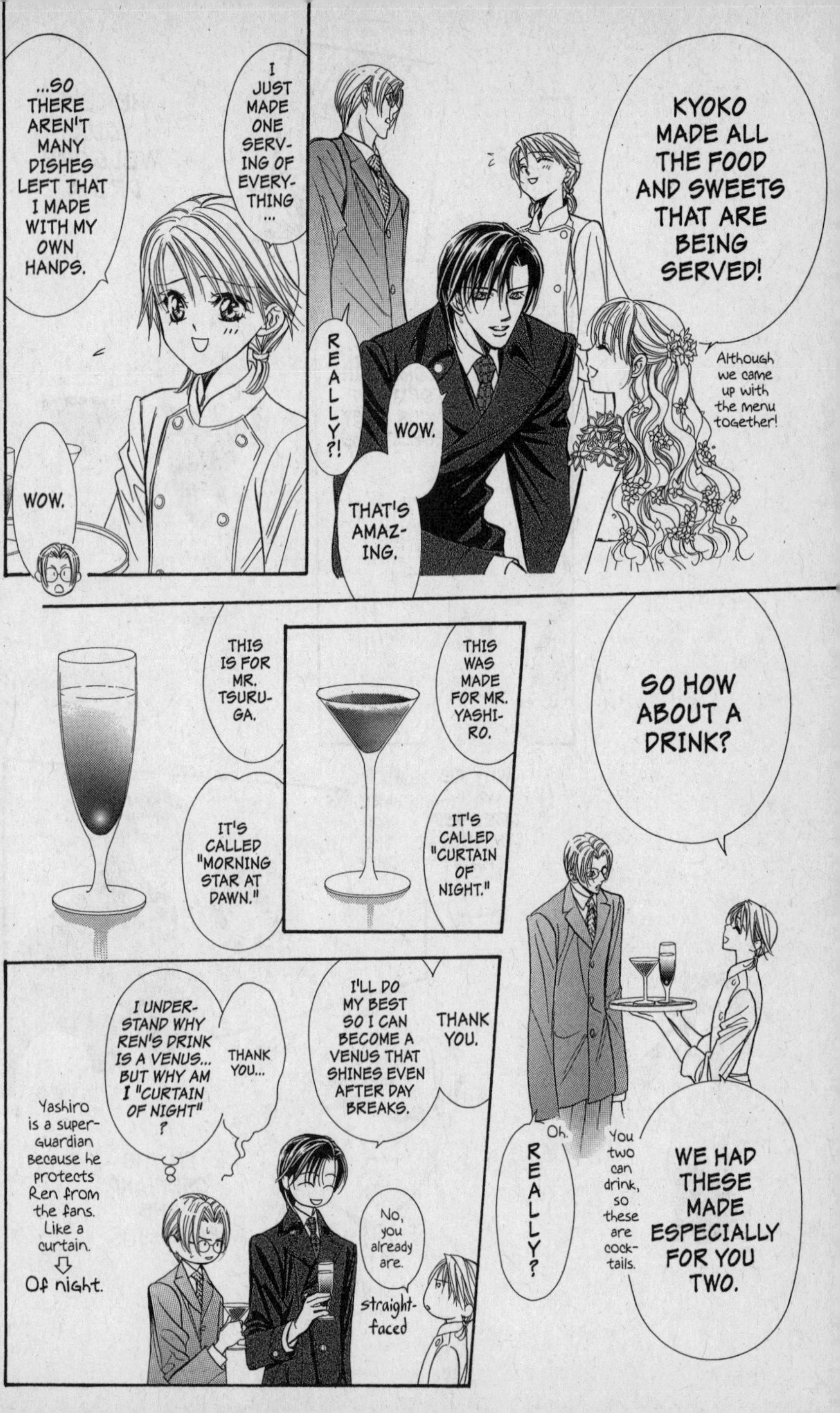
KYOKO MADE ALL THE FOOD AND SWEETS THAT ARE BEING SERVED!
Although we came up with the menu together!
WOW.
REALLY?!
THAT'S AMAZ-ING.
I JUST MADE ONE SERV-ING OF EVERY-THING...
...SO THERE AREN'T MANY DISHES LEFT THAT I MADE WITH MY OWN HANDS.
WOW.
SO HOW ABOUT A DRINK?
WE HAD THESE MADE ESPECIALLY FOR YOU TWO.
You two can drink, so these are cock-tails.
Oh.
REALLY?
THIS WAS MADE FOR MR. YASHI-RO.
IT'S CALLED "CURTAIN OF NIGHT."
THIS IS FOR MR. TSURU-GA.
IT'S CALLED "MORNING STAR AT DAWN."
THANK YOU.
I'LL DO MY BEST SO I CAN BECOME A VENUS THAT SHINES EVEN AFTER DAY BREAKS.
No, you already are.
straight-faced
THANK YOU...
I UNDER-STAND WHY REN'S DRINK IS A VENUS... BUT WHY AM I "CURTAIN OF NIGHT" ?
Yashiro is a super-guardian because he protects Ren from the fans. Like a curtain. ⇩ Of night.

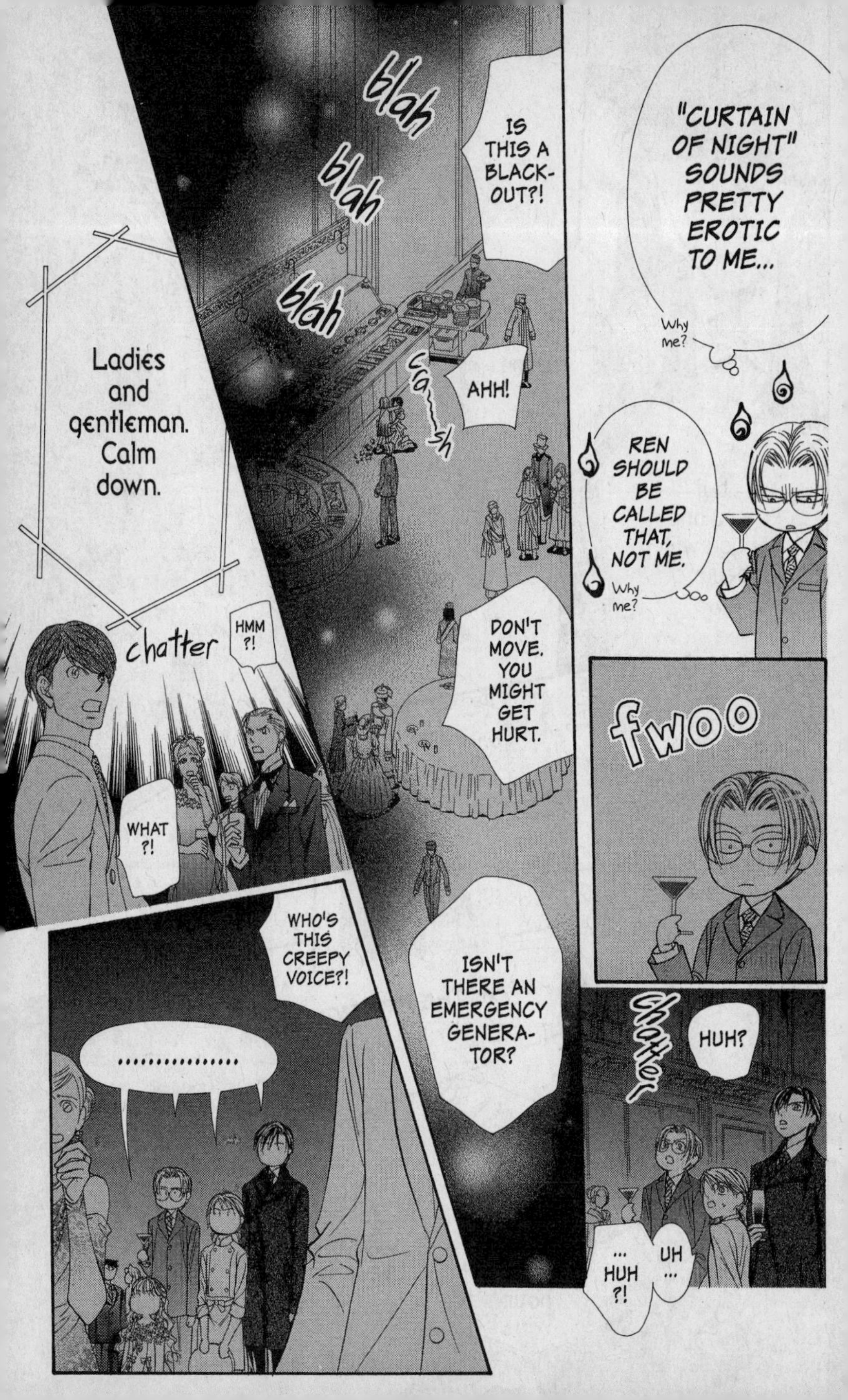
"CURTAIN OF NIGHT" SOUNDS PRETTY EROTIC TO ME...
Why me?
REN SHOULD BE CALLED THAT, NOT ME.
Why me?
fwoo
chatter
HUH?
UH ...
... HUH ?!
IS THIS A BLACK-OUT?!
blah
blah
blah
crash
AHH!
DON'T MOVE. YOU MIGHT GET HURT.
ISN'T THERE AN EMERGENCY GENERA-TOR?
Ladies and gentleman. Calm down.
chatter
HMM ?!
WHAT ?!
WHO'S THIS CREEPY VOICE?!
....

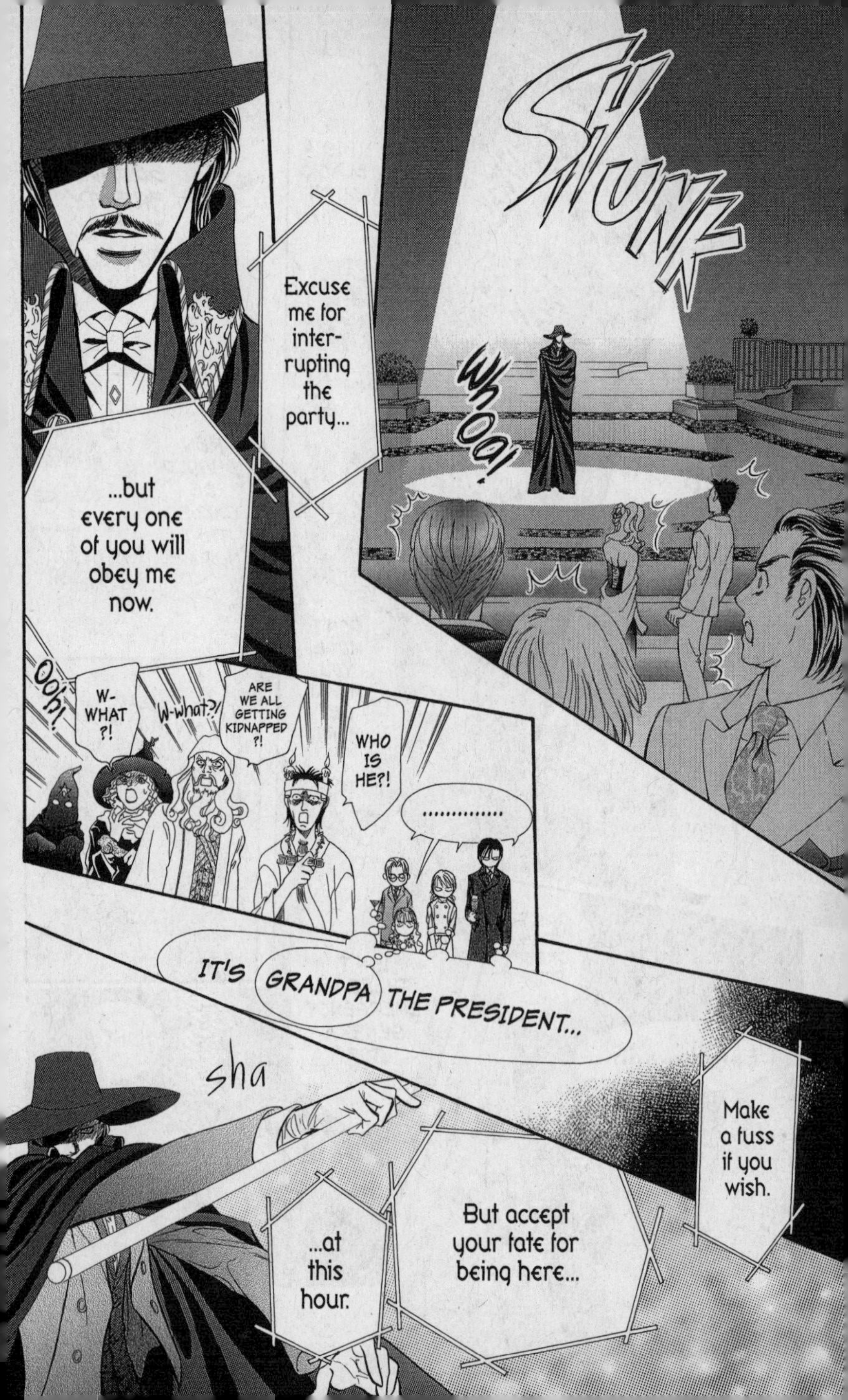
SHUNK
Whoa!
Excuse me for interrupting the party...
...but every one of you will obey me now.
WHO IS HE?!
....
ARE WE ALL GETTING KIDNAPPED?!
W-what?!
W-WHAT?!
Ooh!
IT'S GRANDPA THE PRESIDENT...
sha
Make a fuss if you wish.
But accept your fate for being here...
...at this hour.

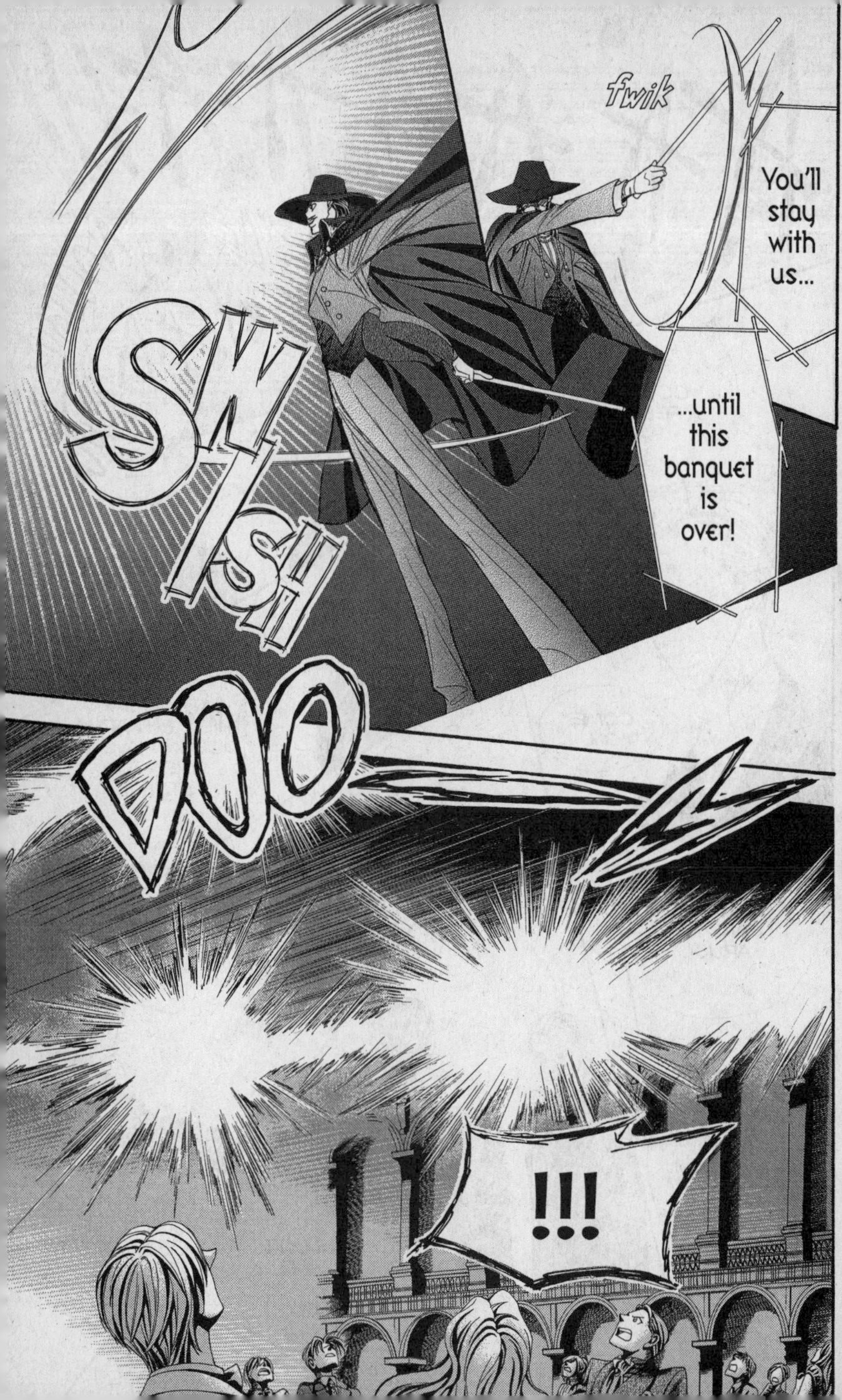
fwik
You'll stay with us...
...until this banquet is over!
SWISH
DOOM
!!!

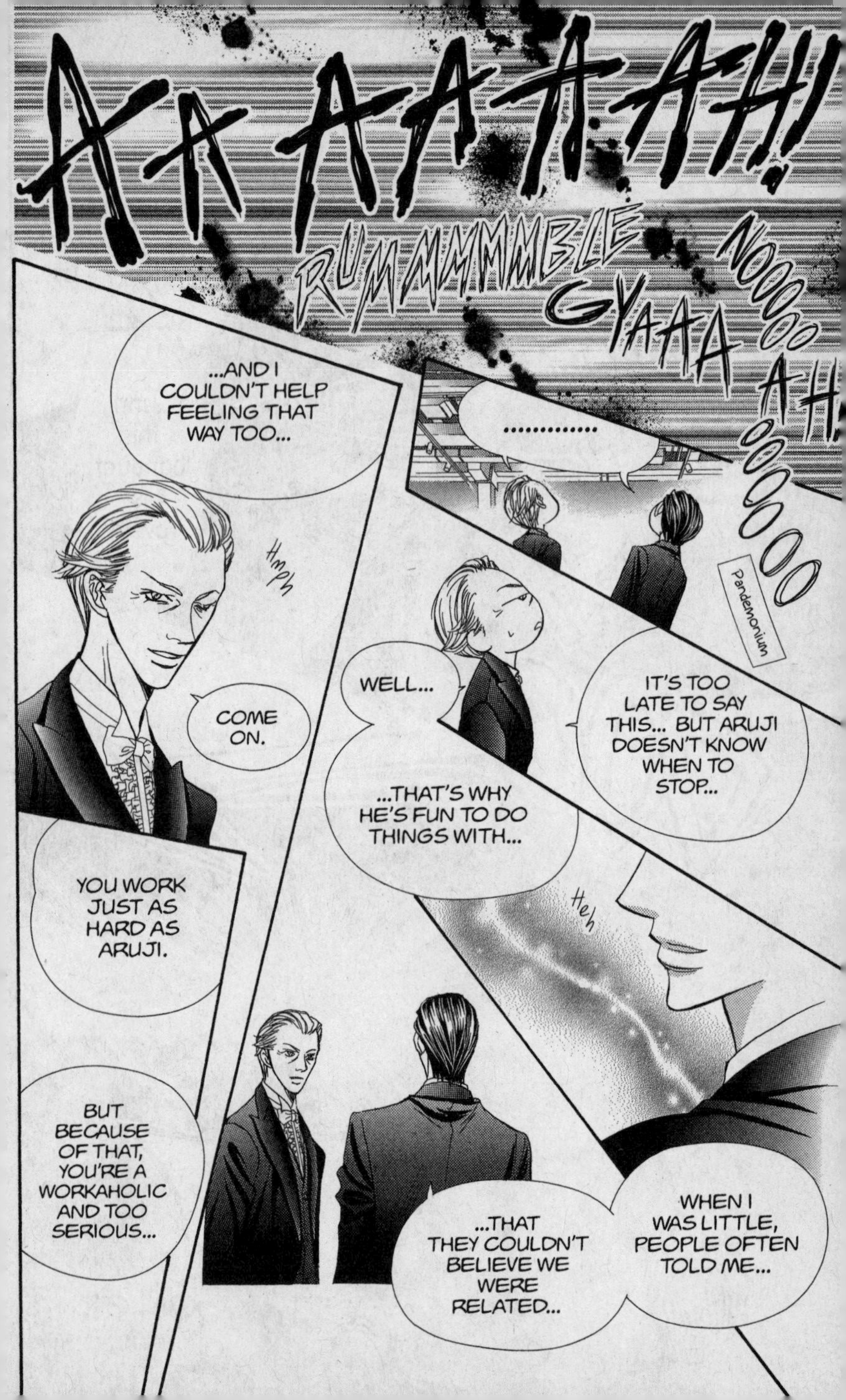
AA-AA-AA-AH!!
RUMMMMMBLE
GYAAA
NOOOOO AH!
OOOOOO
....
Pandemonium
IT'S TOO LATE TO SAY THIS... BUT ARUJI DOESN'T KNOW WHEN TO STOP...
WELL...
...THAT'S WHY HE'S FUN TO DO THINGS WITH...
Heh
WHEN I WAS LITTLE, PEOPLE OFTEN TOLD ME...
...THAT THEY COULDN'T BELIEVE WE WERE RELATED...
...AND I COULDN'T HELP FEELING THAT WAY TOO...
Hmph
COME ON.
YOU WORK JUST AS HARD AS ARUJI.
BUT BECAUSE OF THAT, YOU'RE A WORKAHOLIC AND TOO SERIOUS...

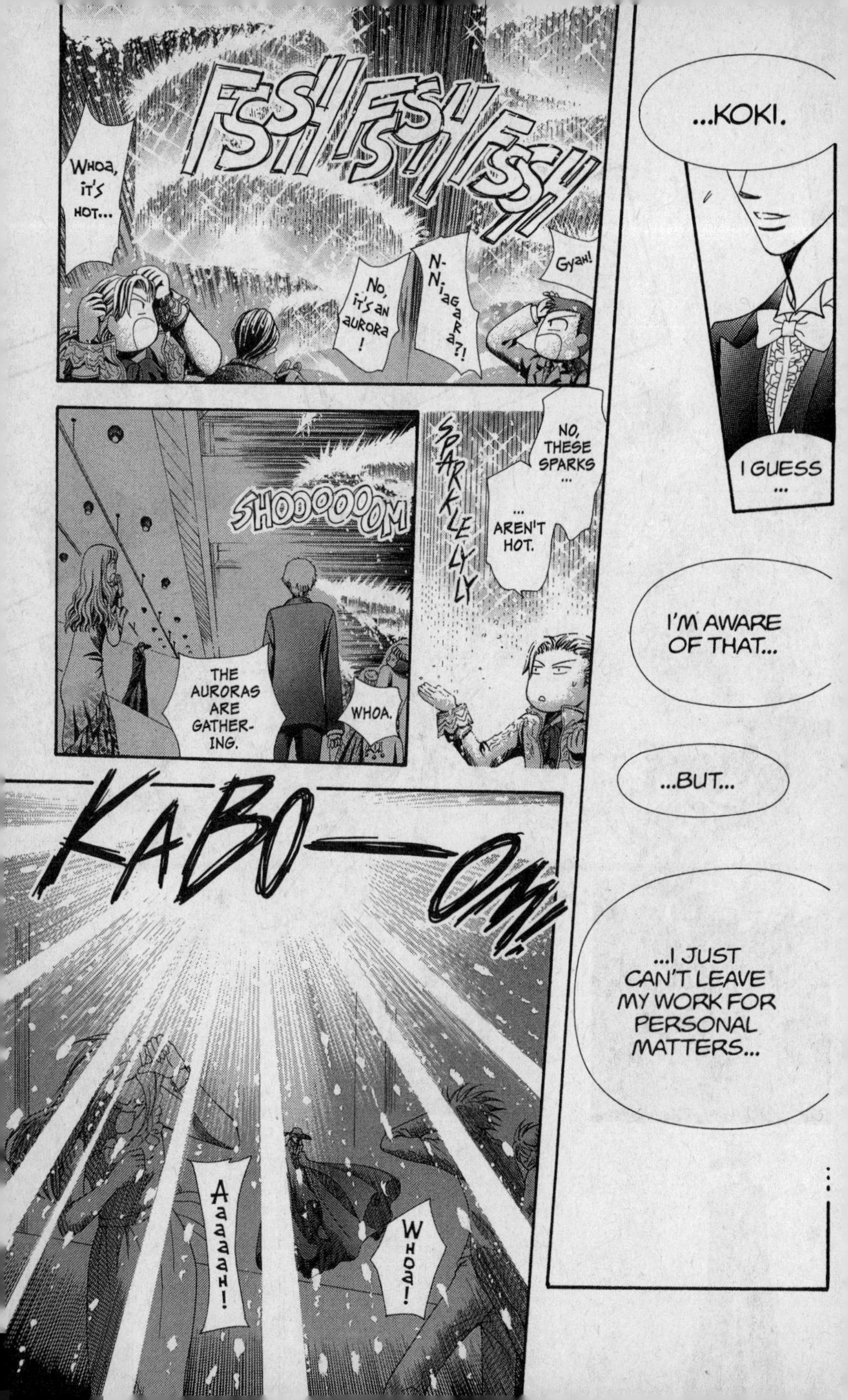
...KOKI.
I GUESS ...
I'M AWARE OF THAT...
...BUT...
...I JUST CAN'T LEAVE MY WORK FOR PERSONAL MATTERS...
...
FSSH FSSH FSSH FSSH
Gyah!
N-Niagara?!
No, it's an aurora!
Whoa, it's hot...
SPARKLELY
NO, THESE SPARKS ...
... AREN'T HOT.
SHOOOOOOM
WHOA.
THE AURORAS ARE GATHERING.
KABO—OM!
Whoa!
Aaaaaah!

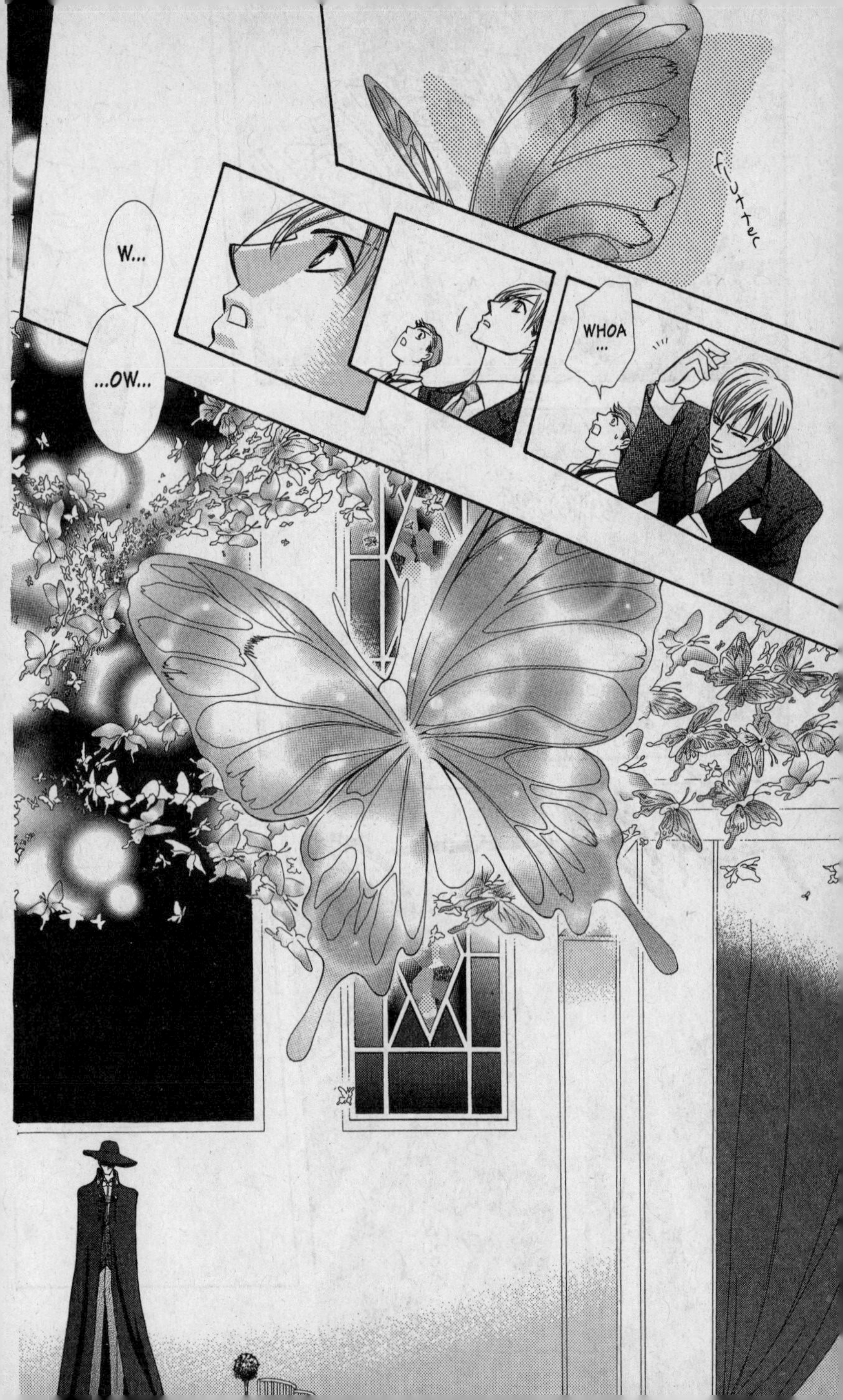
flutter
WHOA ...
W...
...OW...

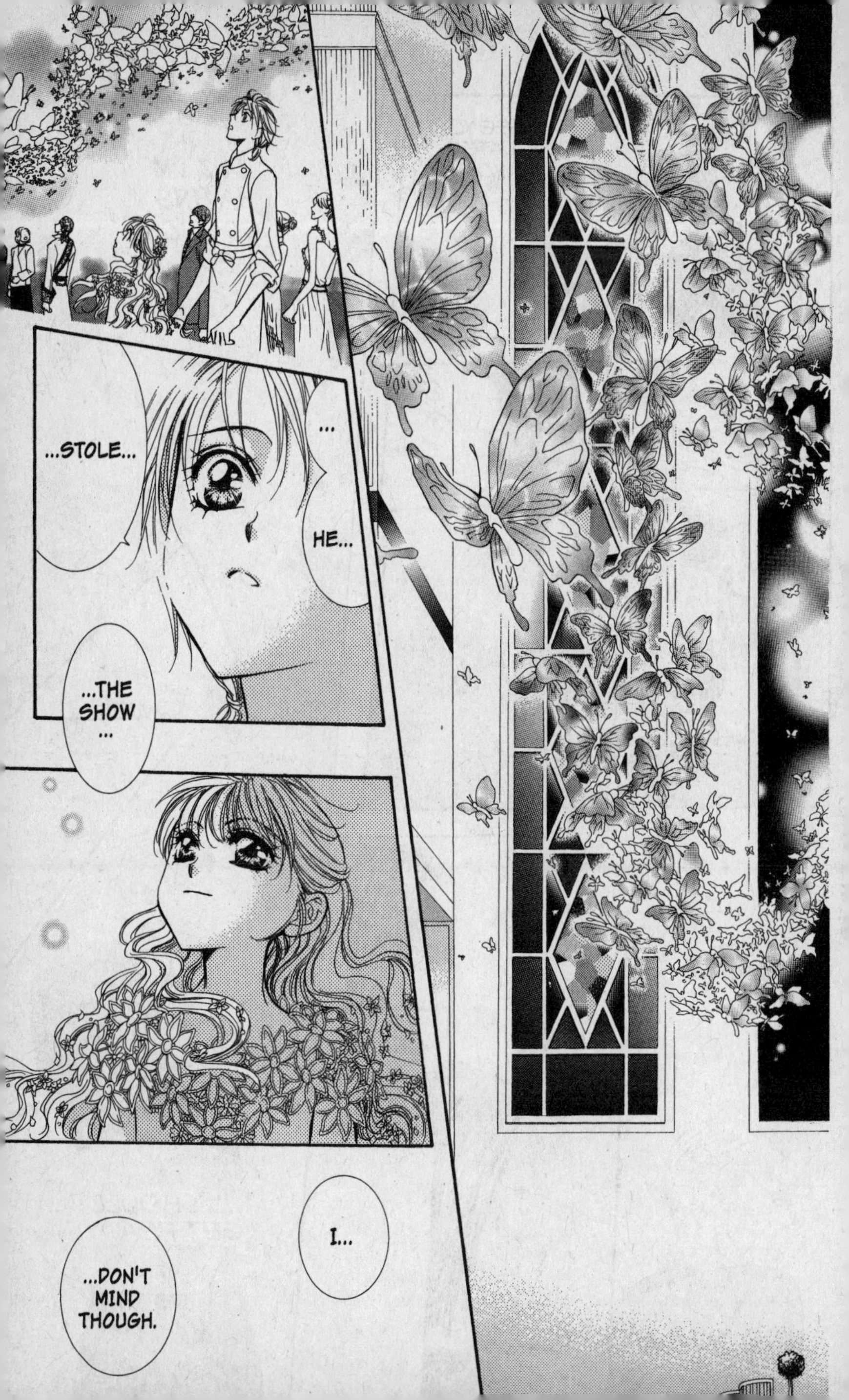
...
HE...
...STOLE...
...THE SHOW ...
I...
...DON'T MIND THOUGH.

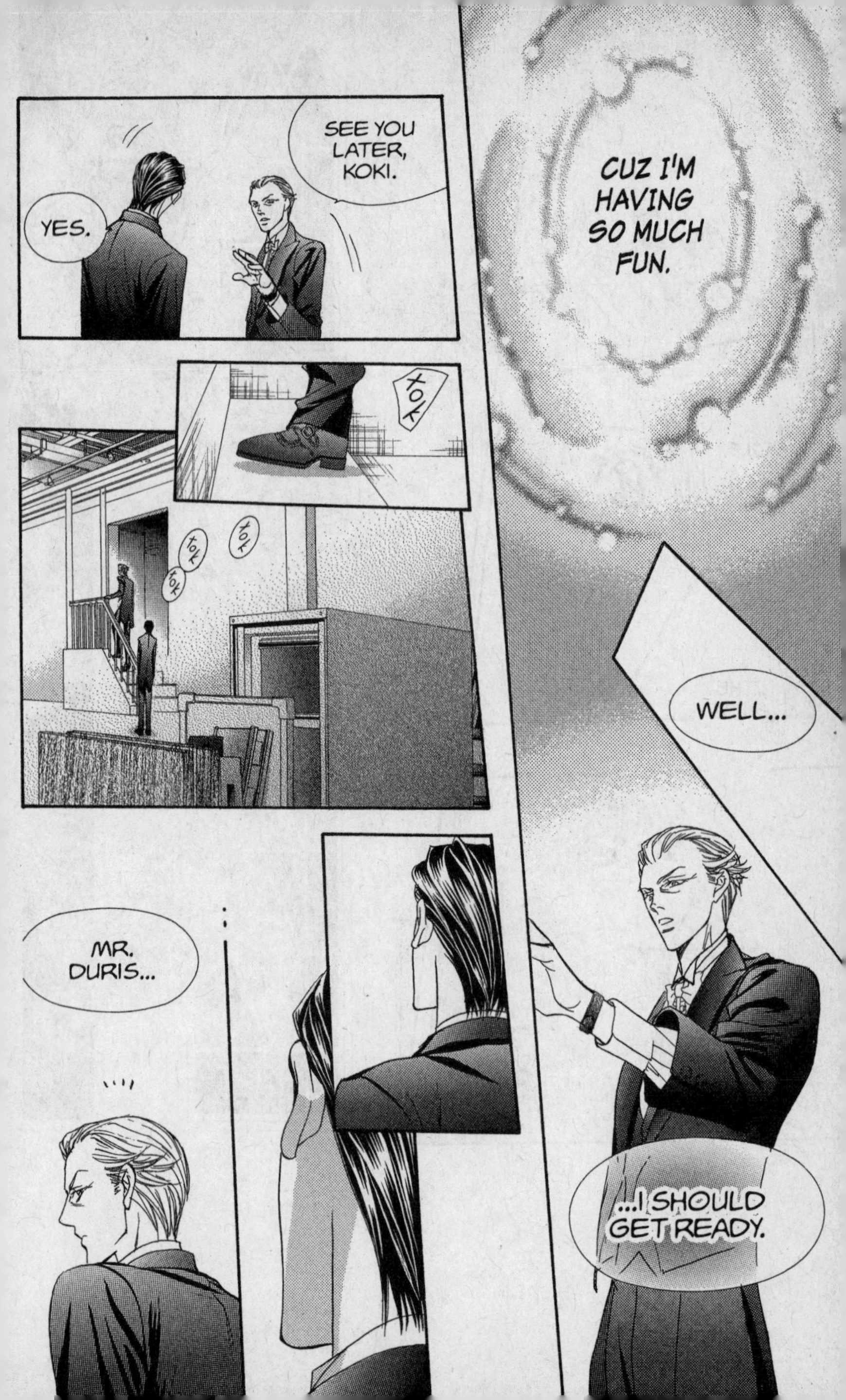
CUZ I'M HAVING SO MUCH FUN.
WELL...
...I SHOULD GET READY.
SEE YOU LATER, KOKI.
YES.
TOK
TOK
TOK
TOK
MR. DURIS...

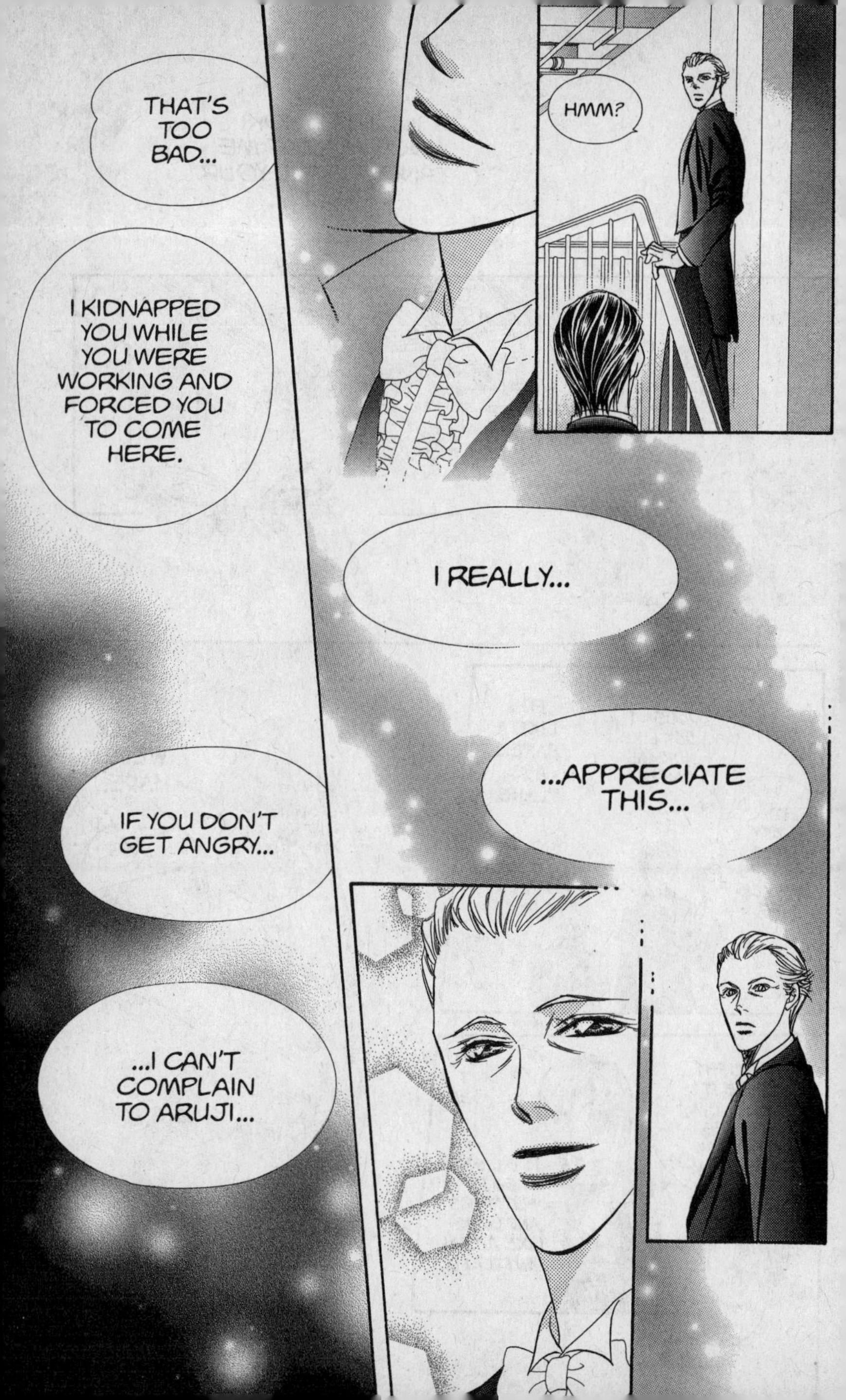
HMM?
THAT'S TOO BAD...
I KIDNAPPED YOU WHILE YOU WERE WORKING AND FORCED YOU TO COME HERE.
I REALLY...
...APPRECIATE THIS...
IF YOU DON'T GET ANGRY...
...I CAN'T COMPLAIN TO ARUJI...

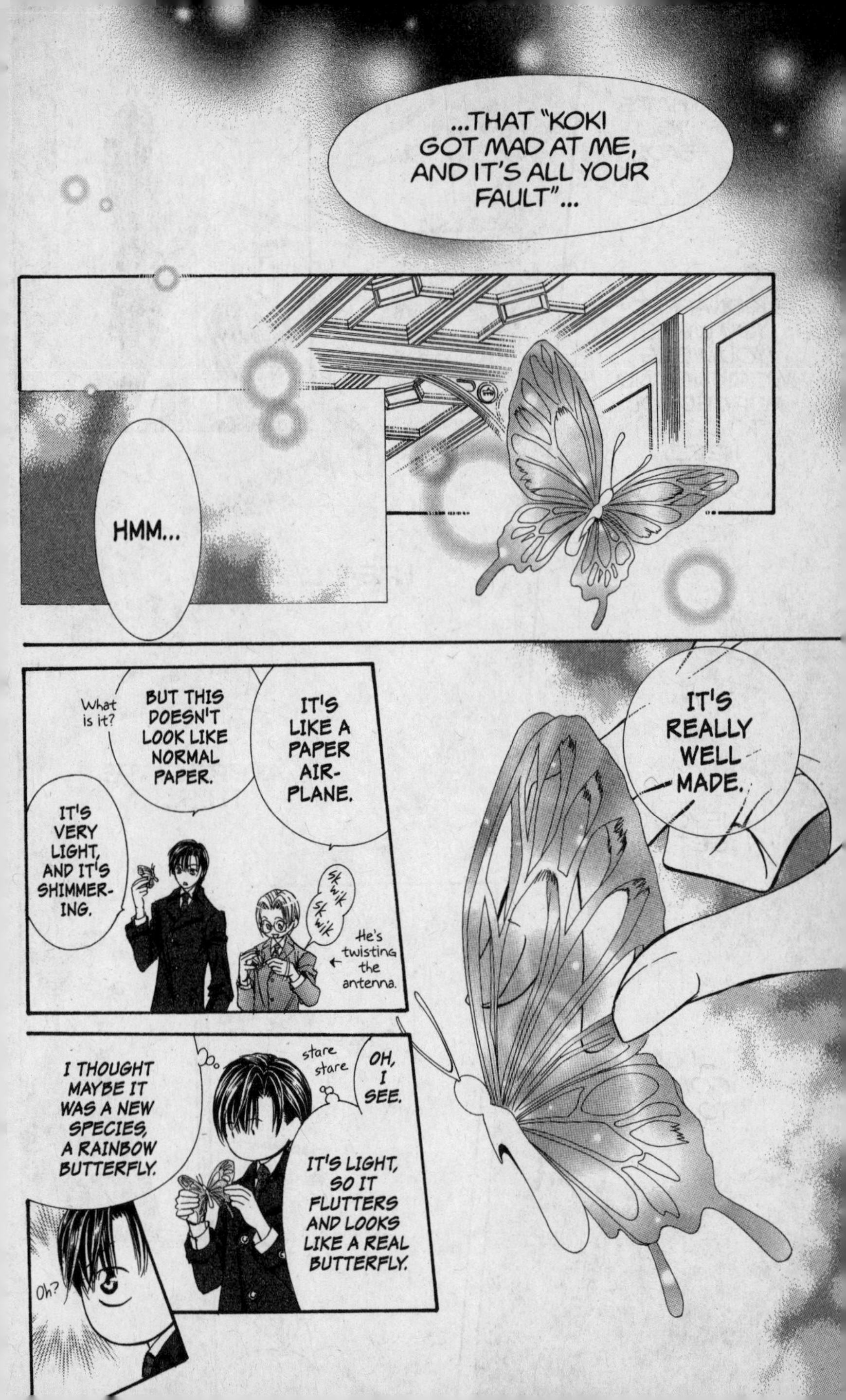
...THAT "KOKI GOT MAD AT ME, AND IT'S ALL YOUR FAULT"...
HMM...
IT'S REALLY WELL MADE.
IT'S LIKE A PAPER AIRPLANE.
BUT THIS DOESN'T LOOK LIKE NORMAL PAPER.
What is it?
IT'S VERY LIGHT, AND IT'S SHIMMERING.
Skwik skwik
He's twisting the antenna.
OH, I SEE.
stare stare
I THOUGHT MAYBE IT WAS A NEW SPECIES, A RAINBOW BUTTERFLY.
IT'S LIGHT, SO IT FLUTTERS AND LOOKS LIKE A REAL BUTTERFLY.
Oh?

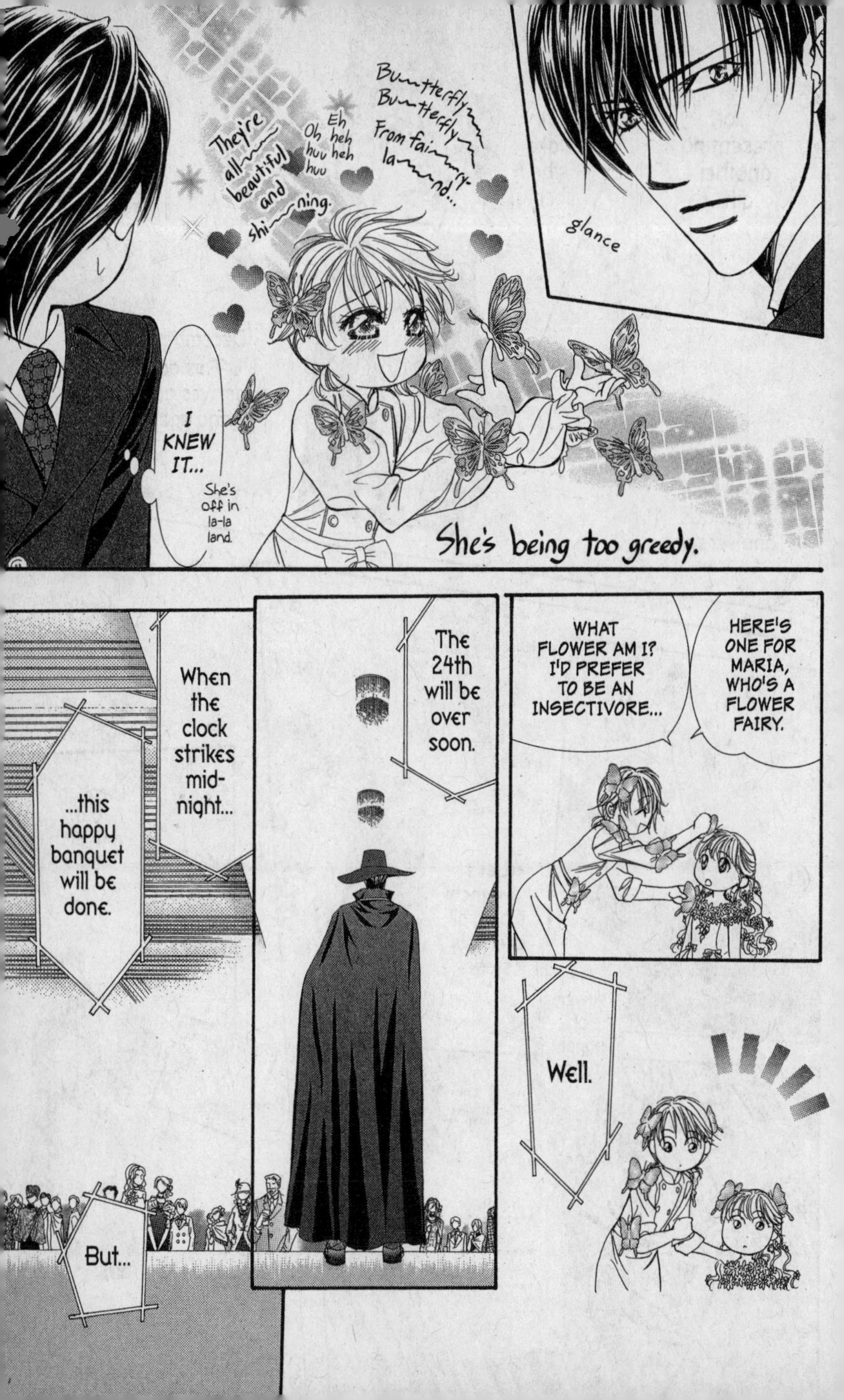
glance
Bu~tterfly Bu~tterfly From fai~ry-la~nd...
Eh heh heh
Oh huu huu
They're all~ beautiful and shi~ning.
I KNEW IT...
She's off in la-la land.
She's being too greedy.
HERE'S ONE FOR MARIA, WHO'S A FLOWER FAIRY.
WHAT FLOWER AM I? I'D PREFER TO BE AN INSECTIVORE...
Well.
The 24th will be over soon.
When the clock strikes midnight...
...this happy banquet will be done.
But...

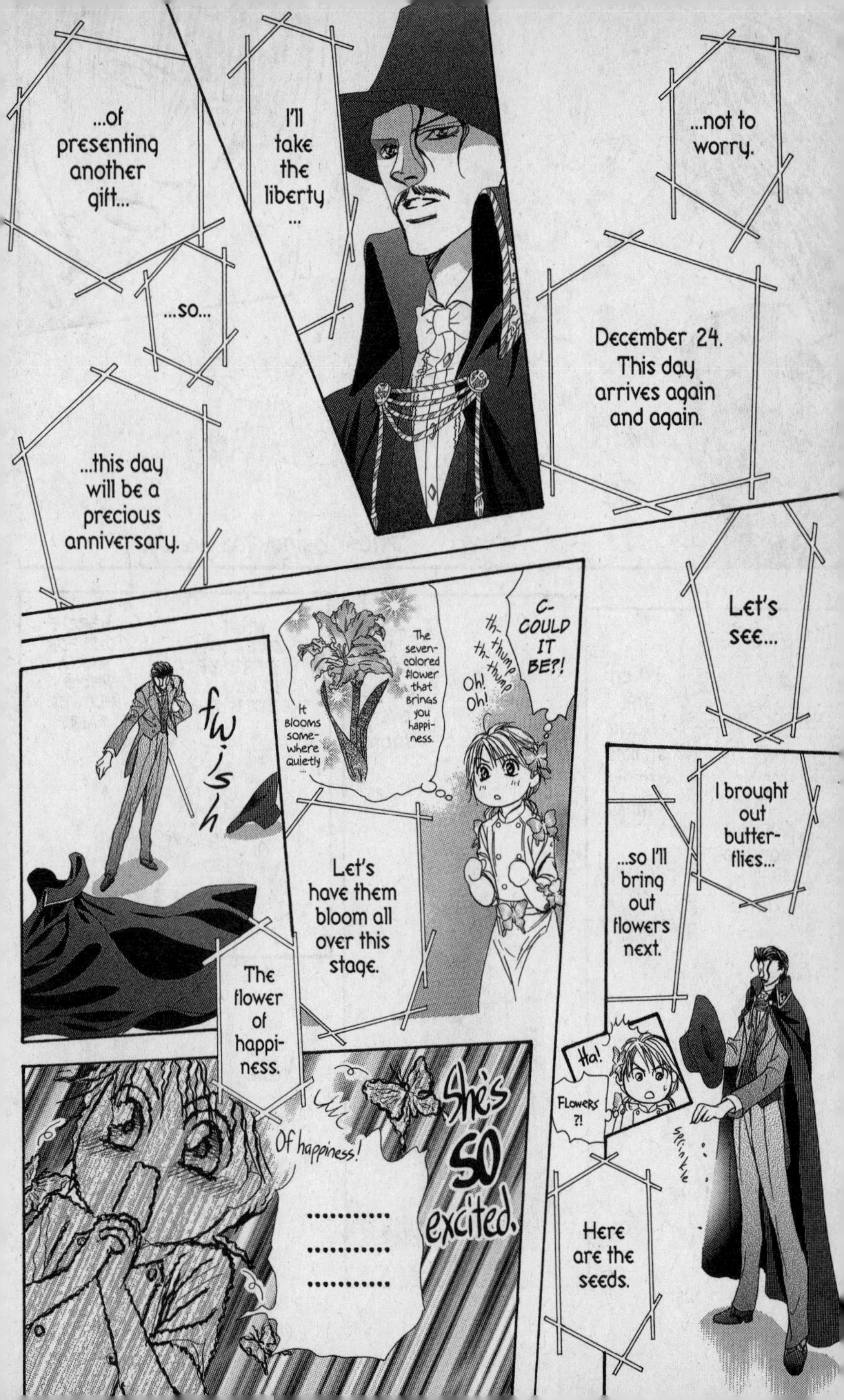
...not to worry.
December 24. This day arrives again and again.
I'll take the liberty...
...of presenting another gift...
...so...
...this day will be a precious anniversary.
Let's see...
I brought out butterflies...
...so I'll bring out flowers next.
Ha!
Flowers?!
sprinkle
Here are the seeds.
C-COULD IT BE?!
th-thump th-thump
Oh! Oh!
The seven-colored flower that brings you happiness.
It blooms somewhere quietly...
Let's have them bloom all over this stage.
fwish
The flower of happiness.
She's SO excited.
Of happiness!
....
....
....

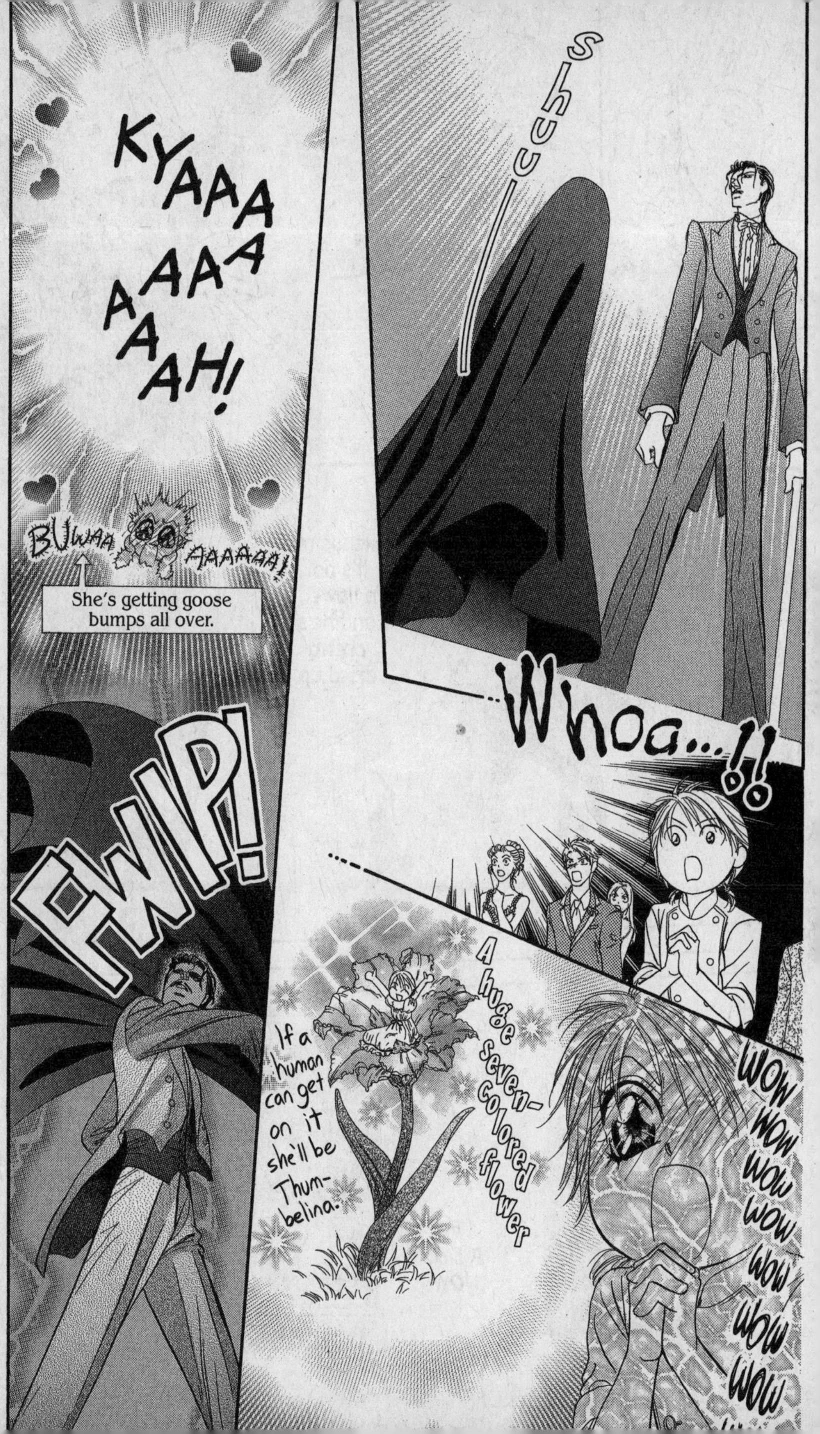
Shuuu—
KYAAAAAAAAAH!
BUWAAAAAAAA!
She's getting goose bumps all over.
Whoa...!!
FWIP!
WOW WOW WOW WOW WOW WOW WOW WOW
A huge seven-colored flower
If a human can get on it she'll be Thumbelina.

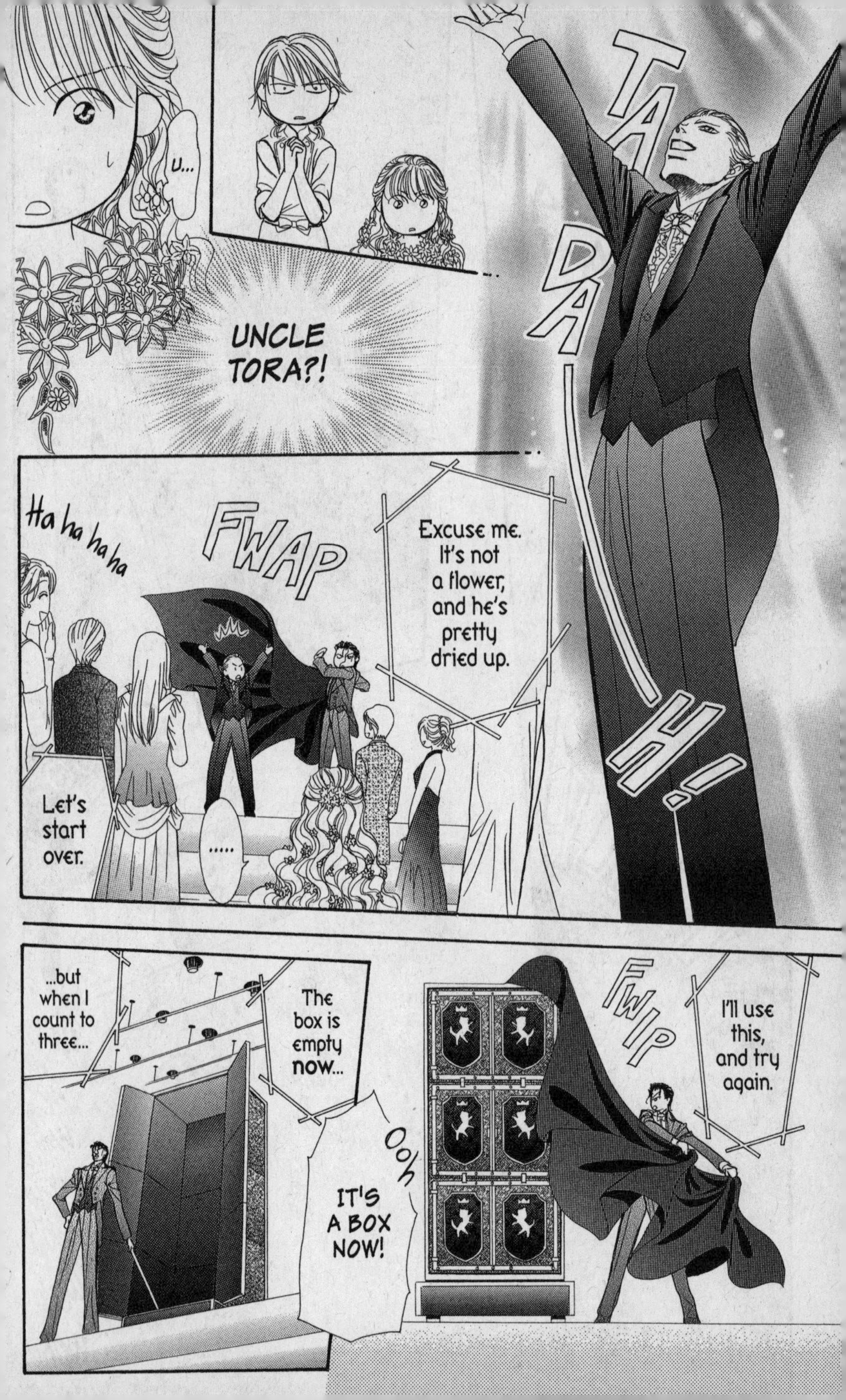
TA-DA-H!
U...
UNCLE TORA?!
Excuse me. It's not a flower, and he's pretty dried up.
FWAP
Ha ha ha ha
......
Let's start over.
FWIP
I'll use this, and try again.
Ooh
IT'S A BOX NOW!
The box is empty now...
...but when I count to three...

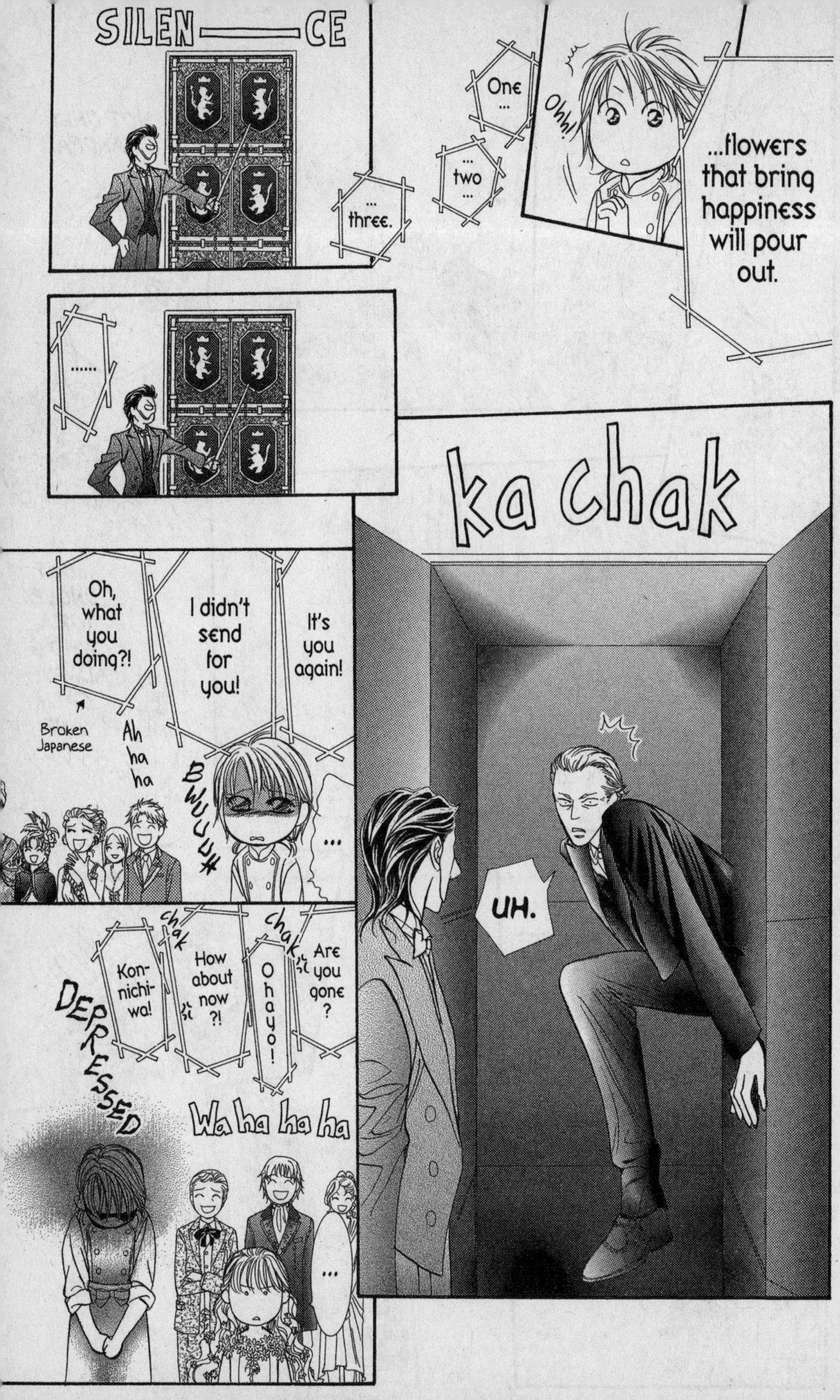
...flowers that bring happiness will pour out.
Ohh!
One ...
... two ...
... three.
SILEN——CE
......
ka chak
UH.
It's you again!
I didn't send for you!
Oh, what you doing?!
Broken Japanese
Ah ha ha
BWUUUH
...
Are you gone?
chak
Ohayo!
How about now?!
chak
Konnichiwa!
DEPRESSED
Wa ha ha ha
...

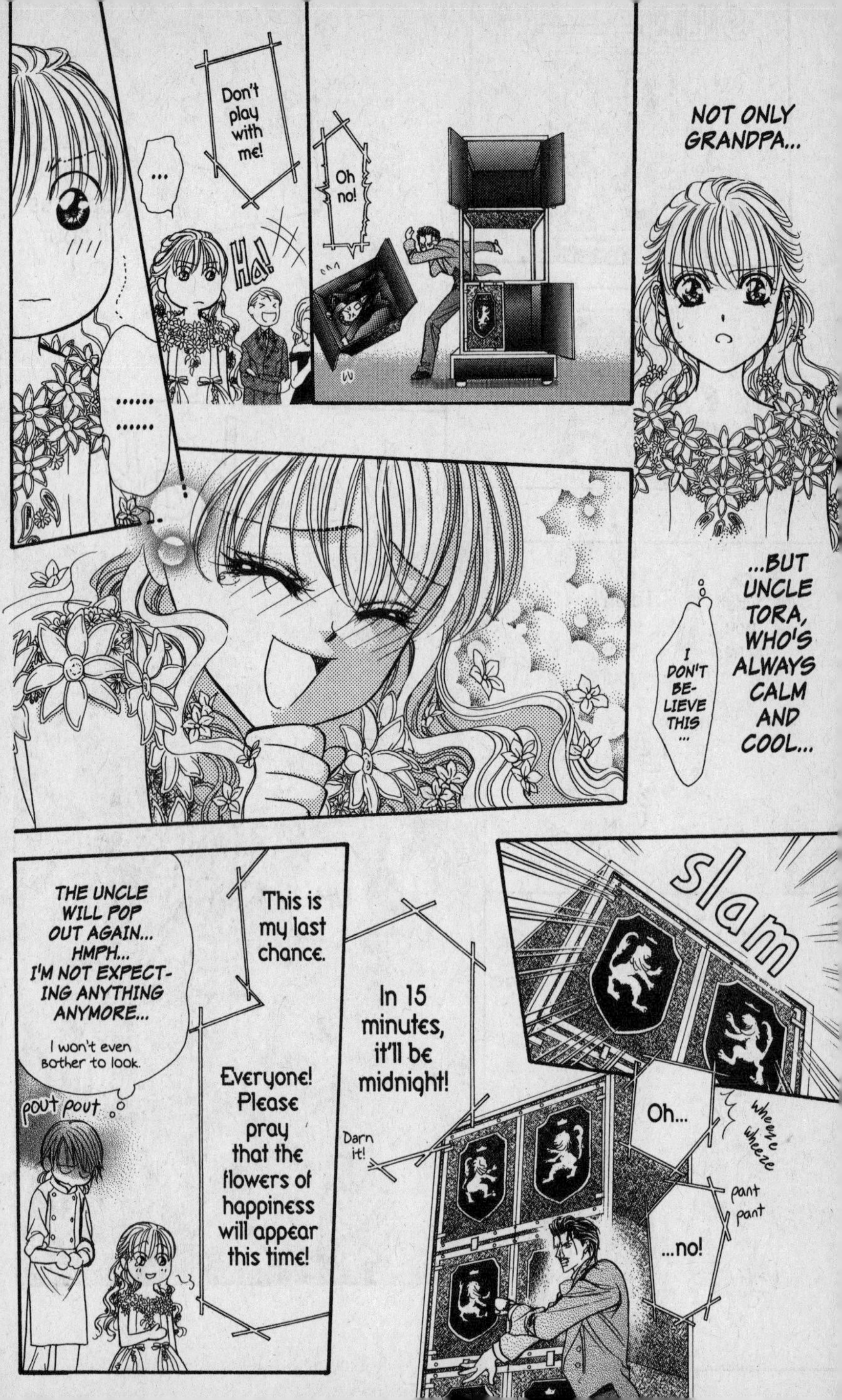
NOT ONLY GRANDPA...
Oh no!
Don't play with me!
...
Ha!
......
......
...BUT UNCLE TORA, WHO'S ALWAYS CALM AND COOL...
I DON'T BE-LIEVE THIS...
slam
Oh...
...no!
wheeze wheeze
pant pant
Darn it!
In 15 minutes, it'll be midnight!
This is my last chance.
Everyone! Please pray that the flowers of happiness will appear this time!
THE UNCLE WILL POP OUT AGAIN... HMPH... I'M NOT EXPECT-ING ANYTHING ANYMORE...
I won't even bother to look.
pout pout

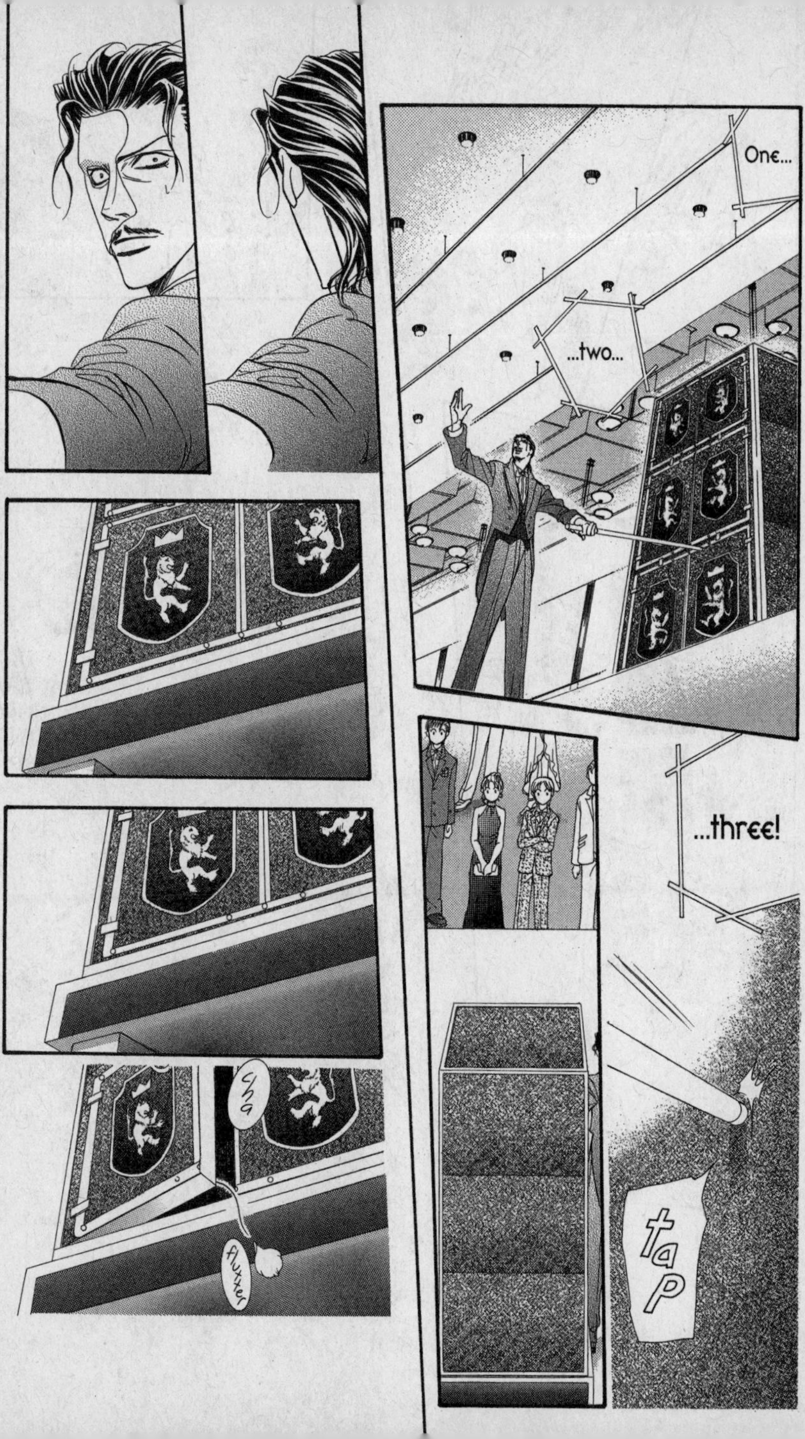
One...
...two...
...three!
tap
cha
fluxxer

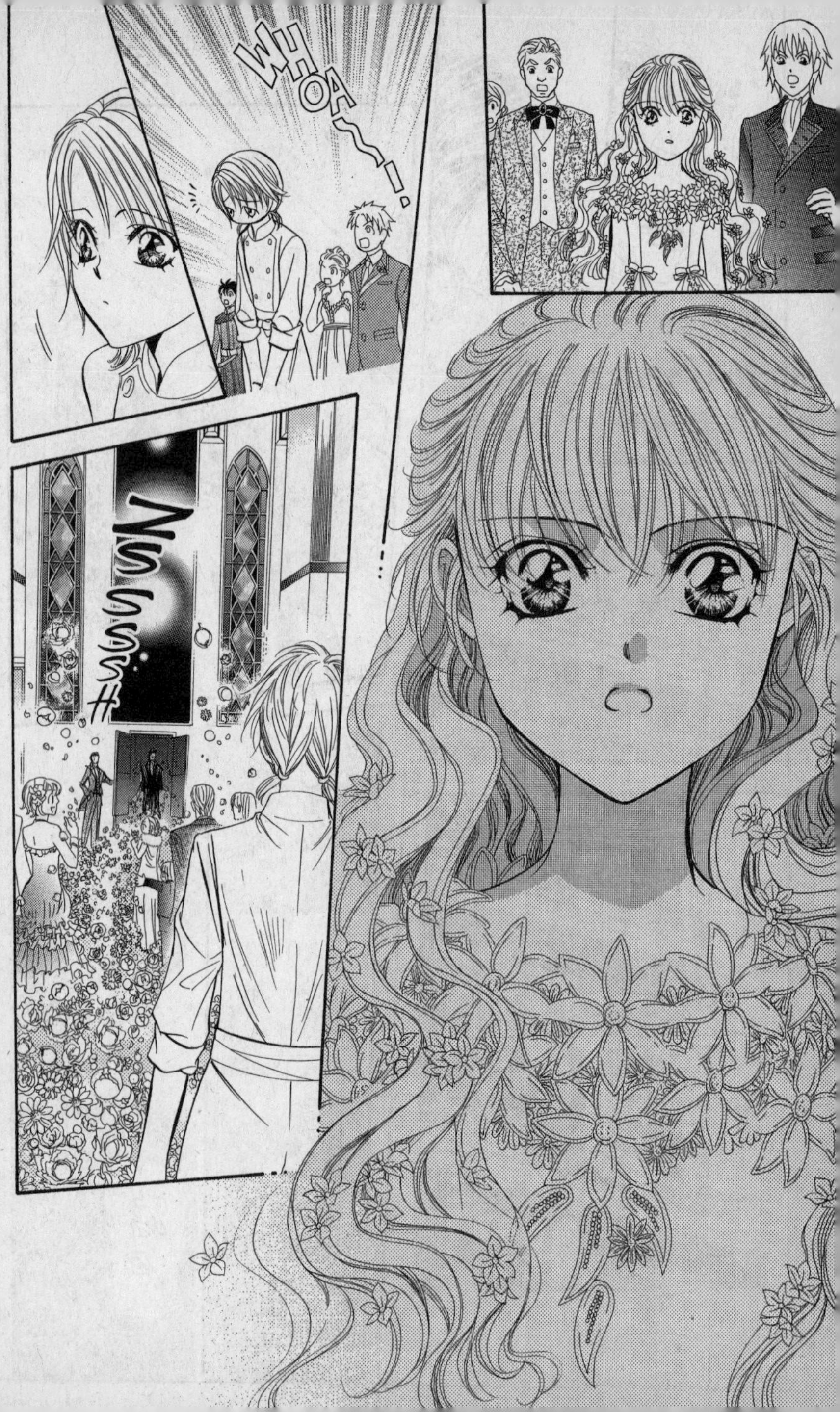
WHOA~~!
SWSSSSH

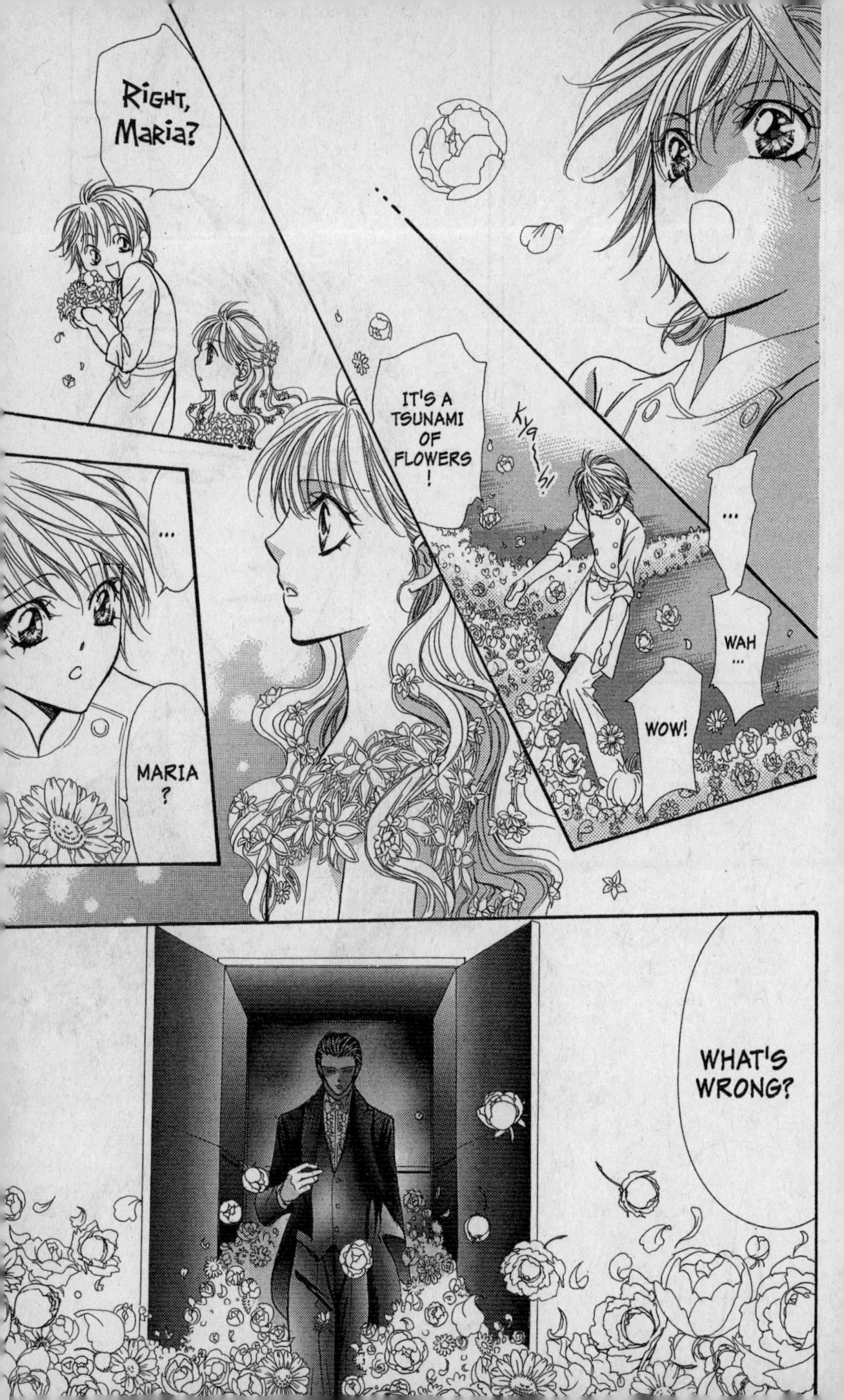
...
WAH ...
WOW!
Kya~h!
IT'S A TSUNAMI OF FLOWERS!
Right, Maria?
...
MARIA ?
WHAT'S WRONG?

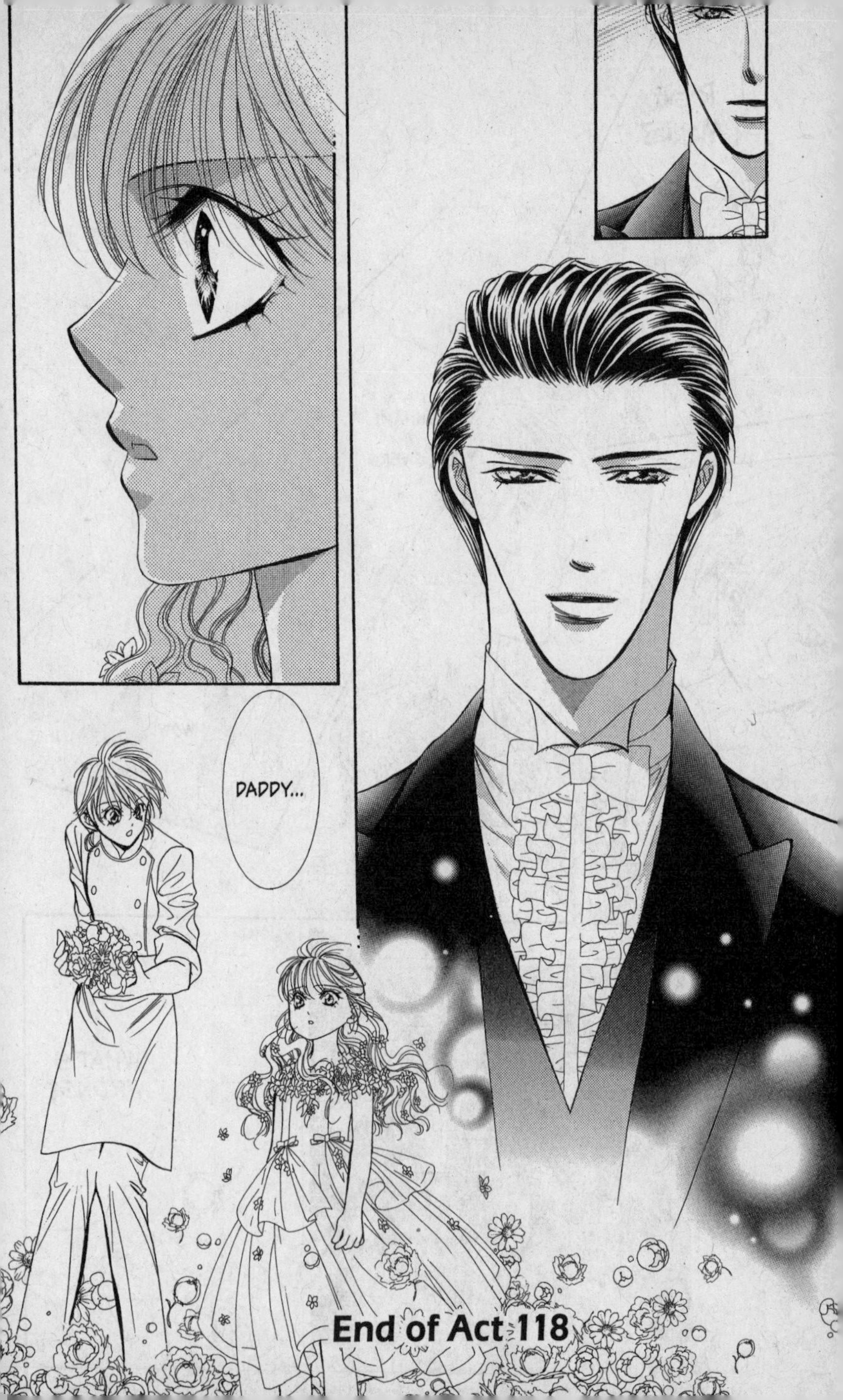
DADDY...
End of Act 118

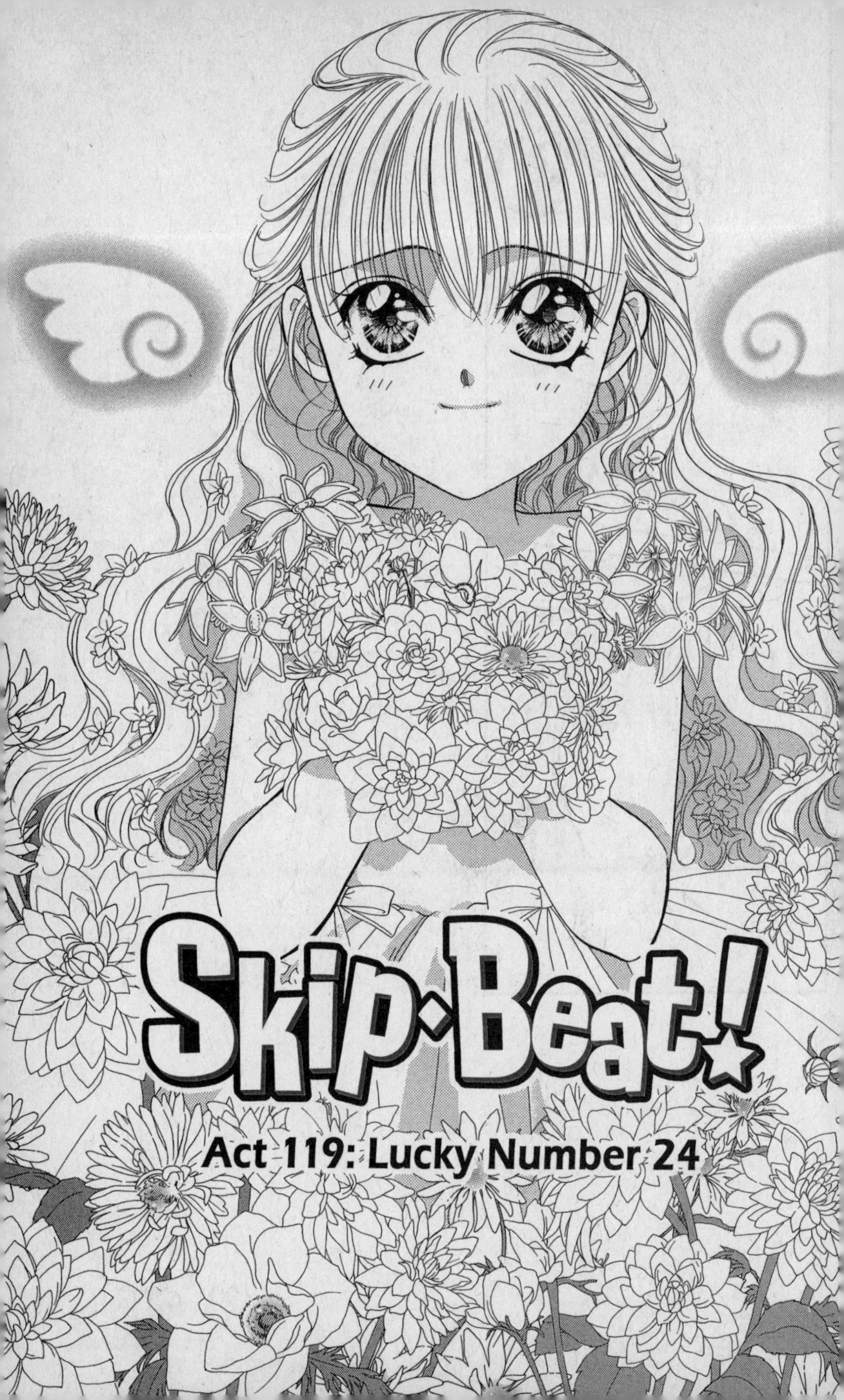
Skip·Beat!
Act 119: Lucky Number 24

WHA
?

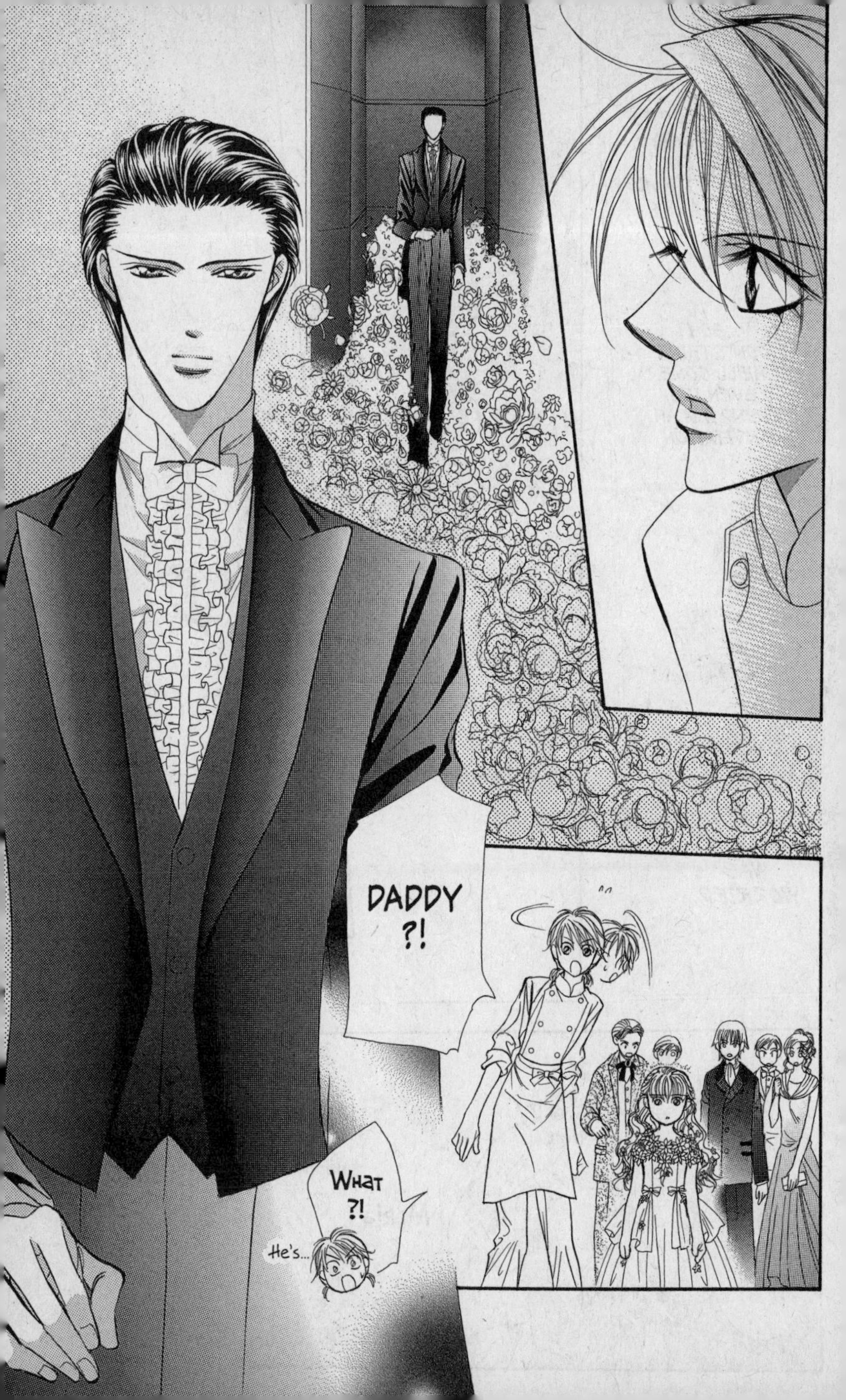
DADDY ?!
WHAT ?!
He's...

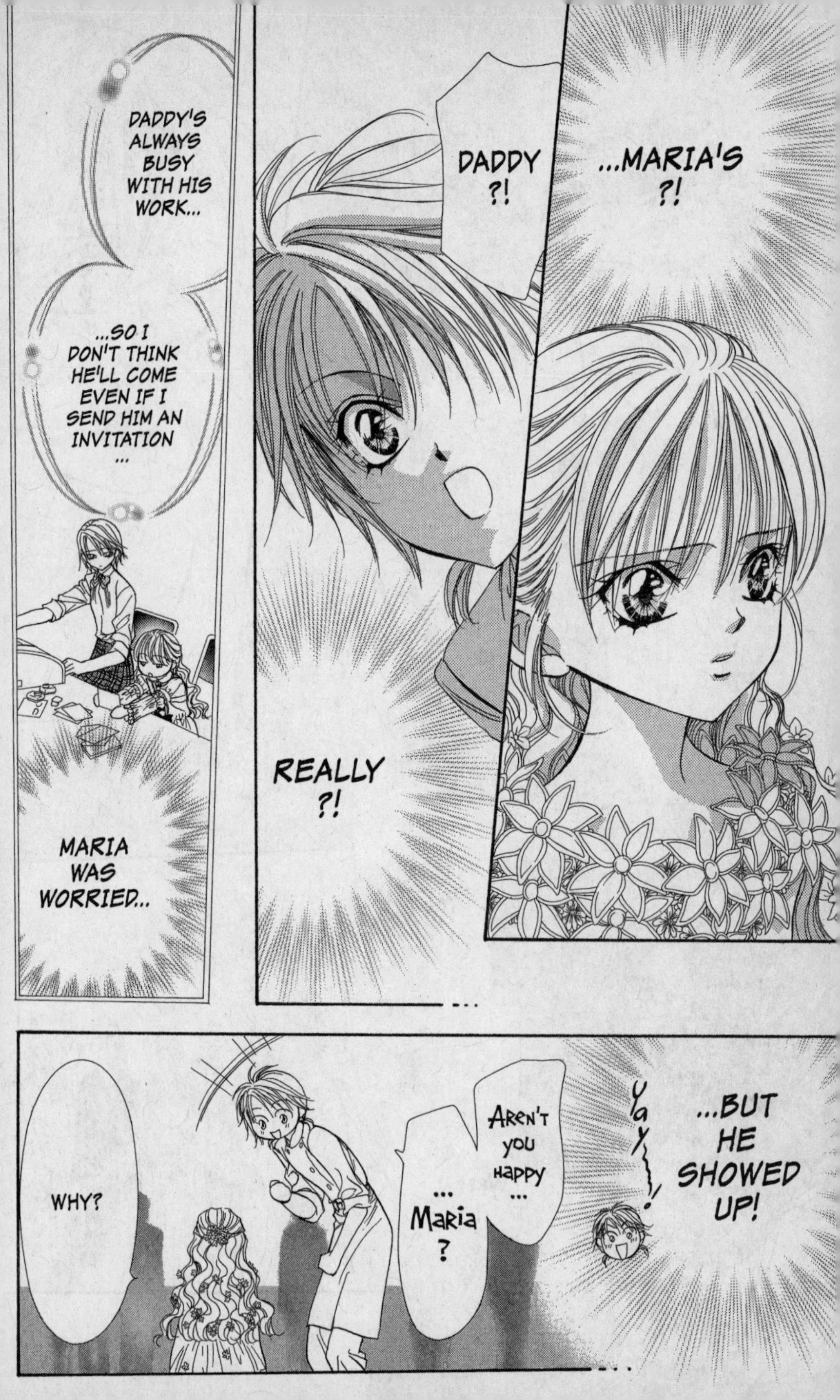
...MARIA'S ?!
DADDY ?!
REALLY ?!
DADDY'S ALWAYS BUSY WITH HIS WORK...
...SO I DON'T THINK HE'LL COME EVEN IF I SEND HIM AN INVITATION ...
MARIA WAS WORRIED...
...BUT HE SHOWED UP!
Yay~!
Aren't you happy ...
... Maria ?
WHY?

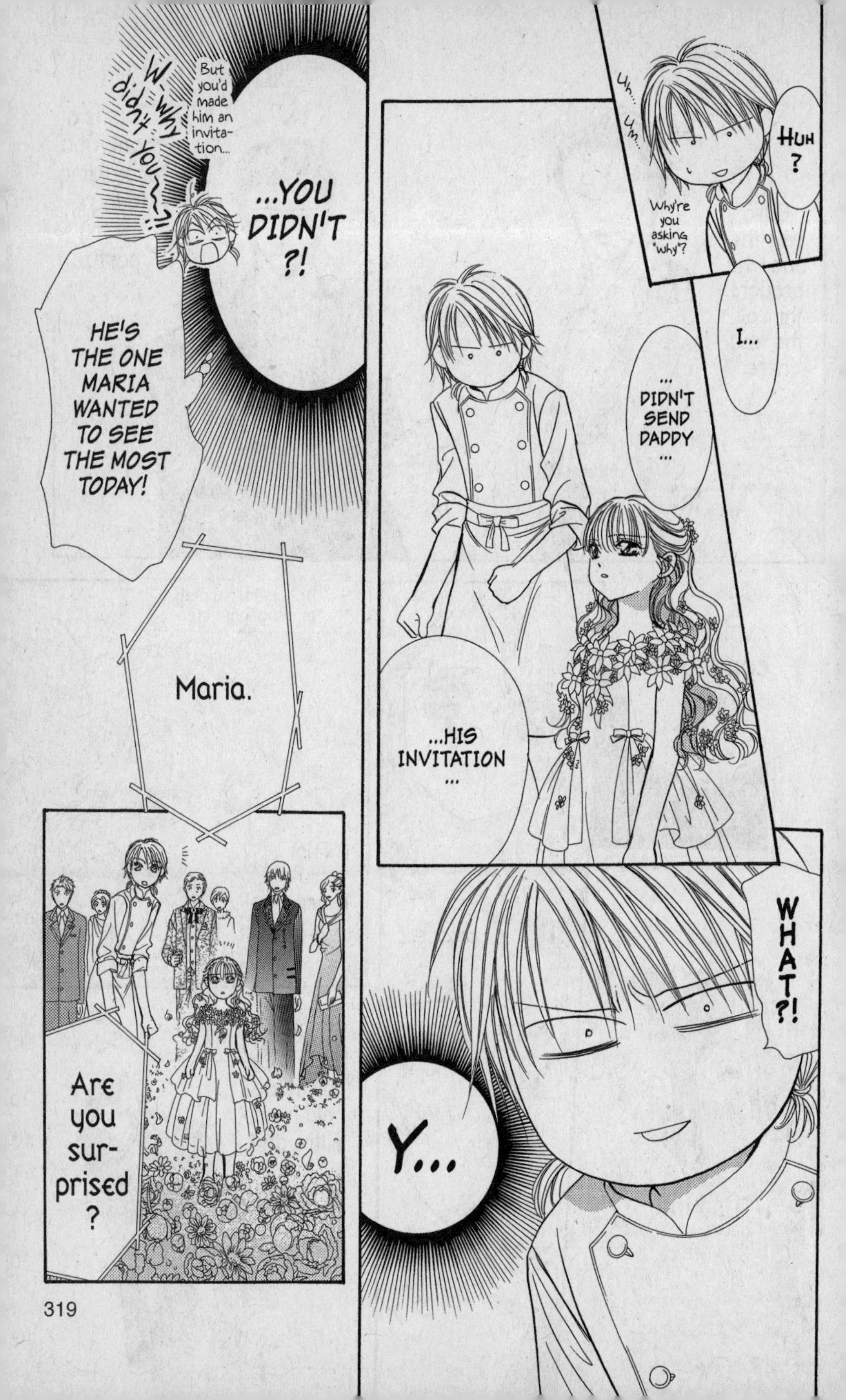
Uh... Um...
Huh?
Why're you asking "why"?
I...
...Didn't send Daddy...
...His invitation...
What?!
Y...
...You didn't?!
But you'd made him an invitation...
W-why didn't you~~?!!
He's the one Maria wanted to see the most today!
Maria.
Are you surprised?

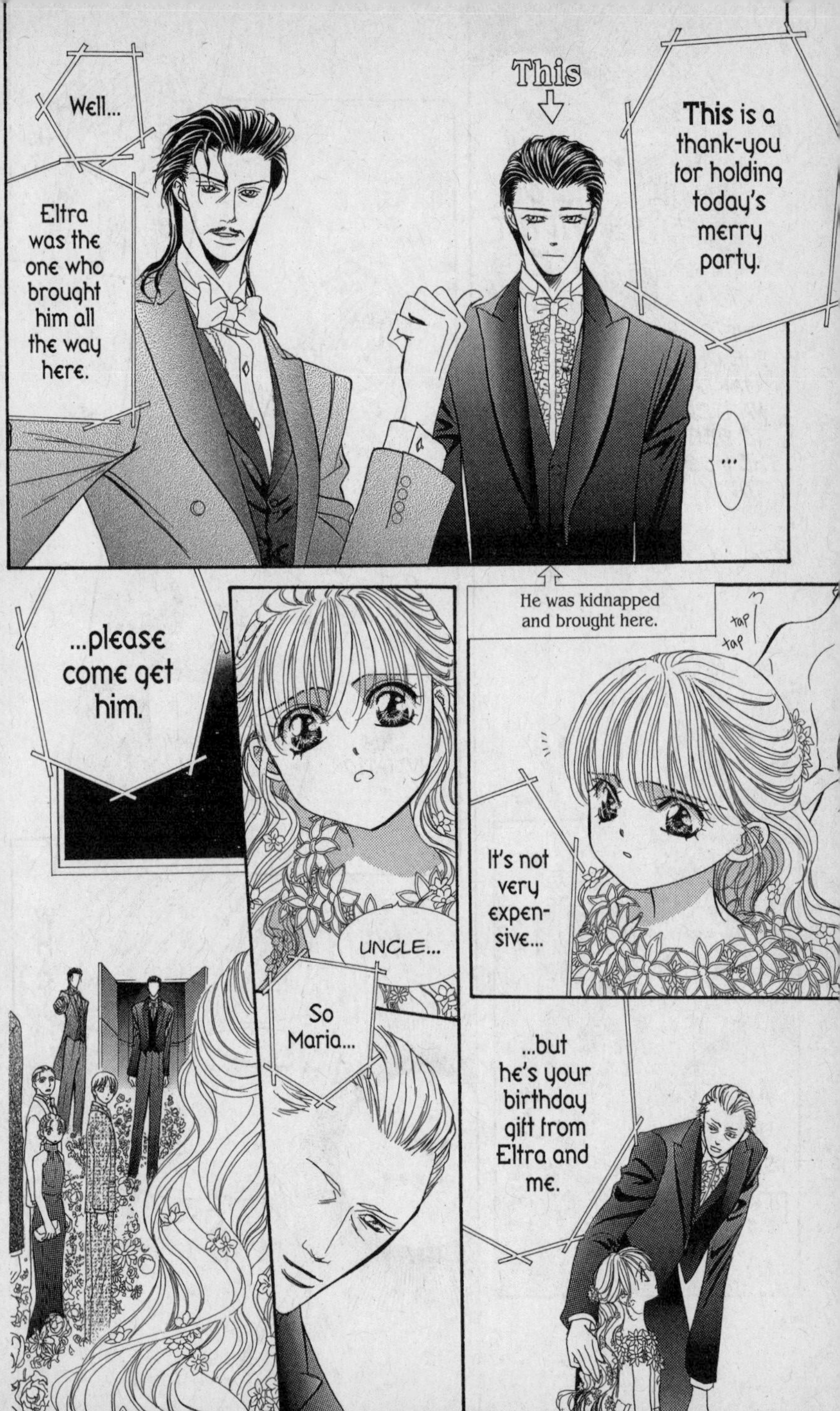
This
This is a thank-you for holding today's merry party.
...
Well...
Eltra was the one who brought him all the way here.
He was kidnapped and brought here.
tap tap
It's not very expensive...
...but he's your birthday gift from Eltra and me.
UNCLE...
So Maria...
...please come get him.

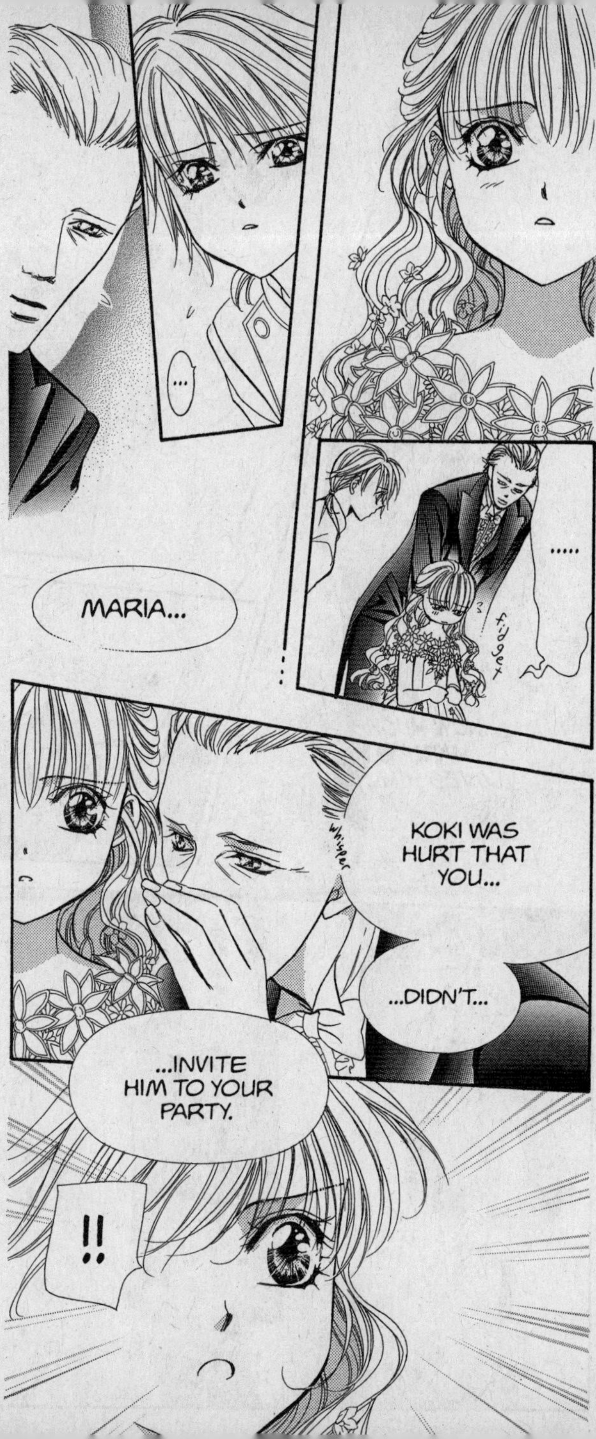
....
.....
fidget
MARIA...
whisper
KOKI WAS HURT THAT YOU...
...DIDN'T...
...INVITE HIM TO YOUR PARTY.
!!

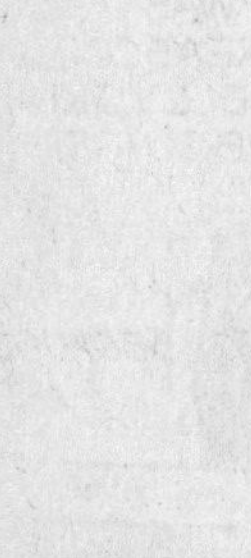

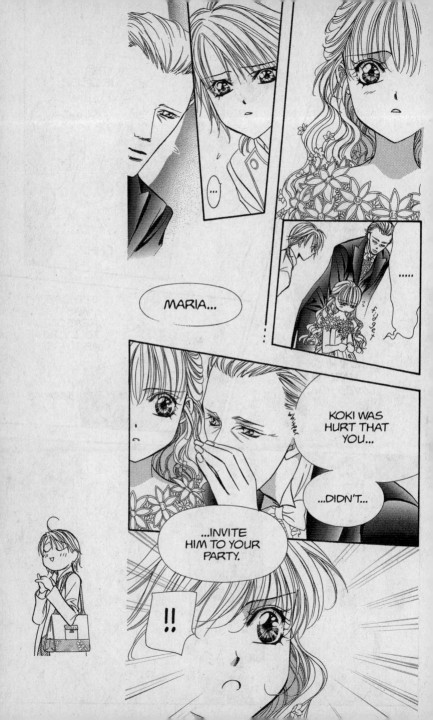

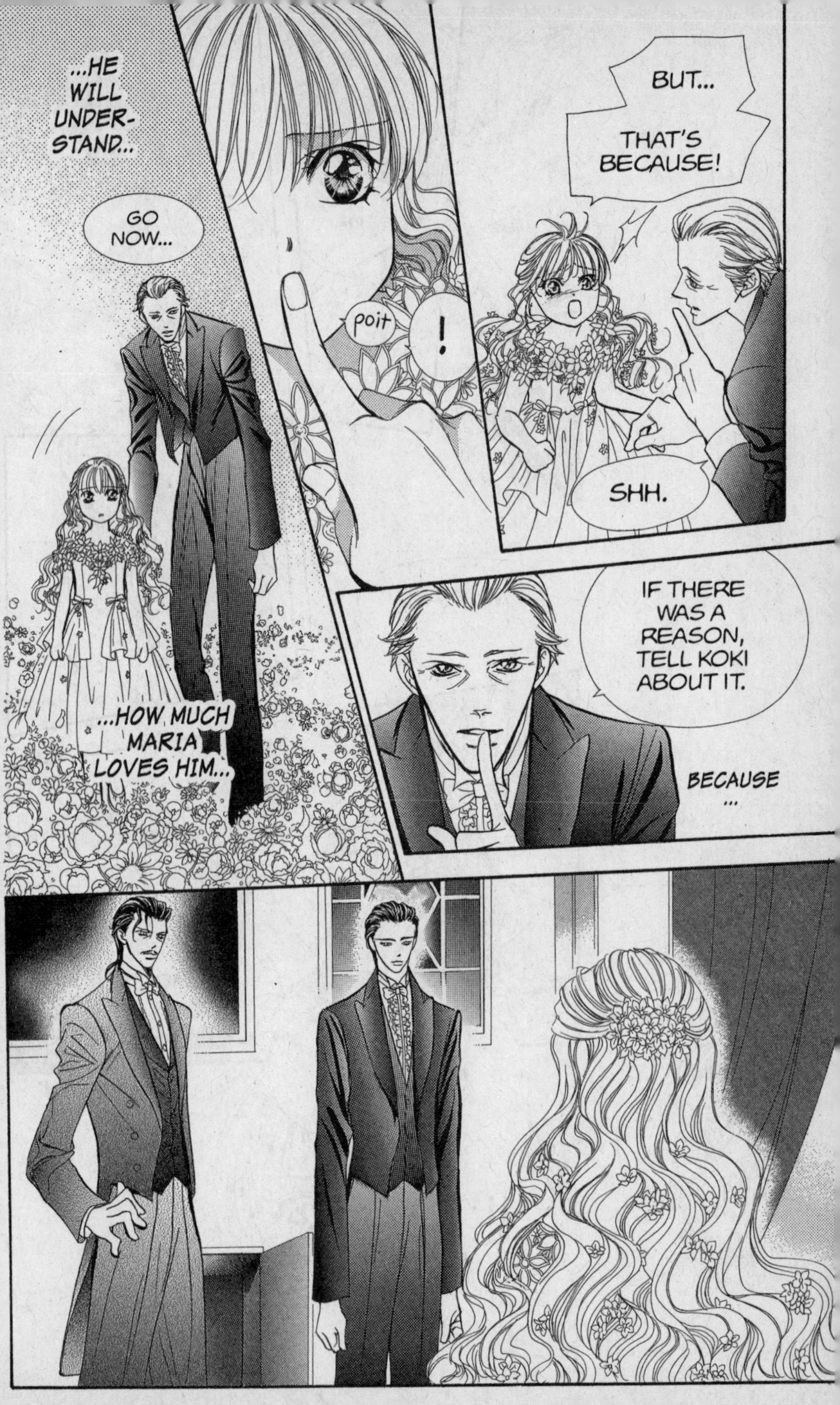
BUT...
THAT'S BECAUSE!
SHH.
poit
!
IF THERE WAS A REASON, TELL KOKI ABOUT IT.
BECAUSE ...
...HE WILL UNDERSTAND...
GO NOW...
...HOW MUCH MARIA LOVES HIM...

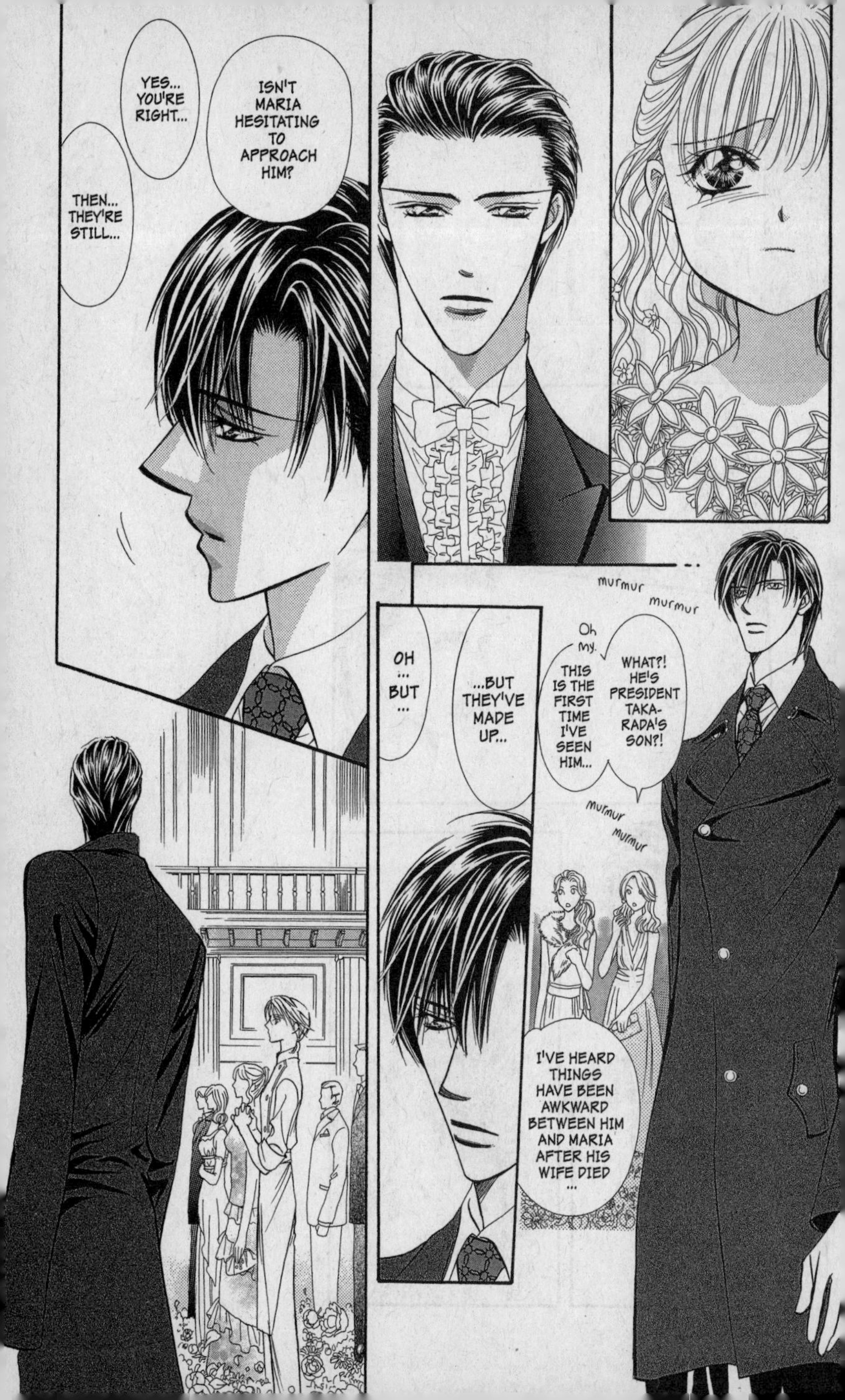
ISN'T MARIA HESITATING TO APPROACH HIM?
YES... YOU'RE RIGHT...
THEN... THEY'RE STILL...
murmur murmur
WHAT?! HE'S PRESIDENT TAKARADA'S SON?!
Oh my.
THIS IS THE FIRST TIME I'VE SEEN HIM...
murmur murmur
I'VE HEARD THINGS HAVE BEEN AWKWARD BETWEEN HIM AND MARIA AFTER HIS WIFE DIED ...
...BUT THEY'VE MADE UP...
OH ... BUT ...

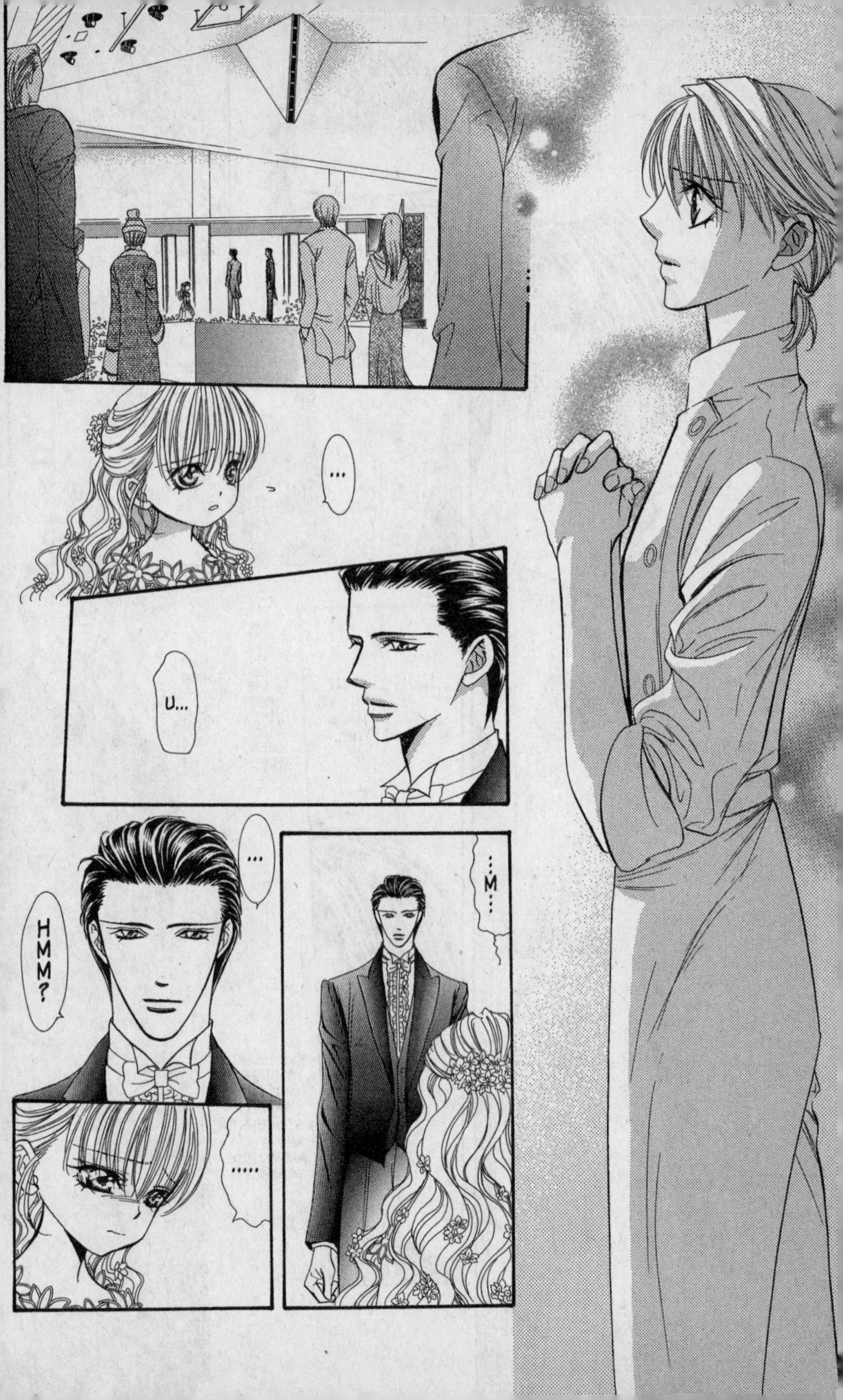
...
U...
...M...
...
HMM?
.....

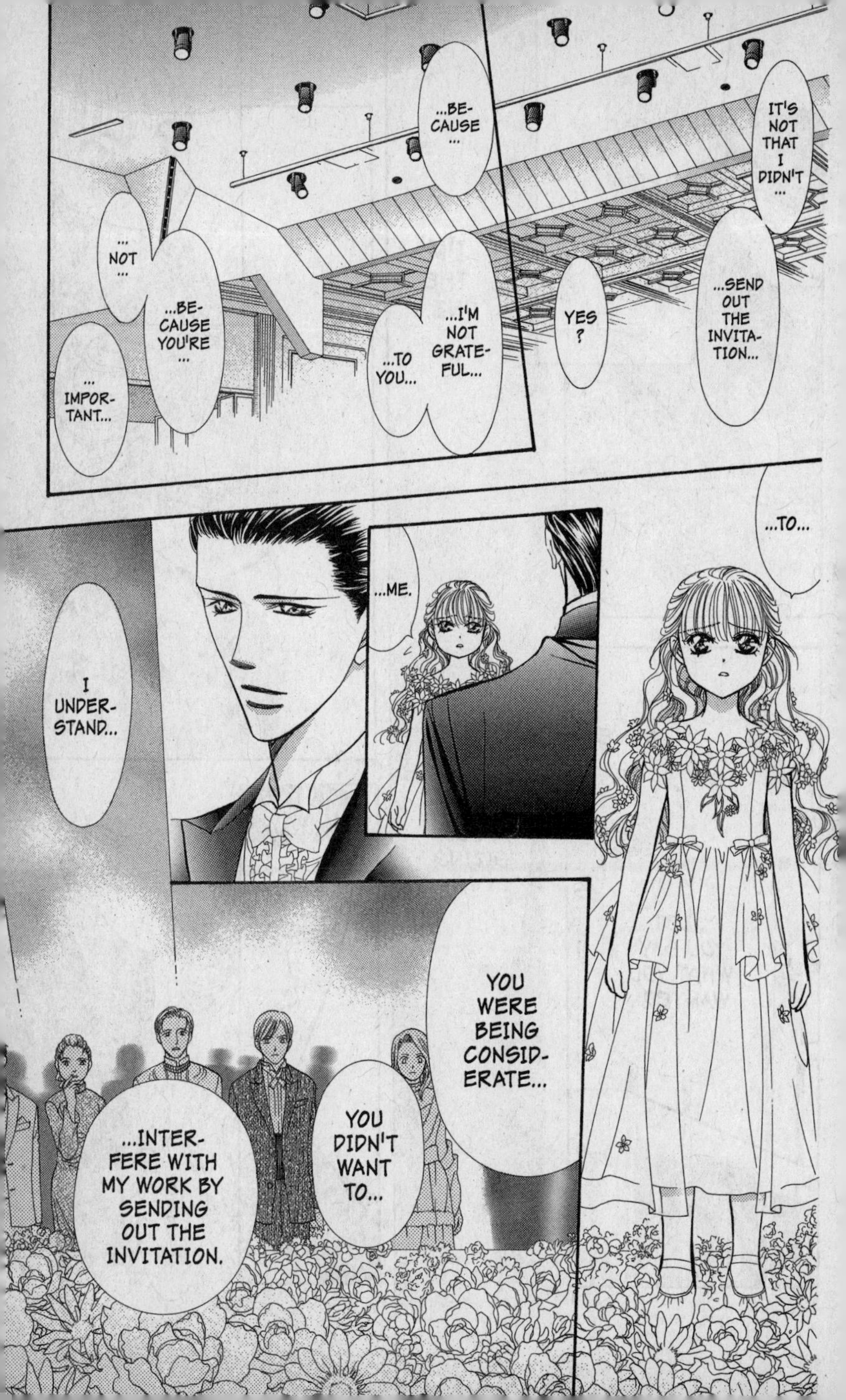
IT'S NOT THAT I DIDN'T ...
...SEND OUT THE INVITATION...
YES?
...BE-CAUSE ...
...I'M NOT GRATE-FUL...
...TO YOU...
... NOT ...
...BE-CAUSE YOU'RE ...
... IMPOR-TANT...
...TO...
...ME.
I UNDER-STAND...
YOU WERE BEING CONSID-ERATE...
YOU DIDN'T WANT TO...
...INTER-FERE WITH MY WORK BY SENDING OUT THE INVITATION.

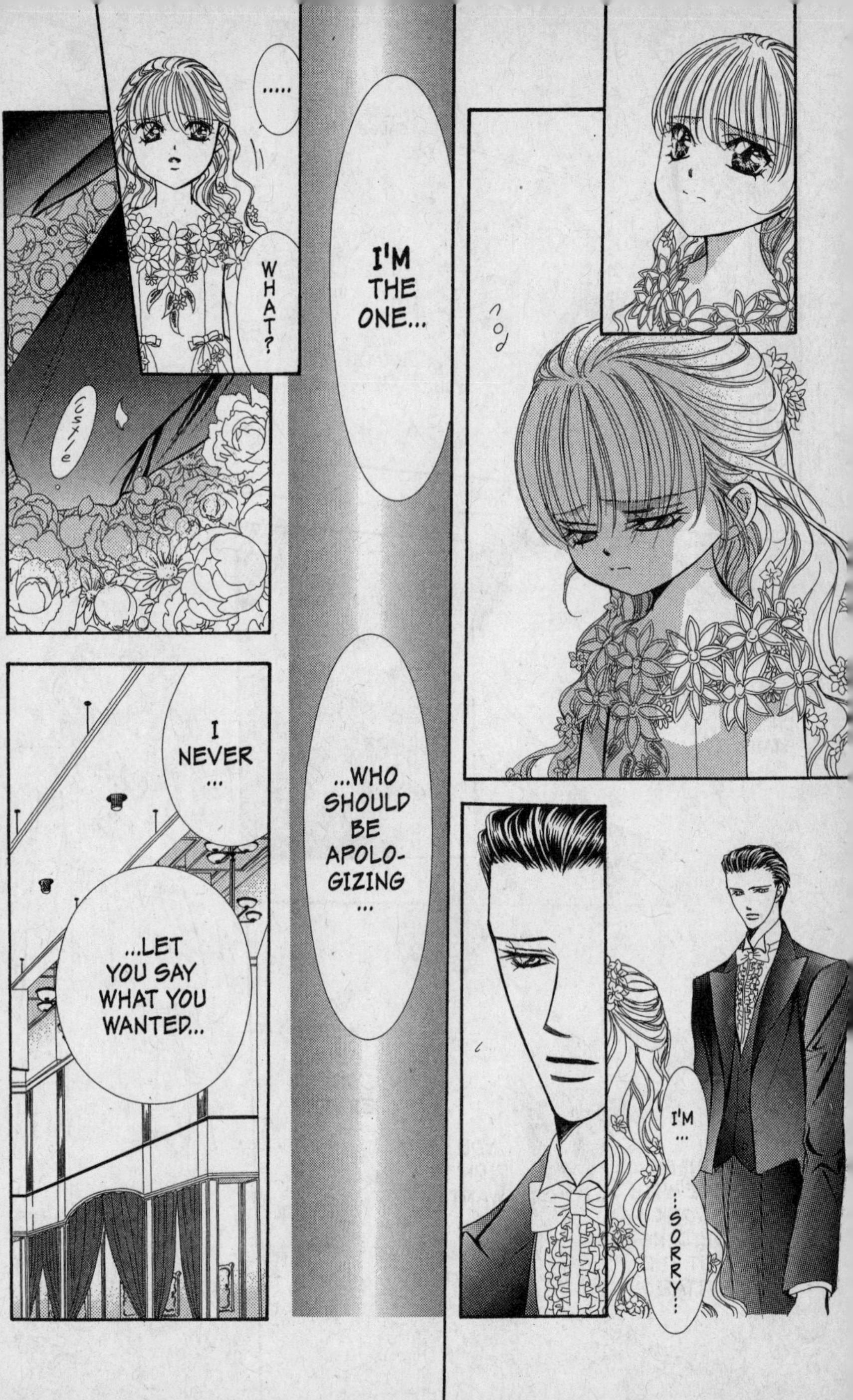
I'M ...
...SORRY...
.....
WHAT?
I'M THE ONE...
...WHO SHOULD BE APOLOGIZING ...
I NEVER ...
...LET YOU SAY WHAT YOU WANTED...

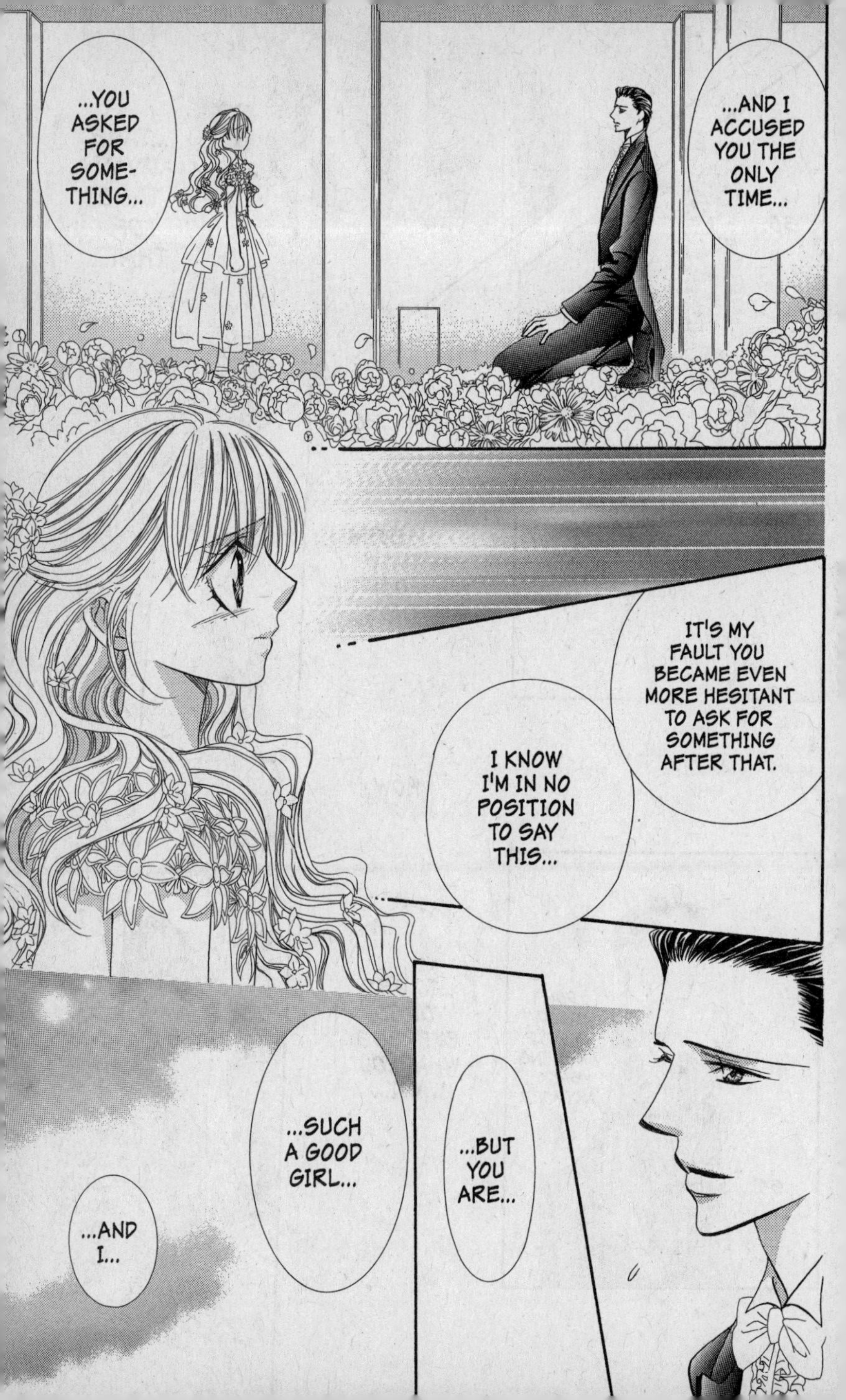
...AND I ACCUSED YOU THE ONLY TIME...
...YOU ASKED FOR SOME-THING...
IT'S MY FAULT YOU BECAME EVEN MORE HESITANT TO ASK FOR SOMETHING AFTER THAT.
I KNOW I'M IN NO POSITION TO SAY THIS...
...BUT YOU ARE...
...SUCH A GOOD GIRL...
...AND I...

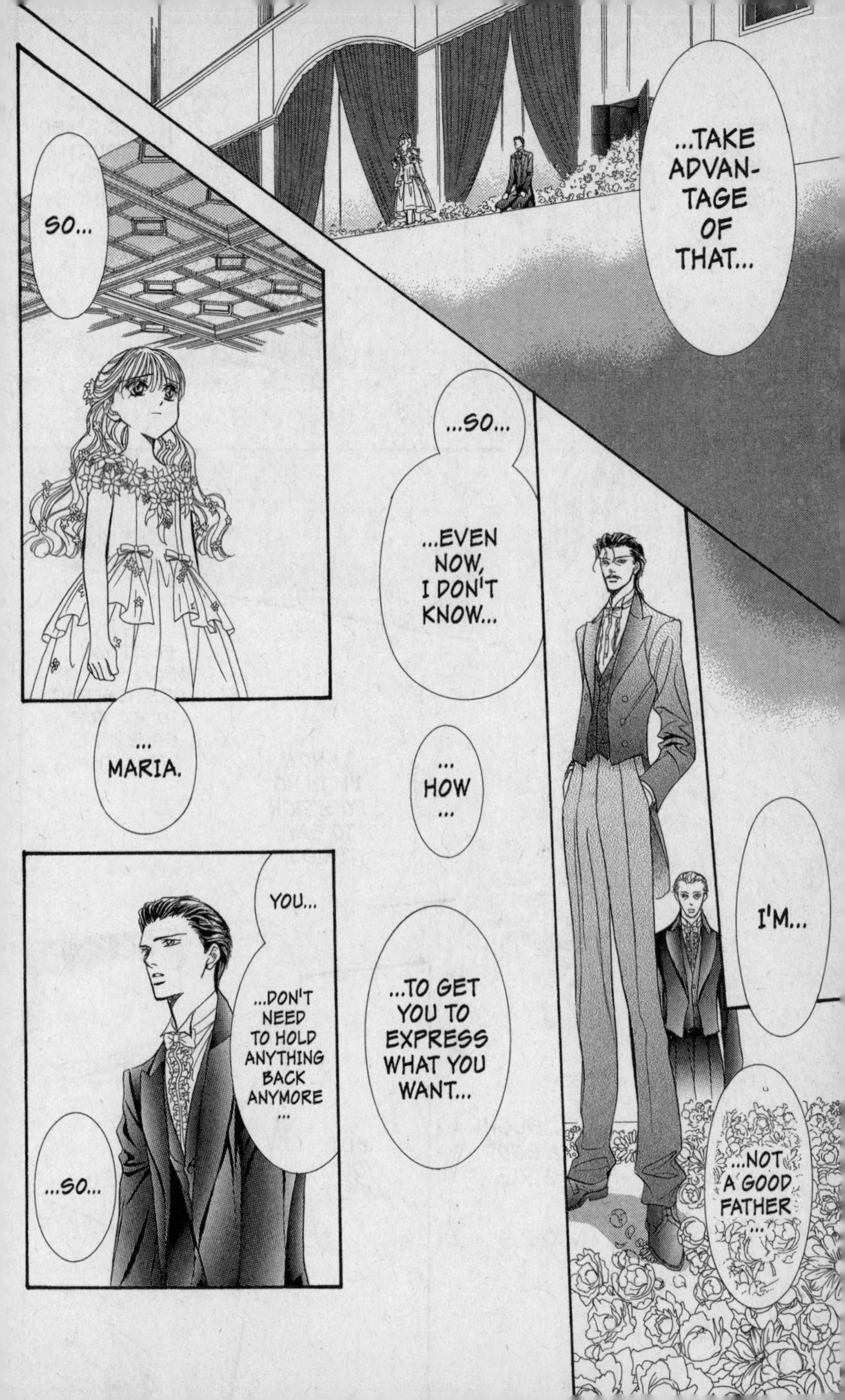
...TAKE ADVANTAGE OF THAT...
...SO...
...EVEN NOW, I DON'T KNOW...
...HOW...
...TO GET YOU TO EXPRESS WHAT YOU WANT...
I'M...
...NOT A GOOD FATHER...
SO...
...MARIA.
YOU...
...DON'T NEED TO HOLD ANYTHING BACK ANYMORE...
...SO...

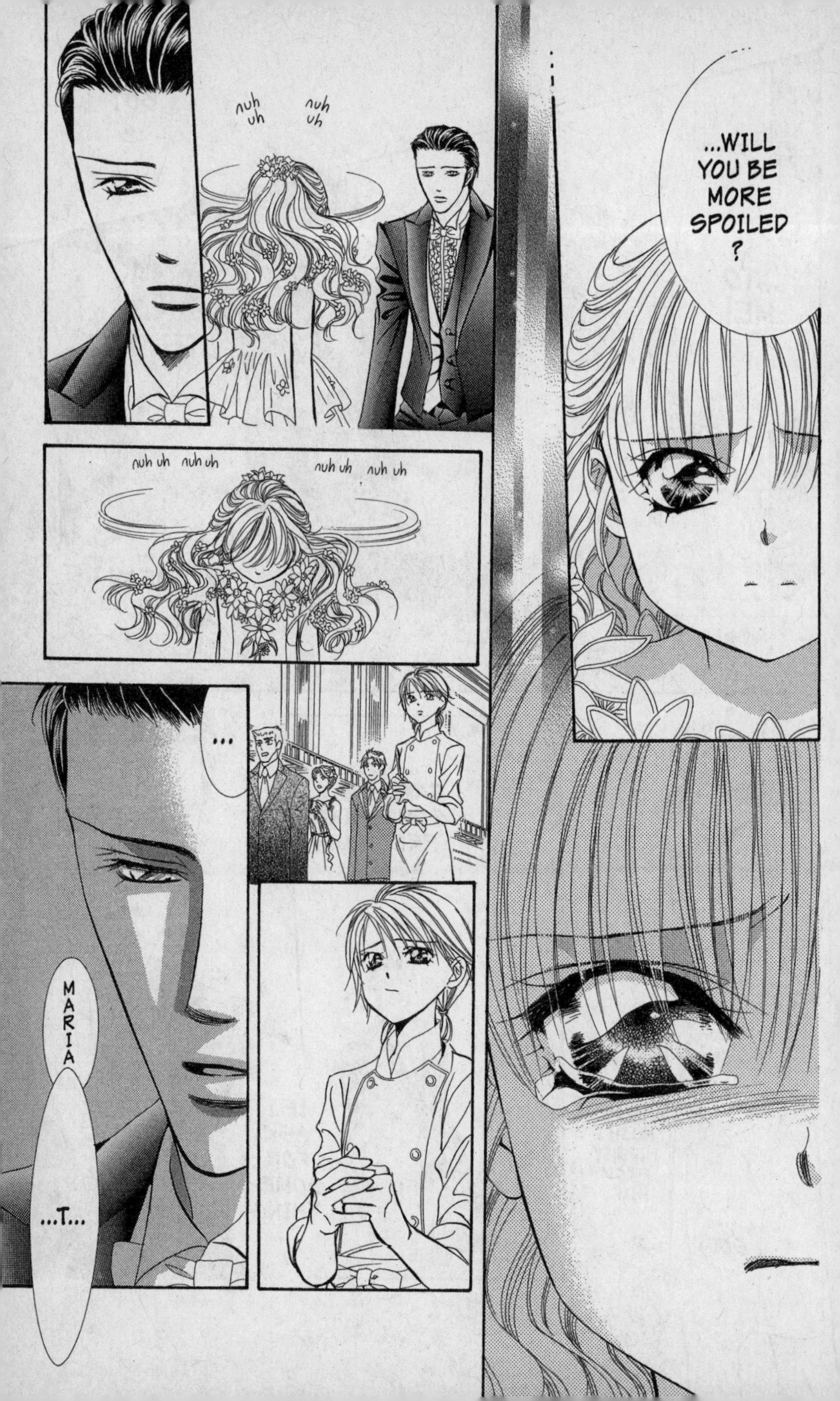
...WILL YOU BE MORE SPOILED ?
nuh uh
nuh uh
nuh uh nuh uh
nuh uh nuh uh
...
MARIA
...T...

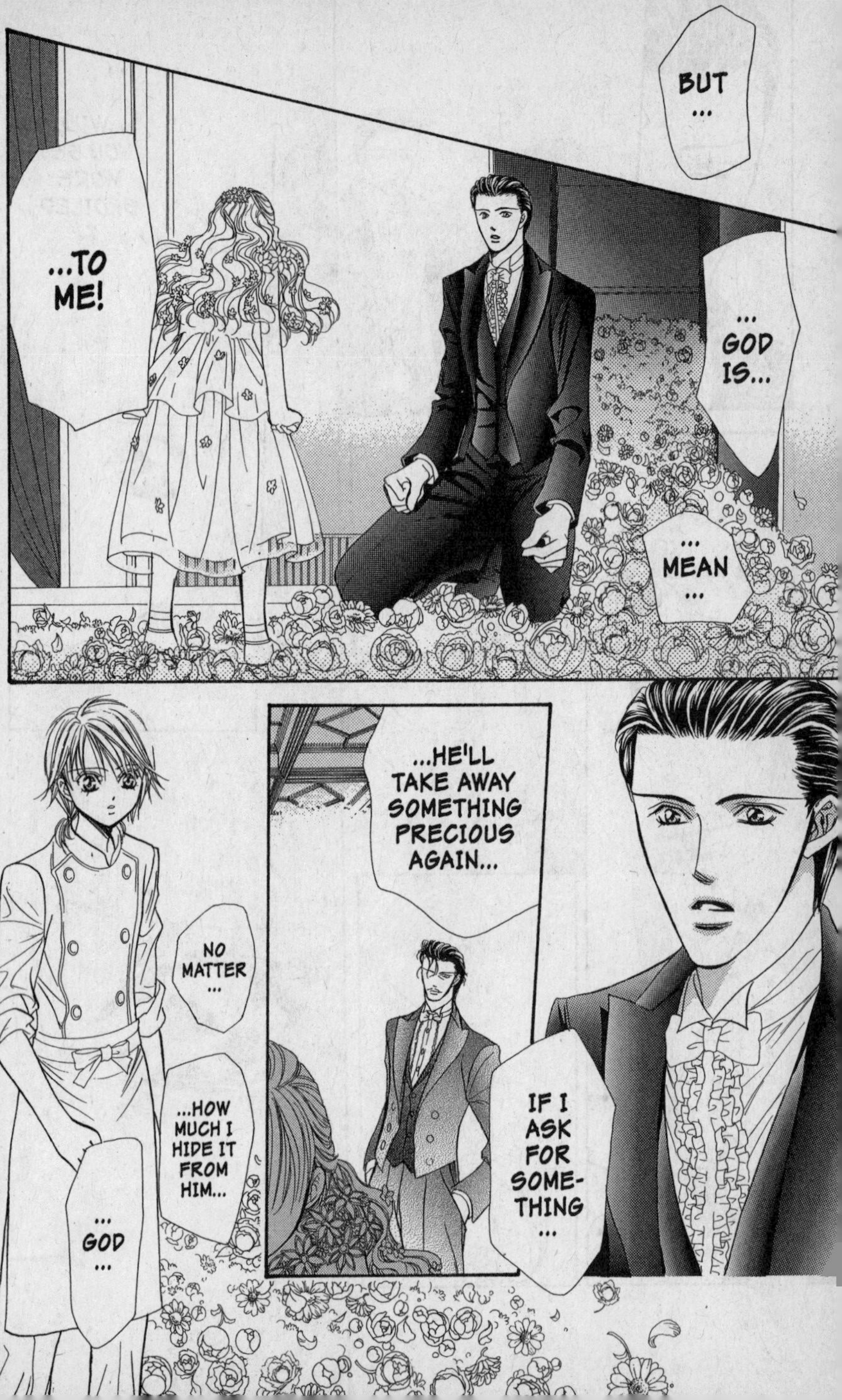
BUT ...
... GOD IS...
... MEAN ...
...TO ME!
IF I ASK FOR SOME- THING ...
...HE'LL TAKE AWAY SOMETHING PRECIOUS AGAIN...
NO MATTER ...
...HOW MUCH I HIDE IT FROM HIM...
... GOD ...

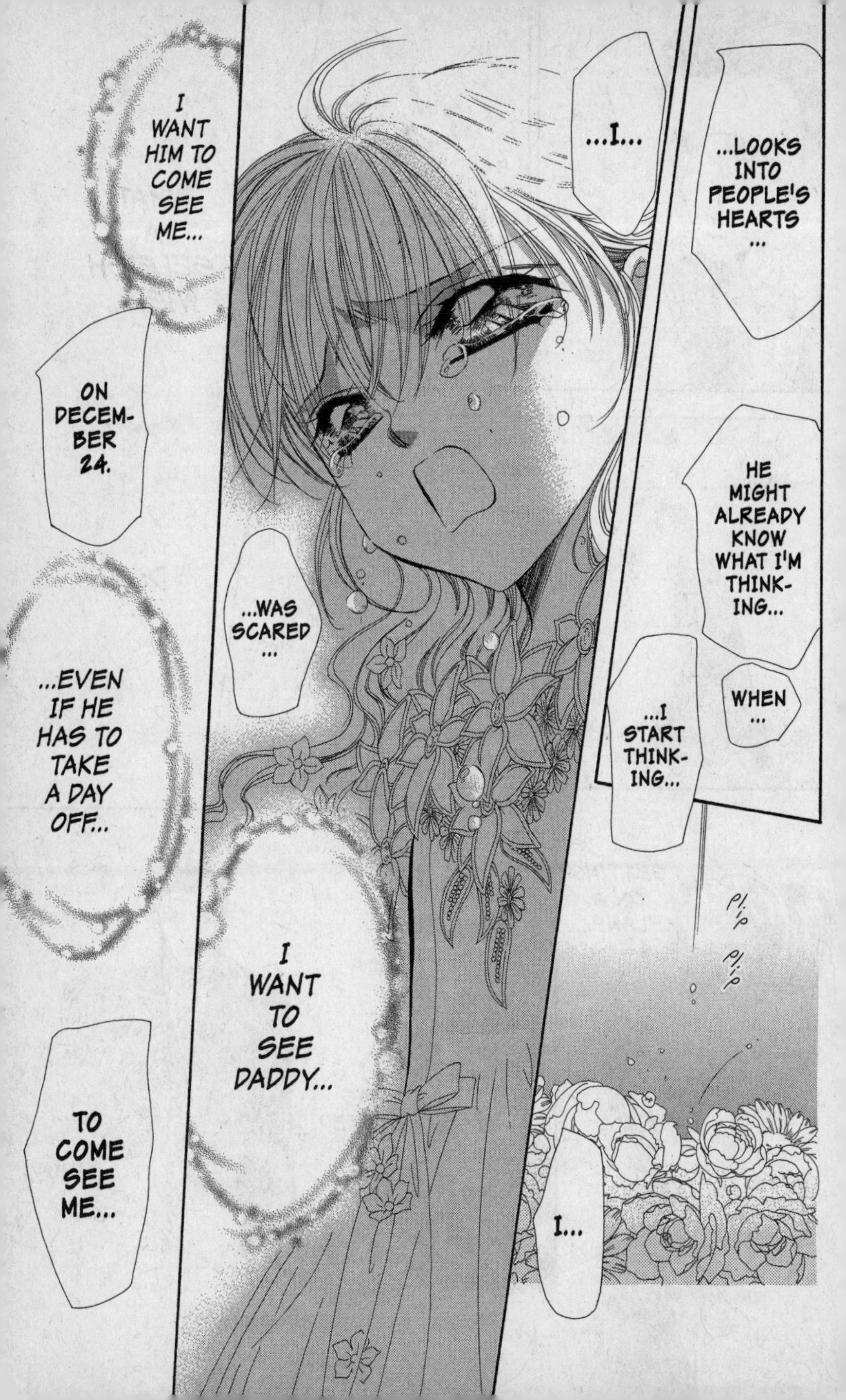
...LOOKS INTO PEOPLE'S HEARTS ...
HE MIGHT ALREADY KNOW WHAT I'M THINKING...
WHEN ...
...I START THINKING...
...I...
...WAS SCARED ...
PLIP
PLIP
I...
I WANT TO SEE DADDY...
I WANT HIM TO COME SEE ME...
ON DECEMBER 24.
...EVEN IF HE HAS TO TAKE A DAY OFF...
TO COME SEE ME...

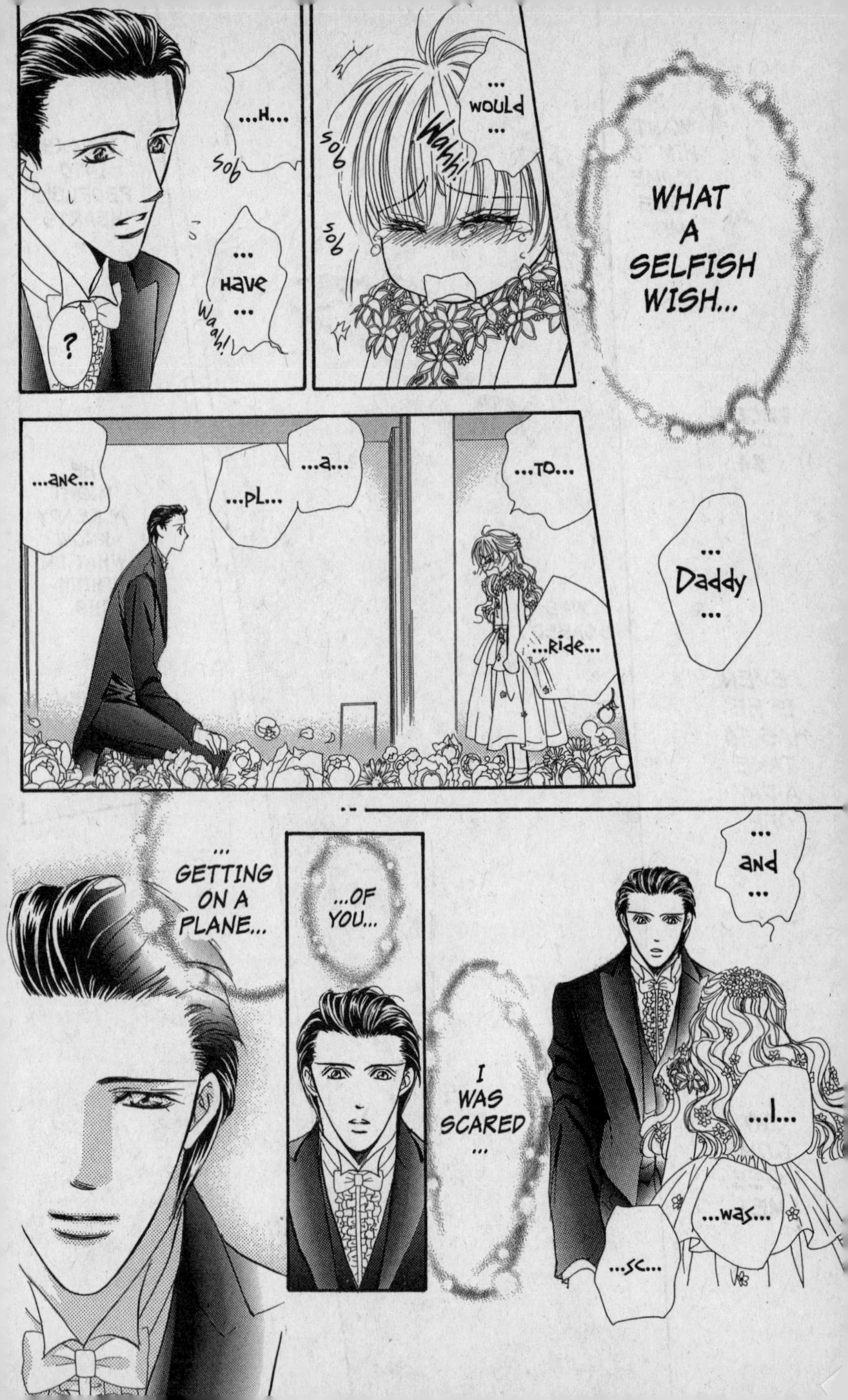
WHAT A SELFISH WISH...
...would...
Waah!
sob
sob
...H...
sob
...have...
Waah!
?
...Daddy...
...TO...
...ride...
...a...
...pL...
...ane...
...and...
...I...
...was...
...sc...
I WAS SCARED...
...OF YOU...
...GETTING ON A PLANE...

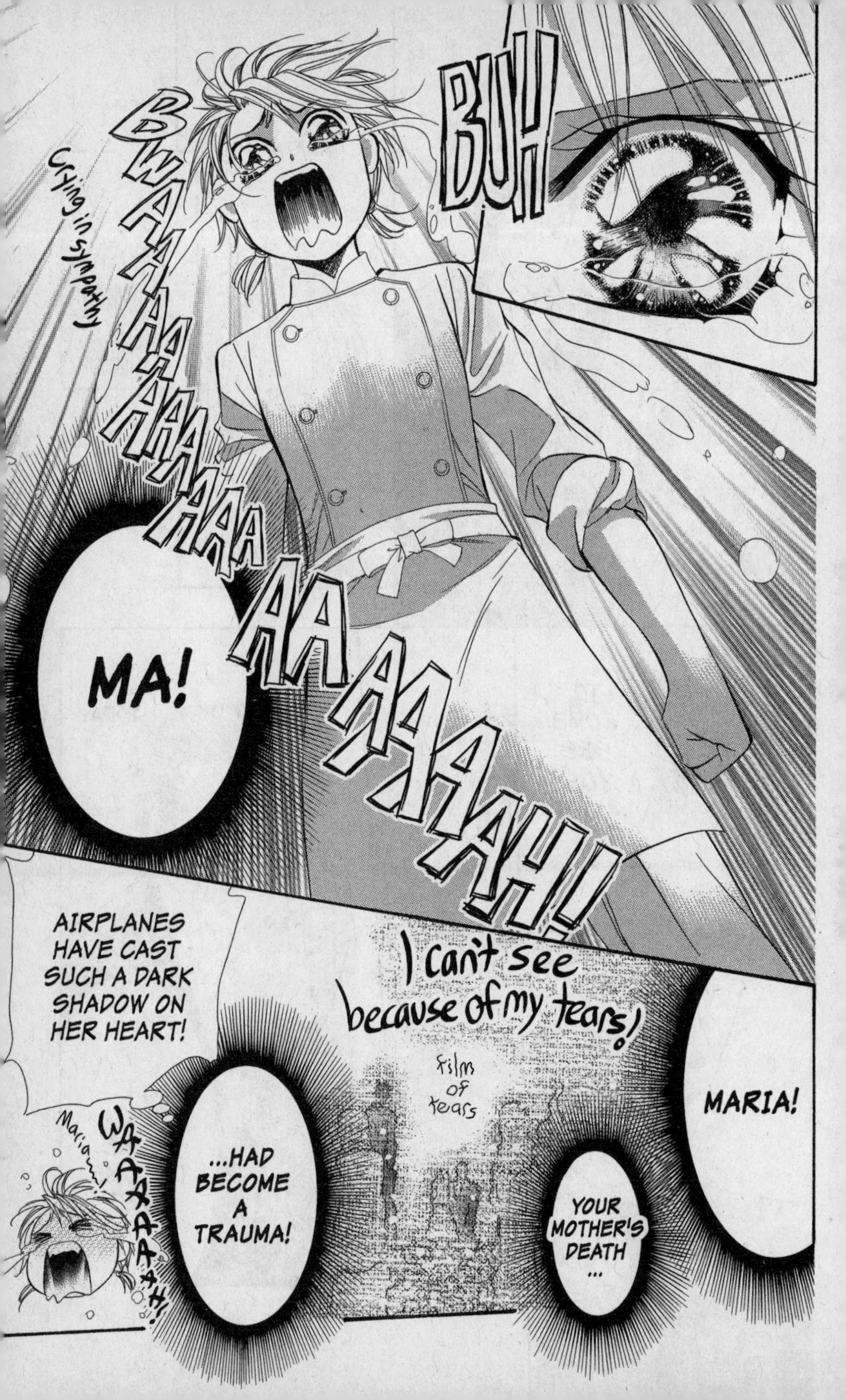
BUH
BWAAAAAAAAAAAAAAAAAAH!!
crying in sympathy
MA!
MARIA!
YOUR MOTHER'S DEATH ...
I can't see because of my tears!
film of tears
...HAD BECOME A TRAUMA!
AIRPLANES HAVE CAST SUCH A DARK SHADOW ON HER HEART!
Maria~!
WAAAAAAAH!!

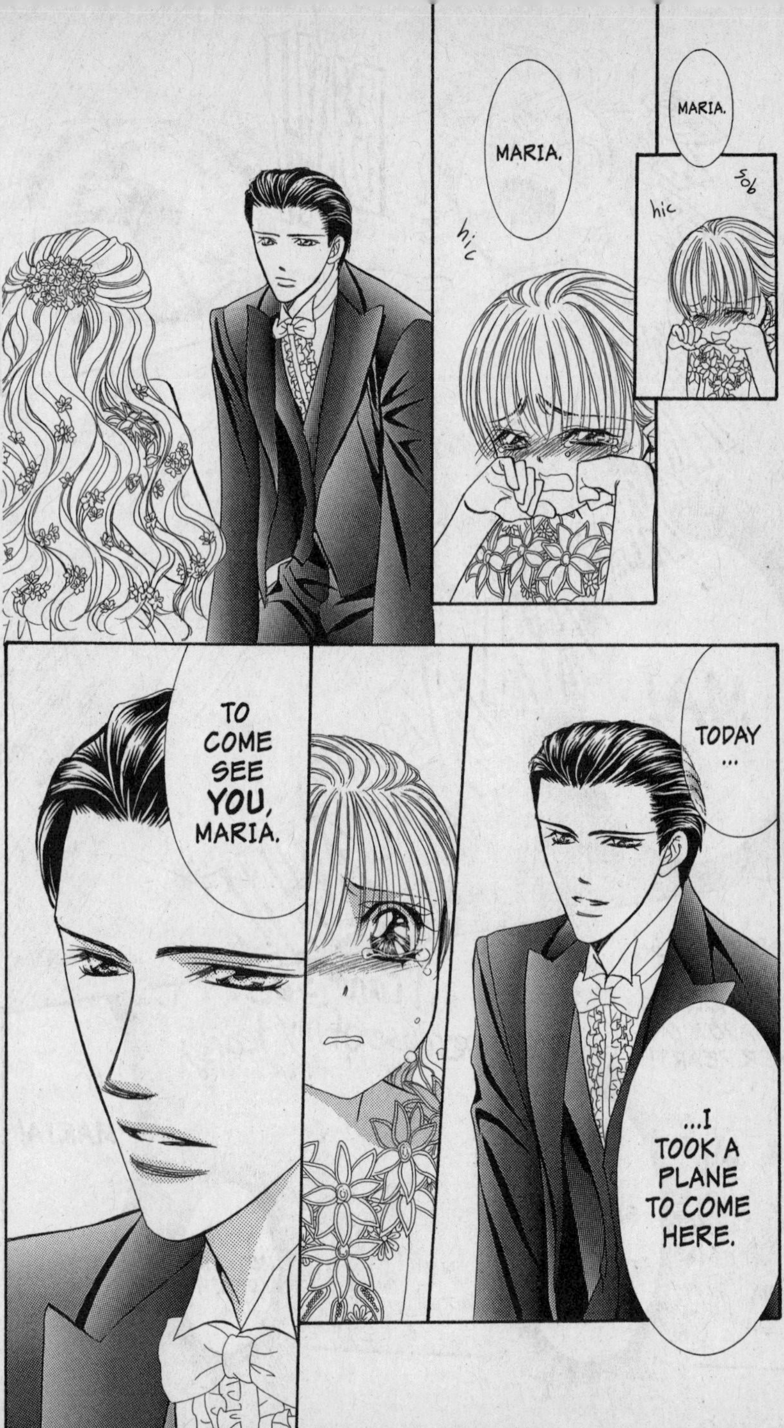
MARIA.
sob
hic
MARIA.
hic
TODAY ...
...I TOOK A PLANE TO COME HERE.
TO COME SEE YOU, MARIA.

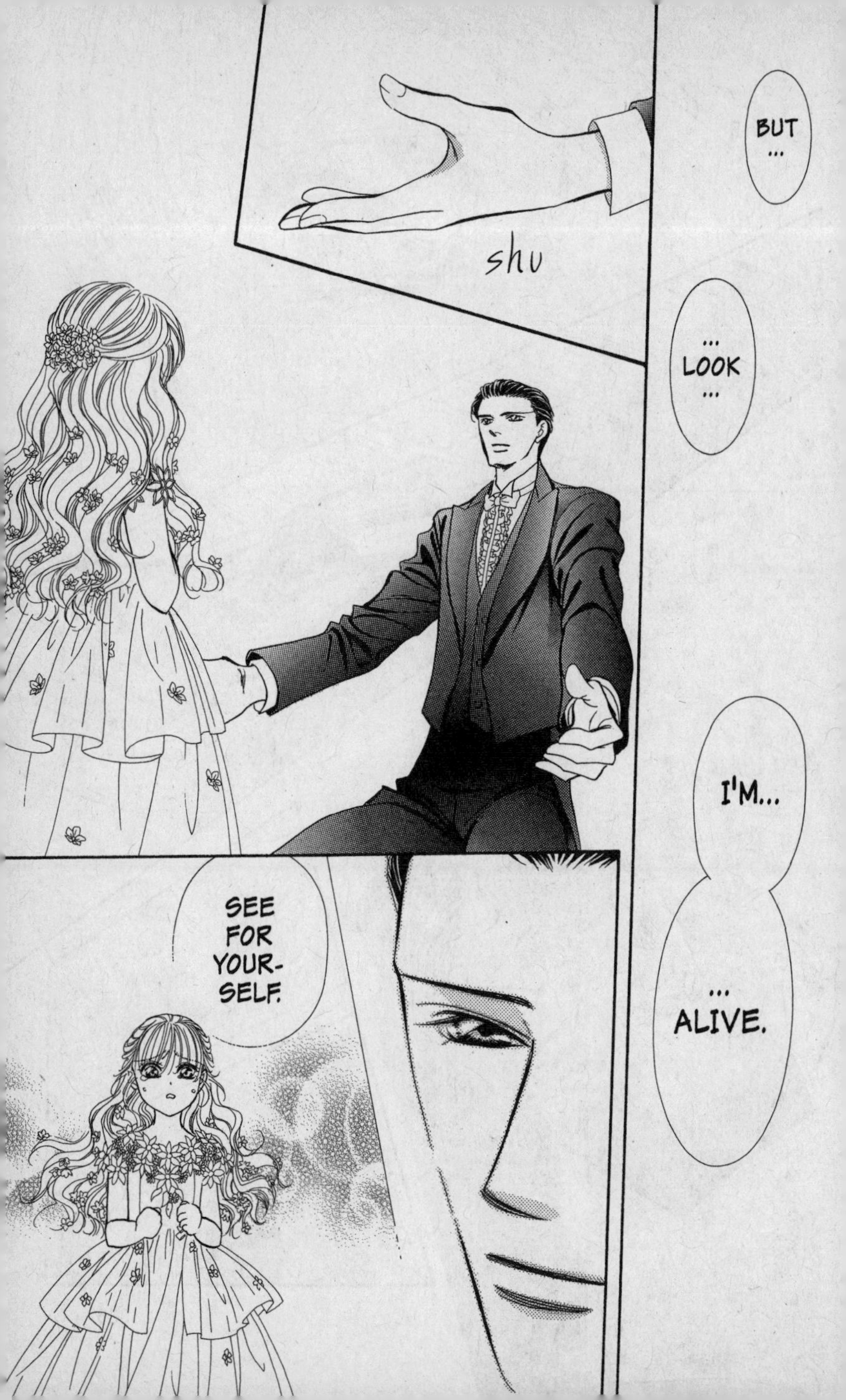
BUT ...
... LOOK ...
I'M... ... ALIVE.
shu
SEE FOR YOUR-SELF.

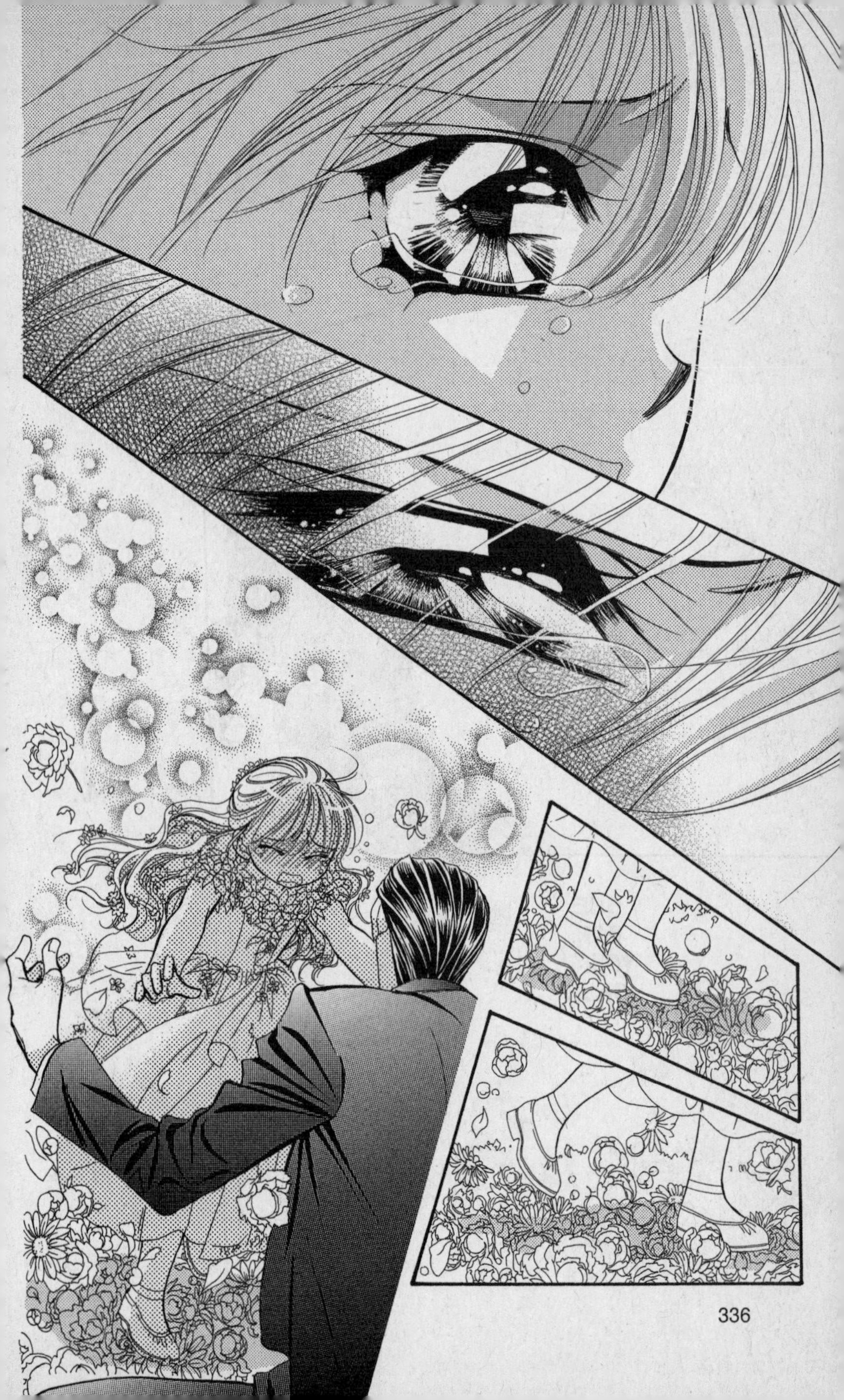

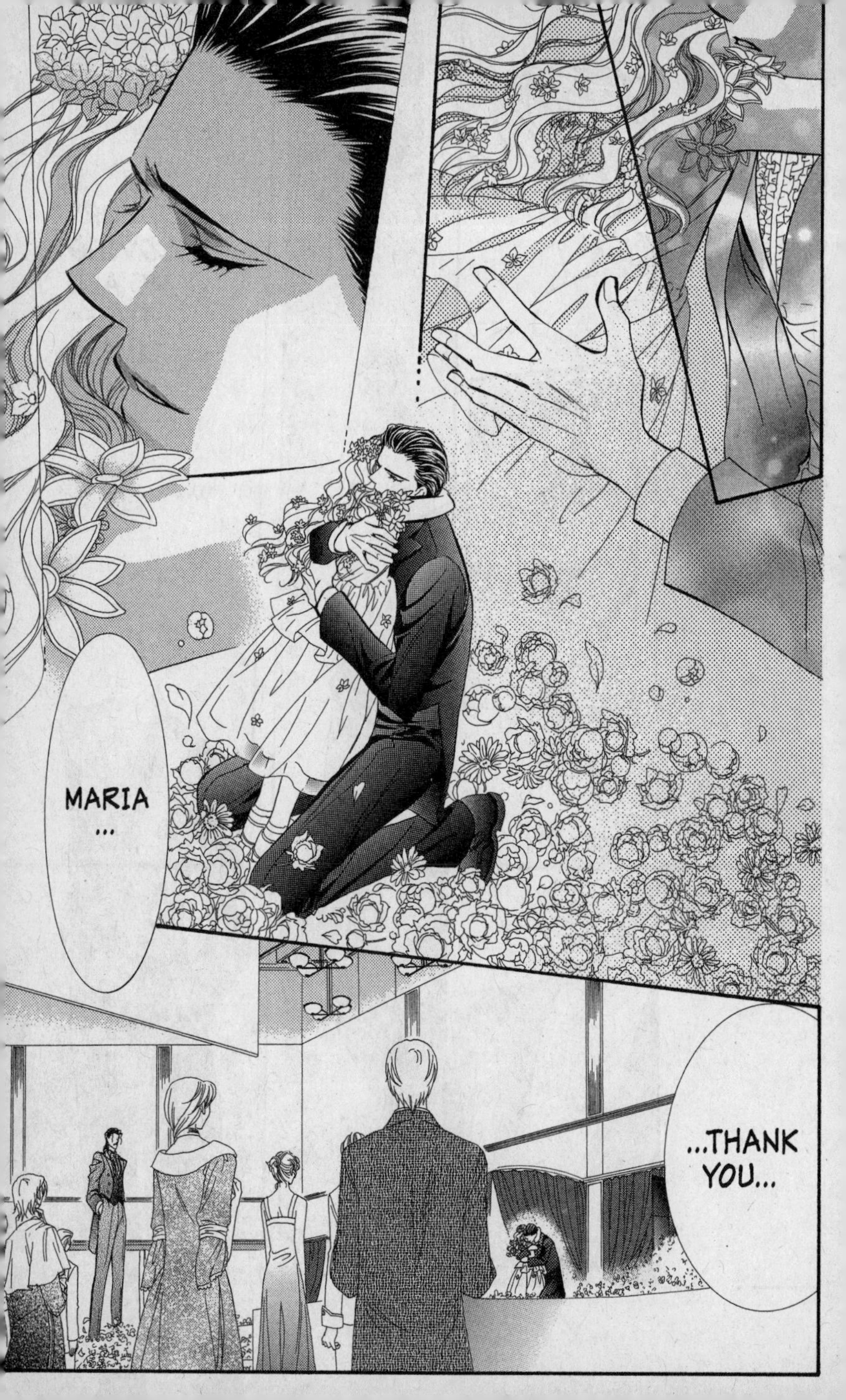
MARIA
...
...THANK YOU...

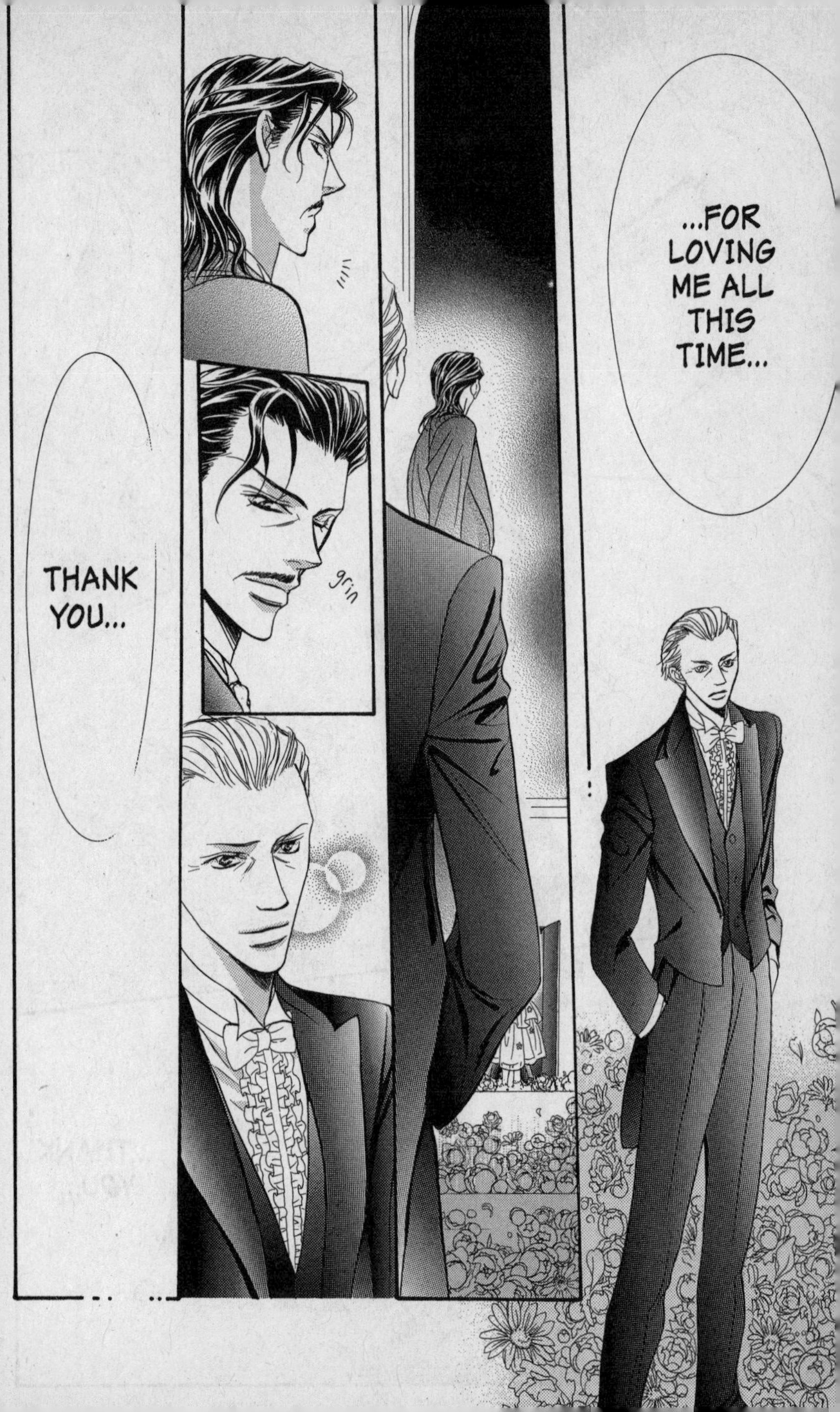
...FOR LOVING ME ALL THIS TIME...
grin
THANK YOU...

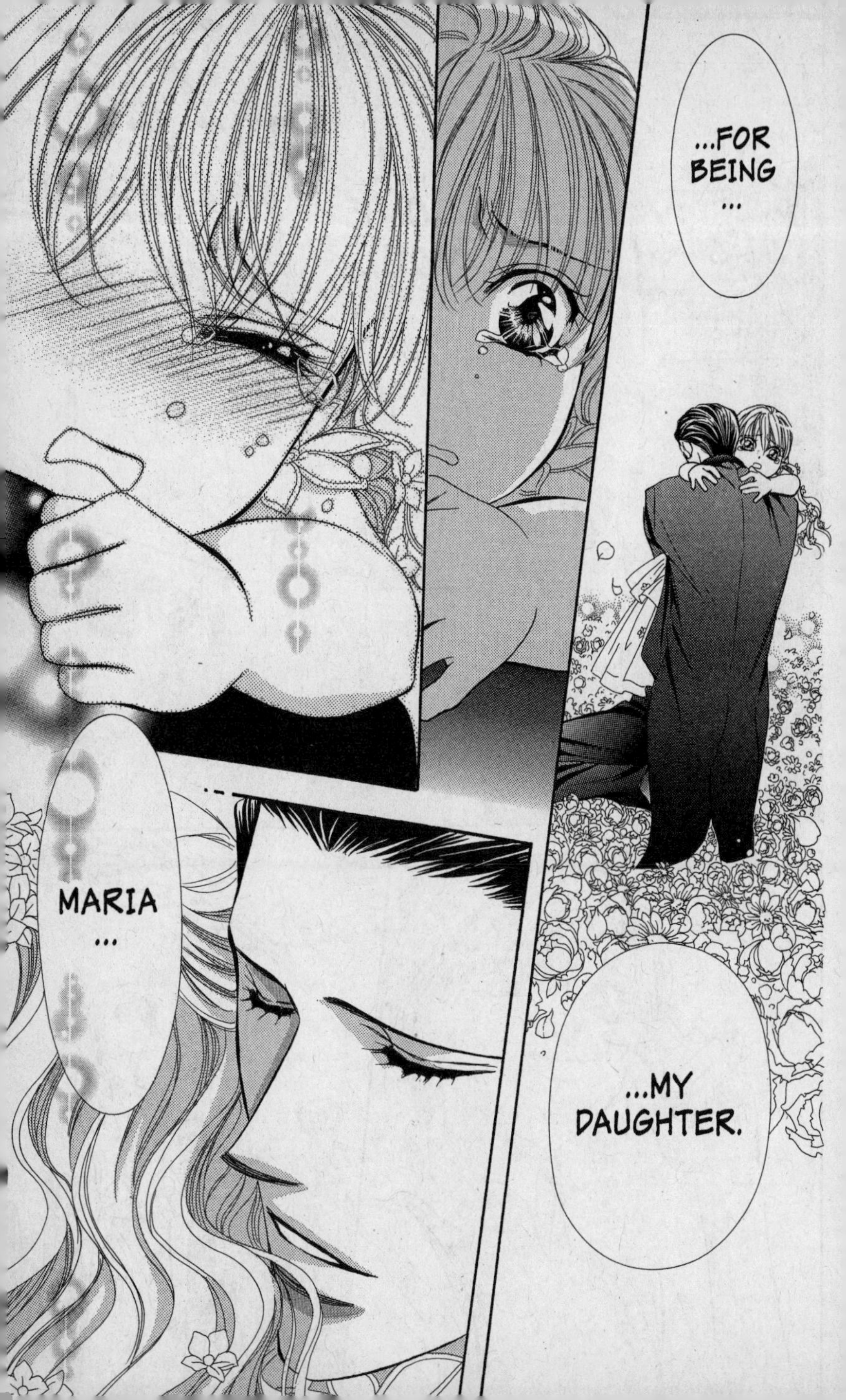
...FOR BEING ...
...MY DAUGHTER.
MARIA ...

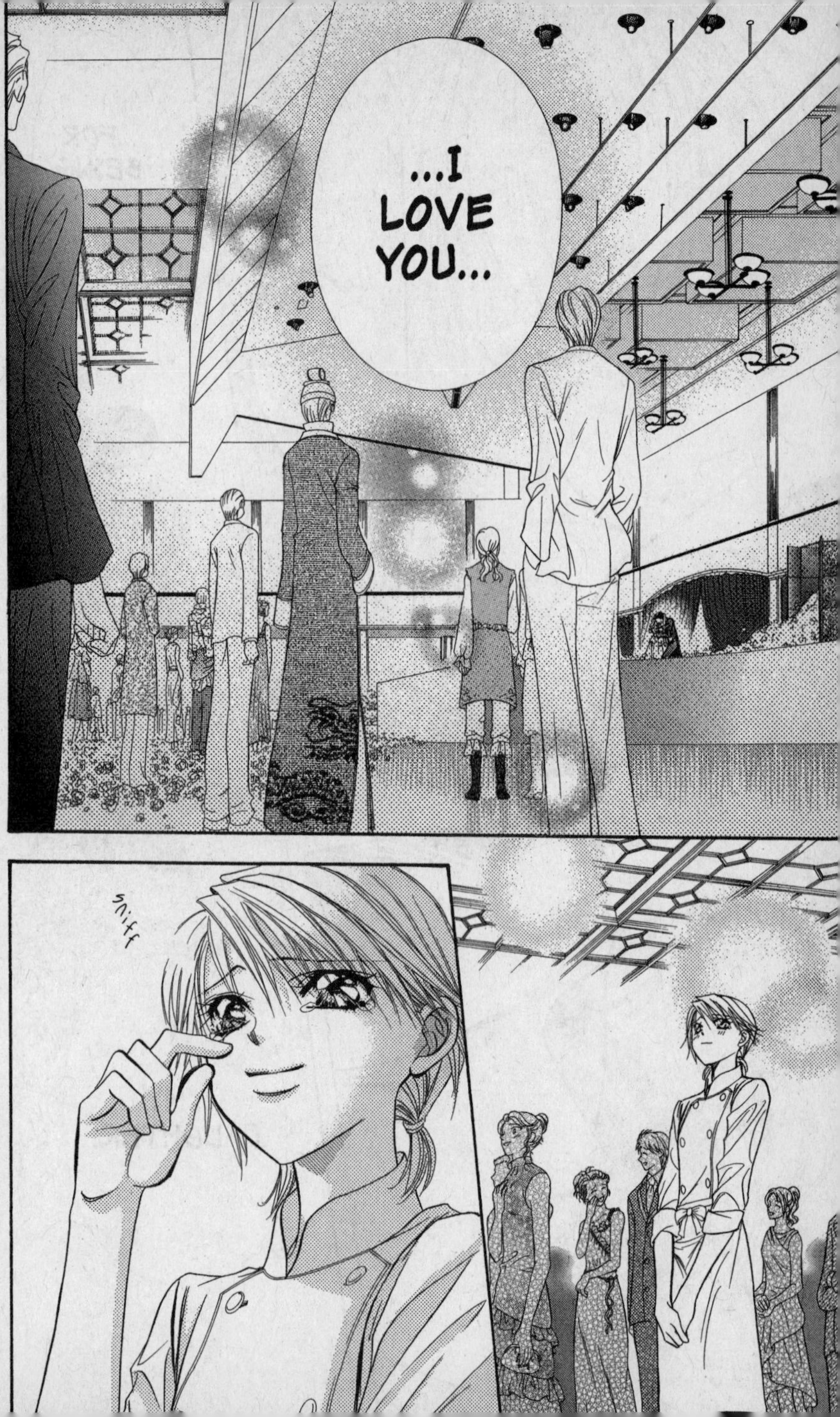
...I LOVE YOU...
SNIFF

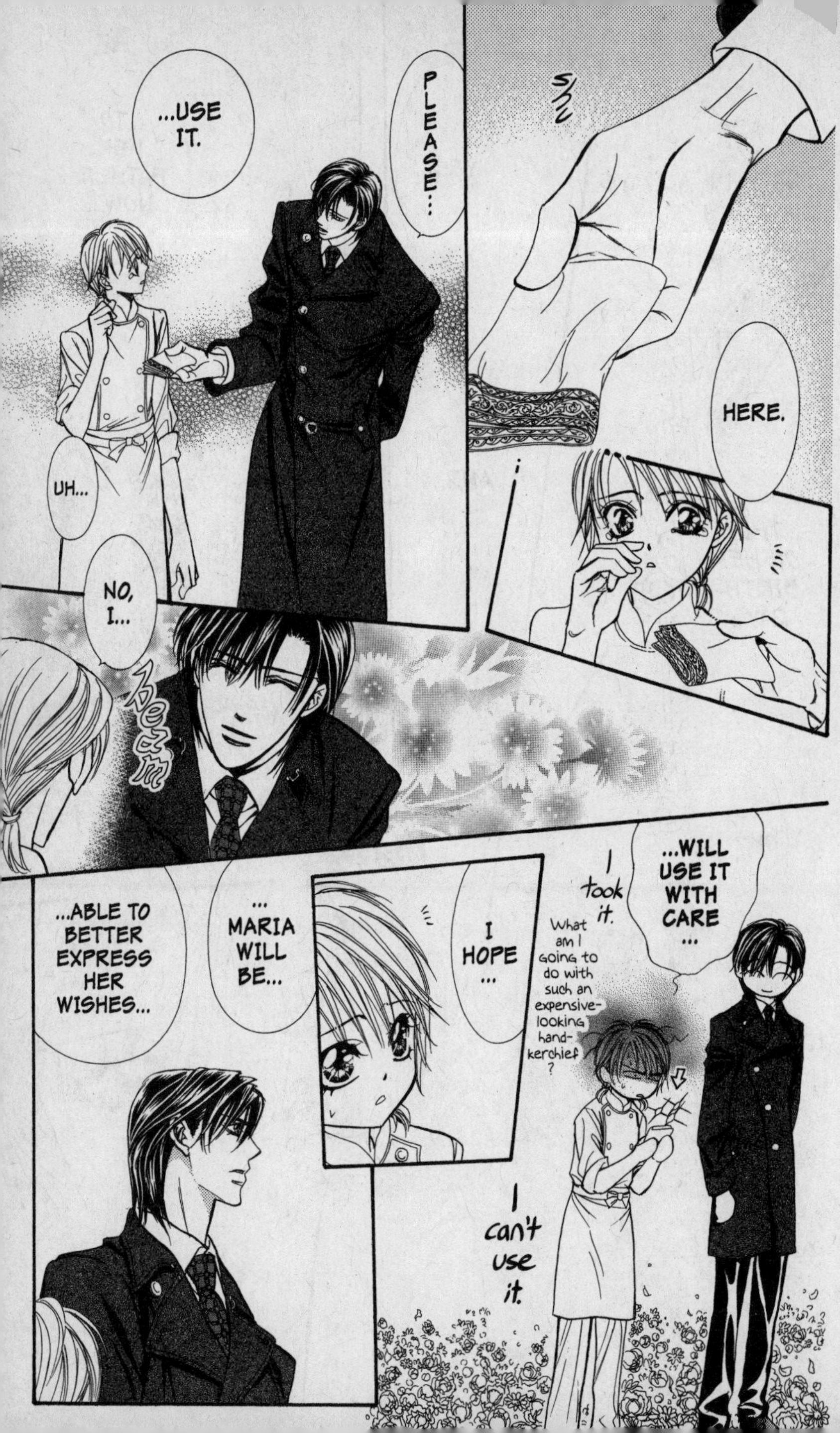

shu
HERE.
!
PLEASE...
...USE IT.
UH...
NO, I...
beam
...WILL USE IT WITH CARE...
I took it.
What am I going to do with such an expensive-looking handkerchief?
I can't use it.
I HOPE...
...MARIA WILL BE...
...ABLE TO BETTER EXPRESS HER WISHES...

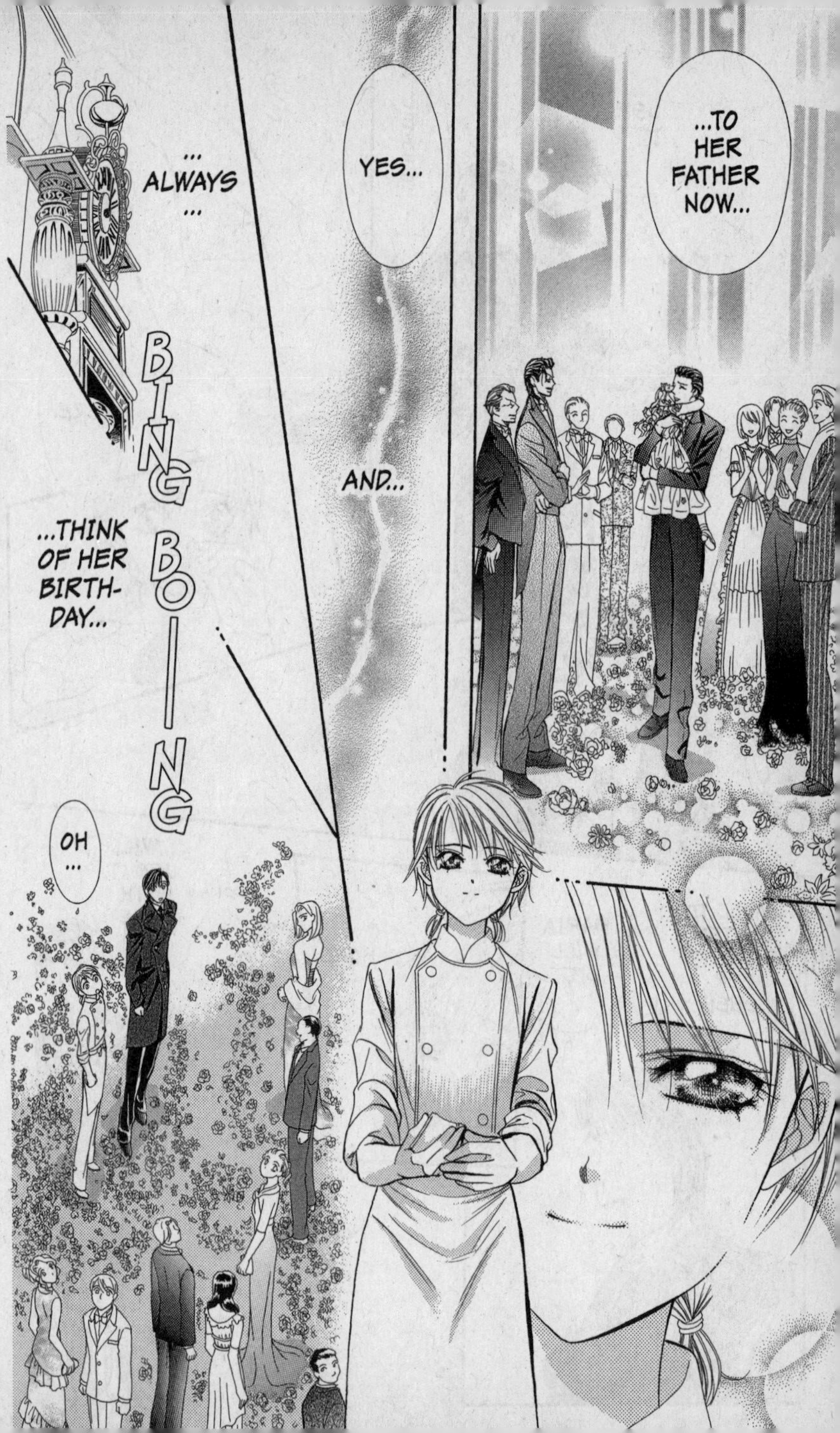
...TO HER FATHER NOW...
YES...
AND...
... ALWAYS ...
...THINK OF HER BIRTH-DAY...
BING BOING
OH ...

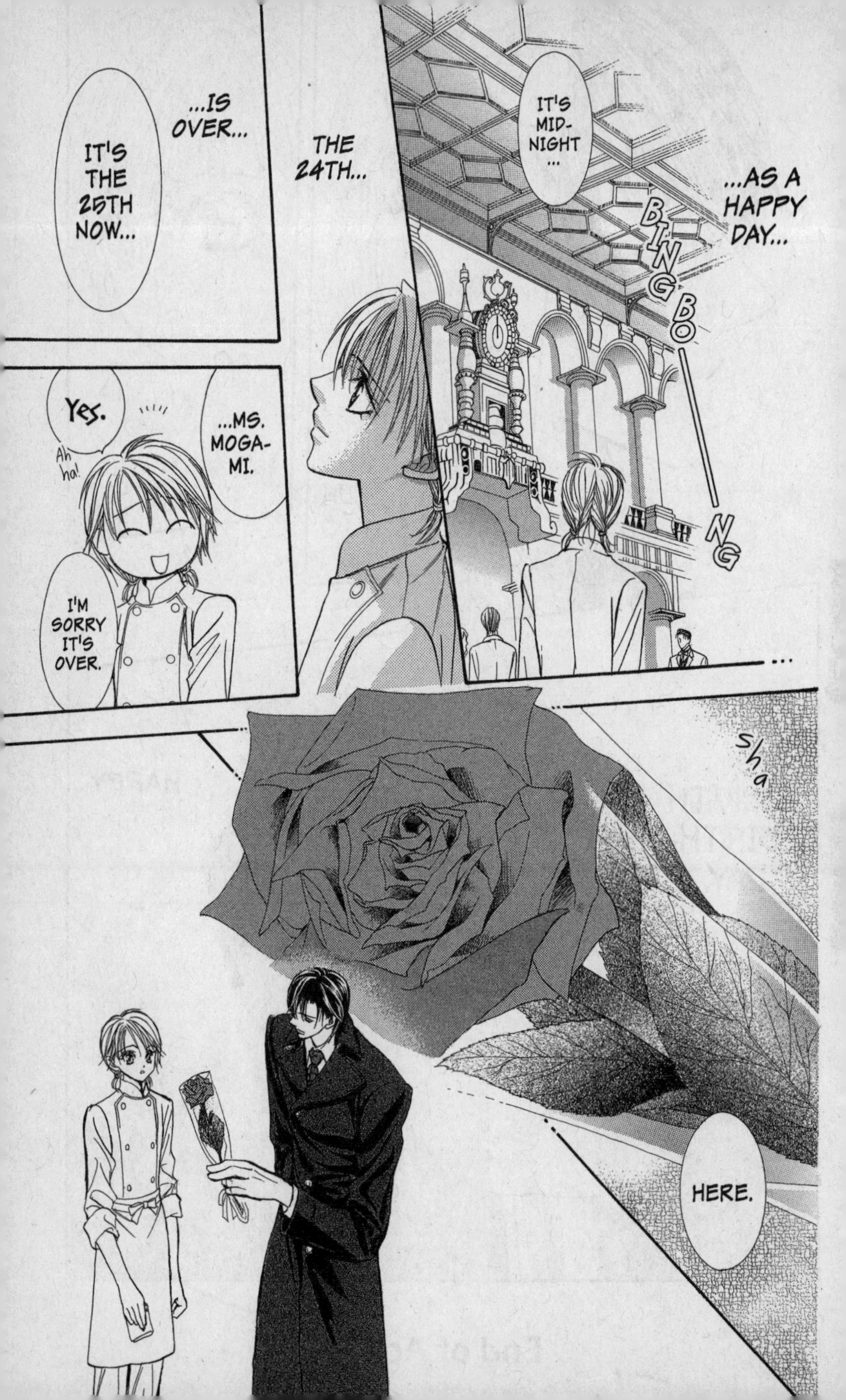
IT'S MID-NIGHT ...
BINGBONG
NG
...AS A HAPPY DAY...
THE 24TH...
...IS OVER...
IT'S THE 25TH NOW...
...MS. MOGAMI.
Yes.
Ah ha!
I'M SORRY IT'S OVER.
Sha
HERE.

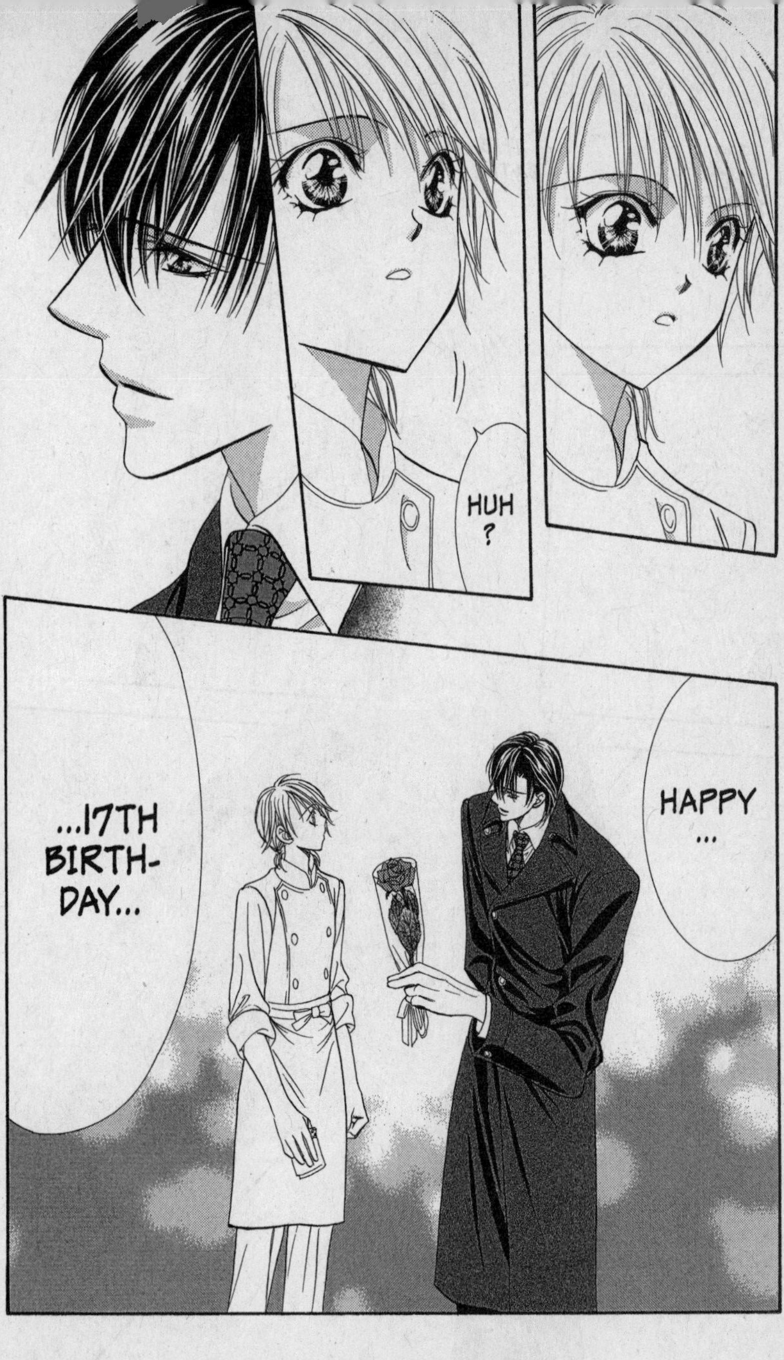
HUH ?
HAPPY ...
...17TH BIRTH-DAY...

End of Act 119

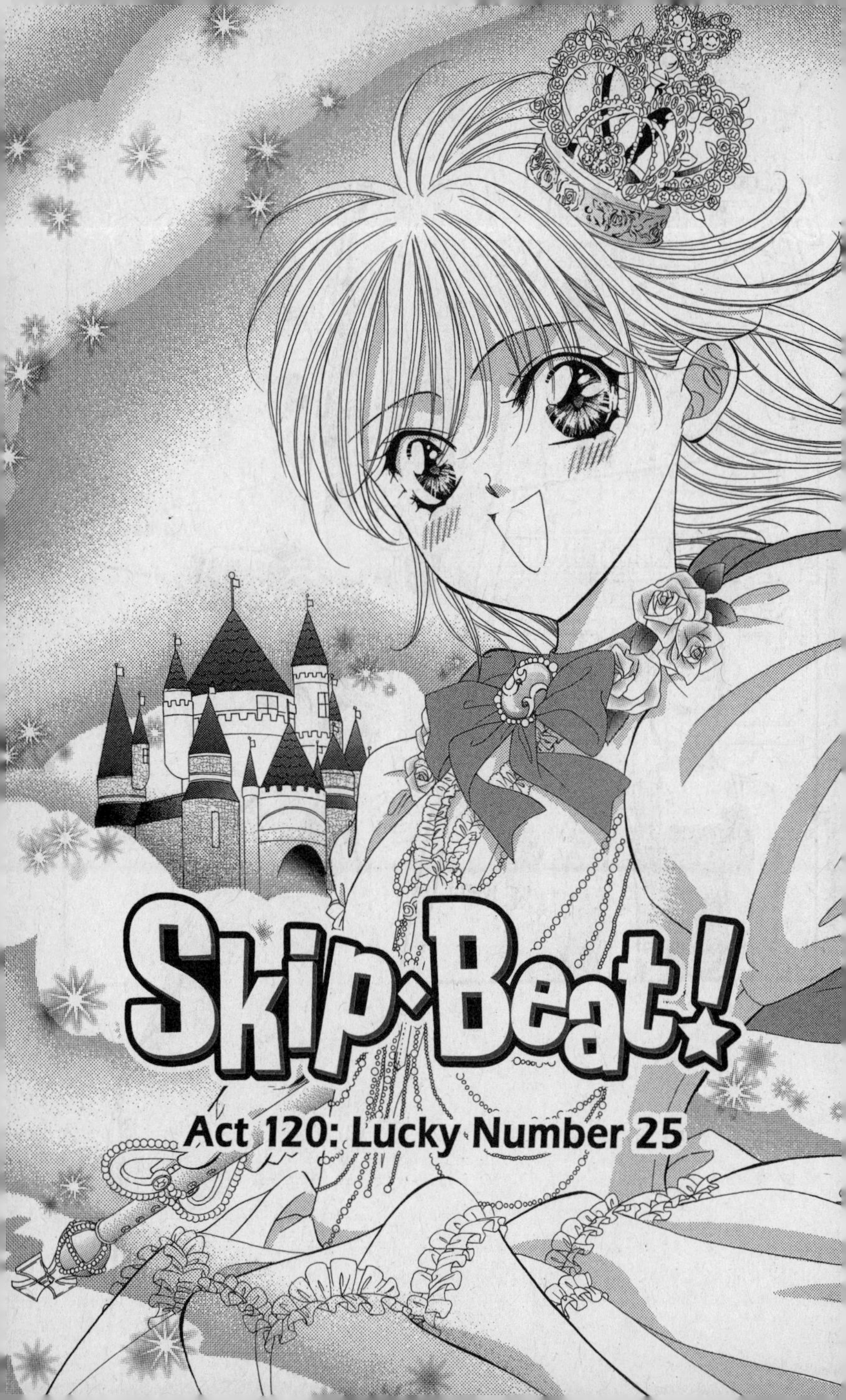
Skip·Beat!
Act 120: Lucky Number 25

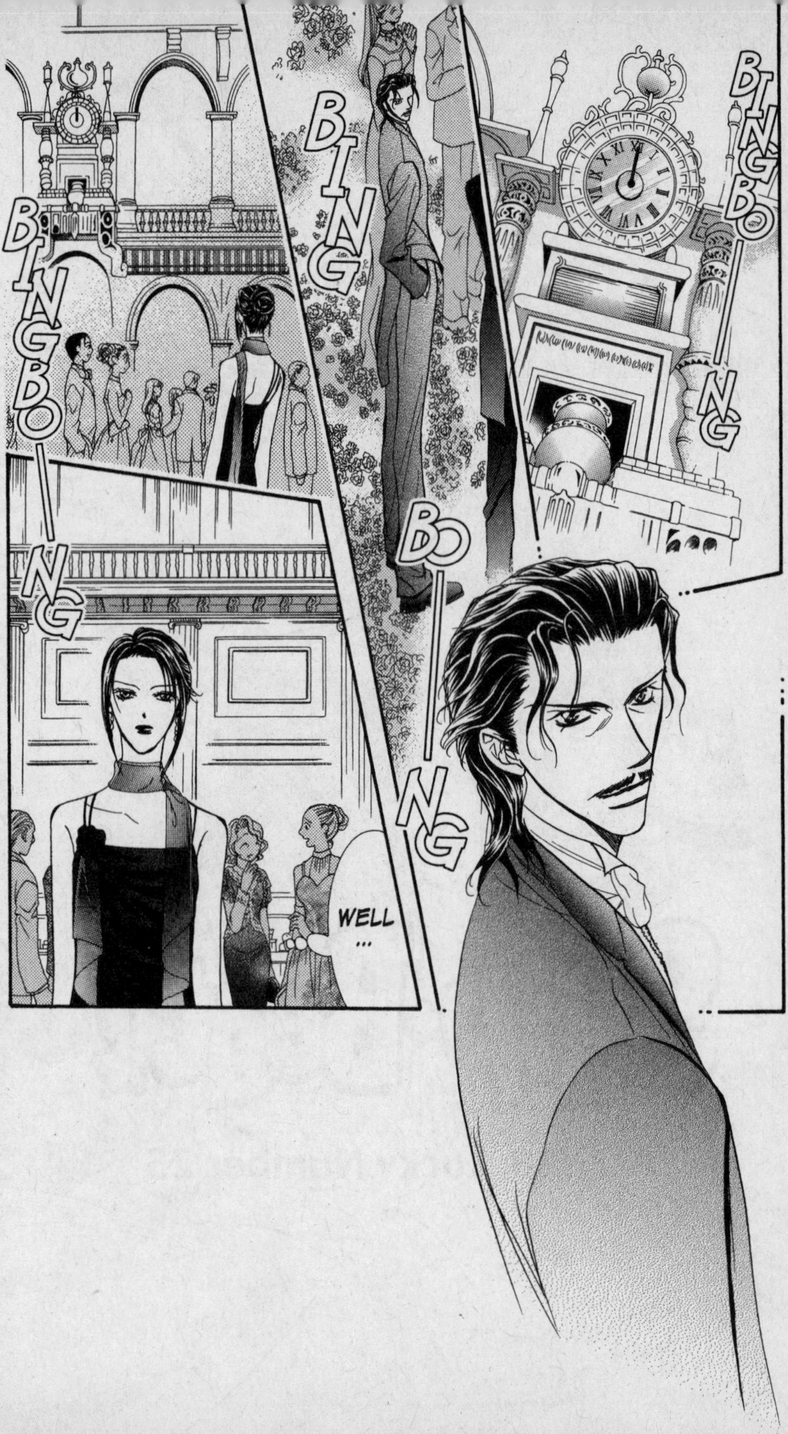
BINGBO-ING
BING
BINGBO-ING
WELL ...
BO-ING

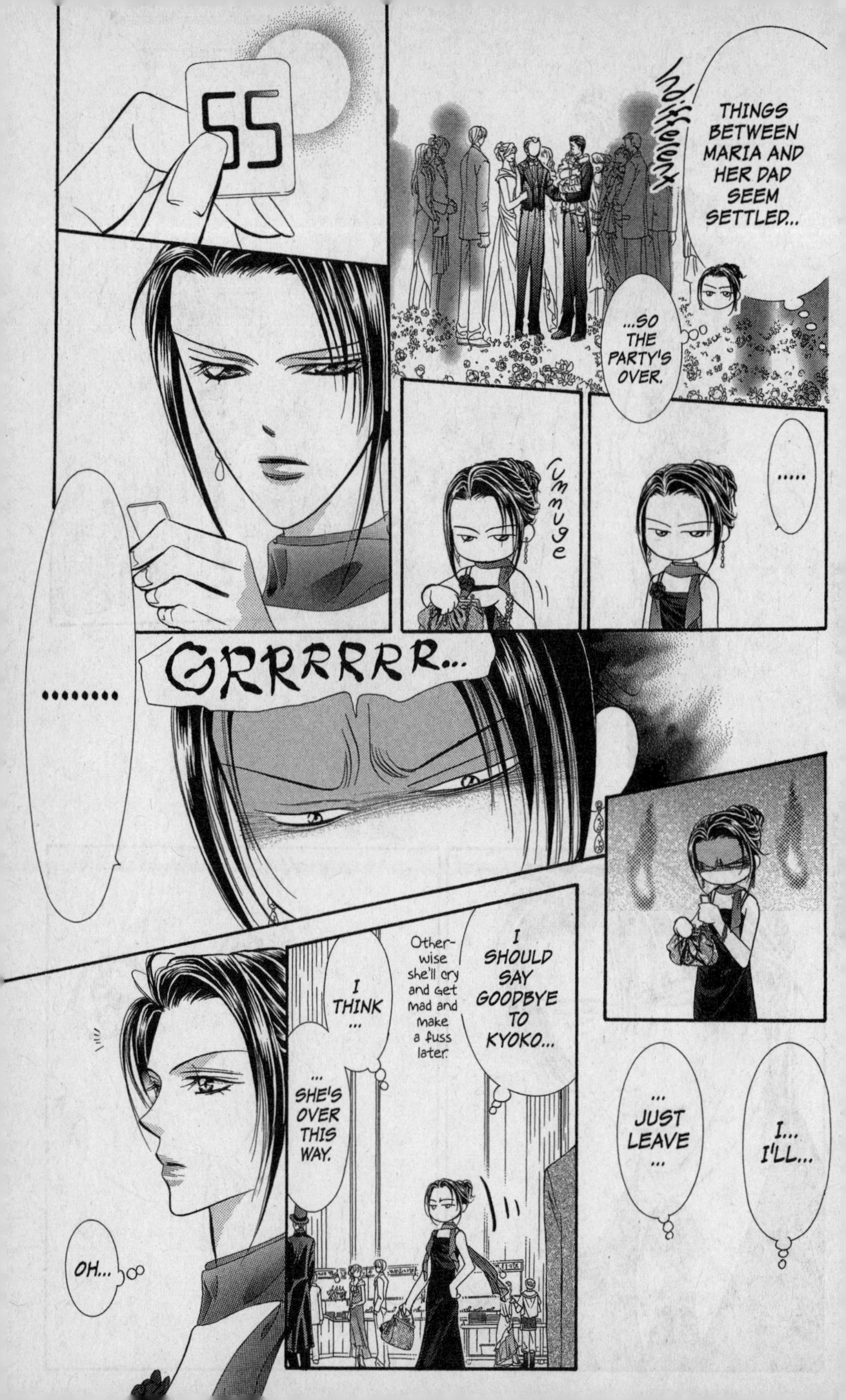
Indifferent
THINGS BETWEEN MARIA AND HER DAD SEEM SETTLED...
...SO THE PARTY'S OVER.
55
.....
rummuge
....
GRRRRRR...
I... I'LL...
... JUST LEAVE ...
I SHOULD SAY GOODBYE TO KYOKO...
Otherwise she'll cry and get mad and make a fuss later.
I THINK ...
... SHE'S OVER THIS WAY.
OH...

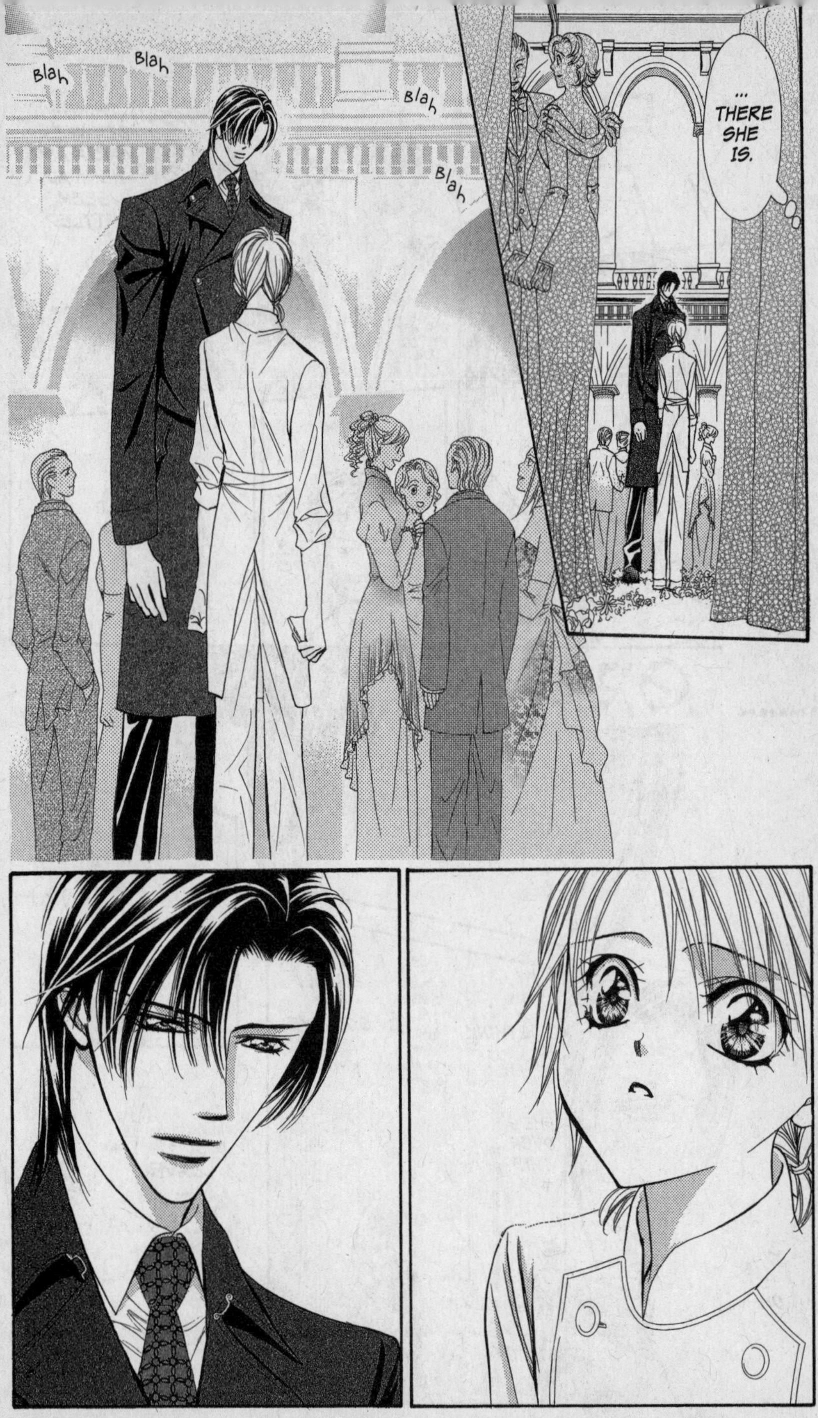
... THERE SHE IS.
Blah
Blah
Blah
Blah

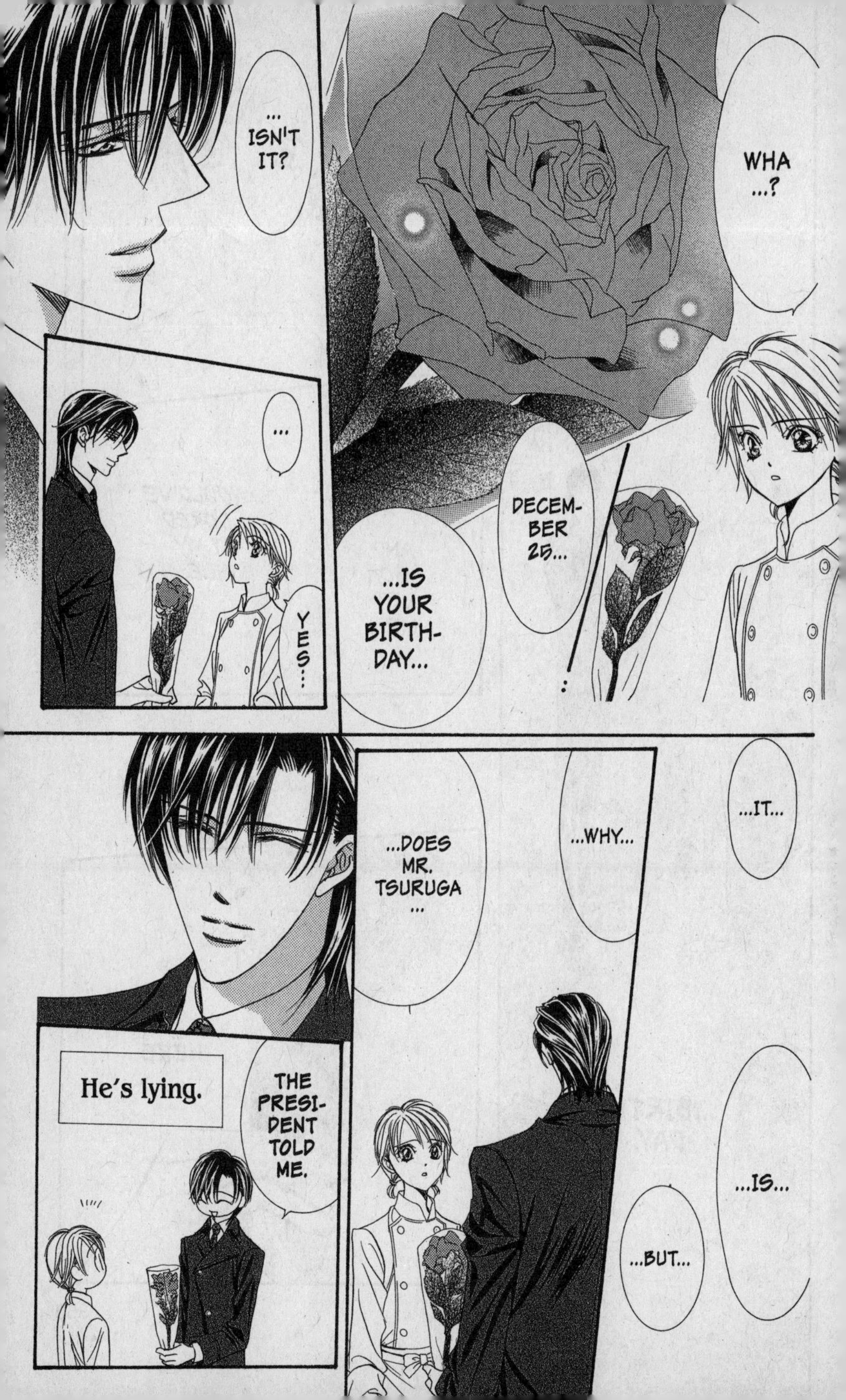
WHA ...?
DECEMBER 25...
...IS YOUR BIRTHDAY...
... ISN'T IT?
...
YES...
...IT...
...WHY...
...DOES MR. TSURUGA ...
...IS...
...BUT...
THE PRESIDENT TOLD ME.
He's lying.

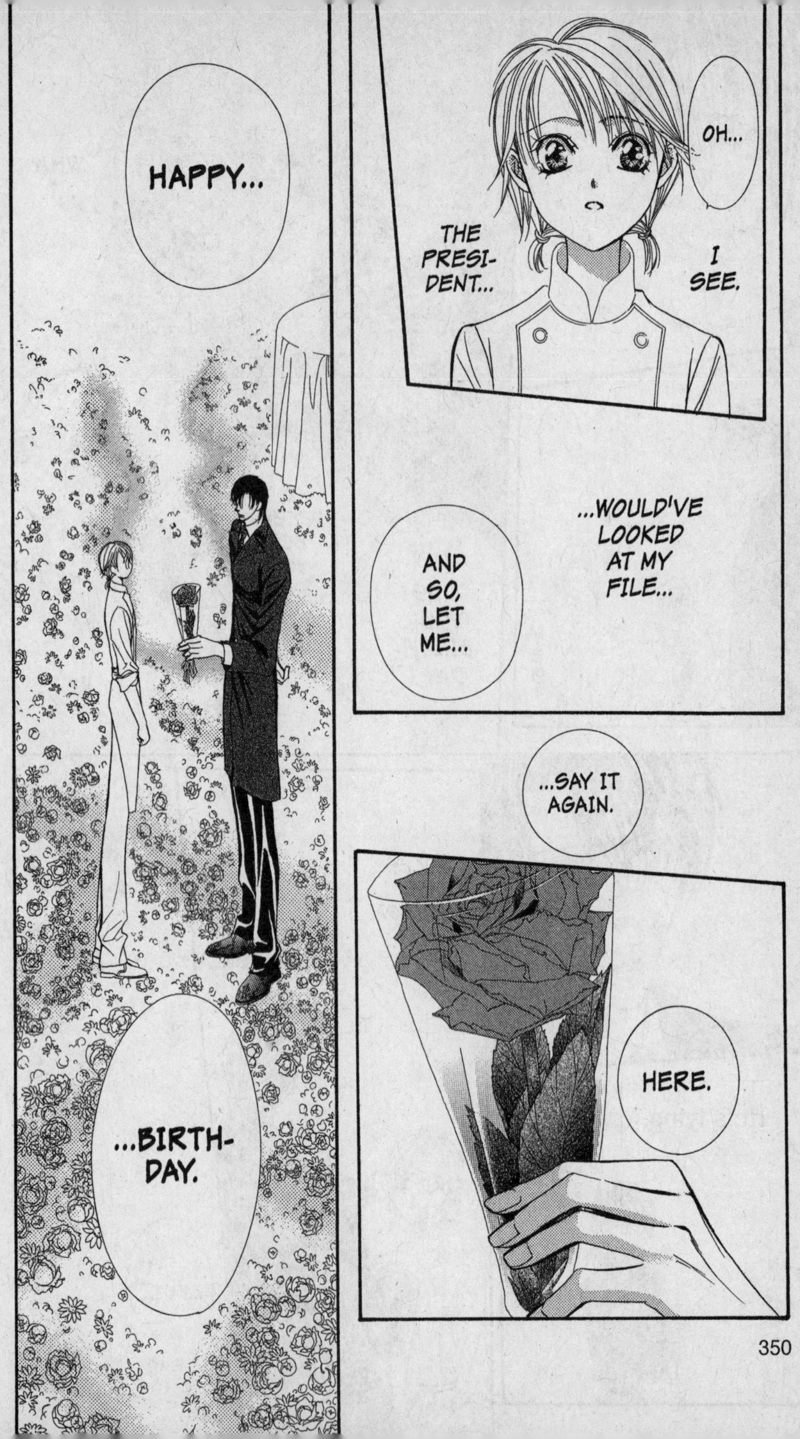
OH...
I SEE.
THE PRESI-DENT...
...WOULD'VE LOOKED AT MY FILE...
AND SO, LET ME...
...SAY IT AGAIN.
HERE.
HAPPY...
...BIRTH-DAY.

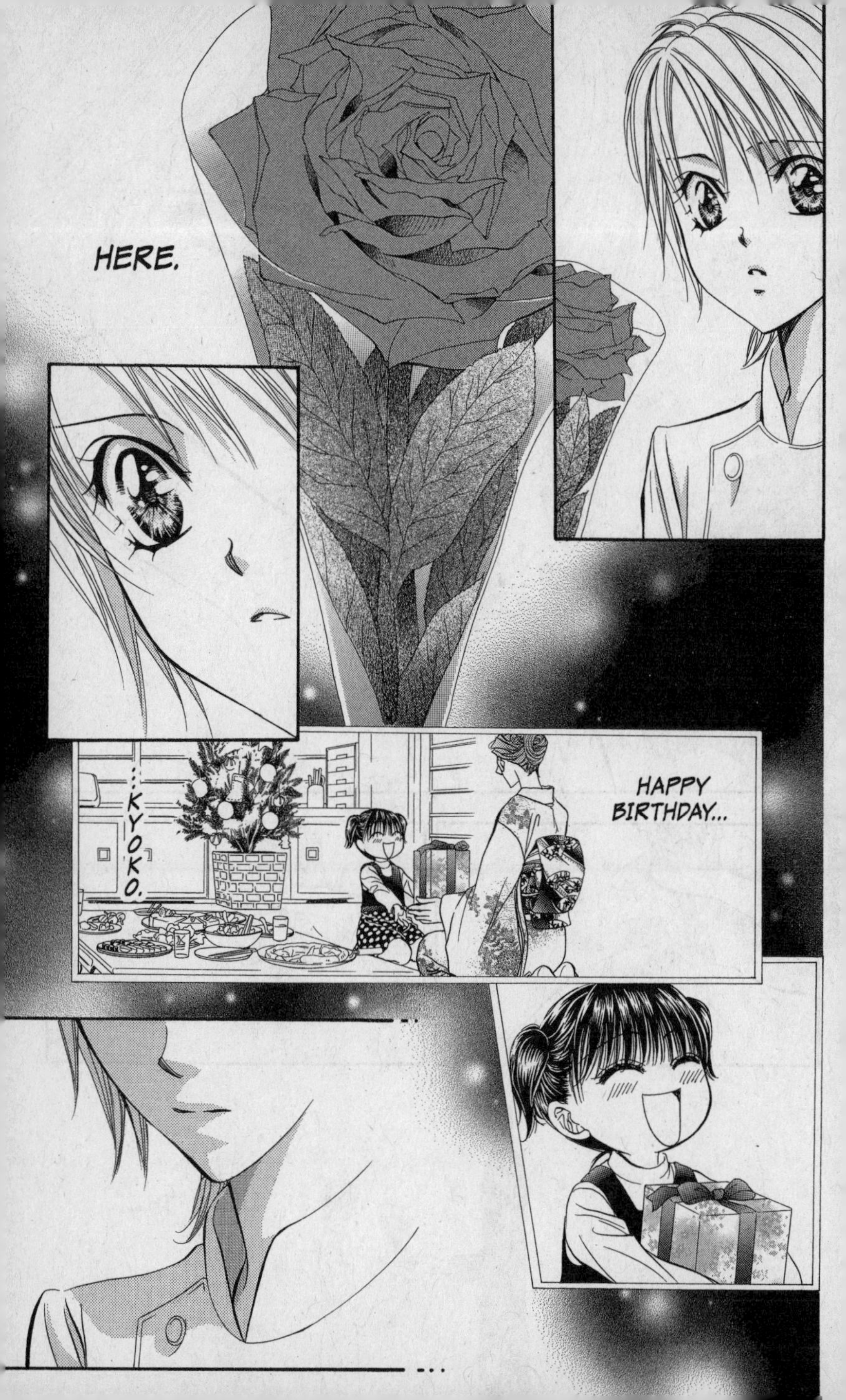
HERE.
HAPPY BIRTHDAY...
...KYOKO.
...
...

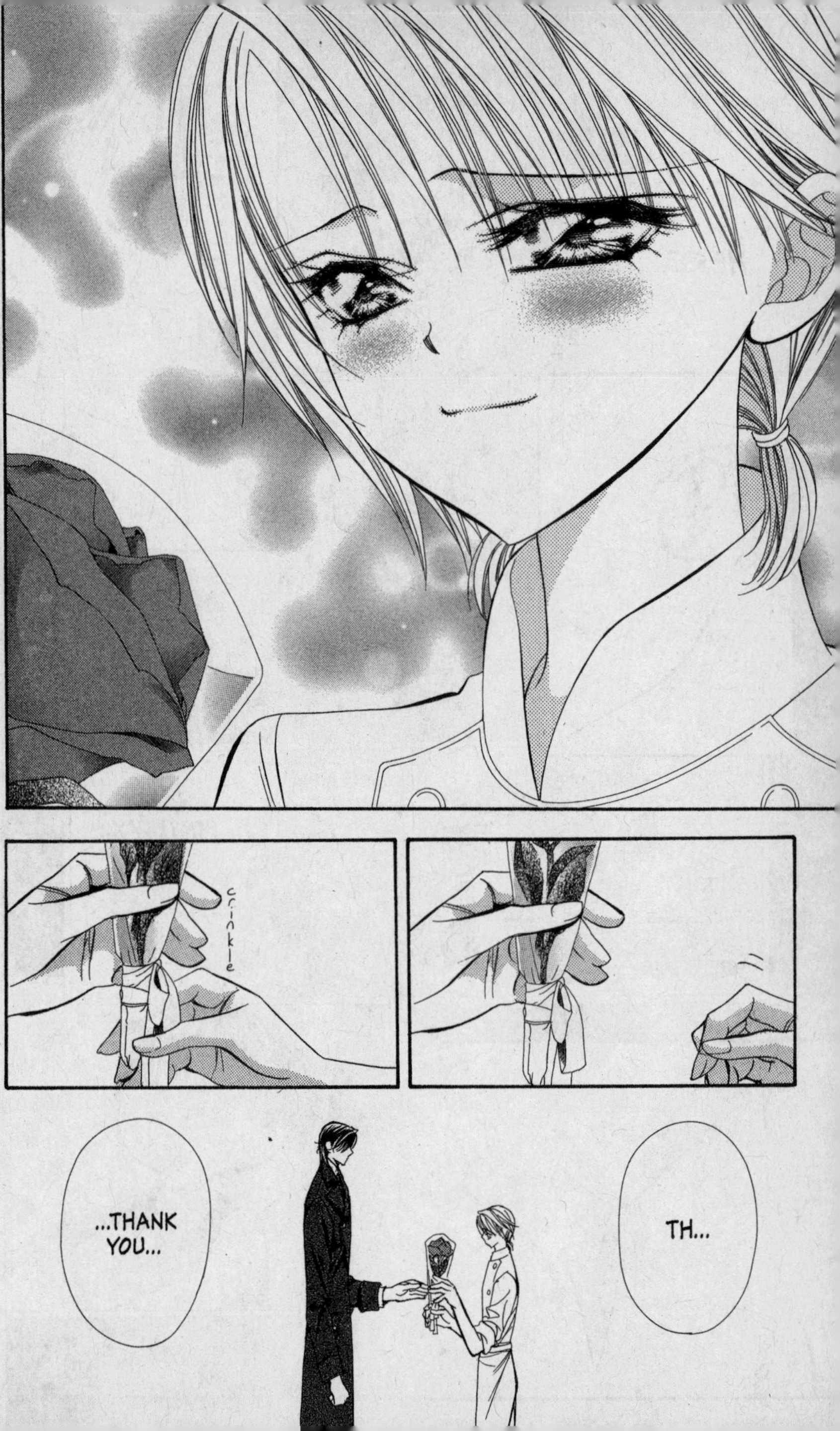
crinkle
TH...
...THANK YOU...

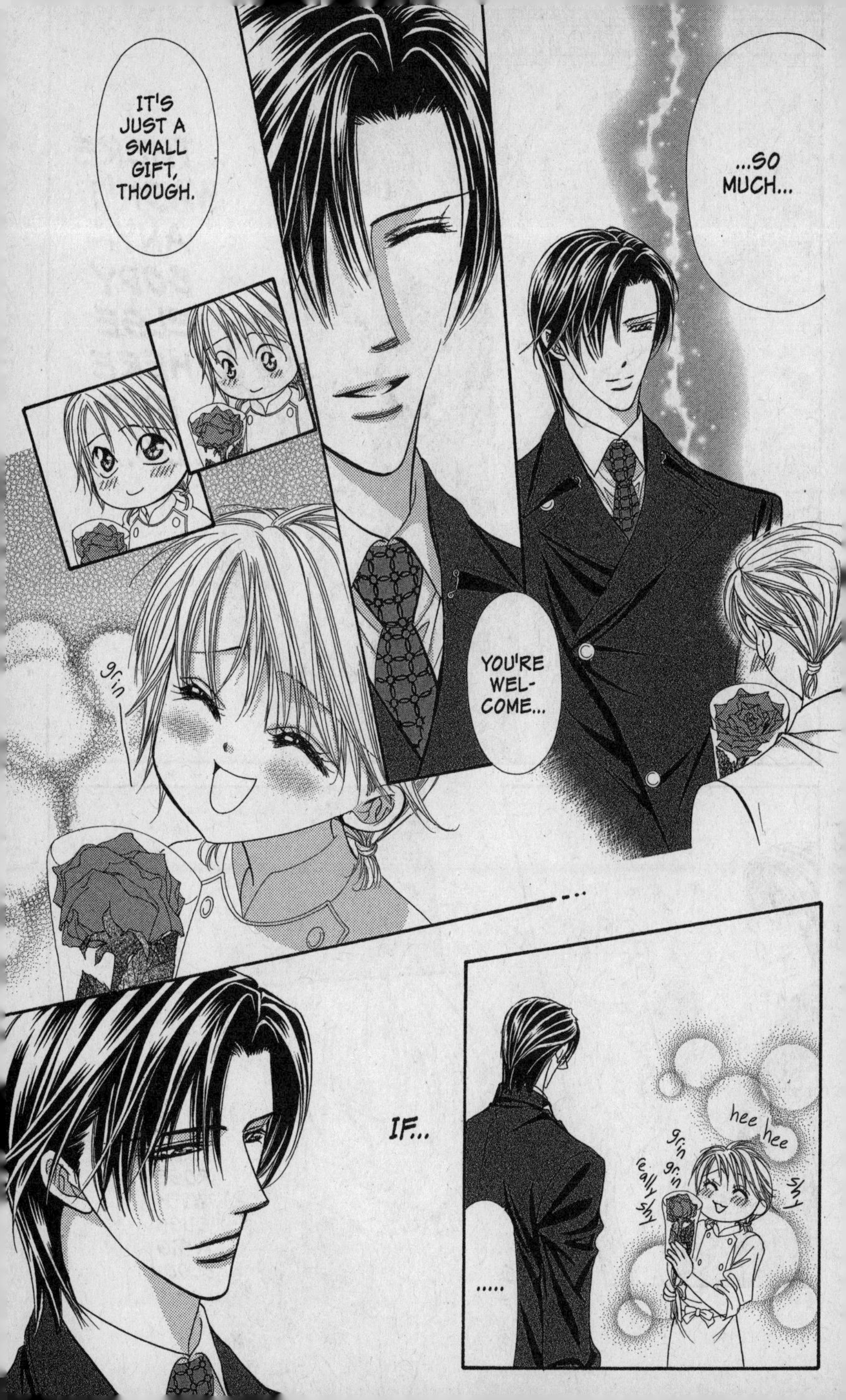
...SO MUCH...
YOU'RE WEL-COME...
IT'S JUST A SMALL GIFT, THOUGH.
grin
hee hee
shy
grin grin
really shy
.....
IF...

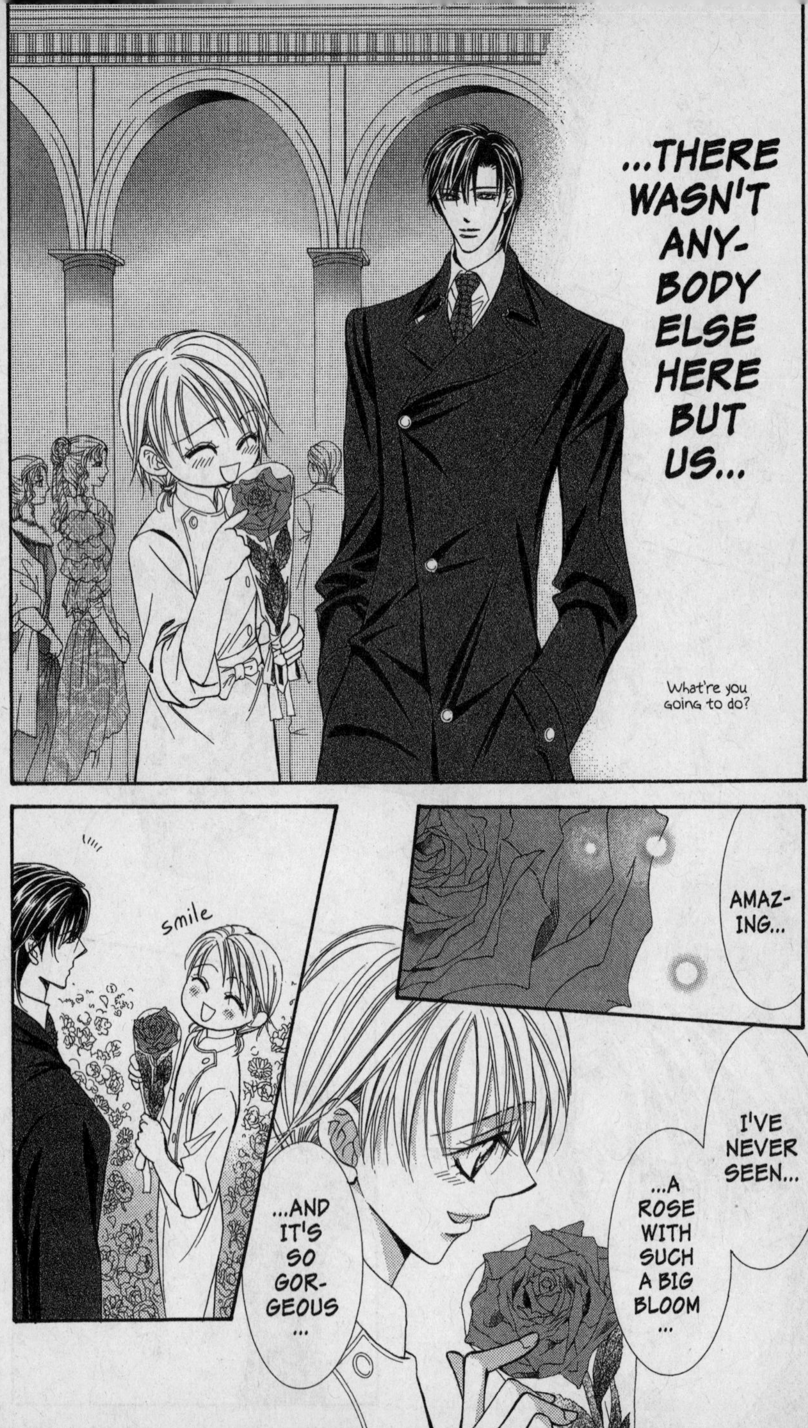
...THERE WASN'T ANY-BODY ELSE HERE BUT US...
What're you going to do?
AMAZ-ING...
I'VE NEVER SEEN...
...A ROSE WITH SUCH A BIG BLOOM...
...AND IT'S SO GOR-GEOUS...
smile

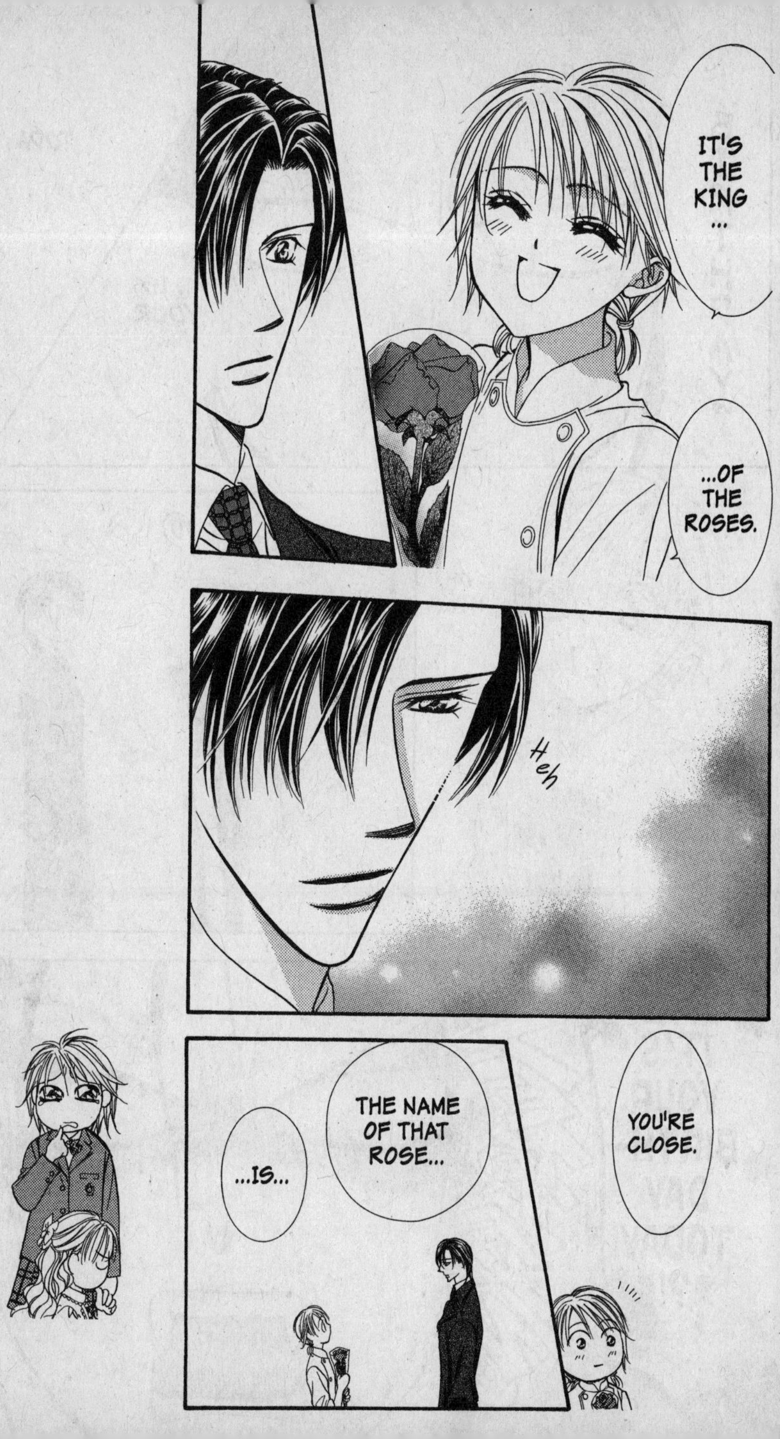
IT'S THE KING ...
...OF THE ROSES.
Heh
YOU'RE CLOSE.
THE NAME OF THAT ROSE...
...IS...

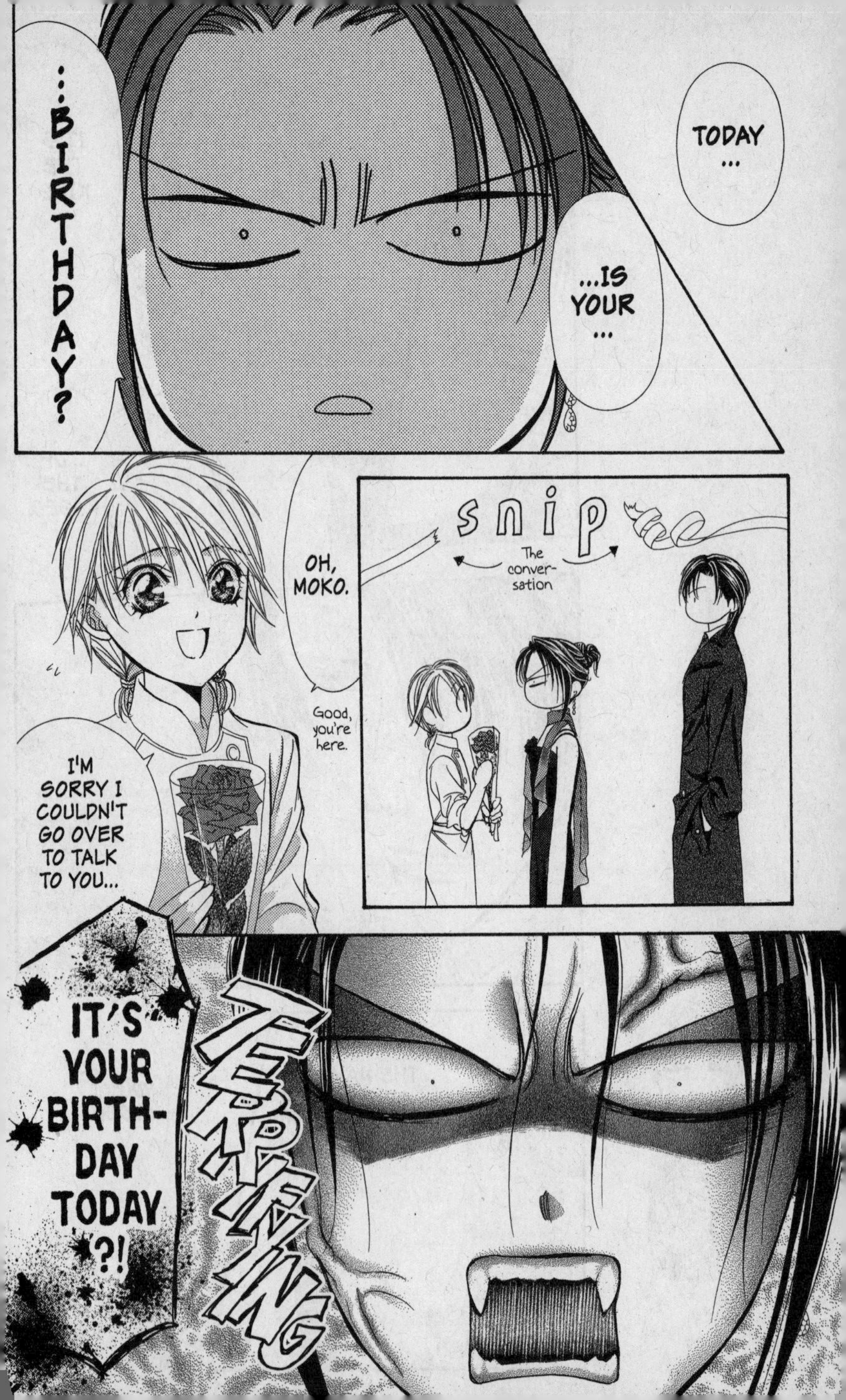
TODAY ...
...IS YOUR ...
...BIRTHDAY?
snip
The conversation
OH, MOKO.
Good, you're here.
I'M SORRY I COULDN'T GO OVER TO TALK TO YOU...
TERRIFYING
IT'S YOUR BIRTHDAY TODAY?!

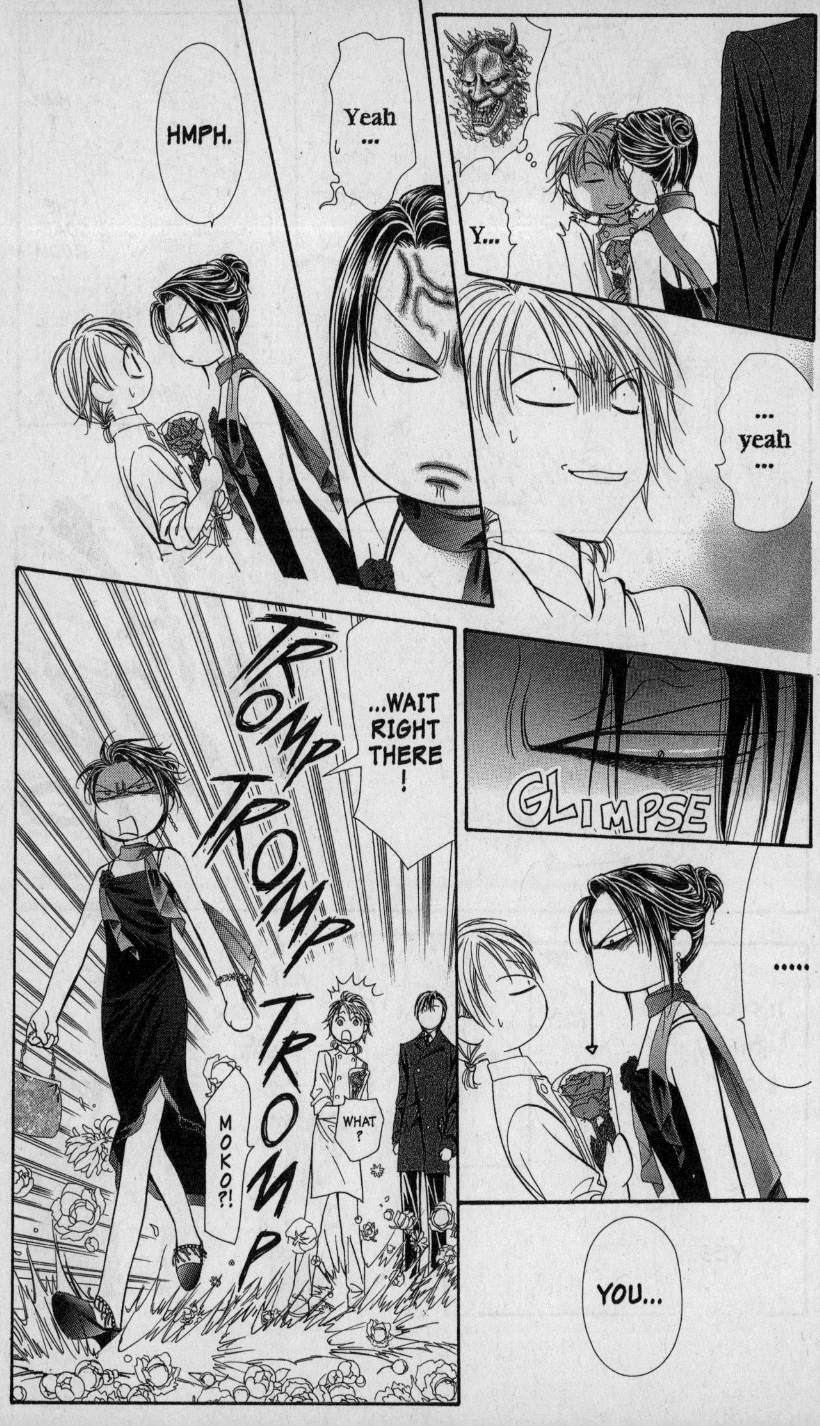

Y...
... yeah ...
Yeah ...
HMPH.
GLIMPSE
.....
YOU...
...WAIT RIGHT THERE !
TROMP TROMP TROMP TROMP
WHAT ?
MOKO?!

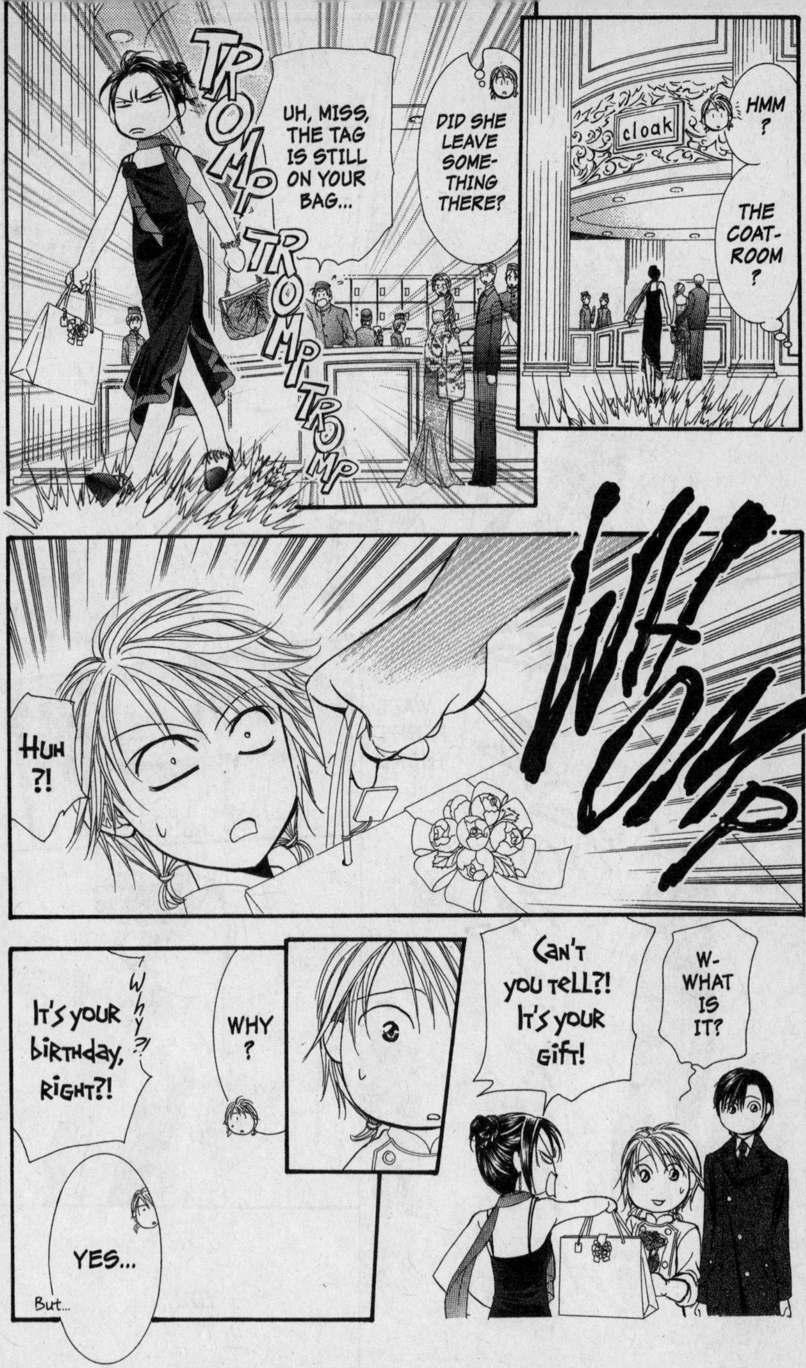
HMM?
cloak
THE COAT-ROOM?
DID SHE LEAVE SOMETHING THERE?
UH, MISS, THE TAG IS STILL ON YOUR BAG...
TROMP TROMP TROMP TROMP
WHOMP
HUH?!
W-WHAT IS IT?
Can't you tell?! It's your gift!
WHY?
Why?!
It's your birthday, right?!
YES...
But...

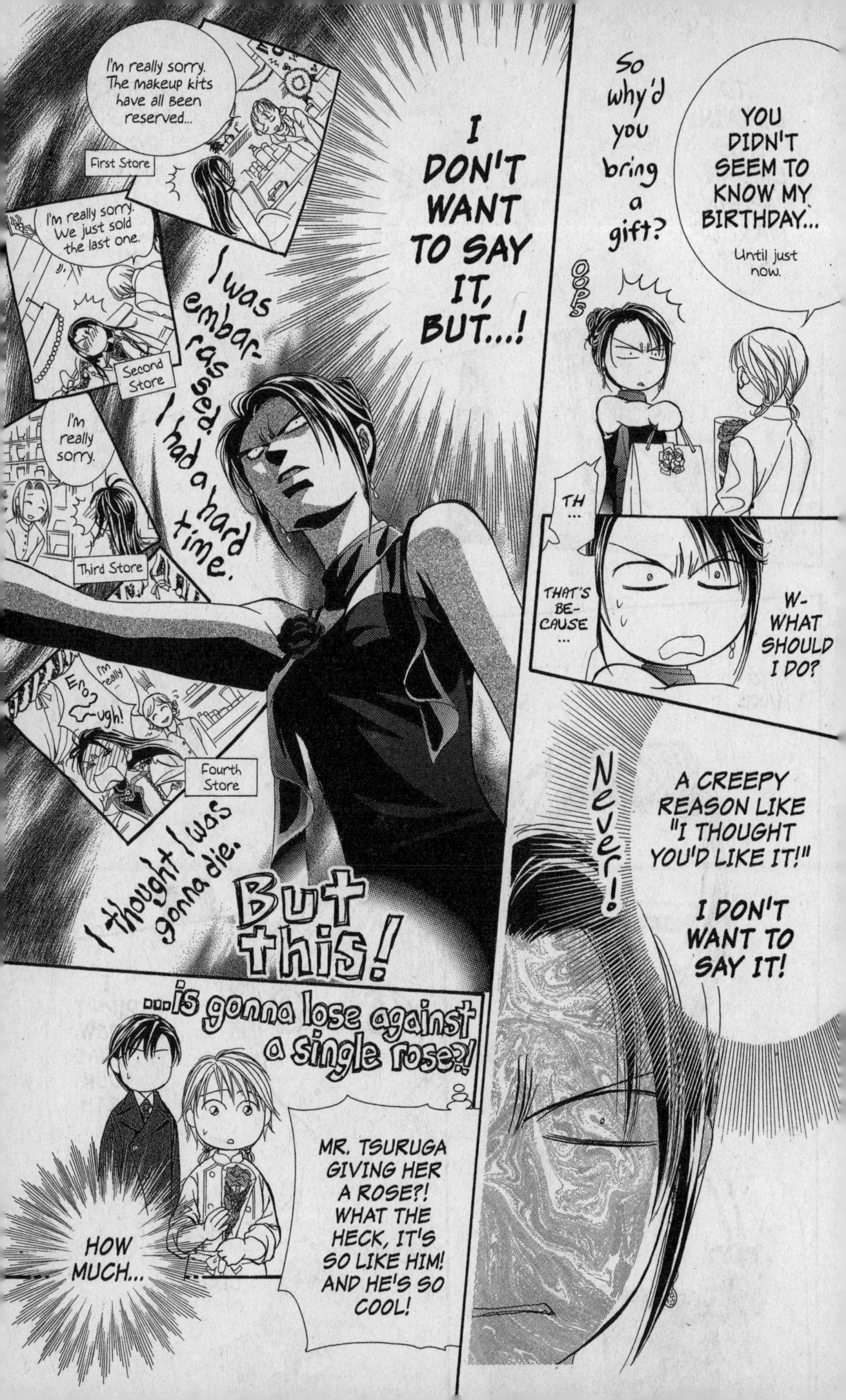
YOU DIDN'T SEEM TO KNOW MY BIRTHDAY...
Until just now.
So why'd you bring a gift?
OOPS
TH...
THAT'S BE-CAUSE...
W-WHAT SHOULD I DO?
A CREEPY REASON LIKE "I THOUGHT YOU'D LIKE IT!"
I DON'T WANT TO SAY IT!
Never!
I DON'T WANT TO SAY IT, BUT...!
I was embarrassed. I had a hard time.
I'm really sorry. The makeup kits have all Been reserved...
First Store
I'm really sorry. We just sold the last one.
Second Store
I'm really sorry.
Third Store
I'm really...
Erg-ugh!
Fourth Store
I thought I was gonna die.
But this!
...is gonna lose against a single rose?!
MR. TSURUGA GIVING HER A ROSE?! WHAT THE HECK, IT'S SO LIKE HIM! AND HE'S SO COOL!
HOW MUCH...

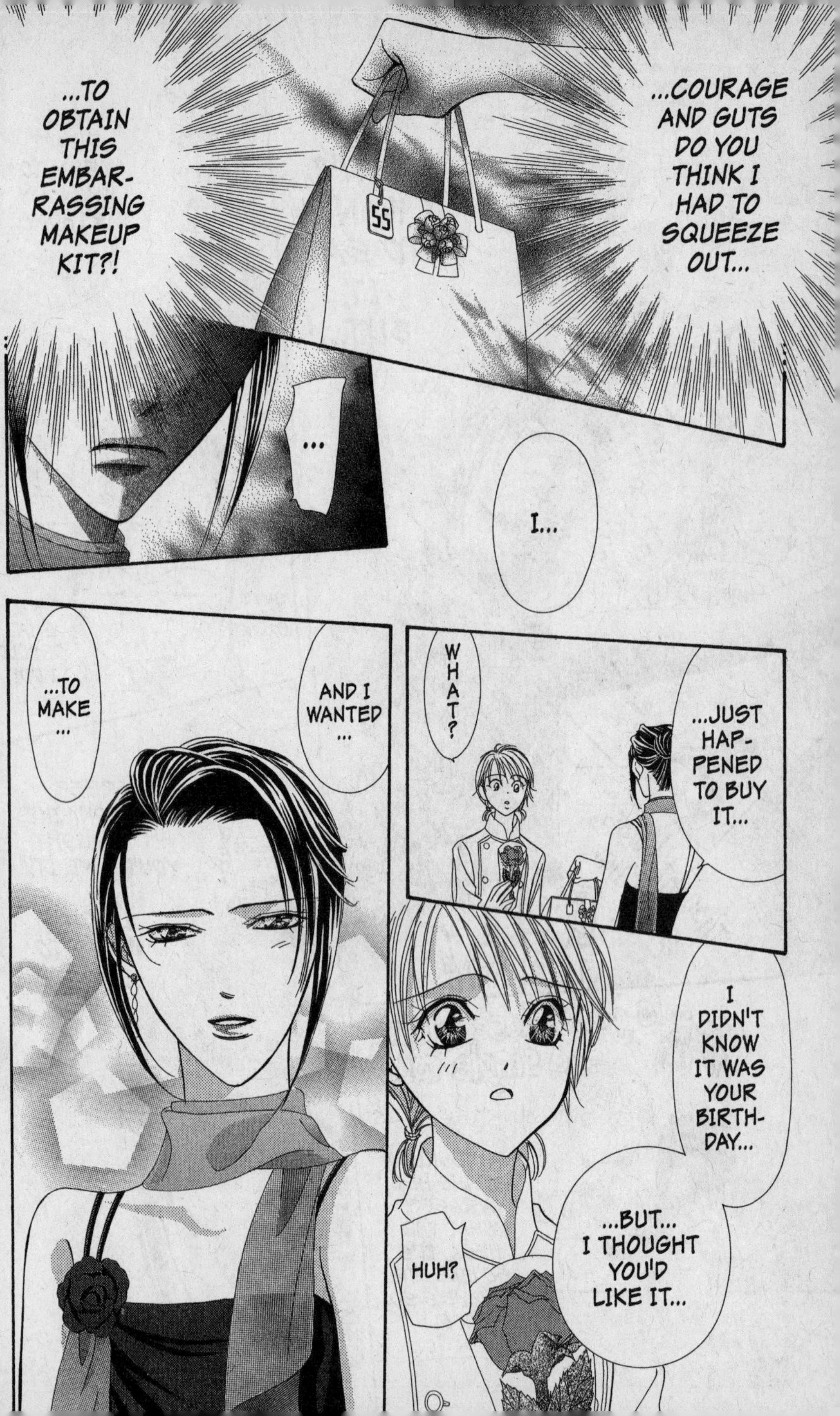
...COURAGE AND GUTS DO YOU THINK I HAD TO SQUEEZE OUT...
...TO OBTAIN THIS EMBARRASSING MAKEUP KIT?!
SS
I...
...
...JUST HAPPENED TO BUY IT...
WHAT?
I DIDN'T KNOW IT WAS YOUR BIRTHDAY...
...BUT... I THOUGHT YOU'D LIKE IT...
HUH?
AND I WANTED...
...TO MAKE...

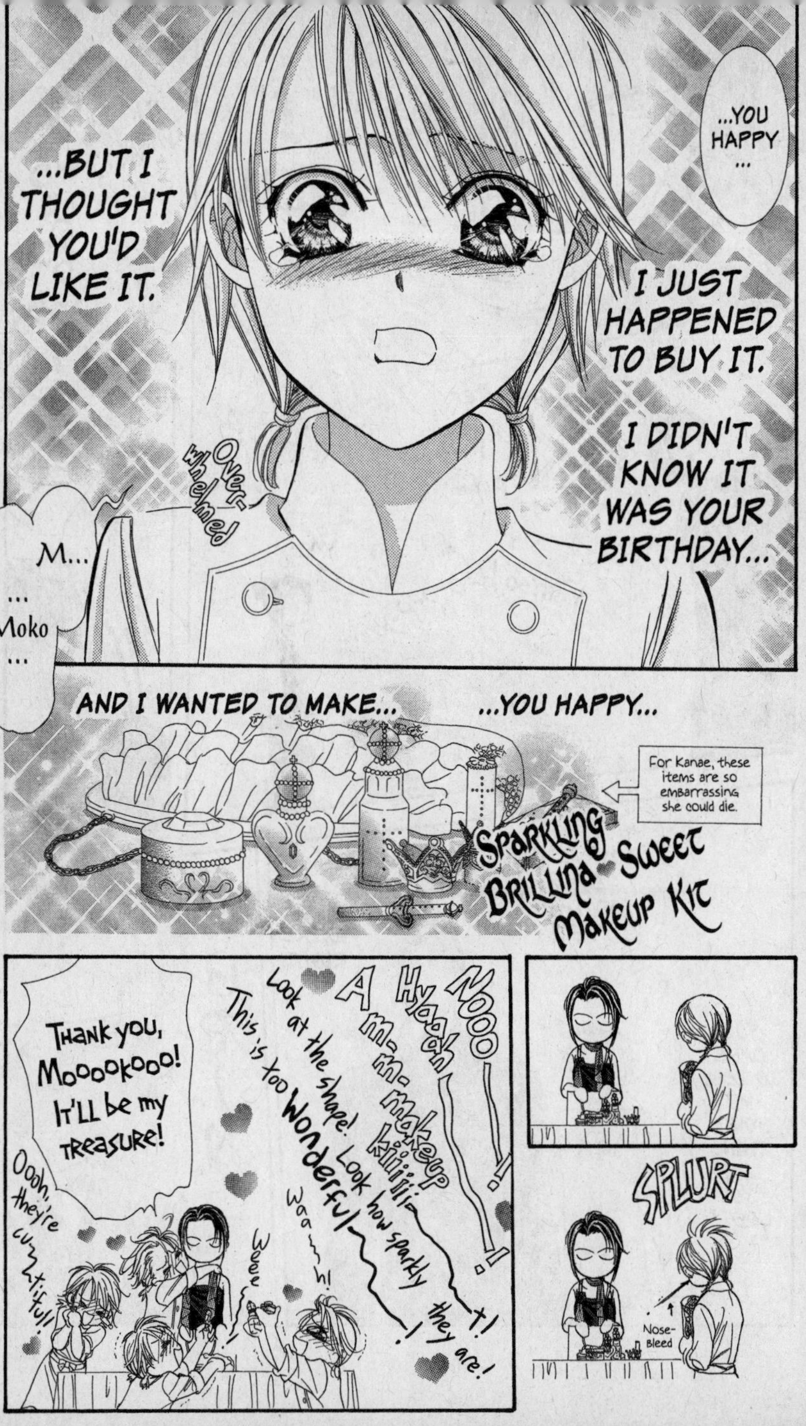
...YOU HAPPY ...
I JUST HAPPENED TO BUY IT.
I DIDN'T KNOW IT WAS YOUR BIRTHDAY...
...BUT I THOUGHT YOU'D LIKE IT.
Over-whelmed
M... ... Moko ...
AND I WANTED TO MAKE...
...YOU HAPPY...
For Kanae, these items are so embarrassing she could die.
Sparkling Brillina Sweet Makeup Kit
SPLURT
Nose-Bleed
Nooo—!
Hyaaah
A m-m-makeup kiiiiit!
Look at the shape! Look how sparkly they are!
This is too wonderful—!
Waa—h!
Weee
Thank you, Moooookooo! It'll be my treasure!
Oooh, they're cu—tiful!

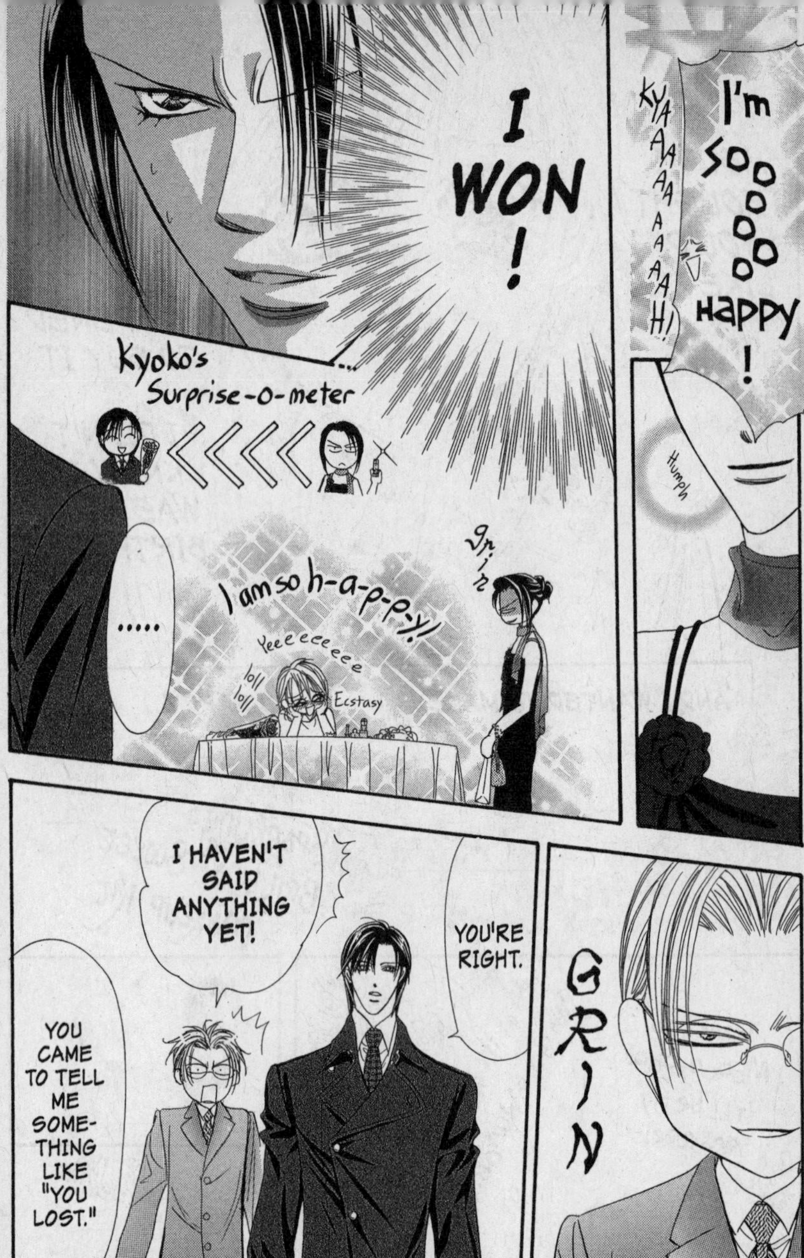
I'm SOOOOOO HAPPY!
KYAAAAAAAAAAH!
Humph
I WON!
...
Kyoko's Surprise-o-meter
grin
I am so h-a-p-p-y!
Yeeeeeeeee
loll loll
Ecstasy
.....
GRIN
YOU'RE RIGHT.
I HAVEN'T SAID ANYTHING YET!
YOU CAME TO TELL ME SOMETHING LIKE "YOU LOST."

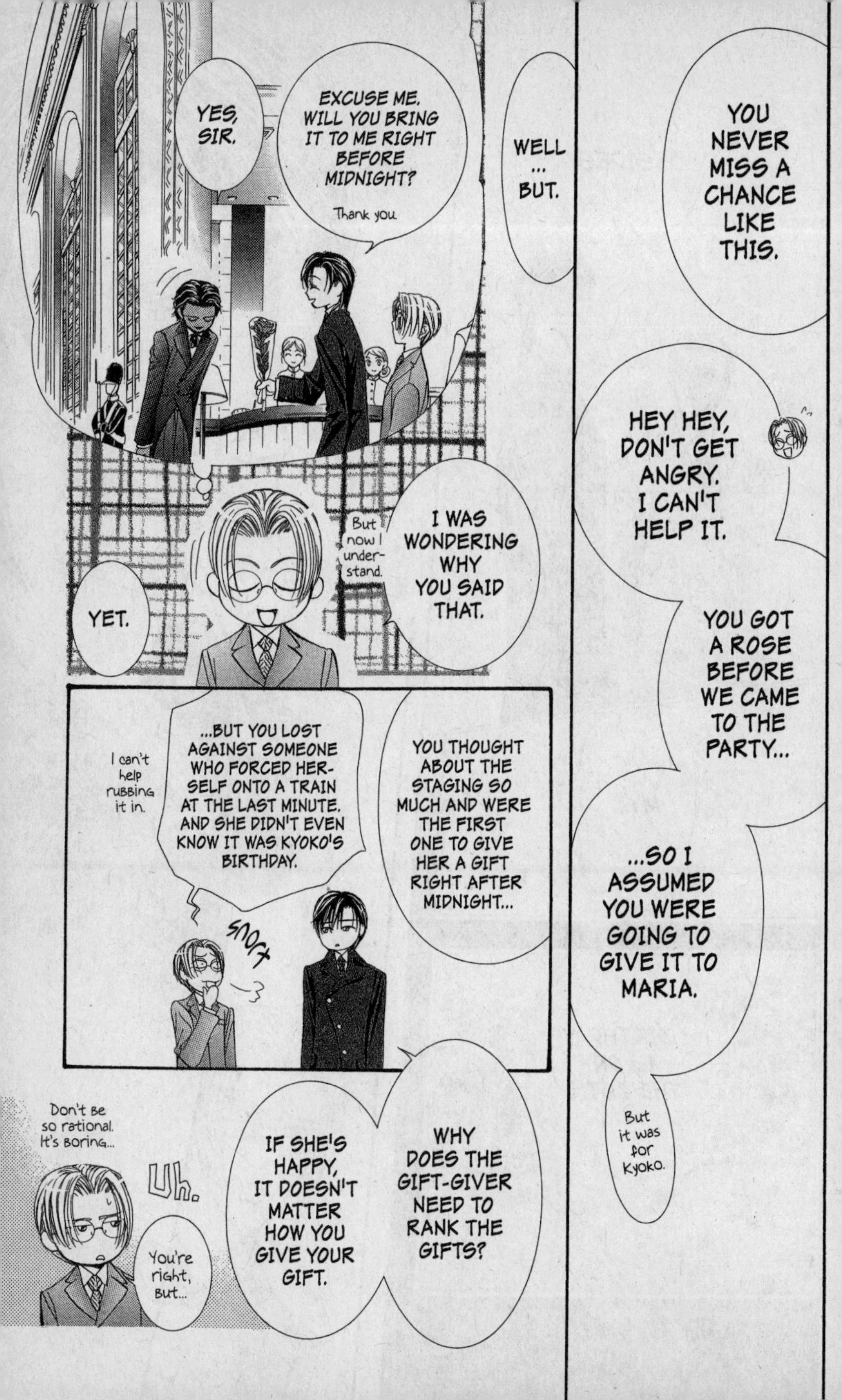
YOU NEVER MISS A CHANCE LIKE THIS.
HEY HEY, DON'T GET ANGRY. I CAN'T HELP IT.
YOU GOT A ROSE BEFORE WE CAME TO THE PARTY...
...SO I ASSUMED YOU WERE GOING TO GIVE IT TO MARIA.
But it was for Kyoko.
WELL ... BUT.
EXCUSE ME. WILL YOU BRING IT TO ME RIGHT BEFORE MIDNIGHT?
Thank you.
YES, SIR.
I WAS WONDERING WHY YOU SAID THAT.
But now I under-stand.
YET.
YOU THOUGHT ABOUT THE STAGING SO MUCH AND WERE THE FIRST ONE TO GIVE HER A GIFT RIGHT AFTER MIDNIGHT...
...BUT YOU LOST AGAINST SOMEONE WHO FORCED HER-SELF ONTO A TRAIN AT THE LAST MINUTE. AND SHE DIDN'T EVEN KNOW IT WAS KYOKO'S BIRTHDAY.
I can't help rubbing it in.
snort
WHY DOES THE GIFT-GIVER NEED TO RANK THE GIFTS?
IF SHE'S HAPPY, IT DOESN'T MATTER HOW YOU GIVE YOUR GIFT.
Uh.
You're right, but...
Don't be so rational. It's boring...

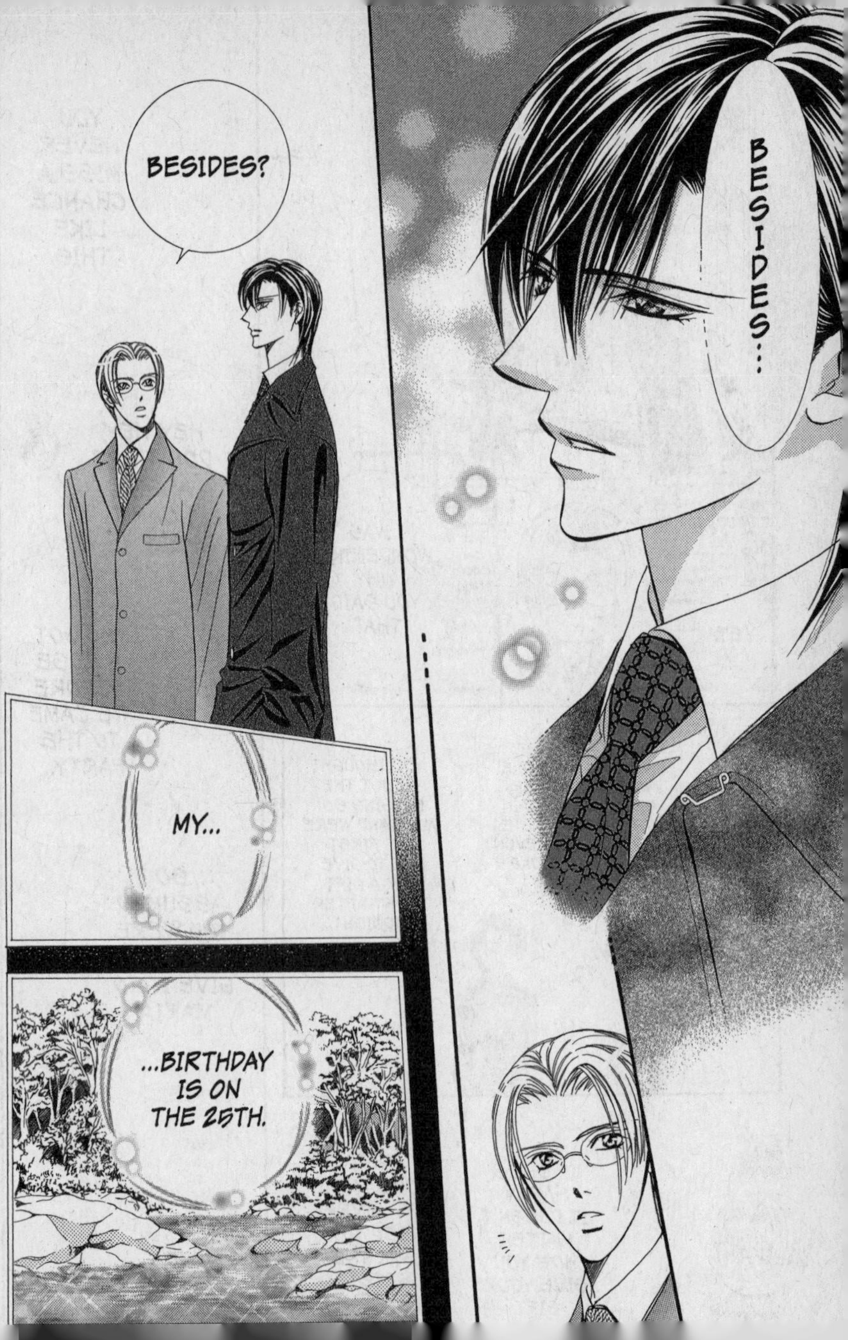
BESIDES...
BESIDES?
MY...
...BIRTHDAY IS ON THE 25TH.

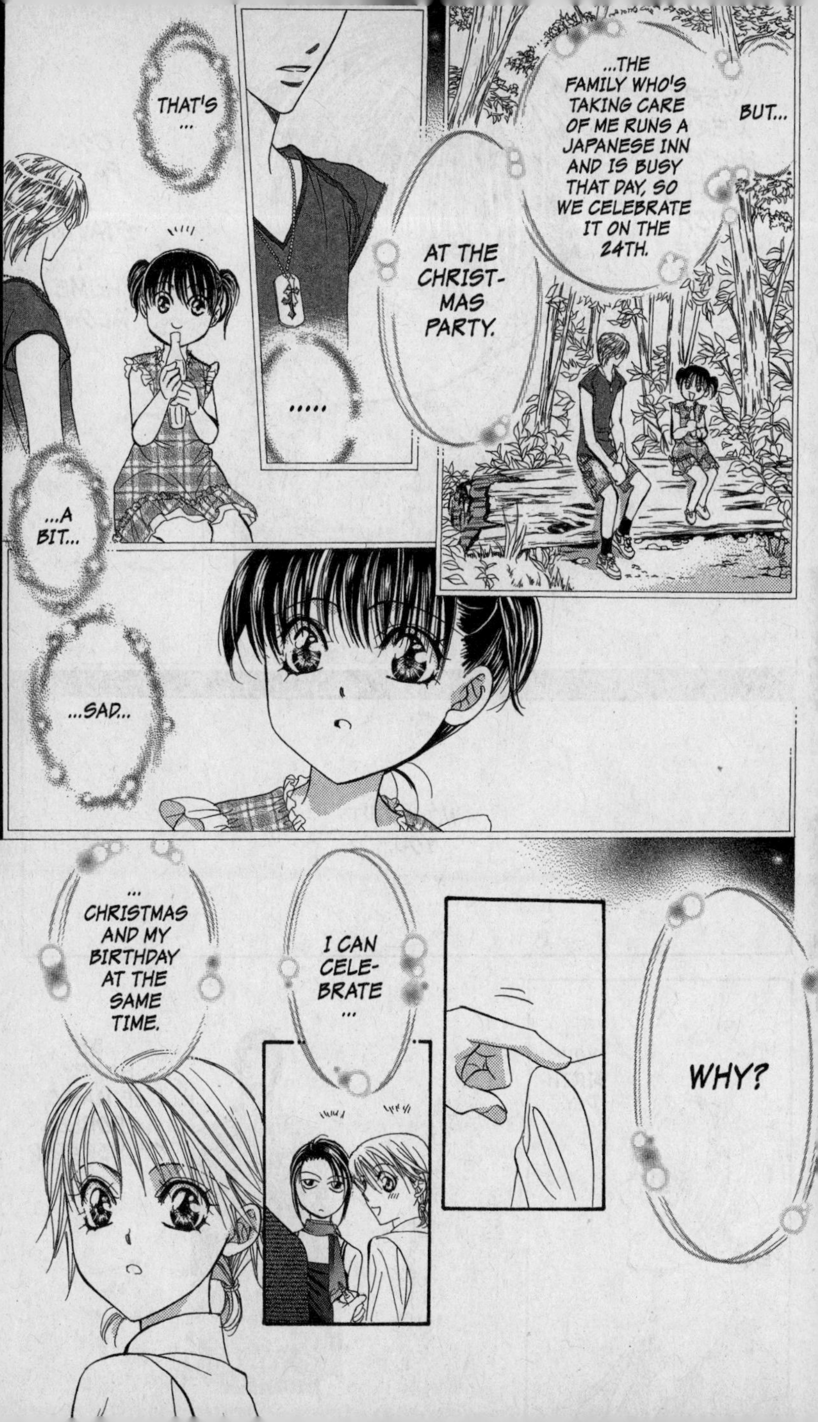
BUT...
...THE FAMILY WHO'S TAKING CARE OF ME RUNS A JAPANESE INN AND IS BUSY THAT DAY, SO WE CELEBRATE IT ON THE 24TH.
AT THE CHRIST-MAS PARTY.
.....
THAT'S ...
...A BIT...
...SAD...
WHY?
I CAN CELE-BRATE ...
... CHRISTMAS AND MY BIRTHDAY AT THE SAME TIME.

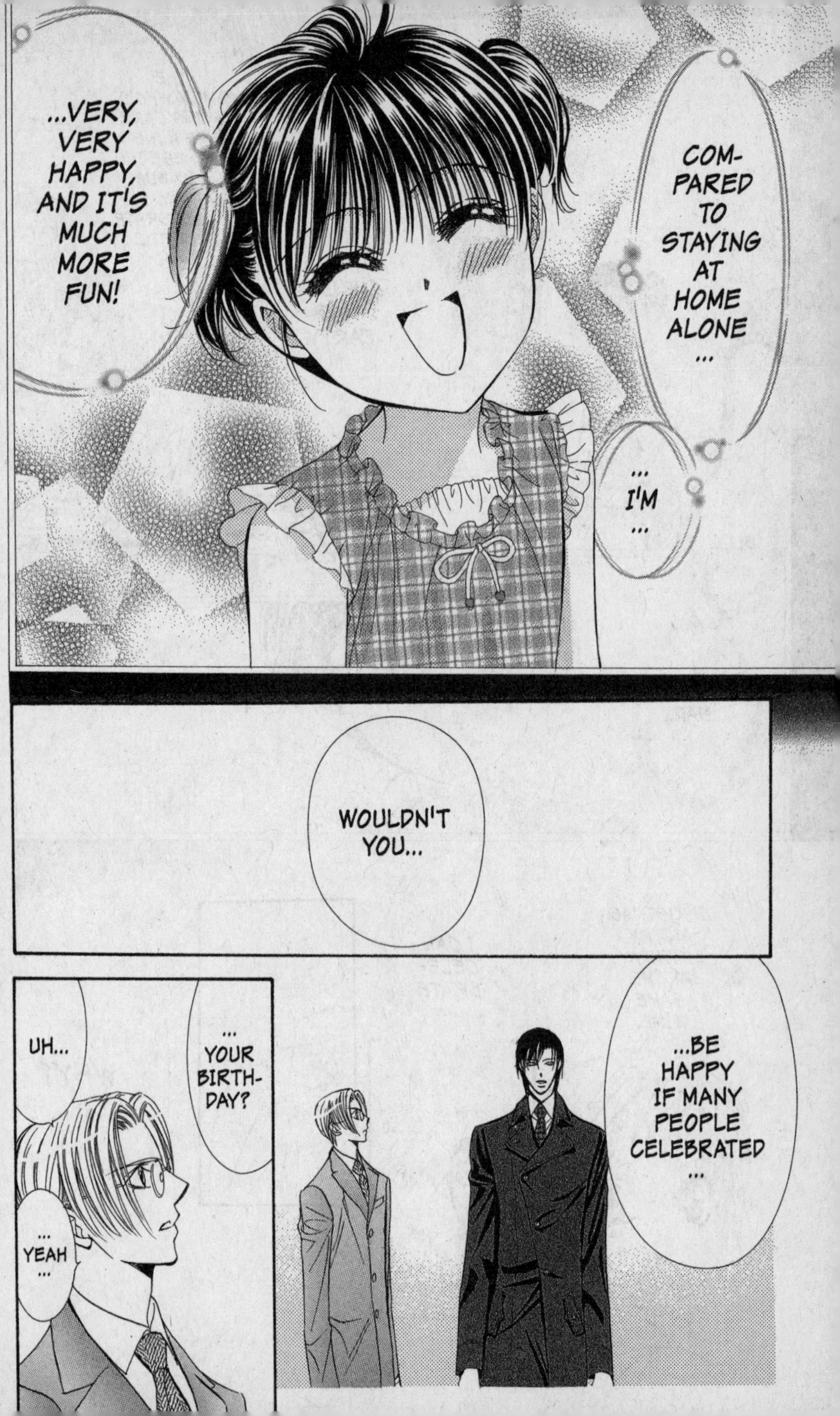
COM-PARED TO STAYING AT HOME ALONE...
...I'M...
...VERY, VERY HAPPY, AND IT'S MUCH MORE FUN!
WOULDN'T YOU...
...BE HAPPY IF MANY PEOPLE CELEBRATED...
...YOUR BIRTH-DAY?
UH...
...YEAH...

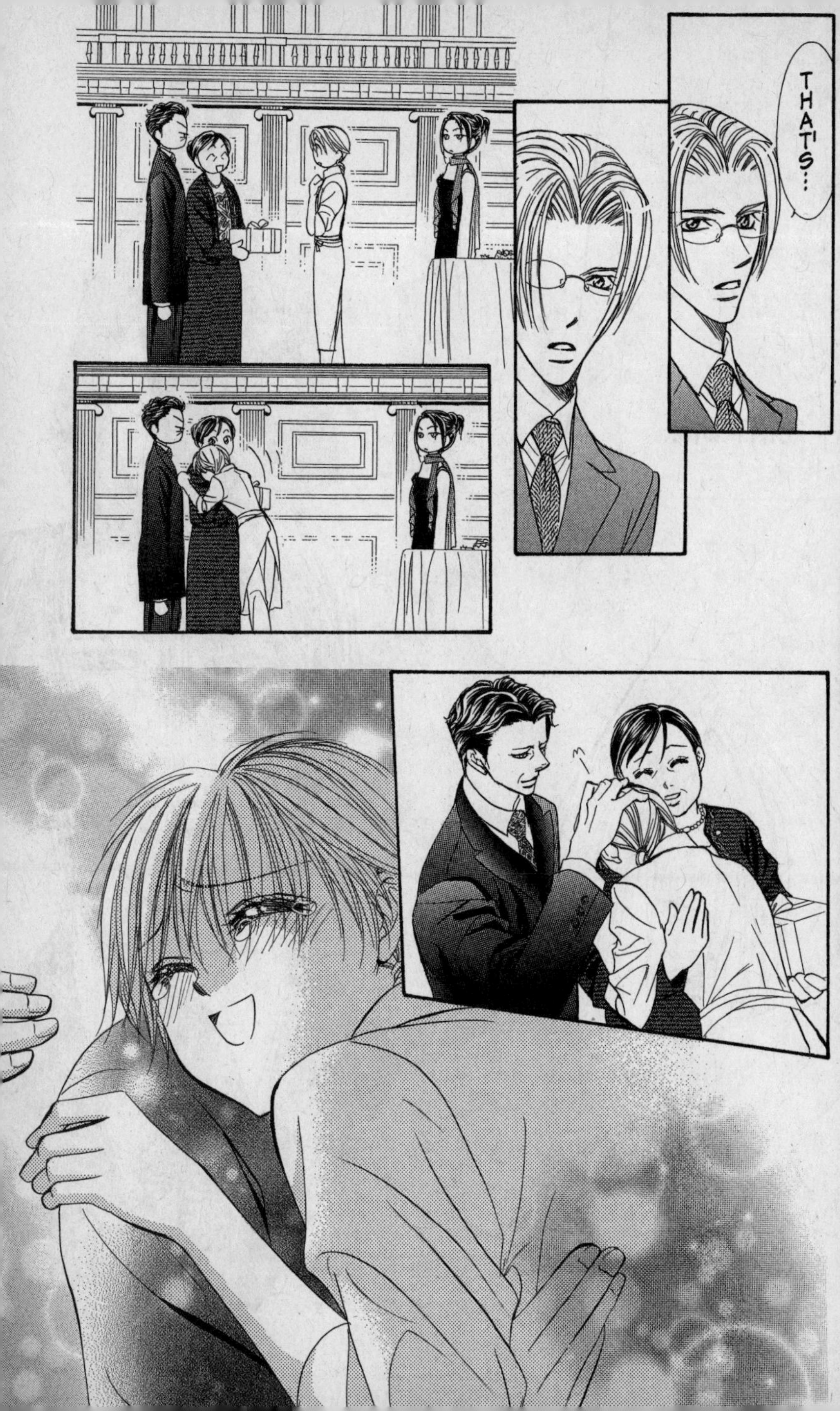
THAT'S...

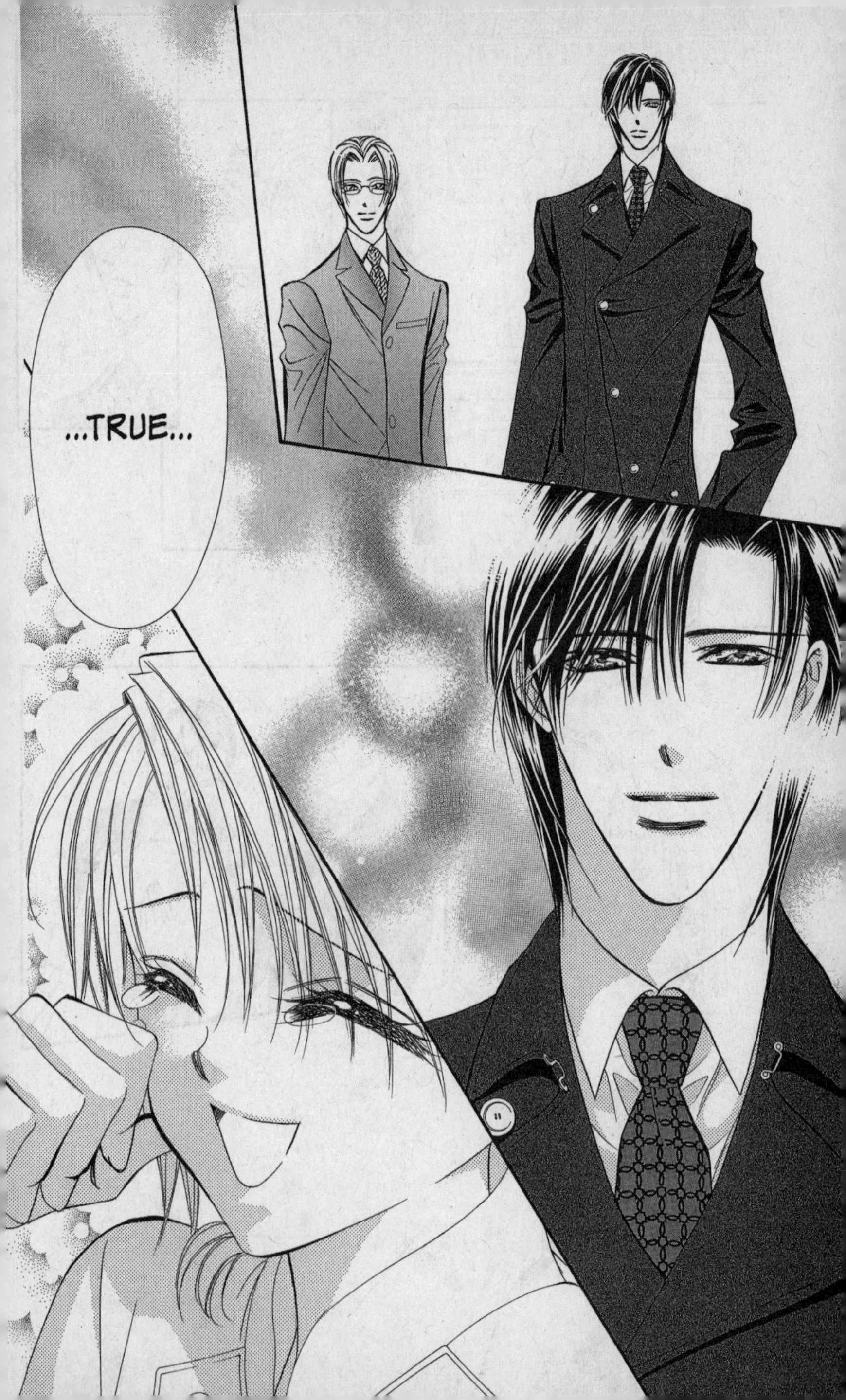
...TRUE...

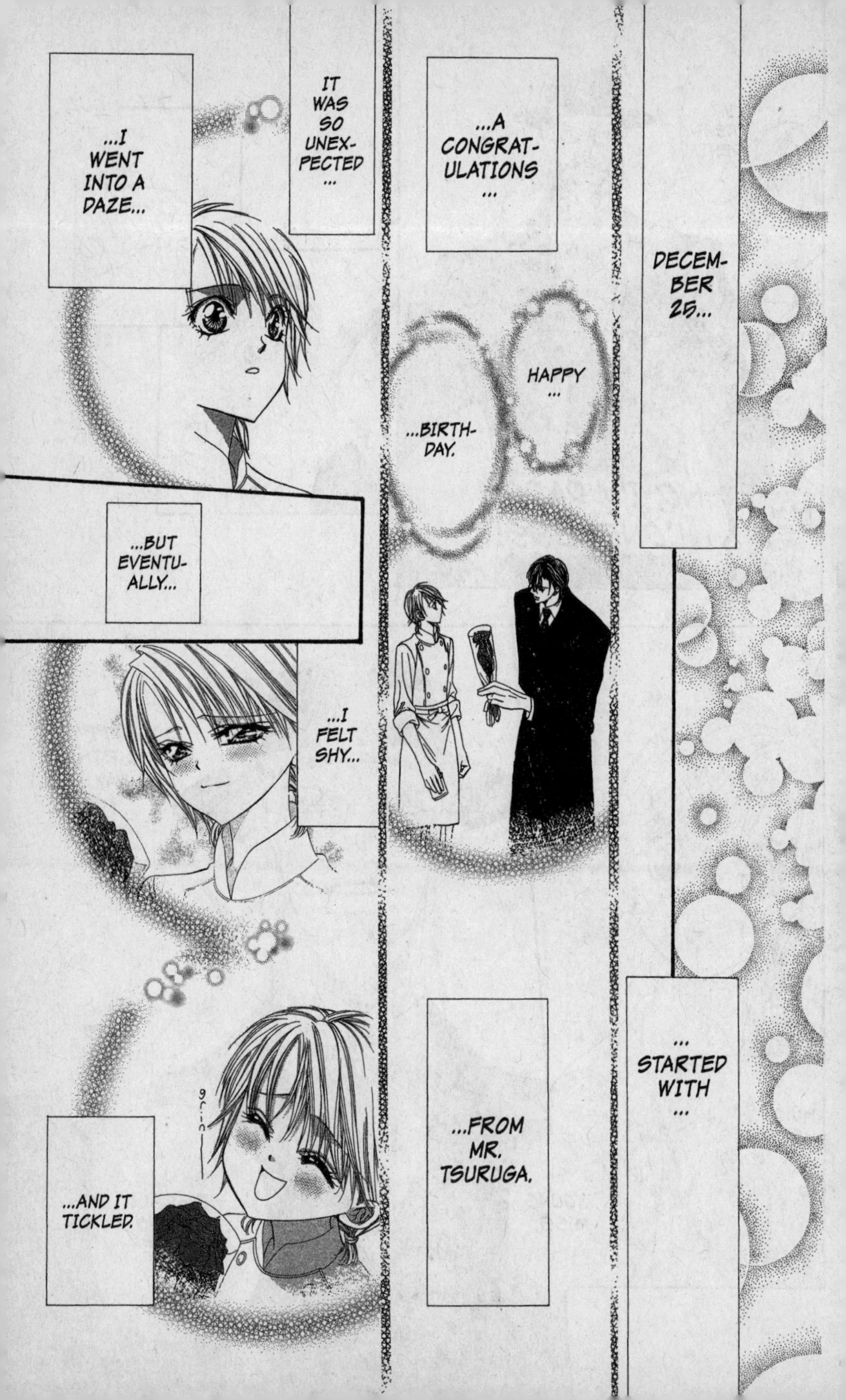
DECEMBER 25...
...STARTED WITH...
...A CONGRATULATIONS...
HAPPY...
...BIRTHDAY.
...FROM MR. TSURUGA.
IT WAS SO UNEXPECTED...
...I WENT INTO A DAZE...
...BUT EVENTUALLY...
...I FELT SHY...
...AND IT TICKLED.

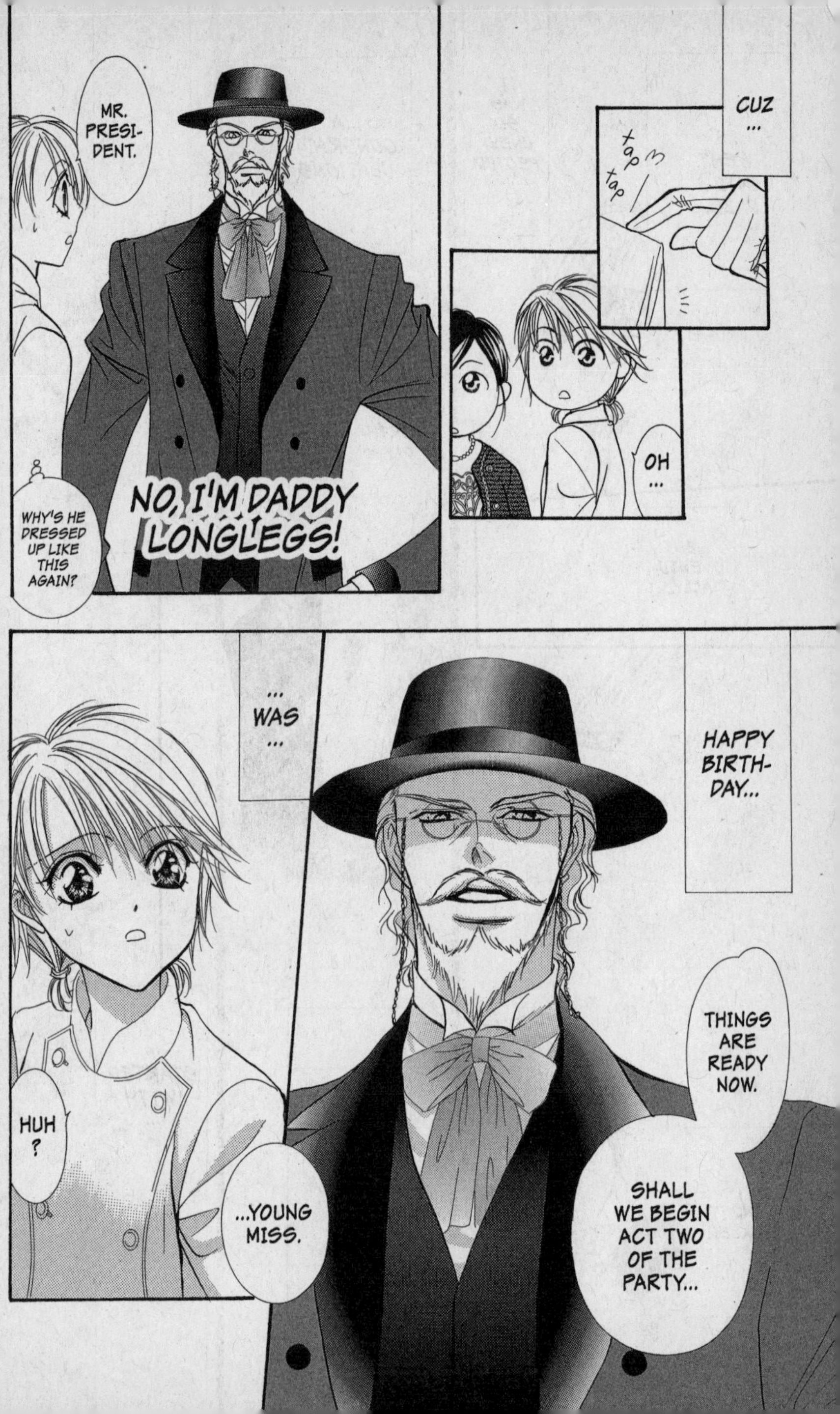
CUZ ...
tap tap
OH ...
MR. PRESI-DENT.
NO, I'M DADDY LONGLEGS!
WHY'S HE DRESSED UP LIKE THIS AGAIN?
HAPPY BIRTH-DAY...
THINGS ARE READY NOW.
SHALL WE BEGIN ACT TWO OF THE PARTY...
...YOUNG MISS.
... WAS ...
HUH?

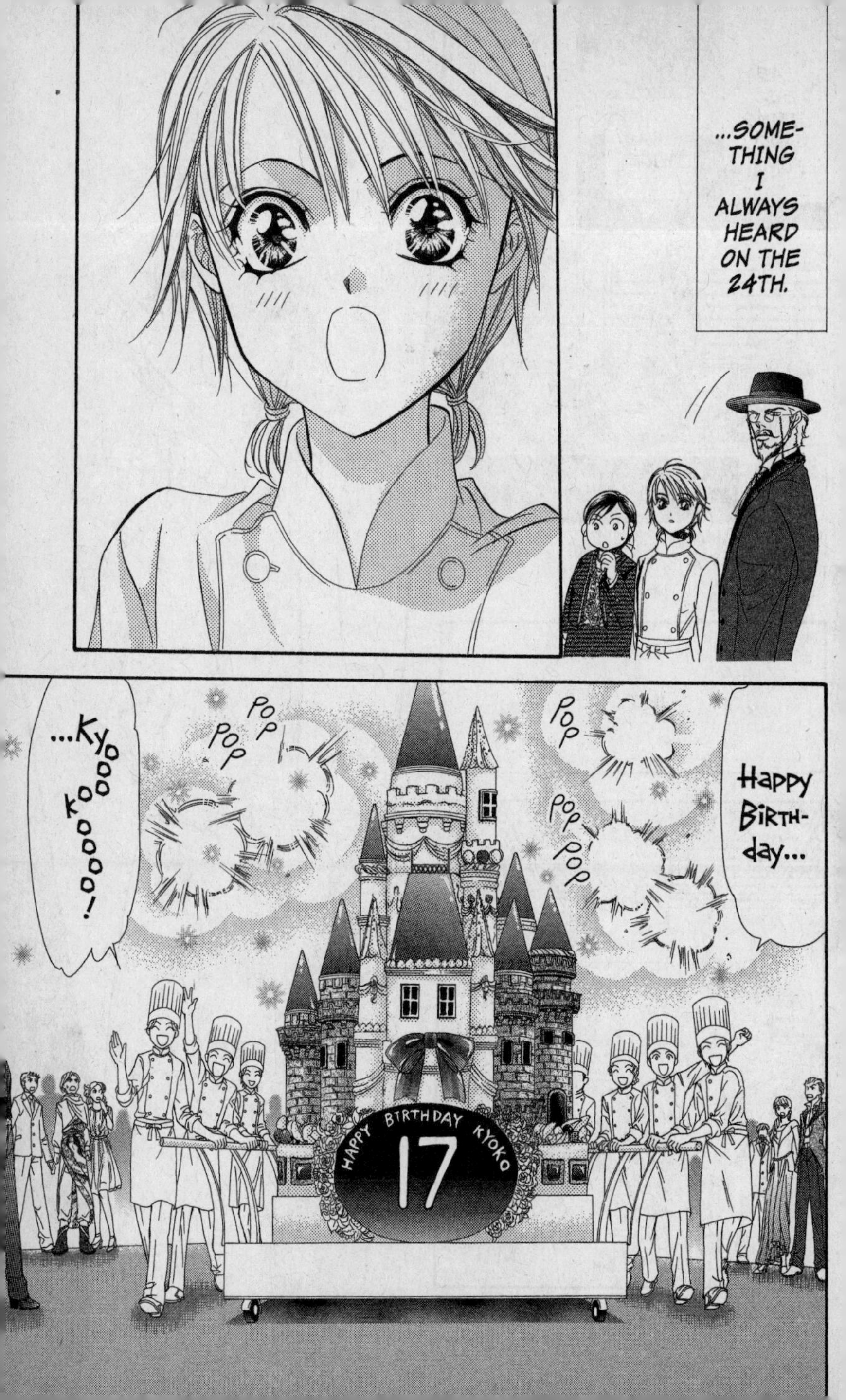
...SOME-
THING
I
ALWAYS
HEARD
ON THE
24TH.
Happy Birth-day...
...Kyoooo koooooo!
POP POP
POP
POP POP POP
HAPPY BIRTHDAY KYOKO
17

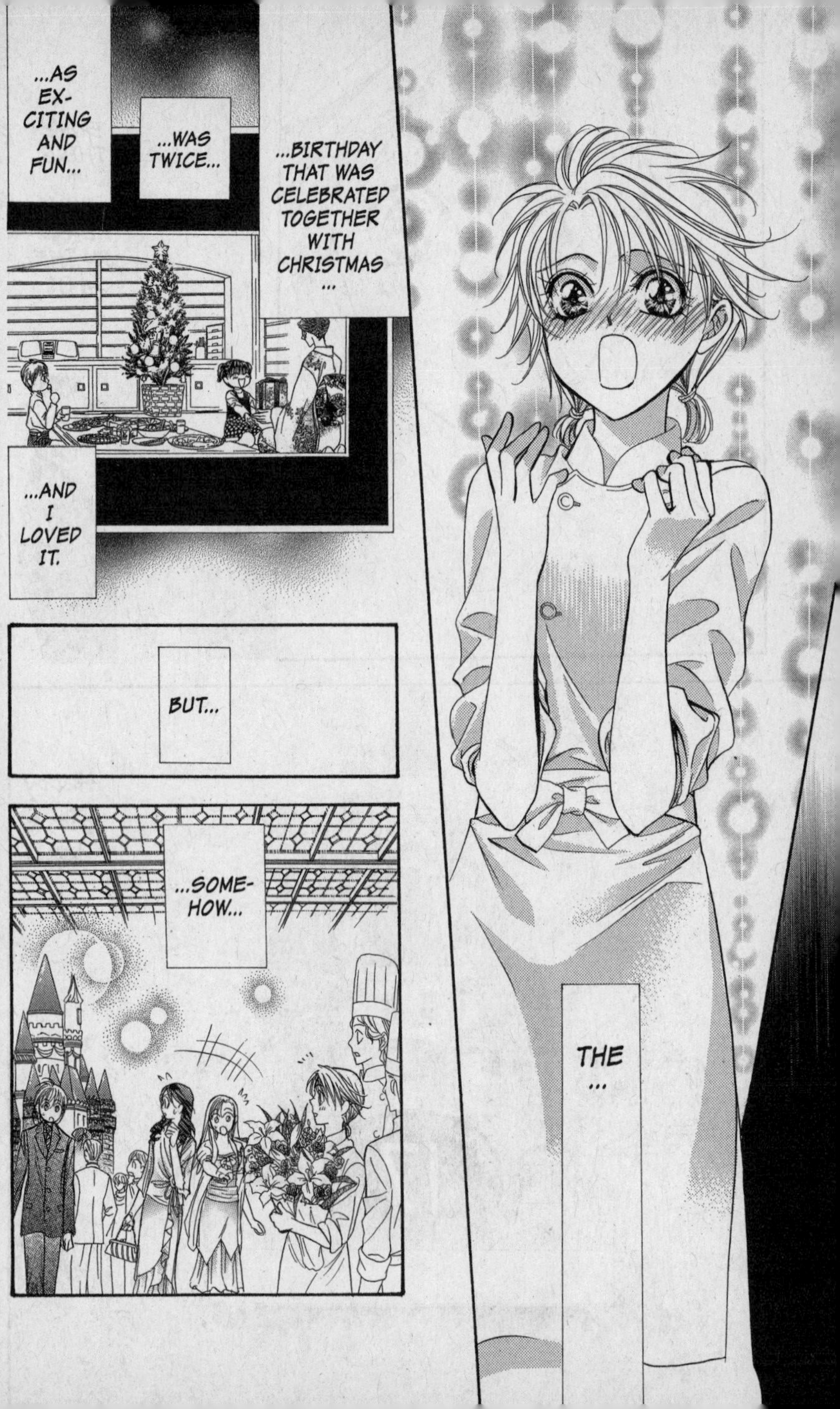
THE...
...BIRTHDAY THAT WAS CELEBRATED TOGETHER WITH CHRISTMAS...
...WAS TWICE...
...AS EX-CITING AND FUN...
...AND I LOVED IT.
BUT...
...SOME-HOW...

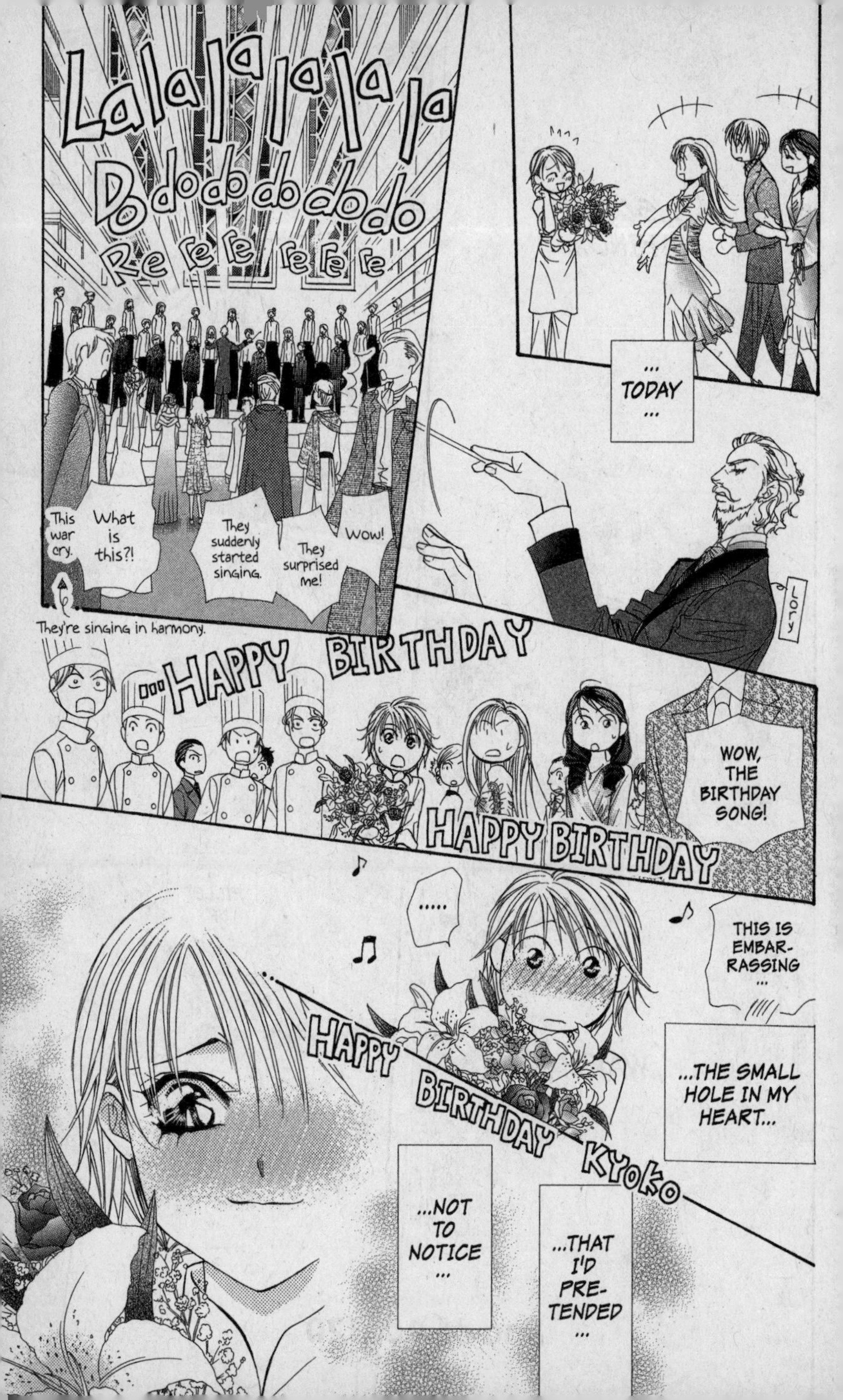
...TODAY...
Lory
Lalalalalala
Dodododododo
Rerererererere
Wow!
They surprised me!
They suddenly started singing.
What is this?!
This war cry.
They're singing in harmony.
...HAPPY BIRTHDAY
WOW, THE BIRTHDAY SONG!
HAPPY BIRTHDAY
THIS IS EMBARRASSING...
.....
HAPPY BIRTHDAY KYOKO
...THE SMALL HOLE IN MY HEART...
...THAT I'D PRETENDED...
...NOT TO NOTICE...

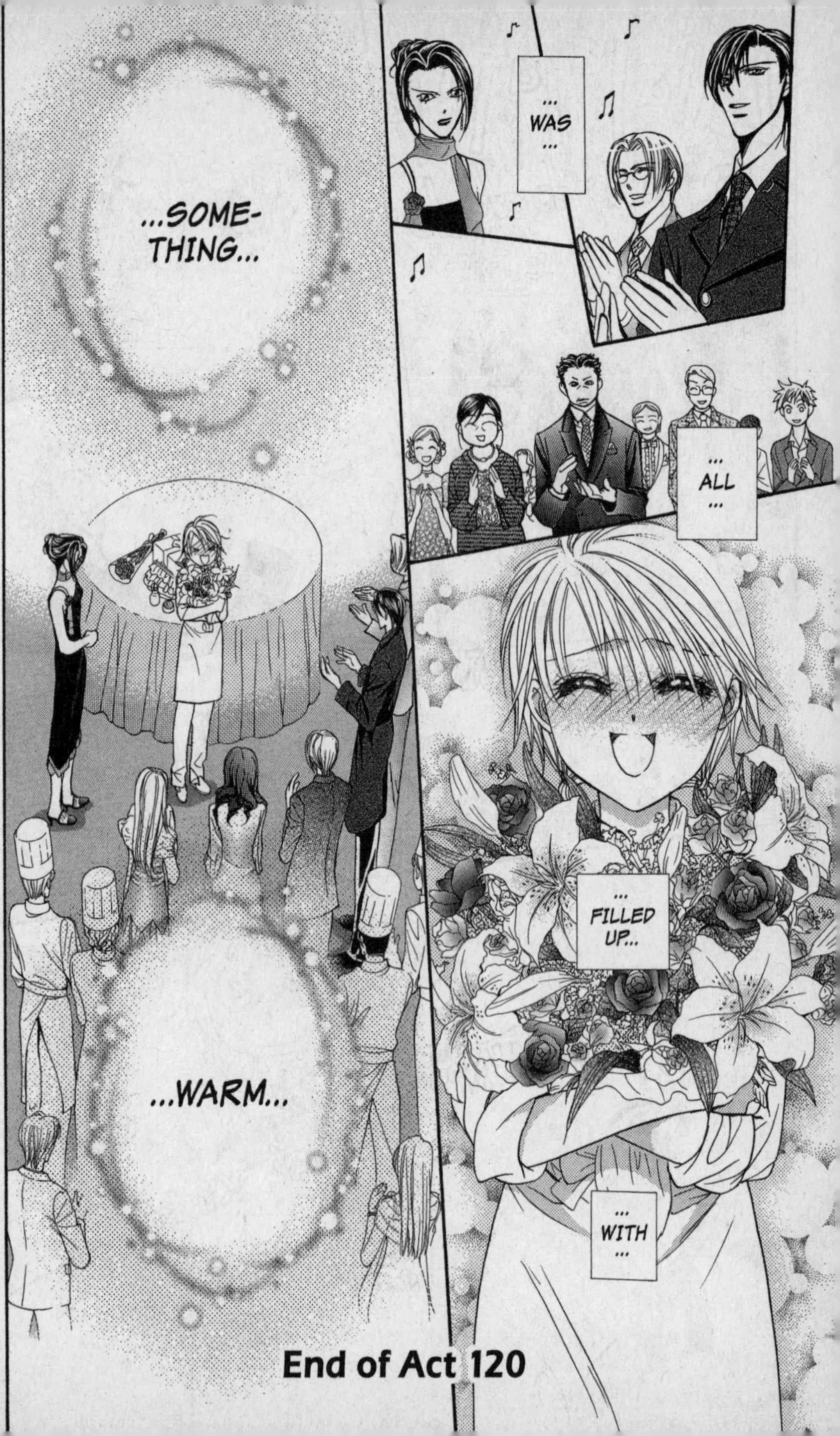
...WAS...
...ALL...
...FILLED UP...
...WITH...
...SOME-THING...
...WARM...

End of Act 120

Skip-Beat! End Notes

Everyone knows how to be a fan, but sometimes cool things from other cultures need a little help crossing the language barrier.

Page 265, panel 8: Tora
This can mean "tiger" depending on the kanji used. In the Japanese, his nickname is spelled phonetically using katakana rather than kanji.

Page 282, panel 3: Yakuza
Moko is reacting to Maria's use of the phrase "good job." In the Japanese, the term she uses can also have the connotation of congratulating someone for finishing a prison sentence.

Page 282, panel 6: The idler
Kyoko is thinking of the character "Tora-san" from the movie series *Otoko wa Tsuraiyo*. In the series, Tora-san wanders all over Japan.

Page 282, panel 6: Tiger
Moko is thinking of the professional wrestler Tiger Mask.

Page 282, panel 7: Toraichi
Now Kyoko is thinking of a company that makes work uniforms for scaffolders. The kanji used for tora is the kanji that means "tiger."

Page 299, panel 3: Niagara
A type of big firework that looks like a waterfall.

Page 357, panel 1: Kyoko's thought balloon
This is a Hannya, a Noh mask with the face of a female demon.

Shojo Beat

Skip·Beat!

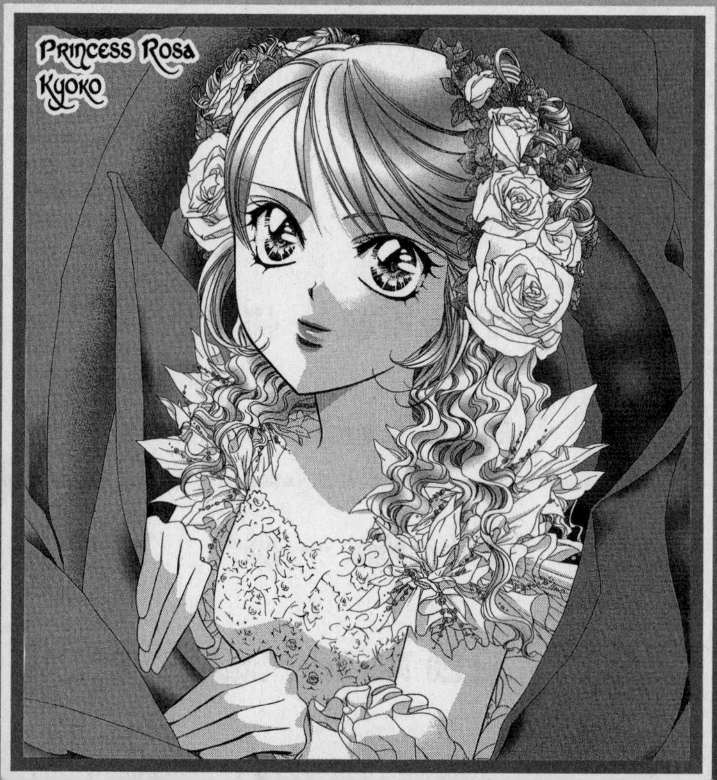
Princess Rosa
Kyoko

Skip·Beat!

Volume 21

CONTENTS

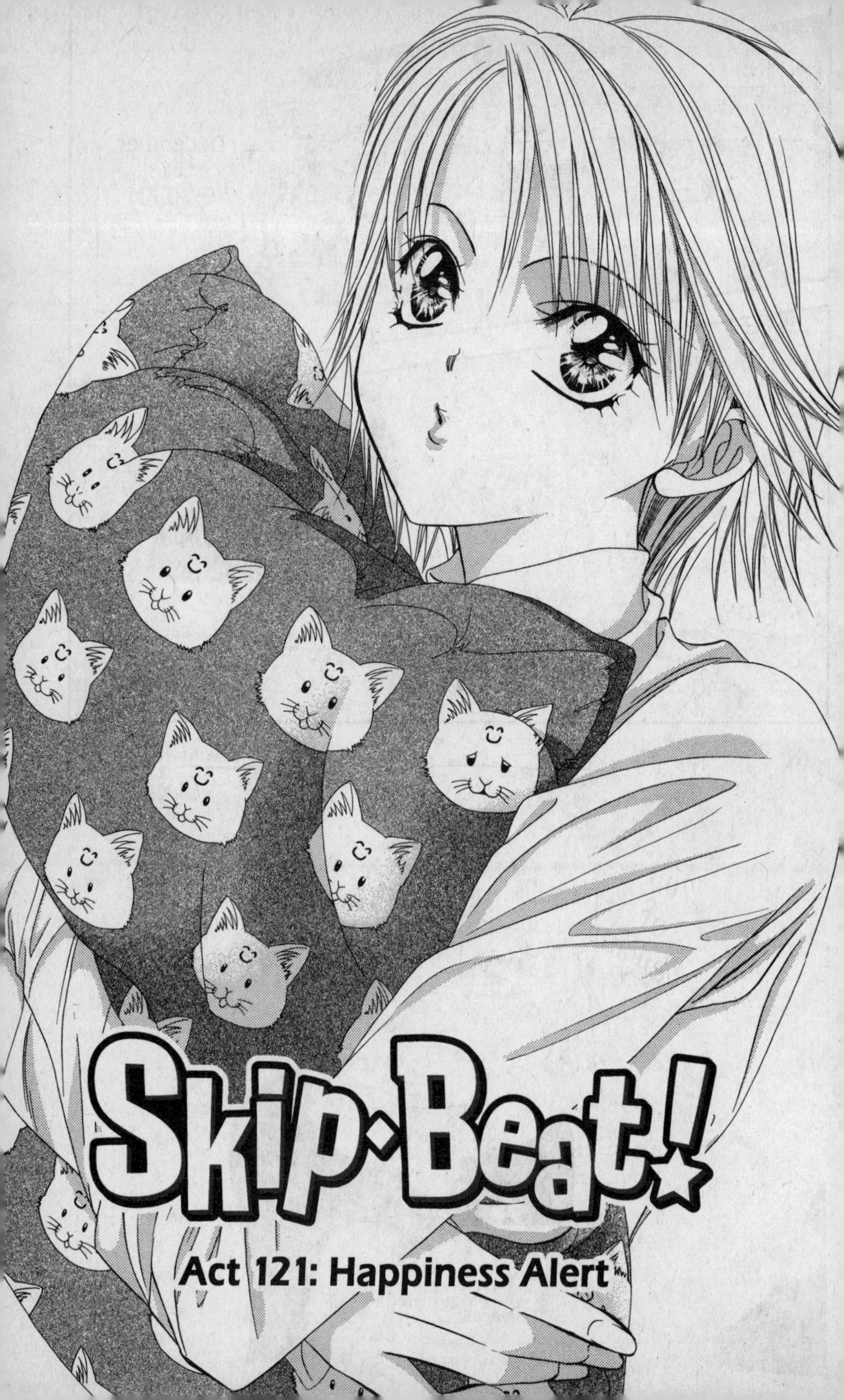
Skip·Beat!
Act 121: Happiness Alert

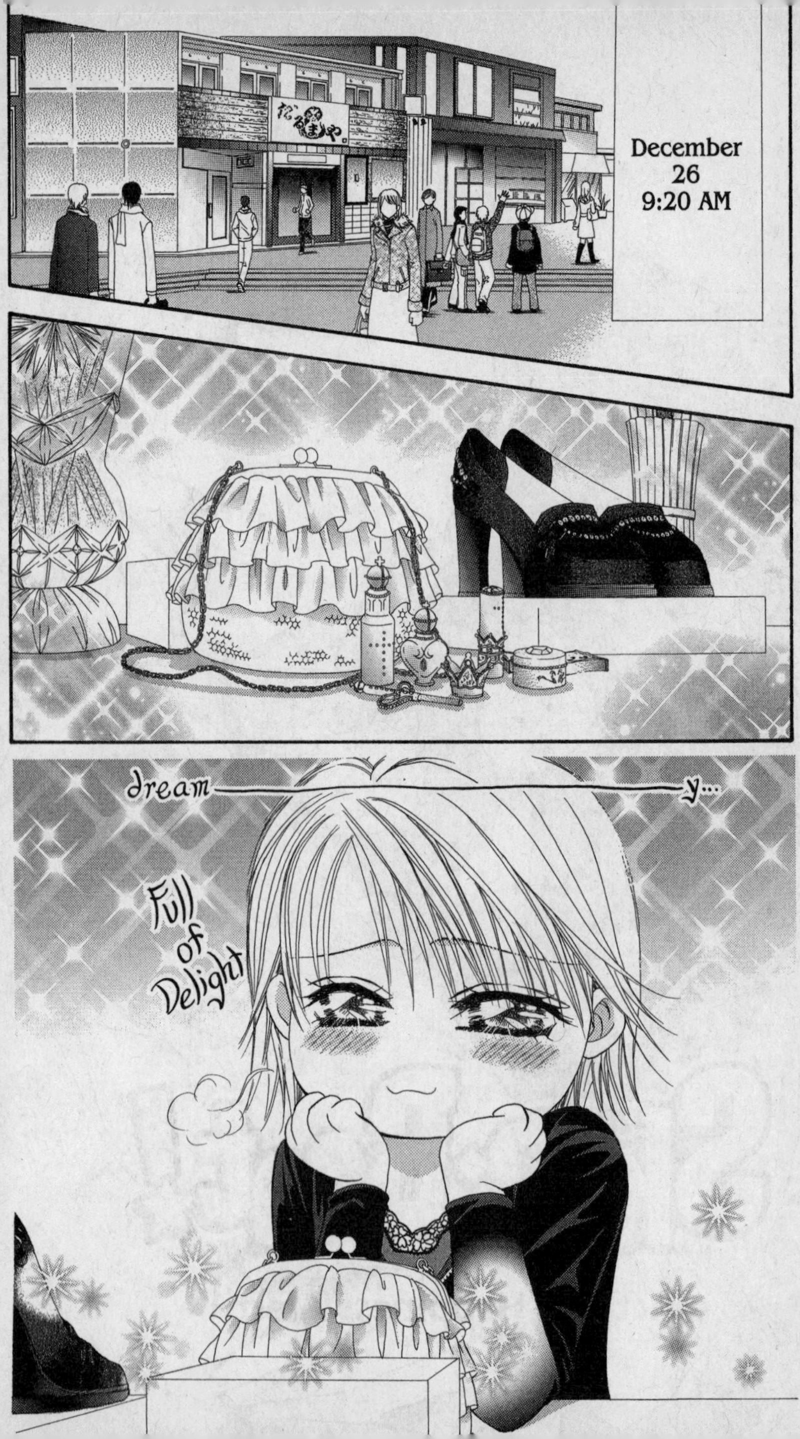
December
26
9:20 AM
dream———y...
Full of Delight

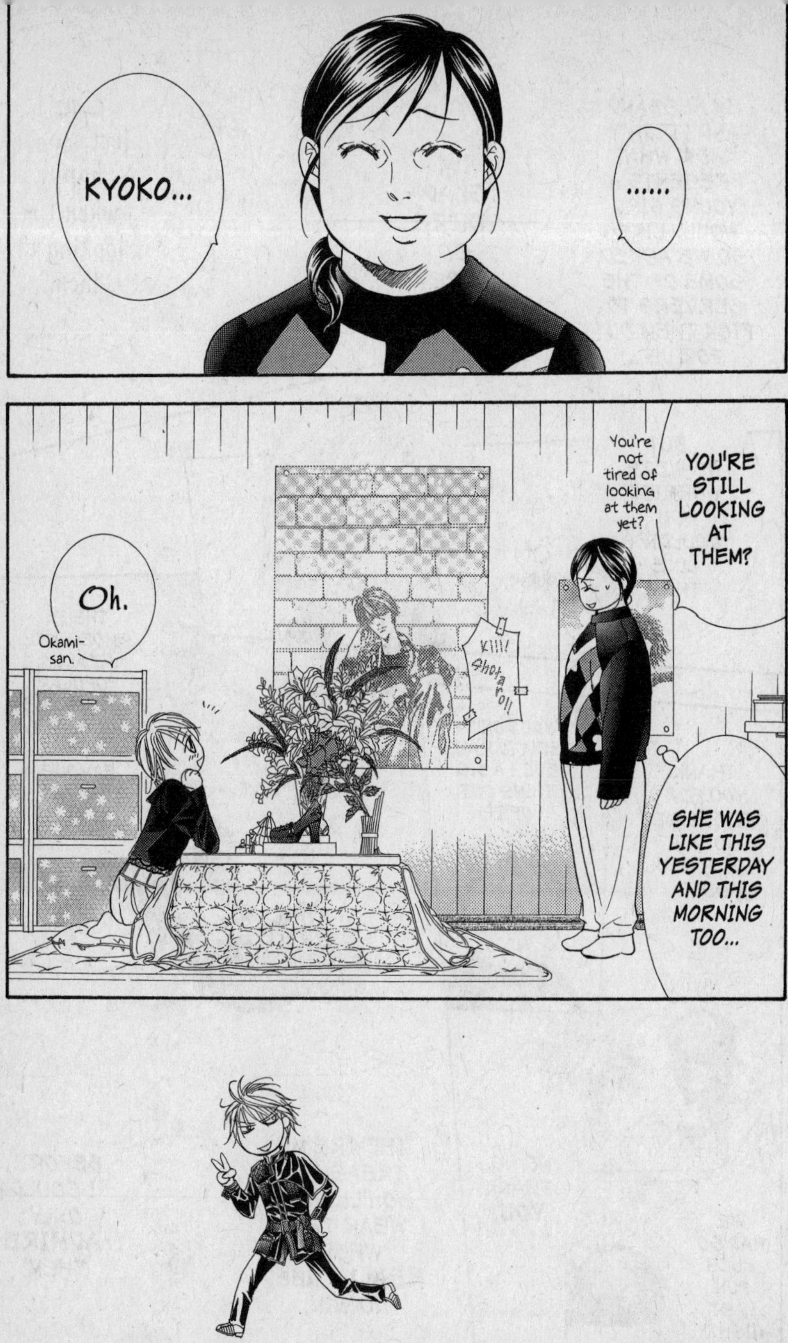
......
KYOKO...
YOU'RE STILL LOOKING AT THEM?
You're not tired of looking at them yet?
SHE WAS LIKE THIS YESTERDAY AND THIS MORNING TOO...
Kill! Shotaro!!
Oh.
Okami-san.

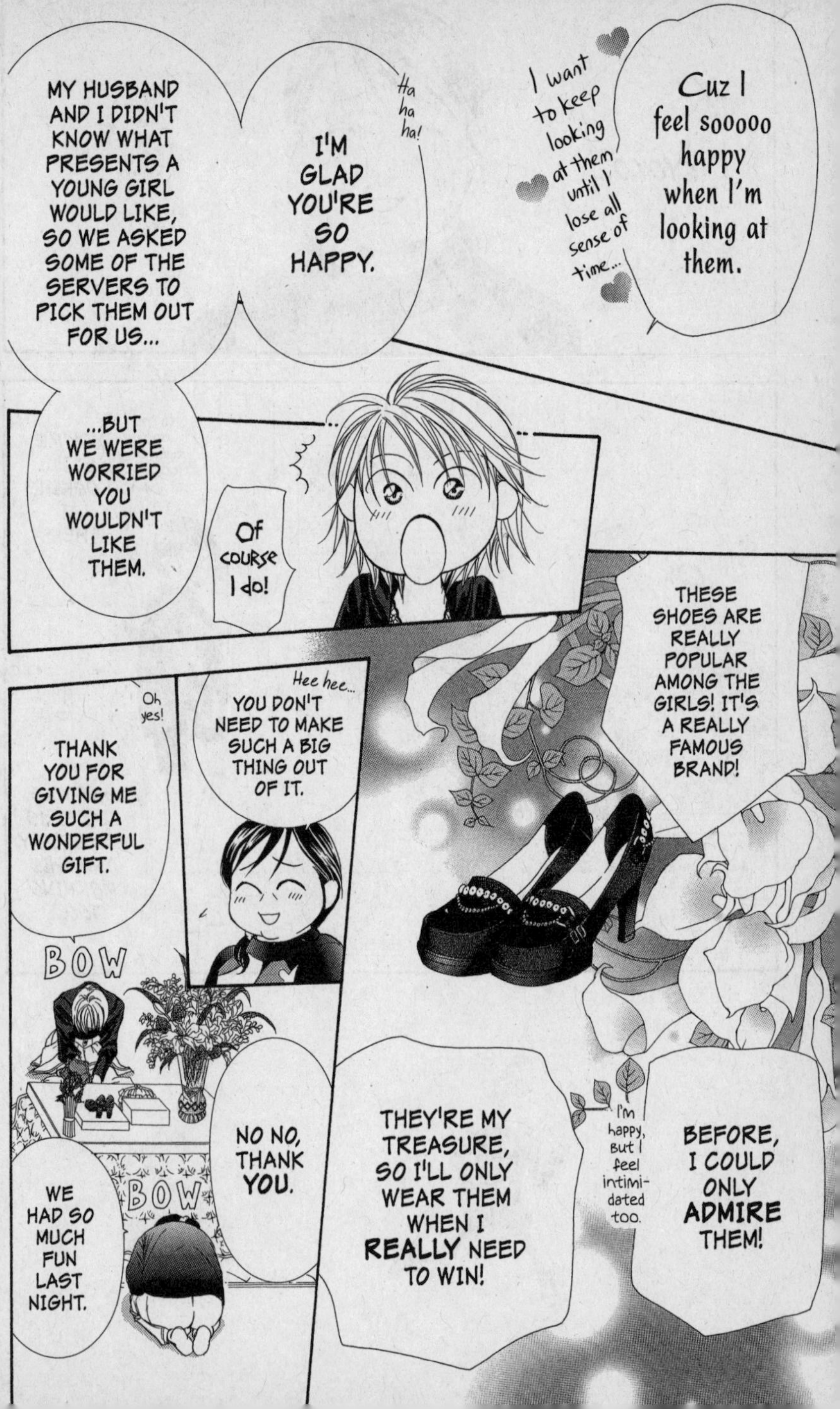
Cuz I feel sooooo happy when I'm looking at them.
I want to keep looking at them until I lose all sense of time...
Ha ha ha!
I'M GLAD YOU'RE SO HAPPY.
MY HUSBAND AND I DIDN'T KNOW WHAT PRESENTS A YOUNG GIRL WOULD LIKE, SO WE ASKED SOME OF THE SERVERS TO PICK THEM OUT FOR US...
...BUT WE WERE WORRIED YOU WOULDN'T LIKE THEM.
...
...
Of course I do!
THESE SHOES ARE REALLY POPULAR AMONG THE GIRLS! IT'S A REALLY FAMOUS BRAND!
BEFORE, I COULD ONLY ADMIRE THEM!
I'm happy, but I feel intimidated too.
THEY'RE MY TREASURE, SO I'LL ONLY WEAR THEM WHEN I REALLY NEED TO WIN!
Hee hee...
YOU DON'T NEED TO MAKE SUCH A BIG THING OUT OF IT.
Oh yes!
THANK YOU FOR GIVING ME SUCH A WONDERFUL GIFT.
BOW
NO NO, THANK YOU.
BOW
WE HAD SO MUCH FUN LAST NIGHT.

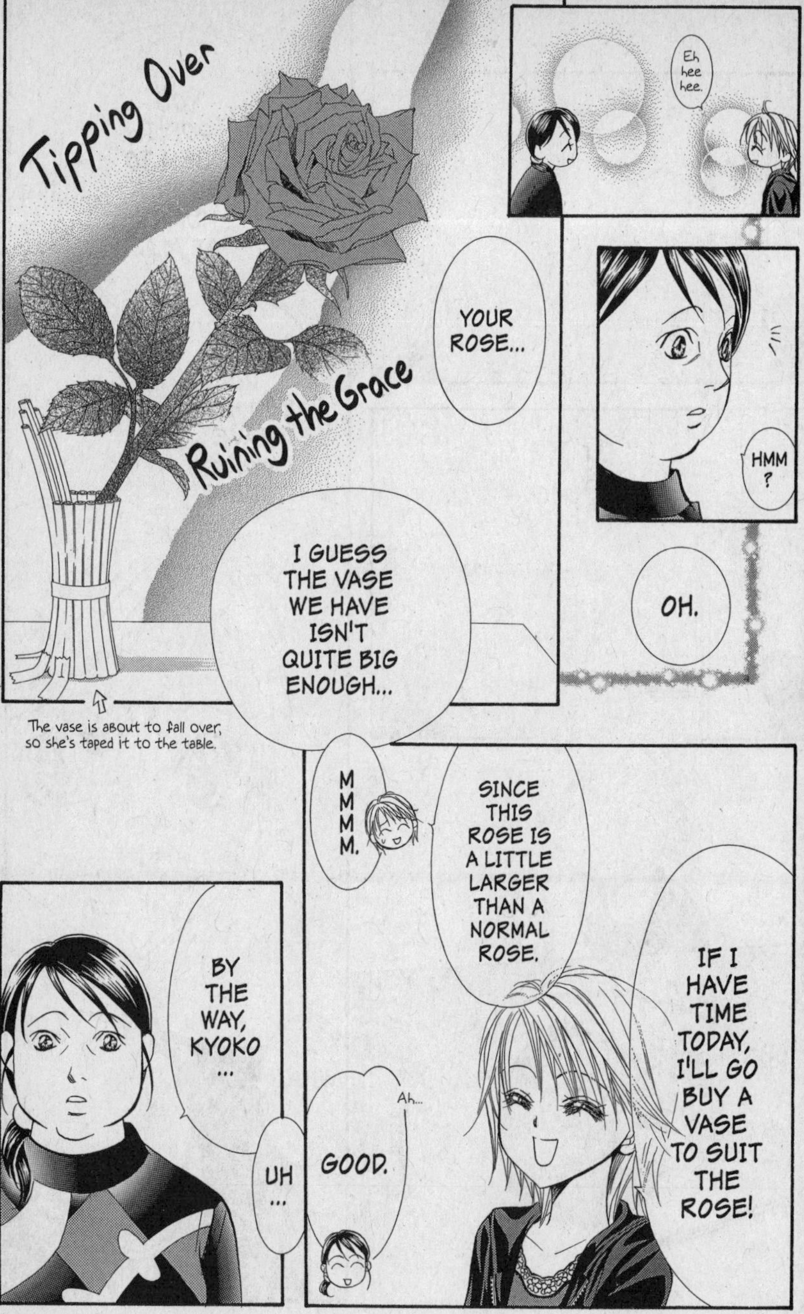

Eh hee hee.
YOUR ROSE...
HMM?
OH.
Tipping Over
Ruining the Grace
I GUESS THE VASE WE HAVE ISN'T QUITE BIG ENOUGH...
The vase is about to fall over, so she's taped it to the table.
IF I HAVE TIME TODAY, I'LL GO BUY A VASE TO SUIT THE ROSE!
SINCE THIS ROSE IS A LITTLE LARGER THAN A NORMAL ROSE.
MMMM.
Ah...
GOOD.
UH...
BY THE WAY, KYOKO...

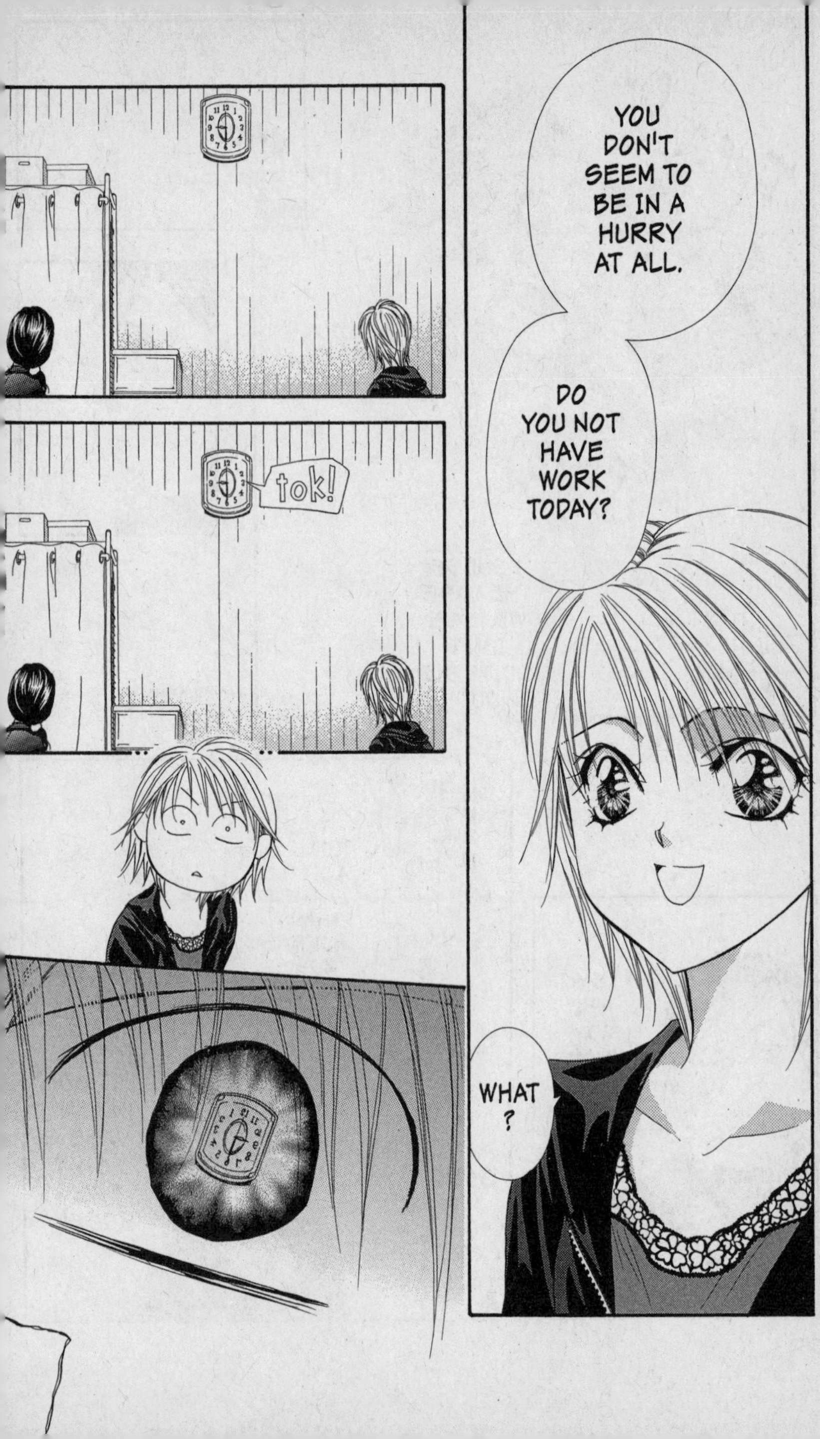
YOU DON'T SEEM TO BE IN A HURRY AT ALL.
DO YOU NOT HAVE WORK TODAY?
WHAT?
tok!

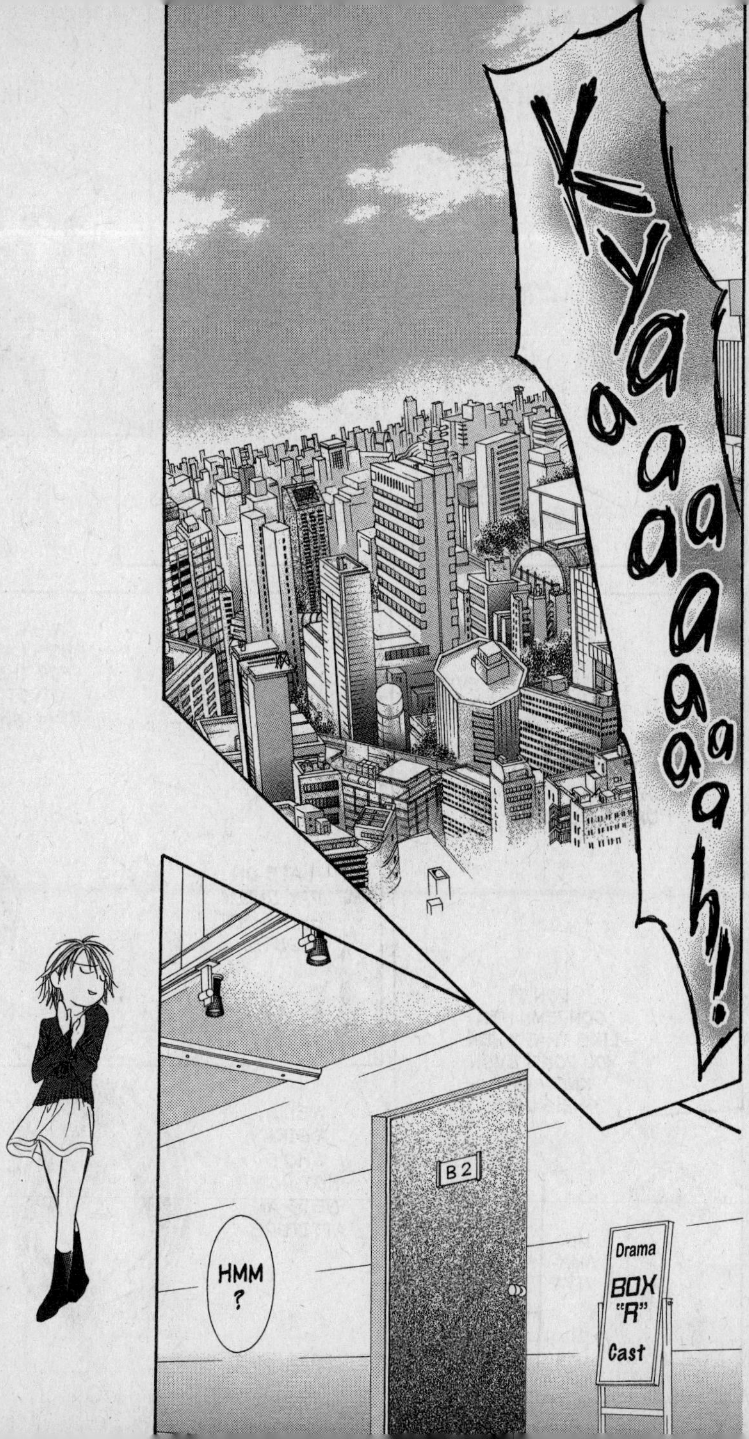
Kyaaaaaaaaaah!!
B2
Drama BOX "R" Cast
HMM ?

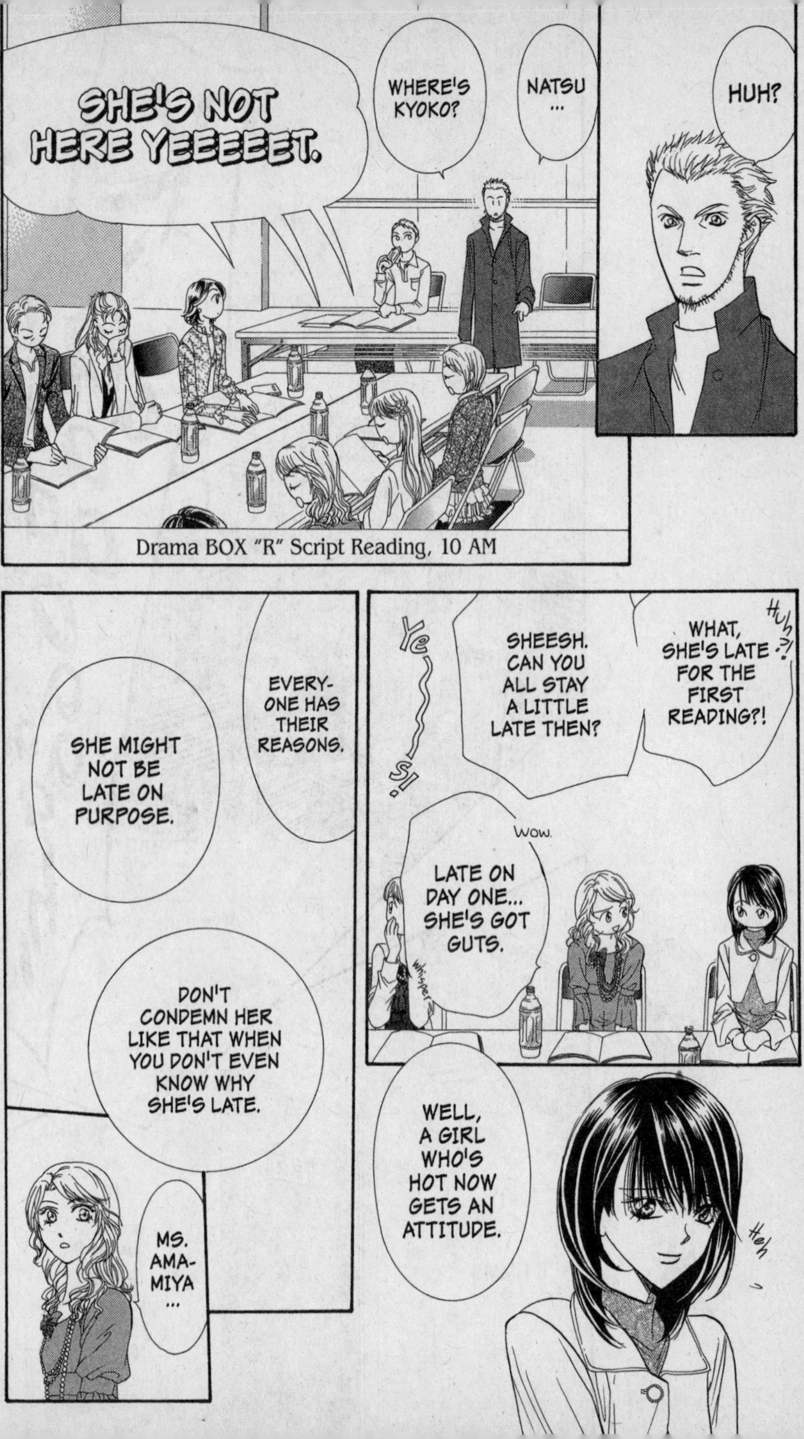
HUH?
NATSU...
WHERE'S KYOKO?
SHE'S NOT HERE YEEEEEET.
Drama BOX "R" Script Reading, 10 AM
Huh?!
WHAT, SHE'S LATE FOR THE FIRST READING?!
SHEESH. CAN YOU ALL STAY A LITTLE LATE THEN?
Ye---s!
Wow.
LATE ON DAY ONE... SHE'S GOT GUTS.
whisper
WELL, A GIRL WHO'S HOT NOW GETS AN ATTITUDE.
Heh
EVERY-ONE HAS THEIR REASONS.
SHE MIGHT NOT BE LATE ON PURPOSE.
DON'T CONDEMN HER LIKE THAT WHEN YOU DON'T EVEN KNOW WHY SHE'S LATE.
MS. AMA-MIYA...

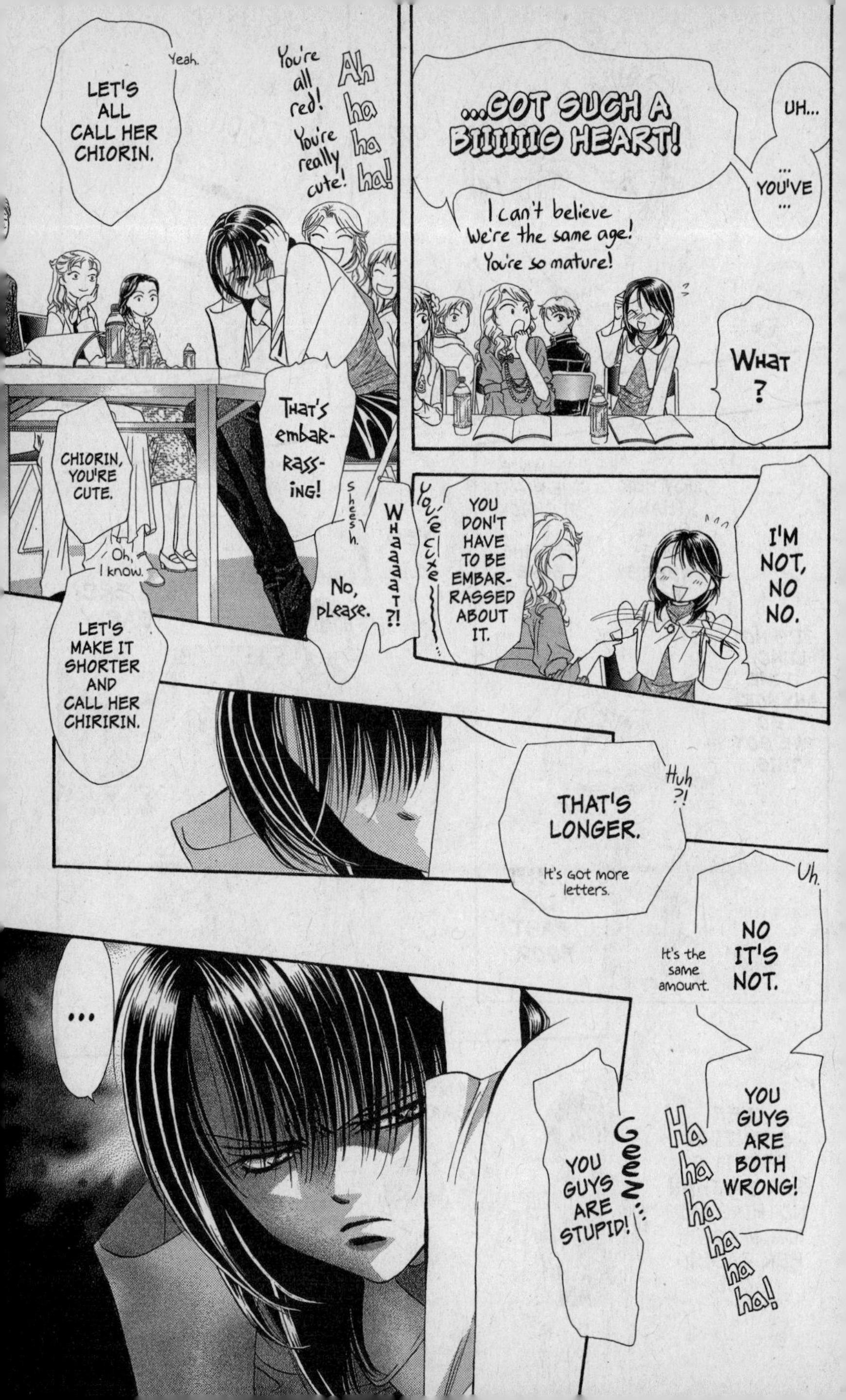
UH...
...YOU'VE...
...GOT SUCH A BIIIIIIG HEART!
I can't believe we're the same age! You're so mature!
WHAT?
I'M NOT, NO NO.
YOU DON'T HAVE TO BE EMBARRASSED ABOUT IT.
You're cute~...
Ah ha ha ha!
You're all red! You're really cute!
Yeah.
LET'S ALL CALL HER CHIORIN.
That's embar-rass-ing!
Sheesh.
Whaaaaat?!
No, please.
CHIORIN, YOU'RE CUTE.
Oh, I know.
LET'S MAKE IT SHORTER AND CALL HER CHIRIRIN.
Huh?!
THAT'S LONGER.
It's got more letters.
Uh.
NO IT'S NOT.
It's the same amount.
YOU GUYS ARE BOTH WRONG!
Ha ha ha ha ha ha!
Geez...
YOU GUYS ARE STUPID!
...

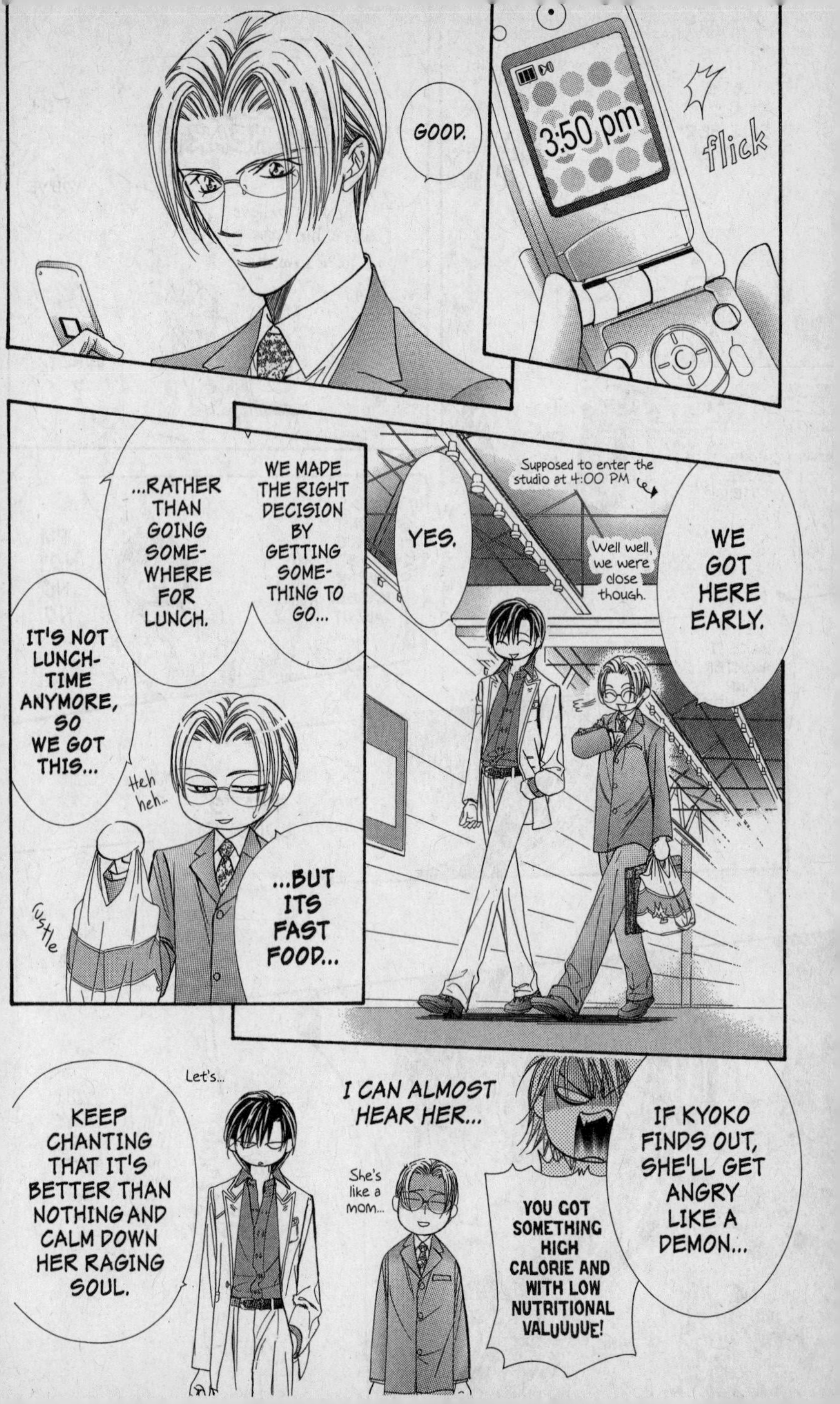
3:50 pm
flick
GOOD.
Supposed to enter the studio at 4:00 PM
WE GOT HERE EARLY.
Well well, we were close though.
YES.
WE MADE THE RIGHT DECISION BY GETTING SOME-THING TO GO...
...RATHER THAN GOING SOME-WHERE FOR LUNCH.
IT'S NOT LUNCH-TIME ANYMORE, SO WE GOT THIS...
Heh heh...
...BUT ITS FAST FOOD...
rustle
IF KYOKO FINDS OUT, SHE'LL GET ANGRY LIKE A DEMON...
YOU GOT SOMETHING HIGH CALORIE AND WITH LOW NUTRITIONAL VALUUUUE!
I CAN ALMOST HEAR HER...
She's like a mom...
Let's...
KEEP CHANTING THAT IT'S BETTER THAN NOTHING AND CALM DOWN HER RAGING SOUL.

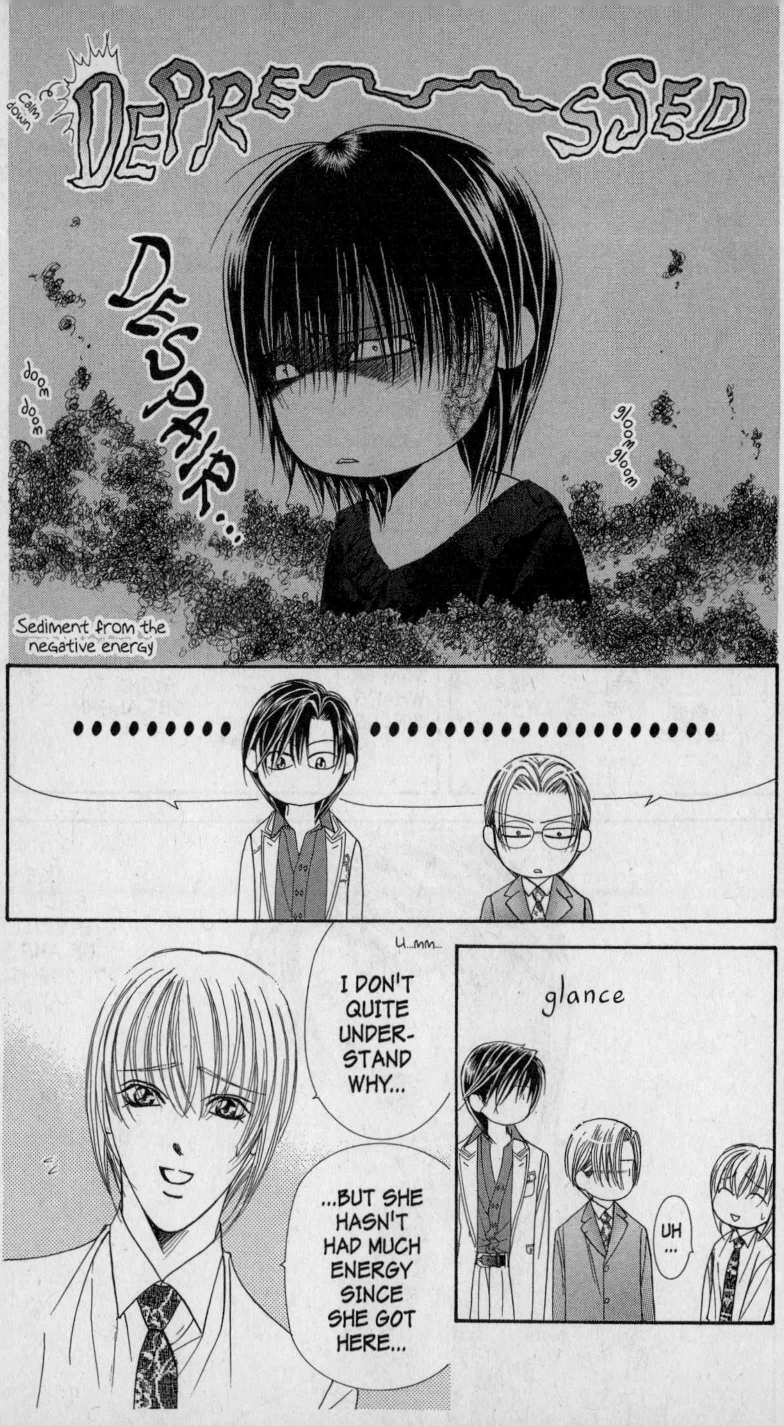
DEPRE~~~SSED
calm down
DESPAIR...
gloom gloom
doom doom
Sediment from the negative energy
....
....
glance
UH ...
u...mm...
I DON'T QUITE UNDERSTAND WHY...
...BUT SHE HASN'T HAD MUCH ENERGY SINCE SHE GOT HERE...

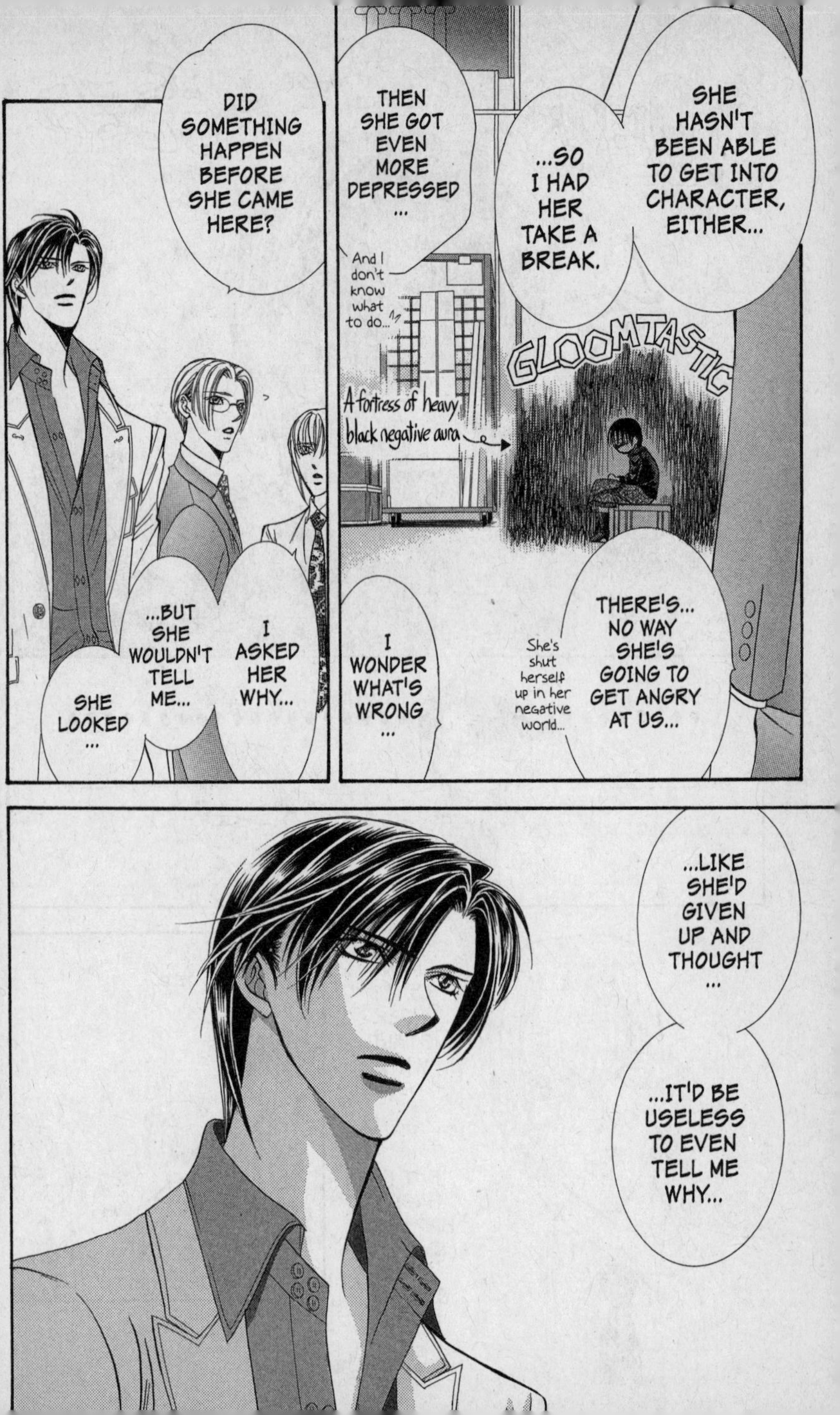
SHE HASN'T BEEN ABLE TO GET INTO CHARACTER, EITHER...
...SO I HAD HER TAKE A BREAK.
THEN SHE GOT EVEN MORE DEPRESSED...
And I don't know what to do...
GLOOMTASTIC
A fortress of heavy black negative aura
THERE'S... NO WAY SHE'S GOING TO GET ANGRY AT US...
She's shut herself up in her negative world...
I WONDER WHAT'S WRONG...
DID SOMETHING HAPPEN BEFORE SHE CAME HERE?
I ASKED HER WHY...
...BUT SHE WOULDN'T TELL ME...
SHE LOOKED...
...LIKE SHE'D GIVEN UP AND THOUGHT...
...IT'D BE USELESS TO EVEN TELL ME WHY...

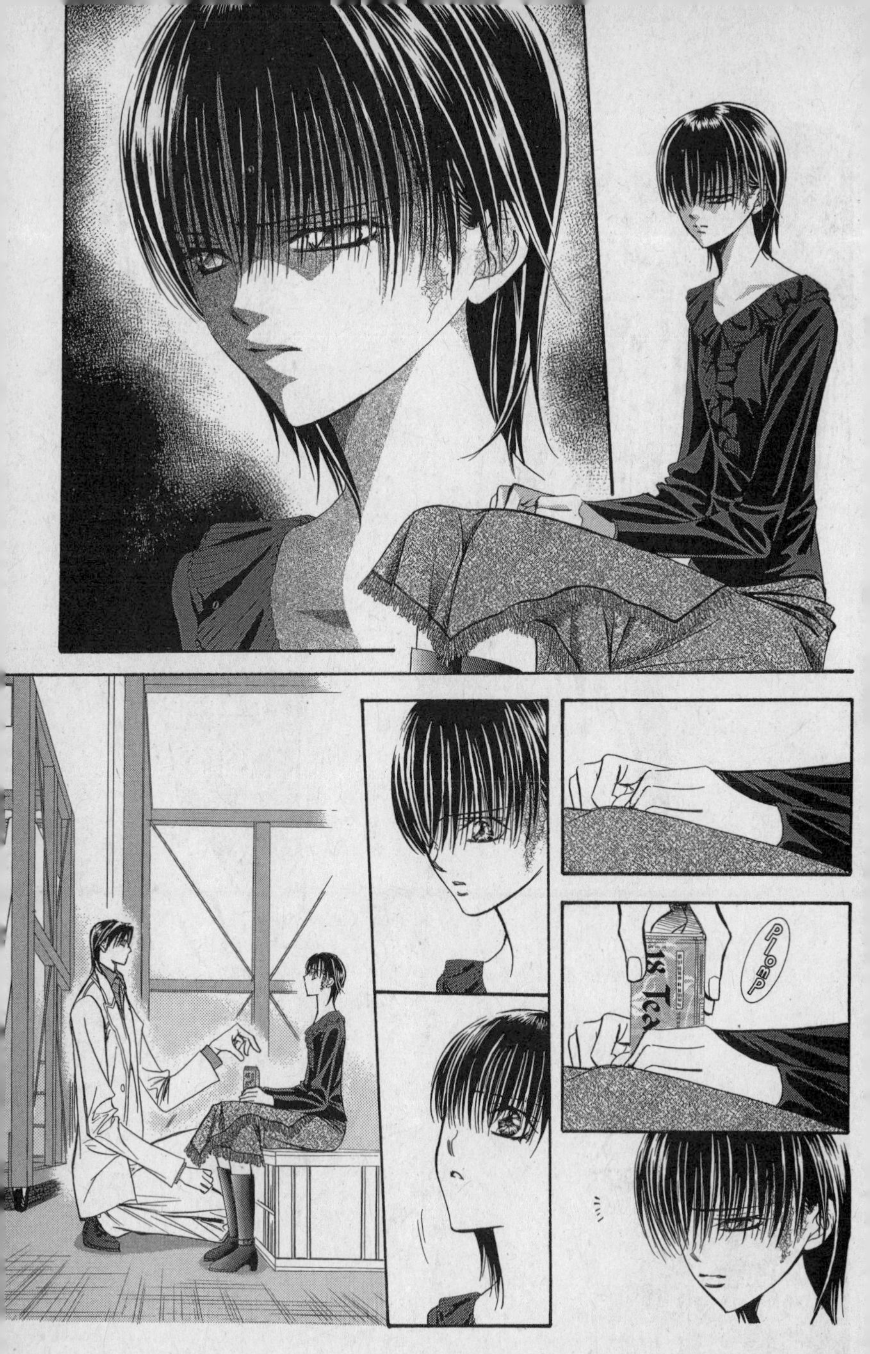
18 Tea
PLOMP

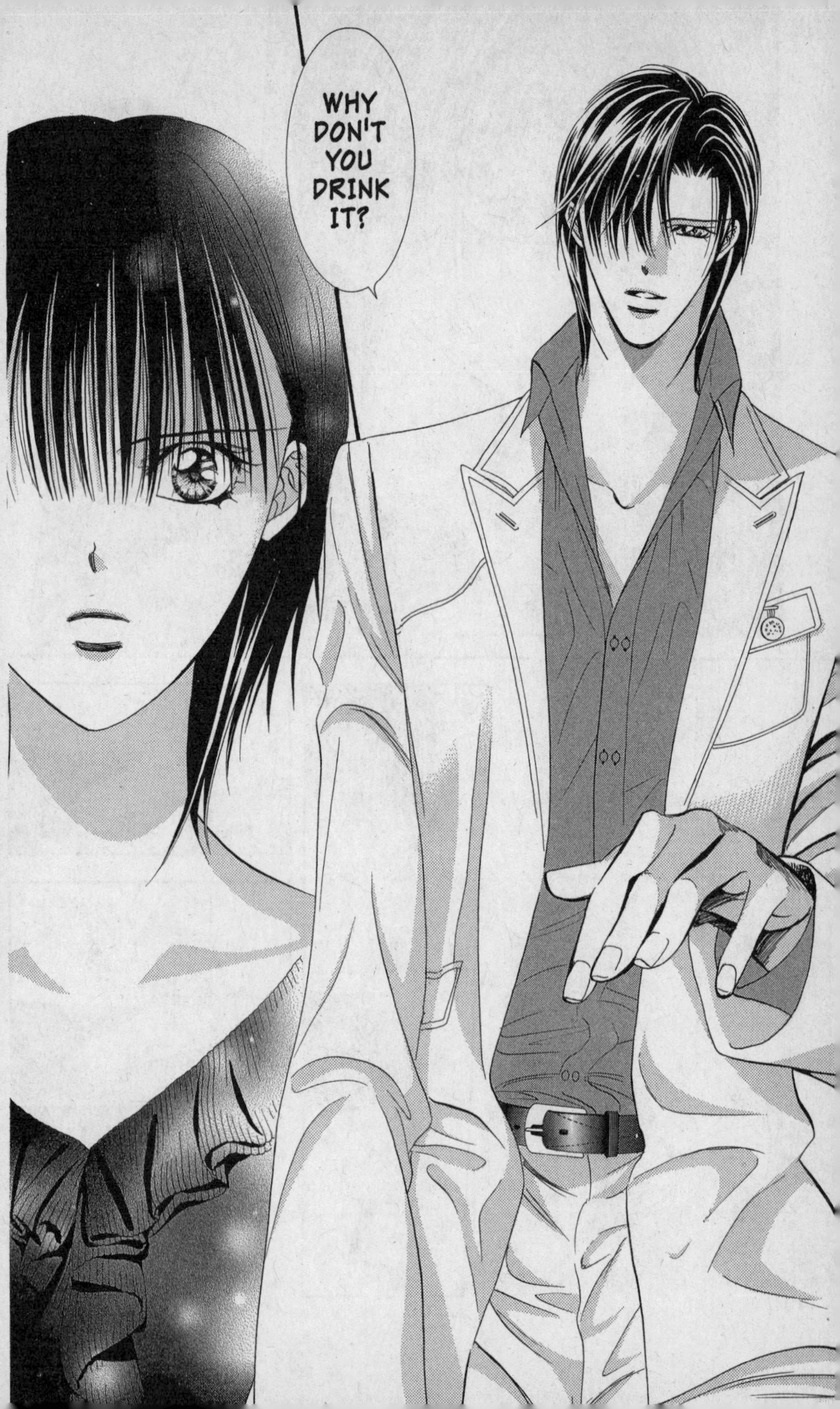
WHY DON'T YOU DRINK IT?

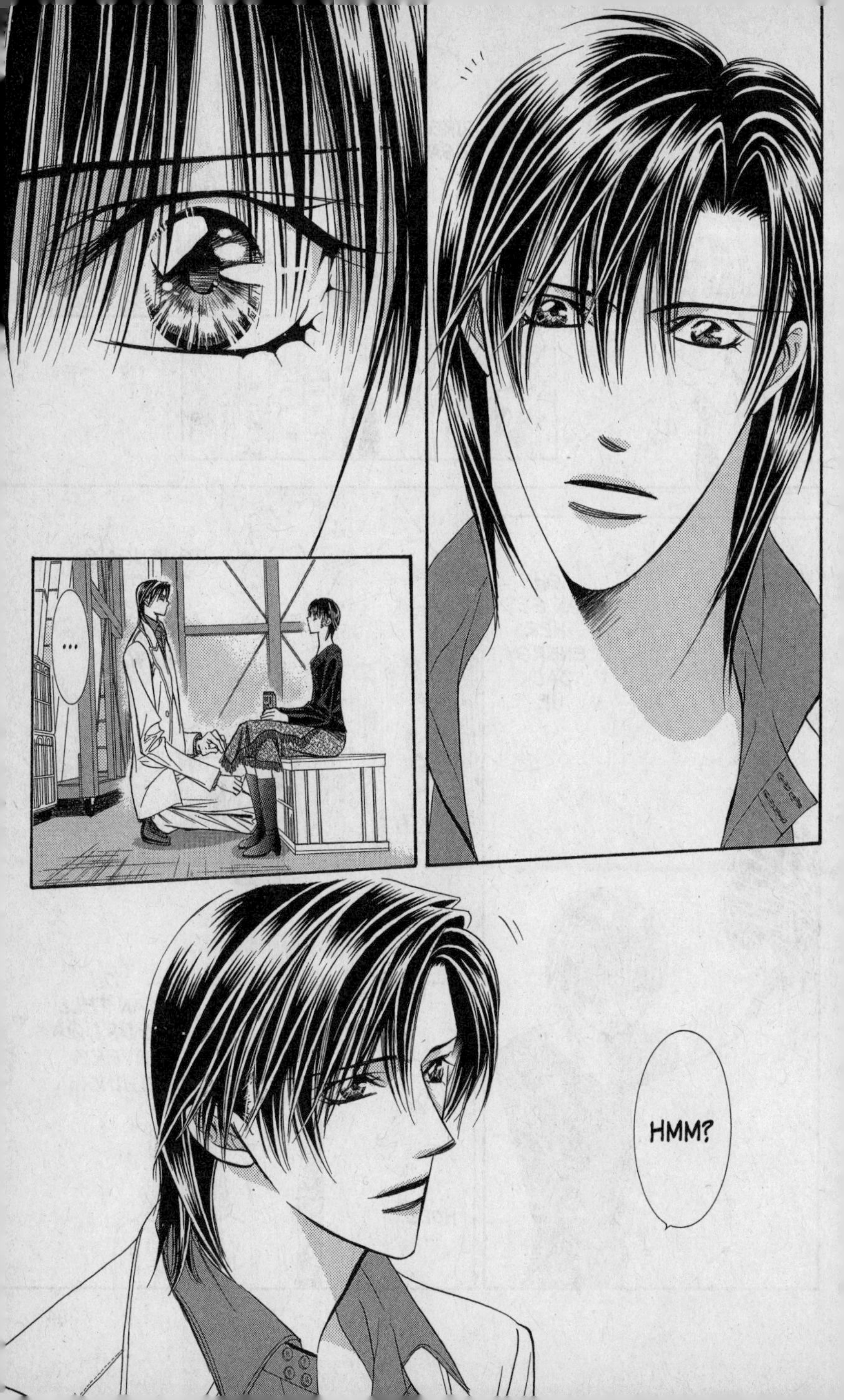
...
HMM?

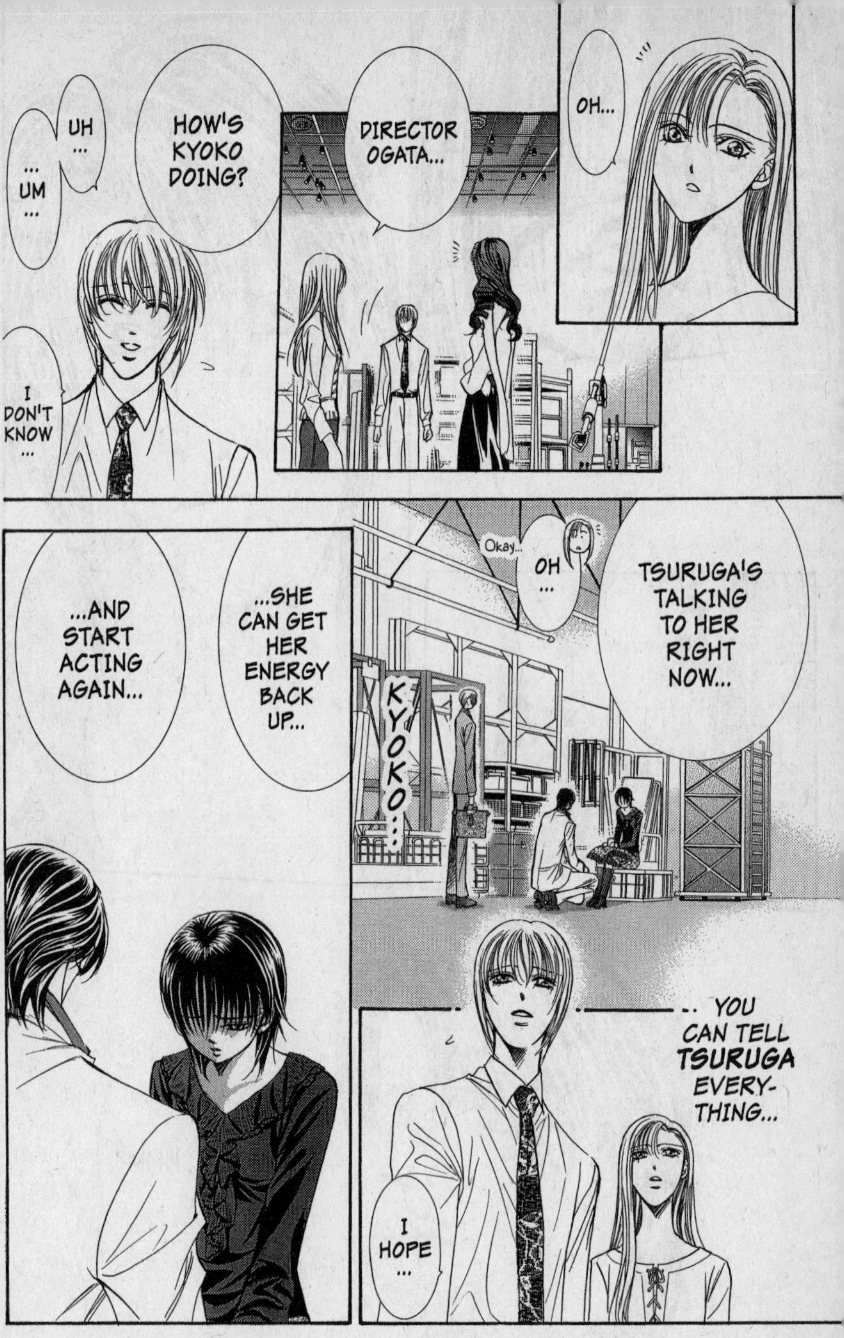
OH...
DIRECTOR OGATA...
HOW'S KYOKO DOING?
UH...
...UM...
I DON'T KNOW...
TSURUGA'S TALKING TO HER RIGHT NOW...
OH...
Okay...
KYOKO...
...YOU CAN TELL TSURUGA EVERYTHING...
I HOPE...
...SHE CAN GET HER ENERGY BACK UP...
...AND START ACTING AGAIN...

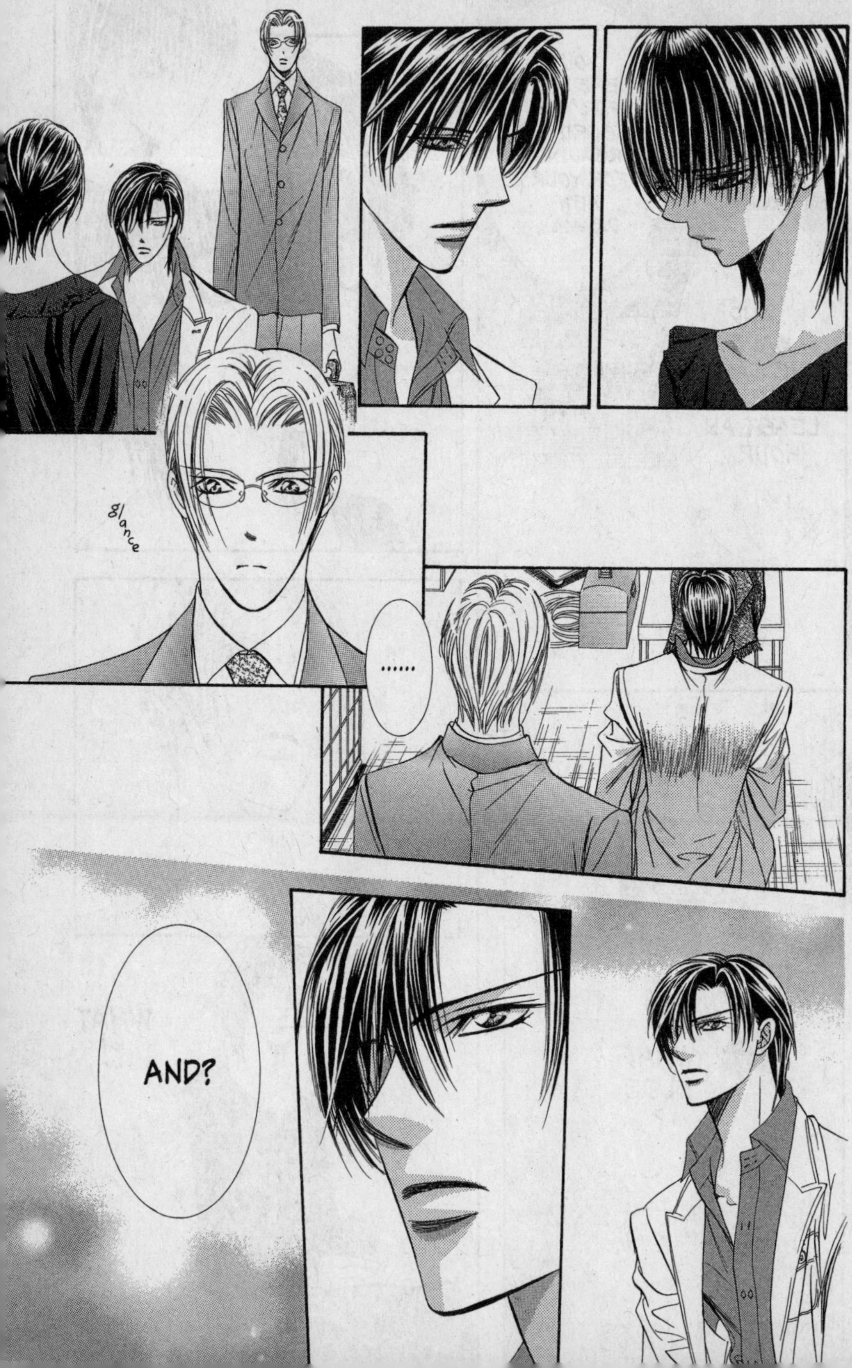
glance
......
AND?

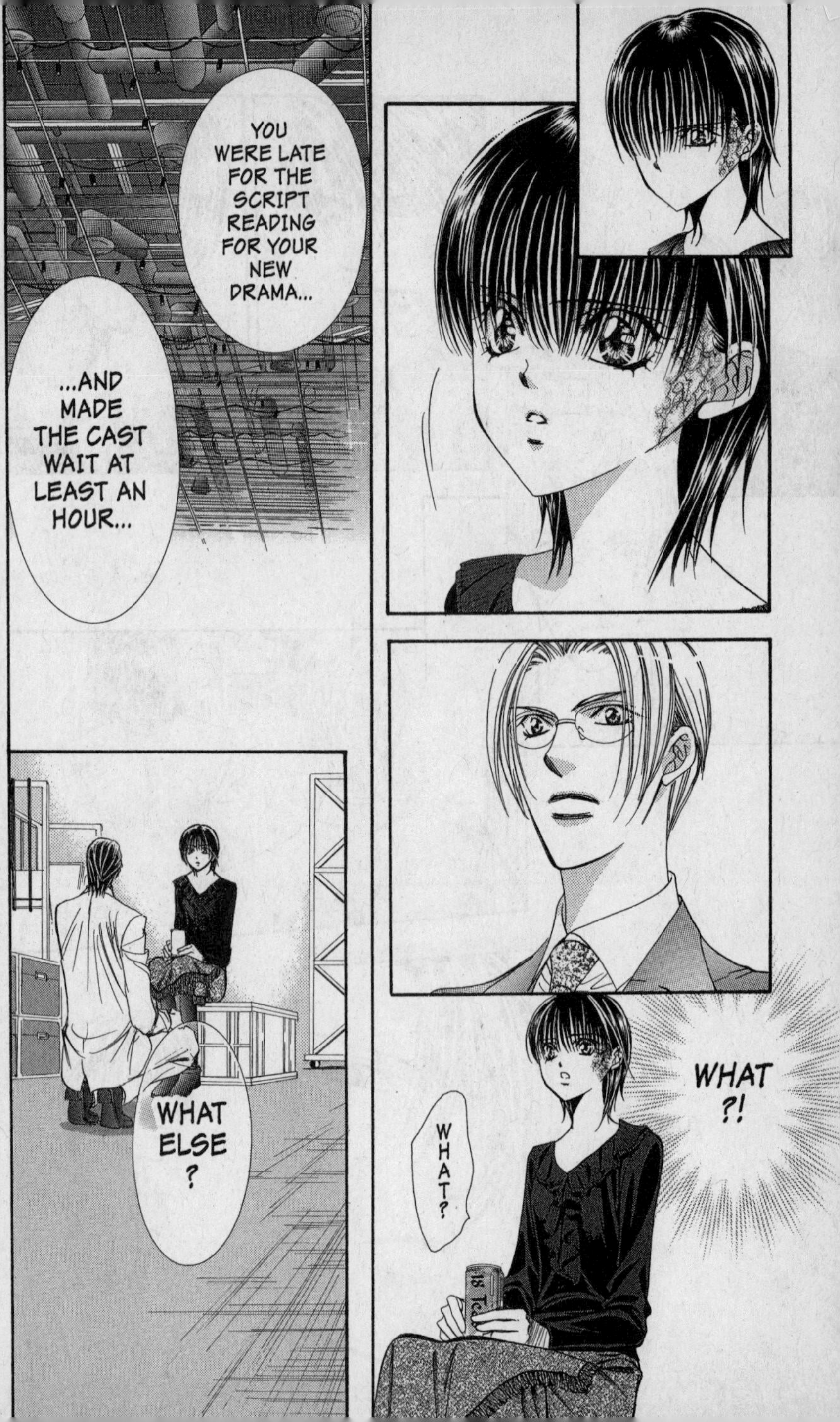
YOU WERE LATE FOR THE SCRIPT READING FOR YOUR NEW DRAMA...
...AND MADE THE CAST WAIT AT LEAST AN HOUR...
WHAT ELSE ?
WHAT?
WHAT ?!

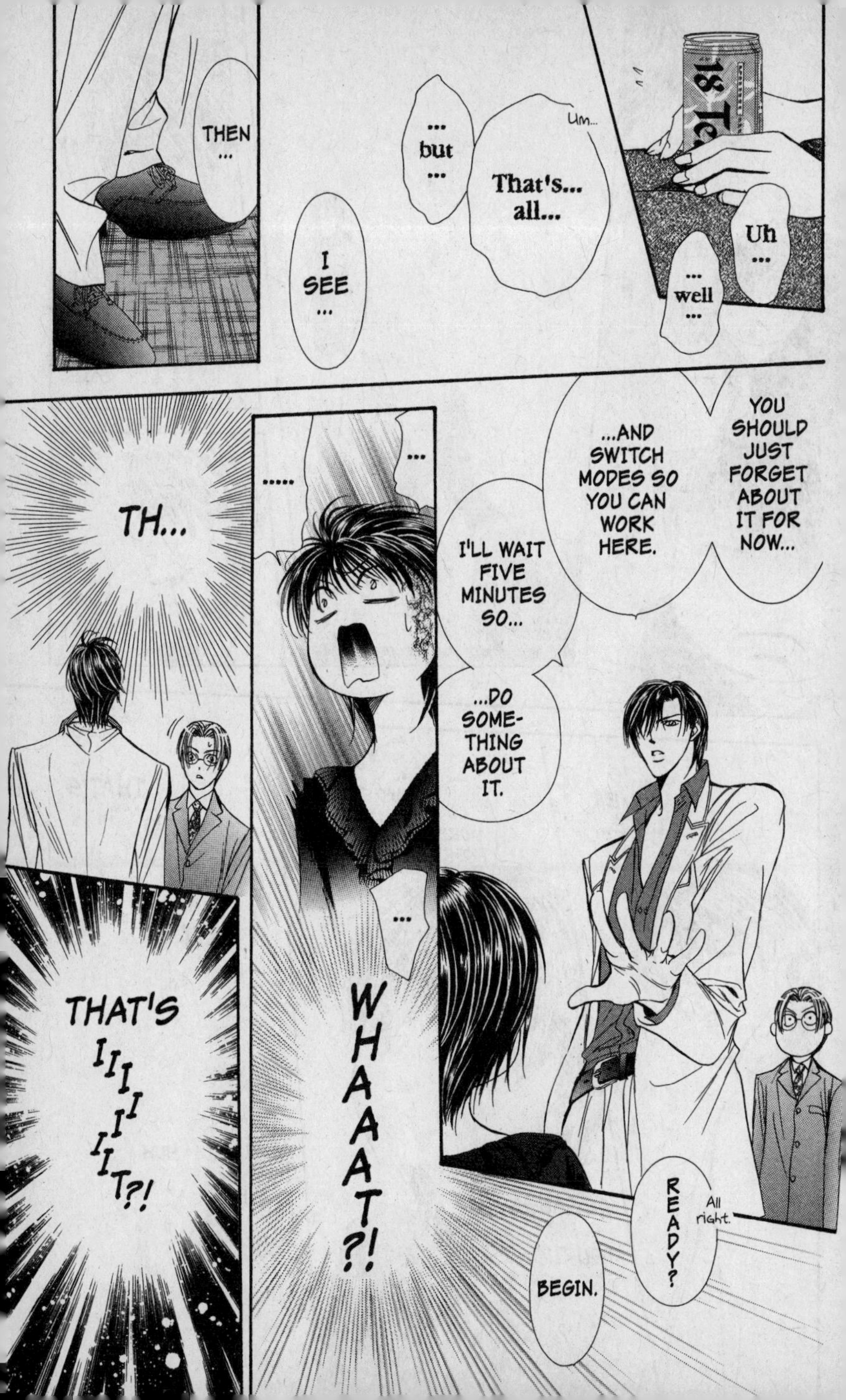
Uh ...
... well ...
Um...
That's... all...
... but ...
I SEE ...
THEN ...
YOU SHOULD JUST FORGET ABOUT IT FOR NOW...
...AND SWITCH MODES SO YOU CAN WORK HERE.
I'LL WAIT FIVE MINUTES SO...
...DO SOMETHING ABOUT IT.
READY?
All right.
BEGIN.
...
......
...
WHAAAAT?!
TH...
THAT'S IIIIIIIT?!

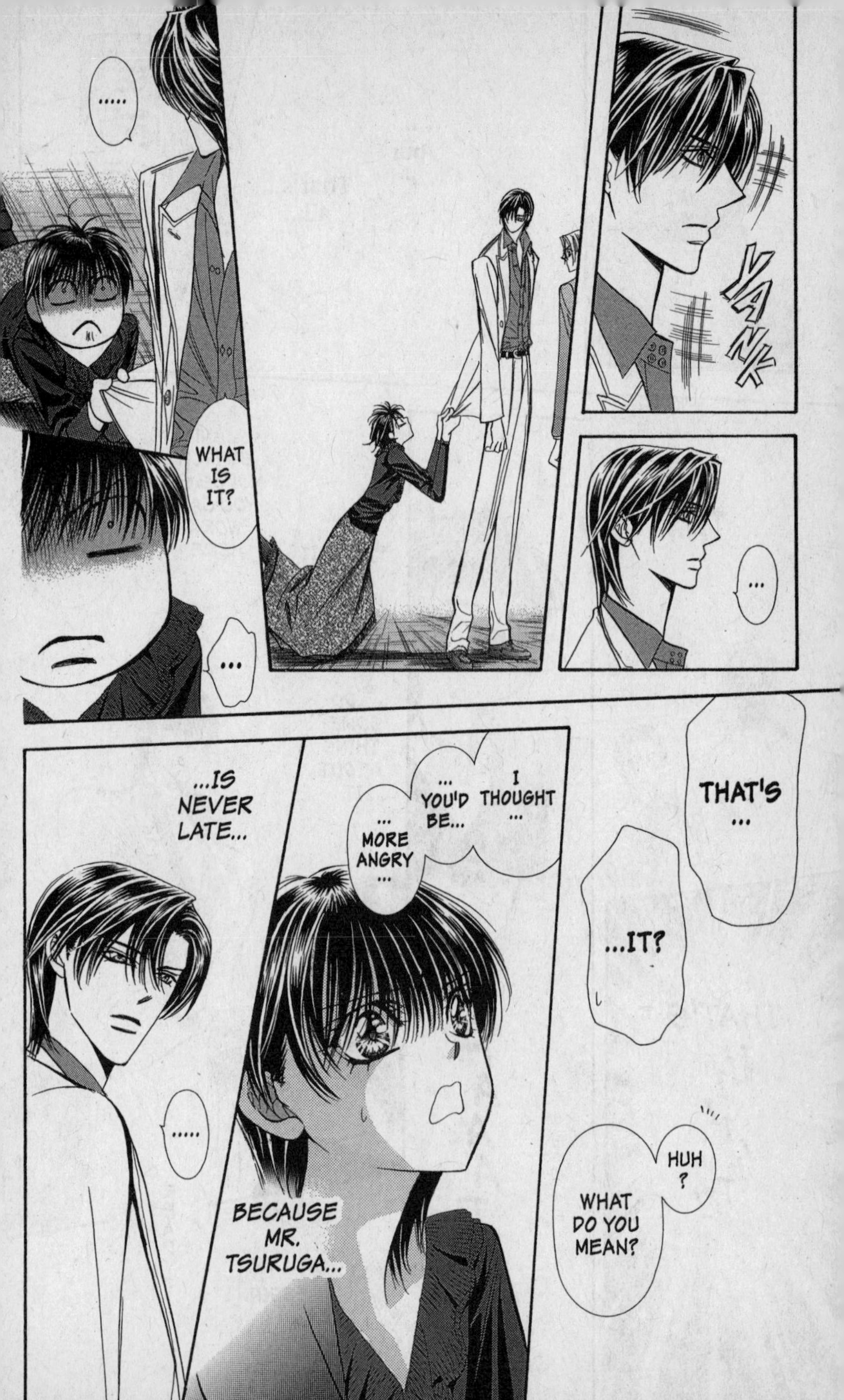
YANK
...
.....
WHAT IS IT?
...
THAT'S ...
...IT?
HUH ?
WHAT DO YOU MEAN?
I THOUGHT ...
... YOU'D BE...
... MORE ANGRY ...
BECAUSE MR. TSURUGA...
...IS NEVER LATE...
.....

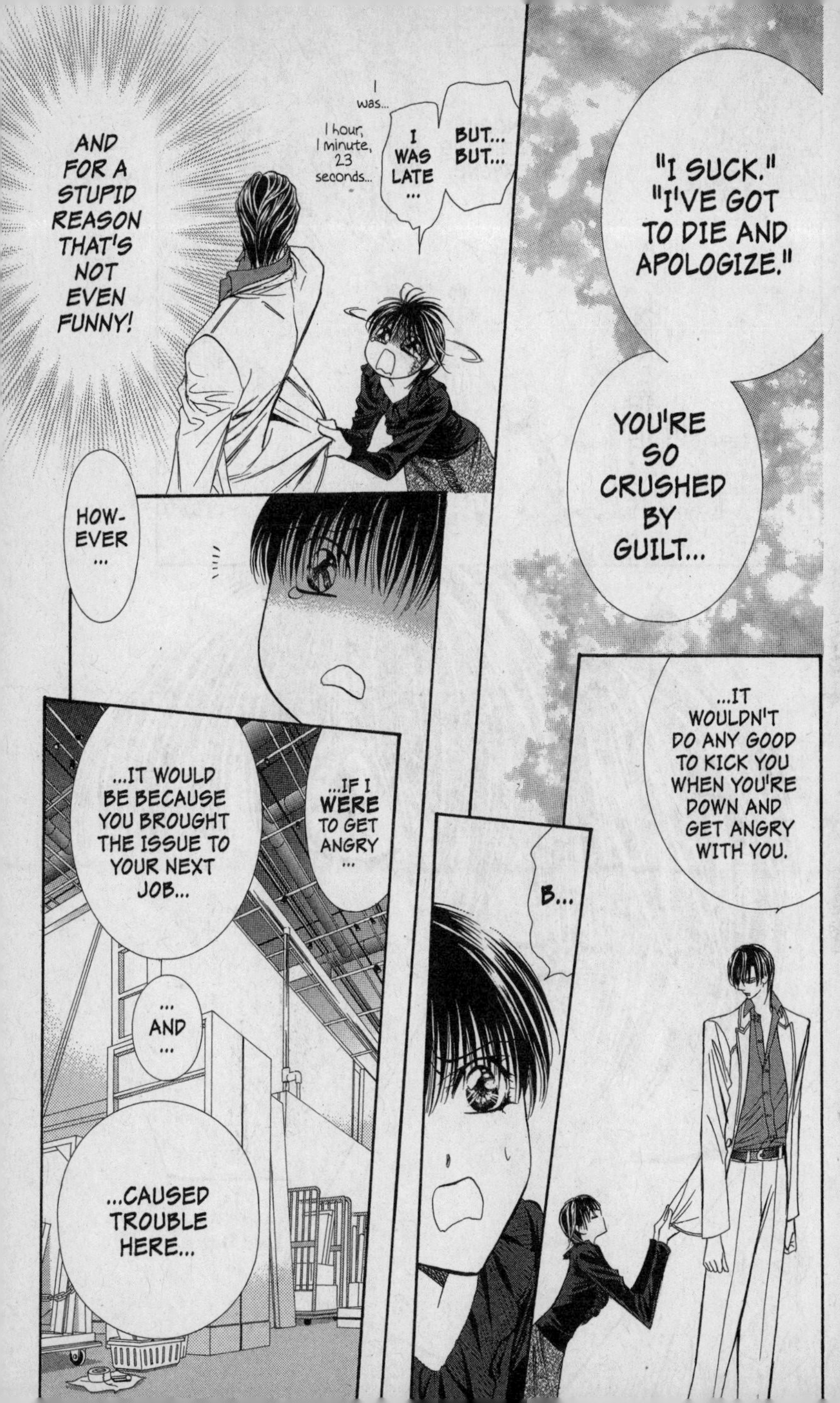
"I SUCK." "I'VE GOT TO DIE AND APOLOGIZE."
YOU'RE SO CRUSHED BY GUILT...
BUT... BUT...
I WAS LATE ...
I was... 1 hour, 1 minute, 23 seconds...
AND FOR A STUPID REASON THAT'S NOT EVEN FUNNY!
HOW-EVER ...
...IT WOULDN'T DO ANY GOOD TO KICK YOU WHEN YOU'RE DOWN AND GET ANGRY WITH YOU.
B...
...IF I WERE TO GET ANGRY ...
...IT WOULD BE BECAUSE YOU BROUGHT THE ISSUE TO YOUR NEXT JOB...
... AND ...
...CAUSED TROUBLE HERE...

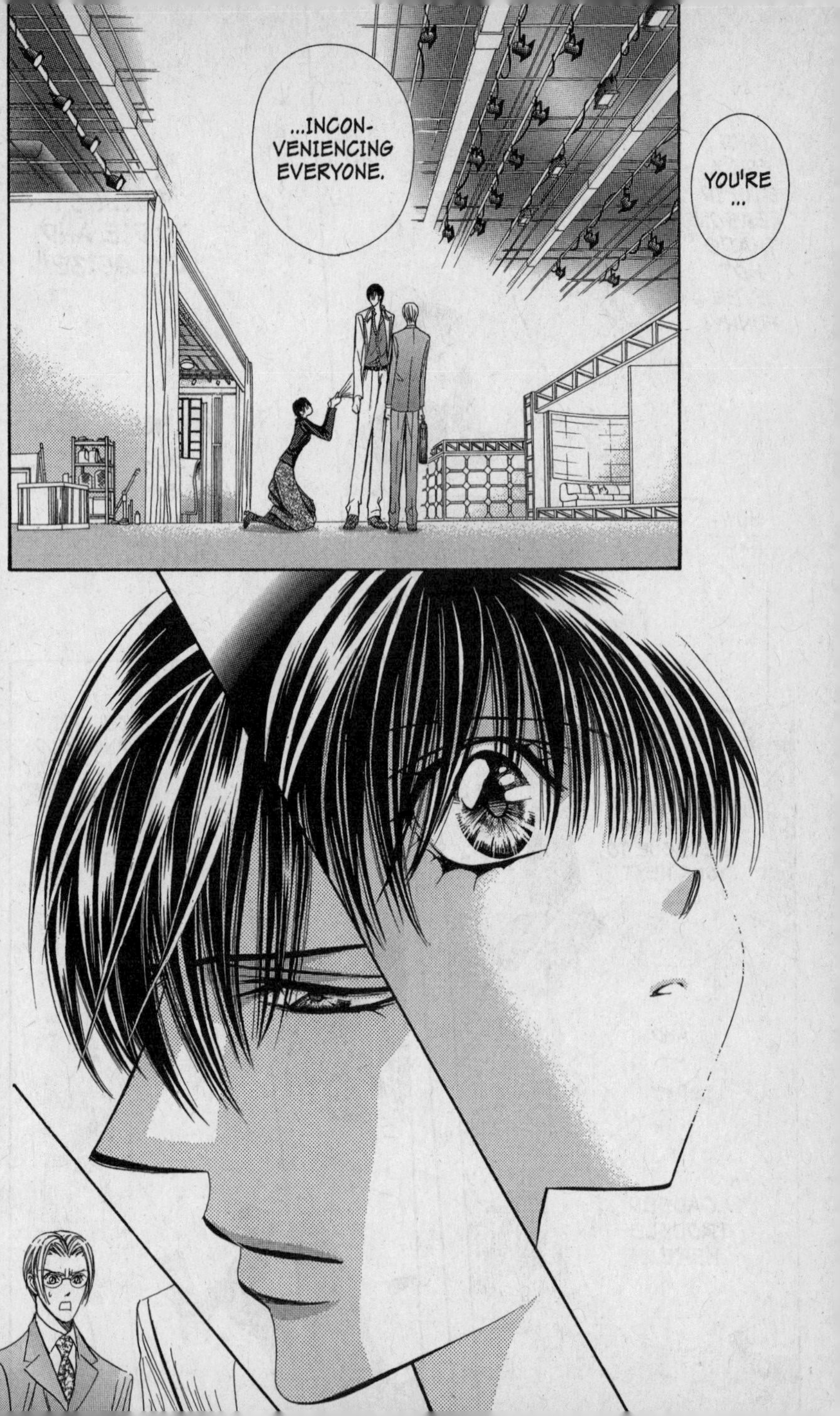
YOU'RE ...
...INCON-VENIENCING EVERYONE.

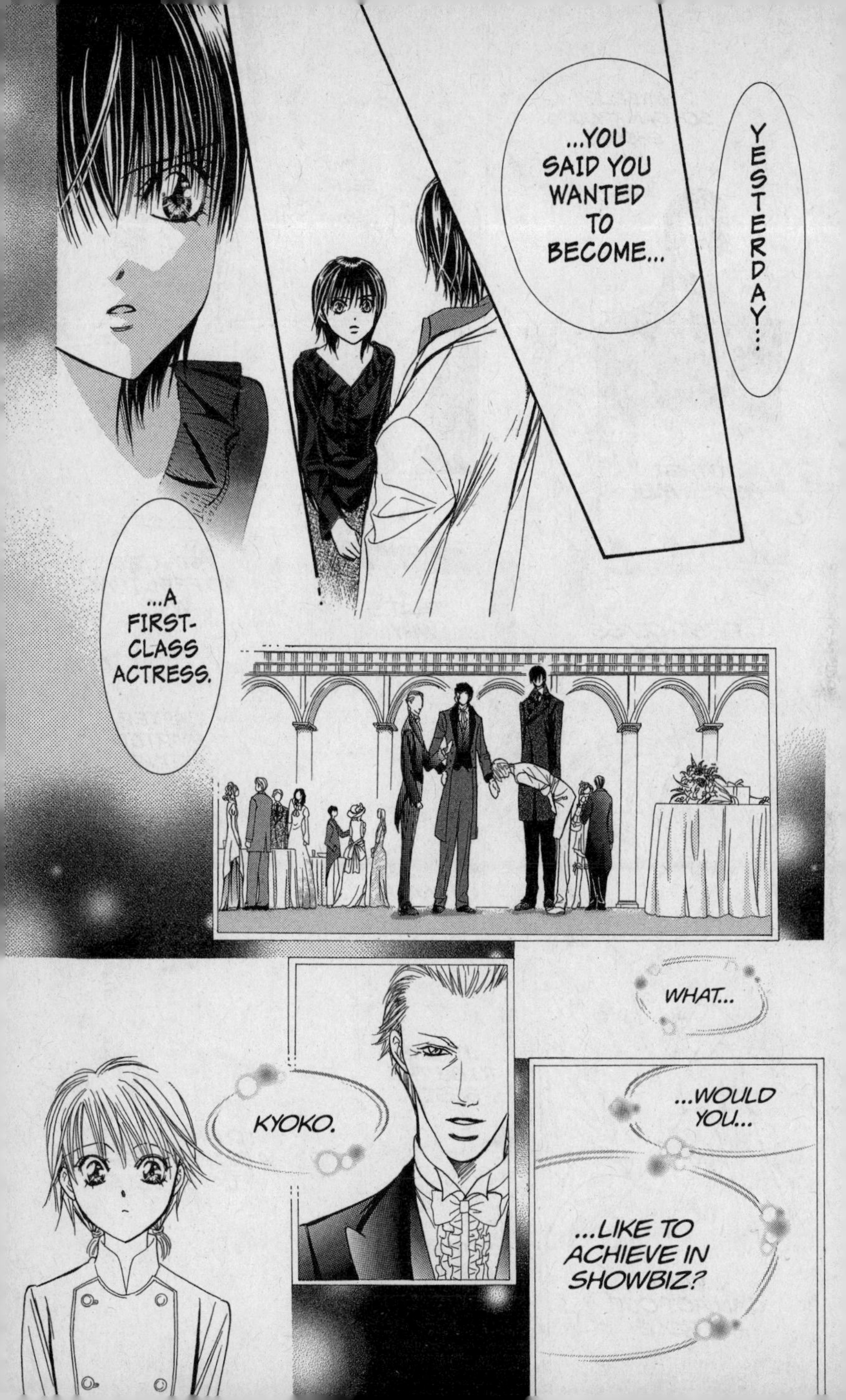
YESTERDAY...
...YOU SAID YOU WANTED TO BECOME...
...A FIRST-CLASS ACTRESS.
WHAT...
...WOULD YOU...
...LIKE TO ACHIEVE IN SHOWBIZ?
KYOKO.

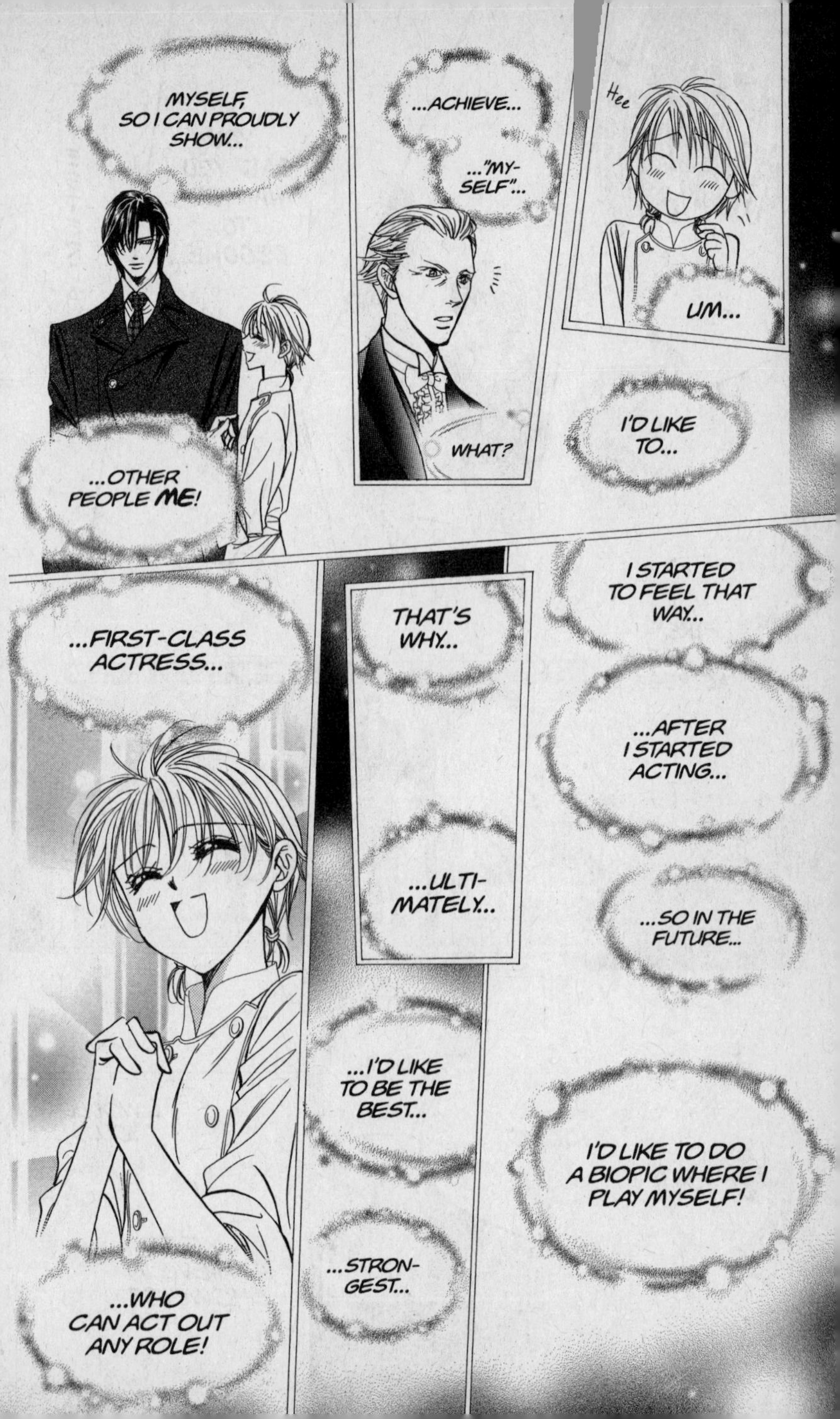
Hee
UM...
I'D LIKE TO...
...ACHIEVE...
..."MY-SELF"...
WHAT?
MYSELF, SO I CAN PROUDLY SHOW...
...OTHER PEOPLE **ME**!
I STARTED TO FEEL THAT WAY...
...AFTER I STARTED ACTING...
...SO IN THE FUTURE...
I'D LIKE TO DO A BIOPIC WHERE I PLAY MYSELF!
THAT'S WHY...
...ULTI-MATELY...
...I'D LIKE TO BE THE BEST...
...STRON-GEST...
...FIRST-CLASS ACTRESS...
...WHO CAN ACT OUT ANY ROLE!

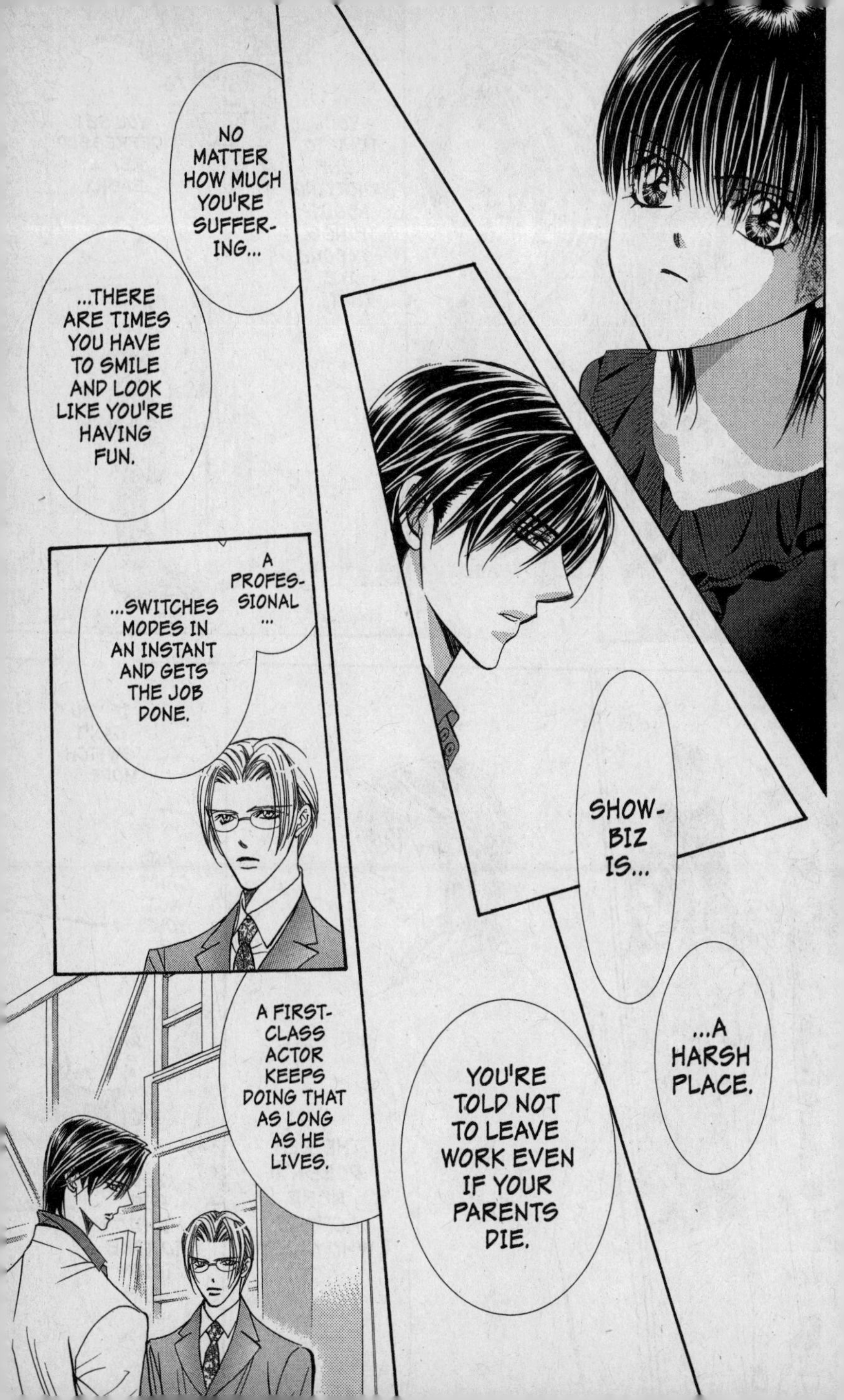
SHOW-BIZ IS...
...A HARSH PLACE.
YOU'RE TOLD NOT TO LEAVE WORK EVEN IF YOUR PARENTS DIE.
NO MATTER HOW MUCH YOU'RE SUFFERING...
...THERE ARE TIMES YOU HAVE TO SMILE AND LOOK LIKE YOU'RE HAVING FUN.
A PROFESSIONAL...
...SWITCHES MODES IN AN INSTANT AND GETS THE JOB DONE.
A FIRST-CLASS ACTOR KEEPS DOING THAT AS LONG AS HE LIVES.

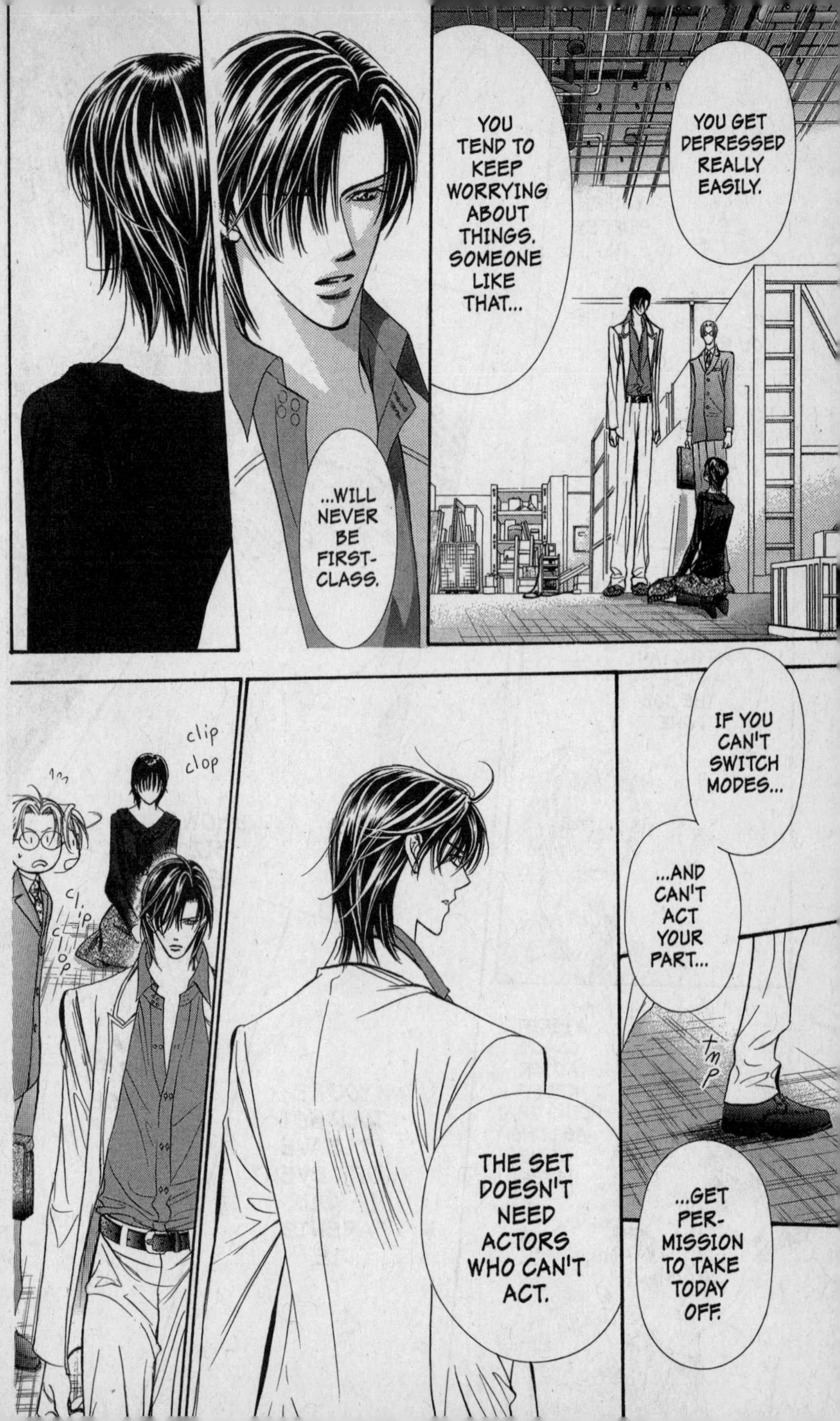
YOU GET DEPRESSED REALLY EASILY.
YOU TEND TO KEEP WORRYING ABOUT THINGS. SOMEONE LIKE THAT...
...WILL NEVER BE FIRST-CLASS.
IF YOU CAN'T SWITCH MODES...
...AND CAN'T ACT YOUR PART...
tmp
...GET PER-MISSION TO TAKE TODAY OFF.
THE SET DOESN'T NEED ACTORS WHO CAN'T ACT.
clip clop
clip clop

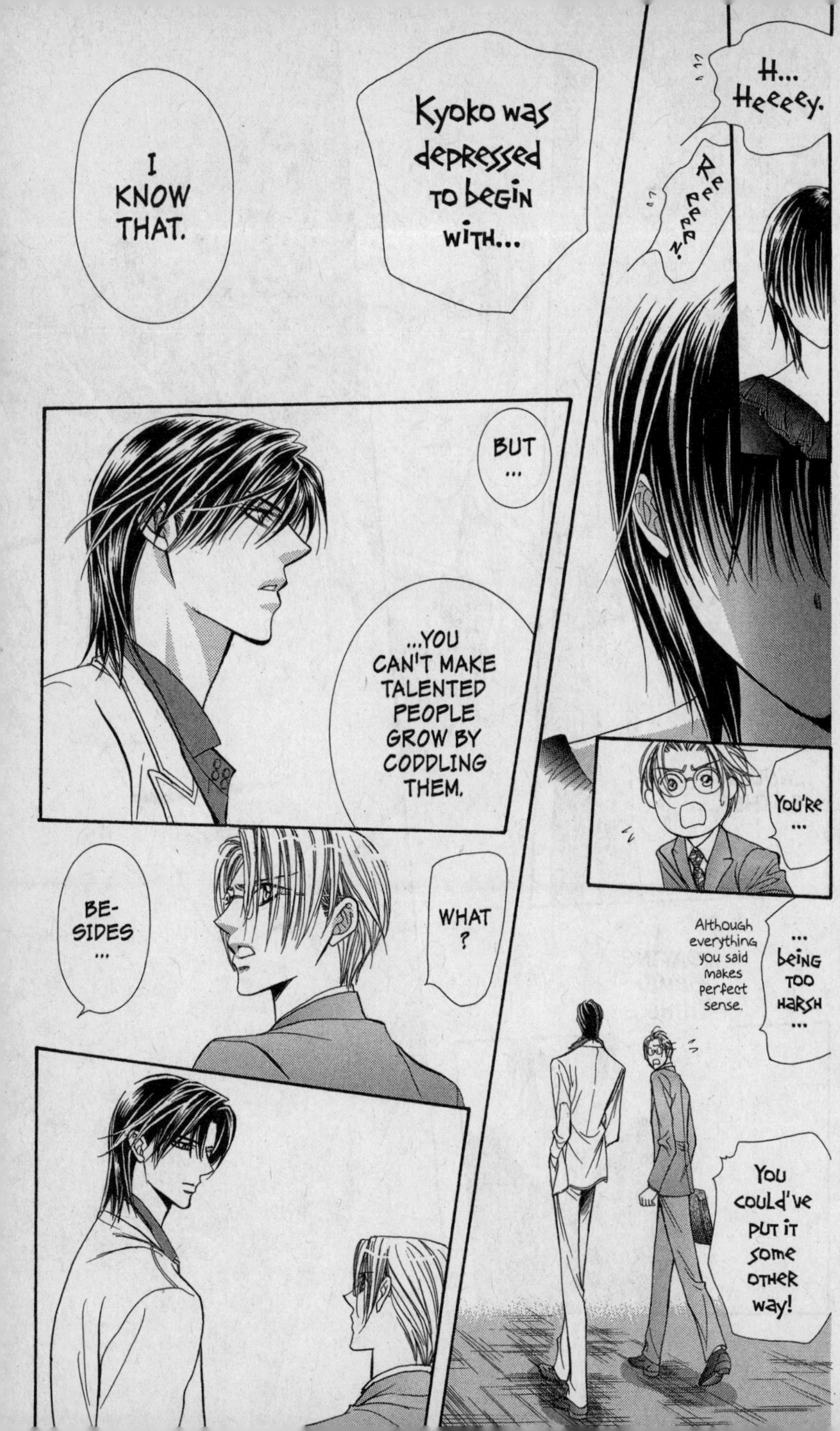
H... Heeeey.
Reeeeen.
You're ...
... being too harsh ...
Although everything you said makes perfect sense.
You could've put it some other way!
Kyoko was depressed to begin with...
I KNOW THAT.
BUT ...
...YOU CAN'T MAKE TALENTED PEOPLE GROW BY CODDLING THEM.
WHAT ?
BE-SIDES ...

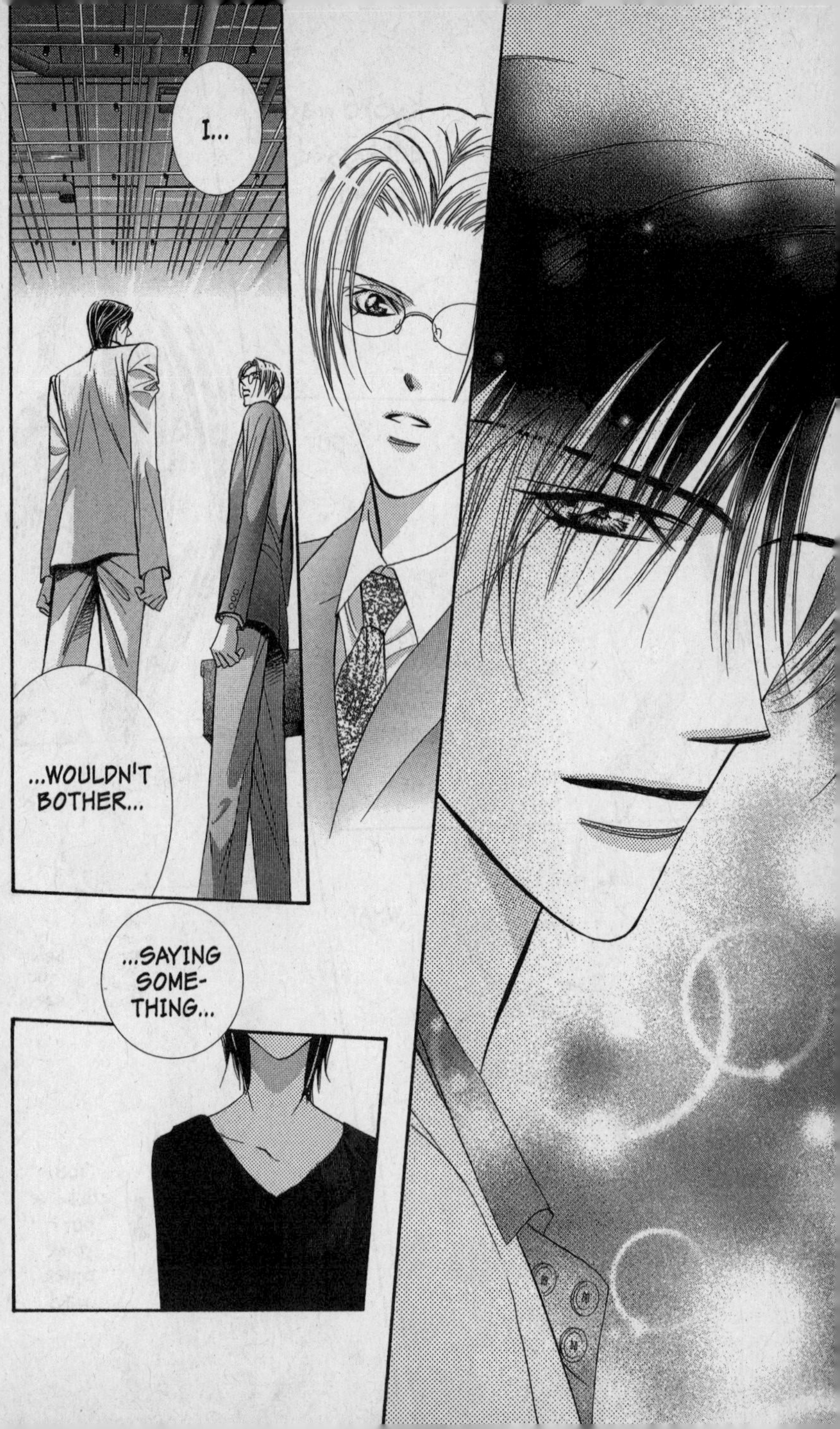
I...
...WOULDN'T BOTHER...
...SAYING SOME-THING...

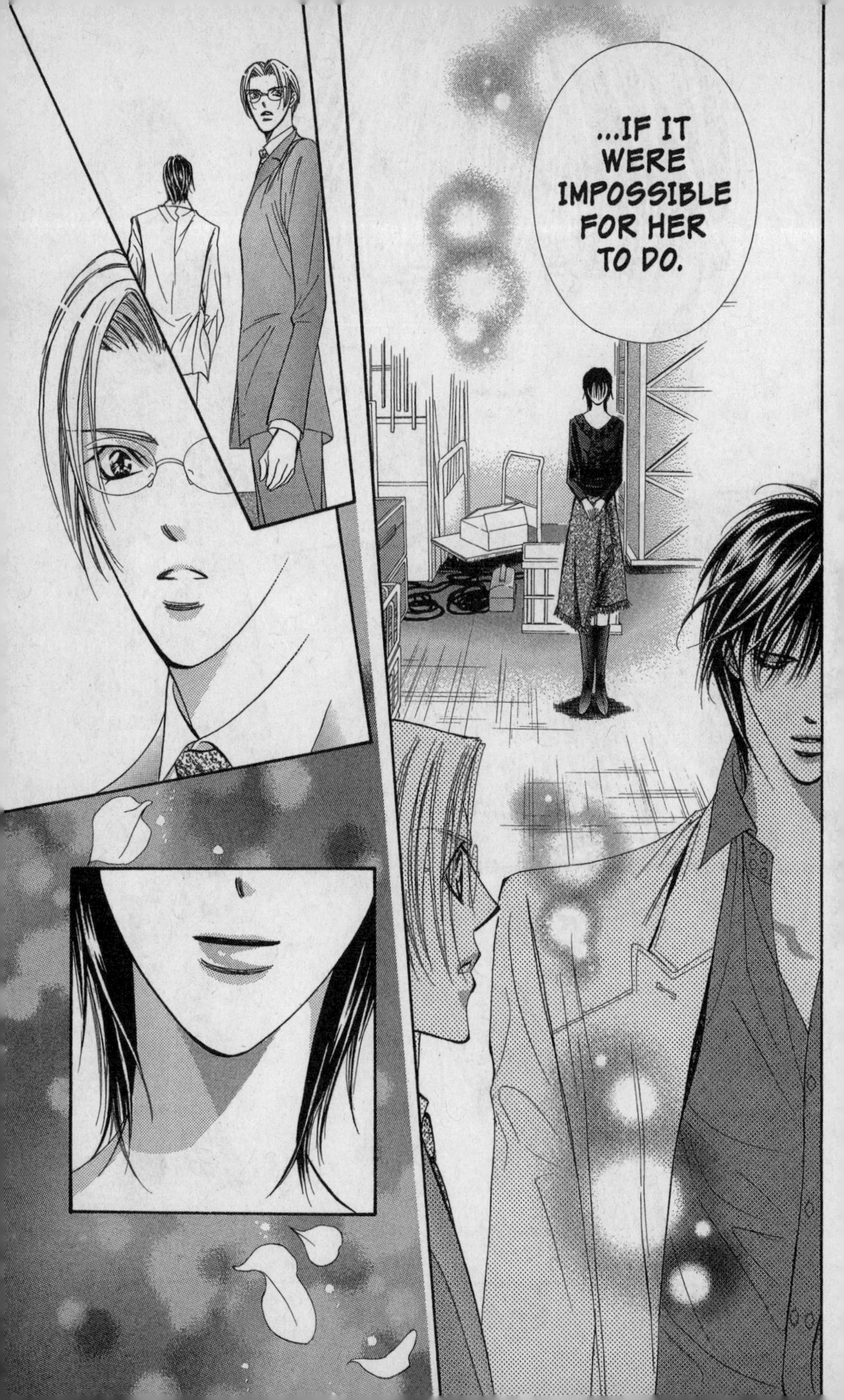
...IF IT WERE IMPOSSIBLE FOR HER TO DO.

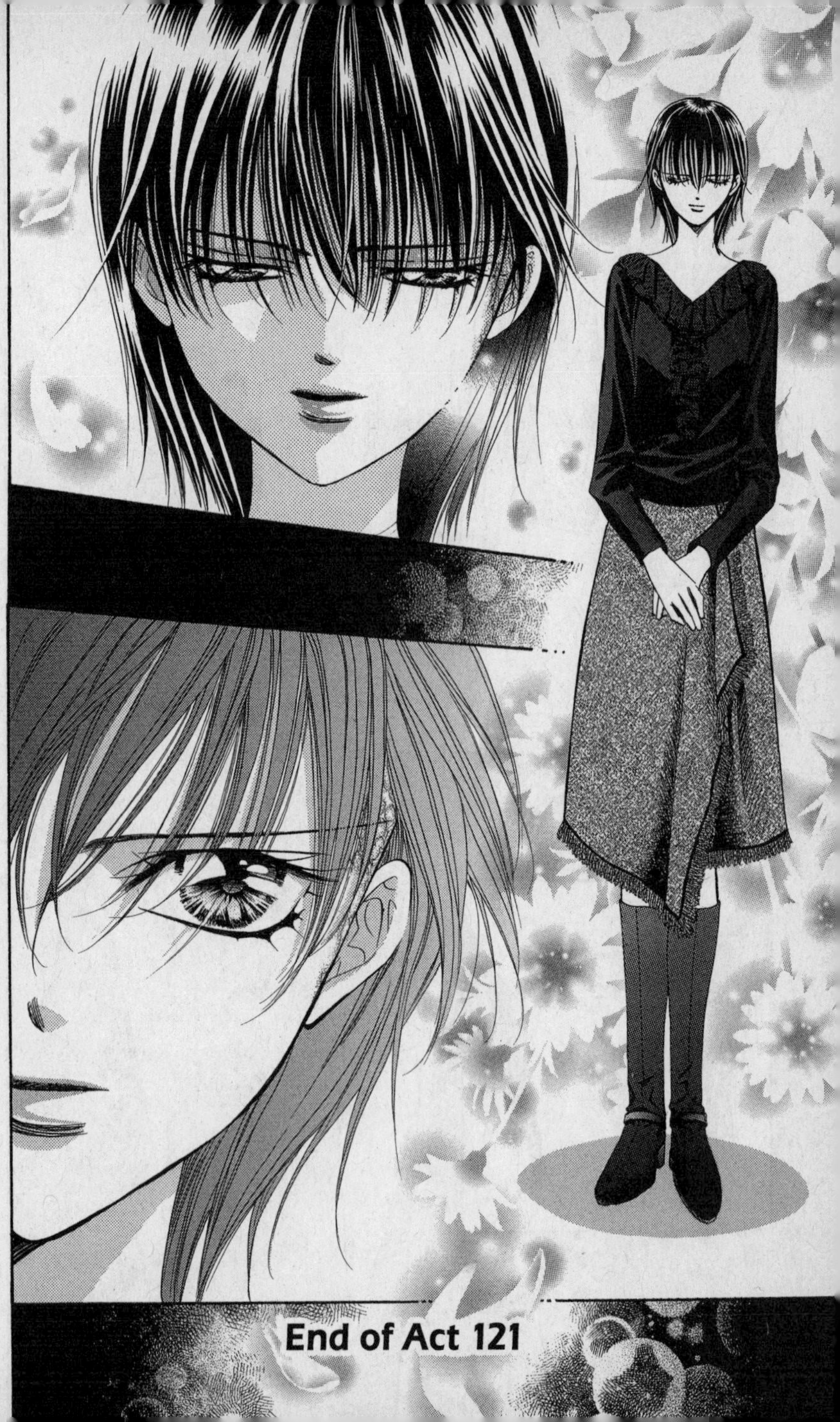
End of Act 121

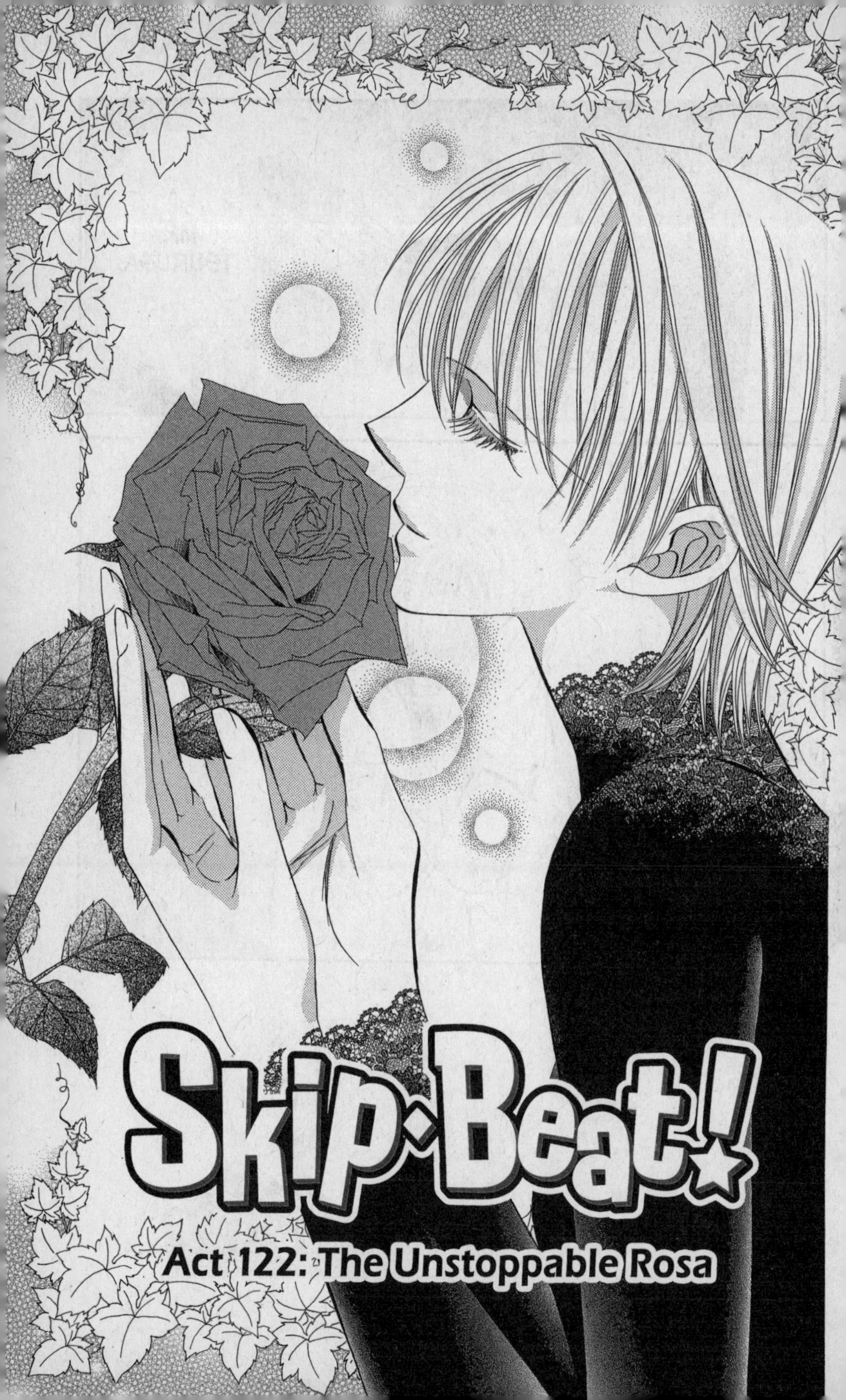
Skip·Beat!
Act 122: The Unstoppable Rosa

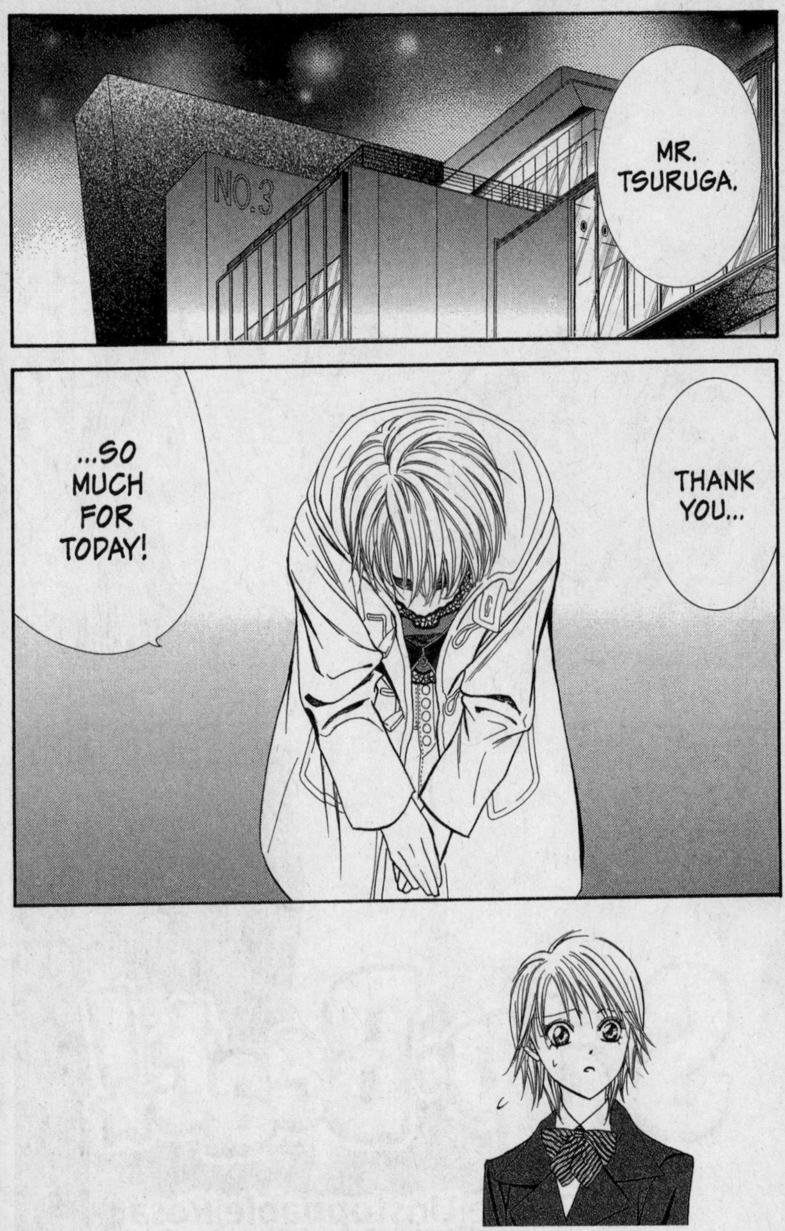
MR. TSURUGA.
THANK YOU...
...SO MUCH FOR TODAY!

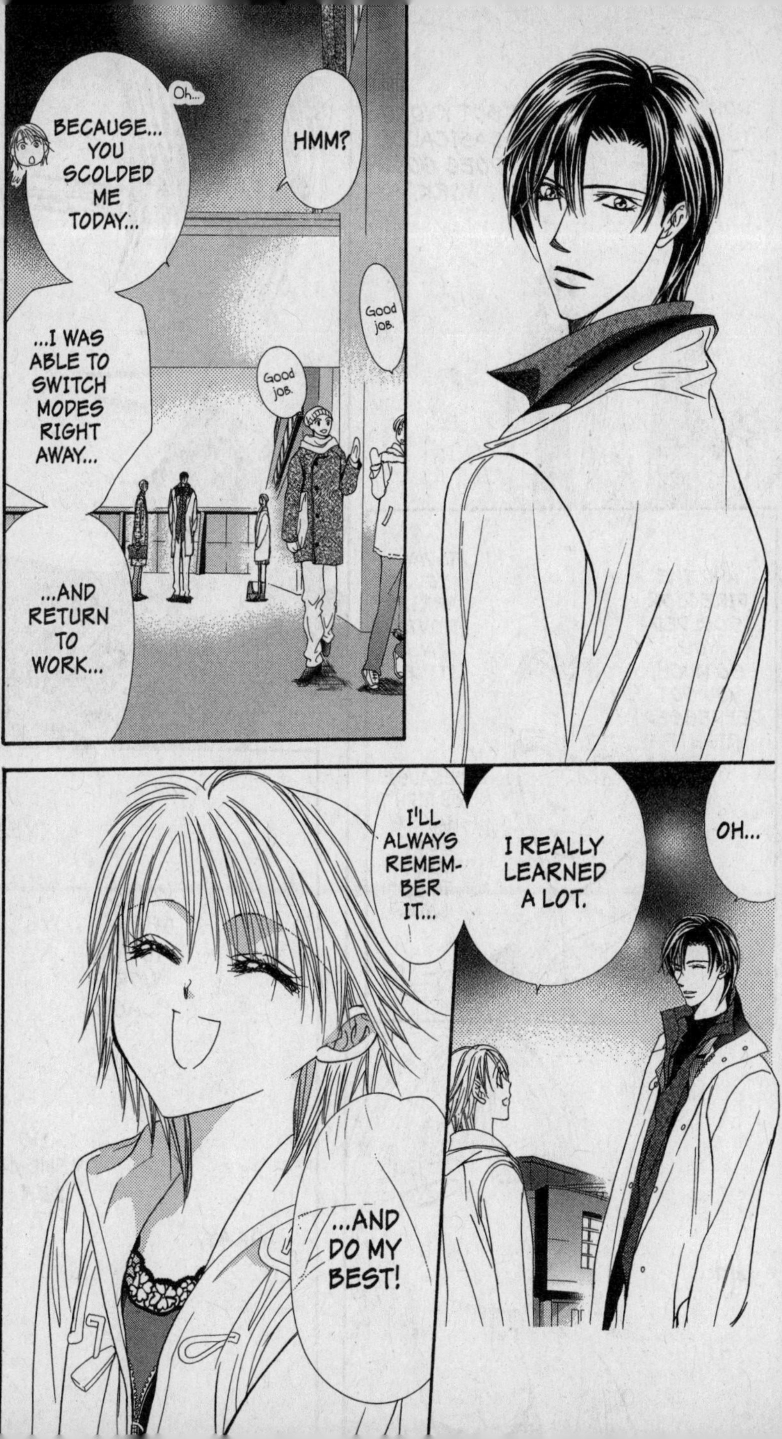
HMM?
Oh...
BECAUSE... YOU SCOLDED ME TODAY...
Good job.
Good job.
...I WAS ABLE TO SWITCH MODES RIGHT AWAY...
...AND RETURN TO WORK...
OH...
I REALLY LEARNED A LOT.
I'LL ALWAYS REMEMBER IT...
...AND DO MY BEST!

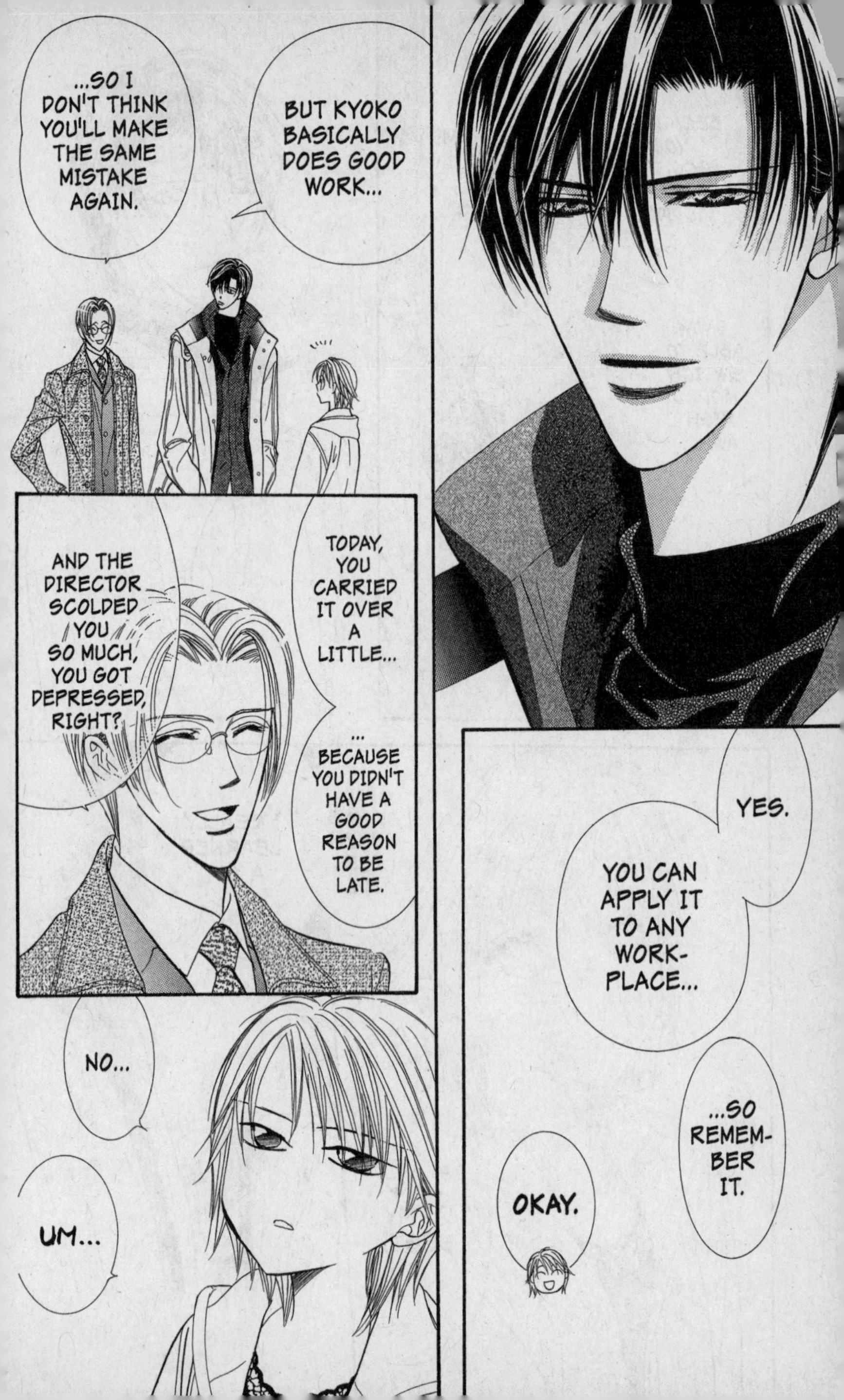
YES.
YOU CAN APPLY IT TO ANY WORK-PLACE...
...SO REMEMBER IT.
OKAY.
BUT KYOKO BASICALLY DOES GOOD WORK...
...SO I DON'T THINK YOU'LL MAKE THE SAME MISTAKE AGAIN.
TODAY, YOU CARRIED IT OVER A LITTLE...
... BECAUSE YOU DIDN'T HAVE A GOOD REASON TO BE LATE.
AND THE DIRECTOR SCOLDED YOU SO MUCH, YOU GOT DEPRESSED, RIGHT?
NO...
UM...

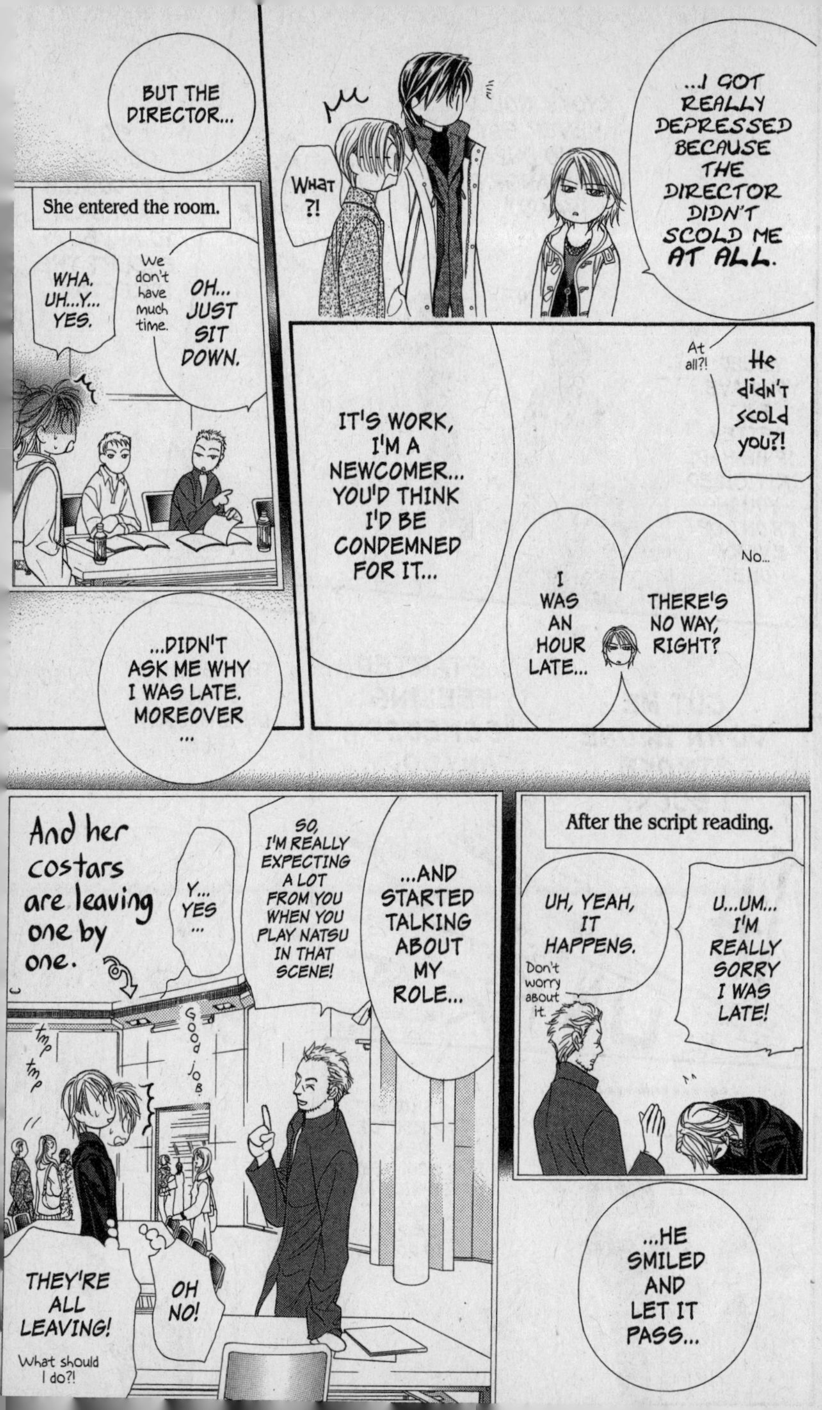
...I GOT REALLY DEPRESSED BECAUSE THE DIRECTOR DIDN'T SCOLD ME AT ALL.
WHAT?!
He didn't scold you?!
At all?!
No...
THERE'S NO WAY, RIGHT?
I WAS AN HOUR LATE...
IT'S WORK, I'M A NEWCOMER... YOU'D THINK I'D BE CONDEMNED FOR IT...
BUT THE DIRECTOR...
She entered the room.
OH... JUST SIT DOWN.
We don't have much time.
WHA. UH...Y... YES.
...DIDN'T ASK ME WHY I WAS LATE. MOREOVER...
After the script reading.
U...UM... I'M REALLY SORRY I WAS LATE!
UH, YEAH, IT HAPPENS.
Don't worry about it.
...HE SMILED AND LET IT PASS...
...AND STARTED TALKING ABOUT MY ROLE...
SO, I'M REALLY EXPECTING A LOT FROM YOU WHEN YOU PLAY NATSU IN THAT SCENE!
Y... YES...
And her costars are leaving one by one.
Good job.
tmp tmp
OH NO!
THEY'RE ALL LEAVING!
What should I do?!

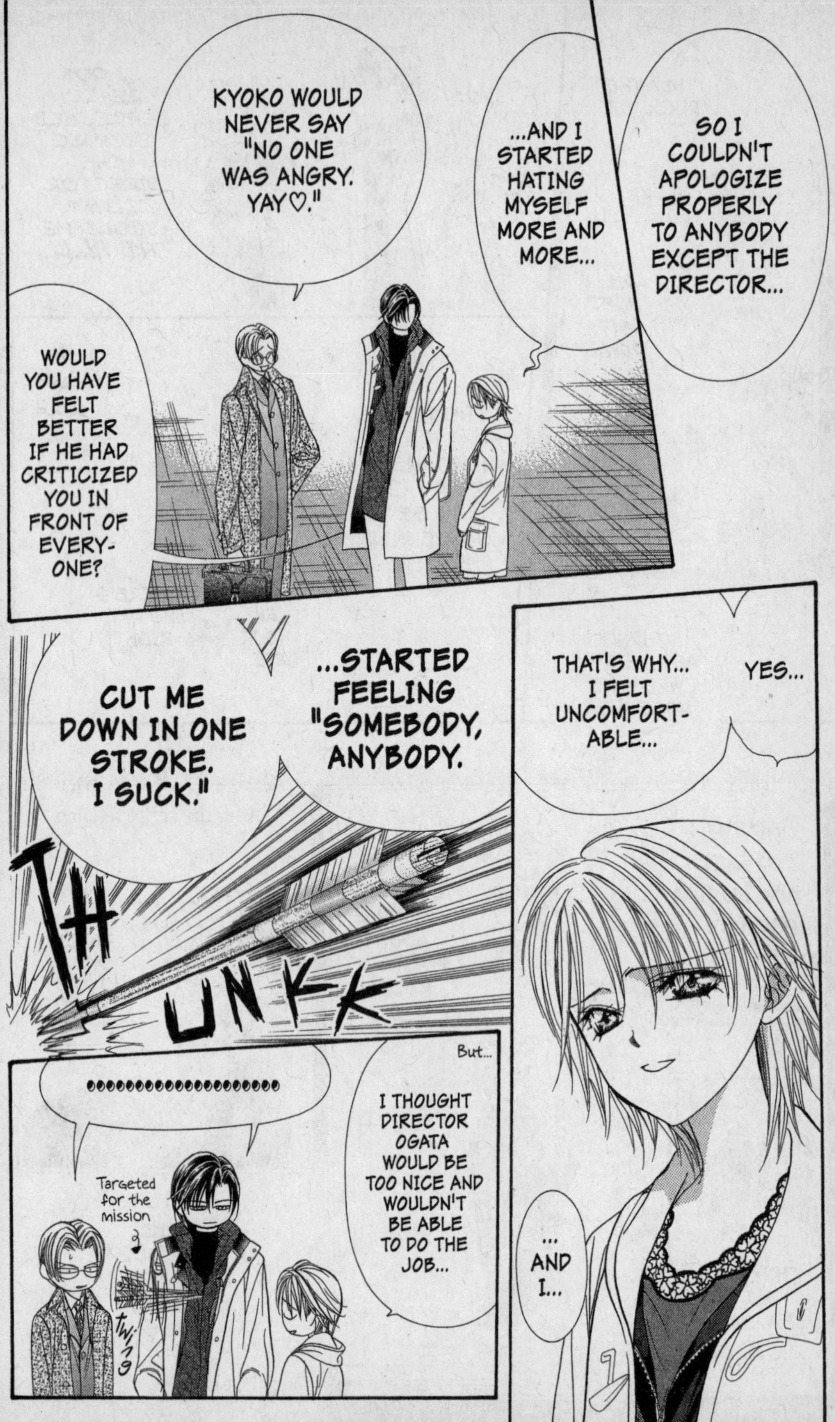
SO I COULDN'T APOLOGIZE PROPERLY TO ANYBODY EXCEPT THE DIRECTOR...
...AND I STARTED HATING MYSELF MORE AND MORE...
KYOKO WOULD NEVER SAY "NO ONE WAS ANGRY. YAY♡."
WOULD YOU HAVE FELT BETTER IF HE HAD CRITICIZED YOU IN FRONT OF EVERY-ONE?
YES...
THAT'S WHY... I FELT UNCOMFORT-ABLE...
...AND I...
...STARTED FEELING "SOMEBODY, ANYBODY.
CUT ME DOWN IN ONE STROKE. I SUCK."
THUNKK
But...
I THOUGHT DIRECTOR OGATA WOULD BE TOO NICE AND WOULDN'T BE ABLE TO DO THE JOB...
••••••••••••••••••••
Targeted for the mission
twing

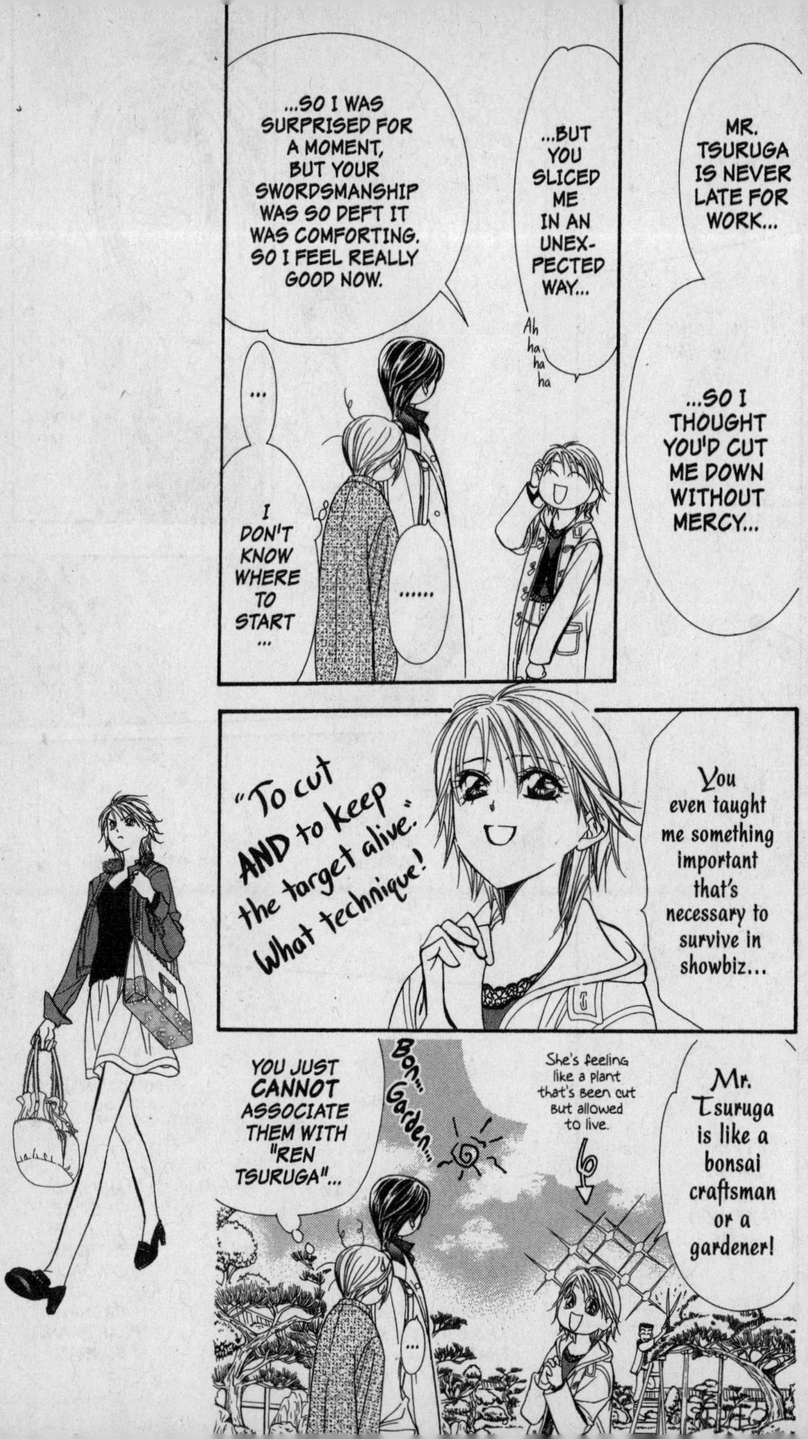
MR. TSURUGA IS NEVER LATE FOR WORK...
...SO I THOUGHT YOU'D CUT ME DOWN WITHOUT MERCY...
...BUT YOU SLICED ME IN AN UNEXPECTED WAY...
Ah ha ha ha
...SO I WAS SURPRISED FOR A MOMENT, BUT YOUR SWORDSMANSHIP WAS SO DEFT IT WAS COMFORTING. SO I FEEL REALLY GOOD NOW.
......
...
I DON'T KNOW WHERE TO START ...
You even taught me something important that's necessary to survive in showbiz...
"To cut AND to keep the target alive." What technique!
Mr. Tsuruga is like a bonsai craftsman or a gardener!
She's feeling like a plant that's been cut but allowed to live.
Bon... Garden...
YOU JUST CANNOT ASSOCIATE THEM WITH "REN TSURUGA"...
...

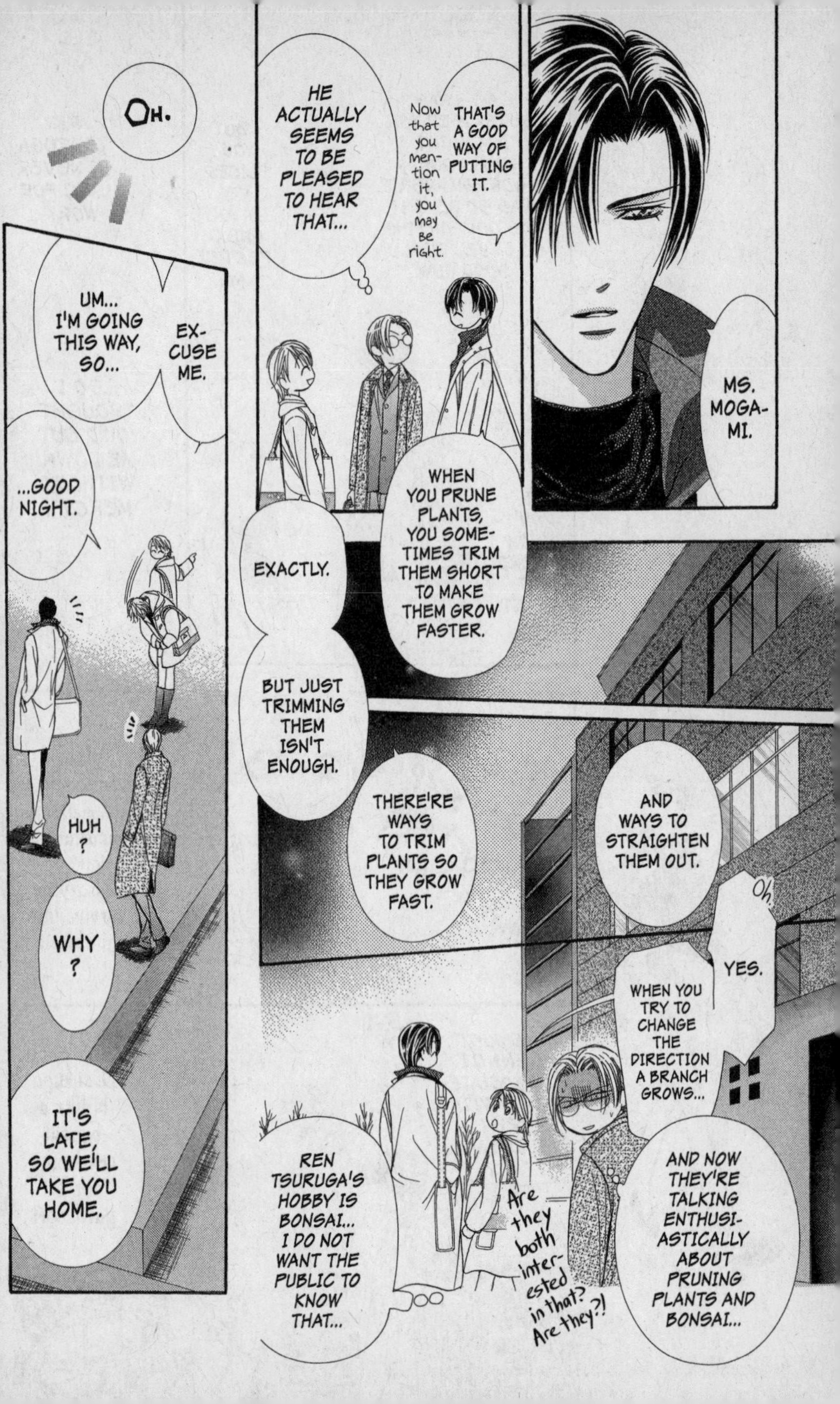
MS. MOGAMI.
THAT'S A GOOD WAY OF PUTTING IT.
Now that you mention it, you may be right.
HE ACTUALLY SEEMS TO BE PLEASED TO HEAR THAT...
OH.
WHEN YOU PRUNE PLANTS, YOU SOMETIMES TRIM THEM SHORT TO MAKE THEM GROW FASTER.
EXACTLY.
BUT JUST TRIMMING THEM ISN'T ENOUGH.
THERE'RE WAYS TO TRIM PLANTS SO THEY GROW FAST.
AND WAYS TO STRAIGHTEN THEM OUT.
Oh.
YES.
WHEN YOU TRY TO CHANGE THE DIRECTION A BRANCH GROWS...
AND NOW THEY'RE TALKING ENTHUSIASTICALLY ABOUT PRUNING PLANTS AND BONSAI...
Are they both interested in that? Are they?!
REN TSURUGA'S HOBBY IS BONSAI... I DO NOT WANT THE PUBLIC TO KNOW THAT...
UM... I'M GOING THIS WAY, SO...
EXCUSE ME.
...GOOD NIGHT.
HUH?
WHY?
IT'S LATE, SO WE'LL TAKE YOU HOME.

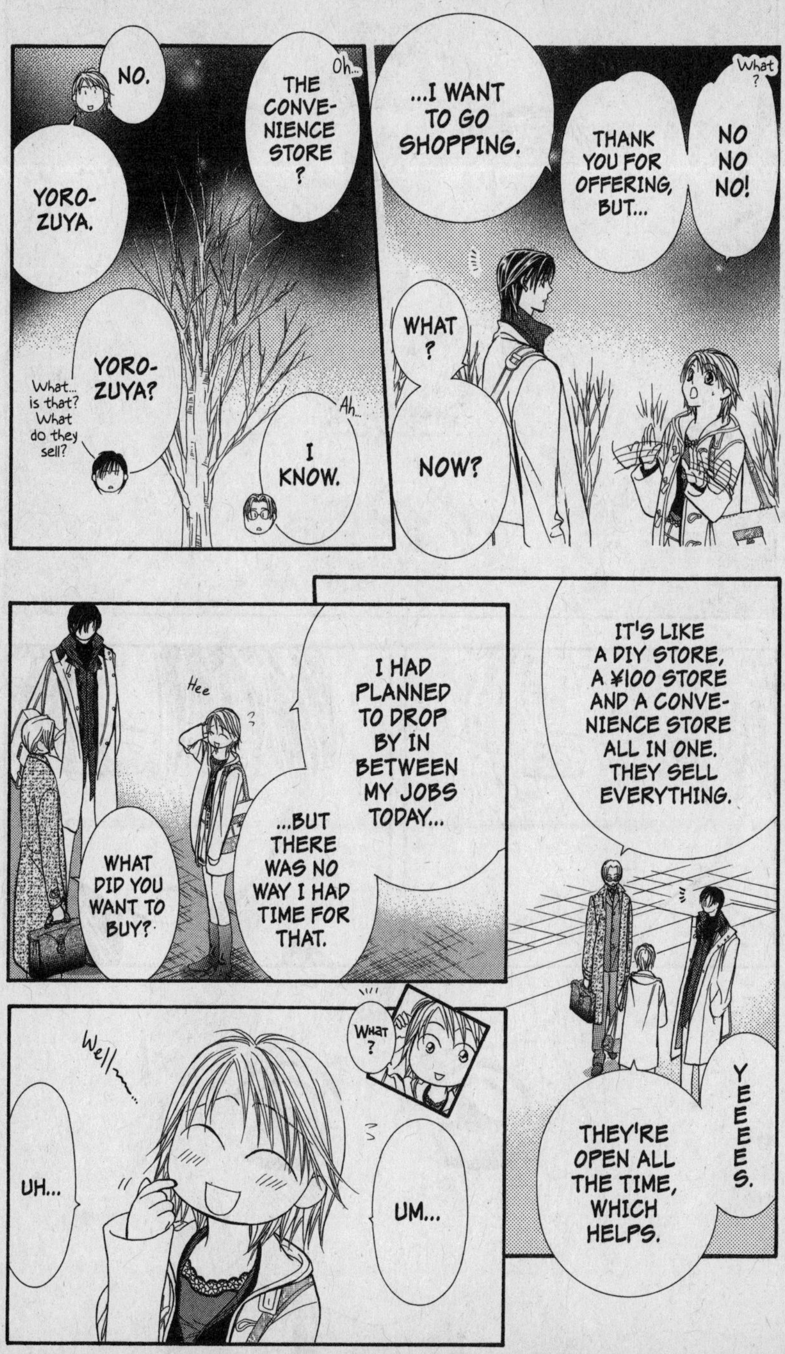
What?
NO NO NO!
THANK YOU FOR OFFERING, BUT...
...I WANT TO GO SHOPPING.
WHAT?
NOW?
Oh...
THE CONVENIENCE STORE?
NO.
YORO-ZUYA.
Ah...
I KNOW.
YORO-ZUYA?
What... is that? What do they sell?
IT'S LIKE A DIY STORE, A ¥100 STORE AND A CONVENIENCE STORE ALL IN ONE. THEY SELL EVERYTHING.
YEEEES.
THEY'RE OPEN ALL THE TIME, WHICH HELPS.
I HAD PLANNED TO DROP BY IN BETWEEN MY JOBS TODAY...
...BUT THERE WAS NO WAY I HAD TIME FOR THAT.
Hee
WHAT DID YOU WANT TO BUY?
What?
UM...
Well~...
UH...

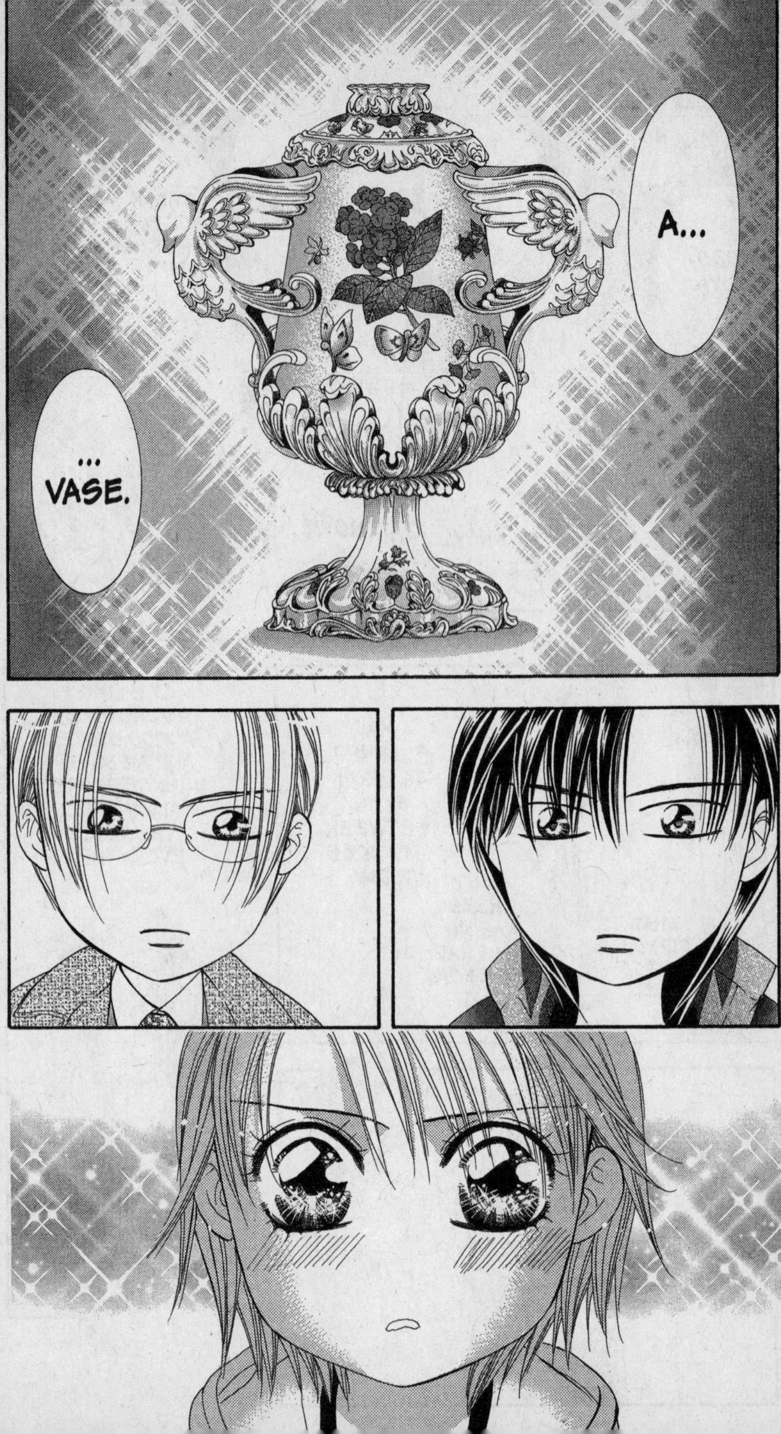
A...
... VASE.

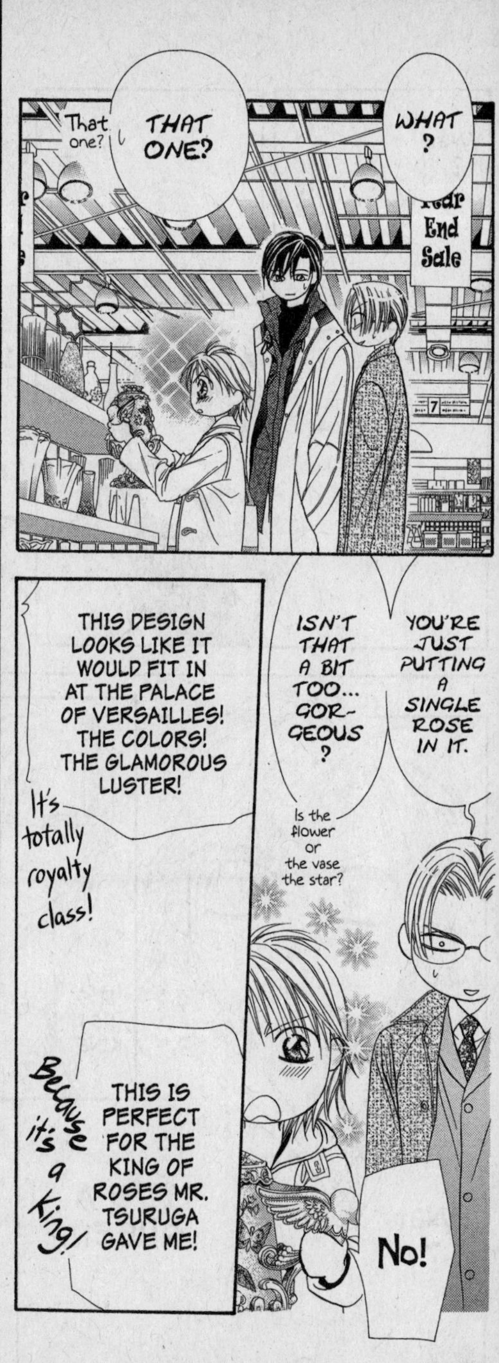
WHAT?
THAT ONE?
That one?
End Sale
YOU'RE JUST PUTTING A SINGLE ROSE IN IT.
ISN'T THAT A BIT TOO... GORGEOUS?
Is the flower or the vase the star?
No!
THIS DESIGN LOOKS LIKE IT WOULD FIT IN AT THE PALACE OF VERSAILLES! THE COLORS! THE GLAMOROUS LUSTER!
It's totally royalty class!
THIS IS PERFECT FOR THE KING OF ROSES MR. TSURUGA GAVE ME!
Because it's a King!
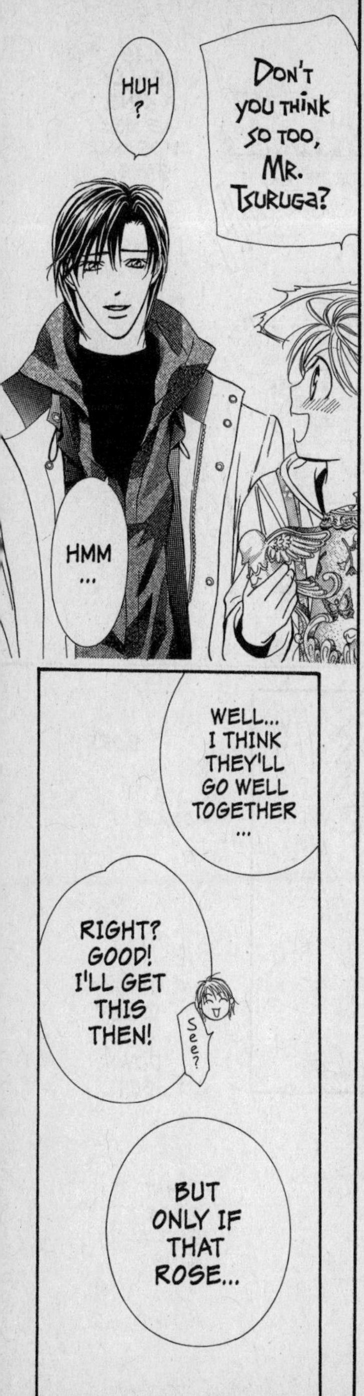
DON'T YOU THINK SO TOO, MR. TSURUGA?
HUH?
HMM...
WELL... I THINK THEY'LL GO WELL TOGETHER...
RIGHT? GOOD! I'LL GET THIS THEN!
See?
BUT ONLY IF THAT ROSE...

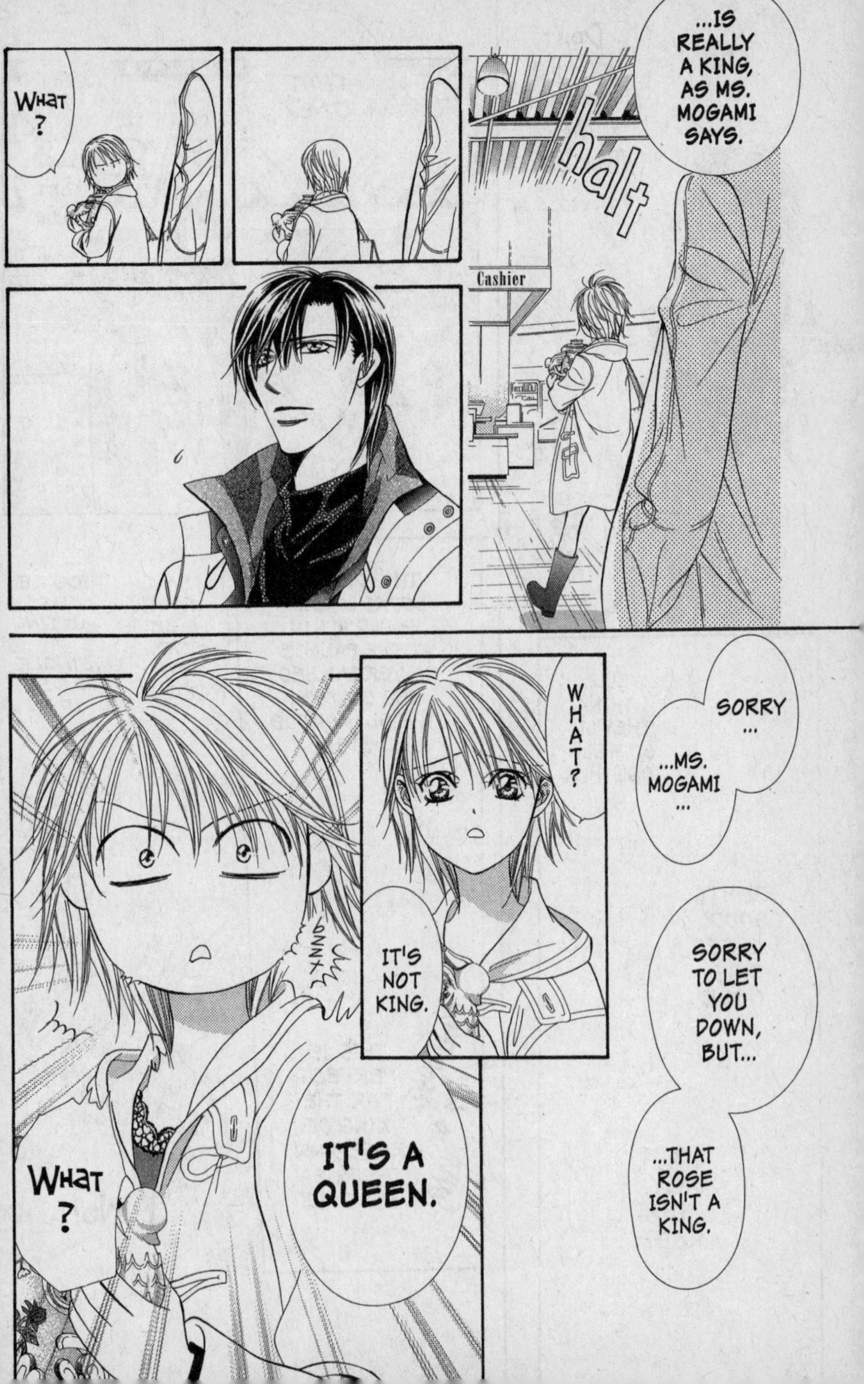
...IS REALLY A KING, AS MS. MOGAMI SAYS.
halt
Cashier
WHAT ?
SORRY ...
...MS. MOGAMI ...
SORRY TO LET YOU DOWN, BUT...
...THAT ROSE ISN'T A KING.
WHAT?
IT'S NOT KING.
IT'S A QUEEN.
WHAT ?

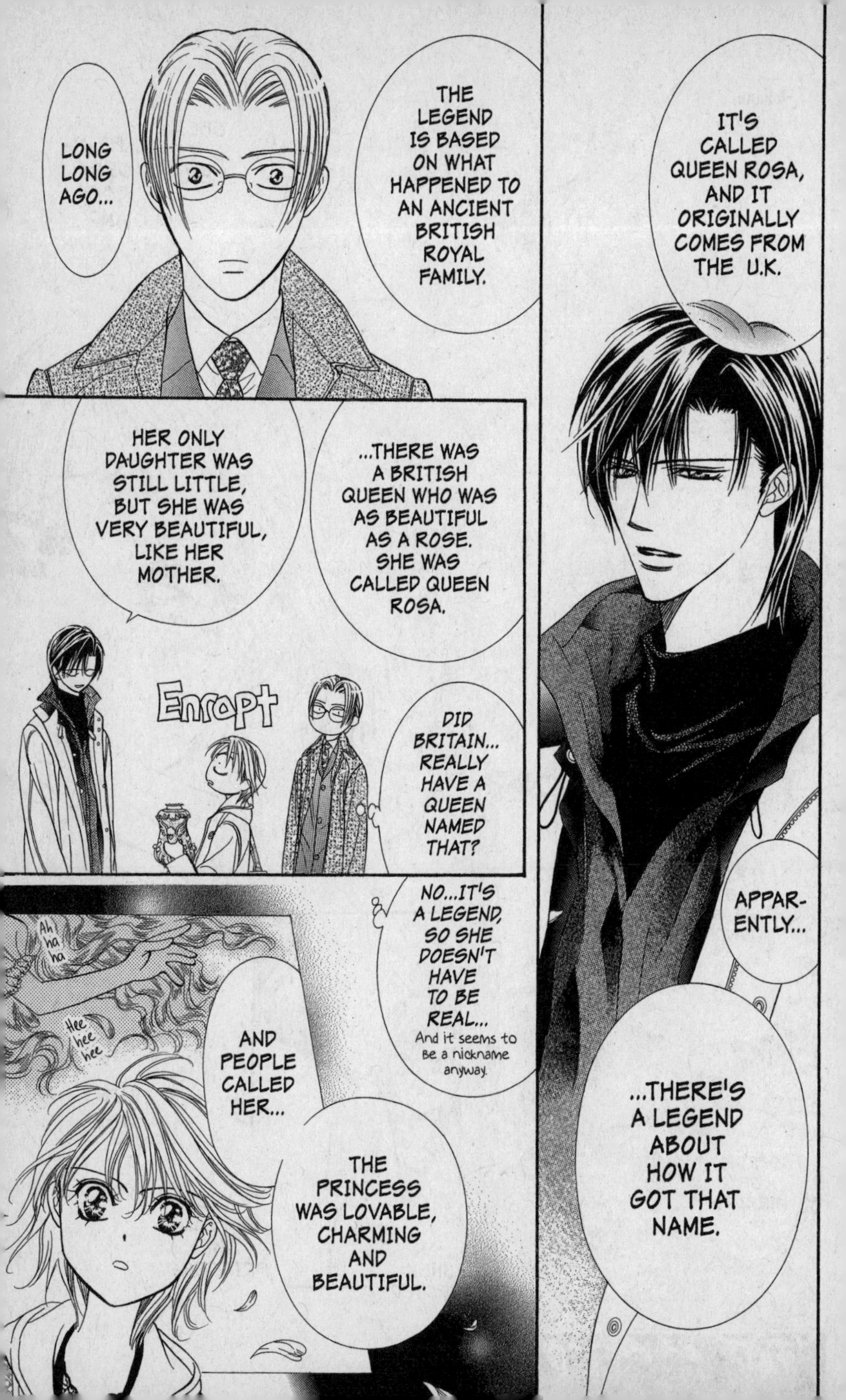
IT'S CALLED QUEEN ROSA, AND IT ORIGINALLY COMES FROM THE U.K.
APPAR-ENTLY...
...THERE'S A LEGEND ABOUT HOW IT GOT THAT NAME.
THE LEGEND IS BASED ON WHAT HAPPENED TO AN ANCIENT BRITISH ROYAL FAMILY.
LONG LONG AGO...
...THERE WAS A BRITISH QUEEN WHO WAS AS BEAUTIFUL AS A ROSE. SHE WAS CALLED QUEEN ROSA.
HER ONLY DAUGHTER WAS STILL LITTLE, BUT SHE WAS VERY BEAUTIFUL, LIKE HER MOTHER.
DID BRITAIN... REALLY HAVE A QUEEN NAMED THAT?
Enrapt
NO...IT'S A LEGEND, SO SHE DOESN'T HAVE TO BE REAL...
And it seems to be a nickname anyway.
Ah ha ha
Hee hee hee
AND PEOPLE CALLED HER...
THE PRINCESS WAS LOVABLE, CHARMING AND BEAUTIFUL.

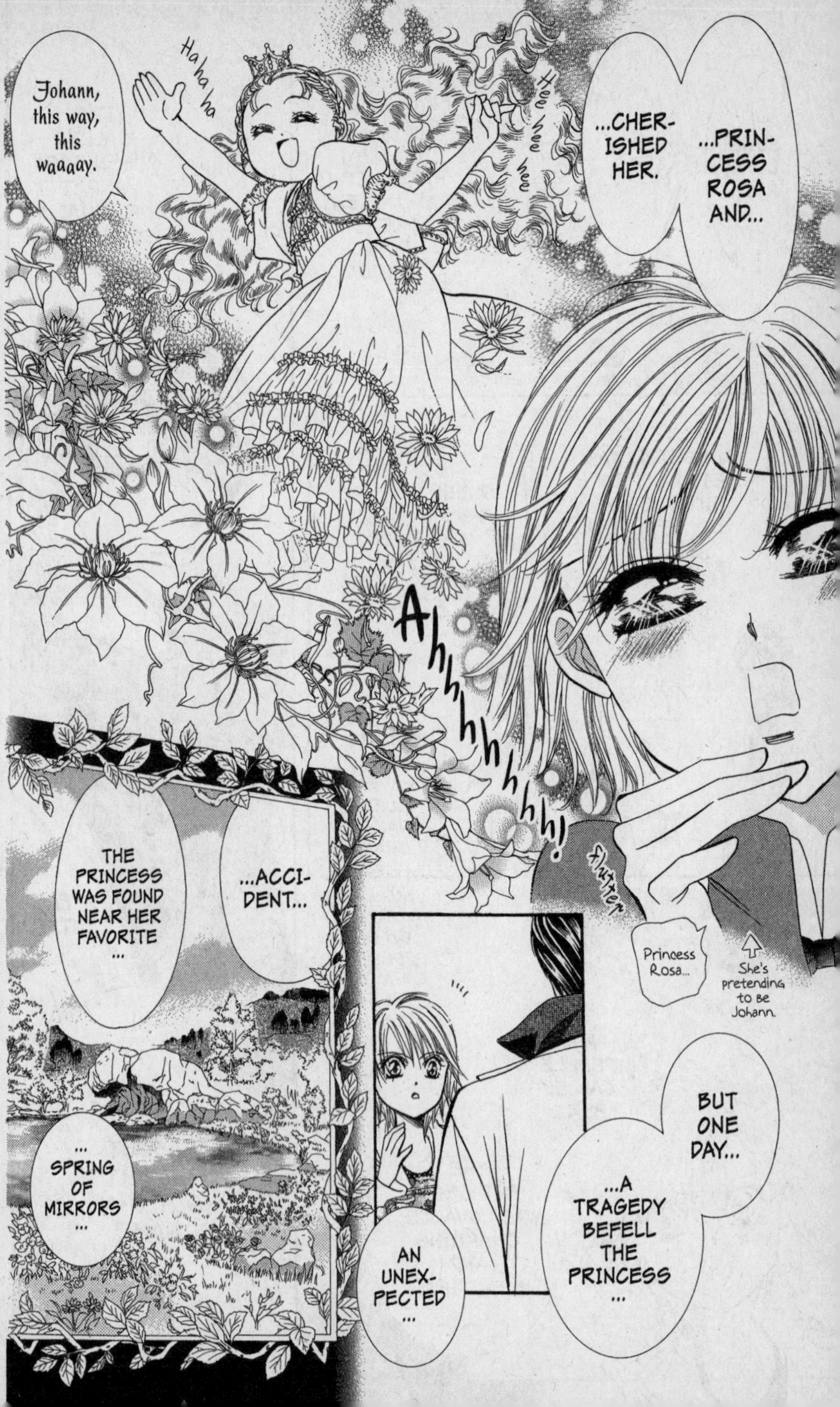
...PRIN-CESS ROSA AND...
...CHER-ISHED HER.
Hee hee hee
Ha ha ha
Johann, this way, this waaaay.
Ahhhhhhhh!
flutter
She's pretending to be Johann.
Princess Rosa...
BUT ONE DAY...
...A TRAGEDY BEFELL THE PRINCESS ...
AN UNEX-PECTED ...
...ACCI-DENT...
THE PRINCESS WAS FOUND NEAR HER FAVORITE ...
... SPRING OF MIRRORS ...

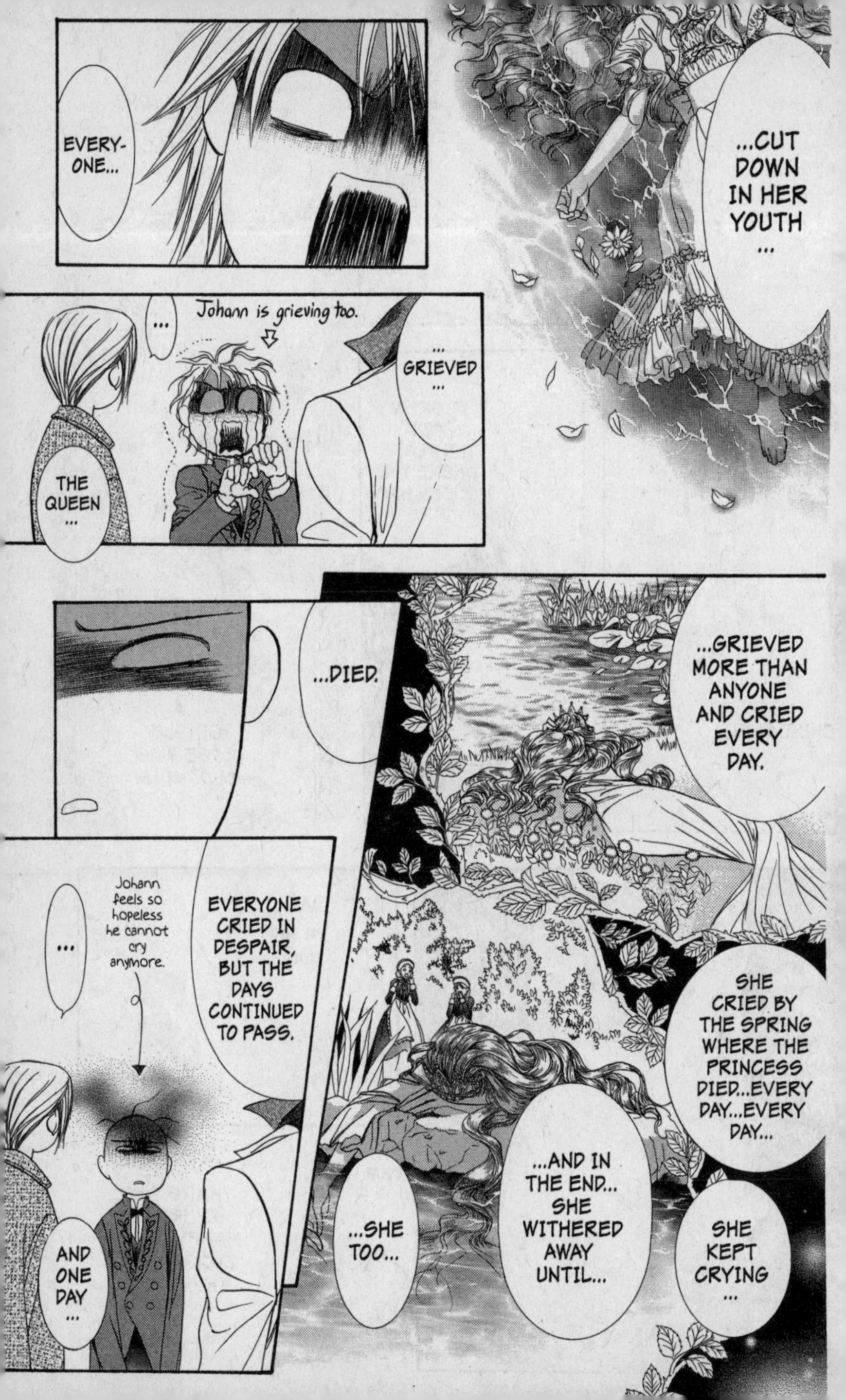
...CUT DOWN IN HER YOUTH...
EVERY-ONE...
...GRIEVED...
...
Johann is grieving too.
THE QUEEN...
...GRIEVED MORE THAN ANYONE AND CRIED EVERY DAY.
SHE CRIED BY THE SPRING WHERE THE PRINCESS DIED...EVERY DAY...EVERY DAY...
SHE KEPT CRYING...
...AND IN THE END... SHE WITHERED AWAY UNTIL...
...SHE TOO...
...DIED.
EVERYONE CRIED IN DESPAIR, BUT THE DAYS CONTINUED TO PASS.
...
Johann feels so hopeless he cannot cry anymore.
AND ONE DAY...

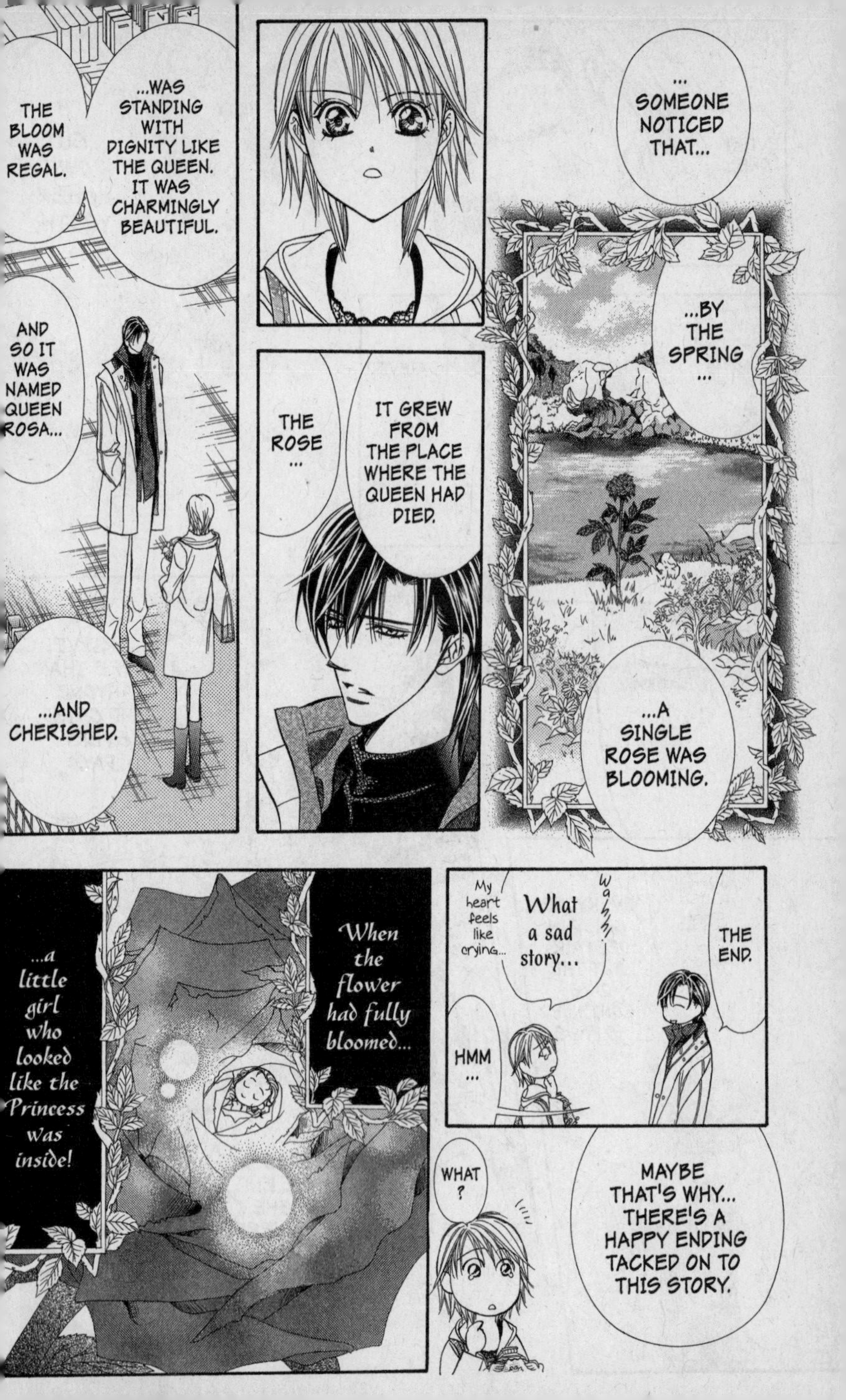
... SOMEONE NOTICED THAT...
...BY THE SPRING ...
...A SINGLE ROSE WAS BLOOMING.
IT GREW FROM THE PLACE WHERE THE QUEEN HAD DIED.
THE ROSE ...
...WAS STANDING WITH DIGNITY LIKE THE QUEEN. IT WAS CHARMINGLY BEAUTIFUL.
THE BLOOM WAS REGAL.
AND SO IT WAS NAMED QUEEN ROSA...
...AND CHERISHED.
THE END.
What a sad story...
My heart feels like crying...
HMM ...
MAYBE THAT'S WHY... THERE'S A HAPPY ENDING TACKED ON TO THIS STORY.
WHAT ?
When the flower had fully bloomed...
...a little girl who looked like the Princess was inside!

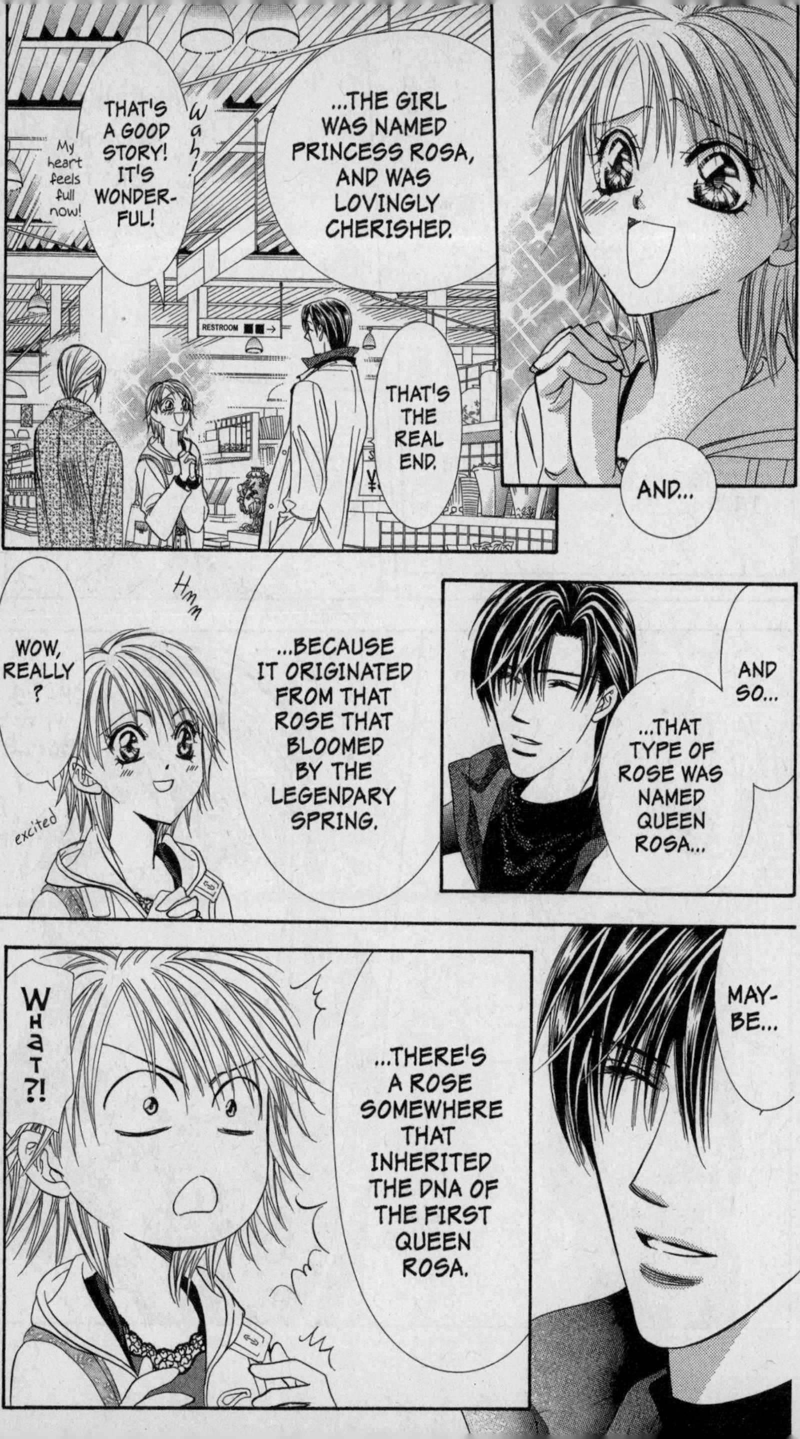
AND...
...THE GIRL WAS NAMED PRINCESS ROSA, AND WAS LOVINGLY CHERISHED.
THAT'S THE REAL END.
THAT'S A GOOD STORY! IT'S WONDERFUL!
Wah!
My heart feels full now!
RESTROOM
AND SO...
...THAT TYPE OF ROSE WAS NAMED QUEEN ROSA...
...BECAUSE IT ORIGINATED FROM THAT ROSE THAT BLOOMED BY THE LEGENDARY SPRING.
Hmm
WOW, REALLY?
excited
MAY-BE...
...THERE'S A ROSE SOMEWHERE THAT INHERITED THE DNA OF THE FIRST QUEEN ROSA.
WHAT?!

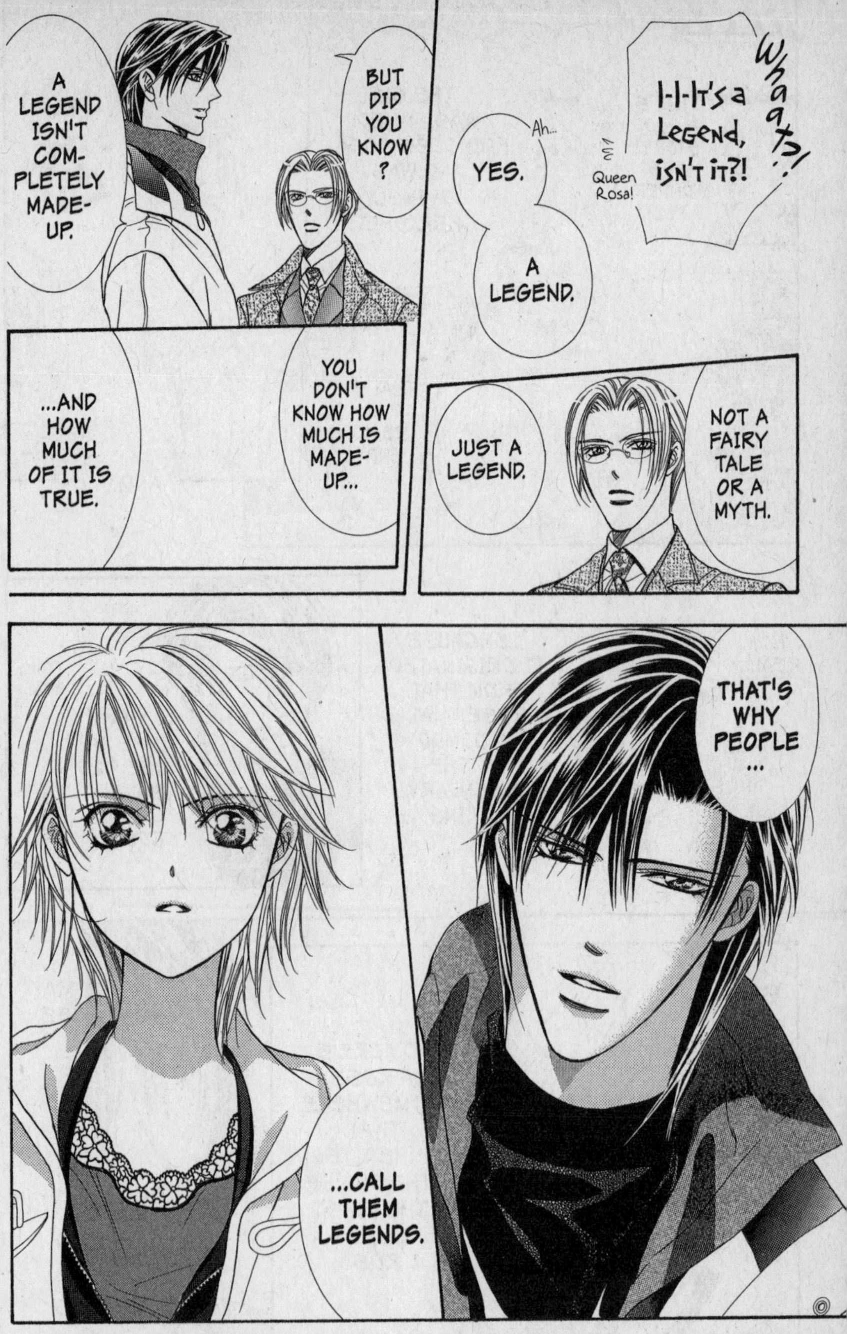
Whaat?!
I-I-It's a Legend, isn't it?!
Queen Rosa!
Ah...
YES.
A LEGEND.
BUT DID YOU KNOW?
A LEGEND ISN'T COMPLETELY MADE-UP.
NOT A FAIRY TALE OR A MYTH.
JUST A LEGEND.
YOU DON'T KNOW HOW MUCH IS MADE-UP...
...AND HOW MUCH OF IT IS TRUE.
THAT'S WHY PEOPLE...
...CALL THEM LEGENDS.

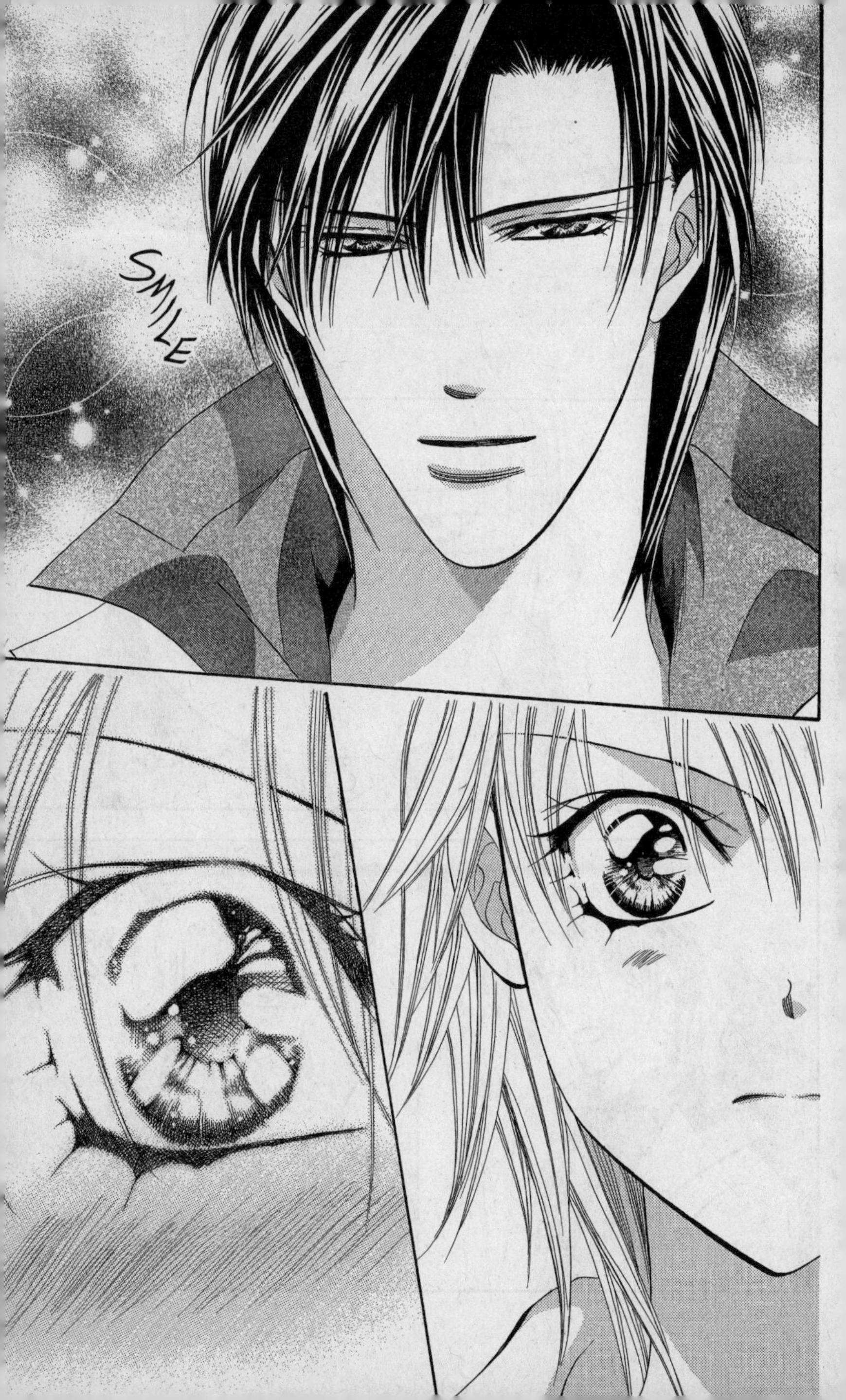
SMILE

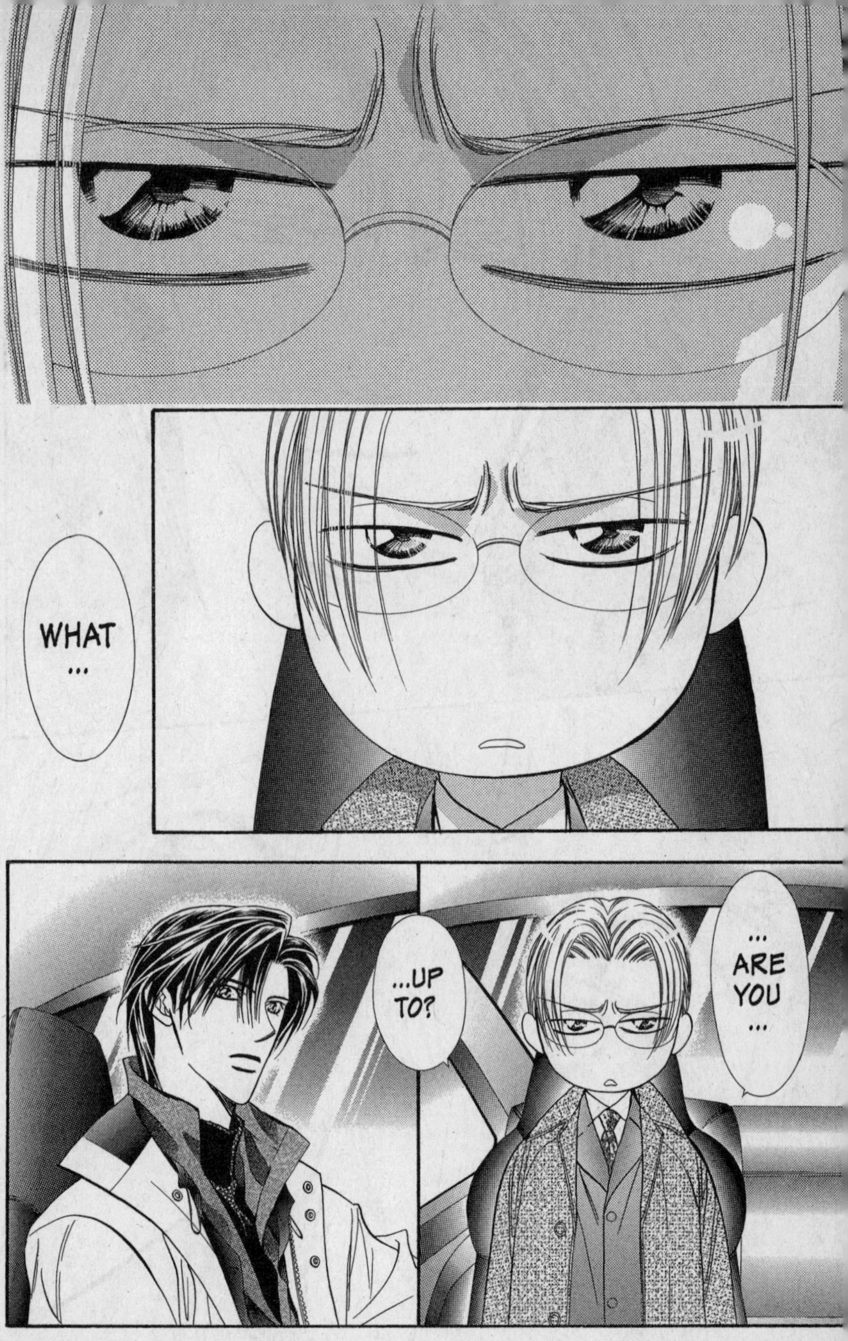
WHAT ...
... ARE YOU ...
...UP TO?

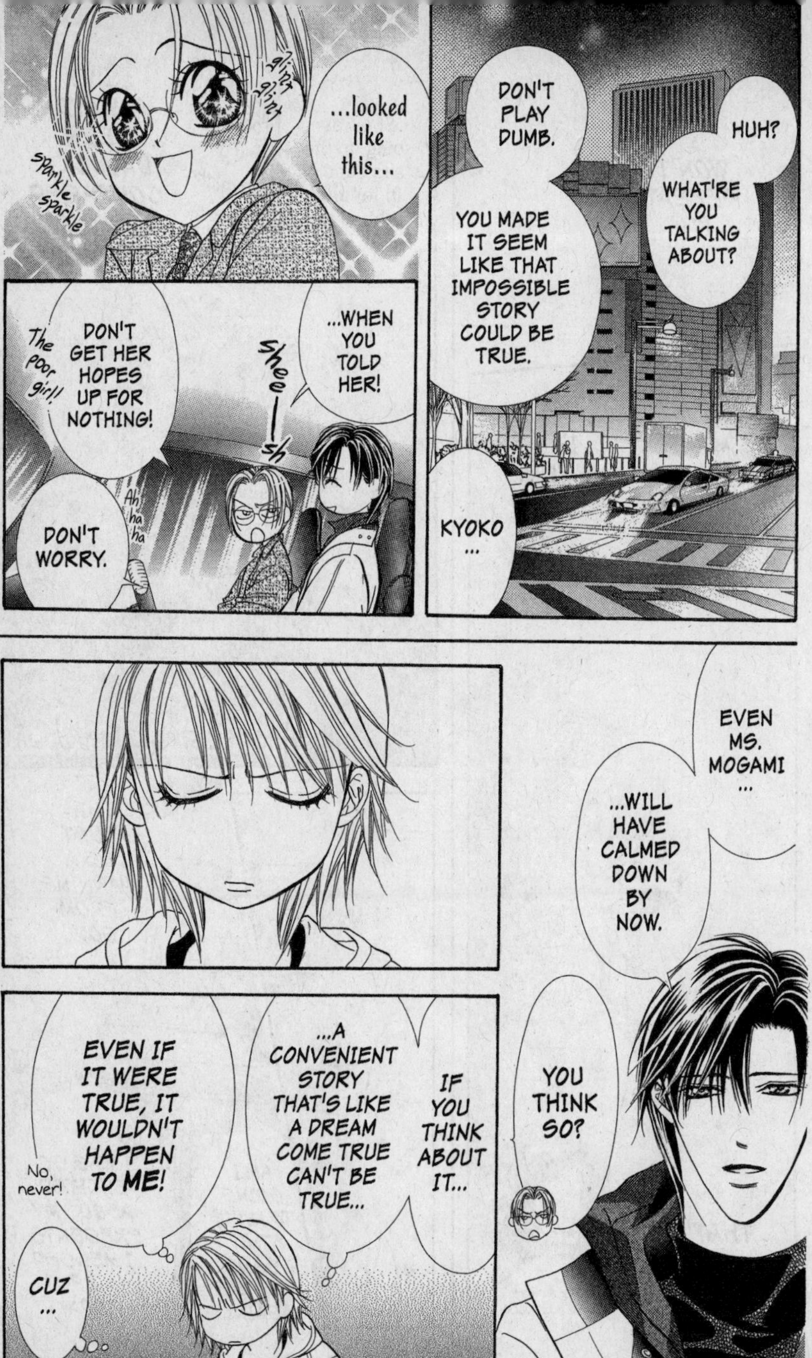
HUH?
WHAT'RE YOU TALKING ABOUT?
DON'T PLAY DUMB.
YOU MADE IT SEEM LIKE THAT IMPOSSIBLE STORY COULD BE TRUE.
KYOKO ...
...looked like this...
glint glint
sparkle sparkle
...WHEN YOU TOLD HER!
shee-ish
DON'T GET HER HOPES UP FOR NOTHING!
The poor girl!!
Ah ha ha
DON'T WORRY.
EVEN MS. MOGAMI ...
...WILL HAVE CALMED DOWN BY NOW.
YOU THINK SO?
IF YOU THINK ABOUT IT...
...A CONVENIENT STORY THAT'S LIKE A DREAM COME TRUE CAN'T BE TRUE...
EVEN IF IT WERE TRUE, IT WOULDN'T HAPPEN TO ME!
No, never!
CUZ ...

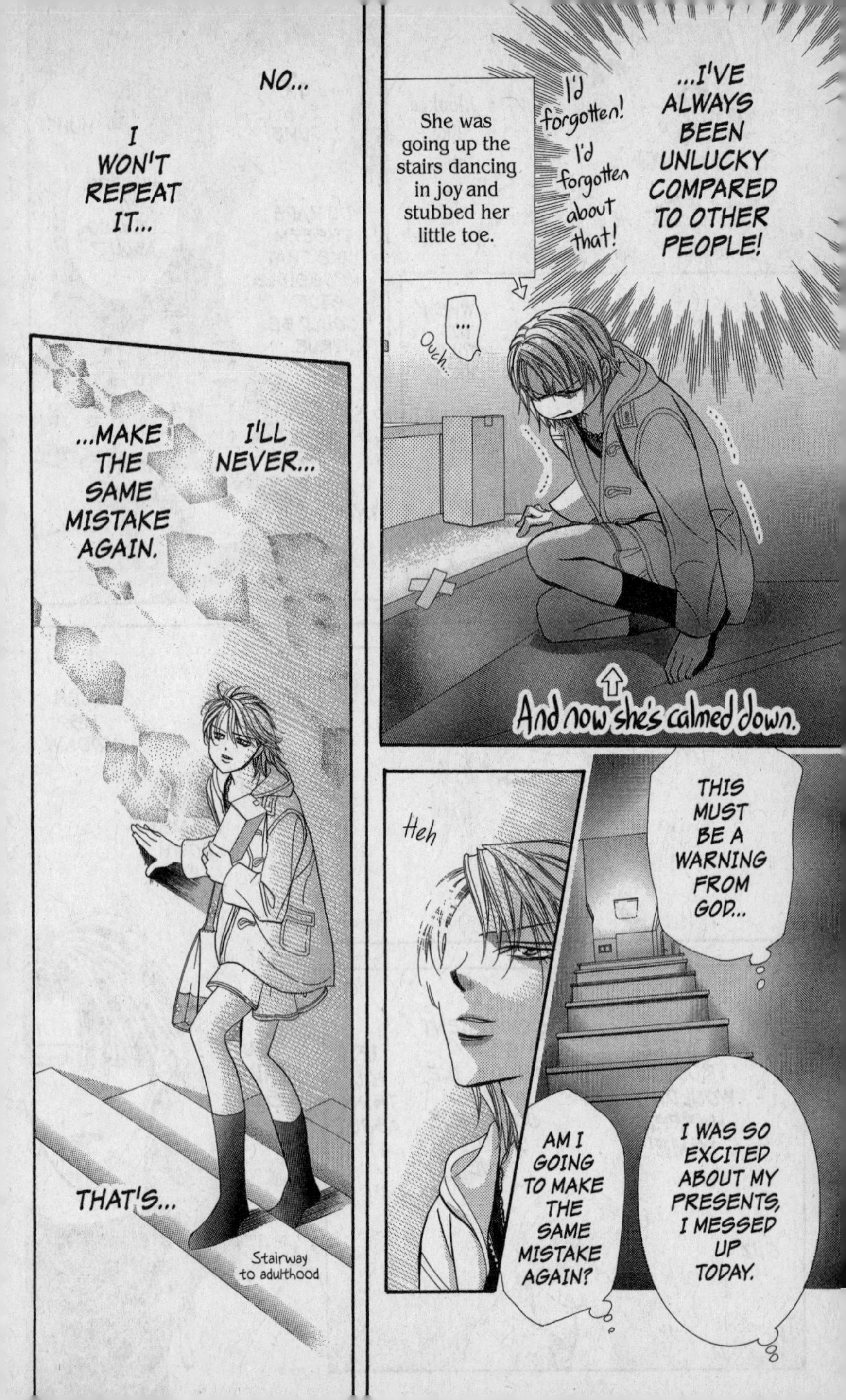
...I'VE ALWAYS BEEN UNLUCKY COMPARED TO OTHER PEOPLE!
I'd forgotten! I'd forgotten about that!
She was going up the stairs dancing in joy and stubbed her little toe.
...
Ouch...
And now she's calmed down.
THIS MUST BE A WARNING FROM GOD...
I WAS SO EXCITED ABOUT MY PRESENTS, I MESSED UP TODAY.
Heh
AM I GOING TO MAKE THE SAME MISTAKE AGAIN?
NO...
I WON'T REPEAT IT...
I'LL NEVER...
...MAKE THE SAME MISTAKE AGAIN.
THAT'S...
Stairway to adulthood

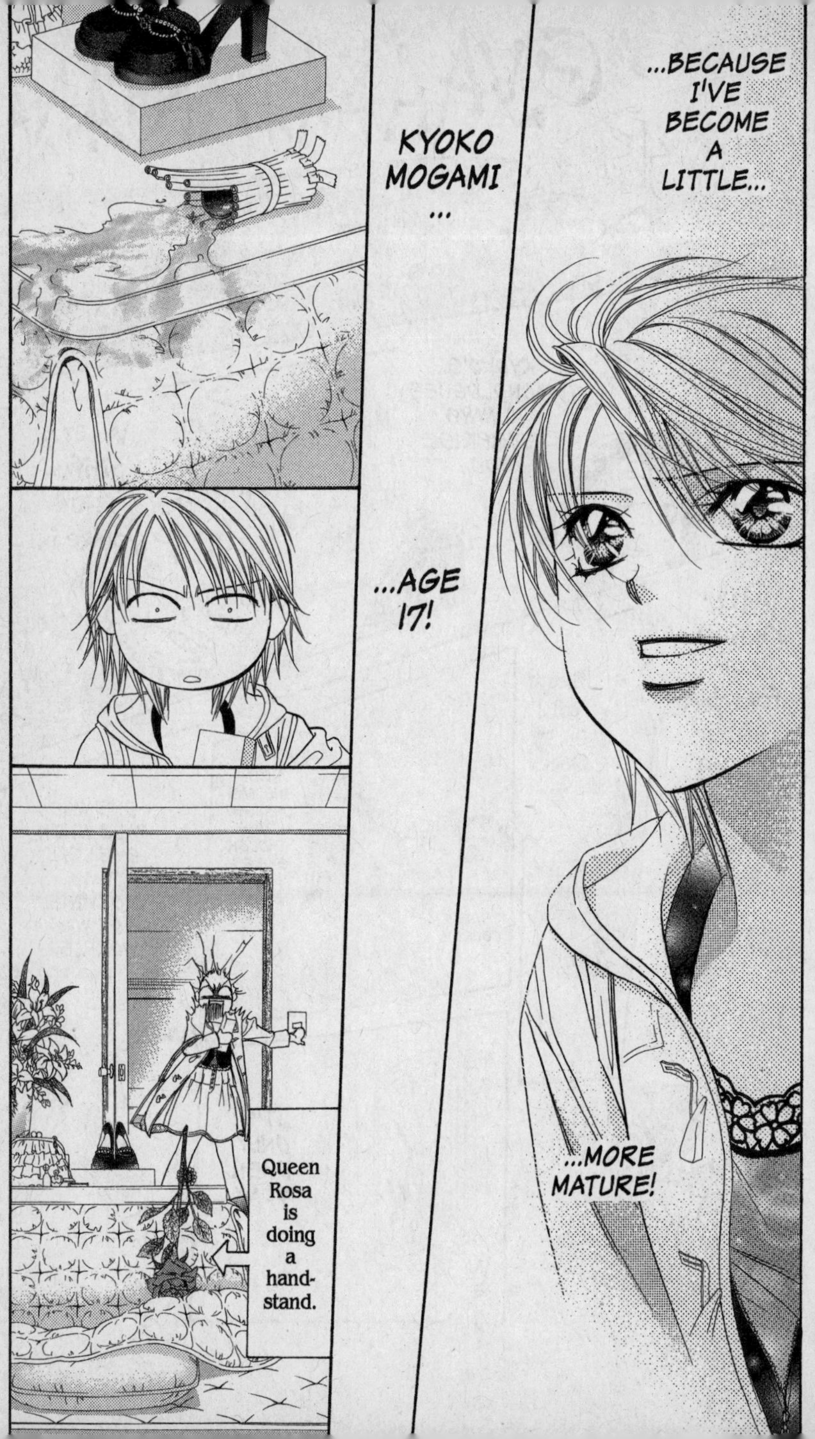
...BECAUSE I'VE BECOME A LITTLE...
...MORE MATURE!
KYOKO MOGAMI ...
...AGE 17!
Queen Rosa is doing a hand-stand.

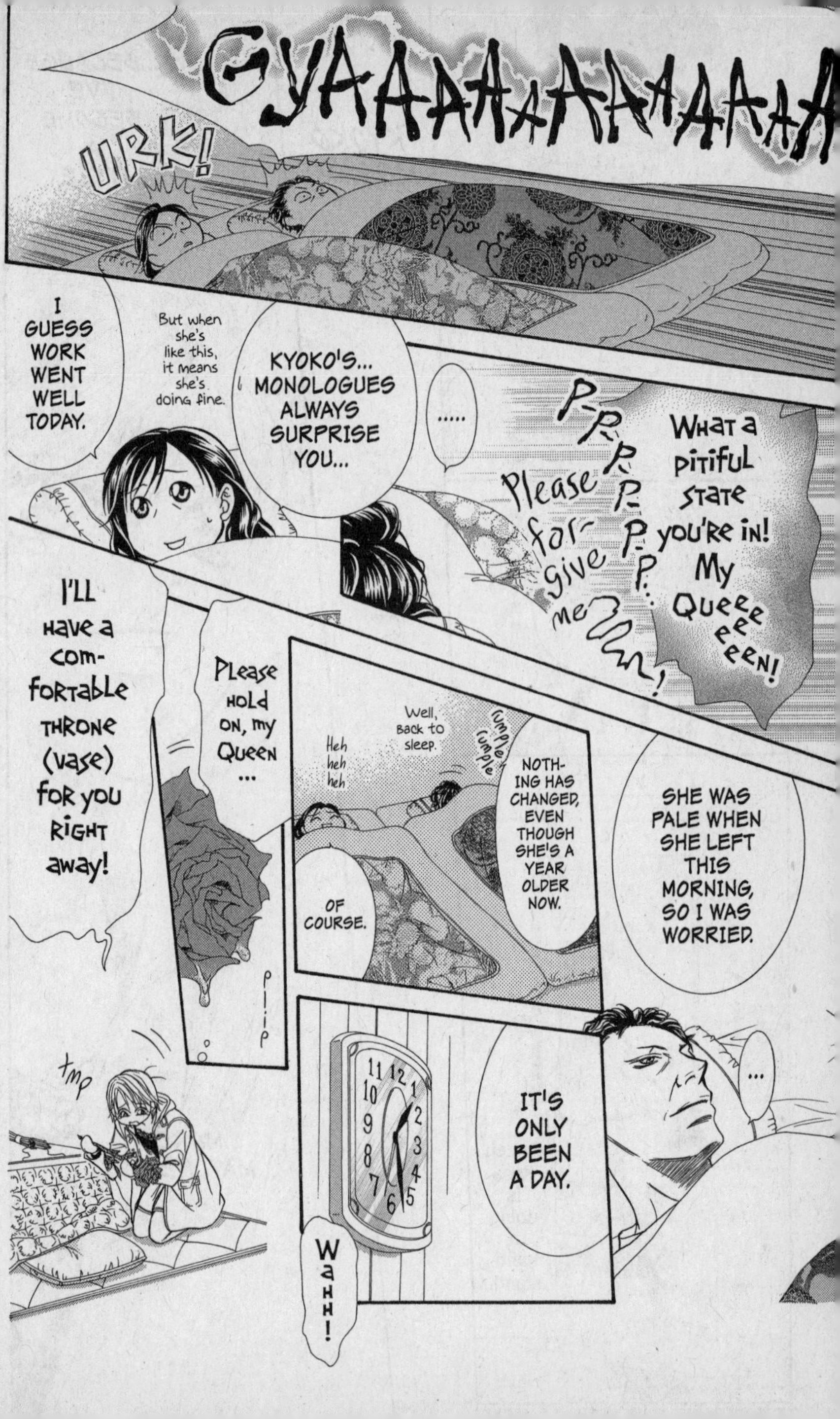

GYAAAAAAAAAAAA
URK!
What a pitiful state you're in! My Queeeeeen!
P-P-P-P-P-P... Please forgive me...!
.....
KYOKO'S... MONOLOGUES ALWAYS SURPRISE YOU...
But when she's like this, it means she's doing fine.
I GUESS WORK WENT WELL TODAY.
SHE WAS PALE WHEN SHE LEFT THIS MORNING, SO I WAS WORRIED.
NOTHING HAS CHANGED, EVEN THOUGH SHE'S A YEAR OLDER NOW.
rumple rumple
Well, back to sleep.
Heh heh heh
OF COURSE.
Please hold on, my Queen...
I'll have a comfortable throne (vase) for you right away!
plip
tmp
...
IT'S ONLY BEEN A DAY.
WAHH!

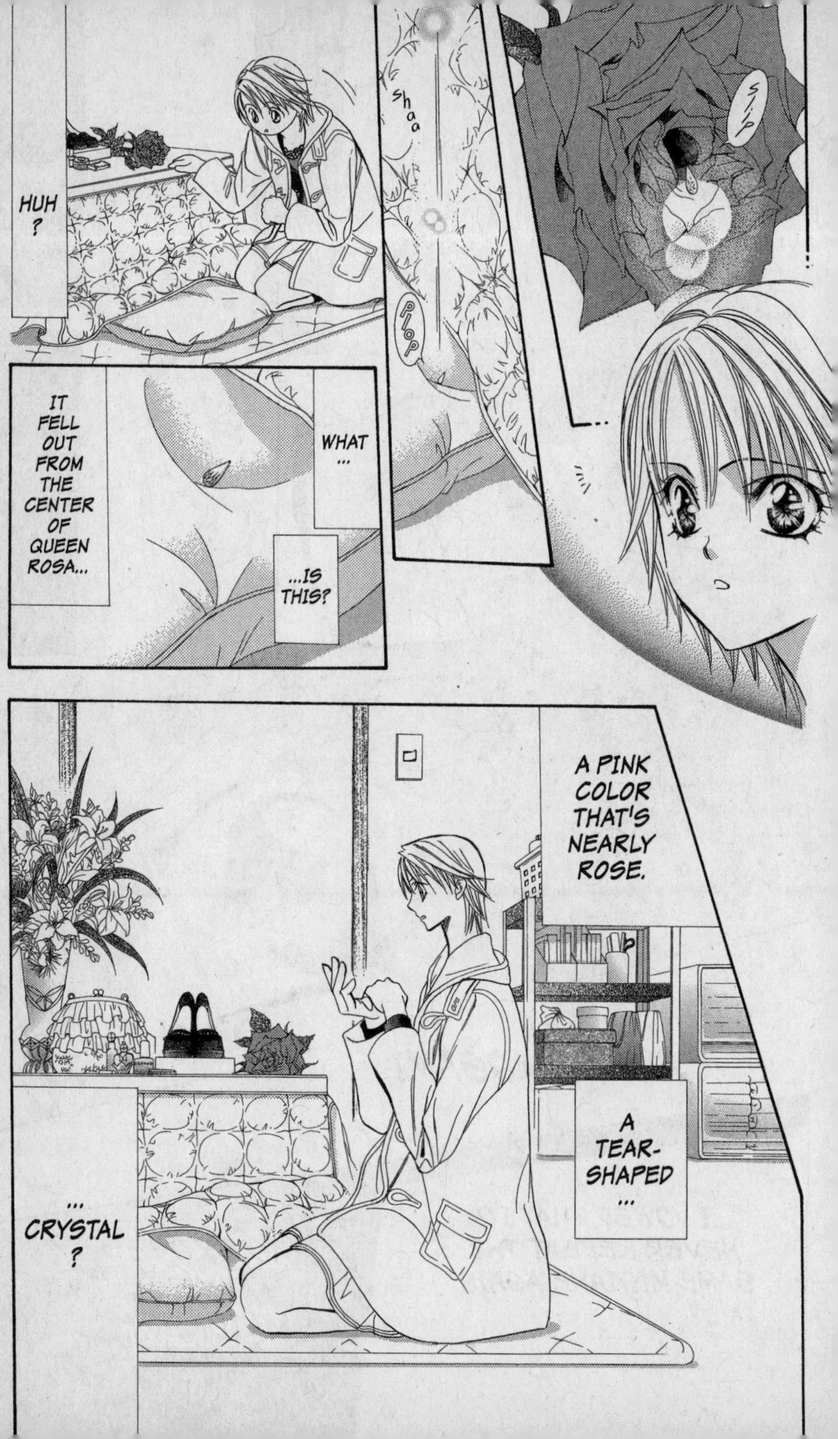
slip
...
shaa
plop
HUH?
...
WHAT...
...IS THIS?
IT FELL OUT FROM THE CENTER OF QUEEN ROSA...
A PINK COLOR THAT'S NEARLY ROSE.
A TEAR-SHAPED...
...CRYSTAL?

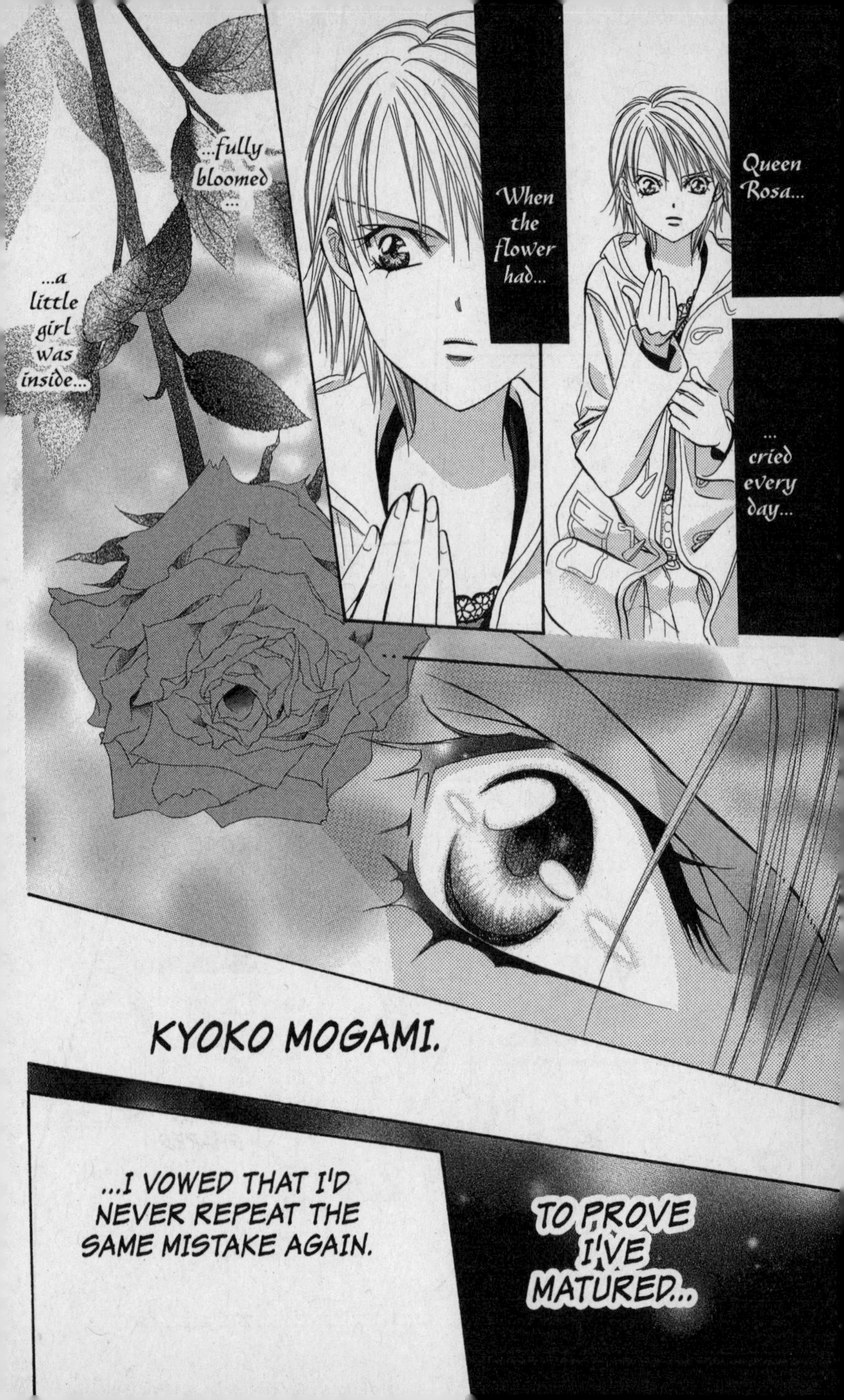
Queen Rosa...
...cried every day...
When the flower had...
...fully bloomed...
...a little girl was inside...
...
KYOKO MOGAMI.
TO PROVE I'VE MATURED...
...I VOWED THAT I'D NEVER REPEAT THE SAME MISTAKE AGAIN.

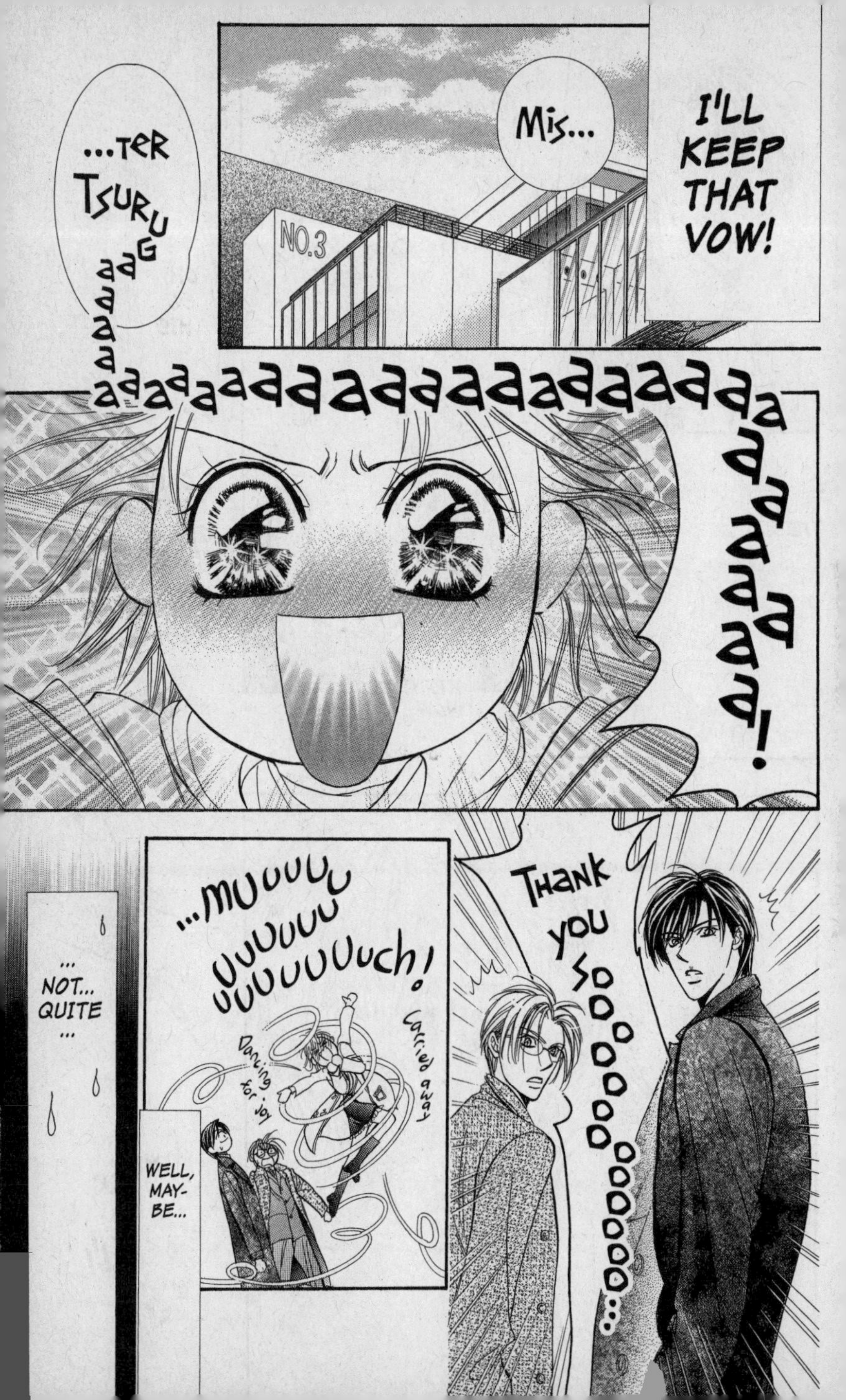
I'll keep that vow!
Mis...
...ter Tsurugaaaaaaaaaaaaaaaaaaaaaaaaaaaaaaaaaaaa!
Thank you sooooooooooooooooo...
...muuuuuuuuuuuuuuuuuch!
Carried away
Dancing for joy
Well, may-be...
... not... quite ...

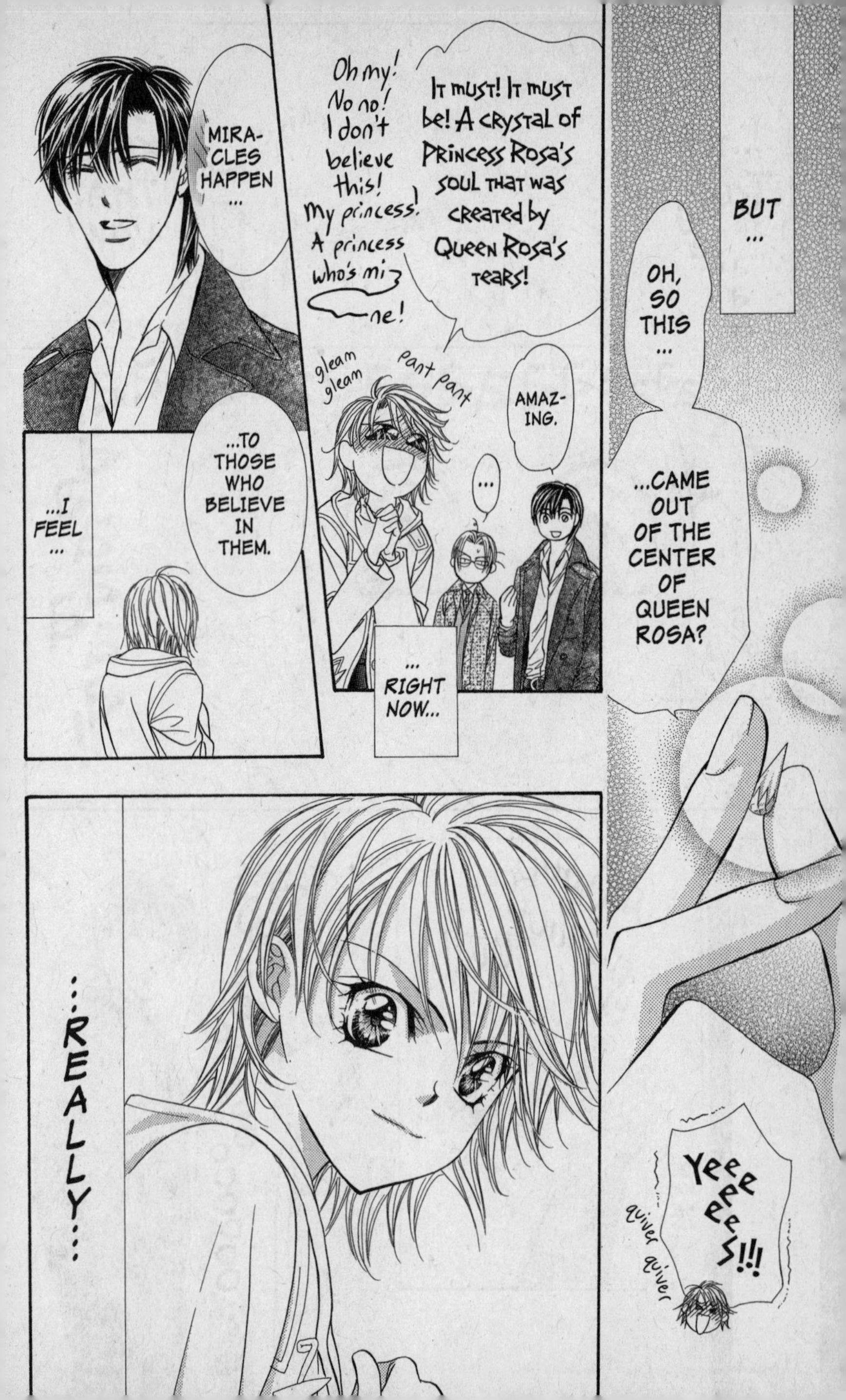
BUT ...
OH, SO THIS ...
...CAME OUT OF THE CENTER OF QUEEN ROSA?
Yeeeees!!!
quiver quiver
It must! It must be! A crystal of Princess Rosa's soul that was created by Queen Rosa's tears!
Oh my! No no! I don't believe this! My princess! A princess who's mi ne!
gleam gleam
pant pant
AMAZ-ING.
...
... RIGHT NOW...
MIRA-CLES HAPPEN ...
...TO THOSE WHO BELIEVE IN THEM.
...I FEEL ...
...REALLY...

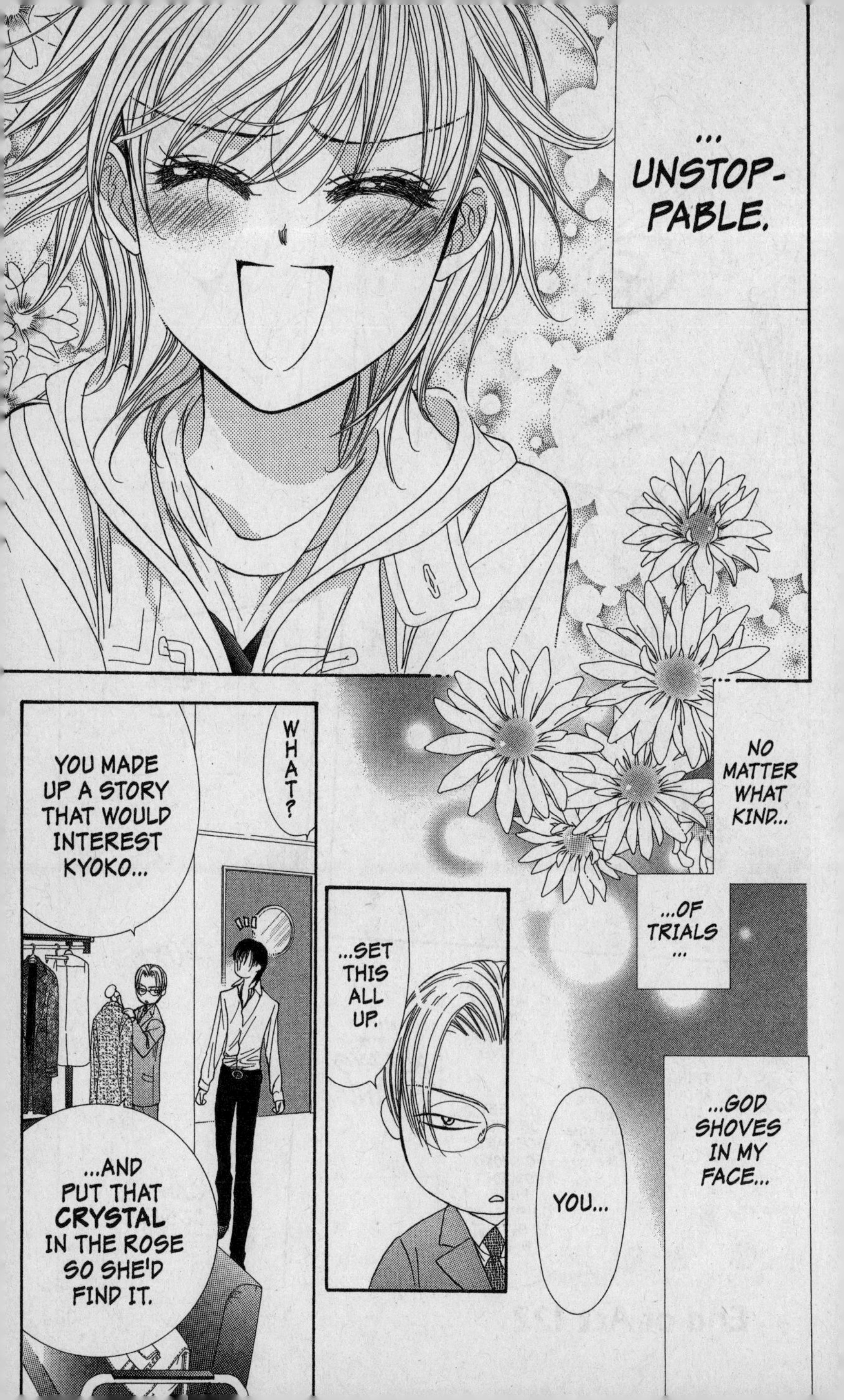
... UNSTOPPABLE.
NO MATTER WHAT KIND...
...OF TRIALS ...
...GOD SHOVES IN MY FACE...
YOU...
...SET THIS ALL UP.
WHAT?
YOU MADE UP A STORY THAT WOULD INTEREST KYOKO...
...AND PUT THAT CRYSTAL IN THE ROSE SO SHE'D FIND IT.

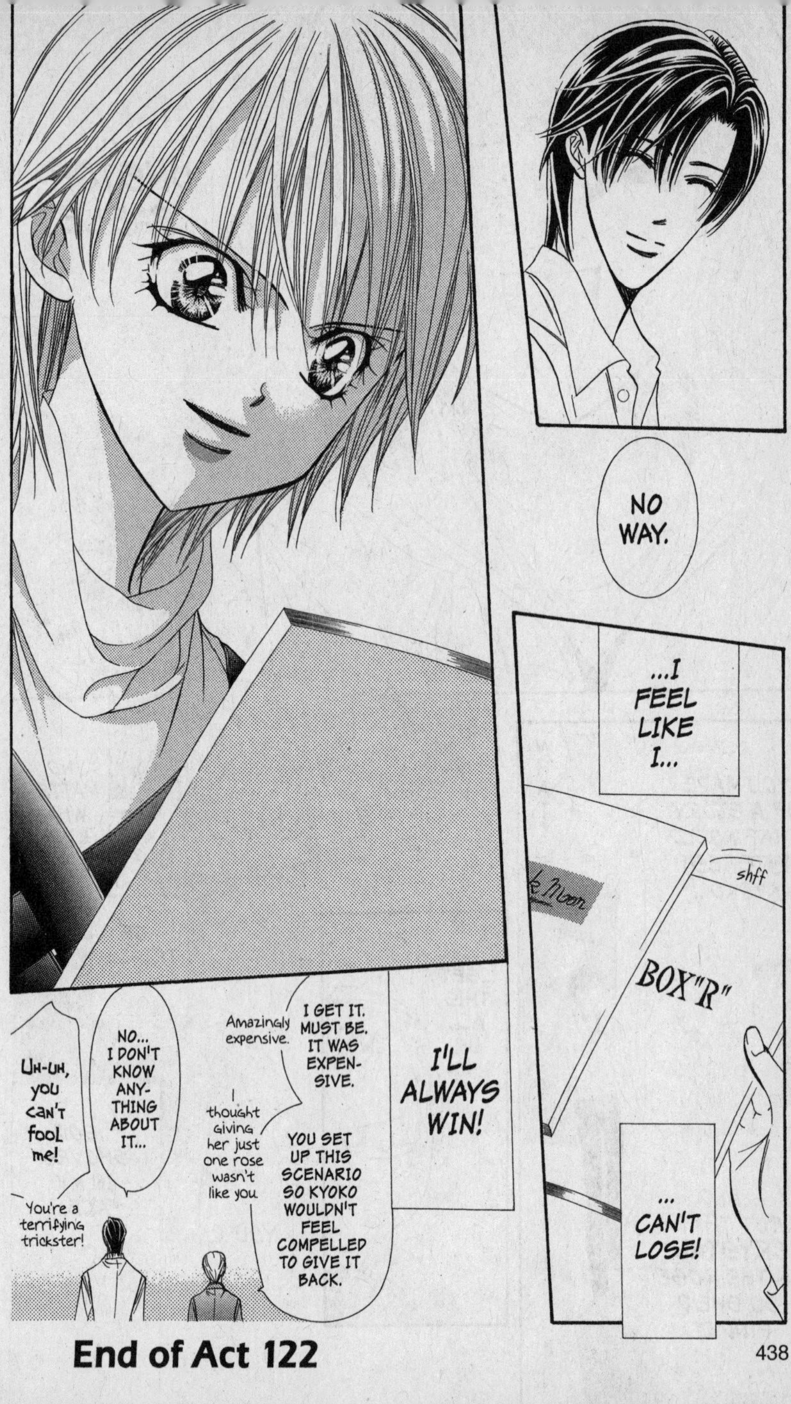
NO WAY.
...I FEEL LIKE I...
shff
BOX"R"
...CAN'T LOSE!
I'LL ALWAYS WIN!
I GET IT. MUST BE. IT WAS EXPENSIVE.
Amazingly expensive.
NO... I DON'T KNOW ANYTHING ABOUT IT...
I thought giving her just one rose wasn't like you.
YOU SET UP THIS SCENARIO SO KYOKO WOULDN'T FEEL COMPELLED TO GIVE IT BACK.
Uh-uh, you can't fool me!
You're a terrifying trickster!

End of Act 122

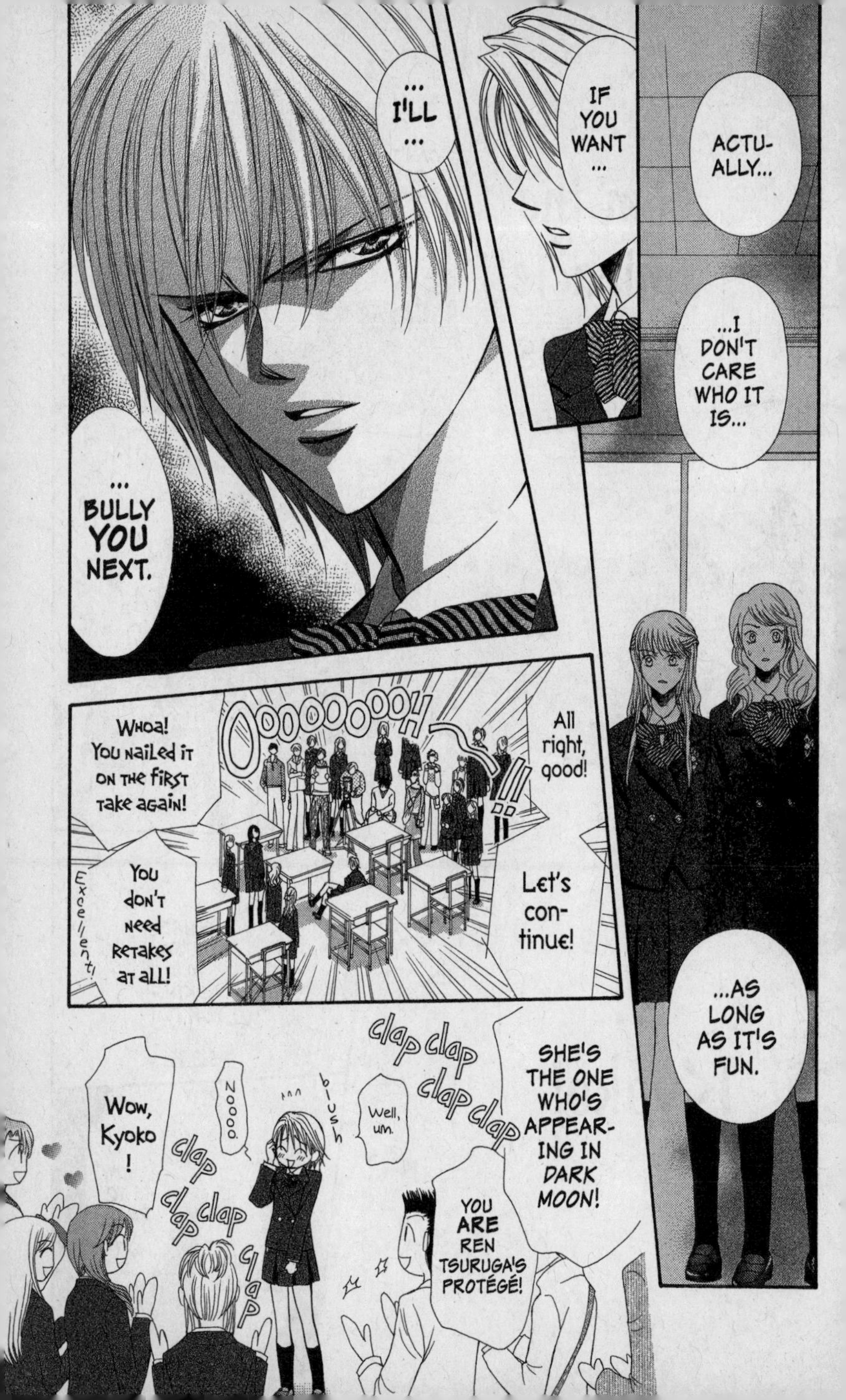
ACTU-ALLY...
...I DON'T CARE WHO IT IS...
...AS LONG AS IT'S FUN.
IF YOU WANT...
... I'LL ...
... BULLY YOU NEXT.
All right, good!
Let's continue!
OOOOOOOOH
!!
Whoa! You nailed it on the first take again!
You don't need retakes at all!
Excellent!
SHE'S THE ONE WHO'S APPEARING IN DARK MOON!
YOU ARE REN TSURUGA'S PROTÉGÉ!
clap clap clap clap
Well, um.
blush
Noooo.
Wow, Kyoko!
clap clap clap clap

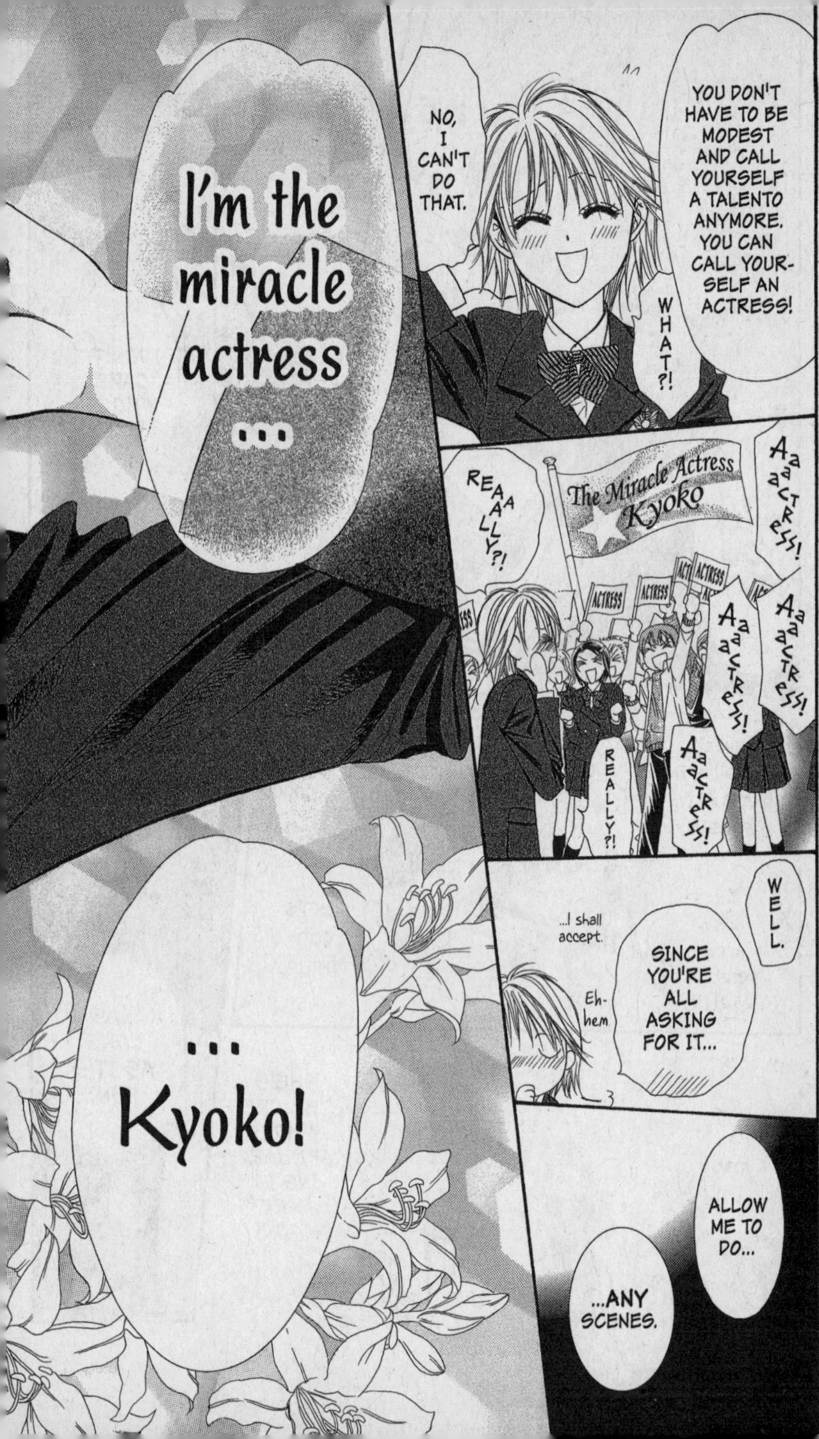
YOU DON'T HAVE TO BE MODEST AND CALL YOURSELF A TALENTO ANYMORE. YOU CAN CALL YOURSELF AN ACTRESS!
NO, I CAN'T DO THAT.
WHAT?!
Aaa actress!
REAAALLY?!
The Miracle Actress Kyoko
ACTRESS
Aaa actress!
Aaa actress!
Aaa actress!
REALLY?!
WELL.
SINCE YOU'RE ALL ASKING FOR IT...
...I shall accept.
Eh-hem
ALLOW ME TO DO...
...ANY SCENES.
I'm the miracle actress...
...Kyoko!

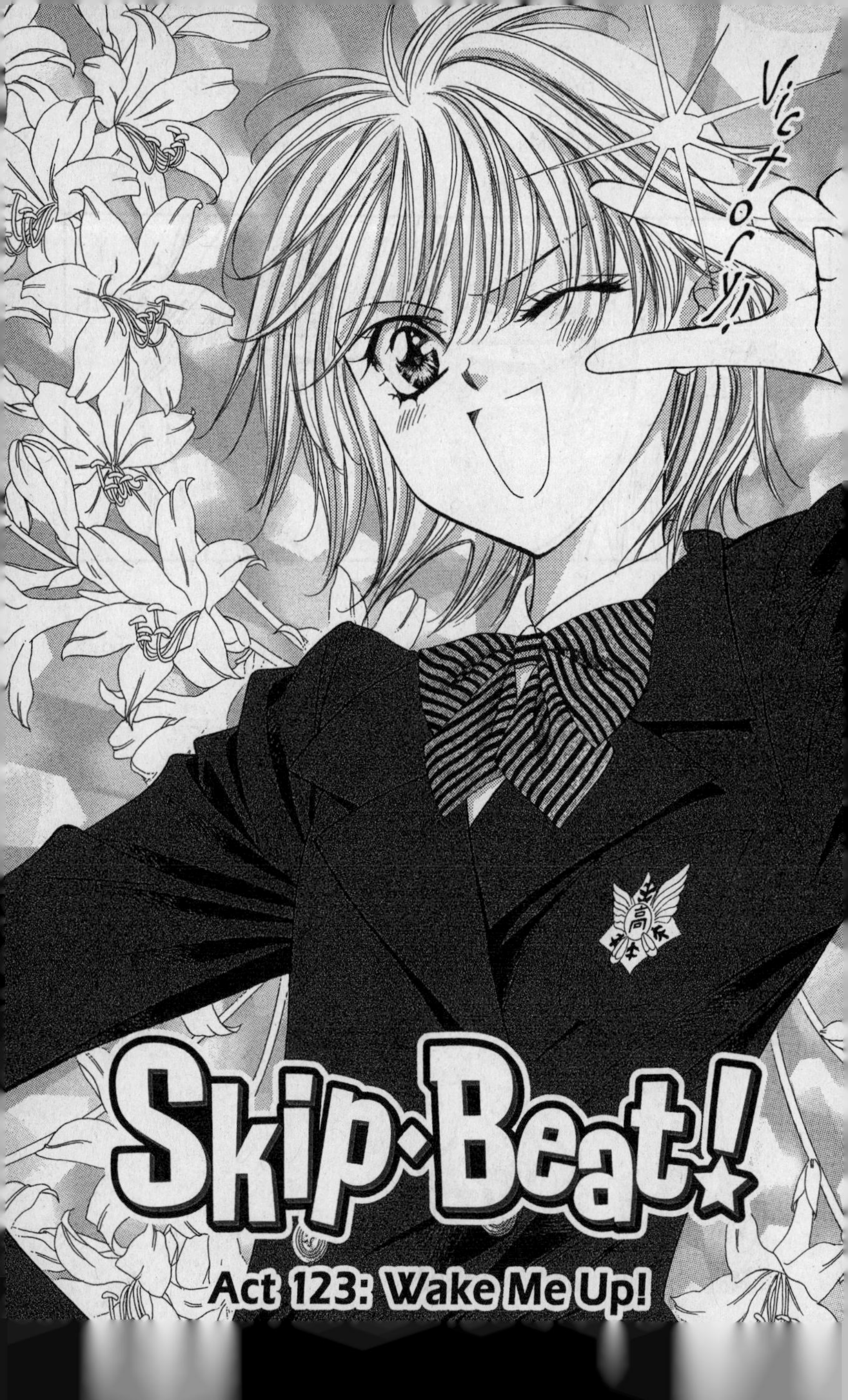
Victory!
Skip·Beat!
Act 123: Wake Me Up!

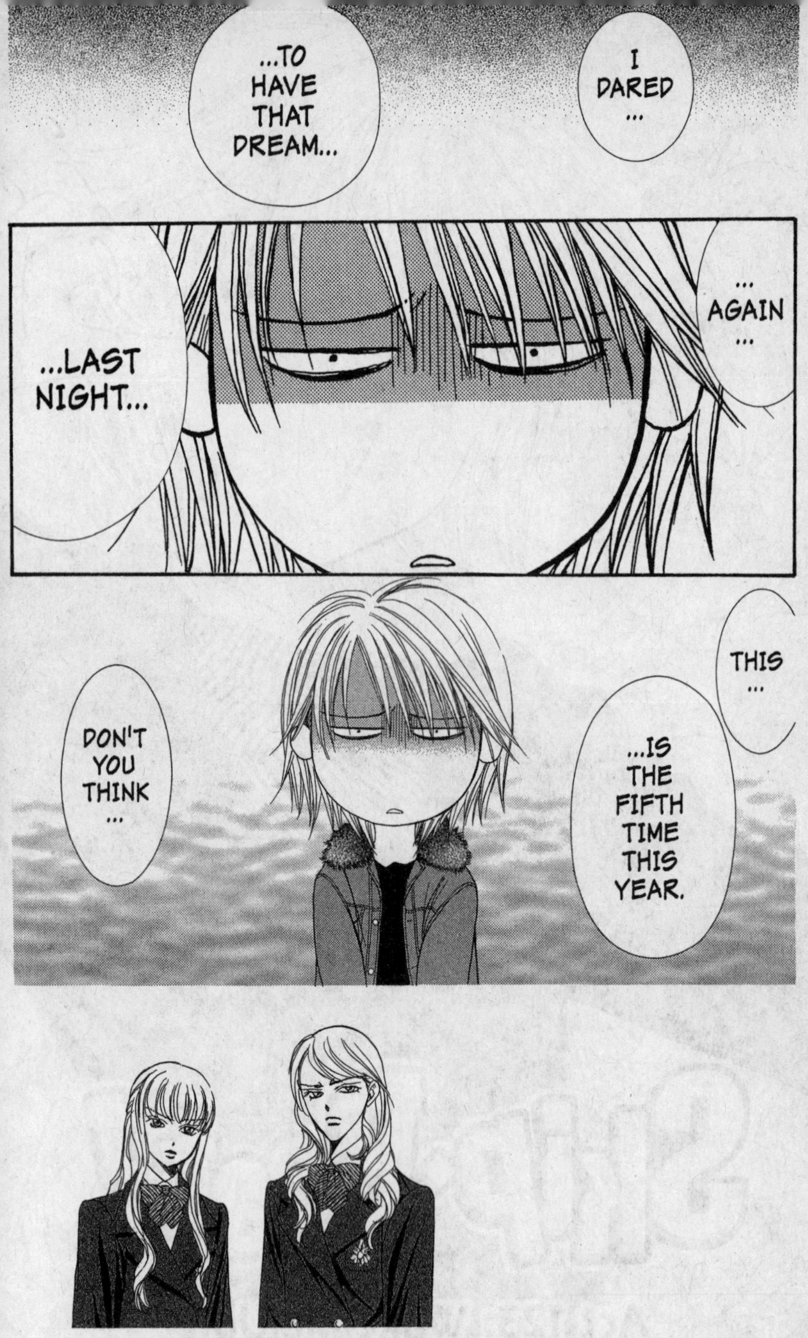
I DARED ...
...TO HAVE THAT DREAM...
... AGAIN ...
...LAST NIGHT...
THIS ...
...IS THE FIFTH TIME THIS YEAR.
DON'T YOU THINK ...

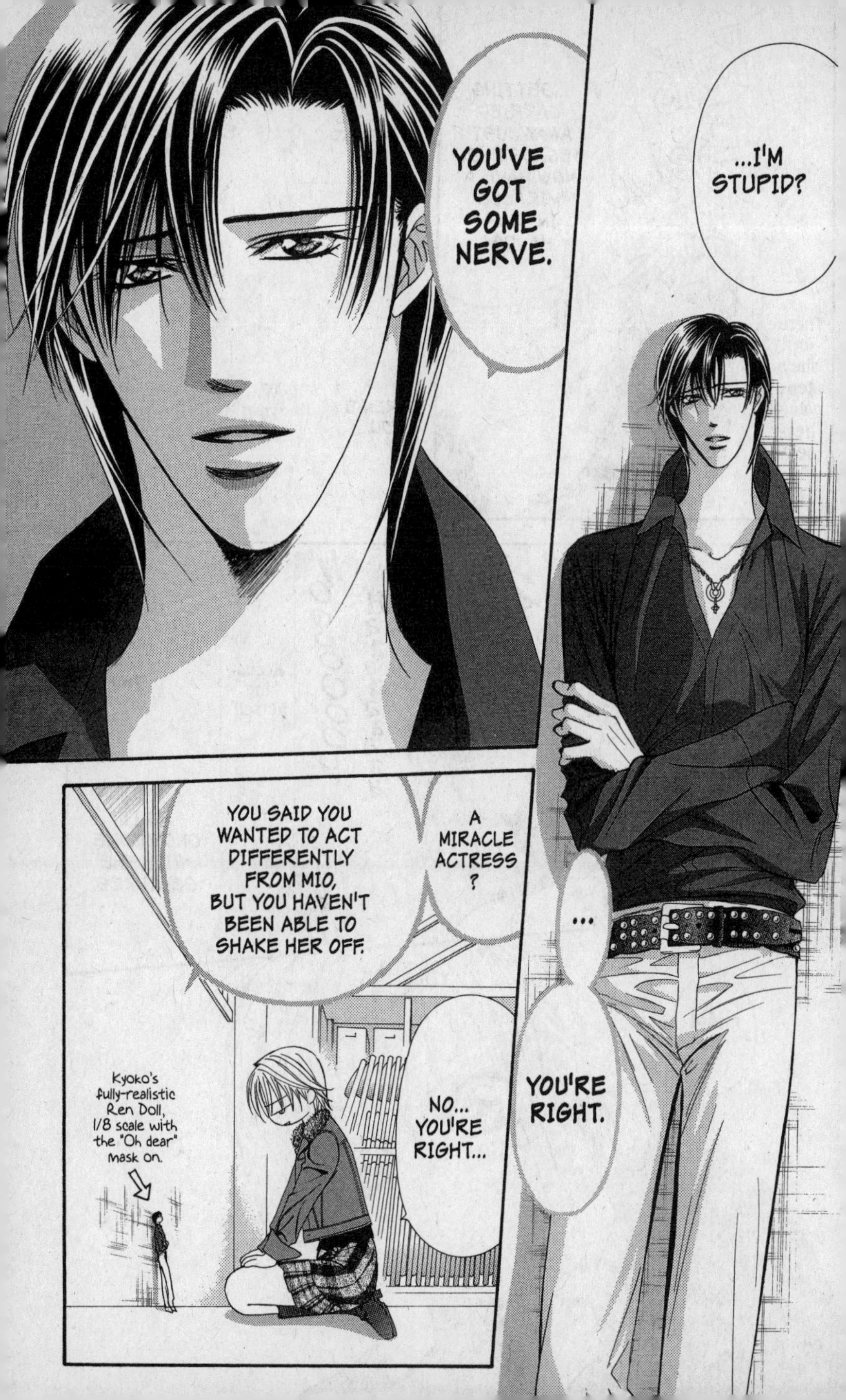
...I'M STUPID?
...
YOU'RE RIGHT.
YOU'VE GOT SOME NERVE.
A MIRACLE ACTRESS?
YOU SAID YOU WANTED TO ACT DIFFERENTLY FROM MIO, BUT YOU HAVEN'T BEEN ABLE TO SHAKE HER OFF.
NO... YOU'RE RIGHT...
Kyoko's fully-realistic Ren Doll, 1/8 scale with the "Oh dear" mask on.

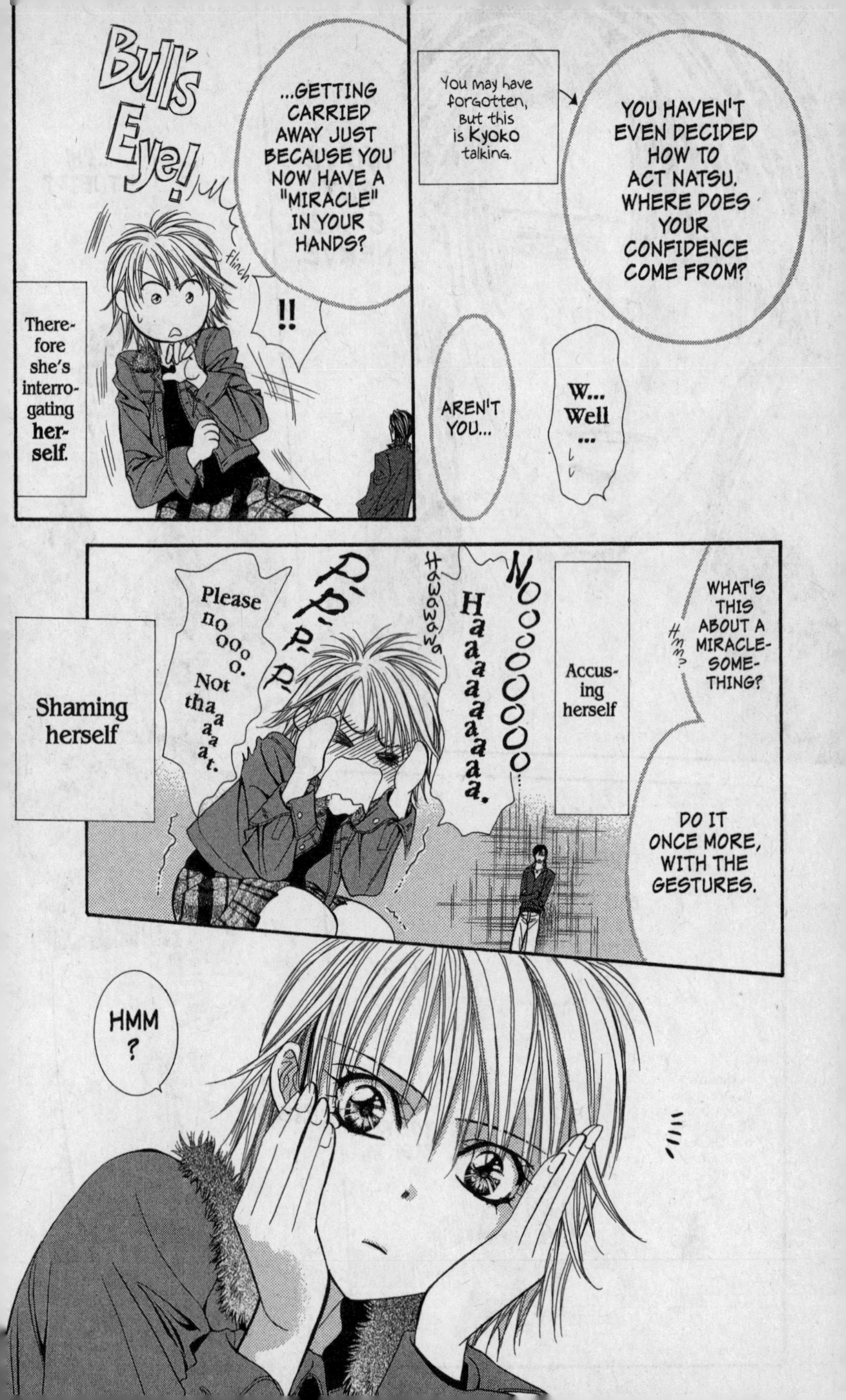

You may have forgotten, but this is Kyoko talking.
YOU HAVEN'T EVEN DECIDED HOW TO ACT NATSU. WHERE DOES YOUR CONFIDENCE COME FROM?
W... Well ...
AREN'T YOU...
...GETTING CARRIED AWAY JUST BECAUSE YOU NOW HAVE A "MIRACLE" IN YOUR HANDS?
Bull's Eye!
flinch
!!
There-fore she's interro-gating her-self.
WHAT'S THIS ABOUT A MIRACLE-SOMETHING?
Hmm?
DO IT ONCE MORE, WITH THE GESTURES.
Accus-ing herself
Noooooooo...
Haaaaaaaaaa.
Hawawawa
P. P. P. P.
Please nooooo. Not thaaaaat.
Shaming herself
HMM ?

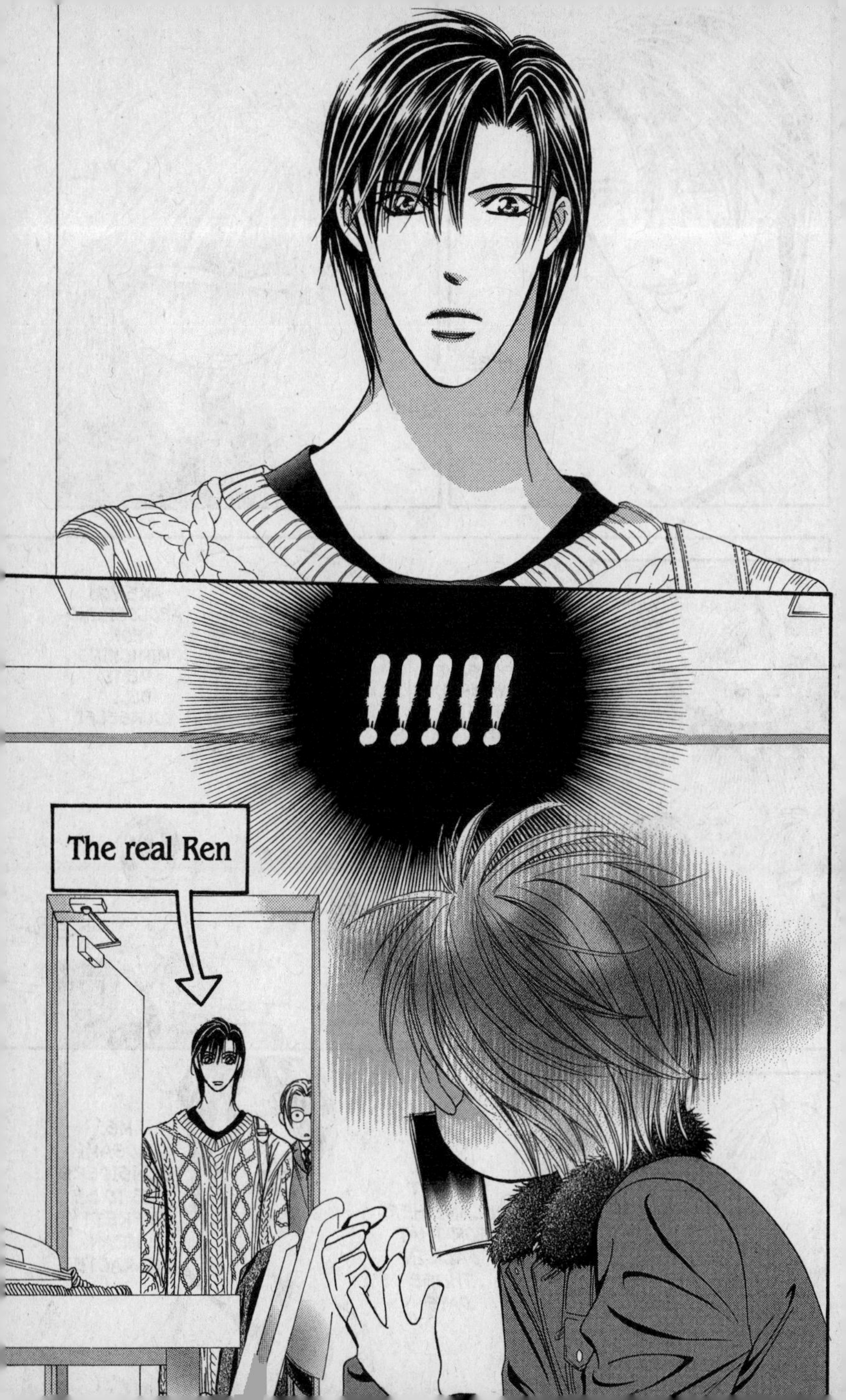
!!!!!
The real Ren

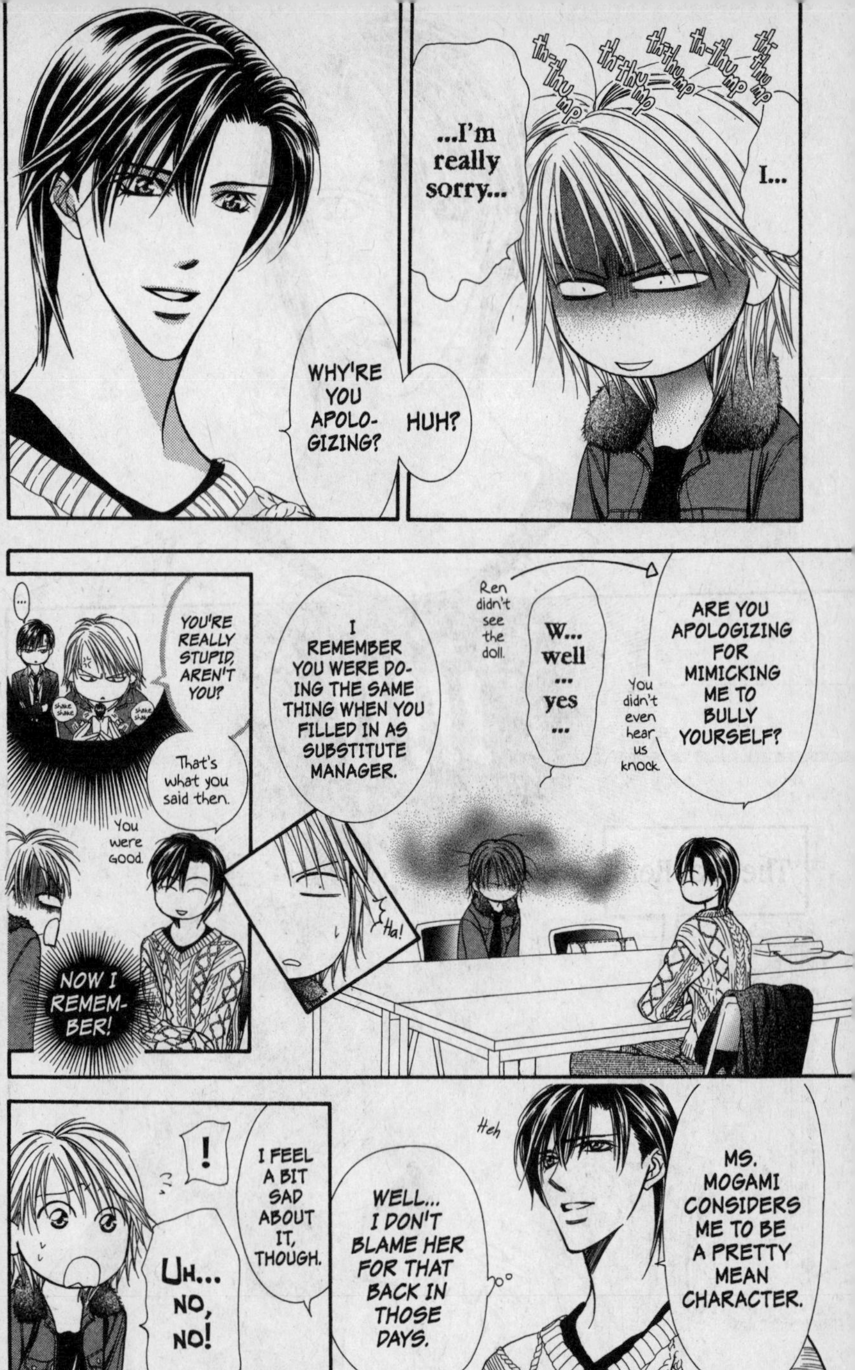

th-thump
th-thump
th-thump
th-thump
I...
...I'm really sorry...
HUH?
WHY'RE YOU APOLOGIZING?
ARE YOU APOLOGIZING FOR MIMICKING ME TO BULLY YOURSELF?
You didn't even hear us knock.
Ren didn't see the doll.
W... well... yes...
I REMEMBER YOU WERE DOING THE SAME THING WHEN YOU FILLED IN AS SUBSTITUTE MANAGER.
Ha!
YOU'RE REALLY STUPID, AREN'T YOU?
...
shake shake
shake shake
That's what you said then.
You were good.
NOW I REMEMBER!
MS. MOGAMI CONSIDERS ME TO BE A PRETTY MEAN CHARACTER.
Heh
WELL... I DON'T BLAME HER FOR THAT BACK IN THOSE DAYS.
I FEEL A BIT SAD ABOUT IT, THOUGH.
!
UH... NO, NO!

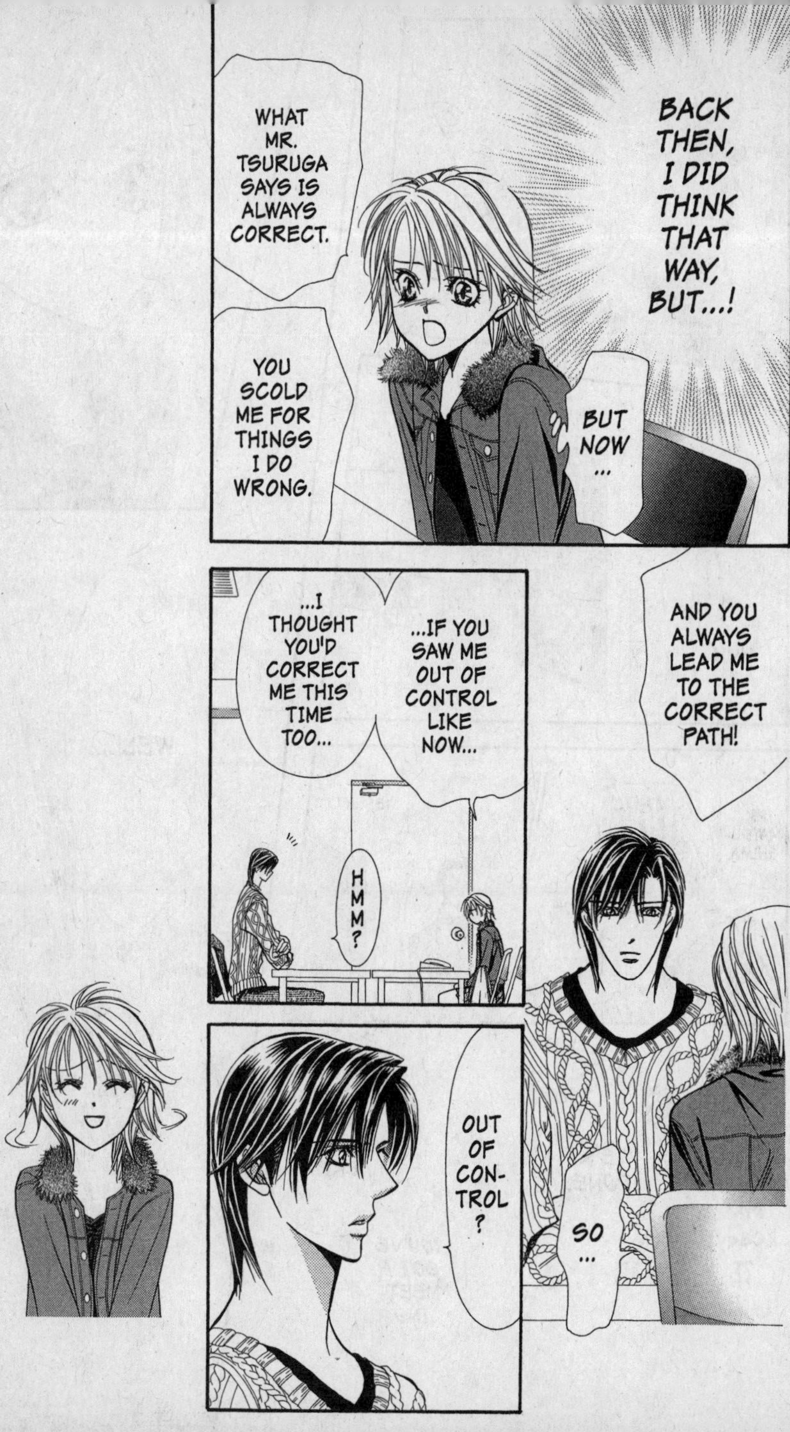
BACK THEN, I DID THINK THAT WAY, BUT...!
WHAT MR. TSURUGA SAYS IS ALWAYS CORRECT.
BUT NOW...
YOU SCOLD ME FOR THINGS I DO WRONG.
AND YOU ALWAYS LEAD ME TO THE CORRECT PATH!
...IF YOU SAW ME OUT OF CONTROL LIKE NOW...
...I THOUGHT YOU'D CORRECT ME THIS TIME TOO...
HMM?
SO...
OUT OF CONTROL?

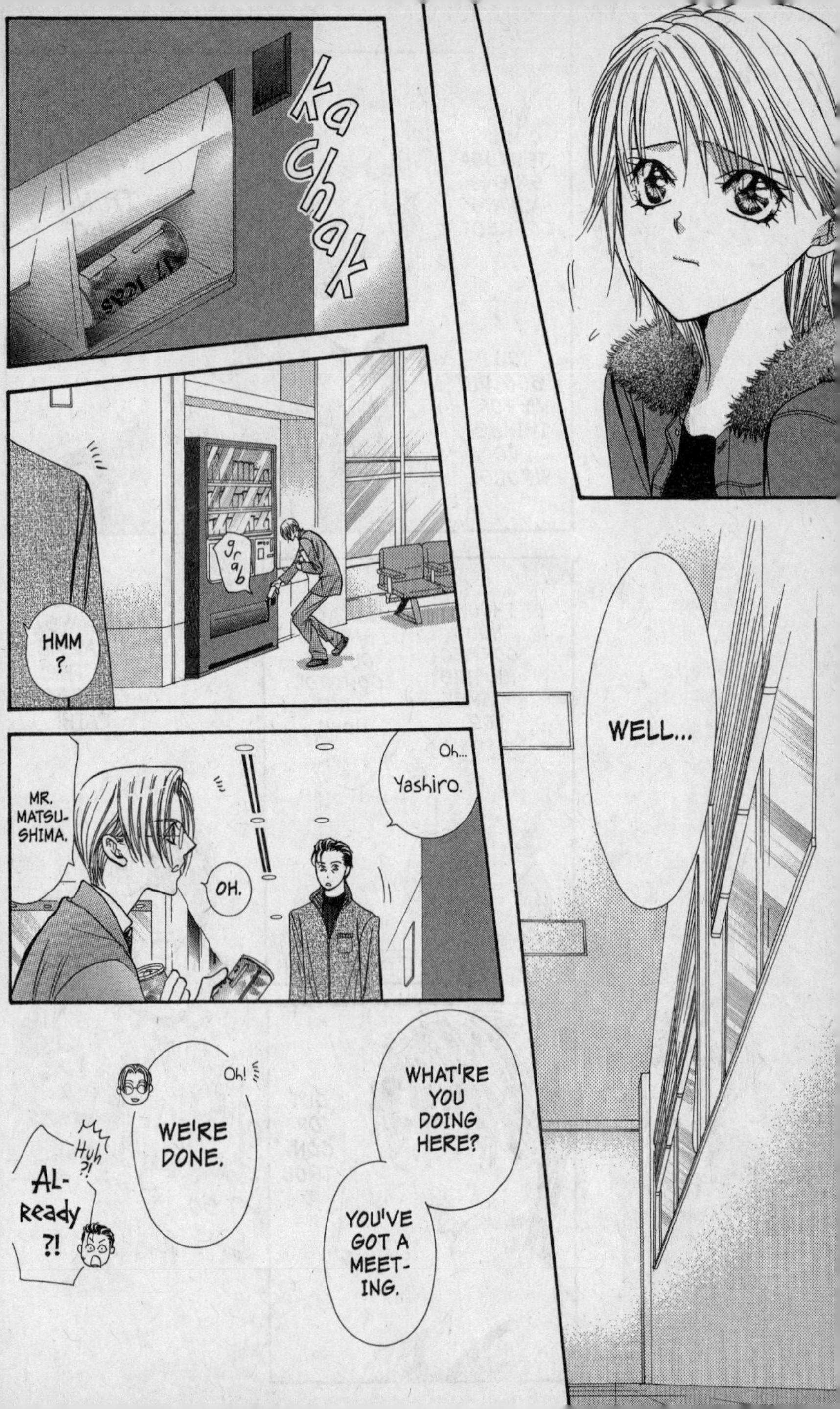
WELL...
ka chak
grab
HMM ?
Oh... Yashiro.
MR. MATSU-SHIMA.
OH.
WHAT'RE YOU DOING HERE?
YOU'VE GOT A MEET-ING.
Oh!
WE'RE DONE.
Huh ?!
AL-ready ?!

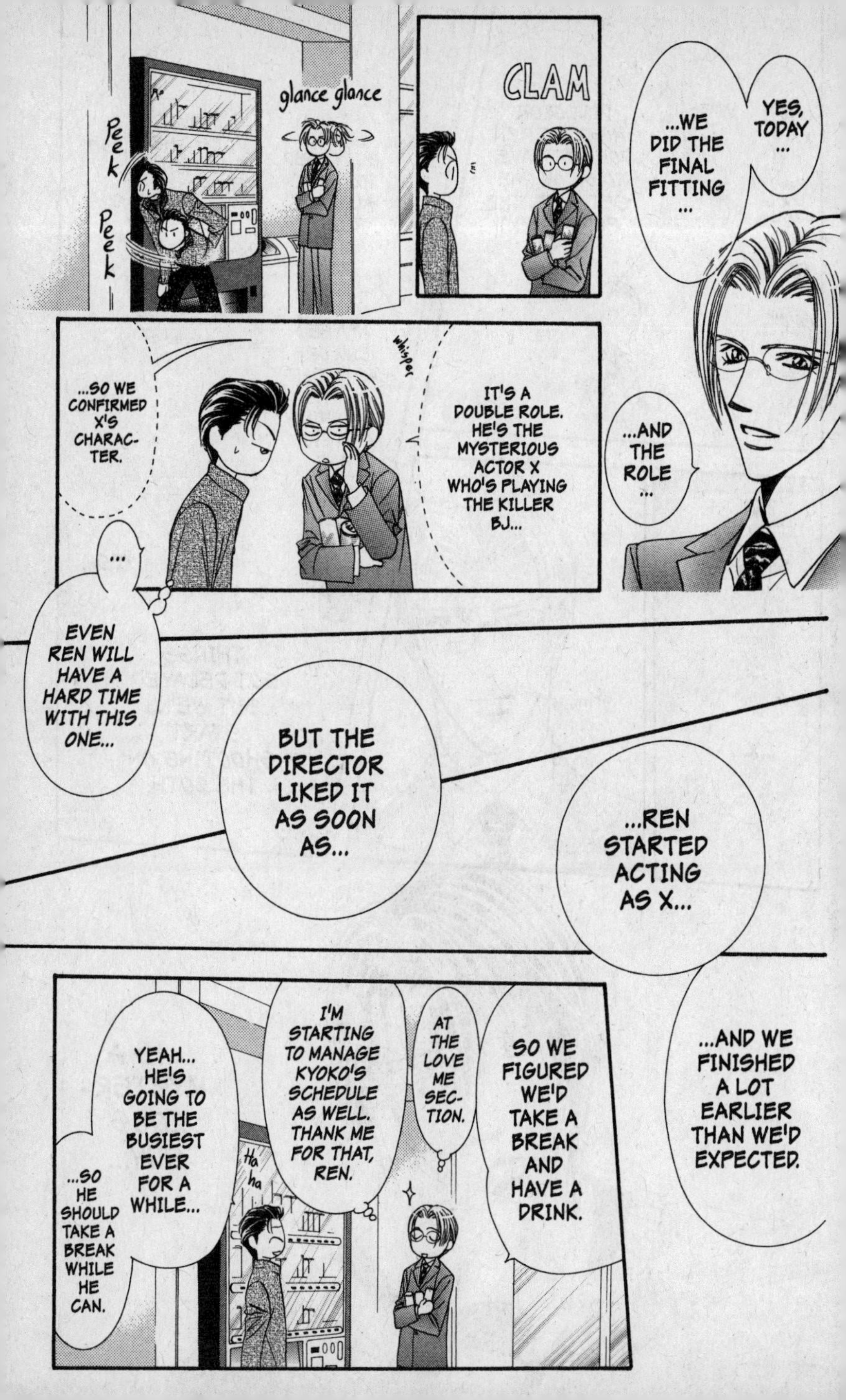
YES, TODAY ...
...WE DID THE FINAL FITTING ...
...AND THE ROLE ...
CLAM
glance glance
Peek Peek
whisper
IT'S A DOUBLE ROLE. HE'S THE MYSTERIOUS ACTOR X WHO'S PLAYING THE KILLER BJ...
...SO WE CONFIRMED X'S CHARACTER.
...
EVEN REN WILL HAVE A HARD TIME WITH THIS ONE...
BUT THE DIRECTOR LIKED IT AS SOON AS...
...REN STARTED ACTING AS X...
...AND WE FINISHED A LOT EARLIER THAN WE'D EXPECTED.
SO WE FIGURED WE'D TAKE A BREAK AND HAVE A DRINK.
AT THE LOVE ME SECTION.
I'M STARTING TO MANAGE KYOKO'S SCHEDULE AS WELL. THANK ME FOR THAT, REN.
Ha ha
YEAH... HE'S GOING TO BE THE BUSIEST EVER FOR A WHILE...
...SO HE SHOULD TAKE A BREAK WHILE HE CAN.

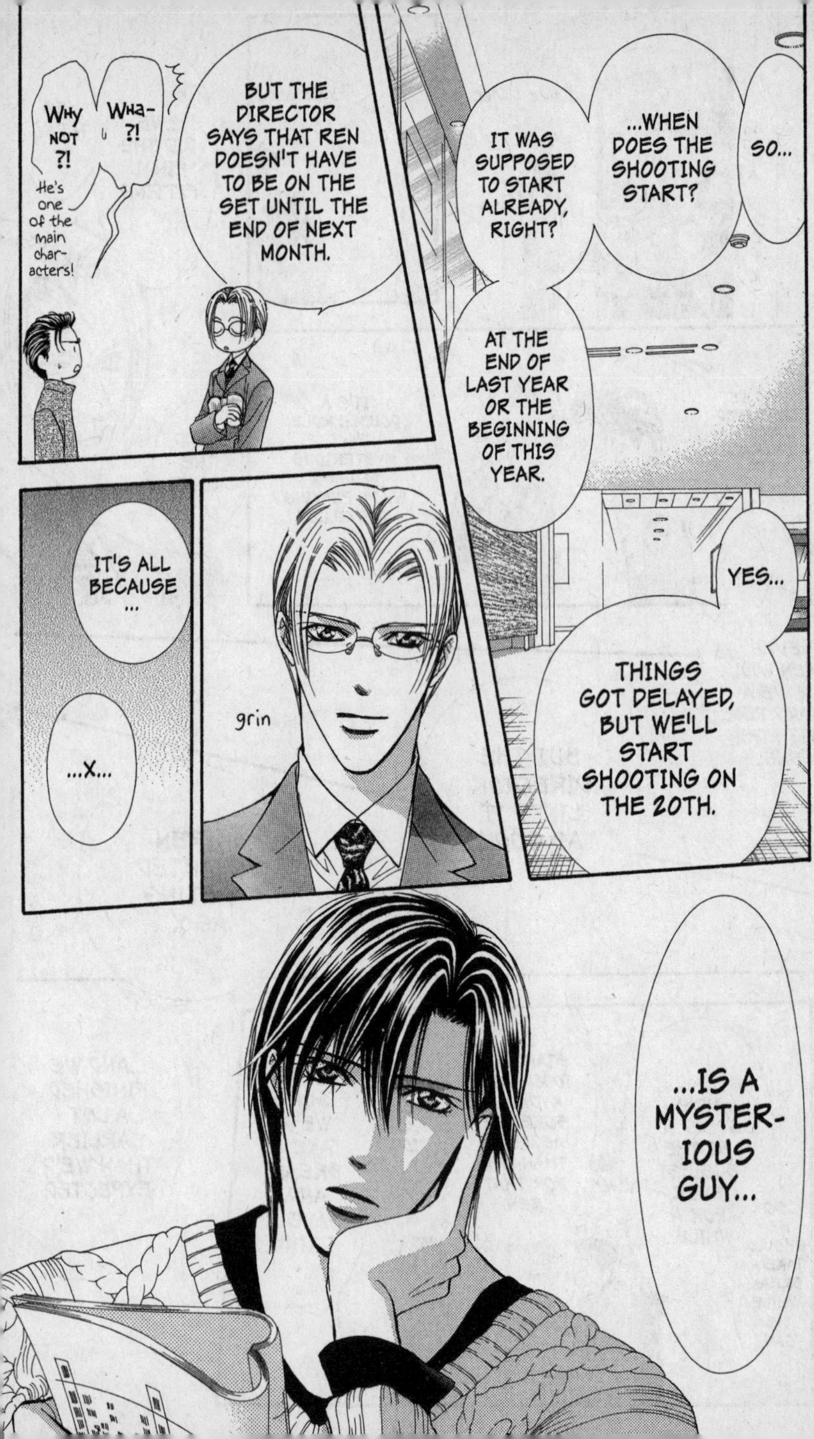
SO...
...WHEN DOES THE SHOOTING START?
IT WAS SUPPOSED TO START ALREADY, RIGHT?
AT THE END OF LAST YEAR OR THE BEGINNING OF THIS YEAR.
YES...
THINGS GOT DELAYED, BUT WE'LL START SHOOTING ON THE 20TH.
BUT THE DIRECTOR SAYS THAT REN DOESN'T HAVE TO BE ON THE SET UNTIL THE END OF NEXT MONTH.
WHA-?!
WHY NOT?!
He's one of the main characters!
grin
IT'S ALL BECAUSE ...
...X...
...IS A MYSTERIOUS GUY...

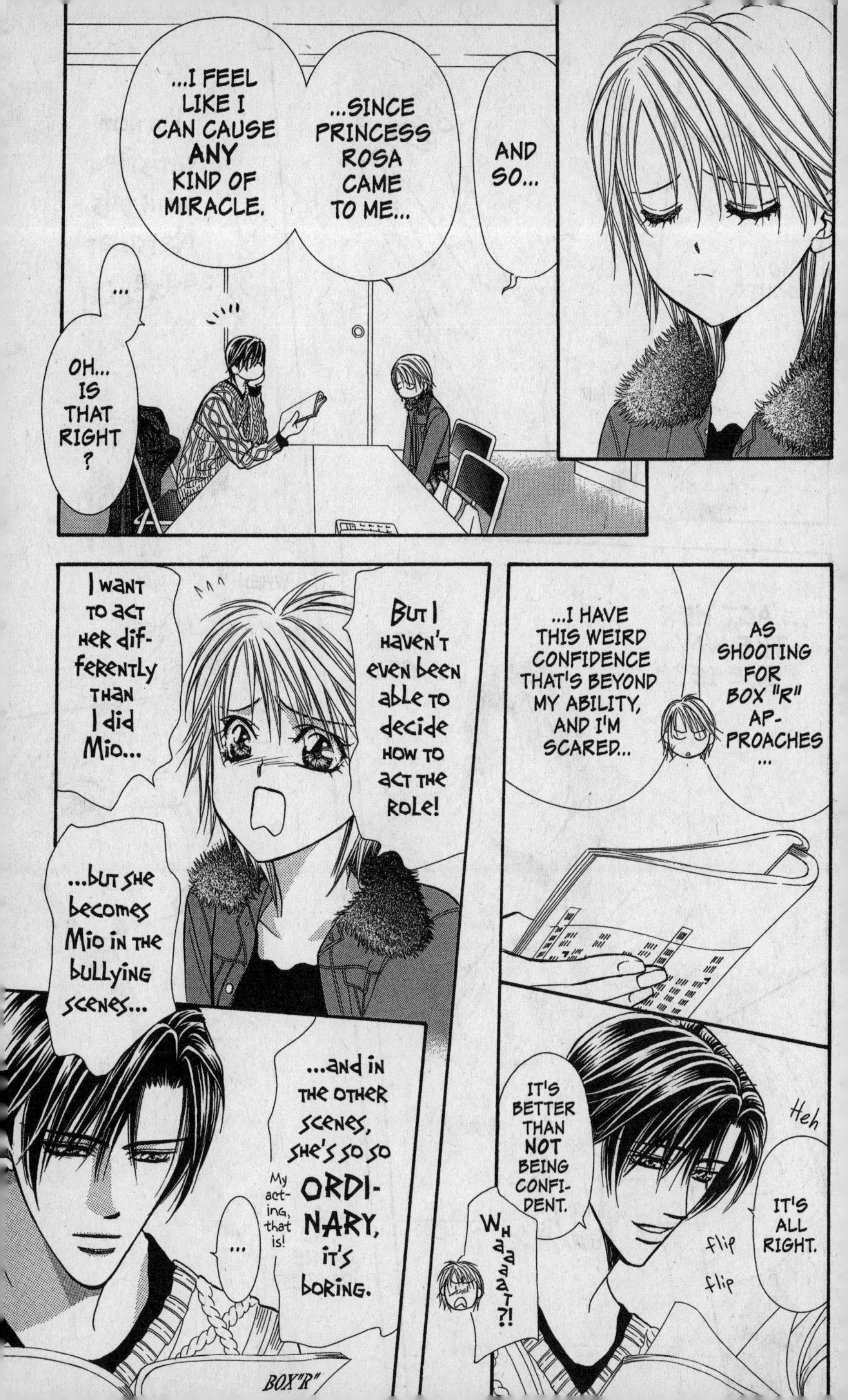

AND SO...
...SINCE PRINCESS ROSA CAME TO ME...
...I FEEL LIKE I CAN CAUSE ANY KIND OF MIRACLE.
...
OH... IS THAT RIGHT?
AS SHOOTING FOR BOX "R" APPROACHES...
...I HAVE THIS WEIRD CONFIDENCE THAT'S BEYOND MY ABILITY, AND I'M SCARED...
But I haven't even been able to decide how to act the role!
I want to act her differently than I did Mio...
...but she becomes Mio in the bullying scenes...
...and in the other scenes, she's so so ORDINARY, it's boring.
My acting, that is!
...
BOX"R"
Heh
IT'S ALL RIGHT.
flip
flip
IT'S BETTER THAN NOT BEING CONFIDENT.
Whaaaat?!

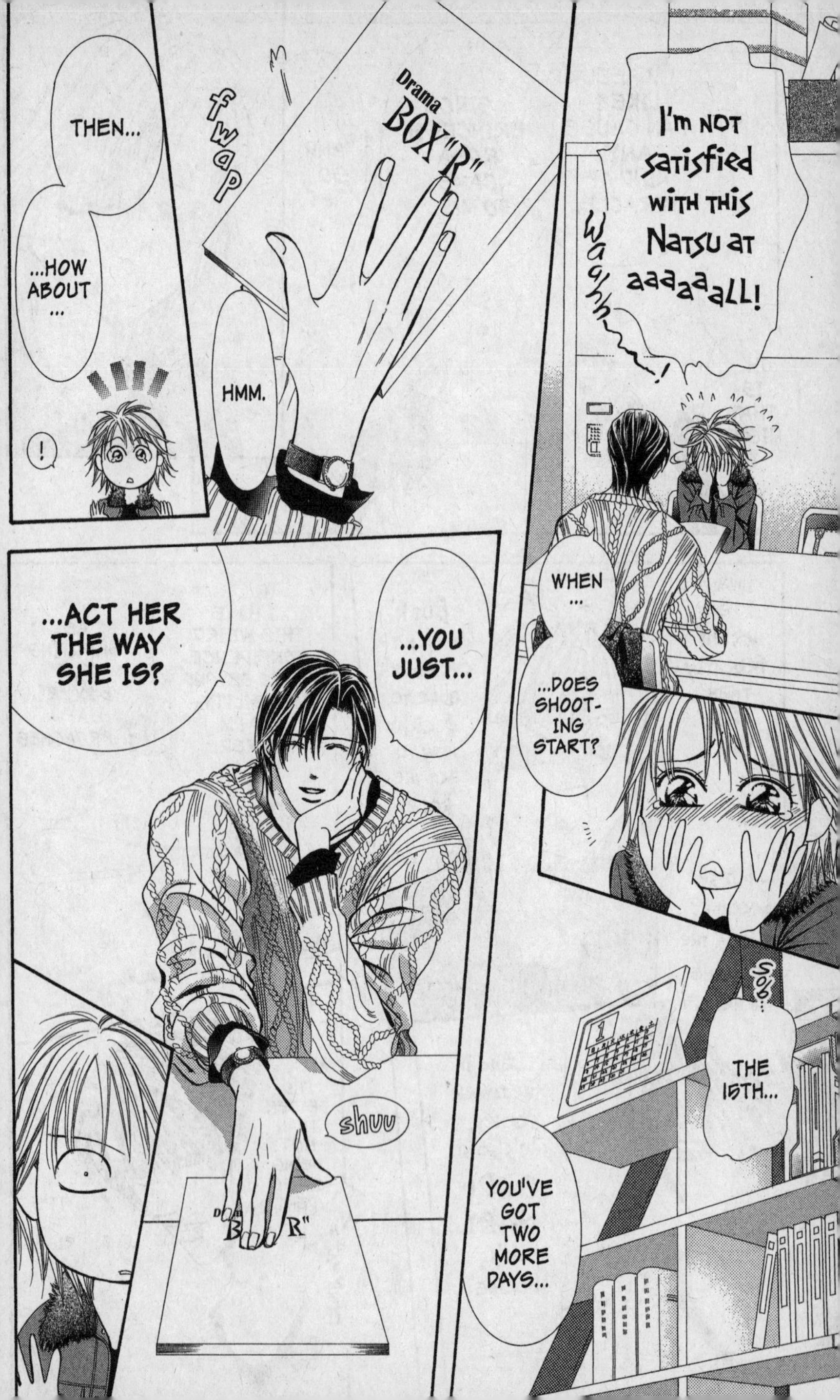

I'm NOT satisfied WITH THIS Natsu at aaaaaaLL!
Waaahh—!
WHEN...
...DOES SHOOT-ING START?
Sob...
THE 15TH...
YOU'VE GOT TWO MORE DAYS...
fwap
Drama BOX"R"
HMM.
THEN...
...HOW ABOUT...
!
...YOU JUST...
...ACT HER THE WAY SHE IS?
shuu

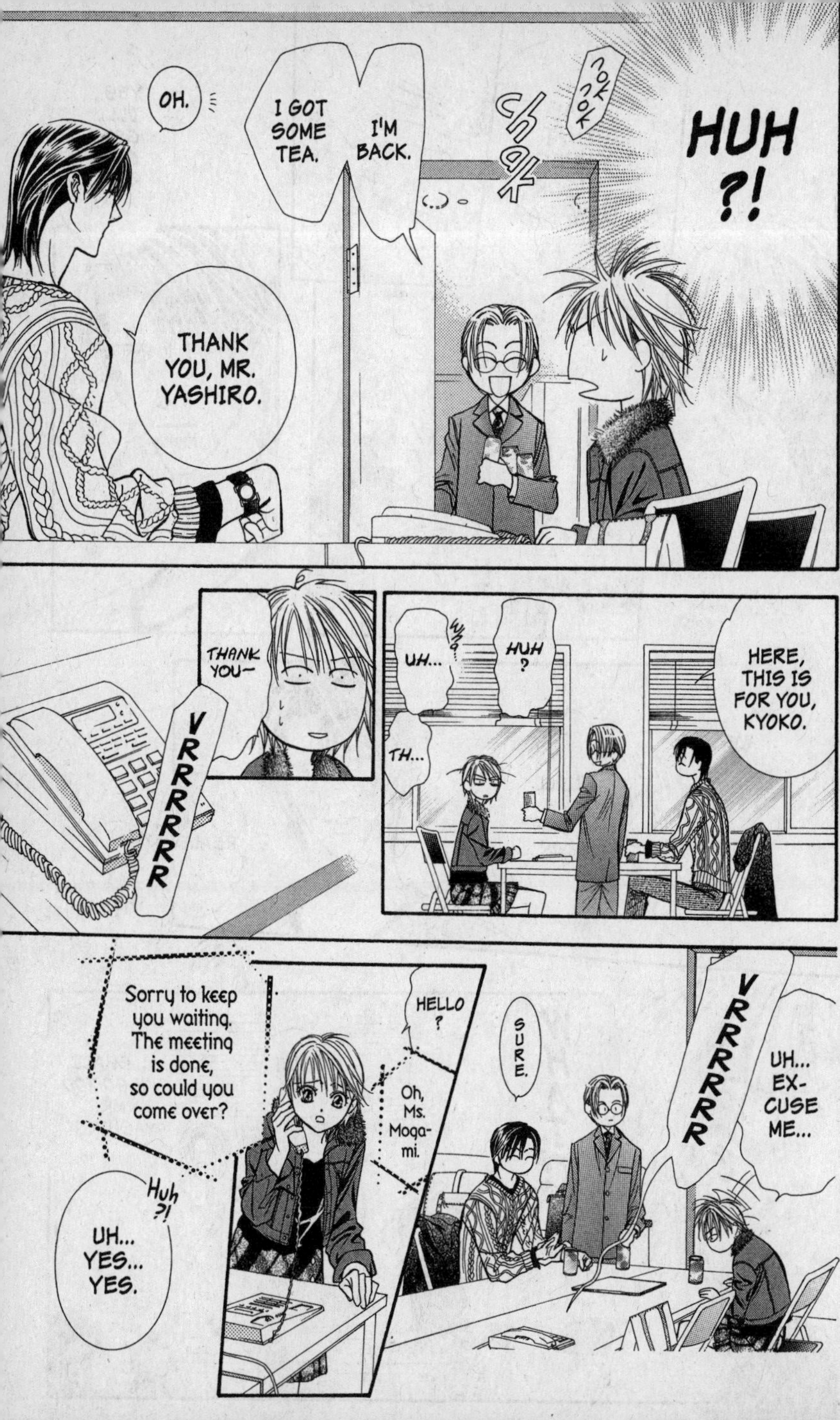
HUH ?!
nok nok
chak
I'M BACK.
I GOT SOME TEA.
OH.
THANK YOU, MR. YASHIRO.
HERE, THIS IS FOR YOU, KYOKO.
HUH ?
UH...
TH...
VRRRRRR
THANK YOU—
UH... EX-CUSE ME...
VRRRRRR
SURE.
HELLO ?
Oh, Ms. Moga-mi.
Sorry to keep you waiting. The meeting is done, so could you come over?
Huh ?!
UH... YES... YES.

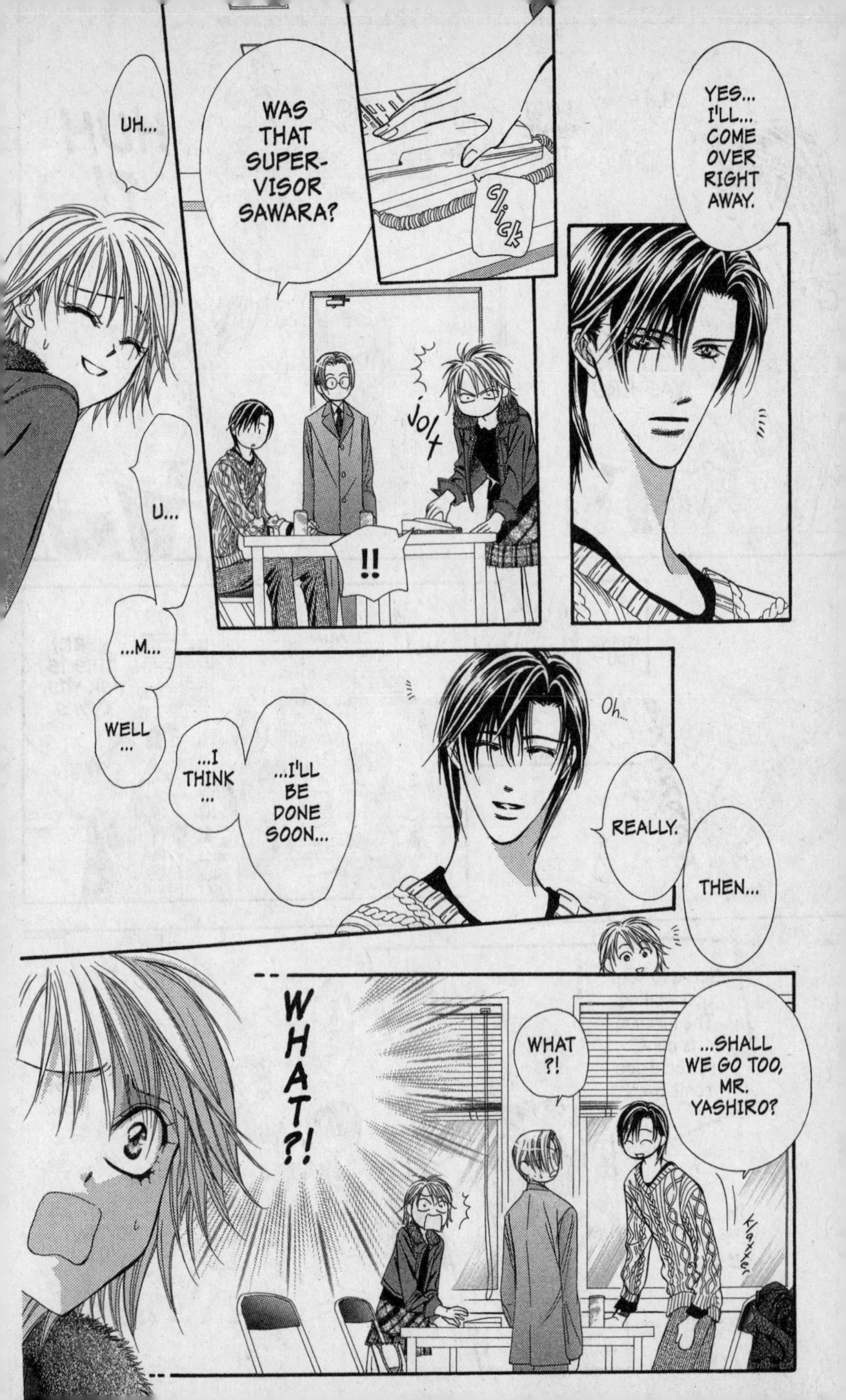
YES... I'LL... COME OVER RIGHT AWAY.
click
WAS THAT SUPERVISOR SAWARA?
UH...
jolt
!!
U...
...M...
WELL...
...I THINK...
...I'LL BE DONE SOON...
Oh...
REALLY.
THEN...
...SHALL WE GO TOO, MR. YASHIRO?
WHAT?!
WHAT?!

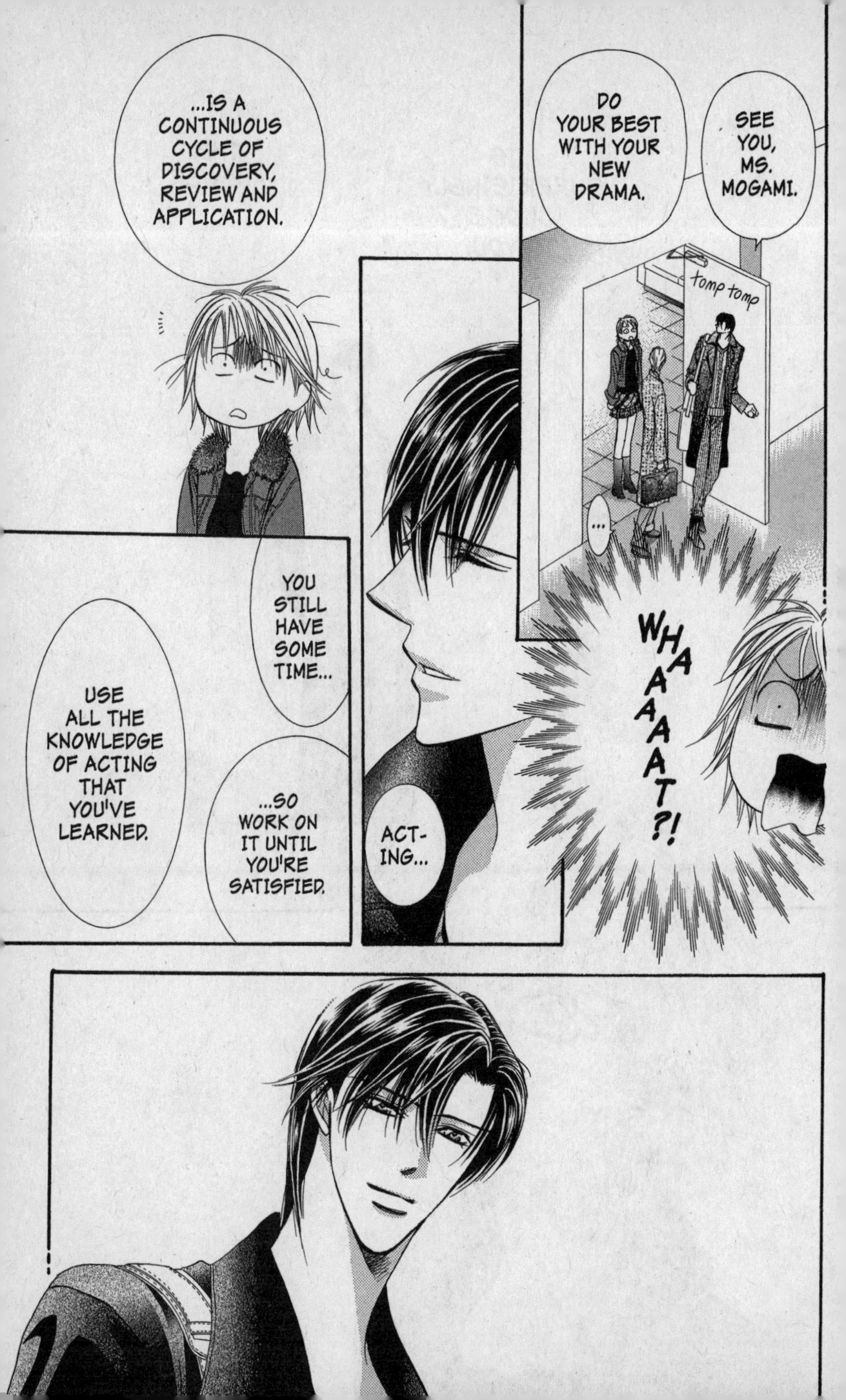
ACT-ING...
...IS A CONTINUOUS CYCLE OF DISCOVERY, REVIEW AND APPLICATION.
YOU STILL HAVE SOME TIME...
...SO WORK ON IT UNTIL YOU'RE SATISFIED.
USE ALL THE KNOWLEDGE OF ACTING THAT YOU'VE LEARNED.
SEE YOU, MS. MOGAMI.
DO YOUR BEST WITH YOUR NEW DRAMA.
tomp tomp
...
WHAAAAAT?!

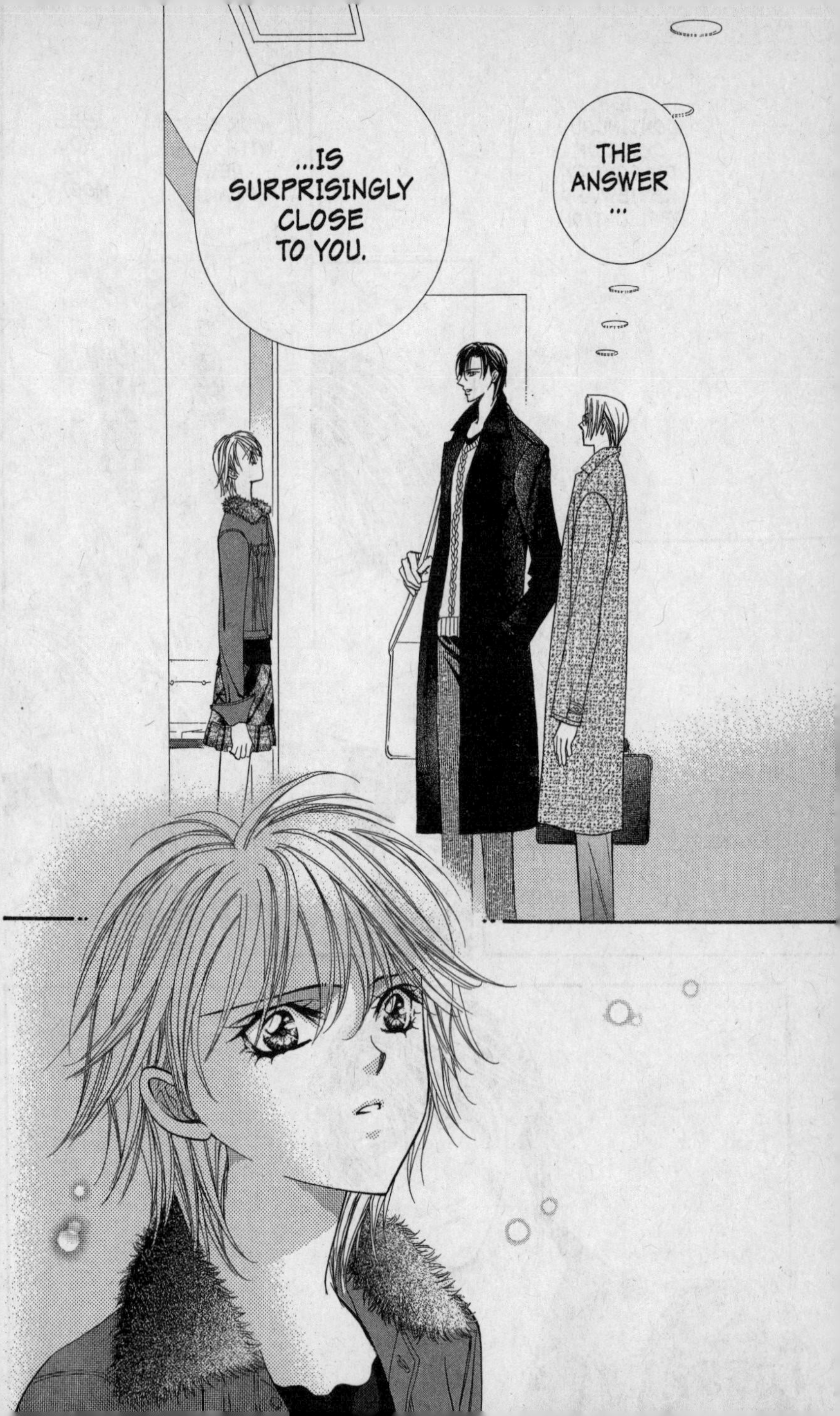
THE ANSWER ...
...IS SURPRISINGLY CLOSE TO YOU.

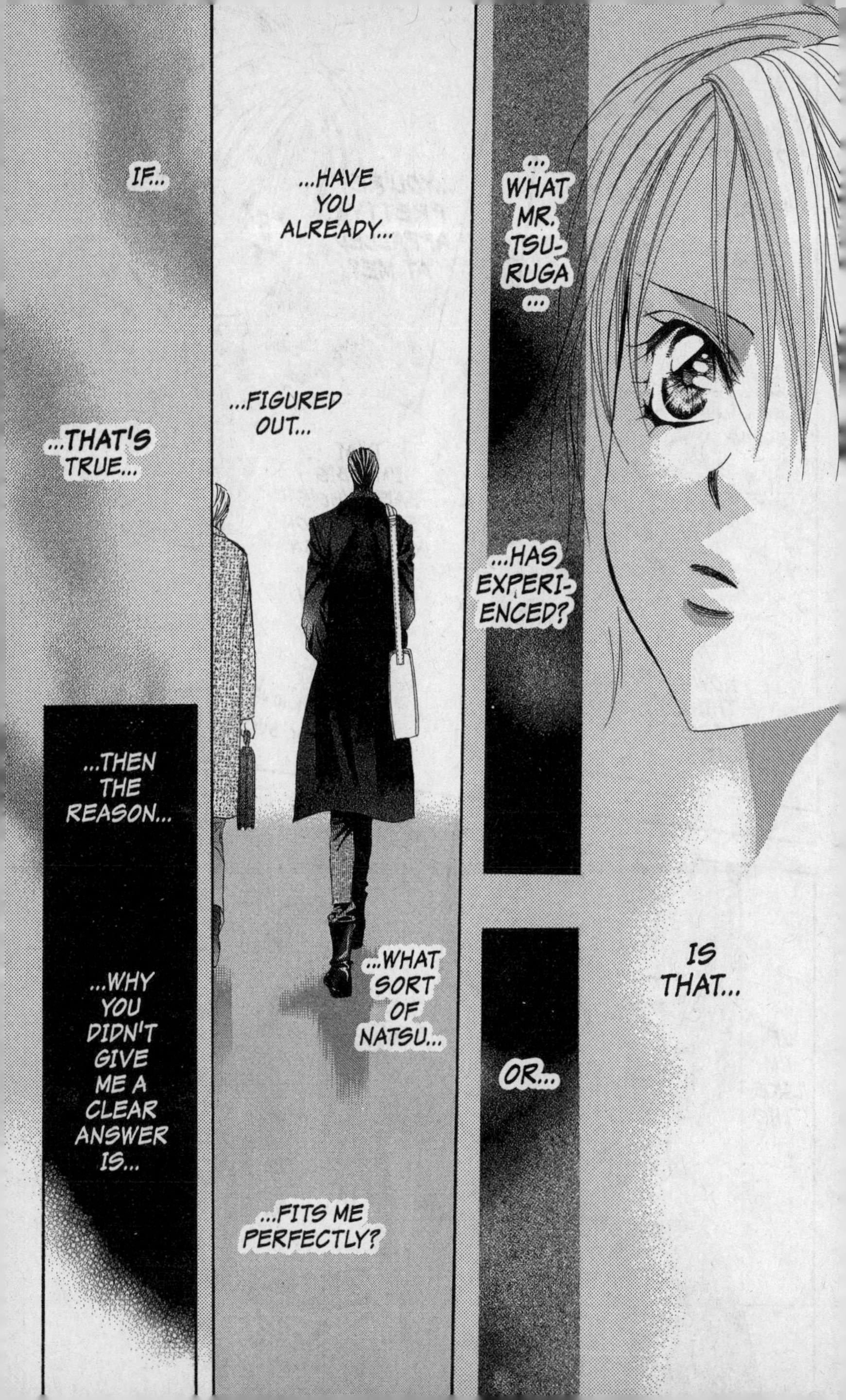
IS THAT...
...WHAT MR. TSURUGA...
...HAS EXPERIENCED?
OR...
...HAVE YOU ALREADY...
...FIGURED OUT...
...WHAT SORT OF NATSU...
...FITS ME PERFECTLY?
IF...
...THAT'S TRUE...
...THEN THE REASON...
...WHY YOU DIDN'T GIVE ME A CLEAR ANSWER IS...

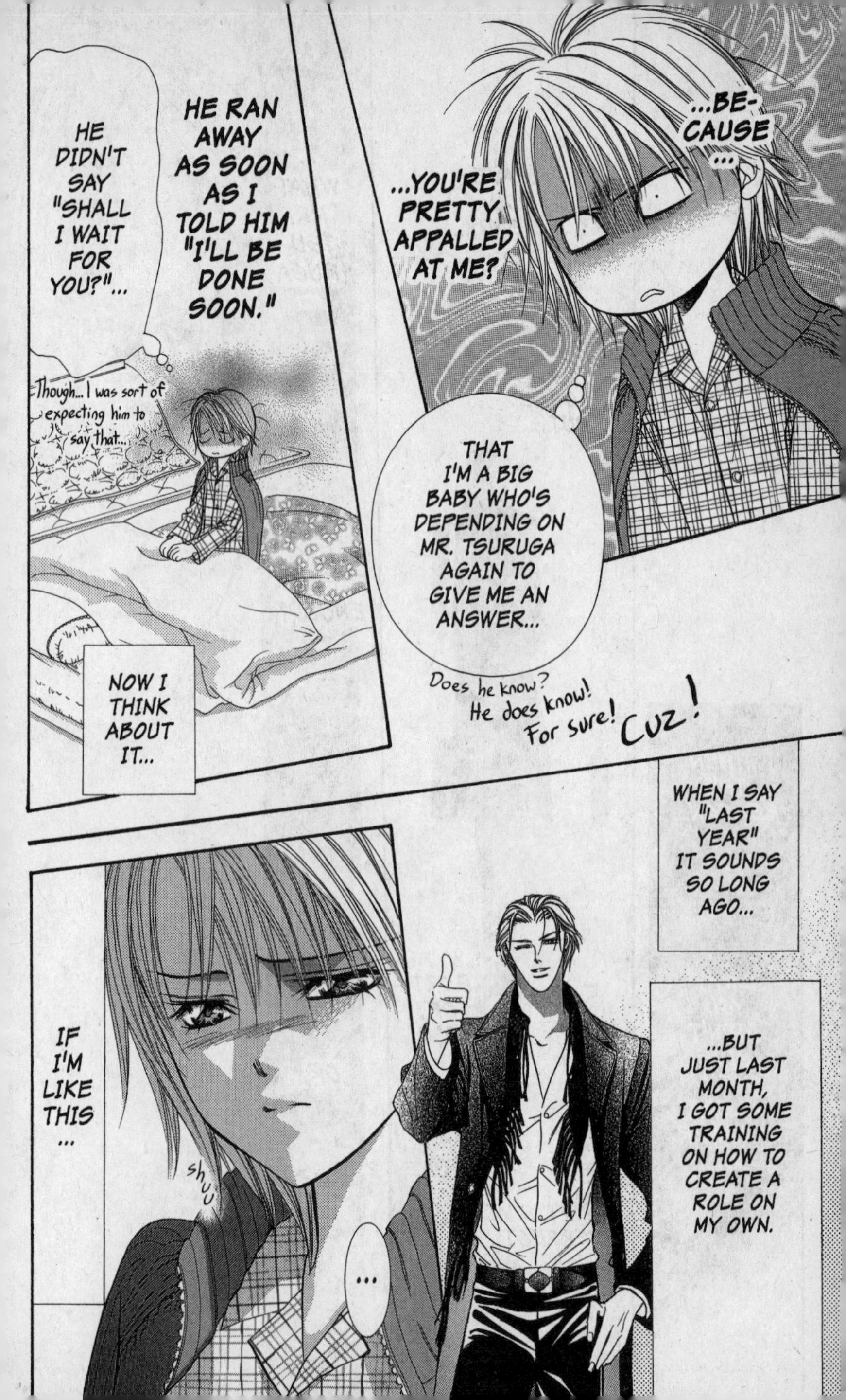
...BE-CAUSE ...
...YOU'RE PRETTY APPALLED AT ME?
THAT I'M A BIG BABY WHO'S DEPENDING ON MR. TSURUGA AGAIN TO GIVE ME AN ANSWER...
Does he know? He does know! For sure! Cuz!
HE RAN AWAY AS SOON AS I TOLD HIM "I'LL BE DONE SOON."
HE DIDN'T SAY "SHALL I WAIT FOR YOU?"...
Though... I was sort of expecting him to say that...
NOW I THINK ABOUT IT...
WHEN I SAY "LAST YEAR" IT SOUNDS SO LONG AGO...
...BUT JUST LAST MONTH, I GOT SOME TRAINING ON HOW TO CREATE A ROLE ON MY OWN.
IF I'M LIKE THIS ...
shuu
...

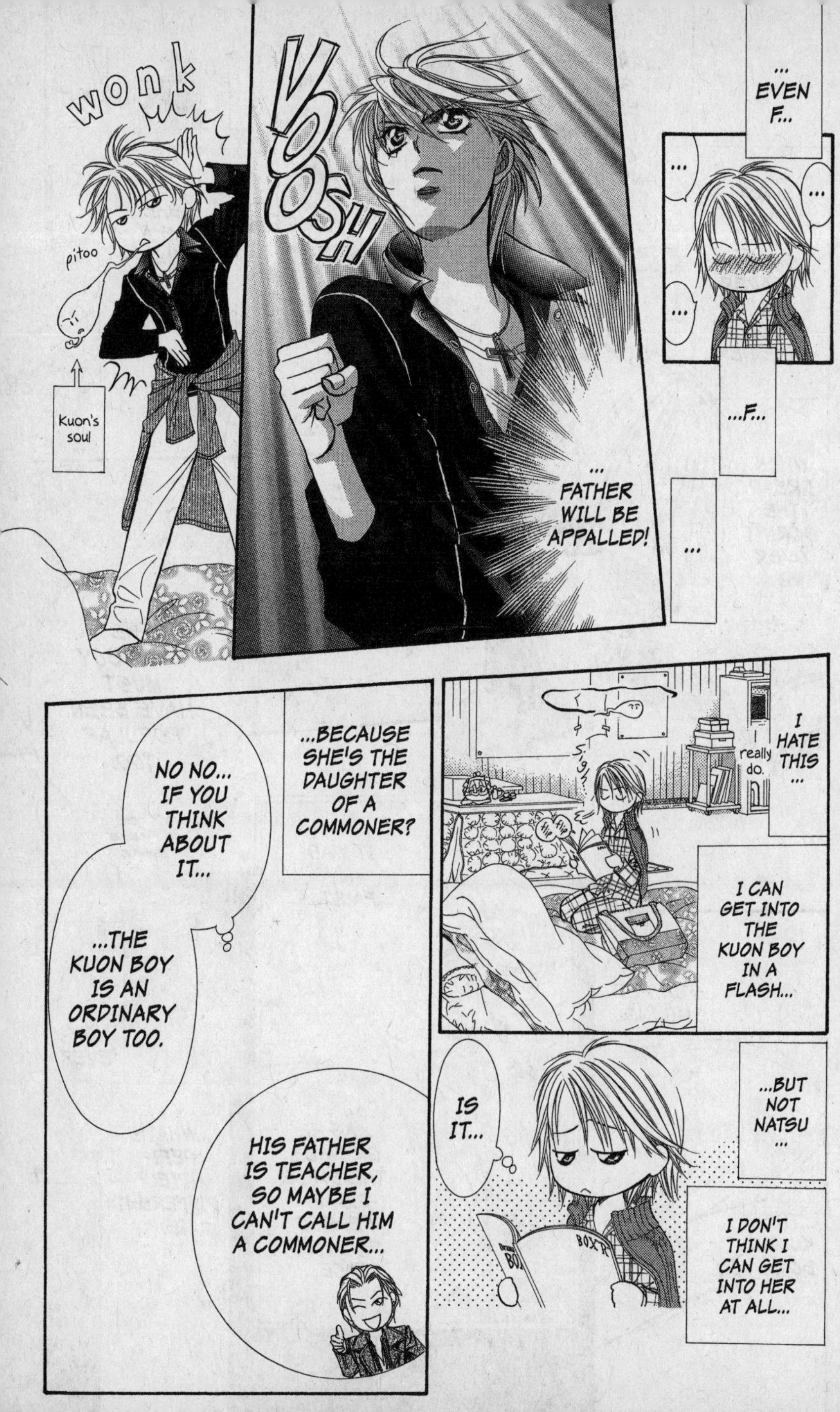
... EVEN F...
...
...
...
...F...
...
VOOSH
... FATHER WILL BE APPALLED!
wonk
pitoo
Kuon's soul
I HATE THIS ...
really do.
sigh...
flip flip
I CAN GET INTO THE KUON BOY IN A FLASH...
...BUT NOT NATSU ...
I DON'T THINK I CAN GET INTO HER AT ALL...
IS IT...
...BECAUSE SHE'S THE DAUGHTER OF A COMMONER?
NO NO... IF YOU THINK ABOUT IT...
...THE KUON BOY IS AN ORDINARY BOY TOO.
HIS FATHER IS TEACHER, SO MAYBE I CAN'T CALL HIM A COMMONER...

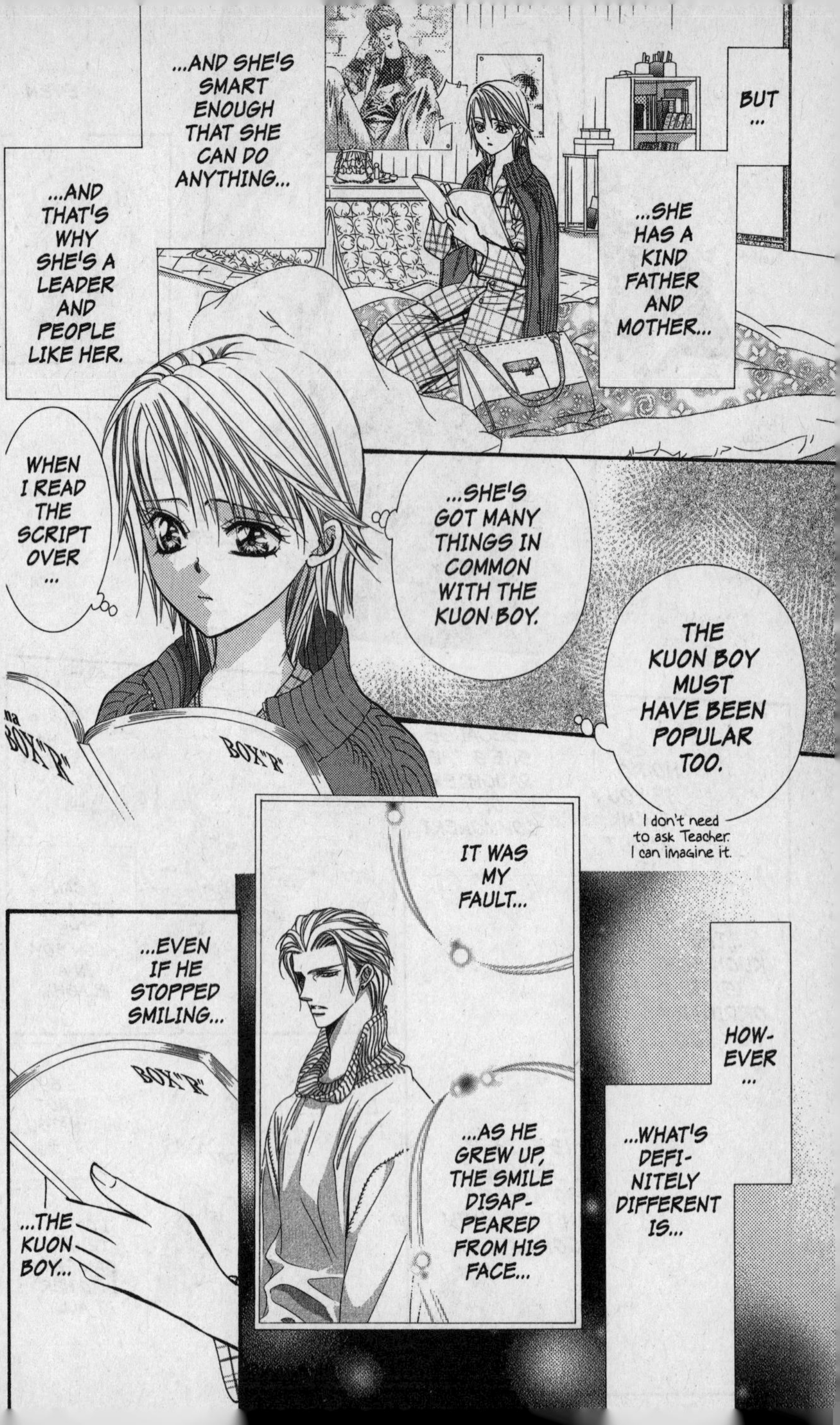
BUT ...
...SHE HAS A KIND FATHER AND MOTHER...
...AND SHE'S SMART ENOUGH THAT SHE CAN DO ANYTHING...
...AND THAT'S WHY SHE'S A LEADER AND PEOPLE LIKE HER.
WHEN I READ THE SCRIPT OVER ...
...SHE'S GOT MANY THINGS IN COMMON WITH THE KUON BOY.
THE KUON BOY MUST HAVE BEEN POPULAR TOO.
I don't need to ask Teacher. I can imagine it.
BOX"R"
BOX"R"
HOW-EVER ...
...WHAT'S DEFI-NITELY DIFFERENT IS...
IT WAS MY FAULT...
...AS HE GREW UP, THE SMILE DISAP-PEARED FROM HIS FACE...
...EVEN IF HE STOPPED SMILING...
BOX"R"
...THE KUON BOY...

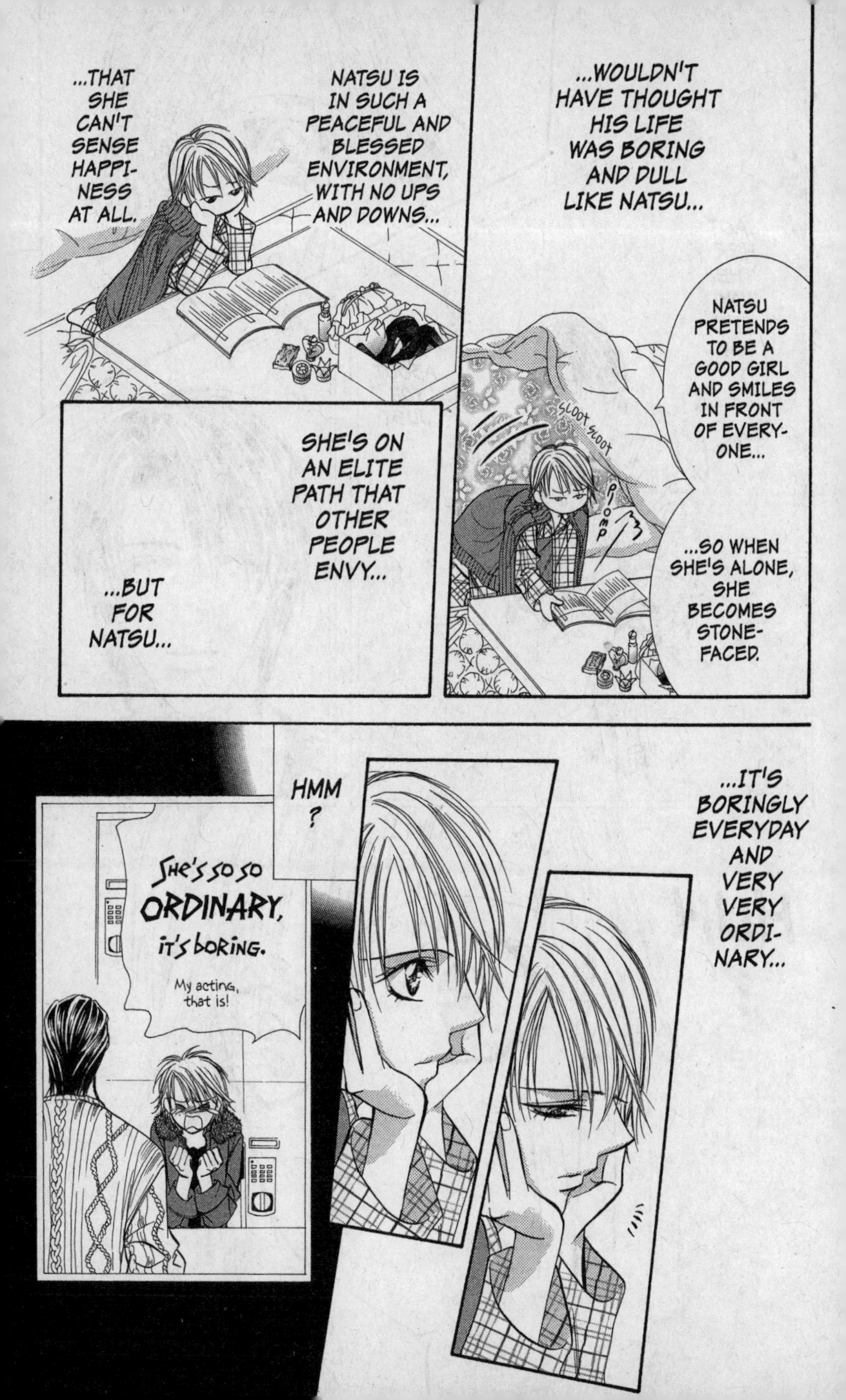

...WOULDN'T HAVE THOUGHT HIS LIFE WAS BORING AND DULL LIKE NATSU...
NATSU IS IN SUCH A PEACEFUL AND BLESSED ENVIRONMENT, WITH NO UPS AND DOWNS...
...THAT SHE CAN'T SENSE HAPPINESS AT ALL.
NATSU PRETENDS TO BE A GOOD GIRL AND SMILES IN FRONT OF EVERYONE...
...SO WHEN SHE'S ALONE, SHE BECOMES STONE-FACED.
SLOOT SLOOT
PLOMP
SHE'S ON AN ELITE PATH THAT OTHER PEOPLE ENVY...
...BUT FOR NATSU...
...IT'S BORINGLY EVERYDAY AND VERY VERY ORDINARY...
HMM?
She's so so ORDINARY, it's boring.
My acting, that is!

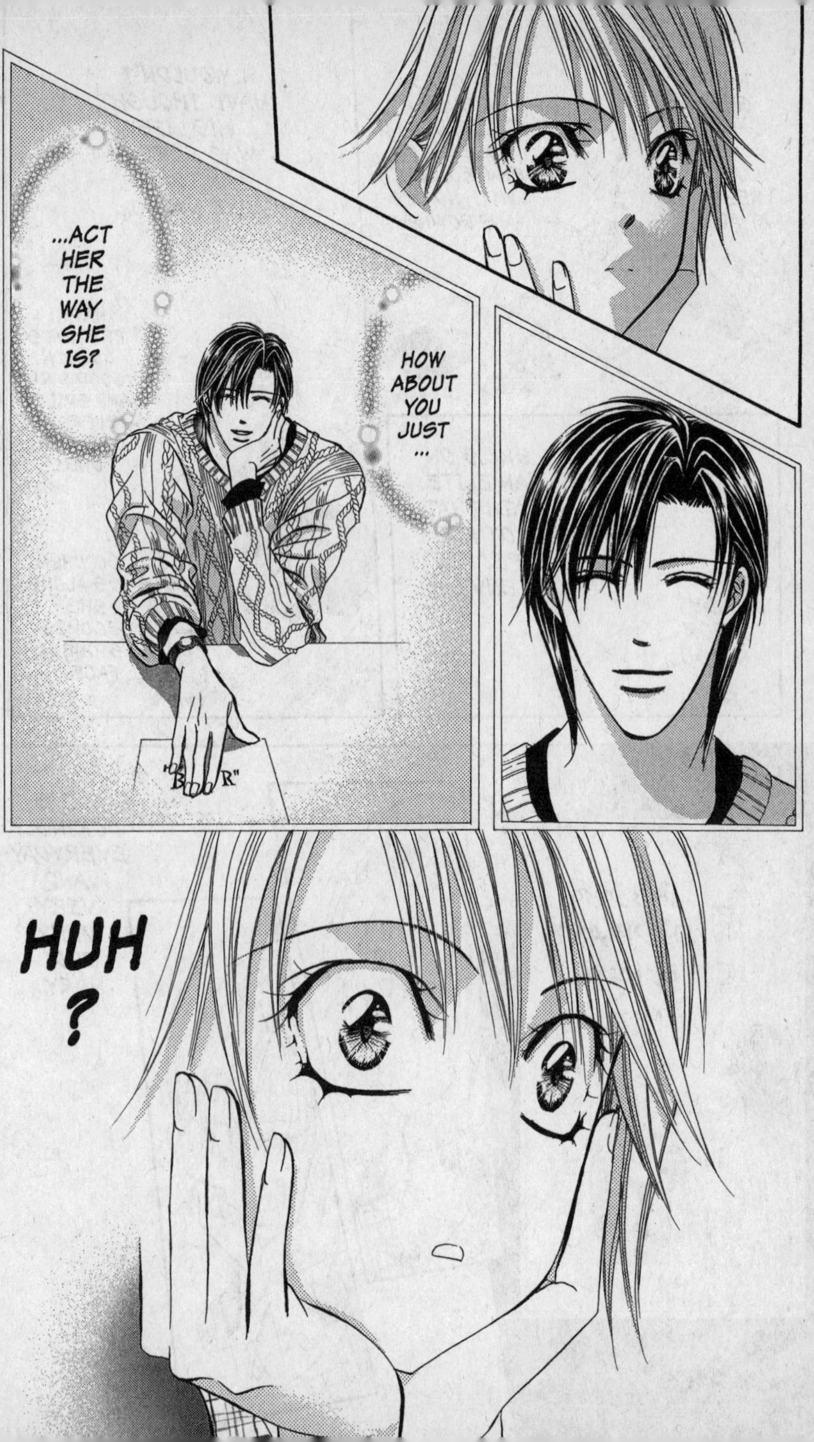
HOW ABOUT YOU JUST ...
...ACT HER THE WAY SHE IS?
HUH ?

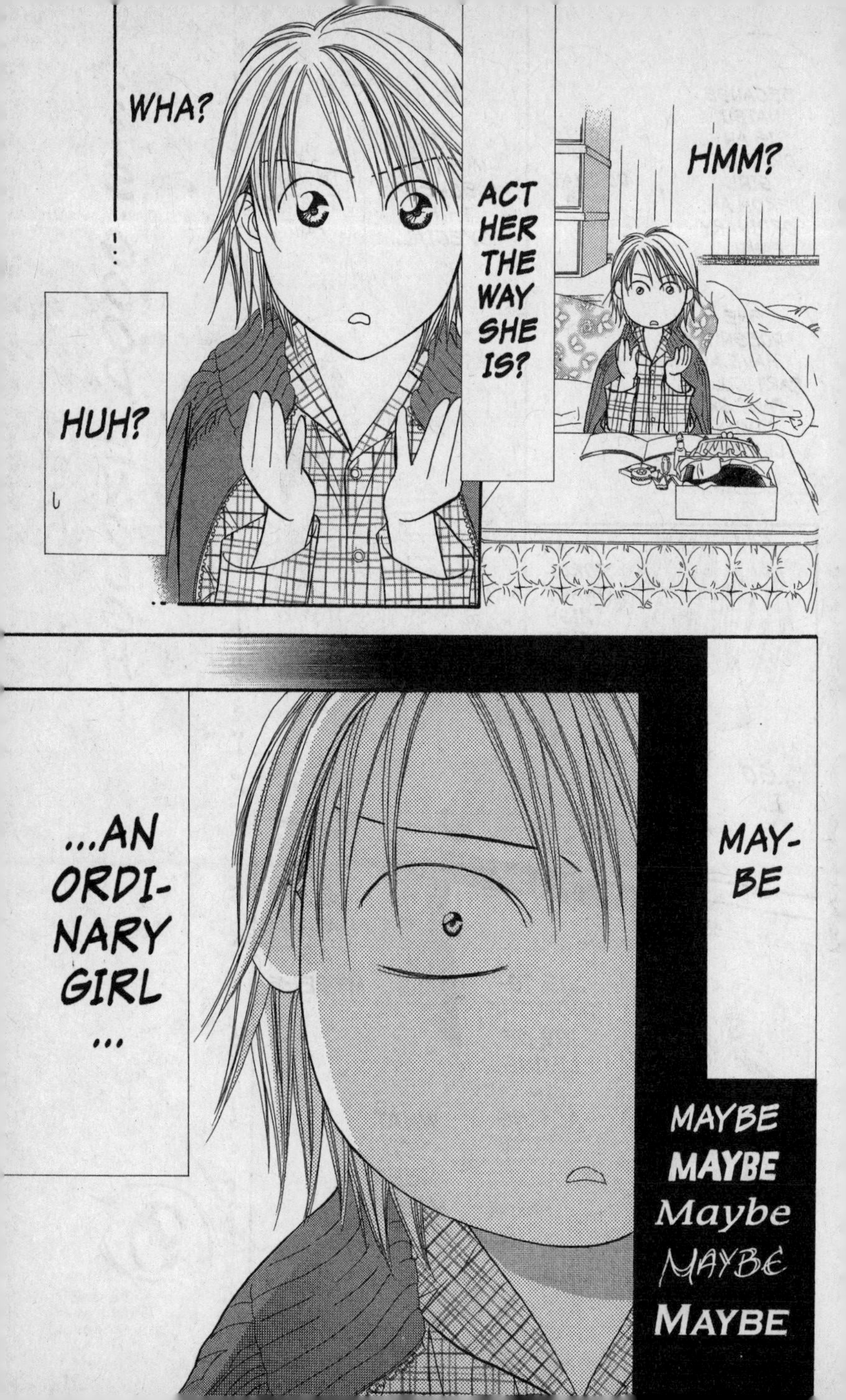
HMM?
ACT HER THE WAY SHE IS?
WHA?
HUH?
MAY-BE
MAYBE
MAYBE
Maybe
MAYBE
MAYBE
...AN ORDINARY GIRL ...

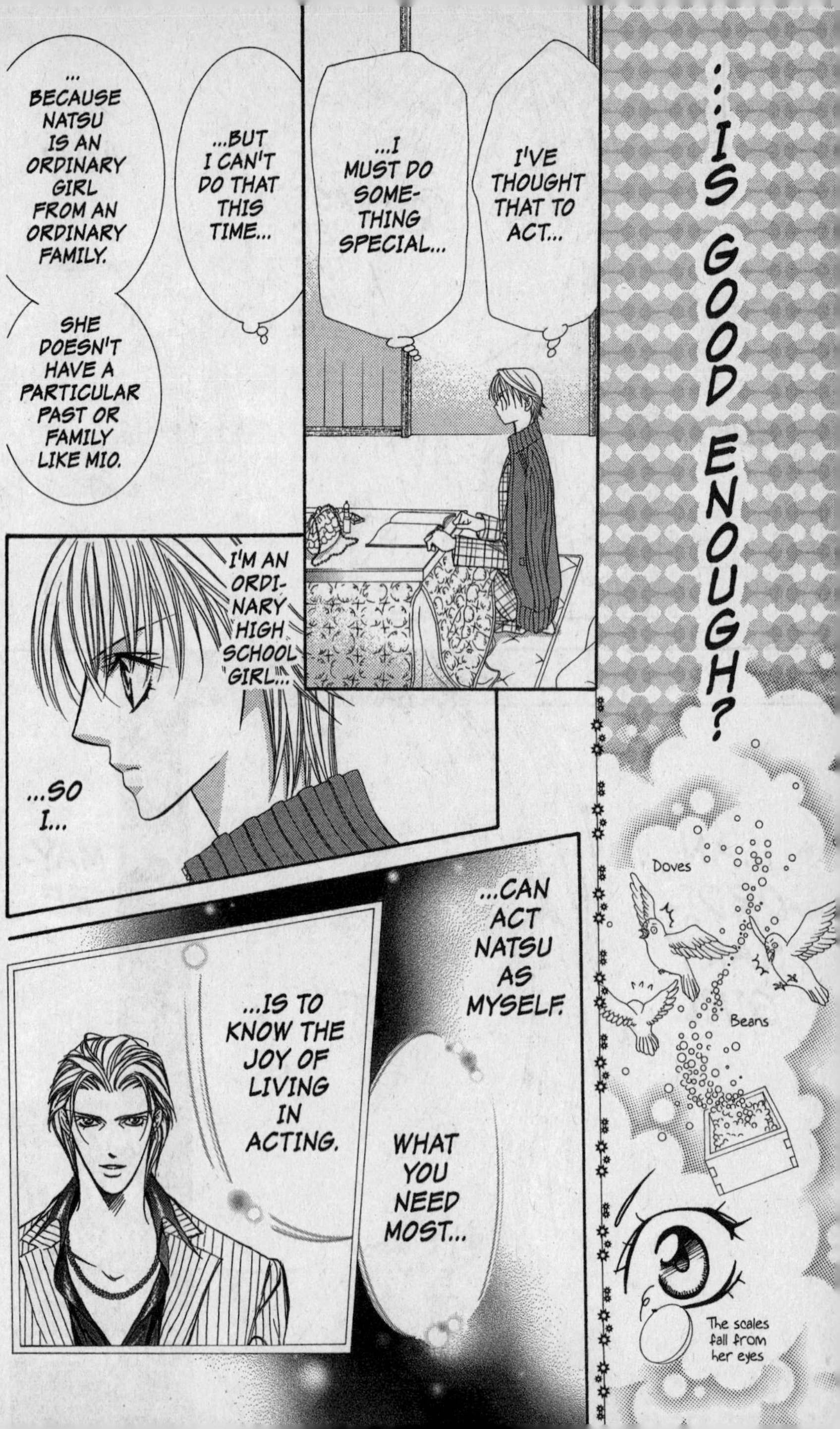
I'VE THOUGHT THAT TO ACT...
...I MUST DO SOME-THING SPECIAL...
...BUT I CAN'T DO THAT THIS TIME...
... BECAUSE NATSU IS AN ORDINARY GIRL FROM AN ORDINARY FAMILY.
SHE DOESN'T HAVE A PARTICULAR PAST OR FAMILY LIKE MIO.
I'M AN ORDI-NARY HIGH SCHOOL GIRL...
...SO I...
...CAN ACT NATSU AS MYSELF.
WHAT YOU NEED MOST...
...IS TO KNOW THE JOY OF LIVING IN ACTING.
...IS GOOD ENOUGH?
Doves
Beans
The scales fall from her eyes

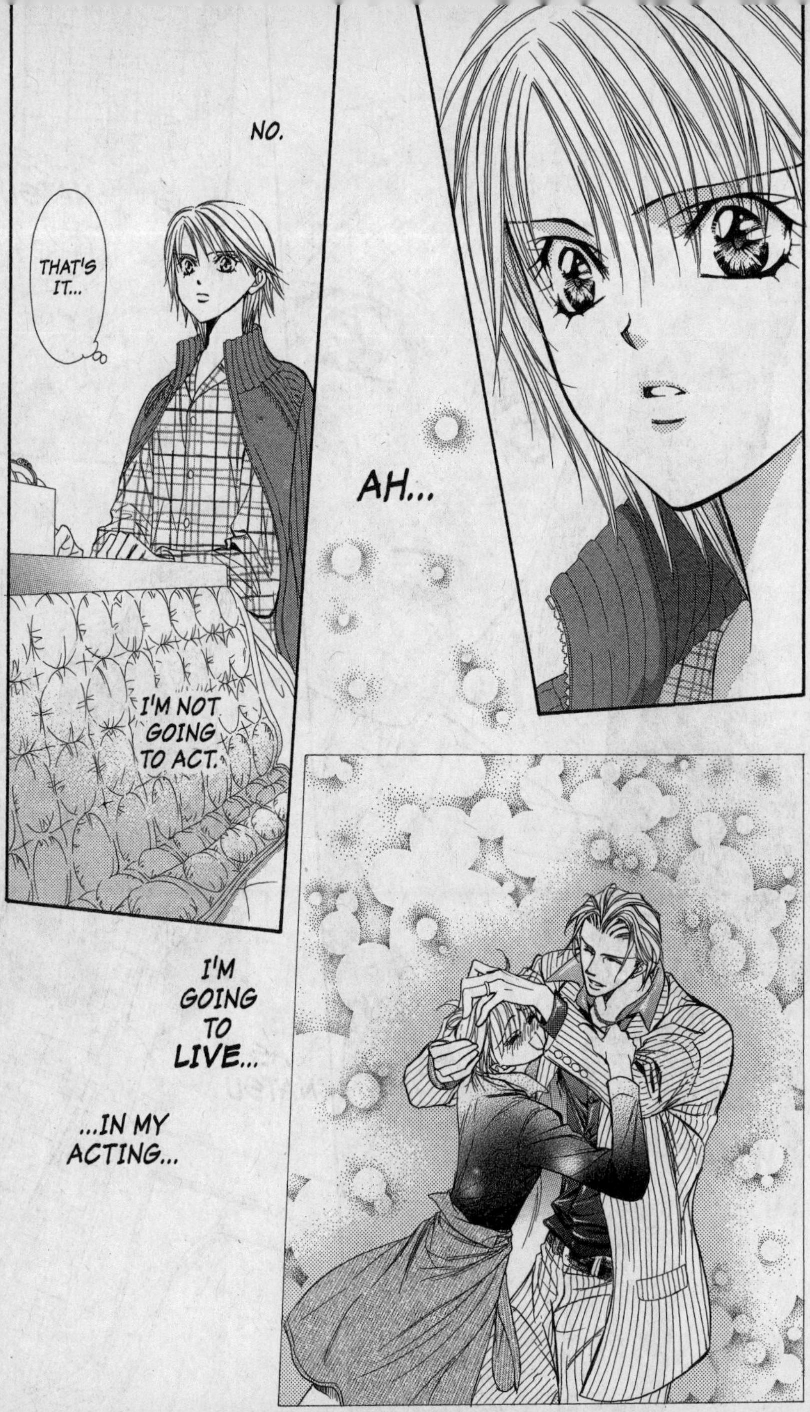
AH...
NO.
THAT'S IT...
I'M NOT GOING TO ACT.
I'M GOING TO LIVE...
...IN MY ACTING...

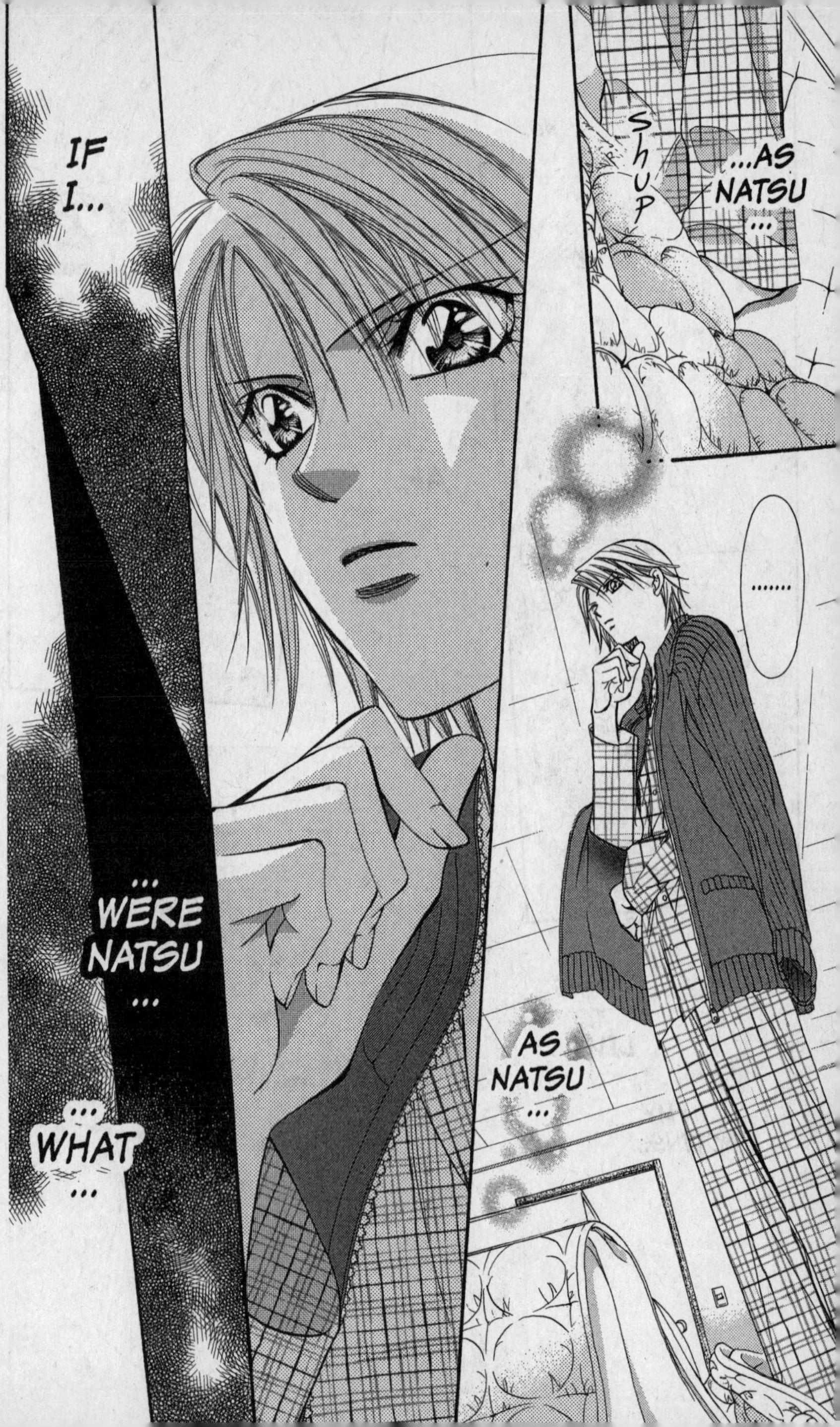
...AS NATSU ...
SHUP
....
AS NATSU ...
IF I...
...WERE NATSU ...
...WHAT ...

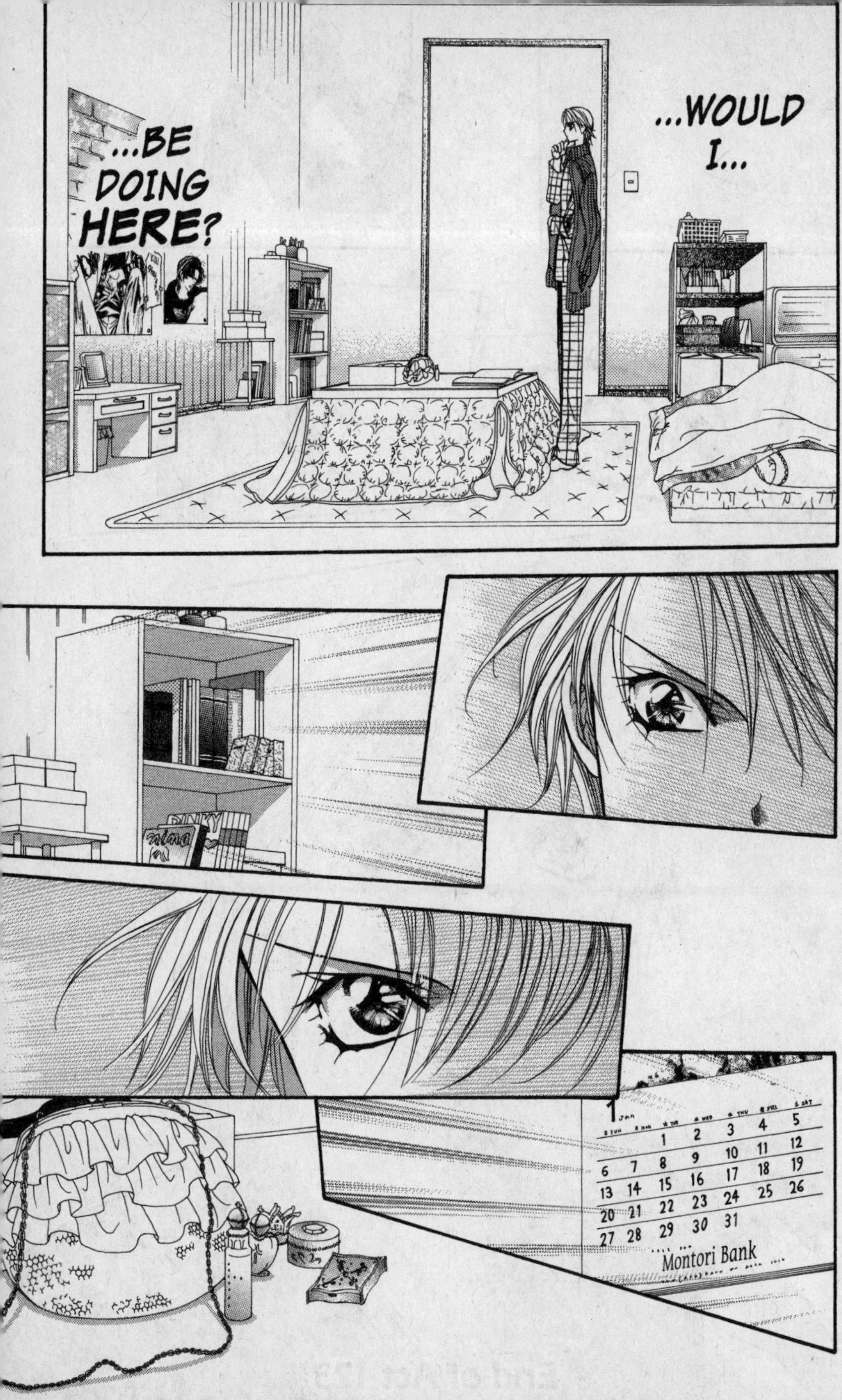
...WOULD I...
...BE DOING HERE?
Montori Bank

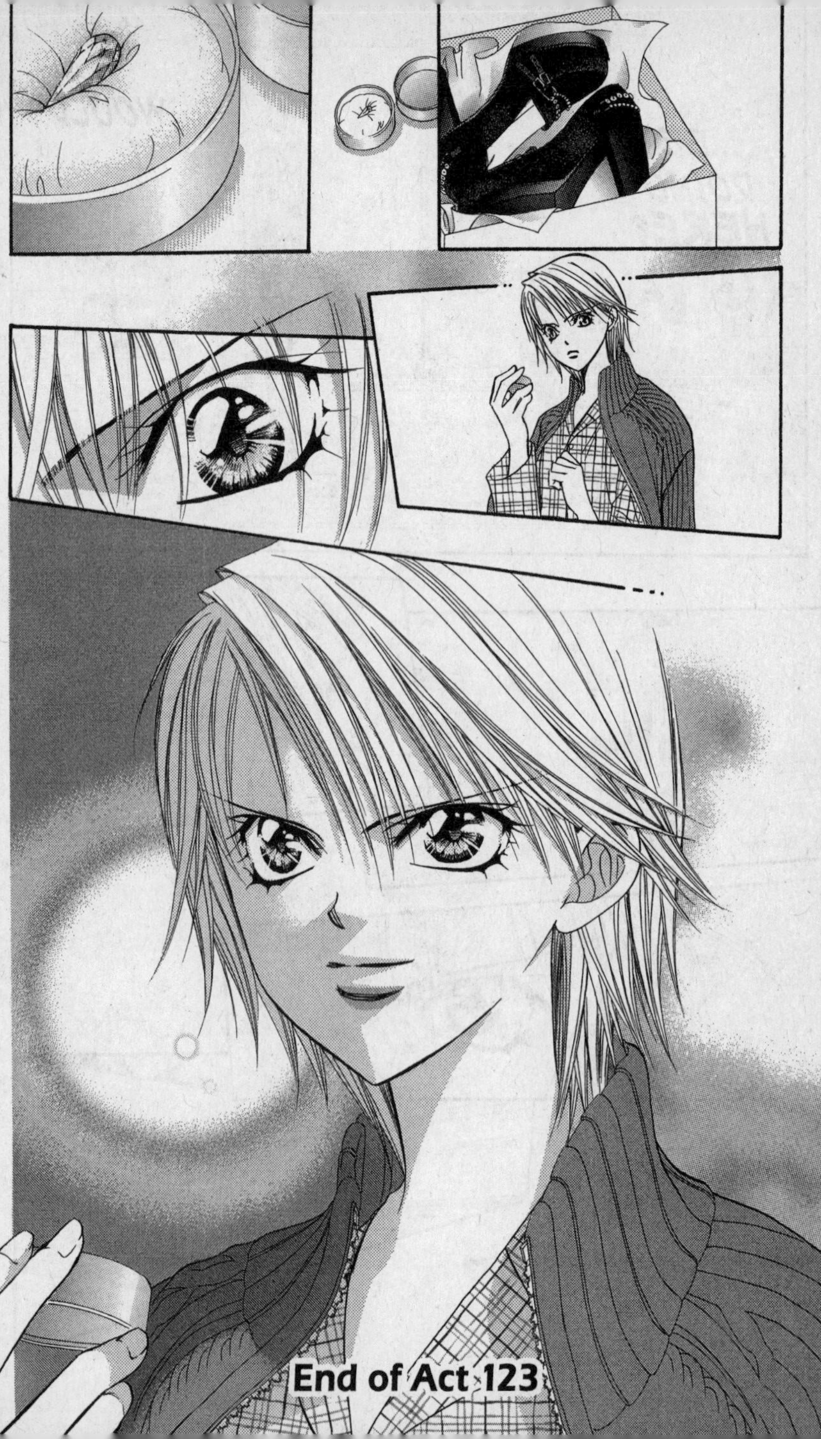
End of Act 123

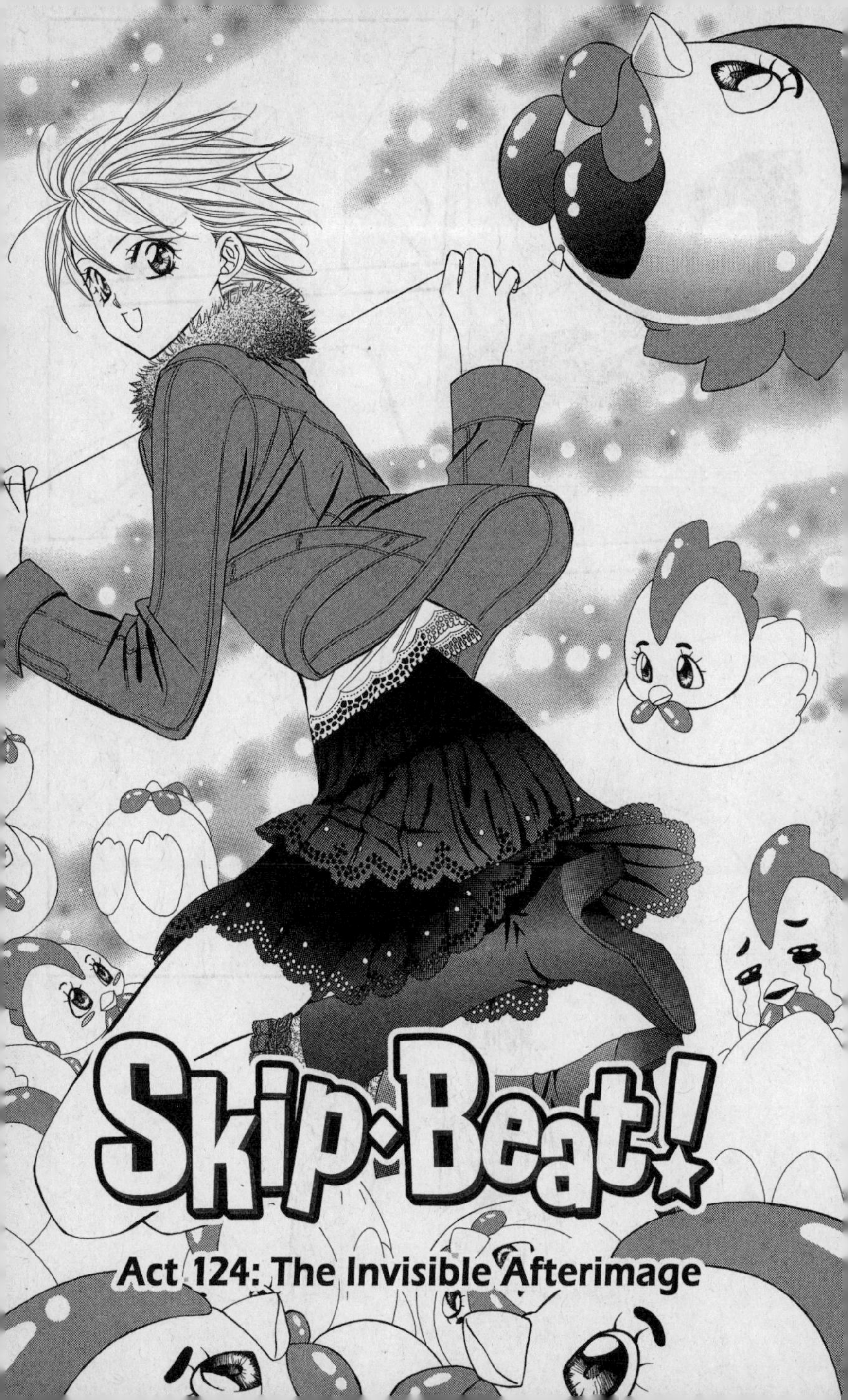
Skip·Beat!
Act 124: The Invisible Afterimage

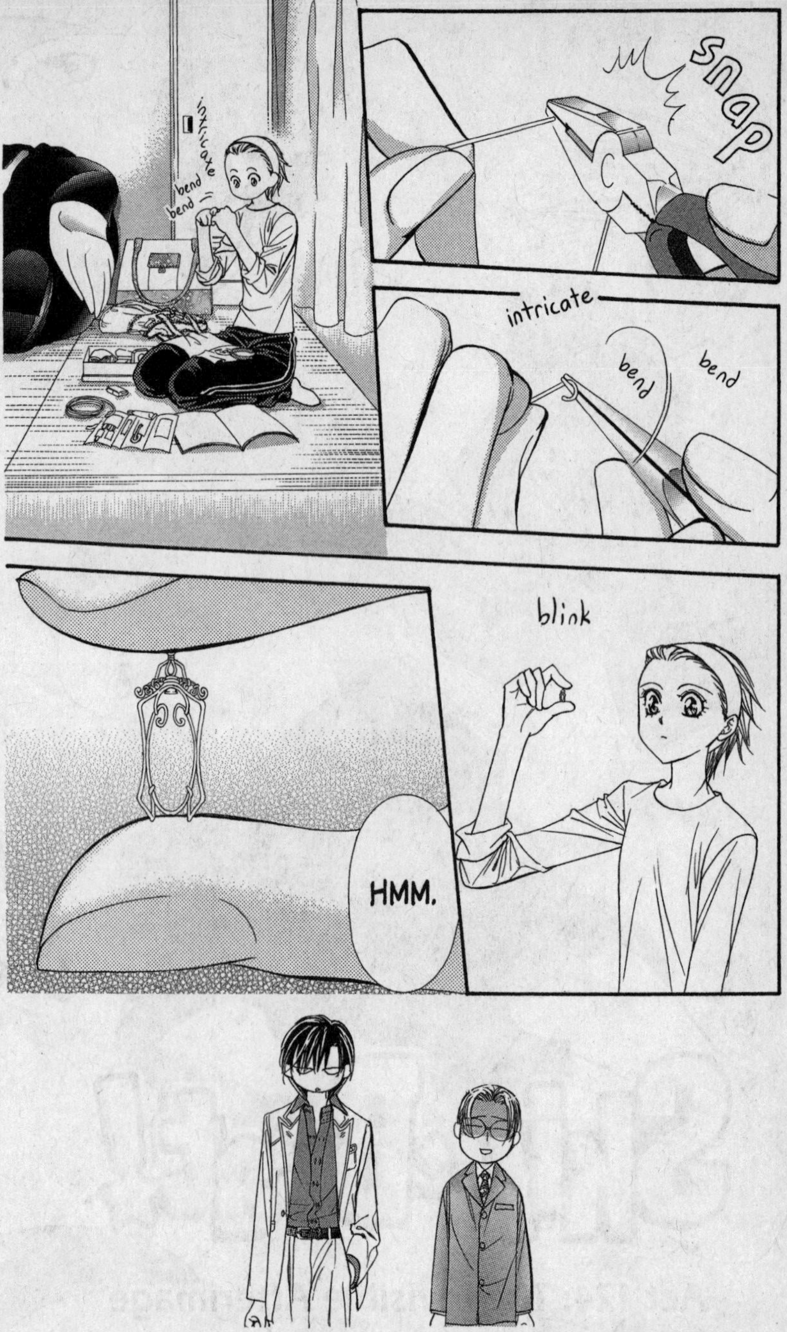
snap
intricate
bend
bend
intricate
bend
bend
blink
HMM.

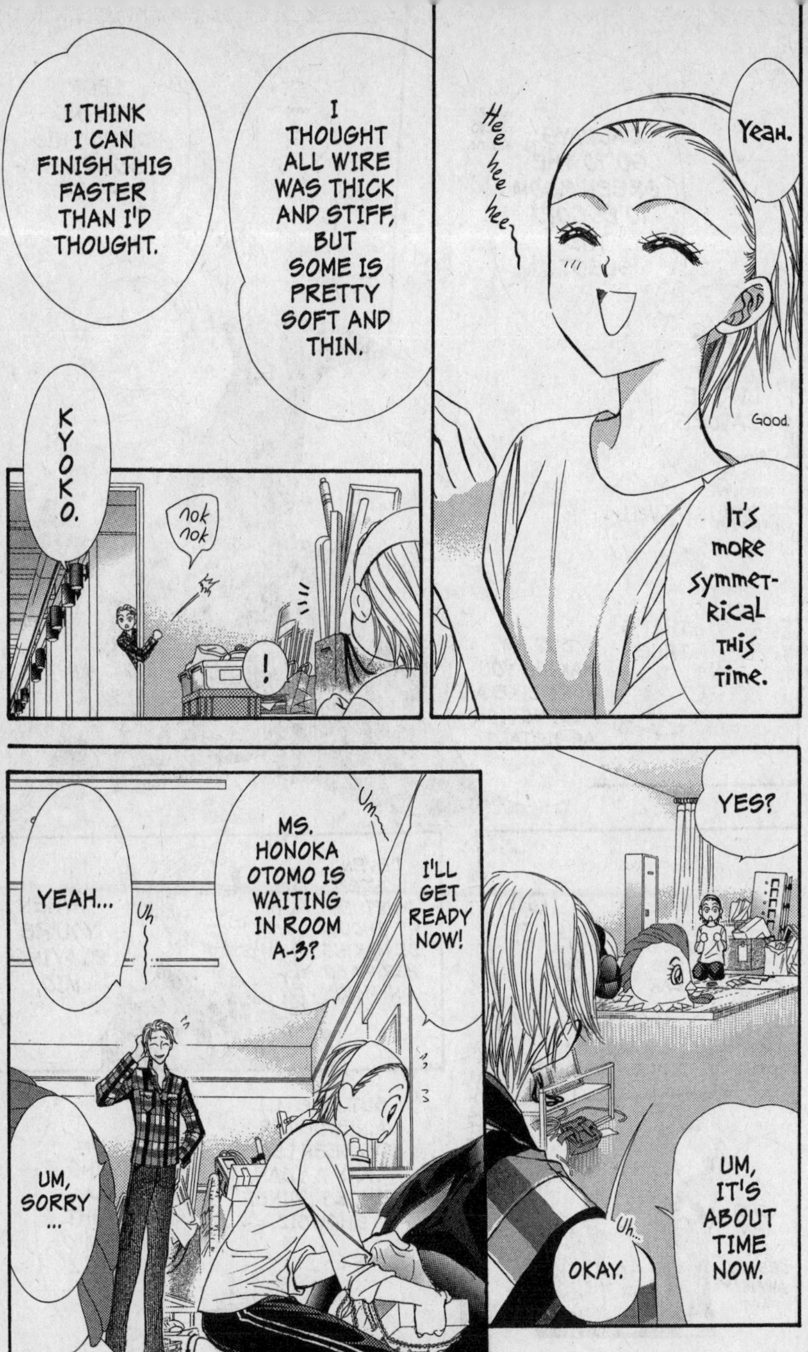
Yeah.
Hee hee hee
Good.
It's more symmetrical this time.
I thought all wire was thick and stiff, but some is pretty soft and thin.
I think I can finish this faster than I'd thought.
Kyoko.
nok nok
!
YES?
UM, IT'S ABOUT TIME NOW.
Uh...
OKAY.
Um
MS. HONOKA OTOMO IS WAITING IN ROOM A-3?
I'LL GET READY NOW!
YEAH...
Uh
UM, SORRY...

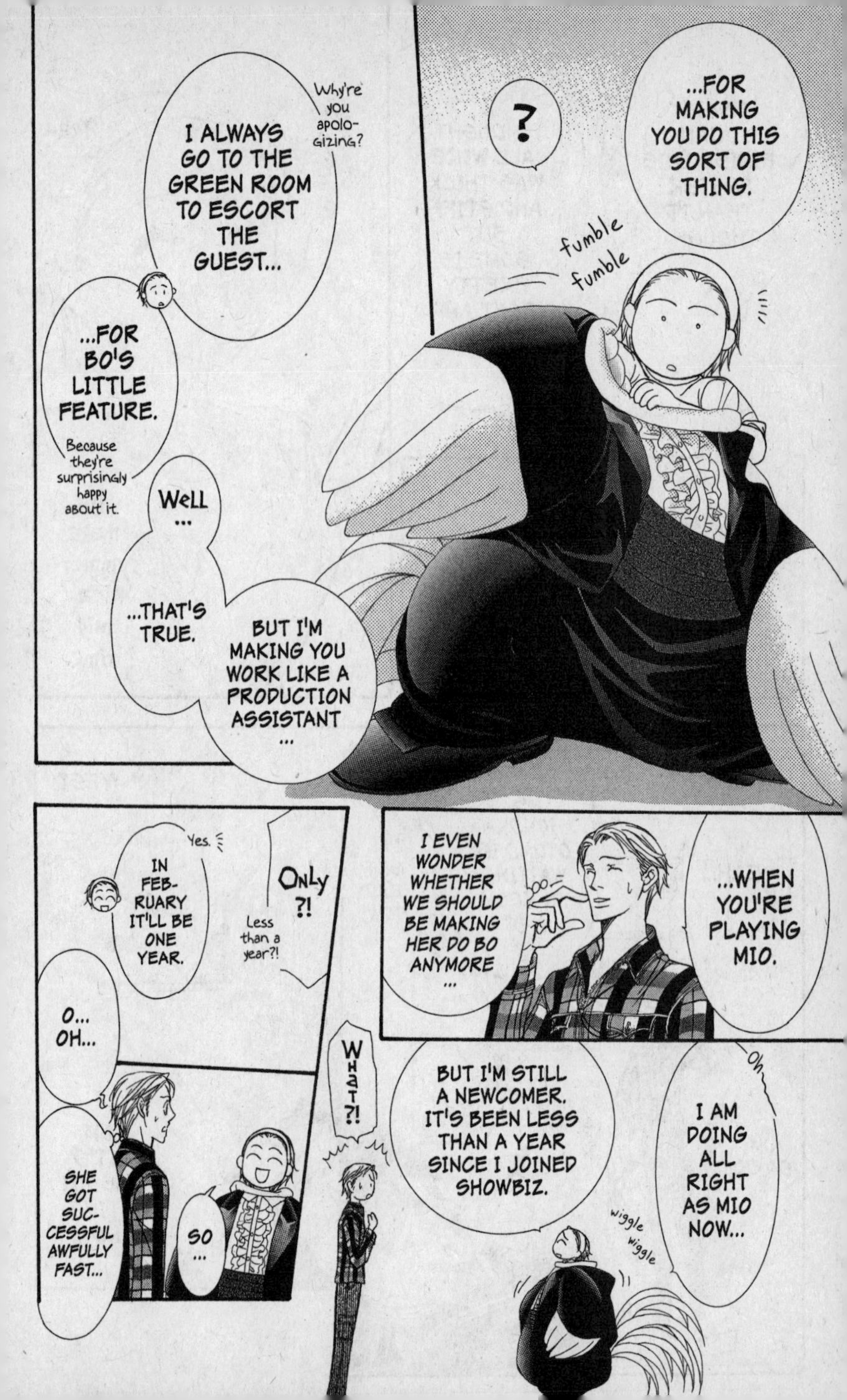
...FOR MAKING YOU DO THIS SORT OF THING.
?
fumble fumble
I ALWAYS GO TO THE GREEN ROOM TO ESCORT THE GUEST...
Why're you apolo-gizing?
...FOR BO'S LITTLE FEATURE.
Because they're surprisingly happy about it.
Well...
...THAT'S TRUE.
BUT I'M MAKING YOU WORK LIKE A PRODUCTION ASSISTANT...
...WHEN YOU'RE PLAYING MIO.
I EVEN WONDER WHETHER WE SHOULD BE MAKING HER DO BO ANYMORE...
Oh
I AM DOING ALL RIGHT AS MIO NOW...
wiggle wiggle
BUT I'M STILL A NEWCOMER. IT'S BEEN LESS THAN A YEAR SINCE I JOINED SHOWBIZ.
WHAT?!
ONLY?!
Less than a year?!
Yes.
IN FEB-RUARY IT'LL BE ONE YEAR.
O... OH...
SO...
SHE GOT SUC-CESSFUL AWFULLY FAST...

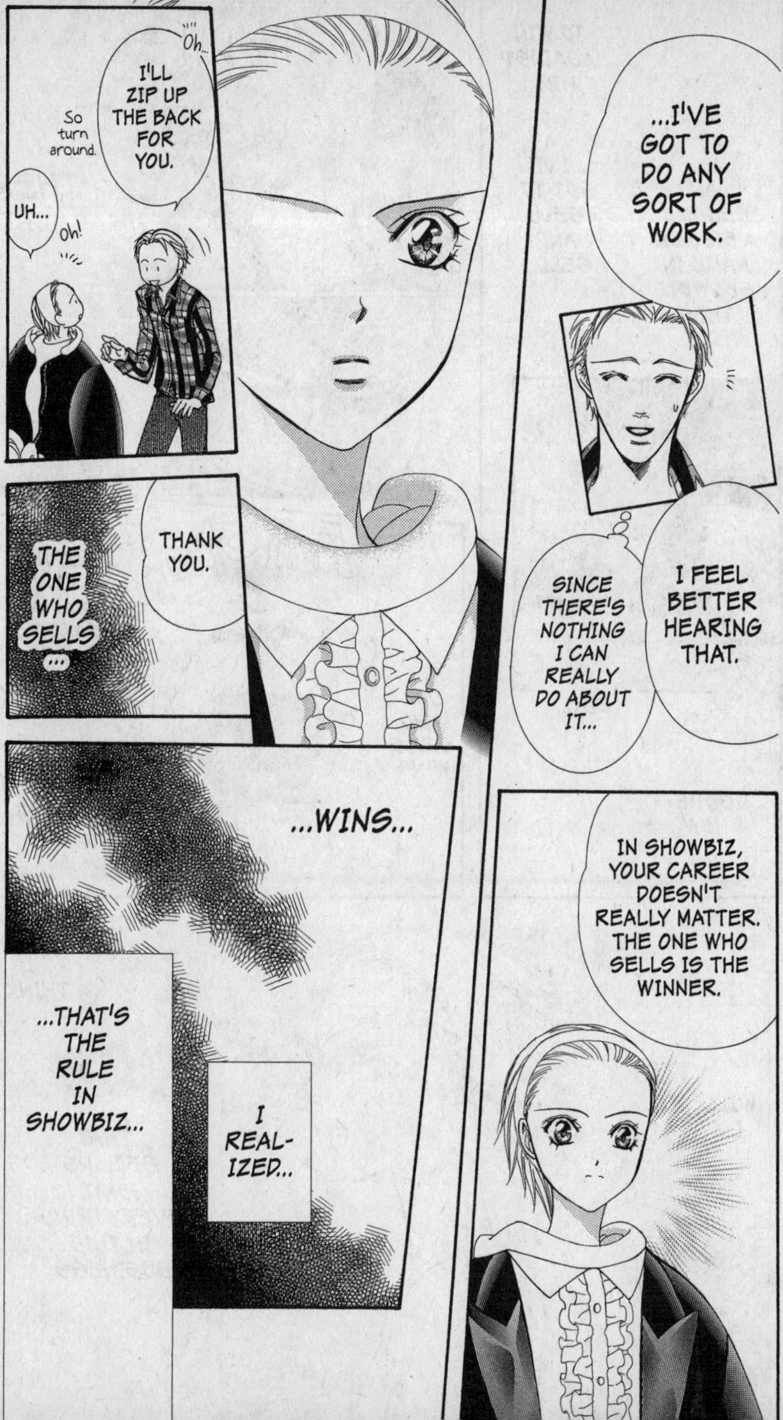
...I'VE GOT TO DO ANY SORT OF WORK.
I FEEL BETTER HEARING THAT.
SINCE THERE'S NOTHING I CAN REALLY DO ABOUT IT...
IN SHOWBIZ, YOUR CAREER DOESN'T REALLY MATTER. THE ONE WHO SELLS IS THE WINNER.
Oh...
I'LL ZIP UP THE BACK FOR YOU.
So turn around.
UH...
Oh!
THANK YOU.
THE ONE WHO SELLS...
...WINS...
...THAT'S THE RULE IN SHOWBIZ...
I REALIZED...

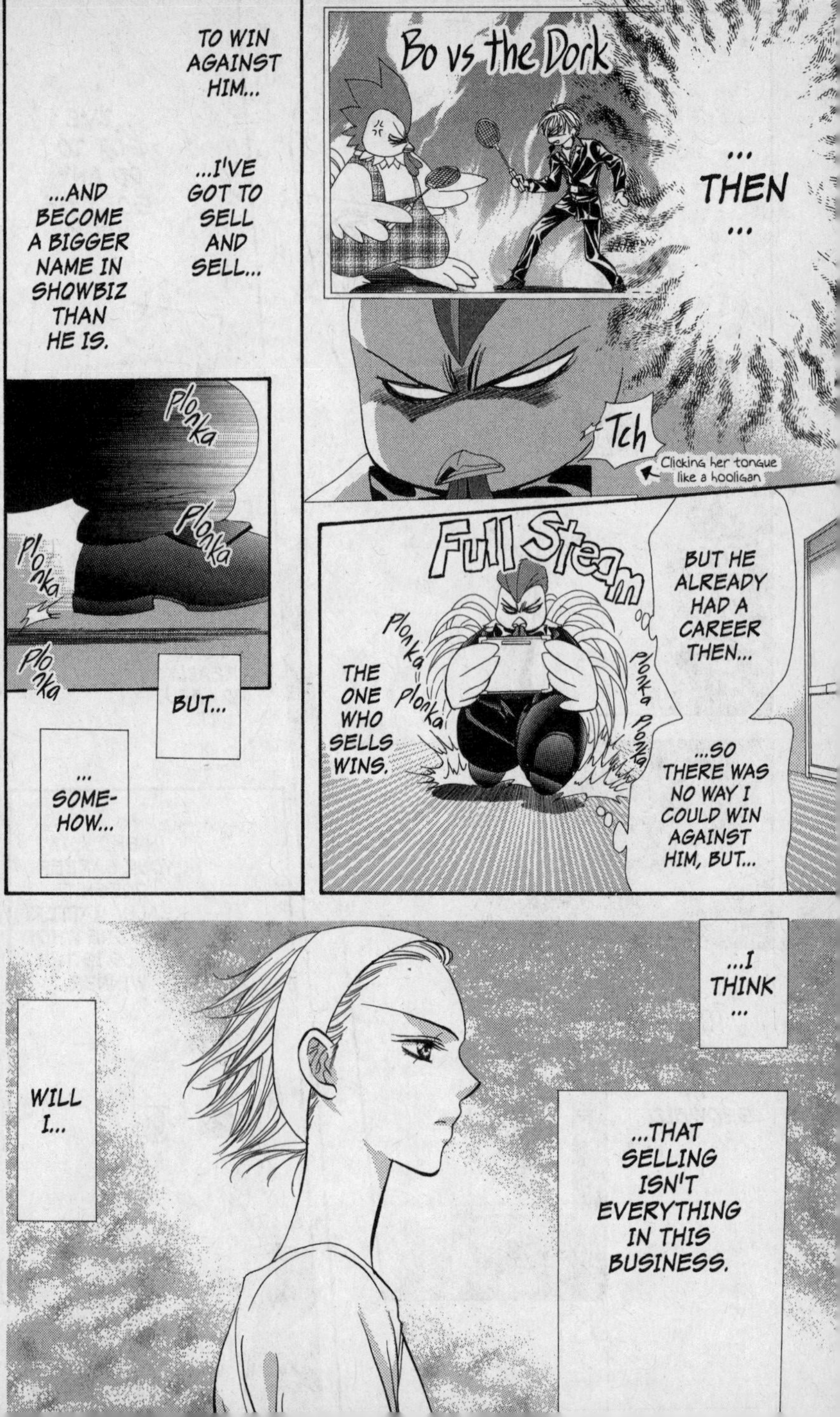
... THEN ...
Bo vs the Dork
Tch
Clicking her tongue like a hooligan
TO WIN AGAINST HIM...
...I'VE GOT TO SELL AND SELL...
...AND BECOME A BIGGER NAME IN SHOWBIZ THAN HE IS.
BUT HE ALREADY HAD A CAREER THEN...
...SO THERE WAS NO WAY I COULD WIN AGAINST HIM, BUT...
Full Steam
Plonka
Plonka
Plonka
Plonka
THE ONE WHO SELLS WINS.
Plonka
Plonka
Plonka
Plonka
BUT...
... SOME-HOW...
...I THINK ...
...THAT SELLING ISN'T EVERYTHING IN THIS BUSINESS.
WILL I...

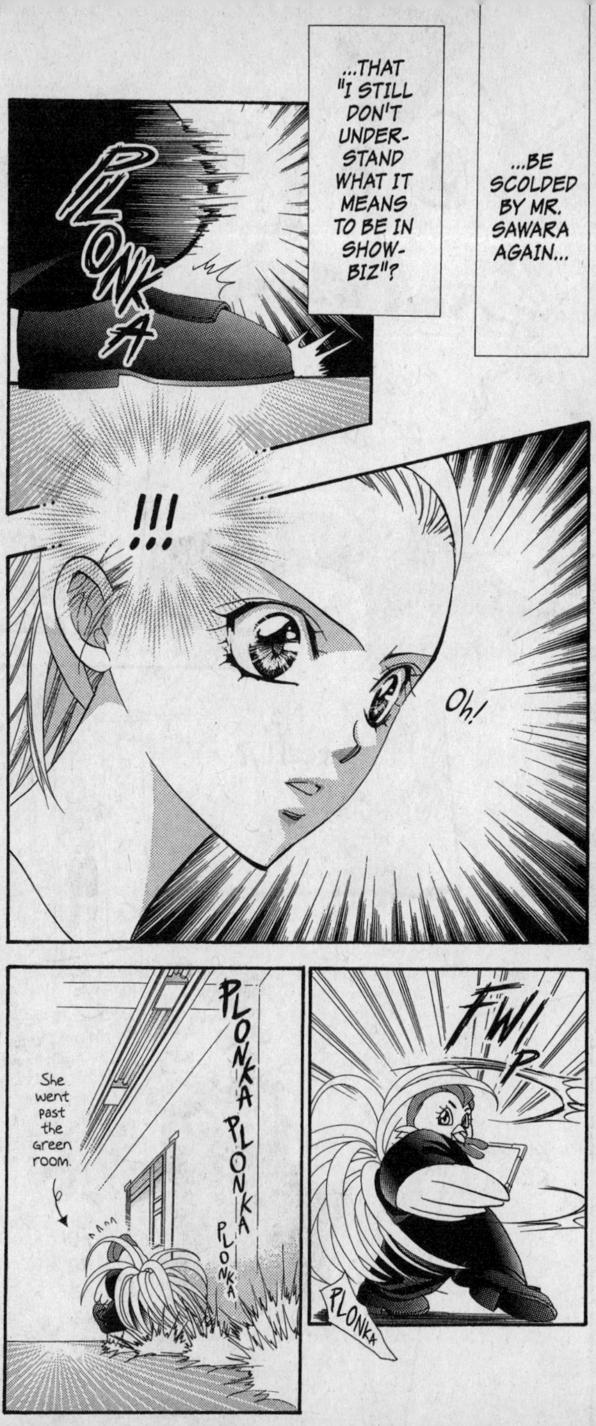
...BE SCOLDED BY MR. SAWARA AGAIN...
...THAT "I STILL DON'T UNDER-STAND WHAT IT MEANS TO BE IN SHOW-BIZ"?
PLONKA
!!!
Oh!
FWIP
PLONKA
PLONKA PLONKA PLONKA PLONKA
She went past the green room.

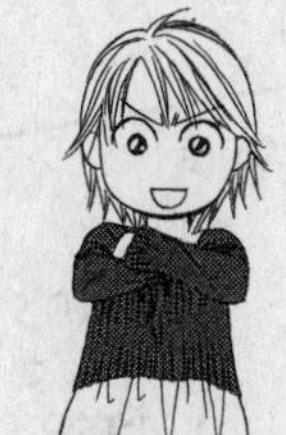

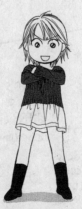

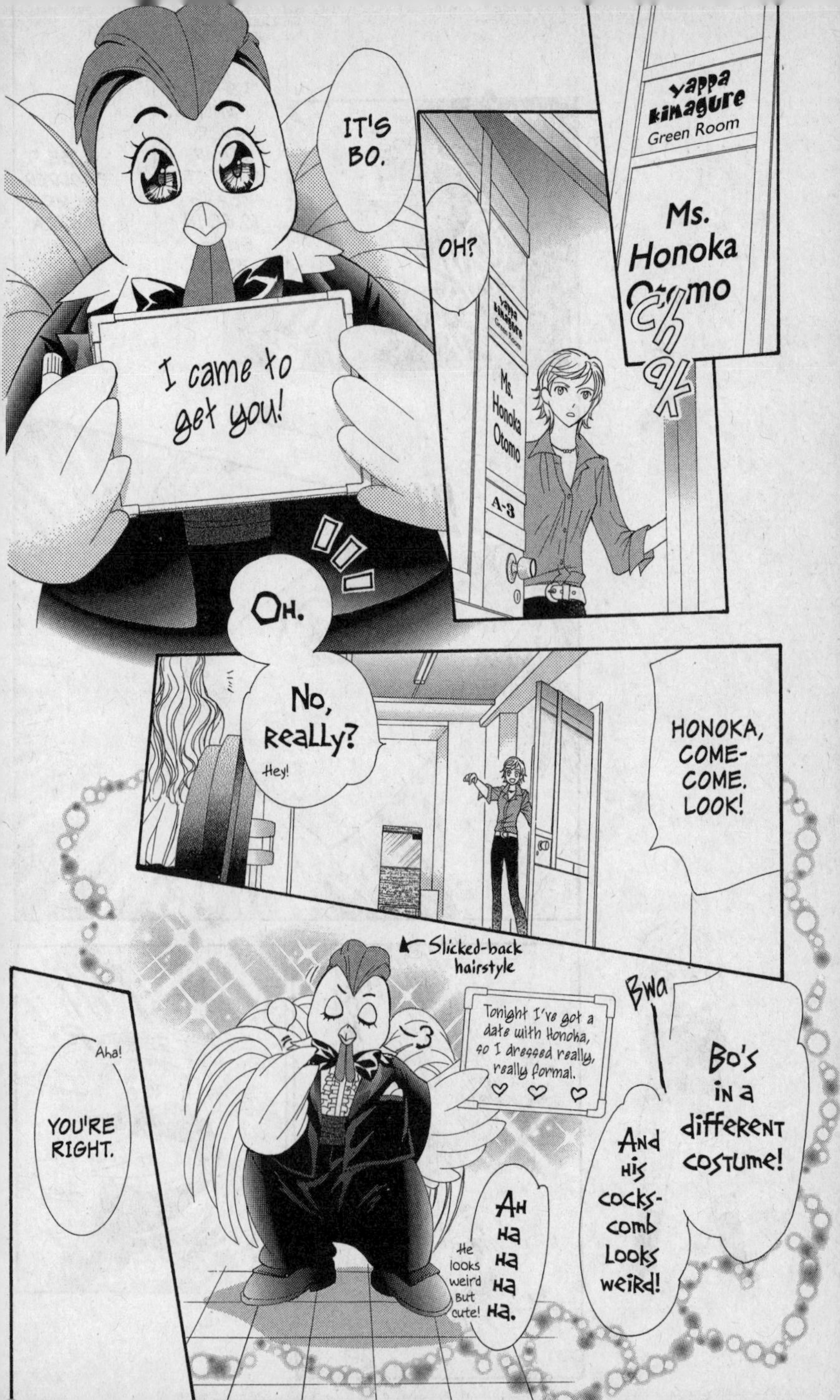
yappa kimagure
Green Room
Ms. Honoka Otomo
Chak
yappa kimagure
Green Room
Ms. Honoka Otomo
A-3
OH?
IT'S BO.
I came to get you!
OH.
HONOKA, COME-COME. LOOK!
No, really?
Hey!
Slicked-back hairstyle
Bwa
Bo's in a different costume!
And his cocks-comb looks weird!
Tonight I've got a date with Honoka, so I dressed really, really formal.
Ah ha ha ha ha.
He looks weird but cute!
Aha!
YOU'RE RIGHT.

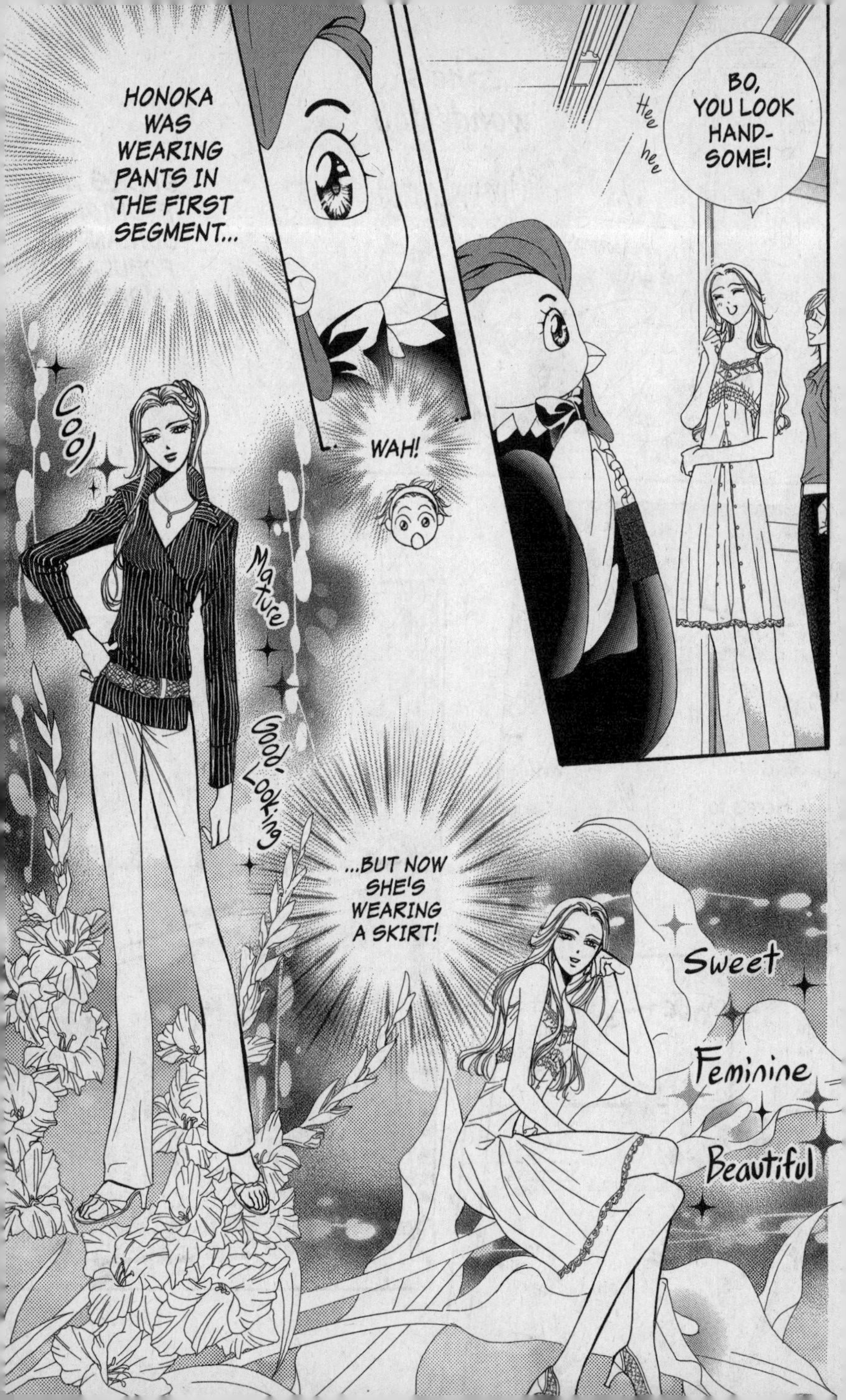

Hee hee
BO, YOU LOOK HAND-SOME!
WAH!
HONOKA WAS WEARING PANTS IN THE FIRST SEGMENT...
Cool
Mature
Good-Looking
...BUT NOW SHE'S WEARING A SKIRT!
Sweet
Feminine
Beautiful

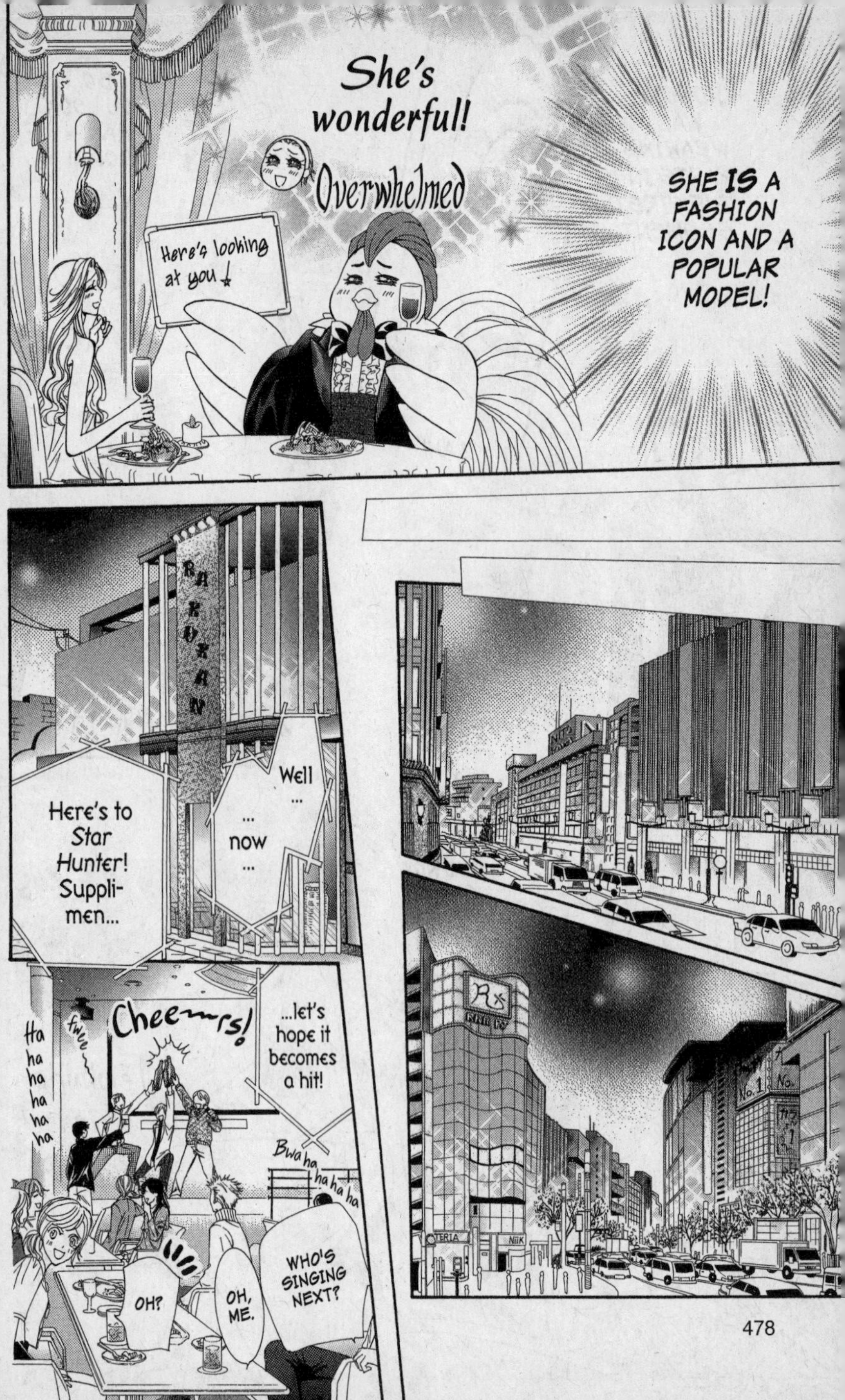
She's wonderful!
SHE IS A FASHION ICON AND A POPULAR MODEL!
Overwhelmed
Here's looking at you
Well ... ... now ...
Here's to Star Hunter! Suppli-men...
...let's hope it becomes a hit!
Cheeers!
fwee~
Ha ha ha ha ha ha
Bwa ha ha ha ha ha
WHO'S SINGING NEXT?
OH, ME.
OH?

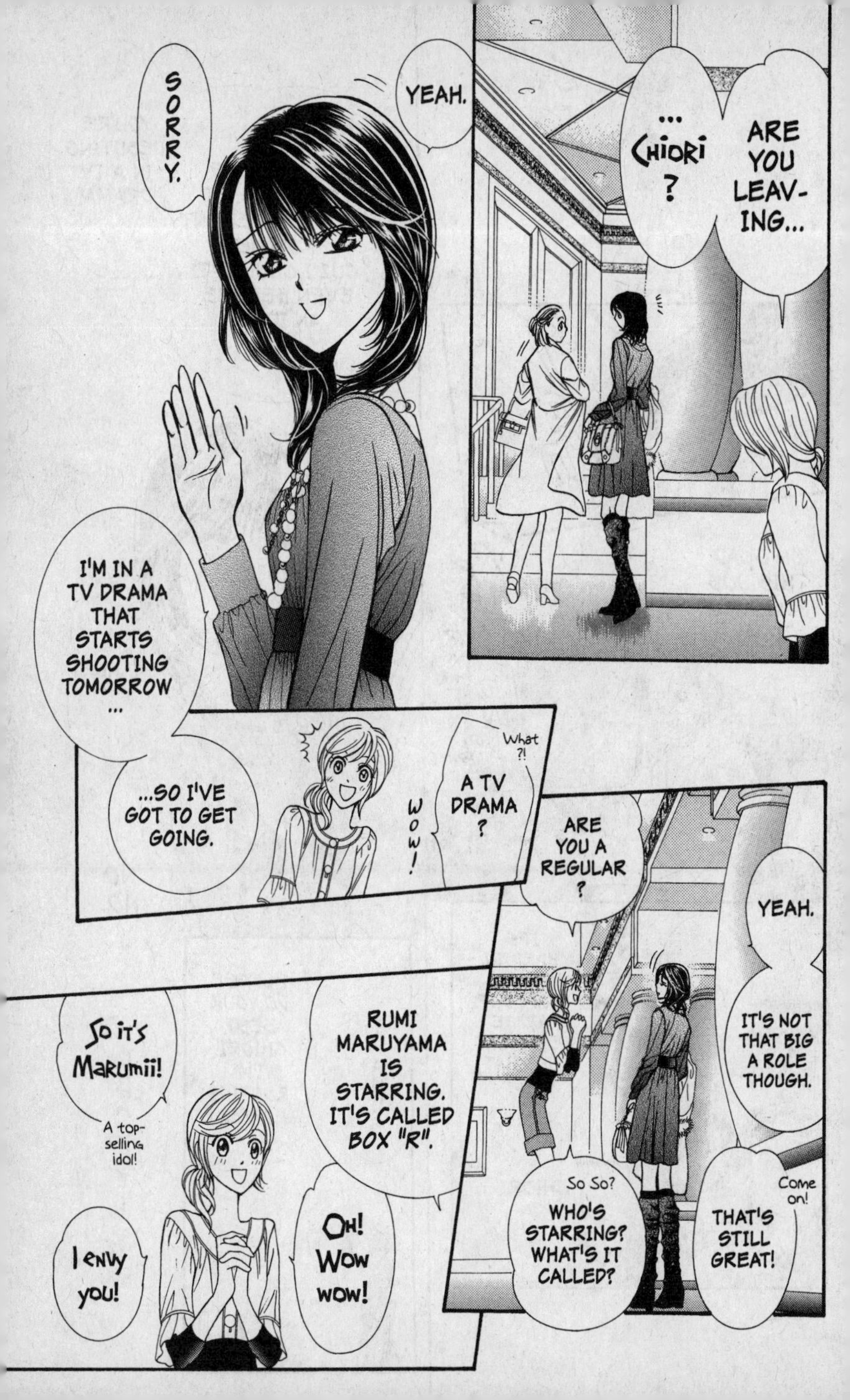
ARE YOU LEAVING...
...CHIORI?
YEAH.
SORRY.
I'M IN A TV DRAMA THAT STARTS SHOOTING TOMORROW...
...SO I'VE GOT TO GET GOING.
What?!
A TV DRAMA?
WOW!
ARE YOU A REGULAR?
YEAH.
IT'S NOT THAT BIG A ROLE THOUGH.
Come on!
THAT'S STILL GREAT!
So So?
WHO'S STARRING? WHAT'S IT CALLED?
RUMI MARUYAMA IS STARRING. IT'S CALLED BOX "R".
So it's Marumii!
A top-selling idol!
OH! WOW WOW!
I envy you!

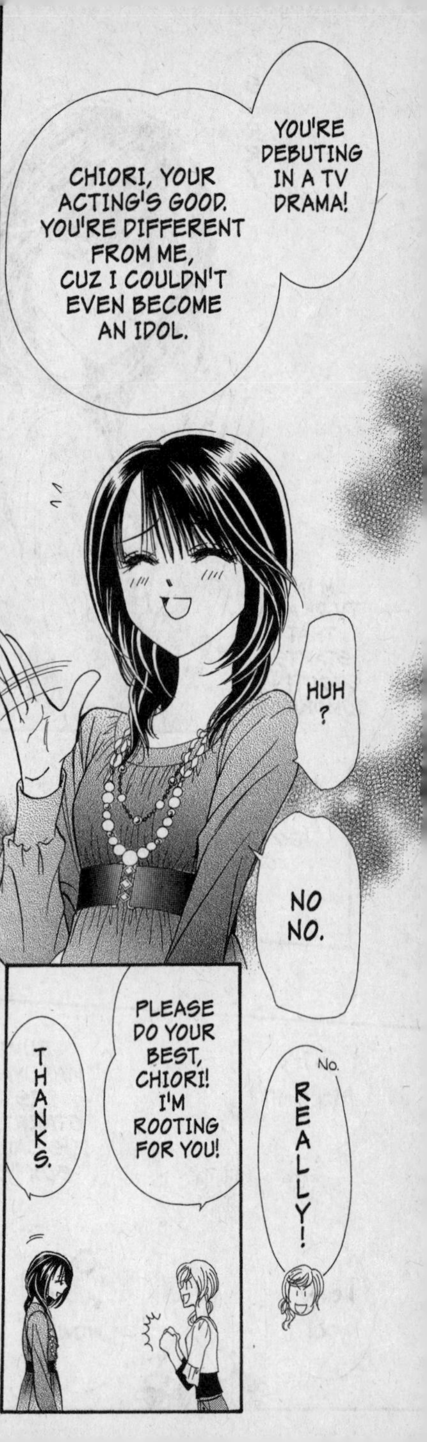
YOU'RE DEBUTING IN A TV DRAMA!
CHIORI, YOUR ACTING'S GOOD. YOU'RE DIFFERENT FROM ME, CUZ I COULDN'T EVEN BECOME AN IDOL.
HUH?
NO NO.
No.
REALLY!
PLEASE DO YOUR BEST, CHIORI! I'M ROOTING FOR YOU!
THANKS.
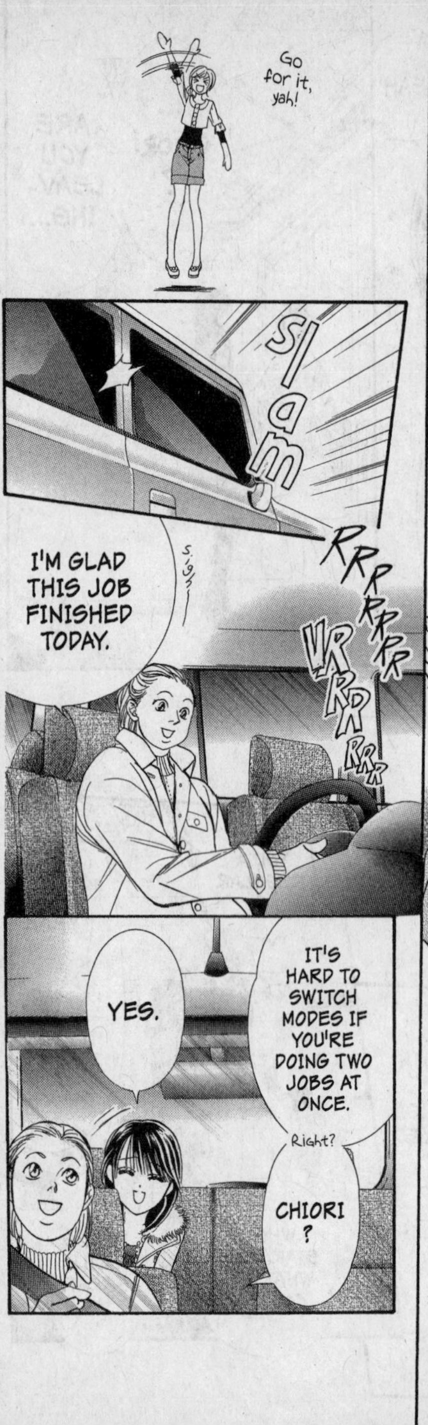
Go for it, yah!
Slam
RRRRRR
VRRRRR
sigh
I'M GLAD THIS JOB FINISHED TODAY.
IT'S HARD TO SWITCH MODES IF YOU'RE DOING TWO JOBS AT ONCE.
Right?
CHIORI?
YES.

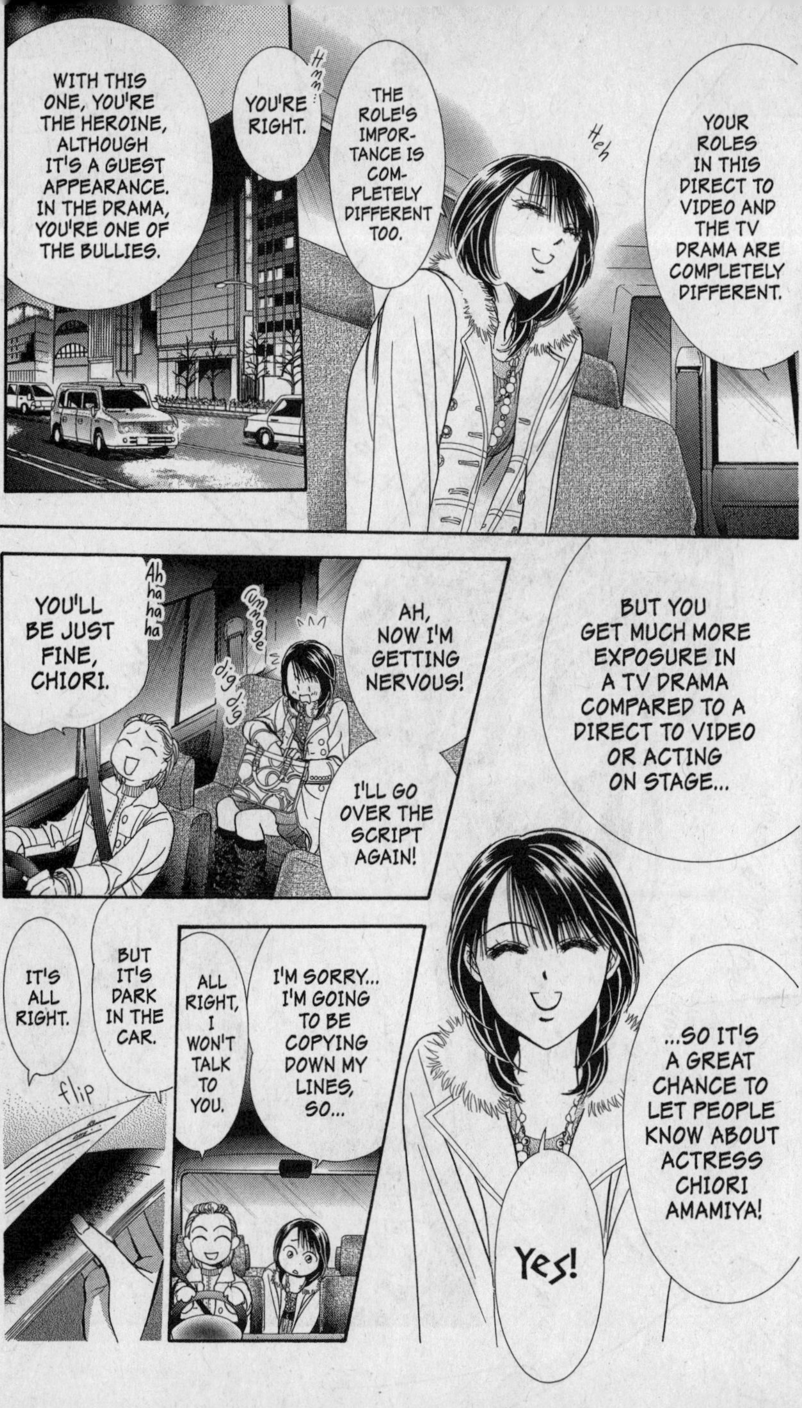
YOUR ROLES IN THIS DIRECT TO VIDEO AND THE TV DRAMA ARE COMPLETELY DIFFERENT.
Heh
THE ROLE'S IMPORTANCE IS COMPLETELY DIFFERENT TOO.
Hmm...
YOU'RE RIGHT.
WITH THIS ONE, YOU'RE THE HEROINE, ALTHOUGH IT'S A GUEST APPEARANCE. IN THE DRAMA, YOU'RE ONE OF THE BULLIES.
BUT YOU GET MUCH MORE EXPOSURE IN A TV DRAMA COMPARED TO A DIRECT TO VIDEO OR ACTING ON STAGE...
...SO IT'S A GREAT CHANCE TO LET PEOPLE KNOW ABOUT ACTRESS CHIORI AMAMIYA!
Yes!
AH, NOW I'M GETTING NERVOUS!
I'LL GO OVER THE SCRIPT AGAIN!
rummage
dig dig
Ah ha ha ha ha
YOU'LL BE JUST FINE, CHIORI.
I'M SORRY... I'M GOING TO BE COPYING DOWN MY LINES, SO...
ALL RIGHT, I WON'T TALK TO YOU.
BUT IT'S DARK IN THE CAR.
IT'S ALL RIGHT.
flip

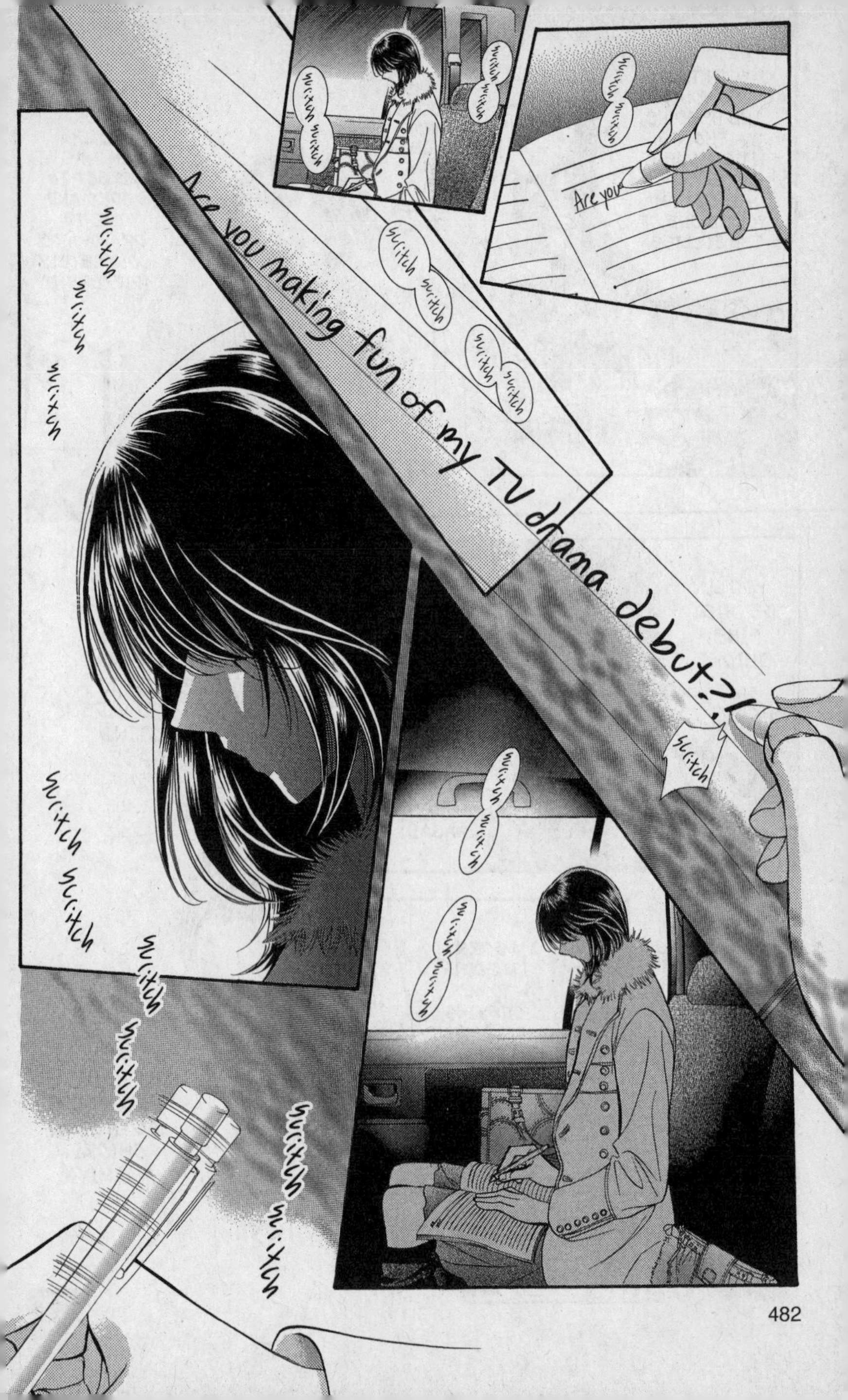
scritch scritch
scritch scritch
Are you
scritch scritch
scritch scritch
scritch
scritch
scritch
Are you making fun of my TV drama debut?!
scritch
scritch scritch
scritch scritch
scritch scritch
scritch scritch
scritch scritch

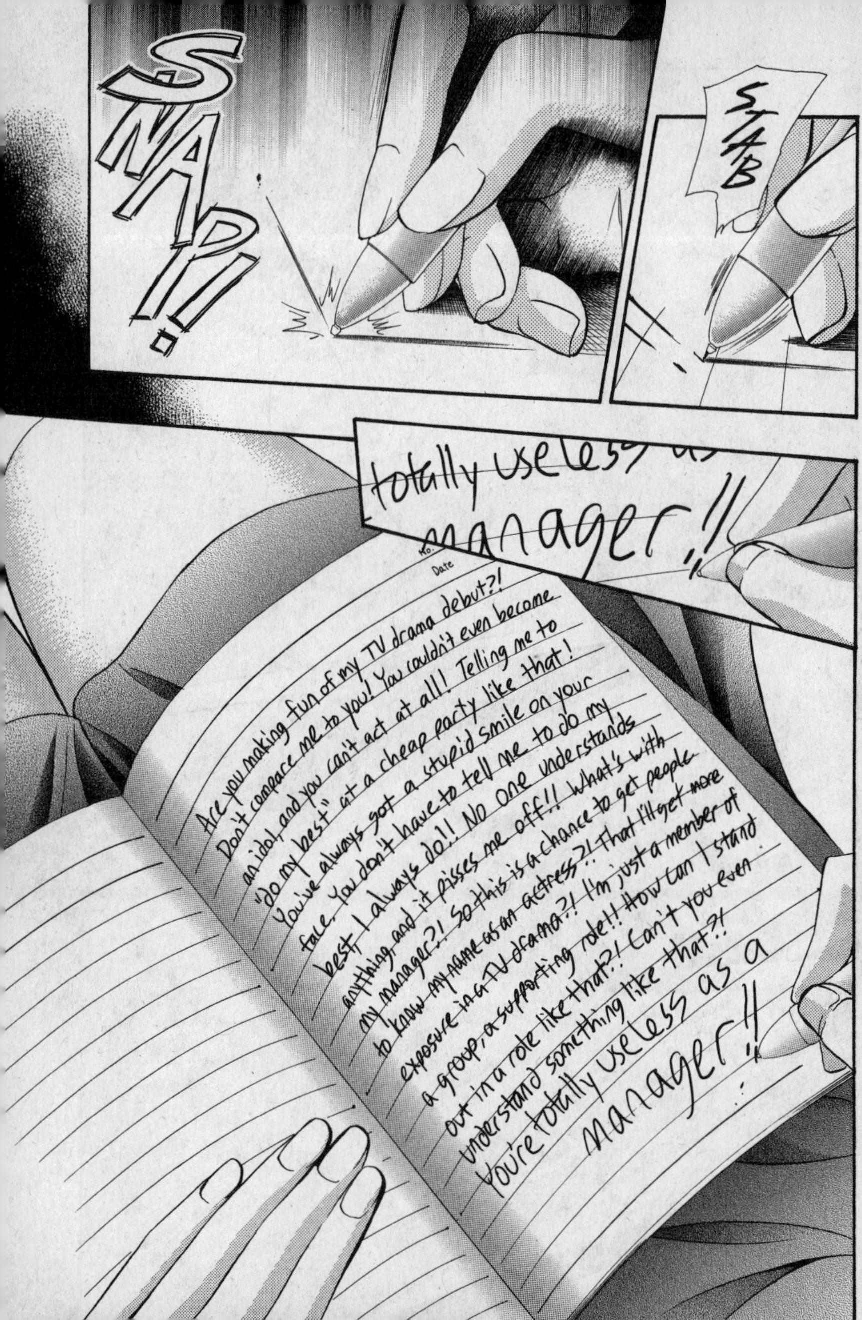
STAB
SNAP!!
totally useless as manager!!
No.
Date
Are you making fun of my TV drama debut?!
Don't compare me to you! You couldn't even become
an idol, and you can't act at all! Telling me to
"Do my best" at a cheap party like that!
You've always got a stupid smile on your
face. You don't have to tell me to do my
best I always do!! No one understands
anything and it pisses me off!! What's with
my manager?! So this is a chance to get people
to know my name as an actress?! That I'll get more
exposure in a TV drama?! I'm just a member of
a group, a supporting role!! How can I stand
out in a role like that?! Can't you even
understand something like that?!
You're totally useless as a
manager!!

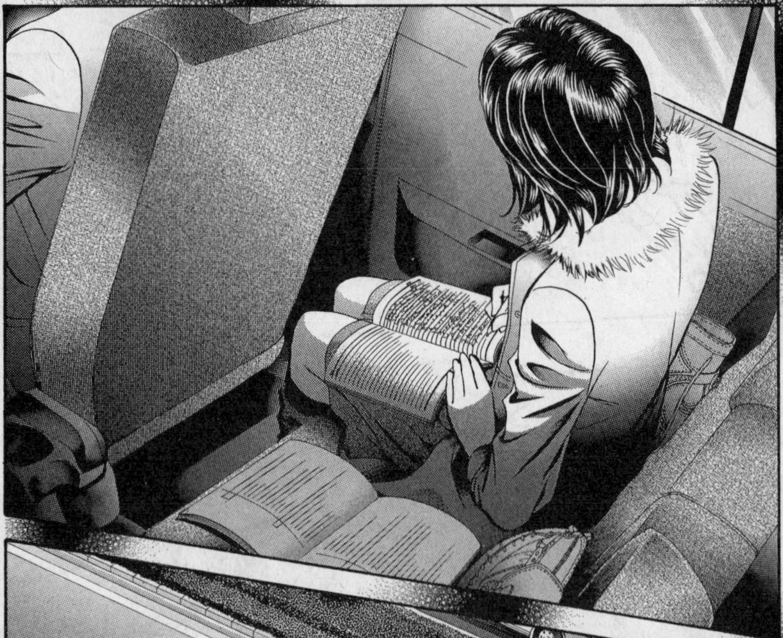
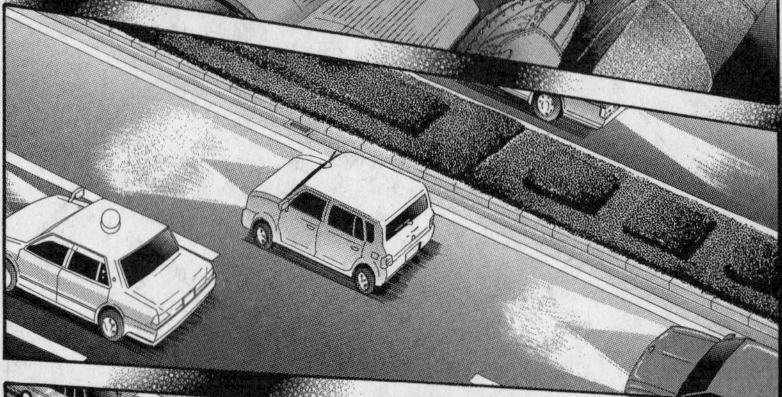
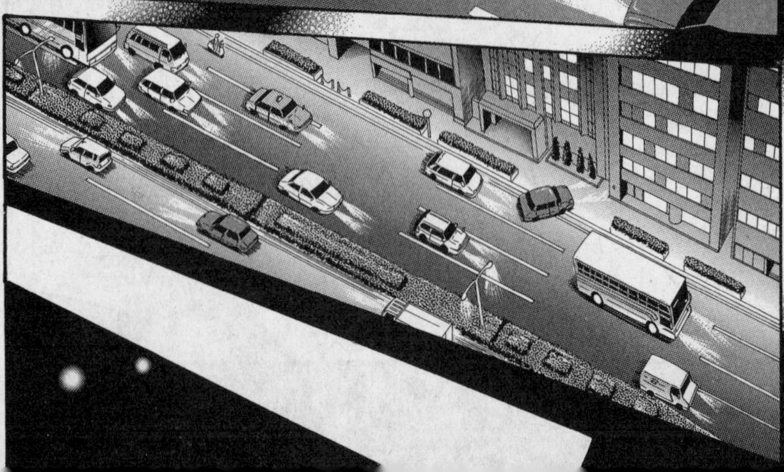

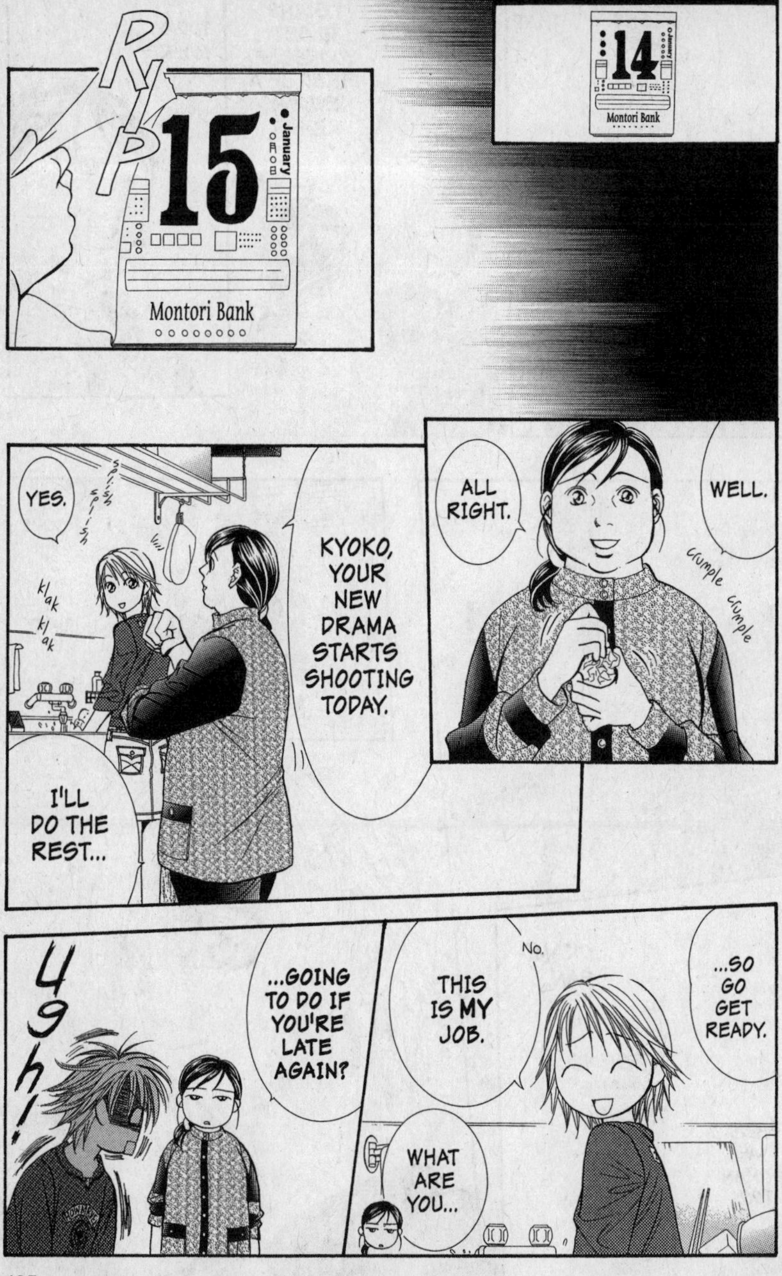
14
January
Montori Bank
RIP
15
January
Montori Bank
WELL.
ALL RIGHT.
crumple crumple
KYOKO, YOUR NEW DRAMA STARTS SHOOTING TODAY.
YES.
splish splish
klak klak
I'LL DO THE REST...
...SO GO GET READY.
No.
THIS IS MY JOB.
WHAT ARE YOU...
...GOING TO DO IF YOU'RE LATE AGAIN?
Ugh!

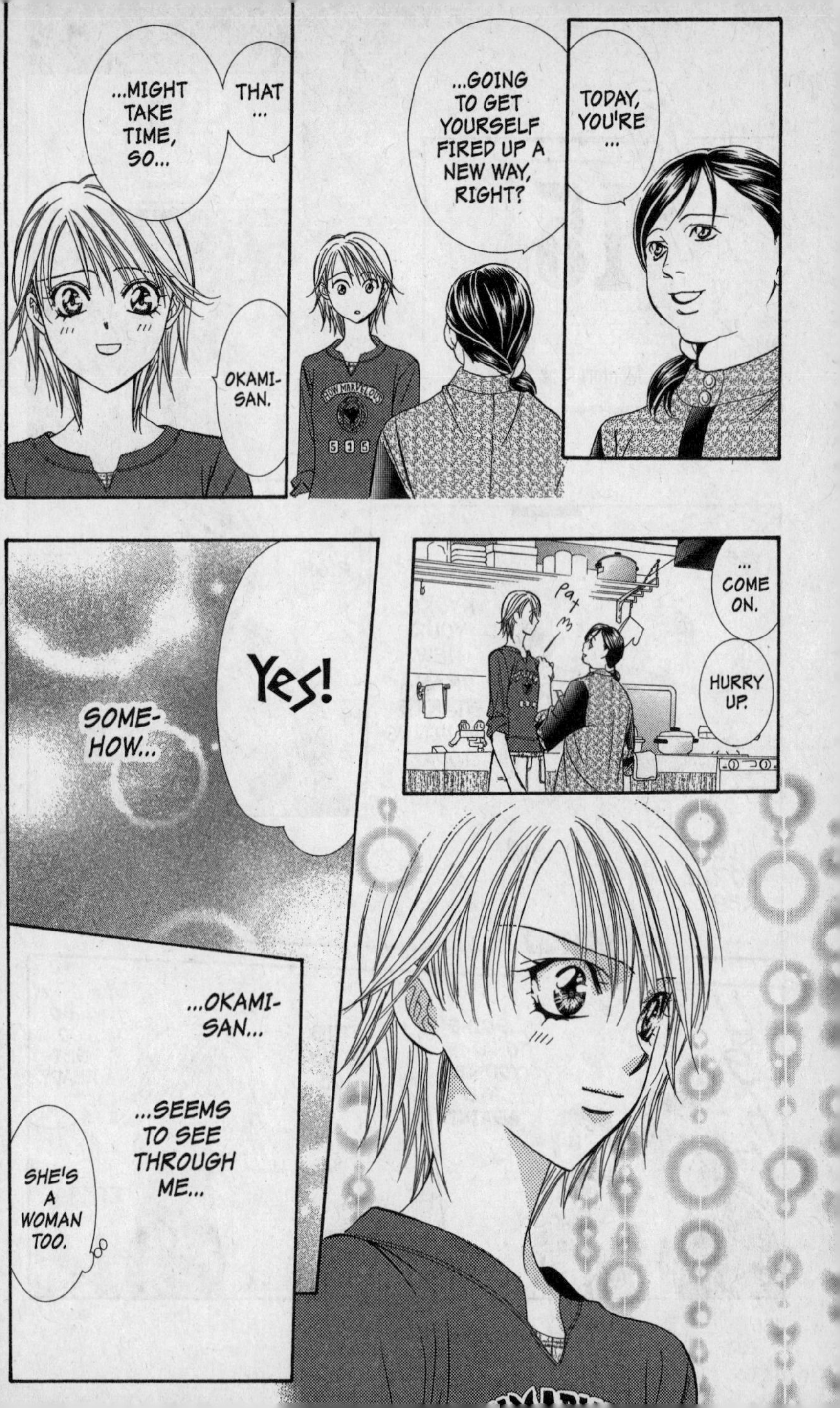
TODAY, YOU'RE ...
...GOING TO GET YOURSELF FIRED UP A NEW WAY, RIGHT?
OKAMI-SAN.
THAT ...
...MIGHT TAKE TIME, SO...
... COME ON.
HURRY UP.
Pat
Yes!
SOME-HOW...
...OKAMI-SAN...
...SEEMS TO SEE THROUGH ME...
SHE'S A WOMAN TOO.

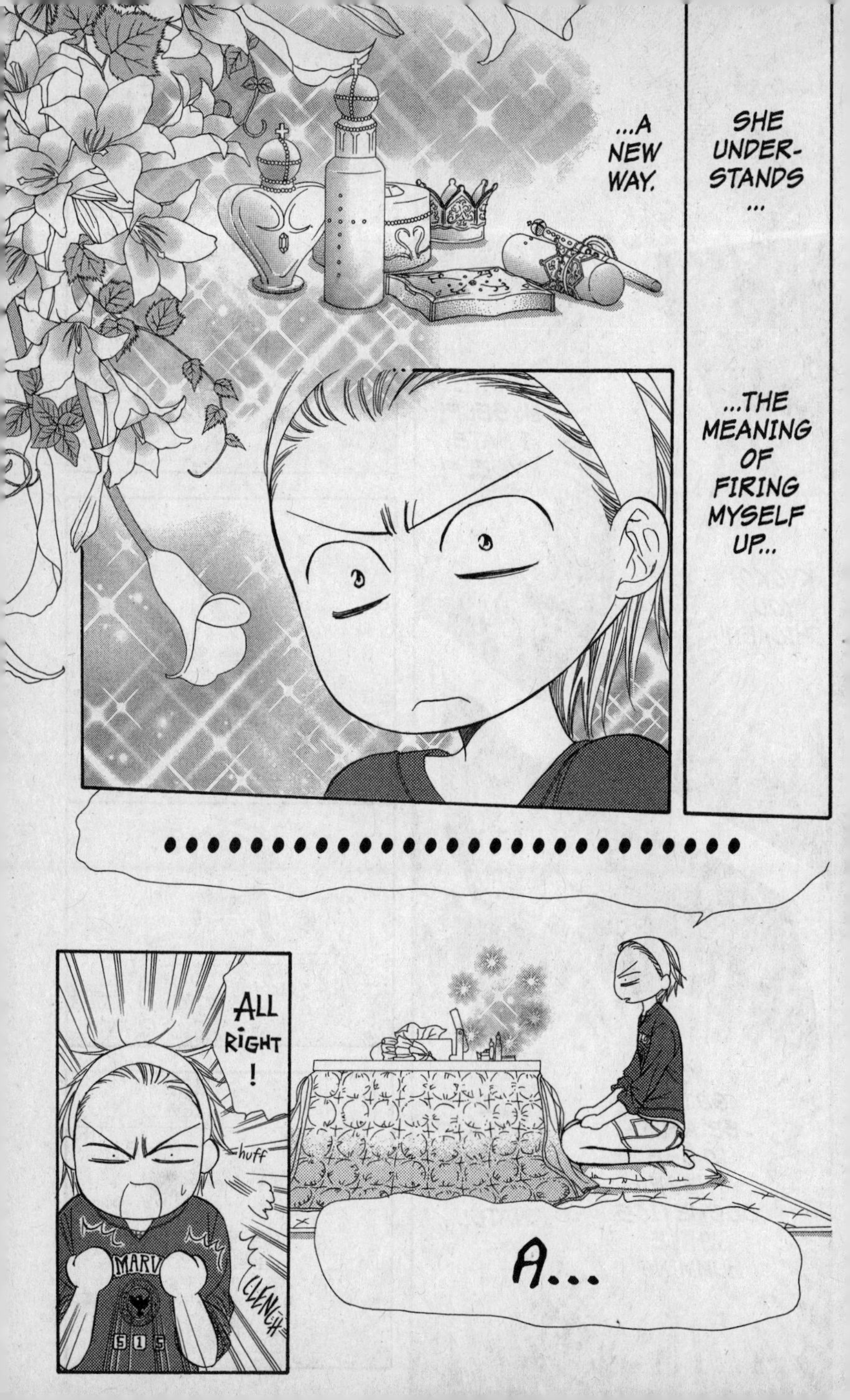
SHE UNDER-STANDS ...
...THE MEANING OF FIRING MYSELF UP...
...A NEW WAY.
••••••••••••••••••••••••••••••••
A...
ALL RIGHT !
huff
CLENCH

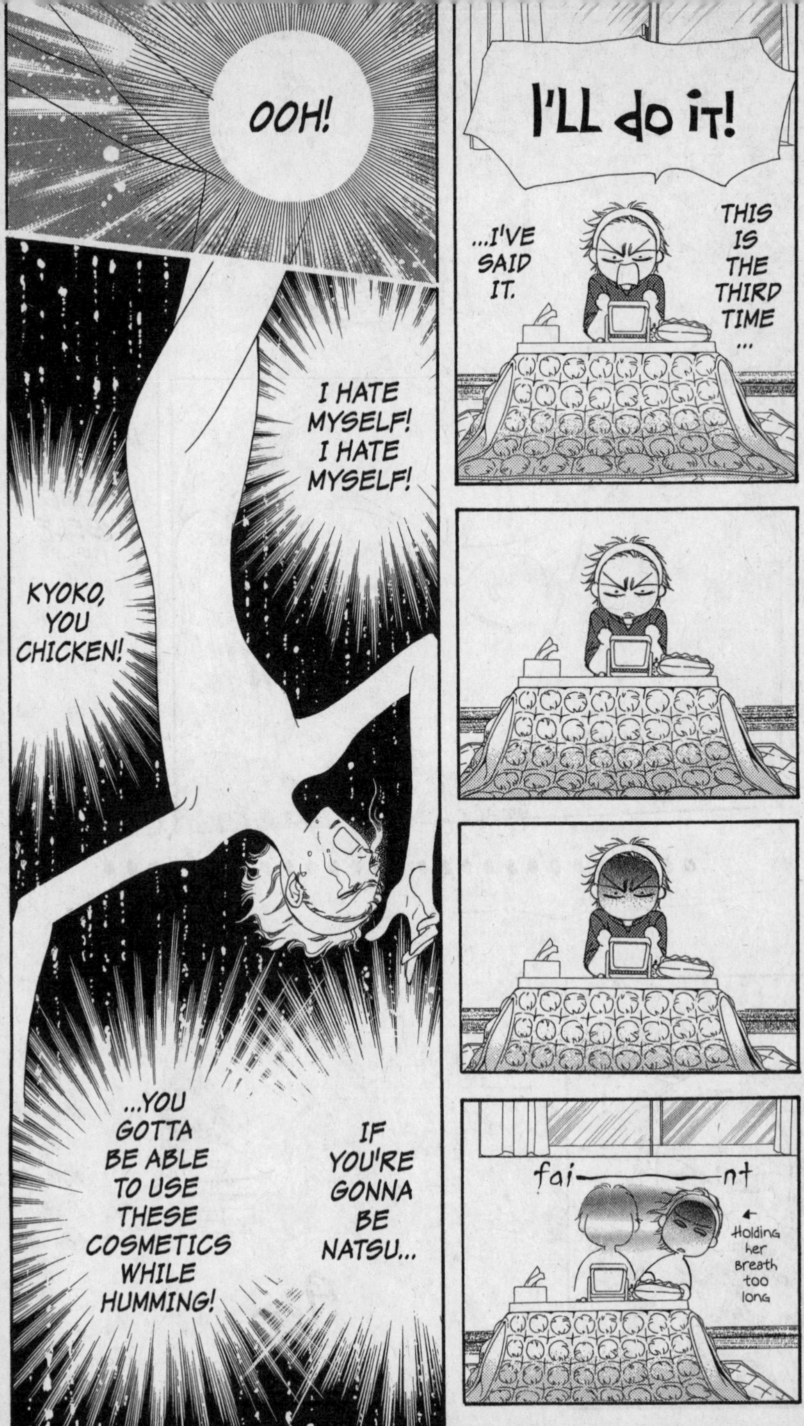
I'LL do it!
THIS IS THE THIRD TIME...
...I'VE SAID IT.
fai———nt
← Holding her Breath too long
OOH!
I HATE MYSELF! I HATE MYSELF!
KYOKO, YOU CHICKEN!
IF YOU'RE GONNA BE NATSU...
...YOU GOTTA BE ABLE TO USE THESE COSMETICS WHILE HUMMING!

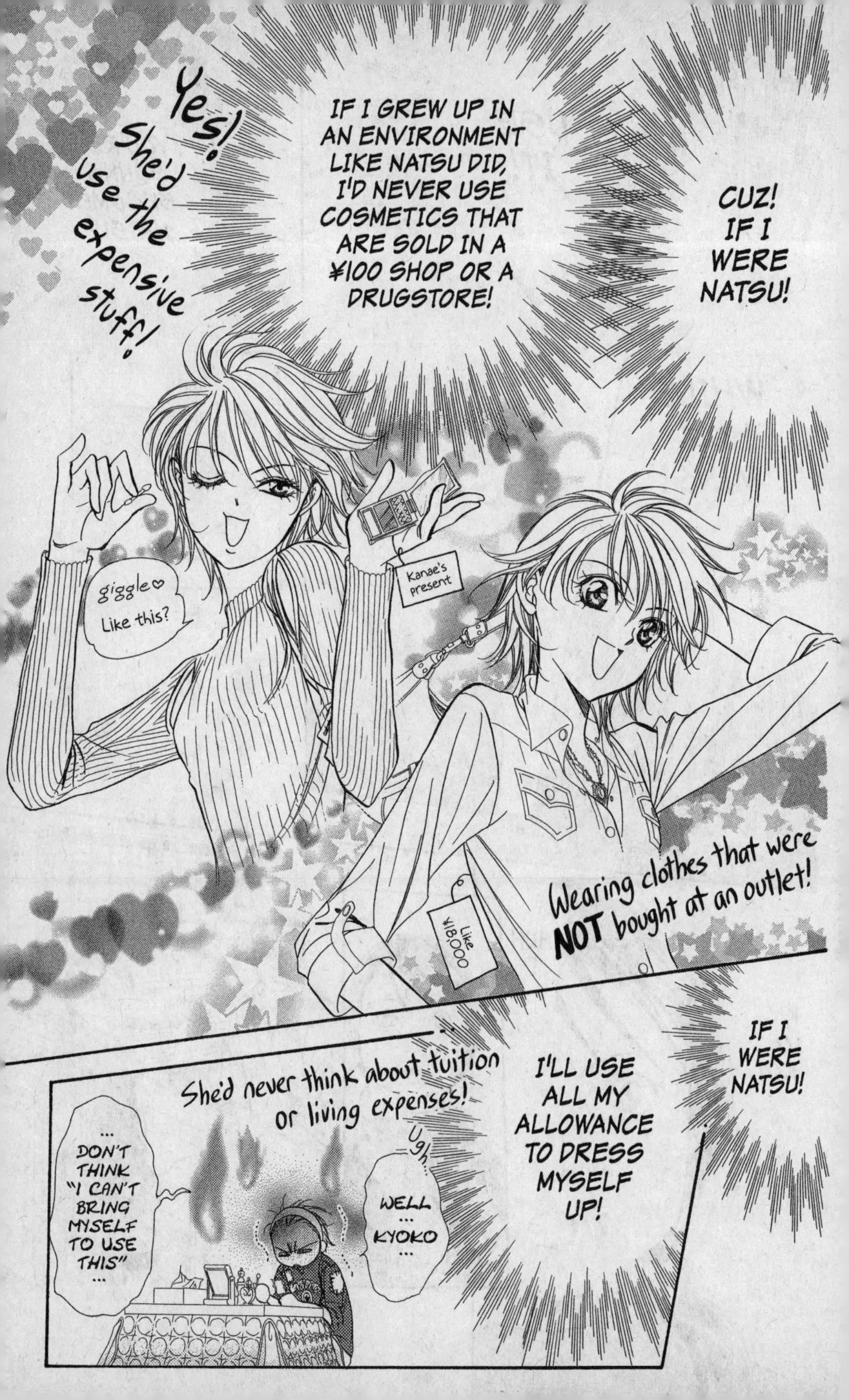
CUZ! IF I WERE NATSU!
IF I GREW UP IN AN ENVIRONMENT LIKE NATSU DID, I'D NEVER USE COSMETICS THAT ARE SOLD IN A ¥100 SHOP OR A DRUGSTORE!
Yes! She'd use the expensive stuff!
Kanae's present
giggle♡ Like this?
Wearing clothes that were NOT bought at an outlet!
Like ¥18,000
IF I WERE NATSU!
I'LL USE ALL MY ALLOWANCE TO DRESS MYSELF UP!
She'd never think about tuition or living expenses!
Ugh...
WELL ... KYOKO ...
... DON'T THINK "I CAN'T BRING MYSELF TO USE THIS" ...

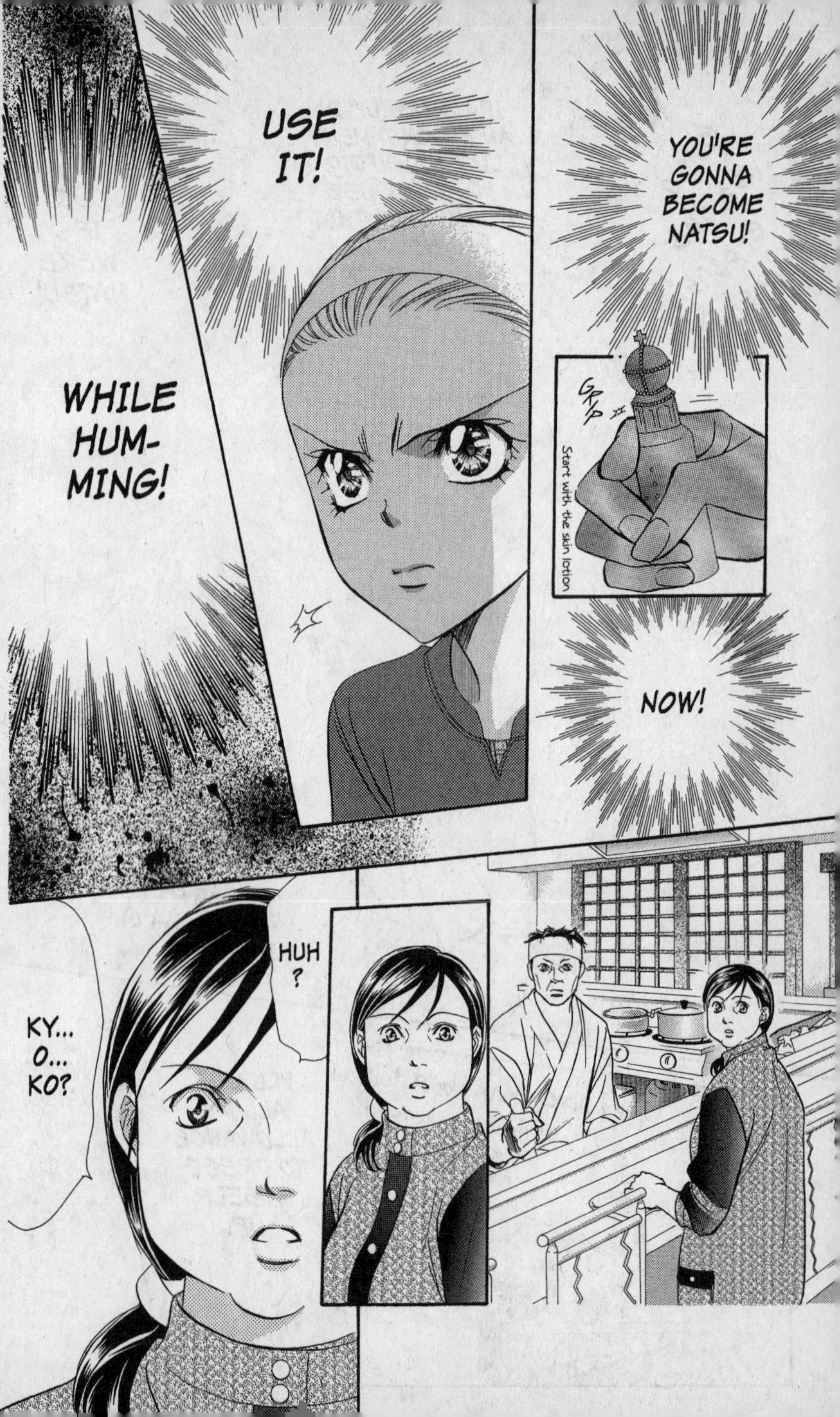
YOU'RE GONNA BECOME NATSU!
GRIP
Start with the skin lotion
NOW!
USE IT!
WHILE HUM-MING!
HUH?
KY... O... KO?

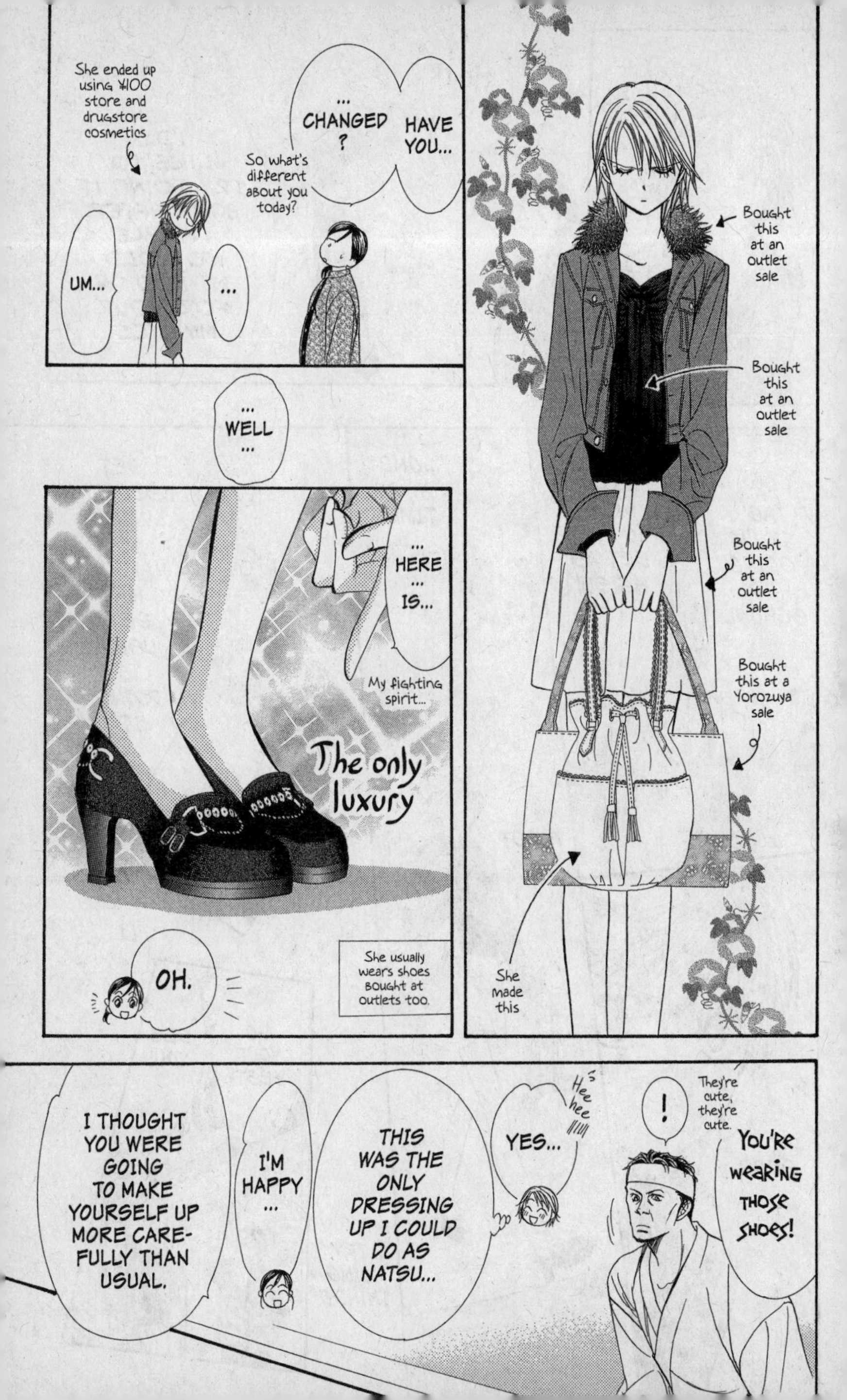
Bought this at an outlet sale
Bought this at an outlet sale
Bought this at an outlet sale
Bought this at a Yorozuya sale
She made this
HAVE YOU...
...CHANGED?
So what's different about you today?
She ended up using ¥100 store and drugstore cosmetics
...
UM...
...WELL...
...HERE...IS...
My fighting spirit...
The only luxury
She usually wears shoes bought at outlets too.
OH.
YOU'RE WEARING THOSE SHOES!
They're cute, they're cute.
!
Hee hee
YES...
THIS WAS THE ONLY DRESSING UP I COULD DO AS NATSU...
I'M HAPPY...
I THOUGHT YOU WERE GOING TO MAKE YOURSELF UP MORE CARE-FULLY THAN USUAL.

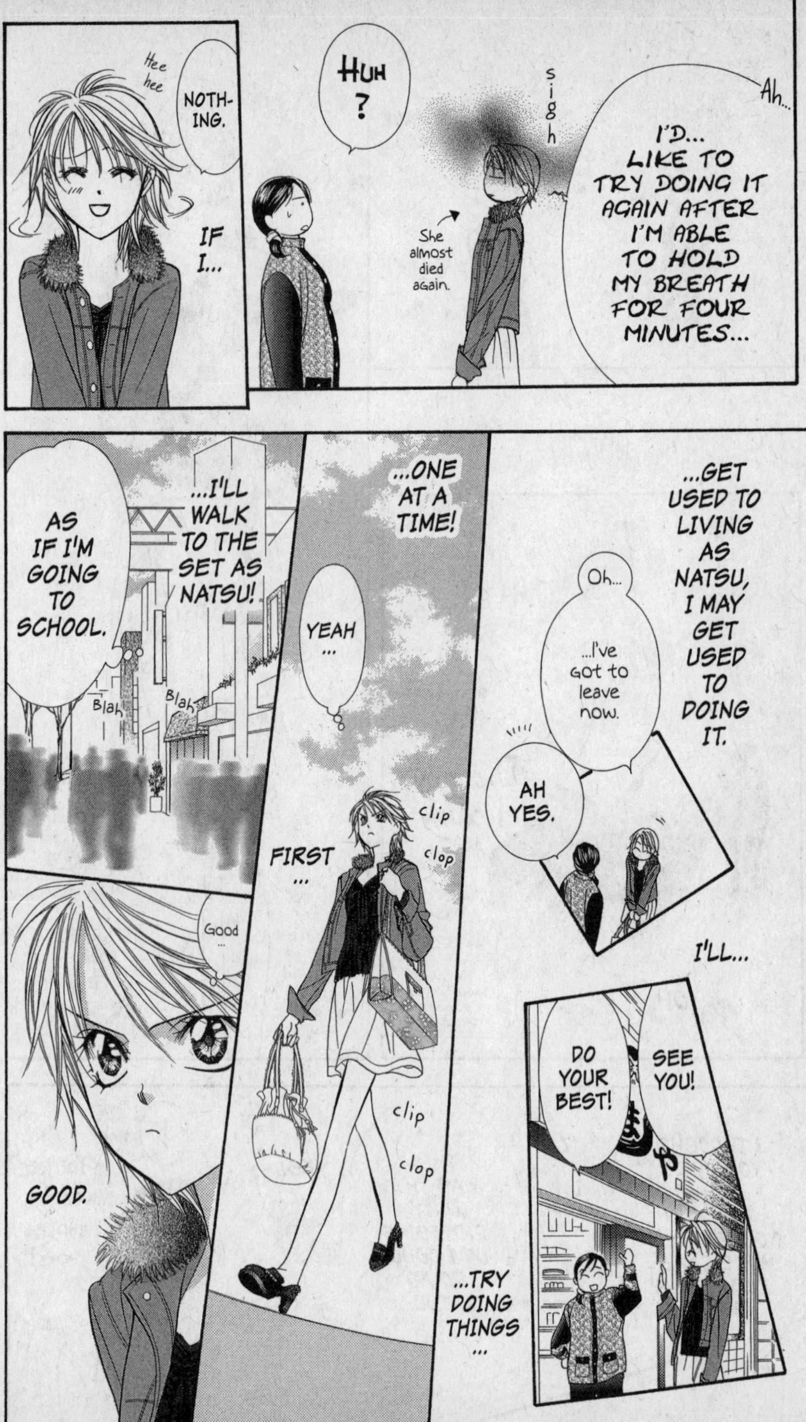

Ah...
I'D... LIKE TO TRY DOING IT AGAIN AFTER I'M ABLE TO HOLD MY BREATH FOR FOUR MINUTES...
sigh
She almost died again.
HUH ?
Hee hee
NOTH-ING.
IF I...
...GET USED TO LIVING AS NATSU, I MAY GET USED TO DOING IT.
Oh...
...I've got to leave now.
AH YES.
I'LL...
SEE YOU!
DO YOUR BEST!
...TRY DOING THINGS ...
...ONE AT A TIME!
YEAH ...
FIRST ...
clip
clop
clip
clop
...I'LL WALK TO THE SET AS NATSU!
AS IF I'M GOING TO SCHOOL.
Blah
Blah
Good ...
GOOD.

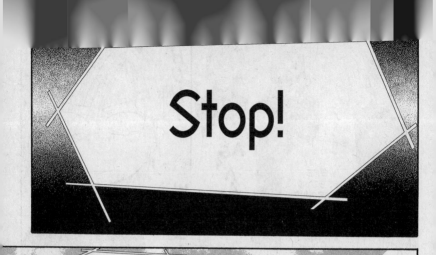

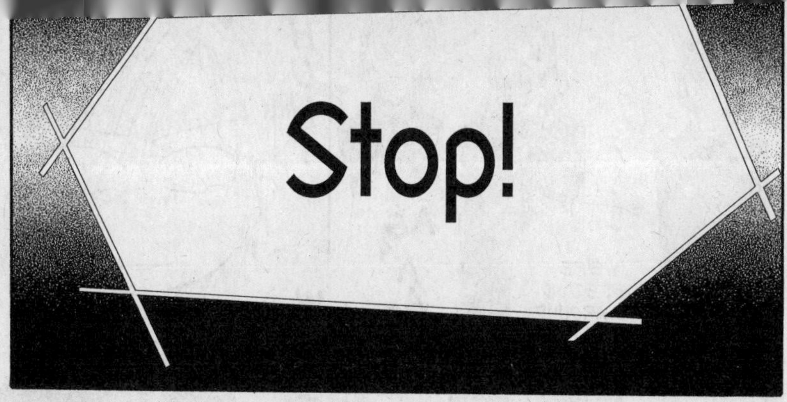
Stop!

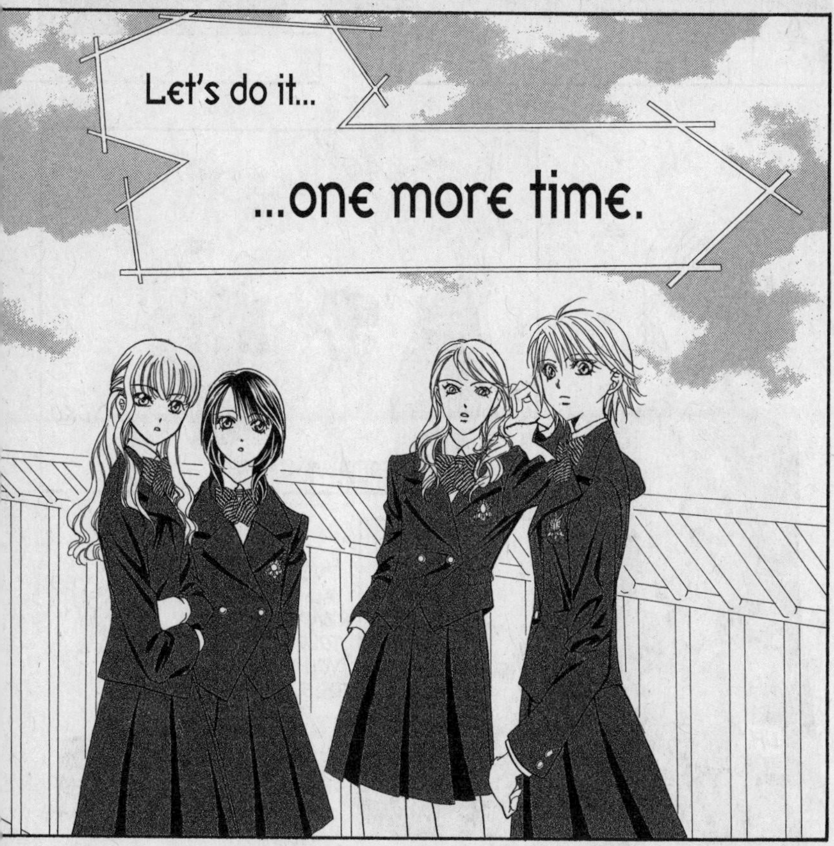
Let's do it...
...one more time.

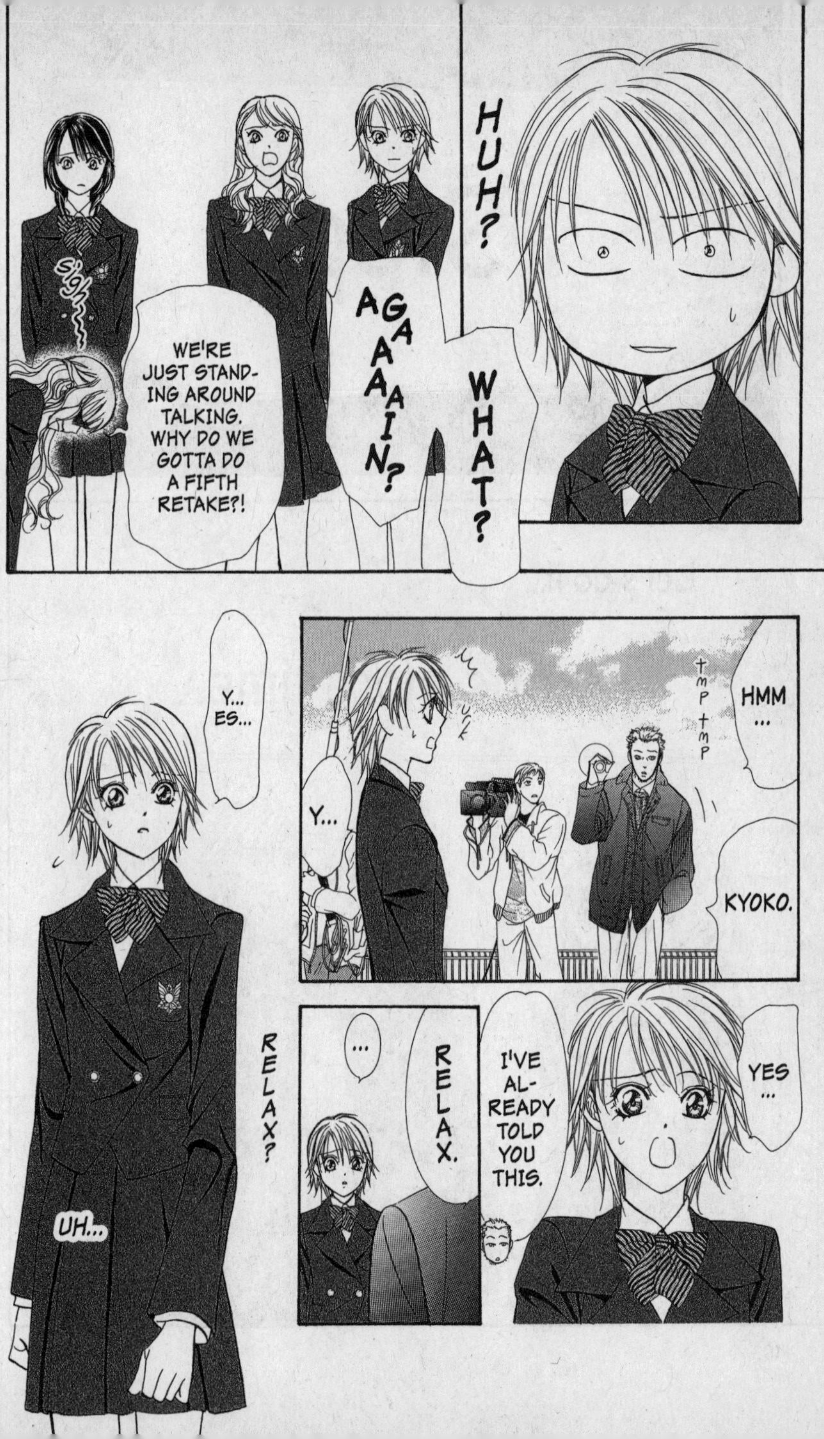
HUH?
WHAT?
AGAAAAIN?
WE'RE JUST STANDING AROUND TALKING. WHY DO WE GOTTA DO A FIFTH RETAKE?!
sigh
HMM...
KYOKO.
tmp tmp
uk
Y...
YES...
I'VE ALREADY TOLD YOU THIS.
RELAX.
...
Y... ES...
RELAX?
UH...

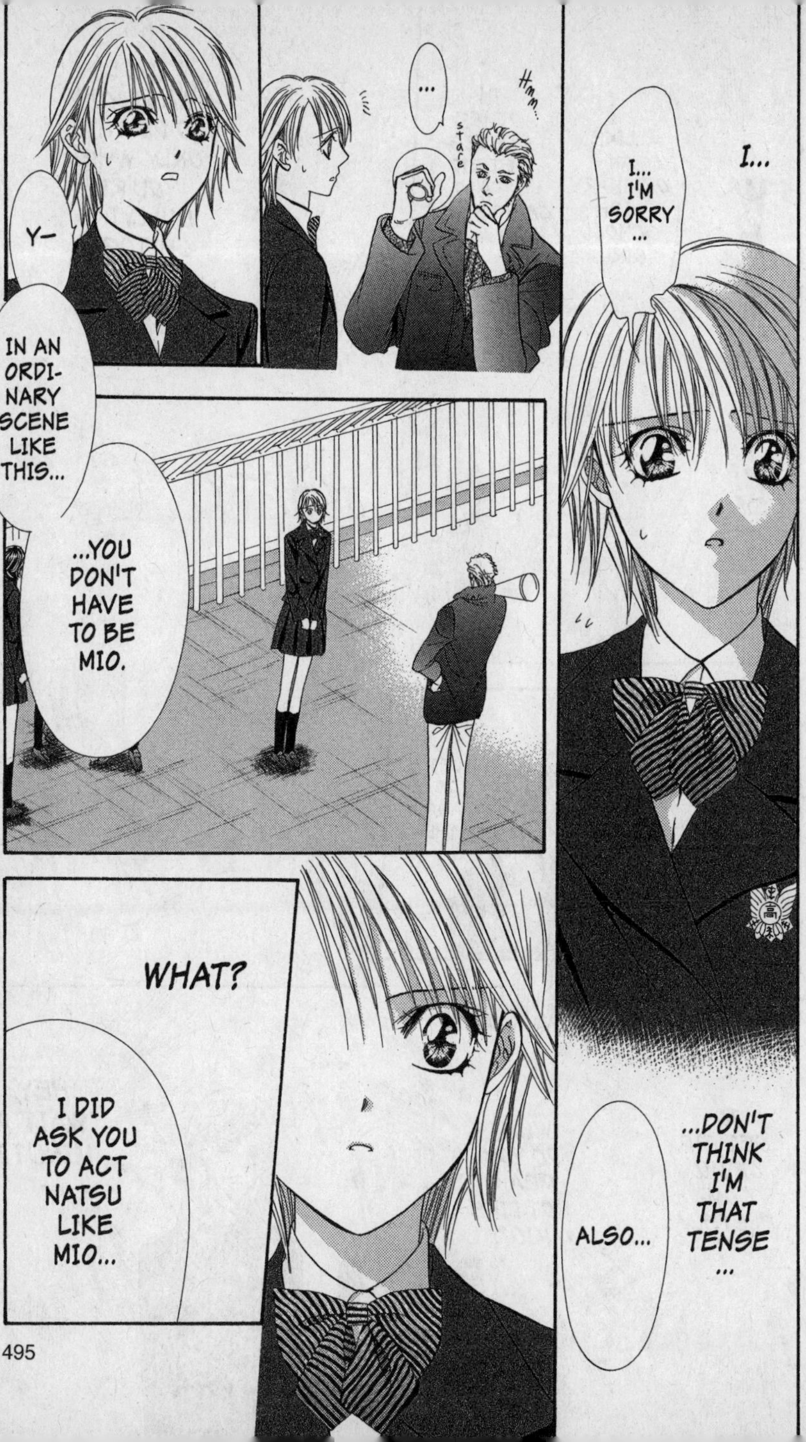

I...
I... I'M SORRY...
...DON'T THINK I'M THAT TENSE...
ALSO...
...
Hmm...
stare
Y—
IN AN ORDINARY SCENE LIKE THIS...
...YOU DON'T HAVE TO BE MIO.
WHAT?
I DID ASK YOU TO ACT NATSU LIKE MIO...

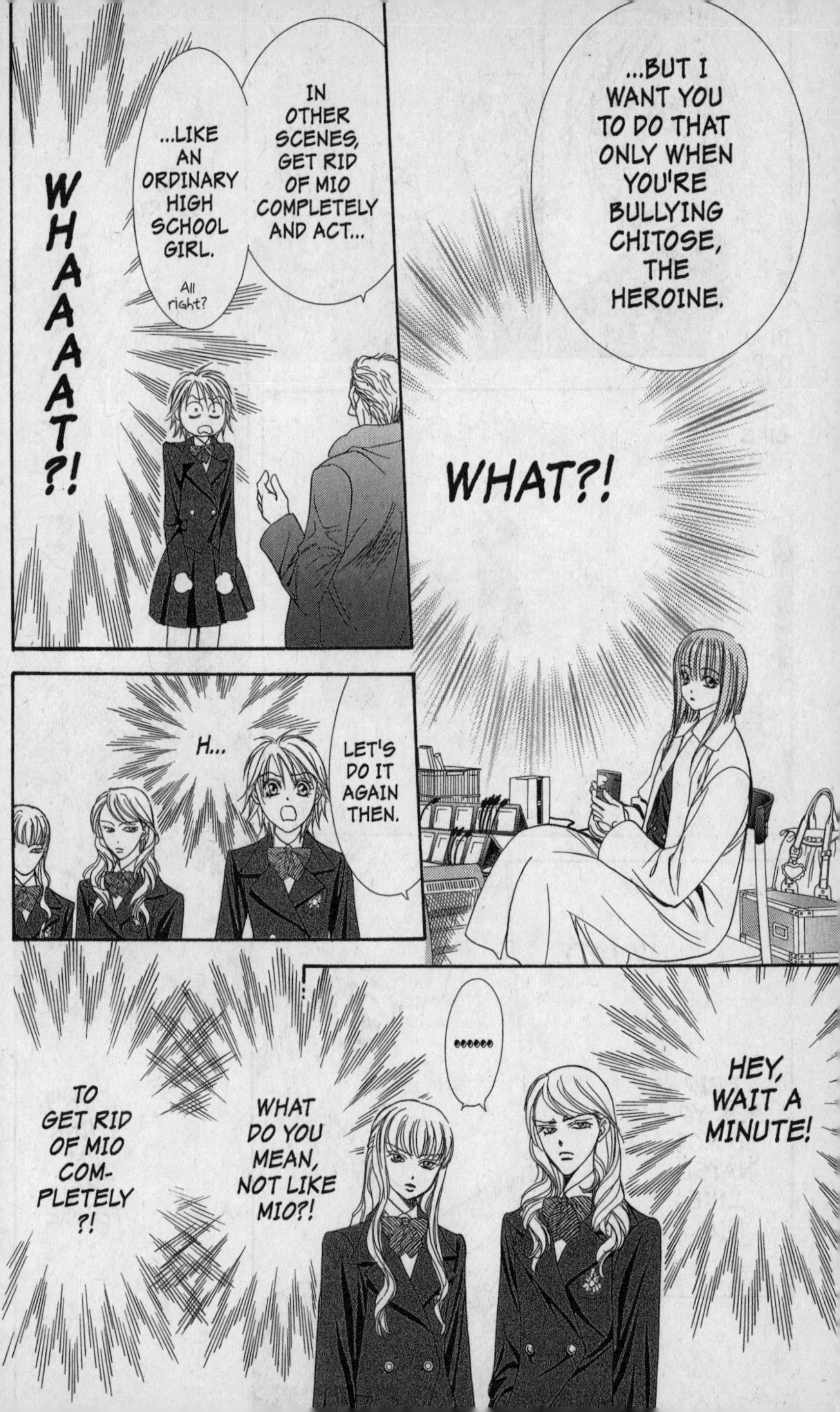
...BUT I WANT YOU TO DO THAT ONLY WHEN YOU'RE BULLYING CHITOSE, THE HEROINE.
WHAT?!
IN OTHER SCENES, GET RID OF MIO COMPLETELY AND ACT...
...LIKE AN ORDINARY HIGH SCHOOL GIRL.
All right?
WHAAAAT?!
LET'S DO IT AGAIN THEN.
H...
HEY, WAIT A MINUTE!
......
WHAT DO YOU MEAN, NOT LIKE MIO?!
TO GET RID OF MIO COM-PLETELY?!

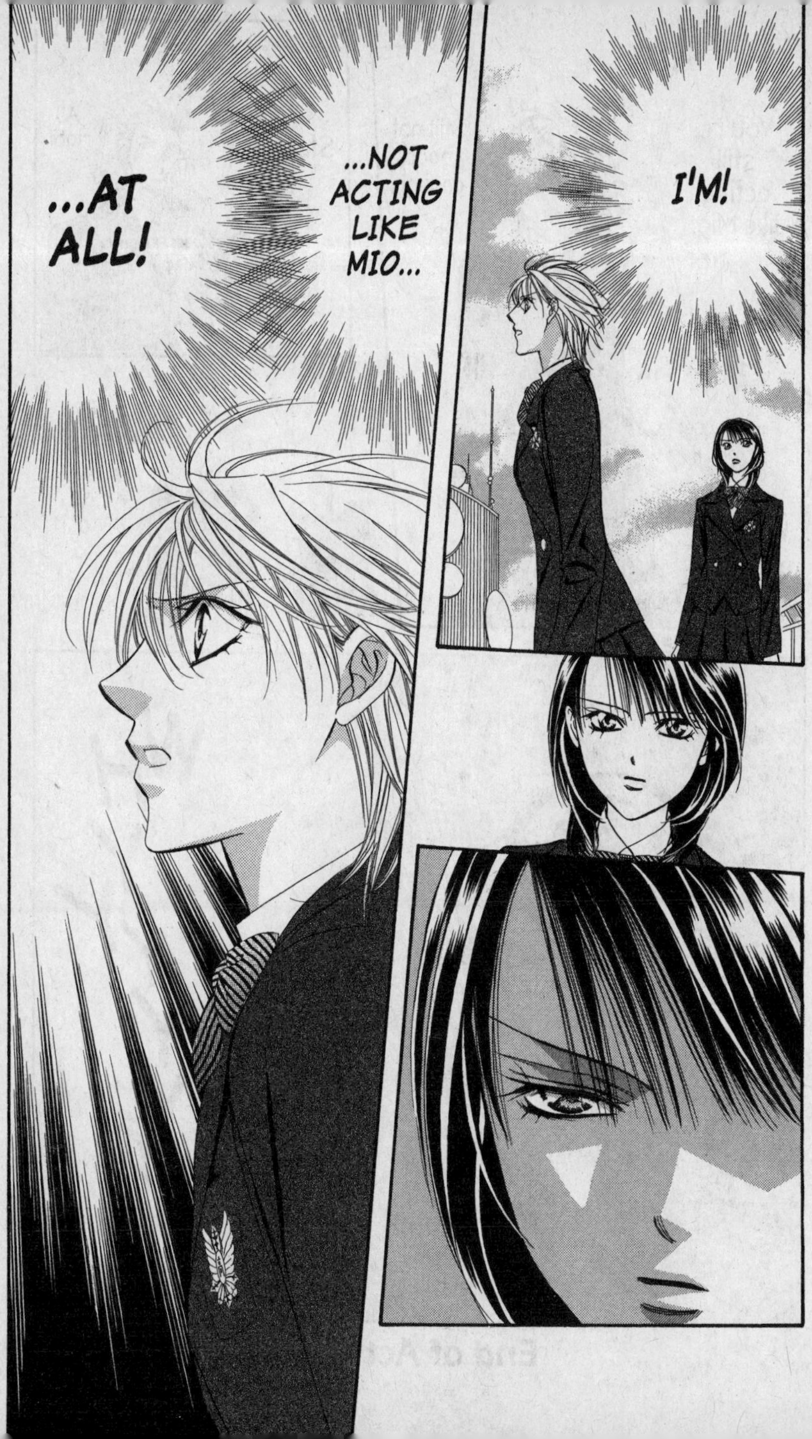
I'M!
...NOT ACTING LIKE MIO...
...AT ALL!

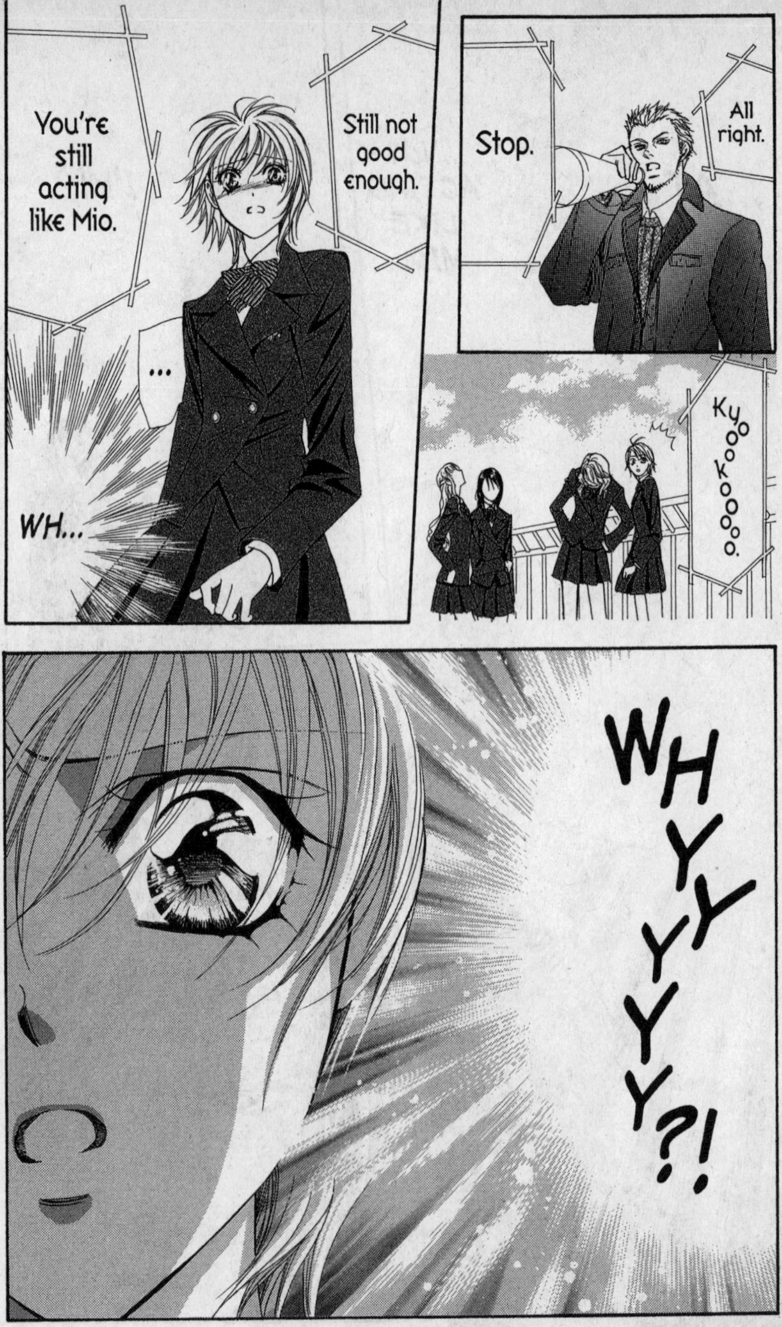
All right.
Stop.
Kyooookoooo.
Still not good enough.
You're still acting like Mio.
...
WH...
WHYYYYY?!

End of Act 124

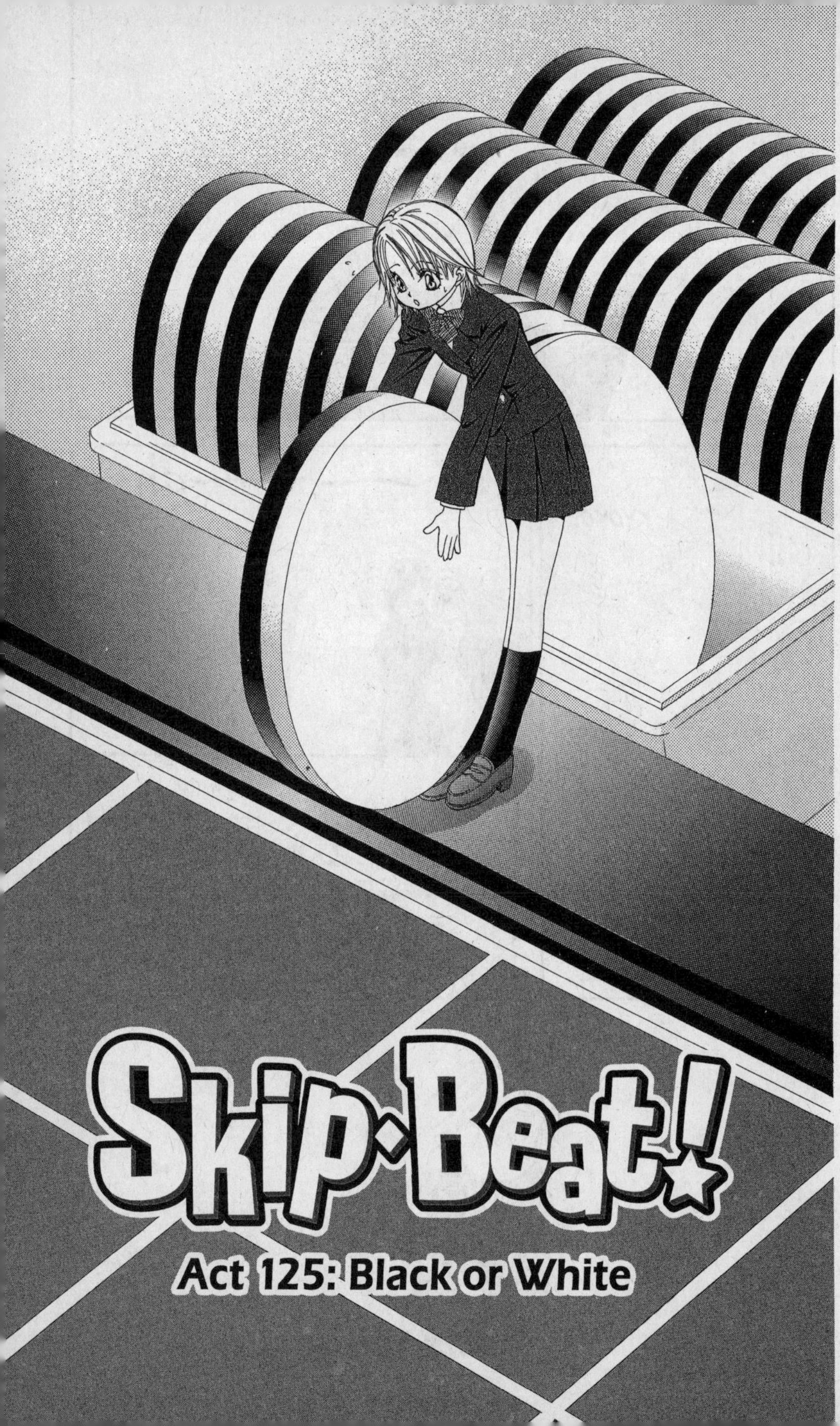

Skip·Beat!
Act 125: Black or White

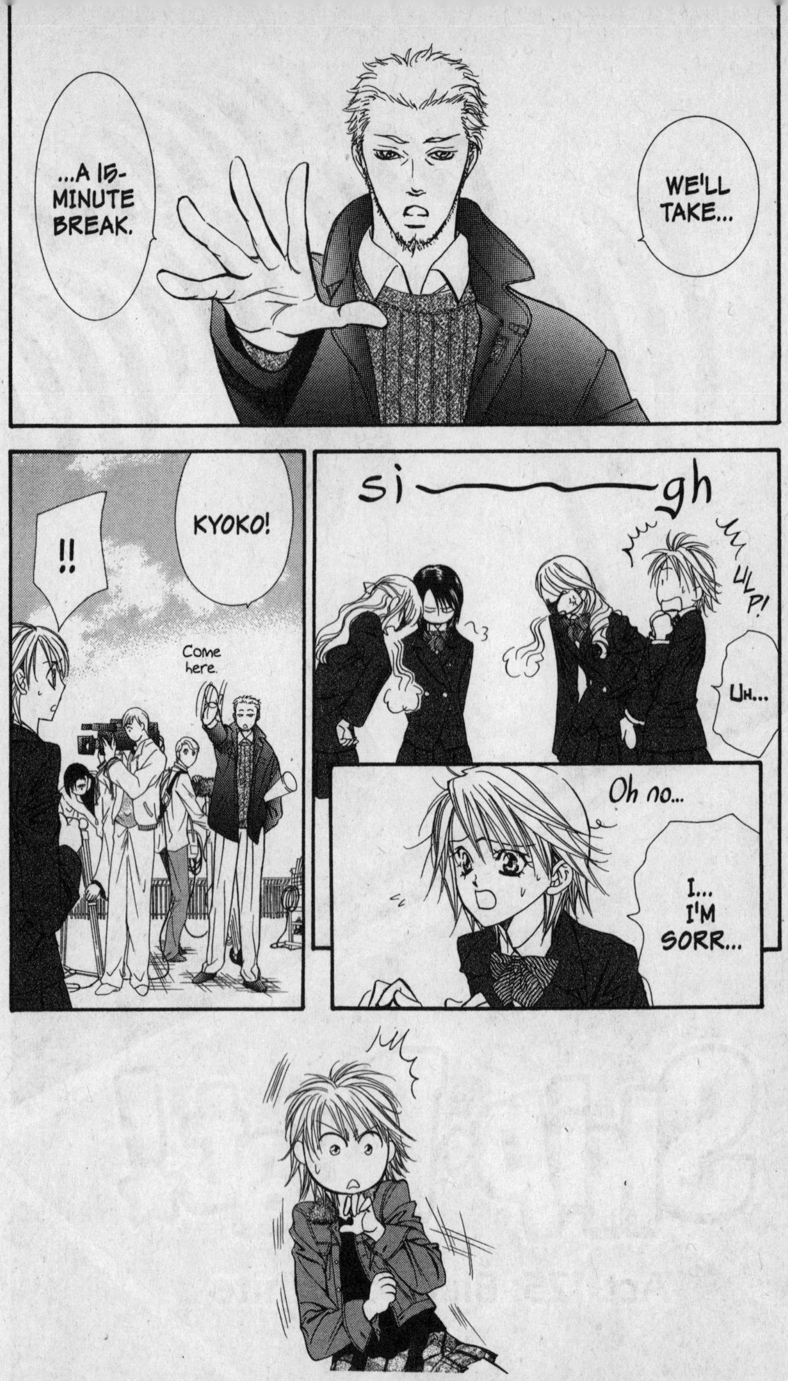
WE'LL TAKE...
...A 15-MINUTE BREAK.
si——————gh
ULP!
Uh...
Oh no...
I... I'M SORR...
KYOKO!
Come here.
!!

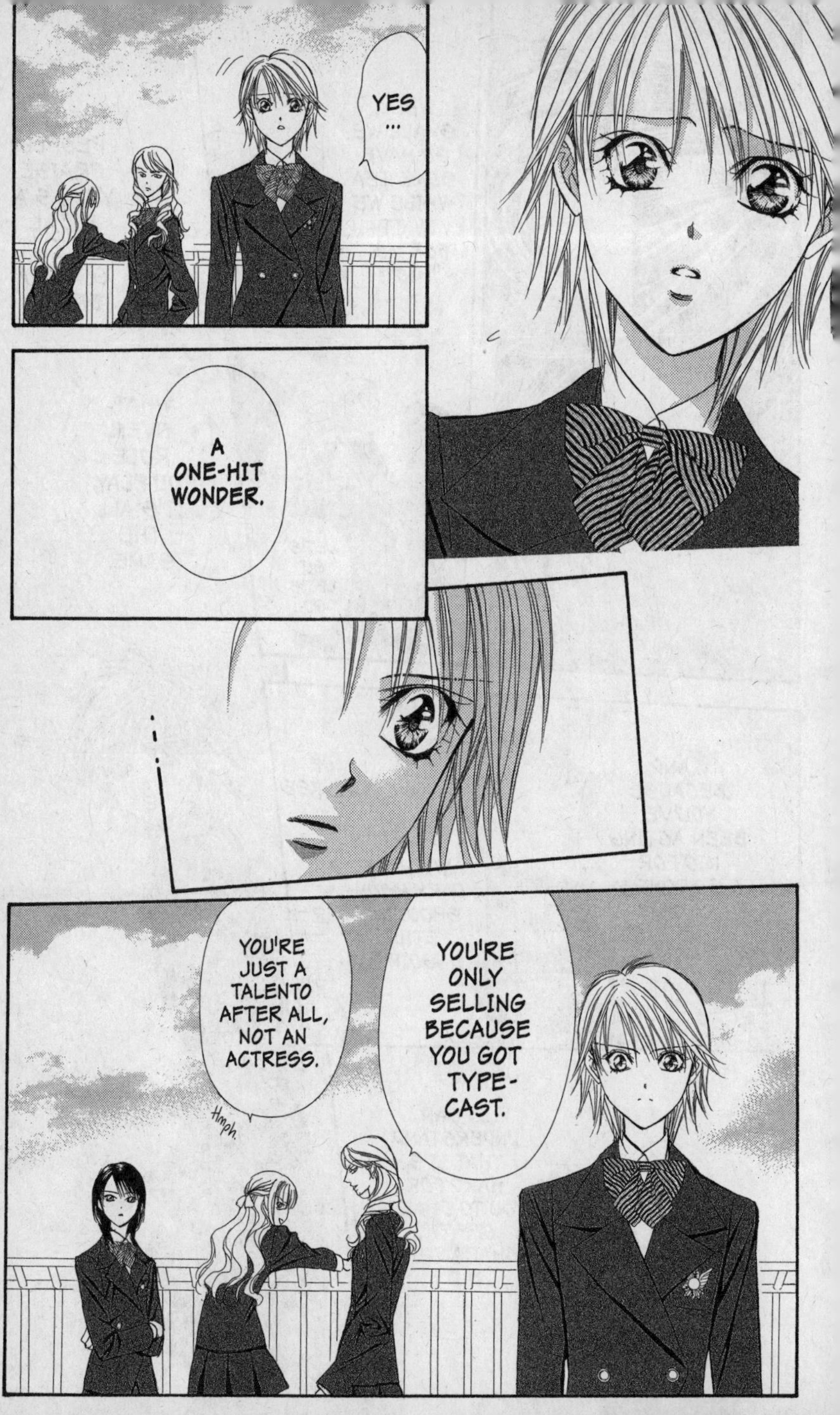
YES ...
A ONE-HIT WONDER.
...
YOU'RE ONLY SELLING BECAUSE YOU GOT TYPE-CAST.
YOU'RE JUST A TALENTO AFTER ALL, NOT AN ACTRESS.
Hmph.

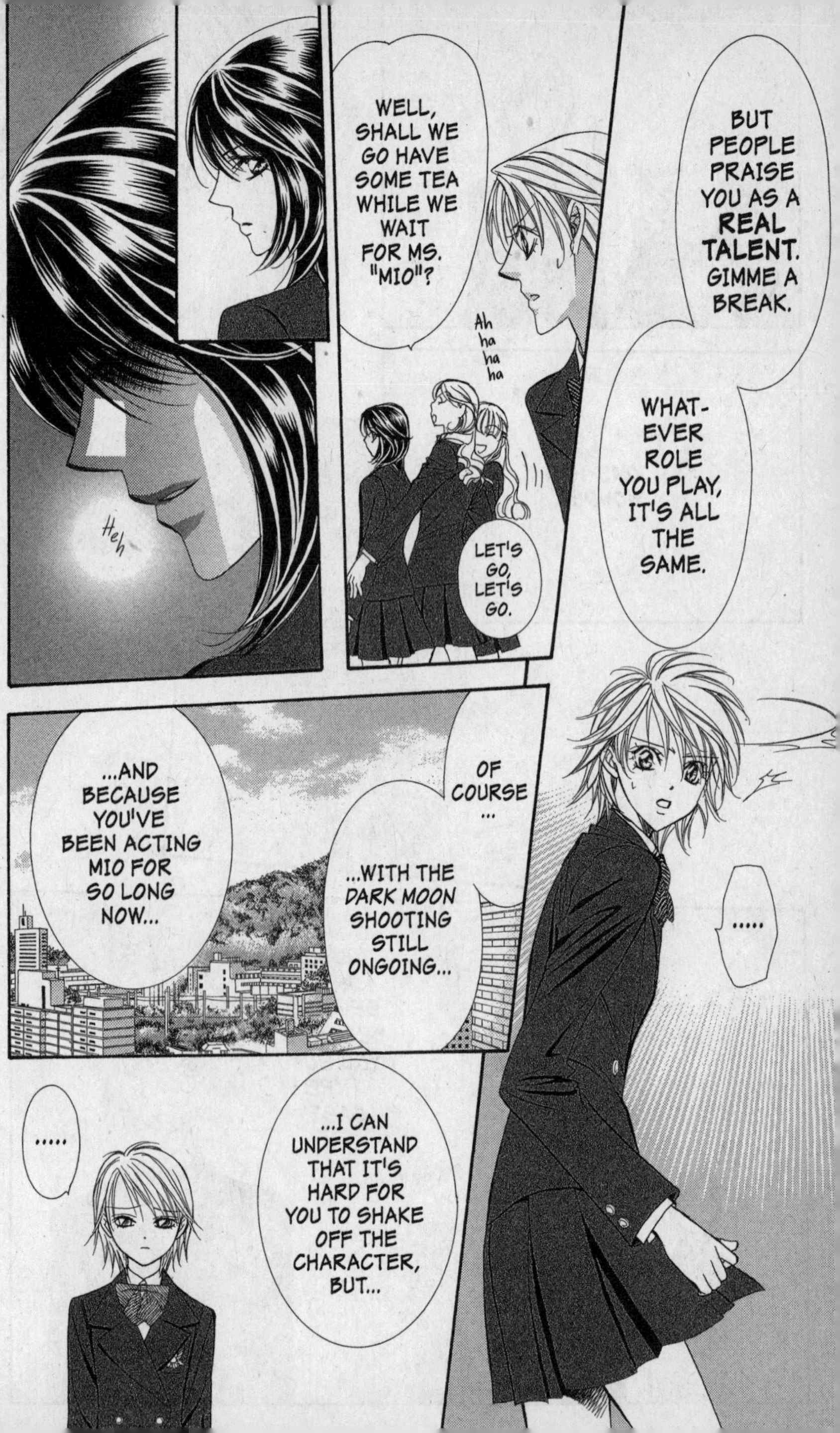
BUT PEOPLE PRAISE YOU AS A REAL TALENT. GIMME A BREAK.
WHATEVER ROLE YOU PLAY, IT'S ALL THE SAME.
WELL, SHALL WE GO HAVE SOME TEA WHILE WE WAIT FOR MS. "MIO"?
Ah ha ha ha
LET'S GO, LET'S GO.
Heh
.....
OF COURSE...
...WITH THE DARK MOON SHOOTING STILL ONGOING...
...AND BECAUSE YOU'VE BEEN ACTING MIO FOR SO LONG NOW...
...I CAN UNDERSTAND THAT IT'S HARD FOR YOU TO SHAKE OFF THE CHARACTER, BUT...
.....

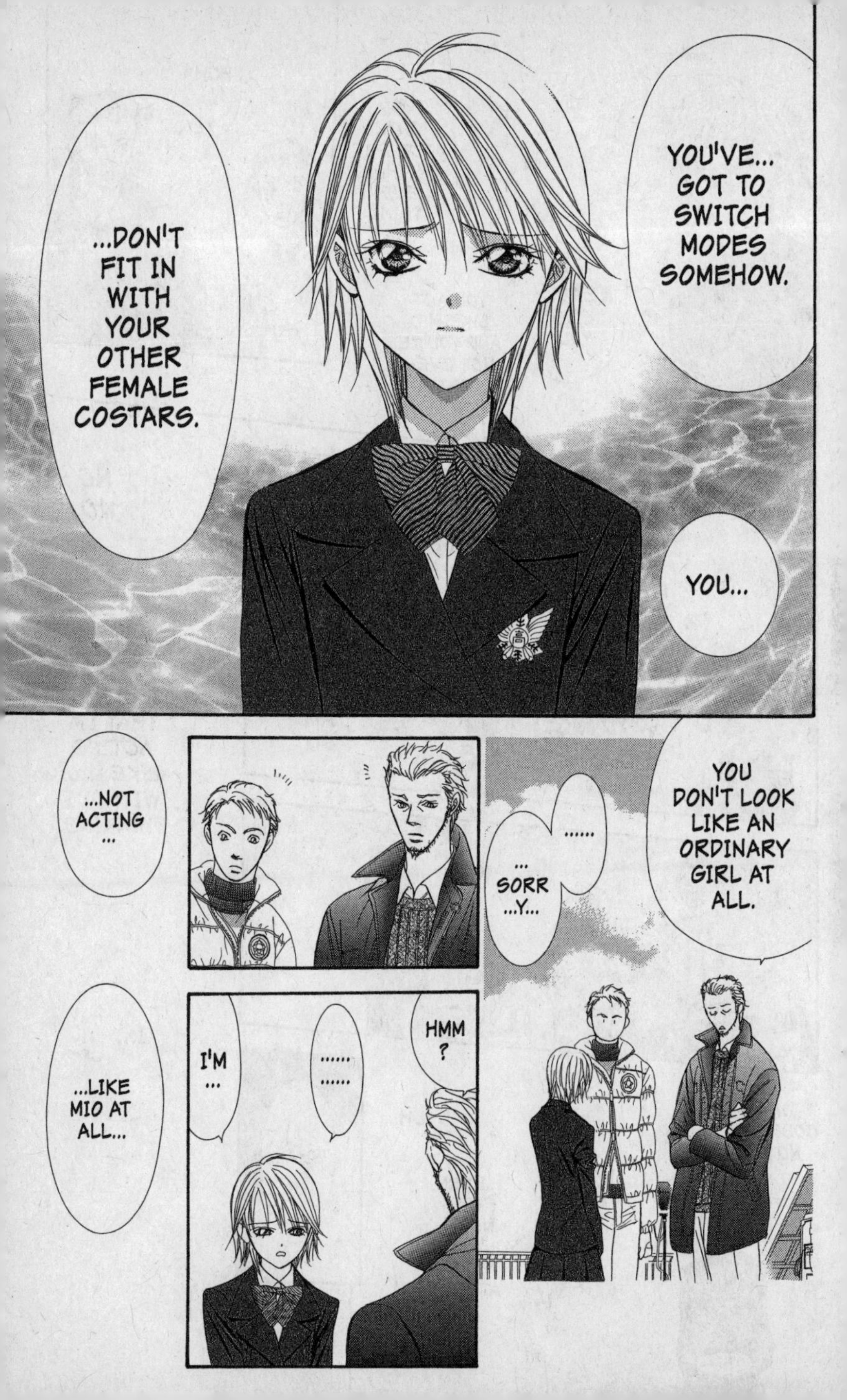
YOU'VE... GOT TO SWITCH MODES SOMEHOW.
YOU...
...DON'T FIT IN WITH YOUR OTHER FEMALE COSTARS.
YOU DON'T LOOK LIKE AN ORDINARY GIRL AT ALL.
......
... SORR ...Y...
HMM ?
....
I'M ...
...NOT ACTING ...
...LIKE MIO AT ALL...

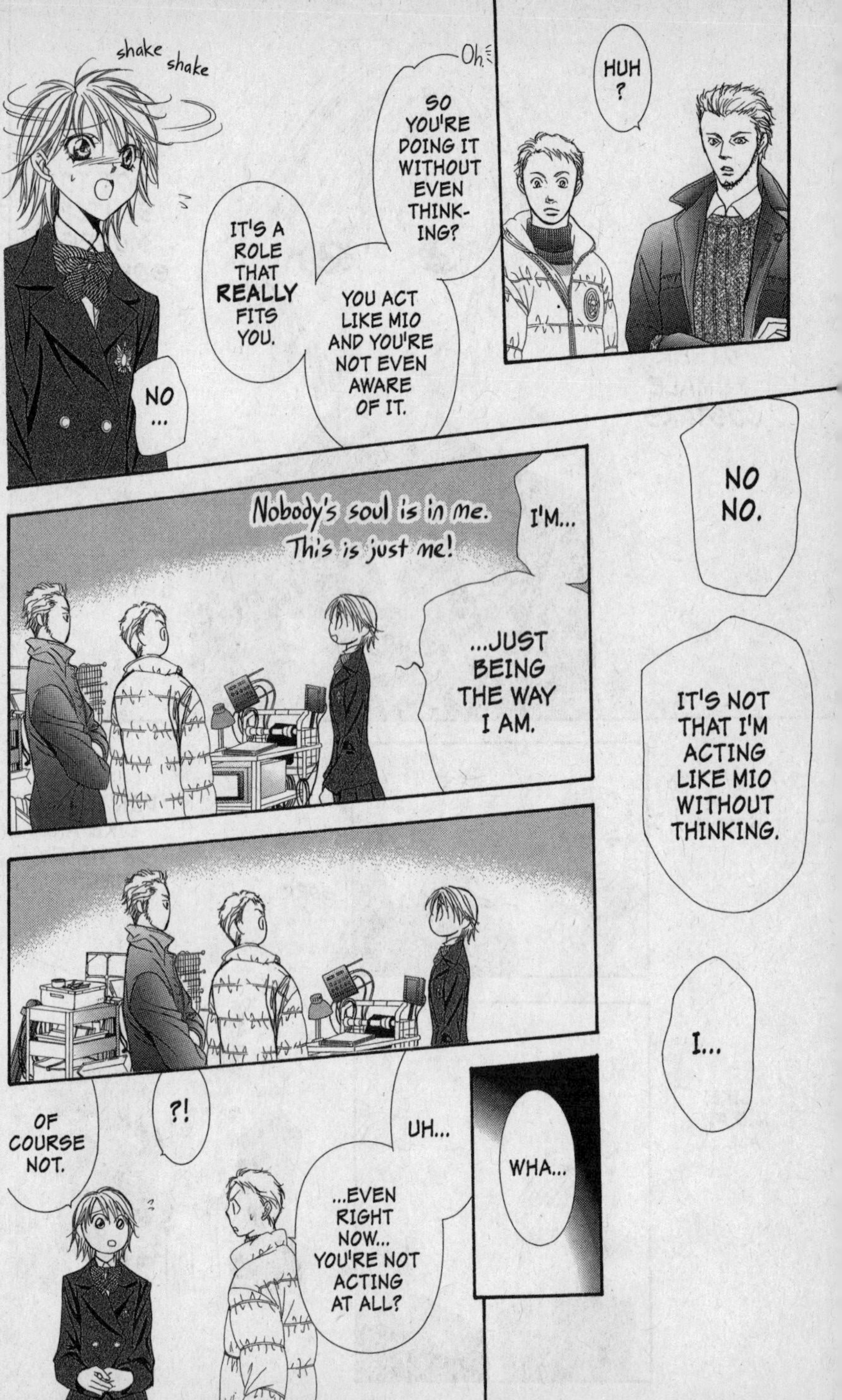
HUH?
Oh.
SO YOU'RE DOING IT WITHOUT EVEN THINKING?
YOU ACT LIKE MIO AND YOU'RE NOT EVEN AWARE OF IT.
IT'S A ROLE THAT **REALLY** FITS YOU.
shake shake
NO ...
NO NO.
IT'S NOT THAT I'M ACTING LIKE MIO WITHOUT THINKING.
I'M...
...JUST BEING THE WAY I AM.
Nobody's soul is in me. This is just me!
I...
WHA...
UH...
...EVEN RIGHT NOW... YOU'RE NOT ACTING AT ALL?
?!
OF COURSE NOT.

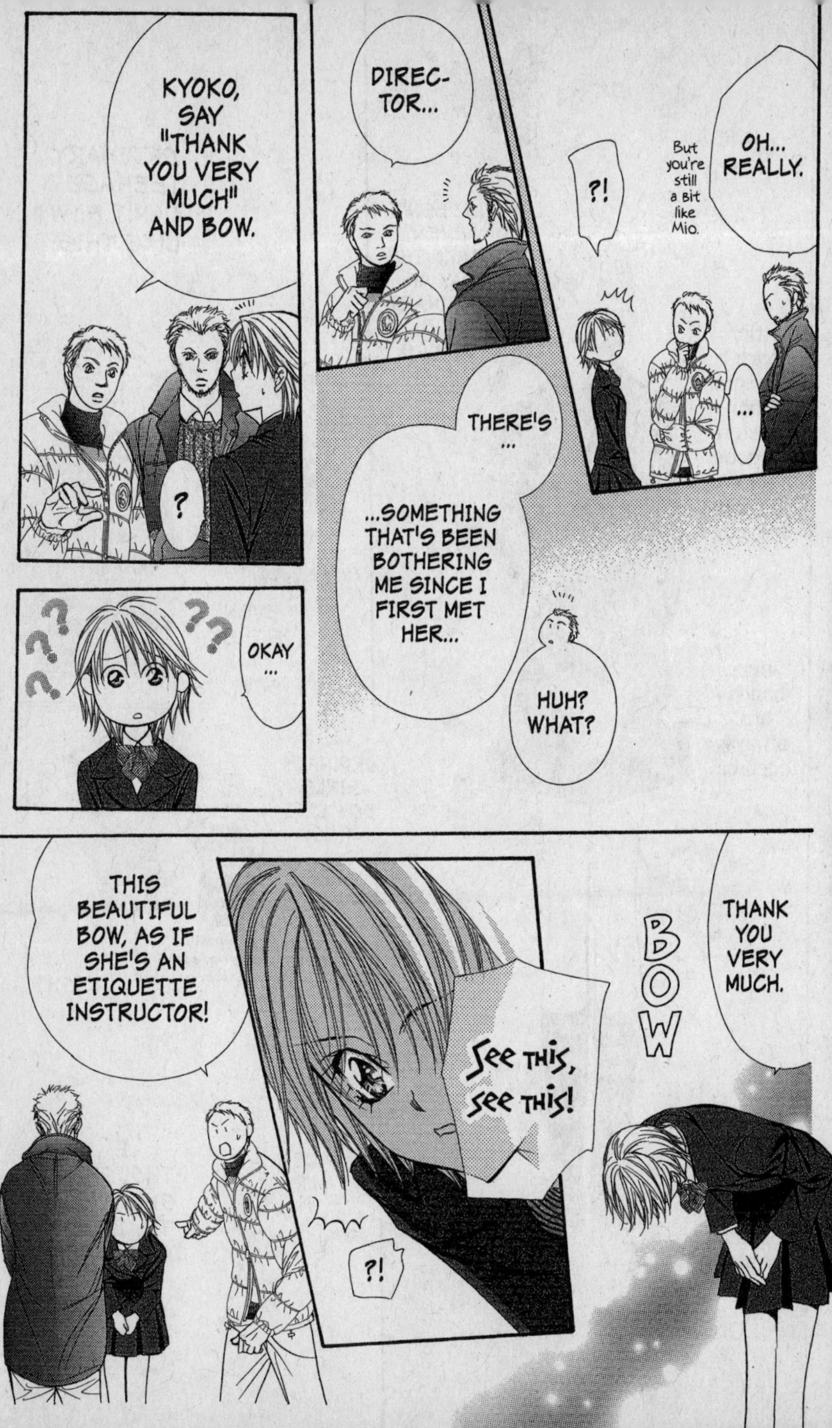
OH... REALLY.
But you're still a bit like Mio.
?!
...
DIREC-TOR...
KYOKO, SAY "THANK YOU VERY MUCH" AND BOW.
?
THERE'S ...
...SOMETHING THAT'S BEEN BOTHERING ME SINCE I FIRST MET HER...
HUH? WHAT?
OKAY ...
THANK YOU VERY MUCH.
BOW
See this, see this!
?!
THIS BEAUTIFUL BOW, AS IF SHE'S AN ETIQUETTE INSTRUCTOR!

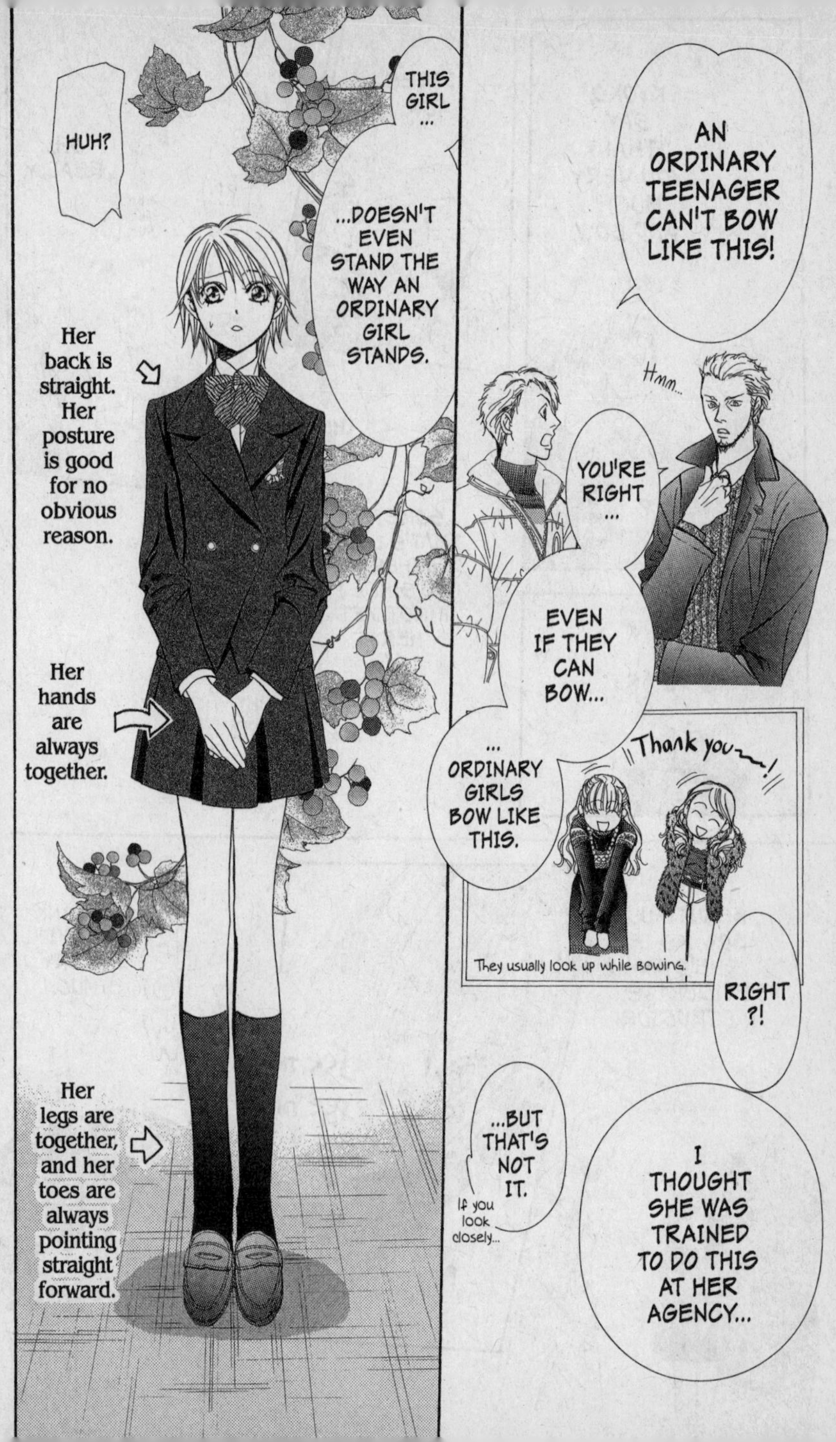
AN ORDINARY TEENAGER CAN'T BOW LIKE THIS!
Hmm...
YOU'RE RIGHT ...
EVEN IF THEY CAN BOW...
... ORDINARY GIRLS BOW LIKE THIS.
Thank you~~!
They usually look up while bowing.
RIGHT ?!
I THOUGHT SHE WAS TRAINED TO DO THIS AT HER AGENCY...
...BUT THAT'S NOT IT.
If you look closely...
THIS GIRL ...
...DOESN'T EVEN STAND THE WAY AN ORDINARY GIRL STANDS.
HUH?
Her back is straight. Her posture is good for no obvious reason.
Her hands are always together.
Her legs are together, and her toes are always pointing straight forward.

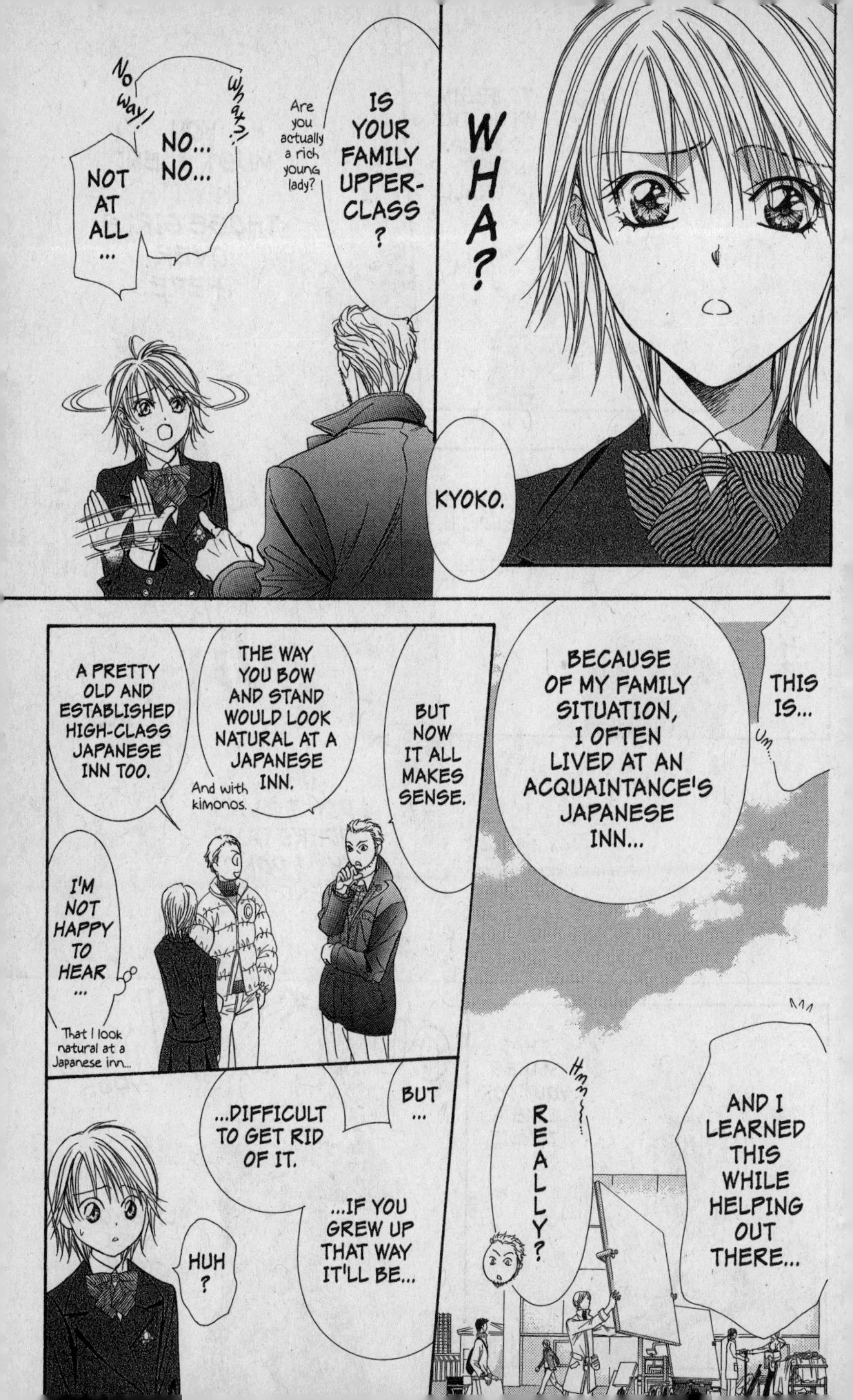
WHA?
KYOKO.
IS YOUR FAMILY UPPER-CLASS?
Are you actually a rich young lady?
What?!
NO... NO...
No way!
NOT AT ALL...
THIS IS...
Um...
BECAUSE OF MY FAMILY SITUATION, I OFTEN LIVED AT AN ACQUAINTANCE'S JAPANESE INN...
AND I LEARNED THIS WHILE HELPING OUT THERE...
REALLY?
Hmm~...
BUT NOW IT ALL MAKES SENSE.
THE WAY YOU BOW AND STAND WOULD LOOK NATURAL AT A JAPANESE INN.
And with kimonos.
A PRETTY OLD AND ESTABLISHED HIGH-CLASS JAPANESE INN TOO.
I'M NOT HAPPY TO HEAR...
That I look natural at a Japanese inn...
BUT...
...DIFFICULT TO GET RID OF IT.
...IF YOU GREW UP THAT WAY IT'LL BE...
HUH?

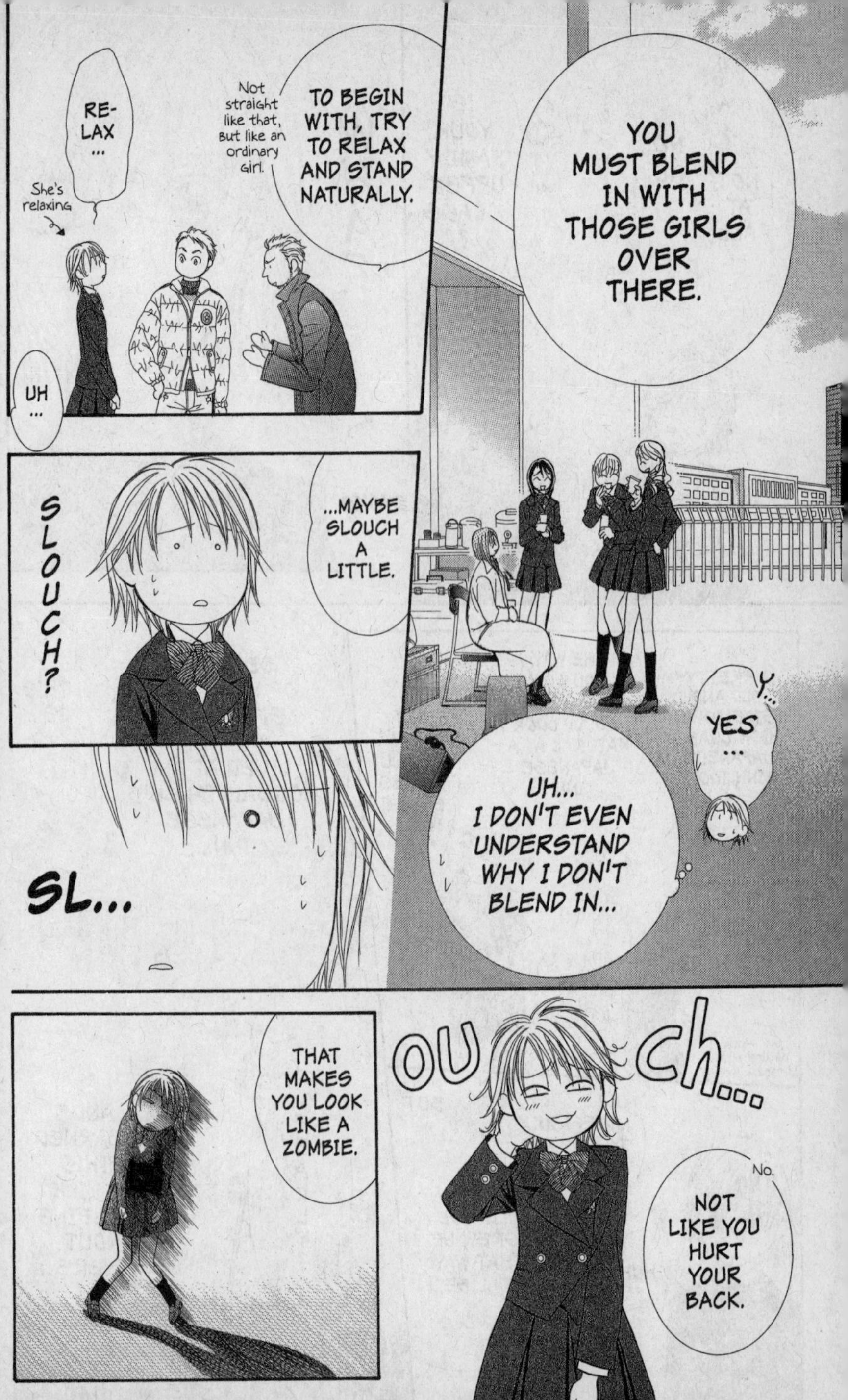
YOU MUST BLEND IN WITH THOSE GIRLS OVER THERE.
Y... YES...
UH... I DON'T EVEN UNDERSTAND WHY I DON'T BLEND IN...
TO BEGIN WITH, TRY TO RELAX AND STAND NATURALLY.
Not straight like that, but like an ordinary girl.
RE-LAX...
She's relaxing
UH...
...MAYBE SLOUCH A LITTLE.
SLOUCH?
SL...
ouch...
No.
NOT LIKE YOU HURT YOUR BACK.
THAT MAKES YOU LOOK LIKE A ZOMBIE.

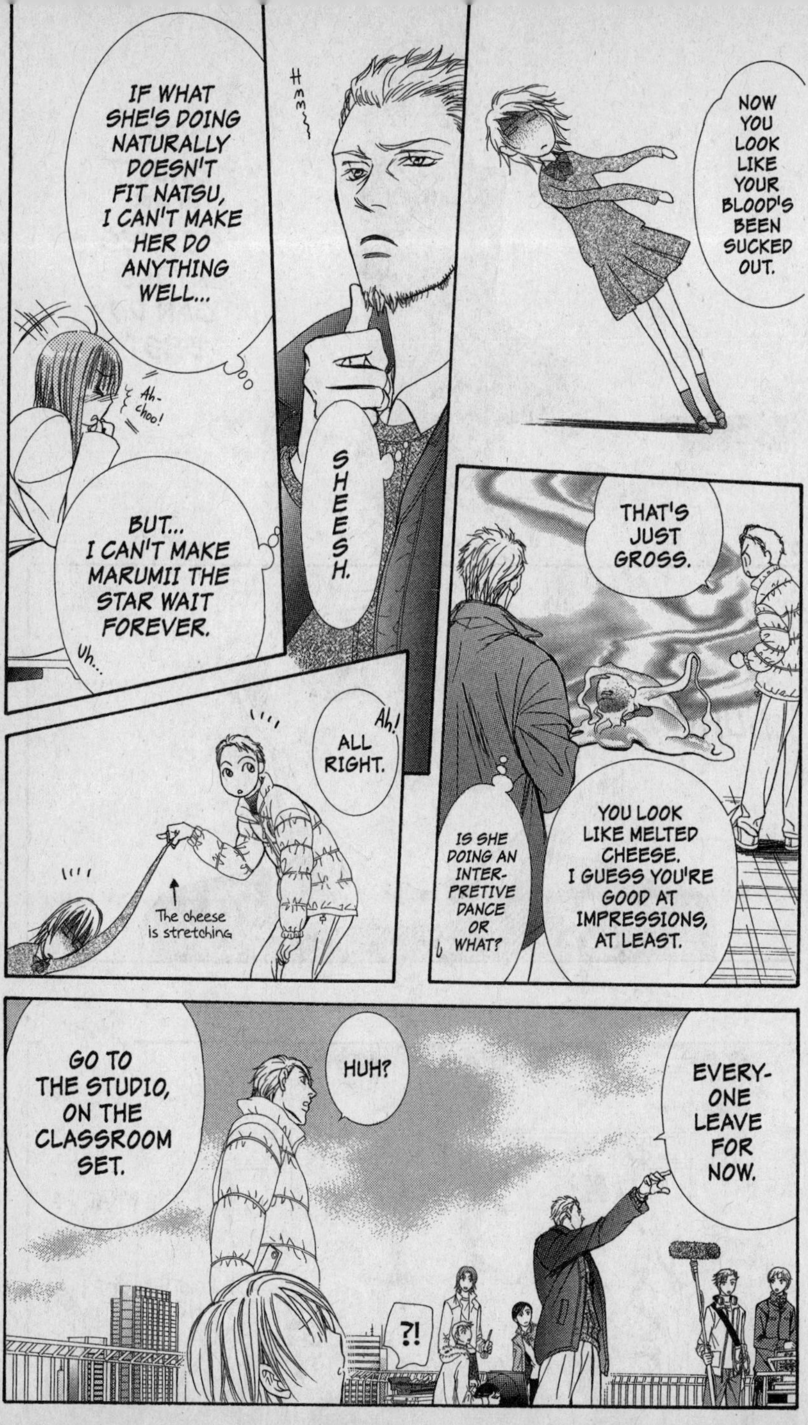
NOW YOU LOOK LIKE YOUR BLOOD'S BEEN SUCKED OUT.
Hmm~
SHEESH.
IF WHAT SHE'S DOING NATURALLY DOESN'T FIT NATSU, I CAN'T MAKE HER DO ANYTHING WELL...
Ah-choo!
BUT... I CAN'T MAKE MARUMII THE STAR WAIT FOREVER.
Uh...
THAT'S JUST GROSS.
YOU LOOK LIKE MELTED CHEESE. I GUESS YOU'RE GOOD AT IMPRESSIONS, AT LEAST.
IS SHE DOING AN INTER-PRETIVE DANCE OR WHAT?
Ah! ALL RIGHT.
The cheese is stretching
EVERY-ONE LEAVE FOR NOW.
HUH?
GO TO THE STUDIO, ON THE CLASSROOM SET.
?!

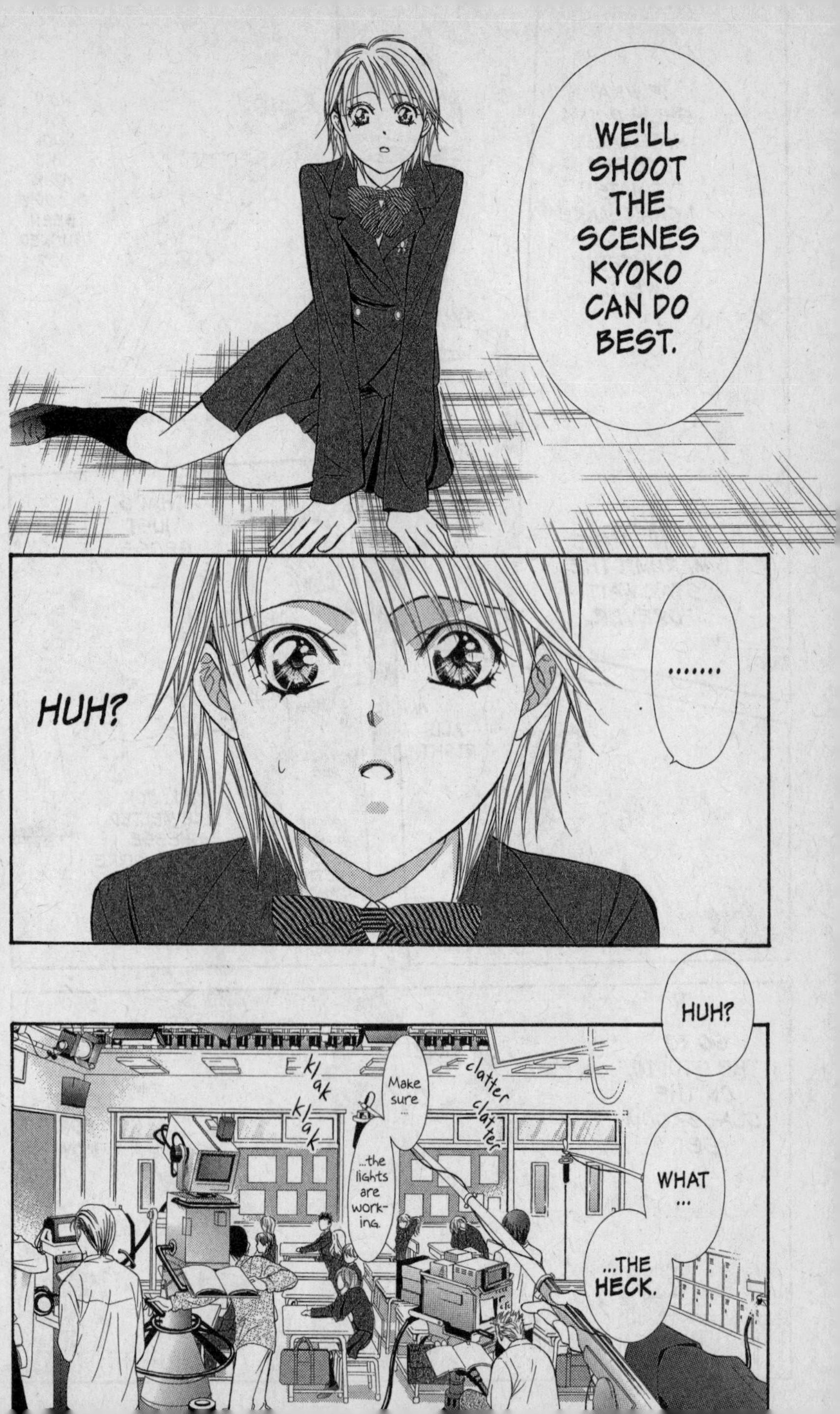
WE'LL SHOOT THE SCENES KYOKO CAN DO BEST.
....
HUH?
HUH?
WHAT ...
...THE HECK.
clatter clatter
Make sure ...
...the lights are working.
klak klak

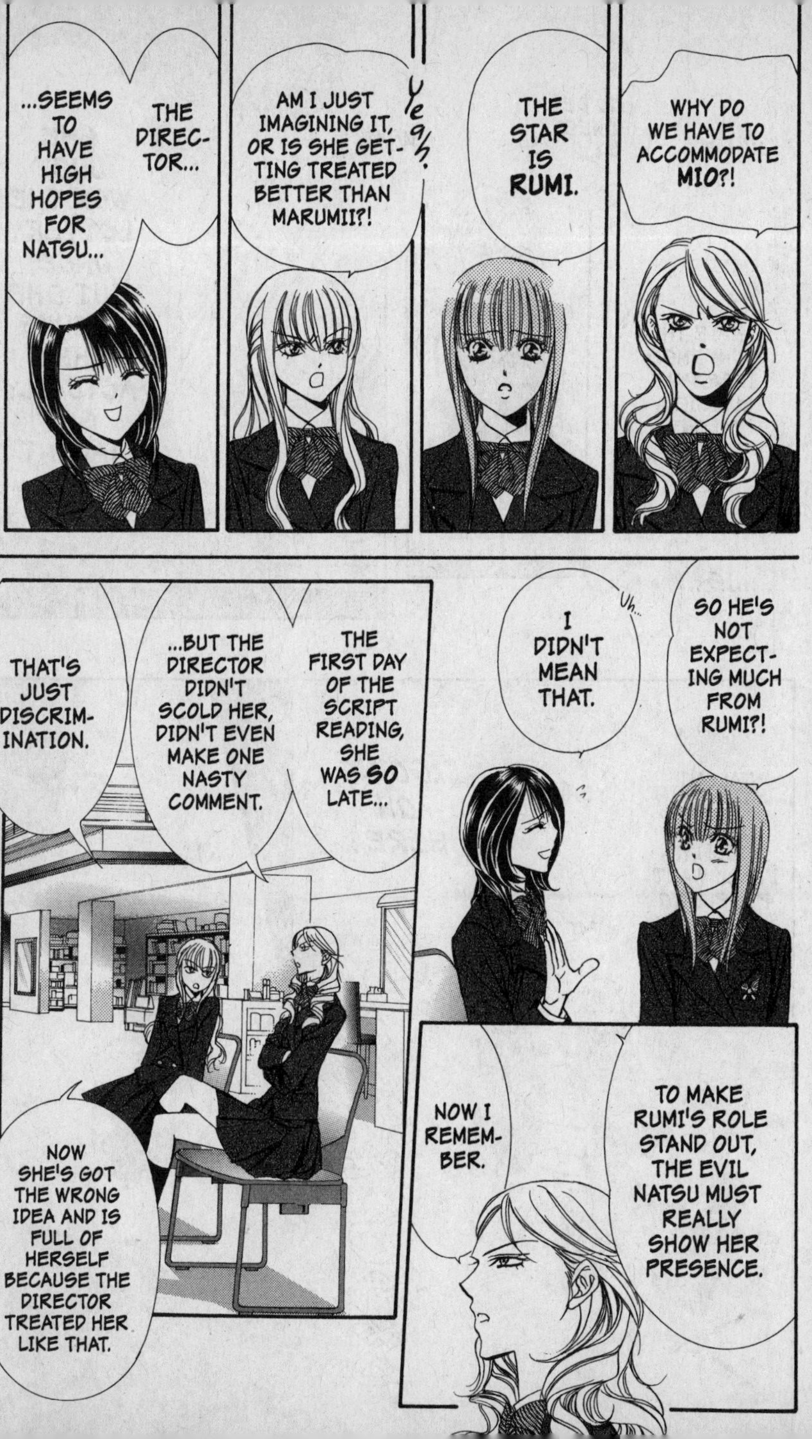
WHY DO WE HAVE TO ACCOMMODATE MIO?!
THE STAR IS RUMI.
Yeah.
AM I JUST IMAGINING IT, OR IS SHE GETTING TREATED BETTER THAN MARUMII?!
THE DIRECTOR...
...SEEMS TO HAVE HIGH HOPES FOR NATSU...
SO HE'S NOT EXPECTING MUCH FROM RUMI?!
Uh...
I DIDN'T MEAN THAT.
TO MAKE RUMI'S ROLE STAND OUT, THE EVIL NATSU MUST REALLY SHOW HER PRESENCE.
NOW I REMEMBER.
THE FIRST DAY OF THE SCRIPT READING, SHE WAS SO LATE...
...BUT THE DIRECTOR DIDN'T SCOLD HER, DIDN'T EVEN MAKE ONE NASTY COMMENT.
THAT'S JUST DISCRIMINATION.
NOW SHE'S GOT THE WRONG IDEA AND IS FULL OF HERSELF BECAUSE THE DIRECTOR TREATED HER LIKE THAT.

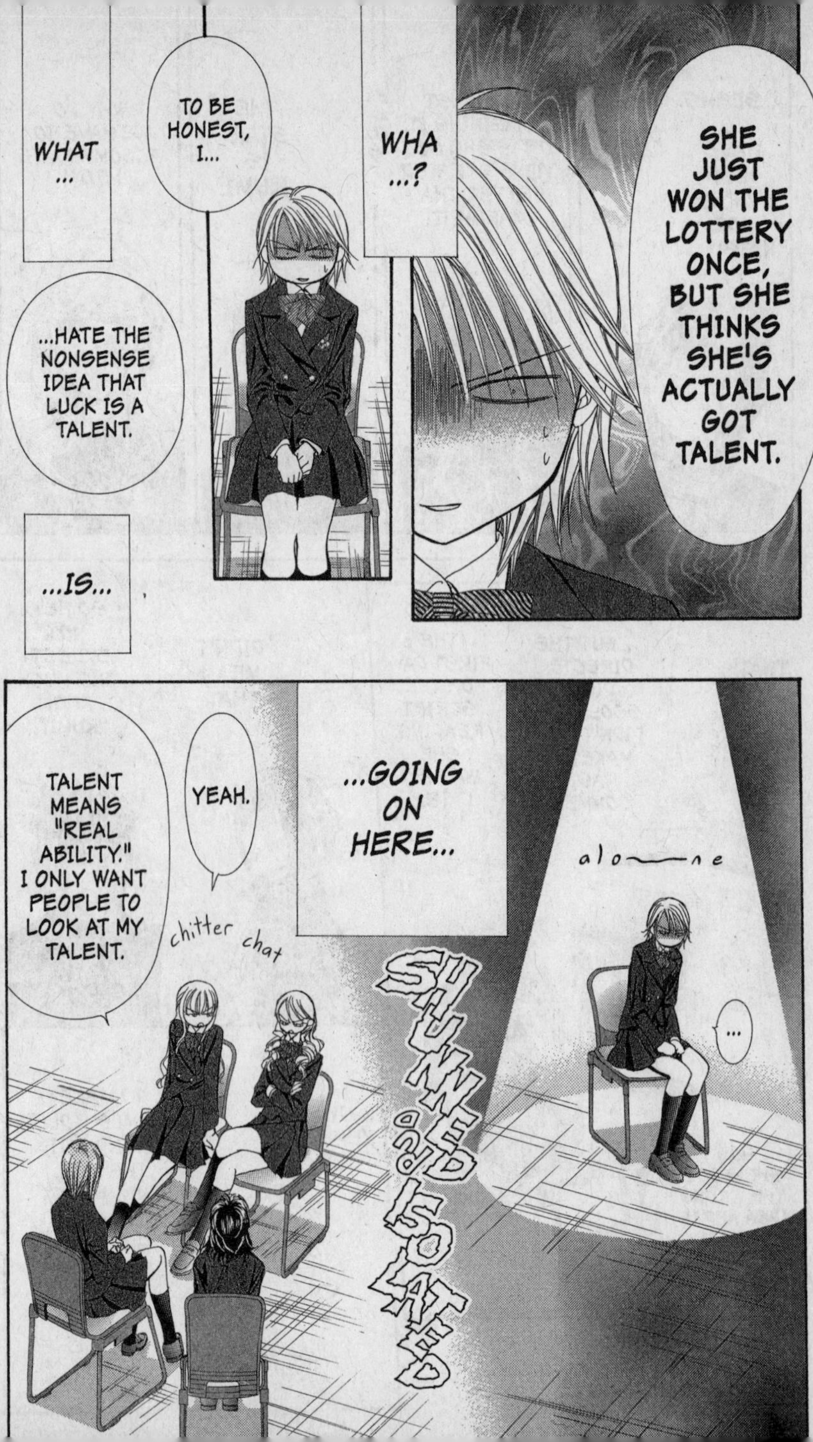

SHE JUST WON THE LOTTERY ONCE, BUT SHE THINKS SHE'S ACTUALLY GOT TALENT.
WHA ...?
TO BE HONEST, I...
WHAT ...
...HATE THE NONSENSE IDEA THAT LUCK IS A TALENT.
...IS...
alo—ne
...
SHUNNED ISOLATED
...GOING ON HERE...
YEAH.
TALENT MEANS "REAL ABILITY." I ONLY WANT PEOPLE TO LOOK AT MY TALENT.
chitter chat

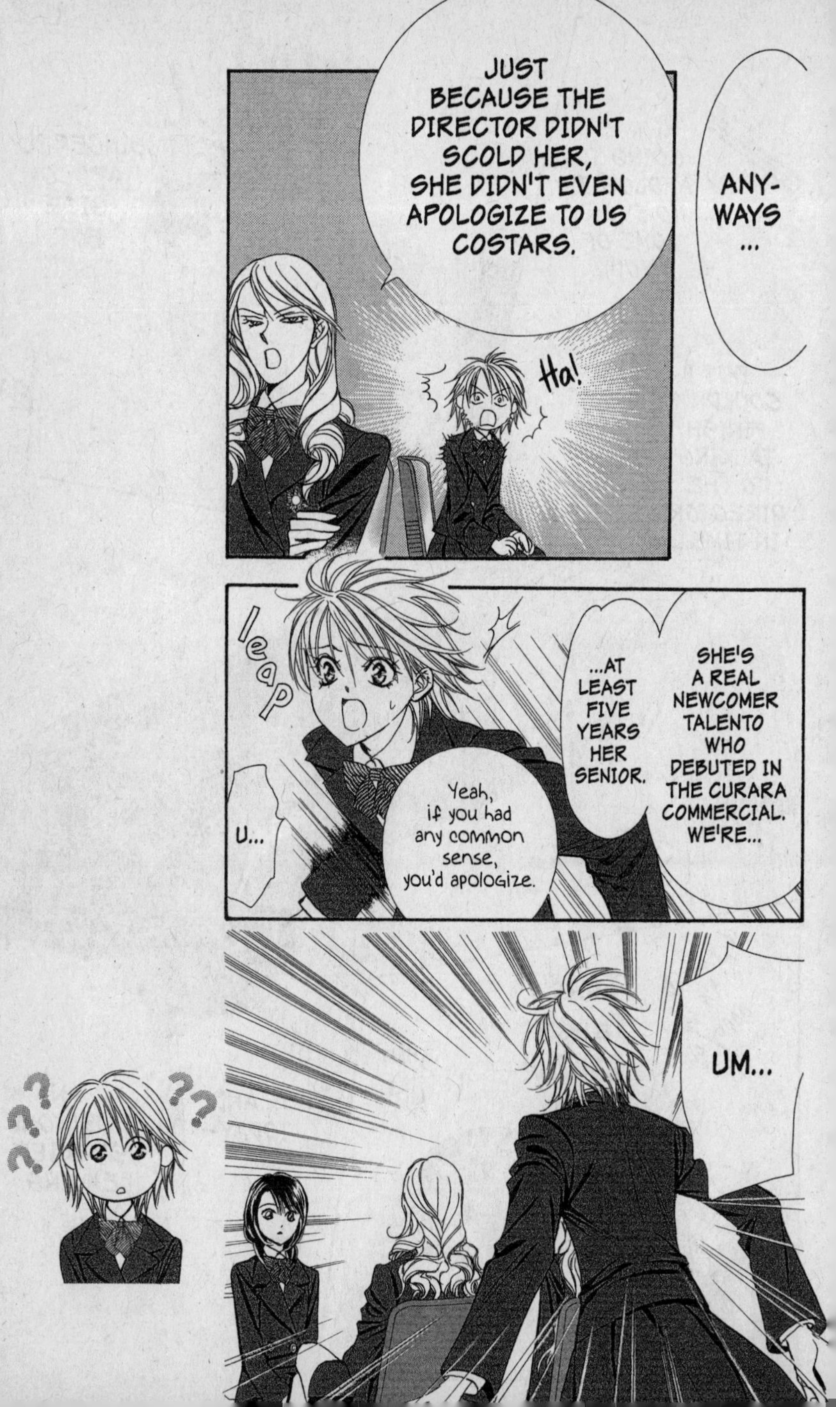
ANY-WAYS...
JUST BECAUSE THE DIRECTOR DIDN'T SCOLD HER, SHE DIDN'T EVEN APOLOGIZE TO US COSTARS.
Ha!
SHE'S A REAL NEWCOMER TALENTO WHO DEBUTED IN THE CURARA COMMERCIAL. WE'RE...
...AT LEAST FIVE YEARS HER SENIOR.
leap
Yeah, if you had any common sense, you'd apologize.
U...
UM...

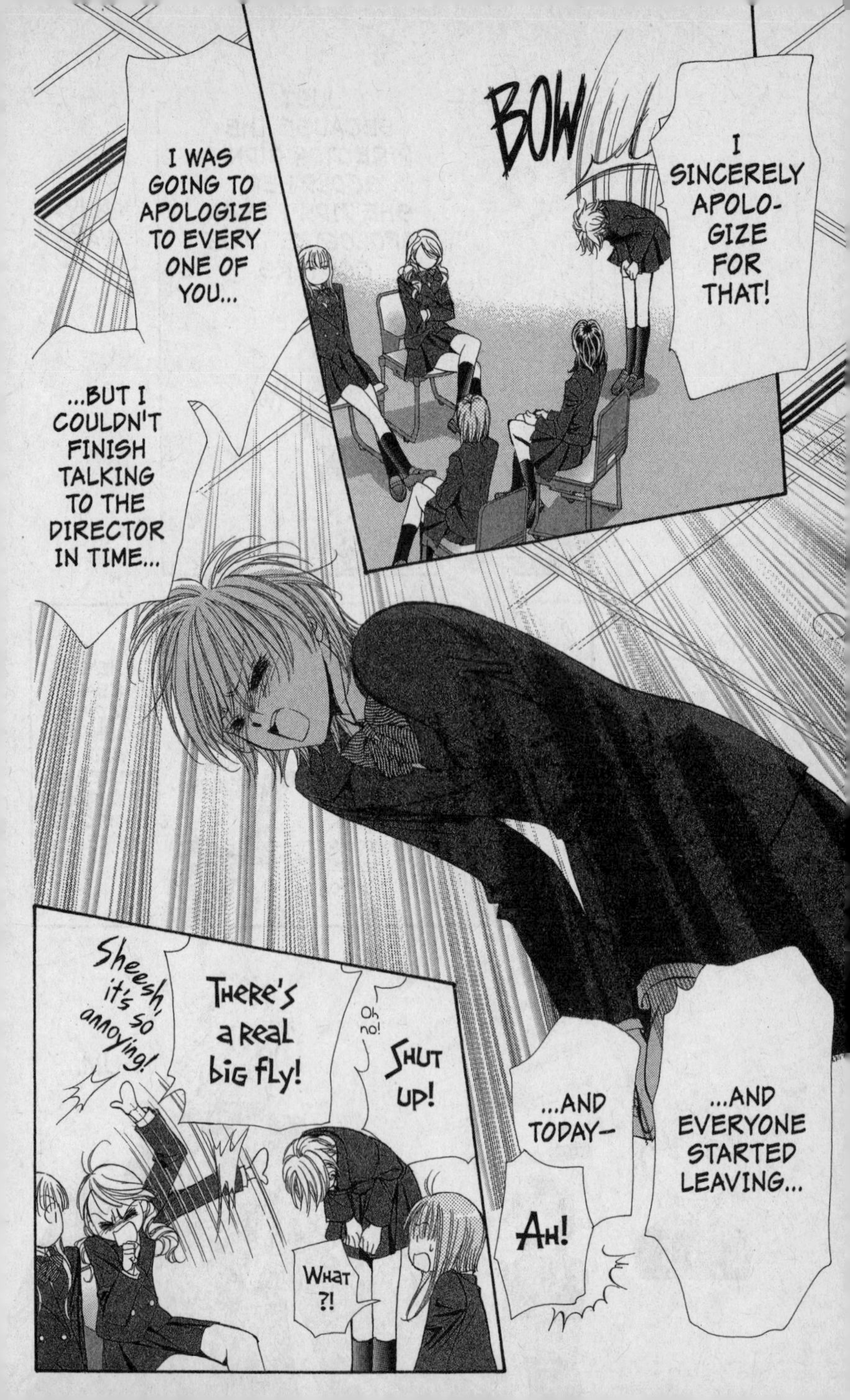
BOW
I SINCERELY APOLOGIZE FOR THAT!
I WAS GOING TO APOLOGIZE TO EVERY ONE OF YOU...
...BUT I COULDN'T FINISH TALKING TO THE DIRECTOR IN TIME...
...AND EVERYONE STARTED LEAVING...
...AND TODAY—
AH!
SHUT UP!
Oh no!
There's a real big fly!
Sheesh, it's so annoying!
WHAT ?!

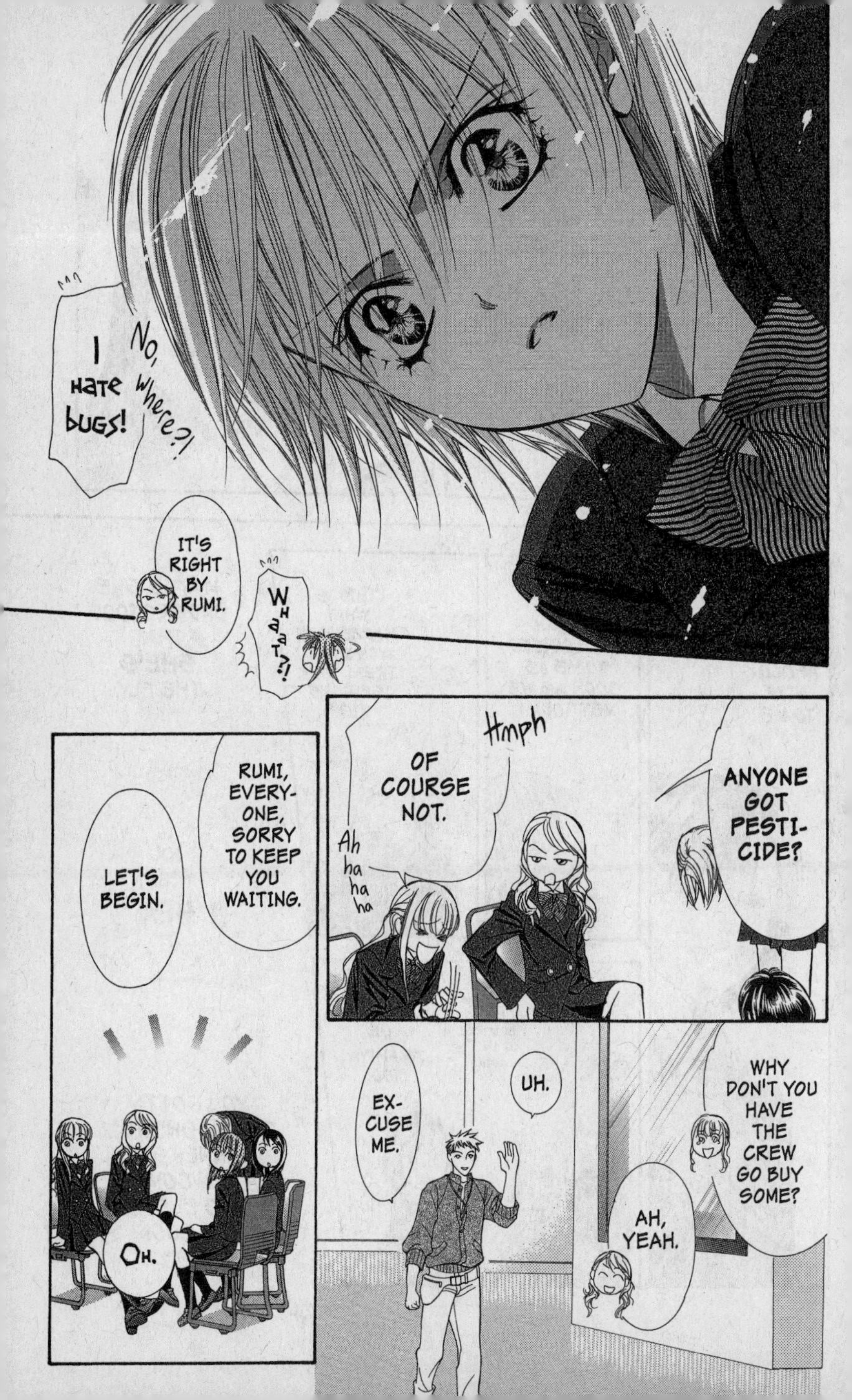
No, where?!
I hate bugs!
It's right by Rumi.
Whaaat?!
Anyone got pesticide?
Hmph
Of course not.
Ah ha ha ha
Why don't you have the crew go buy some?
Ah, yeah.
Uh.
Excuse me.
Rumi, everyone, sorry to keep you waiting.
Let's begin.
Oh.

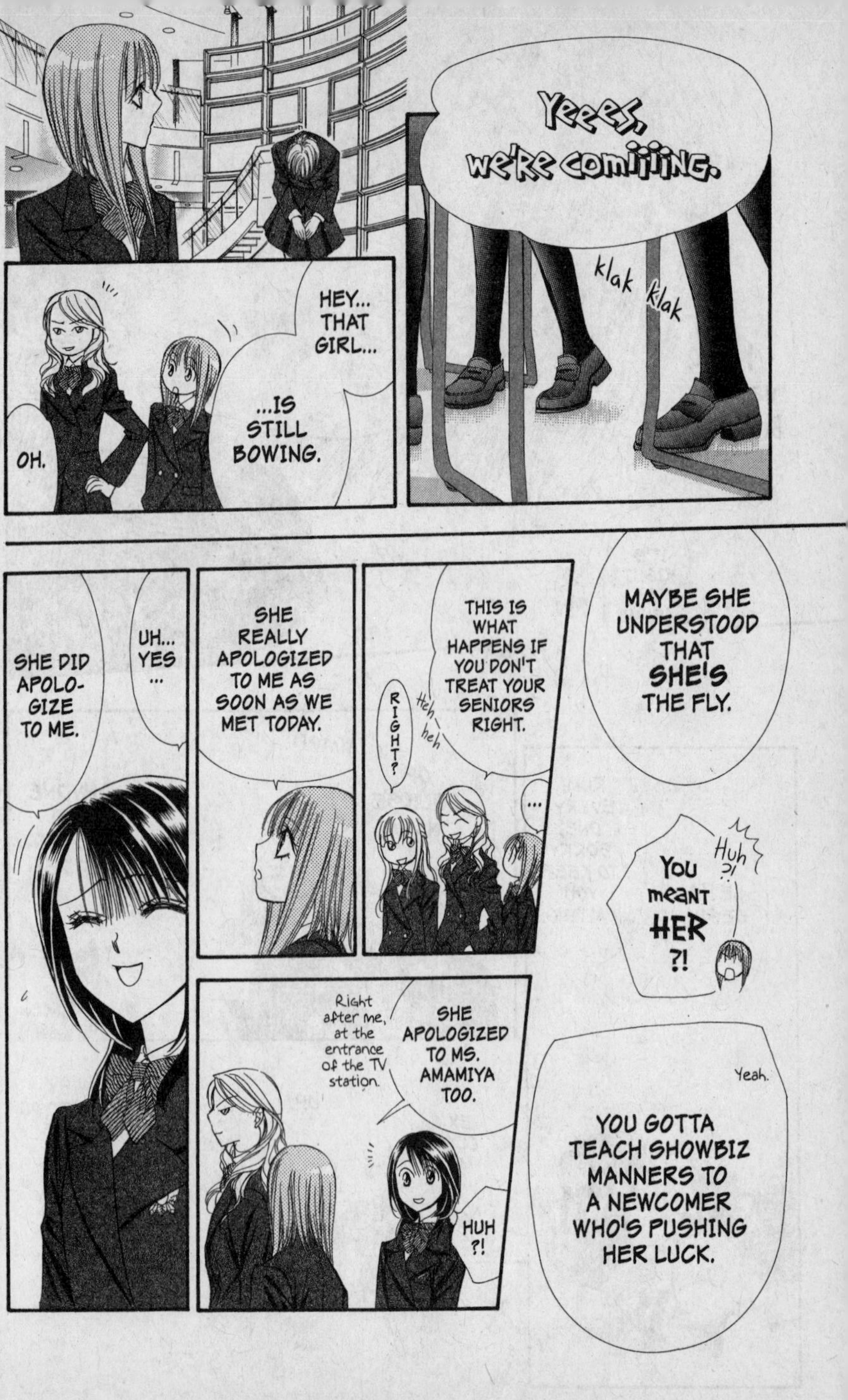

Yeees, we're comiiiing.
klak klak
HEY... THAT GIRL...
...IS STILL BOWING.
OH.
MAYBE SHE UNDERSTOOD THAT SHE'S THE FLY.
Huh ?!
You meant HER ?!
Yeah.
YOU GOTTA TEACH SHOWBIZ MANNERS TO A NEWCOMER WHO'S PUSHING HER LUCK.
THIS IS WHAT HAPPENS IF YOU DON'T TREAT YOUR SENIORS RIGHT.
RIGHT?
Heh heh
...
SHE REALLY APOLOGIZED TO ME AS SOON AS WE MET TODAY.
UH... YES ...
SHE DID APOLO-GIZE TO ME.
SHE APOLOGIZED TO MS. AMAMIYA TOO.
Right after me, at the entrance of the TV station.
HUH ?!

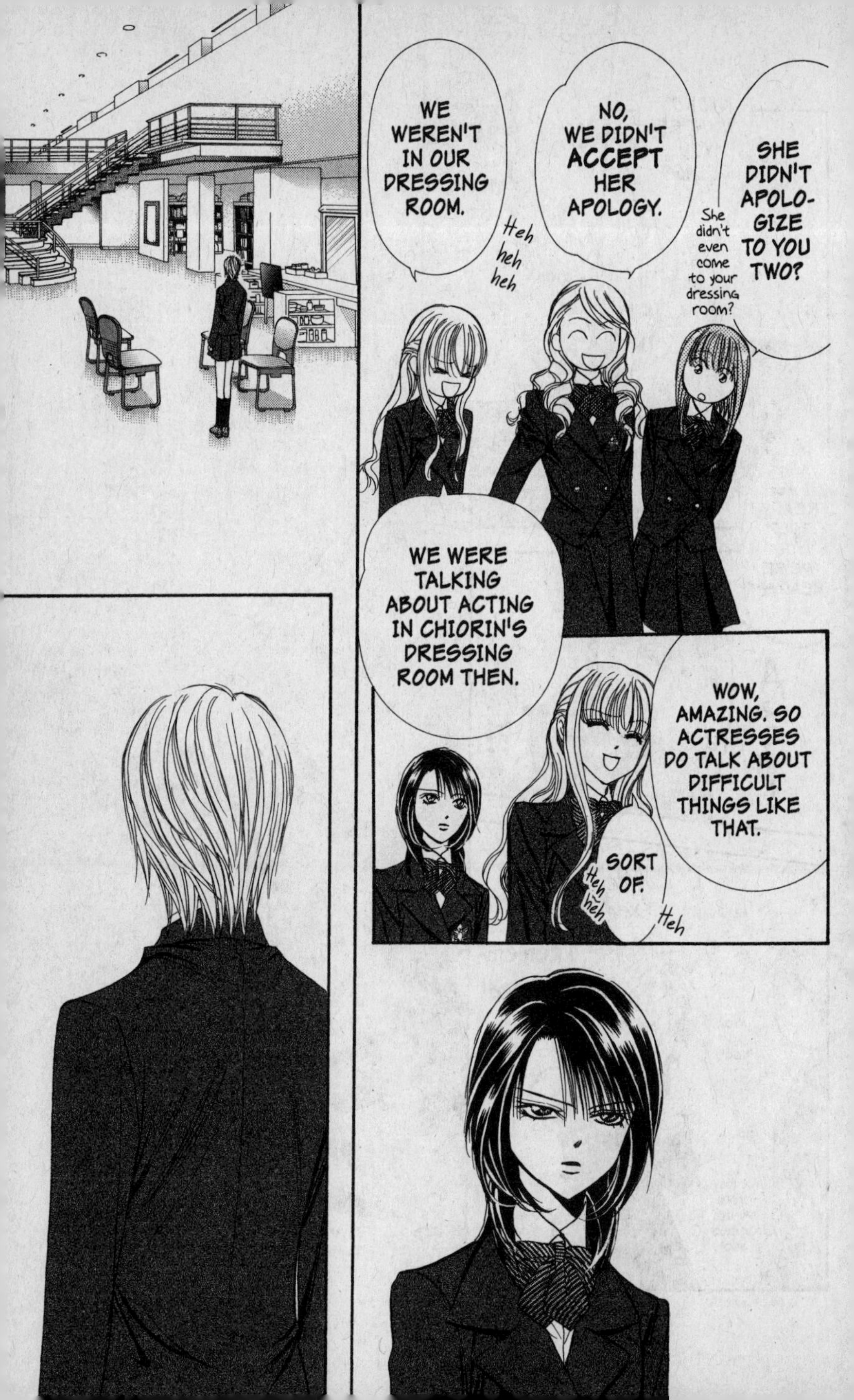
SHE DIDN'T APOLO-GIZE TO YOU TWO?
She didn't even come to your dressing room?
NO, WE DIDN'T ACCEPT HER APOLOGY.
WE WEREN'T IN OUR DRESSING ROOM.
Heh heh heh
WE WERE TALKING ABOUT ACTING IN CHIORIN'S DRESSING ROOM THEN.
WOW, AMAZING. SO ACTRESSES DO TALK ABOUT DIFFICULT THINGS LIKE THAT.
SORT OF.
Heh heh
Heh

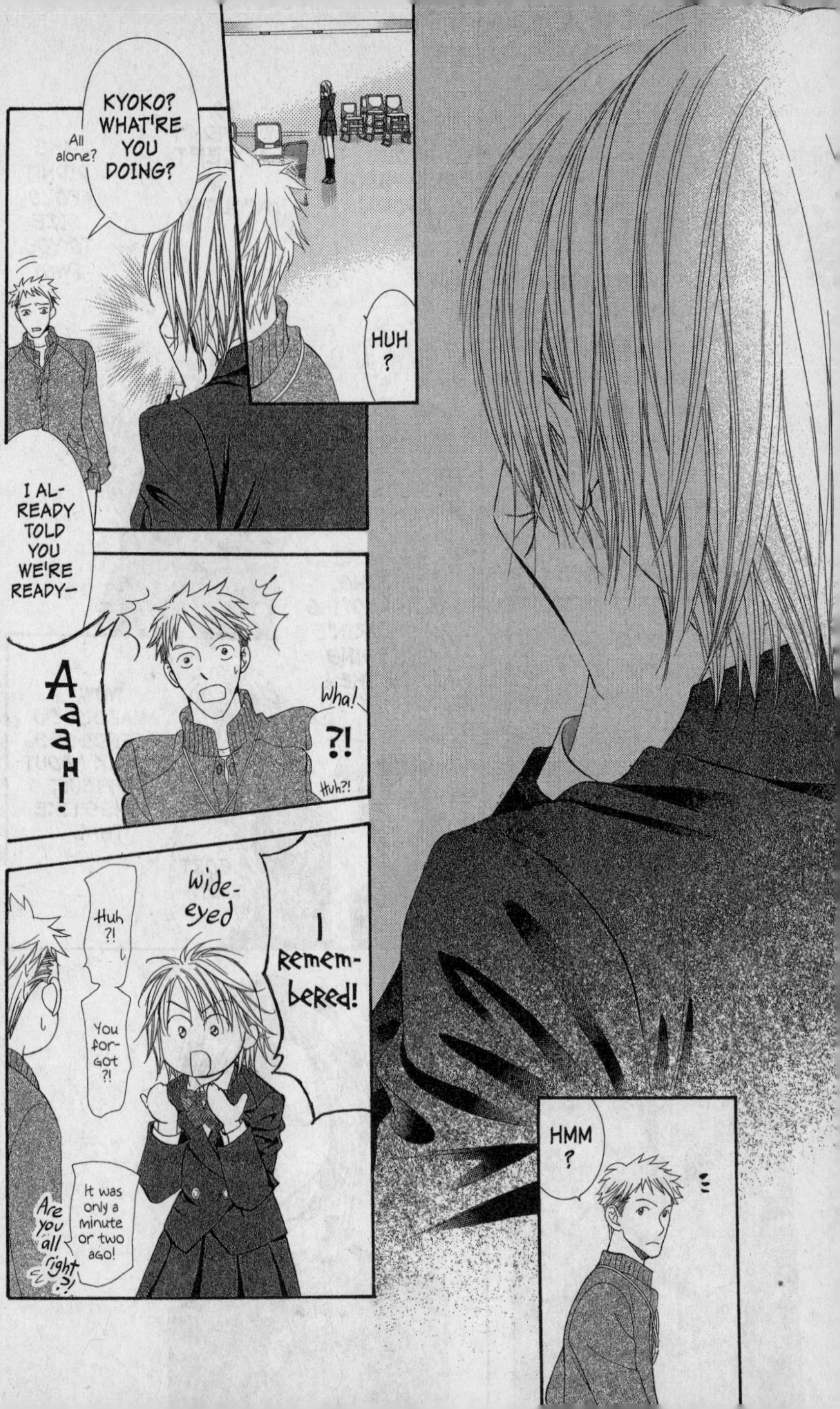

HMM ?
HUH ?
KYOKO? WHAT'RE YOU DOING?
All alone?
I AL-READY TOLD YOU WE'RE READY—
Aaah!
Wha! ?!
Huh?!
I remem-bered!
wide-eyed
Huh ?!
You for-got ?!
It was only a minute or two ago!
Are you all right ?!

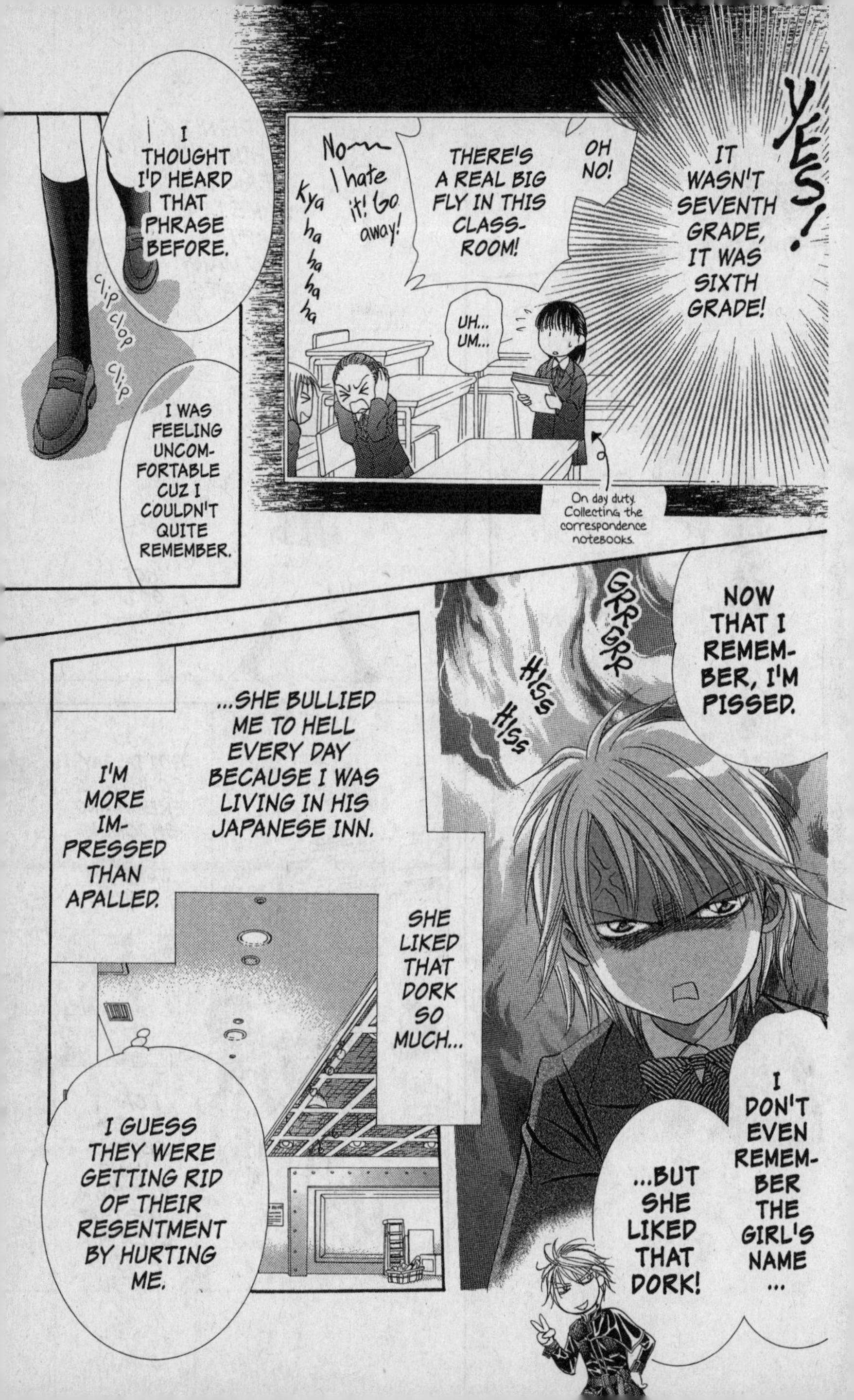
YES!
IT WASN'T SEVENTH GRADE, IT WAS SIXTH GRADE!
OH NO!
THERE'S A REAL BIG FLY IN THIS CLASS-ROOM!
No~ I hate it! Go away!
Kya ha ha ha ha ha
UH... UM...
On day duty. Collecting the correspondence notebooks.
I THOUGHT I'D HEARD THAT PHRASE BEFORE.
clip clop clip
I WAS FEELING UNCOM-FORTABLE CUZ I COULDN'T QUITE REMEMBER.
NOW THAT I REMEM-BER, I'M PISSED.
GRR GRR
HISS HISS
I DON'T EVEN REMEM-BER THE GIRL'S NAME ...
...BUT SHE LIKED THAT DORK!
...SHE BULLIED ME TO HELL EVERY DAY BECAUSE I WAS LIVING IN HIS JAPANESE INN.
I'M MORE IM-PRESSED THAN APALLED.
SHE LIKED THAT DORK SO MUCH...
I GUESS THEY WERE GETTING RID OF THEIR RESENTMENT BY HURTING ME.

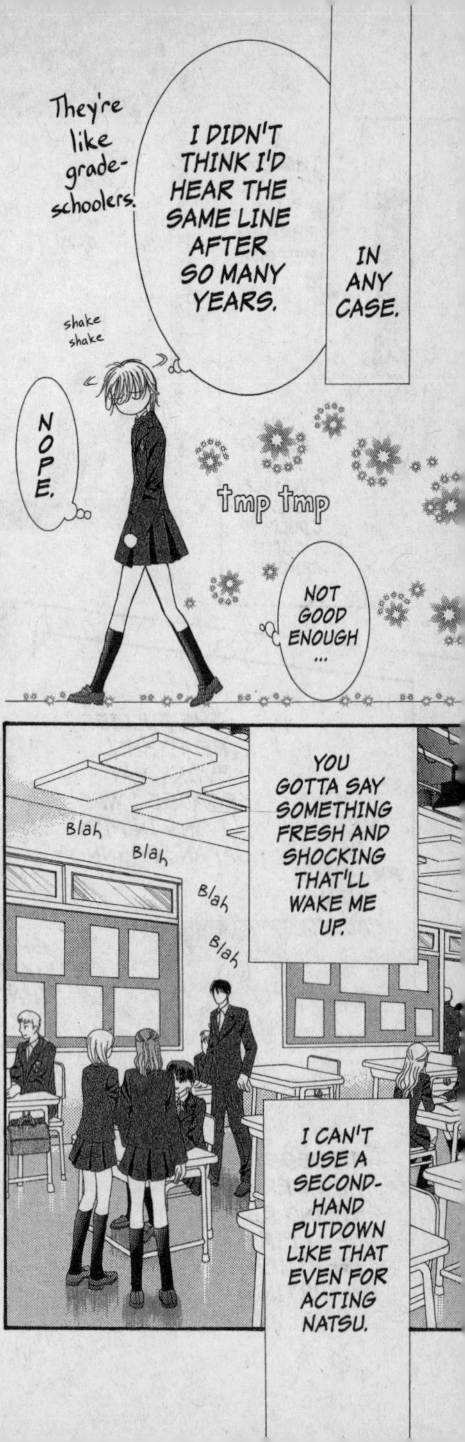
IN ANY CASE.
I DIDN'T THINK I'D HEAR THE SAME LINE AFTER SO MANY YEARS.
They're like grade-schoolers.
shake shake
NOPE.
tmp tmp
NOT GOOD ENOUGH ...
YOU GOTTA SAY SOMETHING FRESH AND SHOCKING THAT'LL WAKE ME UP.
Blah
Blah
Blah
Blah
I CAN'T USE A SECOND-HAND PUTDOWN LIKE THAT EVEN FOR ACTING NATSU.

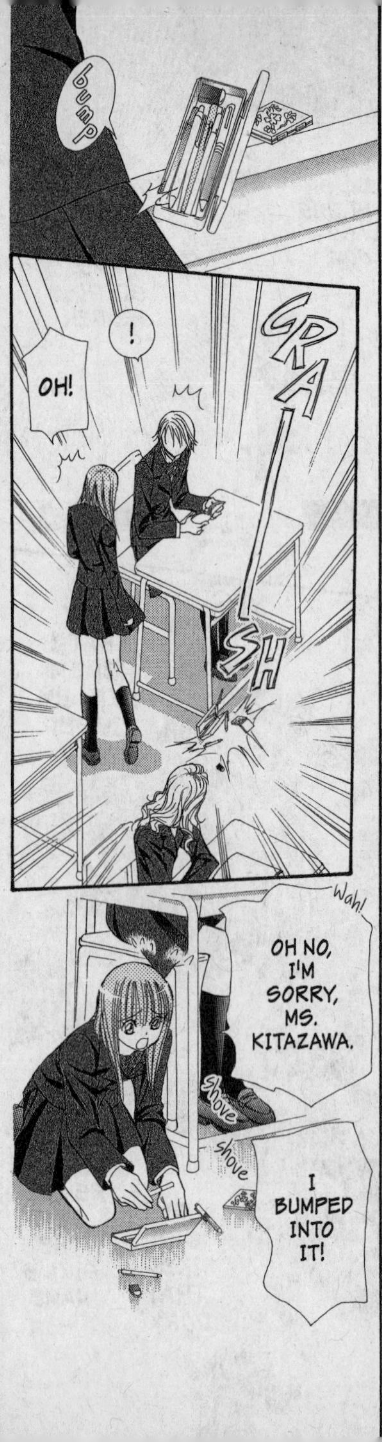
bump
CRASH
!
OH!
Wah!
OH NO, I'M SORRY, MS. KITAZAWA.
shove
shove
I BUMPED INTO IT!

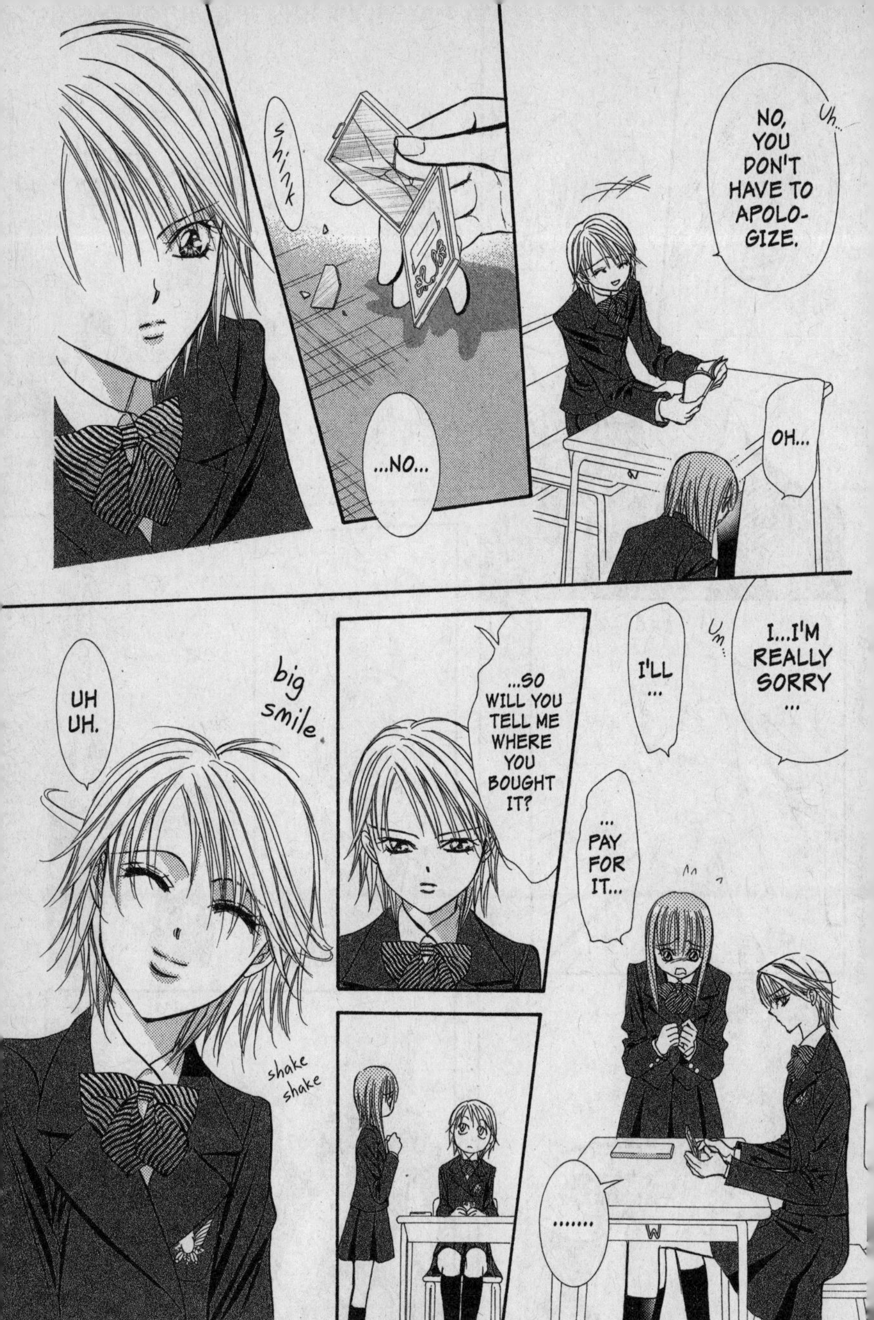
Uh...
NO, YOU DON'T HAVE TO APOLOGIZE.
OH...
shhink
...NO...
I...I'M REALLY SORRY ...
Um...
I'LL ...
... PAY FOR IT...
....
...SO WILL YOU TELL ME WHERE YOU BOUGHT IT?
big smile
UH UH.
shake shake

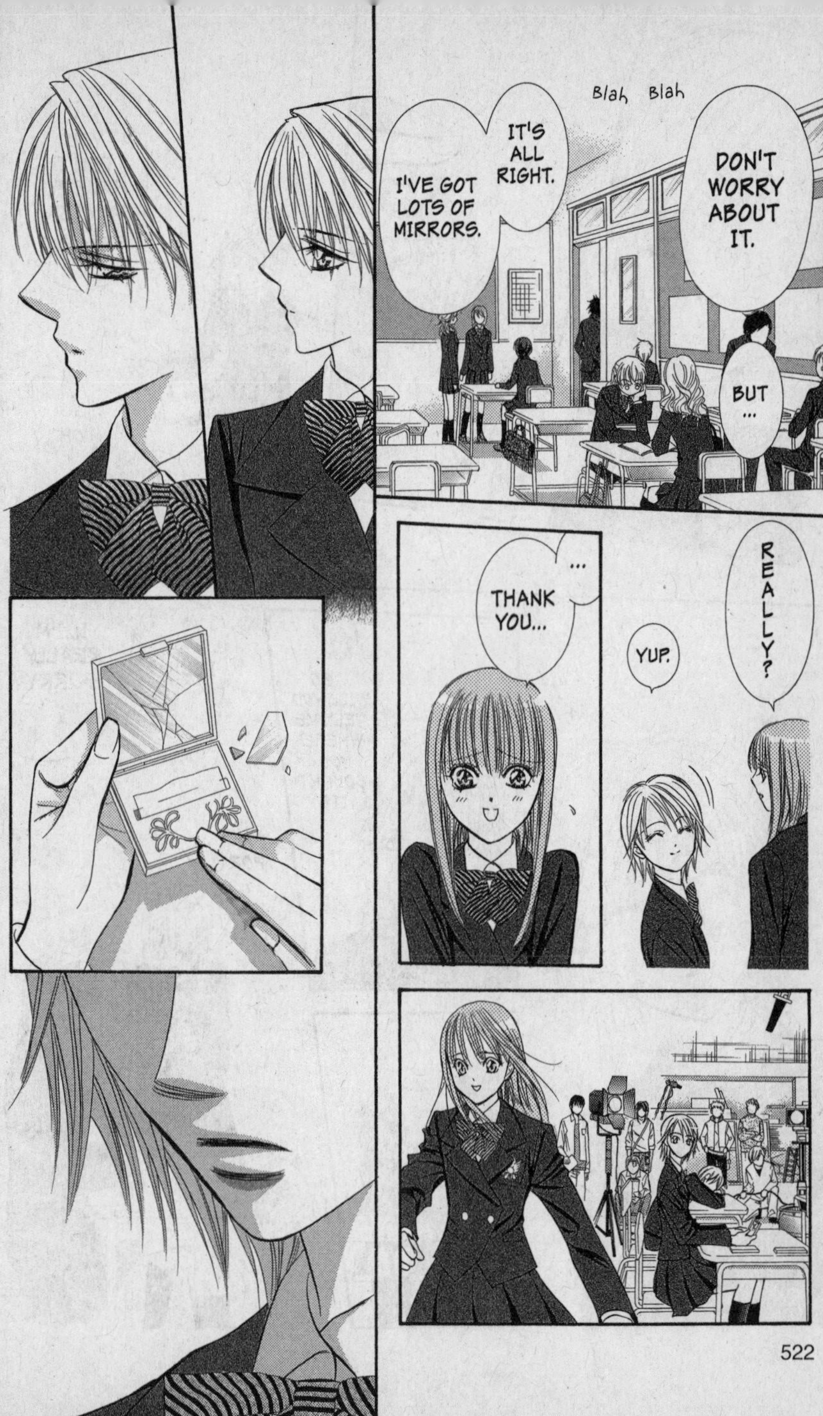
Blah Blah
DON'T WORRY ABOUT IT.
BUT ...
IT'S ALL RIGHT.
I'VE GOT LOTS OF MIRRORS.
REALLY?
YUP.
... THANK YOU...

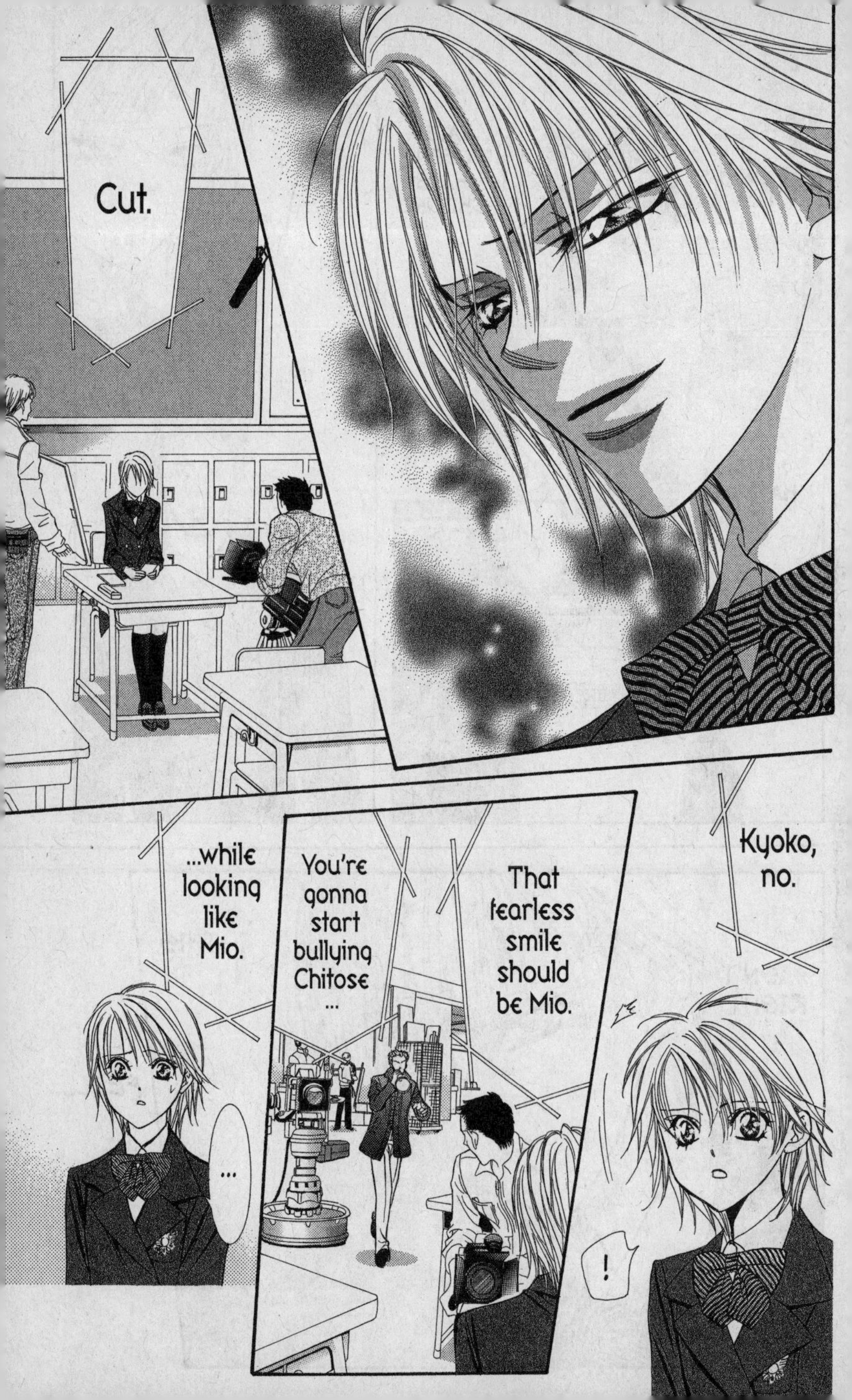
Cut.
Kyoko, no.
!
That fearless smile should be Mio.
You're gonna start bullying Chitose...
...while looking like Mio.
...

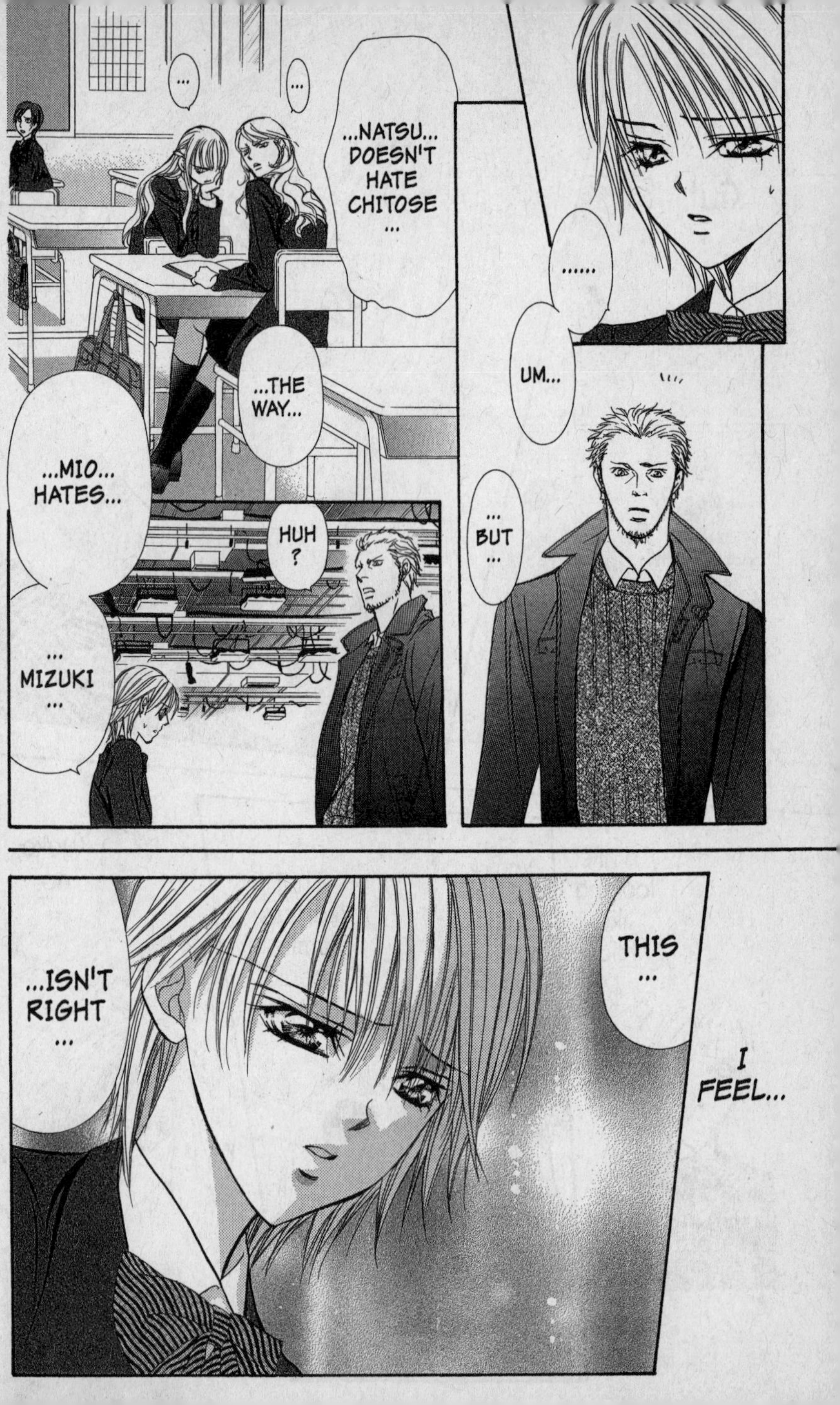
......
UM...
... BUT ...
...
...
...NATSU... DOESN'T HATE CHITOSE ...
...THE WAY...
...MIO... HATES...
HUH ?
... MIZUKI ...
THIS ...
...ISN'T RIGHT ...
I FEEL...

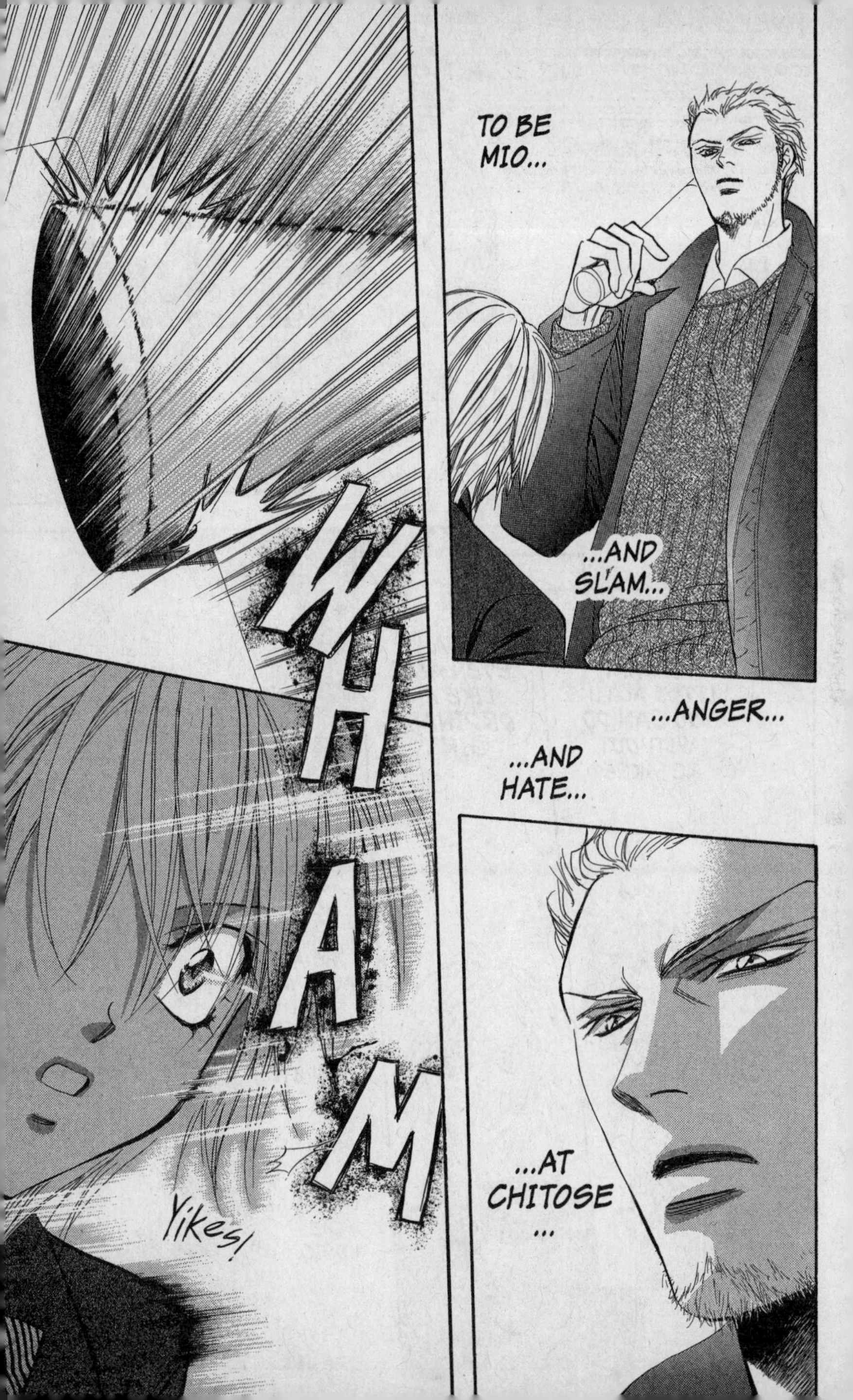
TO BE MIO...
...AND SLAM...
...ANGER...
...AND HATE...
...AT CHITOSE ...
WHAM
Yikes!

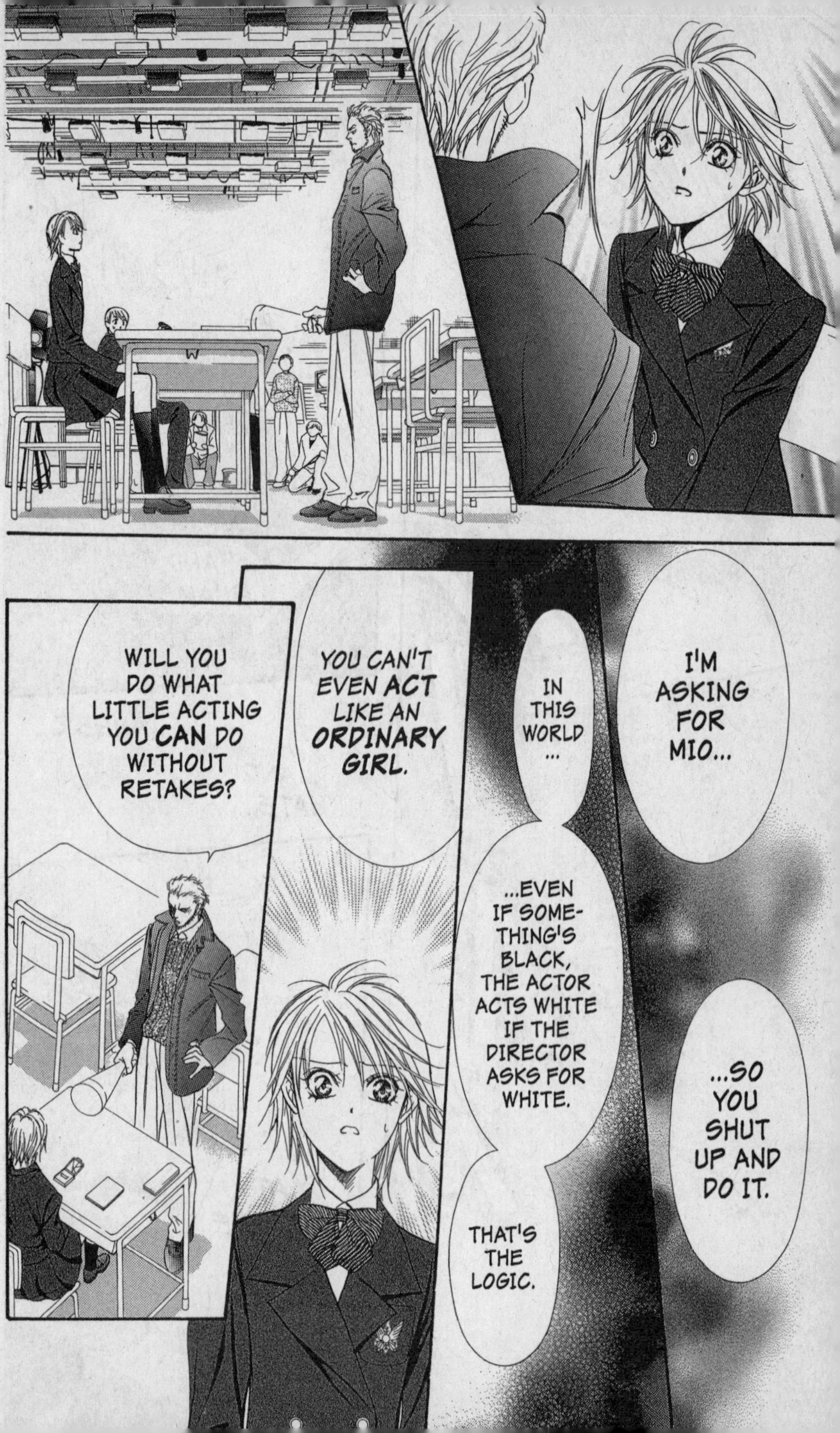
I'M ASKING FOR MIO...
IN THIS WORLD...
...EVEN IF SOMETHING'S BLACK, THE ACTOR ACTS WHITE IF THE DIRECTOR ASKS FOR WHITE.
THAT'S THE LOGIC.
...SO YOU SHUT UP AND DO IT.
YOU CAN'T EVEN ACT LIKE AN ORDINARY GIRL.
WILL YOU DO WHAT LITTLE ACTING YOU CAN DO WITHOUT RETAKES?

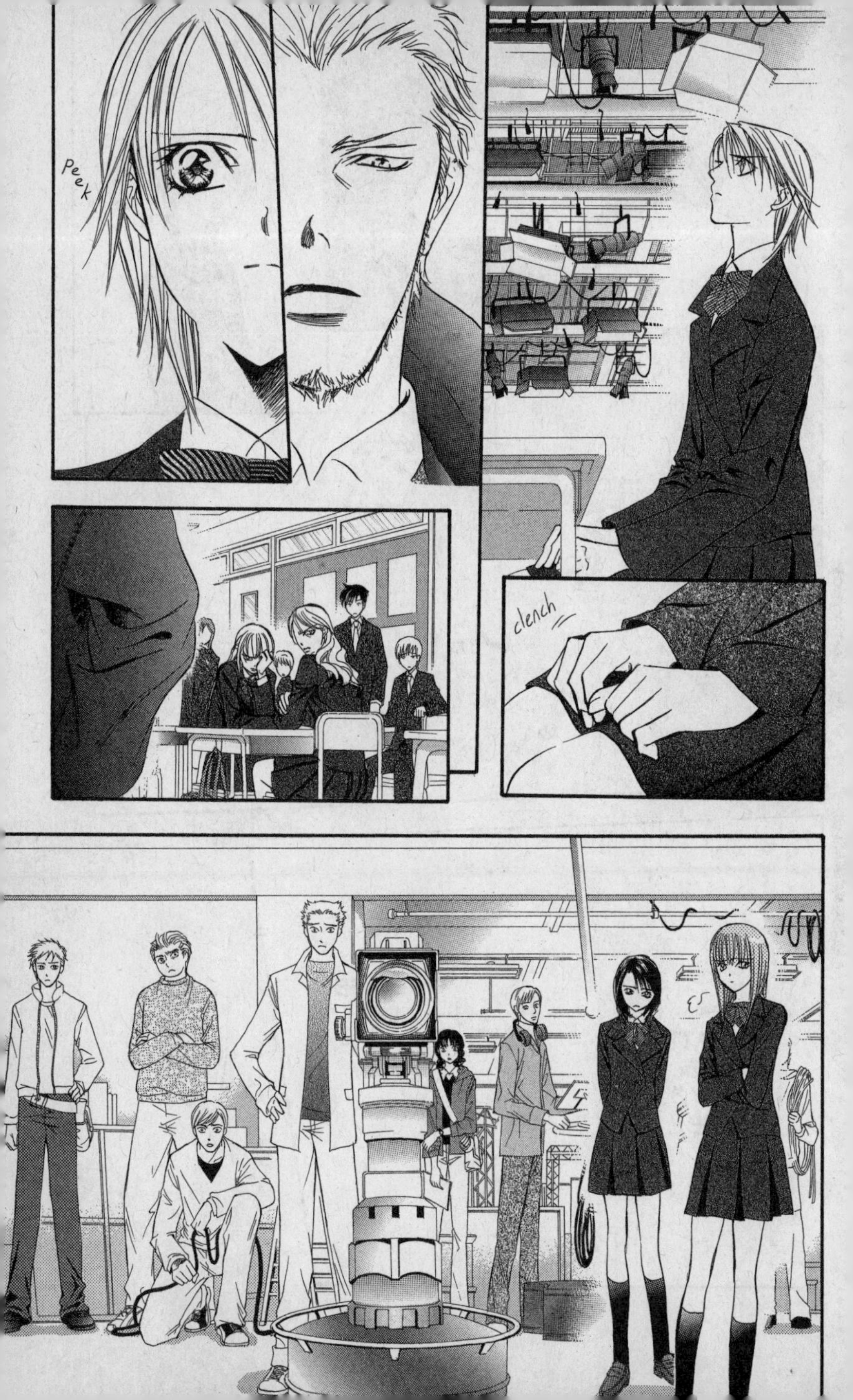
peek
clench

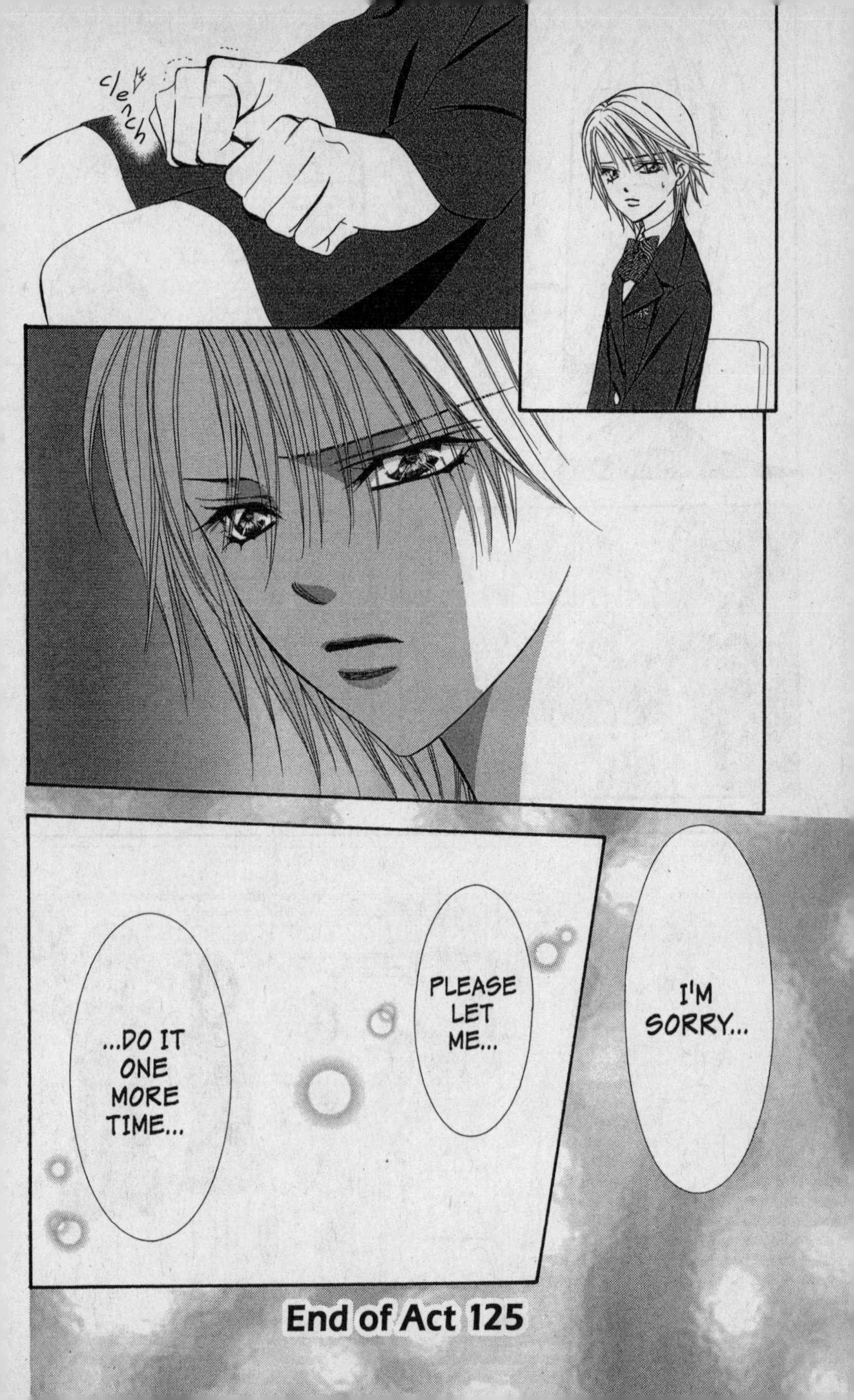
clench
I'M SORRY...
PLEASE LET ME...
...DO IT ONE MORE TIME...

End of Act 125

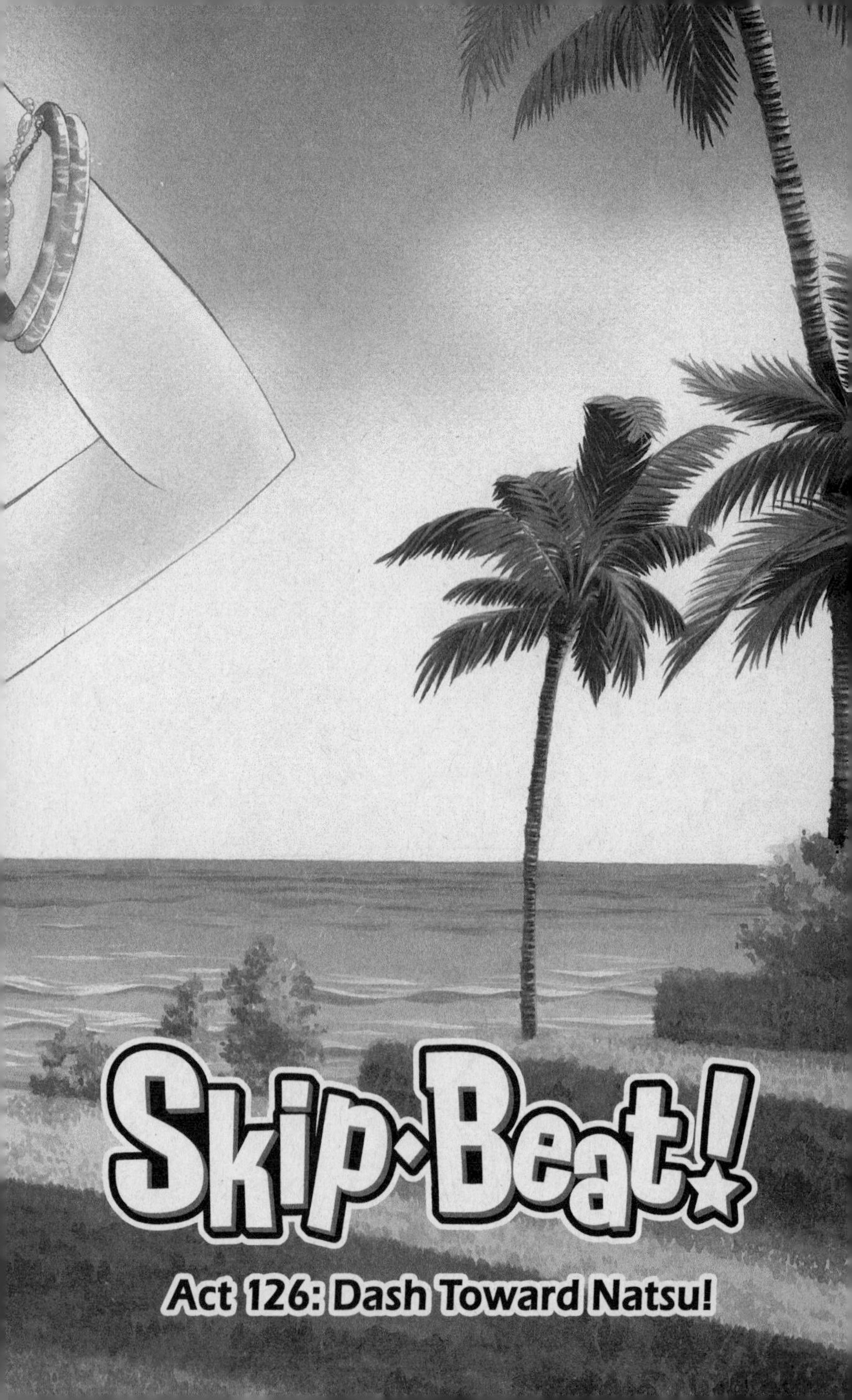
Skip·Beat!
Act 126: Dash Toward Natsu!

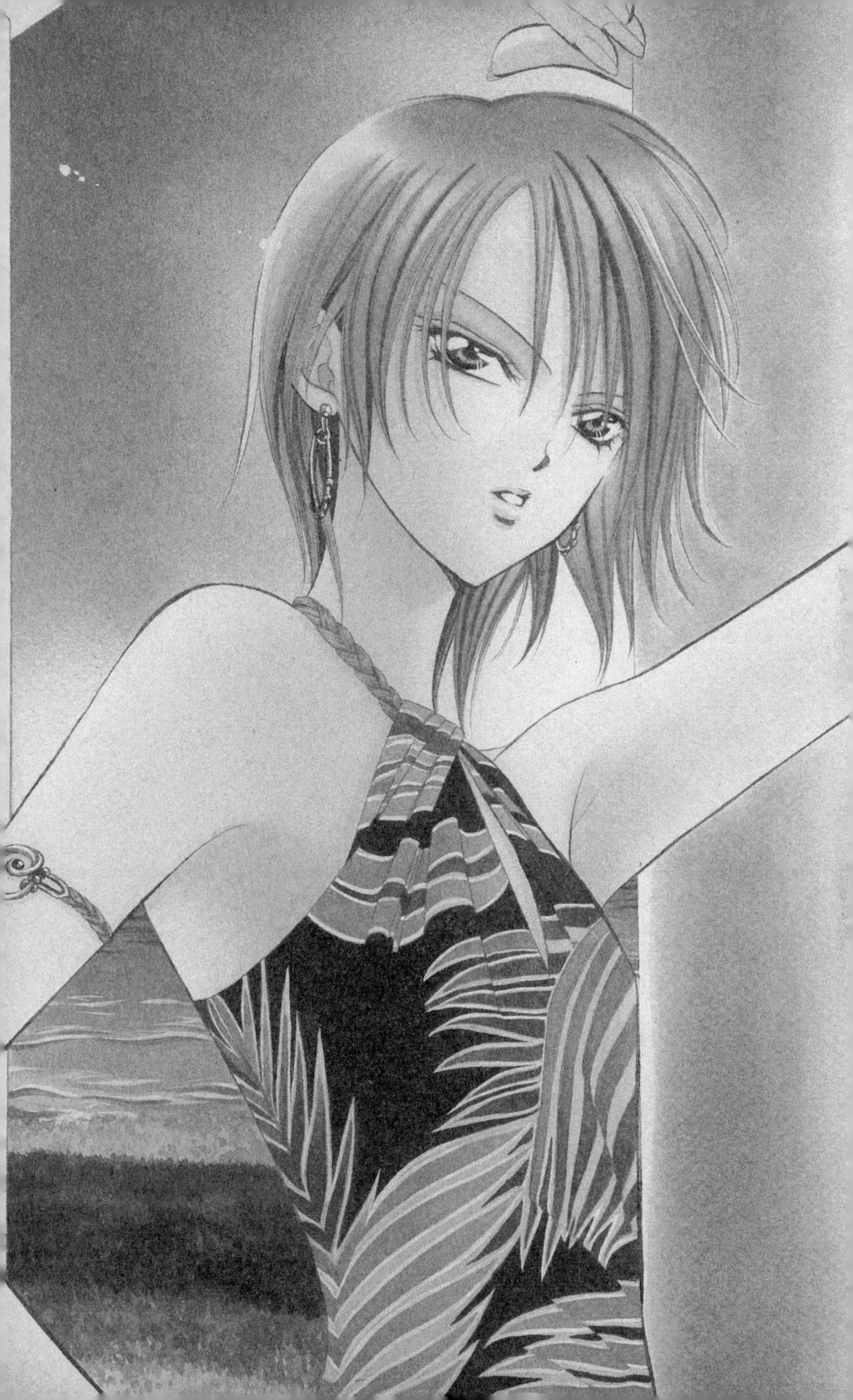

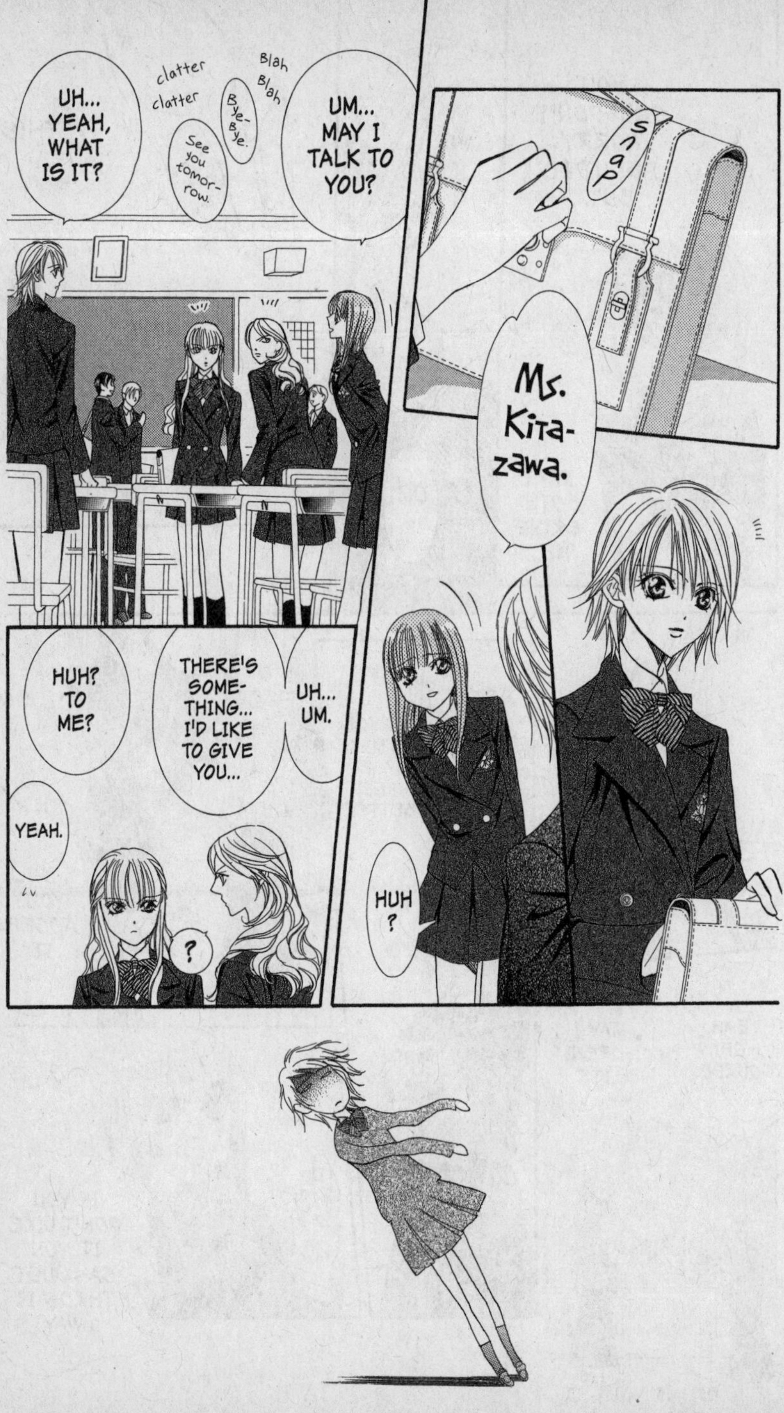
snap
Ms. Kita-zawa.
HUH?
UM... MAY I TALK TO YOU?
Blah Blah
Bye-Bye.
See you tomorrow.
clatter clatter
UH... YEAH, WHAT IS IT?
UH... UM.
THERE'S SOMETHING... I'D LIKE TO GIVE YOU...
HUH? TO ME?
YEAH.
?

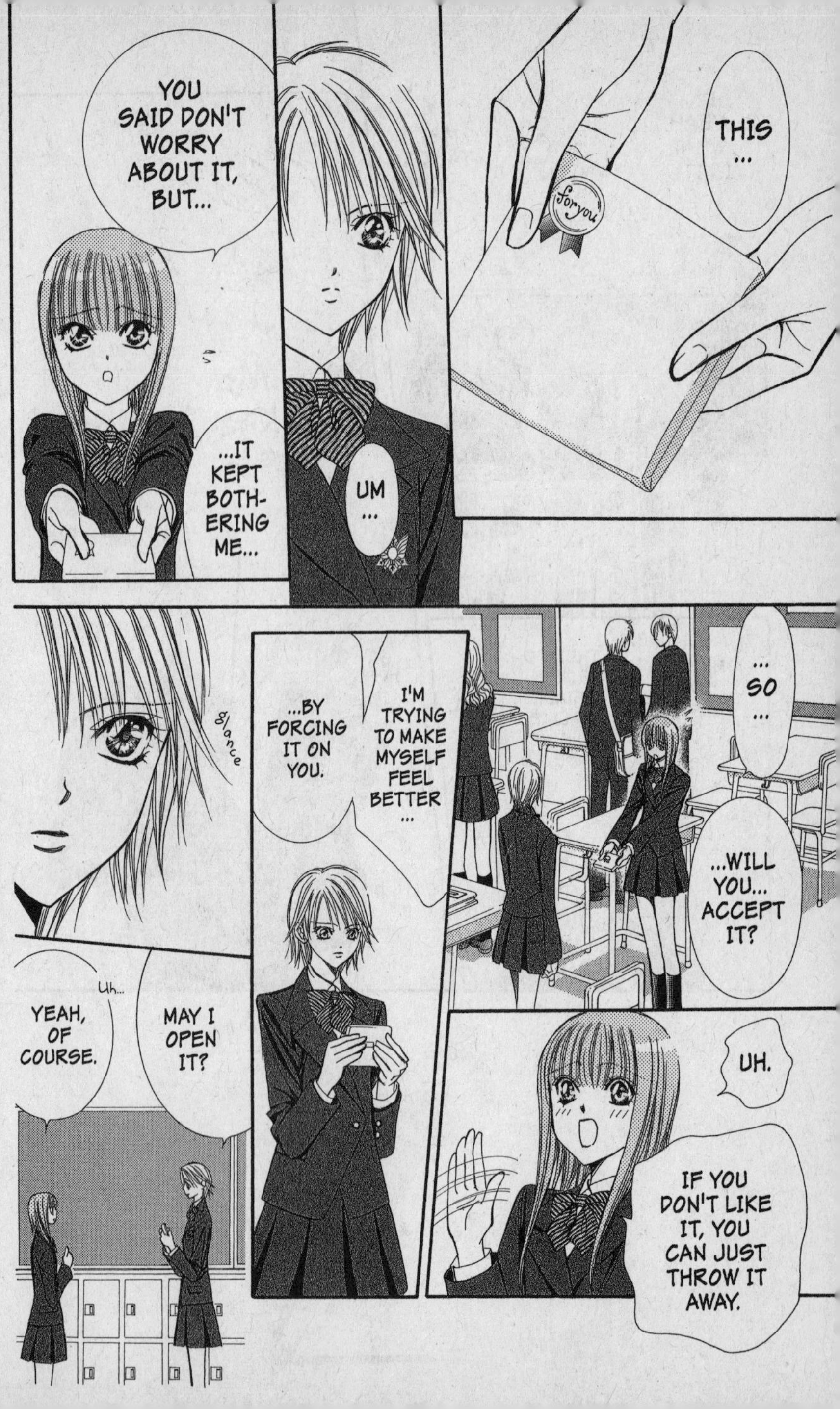
THIS ...
UM ...
YOU SAID DON'T WORRY ABOUT IT, BUT...
...IT KEPT BOTHERING ME...
... SO ...
...WILL YOU... ACCEPT IT?
UH.
IF YOU DON'T LIKE IT, YOU CAN JUST THROW IT AWAY.
I'M TRYING TO MAKE MYSELF FEEL BETTER ...
...BY FORCING IT ON YOU.
glance
MAY I OPEN IT?
Uh...
YEAH, OF COURSE.

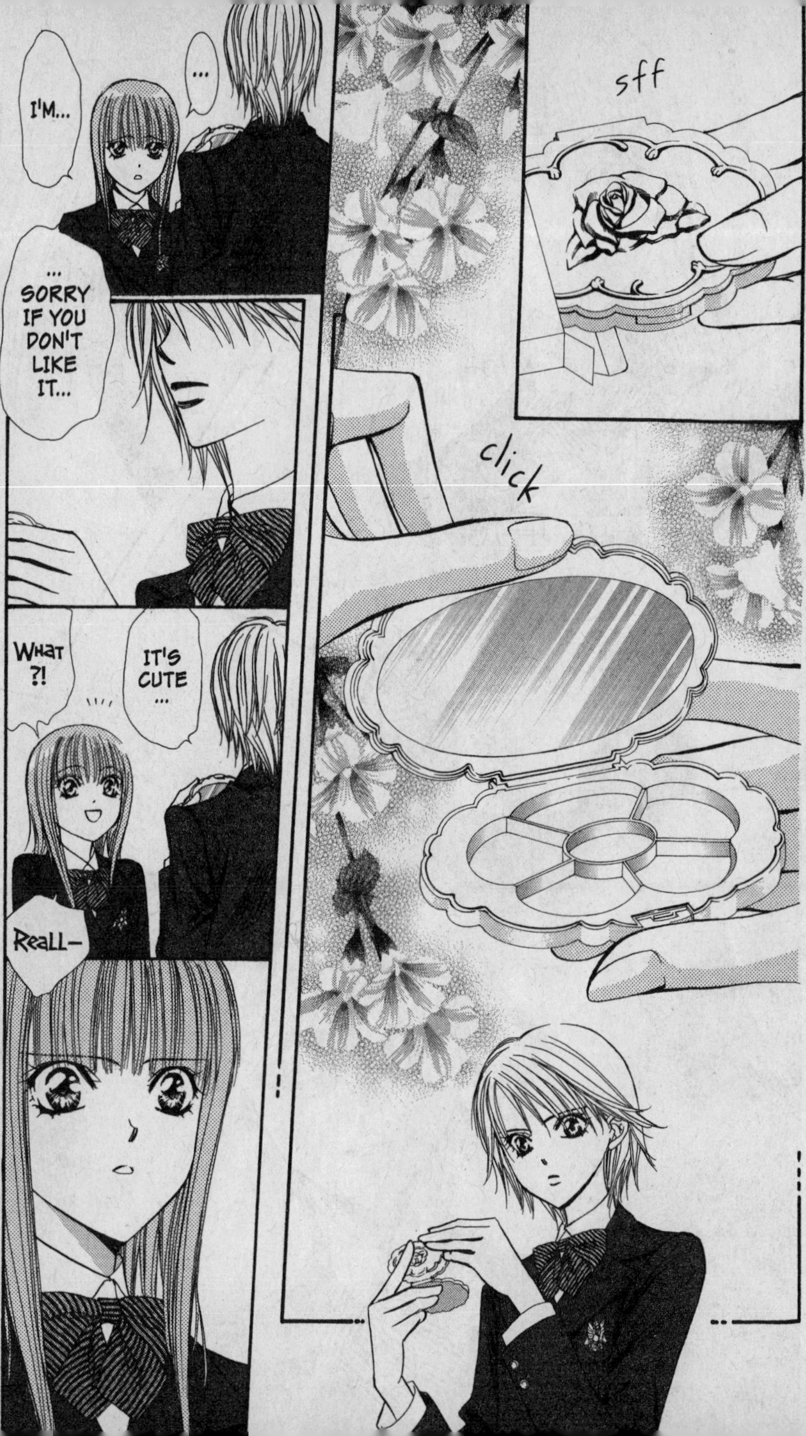
sff
click
...
I'M...
...SORRY IF YOU DON'T LIKE IT...
IT'S CUTE...
WHAT?!
Reall—

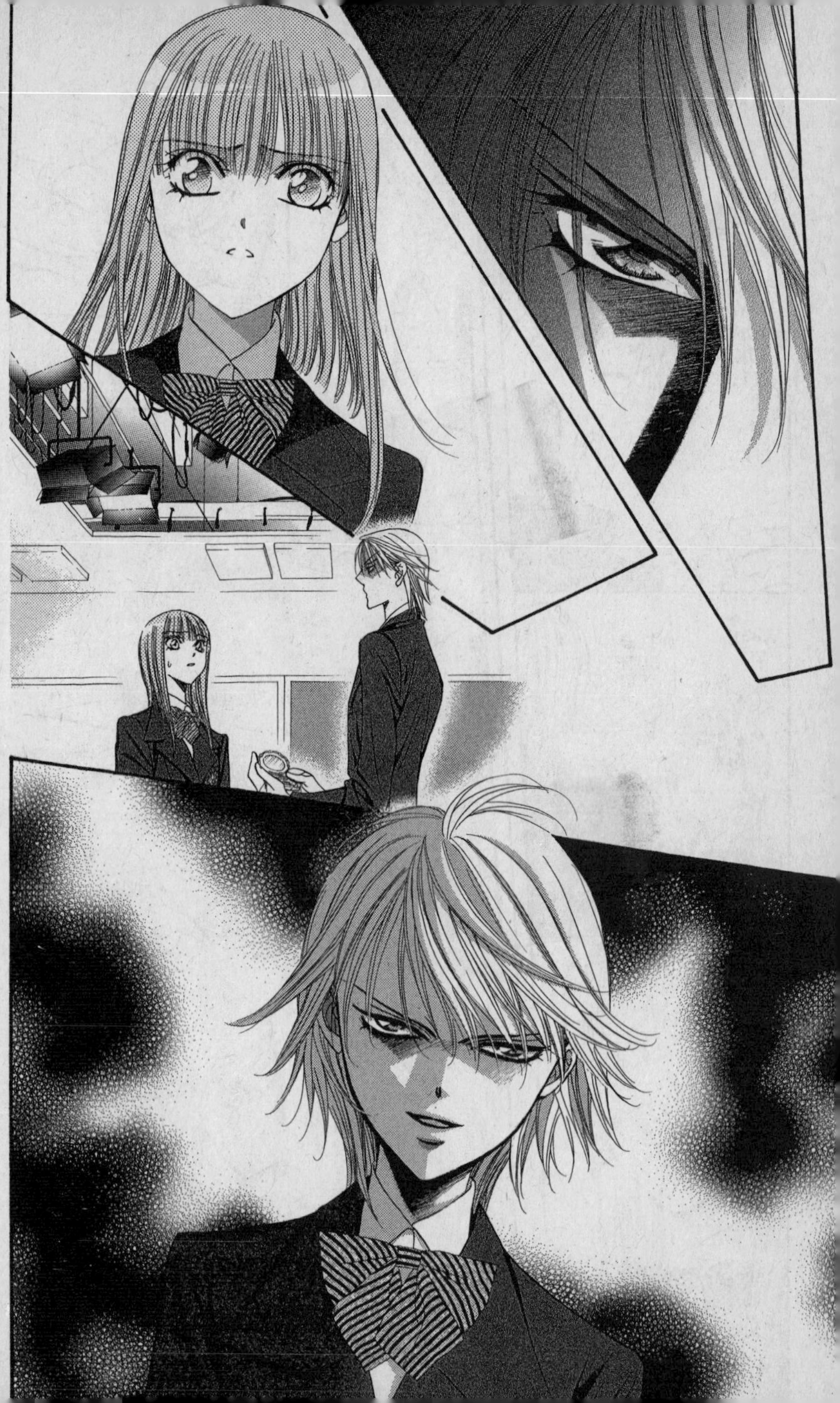

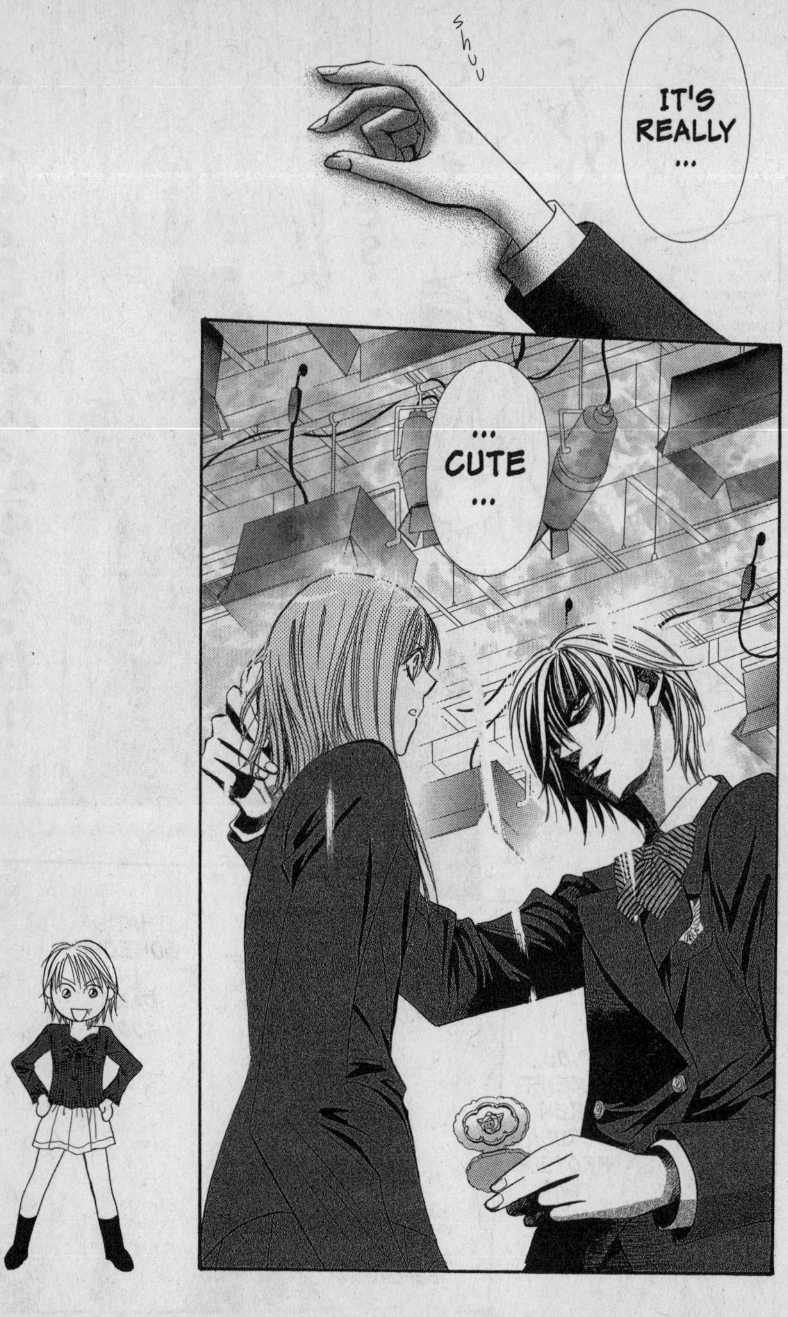
IT'S REALLY ...
shuu
... CUTE ...

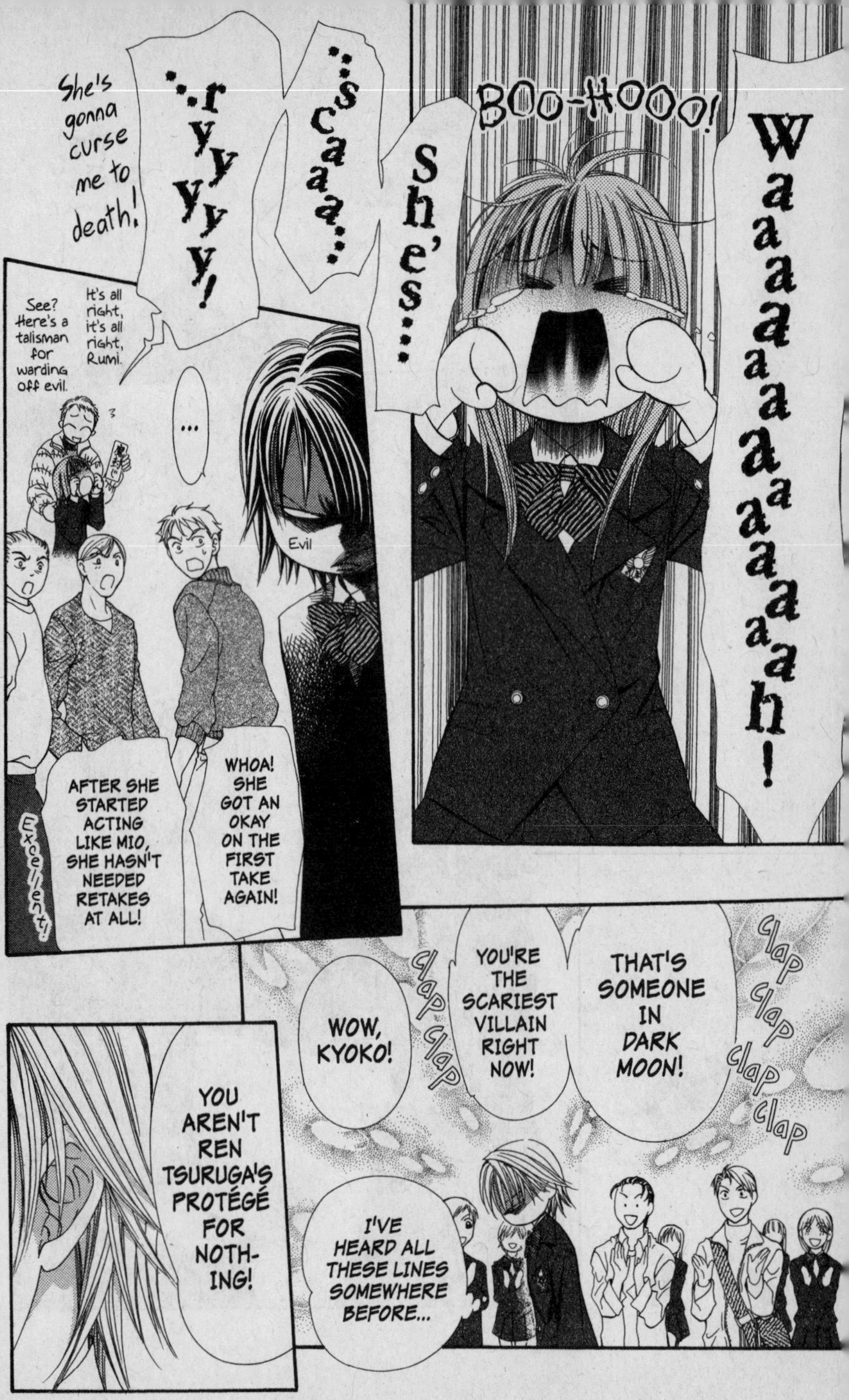
Waaaaaaaaaaaaah!
BOO-HOOO!
She's... scaaa... ryyyy!
She's gonna curse me to death!
...
It's all right, it's all right, Rumi.
See? Here's a talisman for warding off evil.
Evil
WHOA! SHE GOT AN OKAY ON THE FIRST TAKE AGAIN!
AFTER SHE STARTED ACTING LIKE MIO, SHE HASN'T NEEDED RETAKES AT ALL!
Excellent!
clap clap clap clap
THAT'S SOMEONE IN DARK MOON!
YOU'RE THE SCARIEST VILLAIN RIGHT NOW!
clap clap
WOW, KYOKO!
I'VE HEARD ALL THESE LINES SOMEWHERE BEFORE...
YOU AREN'T REN TSURUGA'S PROTÉGÉ FOR NOTH-ING!

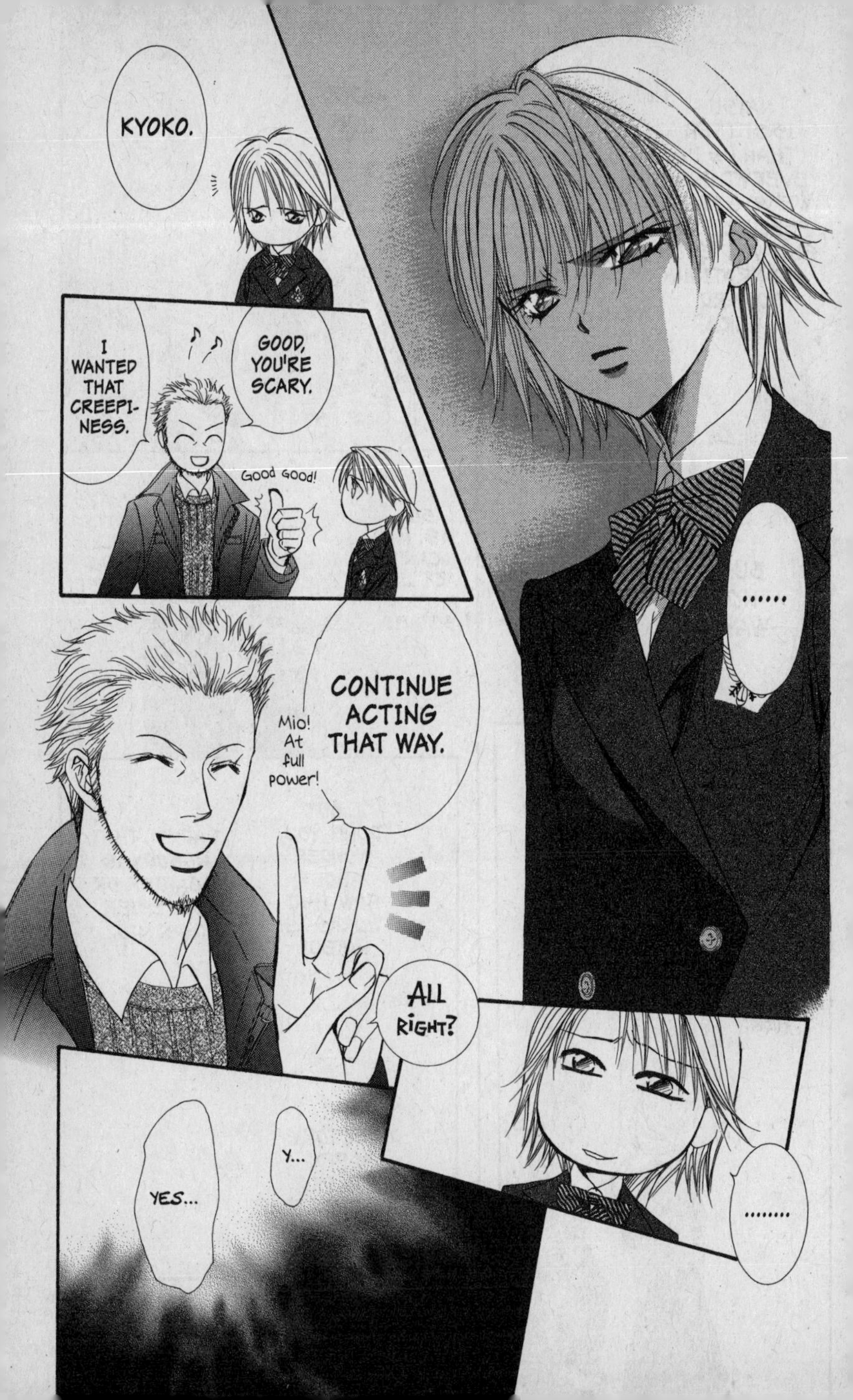
......
KYOKO.
GOOD, YOU'RE SCARY.
I WANTED THAT CREEPINESS.
Good Good!
CONTINUE ACTING THAT WAY.
Mio! At full power!
ALL RIGHT?
....
Y...
YES...

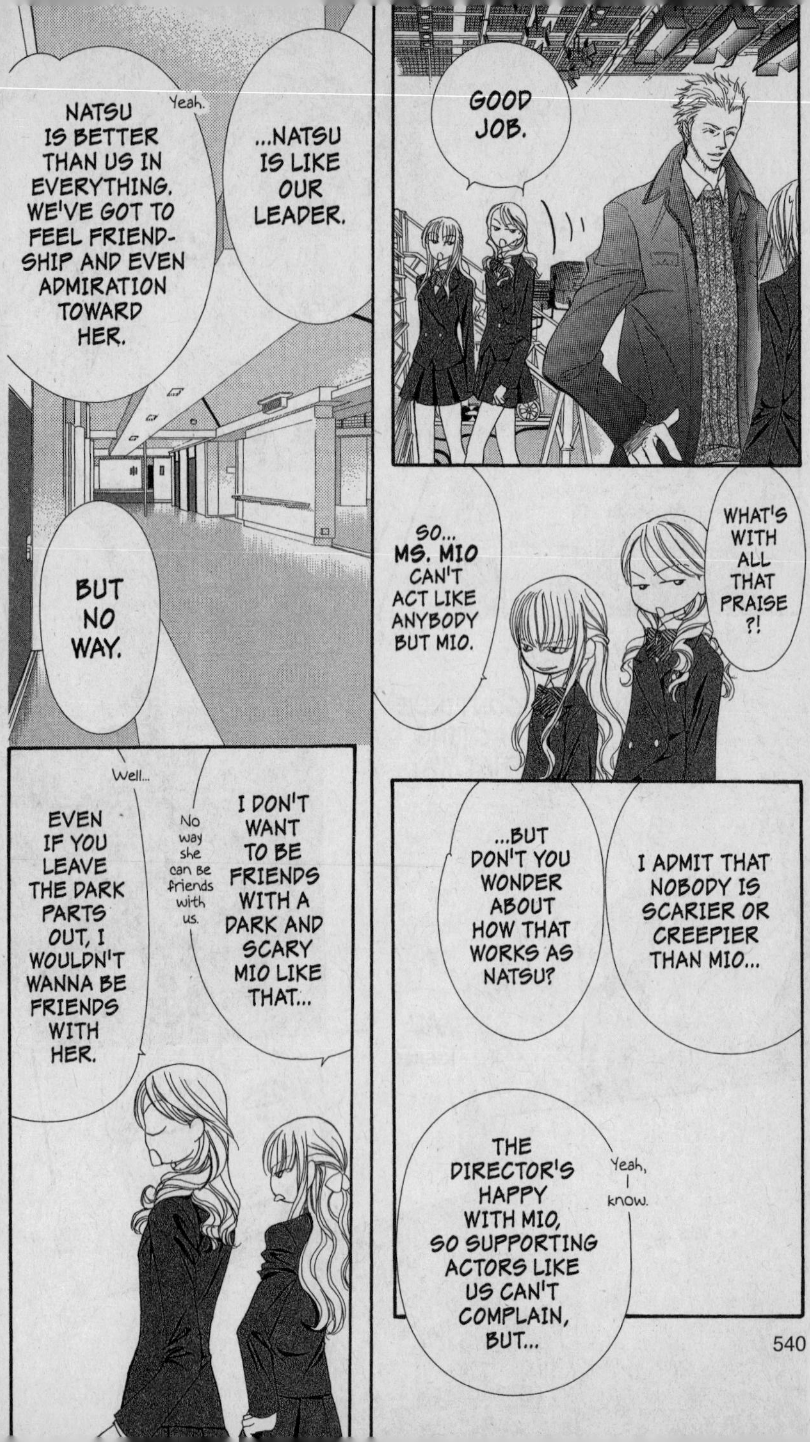
GOOD JOB.
WHAT'S WITH ALL THAT PRAISE ?!
SO... MS. MIO CAN'T ACT LIKE ANYBODY BUT MIO.
I ADMIT THAT NOBODY IS SCARIER OR CREEPIER THAN MIO...
...BUT DON'T YOU WONDER ABOUT HOW THAT WORKS AS NATSU?
Yeah, I know.
THE DIRECTOR'S HAPPY WITH MIO, SO SUPPORTING ACTORS LIKE US CAN'T COMPLAIN, BUT...
...NATSU IS LIKE OUR LEADER.
Yeah.
NATSU IS BETTER THAN US IN EVERYTHING. WE'VE GOT TO FEEL FRIEND-SHIP AND EVEN ADMIRATION TOWARD HER.
BUT NO WAY.
I DON'T WANT TO BE FRIENDS WITH A DARK AND SCARY MIO LIKE THAT...
No way she can be friends with us.
Well...
EVEN IF YOU LEAVE THE DARK PARTS OUT, I WOULDN'T WANNA BE FRIENDS WITH HER.

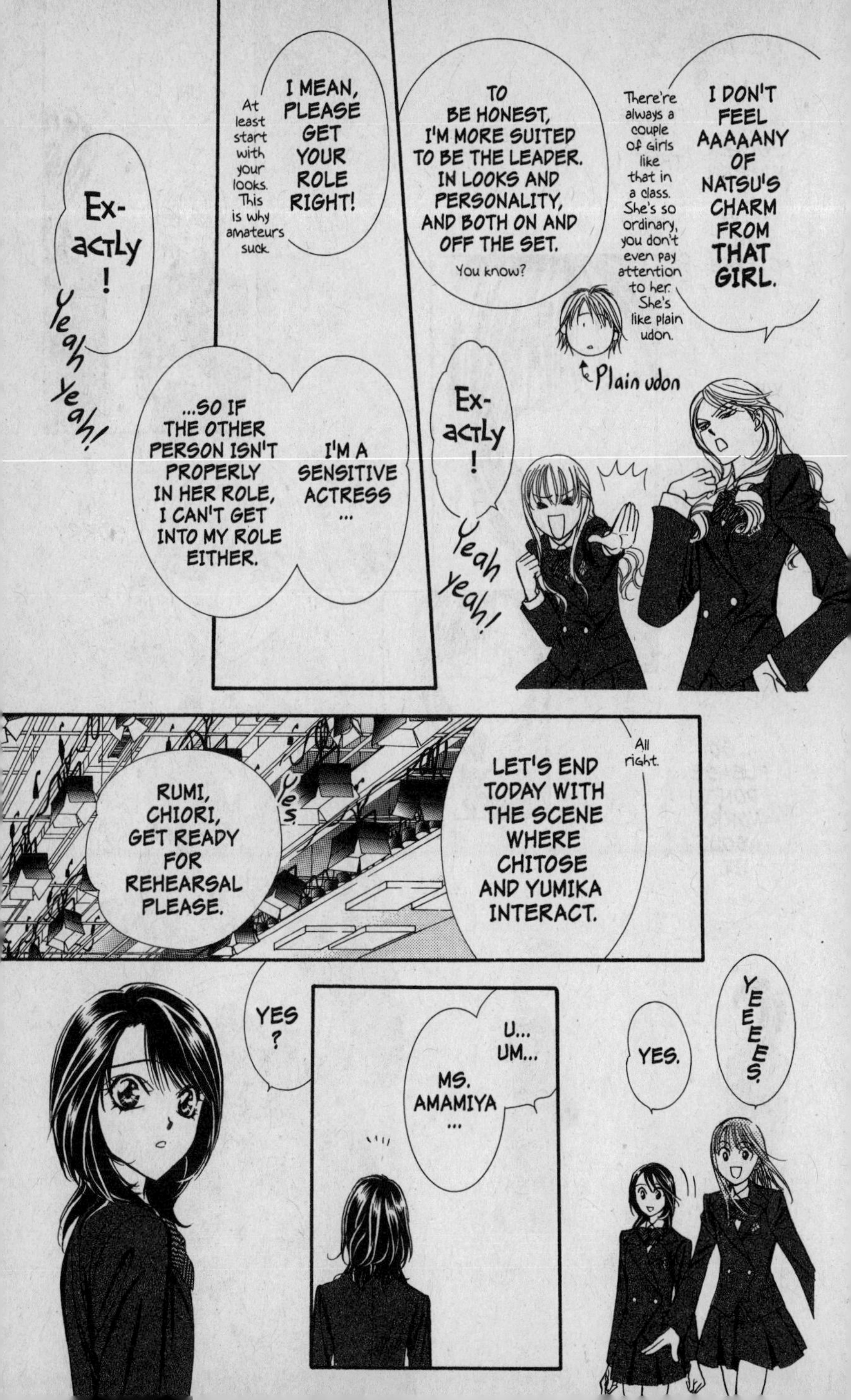

I DON'T FEEL AAAAANY OF NATSU'S CHARM FROM THAT GIRL.
There're always a couple of girls like that in a class. She's so ordinary, you don't even pay attention to her. She's like plain udon.
Plain udon
TO BE HONEST, I'M MORE SUITED TO BE THE LEADER. IN LOOKS AND PERSONALITY, AND BOTH ON AND OFF THE SET.
You know?
Ex-actly!
Yeah yeah!
I MEAN, PLEASE GET YOUR ROLE RIGHT!
At least start with your looks. This is why amateurs suck
I'M A SENSITIVE ACTRESS...
...SO IF THE OTHER PERSON ISN'T PROPERLY IN HER ROLE, I CAN'T GET INTO MY ROLE EITHER.
Ex-actly!
Yeah yeah!
All right.
LET'S END TODAY WITH THE SCENE WHERE CHITOSE AND YUMIKA INTERACT.
Yes.
RUMI, CHIORI, GET READY FOR REHEARSAL PLEASE.
YEEEES.
YES.
U... UM...
MS. AMAMIYA...
YES?

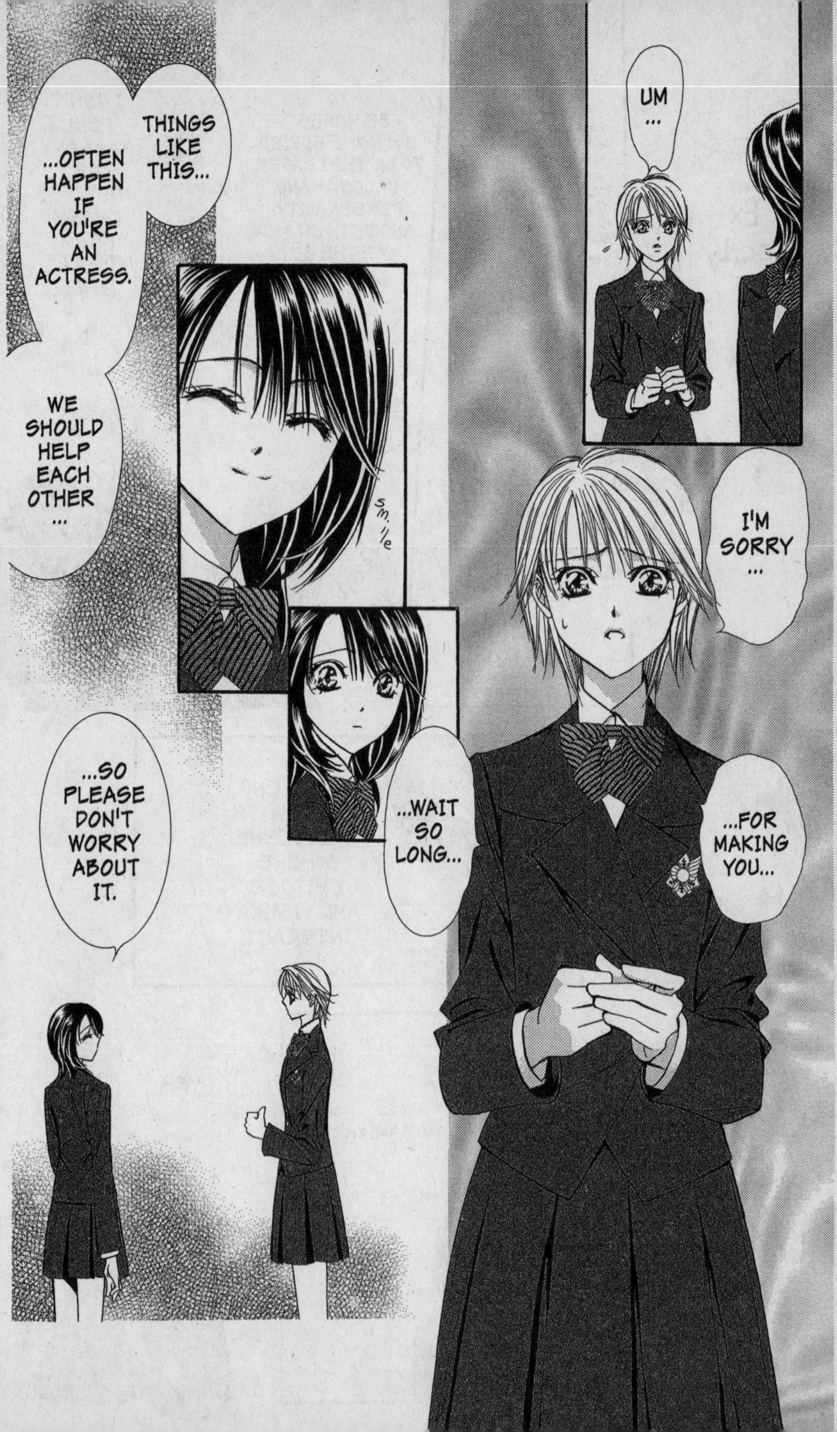
UM ...
I'M SORRY ...
...FOR MAKING YOU...
...WAIT SO LONG...
THINGS LIKE THIS...
...OFTEN HAPPEN IF YOU'RE AN ACTRESS.
smile
WE SHOULD HELP EACH OTHER ...
...SO PLEASE DON'T WORRY ABOUT IT.

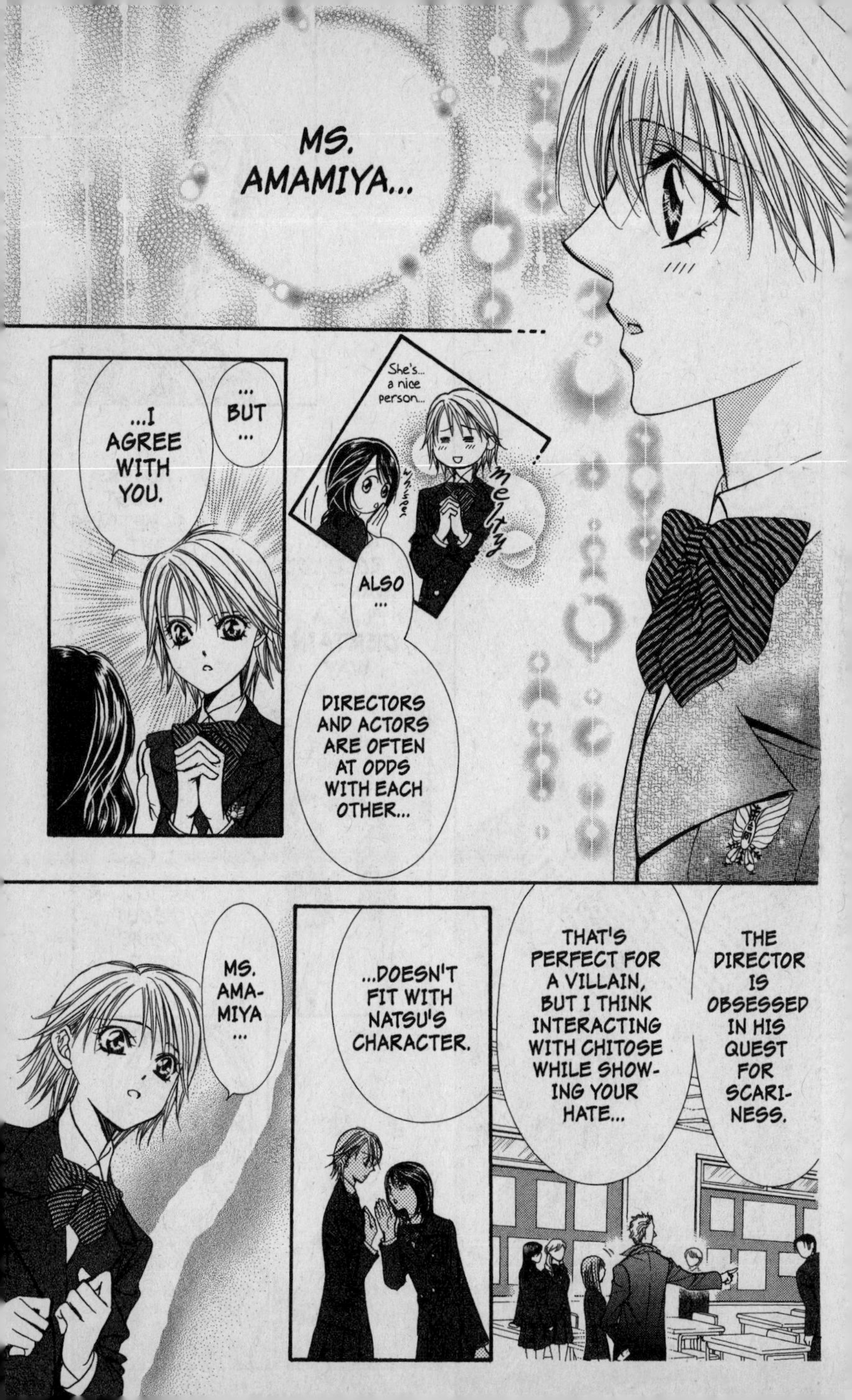
MS. AMAMIYA...
She's... a nice person...
whisper
melty
ALSO...
DIRECTORS AND ACTORS ARE OFTEN AT ODDS WITH EACH OTHER...
...BUT...
...I AGREE WITH YOU.
THE DIRECTOR IS OBSESSED IN HIS QUEST FOR SCARINESS.
THAT'S PERFECT FOR A VILLAIN, BUT I THINK INTERACTING WITH CHITOSE WHILE SHOWING YOUR HATE...
...DOESN'T FIT WITH NATSU'S CHARACTER.
MS. AMA-MIYA...

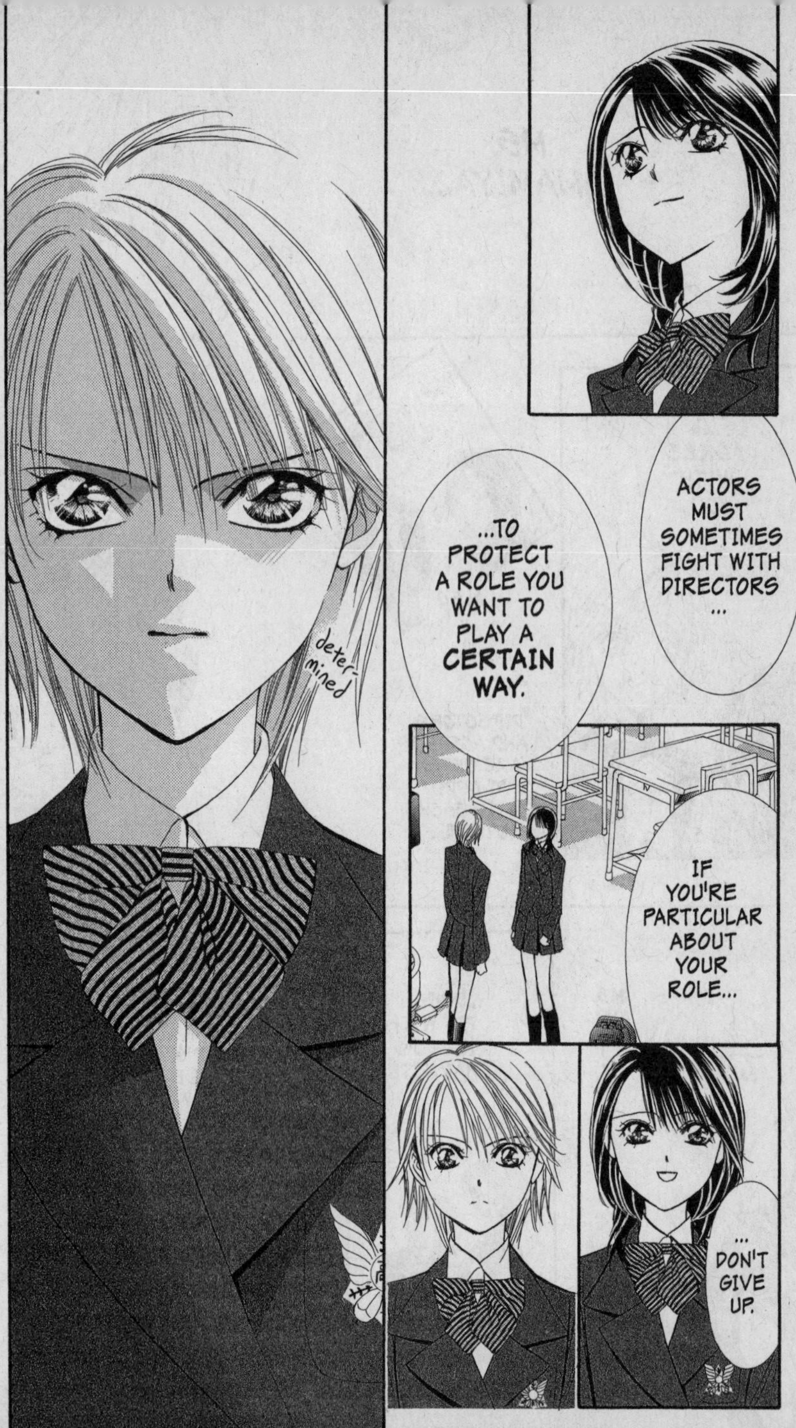
ACTORS MUST SOMETIMES FIGHT WITH DIRECTORS ...
...TO PROTECT A ROLE YOU WANT TO PLAY A **CERTAIN WAY.**
IF YOU'RE PARTICULAR ABOUT YOUR ROLE...
... DON'T GIVE UP.
deter-mined

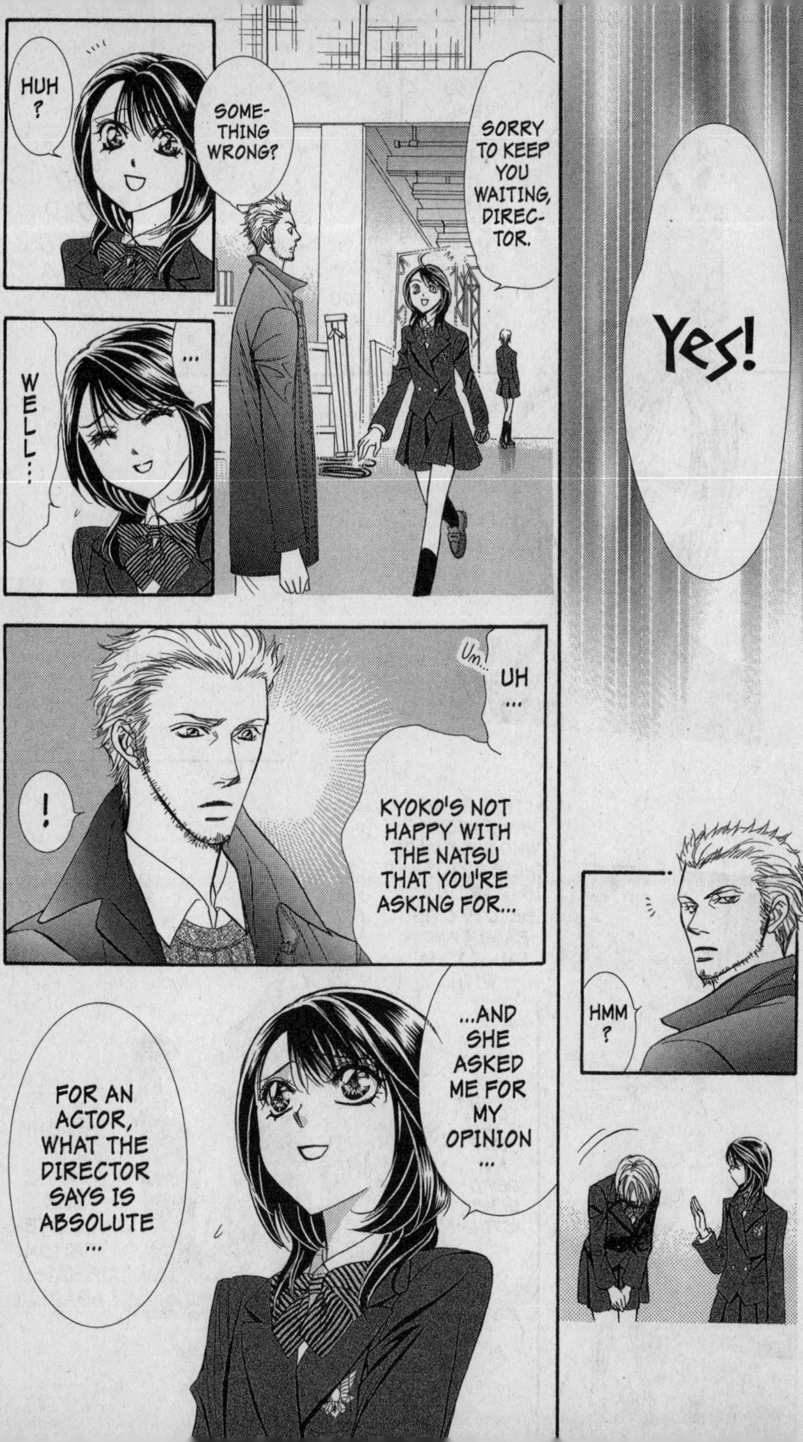

Yes!
HMM?
SORRY TO KEEP YOU WAITING, DIRECTOR.
SOME-THING WRONG?
HUH?
...
WELL...
Um...
UH...
KYOKO'S NOT HAPPY WITH THE NATSU THAT YOU'RE ASKING FOR...
!
...AND SHE ASKED ME FOR MY OPINION...
FOR AN ACTOR, WHAT THE DIRECTOR SAYS IS ABSOLUTE...

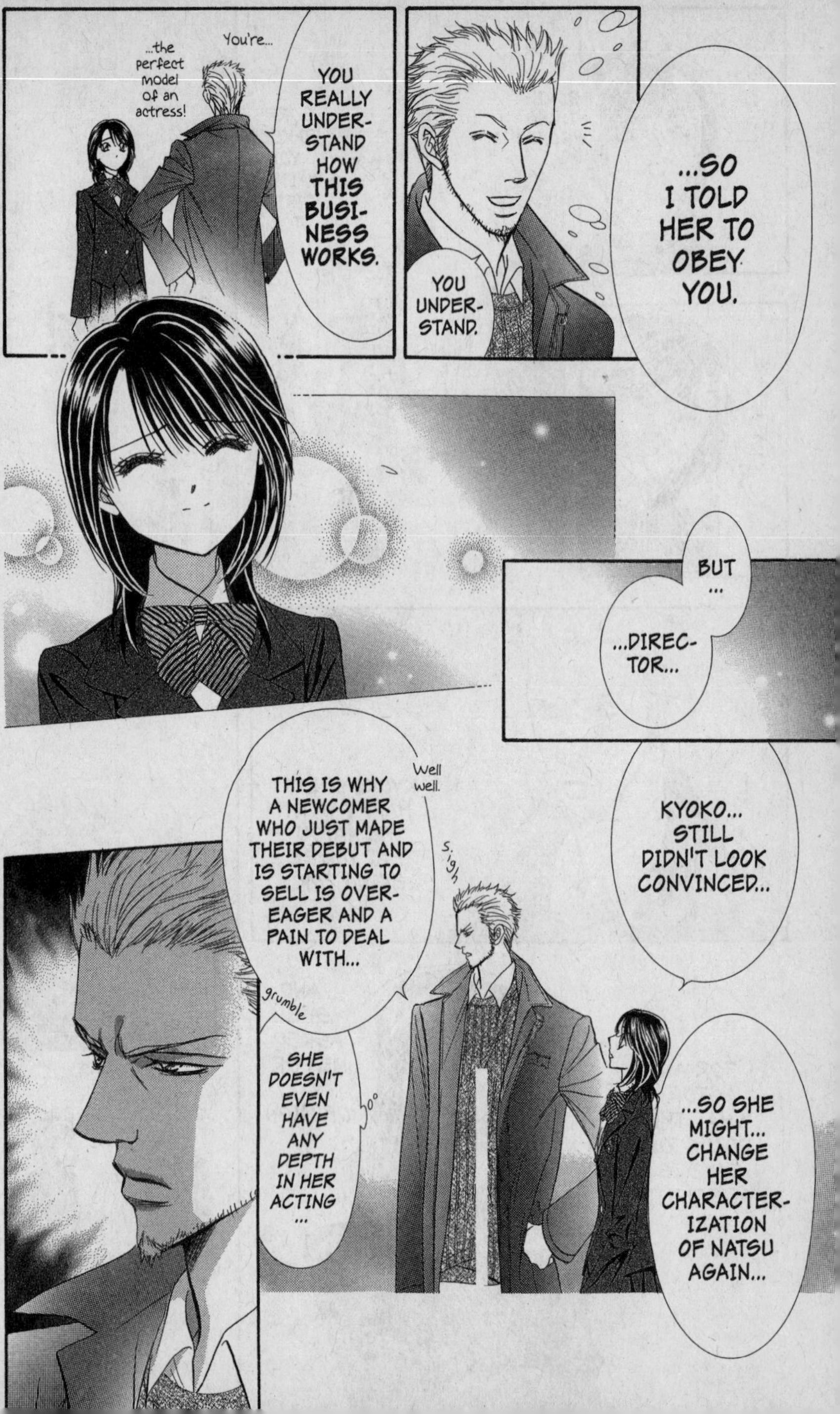
...SO I TOLD HER TO OBEY YOU.
YOU UNDERSTAND.
YOU REALLY UNDERSTAND HOW THIS BUSINESS WORKS.
You're...
...the perfect model of an actress!
BUT...
...DIRECTOR...
KYOKO... STILL DIDN'T LOOK CONVINCED...
...SO SHE MIGHT... CHANGE HER CHARACTERIZATION OF NATSU AGAIN...
Well well.
sigh
THIS IS WHY A NEWCOMER WHO JUST MADE THEIR DEBUT AND IS STARTING TO SELL IS OVER-EAGER AND A PAIN TO DEAL WITH...
grumble
SHE DOESN'T EVEN HAVE ANY DEPTH IN HER ACTING...

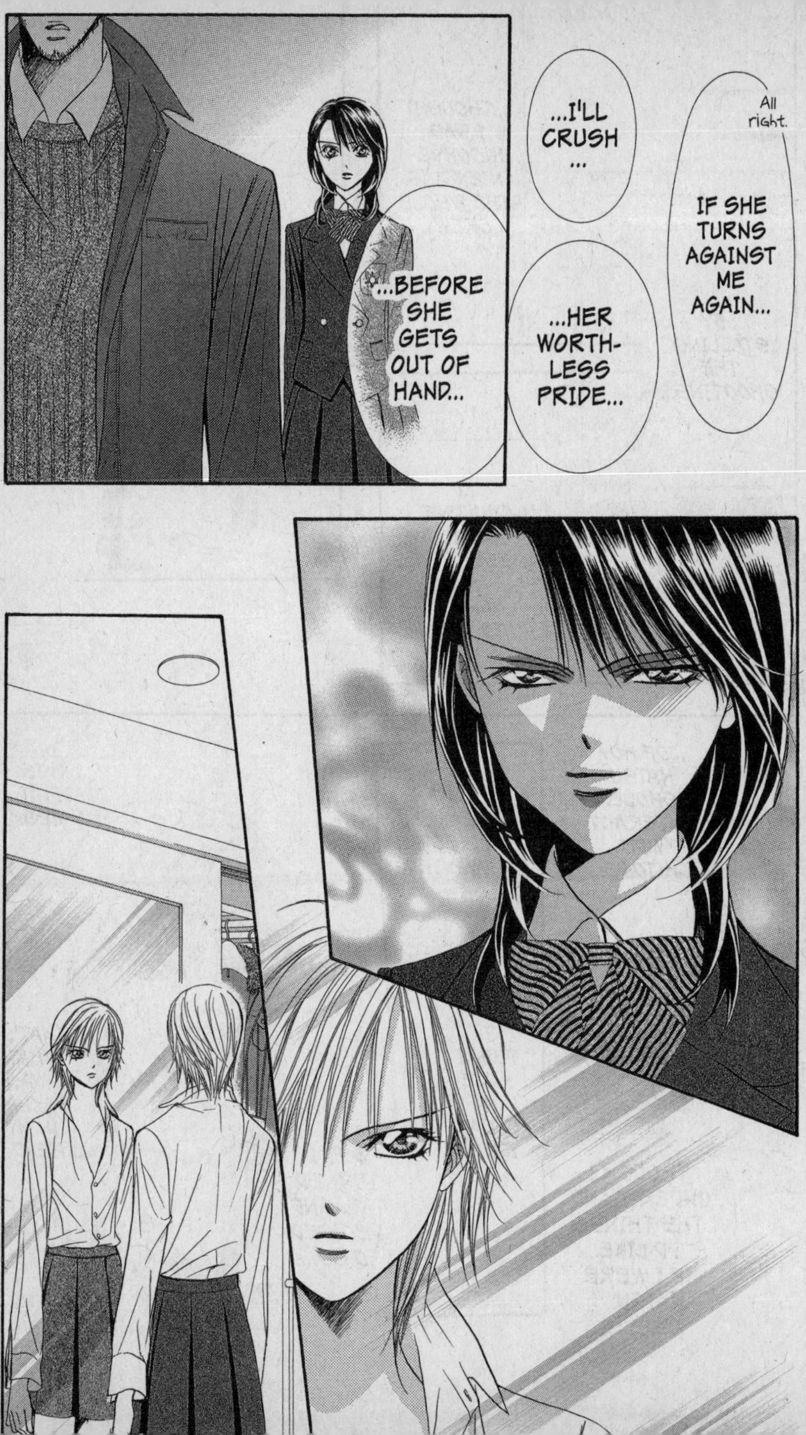
All right.
IF SHE TURNS AGAINST ME AGAIN...
...I'LL CRUSH...
...HER WORTH-LESS PRIDE...
...BEFORE SHE GETS OUT OF HAND...

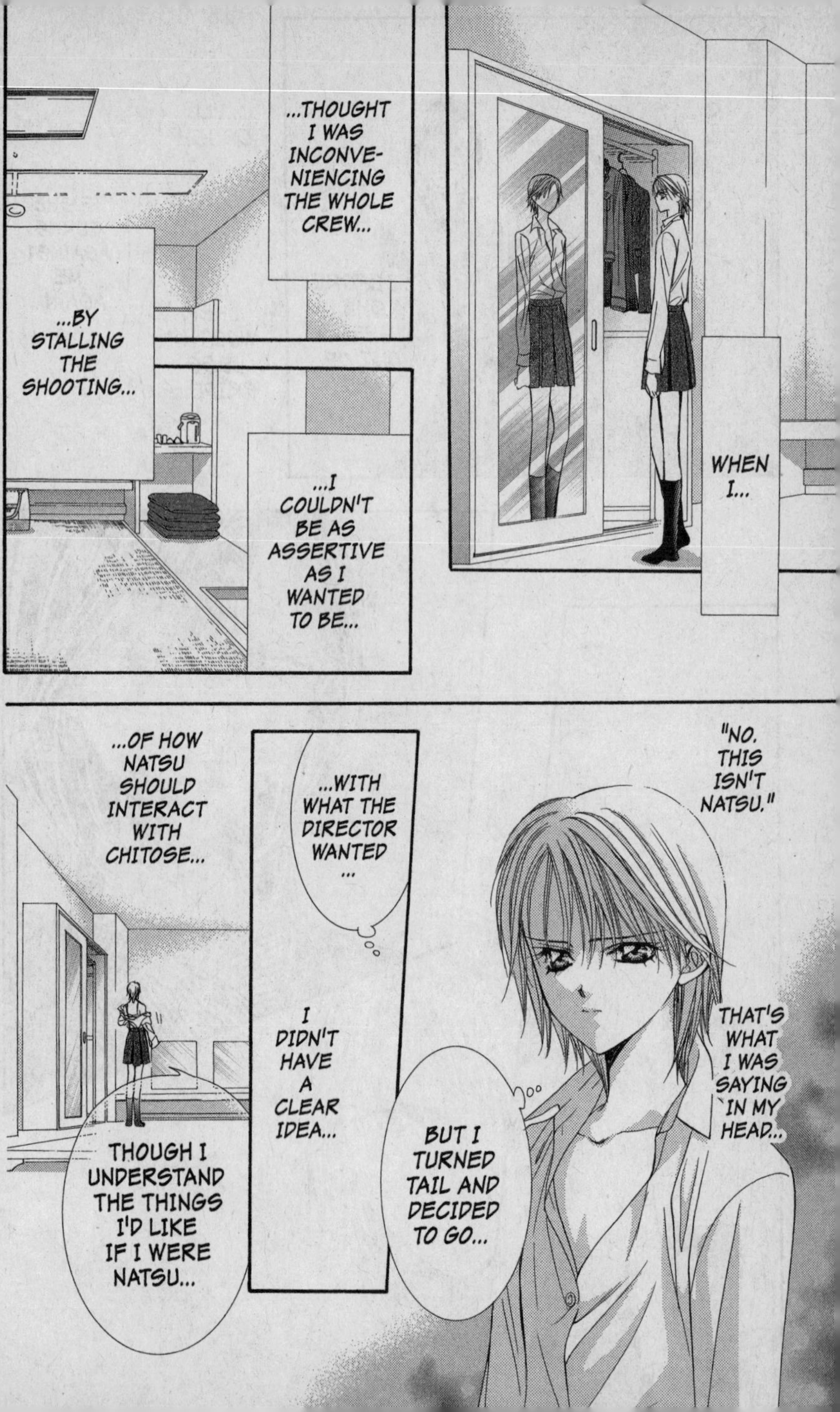
WHEN I...
...THOUGHT I WAS INCONVENIENCING THE WHOLE CREW...
...BY STALLING THE SHOOTING...
...I COULDN'T BE AS ASSERTIVE AS I WANTED TO BE...
"NO. THIS ISN'T NATSU."
THAT'S WHAT I WAS SAYING IN MY HEAD...
BUT I TURNED TAIL AND DECIDED TO GO...
...WITH WHAT THE DIRECTOR WANTED...
I DIDN'T HAVE A CLEAR IDEA...
...OF HOW NATSU SHOULD INTERACT WITH CHITOSE...
THOUGH I UNDERSTAND THE THINGS I'D LIKE IF I WERE NATSU...

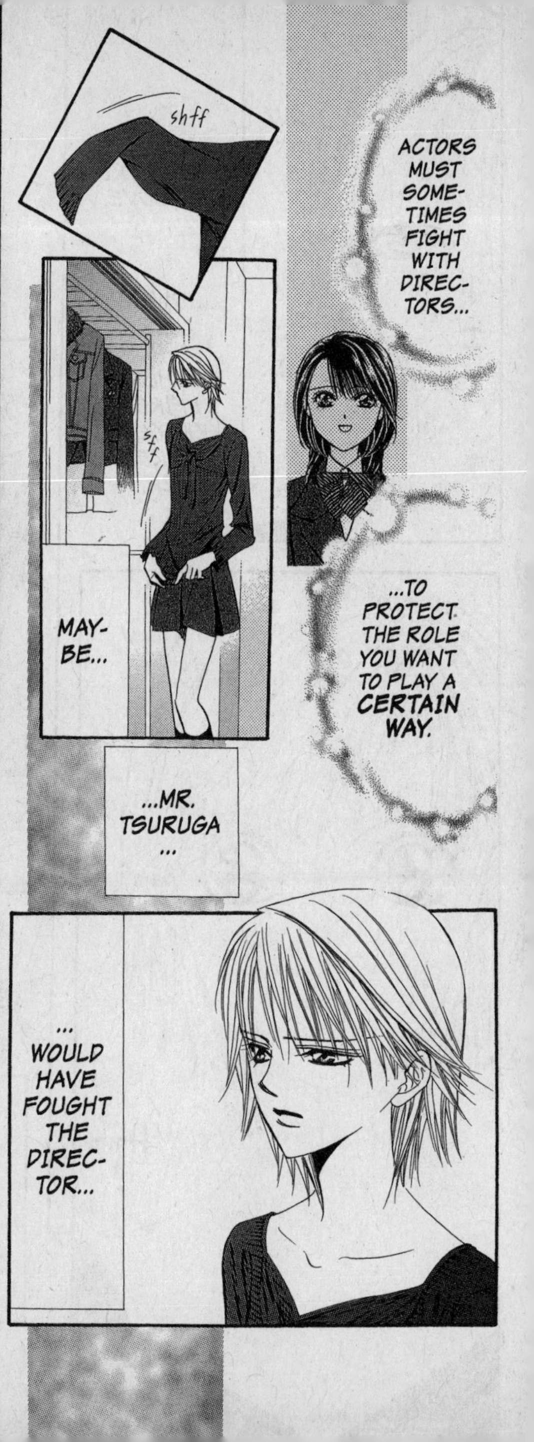
ACTORS MUST SOME-TIMES FIGHT WITH DIREC-TORS...
shff
...TO PROTECT THE ROLE YOU WANT TO PLAY A CERTAIN WAY.
sff
MAY-BE...
...MR. TSURUGA ...
... WOULD HAVE FOUGHT THE DIREC-TOR...
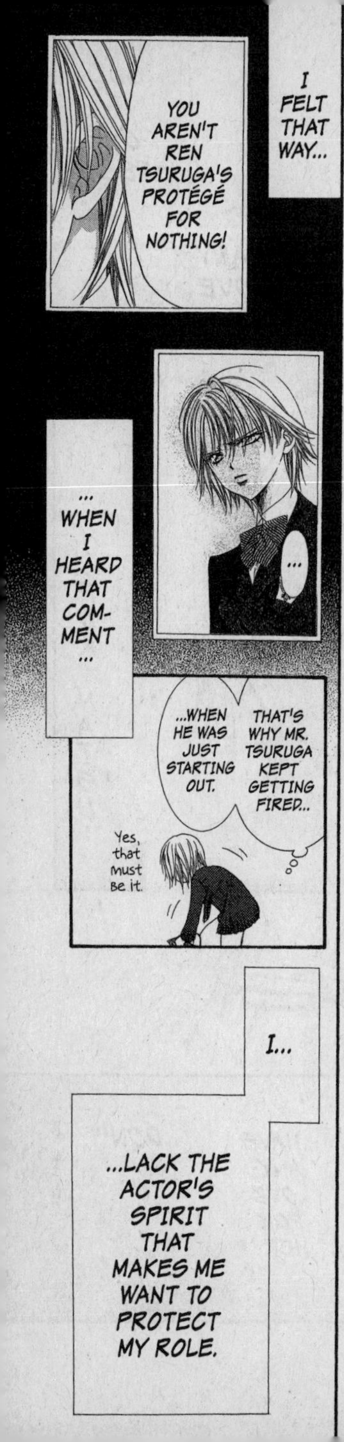
I FELT THAT WAY...
YOU AREN'T REN TSURUGA'S PROTÉGÉ FOR NOTHING!
...
... WHEN I HEARD THAT COM-MENT ...
THAT'S WHY MR. TSURUGA KEPT GETTING FIRED...
...WHEN HE WAS JUST STARTING OUT.
Yes, that must be it.
I...
...LACK THE ACTOR'S SPIRIT THAT MAKES ME WANT TO PROTECT MY ROLE.

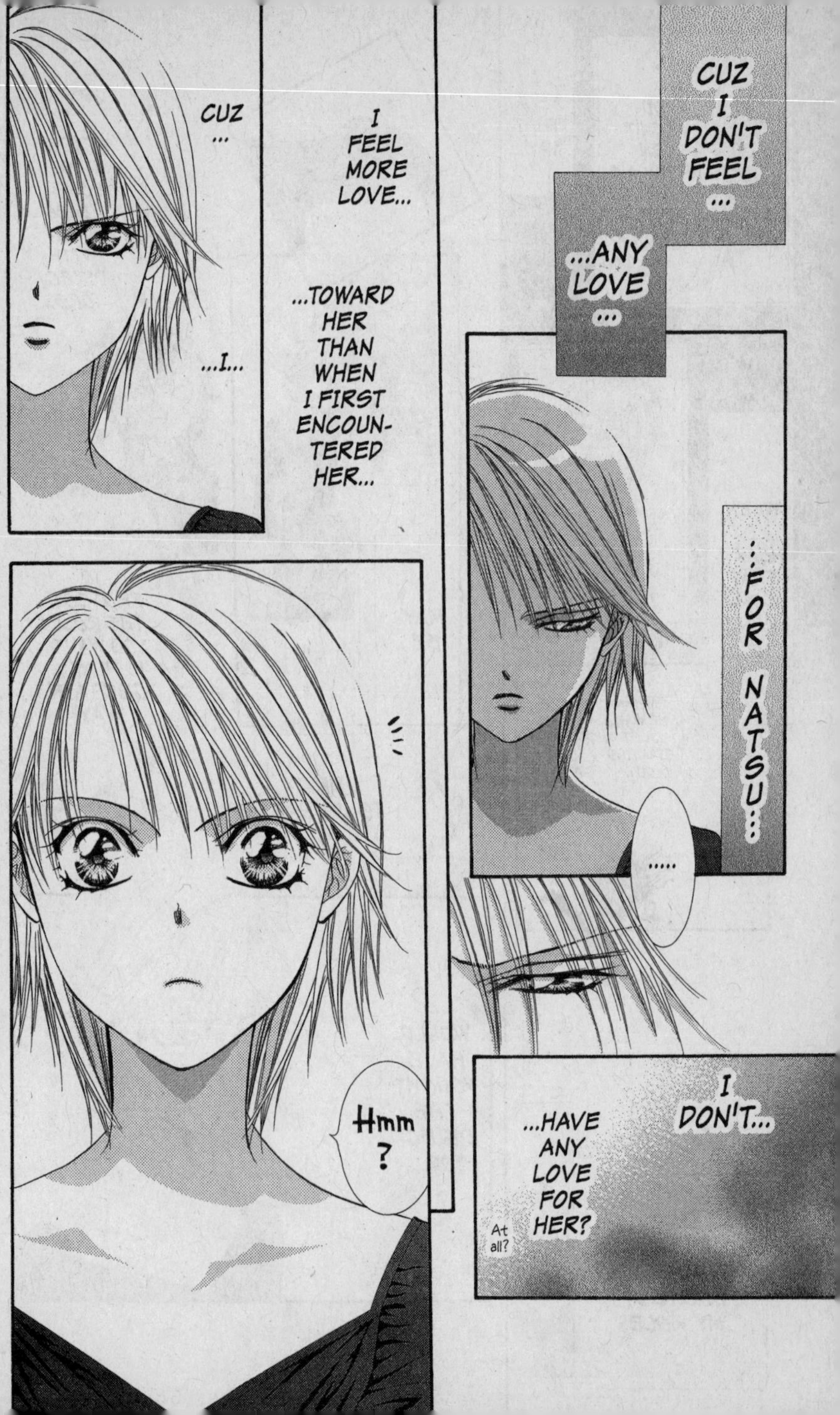
CUZ I DON'T FEEL...
...ANY LOVE...
I FEEL MORE LOVE...
...TOWARD HER THAN WHEN I FIRST ENCOUNTERED HER...
CUZ...
...I...
...FOR NATSU...
.....
Hmm?
I DON'T...
...HAVE ANY LOVE FOR HER?
At all?

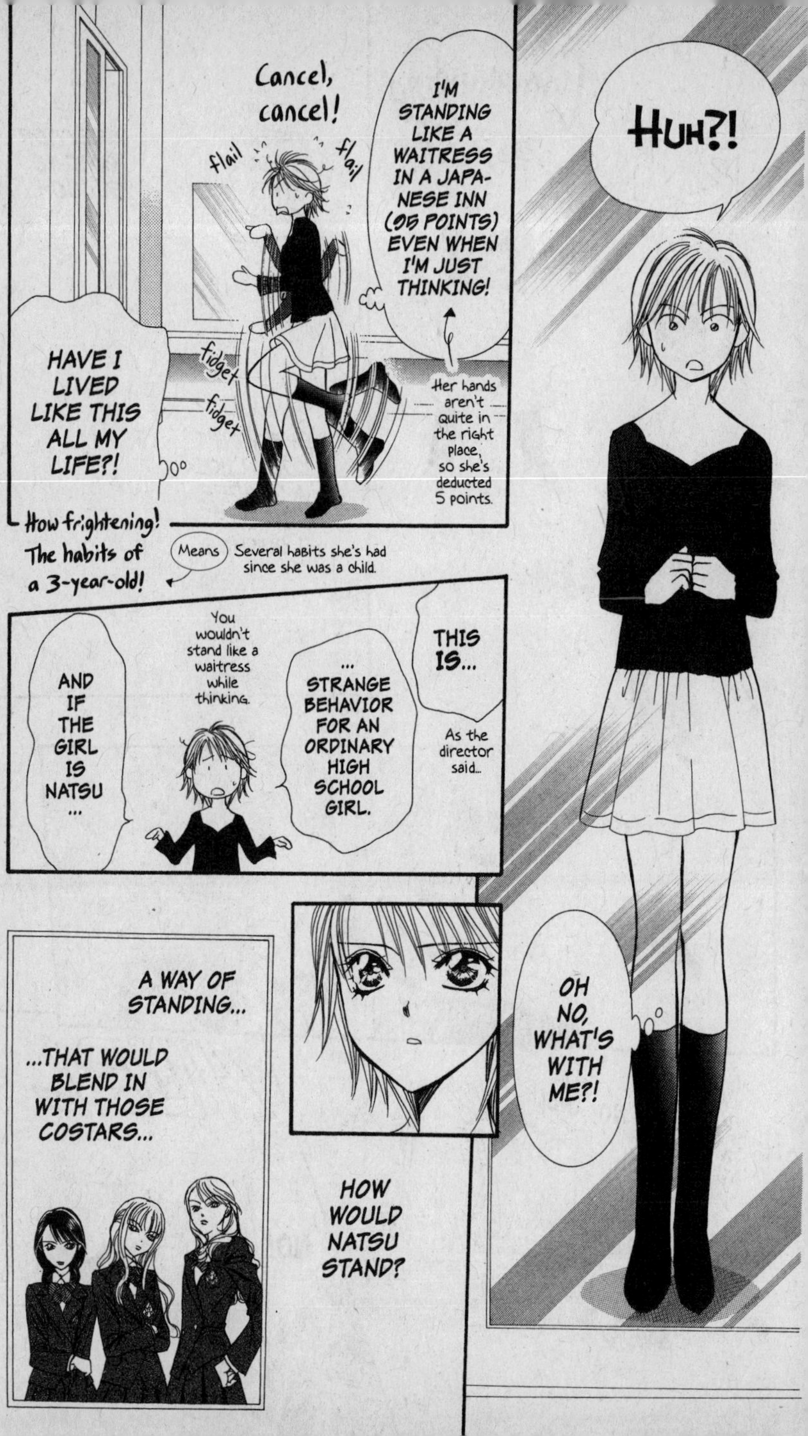
HUH?!
OH NO, WHAT'S WITH ME?!
I'M STANDING LIKE A WAITRESS IN A JAPANESE INN (95 POINTS) EVEN WHEN I'M JUST THINKING!
Her hands aren't quite in the right place, so she's deducted 5 points.
Cancel, cancel!
flail flail
fidget fidget
HAVE I LIVED LIKE THIS ALL MY LIFE?!
How frightening! The habits of a 3-year-old!
Means Several habits she's had since she was a child.
THIS IS...
As the director said...
... STRANGE BEHAVIOR FOR AN ORDINARY HIGH SCHOOL GIRL.
You wouldn't stand like a waitress while thinking.
AND IF THE GIRL IS NATSU ...
HOW WOULD NATSU STAND?
A WAY OF STANDING...
...THAT WOULD BLEND IN WITH THOSE COSTARS...

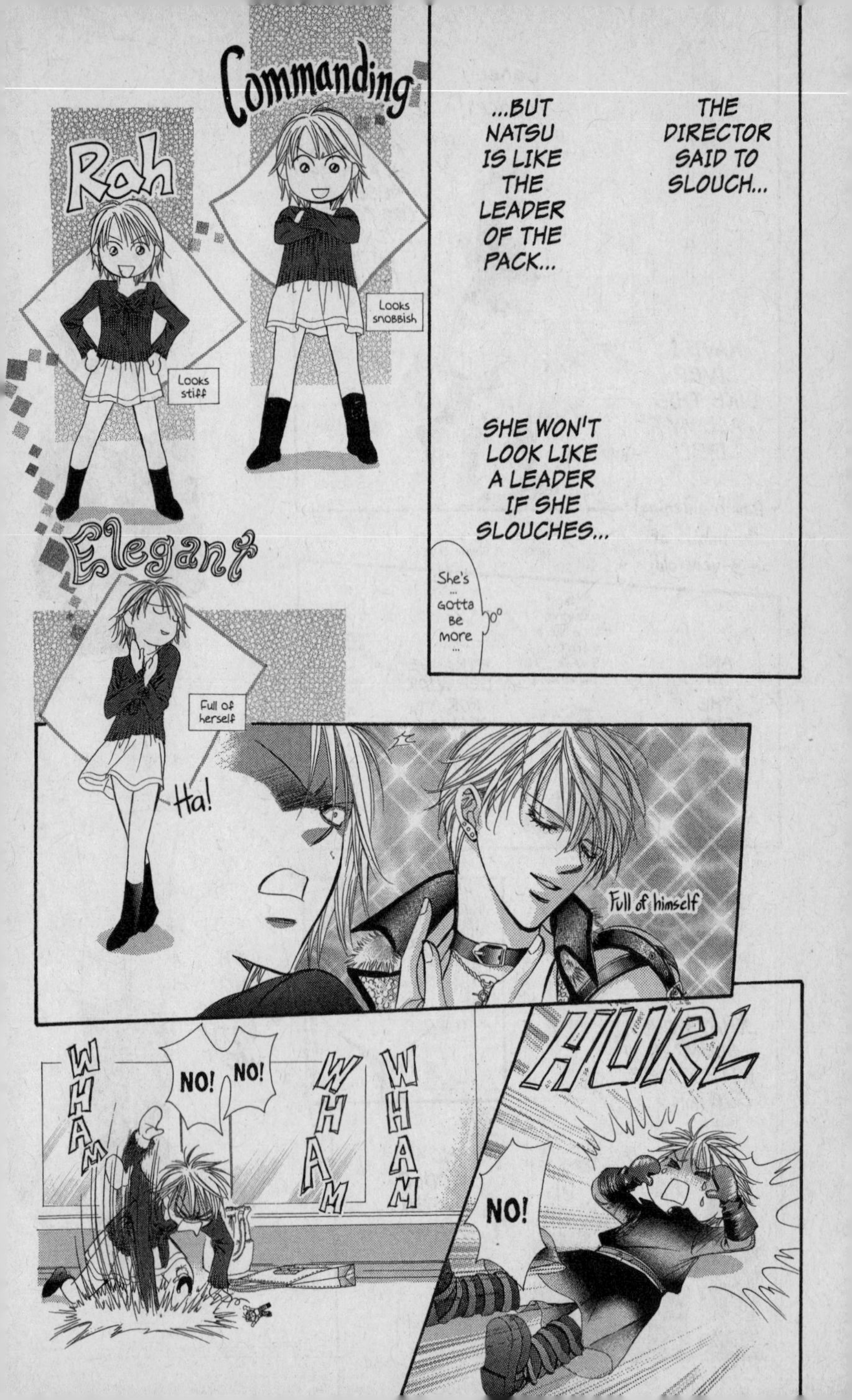
THE DIRECTOR SAID TO SLOUCH...
...BUT NATSU IS LIKE THE LEADER OF THE PACK...
SHE WON'T LOOK LIKE A LEADER IF SHE SLOUCHES...
She's... gotta be more...
Commanding
Looks snobbish
Rah
Looks stiff
Elegant
Full of herself
Ha!
Full of himself
HURL
NO!
WHAM
WHAM
WHAM
NO!
NO!

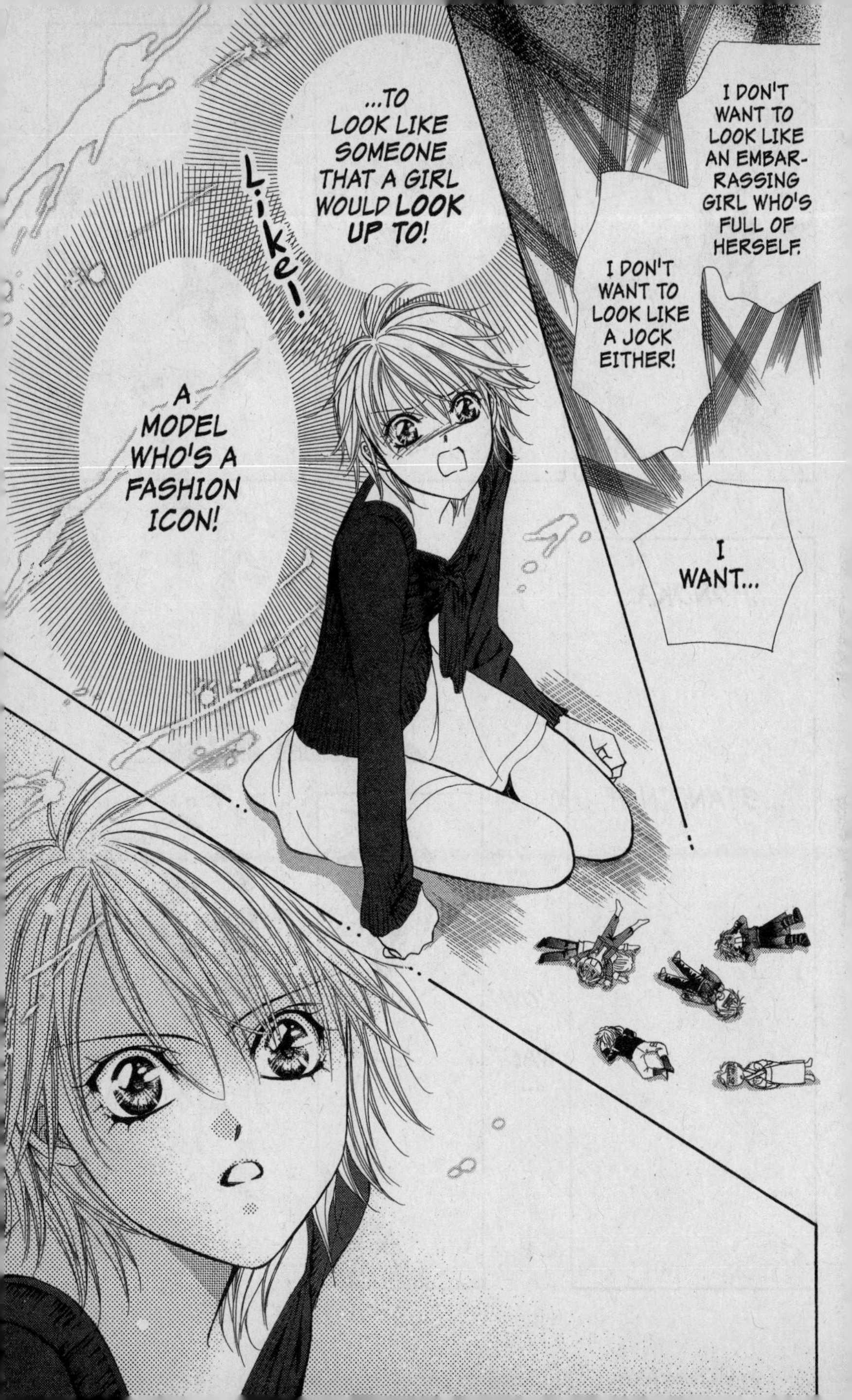
I DON'T WANT TO LOOK LIKE AN EMBARRASSING GIRL WHO'S FULL OF HERSELF.
I DON'T WANT TO LOOK LIKE A JOCK EITHER!
I WANT...
...TO LOOK LIKE SOMEONE THAT A GIRL WOULD LOOK UP TO!
Like!
A MODEL WHO'S A FASHION ICON!

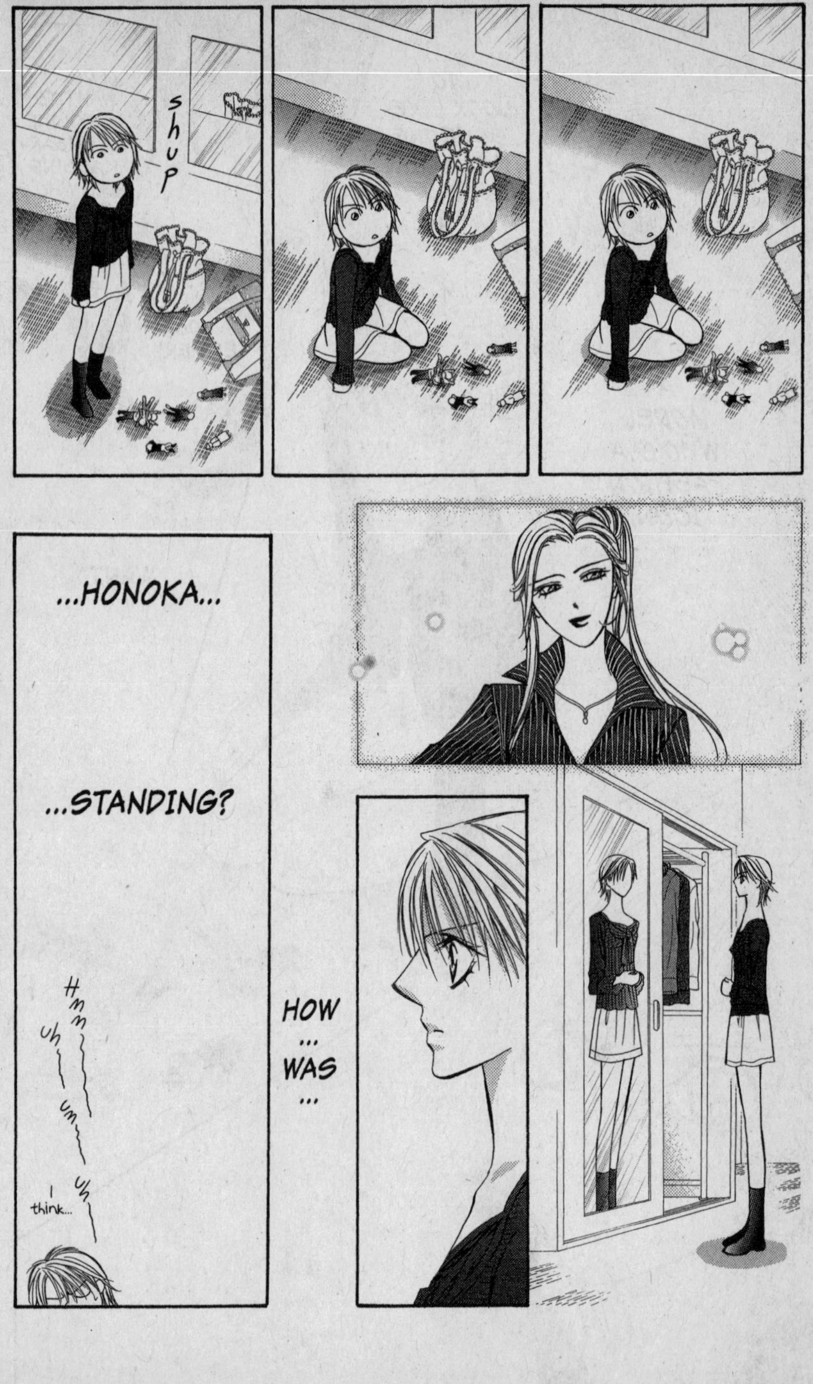
shup
HOW ... WAS ...
...HONOKA...
...STANDING?
Hmm~ uh~ um~ uh~
I think...

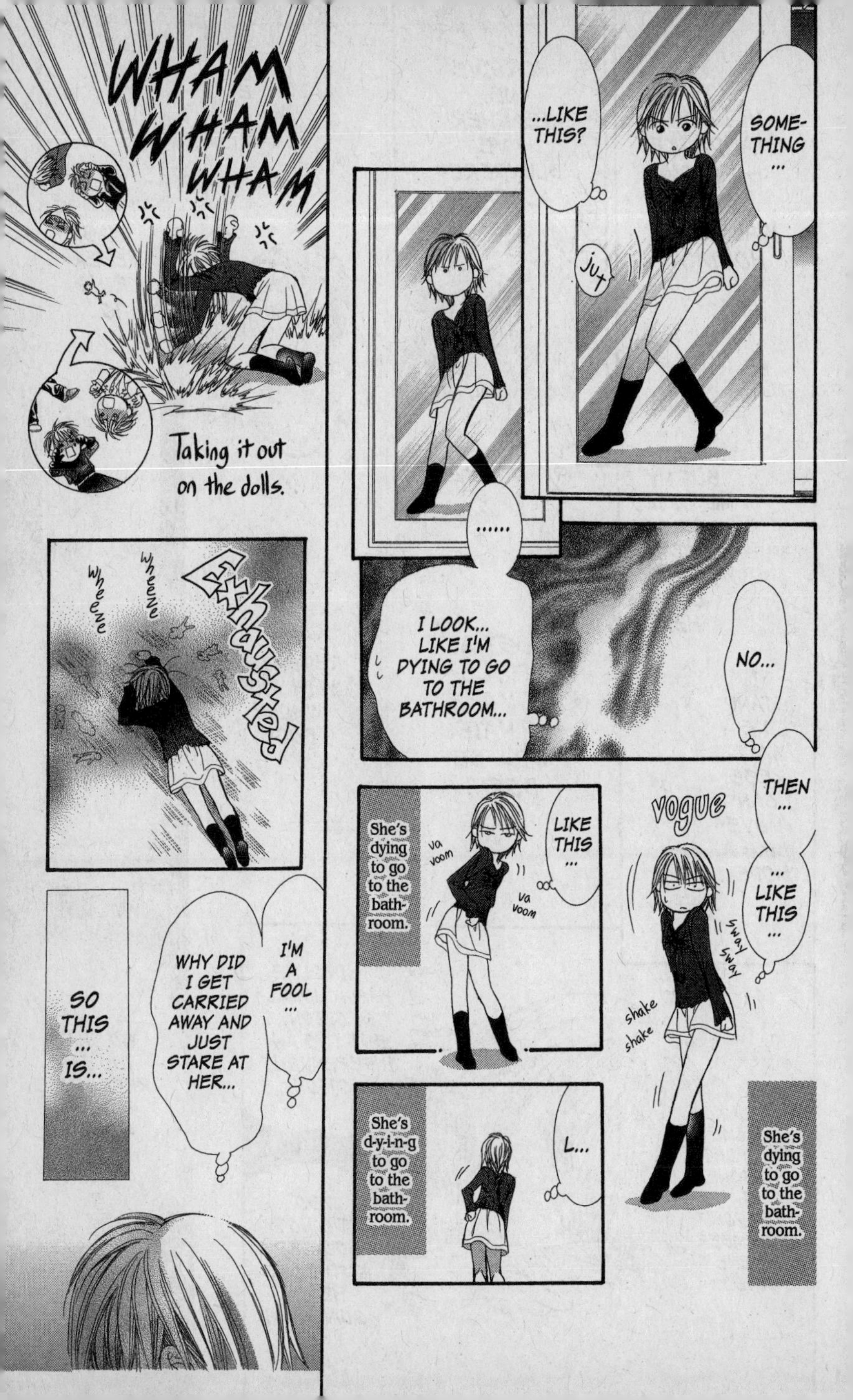
SOME-THING ...
...LIKE THIS?
jut
......
I LOOK... LIKE I'M DYING TO GO TO THE BATHROOM...
NO...
THEN ...
... LIKE THIS ...
vogue
sway sway
shake shake
She's dying to go to the bath-room.
LIKE THIS ...
va voom
va voom
She's dying to go to the bath-room.
L...
She's d-y-i-n-g to go to the bath-room.
WHAM WHAM WHAM
Taking it out on the dolls.
Exhausted
wheeze
wheeze
I'M A FOOL ...
WHY DID I GET CARRIED AWAY AND JUST STARE AT HER...
SO THIS ... IS...

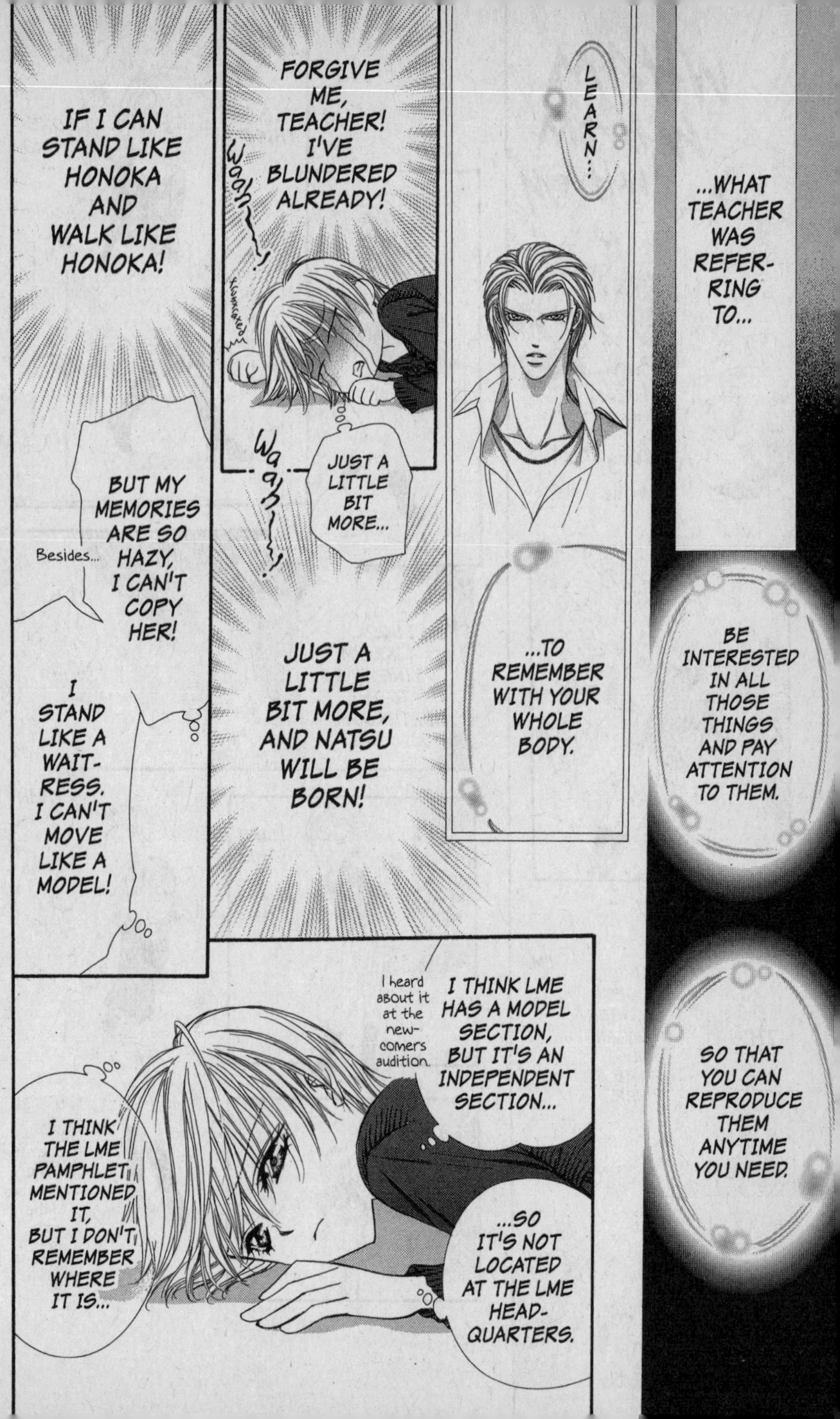
...WHAT TEACHER WAS REFERRING TO...
BE INTERESTED IN ALL THOSE THINGS AND PAY ATTENTION TO THEM.
SO THAT YOU CAN REPRODUCE THEM ANYTIME YOU NEED.
LEARN...
...TO REMEMBER WITH YOUR WHOLE BODY.
FORGIVE ME, TEACHER! I'VE BLUNDERED ALREADY!
JUST A LITTLE BIT MORE...
JUST A LITTLE BIT MORE, AND NATSU WILL BE BORN!
IF I CAN STAND LIKE HONOKA AND WALK LIKE HONOKA!
BUT MY MEMORIES ARE SO HAZY, I CAN'T COPY HER!
Besides...
I STAND LIKE A WAITRESS. I CAN'T MOVE LIKE A MODEL!
I THINK LME HAS A MODEL SECTION, BUT IT'S AN INDEPENDENT SECTION...
I heard about it at the newcomers audition.
...SO IT'S NOT LOCATED AT THE LME HEADQUARTERS.
I THINK THE LME PAMPHLET MENTIONED IT, BUT I DON'T REMEMBER WHERE IT IS...

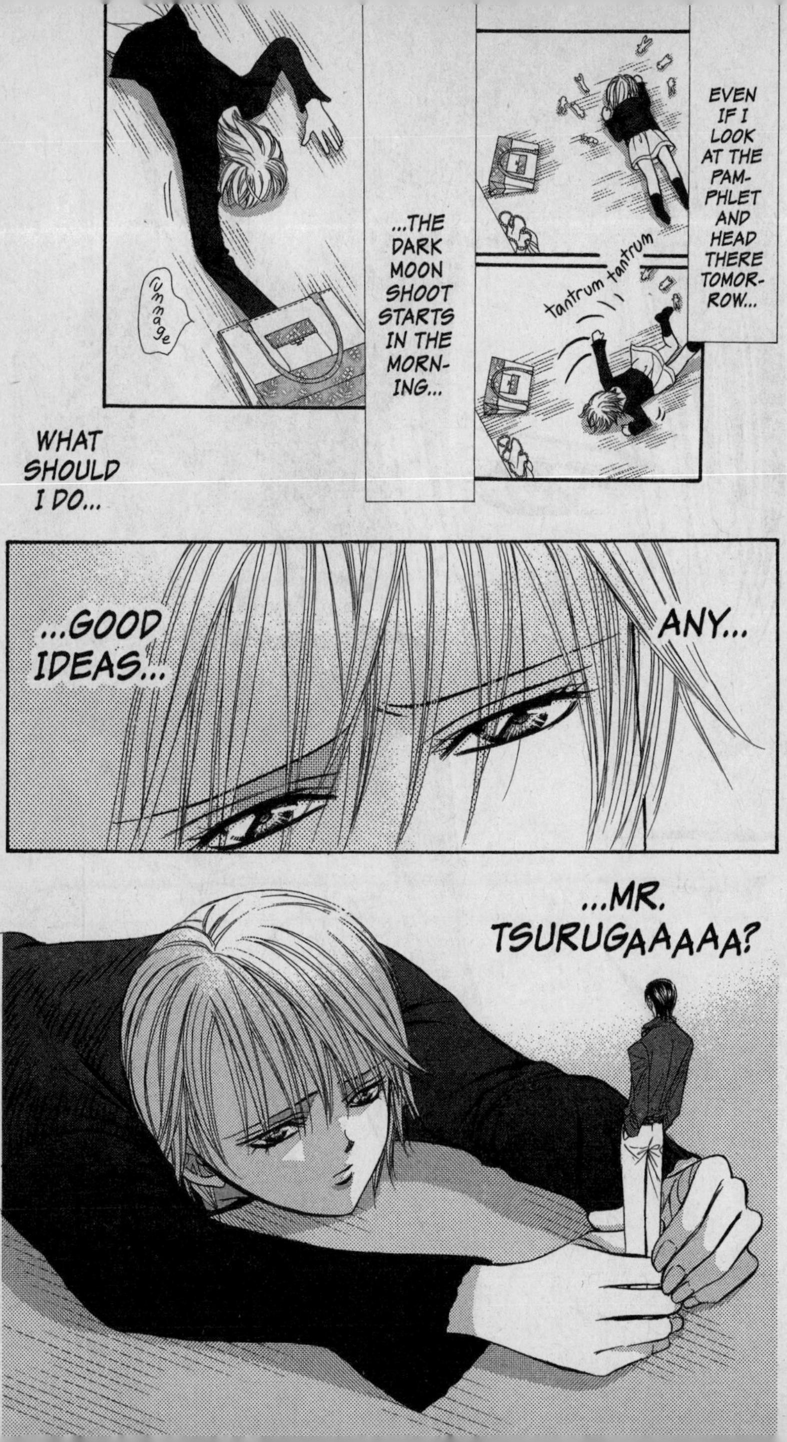

EVEN IF I LOOK AT THE PAMPHLET AND HEAD THERE TOMORROW...
tantrum tantrum
...THE DARK MOON SHOOT STARTS IN THE MORNING...
rummage
WHAT SHOULD I DO...
ANY...
...GOOD IDEAS...
...MR. TSURUGAAAAA?

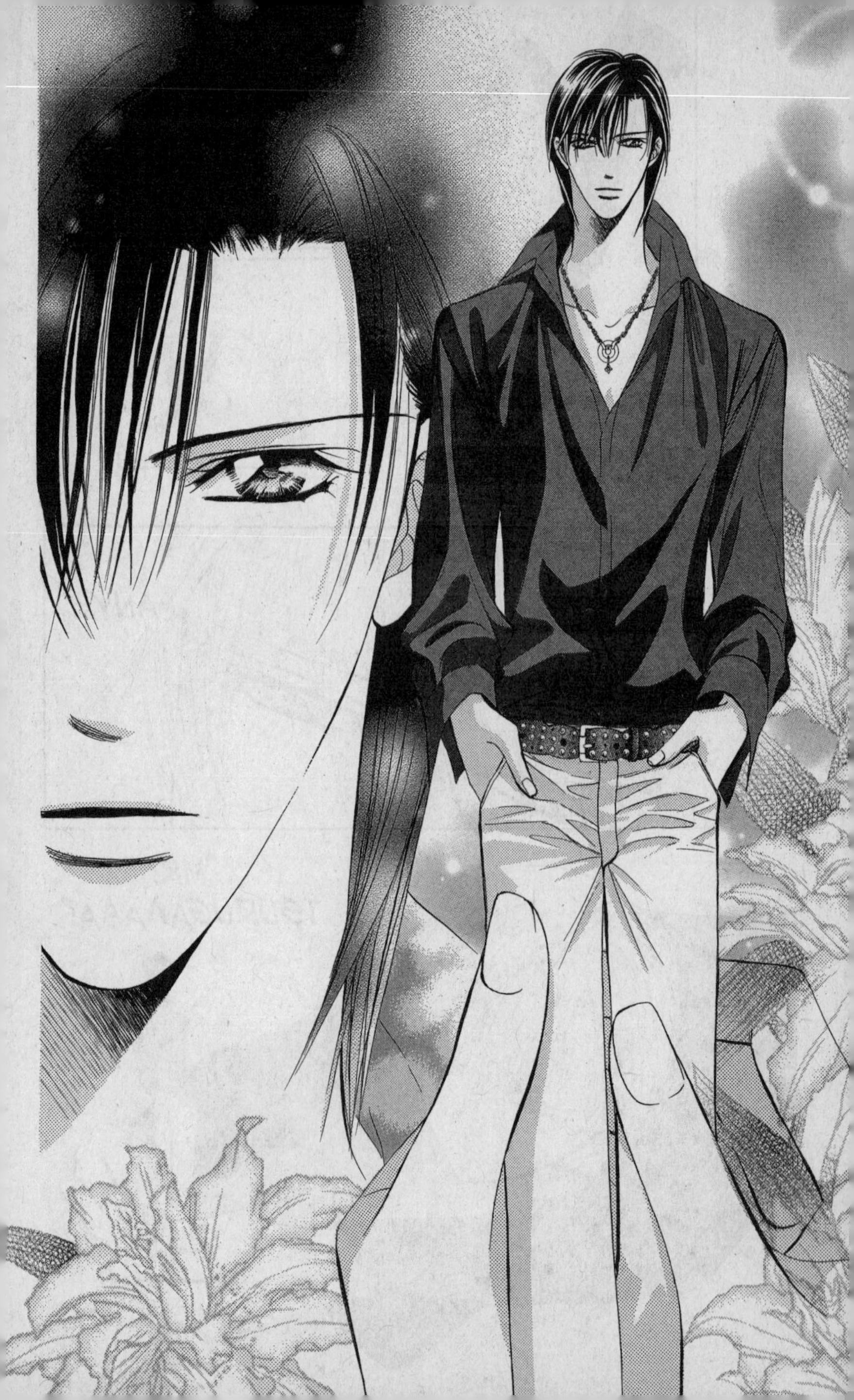

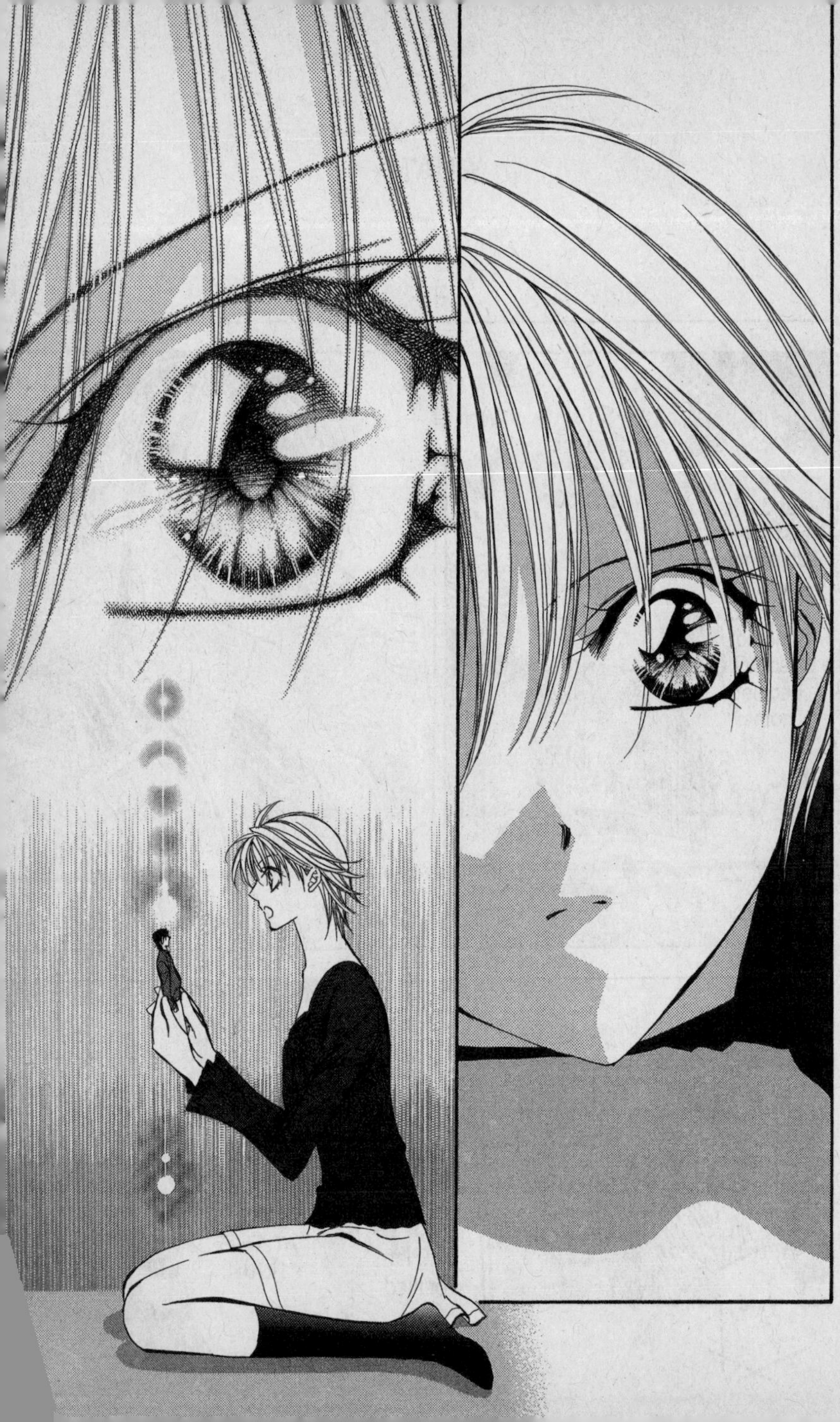

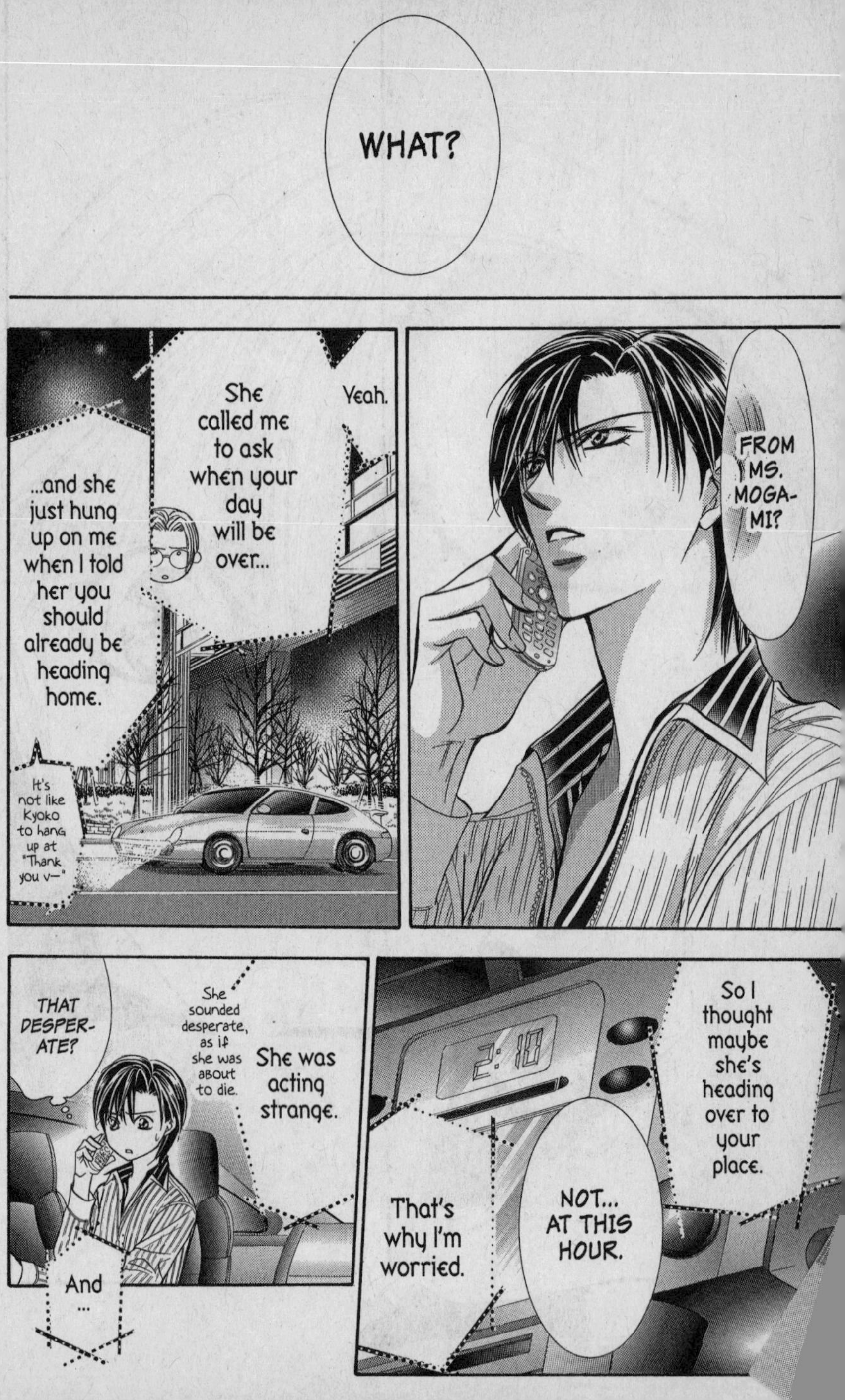
WHAT?
FROM MS. MOGAMI?
Yeah.
She called me to ask when your day will be over...
...and she just hung up on me when I told her you should already be heading home.
It's not like Kyoko to hang up at "Thank you v—"
So I thought maybe she's heading over to your place.
NOT... AT THIS HOUR.
That's why I'm worried.
She was acting strange.
She sounded desperate, as if she was about to die.
THAT DESPERATE?
And ...

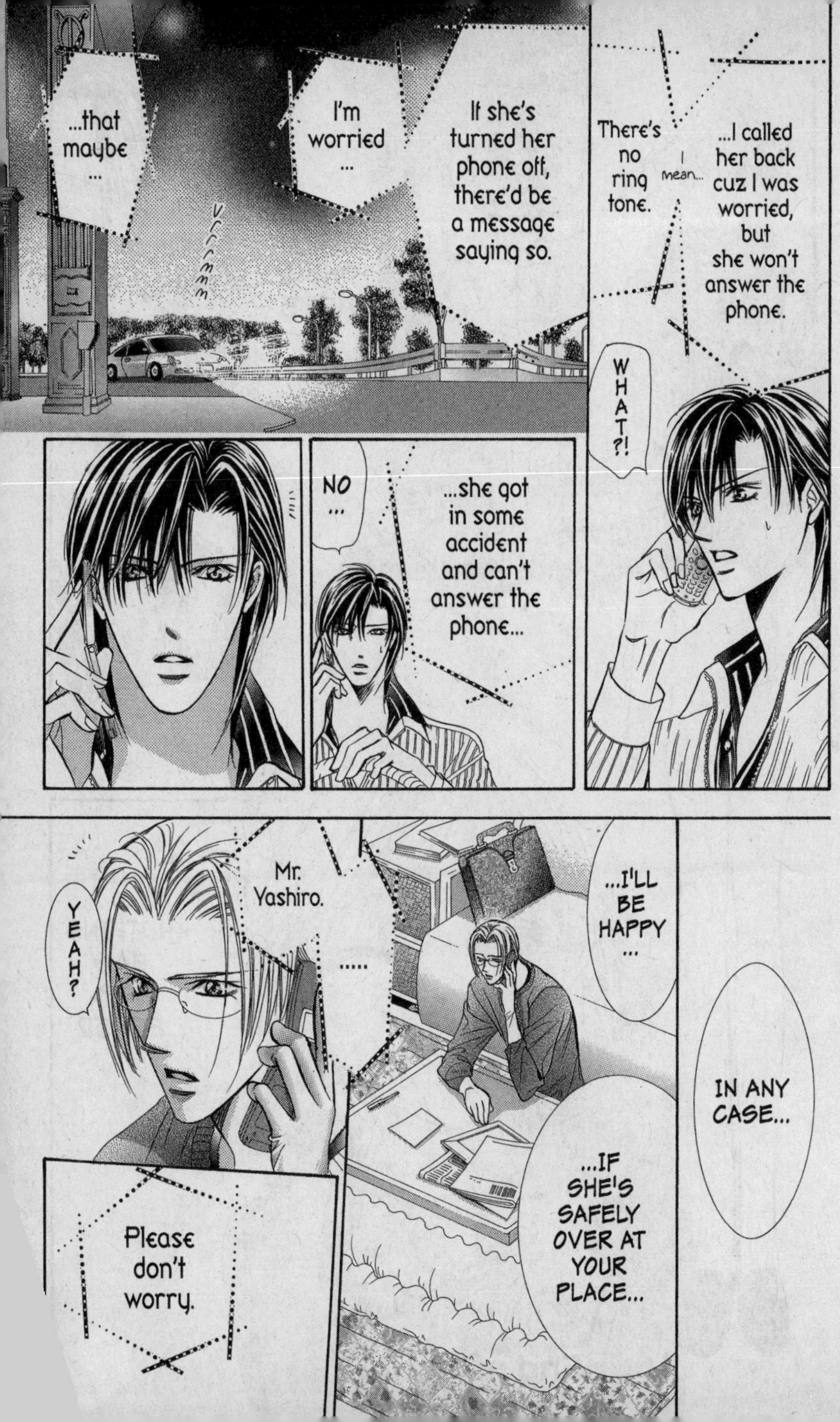
...I called her back cuz I was worried, but she won't answer the phone.
I mean...
There's no ring tone.
WHAT?!
If she's turned her phone off, there'd be a message saying so.
I'm worried...
...that maybe...
Vrrrmmm
NO...
...she got in some accident and can't answer the phone...
IN ANY CASE...
...IF SHE'S SAFELY OVER AT YOUR PLACE...
...I'LL BE HAPPY...
Mr. Yashiro.
.....
YEAH?
Please don't worry.

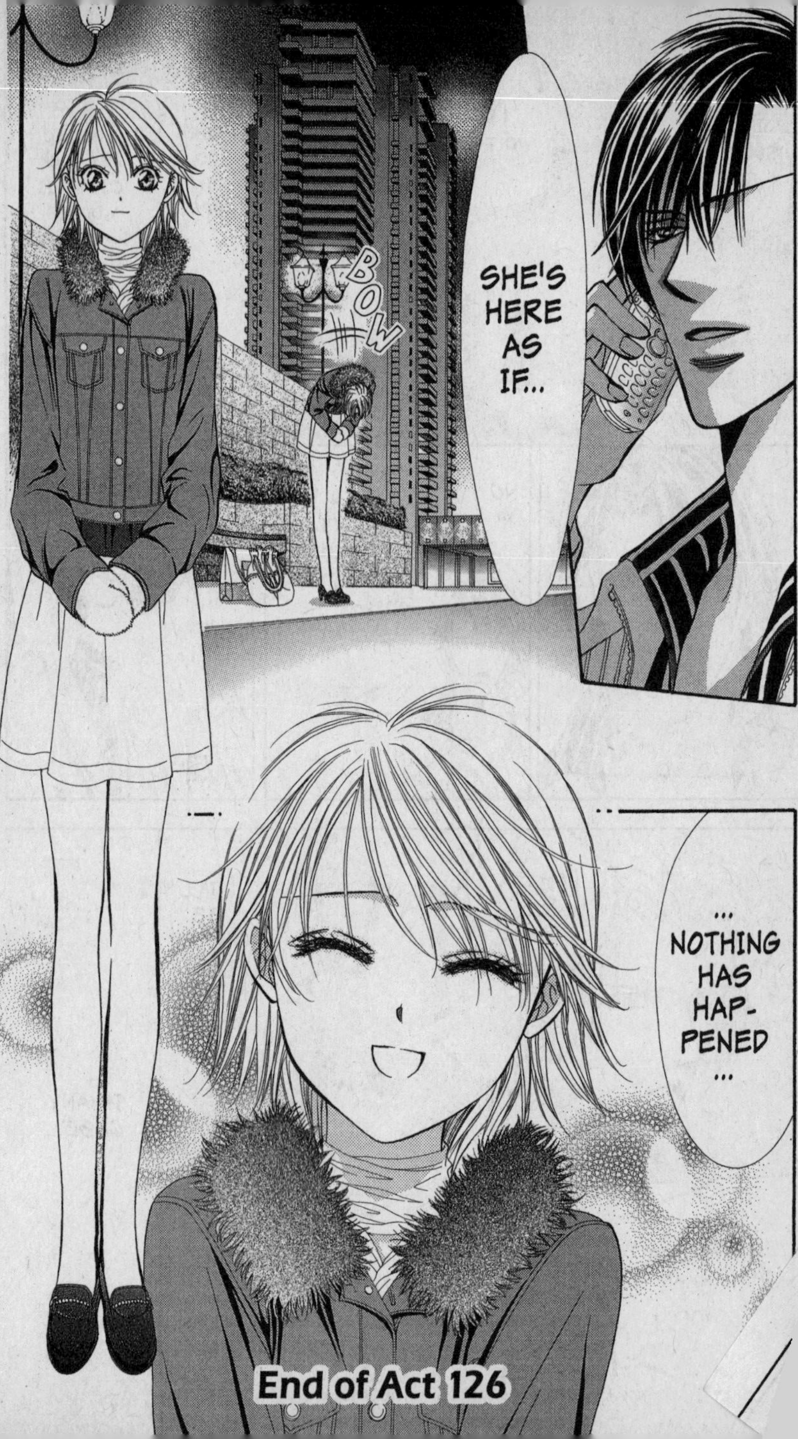
SHE'S HERE AS IF...
BOW
... NOTHING HAS HAP-PENED ...
End of Act 126

Skip-Beat! End Notes

Everyone knows how to be a fan, but sometimes cool things from other cultures need a little help crossing the language barrier.

Page 381, panel 2: Okamisan
In traditional Japanese restaurants, the female manager is called "Okamisan."

Page 387, panel 4: More letters
In hiragana Chiorin (ちおリン) and Chiririn (ちりリン) have the same number of characters.

Page 389, panel 1: (Calm down) Depreeeeeeeeessed
In the original Japanese, the kanji translated as "calm down" and "depressed" can both be read as "chin."

Page 417, panel 2: Yorozuya
Yorozuya means "a dealer in all sorts of articles," and tends to refer to a general store, but here is the name of the store.

Page 440, panel 1: Talento
A "talento" in Japan usually appears on various TV shows and other mass media outlets. They often sing, star in commercials and write for print media as well.

Page 464, panel 1: Doves, beans
In Japanese there is an expression "to look as if a dove got hit by a peashooter," which refers to a puzzled look or a blank look.

Page 481, panel 1: Direct to video
Called V Cinema in Japan, they are low-budget flicks that are made mainly for the video rental market and rarely get shown in theaters. Many V Cinema movies feature the underground world, such as the yakuza.

Page 519, panel 1: Correspondence notebooks
Used for communication between students, teachers and parents.

Page 541, panel 1: Plain udon
Udon in hot broth with minimal toppings, if any.

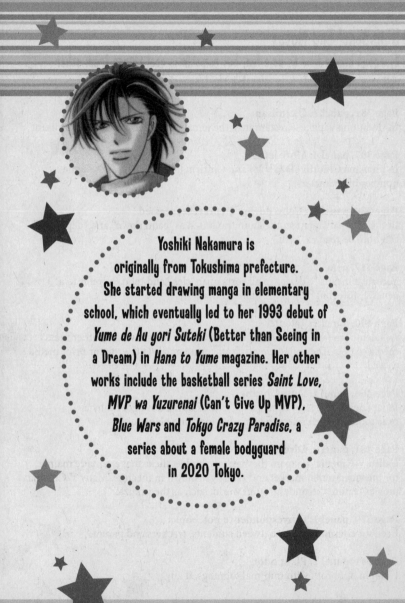

Yoshiki Nakamura is
originally from Tokushima prefecture.
She started drawing manga in elementary
school, which eventually led to her 1993 debut of
Yume de Au yori Suteki (Better than Seeing in
a Dream) in *Hana to Yume* magazine. Her other
works include the basketball series *Saint Love*,
MVP wa Yuzurenai (Can't Give Up MVP),
Blue Wars and *Tokyo Crazy Paradise*, a
series about a female bodyguard
in 2020 Tokyo.

SKIP·BEAT!
3-in-1 Edition
Vol. 7
A compilation of graphic novel volumes 19–21

STORY AND ART BY YOSHIKI NAKAMURA

English Translation & Adaptation/Tomo Kimura
Touch-up Art & Lettering/Sabrina Heep
Design/Yukiko Whitley
Editor/Pancha Diaz

Printed in the U.S.A.

Published by VIZ Media, LLC
P.O. Box 77010
San Francisco, CA 94107

www.viz.com   www.shojobeat.com

10 9 8 7 6 5 4 3 2 1
3-in-1 edition first printing, March 2014

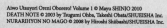

SURPRISE!

You may be reading the wrong way!

It's true: In keeping with the original Japanese comic format, this book reads from right to left—so action, sound effects, and word balloons are completely reversed. This preserves the orientation of the original artwork—plus, it's fun! Check out the diagram shown here to get the hang of things, and then turn to the other side of the book to get started!

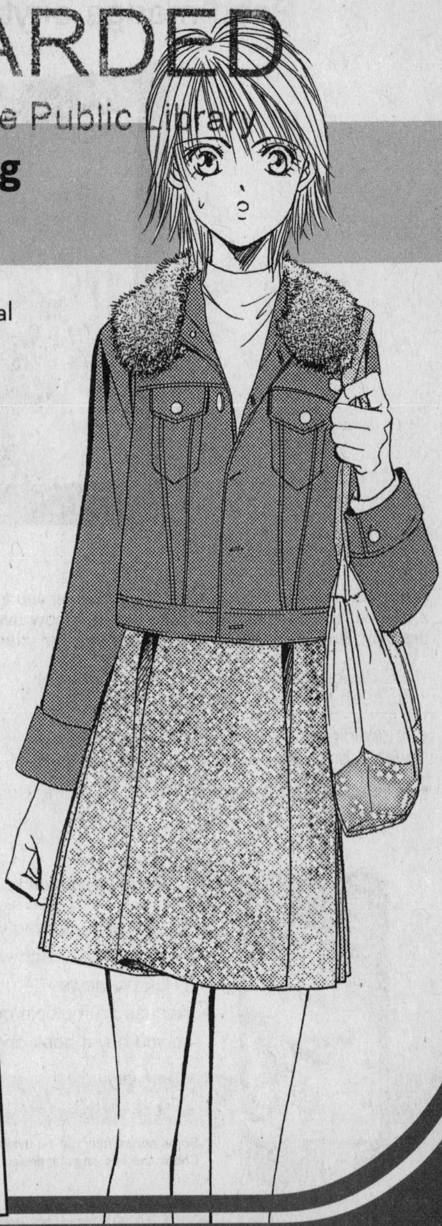

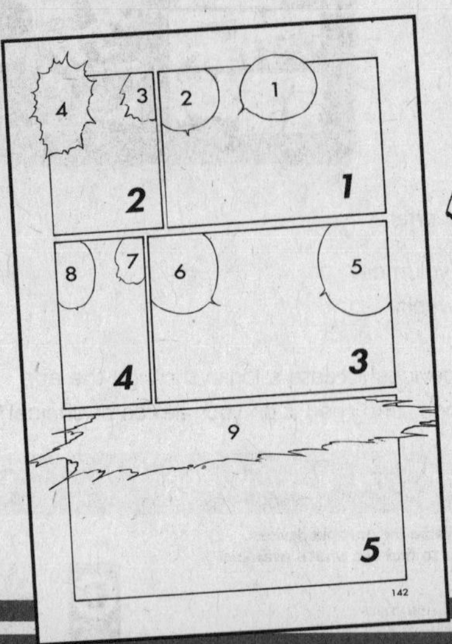
1
2
3
4
1
2
5
6
7
8
3
4
9
5
142